ANNALS OF THE NEW YORK ACADEMY OF SCIENCES

VOLUME 280

October 28, 1976

ORIGINS AND EVOLUTION OF LANGUAGE AND SPEECH*

Conference Organizers

HORST B. STEKLIS, STEVAN R. HARNAD, AND JANE LANCASTER

CONTENTS

*This series of papers is the result of a conference entitled Origins and Evolution of
Language and Speech, held by The New York Academy of Sciences on September 22, 23, 24,
and 25, 1975.

iii

iv

This monograph was aided by contributions from:

- THE GRANT FOUNDATION, INC.
- THE HARRY FRANK GUGGENHEIM FOUNDATION
- WENNER-GREN FOUNDATION FOR ANTHROPOLOGICAL RESEARCH INC.

OPENING REMARKS*

Stevan R. Harnad

Department of Psychiatry
Institute of Mental Health Sciences
CMDNJ-Rutgers Medical School
Piscataway, New Jersey 08854

Our conference title contains a pair of conjunctions of which each appears to introduce a redundancy. We speak of "origins and evolution" and of "language and speech." Actually, both pairs were chosen advisedly.

The question of *evolution* of language has to do with the behavioral and neural precursors, parallels, and continuities in communication, cognition, and allied activities ranging back in human evolution and drawing from evidence sometimes removed from the primates which are of primary concern.

The *origins* question, on the other hand, concerns relatively local conditions in space and time that were specific to that putative period when language actually began.

The distinction between *language* and *speech* is also not unrelated to this first distinction. Some participants in this conference, as you will see, have strong commitments to language as speech; that is, as a special kind of vocalization. Others will be considering different systems of linguistic communication and suggesting that the origins of human language may not have been oral ones at all. The name of Gordon Hewes, who will be chairman of the first session, is particularly associated now with the theory of *gestural* origins, and in fact with the current revival of interest in the question of language origins in general.

As you will surely be told by Prof. Aarsleff in his historical introduction, this topic has been in some disrepute since the middle of the last century because it had so long seemed to produce little more than idle conjecture on the basis of little or no evidence. We think that the situation has changed, and the topic deserves a major and modern reconsideration in the form of this multidisciplinary conference.

Virtually all aspects of our relevant knowledge have changed radically since the nineteenth century. Our concept of the nature of language is totally altered and has become both more profound and more complex. The revolution in linguistics due to Noam Chomsky has provided a very different idea of what the nature of the "target" for the evolutionary process might actually be. We are told that there are features of language that cannot be learned from experience, and we hope it will be possible to consider at this conference what other kinds of origins such features may have had, if this is indeed the case.

Other linguists and logicians will also help to see to it that our formulation of the target is as modern and sophisticated as current knowledge demands. Sessions on perceptual and cognitive substrates will consider the antecedents and bases of language and thinking in both human and nonhuman species. The Artificial Intelligence session will consider the progress that machines are making in this direction. Paleobiologists will examine the evidence from both artifacts and fossils, including the all-important data on the brain of early man. The sessions entitled

*The chairmen gratefully acknowledge the conscientious work of Ellen Marks, Renée Wilkerson, Elvira Flores, Ann Collins, Beatrice Radin, Bill Boland, Annette Tagliaferro, and others at The New York Academy of Sciences.

1

"Behavioral Parallels and Continuities" will consider precursors of language as a communicative system, and there will be a special session on the current work in teaching chimpanzees symbolic communication codes (which some will be equating with language at this conference). Two sessions on the perception and production of speech will examine evolution of the vocal apparatus and the development of speech-related specializations both in speech production and in audition.

The brain will receive special consideration, with the "neural parallels and continuities" session examining mechanisms prior to the encephalization of speech. The sessions on the human brain itself will consider cerebral dominance, functional localization, aphasia and other topics related to the nervous system and language. In the concluding session the entire conference will be overviewed from the point of view of cognition, paleobiology, and the nervous system.

Finally, if we have succeeded in assembling a distinguished and exciting program, it is only because the topic seems to have developed a momentum of its own, one which we hope will testify to the timeliness of this conference.

Part I.   History of Language-Origins Theory

INTRODUCTION

Gordon W. Hewes

Department of Anthropology
University of Colorado
Boulder, Colorado 80302

It has been well over 200 years since an Academy of Science has sponsored an exchange of ideas on this topic; there have been only occasional meetings, symposia, and discussions before and since. In the mid-1740s the abbé de Condillac, Diderot, and Jean Jacques Rousseau used to meet for dinner at the Hôtel De Panier Fleuri at the Palais Royale, where the topic was certainly brought up. But no major scholarly organization deigned to recognize the importance of this matter until the Berlin Academy of Sciences set an essay competition dealing with it in 1769. Of the 34 essays submitted, manuscripts of 24 survive in the Archive of the Academy in East Berlin. Only five of these have ever been published.

It would be very fitting if, as one result of this Conference, our host, The New York Academy of Sciences would ask its colleagues in Berlin to get around to their publication, after two centuries, of the papers submitted in the 1769 competition.

The first prize was won in 1772 by Johann Gottfried Herder. Almost a century after that historic essay contest, the Société de Linguistique de Paris, beset by papers purporting to solve the question of glottogenesis, saw fit to ban in 1866 all further communication on this subject. Still, the prohibition did not completely stifle speculation.

The session we are now beginning may mark a turning point—or perhaps it will be another 200 years before any Academy of Sciences thinks the topic is worthy of such treatment.

AN OUTLINE OF LANGUAGE-ORIGINS
THEORY SINCE THE RENAISSANCE

Hans Aarsleff

Department of English
Princeton University
Princeton, New Jersey 08540

Why a "Conference on Origins and Evolution of Language and Speech" would wish to hear about the history of the subject is a good question. Is this history at all relevant to current study and research? It would be presumptuous for me to say, since I cannot claim to have any close knowledge of the interesting work that has been done in recent decades. This, at least, is certain: since the possession of language and speech has always been considered the chief characteristic of the human species, the question of origin has also been considered fundamental in any attempt to understand the nature of man and what distinguishes him from other animals. Most major philosophers and most philosophical systems have dealt with the problem in one way or another; in fact, so universal has this interest been that its absence, as in Kant, has been cause for wonder. Plato, Aristotle, the Stoics, the Epicureans, the Church Fathers, Thomas Aquinas, Luther, the German mystics, Jacob Boehme and Robert Fludd, Marin Mersenne, John Locke, and, following him, most eighteenth-century philosophers would readily have understood the question in its present formulation, although they would have given quite different answers. A meeting of physicists would hardly schedule a paper on past doctrines concerning the constitution of the solar system; it would simply not appear sufficiently instructive to be worth the time and effort in that context. Is our situation different? It would again be presumptuous for me to say, but given the difficulty of the problem, it is at least possible that we may learn something, both positively and negatively, from a knowledge of past discussion of the question.

The problem is difficult, because it has traditionally been seen as the central question about the nature of man. It has been bound up with other fundamental questions such as intelligence, reason, thought, man's social nature, political philosophy, and the progress of knowledge. In its classic eighteenth-century formulation, the origin of language and speech was the key to the question of the history of thought, of mankind. This complex mixture of speculation and some empirical information that was often cogent is illustrated in Lord Monboddo's great work from the 1770s, *Of the Origin and Progress of Language*. This work shows a feature that is common to all such treatments: it is intimately involved with contemporary assumptions and philosophical doctrines. Arguing against Humean scepticism, Monboddo did not arrive at his discussion of the origin of language until he had devoted two long sections to epistemology and to the social and political nature of man. Yet, he was convinced that the origin of language occupied a central place in what he, according to a typical eighteenth-century formulation, called "the natural history of man," for, as he said, "it is by language that we trace, with the greatest certainty, the progress of the human mind," a view that would have gained the emphatic agreement of Locke, Leibniz, and Condillac.

The eighteenth century did not share the attitude of Dr. Johnson, who found little merit in "Lord Monboddo's strange speculation on the primitive state of human nature"; it was, Johnson said, "all conjecture on a thing useless, even were it known to be true. Knowledge of all kinds is good; conjecture, as to things useful, is good; but

4

conjecture as to what it would be useless to know, such as whether men went upon all fours, is very idle." Unlike Dr. Johnson, we do share the eighteenth century's curiosity about these matters; if at all possible, we do want to know whether men ever went upon all fours, and especially whether the higher primates could learn to speak and why they do not. But seen in the context of his time, Johnson was right to stress that this was all a matter of speculation and conjecture. Some twenty years later, the Scottish philosopher Dugald Stewart called Adam Smith's essay "Considerations Concerning the first Formation of Languages" (1761) an example of "conjectural or theoretical history." The eighteenth century did not fool itself that it was establishing facts about the primitive state of mankind; it sought reasoned plausibilities with the chief intent of separating man's natural endowments from his artificial accomplishments; the chief product of man's art was language, which, in turn, was the foundation of the progress of thought and knowledge. It is one of the curious quirks of history that the nineteenth century became so compulsively historical in the factual sense that it misinterpreted the eighteenth century on this important point, with the significant consequence that linguistic philosophy came to be ridiculed as useless and jejune, "unempirical" speculation quite unworthy of serious attention by right-minded scholars; that is, by university professors who, from the limited but dominant perspective of their chairs in historical philology, collectively saw themselves as the sole legitimate authority on all matters relating to the study of language.

My own business, so to speak, is intellectual history, and it is in this manner that I propose to deal with the subject. This means that I am more interested in what has been said than in the question whether past discussions fit current conceptions; it is often forgotten or ignored that adequate attention to the former problem is the indispensable prerequisite to an informed handling of the latter. Needless to say, in the short time we have, I can only deal with a small part of the wealth of material that is available. After a single example from antiquity, I shall jump to the seventeenth and later centuries.

Nearly 2,500 years ago, Herodotus told the story of an Egyptian king who wished to know which nation was the oldest on earth. He therefore contrived to have two children brought up in isolation from all speech in order to find out what language they would speak if left to their own devices. He was disappointed to learn that the first word they spoke was not Egyptian but Phrygian, thus proving that the Phrygians were the oldest nation. I mention this anecdote because it shows the consistency with which the problem and the experiment designed to solve it have recurred. As late as the eighteenth century, the same experiment was proposed, though it was at the same time admitted that it could not be performed, for obvious reasons. History records several similar experiments, usually with the answer that the language the children spoke was Hebrew. But even if the experiment could not be performed, the same problem drew attention to so-called wolf-children; that is, children who for some reason had lived isolated from other humans, growing up among animals. The most familiar example is perhaps the "Wild Boy of Aveyron," who a few years ago was the subject of a beautiful movie, based on the account of the French doctor, Jean Itard, written in 1801. It is a sign of the philosophical interest in such children that reports began to occur with increasing frequency from the latter half of the seventeenth century; cases were discussed by Leibniz, Condillac, Monboddo, and many others. I am sure it is well known that these children did not speak and never learned to speak if they had lived in isolation beyond the early, speech-learning years of childhood. The communication of deaf-mutes was also a lively subject in the seventeenth century and especially in the latter half of the eighteenth, chiefly owning to Condillac's philosophy of communication and language.

If we jump some two thousand years to the Renaissance, we find a different conception of the problem, which now began to receive much serious attention. Argument and counterargument developed views that led directly to the eighteenth century. The formulation that remained dominant far into the seventeenth century was based on the Old Testament, with a strong admixture of Jewish mysticism as found in the cabalistic doctrines that became known in the west after the expulsion of the Jews from Spain in 1492, a year which for that reason marks a watershed in linguistic philosophy and speculation. It is well known that Genesis contains two profoundly influential linguistic statements: Adam's name-giving in Chapter 2 and the story of the Babylonian Confusion in Chapter 11. The first is the source of the powerful conception of Adam as archetypal man, in every respect, of course, but chiefly in the matter of language. The dominant interpretation of the act of name-giving was turned into a doctrine of the origin of language in this fashion. This act occurred before the Fall when Adam was in a state of perfect, nearly divine knowledge. Thus his "names" bore a natural relation to the animals they named, simply because there must, so it was postulated, have been perfect harmony between word and thing; words could not be merely accidental or based on some sort of agreement that arbitrarily assigned a sound to the animal named. This idea led to the doctrine, heard even late in the seventeenth century, that Adam, also after the Fall, was both the greatest philosopher and the greatest etymologist who ever lived. Since all mankind descended from Adam and Eve, all languages had a single origin and exhibited certain common features. We may find this conception useless or fanciful, but it had great value in stimulating linguistic study, for instance in the search for what we call linguistic universals. It was generally postulated that this first language was Hebrew, a belief which in turn led to a great deal of comparative study that was much more fruitful and competent than the nineteenth century's inordinate pride in its own comparative, historical philology, has allowed us to know. Leibniz, for instance, had great respect for this work, which he knew intimately.

Now, we might think that the Babylonian Confusion put an end to these doctrines. But with some exceptions, that was not the case. The Confusion was open to several interpretations; one of them was that though the single language of mankind had been scattered into mutually unintelligible forms of speech, it was still possible that the original elements of the pre-Babylonian natural language had been preserved in the new languages. Thus, though the present languages could not be seen to be natural in the Adamic sense, they were still not the product of conventional agreement which arbitrarily assigned certain sounds to stand for certain things. This belief raised the hope that determined etymological study might reveal the forms of the original natural language. There were, in fact, people who made vast collections of words in the largest possible number of different languages on the assumption that it would be possible to arrive at the original elements of the Adamic language by some sort of etymological distillation, so to speak. This may seem nearly idiotic, and few seventeenth-century figures put any trust in it, but the need to argue against this doctrine was fruitful.

The conception I have described is properly called mystical, although it pretended to offer something like empirical means to recapture the Adamic protolanguage. But there was another, much more influential and genuinely mystical, linguistic mode, best illustrated by Jacob Boehme. In his moments of God-given inspiration, Boehme claimed that he was given direct insight into the natures of things and that he understood the Adamic language; thus words became, in these moments, direct revelations of the essences of things; that is, language became again genuinely natural, as it was to Adam. Each word revealed the nature of the thing, almost as a chemical formula does to us. In this conception there is a strong admixture of cabalistic lore and Renaissance neoplatonism.

Such claims did not remain confined to the province of religion. On the contrary, if Boehme and such cabalistic figures as Robert Fludd were right, then it would, by this means, be possible to gain real, scientific knowledge of the constitution of things in nature by the proper study of words and language. This seems so utterly fantastic to us that we may hesitate to believe that these views could pose a threat to science, but this is in fact precisely what happened, and for this reason the advocates and practitioners of the new science felt compelled to argue against them. Thus it was seriously maintained by some, also in England, that science must not neglect this potential source of knowledge. If, for instance, the word "gold" could be understood in proper cabalistic fashion, it would give us information about the essence of gold itself. The chief thrust of Locke's *Essay* is an argument against this view, and it was for this reason he argued that we can never know more than what he, defiantly, called the "nominal essence" of gold. This term was defiant because it implied a rejection of the mystical understanding of essence. In this sense it can be said that Locke's *Essay* was a handbook in the epistemology of the new mechanical philosophy, or what we call science, practiced and advocated by the "Royal Society of London for the Promotion of Natural Knowledge."

It is in this light that Locke's argument against "innate notions," as he called them, must be understood, an argument in which the Royal Society found itself involved owing to attacks upon it conducted in these terms, most characteristically by a man named John Webster, whose text used the very terms that occur in Locke's counterargument. It has rightly been said that "Locke certainly considered the doctrine of innateness as having its foundation in the abuse of words." On these points, arguments closely similar to Locke's had previously been advanced both by his close and admired friend Robert Boyle and by Descartes's correspondent Marin Mersenne. Time does not permit closer consideration of Marin Mersenne, who in the first half of the seventeenth century was the influential advocate of mechanical philosophy. A large part of his extensive writings are therefore devoted to argument against the cabalistic doctrines of Robert Fludd, in the same manner that Locke later argued against other statements of the same doctrines. For this reason, Mersenne is the most innovative and influential writer of the first half of the seventeenth century on the nature of language, although there would seem to be no evidence that he directly influenced Locke; the close similarity of their arguments is sufficiently explained by their common opposition to the same doctrines and their common commitment to the same mechanical philosophy.

Like Locke, Mersenne argued forcefully that we can never know the internal constitutions of things, that language is purely conventional (as opposed to natural in the Adamic sense), and that all the knowledge that is open to us in these matters must rely on the external manifestations of things. Like Locke, he took reason to be the fundamental, defining characteristic of man, the source of his uniqueness and all his artificial accomplishments, and the basis of all knowledge that truly deserves the name. Locke was a great admirer of the Port-Royal logic and grammar, a fact that is also evident in the *Essay*. The contrast and conflict between so-called empiricism and rationalism is a nineteenth-century invention, advanced in the context of a conservative reaction against contemporary philosophical doctrines, in the interest of a characteristic Victorian ideology. Further, this view did not remain unopposed during the nineteenth century; Coleridge, who was no mean judge, said that Locke and Descartes held "precisely the same opinions about the original sources of our ideas." Locke's argument against innateness is one among several that were aimed at doctrines well known in the seventeenth century. Locke did not present what has been called a "caricature" of seventeenth-century rationalist philosophy. His discussion of the association of ideas is incontrovertible evidence of his rationalism; to

Locke the association of ideas is what he called "a sort of madness," because it interferes with the rational procedures of genuine knowledge. This distinction was observed during the eighteenth century, very clearly, for instance, by Condillac, who made the same distinction between the involuntary association of ideas on the one hand and the voluntary "connection of ideas" which is governed by reason.

In the *Essay*, Locke did not address himself directly to the problem of the origin of language, but by devoting a separate book, Book III, to what he called "language and words in general," he placed the problem of language at the center of his epistemology; it is a serious error, however, to assume that all Locke had to say about that problem is contained in Book III. The whole tenor of his genetic psychology was an invitation to further exploration. He made some suggestive remarks that bore directly on the subject; for instance, when he observed that he was apt to think that the names of things may very much direct our thoughts to the originals of men's ideas. He repeatedly dismissed the doctrine of natural language, just like Mersenne, for example, when he said that "words . . . came to be made use of by men as the signs of their ideas; not by any natural connexion that there is between particular articulate sounds and certain ideas, for then there would be but one language amongst all men [a point, incidentally, also made by Mersenne and others]; but by a voluntary imposition, whereby such a word is made arbitrarily the mark of such an idea. . . . Words in their primary or immediate signification, stand for nothing but the ideas in the mind of him that uses them, how imperfectly soever or carelessly those ideas are collected from the things which they are supposed to represent." (*Essay* III, ii) In the philosophy and study of language, Locke's influence was immense during the eighteenth century, credited by all who wrote on the subject, including the universal grammarian Du Marsais, who rejected outright the Cartesian doctrine of innateness.

It has already been pointed out that wolf children began to gain increasing attention from the latter half of the seventeenth century. The same is true of the higher primates, though the arguments and speculations derived from this source long remained uncertain, since the information was based not on observation of living specimens but on the anatomy of dead bodies. The most influential text was a book published in 1699, Edward Tyson's learned and much-admired *Orang-Outang, sive homo sylvestris, or the Anatomy of a Pygmie compared with that of a Monky, Ape, and a Man.* For our purposes, the crucial point was Tyson's finding that the ape had organs of speech as perfect as those of man. This led him to the observation, embarrassing to a number of assumptions, that "there is no reason to think that agents do perform such and such actions because they are found with organs proper thereunto; for . . . apes should speak, seeing that they have the instruments necessary for speech." (pp. 51–52) This claim tended to support the uniqueness of man, in line with the Cartesian doctrine that animals are mere machines, a doctrine that proved fruitful by eliciting arguments against its plausibility based on closer observation of the behavior of animals. Tyson's account was given wider currency when it was repeated in Buffon's influential *Natural History.* Strange as it may seem at first, Monboddo enrolled the orang-outang in the species man in order to elevate the special stature of man. Monboddo found support for his argument in the fact that the orang-outang used tools much like man, in this case a sort of walking-stick, which from the late fifteenth century right through Tyson and Buffon remained a conventional detail of the iconography of this primate, pictured in half-upright position supporting himself with this stick. If it is true that orang-outangs use tools, then Monboddo was so far right; but the situation is curious. Since apes had not been reliably observed in their natural habitats, the stick really offered no authoritative evidence at all. In fact, one rather suspects that the stick was introduced, first in 1486, because it would have offended religious doctrine to show a monkey that walked erect on his own two feet alone, for this posture was traditionally taken to be the exclusive privilege of man as a sign of the divine favor which no other creature than man enjoyed.

Let me now turn to the work of Condillac. In 1746 he published, in French, a work called *An Essay on the Origin of Human Knowledge*; he readily admitted his debt to Locke—in fact, the English translation (1756) bore the subtitle, "A Supplement to Mr. Locke's *Essay*." The importance of Condillac can hardly be overestimated. His influence is pervasive on the French *Encyclopédie*, as well as on European thought in general during the latter half of the eighteenth century. In France his influence soon became apparent in the work of Diderot, Rousseau, Turgot, and many others, who acknowledged their indebtedness; in Germany the thought of his *Essay* was debated in the Berlin Academy, leading directly to Herder's prize essay on the origin of language (1772); in Edinburgh it became, indirectly, it seems, the chief impulse for Monboddo's great work. In his later works, Condillac continued to expound and extend the philosophy of the *Essay*.

The core of Condillac's doctrine is this. He posits axiomatically that man is a social creature, thus agreeing with Locke and, for that matter, the Bible; that man has the capacity for sense experience; and that he is rational. These features we cannot explain, but experience shows that we have them. Animals do not have reason, though they are capable of certain rudimentary forms of thought. With these natural endowments, how has man gained the knowledge he has? The answer is that the deliberate use of arbitrary signs, in the form of language and speech, is the indispensable instrument without which man would have remained in the condition of the animals. The crucial element in the origin of human knowledge is the origin of language, a problem that involves the question of the nature of language. His procedure is a search for basic principles, for as Condillac said, "principle is synonymous with beginning." In typical eighteenth-century fashion, he is using the search for origins to separate nature from art. Language is man's greatest and most decisive artificial creation, and it is in turn the foundation of human knowledge.

Condillac's *Essay* is divided into two parts, the first on the operations of the mind, the second on "language and method." The basic argument of the first part is this: Condillac says that he is examining the present state of man; that is, after the Fall, and not before, when it was possible to have ideas prior to the use of the senses. All knowledge must therefore begin with simple perception. If an act of perception is accompanied by consciousness of having a perception, it is attended by attention; this capacity for attention makes it possible for the mind to note changes in its perceptions, in their disappearance and recurrence. When the latter occurs, the result is reminiscence, which is the beginning of experience, for without it every moment would appear to be the first in our existence. It cannot be explained, but is assumed to have its foundation in the nature of the union of body and mind. Attention has the further effect of linking certain perceptions together in such a manner that they become inseparable; one will recall the other. This connection is the source of imagination, memory, and contemplation. Imagination occurs when the attention is so full as to recall the perception of an object as if it were present. Memory occurs when the reproduction is less complete, making present in the mind not all the connected perceptions but only some of them, such as the circumstance in which the object was first perceived. The mind may, for instance, be able to recall the name of a flower or the place where it was first seen, but fail to recall its odor and other details. Both imagination and memory, and by extension contemplation, depend on the connection of ideas which is the product of attention, whose force and selection are governed by the needs that accompany particular situations. Thus situations of strong emotion—such as fear, delight, love—are especially fruitful, a principle also familiar in eighteenth-century aesthetics, in large measure owing to Condillac. As yet, however, both imagination and memory are beyond the active control of the mind, for neither will occur except by the chance enounter of a perception that elicits a particular imagination or memory. It is this circumstance that raises the possibility of an active and deliberate use of signs; if the mind could somehow have a sufficient stock of signs at its disposal, it would also be able to control and master its past experience; it would, so to speak, have a reliable retrieval system.

There are three kinds of signs to consider. First, accidental signs, which are obviously beyond our deliberate control. Secondly, natural signs, "or the cries which nature has established to express the passions of joy, of fear, or of grief, etc." They are uttered involuntarily in the situations that give rise to them; they are, in fact, vocal gestures, of the same order as other natural expressions of the face, arms, hands, or the whole body. If a particular passion and the accompanying vocal gesture have occurred often, they will become linked so that one will elicit the other; "Then it is," says Condillac, "that this cry becomes a sign, but this imagination will not acquire any habit till it has been heard by chance; consequently this habit will be no more in man's power than" is the case with accidental signs. Finally, there is a third kind of sign, "instituted signs, or those which we have chosen ourselves, and bear only an arbitrary relation to our ideas." It is on the use of this internalized stock of signs that all knowledge and its progress depends, for they open the way for the exercise of reflection, which means deliberate and productive control over thought and the materials of past experience. Reflection is given in the nature of man; it is the expression of reason, which, Condillac says, "crowns the understanding." We are capable of higher degrees of reflection in proportion to our reason. From these admittedly small beginnings, the progress of language and knowledge is made possible, the use of arbitrary signs and the capacity for reflection mutually helping each other to higher and higher degrees of intellectual control.

It is at this point that the crucial question of the origin of language enters the argument. Condillac says: "It seems that we would not know how to make use of instituted signs, if we were not already capable of sufficient reflection to choose them and attach ideas to them; how then, it may be asked, can it be that the exercise of reflection is only acquired by the use of signs?" He answers: "I shall meet that difficulty when I give the history of language."

The origin of language is the subject of the second part of the *Essay*. It begins with the second kind of signs, natural cries, which form part of the gestural "language of action" that is natural to man. It is not part of the instituted language and speech, whose origin Condillac seeks to explain; without reason and the innate capacity for reflection, nothing would happen. Since the language of action is natural, it is the same in all, and when heard or observed it elicits the same passion that first occasioned it. Similar situations would occur along with the vocal gestures appropriate to them, so far, involuntarily. By such repetition, the early human creatures would in time gain the power to recall a certain range of such gestures at will and thus also to reproduce them as signs for the information of others; that is, communication. For instance, the sign or gesture indicating fright at the approach of a lion could, by one person who was not directly threatened, be deliberately produced to alert another who was in danger; this act would involve the exercise of reflection, a procedure tantamount to using the original, involuntary sign with the function of a deliberate arbitrary sign. Thus man would gradually, by slow degrees and in the long process of time, as Condillac often emphasizes, come to do by reflection at will what he had previously done by instinct alone. The deliberate use of a few simple signs would extend the operations of the mind and the facility of reflection; the signs would in turn be improved, increase in number, and grow more firmly familiar. The mind and the use of signs would interact to the mutual advantage and progress of both. At this stage it became possible to create the language whose origin Condillac is seeking, the use of deliberately created arbitrary signs. This is the importance of instituted signs, which alone will serve this purpose. Condillac said: "The natural cries served early man as a model for a new language. They articulated new sounds, and by repeating them several times with an accompanying gesture indicating the objects they wished to note, they accustomed themselves to give names to things." He stresses that for a very long time, the language of action would coexist with the new language, both of them simultaneously serving together in the process of communication. This also came to form an important element in Romantic esthetics, for example, regarding poetic meter.

There are several other aspects of Condillac's thought that are interesting, but they do not concern us here; the outline I have given does not exhaust his philosophy of language. In the closing years of the eighteenth century, his philosophy was taken up with special eagerness by the French *idéologues*, who, for a while, until they were suppressed by Napoleon as politically dangerous, exercised considerable influence. When Wilhelm von Humboldt spent two years in Paris in the late 1790s, he was especially close to the *idéologues*, and it is clear that it is to them that he owes both the beginning of his linguistic philosophy as we know it and a number of its fundamental features. This indebtedness has been obscured, ignored, or denied by a scholarly tradition that has found his intellectual background exclusively in German sources. The mention of Wilhelm von Humboldt calls to mind a prominent feature of Condillac's philosophy of language; this feature is that the use of language is creative, in its beginning and continuing in every act of speech. If we were to enroll Condillac in the tradition of so-called empiricism, this feature of creativity would not belong here, according to some recent views. The importance of creativity is even textually evident in Condillac's frequent use of such terms as "generate," "generating," "generation," and similar terms (in their French equivalents, of course). This, you may recall, is a view that has often been associated chiefly or exclusively with Humboldt.

Condillac belongs in the tradition of linguistic philosophy that began in the seventeenth century with such innovative figures as Mersenne and Locke. Although this tradition incorporated some views already familiar in antiquity, it began as a reaction against the mystical linguistic doctrines that were seen to pose epistemological difficulties for the new science. The views represented by Descartes were not new, and they did not conflict with the Locke tradition, as shown by the case of Du Marsais, among others. There is thus an intimate connection between this tradition and the philosophy of the new science. This important aspect of intellectual history has received little attention; indeed, it has generally been ignored or denied, owing to subservience to the nineteenth century.

We can speculate on the reasons why this tradition fell into neglect and even disrepute, a situation that has rightly been seen as an impoverishment of the study and philosophy of language. Briefly said, the nineteenth century became so overpoweringly successful in creating its own mode of philological, historical language study that all linguistic problems that did not fit this mode came to be considered trivial, irrelevant, or worse yet, in the positivistic temper of the times, unscholarly and unscientific. In that century, therefore, professional students of language had little to offer that is relevant to our present concern, the origin of language. In fact, one could say that there was a regression. In Condillac's century, there was little fear that the study of language posed a threat to religious belief, but during the next century it did enter into this set of problems. When other sciences, especially geology, with such works as Sir Charles Lyell's *Principles of Geology*, were felt to cast doubt on fundamental points of Victorian orthodoxy, language and especially its origin were invoked as proof of the evident and necessary intervention of divine power. This situation gave rise to a number of arguments about the origin of language, best known perhaps from the writings of Max Müller, who argued that the origin relied on a special act of divine favor, operative only on that occasion and for that purpose. This argument denied the principle of uniformitarianism, which had become established in geology (and in other moments in history in the other sciences), an especially dangerous principle, it was felt, because it raised doubts about the biblical account of the flood. These controversies are now forgotten, but they were prominent in England during the midnineteenth century, indicated, for instance, by the fact that the British Association for the Advancement of Science, meeting in Oxford in 1847, considered this problem at great length in the attempt to support orthodoxy on arguments derived from the philosophy of language. It is significant that the men who were active on the side of orthodoxy were the same who denigrated Lockean philosophy on conservative grounds. Thus, questions which in the eighteenth century had commanded wide interest and assent among students of language were in the nineteenth century taken over by ethnologists, anthropologists, and by Charles Darwin, who took an active part in this controversy, seen for instance in *The Descent of Man*. William Dwight Whitney wrote extensively on the origin of language, chiefly in often virulent controversy against Max Müller. The effect of this religious controversy and of the new comparative philology was to put the great linguistic tradition of the previous centuries out of court among professional students of language. And so, on the whole, it has remained until recent years; both the school of Bloomfield and later, dominant schools of linguistic study have given little encouragement to serious work on the question of the origin of language.

Still, it would not be correct to say that the eighteenth century was altogether forgotten. It has often been noted that the Linguistic Society of Paris, in the second clause of its bylaws, in 1866 expressly prohibited the discussion of the origin of language. But this prohibition had little effect, and it was deplored by prominent French linguists, notably Michel Bréal, who said he could not imagine that the study of language would retain much relevance and vitality if this question was removed from its domain. Although himself the French translator of Bopp's *Comparative Grammar*, Bréal was also the first and most severe critic of the German school of comparative philology, which he referred to in terms that show he took the period of its dominance to mark a course of increasing narrowness and triviality, even silliness, in the study of language. For Bréal this period covered the fifty years from 1816 to 1866; that is, from Bopp to Schleicher. Bréal spoke with great admiration of the *idéologues* and the eighteenth century. In this revival of respect for the Condillac tradition, he was not alone; among several other well-known exponents of the same admiration was Hippolyte Taine. This is of some importance, for Bréal was one of Saussure's teachers, and Saussure seems also, from other sources, to have been under positive influence of the eighteenth century, a fact that must immediately appear evident to anyone familiar with the literature. Both the doctrine of the linearity of speech and of the arbitrariness of the linguistic sign are fundamental in Condillac and his followers.

To conclude, I have tried to outline the major stages in the history of the philosophy of language since the Renaissance as it bears more narrowly on the problem of the origin of language. The doctrine of natural language typically illustrated by speculation on Adam's name-giving was dominant during the sixteenth and much of the seventeenth centuries. It would be both ungracious and false to think that this tradition of study was useless; on the contrary, within its clear definition of basic views and assumptions, much useful work was done. I have further tried to show how this linguistic philosphy elicited counterarguments and new modes of study, prominently in Mersenne and Locke, and that this new orientation formed the foundation of linguistic philosophy during the eighteenth century. I have paid some attention to Condillac, not merely because he seems to me to hold considerable inherent interest, but also because his importance is now increasingly coming to be realized. I cannot conceive that any history of linguistics, or indeed any intellectual history, will be worth much unless Condillac is granted the prominent place he demands. Finally, I have tried to sketch why the nineteenth century has tended to obscure our view of the accomplishments of the previous centuries, when the subject of this conference was also a vital issue. Behind the course I have followed lies the belief that a good understanding of the history of the study of language will result in some significant revisions in the generally accepted structure of intellectual history. The history of the study of language, like the history of science, is not a small parochial affair that should aim merely to fit the pieces into the sort of history we already have. Among the benefits of this enterprise may be that it will lend respect and perhaps some useful impulses to speculation and study that will enlighten our understanding of the nature of language and the origins and evolution of language and speech.

NOTES AND REFERENCES

GORDON W. HEWES' *Language Origins: A Bibliography*, second revised and enlarged edition (The Hague: Mouton, 1975), in two parts, is a magnificent guide to the extensive literature. TYSON's book has been issued in facsimile (1966, Dawson's, London), with an introduction by Ashley Montagu. There is a relevant essay by the Dutch anatomist PETER CAMPER, "Account of the Organs of Speech of the Orang Outang," with proof of "the true organical reason . . . the absolute impossibility there is for the Orang and other monkies to speak," in *Philosophical Transactions of the Royal Society,* 1779, **69:** 139–159. The English translation of Condillac's *Essay* has been reissued in the series Scholars' Facsimiles and Reprints (1971 Gainesville, Fla.) but the French text is preferable. On wolf children, see LUCIEN MALSON, *Wolf Children and the Problem of Human Nature* (1972, Monthly Review Press), with a list of recorded cases from 1344 to 1961 on pp. 80–82; this volume contains Jean Itard's *The Wild Boy of Aveyron.* (This book was first published in French under the title *Les Enfants Sauvages,* Paris, 1964.) See also FRANK TINLAND, *L'homme sauvage* (1968, Payot, Bibliothèque Scientifique, Paris). On Mersenne, see A. C. CROMBIE's excellent article, with full references, in *Dictionary of Scientific Biography* 9, 1974, 316–322. On JACOB BOEHME, see *ibid.* 2 (1970), 224–224, with bibliography. There is an interesting essay by ROBERT WOKLER on "Tyson and Buffon on the Orang-utan," to appear in *Studies on Voltaire and the Eighteenth Century* as part of the *Proceedings of the Fourth International Congress on the Enlightenment* held in New Haven, Conn., in July 1975. On John Webster, Locke, and related questions see "Leibniz on Locke on Language," *American Philosophical Quarterly* 1 (1964), 165–188. On Condillac and on the nineteenth century, see *The Study of Language in England 1780–1860* (1967 Princeton), especially Chapters 1 and 6. "Locke's Reputation in nineteenth-century England," *The Monist* 55 392–422. "Condillac's speechless Statue," *Studia Leibnitiana.* Supplementa XV—Akten des II. Internationalen Leibniz-Kongresses, Hannover, 17–22. July 1972, Vol. 4. "Thoughts on Scaglione's *Classical Theory of Composition:* The Survival of 18th-century French Philosophy before Saussure," to appear in *Romance Philology* (May 1976). On "Cartesian linguistics," see "The History of Linguistics and Professor Chomsky," 1970, *Language* 46: 570–585; "Cartesian Linguistics: History or Fantasy?", *Language Sciences* No. 17: 1–12, October 1971 and the "Epilogue" to my forthcoming "The eighteenth Century, including Leibniz," to appear in *Current Trends in Linguistics,* Vol. 13, the *Historiography of Linguistics.* On Condillac, see also "The Tradition of Condillac: The Problem of the Origin of Language in the eighteenth Century and the Debate in the Berlin Academy Before Herder," in *Studies in the History of Linguistics,* edited by Dell Hymes (1974, Indiana University Press,) pp. 93–156.

DISCUSSION

Gordon W. Hewes, *Moderator*

Department of Anthropology
University of Colorado
Boulder, Colorado 80302

DR. SHERWOOD WASHBURN (*Department of Anthropology, University of California, Berkeley, Calif.*): I might make an historical comment. Discussions on origins of language have been going on for a long time as has been mentioned and will be repeatedly noted at this conference. In retrospect, it is odd that people thought these discussions could go on without any clear facts on the communication systems of nonhuman primates. In 1929 Yerkes and Yerkes published that it was "incredible" that so many generalizations had been made about the behavior of the great apes without any reliable information. The trustworthy accounts of communication in the great apes are: on the gorilla, Schaller in 1963, with information on communication greatly extended by Fossey in 1972; on the chimpanzee, Goodall 1968; on the orang, MacKinnon, 1974.

It is a sobering thought that *all* the generalizations about the behavior of the apes that have been used in social science were made a hundred years *before* there were any data—that did not worry anyone!

One point this conference might consider is what kind of information is needed about the behavior of the apes before generalizations can be usefully made. Should the sounds be studied as if they constituted an independent system? This is the usual practice, but in Fossey's paper she shows that the sounds may be described as a separate system or as falling in a small number of categories which always include gestures. These are two very different ways of looking at the same information. If scientists had been interested in communication (rather than language), and if they had started with the study of monkey communication, they would have found that gestures and postures were always important, and it would not have been necessary to discover kinesics, proxemics, or the importance of facial expressions. These would have been regarded as the foundations of communicative behavior.

In summary, reliable data on primate communication under natural conditions are recent, and there is still no agreement on how they should be collected or how they should be analyzed. So there is a long way to go before the most basic problems are settled.

DR. MARK LIBERMAN: I hesitate, in a way, to raise this question, since it is not directly related to the history of ideas about the origin of language; but it does bear on some points you made about Condillac that explained to me a fact I have always found puzzling; namely, that in the introduction to his work on chemistry, Lavoisier says, after citing Condillac at length, that he feels he has himself engaged in a fundamentally *linguistic* enterprise, namely the enterprise of giving "names" to chemicals. He actually presents this as the theoretical underpinning, the philosophical basis of what's really the foundation of modern chemistry. I always found that extremely puzzling, for it seemed to me not to relate in any way to what I had always been taught about what the philosophy of science was. What happened to that idea about what science was? Did it disappear completely during the following century? Does it reappear in other ways?

DR. AARSLEFF: You don't need to hesitate to ask that question, it is a good one, and it is immediately related to the problem of the origin of language. It falls, as it were, in the category of what I had in mind when I said that there are many other important problems in Condillac which I didn't have a chance to take up. As I think I said, the entire problem concerns not merely the origin of language, but also the nature of language, the nature of man, the extension of knowledge and even its quality, to so speak, as well as the improvement of teaching in order to secure efficient and correct communication of knowledge. You are right; the fact that Lavoisier credits the idea of the new chemical nomenclature to Condillac is significant, and it is entirely in line with Condillac's intentions. Some twenty years after Lavoisier, the same ideas were taken up by the French *idéologues*; they were radical followers of Condillac, and they wished to apply the same principles generally in an educational program that was designed to secure the advancement of knowledge and the perfectibility of man.

The principle follows from Condillac's basic doctrines. If thought and knowledge depend on the arbitrary signs man has created, on words, then the quality of knowledge, its truth, so to speak, depends on the suitability of the signs. In his later writings, Condillac developed the idea of a "well-made language"; that is, of good terminology as the precondition of good knowledge. This all indicates something that was prominent in the philosophy of language in the 17th and 18th centuries: It was always understood that it was not merely the aim of the philosophy of language to clear up something about the nature of language; it must also be applicable and provide results which, when put into effect, will improve communication, knowledge, science, teaching, and indeed all aspects of life and social living. When in my paper I tried to illustrate what was meant by the Adamic language, I think I said that it worked on much the same principle as chemical formulae do to us. Thus an improved terminology is, so to speak, a substitute for the language that man lost when Adam fell from the world of nearly perfect intellection. There is another example of a great nomenclator in the 18th century; namely, the Swedish botanist Linnaeus, who—on somewhat different principles than Condillac—believed that he was in fact recapturing the language of God. If you take a look at the index to my book *The Study of Language*, you will find a reference to Condillac and Lavoisier on the point you mentioned, as well as to other natural scientists who took up the same problem.

In the paper I also briefly referred to another striking example of the epistemological value of linguistic philosophy; namely, when I mentioned Mersenne, Locke, and the Royal Society. The Royal Society sponsored a very large work on a philosophical language, written by one of its prominent members, John Wilkins, and designed precisely to act as a substitute for the lost Adamic language. It did not meet its aim, but it was in the context of similar ideas and in part owing to Wilkins' work that Leibniz went to work on what we now call symbolic logic. Leibniz was acutely aware that knowledge and correct, even efficient and speedy reasoning depend on proper terms and symbols. In this sense the problem you have raised is indeed related to the philosophy of science.

Thus the problem was well known and seriously studied during the seventeenth and eighteenth centuries; indeed, also earlier. Has the idea now disappeared, or perhaps reappeared? No, I don't think it has disappeared, though it may not enter the perspective of most of us in quite the same obvious fashion as earlier, though I should think that the work of Carnap and other logicians would illustrate continued interest. Even without deeper philosophical searching, it is generally recognized that the maturity and success of new disciplines depend on the development of proper terms that ensure clear and unambiguous understanding of basic ideas. There are several examples of this occurring during the 19th and 20th centuries. One good example is the French mathematician and philosopher of science, Antoine Cournot, who was the founder of mathematical economics, a contribution of obvious importance. For our purposes, Cournot is especially interesting, because he was a great admirer of

Condillac, advocating his ideas at a time when few gave them any serious thought, and owing to this orientation, Cournot seems to have exercised a significant influence on the renewal of linguistics that occurred in France in the late 19th century, with the aim of overcoming the failure of German historical philology to say anything relevant about the philosophy of language. It is easy to perform a simple thought experiment that will illustrate the fruitful interaction of terminology and symbolization with advance in science. If we take a number of typical texts in one of the natural sciences, say physics, and arrange them in chronological order from the early 17th century to the present day, a mere glance at the pages will show the increasing use of special terms, signs, and symbols, all constituting an international language, so to speak, that is independent of the reader's native language. The 17th century was frustrated in its effort to create a general language suitable for all knowledge, but a somewhat similar result has been achieved within individual areas of study and knowledge. On the total spectrum of knowledge, a distinction is sometimes made between the "hard" natural sciences at one end (such as physics and chemistry) and the "soft" sciences at the other, for instance, the social sciences, with biology perhaps somewhere in between. Thus it is reasonable to think that moving the "soft" sciences toward the other end of the spectrum will involve continued efforts to repeat what Lavoisier and Berthollet were the first to do for chemistry.

Now, I may perhaps make a final observation by speculating for a minute on why you hesitated to ask your good question, for this relates directly to a matter that has long interested me, and to which I also referred in the paper. I think you hesitated because there is no ready way of gaining the sorts of information I have been talking about. Nineteenth-century German historical philology was so successful and institutionally powerful that it has contrived, with great self-interest, to make the world believe that there never was a legitimate, "scientific" study of language until it came along, and that it must forever remain the norm. This has largely been believed, and the histories we have all illustrate, even celebrate this ideology. That is why it is so hard to gain reliable and sympathetic knowledge and understanding of what was done in the seventeenth and eighteenth centuries, as well as in other periods. In fact, German historical philology does not merit the exclusive position that it has arrogated to itself in the history of the study of language. If the matters we have been talking about are interesting and fruitful, then they need to be known so that we can discuss them and perhaps even learn from them. Whether they can be known and again enter the realm of available information will depend on a good history of the study of language; that is, a history that does not make advance judgments by letting current doctrine determine who was right and who was wrong. Such a procedure will in any event merely create historical deception, for it will not be able to establish the sort of coherence we expect of history. Put in terms you may be familiar with, this is a question of internal vs. external history of science. I became aware of these problems more than a dozen years ago when I tried to make sense of the study of language in Europe and England over a period of some 200 years, from the seventeenth to the nineteenth centuries. Here the available histories gave small help. In the Introduction to a book on *The Study of Language in England*, published early in 1967, I therefore argued for a reorientation in the history of the study of language. This meant not only taking all modes of language study seriously, without prejudice, but also seeing them within the larger context of intellectual history and the history of science. I think my paper may have suggested that language study tends to be intimately related to the religious, intellectual or philosophical, and scientific concerns of the times, indeed even to political and social concerns, as already evident in the seventeenth century. Thus, in that Introduction, I argued for a new methodology that would apply to the history of the study of language in general, and I tried to illustrate that method in the book. I did this with specific reference to the example of the history of science owing to the distinguished though recent career of that discipline and its success at meeting conceptual problems and scholarly standards that will also have to be met by the history of linguistics if it is to be of any use and interest. As yet, there is little sign that the example has been followed; in fact, the current popularity of the subject has caused the publication of a mass of poorly informed and inferior work that gives little hope for the future. But if the history of the study of language some day meets the standards of the history of science, I have no doubt that many will take interest in the knowledge it makes available, as suggested by your relevant and fruitful question.

DR. HEWES: This has been principally a discussion of the history of the subject of the origin of language in Western thought. As far as I know, intellectual concern with the problem of the origin of language beyond legend or myth is not outstanding in any other major civilization, any other major literature such as Chinese, or even Indic philosophy (where there was, however, a well-developed system of grammar). There are myths about the origin of language, but they do not seem to have provoked the same kind of sharp exegesis as in the West. At the beginning of Prof. Aarsleff's talk there was mention of the blending of Greek and Judaic speculation. Would you agree with me that serious language-origins speculation is a uniquely Western development?

DR. AARSLEFF: Yes, but I feel I know hardly anything about the subject. I have wondered about this question and would, of course, like to know more, but I'm familiar only with the West.

It certainly would be interesting to know whether the Chinese, as a culture entirely separate from that of Western Europe, had anything to say on this subject.

The ancient Near East, of course, had a great deal to say about it, and I would assume that that is why we read about in in Genesis II and XI, for instance, and in fact it would seem that linguistic speculation of the mystical sort that becomes very influential and that has some features we would call Platonic and meta-NeoPlatonic, has its origin or its first base in the Eastern Mediterranean.

There is a great deal on this in the Greek Church Fathers, and much of the information one finds in them will flow into information that becomes available as a consequence of the Renaissance. But this is really all I can say about it. It would be fascinating to have good material for a comparison of what different cultures have done about this problem and which, indeed, have done anything? If one should learn that a major culture, for instance, the Chinese, never had worried about the problem, well, then, that would be very interesting information indeed.

Part II. Formulating the Target (I)

INTRODUCTION

Donald Davidson

Department of Philosophy
The Rockefeller University
New York, New York 10021

Human speech developed from something more primitive, something that was like speech but was not; the same is true, of course, of the history of each person. Apes and other beasts exhibit behavior more or less like human language behavior; less, in their natural state, and more, we are told, when artfully prodded. Although the facts about these prelinguistic and quasilinguistic states and events are not easy to come by, they can be counted on to be revealing. But how much we learn about language from the facts depends not only on expert, patient, and ingenious research, but also on our being able to describe the results of the research without distortion or unjustified assumptions. And here I want to call attention to a difficulty that arises when we try to express what the gestures, cries, babblings, or apparent words or sentences, of language-like behavior *mean*. There are problems enough in giving purely behavioral, phonetic, or syntactic descriptions of prelinguistic phenomena, but I shall fasten on the problem of semantic interpretation.

We tend to assume that we can interpret quasilinguistic behavior, whether in children or chimpanzees, by using some elementary subset of sentences drawn from our own developed language: the idea is that these simple sentences of ours give the meaning of the behavior or signs to be interpreted. But this idea, and the assumptions behind it, are not easy to justify. The general source of trouble is easy to identify: it is that even the simplest sentences of a language depend for their meaning on relations that hold between them and sentences with more complex structure, or sentences based on more sophisticated concepts. Because of the holistic character of the semantic aspect of language, it is wrong to suppose that a sentence (or word) belonging to a natural language would have the same meaning if its linguistic environment were radically impoverished. By the same token, there is no reason to suppose any element of prespeech behavior, or of animal communication, has the same meaning as the utterance of a word or sentence in a developed language.

Philosophy, at least since the time of Kant, has abounded with arguments designed to show that if one or another important part of the system of concepts with which we operate is lopped off, what remains cannot be made intelligible simply as the remainder; we may be quite unable to make clear sense of the truncated structure. The same point holds for language.

Formal semantics provides tools for illustrating the thesis. If a language or system of signs or signals can be treated as having only a finite number of complete message units (sentences, gestures, etc.), then an adequate semantics (at least in the sense of an account of the conditions under which messages are true or in some other way appropriate) does not have to read any structure into the sentences (message units) at all, no matter how prone we may be to think it is there. And so there is no clear justification, in such a case, for supposing we have much idea what such a "language" is about.

Merely adding analogs of the sentential connectives (on a par with conjunction, say, or sentential negation) makes the number of formally distinct sentences potentially infinite. But an adequate semantics still needs not discover any structure in the basic sentences. The only structure required is that carried by the connectives.

18

Even at this stage, then, the observed structure cannot be shown to contain prototypes of names, nouns, verbs, or predicates.

It is only when a language must be interpreted as having the means to express multiple generality—symbols for expressing what "all," "some," "any," and so forth do in English, and employed with scopes that overlap to an arbitrary degree of complexity—that our semantics is forced to impose on the language a systematic relation to objects, whether of people, spirits, stones, actions, or numbers. To put the matter differently, until a language, or language-like structure, is found to have expressive powers very similar to the most highly developed languages, we are apparently at a loss to make clear sense of what its sentences, or utterances, mean, or are about.

These remarks are based on certain assumptions about the right way of doing semantics. There are other approaches to semantics, and perhaps one of these will provide better means for describing the early stages in the development of language. In any case, a target emerges: to develop a nontendentious framework of concepts for the semantic analysis of prelinguistic behavior.

FRAME SEMANTICS AND THE
NATURE OF LANGUAGE*

Charles J. Fillmore

Department of Linguistics
University of California/Berkeley
Berkeley, California 94720

The decision to schedule sessions on "formulating the target" for the first day of this conference, based undoubtedly on the simple wisdom that knowing what a thing is like is a prerequisite to asking how it got that way, was probably also made in the hope that the target-formulating contributions might actually lead to some sort of consensus on the nature of language. Scholars inquiring into the origin of language will surely want to agree on at least some of the details of the last scene of the evolutionary scenario they are trying to construct. Unfortunately, the problem of describing this last scene is a notoriously difficult one: making clear the true nature of language is no trivial assignment, as I think everybody here is well aware.

As a contribution to at least a part of the understanding we need, I will present for your consideration a way of talking about one aspect of the process of communicating in a human language, something I will refer to as "framing." I choose this, not because I find it intrinsically more important than the formal structures of messages or meanings, or more important than the many global properties by which, from a more purely comparative perspective, human languages can be shown to differ from other communicating systems; I choose framing because I think it is important and because I suspect that it might not get mentioned, or that it might not be sufficiently highlighted, in the other papers to be read at this conference.

I mean by framing the appeal, in perceiving, thinking, and communicating, to structured ways of interpreting experiences. It is an alternative to the view that concepts or categories are formed through the process of matching sets of perceptual features with, say, words. I plan in this paper to justify the frames notion, to give a number of examples, mostly from English, of different kinds of frame structures, to suggest informally and intuitively how the frame concept can figure in the explanation of the communication and comprehension processes, and in the end to offer some hedged speculations on how the study of frames might appear in research on evolution toward language and on the evolution of language.

Thinkers who lacked a true evolutionary perspective could find questions like "What is the origin of language?" intelligible in a way that we cannot. We can envy the simplicity and admire the reasonableness of Samuel Johnson's speculations on the question.[1] Dr. Johnson argued as follows. If language was invented, it was invented either by children or adults; it could not have been invented by children, because children do not know enough to invent a language; it could not have been invented by adults, because adults are not pliable enough to learn a language; therefore the appearance of language in the history of mankind has to be due to divine inspiration.

*This work was sponsored in part by the National Science Foundation, grant no. SOC75-03538.

When the question of the origin of language is considered from an evolutionary perspective, it loses much of its clarity and simplicity. Should we be looking for the *first step* in the chain of events that led to what we now see as human language? The first step away from what? Or should we be trying to determine the *last step*, the step by which the final criterial property of language was acquired? What might that have been? Or is it perhaps some kind of a *key step* in this development that we need, that step by which was overcome the last serious barrier to the natural and inevitable sequence of changes that ended in the kind of language we have today? Or, are these the right alternatives? Since there is no evidence whatever on the nature of any of the intermediate stages along the great distance separating present-day language and even the most elaborated of the call systems, and since communication systems appear to have had different histories in different branches of the evolutionary tree, none of these questions may turn out to be useful. Ultimately, I believe, we can be satisfied with nothing short of the whole story, and for that we may need to reconstruct a long and complex chain of events.

Linguistic scholars, who have seldom felt called on to make anything more than slight lip-service acknowledgments of the problem of the origin of language, have generally not troubled themselves very much about these uncertainties. For example, one common suggestion found in the standard treatises and textbooks is that speech ultimately goes back to the involuntary cries of animals; to Sir Alan Gardiner the prototype was the squeal of a trapped rabbit.[2] A part of this story, as in Sapir's version,[3] is that the expressive vocalization, initially inseparable from the experience that caused it, came by some leap of imagination to be used as a name for the experience. This story gives the origin of language an account somewhat similar to the way ritualized movements among some animals are traced back to more directly functional movements appearing in acts of combat or surrender.

At least since the time of Gabelentz (1891)[4] there has been, in treatises on language, a standard list of factors in the development of man that were hospitable to the birth of language: the upright gait, the enlarged brain, the infant's long helplessness, and all the rest. Building pieces of a language-origin scenario around one or another of these has been a favorite and inexpensive pastime of grammarians and philologists for a long time. One such account, using the enlarged brain as the explanatory principle, is given by C. D. Buck.[5] Buck tells us that while many animals, including primitive man, had cries that expressed emotion, primitive man, because his brain was larger than that of any of his competitors, was alone able to gain "an awareness of a connection between the sound and something expressed by it." This account seems to require two magic wands, one for explaining why the size of the brain is relevant to the ability to perceive relationships, and the other for explaining how "an awareness of a connection" makes it possible to go further.

One of the most imaginative of the language-origin stories is found in Otto Jespersen's 1921 book on the nature, origin, and development of language.[6] Jespersen may have been the first to use actual linguistic data in guiding his speculations. He compared what he called "savage" languages with civilized languages, imputing to the primordial language features that predominate in "savage" languages; and he took a number of well-documented principles of language change and applied them backwards. Irregular forms tend in time to get regularized; the primitive language therefore lacked regular or recurring patterns of word formation. Long words tend in time to get shortened, and complex phonetic systems tend to get simplified; the primitive language abounded in very long words pronounced with an exuberant variety of difficult sounds. "Savage" languages tend to have tones; the long and phonetically intricate words in the primitive language were sung, not spoken. Many words for abstract or general concepts in modern languages originally had concrete or specific meanings; words in the primitive language were names of highly specific objects.

The Jespersen scenario begins with people devising individual courtship and battle songs, using in them as wide a variety of sounds as their vocal equipment and their inventiveness would allow them. To the members of a familiarity group, each of these personal songs came to be associated with its singer, as a kind of Wagnerian *leitmotiv*. Within the group, one person could refer to another by imitating his song. The song, thus, became a proper name—and what, Jespersen asks, could be more concrete and specific than a proper name? Once this naming relationship got established within a group, it became possible for people to use a proper name to refer to some trait of the owner of that name, or to remind the group of some event in that individual's history. On this base, then, the processes of analogy and simplification did their work.

Just one of the reasons why all of these stories are unsatisfying is that they end too soon. The last scene has got to be more than a state in which people name things and evoke memories.

Suggestions about the origin of language are frequently embedded in discussions of the essential or criterial features of language. And in the way that many language-origin stories have concentrated on single critical events, many inquiries into language essentials are concerned with the discovery of some single trait or cluster of traits that separates human language from everything else. The attempt to give a "key feature" definition of language has had some of the same kind of history that we see in the definition of man, namely one in which the official definition undergoes changes, not because of new knowledge about the thing being defined, but through the discovery of new facts about the rest of the world. Changes in the definition of man have been forced, not by anybody's having found out anything new about the nature of man, but by observations about sea otters and chimpanzees; in the same way, many proposals on the nature of language have had to be rejected because of discoveries about rhesus monkeys, computing machines, or the language of deaf-mutes.

I think there is much to be gained by separating the effort to characterize language from the effort to determine what is uniquely human in language. The question, "What can folks do that beasts can't?" need not be regarded as a necessary part of the inquiry into the nature of human language. There are certain general dangers in the comparative approach to characterizing language. The comparative approach sometimes invites scholars to take positions on badly understood issues that in any case have no relevance to their main work. The Gardners report their annoyance at the question, "At what point would you be ready to announce that Washoe has a language?".[7] They wisely rejected this question, because no matter what stand they had taken, fruitless polemic and endless misunderstandings would have been the result. Linguists trying to formulate their view on the nature of language would be wise to avoid such a trap.

Linguists, especially those working within the generativist tradition, take as their main goal that of characterizing the set of abilities that together make up an individual's knowledge of his language. In order to separate purely linguistic from other sorts of knowledge, certain abstractions and idealizations are thought to be necessary: the linguist's observations are first of all abstracted away from the contexts in which they occur; that is, they are isolated from the larger behaviors which they interpenetrate; and second, the observations undergo certain "editing" functions to

eliminate mistakes and "noise" caused by factors in the speaker and in the environment that are not related to the speaker's purely linguistic competences. Once these
adjustments are made, the linguist strives to capture the *regularities* detected in his
data by formulating *rules* imputable to his subjects.

The part of linguistic knowledge that can be represented by rules makes up the
grammar of the speaker's language; the part that cannot be so represented—that is,
the part that represents item-by-item knowledge—makes up the *lexicon*. In one part,
at least, a language system can be described by stating the rules of its grammar and by
listing and describing the items in its lexicon.

In this view, what is common across languages, in the form and substance of the
rules, in the contents and organization of the lexicon, in the dependencies and
redundancies in the system, is taken as representing the nature of language in general,
that is, as indicating the universal properties of human language. The parts of this
universal structure that cannot be accounted for by appeal to common experiences or
uniformities in the environment are imputed to innate structures in the human mind,
that is, to capacities innate to the species.

I have no quarrel with this program as far as it goes; but I feel sure that for many
purposes we need to add to this approach an awareness of the importance of the
social functions of language, a concern with the nature of the speech production and
comprehension processes, and an interest in the relationships between what a speaker
says and the context in which he says it.

My effort is to look for what can be known about the workings of language
through a consideration of the processes of communication. A proposal that I favor
is that in characterizing a language system we must add to the description of
grammar and lexicon a description of the cognitive and interactional "frames" in
terms of which the language-user interprets his environment, formulates his own
messages, understands the messages of others, and accumulates or creates an internal
model of his world. The evolution *toward* language must have consisted in part in the
gradual acquisition of a repertory of frames and of mental processes for operating
with them, and eventually the capacity to create new frames and to transmit them. In
considering the evolution *of* language, we may find that degrees of general language
complexity among the attested languages can be described partly in terms of the
relative extent of elaboration of the system of frames and of the ways in which these
are codified in the vocabulary and in the grammatical categories of the language.

There are several notions that make up the background to what I have in mind,
and these are: the concept of context, the concept of prototype or paradigm case, the
notion "frame" or "schema" as it is used in recent work in psychology and artificial
intelligence, and the notion that sometimes goes by the name of "semantic memory."

In discussions of meaning, the notion of context appears in several different
contexts. We can speak of the context of an utterance (or utterance fragment) and
intend by that either the real-world situation in which the utterance is produced or
the other utterances that surround it in a discourse. We can also speak of the context
of the experience or percept that makes up the base of our understanding of a word.
The linguist has good reasons for regarding the description of context, in any of these
senses, as an added complexity in his job of describing a language; but unfortunately,
it has been easy for linguists to think of knowledge of context as an added complexity
for the language-user as well.

It is easy to believe that the following description predicts the scale of complexity
for the language-user. At one level a speaker is able to pronounce, say, the utterance,

"Good morning, sir." At another level he knows that by saying "Good morning, sir" he can succeed in greeting his addressee. That is an additional piece of knowledge, beyond merely knowing how to pronounce the sentence. At a third level he can also know that the greeting is appropriate only during a certain part of the day; that the person greeted with this utterance should be a male adult to whom the speaker owes, or wishes to suggest that he owes, a certain level of deference; and that such a greeting is appropriately addressed to the same person at most once per morning. This "pragmatic" knowledge represents a third degree of complexity. We have, at one level, the ability to produce an utterance; at another level, an awareness of the particular function that can be served by a performance of this utterance; and at a third level, the knowledge of the appropriate and meaningful contexts in which this purpose can be achieved with this utterance.

The important question to ask, of course, is whether complexity for the analyst reflects complexity for the participant. The argument that it in general does not comes from work on behavior and perception. Goldstein and Scheerer have argued from their work with aphasic patients that behaviors separated from meaningful contexts are a greater cognitive challenge than the same behaviors in context;[8] and Rudolf Arnheim reports that art students studying the techniques of realistic painting need to learn to decontextualize the objects of their perception in order to become aware of the "real" nature of their color perceptions, in order to eliminate color constancy effects.[9] In these examples, acts and judgments that require abstraction from context are cognitively more complex than the kinds of acts and judgments that occur naturally in context.

These facts about context and perception are relevant to the theory of language in two ways. First, the meanings of words may, more than we are used to thinking, depend on contexted experiences; that is, the contexts within which we have experienced the objects, properties or feelings that provide the perceptual or experential base of our knowledge of the meaning of a word (or phrase, or grammatical category) may be inseparable parts of those experiences. Second, the process of interpreting an utterance may depend, more than we are used to thinking, on our perception of the context in which the utterance is produced and our memories of the contexts for earlier experiences with the utterance or its constituent parts.

A second notion needed for the concept of framing is that of the prototype or paradigm case. The notion figures importantly in the Philosophical Investigations of Ludwig Wittgenstein,[10] is adumbrated in the writings of the German semantic theorist Karl Erdmann,[11] and plays a role in recent work in psychology on category formation, especially that of Eleanor Rosch.[12] The idea is that in order to perceive something or to attain a concept, what is at least sometimes necessary is to have in memory a repertory of prototypes, the act of perception or conception being that of recognizing in what ways an object can be seen as an instance of one or another of these prototypes. This "situating" process depends not only on the existence of individual prototypes, but also on the character of the whole available repertory of prototypes. A child's seeing a squirrel as a "funny looking kitty" (taken from Woodworth's discussion of "reification"[13]) is one example of this kind of perception; the description of a 170° angle as a "bent stick" is another (that example from Arnheim[9]).

The appeal to prototypes is to be distinguished from the idea of perception according to which the perceiver consults a checklist of criterial properties. In the extent to which knowledge of word meanings involves knowledge of prototypes, a typical device in linguistics for representing meaning, namely, in terms of clusters of semantic features, however well it may serve the purposes of linguistic theory, may not be usable in describing the language-comprehension process.

A particularly important notion, figuring especially in recent work in linguistics, cognitive psychology, and artificial intelligence, is the notion that goes by such names as "frame," "schema," and "scenario." Briefly, the idea is that people have in memory an inventory of schemata for structuring, classifying, and interpreting experiences, and that they have various ways of accessing these schemata and various procedures for performing operations on them. Some of the schemata may be physiologically built in (such as various aspects of the body schema, the identity of the focal hues in the color spectrum, and perhaps what the gestalt psychologists call "good figures"— see Rosch[12]), others may owe their existence to perceived constant cause-effect relationships in the world, while still others may depend for their existence on symbolization.

The concept of frame does not depend on language, but as applied to language processing the notion figures in the following way. Particular words or speech formulas, or particular grammatical choices, are associated in memory with particular frames, in such a way that exposure to the linguistic form in an appropriate context activates in the perceiver's mind the particular frame—activation of the frame, by turn, enhancing access to the other linguistic material that is associated with the same frame.

A language has both interactional frames and cognitive or conceptual frames. The most explicit proposal for including interactional frames in a description of a language is found in Dell Hymes's paper on the ethnography of speaking.[14] The interactional frames amount to a categorization of the distinguishable contexts of interaction in which speakers of a language can expect to find themselves, together with information about the appropriate linguistic choices relevant to these interactions. One simple example is the greeting frame. In some languages a greeting frame specifies that the socially superior initiate the greeting, in some it is the socially inferior, while in others the initiator role is unassigned or is based on other considerations; in all languages the form of a greeting is determined from a restricted inventory of topics and expressions, many of these dependent on highly specific contextual conditions. A part of knowing a language is knowing or recognizing a large number of such frames, and knowing what linguistic choices are relevant for each of them.

Here is an example of a cognitive frame. There is in English, and presumably in every language spoken by a people with a money economy, a semantic domain connected with what we might call the commercial event. The frame for such an event has the form of a scenario containing roles that we can identify as the buyer, the seller, the goods, and the money; containing subevents within which the buyer surrenders the money and takes the goods and the seller surrenders the goods and takes the money; and having certain institutional understandings associated with the ownership changes that take place between the beginning and the end of each such event. Any one of the many words in our language that relate to this frame is capable of accessing the entire frame. Thus, the whole commercial event scenario is available or "activated" in the mind of anybody who comes across and understands any of the words "buy," "sell," "pay," "cost," "spend," "charge," etc., even though each of these highlights or foregrounds only one small section of the frame. Each of these words, so to speak, brings along with it simultaneously a ground and a figure, simultaneously a setting and the piece of that setting to which the word is pointing.

As a second and quite different kind of example of cognitive frames, we can consider (borrowing from Coseriu[15]) the Greek nouns *brotos* and *anthropos*. They both designate man. But the first presents man as one term of a contrast set in which the other is god; the second presents man as one term in a contrast set in which the other is animal. *Brotos* designates man as non-god, *anthropos* designates man as non-beast. Each word simultaneously identifies the creature and the larger framework or context within which the creature is being spoken of.

Another important notion in writings on language understanding is that of a speaker/hearer's ongoing model of the world, this conceived of as some kind of network of interlinked relationships representing bits of knowledge and the ways in which these bits of knowledge are integrated into a more or less coherent model or image of the world. Associated with this concept is the view that in an act of communication, one person affects the content of another person's world model. The term "semantic memory" is used by Quillian for what I have in mind;[16] the word "image" has a meaning something like this in the work of Kenneth Boulding.[17]

This model or image is thought of as including a record of the individual's beliefs about the world, a filtered and partly interpreted record of his past experiences, a current register of information about his position in space, time, and society, together with his version of the world-models of the other relevant people in his environment.

The process of communication can be seen as involving one person saying something that will induce another person to change his model of the world. In Boulding's words, "The meaning of a message is the change which it produces in the images."[17] This process involves appeal to contexts, because current, imagined and remembered contexts make up part of the model; it involves frames, because frames, in the sense I have in mind, provide the building blocks for constructing the pieces of the model; and it involves prototypes, because many of our framing abilities require a knowledge of prototypes.

The proposal I am representing is made up of the concepts I have just reviewed. I will state the proposal in an extreme form, for the enhanced clarity that I hope will attend such a formulation; the necessary hedges and qualifications are to be filled in by the cooperative listener.

Every memorable experience occurs in a meaningful context and is memorable precisely because the experiencer has some cognitive schema or frame for interpreting it. This frame identifies the experience as a type and gives structure and coherence—in short, meaning—to the points and relationships, the objects and events, within the experience.

Individual words are learned within such meaningful contexts, and each word serves to foreground some part of the context. For example, it is probably true that American children first learn the nouns "orange" and "grapefruit" through the experience of eating them in the ways we typically eat them: the one by peeling it and breaking it into its natural segments, the other by cutting it in half and eating it with a spoon. A student in my department reports that a group of seven-year-old children were not willing to accept as anything but an orange a grapefruit she was eating the way one eats an orange. It may be that the first frames these children acquired for these fruits were scenarios that included specific ways of eating them, and that only later are these to be replaced by a naming frame based on context-free perceptual properties.

We sometimes find that a single word has concurrently more than one frame, even though the same history of experiences was responsible for both frames. This appears to be true of the English noun "breakfast." This word identifies the first meal in the day, presupposing a community in which more than one meal is eaten per day and in which one of those is eaten shortly after the end of one's nightly sleep. In the first instance the word is associated with a complex frame made up of the frame for the divisions of the day and a frame for an eating pattern of the kind familiar to us, placing in the foreground the first meal of the day. It is by having this complex frame, with the time of day as an essential element, that a speaker of English can understand a sentence like, "The Wongs always have chicken soup for breakfast." The same word is also associated, however, with a particular familiar combination of foods typically eaten as breakfast, in America this being most typically fried eggs and toast with fairly restricted possibilities for substitution, omission, and extension. It is this frame for the word which makes it possible for a speaker of English to understand a cafe sign that reads, "Breakfast served any time." In short, a meal can satisfy the breakfast prototype in either of two ways and still deserve the name.

In general, a word can be linked to its meaning in any of three ways, and we can refer to these as *functional, criterial,* and *associational.* Identifying "breakfast" with one in a structured pattern of meals is functional; identifying it with a particular collection of foods is associational. Katherine Nelson discusses the child's acquisition of the meaning of the word "ball," which begins with a functional concept, that of a particular set of things played with in particular settings and with particular people, and ends with the criterial concept, having to do with sphericity and bounceability.[18] Wittgenstein discusses the word "disease" and points out that diseases are sometimes identified functionally, by their symptoms, and sometimes criterially, by their causes.[19] We can say either that a certain disease has symptoms shared by other diseases, thus separating the notion from a particular syndrome, or we can say that a certain disease has no known cause, thus separating the concept of disease from a disease's causes.

Given the assumption about framing and word meaning that I have been suggesting, we can say that the process of understanding a word requires us to call on our memories of experiences—selected, filtered, and generalized—through which we have learned the words in their labeling or describing functions. It follows, of course, that the kinds of understandings I have been talking about can be communicated only between people who share the requisite frames. People who eat only one meal a day will not need the word meaning what "breakfast" means; people who believe that all diseases are caused by evil spirits will not have separate frames for diseases according to symptoms and causes. Similarly, in a society which lacks the institution of marriage and which uniformly practices free love, there can be no word for cuckold, or wittol either.

Lexical framing contributes in important ways to the comprehension of sentences and larger utterances. The following examples will show something of how that works. Imagine that two men spend a short period of time in San Francisco, the two doing more or less similar things during their visit. Then suppose that after the experience one of them writes home, "I spent two hours on land this afternoon," and the other writes home, "I spent two hours on the ground this afternoon." The process of understanding the sentence with "on land" requires having a frame for sea voyages and knowing that people engaged in sea voyages spend part of their time "on land" and part of their time "at sea," and knowing that these phrases identify the two states given in the frame. To understand the sentence with "on the ground" is to know about air travel, and to know that the two alternating states in an extended period of air travel are called being "on the ground" and "in the air." In understanding these sentences, we have not merely activated these two-state frames, but we have also made use of the fact that the sentences begin with "I" (first person) and "spent" (past tense) and contain the time-deictic expression "this afternoon." Since the person is speaking of himself within a two-state temporal frame, and since he refers to his being in one of the two states in the past, we conclude that at the time of writing he is in the other state. The one man wrote his letter while at sea, the other wrote his in the air. One of the most characteristic features of intelligent activity is knowing more than you are told (on this point see Lindsay[20]); one of the ways in which people accomplish this in speech understanding is by using knowledge of lexical and grammatical frames.

Many objects, persons, and experiences in the world are framed in terms of their potential role in supporting, harming, or enhancing people's lives or interests. We can know that this is so if we know how to interpret expressions in which such things are evaluated—expressions containing, for example, the word "good" or "bad." We readily understand the phrases "a good chair," "a good steak," and "a good teacher," because we know in what ways a chair or a steak or a teacher can be life-enhancing. We have to work a little harder to understand phrases like "a good leaf," "a good triangle," or "a good widow," because we cannot count on any scenario we might invent as being the one the speaker had in mind. The act of understanding the simple word "good" requires us to find an appropriate dimension of evaluation. If we can do this immediately when the phrase with "good" is given to us out of context, that is a measure of the extent to which the head nouns come with ready-made function-identifying scenarios. That we can sometimes do this successfully by appealing to contextual information that is evidence of the creative aspect of the language comprehension process. In either case, the evidence supports the point of this paper, that the process of language understanding is a creative process and that it depends on the language-user's ability to use language to indicate ways of framing experience.

When I spoke earlier of the commercial event frame and the large collection of words that are linked with this frame, I pointed out that the experience of confronting any one of these words will activate the entire frame. It is obvious, of course, that any sentence containing one of these words could have the effect of introducing other frames, these getting hooked up with the commercial event frame in such a way as to determine some piece of the resulting model of the information in the text. Examples of how the interlinking of different frames works can be seen in the following: consider an event within which one person gives money to another person (equivalent to one of the subevents in the commercial event frame), and consider the words we can use in English for naming that money, or that presentation of money. Almost anything that we call it will introduce a new frame. To get a sense of the variety possible, consider the larger scene that you find yourselves imagining when you know that the money that changed hands was a bribe, or a tip, or ransom, or change, or rebate, or alimony. Each of these words is understood as naming a quantity of money that changes ownership in one kind of event, but it simultaneously locates that event within a larger history about which a number of details are known.

One of the goals of the kind of frame semantics that I am speaking for is that of having a uniform representation for word meanings, sentence meanings, text interpretations, and world models. The word "alimony" links together a frame involving money transfer with a frame that identifies an occurrence in two people's life histories in a fairly specific way. Understanding this word requires knowing the whole scenario; understanding a sentence containing this word requires knowing the scenario and using the lexical contents and grammatical structure of the rest of the sentence to fill in some of the details; understanding a large text containing such a sentence may require situating a scene described by this text as a well-defined part of a larger story or state of affairs. Furthermore, the representation of an individual's model of the world might include information about the people the individual knows that is structured in ways similar to the frames needed for linguistic description.

A frame is a kind of outline figure with not necessarily all of the details filled in. If I tell you that I bought a new pair of shoes, you do not know where I bought them or how much they cost, but you know, by virtue of the frame I have introduced into our discourse, that there have got to be answers to those questions. Comprehension can be thought of as an active process during which the comprehender—to the degree that it interests him—seeks to fill in the details of the frames that have been introduced, either by looking for the needed information in the rest of the text, by filling it in from his awareness of the current situation, or from his own system of beliefs, or by asking his interlocutor to say more.

The ultimate correct theory will have to provide for the ways in which the interpreter of a text acts creatively to build a detailed model of the text, it will have to show how specific lexical items in specific grammatical relation to each other (as suggested by the adjective-noun constructions in which the adjective is "good") constrain the way in which the creative structuring takes place, and it will have to show (as we saw in "alimony") how individual lexical items can bring along with them fairly large pre-packaged complex frames.

We can speak of a single integration of the instruments of a language—phonetic, semantic, syntactic—as a language *system*, using that term independently of whether we have in mind the system of an individual or that of an entire speech community. One aspect of a linguistic system, I have been arguing, consists in the ways in which the language user's cognitive and interactional frames are linked up with linguistic material. One way of examining a linguistic system, then, is that of providing an inventory of the frames that have linguistic reflexes, paying attention to the number of frames, to the areas of special elaboration, to the degree to which complex frames have been prepackaged in lexical meanings, to the structure and complexity of the frames, and so on.

The classification of frame types, for example, can be used in analyzing the vocabulary of a language. This analysis can begin at the one end with lexical items that have relatively simple word-to-world mappings, such as the names of colors or the names of natural kinds, and can continue on to the highly elaborated conceptual frameworks that presuppose subtle sorts of knowledge about the intellectual and institutional life of a people.

We may find from such a survey that certain kinds of frames are missing from language systems whose users lack certain kinds of training. To give a simple example, the word "angle," in connection with its simple perceptual frame, designates a simple two-straight-lines figure of the kind that easily permits closure with a straight line. Such an angle would be described by people who have the more technical frame as an angle between 0° and 180° but not too close to either end. Only people with special training will have this additional abstract or procedural frame for the word, this second frame involving the imaginary rotation of a line around a point and measurement of the arc created by this rotation. This frame for "angle" is the one that lends itself to certain mathematical purposes, but it is no longer a perceptual "given."

Once we have, at least for some domains of thought and action, descriptions of frame inventories, it will than be possible to compare different language sytems with respect to their range of communicative possibilites. If we had any extant primitive languages to work with, we would, of course, wish to compare those with some of the fully developed languages, and learn something about the course of language evolution directly; but unfortunately we do not. Yet there may be other kinds of comparisons we could make that would give indirect evidence, or at least some useful hunches. By studying the developing language system of a child we may be able to get a fairly good idea of which frames are conceptual or developmental prerequisites to which other frames. A study of the cognitive potential of a developing language system will be more reliable if it is based on an examination of frames than if it is based on some superficial measure such as vocabulary size. As we have seen with words like "ball," "angle," and "disease," the measure of the conceptual richness of a language system cannot be predicted from an inventory of its vocabulary.

There are, throughout the world, auxiliary trade languages called pidgins, and in many places creole languages developing, or developed, out of them. It may be fruitful to examine the frame inventories of a creole language before and after creolization. Since pidgins were created as auxiliary languages by people who already spoke fully formed regular languages, there is no compelling reason to believe that the course of the evolution of language followed the kind of development seen in the creolization process, but it is not unreasonable to believe that some insights on the growth and elaboration of a language system could result from such an inquiry.

It should also be possible to use frame analysis for studying what happens to a language when its community acquires a writing system and moves toward civilization. Before the introduction of writing, languages are generally restricted in their use to direct, typically face-to-face, interactions. The more highly developed languages will differ from these in having mechanisms that facilitate more public uses: uses, for example, in which the sender and the receiver know very little about each other's model of the world, in which sender and receiver are separated by space and time, and in which mechanisms exist that compensate for the absence of a shared context and the use of paralinguistic signaling systems. The very least the more advanced languages will have is a vocabulary appropriate for talking about the writing system; but it is likely to have more rigidly codified mechanisms for coreference and anaphora and less dependency on demonstrative elements, and it is likely to have developed grammatical and rhetorical mechanisms for enhancing sustained reasoning.

Another area of research to which an analysis of frames can offer some contribution is the question of whether the possession of language is a necessary condition for the existence of certain cognitive abilities. The correct answer to the question is undoubtedly going to be some version of Arnheim's conclusion that language facilitates but is not necessary for thinking.[9] Given an analysis of frames and their combinability into larger conceptual structures, it ought to be possible to learn which particular styles and strategies of thinking are especially enhanced through the use of language; in that way such issues as whether languageless thought deserves to be called thought can be replaced by more substantive concerns.

Similarly, some clarity could be brought, through frame analysis, to the question of whether the faculty of *abstraction* is in some sense restricted to possessors of human language. After disposing of the narrowest view of abstraction—by which the use of language is the only evidence of abstraction—and the broadest view of abstraction—by which animals at play are engaged in abstraction—attention can be turned to the different senses in which lexical items have been described as abstract. The words people have called "abstract" differ greatly in their frame structure, as can be readily understood by imagining the frames that would be needed for such words as "color," "angle" (in its procedural sense), and "charity." In asking what sorts of abstractions nonhumans are capable of, the many different kinds of "abstraction" will need to be examined separately. As with the question of language and thought, here too is a case where a large and general question needs to be replaced by a set of smaller, more precise questions.

The remarks I have presented in this paper were introduced as offering a contribution to our understanding of the nature of language. In some ways of defining that question I have probably failed. I have felt that an important aspect of the workings of a language is what people go through in the experience of using a language. I suspect that human language must have evolved, and must now be structured, in ways that allow the framing and model-building and coherence-imputing processes in language communication to do their work. Fortunately, it is possible to study these processes without having to worry about which of them are unique to language, or even which of them are unique to man.

ACKNOWLEDGMENT

The author is indebted to Paul Kay for some much-needed advice in the preparation of one portion of this paper.

REFERENCES

1. BOSWELL, J. 1791. Life of Samuel Johnson LL.D. (Year 1783).
2. GARDINER, A. 1951. The Theory of Speech and Language. The Clarendon Press. Oxford, England.
3. SAPIR, E. 1933. Symbolism. *In* Encyclopedia of the Social Sciences.: 565. Reprinted in MANDELBAUM, D. G. 1949. Selected Writings of bedward Sapir. University of California Press. Berkeley, Calif.
4. GABELENTZ, G. v. D. 1891. Sprachwissenschaft. Leipzig, Germany.
5. BUCK, C. D. 1949. A Dictionary of Selected Synonyms in the Principal Indo-European Languages. A Contribution to the History of Ideas. University of Chicago Press. Chicago, Ill.
6. JESPERSEN. J. O. 1921. Language: Its Nature, Development and Origin. Reprinted in 1964. Norton and Company. New York, N.Y.
7. GARDNER, R. A. & B. T. GARDNER. 1969. Teaching sign language to a chimpanzee. Science 165: 664–672.
8. GOLDSTEIN, K. & M. SCHEERER. 1941. Abstract and concrete behavior. Psychol. Monogr. 53: 239. (Cited in Ref. 9.)
9. ARNHEIM, R. 1969. Visual Thinking. University of California Press. Berkeley, Calif.
10. WITTGENSTEIN, L. 1953. Philosophical Investigations. Blackwell. Oxford, England.
11. ERDMANN, K. 1910. Die Bedeutung des Wortes. Aufsätze aus dem Grenzgebiet der Sprachpsychologie und Logik. Leipzig, Germany.
12. ROSCH, E. 1973. Natural categories. Cog. Psychol. 4: 328–350.
13. WOODWORTH, R. S. 1938. Experimental Psychology. Henry Holt. New York, N.Y.
14. HYMES, D. H. 1962. The ethnography of speaking. *In* Anthropology and Human Behavior. T. Gladwin and W. C. Sturtevant, Eds. Anthropological Society of Washington. Washington, D.C. Reprinted in Readings in the Sociology of Language. J. Fishman, Ed.: 99–138. Mouton. The Hague, The Netherlands.
15. COSERIU, E. 1966. Structure lexicale et enseignement du vocabulaire. Actes du Premier Colloque International de Linguistique Appliquée. Nancy, France.
16. QUILLIAN, M. R. 1968. Semantic memory. *In* Semantic Information Processing. M. Minsky, Ed.: 216–270. MIT Press. Cambridge, Mass.

17. BOULDING, K. E. 1956. The Image. University of Michigan Press. Ann Arbor, Mich.
18. NELSON, K. 1974. Concept, word, and sentence: interrelations in acquisition and development. Psychol. Rev. **81:** 267–285.
19. WITTGENSTEIN, L. 1960. The Blue and Brown Books: 25. Blackwell. Oxford, England.
20. LINDSAY, R. K. 1963. Inferential memory as the basis of machines which understand natural language. *In* Computers and Thought. E. A. Feigenbaum & J. Feldman, Eds.: 217–233. McGraw-Hill. New York, N.Y.

A HYPOTHESIS ABOUT THE
UNIQUENESS OF NATURAL LANGUAGE*

Jerrold J. Katz

Linguistics and Philosophy Graduate Programs
The Graduate Center of the City University of New York
New York, New York 10036

Descartes made the following claim:

> ... none are so depraved and stupid, without even excepting idiots, that they cannot arrange different words together, forming of them a statement by which they make known their thoughts; while, on the other hand, there is no other animal, however perfect and fortunately circumstanced it may be, which can do the same.[1]

This claim has fared far better than Descartes's other, more famous claim about the seat of the soul. Research specifically designed to disprove Descartes's claim that language is a uniquely human attribute has left it entirely intact, whereas research undertaken with no motive to confirm or disconfirm the claim has strengthened it.

The Gardners, Premack, and others take issue with Descartes's claim, arguing, on the contrary, that if chimps are so "fortunately circumstanced" as to be in training with the proper psychologists, they can be taught a language or something differing only inessentially from a language. Their empirical results, however, fail to shake Descartes's claim. For example, Washoe and Sarah string words together to make their thoughts known, but they do not form genuine sentences. Nothing in the chimp studies to date suggests that these animals can do anything more significant than a dog or cat does when it rings a bell to communicate its desire to go outside. A chimp does, of course, acquire a far more complex set of discriminations in learning to arrange chips as a signal for food than a dog or cat does in learning to ring a bell, but such a difference in degree does not amount to *the* difference in kind required to refute Descartes's claim. Concluding their examination of Premack's work, Fodor *et al.* express this point as follows:

> ... *all* of what Premack calls productivity in Sarah's use of language consists in her "generalizing" from the trained content. . . . there is no indication that Sarah has ever done the most characteristic thing that a productive syntax permits human speakers to do; namely, use a sentence of a syntactically novel form without being specifically trained on sentences of that form. Productivity in human languages exploits iterative syntactic mechanisms which generate *novel constituent sequences.*[2]

In short, chimps fail to produce the novel constituent structures from which we can infer internalized syntactic rules.

Descartes had empirical support for his claim that language is uniquely human. He pointed out that

> ... men who, being born deaf and dumb, are in the same degree, or even more than the brutes, destitute of the organs which serve the others for talking, are in the habit of themselves inventing certain signs by which they make themselves understood.[1]

Recent work on American Sign strengthens this argument by producing evidence that the "gesture language" of the deaf is not essentially different from spoken natural languages.[3] Since a gesture system can qualify as a natural language, and since

---

*The author wishes to thank Virginia Valian for valuable criticism of an earlier draft.

33

chimps can produce as wide a range of gestural configurations as can humans, it would seem that the best hypothesis to explain why chimps never develop a gesture natural language is simply that they lack the capacity to acquire any natural language.

The question to which Descartes addressed himself is Aristotle's question of what makes human beings unique. The question to which we address ourselves here is what makes natural languages unique. Even if natural language is not uniquely human, it can still differ from other communication systems. For example, if it were to turn out that porpoises have the capacity for natural language, we would still be in the dark about the nature of the communication system we share with porpoises. This can be seen from the following Gedunken experiment. You've just seen the TV broadcast of the first English-Porpoise bilingual performing feats of English-Porpoise translation comparable to any other feats of translation. Do you now know any more about the *nature* of natural language?

Although the two questions are conceptually distinct, they are by no means unrelated. One way to see their relation is to note that those with the same philosophical outlook will answer the two questions in the same way. Rationalists like Chomsky follow Descartes in claiming both that natural language is uniquely human and that natural language is qualitatively different from even the most elaborate and highly ramified associative systems. Empiricists like Skinner are disposed to think that natural languages may well not be uniquely human and that what is special about them, if anything, is merely the great complexity of the associative connections making them up. The reason for these preferences is not hard to see.

Rationalists hold that the acquisition of linguistic competence is to be explained as a process in which innate schemata expressing the form of a grammar are realized as particular hypotheses about the grammatical structure of a language. Empiricists, on the other hand, take the language learner's hypotheses to be determined by the form of the distributional regularities in the available speech sample. Empiricists emphasize the environment by taking the rules of a language to be inductive extrapolations from observed regularities. Thus, the empiricist's case for an environmental basis for natural language would be confirmed if it were the case that the more intelligent the species, the more language it can learn (assuming that conditions are constructed to compensate for such irrelevant things as vocalization limitations). On the other hand, the rationalist's case for a genetic basis for natural language would be confirmed if the presence and absence of language were to coincide with the dramatic species difference between humans and nonhumans.

The uniqueness of language is also relevant to the rationalist-empiricist controversy. If what is unique about natural language is simply its greater degree of associative connections, then empiricist models of learning offer plausible accounts of how languages are learned. If, instead, what is unique about natural languages is something entirely different from a network of associative connections, then some rationalist account postulating innate schemata rich enough to explain the special structure of natural languages will be necessary.

Recent work in transformational grammar shows that a rationalist account of some sort is necessary. This work reveals levels of underlying syntactic and semantic structure that make it unreasonable to suppose that the rules of a language are acquired inductively from distributional relations in the superficial form of actual utterances.† But, beyond saying this, it is not clear what can be said about the relative

---

† The argument, made by Chomsky and others, is, in a nutshell, that the underlying syntactic and semantic structure to a great extent has no reflection in the observable form of sentences, so

contributions of nature and nurture. Research in psycholinguistics based on transformational grammar has had surprisingly little to say about the properties of a model of language acquisition. There is, to be frank, no nativistic acquisition model to which one might turn after rejecting empiricist models. Further, rationalist linguists have had equally little to say about the uniqueness of natural language. There are only scattered suggestions, principally by Chomsky himself. In this paper, I will try to take a small step toward remedying the latter deficiency by putting forth a hypothesis about the uniqueness of natural language that is at least not obviously too weak to work.‡

Chomsky reports that the Cartesians suggested "the creative aspect of language use" as "the essential and defining characteristic of human language." (Ref. 1, p. 19.)

> ... man has a species specific capacity ... which manifests itself in what we may refer to as the "creative aspect" of ordinary language use—its property of being both unbounded in scope and stimulus-free. Thus Descartes maintains that language is available for the free expression of thought or for appropriate response in any new context and is undetermined by any fixed association of utterances to external stimuli or physiological states. (Ref. 1, pp. 4–5).

There are, then, three components to the creative aspect of language use. First, there is *unboundedness*: this is understood as depending on the infinitude of the set of sentences. In principle, a fluent speaker can produce or understand any of infinitely many sentences (thus ones that may never have occurred before). Second, there is *stimulus-freedom*: this is understood as the absence of control over verbal behavior by external stimuli or internal, nonvolitional states. Third, there is *appropriateness*: this is understood as something like "fitting the situation," meaning how suitable or natural the verbalization is in the situation. (The honey bee's waggle-tail dance is appropriate and unbounded, but, presumably, under some strong degree of stimulus-control, whereas the shorthand of a drunken stenographer might be an instance of inappropriateness coupled with unboundedness and no stimulus control.)

All three of these features are significant aspects of language use, but it does not seem likely that any or all of them constitute the uniqueness of natural language. Unboundedness is a consequence of a system's having recursive structure, and since such structure can be exceedingly simple, exceedingly simple systems, too simple to be a natural language, are unbounded. An automaton that just enumerates strings of *a*'s of any length qualifies as unbounded. Stimulus-freedom and appropriateness, moreover, do not even seem particularly matters of language. They seem matters of performance rather than competence and matters of general behavior rather than linguistic behavior. Surely, a schizophrenic who makes inappropriate remarks under rather rigid control of external stimuli need not be taken to have any deficiency in linguistic competence. There is the same reason for saying that there is no deficiency in linguistic competence in such a case as there is for drawing the competence/performance distinction in the first place.

Premack reports that Sarah is capable of the productive use of conjunction.[4] Suppose she can produce strings of the form "Sarah take apple, and candy, and

---

that the language learner who is trying to induce the rules of the grammar from a sample of utterances would have to somehow form a hypothesis about such underlying, unobservable structure from a sample that is too degenerate with respect to this structure to permit such hypotheses as *inductive* extrapolations. The claim is that the only way that we can explain the fact that appropriate hypotheses obviously are considered is to suppose that their form is specified innately, thereby making up for the degenerateness of the evidence.

‡The other deficiency is a problem of far larger proportions. I have nothing to say about it, except insofar as the remarks I will make about the uniqueness of natural language bear on the question of how a model of acquisition should be built.

banana, and . . ." with no upper limit on the number of conjuncts. Suppose also that she does this after having been trained on cases with only two conjuncts. This example, as it is, does not show that Cartesians are wrong in taking creativity to be the uniqueness of natural language, since with just this rule and a finite vocabulary of names Sarah's output is restricted, in principle, to a finite number of sentences. But, now, suppose Sarah's ability were to develop so that she learns a productive rule for names. Say she learns to iterate a chip n times to refer to n of the things to which the chip can refer. The "chip-sentence" "Sarah wants apple apple apple" translates as the English sentence "Sarah wants three apples." With this easily imaginable extension, Sarah's output is, in principle, infinite. Moreover, since her behavior is stimulus-free in the proper sense and appropriate, it would appear that her communication system is creative. The fact that it is clearly not a natural language shows that we must look further for the distinctive characteristic of natural language.

The failure of the Cartesian hypothesis might be due to the fact that we can have infinite output even though there is no abstract structure. We may thus try a related hypothesis, based on the Fodor *et al.*[2] claim that Sarah failed to exhibit constituent structure and thus failed to be using language. Again, we can do a Gedanken experiment. Suppose the same rule for unbounded conjunctions as above, but, instead of the previous rule for producing infinitely many words, suppose Sarah's rule is the $[\Sigma, F]$ grammar G. Sarah's "sentences" now include "Sarah wants apple apple banana banana,"

(G) $\Sigma : Z$
    $F : Z \longrightarrow$ apple banana
    $Z \longrightarrow$ apple Z banana

and so on, but they no longer include strings such as "Sarah wants apple." In describing a grammar such as (G), Chomsky points out that

> . . . we have introduced a symbol Z which is not contained in the sentences . . . This is the essential fact about phrase structure which gives it its 'abstract' character.[5]

Thus, Sarah's strings now exhibit constituent structure. But the introduction of structure here has, if anything, made the case even less likely to qualify as a natural language, since Sarah no longer has the ability to ask for a single fruit or for fruits of the same kind. This criterion for the presence of language thus fails to offer us any better hypothesis.

The unifying theme of all these failures is the attempt to find the uniqueness of natural languages at the syntactic level. Perhaps this is wrong. Perhaps, as philosophers and logicians such as Frege and Tarski have at times suggested,[6,7] it is the fact that natural languages provide their speakers with the potential to express any thoughts that constitutes their distinctive feature. This suggests that the uniqueness of natural language has to do with its *semantic* as well as its syntactic and phonological levels, that it consists in the completeness of the semantic level of language and the power of the syntactic and phonological levels to express the objects at the semantic level.

Such a hypothesis has considerable initial plausibility. First, it has something to say about semantic structure. It would be hard to believe that the unique feature of natural language has as little to do with semantic structure as the syntactic hypotheses suggest. Second, we immediately explain why we feel that in each of our Gedanken experiments Sarah fails to satisfy the real criterion for having a natural language. Third, this hypothesis squares with our notion that competence in a foreign language is being able, in principle, to say or understand anything in the foreign language. Indeed, the only way to know that our English-Porpoise bilingual is genuinely bilingual would be by some test to determine whether any thought we might ask to be translated is properly translated. Fourth, the hypothesis succeeds in making a distinction between natural languages, on the one hand, and systems of animal communication and artificial languages, on the other. The unbounded systems of animal communication with which we are familiar, like that of the honey bee, can now be dismissed as not a natural language, since we know that its "sentences" fail to say anything about anything except the location of food sources and nesting areas (and even fail to express information about elevation). Artificial languages like those in logic and computer sciences are the clearest case of the desirability of characterizing natural languages in terms of expressive power.

Suppose, then, we say that this "effability," as I will call it, is the unique aspect of natural language. We stand to gain a great deal, but, at the outset, I must warn you that when you take something from philosophy you have to be prepared to take the bad with the good. The bad in this case is that, like everything else in philosophy, the notion of effability is controversial and becomes more so when other philosophical notions are brought in to make things more precise.

To make the effability hypothesis more precise, I will state it as (E).

(E) Every proposition is the sense of some sentence in each natural language.[8,9] This means that each of the infinite number of propositions is represented, in each and every language, by the sense of some sentence. Or, put another way, for any and every language, there is no proposition which is not a sense of at least one of its sentences. By the term "proposition" I mean the objects to which principles of logic apply. When one says that every disjunction coupled with the denial of one of its disjuncts implies the other, we are referring to propositions. Logic studies deductive relations among propositons; physics and other sciences study the truth and falsity of particular classes of propositions. The term "sense" refers to one component of the meaning of words, phrases, clauses, and sentences in English, Chinese, and other natural languages. Senses are the primary objects of study in linguistic semantics.§

Having made effability more precise, we are faced with a number of controversial matters. It will be desirable to consider some of them in order to convey something of the justification that can be erected for (E).

The first is that it is a consequence of (E) that the objects of study in linguistic semantics are the things to which laws of logic apply. What does it mean to identify them and how can such an identification be justified? As I will interpret this claim, it identifies propositions with senses of sentences in just the way that water is identified with H_2O. Hence, the justification must proceed in the same way that arguments for theoretical identification proceed in other sciences. We have to show that the identification simplifies the overall ontology of linguistic semantics and deductive logic and eliminates answerless questions about the correlations between the behavior of objects in the one realm and the behavior of the objects corresponding to them in the other.

§It should be observed at this point that the principle (E) does not guarantee us that the propositions will do justice to the range of states of affairs, that there will be no failure on the part of the propositions to represent all the facts. This is discussed in "Effability and Translation." Also, (E) belongs to a special class of principles, which have theoretical terms in them and hence may alter their meaning with changes in the theories where these terms appear. Stating a principle like (E) is thus a matter of theorizing about the future of the theories in question. This is, of course, highly risky, but it may be of some comfort to realize that one's theoretical opposition takes the same risk.

Such a justification is not hard to sketch. There is a tight *prima facie* correspondence between the behavior of senses of sentences and propositions. For example, logicians distinguish between sentences that express a proposition, and so enter into deductive relations in arguments, and sentences that do not.
(1) is an example of a sentence that does enter in to deductive relations and
   (1) Charles drank prune juice
(2) is an example of a sentence that does not. There is a sentence logically
   (2) Charity drinks procrastination
implied by (1), namely, (3), but there is no sentence implied by (2). Linguists
   (3) Charles swallowed a liquid
describe a sentence like (2) as meaningless, as having no sense, and they contrast it with (1). Here is another example of the correlation between propositions and senses. Logicians distinguish between sentences that express a single proposition and those that express more than one. It is common to find them criticizing an argument such as (4)–(5) for committing a "fallacy of ambiguity"
   (4) Charles insulted an old man and woman
   (5) Charles insulted two old people
because its premise expresses more than one proposition. Linguists say that a sentence like (4) is polysemous; that is, that it has more than one sense. Take one further example. Logicians take some sentences to express the same proposition. Thus, they take sentences like (1) and (6) to be freely interchangeable in any
   (6) Prune juice was drunk by Charles
argument perserving validity. Linguists, of course, say that such sentences are synonymous; that is, that they have the same sense.

Supposing this correspondence to continue to hold in further cases, we can say either that there is a correlation, as we say about the pressure and temperature of a gas, or that there is an identity, as we say about water and H_2O. The former commits us to countenancing both propositions and senses of sentences, twice as many things as we have to on the latter choice. Furthermore, the former choice obliges us to offer some explanation of why there is such a correlation. We have answered questions like why it is that whenever a sentence expresses no proposition it has no sense and whenever it has no sense it expresses no proposition; why it is that whenever a sentence expresses more than one proposition it has more than one sense and whenever it has more than one sense it expresses more than one proposition; and why it is that whenever two sentences express the same proposition they have the same sense and whenever two sentences are synonymous they express the same proposition. Such questions are as answerless as the question of why it is that wherever there is water there is H_2O, and wherever there is H_2O there is water. Therefore, the fact that we halve the number of entities in our logicolinguistic ontology and remove the obligation to answer such questions are, other things equal, good grounds for identifying propositions and senses.[10]

One controversial matter is whether things are equal, whether, that is, the correspondence continues to hold. Some philosophers have wondered whether we can speak about senses of sentences in all the ways we speak about propositions.[11] They point out that it is odd to say "She refuted the sense of the sentence," but it is not odd to say "She refuted the proposition." If this oddity had to be explained on the grounds that senses of sentences are not the sorts of things that can be refuted, the correspondence would break, down. But this is not necessary. It can be explained by referring to superficial usage differences that reflect how locutions in logic and linguistics were customarily used prior to raising the question of identification. For example, no translator of the Bible would translate God's command at the beginning of *Genesis* as "Let there be electromagnetic radiation," but this has nothing to do with light not being electromagnetic radiation. (Ref. 8, pp. 123–124.)

Effability logically implies the full intertranslatability of natural languages; that is, (E) entails (T). (T) says that, for any pair of languages,

(T) For any pair of natural languages and for any sentence S in one and any sense σ of S, there is at least one sentence S' in the other language such that σ is a sense of S'.

any sense of a sentence in one language will also be the sense of a sentence in the other language. That (E) entails (T) can be seen from the following argument. Arbitrarily select a pair of natural languages, L_i and L_j, and any meaningful sentence S in L_i. Let σ be any sense of S. By (E), the proposition σ is the sense of some sentence S' in L_j. Since S and S' share a sense, they are translations. To put it less formally, (E) states that every language can express every sentence-sense. If (E) is true, then it must also be true that a sentence-sense expressed in one language can also be expressed in any other. Thus, all languages are intertranslatable.

Since effability entails full intertranslatability, it can be verified on the basis of evidence from comparative linguistics. That is, effability is a testable hypothesis: if there is any proposition that can be expressed in one language but not in another, effability is false. Rationalists do not wish their hypotheses to be empiricist, but they do wish them to be empirical. Keenan has recently argued that some natural languages do not have the same expressive power.[12] I want to examine his argument both to substantiate my claim that effability is empirical and to indicate some of the conceptual pitfalls that have to be taken into account in testing abstract principles against concrete facts.

Keenan sets the stage for his argument by observing that a necessary condition for two sentences to be translations of each other is that they have the same semantic properties and relations; that is, that "they answer the same questions and make the same assertions and presuppositions." (Ref. 12, p. 193.) He then points out that restrictive relative clauses contribute to the presupposition of sentences like (7). (7) presupposes that there is a man who took the addressee's

(7) The man who took your watch is selling it.

watch. Keenan goes on to note that Hebrew allows relative clauses in sentential contexts where English does not, and on the basis of examples of cases such as (8) he claims that English and Hebrew do not coincide in expressive power.

(8) Zot ha-isha she-ami makir et ha-ish she-natan la et ha-sefer.

Keenan argues as follows:

> Translating sentences like (8) containing "impossible" relative clauses into English is a definite problem. The relative clause part cannot, as we have seen, be naturally translated as a relative clause of English. The only alternative we know would factor the information in (8) into two parts, each simpler than (8) itself. We might try, for example, "I know a man that gave some woman a book and this is that woman." But this sentence fails to be an exact translation of (8). For one thing, it asserts "I know some man" whereas this information is presupposed in (8). And, as any translation that factors (8) into distinct conjuncts will similarly assert some of what is presupposed in (8), we can tentatively conclude that there is no translation of (8) into English. (Ref. 12, p. 195.)

Thus, Keenan's argument is that there are some Hebrew relative clause sentences that cannot be translated into English relative clause sentences. If the information in the Hebrew relative clause has to be conveyed by several English clauses, the distinction between what is presupposed and what is asserted is not maintained in English. The English "translation" would not be equivalent in every semantic property and relation to the Hebrew original, and would therefore not be an exact translation.

If Keenan is right about the possible candidates for English translations of (8), effability is false. There would be a proposition; namely, the one that is the sense of (8), which is not a sense of any English sentence. But Keenan's argument does not succeed in showing that effability is false, because the English sentences (9), (10), and (11) have the same sense as (8).

(9) This is the woman such that she was given a book by the man I know

(10) This is the woman who received a book from the man I know

(11) This is the woman who was given a book by the man I know

Why did Keenan overlook these cases? Probably, because they do not seem, in his words, "natural translations" of (8). This is true if the notion of natural translation requires preservation of clausal, phrasal, and morphological strucutre. But, in that case, natural translation is a matter of style as well as semantic content. Natural translation is then distinct from effability and intertranslatability. These latter concepts, as Keenan acknowledges at the beginning, involve a relation between sentences that holds just in case a proposition expressed by one has exactly the same *semantic* properties and relations as a proposition expressed by the other. No doubt, there are translation relations involving further grammatical properties and relations, but these translation relations go beyond the guarantee that translations express the same proposition. They guarantee further that translations express the same proposition in grammatically similar ways. The difference between our notion of "logical" translation and "natural" translation must be carefully considered when highly abstract principles are tested against the facts in comparative linguistics. (Ref. 9, Sections 5, 6, & 7.)

Above, we described the controversy between rationalism and empiricism over the uniqueness of human beings and human natural language. We described the limitations of a syntactic account of uniqueness and proposed a hypothesis that concerns semantic as well as syntactic structure. The effability hypothesis sharply focuses the rationalist-empiricist controversy on the concrete questions of the relation of language to thought and the character of language acquisition. Quine and other linguistic relativists, such as Whorf and Sapir, make the empiricist assumption that the objects manipulated in thought are or correspond directly to the particular sentences learned in acquiring a language. Quine is particularly clear:

> Thus who would undertake to translate 'Neutrinos lack mass' into the jungle language? If anyone does, we may expect him to coin words or distort the usage of old ones. We may expect him to plead in extenuation that the natives lack the requisite concepts; also that they know too little physics. And he is right except for the hint of there being some free-floating, linguistically neutral meaning which we capture, in 'Neutrinos lack mass', and the native cannot.[13]

To make it perfectly clear, Quine adds that it is an illusion to think that less theoretical, so more readily translatable sentences

> . . . are diverse verbal embodiments of some intercultural of some intercultural proposition or meaning, when they are better seen as the merest variants of one and the same intercultural verbalism. The discontinuity of radical translation tries our meanings: really sets them over against their verbal embodiments, or, more typically, finds nothing there.[13]

This is the very opposite of a rationalist view. For rationalists, cases of failure to translate theoretical sentences represent only a temporary inability of speakers, based on their lack of knowledge of the relevant sciences, to make the proper combination of primitive semantic concepts to form the appropriate proposition. That is, the failure represents a temporary vocabulary gap (rather than a deficiency of the language) which makes it necessary to resort to paraphrase, creation of technical vocabulary, metaphorical extension, and so on, in order to make translations possible in practice, as well as in principle.

The empiricist assumption that our concepts come from experience is responsible for the empiricist's view that natural languages are not intertranslatable; similarly, the rationalist assumption that our concepts come from our genes is responsible for the rationalist's view that natural languages are intertranslatable. The well-known doctrine of linguistic relativity, which states that cultural differences produce incommensurate conceptual frameworks, derives neither from the discovery of exceptional facts about exotic languages by linguists like Whorf nor from important breakthroughs in the study of methodology by philosophers like Quine. Rather, the doctrine derives from the empiricism common to these linguists and philosophers.¶

REFERENCES

1. CHOMSKY, N. 1966. Quoted in Cartesian Linguistics: 4. Harper & Row. New York, N.Y.
2. FODOR, J., T. BEVER & M. GARRETT. 1975. The Psychology of Language: 449. McGraw-Hill, Inc. New York, N.Y.
3. BELLUGI-KLIMA, U. & E. KLIMA. This volume.
4. PREMARK, D. A. 1969. A Functional Analysis of Language. Invited Address. American Psychological Association. Unpublished. Washington, D.C. 1969, and 1971. Language in Chimpanzees. Science 172: 30–31, 808–822.
5. CHOMSKY, N. 1957. Syntactic Structures. Mouton & Co. The Hague, The Netherlands.
6. FREGE, G. 1969. Compound Thoughts. Mind 72: 1.
7. TARSKI, A. 1956. Logic, Semantics, and Metamathematics. Oxford University Press, London, England.
8. See KATZ, J. J. 1972. Semantic Theory 164: 18–24. Harper & Row, New York, N.Y.
9. Also see KATZ, J. J., for the more recent and fuller discussion in my Effability and translation. In Meaning and Translation: Philosophical and Linguistic Approaches. M. Guenthner-Reutter and F. Guenthner Eds. Duckworth. London, England. In press.
10. For a more extensive discussion of this identification, see KATZ, J. J. Logic and Language: An Examination of Recent Criticisms of Intensioinalism. In Minnesota Studies in the Philosophy of Science. K. Gunderson & G. Maxwell, Eds. Univ. Minnesota Press. Minneapolis, Minn. In press.
11. For example, see CARTWRIGHT, R. 1962. Propositions. In Analytic Philosophy. R. J. Butler, Ed. Basil Blackwell & Mott. London, England.
12. KEENAN, E. 1974. Logic and Language. In Language as a Human Problem: 187–196. E. Haugen & M. Bloomfield, Eds. Norton. New York, N.Y.
13. QUINE W. V. O. 1960. Word and Object: 76. M.I.T. Press. Cambridge, Mass.

¶Quine is not a linguistic relativist in exactly the same sense as Sapir and Whorf, as he himself points out (Ref. 13, pp. 77–78). His basic point is that it is even mistaken to suppose that the choice between conflicting translations of a sentence is like ordinary choices in science, where there is a right and wrong choice. (See Ref. 13, pp. 75–76 and pp. 205–206.). But, like Sapir and Whorf, Quine bases his more radical doctrine on empiricism (see my "Logic and Language: An Examination of Recent Criticisms of Intensionalism," and my "Where Things Now Stand with the Analytic-Synthetic Distinction," Synthese, 28, 1974, pp. 283–319.

DISCUSSION

Donald Davidson, *Moderator*

Department of Philosophy
The Rockefeller University
New York, New York 10021

DR. WESCOTT: In response to Dr. Katz, it seems to me that there is evidence for linguistic creativity in chimpanzees, specifically, in the case of Washoe, a young female trained by Allan and Beatrice Gardner at the University of Nevada. She was taken walking one day by a pond where for the first time she saw a duck, a kind she had never seen before. She immediately got excited and signed *water bird*, which I think is a very good indication of the kind of spontaneous creativity that we think of in connection with people using human language.

PROF. KATZ: The claim that I was reporting to you made by Fodor, Bever, and Garrett was that chimps exhibit no *syntactic* creativity. Köhler's studies, for example, show that creativity of an *intellectual* sort is something of which chimps are quite capable. They also exhibit creativity of the sort involved in complicated discrimination learning which requires substituting an item into a slot in which that item has never before appeared. These behaviors are conceded to indicate a kind of intellectual creativity of which chimps are certainly capable. But the point in question here was whether there was *syntactic* creativity in the sense in which a linguist uses that notion concerning the structure of sentences.

The argument was that there is no evidence for syntactic creativity. The only sentences used either by Washoe or Sarah that indicate any kind of infinite potential were the conjunctions, but those also happen to be sentences that involve no *constituent structure*. The argument of Fodor *et al.* was that you don't have creativity of the right sort unless you have both the potential infinity and the constituent structure of the sort linguists have described in connection with creativity in syntax, and so far only exhibited by human language.

DR. WESCOTT: What I meant, of course, was lexical creativity. By syntactic creativity, do you mean the creation of new structures?

PROF. KATZ: Yes.

DR. WESCOTT: Well I won't argue that one.

DR. COUNT: I just wanted to substantiate Prof. Wescott's comment with Washoe's feats a little bit more. This happened before 1970. They had been trying to teach her the sign language word for "bib," and she was having a little difficulty, or refusing to use it. I shall have to demonstrate this by an act. She still wanted that bib put around her neck so that she could eat, and they refused to give her anything until she had signed the word for "bib." So this is what she did [performed pantomime of bib]. The Gardners tell me they reported upon this act at the deaf and the dumb school and found out that this is what deaf and dumb people also have used as an appropriate sign for a bib.

PROF. KATZ: I want to make two small comments in response to that. One is that it's hard to see how this kind of behavior is at all different from cases where your dog brings you the ball and drops it in your hand and then starts running down the walk so that you'll throw it to him.

And second, the comparison with sign language is, I think, unfortunate. For although there are these iconic aspects to sign language, they are not really the essential aspects of its syntax. The syntax of Sign is really quite as distinct from these iconic features as the pictures in a rebus are from the words of English. They are

42

used, and can be used the way we use pictures in our written language, but they are not part of the syntax. Sign language has an elaborate syntax which is quite independent of that pictorial aspect of gesture which signers sometimes employ. Prof. Bellugi will talk on that (this volume).

DR. KEENAN: I'd like to respond partially to Prof. Katz's analysis of my example. I certainly would not want to require that a perfect translation criterion stipulate that perfect translations have the same syntactic form across languages, though admittedly that's the most natural place to start looking. Furthermore, the argument that you can't translate adequately one sentence into another in a different language is never really deductively conclusive, given that we don't have the same enumeration of the set of sentences of any language. All I can do is try to find translations, and if you are cleverer than I am, perhaps you can find better ones.

I'd like to ask very briefly a question concerning a point that was unclear in my mind, but which I think you'd probably have a good answer for. If the perfect translatability hypothesis merely requires that the sense of a sentence in one language be the sense of some sentence in another, I think that that will allow that we could have, let's say, a very artificial case of a language containing only one sentence, say, "All men are mortal." I claim that this is infinitely ambiguous. If all the English sentences were mapped onto that sentence, would that, in principle, satisfy your claim? I assume you wouldn't want it to.

PROF. KATZ: No, of course it doesn't. The principle that I enunciated refers to natural languages, and therefore the test is not the construction of some artificial language which has a single sentence in it, but looking at the existing natural languages and seeing whether the principle holds for every one.

Let me say that the question I was trying to raise was really that of the notion of a "good translation." The impression I had was that there were more notions of translation underlying that expression than were apparent at first glance, and that what one wanted was to distinguish first a kind of base notion of logical translation, and then to look at the overlay imposed by the rest of the levels of grammar in order to see what further notions of translation emerged from such an analysis. In the volume to which you and I are both contributing, I attempt to set out different levels of translation such that tighter and tighter conditions can be brought to bear on the pairing of sentences. These more stringent translation relations are based on higher levels of structure in the grammar and other features of language use. I think it would be important to look at translatability theses at different levels to see where the divergence between natural languages breaks down and where it's preserved. My effability claim is just for this base level, referring to a relation defined exclusively by the properties of the semantic level of grammar.

JOHN FIGARILLO: I'd like to ask a question about this translation criterion which you propose. The first speaker seemed to show the importance of schemata and frames. Now, if you have societies that don't share schemata and frames, how are you going to translate in any meaningful sense from one language to the other without reducing sense to a very, very low level?

PROF. KATZ: I disagree with the previous speaker. Although at the beginning of his talk Prof. Fillmore was at pains to say that he was abiding by the competence performance distinction, I think in fact he was not. I think this shows up if you look at the claims he made about societies in which there is no institution of marriage, just free love. In such societies, he wants to say, there is no word in the language for "cuckold," and no word for "divorce." I think that is really a competence/performance confusion. Language *can* have such words, even though the use of the language never has occasion to apply them. If you do abide by the distinction, then the claim I'm making is only about the competence from language to language and not about the performance. You see, I'm *not* saying that in that happy society they do have certain words in their language, but simply fail to have occasion to use them (i.e., the translation of one of our sentences containing our corresponding term). I only claim that the two languages will match in the linguistic meaning of the sentences, but not in any of the situations or bases under which they're applied, or used.

DR. FIGARILLO: Perhaps *breakfast* and *money exchange* might be other cultural features which would be so different that translation would be difficult.

PROF. KATZ: It might be that translation is difficult, but all I'm suggesting is that there would be no barriers to members of that culture constructing a vocabulary in which they talk about things to which they do not ordinarily have occasion in their culture to refer. We do that all the time in various aspects.

DR. FIGARILLO: Yes, but perhaps only because of so much shared culture.

JAN DEBBS: Thinking about what has happened to the chimpanzee population, I find myself bothered by the extent to which we have been employing our own peculiar criteria to phenomena that may not happen to them.

There is no native informant here to listen to a chimpanzee talk according to the model that we are attempting to impose on chimpanzees. There's no certitude that the human capacity to understand chimpanzee metaphor (if there is such a thing) is such that we would recognize such metaphor if it were created.

PROF. KATZ: Two points: one is that of course it is our own natural language that these psychologists are claiming chimpanzees are capable of learning. Number two, it's interesting to contrast the work that's been done on chimpanzees with, for example, Von Frisch and his collaborators' work on bees (see Reid, this volume). Now it seems to me that here is a system which we seem to be able to describe in some detail, despite the fact that it is quite different from anything that we have the ability to use. We are perfectly capable of designing experiments that specify particular properties of that system, and it seems to me that if the chimpanzees did have something more elaborate than what the training studies show, we certainly ought to be able to apply similar methods and reveal what it is. It hasn't been done yet.

PROF. FILLMORE: I wonder if it's true that these psychologists have been claiming that chimpanzees are approaching natural language? I remember the Gardners being very frustrated at hearing the question: "At what point would you say Washoe has a natural language?" They replied: "We do our work without worrying about whether we can answer that question or not." So maybe that part of your claim on their behalf is overstated.

PROF. KATZ: I wasn't claiming that they were saying there was a specific point at which their chimps had a natural language. I was claiming that their thesis was that studies such as theirs would give us evidence to show that chimpanzees were capable of learning a natural language.

DR. SIKLOSSY: I work in artificial intelligence, and I'm quite surprised, or amused, actually, that the polemic which is still going on in my field seems to have a counterpart in this question of language in the chimpanzee. Our game was to show that machines can be intelligent, so we set up tests, and of course when machines passed these tests, then we would set up more difficult tests; and of course we'll just keep playing the game on and on. This really is what is being done with chimpanzees. It's saying: Well, they *can't* do this, and then once they do, somebody will dream up something even harder. I really can't see any great value in this game. I think it leads to a lot of futile polemics, and if one goes back in the history of science one finds similar polemics, such as the claim that one cannot artificially synthesize chemicals which are synthesized by the body. I really wonder whether this methodology is the right way to go.

PROF. KATZ: I think your description is mistaken. It's not that these poor psychologists have shown that chimpanzees can do A, and then the bad linguist comes and says "Ah, but they can't do B," and they do B and the linguist comes back and says, "Ah, but you can't do C," etc. That's a misdescription.

The original claims, as I understood them, were that the chimps were capable of a "productive" use of language, and the claim was for "productivity" in the sense in which linguists use that term. Now it seems to me further that none of the evidence shows that it is a productive use of language. So in fact, results didn't show that chimps could do A. And the linguists are still waiting to have it demonstrated that they *can* do A.

DR. DAVIDSON: I don't know how far we've gone in formulating a target, but it does seem to me that a clear common need has emerged: whether we want to study the relations between different natural languages or assess the relevance of animal communication to the study of natural language. We need some way of characterizing usefully the notion of semantic creativity.

ON THE NATURE OF LANGUAGE

Noam Chomsky

Department of Linguistics
Massachusetts Institute of Technology
Cambridge, Massachusetts 02139

Imagine a creature so magnificently endowed as to be in a position to regard humans rather in the way that we regard fruit flies. Faced with the problem of determining the nature of language, this creature might exploit a variety of means. It might undertake the study of genetic mutations or intrusive experimentation of various sorts. Or, it might investigate the variation in knowledge of language attained as experience available is experimentally controlled. Under the latter approach, the genetically determined human language faculty, which specifies the nature of language, is considered as a function associating knowledge attained with experience available. Taking the "grammar of a language" to be a representation of the knowledge attained, or at least a fundamental component of such knowledge, the language faculty may be regarded as a fixed function, characteristic of the species, one component of the human mind, a function which maps experience into grammar. The method of concomitant variation is a natural way to study such a function directly.

We may construe a general linguistic theory or a theory of "universal grammar" as a hypothesis concerning this acquisition function. *A priori*, one might imagine a range of possibilities. Thus it might be that "generalized learning strategies" involving procedures of induction, analogy, and generalization in some dimensional system exhaust the contents of the language faculty. Or, the course of language acquisition might reflect cognitive growth in other domains, say, constructions of "sensory-motor intelligence." It has been proposed in the past that "taxonomic" procedures of iterated segmentation and classification suffice to determine the grammar of particular languages and thus express "the nature of language."

Alternatively, one might argue that languages have a partially determinate structure as a matter of biological necessity, much as the general character of bodily organs is fixed for the species. Such structure must therefore be spelled out in the theory of the language faculty. The theory of distinctive features is perhaps the most familiar case. It has been proposed that a certain set of features is available in principle for phonetic representation; each language must make its selection from among these, observing certain implicational principles governing such systems. See Reference 1 and much subsequent work. The theory of distinctive features can be regarded as a hypothesis concerning the acquisition function for language. In my view, work of the past years has provided considerable support for a conception of the language faculty along these lines, as a schematism that narrowly constrains the form of the grammar attained, rather than a system of generalized inductive and taxonomic procedures for acquiring knowledge. Thus it seems to me not unreasonable to approach the study of language as we would the study of some organ of the body.

Suppose that a hypothesis is advanced asserting that grammars must have the property P; that is, having the property P results from the structure of the language faculty itself rather than from experience, though relevant experience may be required to "trigger" the proper growth and functioning of a system with the property P. In principle, the hypothesis might be tested in various ways, say, by designing an environment neutral with regard to *P*, and determining whether grammars invariably have the property *P* rather than not-*P*, no less compatible with presented experience, in such an environment. Or, one might design an environment with experience inconsistent with *P* to verify the prediction that the language violating *P* is not learned under normal conditions of time and access to data, or used with normal facility, and so on.

Of course, no such course of inquiry is available to humans investigating human language. Part of the intellectual fascination of the study of human language derives from the fact that it is often necessary to devise intricate and complex arguments to support, or reject, the hypothesis that grammars must meet some condition *P* as a matter of biological necessity. This unavoidable contingency of inquiry in no way deprives the study of language of its empirical character, although it does bear on the force and persuasiveness of particular empirical theories.

Given the actual conditions of inquiry, a natural line of argument is the following. Suppose we find that a particular language has the proprty *P*; that is, speakers' judgments and other behavior conform to *P* where clear and reliable, constructions violating *P* are rejected, and so on. Suppose, furthermore, that *P* is sufficiently abstract and evidence bearing on it sufficiently sparse and contrived so that it is implausible to suppose that all speakers, or perhaps any speakers, might have been trained or taught to observe *P* or might have constructed grammars satisfying *P* by induction from experience. Then it is plausible to postulate that *P* is a property of the language faculty, that languages conform to *P* as a matter of biological necessity. We are assuming, then, that the environment—which we cannot control—is neutral with respect to *P*, and we seek properties for which this assumption is plausible.

A familiar and very simple example of this kind of reasoning concerns the property of "structure-dependence" of linguistic rules. In this case, the argument, which I will not review (see References 2, 3) seems to me quite compelling, and there is a theory of linguistic rules with other virtues as well that accounts for the facts. Thus the argument is that the structure-dependent property of rules is not something that has to be learned, but is a precondition of learning. The language faculty requires that rules be formulated in these terms, though for an organism differently designed, a system violating this principle could serve the functions of language no less well.

Note that in such cases as these we may plausibly postulate that *P* is a property of universal grammar on the basis of investigation of a single language. There is no paradox here. The argument rests on the alleged fact that something is known without relevant experience so that knowledge must be attributed to the language faculty itself, a faculty common to the species. Deep analysis of a single language may provide the most effective means for discovering nontrivial properties of universal grammar.

Of course, the argument is nondemonstrative and is therefore open to refutation by broader inquiry into the same language or other languages. Consider the following case, patterned on the familiar argument concerning structure-dependence of rules.

We find in English two kinds of relative classes, restrictive and nonrestrictive. In (1), the italicized relative clause is restrictive; in (2), nonrestrictive:

(1) People *who go to MIT* like math
(2) John, *who goes to MIT*, likes math

These two types of relatives have quite different syntactic and semantic properties. In particular, restrictives can "stack," giving such sentences as (3), whereas nonrestrictives cannot, so that (4) is ruled out:

(3) People who go to MIT who like math will get jobs
(4) John, who goes to MIT, who likes math, will get a job

It seems implausible that all people capable of these distinctions have sufficient confirmatory evidence to establish the principle governing stacking of relatives. Following the line of argument just outlined, it is therefore reasonable to postulate that as a property of universal grammar, biologically necessary, nonrestrictive relatives cannot stack.

Reasonable, but apparently incorrect. It seems that in Korean and Japanese, for example, such sentences as (4) are quite acceptable. Therefore the hypothesis, though reasonable, is untenable.

Bearing in mind that experience to ground the distinction between (3) and (4) does not seem generally available, we might propose a more abstract hypothesis. Perhaps some other linguistic property, which must itself be learned, determines whether nonrestrictives can stack by virtue of a general principle of universal grammar. We observe, for example, that Korean and Japanese do not distinguish two types of relatives, restrictive and nonrestrictive, and that speakers of these languages often find difficulty in discerning the difference of sense.[4,5] We might therefore postulate that in languages that distinguish two types of relatives, restrictive and nonrestrictive, only restrictives can stack. We are postulating, then, that the language learner must determine from experience whether the language to which he is exposed distinguishes restrictives and nonrestrictives. Given this information, he can appeal to a general principle of universal grammar to establish which relatives can stack, without any experience with stacked relatives. He need not be taught that (4) is excluded and (3) grammatical. Rather, given that English regularly distinguishes (1) from (2), it follows by a general principle that it excludes (4). The conclusion is reasonable, since otherwise we would be hard put to explain why people do not generalize from the stacked relative (3) to the stacked nonrestrictive (4). I note in passing that other learned properties of the language might be suggested as the key to bringing a general principle to bear, in this case.

Our new, more abstract hypothesis is no less empirical than the earlier, simpler one. We know just what evidence would refute or confirm it. Though the direct test of controlling the environment is excluded, we may nevertheless search for relevant evidence among the existing languages or in observation of language acquisition, and perhaps in other ways.

Pursuing a similar line of argument, we may seek universal conditions in any domain of grammar. Suppose, say, that some principle of rule ordering serves to explain some phonetic properties of English. Then—particularly if the evidence is "exotic"—we may reasonably propose that the principle belongs to universal grammar, and then ask whether this conclusion is supported by further inquiry into English and other languages. We will not be surprised to discover, again, that a learned property of language determines when and how the universal principle is applied.

Or, consider the domain of interaction of syntax and semantics. It seems to be a property of certain types of common nouns that they can be used with either abstract or concrete reference. Consider the sentences (5) and (6):

(5) John wrote a book
(6) The book weighs five pounds

In (5), the reference of *book* is abstract. Thus, John may have written the book in his head, committing nothing to paper, but (5) would still be appropriate. Or, if there are two copies of the book before me, I may say of each, "John wrote this book," but I do not conclude that John wrote two books. In contrast, the reference of *book* in (6) is concrete. A specific material object weighs five pounds. If a hardcover and paperback copy of the book that John wrote lie before me, I may say that this book weighs five pounds and that book, three pounds.

We have here what appears to be a systematic ambiguity over a certain category of words, as distinct from the idiosyncratic ambiguity of such words as English *trunk*, which may refer to an oversized suitcase or an appendage of an elephant. Typically, in such cases of systematic ambiguity, we can combine the two senses in a relative construction, as in (7) or (8):

(7) (i) John wrote a book that weighs five pounds
   (ii) The book that John wrote weighs five pounds
(8) (i) John wrote a book, which weighs five pounds
   (ii) This book, which John wrote, weighs five pounds

Such combinations are excluded in other cases of ambiguity. For example, in sentence (9), the phrase *flying planes* may be construed as referring to objects that fly, which are dangerous, or to the act of piloting, which is dangerous:

(9) Flying planes can be dangerous

In this case, the ambiguity of *flying planes* is syntactically determined, not a general property of phrases with a certain semantic function or character. In this case, of course, we cannot combine the two senses in a relative construction. Sentence (10) is excluded, and in (11), we must construe the head of the relative to be *planes* rather than *flying planes:*

(10) Flying planes, which is a nuisance, are dangerous
(11) Flying planes, which are a nuisance, is dangerous

In general, relativization seems to be free in the case of systematic ambiguity, as in (7), (8). Consider, for example, such words as "temperature" which designate functions of some sort. Thus we can say (12), meaning that the function is increasing over a certain interval including the present:

(12) The temperature is rising rapidly

But such terms can typically be used also to designate a value of the function at a given time and place, as in (13):

(13) The temperature was 70° here at sunrise

There are problems in determining the meaning of such expressions (see References 6, note 12, and 7). But again we find that the two senses can be combined, as in (14):

(14) The temperature, which was 70° here at sunrise, is rising rapidly

Presumably the systematic ambiguity of words such as *book, temperature,* and others (Reference 8, p. 19 ff for some examples) is determined in the lexicon, perhaps by means explored in Reference 9 or 10. Thus, we have a single formal element with a fixed range of meaning, and relativization is possible, despite a shift of sense. But in the case of *flying planes* (syntactically determined ambiguity) or *trunk* (idiosyncratic ambiguity) we have two formal elements, in each case, with the same phonetic form. Relativization is impossible in such cases.

One might imagine that the constraint has something to do with "semantic incoherence" or the like, but this is far from clear. Notice that nonrestrictives have a sense rather like conjunction. Thus the pairs (i) and (ii) of (15)–(17) are close in meaning:

(15) (i) John, who goes to MIT, likes math
    (ii) John likes math and John goes to MIT
(16) (i) The temperature, which was 70°, is rising
    (ii) The temperature is rising and the temperature was 70°
(17) (i) This book, which John wrote, weighs five pounds
    (ii) This book weighs five pounds and John wrote this book

Why, then, does not (18)(i) have approximately the meaning of (18)(ii), and (19)(i) approximately the meaning of (19)(ii):

(18) (i) Flying planes, which is a nuisance, are dangerous
    (ii) Flying planes are dangerous and flying planes is a nuisance
(19) (i) Jumbo waved his trunk, which was full of clothes
    (ii) Jumbo waved his trunk (of an elephant) and the trunk (container) was full of clothes

There is nothing incoherent about (18)(ii) and (19)(ii). We might ask, then, why we do not generalize from (15)–(17) to the absurd (18)–(19). It seems that a general principle of syntax-semantics interaction is involved, and again it seems plausible to attribute it to universal grammar, although much remains obscure in this case.

Let me turn now to some more complex cases. Consider the operation of question-formation. A rule of "wh-movement" forms the sentence (20) by preposing the wh-word of (21):

(20) Who did John see
(21) John saw who

We ignore here a number of irrelevant details. The wh-word may be deeply embedded, as in (22) deriving from (23):

(22) Who did Mary believe that Bill wanted her to see
(23) Mary believed that Bill wanted her to see who

But if the wh-word is in a sentence embedded within a noun phrase, it cannot be extracted. Thus we cannot derive (24) from (25):

(24) Who did Mary believe the claim that John saw
(25) Mary believed the claim that John saw who

The latter fact follows from a general condition that Ross calls the complex noun phrase constraint (CNPC; cf. Reference 11), which implies, in particular, that a word cannot be extracted from a sentence embedded within a noun phrase, to a position outside that noun phrase.

Again, it is difficult to imagine that everyone has received relevant instruction or been exposed to relevant experience. Nor is there any "semantic incoherence" or other similar defect in (24); were it a well-formed sentence, we would know exactly what it means. Thus it seems plausible to attribute CNPC to the language faculty itself. Otherwise, it is hard to see why some, or all, speakers would not simply generalize the rule of wh-movement to the case of a sentence within a noun phrase.

In this case, the constraint CNPC seems so special and artificial that we might search for some deeper and more natural principle from which it follows. I have argued elsewhere [12,3] that we can explain this and other constraints on the assumption that all transformational rules are *bounded* and *cyclic*; that is, they apply within a sentence or noun phrase or across adjacent phrases of the type sentence, noun phrase, but not across more widely separated domains. It can be shown that many crucial instances of CNPC follow from this general principle of rule application if we add an empirical observation: that sentences, but not noun phrases, have a *complementizer* position that can be filled by the *wh*-word or by other words such as *that* ("that John left surprised me") or *for* ("for John to leave would be a mistake");[13,14]

The explanation is controversial. If it is on the right track, as I believe, it illustrates again the expected interaction between general principles that belong to the language faculty and that determine the nature of language, and specific facts that must be learned. In this case, the general principle is the principle of bounded cyclicity, and the fact that must be learned is that English sentences have a complementizer position that can be filled by a *wh*-word, as in (20), (22), or (26) (from (27)), although we cannot, of course, derive (28) from (29), noun phrases having no complementizers:

    (26) I wonder [who John saw]
    (27) I wonder [COMP John saw who]
    (28) I saw [who John's picture of]
    (29) I saw [John's picture of who]

Let us explore the domain of syntax-semantics interaction a bit further. Consider English reciprocal constructions. We have, basically, two types, as in (30), (31):

    (30) Each of the men saw the others
    (31) The men saw each other

These seem close to synonymous at first glance. In general, we can replace the pair (*each of the men, the others*) by the pair (*the men, each other*) with little if any change of sense. Such substitution gives (31) from (30) in the context (32):

    (32) . . . saw . . .

But such substitution without change of sense is not always possible. Consider the two discourses (33) and (34):

    (33) Each of the women saw some of the films. Each of the men saw the others.
    (34) Each of the women saw some of the films. The men saw each other.

In (33), the phrase *the others* may refer to the films not seen by the women. In (34), the phrase *each other* must refer to the men. Thus substitution of the pair (*the men, each other*) for (*each of the men, the others*) in (33) radically changes the sense. The point is that the phrase *each other* must have its antecedent within the same sentence, while the phrase *the others* need not. The sentences (30) and (31) may have close to the same meaning, but (30) has a broader range of meaning. The reference of *each other* is fixed by a principle of (sentence-) grammar, but the reference of *the others* is not, though the principle governing it may apply within a sentence.

This distinction has an interesting range of consequences. Consider, for example, the sentence (35):

    (35) Each of the candidates wanted [John to vote for the others]

Suppose that we replace the pair (*each of the candidates, the others*) by the pair (*the candidates, each other*). Then we derive (36):

    (36) The candidates wanted [John to vote for each other]

But (36) is no sentence of English. Again, the problem is not semantic. If compelled to assign it a sense, we would, presumably, select the perfectly sensible (35). We might suppose that the problem is that *each other* must find its antecedent within the same sentential structure, that is, within the brackets in (36). But this condition is too strong, as we can see from (37):

(37) The candidates wanted [each other to win]

In the sentences (35), (36), (37), the bracketed phrases are sentential.[14] But only (35) and (37) are well formed. (36) is not. It is fair to ask why not. Why does the speaker not generalize, noting that the substitution of phrases is permissible in (30), (31), or in (38), (37):

(38) Each of the candidates wanted [the others to win]

Why is the substitution impermissible in (35), contrary to the natural generalization? It is difficult to believe, again, that this is the result of specific training or experience, in each (or any) case. Language learners are not corrected for such mistakes as (36); nor do they actually make such mistakes. In fact, relevant examples are rare, and a person might well live most or all of his life without coming across any, although he would make the proper distinctions on first presentation with a relevant example, so it appears.

The answer to the problem, I believe, lies in still another general condition on grammar that I have called elsewhere the "specified subject condition (SSC)."[12,3] The condition entails that a phrase X within a phrase P cannot be related to a position outside of P if P contains a subject distinct from X (or, in fact, distinct from the occupant of the outside position, in a well-defined sense). Thus if the bracketed expression in (39) is a P, then Y cannot be related by rule to X if Z is the subject of P:

(39) $\ldots Y \ldots [Z \ldots X \ldots]$

In (36), *the candidates* is Y, *John* is Z, and *each other* is X. Therefore the rule of reciprocal interpretation cannot apply to the pair (*the candidates, each other*), by SSC. But the principle SSC is a principle of (sentence-) grammar. Therefore it does not apply to the case (35). Similarly, it is inapplicable in (37) because *each other* is itself the embedded subject.

The principle SSC applies much more broadly. Consider again *wh*-movement. We have (40) but not (41):

(40) Who did you hear stories about
(41) Who did you hear [John's stories about]

((40) may also be blocked in a style that imposes more stringent conditions on "stranded prepositions," but this is irrelevant here). The reason, I think, is that the bracketed noun phrase of (41) has a subject, *John*, while the phrase *stories about who*, which underlies (40), has no subject. Therefore SSC blocks *wh*-movement in (41), but not (40). We are relying here on a generalization of the notion "subject" of traditional grammar, a generalization which I believe is independently well motivated.[8] Both this extended notion of "subject" and the general principle SSC are fair candidates for universal grammar. That is, it seems to me quite reasonable to propose that they are determined by the language capacity itself.

Consider one final case, one step more complex. Consider the sentences (42), (43):

(42) John seemed to each of the men to like the others
(43) John seemed to the men to like each other

Here again, substitution of (*the men, each other*) for (*each of the men, the others*) in (42) is impossible. Why is this so?

Notice that the verb *like* in (42), (43) does not have a subject before it as it does in (44):

(44) The men wanted [Bill to like each other]

Thus (44) has the form of (39); the rule of reciprocal interpretation is blocked because of the presence of the subject *Bill* (= Z of (39)). But in (43), there is no subject corresponding to *Bill* of (44). Nevertheless, (43) is no more grammatical than (44).

In traditional terms, the verb *like* in (43) does indeed have a subject, namely, an "understood subject." *John* is the "understood subject" of *like* in (43). Apparently, this mentally present but physically absent subject behaves just as the physically present subject *Bill* does in (44), bringing SSC into operation. Thus we may think of (43) as having the abstract structure (45):

(45) John seemed to the men [Z to like each other]

Here Z is the null subject, interpreted as referring to John. But (45) has the structure (39), so that SSC blocks the reciprocal rule.

Again, there is no logical necessity for a language to be designed in such a way that phonetically null mentally present subjects behave just as physically present subjects do. If language were designed differently, (43) would have approximately the meaning of (42), just as (31) has approximately the meaning of (30) and (37) approximately the meaning of (38). The language would be no less well designed for communication or expression of thought (for a creature designed to handle this language). Again, a person might live most or all of his life without ever being exposed to relevant evidence (let alone training) that would indicate to him that the natural generalization is (for some reason) blocked in (43). Thus, it seems absurd to claim that experience provides the basis for these judgments. Nor do they seem to be explicable in "functional" terms on grounds of communicative efficiency or the like.

Rather, it seems that once again, the facts reflect a biologically given precondition for learning. The child learning English simply imposes the requirement that mentally present subjects function as though they were physically present. He does this even in the absence of relevant evidence, so it appears. A theory of universal grammar—that is, a theory of the language faculty—must seek an explanation as to why this is so. The answer, I think, lies in the "trace theory of movement rules," which requires that when a phrase is moved by transformation it leaves behind a phonetically null but morphologically real element "trace" (a so-called "zero morpheme") that functions semantically as a kind of bound variable. Other rules of syntax and morphology have no way of knowing that this element will (ultimately) be phonetically null. Hence it operates as a specified subject, and in other ways in the system of rules, while playing an essential role in semantic interpretation.

Space does not permit a discussion of syntactic and semantic consequences of the trace theory.[3,12,15,16] I will describe briefly a curious phonetic effect of trace, which gives independent evidence that it is morphologically nonnull. Consider the sentences (46), (47), (48):

(46) Who do you want to hit
(47) Who do you want to see Bill
(48) Who do you want to choose

These derive, respectively, from (49), (50), (51):

(49) You want to hit who
(50) You want who to see Bill
(51) (i) You want who to choose
(ii) You want to choose who

Thus (48) is ambiguous as between the two interpretations (51)(i), (51)(ii).

It has been observed by a number of people that in (46) and sense (51)(ii) of (48), the sequence *want to* can be elided to *wanna*; but this is impossible in (47) or in sense (51)(i) of (48). Thus consider (52), (53), (54):

(52) Who do you wanna hit
(53) Who do you wanna see Bill
(54) Who do you wanna choose

Sentence (54) can mean only (51)(ii) and (53) is impossible. Why is this so?

Notice that under the trace theory, we have the abstract structures (55), (56), (57), corresponding to (49), (50), (51), respectively:

(55) Who do you want to hit t
(56) Who do you want t to see Bill
(57) (i) Who do you want t to choose
(ii) Who do you want to choose t

In each case, t is the trace left by *wh*-movement. There is a rule attaching *to* to a preceding occurrence of *want* in certain styles. The resulting phonological word then reduces to *wanna*. Obviously, the rule will not apply if there is intervening morphological material, as in (58):

(58) John will want Bill to go

For exactly the same reason, the attachment rule will not apply in (56) and (57)(i). It follows that *wanna* can appear in (46) but not (47), and that when it appears in (48), we know that (48) was derived from (57)(ii) rather than (57)(i) and therefore means (51)(ii) rather than (51)(i).

Although the trace is phonetically null, it is syntactically and morphologically real and enters into the computations that determine the form and meaning of sentences no less than the zero plural of *sheep*. See References 17 and 18 and references cited there. Note that I have not explained why the understood subject of *hit* does not block elision in (46), or the understood subject of *choose* in (51)(ii)). Here lies another tale.

The trace theory too is controversial and not without its problems. But it does serve to explain quite a range of apparently unrelated facts and it lays the basis for other promising developments in linguistic theory, I believe. If it proves to be correct, or perhaps to be a special case of a still more adequate theory, then again we will have evidence concerning the intrinsic structure of the language faculty, a species property that fixes the essential nature of language.

Examples such as these only scratch the surface of the problem, needless to say. I offer them to illustrate a certain pattern of argument that has proved quite productive and that offers a great deal of promise for the future as well, in that its potentialities have barely been tapped. We might wish that more direct tests could be devised for hypotheses concerning universal grammar. But even in their absence, strictly linguistic investigation can lead us to some plausible general principles of some subtlety, principles that we may hope to relate to the results of other lines of investigation into the nature of language.

REFERENCES

1. JAKOBSON, R., G. FANT & M. HALLE. 1963. Preliminaries to Speech Analysis. MIT Press. Cambridge, Mass.
2. CHOMSKY, N. 1965. Aspects of the Theory of Syntax. MIT Press. Cambridge, Mass.
3. CHOMSKY, N. 1976. Reflections on Language. Pantheon. New York, N.Y.
4. KUNO, S. 1973. The Structure of the Japanese Language. MIT Press. Cambridge, Mass.
5. ANDREWS, A. 1975. Studies in the Syntax of Relative and Comparative Clauses. Ph.D. dissertation. MIT. Cambridge, Mass.
6. CHOMSKY, N. 1975. Questions of form and interpretation. Linguistic Analysis 1(1): 75–109.
7. HACKING, I. 1975. All kinds of possibility. Philos. Rev. 84(3): 321–37.
8. CHOMSKY, N. 1972. Studies on Semantics in Generative Grammar. Mouton. The Hague, The Netherlands.
9. KATZ, J. J. 1972. Semantic Theory. Harper and Row. New York, N.Y.
10. JACKENDOFF, R. S. 1972. Semantic Interpretation in Generative Grammar. MIT Press. Cambridge, Mass.
11. ROSS, J. R. 1967. Constraints in Variables in Syntax. Ph.D. dissertation. MIT. Cambridge, Mass.
12. CHOMSKY, N. 1973. Conditions on transformations. In A Festschrift for Morris Halle. S. Anderson & P. Kiparsky, Eds. Holt, Rinehart and Winston. New York, N.Y.
13. BRESNAN, J. 1970. On complementizers: towards a syntactic theory. Foundations of Language 6: 297–321.
14. BRESNAN, J. 1972. The Theory of Complementizers in English Syntax. Ph.D. dissertation. MIT. Cambridge, Mass.
15. WASOW, T. Anaphoric Relations in English. To be published.
16. FIENGO, R. W. 1974. Semantic Conditions on Surface Structure. Ph.D. dissertation. MIT. Cambridge, Mass.
17. SELKIRK, E. 1972. The Phrase Phonology of English and French. Ph.D. dissertation. MIT. Cambridge, Mass.
18. LIGHTFOOT, D. 1975. Traces and Doubly Moved NPs. Mimeograph. McGill University, Montreal, Quebec.

DISCUSSION OF THE PAPER

DR. VON GLASERSFELD: I may have misunderstood what Professor Chomsky said, but the last example, "Who do you want to see Bill," surely is a perfectly good English sentence?

DR. CHOMSKY: It's a perfectly good English sentence, but you can't run together the words "want" and "to" to give the elided "wanna." That is, you can't say, "Who do you wanna see Bill?" That's the point. It's a phonetic point. The sentence is fine, but it can't have that phonetic realization.

DR. VON GLASERSFELD: I wouldn't be able to judge that.

MARY SMITH (Univ. of Connecticut, Storrs, Conn.): Do you have any evidence for other languages that this sort of subject constraint is really built in?

DR. CHOMSKY: Well, I personally don't, because I don't know any other languages well enough to work on them. But there is some work on other languages that has brought out some very interesting evidence, I think. For example, there is a Brazilian linguist named Carlos Quicoli who has been working recently on Portuguese clitic movement, movement of pronominal elements from their original position to attach to verbs; and I think he's got some very striking evidence that it observes the specified subject condition. Jean-Roger Verneaud, a French linguist, has presented some evidence from French, again bearing on the same things. There is further evidence in an important new book by Richard Kayne, and there are other things of that sort.

I should say, incidentally, that it would be important, of course, to try to find out whether there is negative evidence. I don't know of any clear cases but that may be through lack of looking. If there is contrary evidence, of course, that means that the condition can't be right as formulated, because it's intended to be a universal condition.

But I think one would expect that relevant evidence will not be easily obtained in other languages any more than it is easily obtained in English. That is, any bit of evidence that is to be relevant to a principle of this degree of abstractness has to be presented within a pretty rich framework of analytic assumptions; so that a superficial investigation of a language won't tell you very much.

For example, you may superficially find sentences that seem to support or to reject the theory. But it won't tell you much unless you really show what rules are involved that generated those sentences. And that requires independent evidence and study of some depth. Thus, a condition on rules can only be confirmed or refuted by rules, not by observed phenomena, as a point of logic.

DR. LOUIS LEVIC: (*Univ. of Wisconsin, Madison, Wis*): If these things are built in, why does someone like Professor von Glasersfeld have difficulty figuring on your example?

DR. CHOMSKY: The difficulty he had was because he didn't know, and couldn't know as a nonnative speaker, that there is an elision rule in English that forms "wanna" from "want to." The fact that you can elide "want to" to "wanna" is not built in. Okay? In other words, there could very well be a dialect of English in which that's just false. Similarly, it's not built in that the word "want" begins with "wa" instead of "pa", let's say.

DR. LEVIC: I see now that you wanted to use that as an example in your argument, but—

DR. CHOMSKY: The argument is that given this rule, which has to be learned, we see that in fact this rule observes some very strange conditions. It applies in some cases and it doesn't apply in other cases.

Now, the question we have to ask is how do we know, how does anybody who knows the language know, that you can apply the rule in some cases and not in other cases? Well, if you don't even know that the rule applies, of course the question doesn't arise. But for a speaker of English who knows that there is such a rule, who knows you can say "I wanna go", let's say, the question arises, how does he also know that you can't say "who do you wanna see Bill?" And the answer, I think, is in this condition.

DR. LEVIC: Okay, that's just for the elision rule, but for the other rule you would expect that anybody who's learning English should be able to pick that up.

DR. CHOMSKY: Which other rule do you mean?

DR. LEVIC: The reciprocal rule, with the senses you gave.

DR. CHOMSKY: Well, there, too, is a learned element. Don't forget, all of these things are going to involve interaction of learned elements and fixed principles. So in the case of the reciprocals there is a learned element; namely, that "each other" and "the others" differ, in that "each other" is governed by rules of sentence grammar and "the others" is not governed by rules of sentence grammar. I don't think there is any way to know that, by one's biological constitution.

But given that you know that, many consequences follow by virtue of principles that I think are part of one's biological constitution. So from this point of view, one would be studying language exactly in the way you'd study an organ, say, the heart. Some aspects of each human heart depend on the embryological environment, let's say the nutritional level or something. I don't know what. But other aspects of it don't. And we want to try and sort those out.

Well, in general it's very tricky to sort them out in the case of a developed organ. What I was trying to illustrate is a pattern of reasoning which I think enables us in interesting cases to sort out these factors.

S. HARNAD: Let me just ask a question which everyone else who has been faithfully attending these sessions is surely burning to ask. If some rules you have described constitute universal constraints on all languages, yet they are not learned, nor are they somehow logically necessary *a priori*, how did language get that way?

DR. CHOMSKY: Well, it seems to me that would be like asking the question how does the heart get that way? I mean, we don't learn to have a heart, we don't learn to have arms rather than wings. What is interesting to me is that the question should be asked. It seems to be a natural question; everyone asks it. And I think we should ask why people ask it.

My feeling is that if, say, the Martian scientist that I was imagining were to look at earthlings and investigate them, he would have no reason to doubt that language is as much an organ of the body as the eye or the heart or the liver. It's strictly characteristic of the species, has a highly intricate structure, developed more or less independently of experience in very specific ways, and so on. It has all the general properties of an organ of the body.

Why does it seem so strange to us to think in those terms? In other words, why does it seem so strange to us to consider human beings in the mental aspects of their life as we would consider any object of the natural world? Why is it so natural to insist on a dichotomy in accordance with which we treat the physical development of human beings as if humans belong to the physical world, but not their mental development?

My own feeling is that what we have here is a kind of inversion of a historical tradition that really ultimately has religious and other roots. Traditionally it was regarded as impossible, for all sorts of reasons, to study the human soul by the methods of science.

Now, what's interesting to me is that precisely within those tendencies in science that tried to be naturalistic, that tried to defend science against religious barbarism and so on, precisely in those branches of science the same curious refusal to deal with the facts persisted, so that the question you raise seems to pose an overwhelming paradox to an investigator. The problem seems overwhelming of explaining the growth of this particular mental organ, human language, through the interaction of a genetically determined system with experience, although analogous questions about other organs do not seem to arise with the same force.

I think the question arises in the case of language exactly as it does in the case of the eye, or the heart, or sexual organs (to pick something that matures long after birth), and so on.

There is every reason to suppose that this mental organ, human language, develops in accordance with its genetically determined characteristics, with some minor modifications that give one language or another, depending on experience. But then, one would say the same about any bodily organ as far as I can see.

DISCUSSION PAPER:
INDUCTION, EVOLUTION,
AND ACCOUNTABILITY

Stevan R. Harnad

Department of Psychiatry
Institute of Mental Health Sciences
CMDNJ-Rutgers Medical School
Piscataway, New Jersey 08854

The problem seems to have to do with the process called "induction." Let us adopt a simple definition and let intuition supply the rest. Induction involves the extraction of information from certain inputs. It involves real time, an initial state in which certain information is demonstrably absent, and a final state in which the information is demonstrably present. In between is something very like trial and error. The extent to which this trial and error is constrained by factors other than pure chance is determined by initial conditions. Furthermore, the extent to which induction is constrained by factors other than pure chance is precisely the extent to which it is not induction. So anyone speaking about "pure" induction must have something else in mind, because according to the present definition, some sort of structurally constrained initial conditions must obtain if an initial state is to be specified at all.

There is no question but that the above definition strongly equates inductive processes with statistical processes. Alternative contenders will have to come forward and be equally specific.

Now, the central question that motivates such close scrutiny of induction: When is it incumbent upon a scientist to give an inductive explanation of an empirical phenomenon? Otherwise stated, what must be explained in terms of "how it got that way" (as opposed to what can be accounted for by a state description *simpliciter*)?

Of course, "a state-description *simpliciter*" is usually neither a simple nor a simplistic matter. For example, if such a description is not to be just an empty phenomenology, it must make reference to certain *alternative states*, not actual but "possible" ones, and the state description must specify the constraints that *generate* the actual states rather than the possible states. It is the rules that exclude or forbid the alternative-states which give power and substance to a generative state description.

Now to return to the question of what demands an inductive explanation rather than a "mere" (possibly generative) state description. Perhaps it would be simpler to state what does *not* demand an inductive explanation, for I claim that what *does* demand such an explanation constitutes by far the larger class.

As an example of what does not require inductive explanation, I offer a *reductio* in the form of an absurd question: Surely it makes no sense to ask, in general, "how the universe 'learned' its laws"! The primary laws of physics (whatever they will ultimately turn out to be), as well as cosmological initial conditions, are the structural constraints on the "initial state" of the universe, and they are not to be accounted for inductively; and this for totally nonmysterious, logical, and methodological (if one can speak of a methodology of theoretical explanation) reasons.

Second, the "laws" of logic are themselves not to be accounted for inductively. They too are "givens."

But it seems to me the buck stops here. When we turn to cosmology, evolution, learning, and other statistical phenomena it makes sense, indeed it is quite necessary, to ask how a particular state of affairs "got that way"; indeed, how it "learned" (by trial and error) to be that way.

We may have a very elaborate and sophisticated state description of phenomena in the latter classes (*viz.* cosmology, evolution, etc.), even generative accounts that specify rules which exclude the empirically nonexistent, but "logically possible" alternative states. And yet we are still entitled, in fact driven, to ask *how* (which is here synonymous with "why") things actually got that way.

It is quite likely that for a particular empirical phenomenon not all inductive questions will be answerable "*in situ*," so to speak; i.e., some properties (or rules) will be "given" as structural constraints as far as that particular phenomenon is concerned. But that only means that the inductive burden must be shouldered at some earlier point in real time.

For example, if a particular behavior is not learned by an organism in ontogeny, then it was "learned" by evolution. And if that is not the case either, then it must be due to some physical conditions. If these physical conditions were not themselves due to essentially statistical processes, then they are direct consequences either of physical initial conditions or of logical first principles. If, however, this final pair of constraints is to be the explanation, then something more than retroactive hand-waving is surely called for. The simple *absence* of an acceptable inductive explanation at a particular time is (like Wang's "photograph" of the platypus not laying eggs, DISCUSSION, this annal) surely no ground for claiming that it is not possible. Either the causal link with physical initial conditions must be explicitly specified, or it must be logically demonstrable that an inductive account would be self-contradictory.

Very rarely, I claim, do empirical phenomena qualify to be exempted by either of the above criteria from being answerable to induction. Structural descriptions, and especially generative ones, can be very satisfying in themselves, particularly if they yield a challenging and elegant internal structure. But that does not render them immune to the question: "Yes, but how did they [i.e. the phenomena] get that way?"—if, that is, the description aspires to lay claim to some empirical validity.

Furthermore (and this is only conjecture now) I suspect that the *alternative states*, which are the real backbone of a generative-structural account, are the ones that could most stand some inductive scrutiny. After all, they are dangerously close to the "modal arguments" of philosophers, in which some "possible world" is deemed worthy of consideration (and even ascribed some ontological status) simply on the grounds that it *seems logically possible*. But "seems logically possible" is a pretty weak sort of claim to fame. Trisecting an angle and squaring a circle (to give analytical examples) "seemed to be possible" to many, and now it turns out that they are not (and never have been). Synthetic examples abound, too: according to current physical law, it is not possible for matter to travel faster than light, nor to know at once the electron's precise momentum and position, even though these phenomena seem perfectly possible. Moreover, the "possible worlds" in which one is imagining these putative possibilities invariably involve tampering with (tentative) primary physical laws and initial conditions, which may itself be no more feasible, from the point of view of designing alternative universes, than squaring the circle.

There are, in all likelihood, many systems-constraints, derivative from physical conditions, which one is in fact hopeless in seeking to imagine away. It is, for example, not a "remarkable coincidence" at all that certain biological organs, e.g. the eye, whether arrived at by parallel or convergent evolution, share a number of essential properties, in all organisms that possess them. These invariances are probably due to constraints upon the transduction of light as it occurs in the universe (as well as to certain optimization factors). The number of actual alternatives is strongly constrained, regardless of what our imaginations seem to tell us. And the design-principles of an eye are not derived by positing rules that exclude imaginary (as opposed to actual) alternatives, thereby generating the real eye, but by examining *how evolution actually selected among the actual alternatives (by induction).* He who asks what disqualified the imaginary alternatives is asking a question, not about visual physiology, but about optics, cosmology, and perhaps ultimately, logic.

There are certainly logical and methodological (and even empirical) problems with the classical theory of evolution. The logical problem, of a kind of circularity, can be telescoped in the phrase "the survival of the survivor." This formulation appears to offer neither information nor refutability. Furthermore, the historical methods to which one is constrained by evolutionary thinking present methodological limitations. Finally, the new "random drift" theories suggest that genetic change is not entirely under the control of "selection pressures," as was once thought. Nor is it often evident whether one is dealing with positive evolutionary selection or with more general systems-constraints. But all these limitations notwithstanding, evolutionary thinking is the only inductive approach to "received" biological states, and, to my knowledge, there appear to be no nonmagic alternatives. Hence it is incumbent upon any scientist who is studying a biological system, no matter how sophisticated, to be an evolutionist, and advert, at least in principle, to the question of "how it got that way."

It is explanations of the sort that are *in principle* refractory to an inductive account (either in terms of ontogeny, phylogeny, or physics) which must be regarded with some suspicion. At best, their refractoriness may be due to logical or cosmological factors. But at worst it may be due to a modal fantasy which generates its own rules and is answerable to none. In such a case, one perhaps has grounds for concluding that such an approach is not dealing with the real world at all, not even as an alternative.

LANGUAGE CHANGE*

William S-Y. Wang

Department of Linguistics
University of California at Berkeley
Berkeley, California 94720

For most of us, the insight that things can have names comes too early in life for it to leave a clear trace in our memory. In the case of Helen Keller, however, it came when she was nearly seven years old, at a much more developed stage of understanding and memory capacity. The impact the sudden insight had on the development of her intellect has been eloquently documented in her own writings. After that magical instant when she abruptly realized that the substance "water" could be represented by an arbitrary sequence of finger movements, new words came to her eagerly, rapidly, and in great abundance. That first word is the all important step—the realization that something may be represented by something else quite unrelated to it in physical, emotional, or any other dimensions.

Phylogenetically, this insight of symbolization came in early man perhaps in just as sudden a fashion. We may never know for sure whether the first "words" were gestural or by sound, or by some combination of modalities. It appears likely, however, that *language*, the systematic use of arbitrary symbols whatever their modality, predates *speech*, where the symbols are specifically acoustic, by a considerable margin, a view that has been advocated by many scholars in the past and recently synthesized by Hewes.[1] *Writing*, which is largely derivative from speech, emerged much later still.

Once this access to symbolization has been achieved, the increase of the lexicon from the first spoken word to several dozen or perhaps even several hundred probably took place at an extremely rapid pace as well. Early man was faced with the additional problem, of course, of inventing a lexicon, whereas ready-made words were available to Helen Keller as they are to normal children. This problem would seem to be relatively minor once the conceptual achievement is made that the physical properties of the symbol are independent of the characteristics of the object symbolized.

This was the emergent state of language. But more than the lexicon emerged—there also had to develop, in ways we do not understand at all as yet, the components of a language system. Once there was a total system, language would be in a steady state and would exhibit a different behavior.

Two critical developments had to take place. On the one side, in order to accomodate a growing lexicon, the words themselves had to be split up into lesser elements. By systematically utilizing the combinatorial possibilities of these elements, a large lexicon could be organized that was viable in terms of ease of production and distinctness of perception. In short, this led to the evolution of phonology, where the elements include syllables, segments, and features. The evolution here is clearly limited by and influenced by the biological mechanisms that produce and perceive sounds.

On the other side, as communication became more complex, there was a growing pressure to put words together in various ways. The particular way in which words

*This work was sponsored in part by the National Science Foundation through grant no. BNS76-00017.

61

got put together came to bear information in itself, in terms of the sequential order of the content words, and also in terms of the function words that must have developed later to indicate the relations among the content words. This led to the evolution of syntax and morphology. Here we would expect the evolution to interact with the more central mechanisms of the nervous system, such as those which subserve memory and reasoning.

We do not know, of course, how long it took spoken language to make the transition from the emergent state to the steady state, or even whether the time schedule for this transition is comparable across the different focal regions of the world in which language is presumed to have been evolving. But it seems that the processes of language change must be fundamentally quite different before and after the steady state is reached. In the emergent state, change probably involved mostly addition—of new sound patterns, of novel morphological and syntactic constructions, and so on. These additions were created to cover areas of culture where language had not yet reached. These were one-shot changes whose appearance must have differed sporadically from speech community to community. After the steady state is reached, the changes are mostly replacements—that is, the substitution of one communicative device by another. These replacement processes are very few in number of types, and they recur frequently across time and space.

As far as current methods of linguistic analysis can determine, all known languages have reached the steady state. This includes languages of extremely isolated communities where speakers are few and material culture very simple, such as the Tasaday language "discovered" in a Philipine forest in 1971.[2] Remarks such as the following that may have impressed 60 years ago do no more than amuse now: "Even to this day there are said to be some low tribes in South America whose spoken language is so imperfect that they cannot converse in the dark."[3]

It has been often observed that all languages are "cut from the same pattern." Indeed, one solid result from these six or seven decades of extensive field work in linguistics on many hundreds of far-flung languages is the knowledge that languages all have a great deal in common, regardless of level of culture, genetic grouping, or size of speech community. The same methods of analysis can be used on any human speech to yield comparable results.

Likewise, all languages are said to have about the same degree of complexity. Hockett, for example, makes the claim that "rough computation shows that the measure of redundancy in English is approximately 50%, and there is some reason to believe that this figure holds for languages in general."[4] A language has many components (lexical, phonological, syntactic, etc.) which individually may be more or less complex; but these components create a total complexity that so far has resisted precise, nonarbitrary measurement. I know of no adequate method for computing the overall complexity of any language. Impressionistically, nonetheless, they tend to balance each other out within a language, so that the total difference in complexity between languages may be relatively small. This was put in picturesque terms by Sapir as he wrote, "When it comes to linguistic form, Plato walks with the Macedonian shepherd, Confucius with the head-hunting savage of Assam."[5]

This lack of correlation between cultural and linguistic complexity was observed very early by Alfred Russel Wallace during his visit to Southeast Asia. When he wrote of language that, "an instrument has been developed in advance of the needs of its possessor,"[6] he was already disputing the explanatory adequacy of natural selection as *the* force behind language evolution; and this was two years before *The Descent of Man* was published by Darwin. Furthermore, cultural institutions such as schools or writing appear to be completely unnecessary for sensitivity toward language use. In Bloomfield's study of the illiterate Menomini, for instance, a community of some 1700 speakers, he found that they were quite able to make observations such as "one person speaks well and another badly," that "such-and-such a form of speech is incorrect and sounds bad, . . ."[7]

In any case, in the evolution toward language, once the major holes have been filled and language has passed into its steady state, the processes of change become more orderly and studiable. The emergence of writing, some time over five millenia ago, has had curiously little effect on how the spoken language changes, as far as can be discerned at present. One might think that once a derivative system has been provided to capture the fleeting sounds of the spoken word, and once various perceptual and memory constraints are bypassed, then significant changes in language structure would come about. But there appears to be no correlated structural difference between languages with and without writing systems.

Furthermore, the processes of change appear to be the same for written and unwritten languages. The phonological dimension of this claim was remarked upon by Sapir in 1931[8] when he considered Bloomfield's historical results from Algonkian and his own from Athabaskan and compared them with processes found in the written languages of the Indo-European family. His conclusion that the same processes are at work in both types of languages has been further buttressed not only by more work on Amerindian and Indo-European languages, but also by the recent achievements in the historical analysis, especially of unwritten languages in Africa and of the richly documented dialects of China.[9]

Yet it would be wrong to think that writing exerts no influence on the development of the spoken language. In the Swedish spoken in Stockholm, for instance, the "d" that is spelled at the end of many words was mostly not pronounced in the sixteenth and seventeenth centuries. Presumably, however, due to the rise of literacy and mass media in recent decades, there has been a reversal of a typical phonological process and the "d" is now actually pronounced in many words in which it was silent before.[10] The typical process in phonological change, of course, is for final consonants to become silent, as can be easily seen by comparing French pronunciation with its spelling.

It should also be noted that influence on spoken language need not be restricted to writing systems of the alphabetic type. In an extensive investigation of the history of Cantonese, Hashimoto has been able to find a number of instances in which the phonological development of a word has been made irregular or exceptional because of the shape of the Chinese character that represents it. Such cases she referred to as "analogical reading."[11]

In saying earlier that the processes of change in spoken language are very few in number of types, we were restricting these processes to just those which are caused by intralinguistic factors. These are factors that are embedded either in the structure of the particular language undergoing change or in the biological make-up of its user. Recent work on this historical change in American Sign Language indicates that sign languages are probably subject to similar sorts of intralinguistic constraints, even though they operate via another modality.[12]

The influence of writing, such as in Swedish and Cantonese, would be an extralinguistic factor. Other extralinguistic factors include language contact as well as various forms of social movement and pressures within the language community itself. A reasonable strategy at present in the study of language change seems to be to first separate out the extralinguistic factors as much as possible, and then to try to extract whatever lawfulness we can from the intralinguistic factors.

Investigations of language change have largely proceeded along three separate but interdependent lines: in syntax-morphology (i.e., in how morphemes combine into words and then into sentences), in semantics (in how words change their meaning), and in phonology (in how words change their pronunciation). Of these perhaps the first line of inquiry is the least explored. There are various global conjectures regarding the interplay between morphology and syntax. It is intuitively clear that reducing the complexity in one area frequently results in increasing that in the other area. There is the conjecture, for instance, that language change proceeds along a cycle, from complex morphology—simple syntax to simple morphology—complex syntax, and then back to complex morphology—simple syntax.[13] If such a cycle exists, its average period probably would easily exceed 1000 years. Since there are so few languages in the world with documented histories surpassing 1000 years, the prospect of obtaining conclusive evidence for such global claims cannot be very promising at present.

There are some relatively straightforward observations to be made, however, on syntactic change. Here is an abbreviated example illustrating syntax simpliciation.[14] In Chinese the yes-no question is formed by (A) joining an affirmative sentence with its negative counterpart, followed by (B) deleting certain shared elements. So for the question "Are you coming?" (A) would yield (1) YOU COME YOU NOT COME, and (B) would yield (2) YOU COME NOT COME. For the question "Do you buy books?", (A) yields (3) YOU BUY BOOKS YOU NOT BUY BOOKS; and (B) yields either (4) YOU BUY BOOKS NOT BUY, or (5) YOU BUY NOT BUY BOOKS. That is, from (B) we have the option of deleting either the second noun object, or the first noun object. Up to this point the data is uniform.

That syntactic change comes in questions containing certain perfective aspect markers, such as "Have you bought books?" Applying (A), we get (6) YOU HAVE BUY BOOKS YOU HAVE NOT BUY BOOKS. Using the same procedure for (B) would yield (7) YOU HAVE BUY BOOKS NOT HAVE as well as (8) YOU HAVE NOT HAVE BUY BOOKS. The point of interest is that whereas both of these sentences are fine for most Chinese speakers of my generation, the second of these two is considered ungrammatical by older generations of the same dialect. The underlying structure for (7) and (8) is shown in FIGURE 1, illustrating the two methods of deletion. The asterisk on (8) indicated that (8) would be judged ungrammatical by the older generation, but grammatical by the younger generation.

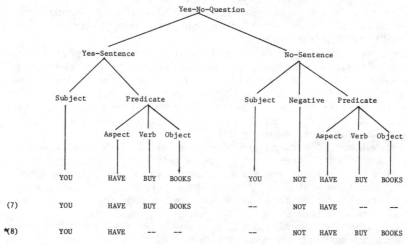

FIGURE 1. Underlying structure for (7) and (8), illustrating the two methods of deletion.

Without the aspect marker there was no such difference between generations. For the syntax of the older generation, therefore, the condition for deleting from the predicate must contain an extra restriction. It must stipulate that deletion cannot be from the first predicate if the predicate contains aspect markers of a certain type. For the syntax of the younger generation there is no such restriction, and deletion from either predicate is always possible. It is reasonable to suggest that since the extra restriction served no functional use, it was simply eliminated from the syntax as the language changed from one generation to the next. This results in reducing the burden on the memory, and the effort that is required to compute, so to speak, the syntactic structure of yes-no questions.

A more complex example of syntactic change is one studied by Bever and Langendoen, tracing the developments in relative clause formation in English over the past 1000 years.[15] These developments were investigated specifically in connection with two importantly related changes: (A) the disappearance of inflections first in nouns, then in verbs, and (B) the appearance of restrictions on certain relative clause markers. Although the details of their example are too rich to be repeated here, the authors make an interesting point by viewing the developments as a "historical competition between what makes a language easy to understand and what makes it easy to learn." The simplification of morphology, they claim, although it makes the language easier to learn, has the adverse effect of leaving too many sentences undermarked at their clause boundaries. In order to reduce ambiguities for the listener, relative clauses become better and better marked. The notion that language is in a state of flux because it has to satisfy simultaneously requirements from different sources—in this case the learner and the listener—is a pivotal one for understanding language change, and I will return to it in another context.

The study of semantic change has accumulated a sizable literature over the past century, but the bulk of it remains mostly anecdotal and unsynthesized. The basic findings are not surprising, even though it took decades of painstaking scholarship to support them with a documented data base. In every language there is homophony, and there is polysemy. In historical change, the semantic range of a word may expand or contract; its sense may shuttle between the concrete and the abstract, between the specific and the vague, between the complimentary and the derogatory, and so on. To give just one example, Nelson Francis[16] noted that the word "enormity" over recent decades has expanded its semantic range and lost its negative connotation. Whereas its application was restricted to contexts like "debt" or "crime," its current usage is no longer restricted in this way; it has become completely synonymous with "enormousness," and simply denotes "large."

Few substantive efforts have as yet been made to look for cross-language commonalities and to raise the biologically or psychologically relevant questions such commonalities must imply. Can it be just an accident that we use the same adjective, "high," to refer to such disparate phenomena as: (1) extending upward, as in *high mountain*, (2) elated, as in *high spirits*, and (3) fast vibrations, as in *high soprano voice*. The question becomes even more intriguing, for words in other languages are frequently polysemous in the same way. In Chinese, for example, the adjective GAO includes precisely these three meanings, i.e. GAO SHAN, GAO XING, and GAO YIN, respectively.

One important line of cross-language research that has recently opened up new perspectives is on how humans categorize the color continuum. Kay[17] has provided a useful review of this work and examined the implications of the results for language variation and change. Investigations in this area have revealed some basic tendencies in the color vocabulary of a wide diversity of languages, drawn from material cultures that range from the very simple to the highly technological. Furthermore, it appears that the categorization data can be rather directly related to known neurophysiological properties of the visual system. Research along this line, where attention is given not only to language-specific semantic observations, but also to universal tendencies as well as to their biological bases, it seems to me, would offer the best hope toward understanding how meaning is structured, and how semantic change actually takes place.

The area of language change that has been by far the most intensively studied is phonology. Samuels has recently provided a comprehensive overview of the current work in this area.[18] In fact, in most accounts of the history of linguistics, modern linguistics grew out of the nineteenth century concern with the study of phonological change and reconstruction. In recent years our perspective on this area has been broadened by considering the question of sound production and sound change within a biological framework.

It has been demonstrated for some decades, from the work on comparative anatomy of the larynx by V. E. Negus [19] and others, that the larynx occupies a much lower position in the human adult than it does either in other primates or in very young human infants. This descent of the larynx, both phylogenetic and ontogenetic, creates a relatively large oropharynx as well as modifies the general geometric configuration of the tongue. Research in this area has been extended in several ways by Philip Lieberman[20] and his colleagues. They reconstructed the larynx positions of various fossil men. Using the techniques of acoustic phonetics, they computed the range of sound that various types of vocal tracts could produce. The range of sounds that could have been produced by those fossil men with high larynx positions was too limited to service speech as we know it today; consequently, it is tempting to conclude that they could not have had spoken language. The descent of the larynx is an adaptation to the larger inventory of consonants and vowels that is needed to support a viable spoken language.

The conclusions contained in the last two sentences need to be carefully qualified before they can be confidently accepted. It is not at all clear how to draw the line between what is and what is not a viable inventory to support spoken language. Let us merely note for now that English and most well-known European languages are on the rich side of segmental distinctions. Many languages make do with much less. Polynesian languages, such as Hawaiian, are well known for their low phoneme inventory as well as simple syllable patterns. Language may lose phonological distinctions on a massive scale, with no apparent ill effects. Certain southwestern dialects of Mandarin Chinese, for instance, have preserved only a small fraction of the number of distinct syllables found in their presumed ancestor—the Middle Chinese of ca. 600 A.D. Li-Jiang,[21] as an example, has only 500 some distinct syllables, whereas Middle Chinese is presumed to have had approximately 3500—a phonological attrition of over 80%! At any rate, to use the presence of a large phonetic inventory as the *sine qua non* of spoken language is somewhat one-sided, since spoken language is a totality of components of which the phonetic is only one.

Furthermore, while the descent of the larynx has resulted in a much greater capacity in our productin of consonants and vowels, it is not obvious that the production of these distinctions was the exclusive or even primary factor that motivated the descent. If we accept as a working hypothesis that human speech could have evolved from some complex inventory of vocal calls, not totally unlike that of some contemporary nonhuman primates, as recently discussed by Peter Marler,[22] then we must pay some attention to the fact that a lower larynx position is also favored for yielding a larger range of pitch and volume. We need only monitor someone's throat when he sings to note that the larynx makes wide vertical and horizontal excursions to enable large pitch changes.

It is quite likely that the gravitational pull on the entire respiratory structure, including, of course, the larynx, increased significantly when early man assumed an upright posture. It is known from radiological observations, for instance, that the vertical position of the bronchial bifurcation may vary over a range of some two cm with respiratory activity. Approximately the same amount of displacement is observable between the standing position and the lying position. The possibility exists, therefore, that the larynx descended for purely passive, mechanical reasons when the human body adjusted to the erect posture. If this is the case, then the changes in gross anatomy must have *preceded* the fine neural control of the laryngeal and supralaryngeal movements. Such a precedence relation has also been argued in the case of the evolution of the primate forelimb, where the anatomy of the digits evolved considerably before many of the neural and functional controls of these digits.

It is not impossible, at any rate, that an early consequence for the descent was to increase the suprasegmental distinctions,[23] and that the segmental distinctions gradually were added in as the accompanying facial gestures left their traces in the acoustic signal. In time, of course, the segmental distinctions became primary because they provide a much richer set of perceptual dimensions, and the suprasegmental signals faded into the background to serve as carriers. The relative chronology of the evolution of phonology, then, consists of three overlapping phases, from gesture to suprasegmentals to segmentals. Gestures and suprasegmentals persist to this day, of course, the latter most prominently in intonation systems, which are found in all languages.[24]

After language has reached its steady state, phonological changes become quite straightforward. Again they constitute only a small number of types that recur frequently in time and in different regions of the world. Most of these types have been observed in many language contexts over the past century, and have been given standard names, such as palatalization, nasalization, rhotacization, umlaut, and others. As our techniques improve for investigating the historical and the physiological bases of such phonological changes, we are acquiring a better understanding of why such changes take place. Often it turns out that the change is motivated by ease of articulation or by distinctness in perception, or by the interaction of these two requirements.

I would now like to report briefly an experiment[25] we have just completed to illustrate this last point, i.e., the interaction between production and perception. The experiment involves the perceptual boundary between two phonemes of tone. Chinese is known as a tone language because words are differentiated not only by vowels and consonants, but by the pitch of the voice as well. This point is illustrated in the following figure, in which the four tones of the Peking dialect are shown (FIGURE 2).

Consider the vowel /i/ as in the English word "bee." When it is pronounced with a level tone it means "clothing"; with a rising tone it means "aunt." To find out where the boundary is between the level tone phoneme and the rising tone phoneme, we synthesized on a PDP-11 computer a set of 11 stimuli, where the first stimulus begins at 105 Hz and rise to 135 Hz. The second stimulus begins at 108 Hz and rises to 135; the third begins at 111 Hz and so on, until the eleventh stimulus is level at 135 Hz. So the Δf between every adjacent stimulus is 3 Hz, a rather large difference in psychophysical terms (FIGURE 3).

There were two tasks: identification and discrimination. For the identification task, the stimuli were presented singly in random order. For each stimulus, Chinese subjects responded by circling one of the two Chinese characters on the answer sheet—one meaning "clothing" and the other meaning "aunt." American subjects responded by circling either L for "level" or R for "rising." For the discrimination task, each presentation contained a sequence of three stimuli in an ABX paradigm. The subject had to judge whether the third stimulus was the same as the first or as the second.

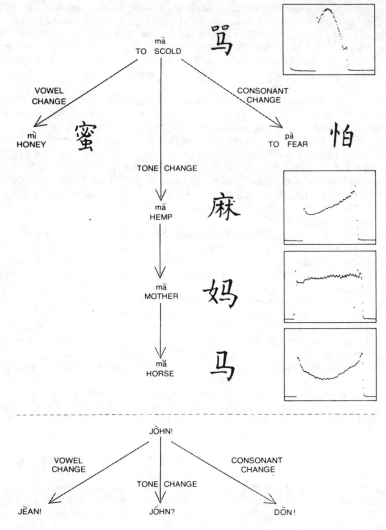

FIGURE 2. TONES are used to alter the meaning of Chinese words. Standard Chinese has only four tones: falling (as in *mà*), rising (*má*), level (*mā*) and dipping, or falling and then rising (*mǎ*). The oscillograph traces at right show the fundamental frequency of the author's voice as he spoke the words. In English, on the other hand, variation in tone is used to convey different moods; the meaning of the word being spoken does not change. In Chinese changing tone has same kind of effect on meaning of word as changing a vowel or a consonant. (By permission of Sci. Amer.[26])

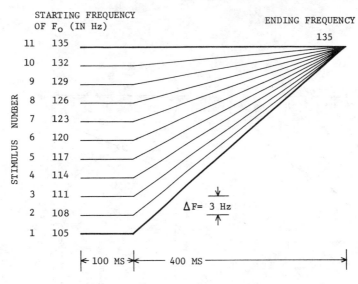

FIGURE 3. Schematic diagram of F_0 patterns.

Typically, there is agreement between the location of the crossover point of the identification curves and that of the peaks in the discrimination curves; that location is the perceptual boundary.

The results can be seen in FIGURE 4. In these graphs, the curves with the circles are based on identification task, and the curves with the "plus" signs are based on ABX discrimination. Stimulus number 1 is maximally rising, and number 11 is level.

For American subjects, the boundary is quite close to the level tone, as is shown in the lower-right graph. Presumably, they are responding to the psychophysical difference between the level tone and the ten other stimuli. The Chinese subjects, however, show variation in the degree to which they are influenced by their native language. The subjects in the upper-left graph, who have not participated in psychophysical experiments before, show just the linguistic boundary, which is consistently below stimulus 8, in which the starting frequency is 126 Hz. The subjects in the lower-left graph, who are familiar with psychophysical experiments, show a linguistic boundary *and* a psychophysical boundary as well. The trained subjects in the upper right graph, which consists of two of the experimenters, show only the psychophysical boundary.

It is clear from these data that for the listener unbiased by his language, the easiest stimulus to distinguish from the rest is the *real* level tone. Even for Chinese speakers whose psychophysical experience can allow them to overcome the suppressive effect of their language background, the boundary shows up between the real level tone and the remaining stimuli.

The question arises naturally as to why the phoneme boundary does not fall on the psychophysical boundary. Would it not be most efficient for a phonmeme boundary to fall on a boundary that already exists for psychophysical reasons? The answer to this question can be had by considering not just the requirements of the hearer, but the requirements of the speaker as well. It turns out that the pitch of the voice is subject to a certain amount of perturbation as a function of the consonants and vowels that are pronounced with it. To require each phoneme of level tone to be

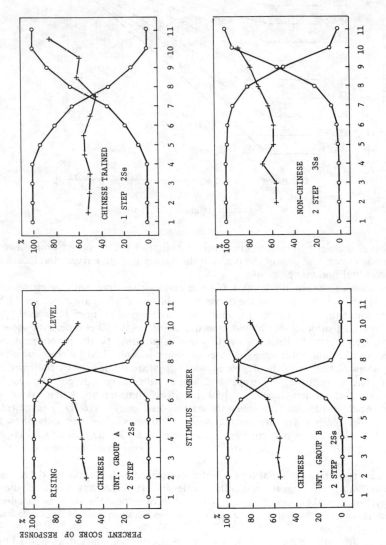

FIGURE 4. Four tones of the Peking dialect.

produced with a perfectly level pitch is to require the speaker to make a diversity of tremendously delicate compensatory movements to neutralize these segmental perturbations. Clearly, these requirements are much more difficult to meet than simply to shift the perceptual boundary a little bit to allow for some freedom in the articulation.

Human speech is an instrument that is subject to the interplay among many demands and requirements. Some of these requirements are biological in nature, others are social. The linguistic system must not yield too much to the ear, else demands become excessive for the larynx or the tongue. An elaborate morphology of case markers favors the user in keeping track of where he is in the sentence. But when it becomes too complex for the memory of the learner, be it the child or the foreigner, the morphology levels out to give way to syntax. And repeatedly in history, whenever a language is washed over by huge waves of words and sounds from another language, it must restore some semblance of order by adjusting its structure to accomodate many of these new elements.

As the biological or social context alters, new requirements arise, and different priorities are given to old requirements. As a function of all this flux, language change may be viewed as an elaborate minimax game whose goal is an optimum response to these diverse requirements. Built somehow into our neural mechanisms that serve language is the plasticity that allows for these fluctuations and change. Some exciting advances are taking place in these last several years on how these mechanisms work. In time, we hope, this new knowledge will contribute toward a biological base upon which explanatory theories of language change can eventually be constructed.

ACKNOWLEDGMENTS

I should especially like to thank A. M. Liberman, H. H. Srebnik, and M. L. Streeter for sharing their thoughts with me.

REFERENCES

1. HEWES G. W. 1973. Private communication and the gestural origin of language. Current Anthropol. **14:** 5–32.
2. NANCE, J. 1975. The Gentle Tasaday. Harcourt Brace Jovanovich, Inc. New York, N.Y.
3. SCIENCE PROGRESS. 1914. Vol. **8:** 524.
4. HOCKETT, C. F. 1958. A Course in Modern Linguistics. Macmillan Co. New York, N.Y.
5. SAPIR, E. 1921. Language. Harcourt Brace and World, Inc. New York, N.Y.
6. WALLACE, A. R. 1869. Geological climates and the origin of species. Quart. Rev. **126:** 359–394.
7. BLOOMFIELD, L. 1927. Literate and illiterate speech. Amer. Speech. 2.10: 432–439.
8. SAPIR, E. 1931. The concept of phonetic law as tested in primitive languages by Leonard Bloomfield. *In* Methods of Social Science: A Case Book. Stuart A. Rice, Ed.: 297–306. University of Chicago Press. Chicago, Ill.
9. CHEN, M. Y. & W. S-Y. WANG. 1975. Sound change: actuation and implementation. Language **51:** 255–281.
10. JANSON, T. 1976. Reversed lexical diffusion and lexical split: loss of -d in Stockholm. *In* the Lexicon in Phonological Change. William S-Y. Wang, Ed. Mouton. The Hague, The Netherlands.
11. HASHIMOTO, A. O.-K. YUE. 1972. Phonology of Cantonese. Cambridge University Press. Cambridge, England.

12. FRISHBERG, N. 1975. Arbitrariness and iconicity: historical change in American sign language. Language **51**: 696–719.
13. HODGE, C. 1970. The linguistic cycle. Language Sciences **13**: 1–7.
14. WANG, W. S-Y. 1965. Two aspect markers in Mandarin. Language 41–3: 457–470.
15. BEVER, T. G. & D. T. LANGENDOEN. 1972. The interaction of speech perception and grammatical structure in the evolution of language. *In* Linguistic Change and Generative Theory. Stockwell and MacCaulay, Eds.: 32–95. Indiana University Press. Bloomington, Ind.
16. FRANCIS, N. 1973. *In Lexicography in English*. Ann. N.Y. Acad. Sci. **211**: 164.
17. KAY, P. 1975. Synchronic variability and diachronic change in basic color terms. *In* Language in Society. **4**: 257–270.
18. SAMUELS, M. L. 1972. Linguistic Evolution. Cambridge University Press. Cambridge, England.
19. NEGUS, V. E. 1949. The Comparative Anatomy and Physiology of the Larynx. Hafner.
20. LIEBERMAN, P. 1975. On the Origins of Language. MacMillan Co. New York, N.Y.
21. CHEN, M. Y. 1973. Cross-dialectal comparisons: a case study and some theoretical considerations. J. Chinese Linguistics. 1.1: 38–63.
22. MARLER, P. 1965. Communication in monkeys and apes. *In* Primate Behavior. I. DeVore, Ed.: 544–584. Holt, Rinehart and Winston. New York, N.Y.
23. LEHISTE, I. 1970. Suprasegmentals. MIT Press, Cambridge, Mass.
24. BOLINGER, D. L. 1964. Intonation as a universal. *In* Proc. Ninth Int. Cong. Linguistics.: 833–844. Mouton. The Hague, The Netherlands.
25. CHAN, S. W., C. K. CHUANG & W. S-Y. WANG. 1975. Cross-linguistic study of categorical perception for lexical tone. J. Acoustical Soc. Amer. **58**: S119.
26. WANG, W. S-Y. 1973. The Chinese language. Sci. Amer. 228: 50–63.

THE LOGICAL DIVERSITY OF NATURAL LANGUAGES

Edward L. Keenan

Department of Linguistics
The University of California at Los Angeles
Los Angeles, California 90024

INTRODUCTION

I will discuss in this paper a conception of language universal which differs from what I'll call the Current View in generative grammar both as regards the methodology for determining universals and as regards the relation between language and mind.

On the Current View, language universals (Us) are conceived of as constraints on the form (and substance) of possible human languages (Ls). These constraints can be represented as overt properties of grammars, given that a L can itself be represented by a grammar. Since each L satisfies the universal constraints, the Us are represented in the grammar of each L and can be determined by studying the grammar of only one L. Properties that vary from L to L are, of course, *prima facie* not candidates for being Us. And since surface structures of Ls are obviously different, it follows that Us are stated at some abstract, underlying level of structure. At that level Ls are all very similar, if not identical. Finally, Us are explained as direct reflections of our innate linguistic competence, which does not vary across speakers of different Ls.

On the view I am proposing however, Ls are held to be distinct in syntactically and semantically significant ways. Us are not in general representable as overt properties of each grammar, so overt properties of grammars do not in general determine innate mental structures. Rather, Us are determined by the pattern of cross-L variation with respect to a given property. Constancy across Ls is merely the special case of zero variation. Further, the cross-L variation need not be determined at a deep level of analysis; shallow or surface levels are often sufficient. Nonetheless, variation-based Us do determine constraints on the form (and substance) of possible human Ls, and may well be explained in terms of the cognitive similarity of L users, although little concerning the Us I will discuss suggests that that similarity extends to the level of innate linguistic capacity.

Before substantiating my proposal I would like to explain why it is a plausible point of view. It is so because, in my opinion, any particular L greatly underrealizes what is universally possible. That is, the constraints on the forms of its structures are normally much stronger than the universally valid ones. To determine the universal constraints, we have to compare the particular constraints of a variety of Ls and then determine what common ground they cover. We will not generally need to state the Us in the grammar of any particular L because the constraints we need anyway will entail the Us and make their statement unnecessary and unmotivated. Advocates of the Current View often assume that the grammar of any particular L will realize to some significant extent what is universally possible.* That is why it is plausible, in that view, to consider that it might be possible to "read off" Us from particular grammars.

---

* For example in Katz (Ref. 9, p. 109) we find: "That is, each linguistic description has a common part consisting of the set of linguistic universals and a variable part consisting of the generalizations that hold only for the given language." In discussing the universal part, Katz (p. 110) goes on to say that ". . . such facts are stated just once in the theory of language as

73

I will illustrate my point with two logically different types of examples. In the first, the universal constraint may well occur in the grammars of some Ls, but will not occur in all. Consider e.g. the coordinate structure constraint (CSC) proposed in Ross.[22] It says, roughly, that operations that form complex structures from simpler ones by moving elements must be constrained so that an element that occurs within a single member of a coordinate structure cannot be moved out of the entire coordinate structure. For example, given a sentence like *John saw the man and the boy* we cannot relativize on *boy* yielding *the boy that John saw the man and* since that would involve moving a member of a single conjunct outside the whole conjunction.

However, in many Ls, probably most, the positions that can be relativized are so highly constrained as to make the statement of the CSC on relative-clause formation unnecessary. For example, in many of the Western Malayo-Polynesian Ls such as Tagalog and Malagasy, the language of Madagascar (see Keenan,[10,14]), only subjects of main clauses can be relativized. Now, since no single member of a coordinate structure can be the subject of the entire construction in which the coordinate structure occurs, it follows that no single member of a coordinate structure can be relativized. We are unmotivated, then, to state the CSC for relative-clause formation in these Ls. Furthermore, at least in Malagasy, the other complex structures that are formed by movement are also constrained by the "subjects only" condition (or in some cases a slight weakening of it, but it is still required that a moved constituent bear a major relation to its root S), so there is no motivation at all for the CSC to appear in the grammar of Malagasy, although Malagasy does, of course, conform to the CSC. To determine that the CSC is (plausibly, at least) a universal constraint on grammars, we need to investigate operations like relative-clause formation in a variety of Ls and then observe that despite the different ways of restricting the relativizable positions in different Ls, it always works out that single members of coordinate structures cannot be relativized by a movement process.

The second type of case concerns Us in which it is necessarily the case that each possible L presents a more specific version of the constraint than is universally valid. In this case, then, the U will not appear in the grammar of any L! Examples of such universal constraints are ones that express dependencies between properties of grammars, such as conditional claims of the form: "If a L (or a grammar) has a property P then it necessarily has some other property Q." Clearly, such claims constrain the form of possible human Ls, since they rule out Ls that have P but do not have Q. But a given L may satisfy the conditional constraint in any of three mutually exclusive ways: it may have both P and Q, or only Q without P, or else neither P nor Q. Further, any one of these ways is stronger than the conditional universal in the sense that, if generalized to hold of all possible languages, it entails the conditional claim but is not entailed by it. For example, if all languages have both P and Q (or all languages have only Q but not P, etc.), then trivially any language that has P has Q. But the conditional claim itself of course does not entail that all languages have both P and Q (or that all have only Q, etc.).

In general, then, to substantiate a conditional universal we must determine that for a "fair sample" of possible languages some have both P and Q, others have Q

<hr>

facts about language, thereby making numerous particular statements of them unnecessary." It appears clear in Katz's view, then, that linguistic universals would appear in the grammars of particular Ls if they were done in isolation. That Katz's view of universals and language variation is different from the one I am proposing is made clear by the final sentence of the paragraph from which the previous quotes were taken (p. 110). "The farther we thus empirically limit the logically possible diversity in natural languages, the richer the theory of universal structure given in the theory of language."

but not P, and others have neither P nor Q. But no language in the sample has P without having Q. So it is clearly the pattern of variation that determines the U here.

I will now support my claims concerning language diversity and variation-based universals, drawing on data from three different subsystems of grammar: the promotion system (e.g. Passives), the cross-reference system, and the relative-clause formation system.

THE PROMOTION SYSTEM

Among the syntactic operations that form complex structures from simpler ones, Ls may have ways of assigning some NPs the grammatical properties of others. Thus in English the Passive transformation (regardless of how it is formally defined) has the effect of presenting the direct object (DO) of the active sentence as the subject of the derived sentence. In such cases I will say, without further attempt at formal definition, that Passive in English *promotes* DOs to subjects. English can also promote a few indirect objects (IOs) to subject. Thus from *John gave the toy to Mary* we can form *Mary was given the toy by John.* Plausibly, in such cases the IO *Mary* is first promoted to DO, *John gave Mary the toy*, and then passivized to subject. This promotion possibility, however, is quite limited. Only a few common verbs like *give, tell*, and *teach* allow it. Many verbs that take IOs such as *add, introduce, contribute, dedicate*, etc., cannot promote IOs to DO or to subject. (*John added a book to the pile, *John added the pile a book, *The pile was added a book by John*).

Now, Ls vary enormously with regard to which NPs they can promote to which positions. Many Ls lack such promotion devices entirely. Thus, many Chadic languages like Hausa,[18] many Kwa languages like Urhobo, and many Melanesian languages like Arosi[1] have no Passive. If our study of universal grammar were based on only those languages, it is hard to see how we would be motivated to posit promotion rules as a possible rule category for human Ls. On the other hand, many Ls can systematically promote most major (nonsubject) NPs to subject. Thus Malagasy and Philippine languages usually have from four to eight "voices" which function to promote locatives, instrumentals, benefactives, temporal NPs, and so on, to subject. For example, given the active sentence (1) in Kalagan,[3] a typical Philippine language in this respect, all of the nonsubject NPs can be promoted to subject:

(1) a. kumamang aku   sa   tubig na   lata adti balkon
      +active   +nom
      get   I   obj water with can on   porch
      'I'll get the water on the porch with the can'

    b. kamangin ku   ya   tubig na   lata adti balkon
      +pass   +agent subj water with can on   porch
      'The water will be gotten by me on the porch with the can'

    c. pagkamang ku   ya   lata sa   tubig adti balkon
      +inst   +agent subj can obj water on   porch
      'The can will be gotten water with by me on the porch'

    d. kamangan ku   ya   balkon sa   tubig na   lata
      +loc   +agent subj porch   obj water with can
      'The porch will be gotten water on by me with the can'

Similarly, in many Bantu languages locatives, as well as DOs and IOs, can be promoted to subject.

Chicewa (Bantu; ex. from Trithart[26])
(2) a. John a- na- mu-on- a   Mary ku sukulu
John he-past-she-saw-indic Mary at school
'John saw Mary at school'

b. Ku sukulu ku- na- on- edw-a-   ko Mary ndi John
at school there-past-see-pass-indic loc Mary by John
'School was seen Mary at by John'

Kinyarwanda (Bantu; ex. from Gary[4])
(3) a. Yohani ya- 0- ic- e   impyisi mu ishyamba
John   he- past-kill-asp hyena in forest
'John killed a hyena in the forest'

b. Ishyamba ri-0   ic- iw- e   mo impyisi na Yohani
forest   it-past-kill-pass-asp-loc hyena by John
'The forest was killed in a hyena by John'

Note that in each of the promotions illustrated in (1)–(3) the derived subject has the position, case (where marked at all), and verb agreements of a subject, and the verb is marked differently, according as the promoted NP is a DO, instrumental, locative, etc.

Promotion possibilities then vary across Ls, but the variation is not random. Some positions are harder to promote to subject than are others. We have, for example, the following universal constraint: If a L can promote locatives to subject then it can promote DOs to subject, but not conversely. In fact, the available evidence (but more is needed, see Keenan and Comrie,[17] Trithart,[26] and Johnson[8] for discussion) indicates that the Case Hierarchy below expresses the relative difficulty of promotion to subject (for major NPs of main clauses):

Case Hierarchy

Subject > DirObject > IndObject > Benefactive > Other Oblique NPs

Thus, if a language can promote an NP low on the hierarchy to subject, then it can promote all intermediate positions to subject; but all the converses fail: Some Ls, e.g. French, can subjectivize only DOs; others, e.g. English, can cover some IOs as well. Japanese (Shimizu[24]) and Iban (Keenan and Comrie[17]) can subjectivize DOs, IOs, and Benefactives; and Philippine and Bantu languages as discussed above, can subjectivize almost all major NPs.

The Case Hierarchy also determines the relative difficulty of promotion to DO. Some Ls, like English, can promote IOs to DO. But Bantu is again more generous, frequently allowing instrumentals and some locatives to be promoted to DO.

Luganda
(4) a. John yatta enkonko na- ekiso
John killed chicken with-knife
'John killed a chicken with a knife'

b. John yatt-is- a ekiso enkonko
John kill- inst- knife chicken
'John killed-with a knife a chicken'

But if a L can promote oblique NPs to DO then it can promote Benefactives and IOs and DO.

Furthermore, promotion to DO is universally harder than promotion to subject. Thus if a L has rules that promote NPs to DO, then it necessarily has rules which promote NPs to subject.

Note, however, that difficulty of promotion is not directly proportional to the distance between two NPs on the Case Hierarchy. It is not, for example, easier to promote locatives to DO that it is to promote them to subject. (Philippine languages promote them to subject, but not to DO.)

The conditional universals we have stated here clearly determine constraints on the form of possible human languages. They may have certain types of promotion rules only if they have others. Exactly why human gramntars should be constrained in this way is not clear. The answer will depend in part on what kind of information is coded in notions like "subject," "direct object," etc. (see Keenan[15] for discussion). So whether the promotion constraints reflect our innate linguistic competence or not is completely open.

The primary purpose of this discussion of promotion systems has been to establish that L variation is not merely random or accidental. Rather, it is regular and determines constraints on the form human Ls can take, and therefore is a proper object of scientific inquiry. It is tempting, however, to dismiss the variation we have discussed so far as somewhat inessential. After all, if English lost the Passive, the rest of the syntax would not be radically affected. Nor would English suffer a loss of expressive power, since Passives and Actives are more or less paraphrases.

However, the role of promotion systems in other languages is often much more crucial to the rest of the syntax than it is in English. To consider only one example, in Malagasy and the Philippine languages we find that the relative clause (RC) forming system depends crucially on the promotion system. In those Ls only subject NPs can be relativized. Thus we cannot even directly say *the man that John saw*, where *man* functions as the DO of *saw*. To relativize on *man* we must first promote it to subject, and say *the man that was seen by John*.

Malagasy
(5) a. mijery ny olona Rajaona
     see   the person John
     'John sees the person'

   b. jeren-dRajaona ny olona
     seen by-John   the person
     'The person is seen by John'

   c. *ny olona izay mijery Rajaona
     the person that see   John
     'the person that John sees'

   d. ny olona izay jeren-dRajaona
     the person that seen by-John
     'the person who is seen by John'

These Ls do not use pronouns (relative or other) to mark the position relativized. The semantic role that the head of the RC plays in the restricting clause is coded in the verb voice. If the verb of the restricting clause is passive in form, then the head NP is the underlying DO of the verb, since we must passivize the verb to make the constituent we want relativize a subject. Similarly, if the restricting verb is, for example, instrumental in form, then the head NP is an underlying instrumental, and so on. If we lost the promotion system in these Ls, the means of forming RCs (and Wh-questions, and coreferential deletions, etc. (see Keenan[14] for discussion), would have to change.

Furthermore, the logical similarity between Actives and Passives is not quite perfect, as Chomsky pointed out some time ago. Thus, to use his example, *everyone in this room speaks two languages* is, it seems to me, vague (not ambiguous), according as it is the same two languages or not. The sentence is simply not explicit on that point. But *two languages are spoken by everyone in this room* has a reading, the preferred or only one for many speakers, in which it clearly does require that we all speak the same two languages. And this fact is no accident. It is universally the case that, other things being equal (and there are very many such other things, see Ioup[6] for discussion), subjects have wider scope, logically speaking, than nonsubjects. This is even true for those few Ls like Malagasy and Gilbertese (see Keenan[13] for examples) in which the subject follows the object in the unmarked word order.

Consequently, Ls vary with regard to logically significant operations (although we cannot conclude from this that they vary with regard to basic expressive power, since Ls with limited promotion devices may, and usually do, have other devices for forcing nonsubjects to have wider scope than subjects).

THE CROSS-REFERENCE SYSTEM

I should like now to consider a type of cross-language variation in which the *prima facie* case that Ls differ in logical expressive power is more impressive. The variation concerns the possibilities of stipulating different NP positions as being either *positively coreferential* (i.e., as referring to the same object), or *negatively coreferential* (i.e., as referring to different objects).

If the potentially coreferent NPs occur within the same clause there are, to my knowledge, three possible ways to stipulate their positive coreference. First, a marked or "reflexive" form of the verb may be used, as in Russian, Bantu generally, Dyirbal, Blackfoot, Turkish, and many other Ls.

Shona (Bantu)
(6) a. John akarowa murume
        John struck   the man

    b. John akamurowa
        John struck-him ($\neq$ John)

    c. John akazvirowa
        John struck-self

Second, in a very few cases, notably Eskimo, one of the NPs can simply be omitted.

Eskimo (Woodbury[30])
(7) a. iNmi-nut tuqup-puq
        self-abl:sg kill-ind:3sg
        'He killed himself'

    b. tuqup-puq
        kill- ind:3sg
        'He killed himself' or 'He died' or 'He was killed'

And third, a marked form of a pronoun may be used, as in an English sentence like *John hit himself*. The reflexive pronoun forces us to understand that the person hit and the person doing the hitting are the same. By contrast, we infer from sentences like *John hit him* or *John hit Bill* that the hitter and the hittee are different. Note that the logical form of a sentence like *John hit himself* and that of *John hit him* are different, since the conditions under which they are true are not necessarily the same. Some Ls, however, do not syntactically codify this logical distinction. Thus, in many Polynesian languages such as Gilbertese and Tahitian, the same sentence is used in either case, the difference in meaning being left up to context.

> *Gilbertese* (ex. from Keenan[12])
> (8) E- tara-ia   Teerau
>   he-hit- him/himself Teerau
>   'Teerau hit him' or 'Teerau hit himself'

Similarly, in some Indo-European Ls this logical distinction is also ignored.

> *Fering* (a N. Frisian dialect; ex. from K. Ebert, personal communication)
> (9) John hee ham   ferreet
>   John has him/himself betrayed
>   'John has betrayed him' or 'John has betrayed himself'
>
> *Middle English* (Chaucer, *The Knight's Tale*, ex. from Keenan[12])
> (10) a. He leyde hym, bare the visage, on the beere (v. 2877)
>   (He = Theseus, hym = Arcite, as is clear from context)
>
>   b. At Thebes, in his contree, as I seyde,
>   Upon a nyght in sleep as he hym leyde (v. 1384)
>   (he = Arcite, hym = Arcite)

These Ls, then, are logically less expressive than contemporary English, since it expresses a logical distinction which they do not.

On the other hand, English does not normally stipulate the coreference between subjects and possessors of objects. Thus the syntax of *John wrecked his car* allows that it be John's car or that it be someone else's. The reference of *his* depends on context, just as did the reference of the object pronouns in Gilbertese, Fering, and Middle English. But many Ls, such as Swedish, Latvian, Russian, Finnish, Japanese, Hindi, and Turkish, distinguish between reflexive and nonreflexive possessors.

> *Swedish* (McClean[19])
> (11) a. Lars har sin   bok
>   Lars has his(=Lars) book
>
>   b. Lars har hans   bok
>   Lars has his(≠Lars) book
>
> *Japanese*
> (12) a. Taroo wa zibun   no inu o   butta
>   Taroo tpc his(=Taroo) gen dog DO hit
>   'Taroo hit his (Taroo's) dog'
>
>   b. Taroo wa kare   no inu o   butta
>   Taroo tpc his(≠Taroo) gen dog DO hit
>   'Taroo hit his (someone else's) dog'

Note that in these examples both positive and negative coreference is stipulated. In the forms with the reflexive *his* the possessor must be the subject, and in the nonreflexive forms the possessor must be someone other than the subject. English appears to lack this discriminating power, and so is less expressive logically than Swedish, Japanese, and others.

One might argue, however, that although English normally does not stipulate coreference of subjects and possessors of objects, it can do so, if necessary, by using the form *own*, as done in the glosses above. Thus in *John wrecked his own car* it is clearly John's car that was wrecked, not someone else's. However, the use of *his-own* is not quite equivalent to the reflexive possessives cited above, since *own* forces the meaning of permanent possession rather than temporary possession, and thus contrasts with a mere *his* in contexts like: *the students were given ballpoint pens to write their exams with, but John didn't use his because he preferred to use his own*. Further, even though *his-own* may be used to force positive coreference in some cases, there seems to be no systematic way of forcing negative coreference. Clearly the absence of *own* in *John wrecked his car* does not force the nonreflexive reading. What English would need here would be a form like *his-else* corresponding to *his-own*. But English lacks such a form.[†]

Further, when the potentially coreferent positions occur in different clauses, one subordinate to the other, English is even less well adapted to stipulating their coreference. It has basically two means for doing so. One, it can repeat a full NP, marked perhaps with an anaphoric marker like *the* or *that* as in *While John was explaining the problem to a student, the student was working a crossword puzzle*. Second, English may delete a positively coreferent NP (triggering perhaps other changes in the sentence as well), as in *John was preparing his lecture while walking in the garden*, where it is clearly John who is doing the walking in contrast to *John was preparing his lecture while he was walking in the garden*, where *he* might refer to John or it might refer to someone else identified in the discourse. A slightly different type of example would be *John expects to be elected*, where clearly John has an expectation about himself, in distinction to *John expects him to be elected*, where the expectation is clearly about someone else. But notice here that the coreferent positions do not occur across clause boundaries in surface, but rather they are the surface subject and object of *expect*. So raising subordinate positions to main clause ones, where coreference is more naturally stipulated in English, is another option English may use.

Noun marking and deletion are probably universal means of stipulating positive coreference across clause boundaries, but other strategies are also in common use, and can often apply in cases where the English strategies cannot. I shall discuss three such strategies: *pronoun marking, case marking*, and *switch reference marking*.

[†]Of the many ways we might attempt to stipulate negative coreference, all I have tried seem to me to fail to be equivalent to the Swedish and Japanese type cases. Thus *John wrecked a car which belonged to someone other than him* fails to identify the car and as well leaves the reference of *him* unclear, whereas the Swedish version of *John wrecked his* ($\neq$ *John's*) *car* identifies the possessor of the car and makes it clear that it is not John. Similarly, *John wrecked the car, which didn't belong to him*, presupposes that a car has been previously identified and is still vague with regard to the reference of *him*. Another alternative, *John wrecked his, someone else's, car* fails for several reasons. First, the reference of *else* is not unequivocally John, we might mean someone else already identified in the discourse. Further, the sentence is pragmatically redundant in a very bizarre way. For the use of *his*, not coreferential with John, presupposes that the speaker and addressee know who is being referred to. And given that the use of proper names like *John* presupposes that the identity of the referent is known to the participants in the discourse, the added assertion *someone else's* is only redundant. It provides less information than what is already presupposed by the use of *his*. Finally, as per our translation of (12b), *John wrecked his (someone else's) car* fails to paraphrase the intended sentences in Japanese and Swedish because it actually talks, metalinguistically, about some of the words in the sentence; namely, the reference of *his*. But the Swedish sentences do not talk about their own words, and so differ in meaning in a very big way from the proposed English translation.

Pronoun Marking

English does not systematically stipulate the coreference of subjects of verbs of thinking and saying and the subjects of their sentential complements. Thus the syntactic form of *John thinks that he will win* allows that *he* refer to John or to someone else already identified in the discourse. But many Ls such as Japanese, Korean, Yoruba (Kwa), and Kera (Chadic) stipulate positive and, generally, negative coreference of these positions by the use of marked vs. unmarked pronominal forms.[‡]

> *Japanese* (ex. from Mat Shibatani, personal communication)
> (13) a. Taroo wa zibun ga   katu to   omotte iru
>   Taroo tpc self   subj win COMP think   be
>   'Taroo thinks that he (= Taroo) is winning'
>
>   b. Taroo wa kare ga   katu to   omotte iru
>   Taroo tpc he   subj win COMP think   be
>   'Taroo thinks that he (likely ≠ Taroo) is winning'

> *Yoruba*
> (14) a. Ojo ro   pe   ȯn   mu sasa
>   Ojo thinks that he(= Ojo) is   clever
>
>   b. Ojo ro   pe   ȯ   mu sasa
>   Ojo thinks that he(≠ Ojo) is   clever

> *Kera* (ex. from K. Ebert, personal communication)
> (15) a. Golsala dig   minti to   bɨ cuuru
>   Golsala thinks that   he(= Golsala) is intelligent
>
>   b. Golsala dig   minti wɨ   bɨ cuuru
>   Golsala thinks that   he(≠ Golsala) is intelligent

Again, it might be argued that although English does appear to lack the means to stipulate the negative coreference of these positions, it can stipulate their positive coreference if necessary. We can, for example, simply mark the embedded subject with a kind of emphatic reflexive, as in *John thinks that he himself should go*. But this use of the reflexive does not in general force coreference with the matrix subject, as is clear from examples like *The president wanted to send the prime minister to the meeting, but his secretary thought that he himself should go*. Clearly *he himself* here does not refer to *his secretary*. A possibly more general alternative would be to simply repeat, in apposition, the matrix subject, as in *John thinks that he, John, should go*. But this solution will not work when the matrix subject is any of several types of quantified NP. Thus we cannot paraphrase the intended meaning of *everyone thinks that he should go* by anything like *everyone thinks that everyone should go* or *everyone thinks that that person should go*. Similarly, if the subject is *most people, no one*, etc. But the Japanese type languages can stipulate both positive and negative coreference in these cases. (In fact, the judgement of negative coreference in sentences with the nonreflexive pronouns is much clearer than in the simpler cases like (13),

> *Japanese* (ex. from Mat Shibatani, personal communication)
> (16) a. Daremo ga   zibun ga   katu to   omotte iru

[‡] Across clause boundaries the use of the *kare* series of pronouns in Japanese may or may not definitely stipulate negative coreference. In the simple cases like (13b) some speakers find that *kare* can corefer to the matrix subject. But in cases like (16b) the use of *kare* definitely does stipulate negative coreference.

Everyone subj self   subj win COMP think   be
'Everyone thinks that he (himself) is winning'

b. Darema ga kare   ga katu to   omotte iru
   Everyone subj he(definitely = other) subj win COMP think   be
   'Everyone thinks that he (someone previously identified) is winning'

So again we have a case where some Ls make a logical distinction that English doesn't.

Case Marking

The possibility of using case marking to stipulate coreference is perhaps not widely recognized. The following example from Classical Greek, provided by E. J. W. Barber (personal communication) is a magnificent illustration of this strategy.

(17) a. élthōn-θ
        coming-nom

     b. élthont-a   eis těn pólin, ho   didáskal-os édeixe
        coming-acc   into the city the teacher- nom showed
                                            nom

     c. élthont-i   tòn paîd-a   tô̂ sōkrát-ē
        coming-dat   the child-acc the Socrates-dat
                       acc   dat

     d. élthont-os
        coming-gen

'Coming into the city, the teacher showed the child to Socrates'

The main clause of (17), *the teacher showed the child to Socrates*, contains three NPs: a nominative, an accusative, and a dative. The subordinate verb, *come*, which lacks an overt subject, takes the case marker of whatever NP in the matrix clause is understood to function as its subject. Thus (17a) means that the person who was coming into the city was the teacher, (17b) means it was the child, and (17c) means it was Socrates. Thus matching of case markers here forces positive coreference. English can, perhaps, also stipulate the positive coreference in these cases by repeating full NPs, e.g. *While the teacher was coming into the city the teacher showed the child to Socrates* (although such a sentence could perhaps be used in a situation in which two different teachers had been previously identified).

But Greek affords us an additional possibility—the absolute construction illustrated in (17d). Here the use of the genitive case marker on the subordinate verb stipulates that the subject of that verb is *not* coreferential with any of the NPs in the matrix, but must be understood to refer to someone else previously identified. Thus the condition expressed by the subordinate clause is absolute, i.e., not dependent on anything in the matrix clause.

The possibility of stipulating negative coreference here is, it seems to us, lacking in English. Notice, however, that many of the daughter Ls of Indo-European developed absolute constructions that functioned to stipulate negative coreference. In Latin the absolute case marker was the ablative (its role in stipulating negative coreference is discussed briefly in Winter[28]), in Gothic and old Slavic it was the dative, and in Sanscrit it was a locative.

Further, the possibility of stipulating positive coreference by case marking is not limited to Indo-European Ls. Ken Hale (personal communication) provides the following example from Walbiri, an Australian L:

(18) kudu-ŋku maliki-θ   paka- ɳu , wanti-njtja-wanu- lu
     child-erg dog- abs strike-past, fall- inf- COMP-erg
     'The child hit the dog, after falling'

Here the use of the ergative case marker on the subordinate verb *fall* unequivocally indicates that its subject is the ergative NP in the main clause. Thus (18) can only mean that it was the child that fell. If the ergative marker on the verb is replaced by the absolutive marker, θ, then it is naturally interpreted to mean that it was the dog that fell (although the other interpretation is perhaps also possible, so the coreference is not unequivocally stipulated in this case, whereas in (18) it is).

Switch Reference

It is characteristic of several language groups that subordinate verbs may carry one of two affixes according to whether their subject is either the same in reference or different in reference from some NP in another clause. This is a typological trait of the Ls of the Eastern New Guinea Highlands Stock[20] such as Fore,[23] Kafe-Kamano, and Bena-Bena.[30] It is also typologically characteristic of the Hokan phylum of American Indian Ls (see Jacobsen,[7] Winter,[28] and Munro[21] for discussion) and occurs as well in some Uto-Aztecan Ls e.g. Hopi.[27]

We consider first some cases from American Indian Ls: (in the examples below we use *ds* to abbreviate *different subject*, and *ss* for *same subject*.)

   Hopi (ex. from Pam Munro, personal communication)
   (19) a. pam navoti:ta (pam) mo:titani-q
           he thinks   (he) win   -ds
           'He thinks that he (=someone else) will win'

        b. pam navoti:ta (pam) mo:titani-qaʔe
           he thinks   (he) win   -ss
           'He thinks that he (himself) will win'

The use of the *different-subject* marker on the subordinate verb in (19a) clearly means that the subject of *win* is not the same as the subject of *think*, whereas the use of the *same-subject* marker in (19b) clearly means that the subject of *win* is the same as the person doing the thinking. Similar claims hold for the Mojave (Yuman family, Hokan phylum) sentences below, again provided by Pam Munro, (personal communication).

(20) ʔi:pa-č̣   su:paw-mpoč piʔipa:-nʸ   iyu: { -m / -k / -ds / -ss }

     man- subj know -neg   person- dem see-

     'The man doesn't know who he saw'

If the suffix *-m* is chosen on the subordinate verb *see*, then the subject of *see* must be different from the matrix subject *man*, and thus the man's lack of knowledge concerns someone other than himself. But if the suffix *-k* is chosen, then the subject of *see* is necessarily the same as the subject of *know*. Similarly,

(21) ʔi:pa-nʸ -č   ʔava:-lʸ nʸa -iyem $\begin{cases} \text{-m} \\ \text{-k} \end{cases}$, yakapit-pč

man- dem-subj house-loc when-come $\begin{cases} \text{-ds} \\ \text{-ss} \end{cases}$, drunk   tense

'When the man came to the house, he was drunk'

Again, if the subordinate verb *come* is suffixed with *-m*, then the man who came is different from the person who was drunk. But if the suffix *-k* is chosen, then the man who came and the person who was drunk are the same.

The data from Hopi and Mojave clearly indicate that those Ls can stipulate negative coreference in a way not possible in English. Furthermore, the use of *ss* markers seems a more effective way of stipulating positive coreference than the English strategies, since it works as well if the controller NP is quantified. Thus parallel to (21) from Mojave we have:

(22) ʔipač-č   pay nʸa- u:θew   -k yakapi:tč -m
men -subj all   when-drink + pl-ss drunk + pl-tns
'When all the men were drinking, they got drunk'

In English however, we cannot generally stipulate positive coreference in this construction by repeating full NPs. Thus *Everyone got drunk after he returned* is not paraphrasable by *Everyone got drunk after everyone returned*. The deletion strategy may be somewhat more effective, since the sentence *Upon returning, everyone got drunk* seems to imply that the subject of *return* and that of *get drunk* are the same. But even here it can be argued that the subject of *return* is only vaguely specified. Thus, in a context like *Pat and Mickey had had a bloody hard day on the job, so upon returning to their wives, everybody got drunk*, it seems that the subject of return is only *Pat and Mickey*, but the subject of *get drunk* includes their wives as well.

The use of switch reference marking in New Guinea Ls is even more striking in certain respects than in the American Indian Ls. Here it is common in narrative discourse for main clauses to be preceeded by up to twenty subordinate clauses (called "medial" forms in the literature). The subordinate verbs carry different markers according to whether or not their subject is different from that of the next clause in the sequence, regardless of whether the next clause is a main clause or not. Further, the switch reference markers may encode information about the relative times of the actions expressed in the two clauses. And in addition, it often happens that the subordinate verb carries an affix which agrees in person and number with the subject of the following clause, regardless of whether it is the same or different. So subordinate verbs often agree with two subjects: their own, and that of the next clause. (In the examples that follow, matching subscripts indicate sameness of reference, different subscripts different reference.)

Fore (Scott[23])
(23) a. kana- ogá-   na$_i$ wa-tä- y$_i$- e
    come-ds:3sg:past 3sg go- past-3sg-indic
        coord. act.
    'He came and he went'

   b. kana- nta-   ná$_i$ wa-tä- y$_i$- e
    come-ss:3sg:pàst 3sg go- past-3sg-indic
        coord. act.
    'He came and he went'

In (23a) the use of the *ds* marker unequivocally means that the person who came is not the same as the person who went, whereas these two are the same in (23b).

Kafe-Kamano (ex. from Harold Levine, personal communication)

(24) a. Ónihava$_j$ hóyaf- ínti bu-i$_j$- ge-no$_i$ Toiso$_i$ a- gé- ´n- e
Onihava$_j$ garden-into go-he$_j$-ds-he$_i$ Toiso$_i$ him-see-past-Emph
'Onihava went into the garden (and) Toiso saw him'

b. Ónihava$_j$ hóyaf- ínti bu-i$_j$- no$_j$ a- gé- ´n- e
Onihava$_j$ garden-into go-he$_j$-he$_j$ him-see-past-Emph
'Onihava went into the garden (and) saw him'

Note here that change of subject is overtly marked (24a), but sameness of subject is indicated by the absence of a switch marker. Note also that while both the Fore and Kafe sentences are translated by coordinate structures in English, the first clause in each case is clearly marked as being not a main clause by virtue of the anticipatory subject marking. So the first clauses of (23) and (24) cannot stand alone as main clauses.

Some Universals of Coreference?

Although the diversity of means Ls use to stipulate coreference makes any generalizations at this point somewhat tentative, the following two "universals" are largely consistent with the data at my disposal.

(1) If coreference, either positive or negative, can be controlled by any NPs in a language, then, in general, subjects of main clauses may control coreference.

(2) If a language can stipulate the negative coreference of two positions then it can stipulate their positive coreference as well.

(1) states that we cannot have human Ls in which only e.g. direct objects control coreference.[§] And (2) states that no L can stipulate only negative coreference. It appears, then, that, like promotion systems, variation in the cross-reference system of a L is regular, and a proper object of scientific investigation.

RELATIVE CLAUSES

I want finally to consider certain types of variation found in the relative clauses (RC) forming system across Ls. Ls differ both with regard to the NP positions which can be relativized and with regard to the means (=strategies) used to relativize them. And the two types of variation are not independent; some strategies are more effective than others in that they can relativize positions which the others cannot.

Consider first the *verb-coding* strategy discussed earlier for Malagasy and the Philippine Ls. There, recall, only surface subjects could be relativized. Thus, if the subordinate verb in the RC is, for example, passive, then the position relativized represents an underlying direct object, since it was necessary to passivize the verb to

---

[§] An interesting potential counterexample here is reported for Angaataha (Huisman[5]), one of the New Guinea Ls. Here the switch reference markers have apparently only a switch location function. One marker indicates that the location of the action of the next clause coming up is the same as that of the clause which carries the marker, and another marker indicates that the location will change in the next clause. But not enough information is available concerning stipulation of coreference to subjects to allow us to say that Angaataha can stipulate coreference between locatives but not to subjects.

promote it to the relativizable slot. Similarly, if the verb is in a locative form the position relativized is an underlying locative, and so on. So it is the verb form that codes the semantic relation between the head NP and the restricting clause.

But verb-coding strategies are inherently limited, since universally the number of verb voices is less than the number of distinct semantic relations that NPs may bear to verbs. Thus, NPs bearing different semantic relations to the verb will be promoted to subject using the same verb voice, and consequently RCs formed on those subjects will be inherently vague or ambiguous. This is particularly clear when NPs bear different *locative* relations to the verb. Thus the Malagasy sentences (25a) and (25b) differ only in their locative prepositions *on* and *under*.

> (25) a. nametraka mofo teo　ambony ny latabatra Rabe
>   placed　　bread there on top of the table　　Rabe
>   'Rabe placed the bread on top of the table'
>
> b. nametraka mofo teo　ambany ny latabatra Rabe
>   placed　　bread there under　the table　 Rabe
>   'Rabe placed bread under the table'

However, when *table* is promoted to subject in either case, the verb goes in the same form, *table* moves to subject position (sentence final) and becomes nominative, losing its preposition. So the derived sentence is the same in both cases:

> (26) nametrahan-dRabe mofo ny latabatra
>   placed by-　 Rabe bread the table
>   '?? The table was bread put by Rabe'

So the exact locative relation between *table* and *put* cannot be expressed in this sentence. But this is the only one that *table* can be relativized from. Consequently the RC preserves the vagueness (or ambiguity) of (26).

> (27) ny latabatra izay nametrahan-dRabe mofo
>   the table　　that placed by-　Rabe bread
>   'the table where Rabe put the bread'

Thus, in many cases where English has two logically distinct RCs, e.g. *the table under which Rabe put the bread* and *the table on top of which Rabe put the bread*, Malagasy and the Philippine Ls have only one; so English codifies a logical distinction that those Ls don't.

On the other hand, the RC forming strategies used in English are generally less effective than the *noun-coding* strategies characteristic of many Ls in which the surface RC presents a nominal element in the position relativized. The nominal element is a pronoun in Welsh, Czech, Persian, Semitic generally, many Polynesian and Melanesian Ls (Tongan, Fijian), etc. (See Keenan and Comrie[17] for discussion.)

Hebrew
> (28) ha- isha　　she- Yon natan la　　et　ha- sefer
>   the woman that John gave　 to her DO the book
>   'the woman that John gave the book to'

On the other hand, in Ls as diverse as Walbiri and Mabuaig in Australia, Hindi, Kannada, Hittite, medieval Slavic, and Bambara (W. Africa), the position relativized is marked by a full NP. In those Ls a RC can be formed from a sentence simply by adding a morphological marker to the NP which defines the domain of relativization. Thus, from (29a) in Bambara we can form the RC in (29b).

(29) a. cἕ ye mùsò yè
man past woman see
'The man saw the woman'

    b. cἕ yè mùsò min yè
man past woman rel see
'the woman that the man saw'

Now noun-coding strategies generally permit the formation of a larger class of RCs than strategies that present no NP in the position relativized (and which I will call for the nonce *deletion* strategies). To take just one example, Ls that use noun-coding strategies can frequently (but not always) relativize into single members of coordinate NPs. Thus from (30a) in Hebrew (ex. from Cole *et al.*[2]) we can form (30b).

(30) a. ha- ish ve- Miriam xaverim tovim
the-man and-Miriam friends good
'The man and Miriam are good friends'

    b. ze ha- ish she- hu ve- Miriam xaverim tovim
this the-man that-he and-Miriam friends good
'This is the man that he and Miriam are good friends'

And from (31a) in Kannada (ex. constructed from Cole *et al.*[2]) we can form (31b).

(31) a. sōfa mattu kurciya naduve avaru mējannu iṭṭiddāro
sofa and   chair-gen between they table-acc placed-have
'They have placed a table between a sofa and a chair'

    b. yāva sōfa mattu kurciya naḍuve avaru mējannu iṭṭiddāro
rel   sofa and   chair-gen between they table-acc placed-have
adu haḷeyadu
that old-is
'the sofa which they have placed a table between (it) and a chair is old'

Further, many Ls (see Keenan and Comrie[17] for details) that normally use deletion strategies to form RCs have recourse to noun coding strategies when relativizing "difficult" positions e.g. possessor NPs, as in *Here comes the student that I can never remember his name*, and NPs in embedded questions, as *This is the road that I don't know where it goes*. For a more detailed analysis of the range of positions that can be relativized by the pronoun-retaining strategies, see Keenan[13] and Keenan and Comrie.[17] For the noun-retaining strategies see Cole *et al.*[2] and Keenan and Bimson.[16]

Some Universals of RC Formation

1. If a L can relativize any NPs it can relativize main clause subjects.
2. If a language L uses noun-coding strategies in RC formation to a greater extent than another language L', then the class of relativizable NPs in L is greater than or equal to that in L'.

(2) above is a way of formulating the intuition that noun-coding strategies yield "lots" of RCs (relative to the "norm" for Ls). But it is logically different from the simple conditional universals we have considered up to now. For it says that properties of some Ls are not independent of those of others! That the grammar of one L should be constrained by that of another may seem outlandish, but quite generally, I think, statements of functional equivalence of different syntactic processes will have this comparative quality. Consider for example the oft-cited, and largely correct, claim

that case-marking Ls have relatively free word order. Note that both case marking (understood to cover the use of prepositions and postpositions) and word-order freedom are matters of degree. Some Ls (e.g. Machiguenga; Peru, see Snell and Wise[25]) case mark practically no major NPs, whereas others, e.g. Tongan (Polynesia), case mark all major NPs. And in some Ls (Walbiri; Australia) word order is totally free, whereas in others (e.g. French) it is fixed. Given that, we may formulate the trade-off between word-order freedom and case marking as follows: If L case marks to a greater degree than L', then the word-order freedom of L is greater than or equal to that of L'.

CONCLUSION: EXPLAINING VARIATION-BASED UNIVERSALS

The primary purpose of this paper has been to substantiate the claim that Ls vary in interesting ways, that the variation is regular, and that it determines universal constraints on the form of possible human Ls. But we have offered no explanation for this variation. And indeed, an explanation for even a part of it would go beyond our current knowledge. So I would like to close by suggesting a line of research which, if pursued, could in my opinion lead to explanations of some of the variation we have discussed.

The starting point for this research would be the Principle of Autonomous Reference (PAR), which I will define below. The PAR is, at the moment, little more than a personal impression based on work in a variety of Ls. It clearly needs conceptual refinement and systematic empirical corroboration. Further, by itself it does not explain the variation in question, but requires in each case supplementary assumptions concerning the nature of language—assumptions that are, again, in need of conceptual clarification and empirical corroboration.

Principle of Autonomous Reference (PAR)

In the basic sentence types of a L a combination of case-marking, position, and verb agreements function to identify exactly one NP as being in principle autonomous in reference.

By *basic sentences* I mean those whose syntactic form is not given as a function of that of other sentences. By *autonomous in reference* I mean an NP used to refer to some object or concept, and whose referent is identifiable to the addressee at the moment of utterance. It other words, in the context of utterance, the information in the NP itself is sufficient to tell the addressee(s) what object or concept is being referred to. Thus the reference of such an NP cannot be made to depend on the reference of some NP that follows it in the discourse. Either it refers directly to some object physically present in the discourse, or it corefers to an object already identified (or at least known to exist).¶

Note, of course, that in any given sentence many NPs may, in fact, be autonomous in reference (e.g. in *John loves Mary* both *John* and *Mary* are in fact autonomous in reference). But only one NP in basic sentences *must* be. Others *may* depend on it for their reference (as happens in *John loves himself*, where the identity of the person loved is specified as being the same as that of the one doing the loving).

¶Three weak points in this definition and subsequent claims are: 1) We need operational tests for degree of basicness; 2) the notion of reference is not defined; and 3) the criteria used to determine which NPs are subjects must be established on universal grounds. See Keenan[15] for discussion.

Now generally speaking, the NPs we identify as subjects of basic sentences are the autonomously referring expressions (AREs) of those sentences. Further, the surface coding properties (case-marking, etc.) of basic subjects also identify main clause subjects of complex sentences, and these subjects are AREs as well.

The "fact" that main clause subjects are AREs might be used in the partial explanation of the variation we have discussed in the following cases:

First, it gives some explanation as to why Ls should have promotion to subject rules. Namely, such rules serve to present NPs as autonomous in reference when they are not necessarily so in basic sentences. It is thus no accident that our judgment of relative scope of quantifier NPs changes when a sentence is passivized. For notice that in an active sentence like *every boy kissed some girl* the "reference" of *some girl* depends on that of *every boy* in the sense that the truth of the sentence requires that for each boy there be some girl whom he kissed. The choice of girl however, may vary with (that is, depend on) the choice of boy. But, in the passive sentence *some girl was kissed by every boy*, we must identify some girl independently of a choice of a boy, and then establish that every boy kissed that girl. Further, if we could show that DOs fail to have any characteristic semantic or pragmatic property, like autonomous reference, we would have a basis for explaining why it is more usual across Ls to have promotion to subject rules than promotion to object rules.

Second, the "fact" that subjects are AREs may partially explain why subjects are the easiest NPs to relativize across Ls. For notice that in general, head NPs of RCs are also autonomously referential. That is, the class of objects they specify must be understood independently of the reference of any NP in the restricting clause. Even if the restricting clause precedes the head, the normal order in SOV Ls, we cannot make the reference of the head depend on anything in the restricting clause, e.g. by pronominalizing it (see Keenan[13] for further exemplification and discussion). So when we relativize on a given NP position, we force that position to be autonomously referential. But because subject NPs already have that property, RC formation on subjects changes relatively little our understanding of the way we understand the sentence relativized into. But when objects are relativized, they are forced to have a property they do not necessarily have: autonomous reference. Perhaps RC formation on objects is therefore universally harder than on subjects, since it distorts the meaning of the sentence relativized into more than RC formation of subjects. Further, object RCs have of necessity two AREs in surface: the head NP and the subject of the restricting clause, whereas subject RCs have only one ARE, of necessity. This explains why the pronoun *he* in *the man who he saw* cannot be understood to necessarily corefer to *man*, for *he* is a subject of a clause of which *man* is an object, and subjects must refer independently of objects. For further discussion of this point see Keenan.[13]

And third, if subjects are generally AREs, it is natural that they should be universally among the controllers of coreference. For if the reference of a subject is always well defined, then the reference of another NP will also be well defined when it is given as a function of that of a subject.

In conclusion, let me just reiterate that our discussion of the PAR and its role in explaining variation-based universals is intended only as suggestive of further research and is not intended as complete in itself. The primary purpose of this paper has been merely to establish certain patterns of language variation and the constraints they determine on human languages.

References

1. CAPELL, A. 1971. Arosi Grammar. Pacific Linguistics. **20** (Series B). The Australian National University. Canberra, Australia.

2. COLE, P. W., S. HARBERT, S. HASHIMOTO, C. NELSON, D. SMIETANA & S. SRIDHAR. 1975. Noun Phrase Accessibility and Island Constraints. Presented at the Parasession of the XIth Regional Meetings of the Chicago Linguistic Society. Chicago, Ill.
3. COLLINS, G. 1970. Two Views of Kalagan Grammar. PhD dissertation. Indiana University. Bloomington, Ind. Unpublished.
4. GARY, J. O. 1974. Promotion Rules in Kinyarwanda. Dept. of Linguistics. University of California at Los Angeles. Unpublished.
5. HUISMAN, R. D. 1973. Angaataha Verb Morphology. Linguistics 110: 43–54.
6. IOUP, G. 1973. Some Universals of Quantifier Scope. Presented at Second Conf. on New Ways of Analyzing Variation. Georgetown University. Washington, D.C.
7. JACOBSEN, W. H. 1967. Switch-reference in Hokan-Coahuiltecan. In Studies in Southwestern Ethnolinguistics. D. Hymes, Ed. Mouton. The Hague, The Netherlands.
8. JOHNSON, D. 1974. Relational constraints on grammars. Preprint. Mathematical Sciences Dept. T. J. Watson Research Center, IBM. Yorktown Heights, N.Y. Unpublished.
9. KATZ, J. 1966. The Philosophy of Language. Harper and Row. New York, N.Y.
10. KEENAN, E. L. 1972. Relative clause formation in Malagasy and some related and some not so related languages. In The Chicago Which Hunt: 169–190. Chicago Linguistic Society. Chicago, Ill.
11. KEENAN, E. L. 1972. On semantically based grammar. Linguistic Inquiry 3(4): 413–461.
12. KEENAN, E. L. 1973. Logical expressive power and syntactic variation in natural language. In Formal Semantics of Natural Language. E. L. Keenan, Ed. Cambridge University Press. Cambridge, Mass. To be published. Presented at Cambridge Colloquium on Formal Semantics.
13. KEENAN, E. L. 1974. The Functional Principle: generalizing the notion of 'subject of'. In Papers from the Xth Regional Meetings of the Chicago Linguistic Society: 298–310.
14. KEENAN, E. L. 1975. Remarkable subjects in Malagasy. In Subject and Topic. C. Li, Ed. To be published.
15. KEENAN, E. L. 1975. Towards a universal definition of 'subject of'. In Subject and Topic. C. Li. Ed. To be published. Presented at winter meetings Linguistic Society of America.
16. KEENAN, E. L. & K. BIMSON. 1975. Perceptual complexity and the cross-language distribution of relative clause and NP-question types. In Functionalism: 253–260. The Chicago Linguistic Society. Chicago, Ill.
17. KEENAN, E. L. & B. COMRIE. Noun-phrase accessibility and universal grammar. Linguistic Inquiry. To be published. Presented at winter meetings of Linguistic Society of America, 1972.
18. KRAFT, CH. H. & A. H. M. KIRK-GREENE. 1973. Hausa. Teach Yourself Books. English Universities Press, Ltd.
19. MCCLEAN, R. J. 1969. Swedish. Teach Yourself Books. English Universities Press, Ltd.
20. MCKAUGHAN, H. 1973. The Languages of the Eastern Family of the East New Guinea Highland Stock. Vol. 1. University of Washington Press, Seattle, Wash.
21. MUNRO, P. 1974. Topics in Mojave Syntax. Ph.D. dissertation. University of California at San Diego.
22. ROSS, J. R. 1967. Constraints on Variables in Syntax. Ph.D. dissertation. Dept. of Linguistics. Massachusetts Institute of Technology. Cambridge, Mass.
23. SCOTT, G. 1973. Higher Levels of Fore Grammar. Pacific Linguistics 23 (Series B). The Australian National University. Canberra, Australia.
24. SHIMIZU, M. 1975. Relational grammar and promotion rules in Japanese. In Papers from the XIth Regional Meeting of the Chicago Linguistic Society: 529–536. Chicago, Ill.
25. SNELL, B. & R. WISE. 1963. Noncontingent declarative clauses in Machiguenga (Arawak). In Studies in Peruvian Indian Languages: 1. Summer Institute of Linguistics of the University of Oklahoma. Norman, Okla.
26. TRITHART, L. 1975. Relational grammar and Chicewa subjectivization rules. In Papers from the XIth Regional Meetings of the Chicago Linguistic Society: 615–625. Chicago, Ill.
27. VOEGELIN, C. F. & F. M. VOEGELIN. 1974. Some recent (and not so recent) attempts to interpret semantics of native languages in North America. Indiana University. Bloomington, Ind. Unpublished.

28. WINTER, W. Switch-reference in Yuman languages. University of Kiel. Kiel, Germany. No date.

29. WOODBURY, A. 1975. Ergativity of grammatical processes: a study of Greenlandic Eskimo. M.A. Thesis. Dept. of Linguistics. University of Chicago. Chicago, Ill.

30. YOUNG, R. A. 1971. The verb in Bena-Bena: its form and function. Pacific Linguistics: **18** (Series B). The Australian National University. Canberra, Australia.

DISCUSSION

Patrick Suppes, *Moderator*

Stanford University
Stanford, California 94305

JOANN GORMETT (*New York University, New York, N.Y.*): I have a question for Dr. Wang. You referred to the emerging state of language and the steady state of language, and I wanted to know what evidence you have for an emerging state, since everything we seem to know about language is about a steady state?

DR. WANG: The distinction between the emerging state and the steady state is more or less the same distinction that Chuck Fillmore used when he talked about evolving *toward* and evolving *of*. Denying some such distinction, it seems to me, would force us to conclude that language emerged instantly in its full splendor, a picture which most of us probably would not find plausible.

It is certainly suggestive to find that all the linguistic changes that have been attested for a diverse range of languages constitute actually a very small number of types. These types make up a minuscule fraction of the large number of logical possibilities that one can easily construct. We might speculate that during the emerging state language change must have been much more sporadic and haphazard, and much less constrained. The fact that changes now proceed along relatively well-defined grooves leads me to believe that the evolution of language has reached some kind of plateau.

I know of no direct evidence for the existence of emergent states—nor is it likely that we'll ever get it. Making the distinction between the two states seems to me both reasonable at this point and useful in that it makes the problem a little more researchable.

DR. KEENAN: Prof, Wang, although you did give a few examples of differences, between languages that had writing systems and those that didn't, I have a general impression, which I cannot justify statistically. This concerns languages that are always spoken in a face-to-face situation—they're unwritten, they tend to be spoken by small populations,—I'm thinking particularly of languages in New Guinea, say, where the populations usually run from about 500 to 3,000 or 4,000. It is my impression that languages of this sort have better developed deixis systems than languages with long-established writing traditions. By deixis systems I mean those elements of the language which, by their nature, reference elements of the context of discourse. So it's not uncommon in those languages to find, for example, that you have a very elaborate series of demonstrative adjectives and pronouns. They're marked differently according to whether the object referred to is or is not visible to the speaker or hearer. You've sometimes got one series of "*this*" that refer to *this up in the north*, another series for *this down in the south*, you may have upriver "*this*," downriver "*this*." You sometimes have markers on verbs which indicate that the evidence in support of the assertion is directly present in the situation; you sometimes get numeral systems where the names of the numbers are exactly the names of ordinary body parts, and so on. In addition, of course, the first and second person pronoun systems often are proliferated. You often get duals, and you often get inclusive and exclusive forms of pronouns.

Now, it seems to me that there's some tendency for this system, the deixis system, to be lost over time, when the language becomes written, and spoken by a large group of people where you often speak in a different context from the one in which the

92

people who read your utterances are present. Often, for example, the demonstrative adjectives evolve into definite articles, and so on. I don't know whether anyone else would share that impression, and I'm certainly not sure how reliable it is statistically.

DR. WANG: I think that's a very valuable comment. Was it Robert Benchley who once said you can't prove that a platypus does not lay eggs by showing photographs of a platypus not laying eggs?

I think you know at this point when we say that we don't find such a correlative difference, it largely means that we haven't found it yet; it does not necessarily mean it doesn't exist. The impression one gets by scanning the literature on, let's say, the American Indian languages that have never been written down and comparing it with the literature on Chinese and the European languages is that there is no correlative difference of *types* of language change with presence or absence of writing. But I think what Ed Keenan just said regarding the communicative needs depending on the makeup of the speech community sounds quite reasonable to me. If anybody in the audience has relevant evidence, I think we'd all like to hear about it.

DR. COUNT: This conference, after all, is one on the origin and evolution of speech, and as I sat listening to Prof. Keenan I was trying without success to make translations or maps from the various categories and logical considerations that he was making into a framework of the origin and the evolution of speech. Can he by any chance develop a theory or a program for converting this into something about the hypothesis of the origin and evolution of the human speech function?

DR. KEENAN: My talk related to the origin of language in the following somewhat remote sense. A good many linguists think that the origin of language, either ontogenetically or phylogenetically, is located within a sort of innate mechanism of the human species. This has suggested a definite methodology for determining what the inherent linguistic structures are. The methodology has been that you can study intensively *one* language and determine what the innate structures will look like, at least to some extent.

I'm suggesting that this really isn't quite so; that because languages select only a very small number of the logically possible, or humanly possible, syntactic structures, we actually have to look at the pattern of variation across languages to determine what the universal constraints on the admissible structures in human language are. So I'm suggesting an addition, if you will, to the methodology for determining the origins of language in that sense.

I'd also be willing to hazard a few guesses however, about how the types of universals I've discussed would relate to the historical development of languages. If it's required, for example, that a language generally obey a constraint of the form: *if it has P then it has Q*; then we might expect that a language will develop Q historically prior to developing P, because if it didn't, it would have to go through a stage where it had P but didn't have Q. And again, although my evidence is impressionistic, and I didn't discuss it because of the very point that Prof. Wang made—we just don't have historically accurate records for enough languages in this regard—it does seem to me that some languages, in effect, behave this way historically. That is, they somehow set themselves up to change their surface forms in fairly dramatic ways. I could give one example here, although maybe it wouldn't be terribly intelligible: There's a fairly well-documented drift toward *ergativity* among the Polynesian languages. Maori is not an ergative language, but it's just about ready to become one. In effect, what could very easily happen in Maori is that the distinction between active and passive could be lost, the noun phrases retaining the morphology appropriate to the passive sentence. So that what would now come to be interpreted as the new subject would carry the old passive agent marker on it, and the language would be ergative.

If you tried to do that in English—that is, if you tried to get rid of the actives and use passives as basic—you'd have to change an enormous amount of the rest of the system; you'd have to change the way reflexivization works, the way imperatives work, *et cetera*, but all those things in Maori are sitting pretty. They already work the right way. So we can, in effect, affect a change in the surface case marking system in Maori without changing drastically the rest of the system. This might illustrate the application of conditional constraints on grammars that might prove useful, but it would take an awful lot of good historical evidence to document that languages actually evolved that way.

DR. DAVIDSON: This is a question for Ed Keenan. What I want to know is something more about what you mean when you say that languages differed logically in significant ways. I can think of two possibilities.

The evidence that you present seems to show only that logical differences and similarities are brought out by syntactically different devices in different languages. It doesn't follow from that that there are differences in the underlying *logic*, but only that some logical *forms* can be expressed in one language and not in another.

So my question is: Do you think your evidence supports the stronger conclusion that there *are* real differences in the underlying logic itself?

DR. KEENAN: Yes, I do think the evidence supports the conclusion. Consider the Hopi examples 19a and b in the text. The sentences were roughly, *he thinks that he will win*, where, in one case, it has to be the thinker who's thinking about himself and in the other case it has to be somebody else who is being thought about. Now these two sentences are logically distinct because they are not true in the same conditions, and I'm claiming that English does not present us with a pair of sentences which codify exactly that logical distinction; that is, whose truth conditions differ in *exactly* the same way. So in that sense there's a basic distinction in logical expressive power.

Stated differently, I can form sentences in Hopi that have logical consequences for which there's no sentence in English to exhibit exactly the same pattern of logical consequence.

In the written version of the paper I explored more attempts to translate the Hopi sentences into English, and in each of the cases I could think of I found that the attempts to do so were either insufficient or else they overstated the case; that is, they brought in new information that wasn't present in the original Hopi sentences.

Finally, as I mentioned in the discussion earlier, this is not ultimately a convincing argument, because maybe I just haven't been clever enough at thinking up translations. However, I've thought a lot about it, and I still didn't come up with any.

DR. STEVEN DAVIS: Can I pursue the question that was just asked? Do you take it that translation has to be sentence to sentence? Why couldn't the translation go from sentence to several sentences? Still, you wouldn't have a difference in underlying logical form or underlying possibilities for logical expressibility.

DR. KEENAN: I think that in general you would. In the kind of elicitation work I do with many speakers of other languages I'll present a certain type of complex structure in one language, and they'll give me three or four sentences' discussion of the fact.

Now the three- or four-sentence "textlet" inevitably presents additional information not in the original one. It will, for example, raise to the level of explicit assertion a lot of material that's presupposed in the original one.

Thus you can, so to speak, make a stab at a translation and get something that's going to do the job for you in some appropriate context, because the differences in the meaning of the two sentences aren't important enough in that context to worry you. So I'm not claiming that there's an enormous practical problem here. But I am claiming there's a theoretical problem in *exact* translation.

In fact, I might even accept that there is a practical problem as well. Having once worked as an interpreter, I can vouch that there's always a problem of getting a sufficiently accurate translation. It's the bugaboo that's always around and you are, nine times out of ten, in the position of saying something that is only approximately right and it will more or less do the job, but you feel that it isn't exactly right. Now, you are claiming that you can always find something that's *exactly* right, and that seems to me an article of faith for which I don't have any impressionistic or systematic empirical justification.

DR. KIPARSKY: I wanted to add one example, not a particularly exotic one, to Ed Keenan's cases of languages differing in logical expressive power. The way to make comparatives in English involves essentially having two sentences which are interrelated in certain ways. "John runs faster than Bill," is really something like "John runs faster than Bill runs fast."

There are a large number of languages that express this in a different way, saying something like "John exceeds Bill in running," or "John exceeds Bill in regard to running," or in "speed of running." Now consider the problems that speakers of those languages have with translating an English expression like, "My house is bigger than your house." "My house is longer than your house is wide." It's extremely difficult if you ask a speaker of, say, Ibo, to translate that. You get no answer.

Now one way in which that might be done is by two sentences with some sort of explicit measure system: "My house is so big, and your house is bigger than that." However it turns out that Ibo in particular has no measure system other than the measures from English that could be used for that purpose!

DR. KEENAN: The comparatives are a very interesting case which I almost thought about choosing for historical purposes. It certainly is correct that languages vary enormously with regard to comparative constructions, and it seems to me that nine times out of ten the construction that's used to express comparison is almost always in some generative sense a kind of derived structure. (Although in some languages the object of comparison is thoroughly integrated into the normal surface forms, and will take a normal preposition like *from* or *against*, or a normal case marking, or whatever.)

In the second alternative you mentioned, the object of comparison would be treated as a direct object of a verb like *exceed* or *surpass*. In other languages like Fijian, according to traditional sources, the only way to express comparison is simply to use two full sentences, e.g. *John is big, Bill is small*, and that has to make do for the comparison. And the variation we get in comparatives there is almost too big to talk about when you consider comparatives like *this yacht is longer than I thought it was*, (an example due to Bertrand Russell, if I'm not mistaken). One has the impression that languages are scrambling like mad to express comparison in a grammaticized way, but they have achieved different degrees of success. Hence comparatives are systematically difficult to translate across languages.

DR. WANG: I'd like to add briefly to Paul Kiparsky's point. The examples he gives for reduction in comparatives have the form $S_1 = NP_1 + VP_1$ and $S_2 = NP_2 + VP_2$. That is, when both the NP's and the VP's are different, many languages cannot coalesce the two sentences into one comparative sentence, whereas English syntax allows a sentence like "She is more beautiful than he is rich," Chinese would need several cross-referencing sentences to express the same idea.

In general, when the VP's are the same, languages appear not to have constraints in forming comparative sentences, like "She is more beautiful than Annabelle." It is when the VP's are different that languages like Chinese do not allow reduction; e.g., sentences like "She is more beautiful than rich" are not possible. *A fortiori* we would expect the constraint to work against cases where the NP's are also different. In any case, it would be of great theoretical interest to know if this unequal reduction of NP and VP in comparative constructions is universal, and to speculate on why it should be so.

ART WEAVER (*Brooklyn College, Brooklyn, N.Y.*): Prof. Wang, how come you get what looks very much like strong categorical perception with something that's a continuum?

DR. WANG: I think there is gradually a body of evidence accumulating which shows that with speech continua, even vowels, there is categorical perception. So it's not surprising that with something like tones, which constitute a continuum, you also get categorical perception. The trick is to get the subject to attach linguistic *labels* to the stimuli—labels do not vary continuously. (See Marler's and Liberman's chapters, this annal.)

Part III. Protolanguages and Universals

HISTORICAL LINGUISTICS AND THE ORIGIN OF LANGUAGE

Paul Kiparsky

Department of Linguistics
Massachusetts Institute of Technology
Cambridge, Massachusetts 02139

The membership of the Linguistic Society of Paris, which decreed the infamous ban on the topic of our present conference, consisted mainly of historical linguists, including some of my teachers and their teachers. I rather sympathize with their skepticism about the relevance of reconstructed protolanguages to the problem of the origin of language. I will first discuss here some possible forms that this relevance *might* take, and come up with on the whole rather pessimistic conclusions. In a more positive vein, I will then turn to some ways in which historical and comparative linguistics can, in my opinion, more usefully guide speculation on the origin of language: by using language change as a source of scenarios for the way early language might have grown.

It will be useful to distinguish between two aspects of having language—having an internal system of semantic representations, or "language of thought," [1] and having a system of signs for expressing thoughts. On this view, there are really two questions about the origin of language. One, the development of man's capacity to have things to say, could be considered a chapter in the evolution of man, and it is one I will not touch on here. The origin of external forms of linguistic expression might, on the other hand, belong to the history of man; at any rate, it is a topic on which linguistic history could possibly bear.

To begin with, it is necessary to form a realistic estimate of how far the comparative method can take us back. The time span over which we can hope to reconstruct anything at all about protolanguages, however generously we set it at, say, 10,000, or even 20,000 years, is still a very small fraction of the period during which language has presumably been spoken by man. Therefore, protolanguages as reconstructed cannot possibly be identified with any original stage of language.

Still, there are several ways in which protolanguages could conceivably give us a glimpse of an earlier stage of linguistic development. We might ask first whether the structures of early languages as reconstructed by comparative linguistics tend to converge in any way toward some particular typological features or configurations of features. We might then extrapolate from any such backward convergences and draw conclusions about earlier stages of linguistic development.

A second question is whether any reconstructed languages have structural features not found in languages today. Any such anomalous features, even if found merely in a few languages, might then have to be taken seriously as potential relics of earlier forms of language.

As a putative example of the first case—that is, convergence of early languages—I would like to discuss the claim that they were more complex than languages of the present time. Jespersen [2] postulated a general, fixed tendency of linguistic change toward simplification, or "progress in language."

There is, in fact, no known single, overall measure of linguistic complexity. For one thing, it is obvious that learning, perception, and production impose conflicting requirements that hold each other in balance at any point of time. Moreover, no way of comparing complexity in syntax, morphology, and phonology has been found.

What Jespersen seems to have had in mind is primarily the morphological complexity of words. He meant not merely the number of morphemes per word, but also something that in an explicit grammar would appear as the amount of arbitrary information that must be recorded about the lexical items of a language; for example, about gender, declensional or conjugational classes, and the case government of verbs.

Complexity in this sense certainly seems to be an important dimension along which languages differ widely. And Jespersen was absolutely right in seeing a tendency toward simplification in the Indo-European languages. The protolanguage had a richer set of morphological distinctions than any of its numerous descendants. No modern Indo-European language preserves anything close to the intricate system of moods, voices, tenses, and aspects in the Indo-European verb, and all have significantly reduced the noun morphology as well, involving the distinctions of gender, number, and case (though in Lithuanian much has been retained and even some new cases have arisen). Moreover, this simplification of morphology has proceeded as a steady drift in each of the separate branches over thousands of years. Interestingly enough, however, this tendency appears to have begun only about 5,000 years ago. Internal reconstruction—that is, projection backwards on internal evidence within the grammar of the Proto-Indo-European language itself—rather clearly reveals a still earlier period in which the complex morphology was in the process of being built up by the addition of enclitics. For example, the split between primary and secondary tenses including the so-called injunctive transparently arose from the addition of a particle to verb forms in order to denote present time. If such recent interpretations as Watkins'[3] are right, this morphological building-up must have been quite as extensive as the simplification that followed.

In fact, then, though there is drift in language change, the direction of drift is not fixed for all time. It is possible to speculate about the case at hand as follows. There are indications that the complexity of a language is, in a gross way, limited by its range of use. Highly complex languages tend to be spoken by small, homogeneous, and often sedentary populations. The spread of a single language over great areas, and especially its adoption by conquered populations, usually brings with it a drift toward structural simplification. If this is the case, then it might not be an accident that the comparative method, which yields a reconstruction at the point at which the protolanguage began to split up into dialects, shows us Indo-European at the height of morphological complexity. That point is precisely the end of the tribal period, during which the language apparently developed an increasingly elaborate morphology, and the beginning of a period of expansion and conquest, when its branches separated and began to acquire simpler morphologies.

The drift toward linguistic simplification has become dramatically accelerated in the capitalist period. Large populations of workers are moved for cheap labor, creating linguistically heterogeneous speech communities among which pidgin and creole languages[4] are quickly formed, as in the Caribbean plantations and more recently in the mines of Rhodesia and South Africa. Creolization is now the major source of new languages, since the formation of large states and widespread communication has slowed down and perhaps put an end to the proliferation of languages by the usual means of dialect split and differentiation. Tribal languages are disappearing much more rapidly than new languages are arising from creolization, so that the number of languages in the world probably peaked some centuries ago at about three thousand.

To summarize, then, Jespersen was right in identifying drift toward simplification as a dominant tendency in the recent history of major languages, but wrong in projecting it back to the beginnings of language. General considerations relating the complexity of a language to the communicative use to which that language is put, as well as internal reconstruction in at least one well-studied linguistic family, suggest that up to about 5,000 years ago the overall direction of development may well have been precisely in the direction opposite to that envisaged by Jespersen. At least one apparent case of convergence, then, turns out on closer examination to be illusory. This is rather fortunate, since the hypothesis of constant simplification would cause obvious problems at the other end.

The effect of these considerations is to diminish the prospects of settling the issue of monogenesis on historical grounds, if not to eliminate them entirely. Over some sufficiently long period of time, any language could change into any other. As a model of the problem, picture a space with clusters of different-colored dots on it. Now let each dot go off on a random walk. Over time the dots will approach random distribution; i.e., hypotheses about their original clustering become less and less confirmable. Suppose, furthermore, the clusters are contained in a frame within which each dot must stay. The effect will be to further decrease the time during which the original distribution can be empirically ascertained. In language, the rate of movement appears to be sufficiently large, and the size of the frame (universal grammar) sufficiently small so that in some 10,000 or 20,000 years any language could presumably change into any other.

Monogenesis is sometimes adduced as an explanation for linguistic universals (Ref. 5 and Wescott, this annal). To take a concrete example, the fact that in the basic word order Subjects precede Objects, apparently in all languages, would be accounted for by assuming that a hypothetical proto-World language had this order, and that none of its descendants happened to switch it around. But this idea is quite untenable, for several reasons. First, it cannot be even made coherent for any *implicational* universals. Consider e.g. Jakobson's observation that languages do not have the feature configuration $\begin{bmatrix} m & F_1 \\ m & F_2 \end{bmatrix}$ without also having the feature configurations $\begin{bmatrix} u & F_1 \\ m & F_2 \end{bmatrix}$ $\begin{bmatrix} m & F_1 \\ u & F_2 \end{bmatrix}$, and $\begin{bmatrix} u & F_1 \\ u & F_2 \end{bmatrix}$, where 'u' and 'm' stand for unmarked and marked specifications of features. For example, no language appears to have the set of consonants /bh dh gh/ without also having the sets /b d g/, /ph th gh/, and /p t k/. There is no property ascribable to a putative original language that could possibly explain why, through a myriad of phonetic changes in which these sets of sounds come and go in the phonological inventories of languages, Jakobson's law continues to hold. This law, and other universals of language, must therefore rather be considered as an intrinsic property of language.

A more subtle difficulty with monogenesis as an explanation for linguistic universals is this. The hypothesis amounts to saying that what linguists consider universals are merely certain stable structural properties of the original language that have not yet had time to change. But then we ought to find that what on this hypothesis are subfamilies (such as Indo-European) are distinguished by other structural properties, also stable, although relatively less so than the "universals" that were characteristic of the protolanguages from which *they* are derived. But this is just what is *not* the case, as far as we now can tell. All typological divisions so far proposed yield insufficiently stable categories to be useful as criteria for membership even in the relatively shallow families that the comparative method can establish. For example, we find *within* both Indo-European and Finno-Ugric two of Greenberg's major word-order types, SVO and SOV, not to speak of nearly the whole gamut of morphological types. But if even the most fundamental and typologically most interesting nonuniversal properties so far proposed fluctuate so relatively easily, we must doubt the existence of any such superstable but nonintrinsic properties of language as this hypothesis supposes apparent language universals to be.

Of course, insofar as universals are evidenced in the child's language acquisition and in psycholinguistic research, the possibility of even entertaining such a monogenetic explanation for them immediately disappears.

This is not to say that we might not eventually find a way of drawing on typological features to establish more distant linguistic kinship than the comparative method allows us to do. Using a large number of syntactic and morphological properties, chosen for their relative stability and immunity to borrowing as determined by the study of languages with known histories, one might derive a measure of structural resemblance that might have genetic significance. If at least some aspects of grammatical structure tend to be relatively more persistent than even basic vocabulary, this method might tell us more than Swadesh's now widely abandoned glottochronology. Sapir[6] considered his most abstract typological properties ("pure-relational," "complex-relational," etc.) as being relatively stable, and there are hints that he used them in historical work, if not to support hypotheses about distant genetic relationships, then at least to suggest them (for example, the possible link between Athapascan and Sino-Tibetan).

Another question that falls under this first rubric, namely, could protolanguages tell us anything about the origin of language, is whether protolanguages ever show features that are anomalous or not found at all in present-day languages, and thus might be pointers to earlier stages of linguistic development. The first point to keep in mind here is that in the great majority of cases, historically reconstructed linguistic systems conform in every way to those we know from presently spoken languages. However, in some cases there are alleged discrepancies. I will just mention one particularly striking and rather well-known example. The Indo-European protolanguage has sometimes been reconstructed with just one vowel or even no vowels at all. This state has been considered archaic, and compared to Kabardian and certain other Caucasian languages which Kuiper[7] also analyzed as vowelless. Bolinger[8] also holds early language to have been primarily consonantal, citing Kabardian as a survival and referring to Lieberman's[9] observations about the restricted vowel repertoire available to Neanderthal man because of his short pharynx (see also this annal).

This is not too convincing, because it seems to be based on a couple of confusions. In the first place, the analysis of Proto-Indo-European as a language with one or no vowels is simply a descriptive trick based on treating the high vowels *i* and *u*, whose existence no one denies, as underlying consonants, on the basis of arguments that are disputable, to say the least. For Kabardian, too, it has been argued that it must be considered to have at least two vowels.[10]

Second, the argument is specious from the phonetic point of view, since no one denies that Indo-European, whatever its underlying phonological system, had *phonetically* at least the five vowels *i e a o u*, thus involving what is precisely the most common repertoire of vocalic articulations in the languages of the world.

In general, it is really a rather remarkable fact that protolanguages turn out to resemble modern languages rather exactly. The significance of this conclusion is sometimes denied, with the objection that linguistic uniformitarianism is a *methodological* principle in comparative grammar and that protolanguages preserve universals merely by virtue of the linguist's a priori rejection of any proposed reconstructions that do not conform. Most comparativists would claim, however, and I would agree, that this methodological principle is empirically justified because there are no clear cases in which insisting on it forces the comparativist into a reconstruction that is overly complicated or on internal grounds unsatisfactory.

My conclusions so far have been on the negative side. There is, however, a different way in which historical linguistics could be, and indeed to some extent already has been, brought into the question. For some of the well-attested processes of language-change are prime candidates for a role in the origin of language. The process I would like to discuss here briefly is that of *reanalysis*. It can be illustrated with the following syntactic observation. A well-traveled one-way street in historical syntax leads from coordination to the subordination of sentences. That is, most types of embedded clauses were at one time main clauses. This is why virtually all subordinating conjunctions, such as *if* or *that* in English, are developed from various types of pronouns.

The basis of these developments is that the content of coordinate structures can be identical with or overlap with subordinate structures. For example, the work of an if-clause can, to some extent, be done by a question. The sentence *if you have it, then show it to me* can be approximated by the two sentences *Do you have it? Then show it to me.* This kind of semantic or at least pragmatic near-equivalence can prepare the ground for syntactic reanalysis. The corresponding kind of question has in German become semantically a real conditional—*Hast du es, dann zeig es mir.* It requires no reply, has comma intonation, and generally functions like an *if*-clause, except that it still shows in its surface structure the earmarks of its interrogative origin. The English counterfactual type *Had you done it, we'd be all right* shows a similar situation.

This kind of language change might be compared to evolutionary adaptation in organisms, e.g. leaves being recruited as tendrils by a climber. Far more than biological organisms, language shows a striking plasticity in this regard. Linguistic change of this type can be completed in a few generations. The reason has to do with a quite crucial factor in shaping linguistic development, namely, the *discontinuous transmission* of language.

Consider first as a hypothetical illustration a language where the verb appears at the end of a sentence. A child learning this language will naturally establish deep structures, with the verb at the end corresponding to the surface structures he encounters. Now suppose a syntactic transformation is added to this language moving the finite verb of main clauses into second position, making it like modern German. At this point a child learning the language might (I don't claim it *must*) analyze it in a quite different way. Rather than taking the verb-final order of subordinate clauses as basic and having a verb-second rule, the child might take the order of main clauses as basic and have the inverse transformation which moves the verb to the end in subordinate clauses. The potential importance of this kind of possible reanalysis derives from the fact that it may in turn have consequences elsewhere in the system. For example, basic word order is a fundamental typological property of languages which, as Greenberg has shown, impinges on many other areas of grammar.

So the crucial fact is that each speaker must recreate the linguistic system for himself, and in doing so may arrive at a different grammar than that which produced the data he encountered. Reinterpretation is possible insofar as the learner's data permits multiple analyses within the framework in which he approaches the data. What I am now suggesting is that this reinterpretation could go in the direction of greater communicative adequacy.

It is clear that the reanalysis of main clauses as embedded clauses suggests a mechanism by which an overt recursive syntax could have become elaborated. In fact, some early comparativists, dizzy with success in deriving much of subordination from coordination, jumped to the conclusion that sentential subordination is a rather recent development. The fallacy is that the new subordinate clauses we see developing in this way might merely be replacing old ones that have become lost. It would be just as wrong to conclude, for example, from the fact that the progressive and perfect in English are comparatively recent formations, that its ancestor lacked an aspect system. In fact, of course, Indo-European did have the corresponding aspect categories, expressed by verb inflection, which have merely been recreated in English by means of auxiliary verbs. Since new formal devices may express old content, the mere fact of their introduction can never be used for glottogenic conclusions.

However, the scenario might very well be right for some earlier stage, undoubtedly far antedating, say, PIE. Given a stage of overt linguistic development with no subordinate clauses, and a stage of mental development ready to integrate more complex syntactic structures, the origin and growth of syntactic embedding could have involved just the kind of reinterpretation of juxtaposed sentences that we know to be a process in linguistic history.

Going further back, most hypotheses of the origin of language, starting, of course, with the account in Genesis, take naming to be the crucial step. The primitive signs in such a system might be vocal or gestural. An important question would be whether the signs are interpreted in relation to each other, and if so, how. Such a stage might be truly asyntactic, with successive signs related at best associatively. Some animal systems are probably of this sort. With a more developed internal representation of thought, however, such a superficially asyntactic stage might constitute a rather rich although highly ambiguous system of expression, comparable to early child language and in some respects to sign language. Many students of child language have argued rather plausibly that the one-word or two-word utterances of the two-year-old are to be properly construed as multiply ambiguous expressions showing underlyingly the same syntactic relations as adult language. To take the familiar example, *Daddy briefcase* might stand for *That's daddy's briefcase*, *Daddy has a briefcase*, *I'm giving Daddy the briefcase*, and so on. Whatever were the prior stages, early language can be assumed to have gone through a similar stage.

In children, this stage contains at least some deictic pronouns (*this, that, these*, etc.). If we assume the same was true for early language, then this deictic system could have served as the basis for the development of an overt syntax. It appears that agreement, which serves to index grammatical relations, most commonly originates in the attachment of pronouns to the verb. Languages commonly express *John likes Mary* as *John Mary he-likes-her*. The personal endings of Indo-European and still more transparently in Finno-Ugric are originally enclitic pronouns. And it is generally true that any noun category, with respect to which a language has verb agreement, is overtly marked in the pronoun system of that language.

So here again is a case where known processes of change can be assumed to have played a constitutive role. This is not to claim, however, that *everything* in language could have been built up in this way. Thus, the origin of derivational morphology, insofar as it cannot be traced to grammaticalized compounding, seems quite mysterious.

Finally, I should like to turn briefly to the question whether languages ever make the kinds of false starts that biological species do. There do seem to be cases where they evolve means of expression that are insufficiently extendable and that must eventually be aborted in favor of new ones. For example, the rather elaborate number inflection of many preliterate languages, with not only singular and plural, but also dual and even sometimes trial, may function originally in lieu of a system of numeral quantification, which is still lacking or just being introduced in some Australian languages of this type.[11] As soon as numerals develop, dual and trial inflection becomes redundant and nonfunctional (the plural still serves as a convenient expression for "more than one"). In Indo-European languages, for example, the original dual has made a rather rapid exit (again, with the exception of Lithuanian).

Another example would be comparative constructions. Many languages do not say *John runs faster than Bill* (which is syntactically derived from something like *John runs faster than Bill runs fast*), but rather say something like *John exceeds Bill in running* (or *in the speed of his running*). There is a real problem in such languages in comparing *different* dimensions of things with respect to the same measure, as in *John's house is wider than Bill's house is long*, or *John has more friends than Bill has enemies*. To the extent that a language is called on to express such ideas, it will have to develop a new syntax for comparatives.

REFERENCES

1. FODOR, J. A. 1975. The Language of Thought. Crowell. New York, N.Y.
2. JESPERSEN, O. 1921. Language: Its Nature, Development, and Origin. Reprinted 1964. Macmillan. New York, N.Y.
3. WATKINS, C. 1969. Indogermanische Grammatik. III. 1. Winter. Heidelberg, Germany.
4. HYMES, D. 1971. Pidginization and Creolization of Languages. Cambridge University Press. Cambridge, England.
5. PUTNAM, H. 1967. The Innateness Hypothesis and explanatory models in Linguistics. Synthèse **17**: 20–28.
6. SAPIR, E. 1921. Language. Harcourt. New York, N.Y.
7. KUIPERS, A. H. 1960. Phoneme and Morpheme in Kabardian. Mouton. The Hague, The Netherlands.
8. BOLINGER, D. 1975. Aspects of Language. Harcourt, Brace, Jovanovich. New York, N.Y.
9. LIEBERMAN, P. 1975. On the Origins of Language: An Introduction to the Evolution of Human Speech. Macmillan. New York, N.Y.
10. HALLE, M. 1970. Is Kabardian a vowel-less language? Foundations of Language **6**: 95–103.
11. HALE, K. 1975. Gaps in grammars and cultures. To appear in volume in honor of Prof. C. F. Voegelin. Peter DeRidder Press. Antwerp, Belgium.

PROTOLINGUISTICS: THE STUDY OF PROTOLANGUAGES AS AN AID TO GLOSSOGONIC RESEARCH

Roger W. Wescott

Department of Anthropology
Drew University
Madison, New Jersey 07940

As used here, the term "protolinguistics" will mean the analytic and comparative study of protolanguages. Protolanguages, in turn, will mean reconstructed ancestral languages, ranging from such relatively firm constructs as Proto-Indic (the archaic Prakrit ancestral to Hindi and Bengali) to such relatively speculative constructs as the Universal Proto-Speech of the Upper Paleolithic Period, which I have elsewhere postulated as ancestral to all contemporary spoken languages.[1]

Nearly all historical linguists employ the term "protolanguage," and many cite hypothetical forms from reconstructed tongues. Yet a minority of these scholars deny that linguistic reconstructions are approximations of the actual sound and shape of dead languages and hold instead that such reconstructions are merely abstract formulae conveniently relating attested languages to one another. My own view of this matter is optimistically majoritarian. While I recognize that all reconstructions are tentative—and will argue below that most protolinguists persist in making avoidable reconstructive errors—I nevertheless believe that reconstructed languages do recapture, in large part, at least, the substance of vanished languages. As an example, I would cite Proto-Romance, the reconstructed ancestor of French, Italian, and Rumanian. As estimated by Robert Hall, its overall correspondence to recorded Classical Latin is about 85%.[2] This congruence, I would say, is no more than we should expect of a diglossic situation in which the speech of literates diverges markedly from that of illiterates.

No discussion of language origins can avoid the question of monogenesis, that is, whether all known spoken languages have a single common origin. Oddly enough, most linguists have taken the position that, in the absence of irrefutable evidence on either side of the question, the burden of proof in the matter rests with the monogeneticists. I say "oddly" because, as an anthropologist, I am keenly aware that in regard to the analogous question of the origin of life, biologists have taken precisely the opposite position, assuming monogenesis and assigning the burden of proof to polygeneticists. Regarding linguistics as a branch of anthropology and anthropology in turn as a branch of biology, I am inclined to follow biological precedent in this matter and assume monogenesis until polygenesis is demonstrated. This inclination is strengthened by my ethnological knowledge of the fact, for example, that the alphabet, although now global in extent and multifarious both in form and in the order of its constituent letter, originated once and only once in the Eastern Mediterranean region early in the first millennium B.C.

Just as we know the vertebrates and the alphabet to have radiated and differentiated over space and time, we can reasonably infer, I think, that speech did the same thing. If this is so, we can further infer that protolanguages resembled one another more than contemporary languages resemble one another and that the earlier the protolanguages were, the more alike they were—back to the point at which they converged. This point I would locate in the Upper Paleolithic Period (between 20,000 and 50,000 years ago). I place it before the subsequent Mesolithic Period because I believe that fewer than 20 millennia would not have produced the linguistic diversity we observe today; and I place it after the preceding Middle Paleolithic because I believe that our hominid predecessor, Neanderthal Man, though capable of manual language, was incapable of vocal language.

Indirect evidence favoring this view comes from the documented history of well-known language families such as Indo-European. Here we find that the earliest recorded forms of most languages are patently more similar than are their contemporary forms. A particularly graphic illustration of this tendency is provided by Avestic, the Zoroastrian scriptural language of the ancient Iranians, and Sanskrit, the Hindu scriptural language of the ancient Indo-Aryans. These two languages were so similar that by performing relatively minor phonological transformations, one could readily convert an Avestic text into a Sanskrit text without any change in vocabulary or word order. No such ready conversion, needless to say, could be performed between modern Pushtu and modern Hindi.

Since the Indo-European languages are the world's most thoroughly analyzed language family and Proto-Indo-European is the most extensively reconstructed protolanguage, we will begin our protolinguistic exposition with Indo-European. I assume that Proto-Indo-European (hereafter PIE) was spoken by a congeries of neolithic tribes moving rather freely, perhaps as transhumant pastoralists, between central Europe and eastern Turkestan during the 3rd millennium B.C. Its system of 23 segmental phonemes I reconstruct (following Winfred Lehmann but deviating from his exposition of vowels and "laryngeals"[3]) as follows:

p	t	k	k^w
b	d	g	g^w
b^h	d^h	g^h	g^{hw}
	s		
m	n		
	r		
	l		
i		ə	u
e		a	o

Here it should be understood that i, $ə$, and u are glides rather than vowels (and hence that they pattern as sonorants, like the linguals and nasals) and that length is a prosodic feature that may combine with any nonobstruent.

Since the discovery of Hittite in the 1920s, it has become clear—as both structuralists and monogeneticists had previously suspected—that pre-Indo-European had had at least one and possibly several dorsal obstruents. If we define PIE as the protolanguage ancestral to English, Spanish, Russian, and Hindi, then, following Edgar Sturtevant,[4] we may posit an earlier protolanguage ancestral both to PIE and to such Anatolian languages as Hittite, Luwian, Palaic, and (perhaps) Armenian, and call it "Proto-Indo-Hittite" (hereafter PIH). PIH was probably spoken by a horticultural people in the circum-Caucasian area in the 4th millennium B.C. A plausible inventory of its 20 or so segmental phonemes follows:

p	t	k	ʔ (?)
p' (?)	t'	k'	
p^h	t^h	k^h	
	š	x	h (?)
m	n		
	h		
	l		
w	y		
o	e		

Three of these phonemes are of doubtful status. These are the glottalized bilabial stop, which yields no certain reflex in Anatolian and only the rare voiced bilabial stop in PIE; and the voiceless glottal stop and the voiceless glottal fricative, which are absent from both Anatolian and PIE but can be inferred for their parent tongue on the basis of internal evidence in each.

The firmer sound-correspondences between Anatolian and IE (the former illustrated exclusively from cuneiform Hittite) follow:

Phoneme	Hittite	Indo-European*
p	paxur, "fire"	PIE pūr-
pʰ	parkuš, "pure"	bʰreg-, "white"
t	titami, "stand"	stistāmi
t'	teik-, "show"	deik-
tʰ	tehi, "place"	dʰē-, "put"
k	kwiš, "who?"	kʷ is
k'	kenu, "knee"	genu
kʰ	kwenzi, "strike"	gʷʰ enti
š	šiptam-, "seventh"	sept(o)m-
x	xanti, "in front"	anti-
m	mal-, "grind"	mol-
n	newaš, "new"	neuos
r	pra-, "forth"	pro-
l	lak-, "lie down"	logʰ-, "lay"
y	yukan, "yoke"	iugom
w	weš, "we"	ue-
e	ešmi, "am"	esmi
o	arpa-, "misfortune"	orbʰo-, "bereft"

*IE meanings are given only when they differ from Hittite meanings.

Once we leave Indo-Hittite, agreement about cognation between Indo-European and other languages falls off precipitously. Nonetheless, striking lexical correspondences persist. Outside the Anatolian family, the largest number of cognates (in proportion to total vocabulary) appears to come from Etruscan, a language isolate from pre-Roman Italy,[5] which seems to have had about 20 segmental phonemes.[6] The protolanguage that was ancestral to PIH and Etruscan is one that I would call (on the analogy of other Indo-hyphenations) Indo-Etruscan and assign to incipiently horticultural peoples of western Eurasia from the 5th millennium B.C.

The more persuasive sound-correspondences between Etruscan and PIH (the latter illustrated from various IH languages) follow:

(proto-)phoneme	Etruscan	Indo-Hittite†
p	φel, "container"	Greek péllā, "bowl"
t	tecum, "earth"	Hittite tekan
k	cap, "take"	Old Irish gaibid
s	se-, "six"	Latin sex
x	hanθ, "in front"	Hittite xanti
m	man-, "think"	Sanskrit mányatē
n	nep-, "humid"	Greek népʰos, "cloud"
r	tur-, "give"	Greek dõron, "gift"
l	lautn, "family"	Lithuanian liáudis, "people"

†IH meanings are given only when they differ from Etruscan meanings.

y	ecnia, "offering"	Sanskrit yajñá, "sacrifice"
w	var-, "water"	Sanskrit vắri
e	eme, "I"	Greek emé-ge, "me"
a	am-, "love"	Latin amo

In the preceding table, the three capital letters in the first column represent what Swadesh called "protophonemes"; that is, sound-classes that resemble morphophonemes in containing phonetically similar phonemes but differ from morphophonemes in that their phonemic realizations are semantically rather than morphologically conditioned. (As we move back in time, the number of such phonosemic stop variants in each articulatory position becomes increasingly more difficult to specify. Even PIE poses problems here. Although most Indo-Europeanists follow the Greek model and reconstruct three manners, a substantial minority follow the Indic model and reconstruct four. Moreover, it remains possible that both groups are wrong and that we ought, instead, to follow the Slavic model and reconstruct two manners of articulation—or even, following the Tocharian model, only one for each articilatory position. Anatolian evidence is of little help in this inquiry, since Hittite and Lycian may be interpreted as having had either one or two manners of occlusion. And Etruscan, though it clearly had two manners, shows no consistent pattern of correspondence between these and the manners of Indo-European. Uralic, finally, resembles PIE in the reconstructive difficulties it poses: a majority of Uralicists posit only one articulatory manner for each occlusive position in Proto-Uralic, hereafter PU. But a minority posit three.)

If we exclude isolates like Etruscan and seek cognation between Indo-Hittite and a language family of comparable complexity, we find that the family offering the largest number of plausible lexical correspondences is Uralic, which embraces (among other languages) Finnish, Hungarian, and Samoyed. The protolanguage that was ancestral to PIH and PU is one which I would call Indo-Uralic and assign to a hunting and gathering people of western Eurasia from the 6th millennium B.C.

The more persuasive sound-correspondences between PU and Proto-Indo-Etruscan (the latter illustrated from PIE, PIH, and Etruscan) follow.

∧	Proto-Uralic	Indo-Etruscan
p	per-, "far"	PIE per-, "traverse"
t	te-, "thou"	PIE te-. "thee"
k	ku-, "who?"	PIH kwi- ‡
s	sen, "he"	PIE se-, ne-
m	man-, "guess"	Etruscan man-, "think"
n	nimi, "name"	PIE nEm-
r	utar-, "udder"	PIE uTer-
l	kol-, "pale"	PIH KEL-, "bright"
y	kar-, "herd"	PIE ker-
w	vet-, "water"	PIE uEd-
e	met-, "honey"	PIE med^h-
a	kap-, "hoof"	PIE kap-, "hoof; goat"

‡Unmarked PIE & PIH meanings are as in PU.

Beyond Uralic, no language or language group presents large numbers of conspicuous lexical cognates with Indo-European. But strong, if indirect, genealogical links have recently been forged between IE on the one hand and Dravidian and Elamite on the other by Stephen Tyler[7] and David McAlpin.[8] More specifically, Tyler has demonstrated extensive lexical correspondences between PU and Proto-Dravidian (hereafter PD); whereas McAlpin has done the same for PD and the various stages of Elamite, from Proto-Elamite (in this case a hieroglyphically recorded rather than a reconstructed language) through Middle Elamite to Achaemenid Elamite. In effect, they have established a linguistic chain that links IE with Elamite through the intermediacy of Uralic and Dravidian, respectively.

This genealogical chain, of course, is reminiscent of Holger Pederson's Nostratic hypothesis, according to which Indo-European, Hamito-Semitic, Ural-Altaic, Dravidian, and Kartvelian (or southern Caucasian) form a single linguistic macrophylum.[9] From a monogenetic point of view, the shortcoming of the Nostratic hypothesis is not that it is false—since all spoken languages are necessarily cognate—but rather that it is misleading, at least insofar as it implies that Eurasian languages have something in common with one another that they do not have in common with African, Oceanian, and American languages. For it is virtually certain that the reasons why the kinship of Indo-European with Semitic and Uralic is so widely perceived are, first, that the regional contiguity of the three families makes their cognation relatively easy to believe in and, second, that the thoroughness with which they have been analyzed makes it comparatively easy to pick out shared lexical items among them.

As a discipline, comparative protolinguistics, it should be admitted, remains relatively weak. But this weakness, I believe, is due far more to its underdeveloped state than to any inherent inadequacy in either linguistic reconstruction or in comparative methodology. To strengthen comparative protolinguistics, I recommend at least two methodological reforms. The first of these is utilization, by comparativists, not only of lexicons in the conventional sense—that is, of inventories of free morphemes or "words"—but also of what I call "morphicons," or inventories of bound morphemes or affixes.[10] In fact, I would go further and assert that morphicons should not be used merely to supplement lexicons; I should say, rather, that wherever possible, morphicons should be used in preference to lexicons, and that it is the lexicons which should be regarded as evidentially secondary.

My reason for preferring morphicons to lexicons is that affixes are far less often borrowed than are words. In the case, for example, of the relation of Indo-European to Uralic, skeptics can always argue that lexemes like PU met-, "honey," and utar-, "udder," were loanwords from PIE. But they find it much harder to dismiss such verb suffixes as the PU/PIE preterit -s- or agential -nt- in the same way.[11]

The second methodological reform that I would propose for comparative protolinguistics (as for comparative linguistics generally) is abandonment of the widespread practice of using Morris Swadesh's lexicostatistic protocols as devices for demonstrating interlanguage cognation. Although I yield to none in my admiration for Swadesh as a linguistic prehistorian, I find that it is insufficiently appreciated by linguists and anthropologists that the primary purpose of glottochronology as a technique is to specify degrees of lexical divergence between languages whose kinship is established or generally assumed. Were this not so, it would be pointless to stipulate, as Swadesh did, that such obvious cognates as English *hound* and German *Hund* may not be lexicostatistically equated because of their recent loss of synonymy. Between languages whose kinship is in doubt, such pairs as *hound* and *Hund*—not to mention others whose divergence is more pronounced—must be coupled if cognation is ever to be demonstrated.

For this reason, I prefer to compare protolanguages and other languages of uncertain mutual relationship in terms of what I call the "semantic cluster" principle. This principle is based on recognition of the fact that many of the terms in Swadesh's and other word-lists comprise or (more often) help comprise relatively self-contained semantic subsystems. Among these subsystems, or semantic clusters, are personal pronouns, numerals, kinship terms, names of body parts, and color terms. Of the clusters just cited, pronouns are probably the most persistent, both because they are oldest (as evidenced by their greater proneness to become bound forms) and because they are least subject to borrowing.[12]

Semantic clusters, however, must be used with care. For each is a subsystem composed of infrasystems with characteristics that are sometimes disparate. Thus, third-person pronouns, for example, are less persistent than others because they are more likely to interdigitate or merge with demonstratives. High numbers are less persistent than low numbers because high numbers are more subject to borrowing. Nursery terms for mother and father, on the other hand, are persistent to excess: that is, they are apparently universal,[13] a fact that makes them useless for subgrouping purposes. Terms for excretory or procreative organs may be subject to verbal taboos that lead either to deformation or to borrowing. And terms for subtle hues or shades are especially likely to be loanwords.

In addition to such major semantic clusters as kinship systems and color terminologies, there are also minor clusters consisting of two or three forms each and constituting antonymous polarities. These antynomies may be either dipolar, as in the case of the dyad *this* vs. *that*, or tripolar, as in the case of the triad *male* vs. *female* vs. *neuter*. Minor clusters tend to be more persistent when they fall within the ambit of major clusters, as in the case of the dipolarity *I* vs. *thou* or the tripolarity *white* vs. *black* vs. *red*.

Lexical persistence, finally—at least insofar as it can be detected with assurance— consists not only of semantic persistence but also of phonic persistence. Yet, surprisingly, few explicit studies have been made by historically oriented investigators of the relative diachronic durability of phonemes or of distinctive features. The only one that I can locate was made sixteen years ago by a jurist and philologist named Arthur Diamond. Diamond, having surveyed the Indo-European, Semitic, Polynesian, and Bantu languages, concluded that the overall order of decreasing consonant persistences is as follows:

1. nasals
2. voiceless stops
3. voiced stops
4. voiceless fricatives
5. voiced fricatives
6. linguals [14]

For vowels, Diamond's order of persistence is:

1. low central vowels
2. high front and back vowels (including glides)
3. all other vowels [14]

And, for obstruent and nasal articulatory positions, his order of persistence is:

1. labial
2. apical
3. dorsal,

although he notes that, among stops, apicals are more persistent than labials.[14]

If Diamond's analysis is sustained when a larger number of language families is surveyed, it would seem that the labial nasal /m/—which is found in nearly all languages outside the Salishan and Iroquoian groups [15]—is the most widely resistant of all phonemes to diachronic change, presumably because of the great visual and tactile palpability of labials and the distinctiveness of nasality, which is the only nonoral consonantal manner.

In reconstructing the phonemic inventories of protolanguages, it is, of course, necessary to do as most Indo-Europeanists have done, namely, to postulate a sufficiently large number of phonemes to account for the diversity of reflexes in all attested daughter languages. But there is a real danger that in so doing, protolinguists will overdifferentiate the aboriginal phonemes and produce an inventory that is intrinsically improbable. By this I mean not so much that they will produce a total number of phonemes that is incredibly high (although this may in fact happen) as that they may produce numerical proportions between types of phonemes that violate linguistic universals of the type now being established by linguists at Stanford University.[16]

An example of such dubious reconstruction is provided by Björn Collinder in his *Comparative Grammar of the Uralic Languages*, in which he postulates 23 consonant phonemes for PU.[17] What is implausible here is not the total inventory but the fact that Collinder posits more sibilants than stops, more nasals than stops, and even more linguals than stops in PU, despite the fact that "implicative universals" expressly veto all three of these proportions.[18]

On the other hand, we should not fall into the alternative error of assuming that the phonological and other traits typical of contemporary languages must have been typical of all or even most languages throughout prehistory. To begin with, it seems inherently improbable that speech sprang fully fledged from either a closed hominoid call-system[19] or an open proto-hominid gesture language.[20] Whatever its source, speech almost certainly developed by stages, even if its evolution was discontinuous in pace.[21]

More precisely, there is evidence that the rate of diachronic sound change (of the type described by such formulae as Grimm's Law) accelerated steadily from the Upper Paleolithic Period till the spread of literacy following urbanization. This evidence consists chiefly of the striking genetic and typological resemblances between protolanguages, which one could scarcely expect to encounter if sound change had always been as rapid as it evidently was during the last few millennia B.C.

Another persistent and even more unidirectional trend has been the steady growth of what George Trager calls "microlanguage"—that is, language that is grammatically structured to a high degree—at the expense of all other domains of what he calls "macrolanguage."[22] The three other domains of Trager's macrolanguage are what he calls "prelanguage," "paralanguage," and "metalanguage." Prelanguage consists of primate calls and infant babblings, paralanguage of extragrammatical interjection and speech-deformation, and metalanguage of song and other verbal or verbalized arts. Although Trager himself has not proposed any unitary term for the three nonmicrolinguistic domains of macrolanguage, my own term for this threefold collectivity is "allolanguage."[23] I describe allolanguage as a language that is alien to the type of speech and writing most easily generated or analyzed by Transformational methods.

The divergence between microlanguage and allolanguage, moreover, is one that seems to me to be capable of accounting for some of the difficulties linguists experience in reconstructing protolanguages. In the case of PIE/PIH, two such difficulties are the apparently sporadic occurrence in it of geminated stops and of $i \sim a \sim u$ vowel apophony. Examples of the former are: PIE pipp-, "to peep"; atta, "dad"; and bʰukkos, "stag." Examples of the latter are kin- = kan- = kun-, "dog." Although PIE gemination was probably solely "expressive" and hence allolinguistic, contemporaneous Dravidian geminates were phonotactically "normal," and hence microlinguistic. And the PIE vocoid apophony which was probably also allolinguistic (and remains so in English echoic sequences like *clink*, *clank*, *clunk*) became microlinguistic in Proto-Germanic (and remains so in English verbal paradigms like *drink*, *drank*, *drunk*).

A third long-range linguistic trend has been the emergence of vowels, first from subphonemic to phonemic status and then from a position of rough parity with consonants to one of segmental primacy. The chief evidence for a prehistoric situation in which only consonants were phonemic is the fact that even today there are languages, such as Wishram (a Chinookan Penutioid vernacular of Oregon), that can be analyzed as being univocalic, and systemically, therefore, vowelless.[24] And there are many other languages—perhaps as many as 10% of contemporary vernaculars—that have fewer than the five to twelve vowel phonemes that characterize a majority of the world's languages. These include Abkhazi, a North West Caucasian language, which has two vowels; Iatmul, an Indo-Pacific language of New Guinea, which has three vowels; and Manobo, an Austronesian language of the Philippines, which has four vowels. What is striking about these languages is that nearly all of them come from such refuge areas as mountain ranges, small islands, polar regions, or isolated continents. This fact, in turn, dovetails nicely with the observation that protolanguages generally seem to have had fewer vowel phonemes than their daughter languages. Proto-Semitic, for example, probably had only three microlinguistic vowels, and PIH only two.

The sense, on the other hand, in which vowels may be said to have reached not only parity with consonants but primacy among segmentals is that most contemporary languages require vowels in all syllables and permit both syllables and words that consist of vowels only.

A fourth long-range linguistic trend is one that I call "optimization of phonemic inventories." By this I mean not only that the size of phonemic inventories, like the pace of sound change, seems to have reversed its evolutionary direction but also that, in the case of phoneme numbers, there seems to have been (in effect) an effort to strike an optimal mean between the extremes of too few and too many phonemes. Among living languages, phonemic inventories run from a minimum of about 10 to a maximum of about 100 segmental phonemes, with an average of 25 to 30. We may assume, I think, that a lack of oral dexterity kept Upper Paleolithic phonemic inventories small. By the Mesolithic Period, however, it is likely that increasing dexterity had led to inventories that averaged numbers near the contemporary upper limit. Evidence for this phonemic amplitude comes both from typological surveys of contemporary languages and from reconstructive work in protolinguistics. In the former case, we note that the phonemic inventories of many "refuge area" languages—ranging in location from Africa's Kalahari Desert to North American Indian reservations—have segmentals ranging in number from more than 40 to more than 100. In the latter, we note that, particularly in the case of the so-called "laryngeals" of Indo-Hittite, many of the peculiarities of the historical languages can be most readily explained by assuming the existence in PIH of dorsal obstruents that were subsequently lost.[25]

This observation leads directly to identification of a fifth and final long-range phonological trend in the evolution of speech. Like the preceding trend, it is curvilinear and optimizing, rather than rectilinear and maximizing, in nature. This fifth trend is a shift of positional primacy initially from labiality to dorsality and later from dorsality to apicality. Both the study of human speech ontogeny and that of primate phonation suggest labial primacy, probably because the lips are visually and tactilely the most accessible of speech organs. Later, however, when the consonantal inventory expanded, expansion apparently occurred primarily in the postapical or dorsal region. Evidence for this inference comes from refuge-area languages, where we find a strikingly high proportion of clicks, pharyngeals, and glottalized obstruents. Vestiges of both Upper Paleolithic labiality and Mesolithic dorsality may well be detectable in scattered survivals of labial trills and various glottalics among the world's languages, the latter being commoner than the former because of the greater recency of dorsal than of labial dominance.

Today, however, an overwhelming majority of the world's languages show apical dominance either in the sense that gaps in their obstruent systems are usually preapical or postapical rather than apical or in the sense that their sonorant systems—and especially their lingual subsystems—are primarily or exclusively apical. This development, if not an optimizing one, is certainly a medianizing one.

Thus far, we have written as though the problem of reconstructing protolanguages were minor, and the only serious question that of relating protolanguages to one another. But in fact this is not so. Although nearly all linguists, for example, concede the genealogical unity of the Semitic, Egyptian, Berber, Cushitic, Omotic, and Chadic language groups, they have proved unable as yet to reconstruct Proto-Afro-Asian, the presumed parent language of the entire family. The same is true of Proto-Congo-Kordofanian, the presumed parent language of the Atlantic, Voltaic, Adamawa, Kwa, Bantoid, and Kordofanian groups. The chief reason for these lacunae is the predominant irregularity of sound correspondences between the recorded languages of these groups.

More precisely, what linguists have discovered is that, although exact phonemic correspondences between most African languages cannot be established, lexical cognations can, because corresponding phonemes in related languages usually share phonetic features. In other words, sound correspondences in these and other language families of great internal time depth must be formulated either subphonemically, in terms of articulatory or acoustic features, or transphonemically, in terms of morphophonemes.

An example of such nonphonemic sound correspondences is provided by the Niger-Kordofanian lexeme for "goat":

Group	Language	Form
Atlantic	Fulani	be'-
Voltaic	Mossi	bū-
Kwa	Yoruba	ewúrέ
	Igede	emū̄ ¯
Ijaw	Proto-Ijaw	òbórí
Bantoid	Tiv	ìvó
	Jukun	bína
	Proto-Bantu	ḅulî

Here the familial proto-form should probably be written as a noun-base, -BEN-, where B represents any voiced labial consonant, E any non-low vowel, and N any apical sonorant. The reason why we cannot—and should not—be more precise than this is that the cross-language correspondences b ~ ḅ ~ v ~ m ~ w, i ~ e ~ ε ~ o ~ u̦ ~ u, and n ~ r ~ l in other lexemes do not occur in a consistent and predictable manner but rather in a capricious and unpredictable manner.

It is, however, unlikely that there was never any reason for these phonic variations. Instead, it is probable that alternations of this kind are remnants of a nongrammatical but semantically systematic type of apophony. In the case of the labial series, the opposition of stop and fricative is paralleled by such English pairings as *pooh ~ fooey*, that of stop and nasal by English *pa ~ ma*, and that of stop and glide by English *pow* ∼ *wow*. Although the putatively aboriginal meanings of these labial sound contrasts remain obscure, those of the apical contrasts are partially discernible on the basis of onomastic patterns that persist in modern languages. In such pairs as *Sarah* ∼ *Sally* and even more in such triads as *Henry* ∼ *Harry* ∼ *Hal*, we observe an incompletely fossilized phonosemic system of augmentation and diminution, in which the lateral diminishes, the vibrant augments, and the nasal maintains neutrality of size. Outside the domain of proper names, the same threefold opposition may be preserved in English *hound* ∼ *horse* ∼ *whelp*, if we assume that horses were first thought of if not as oversized dogs, at least as weighty coursers.[26]

In addition to fossilized patterns of apophony, archaic languages probably also had patterns of affixation that likewise serve to obscure regular sound correspondences across languages. Among these are sonorant infixations of two types: prenuclear (occurring before the syllabic peak) and postnuclear (occurring after the syllabic peak). Although they have evidently ceased to be microlinguistically productive, they remain productive in allolanguage. Examples from PIE microlanguage and English allolanguage follow:

Optional infix	PIE	English
(E)i	pek- ∼ peik-, "to fleece"	grip ∼ gripe
(E)u	$b^h eg^u$- ∼ $b^h eug$-, "to flee"	crackle ∼ croak
l(E)	kEu- ∼ klEu-, "to hear"	beep ∼ bleep
r(E)	$b^h eg$- ∼ $b^h reg$-, "to break"	caw ∼ crow
(E)n	$g^h ed$- ∼ $g^h end$-, "to take"	click ∼ clink
n(E)	$megh$- ∼ men(e)g^h-, "large"	kick ∼ knock [27]

Consonantal apophony and sonorant infixation, whether acting sequentially or in concert, may easily obscure ancient cognations that would otherwise be patent. An example of apophonic obscuration is the formal contrast between PIH kan-,[28] Proto-Cushitic kar-, and Proto-Semitic kal-, all meaning "dog." And an example of infixative obscuration is the treble contrast between PIE kuon- and PU koir-, also meaning "dog," in which PIE exhibits prenuclear infixation, selection of an augmentative glide, and preservation of a neutral sonorant, but PU exhibits postnuclear infixation, selection of a diminutive glide, and substitution of an augmentative sonorant. (It is possible, of course, to reformulate the distinction between apophony and infixation as a distinction between two different kinds of infixation: replacive in the case of kan- ∼ kar- ∼ kal- and additive in the case of kuon- ∼ koir- ∼ koN-.)

Yet, whether or not we define apophony as a type of infixation, resorting to it as an explanatory device does not solve all the problems of protolinguistics. On the contrary, apophony may create new problems, the most conspicuous of which is ambiguity. In the realm of vowel alternation, we know that apophony may be either horizontal (as in the case of English *gleam* ∼ *gloom*) or vertical (as in the case of English "*squish*"/skwiš/ ∼ *squash*/skwaš/.[29] The same is true in the realm of consonant alternation (as in the cases of English *grip* ∼ *grab* and *damp* ∼ *dank*, respectively).[30] If carried to its logical extreme, this principle obviously allows us— ultimately—to equate any speech sound with any other speech sound by resorting to horizontal, vertical, or, combining the two, diagonal apophony (of the kind that occurs in English *squeak* ∼ *squawk* or *Betty* ∼ *Bessy*.)[31]

My tentative solution to this problem hinges on the observation that even today, most consonant alternation is vertical rather than horizontal (presumably because the average consonant inventory has more manners than positions), whereas most vowel alternation is horizontal rather than vertical (presumably, again, because the typical five-vowel inventory can readily be arranged in a front-to-back sequence but not in a high-to-low one). If we may assume that archaic consonantal apophony was wholly vertical and that later nonvertical alternations were due to analogizing feedback from the subsequently developed vowel system, our problem is reduced to one of separating evolutionary linguistic strata.

A similar problem arises with regard to the question of distinguishing early base consonants from infix consonants. This problem persists in some contemporary forms, such as English *chirp*, which can be derived, with equal plausibility, either from *chip* (with a lingual infix) or from *chirr* (with an occlusive suffix). In most cases, to be sure, such alternative etyma will not spring to hand. But this fact attests only to fortuitous defects in the linguistic record, not to a lack of aboriginal morphological ambiguity. Perhaps, however, the earliest UPS bases consisted exclusively of obstruents, sonorants having been restricted to infixes. And it may be, too, that when external affixes came to outnumber internal affixes, suffixes were wholly or predominantly syllabic—specifically, diphonemic, consisting of a vowel followed by a consonant. Either way, protolinguistic etymologies would be partially if not wholly disambiguated.

Etymological ambiguity of a slightly different kind besets the linguist who seeks to establish cognations between protolanguages. For, because protolanguages become increasingly similar the further back one traces them, the more difficult it becomes to distinguish inherited from borrowed vocabulary in any given protolanguage. The protolinguist's problem here is a little like that of the historian of English who, though he has no difficulty isolating French elements in Middle English, is sometimes uncertain whether to ascribe non-Romanic elements to Old English or to Old Norse, since the latter two were often indistinguishable. The protolinguist's problem, however, is of course the more difficult, since he has no documentary evidence to assist him. An example of this kind of difficulty is the obvious identity of PIE *g^wou-*, PU *ku-*, Proto-Turkic *ko-*, Proto-Bantu *-go*, and Sumerian *gu-*, all meaning "cattle." If the implied meaning was "domesticates," the chances are that all these protoforms were loans from Sumerian or a nearby language; but if the implied meaning was merely "bovines," the chances are that most if not all of them are cognates.

A special case of this difficulty is supplied by prehistoric pidginization. If, for example, Proto-Germanic was in fact an Indo-European pidgin spoken as a second language by native speakers of Uralic, one could argue either that its vocabulary was borrowed from Indo-European or that its structure was borrowed from Uralic.

A particularly puzzling example of apparent cognation is provided by a North American language. In Lake Miwok, a Penutian language of northern California, the personal verb inflections are:

> 1st person singular—m, plural—maš
> 2nd person singular—s, plural—toš
> 3rd person singular—ṭ, plural—p

If we assume that Miwok -p and PIE -nt are alternative assimilations of an earlier *-mt (as we assume that the PIE accusative plural ending -ns is an assimilation of earlier *-ms), then the correspondence between Lake Miwok and Indo-European becomes almost unbelievably close. Few can say whether this closeness is due to a special link between Indo-European and the American Indian languages, as Mary Le Cron Foster thinks;[32] to prehistoric Pacific crossings from the Old World to the New, as various diffusionists suggest;[33] or to the kind of improbable coincidence that Carl Jung called "synchronicity." But, whichever it is, this is the kind of detailed transfamilial parallel that arrests our attention and invites us to rethink linguistic prehistory.

Some protolinguistic problems, finally, are due almost exclusively to lack of information. One such lacuna is the question of unidirectionality in sound change. It is, for example, assumed by most historical linguists that palatized velar stops readily become prepalatal affricates or sibilants and that sibilants readily become dorsal fricatives—as in Sanskrit satám, "hundred," from PIE kmtóm or Classical Greek heptá, "seven," from PIE septḿ—but the reverse changes rarely, if ever, occur. Unfortunately, however, no broad empirical survey of the subject has (to the best of my knowledge) ever been made. And until it is made, we will be compelled to make do with impression and speculation. Let us hope that conscientious collection of evidence may soon remove us from this limbo.

NOTES AND REFERENCES

1. WESCOTT, R. W., Ed. 1974. Language Origins: Chap. 6, The Origin of Speech: 115–116. Linstok Press. Silver Spring, Md.
2. HALL, R. A., JR. 1974. An External History of the Romance Languages. The Reconstruction of Proto-Romance: 16–17. American Elsevier. New York, N.Y.
3. LEHMANN, W. H. 1952. Proto-Indo-European Phonology: 99. University of Texas Press. Austin, Texas.
4. STURTEVANT, E. H. 1942. The Indo-Hittite Laryngeals. Linguistic Society of America. Baltimore, Md.
5. Etruscan or a closely related vernacular was apparently also spoken on the Aegean island of Lemnos. Vladimir I. Georgiev (Introduzione alla Storia delle Lingue Indeuropee, Edizioni dell' Ateneo, Rome, 1966) believes that Etruscan was a later form of Hittite.
6. CARNOY, A. 1955. Dictionnaire Etymologique du Proto-Indo-Européen. Université de Louvain. Belgium.
7. TYLER, S. A. 1968. Dravidian and Uralian: The lexical evidence. Language 44(4).
8. MCALPIN, D. W. 1974. Toward Proto-Elamo-Dravidian. Language 50(1): 89–101.
9. PEDERSEN, H. 1903. Tuerkische Lautgesetze. Zeitschrift der Deutschen Morgenlaendischen Gesellschaft. Band 57: 560.
10. WESCOTT, R. W. A Bini morphicon. In Linguistic and Literary Studies in Honor of Archibald A. Hill. Edgar Polomé, Ed. Pieter de Ridder Press. Lisse, The Netherlands. In press.
11. KERNS, J. C. 1967. Eurasiatic Pronouns and the Indo-Uralic Question. Fairborn, Ohio.
12. DYEN, I., A. T. JAMES & J. W. L. COLE. 1967. Language divergence and estimated word retention rate. Language 43(1): 150–171.
13. MURDOCK, G. P. 1959. Cross-language parallels in parental kin terms. Anthropological Linguistics 1(9): 1–5.
14. DIAMOND, A. S. 1959. The History and Origin of Language: Chap. 15, The Earliest Words, 197–199. Philosophical Society. New York, N.Y.
15. HOCKETT, C. F. 1955. A Manual of Phonology. (Memoir 11. Int. J. of Am. Linguistics 21(4): 19.
16. GREENBERG, J. H., et al. (Committee on Linguistics.) 1969—. Working Papers on Language Universals. Stanford University. Stanford, Calif.
17. COLLINDER, B. 1960. A Comparative Grammar of the Uralic Languages. Almqvist and Wiksell. Stockholm, Sweden.
18. GREENBERG, J. H. 1968. Anthropological Linguistics: An Introduction: Chap. 8, Synchronic Universals. Random House. New York, N.Y.
19. HOCKETT, C. F. 1959. Animal "languages" and human language. In The Evolution of Man's Capacity for Culture. James N. Spuhler, Ed. Wayne State University Press. Detroit, Mich.
20. HEWES, G. W. 1973. Primate communication and the gestural origin of language. Current Anthropol. 14(1): 5–24.

21. WESCOTT, R. W. 1967. The Evolution of Language: Re-opening a closed subject. Studies in Linguistics **19:** 67–82.
22. TRAGER, G. L. 1955. Language. *In* Encyclopaedia Britannica. Chicago, Ill.
23. WESCOTT, R. W. 1975. Allolinguistics: exploring the peripheries of speech. *In* The Second LACUS Forum. Adam Makkai and Valerie Becker Makkai, Eds. Hornbeam Press. Columbia, S.C.
24. HOCKETT, C. F. 1963. The problem of universals in language. *In* Universals of Language. Joseph H. Greenberg, Ed. M.I.T. Press. Cambridge, Mass.
25. WINTER, W., Ed. 1965. Evidence for Laryngeals. Mouton. The Hague, The Netherlands.
26. For fuller treatment of the subject of archaic apophony, see WESCOTT, R. W., 1974, Types of apophony in proto-speech. *In* Language Origins, Roger W. Wescott, Ed. Linstok Press. Silver Spring, Md.
27. The initial k of *knock* is still pronounced in Scottish English. In American English, it is also preserved in the allolog *konk*.
28. Although most Indo-Hittite languages exhibit reflexes of the form kuOn-, an allolog kan- is indicated by Latin canis, Middle Irish cano, "wolf-pup," and Thracian kandáōn and Lydian kandaúlēs, "dog-slayer."
29. WESCOTT, R. W. 1970. Types of vowel alternation in English. Word **26**(3).
30. WESCOTT, R. W. 1971. Labio-velarity and derogation in English: a study in phonosemic correlation. American Speech **46**(2).
31. Here the nickname *Beth* is assumed to stand in the vertically apophonic relation to the allolog *Betty*.
32. FOSTER, M. LE C. 1971. American Indian and Old World languages. Presented at ann. mtg. Amer. Anthropological Assn. New York, N.Y.
33. Notably George F. Carter, Edwin Doran, Jr., and Jonathan D. Sauer. 1971. *In* Man Across the Sea: Problems of Pre-Columbian Contacts. Carroll L. Riley and J. Charles Kelley, Eds. University of Texas Press. Austin, Texas.

DISCUSSION OF THE TWO
PRECEDING PAPERS

Paul Kay

Department of Anthropology
University of California
Berkeley, California 94720

Please interpret the brief remarks I have to make in terms of two factors that limit their probable cogency: 1) that I didn't have a chance to read the papers beforehand (although I got a chance to speak with Prof. Kiparsky and a chance just to glance at Prof. Wescott's paper) and 2) that I've never worked in historical linguistics. My overall reaction is somewhat more sympathetic to Kiparsky than to Wescott, and I will follow his format somewhat in first talking briefly about some difficulties in using the methods of historical linguistics for research on the origin of language and then trying to think of something somewhat more hopeful at the end.

As I understand it, the classical comparative method in historical linguistics is concerned with the study of sound-meaning correlations between languages. That is, we have word A in language X, and word B in language Y, and A sounds somewhat like B and A means somewhat the same thing as B. The study of the historical relationship between languages X and Y involves the study of many correlations like that between A and B.

Two methodological problems crop up immediately, one having one to do with sound and one with meaning. Taking the meaning one first, how do we decide when the meanings of two words in the languages being compared are sufficiently close to count as a "correlation" should one decide the sounds are also similar enough? It would be nice if we had both a precise way of measuring similarity of meaning and also an empirically motivated cutoff point. Then we might be in a position to say, for example, "If the meanings are more similar than 3.28 meaning units, that counts for doing a reconstruction. Otherwise not."

Everybody knows that's not the case. What is the case? Students of well-studied and/or philologically well-documented language families have had a lot of practical experience with semantic change, and someone who is steeped in the tradition of, say, Indo-European studies gets a very good feeling for when two meanings are sufficiently alike to worry about whether the words are phonetically similar. In making such decisions one is liable to two types of error, analagous to statistical errors of Type I and Type II. One may mistakenly conclude that the meanings are close enough to count, which is analogous to a Type I error, or one may mistakenly conclude that the meanings are not close enough, analogous to a Type II error. Now, in entering upon the field of language origins the historical linguist is attempting to extrapolate from his experience with changes of meaning on a five-to-ten-thousand year scale to judgments whether two words may be descended from a common meaning 50,000 or more years ago. The risk of Type I error seems high. We run a serious risk of saying, "Well, it means 'moon' in language X and it means 'light' in language Y, and, well, since the sounds look alike and we could expect 'a lot' of meaning drift in that time, let's guess the two are cognate." In any case, whether the greater probability of error is of Type I or Type II, the fundamental problem is that our seat-of-the-pants expertise for deciding when things are close enough in meaning is based on evidence from languages never separated for more than 10,000 years, and I don't think we can reasonably extrapolate to languages separated by 50,000 or

100,000 or 1,000,000 years, or however far back we must go to talk about the original or primordial language.

The same applies to sound, although I think here perhaps the risk of the Type II-type error is the greater. If you look at words in established language families you find many that are known to be cognate but that don't sound at all alike, such as English *foot* and French *pied*. This shows that sound change can sometimes be very fast, and so we would expect much of the similarity in languages with no closer parent than the primordial language (if there was such a thing) to be totally obliterated, leading to a lot of Type II error.

In any case, we have the problem of extrapolating about what's close enough to count as a sound-meaning correspondence from expertise established in a 5,000–10,000 year or shorter time span, corresponding to philologically documented languages, to a time depth which is (1) highly uncertain and (2) at least an order of magnitude greater. I don't think we have any good principles on which to base such extrapolations, or maybe I should put it less negatively and say principles on which to base such extrapolations should be an object of interest to people who want to make these extrapolations.

Another problem with extension of the classical comparative method to a hypothetical ultimate protolanguage is the question of borrowing. The standard way, as you know, of distinguishing between cognatehood and borrowing in comparative historical linguistics is that, on that basis of systematic sound correspondences, one in effect reconstructs the phonology of the protolanguage. Then, to oversimplify, if there are similarities in sound and meaning between two words that do not obey the sound laws that have been established, we conclude that they have resulted from borrowing. Now Prof. Wescott has explicitly—and others in this area have implicitly—given up the notion of establishing, exact sound correspondences, and, in effect, of establishing the phonology of the protolanguage. But if one gives up that rigorous test, there is no real way to tell cognate from borrowed words.

A final methodological problem is that when one finds fairly loose but nevertheless impressive sound-meaning correspondences between pairs of languages like French and Turkish or Russian and Shawnee, one cannot help wondering to what extent these may be caused by some kind of universal sound symbolism rather than descent from a common ancestor. There is a fairly large amount of suggestive evidence that there is some degree of universal sound symbolism operating in languages (although almost all the experiments on one side of that issue have competing experiments that seem to come out on the other side). Still, the problem remains: how does one separate global similarities due to inherent tendencies of sound symbolism from those due to common genetic heritage? There are all these difficulties in using the classical methods of comparative linguistics in a time frame that is very different from that of the data from whose consideration the principles of that method were derived.

Now, on the positive side there seems to me to have been some recurrent themes today that yield some very tentative suggestions regarding long-term developmental trends in languages as we know them, although I wouldn't, even speculatively, project them backwards toward some very early period at which language was just emerging.

Prof. Kiparsky talked about the idea of reanalysis as an important mechanism of linguistic changes, an actual mechanism, and we have looked at some examples of reanalysis and I thought maybe we could classify some of them.

One thing that both Prof. Kiparsky and Prof. Keenan before him talked about is a set of examples like that in which demonstratives in historically attested cases are reanalyzed into relative pronouns, and in fact, one might make the wild speculation that there is a general tendency for deitic elements to change into anaphoric elements.

If this were found to be the case, it would be a type of unidirectional linguistic change that we could motivate extralinguistically. In small, homogeneous speech communities there is a maximum of shared background between speakers, which is the stuff on which deixis depends. As society evolves toward complexity and the speech community becomes less homogeneous, speakers share less background information, and so one would need to build more of the message into what was actually said resulting in an upward shift in the relative selective advantage of anaphoric to deictic processes.

Another possibility suggested by some things I heard today involves a shift from lexical realization of semantic material to the encoding of that material grammatically, and this can be seen in at least one contemporary study of the creolization process by Gillian Sankoff and Suzanne Laberge in Tok Pisin. They found that for pidgin speakers of Tok Pisin, future time is indicated by an adverb that is a lexical item that occurs once at the beginning of the discourse. For the children of these speakers, who speak the language as a creole—that is, as a native language—that item has become shortened to a single phone and has changed from a discourse initial word to a preverbal affix on each verb in the discourse. In other words, it has changed overnight from a lexical to a grammatical element. There might be something suggestive to look for here.

I'll just say, finally, that if we try to relate these hypothesized kinds of long-run change (if such really exist) from deitic to anaphoric and from lexical to grammatical, we can see that they are motivated by two functional exigencies. The movement of deitic to anaphoric expression may be interpreted as one that is essentially benefiting the hearer. In a situation in which the hearer cannot make a deitic connection, one builds in the context and refers to it anaphorically. The conversion from lexical to grammatical expression of semantic material might be thought of as a parallel convenience to the speaker. This appears to be the case when you get a language that is spoken only as a second language changing to a creole, which is the first language. The native speakers of that language grammaticize, if you will, information that is treated lexically by speakers who speak the language as the second language.

DISCUSSION PAPER: MATHEMATICAL LINGUISTICS, LOGIC, AND THE DEVELOPMENT OF LANGUAGE AND REASONING IN THE CHILD

George Epstein and Stuart C. Shapiro

Department of Computer Science
Indiana University
Bloomington, Indiana 47401

INTRODUCTION

In recent years there has been increasing interest in the development of language and reasoning in the child and its relation to mathematical linguistics and logic. Major sources for this twofold interest are work by Chomsky[5] and by Inhelder and Piaget.[18]

There are great difficulties in connecting a child's reasoning as described verbally by the child, with some particular formal logic. These difficulties are compounded if it is assumed *a priori* that that logic must be the classical two-valued logic with which we are most familiar. This is quite evident when one considers the early years of the child's development, or even the preoperational stage of the child before binary logical operations can be performed.[32,33]

In a recent personal conversation, Wescott has suggested that the same considerations that focus interest on protolanguages, as in Ref. 35, might also focus interest on "protologics"; that is, on source constructs from which certain classes of other logics might stem. Such a protologic would find immediate application in research in artificial intelligence, where it would suggest a basic natural logic on which to develop a model of adult human reasoning and language understanding. While the search for such protologics must be conducted elsewhere (see Ref. 21), an obvious preliminary is to look at the case for contemporary children.

This paper discusses some examples of nonclassical logics which might be incorporated into a mathematical linguistic system related to the development of language and reasoning in the child. Arguments for such strong bonds between the linguistic and logic systems may be found elsewhere (e.g., Refs. 14, 20).

POSTLANGUAGE PRODUCTION RULES FOR MULTIPLE-VALUED LOGIC

Consider those language production rules which involve logical connectives of propositional calculus.[19,34] In what follows, read $\alpha \supset \beta$, $\alpha \, \& \, \beta$, $\alpha \cup \beta$, $\sim\alpha$, $\Box\alpha$, $\vdash\alpha$, W[α], and Lα, as α leads to β, α and β, α or β, it is not the case that α, it is the case that α, α is a theorem, α is a well-formed formula, and α is a propositional variable, respectively. Where clarity allows, we write Wα instead of W[α]. The remaining two symbols p, 1 are used to generate the propositional variables p, p1, p11, p111, p1111, ..., which we denote briefly by p_0, p_1, p_2, p_3, p_4, ..., whenever convenient.

The single axiom Lp and the following production rules yield a logic that cannot have more than two values:

1. L$\alpha \rightarrow$ Lα1
2. L$\alpha \rightarrow$ Wα

120

3. $W\alpha \to W \sim \alpha$

4. $W\alpha \to W\square\alpha$

5. $W\alpha, W\beta \to W[\alpha \supset \beta]$

6. $W\alpha, W\beta \to W[\alpha \& \beta]$

7. $W\alpha, W\beta \to W[\alpha \vee \beta]$

8. $W\alpha \to \vdash \alpha \supset \alpha$

9. $W\alpha, W\beta, W\gamma \to \vdash (\alpha \supset \beta) \supset (\gamma \supset (\alpha \supset \beta))$

10. $W\alpha, W\beta, W\gamma \to \vdash (\alpha \supset (\beta \supset \gamma)) \supset ((\alpha \supset \beta) \supset (\alpha \supset \gamma))$

11. $W\alpha, W\beta \to \vdash (\alpha \& \beta) \supset \alpha$

12. $W\alpha, W\beta \to \vdash (\alpha \& \beta) \supset \beta$

13. $W\alpha, W\beta, W\gamma \to \vdash (\alpha \supset \beta) \supset ((\alpha \supset \gamma) \supset (\alpha \supset \beta \& \gamma))$

14. $W\alpha, W\beta \to \vdash \alpha \supset (\alpha \vee \beta)$

15. $W\alpha, W\beta \to \vdash \beta \supset (\alpha \vee \beta)$

16. $W\alpha, W\beta, W\gamma \to \vdash (\alpha \supset \gamma) \supset ((\beta \supset \gamma) \supset ((\alpha \vee \beta) \supset \gamma))$

17. $W\alpha, W\beta, W\gamma \to \vdash (\alpha \& (\beta \vee \gamma)) \supset ((\alpha \& \beta) \vee (\alpha \& \gamma))$

18. $W\alpha \to \vdash \alpha \supset \sim \sim \alpha$

19. $W\alpha, W\beta \to \sim \sim (\alpha \supset \beta) \supset (\alpha \supset \beta)$

20. $W\alpha, W\beta \to \vdash (\alpha \supset \sim \beta) \supset (\beta \supset \sim \alpha)$

21. $W\alpha, W\beta \to \vdash \sim \alpha \supset (\alpha \supset \beta)$

22. $W\alpha \to \vdash \square\alpha \supset ((\alpha \supset \alpha) \supset \alpha)$

23. $W\alpha \to \vdash ((\alpha \supset \alpha) \supset \alpha) \supset \square\alpha$

24. $W\alpha \to \vdash \square\alpha \vee \sim \alpha$

25. $\vdash \alpha, \vdash \alpha \supset \beta \to \vdash \beta$

It will be seen below that production rules for non-2-valued logics are obtained easily from the above by simply altering production rule 24 (without alterations elsewhere), which here is equivalent to the rule corresponding to the classical law of the excluded middle $W\alpha \to \vdash \alpha \vee \sim \alpha$. Note that in this case the unary operator $\square$ simply reduces to the identity operator. In a full system, of course, there would be other linguistic production rules (see Refs. 19, 34).

Rule 24 indicates a bipartite expression with terms $\square p$ and $\sim p$, and suggests for consideration $2^{2^1} = 4$ possible disjunctions of these terms, viz., $\sim p \& \square p, \sim p, \square p,$ $\sim p \vee \square p$. Consideration of two variables, p_1 and p_2, yields 4 terms which through rule 17 are seen to be $\square p_1 \& \square p_2, \sim p_1 \& \square p_2, \square p_1 \& \sim p_2, \sim p_1 \& \sim p_2$, and suggest for consideration $2^{2^2} = 16$ possible disjunction of these terms.[24] Consideration of these full 16 possibilities by Post and Wittgenstein in this century was preceded by a long history of work in which fewer than 16 possibilities were considered. The work of Inhelder and Piaget[18] considers these full 16 possibilities.

Inhelder and Piaget[18] perform experiments in which certain factors $F_1, F_2, \ldots, F_T$ are assumed to play a part in effecting experimental outcomes. A simplifying assumption is that only one factor F_S plays a part, for some S satisfying $1 \le S \le T$, and that factors are investigated in pairs (F_i, F_j), for $i = 1, 2, \ldots, T; j = 1, 2, \ldots, T$. F_i is then associated with p_1 and F_j with p_2, to obtain each of the 16 possibilities mentioned above.

Inhelder and Piaget establish connection to the full 16 possible disjunctions and classical two-valued logic through these experiments and their protocols (Ref. 18, pp. 102–104). For example, in one protocol the experiment concerns apparatus in which there are several boxes and a hidden magnet with other factors including weight, color, distance, and content. The disjunction:

$$(\square p_1 \& \sim p_2) \vee (\sim p_1 \& \square p_2) \vee (\square p_1 \& \square p_2) = \square p_1 \vee \square p_2$$

occurs in this protocol when p_1 corresponds to the factor F_i of distance and p_2 corresponds to the factor F_j of content, the subject stating, "It's either the distance or the content." (Possibly both.) (Ref. 18, p 102). Connections with each of the other 15 disjunctions (using appropriate values of i, j for the factors F_i, F_j) are obtained in similar manner. See also (Ref. 24).

It is clear that this approach assumes *a priori* that connections are to be made with two-valued logic, and that this assumption may tend to bias the protocols toward the establishment of such connections. Some evidence for this is given by Lovell.[22] In what follows we present Post language-production rules for non-two-valued logics, and show their use for such experiments and protocols.

Replacement of rule 24 with rule 24_t given by:

$$24_t \quad W\alpha, W\beta \rightarrow \vdash \sim (\sim \Box \alpha \& \beta) \vee (\alpha \supset \beta)$$

yields a logic with, at most, three values (see condition (7) of Ref. 11). Replacement of rule 24 with rule 24_m given by:

$$24_m \quad W\alpha, W\beta, W\gamma \rightarrow \vdash (\alpha \supset (\beta \cup \gamma)) \supset ((\alpha \supset \beta) \vee (\alpha \supset \gamma))$$

yields a multiple-valued logic whose number of values need not be bounded. Axioms corresponding to this last system may be found in Refs. 12, 13.

The immediate interest here is with a law of included middle which is a consequence of *either* of these replacements. For the single variable p, this law includes a middle term between the terms $\sim p$, $\Box p$ of the law of excluded middle, and is given by:

$$\sim p \vee \sim (\sim p \vee \Box p) \vee \Box p.$$

Here the included middle term is $\sim (\sim p \vee \Box p)$. This term must be taken into account if either rule 24_t or rule 24_m is used instead of rule 24. Rule 24_t yields a simplifying case in which there is at most one extra value, e, for which $\sim (\sim p \vee \Box p)$ holds, as there is one value t (truth) for which p holds, and one value f (falsity) for which $\sim p$ holds. The presence of additional extra values $e_1, e_2, \ldots$ when rule 24_m is used, does not alter these ideas as the above law of included middle still holds (further details for such systems may be found in Refs. 7, 10, 12, 27).

Results for two variables p_1, p_2 are now obtained as they were in the previous section. Since there are three terms in the above law of included middle, these now generate $3^2 = 9$ conjunctions; namely, $\sim p_1 \& \Box p_2$, $\sim p_1 \& [\sim (\sim p_2 \vee \Box p_2)]$, $\sim p_1 \& \Box p_2$, $[\sim (\sim p_1 \vee \Box p_1)] \& \sim p_2$, $[\sim (\sim p_1 \vee \Box p_1)] \& [\sim (\sim p_2 \vee \Box p_2)]$, $[\sim (\sim p_1 \vee \Box p_1)] \& \Box p_2$, $\Box p_1 \& \sim p_2$, $\Box p_1 \& [\sim (\sim p_2 \vee \Box p_2)]$, $\Box p_1 \& \Box p_2$. It is easily seen that the number of possible disjunctions of these nine conjunctions is $2^{32} = 512$. Further details may be found in Ref. 8.

There is similarly an easy extension for the work of Inhelder and Piaget. It is evident that these 512 disjunctions contain the 16 disjunctions of the previous section. Although it is not clear that the simple experiments of Inhelder and Piaget are appropriate for such extension (for one thing, the conditions of each experiment were time invariant), it is easy to observe that no distinction was made between factors F_j, which were untested as opposed to factors F_k, which were tested and subsequently excluded from the experiment at hand. In other words, $\Box p_1$ could just as easily be the result of an exclusion of a tested factor, obtained through $[\Box p_1 \& \sim p_2] \vee (\Box p_1 \& \Box p_2) = \Box p_1$, as the result of failing to take p_2 into account. In the system of this section, $[\Box p_1 \& \sim p_2] \vee [\Box p_1 \& \Box p_2]$ does not so reduce. There is provision for expressing the extraneity of an untested factor through $\sim (\sim p_2 \vee \Box p_2)$, or through a third value e for which $\sim (\sim e \vee \Box e)$ evaluates to the value t.

Regardless of whether this extension is appropriate for these simple experiments, some such extension is required to account for the fact that children face experiments and decision-making situations that daily become more and more complex in nature.

The fact that there may be as many as 512 possible disjunctions to consider for two propositional variables in the three-valued case, as opposed to 16 possible disjunctions for two propositional variables in the two-valued case, may be discouraging for those who incline toward the fewer and easier number, but should be more than sobering for those who reject the balance of these 496 possibilities in experiments or decision-making situations as a matter of simple convenience, or on the assumption that these possibilities are irrelevant or without ramifications.[8]

Yet a different alteration in the above production rules yields a system of rules for a relevance logic that is related to computerized question-answering (QA) systems.[3,31] This is presented in the next section.

Let us make some observations about the systems given above. First, observe that each production rule contains exactly one occurrence of the production symbol $\rightarrow$, whereas there is no such limitation on the number of occurrences of the symbol $\supset$ on the right-hand side of these rules. Second, contradictions lead to any proposition variable whatever, the corresponding rule being $W\alpha, W\beta \rightarrow \vdash (\alpha \& \sim\alpha) \supset \beta$. Third, the Hasse lattice diagrams for the logical multiple values in these systems are as follows:

$$
\begin{array}{ccc}
\bullet\, e_1 = t & \bullet\, e_2 = t & \bullet\, e_3 = t \\
\bullet\, e_0 = f & \bullet\, e_1 = e & \bullet\, e_2 \\
& \bullet\, e_0 = f & \bullet\, e_1 \\
& & \bullet\, e_0 = f
\end{array}
$$

The relevance logic about to be given offers a counterpoint to each of the above observations. This is the so-called relevance logic of tautological entailments (Ref. 1, Ch. III) with the corresponding four-valued Hasse diagram:

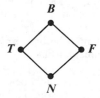

This uses denotations for the values as suggested in Ref. 2.

In what follows there is exactly one occurrence of the symbol $\supset$ on the right-hand side of any symbol $\vdash$. This captures the corresponding property of the symbol $\rightarrow$ within these same rules, as well as the property of single step-by-step reasoning shown by children within the protocols of Inhelder and Piaget. Also, contradictions do not lead to any proposition variable whatsoever. That is, in what follows, the corresponding rule $W\alpha, W\beta \rightarrow \vdash (\alpha \& \sim\alpha) \supset \beta$ does not hold, although the rule $W\alpha \rightarrow (\alpha \& \sim\alpha) \supset \alpha$, for example, does. It is supposed that some such relaxing of the rule $W\alpha, W\beta \rightarrow \vdash (\alpha \& \sim\alpha) \supset \beta$ is required to prevent the breakdown of these formal systems in the presence of contradictions that occur during the prelogical stage, or even later. The single axiom is again Lp and production rules are as follows:

1. $L\alpha \rightarrow L\alpha 1$
2. $L\alpha \rightarrow W\alpha$
3. $W\alpha \rightarrow W \sim \alpha$
4. $W\alpha, W\beta \rightarrow W[\alpha \& \beta]$
5. $W\alpha, W\beta \rightarrow W[\alpha \lor \beta]$
6. $W\alpha, W\beta \rightarrow \vdash (\alpha \& \beta) \supset \alpha$
7. $W\alpha, W\beta \rightarrow \vdash (\alpha \& \beta) \supset \beta$
8. $W\alpha, W\beta \rightarrow \vdash \alpha \supset (\alpha \lor \beta)$
9. $W\alpha, W\beta \rightarrow \vdash \beta \supset (\alpha \lor \beta)$
10. $W\alpha, W\beta, W\gamma \rightarrow \vdash (\alpha \& (\beta \lor \gamma)) \supset ((\alpha \& \beta) \lor \gamma)$
11. $W\alpha \rightarrow \vdash \alpha \supset \sim \sim \alpha$
12. $W\alpha \rightarrow \vdash \sim \sim \alpha \supset \alpha$
13. $\vdash \alpha \supset \beta, \vdash \beta \supset \gamma \rightarrow \vdash \alpha \supset \gamma$
14. $\vdash \alpha \supset \beta, \vdash \alpha \supset \gamma \rightarrow \vdash \alpha \supset (\beta \& \gamma)$
15. $\vdash \alpha \supset \gamma, \vdash \beta \supset \gamma \rightarrow (\alpha \lor \beta) \supset \gamma$
16. $\vdash \alpha \supset \sim \beta \rightarrow \vdash \beta \supset \sim \alpha$

The only theorems that involve the logical operation $\supset$ alone are of the form

$$\vdash p_i \supset p_i, \qquad i = 0, 1, 2, \ldots$$

As above, there is associativity and commutativity for each of the operations $\&$, $\lor$, with distributivity of each operation across the other, and again both of DeMorgan's laws hold for these two operations. However, $\vdash (p_1 \& (\sim p_1 \lor p_2)) \supset p_2$ does not hold, and $\vdash p_1 \supset (p_2 \lor \sim p_2)$ also fails to hold. Again, in a full system there would be other linguistic production rules.[19,34]

Here we focus attention on the four-valued Hasse diagram just given. In simplest terms, consider any question-answering or interactive system in which T represents that one component (human, entry of computer memory, etc.) of the system has received information that p is *true*, F represents that one component of the system has received information that p is *false*, B represents that one component of the system has received information (from two or more sources) that p is *both* true and false, and N represents that one component of the system has not received any information (from any source) whether p is true or false (that is, *none* of true or false has been received).

This is of interest not only for complex systems involving one or more computer subsystems,[2,31] but also for experimental situations with children in which the testing of irrelevant as well as relevant factors is encouraged, or where the experiment is such that contradictory test results are generated.

It is the actual case that such situations cannot be ignored by real-life experimenters in a laboratory. As a simple example, the time-invariance hypothesis for an experiment may fail just because the conditions of the experiment were accidentally changed by some third party during the temporary absence of the experimenters. Under this circumstance, what was relevant may become irrelevant, what was irrelevant may become relevant, and new experimental outcomes may contradict old experimental outcomes.

The logic just described, however, is only one of various kinds of relevance logics that might have been considered in this section. The system in Ref. 4, for example, does not fix any limit on the number of occurrences of the logical operation $\supset$. There are, in fact, numerous variations for the systems (see Refs. 6, 9, 29 for multiple-valued logics and Ref. 1 for relevance logics). There are still other kinds of nonclassical logic that have not been mentioned, for reasons of brevity. There are a number of systems that are obtained through the introduction of unary operations which obey certain production rules because of semantic or hypothesized interpretations of these operations. In particular, the operation $\square$ appears in modal logics.[16] These are discussed by Lakoff[20] and Hintikka.[15] Among other logics, we mention temporal logics,[26,30] spatial logics (Ref. 28, 229–249) and epistemic logic (28, 40–53). See Refs. 25, 17, and 23, respectively, for work by Piaget in these areas.

SUMMARY

We have suggested that it is unnecessary to use the classical two-valued logic alone, when establishing relations to the development of language and reasoning in the child. We have presented some alternatives.

REFERENCES

1. ANDERSON, A. R. & N. D. BELNAP, JR. 1975. Entailment. Princeton University Press. Princeton, N.J.
2. BELNAP, N. D., JR. A useful four-valued logic. Modern Uses of Multiple-valued Logic. J. M. Dunn and G. Epstein, Eds. D. Reidel. Dordrecht, The Netherlands. To be published.
3. BELNAP, N. D., JR. How a computer should think. Contemporary Aspects of Philosophy— Proceedings of the Oxford International Symposium. To be published.
4. BELNAP, N. D., JR. & J. R. WALLACE. 1966. A decision procedure for the system E_I of entailment with negation. Z. mathematische Logik und Grundlagen der Mathematik 11. 277–289.
5. CHOMSKY, N. 1956. Three models for the description of language. PGIT 2(3): 113–124.
6. DUNN, J. M. & G. EPSTEIN, Eds. Modern Uses of Multiple-Valued Logic, D. Reidel. Dordrecht, The Netherlands. To be published.
7. EPSTEIN, G. 1960. The lattice theory of post algebras. Trans. American Math. Society 95(2): 300–317.
8. EPSTEIN, G. 1960. Decisive Venn diagrams. Proc. 1976 Intern. Symp. Multiple-Valued Logic. Logan, Utah: 142–149.
9. EPSTEIN, G., G. FRIEDER & D. C. RINE. 1974. The development of multiple-valued logic as related to computer science. Computer 9: 20–32.
10. EPSTEIN, G. & A. HORN. 1974. Chain-based lattices. Pacific J. Math. 55(1): 65–84.
11. EPSTEIN, G. & A. HORN. 1974. Finite limitations on a propositional calculus for affirmation and negation. Bull. Section of Logic. Polish Academy of Sciences 3(1): 43–44.
12. EPSTEIN, G. & A. HORN. 1974. P-algebras, an abstraction from Post algebras. Algebra Universalis 4(2): 195–206.
13. EPSTEIN, G. &. A. HORN. Logics which are characterized by subresiduated lattices. Zeitschrift für mathematische Logik und Grundlagen der Mathematik. To be published.
14. HARRIS, Z. S. 1971. Structures Mathématiques du Language. Dunod. Paris, France.
15. HINTIKKA, K. J. J. 1973. Grammar and logic: some borderline problems. Approaches to Natural Language. K. J. J. Hintikka, J. M. E. Moravcsik, and P. Suppes, Eds. D. Reidel. Dordrecht, The Netherlands.
16. HUGHES, G. E. & M. J. CRESSWELL. 1968. An Introduction to Modal Logic. Methuen and Co. London, England.
17. INHELDER, B. & J. PIAGET. 1956. The Child's Conception of Space. Routledge and Kegan Paul. London, England.
18. INHELDER, B. & J. PIAGET. 1958. The growth of logical thinking from childhood to adlescence: an essay on the construction of formal operational structures. Basic Books. New York, N.Y.
19. KORFHAGE, R. R. 1966. Logic and Algorithms: 144–151. John Wiley and Sons. New York, N.Y.
20. LAKOFF, G. 1970–1971. Linguistics and natural logic. Synthese 22: 151–271.
21. LEVI-STRAUSS, C. 1966. The Savage Mind. University of Chicago Press, Chicago, Ill.
22. LOVELL, K. 1961. A follow-up study of Inhelder and Piaget's The growth of logical thinking Br. J. Psychol. 52: 143–153.

23. PIAGET, J. 1929. The Child's Conception of the World. Harcourt, Brace and World. New York, N.Y.
24. PIAGET, J. 1949. Traité de Logique: 229–238. Librairie Armand Colin. Paris, France.
25. PIAGET, J. 1955. The development of time concepts in the child. Psychopathology of Childhood. P. H. Hoch and J. Zubin, Eds. Grune and Stratton. New York; 21.4.
26. PRIOR, A. N. 1967. Past, Present, and Future. Oxford Press. London, England.
27. RASIOWA, H. 1974. An Algebraic Approach to Non-classical Logics: 132–164. North-Holland. Amsterdam, The Netherlands.
28. RESCHER, N. 1968. Topics in Philosophical Logic. D. Reidel. Dordrecht, The Netherlands.
29. RESCHER, N. 1969. Many-valued Logic. McGraw-Hill, Inc. New York, N.Y.
30. RESCHER, N. & A. URQUHART. 1971. Temporal Logic. Springer-Verlag. New York, N.Y.
31. SHAPIRO, S. C. & M. WAND.   . The relevance of relevance. Working paper. Computer Science Department, Indiana University, Bloomington, Ind. 47401.
32. SINCLAIR DE ZWART, H. 1967 Acquisition du Language et Développement de la Pensée. Dunod. Paris, France.
33. SINCLAIR DE ZWART, H. 1969. Developmental psychology. Studies in Cognitive Development. D. Elkind and J. H. Flavell, Eds. Oxford Press. London, England.
34. WALL, R. 1972. Introduction to Mathematical Linguistics. Prentice-Hall. Englewood Cliffs, N.J.
35. WESCOTT, R. W. This annal.

DISCUSSION

George Epstein, *Moderator*
Department of Computer Science
Indiana University
Bloomington, Indiana 47401

ISADORE DYAN (*Yale University, New Haven, Conn.*): After hearing the two papers, one can only sympathize with the members of the *Societé de Linguistique*.

I suspect that there is very little chance that we will be able to utilize our systems of reconstruction in such a way as to give us some idea of how languages originated. The reconstructions that we get nearly always present us with a language very much of the same type as the ones we see today.

FRANKLIN HOROWITZ (Formerly of *Rutgers University, New Brunswick, N.J.*): Dr. Kiparsky spoke of the two stages in the development of Indo-European where there was an earlier simple structure which became more complex and has since become less complex; but isn't that really a function of the difference between *comparative methods* and *internal reconstruction*? In the comparative method we project onto the protolanguage features of various dialects which may never have existed concomitantly; and in the case of internal reconstruction (to the extent that we can apply it), we reconstruct earlier regularity out of later irregularity.

PROF. KIPARSKY: Yes, it's a really difficult question, and a nice point. Let's imagine, however, that the situation had been the reverse. It seems to me that one can certainly recover more complex earlier stages on the basis of internal reconstruction, and that's very commonly done in historical linguistics.

For example, let's say we just had Latin; then, by looking at Latin morphology on the basis simply of internal reconstruction, we could tell a lot about an earlier, more complex stage that must have antedated Latin. So it's not true that the two procedures necessarily lead you in those opposite directions. But I do think that something is inevitably lost in any kind of reconstruction. And that may make the results rather more fuzzy than we would like them to be.

GLEN GILBERT (*Southern Illinois Univ., Carbondale, Ill.*): Prof. Wescott, I think that the notion of a protolanguage, or should I say the attraction of a protolanguage, is becoming increasingly untenable, if we can believe Richard Leakey's recent discovery that at Lake Rudolph *Homo erectus* remains dating to perhaps three million years before the present have been found.

I think, with regard to any notion of great jumps in language abilities such as you've postulated between two forms of *Homo sapiens*, that the burden of proof lies on anyone who is to establish such a claim, and that with each passing year the development of language seems much less a matter of discrete jumps than of a long-term continuum. Therefore, I think that we're being driven against our will onto much more of an agnostic position than we could have taken even a few years ago, and your idea startles me.

PROF. WESCOTT: Let me begin by saying that I don't think the idea of a continuity of evolution is incompatible with the idea of jumps in evolution. In fact, I think that practically all real evolutions have been jerky in nature.

There's no question in my mind that we and all of our close relatives are very complex in our communicative system and have always been. The question is: at what point did we reach particular achievements such as the development of a grammatical system or the development of a system which we could call a natural language in any sense? And here I don't think it's at all out of order to look back speculatively. I think it is a justifiable position that all contemporary languages resemble one another much more than they need to. This isn't only my view; it's the view, for example, of Charles Hockett of Cornell. He thinks what's really startling is that all languages are as much alike as they are, not that they're so different. So I believe it is quite possible that in the distant past we had other communicative systems which were very close to language as we now know it. But I don't think that the evidence points to indefinite antiquity for all known languages or language groups. I think the evidence points in the other direction, to a relatively slight antiquity.

I would say the same thing of the communicative systems of many higher mammals, including dolphins, and elephants. They're very complex and highly developed, but I don't think their signalings constitute language in the narrow sense.

PROF. KIPARSKY: I'd just like to make a comment on the question of *monogenesis*. The argument that it's necessary to assume a single protolanguage to account for resemblances between existing ones runs into the problem that the variations within families of closely related languages is extremely large, in some cases as large as the variation across what we know to be closely related families of languages.

That is, the differences between, say, English and Morati, or Morati and Tocarian, or some distant pair of Indo-European languages, are about as large as the differences between any two languages.

This is true of all the typologically interesting properties one may pick: verb second, type of phonology, etc. So if the resemblance among all languages of the world were going to be explained by a common ancestor, then one would have to find a way of dealing with the fact that the resemblance doesn't seem to correlate with the depth of actual relationships as we know them.

PROF. WESCOTT: I think Dr. Kiparsky has just given an excellent argument for monogenesis, because we know that Morati, Tocarian, and English are related. I think the burden of proof is now with you.

DR. KIPARSKY: You've completely missed my point. I'm sorry.

DR. EPSTEIN: Well, restate your point.

DR. KIPARSKY: Okay. If we were going to account for the resemblances between, say, Finnish and English on the basis of assuming that they were once the same language, then you'd have to postulate some grade of divergence. The fact is, however, that languages which we know to have been the *same* language at a relatively recent time, say 5,000 years ago, like English and Morati, differ far more from each other structurally than Finnish and English, which are not as closely related. This suggests that the tracks of original identity get lost rather fast and that actual variation somehow extends all over the map within a matter of something like 10,000 years.

Part IV. Perceptual and Cognitive Substrates (I)

INTRODUCTION

Sam Glucksberg

Department of Psychology
Princeton University
Princeton, New Jersey 08540

In this post-Darwinian age it is, I should think, appropriate for students of language and language behavior to consider seriously the phylogenetic continuities and potential precursors of human language. The three papers this evening share a common theme. While only humankind displays language, at least in the oral-acoustic mode, there should be important and interesting precursors, or perceptual, cognitive, and social substrates present in other animal species that are necessary (though not sufficient) for the phylogenetic development of language. These substrates should be discernible, if anywhere, in our closer evolutionary relatives, notably the primates in general and the apes in particular.

During the recently ended era of radical behaviorism, it was fashionable, if not *de rigeur*, to view virtually all animal behavior in terms of stimulus-response mechanisms of varying complexity. All behavior would, it was believed, be ultimately reducible to the "laws" of Pavlovian and operant conditioning. Human behavior was, of course, included in this optimistic program, with the noteworthy exception of those behaviors mediated by language—or to put it into the technical jargon of the time, verbal behavior and verbally mediated behavior. The surface manifestation of this metatheoretical view is clearly exemplified by Edward Chase Tolman's classic statement on the importance and relevance of studying maze-learning in the albino and hooded rat. If we could only understand the determinants of the laboratory rat's behavior at a choice-point in a maze, we would then understand most of what would be worth understanding about the behavior of all animals, including ourselves.

A logical extension of this view is, in retrospect, clear. If, indeed, human capacities, abilities, and mental processes are limited to stimulus-response processes—with the addition of mediating processes and, of course, language—then other animals must surely be as limited as we. If humans could not, in principle, have purposes, beliefs, or could not engage in complex information-processing activities, how then could the lower animals? In this context, Kohler's demonstration of "intelligent, insightful" problem solving by apes and Meier's demonstration of inferential behavior in the rat were, perhaps, undeniable, but at the same time philosophically out of tune and inexplicable. Such "facts" could not be fit into the general scheme of things, and so the work was not followed up or exploited by others in the field. Similarly, Bartlett's work on memory in the 1930s lay fallow until the resurrection of cognitive psychology in the late 1950s.

As the papers in this session illustrate, we are now willing to entertain the possibility that animals other than humans engage in complex perceptual, cognitive, and communicative activities. Paradoxically, perhaps, our current willingness—if not overwillingness—to attribute human-like intelligent activity to other species can be attributed, at least in part, to our recently returned willingness to attribute such activity to ourselves! The return to cognition spurred by such figures of the last two decades as Noam Chomsky, George Miller, Ulric Neisser, and Donald Broadbent, not only restored to humanity those attributes of perception, memory, and cognition that we had until then reserved for electronic computing machines, but also permitted us to consider whether other animals had been grossly underestimated and oversimplified as well.

Our willingness to attribute complex functioning to nonhuman animals should not, of course, lead us to accept uncritically all claims of the form, Animal Species A has abilities X, Y, and Z. We had been blinded, in the past, to the behavioral complexities displayed by both human and nonhuman species. Now that the pendulum has swung in the other direction, we should be wary of uncritical acceptance of claims for complex functioning unsupported by empirical evidence, and of potentially misleading and spurious parallels or analogs of human linguistic functioning. The principle of parsimony and Lloyd Morgan's canon are still, I believe, useful guidelines.

In this context, the three papers we will hear tonight provide provocative suggestions on some possible phylogenetic continuities between (1) verbal and nonverbal communication systems; (2) the perceptual integration capabilities of humans and nonhuman primates, and (3) skilled activity in general and language activities in particular.

COMMUNICATION AND COGNITIVE ORGANIZATION IN HUMANS AND OTHER ANIMALS

Emil W. Menzel and Marcia K. Johnson

Department of Psychology
State University of New York at Stony Brook
Stony Brook, New York 11794

Chomsky[1] once remarked that if animal communication has any fundamental properties in common with human language, the place to look for these properties is not at the level of ethological displays (i.e., the motor aspects of performance) or linguistic analysis, but rather at the level of perceptual and cognitive organization (see also Count;[2] Eisenberg;[3] Osgood.[4]) In this paper we shall consider those aspects of human and nonhuman communication which seem most interesting from a functionally oriented, cognitive, and comparative point of view.

A FUNCTIONAL POINT OF VIEW

First of all, all communication systems may be viewed as means to an end. They are mechanisms whereby humans or nonhumans solve the basic problems of coordinating and regulating their societies; discriminating each other's specieshood, sex, age, social background, group membership, emotional and motivational states, and the state of other objects and events in the environment; transmitting the capacity for similar accomplishments to subsequent generations; and thus ultimately securing all of the requisites for the survival and reproduction of the phenotype. Inasmuch as all living species are, almost by definition, capable of achieving their basic goals under natural conditions, it seems chauvinistic to ask whose communication systems are the "best," or to attempt to train animals in our languages before learning theirs.

Communication is Part of the General Information Processing Activities of an Organism

Communication is embedded in the general perceptual and cognitive activities of the organism, and these activities have the primary characteristic of being adaptive and purposeful. To separate communication from the overall information pickup and transmission capabilities of the individual would be a tour de force on the part of the human observer. Obtaining information from language or other specialized signal systems must share common features with obtaining information from any source.

Meanings Have Multiple Signs and There Are Multiple Meanings for Signs

Communication is symbolic, but the symbols do not correspond to meanings in any simple one-to-one fashion. An animal moving through the woods might hear a

131

single vocalization or the sound of several footsteps, or see a footprint in the sand, or smell the slight trace of urine or body odor in the air. Any number of these "sign stimuli" might stop him in his tracks, cause him to hypothesize or conclude that "something is out there," and that "it is probably over there rather than elsewhere," and "it is an X animal rather than a Y," and so forth. It is not the stimulus as such, but what that stimulus might *represent* which makes the stimulus biologically or cognitively significant. There is probably no one "innate releasing stimulus" for any particular hypothesis, and the same general conclusion can be reached in a host of different ways. Conversely, the "same" nominal stimulus can often represent a number of objects or events. What is a *snake*? It depends on whether you are talking to a student of biology, a fundamentalist preacher who is about to baptize you, a two-year-old child who is about to set foot in a Louisiana swamp, your psychoanalyst, a dance leader, a crapshooter. Neither the calls of monkeys nor the words of people *directly* stand for things. As Olson[5] and others have suggested, words serve to provide information relative to a given set of alternatives. This reduces the likelihood that a dictionary approach—assigning signs to meanings in a direct one-to-one fashion—will be adequate for characterizing any communication system.

The Importance of "Triangulation"

In the everyday world information comes from multiple sources, and except perhaps for organisms with split brains[6] or those in highly specialized laboratory experiments,[7] various channels function together as a coordinated, if not in some sense a unified, information-getting system. As Hornbostel (quoted by Gibson,[8] p. 54) put it, "it matters little through which sense I realize that . . . I have fallen into a pigsty." Many different forms of stimulus energy can all carry the same information; and information about the world can be obtained with any cue system alone or with many combinations of cues working together. D. T. Campbell[9] gives the latter process a very apt name: "triangulation." The most obvious form of triangulation is intramodal binocular vision or the ability to integrate the information received by each eye separately into a single percept. Other forms of triangulation would include the integration of information from verbalizations and gestures, visual and auditory cues, and so on.

The Importance of Cognitive Structures

A fundamental characteristic of information processing in general, as well as of language, is that two or more individuals do not reach the same understanding without similar cognitive structures. This is, of course, because the meaning of a message depends on the cognitive structure or schema to which it is referred (e.g. Bransford & Johnson.)[10] *Move out of the way* means one thing if someone is trying to run a vacuum cleaner around you and another if a large truck is coming toward you. Similarly, the sound of leaves rustling probably means one thing if you know a friend is near the source of the noise and another if you have reason to believe that a predator might be near. Thus, not only is there "triangulation" of information from various sources, but also there is considerable "filling in" or redintegration on the basis of the cognitive structures which are active at any given moment. Probable inferences based on past experience and reasonable hypotheses in any given situation are an integral part of information utilization (e.g., Kintsch;[11] Johnson *et al.*;[12] Johnson).[13]

Taking into Account the Cognitive Structure of Someone Else

In ordinary human discourse, the appropriate cognitive organization may be given by the immediate environment, as in the *Move out of the way* example. Or it may be given by experience and conventions; to use John Searle's example, *Could you pass the salt?* does not ordinarily mean *are you able to pass the salt?* but rather *Please pass the salt.* However, environmental cues and the habits of conventions are often only partial cues to meaning. Frequently, much of the appropriate cognitive structure must be established during the interaction of speaker and listener.

One of the most interesting aspects of practical communication situations is that people continually assess and take into account the cognitive competencies and cognitive structures of others and tailor their communications accordingly. If you were looking for the TWA gate at Kennedy Airport, you would be more likely to ask a person in an airport uniform than a randomly selected passerby. If you wanted to buy marbles, you would be more likely to ask a child where to go than to ask an adult. Similarly, if the airport guard or child were giving you directions, he or she would very likely start by determining something about your current state of knowledge about the environment. "Well, do you know where the airport restaurant is? Good. Turn left there and it's about three gates down."

An ongoing series of studies by David Goldstein and some of his colleagues indicates that children communicate more effectively the more familiar they are with the environment they are communicating about (Goldstein & Kose, personal communication). More importantly, children are more likely to use gestures in interactions with younger children than in interactions with adults (Goldstein et al., personal communication); and the length of children's verbalizations is affected by the age of the listener (Shatz & Gelman [14]). Apparently, by the age of four or five, if not sooner, children are beginning to tailor their communication to fit the presumed cognitive outlook of their listeners. As adults, many specific features of our communications (e.g., word choice, gestures, length of sentences, tone of voice, our rate of speech) are determined partially by the presumed capacities and actions of someone else.

Successful Communication Is Based on the Above
Characteristics of the Process

In general, successful communication depends on accurate assumptions about the cognitive organization of others and creative ways of using the entire communication process—making gestures, facial and body expressions, drawing pictures, making analogies, in addition to "straight" verbalization. This point is important not only in people-to-people exchanges, but also in people-to-animal exchanges. Most behavioral work with animals (like that with human infants) is largely a communication problem. Since we cannot verbally question an octopus about whether he can tell the difference between black and white, we have had to find some other ways to ask such questions. The most successful behavioral researchers are probably those who have particularly good intuitions about the way the world might look from someone else's point of view. As Konrad Lorenz put it, the first requirement of good research is that you be thoroughly familiar with your animal.

Since successful communication depends on accurately assessing the available cognitive structures of other beings, and animals integrate information from various sources, it is misleading to think of communication as one individual transmitting information to another who knows absolutely nothing about the intended message.

The more two individuals share common structures, assumptions, knowledge, and values, the more efficient their communication. This is one reason why it is easier to teach a human language to a chimpanzee than to a rhesus monkey. Perhaps this is partly why animal communication systems appear less elaborate than our own. In their societies, more information is shared information. Thus there is less variability in psychological organization to overcome.

In any event, if successful people-to-people and people-to-animal communication depends on accurate assumptions about the cognitive structure of other beings, it is probably not too far-fetched to assume that communication between animals involves similar assumptions about how the world looks to someone else.

LOOKING AT ANIMALS COLLECTING AND TRANSMITTING INFORMATION

With this background of assumptions, consider a "simple" interaction between an animal and an unknown object or being. Suppose that a normal, free-ranging monkey is strolling through the woods and suddenly comes into sensory contact with an object. How would he go about sizing up the situation? How would he know whether he was dealing with another living being, and if so, how would he determine its intent? If it were a conspecific, how would he determine whether it knows better than he does the lay of the land, the whereabouts of food, predators, and the rest of the social group?

Intentional Triangulation and Testing Hypotheses

Even if our monkey could conceivably be viewed as a "passive receiver" at the instant he perceives the first signal or cue (a glimpse, an odor, etc.), he does not remain passive for long. In nature, few situations can be sized up with certainty on the basis of a single distal cue; and in most cases the monkey will accordingly not "automatically" race toward or away from the source of the signal, but rather he will seek out additional information, or indulge what Pavlov called the "what is it?" reflex. He might turn his head this way and that, send out an answering call, sniff the air further, possibly climb a tree to scan the area visually. In this way, whatever "hypothesis" or "question" was posed initially can be further probed or checked out. We doubt very much that monkeys, like theorists (e.g., Marler[15]), sort various signals or cues into different categories according to what sensory modality is involved. They are, in other words, probably even less aware of and interested in their raw sensations as such than are human beings.

The Problem of Context

The extent to which our monkey will continue to indulge his curiosity depends upon many factors in addition to his initial hypothesis about the object. It depends, for example, upon his general familiarity with this particular portion of woods, whether or not the area includes large vertical structures that might provide cover or escape, how far away he is from his companion, how hungry he is, and so on. Those scientists who relegate such considerations to a garbage-pail category of "contextual factors" and focus their attention on "signals as such" should ask themselves: How do we, as observers, know which stimuli are "context," *psychologically speaking*, and how do we know which stimuli are at the "core" of the animal's attention, at any given instant? As Floyd Allport [16] has shown, the "core vs. context" distinction might be useful in informal discussion, but it is based on inadequate theories of cognitive structure and meaning (see also Menzel [17]).

To give an illustration, consider why it is so difficult to do good auditory "playback" experiments on primates, if not on many other higher mammals. If you record the "alarm call" of some bird species and play it back on a high-fidelity tape recorder, birds of that species will often respond very much as they would to the live event. Try the same experiment on a rhesus monkey or a chimpanzee, however, and he will probably glance at the recorder, then at you, and soon go on about his business. There are at least two ways in which the experiment could be changed to increase the chances of getting a "better" outcome; either add further cues that would tend to support the same hypothesis, or eliminate those cues (starting with the visible presence of a human being and a strange looking gadget) which might give rise to alternative hypotheses. Thus, for example, if the call came from behind some bushes that might easily conceal both a monkey and something about which a monkey might well become alarmed, and if the call were the voice of a known individual who was not in sight but whom the subject had seen walking over toward those bushes a few minutes earlier, and if, moreover, the subject himself had heard a leopard growling within the last several hours, we would predict without hesitation that his response would be less sanguine. It is not merely what animals know but what they don't know (and are capable of hypothesizing) that gives the signal its specific meaning. The call constitutes an "alarm cry"—i.e., it has the customary "dictionary" meaning which the Darwinian student of animal behavior has tried to assign it—only under certain sets of circumstances. With animals, as with people, we have to take into account what Orne [18] calls "communication by the total experimental situation."

Novelty: Assimilating Something New

Back to our monkey in the woods. In the interest of brevity, we will henceforth concentrate our attention on visual cues. Certainly the monkey would take into account whether the object looks like other objects with which he is already familiar, particularly in this part of the forest. There is a fairly high positive correlation between the phyletic status of the animal and the length of time he will spend in exploring a strange object (Glickman & Sroges [19]) and with most (but by no means all) classes of objects, the young will continue to respond longer than will adults. From our point of view, this cannot be attributed simply to motivational differences. Confronted with something new or unusual, animals attempt to make some sense of it, to organize it within a known framework, to discover what it is and what it does and what it might be good for. The more complicated the object and the more complicated the perceiver, the more possibilities there are to be explored. Adults of a given species might explore simple objects less than a youngster would, because they can evaluate such objects more quickly.

Assessing Someone Else

Apparent Size.

Generally speaking, objects that look large are approached much more tentatively than are objects that look smaller. For example, the same object usually produces quite different reactions according to whether it is standing upright or lying on its side, and the upright position usually produces greater caution. It is striking that so many of the visually-mediated "aggressive displays" of so many different species are based on the simple principle of "making oneself look bigger" (via sitting up vs. lying down, standing bipedally vs. standing quadrupedally, showing piloerection, and so on). Conversely, one way to get a timid animal or child to approach is to stoop down or otherwise make yourself look smaller. A puzzling problem is why even presumably intelligent animals such as monkeys and men, who show excellent size constancy in other situations, often do not see through such tricks.

Visual Capacity.

Of all the static visual cues that lead a monkey to respond to an object as if it were a living being, one of the most important is anything that looks like eyes. Two buttons attached to a rectangular piece of fur, for example, will produce a much more pronounced reaction than the fur alone. To be really effective the buttons should be located together on one end of the rectangle. A monkey will characteristically circle the object and then make his first close approach from the "tail end" of the object—that is, the end opposite from the eyes. Using a doll as the test object, one can in fact often cause the direction of the monkey's approach to vary simply by having the doll's eyes either opened or closed. A radio-controlled doll which would open its eyes and rotate its head toward the monkey as he was sneaking in cautiously from the rear would probably produce a striking effect. It should go without saying that similar behaviors occur if the test objects are other living beings, particularly other monkeys; the phenomenon of "gaze aversion" is by now very well known. One of us (Menzel) kept a record for about two months of all the times that he was approached and threatened by free-ranging rhesus monkeys as he was sitting passively in the woods. The data of principal interest were the direction of approach and the monkey's location when he sounded his first threat vocalization. A large majority of the monkeys (especially the smaller ones) made their approach from the rear, and in addition, many of these came in from overhead. They approached much closer, too, than those who did not come in from outside the test person's field of vision.

We could add many more examples of such behaviors, but perhaps their major point is already clear. Not only does the monkey seem to know the layout of the environment and his own behavioral and information-processing potentials, but also, he seems to be making hypotheses or somehow taking into account what behavioral and perceptual capacities *the other being* might possess. Was this indeed not true almost from the start, when our imaginary monkey received its first cue about the presence of the object? From a phenomenological point of view we might be stretching the data in putting forth such a claim; but from an evolutionary and functional point of view the claim is most plausible. In other words, we would argue that *most* species-specific behaviors, if not most morphological characteristics of living things (such as the eye-spots of a moth which frighten off predatory birds, and the bright colors of flowers which attract bees) in some way "take into account" the perceptual and cognitive organization of other living beings. Just where in the foregoing description of the monkey's behavior one is actually warranted in positing phenomenological knowledge or understanding on the monkey's part is a matter that future research will have to settle, but we are convinced that the question is not a trivial one (Bastian & Bermant[20]).

Behavior Potentials

Up to now we have said nothing about motion, and this is undoubtedly the most important single visual feature that gets and holds an animal's attention and assists him in distinguishing between a living being, a dead animal, and an inanimate object. Indeed, the general attention-getting value of movement most likely evolved in the first place because moving things are so apt to be either living beings or objects that are being acting upon by living beings; that is, certain types of movement are a fairly reliable sign of life, and hence of food, danger, or something else that might be of biological significance. A pile of leaves or a series of bushes that rustle and stir in a regular progression (as if they were being moved by a live animal burrowing or walking through them) will frequently be investigated, and the monkey does not investigate all points along this line of movement, but only the *last* point.

Even more pertinent to our present discussion, monkeys are capable of learning very quickly to discriminate between two static objects, one of which will move in one way (suddenly and rapidly toward you) when it is approached and another of which will move in a different way (slowly and away from you). In other words, the animals seem to learn a particular object's *potential ability* to move in a particular way; the object does not have to be moving at any given instant to produce its differential effect. It would be very surprising to us if normally raised monkeys could not, like people, take into account the following sorts of facts when they confront "new" animals: if the beast has wings and feathers, it is probably capable of traveling through the air; if it has no appendages at all, it probably cannot travel through the air; if it has big teeth, it can probably bite; and, in general, the more it looks like me, the more likely it can do whatever I can do.

While the general nonrandomness of an object's movement and the suddenness and directionality of this movement are highly effective determinants of a monkey's response, these animals seem also to be highly sensitive to whether or not the object's movement (and, of course, its other behaviors) are nonrandom *specifically with respect to their own behavior.* For example, a radio-controlled doll that moves its head up and down on a randomly determined schedule would probably be much less apt to inhibit a monkey from taking food that lay at the doll's feet than another doll that performs precisely the same movements but "looks down" only when the monkey is about to put his hand on the food.

Many aspects of the stalking behavior and play of mammals have some of the characteristics we have discussed so far. Consider, for example, how a monkey tries to sneak up on another animal for a "surprise attack." Not only will he move slowly, silently, and low to the ground, circle in from the rear if possible, and keep trees, rocks, bushes, or any available visual barrier between himself and the victim, but also, he will continually keep a watch on what the victim is doing. If he steps on a dry leaf he will freeze and watch the victim, and if the victim pricks up its ears, he will probably take greater care not to make any noise. If the victim starts visually to scan the area in the monkey's direction, the monkey might move quickly and duck behind a tree. If the victim plops down on the ground and closes its eyes, the monkey moves in faster than before, and so on.

Certainly it is not farfetched to say that the monkey perceives the correlation or the lack of correlation between his own behavior and that of the other animal (*and vice versa*) and varies his behavior appropriately. Is it possible that he also tries to guess what the other animal is hypothesizing, or even, conceivably, to control the other animal into hypothesizing one thing rather than another? Such a question might at first glance seem absurdly anthropomorphic. However, as Norbert Wiener suggested many years ago in his classical description of a fight between a mongoose and a snake, a principal advantage that the "higher" animal has is that he can use higher orders of information and feedback than the "lower" animal. In a fight he can correct his own moves in midcourse according to cues received from the other animal, rather than responding on an all-or-none basis; he can feint in one way to draw the other animal out, and then utilize this "opening"; he can keep himself in a favored location and gradually maneuver the other animal into a corner; he can learn what the other animal's potentials for certain types of movement will be as it gets more and more tired, and so proceed on the principle of first wearing the other animal down before the killing move is made. By the objective criteria that authors such as Tolman,[21] Sommerhoff,[22] and Rosenblueth et al.[23] have proposed, not only monkeys and mongooses but possibly even the snake could be said to know something about other animals' behavior potentials, hypotheses, and intentions.

Communicating about Others, Objects, Intentions, and the Environment

A still more complicated form of interaction is that which involves a third party in addition to the sender and the receiver. Can animal A perceive the fact that animal B's behavior is nonrandom with respect to animal C or with respect to an object? Since such behavior may be said to involve communication about the environment, and since it has been an accepted dogma for many years that animals other than man do little if any communicating about the environment, there are many authors who would be understandably skeptical about the ability of monkeys on this score. Consider, however, the following examples, which we are sure almost every field observer of primates has seen:

1. A human observer stares hard at an infant, then leans down to pick up a rock. The infant's mother, who is 20 yards off, starts to threaten the observer.

2. Monkey A, Monkey B, and a big ripe banana are all located 20 feet from each other, like three points of an equilateral triangle. Monkey A happens to see the banana first and starts for it. Monkey L, who is dominant to A, looks up at A, then immediately spots the banana too, and gives a gruff vocalization and gets up and starts for the same goal. A stops short at B's vocalization, glances once or twice between B and the banana, and sits down and grimaces at B.

3. Monkey A and Monkey B are sitting a few yards apart. Monkey A spots something behind a bush and cocks his head and stares toward the bush. Monkey B immediately stares in the same direction, then gets up and walks over and looks behind the bush.

We could, of course, extend this sort of analysis to four-party, five-party, or N-party interactions, and ask how many independent factors a monkey is capable of taking into account simultaneously before responding, but unfortunately there is very little empirical data available on such "higher order" situations. A majority of the available studies of primate behavior focus attention on simple dyadic relations (see Kummer et al.[24] for a cogent critique). It is, however, safe to predict that although probably all species of primates are capable of taking into account two or three independent factors, various species of primates would differ greatly in the sheer number of independent factors they could handle simultaneously.[25]

Perhaps the major point that we are trying to make here is that any statement to the effect that "animals other than man are capable only of communicating their internal emotional states and cannot convey information about objects" is predicated upon a false dichotomy and a very narrow view, even of emotional and expressive behavior. As Michotte[26] pointed out some years ago, human beings, if not other animals also, characteristically perceive "emotion" as a modification of a signaler's behavior *in regard to* oneself or *in regard to* some object or event. That is, we judge the character and meaning of another being's internal state not merely from his motor patterns and vocalizations and other molecular reactions, but also from the relation of these reactions to the rest of the environment.

When we see an individual acting excited or even just walking rapidly in a straight line, we tend to assume that the individual is not performing some isolated activity, but rather that his behavior has some external referent or cause, if not some goal or purpose. A whole group of monkeys startles and leaps for the trees when one member does so, not because of what the leader's behavior portends about his internal state, but because of what such behavior might portend (or has in the past portended) about the environment and the receiver's odds of survival. A chimpanzee heads over in the direction of another chimpanzee who is giving loud "food calls" not because the calls indicate how happy the signaler is (and happiness is contagious), but because of what the calls suggest about the receiver's odds of getting something for himself.

Chimpanzees that have seen a member of their group orient toward an object which they themselves cannot see will often search the field in the indicated direction. It is not necessary that the signaler accompany them or even that he be in the situation at the time of group response. Moreover, there can be a considerable temporal delay between the leader's signal and the followers' response. Further, the followers react quite differently if the hidden object is a snake than if it is a pile of food, and they can similarly discriminate the difference between a large vs. a small pile of food or a preferred vs. a less preferred type of food.[28]

To give one more example, consider a group of semidesert-dwelling hamadryas baboons that sleep every night on one of several cliffs but that forage up to several miles from these cliffs during the day.[29] Assume that on a given day the group is at a position from which each cliff lies in a different direction, and that the leader of the group starts to glance alternately toward the setting sun, the cliffs, and the other animals, and then strides off in the direction of one of the cliffs. Would it really be so remarkable if the other adult group members could predict the leader's (and the group's) destination an hour or so and a few miles in advance? Does the leader actually need a vocal or gestural language to get across to the human observer or to his followers that it is late in the day and time to move out, and that he intends to spend the night at the same place the group put up a few nights ago?

It seems to us that one function of communication is to reduce the others' uncertainty in situations that are not already clear, and that the more information the sender and receiver already have in common and the better they can evaluate each other's knowledge and momentary predispositions, and the greater the number of alternative ways they have for filling in the few remaining blanks of information, the less necessary is any particular "signal."

According to Suzanne Langer,[30] two of the clearest suggestions of symbolization in nonhuman species, and hence two of the clearest precursors of language-like processes are (1) the "mere sense of significance" that animals attach to strange-looking objects and new situations and (2) expressive movements and "dances." Maybe she did not go far enough. Almost any motor behavior, even simple locomotion, is "symbolic" in the sense that it usually has some external referent or "refers to" objects and events that the animal has either encountered in the past or expects to encounter in the future. Actions may also be said to possess most of the formal design features by means of which other investigators have tried to characterize language. The ability of nonverbal animals to "tell" each other the nature and location of objects and events is limited only by the richness of a signaler's behavioral organization and a receiver's knowledge of the signaler and the common environment in which they are operating.

Summary and Conclusions

Our major goal has been to indicate some primary features of a cognitively oriented, functional account of communication. In summary, we have argued that communication is part of the general perceptual and cognitive activities of an organism. Before we can predict how a "word" or a "signal" will be comprehended in a particular situation by a particular receiver, we must presuppose a good bit about the psychological organization of the receiver. Specialized signals supplement and complement the information that is available from other sources, including internal schemata and hypotheses. Some of the most interesting of these hypotheses involve assumptions about the perceptual and cognitive capacities of someone else. Sometimes these assumptions may be wrong, but many animals, and especially primates (including us) seem to be able to correct them even in the midcourse of an action on the basis of feedback from another individual. Where language leaves off and nonlanguage begins, or where "cues" leave off and "context" begins, is an open question, and in our opinion it is not a very central one.

These considerations suggest that it is time to question, if not lay to rest, many of the assumptions that still linger on in the area of animal communication, especially the assumptions that there are one-to-one correspondences between particular signals and particular meanings (the principle of the dictionary and the ethogram), that the relative communicative ability of species can be measured in terms of how many different signals they make (vocabulary size), that nearly all nonhuman communication patterns are involuntary and nonintentional, that the hallmark of human language is the ability to indicate objects rather than purely internal states, that without language animals can convey nothing about the past or the future or about objects that are not present to the senses. In particular, we would argue that any theory of communication that ignores the ability of animals to use many different interchangeable means for getting across the same general message (which ability has been called "paraphrasing" and "translation" in linguistics, "means-ends-readiness" in the area of problem solving, and "equifinality" in biology) is of little value for understanding primate communication or its biological roots or its cognitive base.

Some investigators have argued that sentences or propositions rather than words or phonemes are the appropriate units for a structural analysis of verbal language. For a functional analysis of language and communication in general, the more appropriate units are the larger events in which sentences *and* nonverbal cues occur. The amount of information conveyed by a signaler to a receiver cannot be specified from any more molecular form of analysis.

The more we think about the fact that communication is part of the general information-processing activities of an organism, the more obvious it becomes that beneath the "deep structure" of human language and human thought there are indeed "deep-deep" structures that we share with other species, and that it is on these structures that our linguistic abilities are predicated.

References

1. Chomsky, N. 1967. The general properties of language. *In* Brain Mechanisms Underlying Speech and Language. F. L. Darley, Ed. Grune & Stratton. New York, N.Y.

2. COUNT, E. W. 1973. Being and Becoming Human. Van Nostrand-Reinhold. New York, N.Y.

3. EISENBERG, J. 1973. Mammalian social systems: are primate social systems unique? *In* Symposia Fourth Inter. Congr. Primatology. Vol. 1. Precultural Primate Behavior. S. Karger. Basel, Switzerland.

4. OSGOOD, C. E. 1971. Where do sentences come from? *In* Semantics: An Interdisciplinary Reader in Philosophy, Linguistics, and Psychology. D. D. Steinberg and L. A. Jacobvitz, Eds. Cambridge University Press. Cambridge, Mass.

5. OLSON, D. R. 1970. Language and thought: Aspects of a cognitive theory of semantics. Psych. Rev. **77:** 257-273.

6. GAZZANIGA, M. 1967. The split brain in man. Sci. Am. **217:** 24-29.

7. HELD, R. 1965. Plasticity in sensory-motor systems. Sci. Am. **213:** 84-94.

8. GIBSON, J. J. 1966. The Senses Considered as Perceptual Systems. Houghton-Mifflin. New York, N.Y.

9. CAMPBELL, D. T. 1966. Pattern matching as an essential in distal knowing. *In* The Psychology of Egon Brunswik. K. R. Hammond, Ed. Holt, Rinehart and Winston, Inc. New York, N.Y.

10. BRANSFORD, J. D. & M. K. JOHNSON. 1973. Consideration of some problems of comprehension. *In Visual information processing.* W. Chase, Ed. Academic Press. New York, N.Y.

11. KINTSCH, W. 1972. Notes on the structure of semantic memory. *In* Organization and Memory. E. Tulving and W. Donaldson, Eds. Academic Press. New York, N.Y.

12. JOHNSON, M. K., J. D. BRANSFORD & S. K. SOLOMON. 1973. Memory for tacit implications of sentences. J. Exp. Psychol. **98:** 203-205.

13. JOHNSON, M. K. 1975. Constructive aspects of memory: historical antecedents. Presented at 83rd Ann. Conv. Am. Psychological Asso. Chicago, Ill. September.

14. SHATZ, M. & R. GELMAN. 1973. The development of communication skills: modifications in the speech of young children as a function of listener. Monogr. Soc. Res. Child Dev. No. 152.

15. MARLER, P. 1965. Communication in monkeys and apes. *In* Primate Behavior. I. DeVore, Ed. Holt, Rinehart and Winston. New York, N.Y.

16. ALLPORT, F. H. 1955. Theories of Perception and the Concept of Structure. John Wiley & Sons, Inc. New York.

17. MENZEL, E. W. 1969. Naturalistic and experimental approaches to primate behavior. *In* Naturalistic Viewpoints in Psychological research. E. Williams and H. Rausch, Eds. Holt, Rinehart and Winston. New York, N.Y.

18. ORNE, M. T. 1973. Communication by the total experimental situation: Why it is important, how it is evaluated, and its significance for the ecological validity of findings. *In* Communication and Affect. P. Pliner, L. Krames, and T. Alloway (Eds.), Academic Press. New York, N.Y.

19. GLICKMAN, S. E. & R. W. SROGES. 1966. Curiosity in zoo animals. Behaviour **26:** 151-188.

20. BASTIAN, J. & G. BERMANT. 1973. Animal communication: an overview and conceptual analysis. *In* Perspectives on Animal Behavior. G. Bermant, Ed. Scott, Foresman. Glenview, Ill.

21. TOLMAN, E. C. 1951. Behavior and Psychological Man. University of California Press. Berkeley, Calif.

22. SOMMERHOFF, G. 1950. Analytical Biology. Oxford University Press. Oxford, England.

23. ROSENBLUETH, A., N. WIENER & J. BIGELOW. 1943. Behavior, purpose and teleology. Philosophy of Science **10:** 18-24.

24. KUMMER, H., W. GÖTZ & W. ANGST. 1974. Triadic differentiation: an inhibitory process protecting pair bonds in baboons. Behaviour **59:** 62-87.

25. NISSEN, H. W. 1958. Axes of behavioral comparison. *In* Behavior and Evolution. A. Roe and G. G. Simpson, Eds. Yale University Press. New Haven, Conn.

26. MICHOTTE, A. 1950. The emotions regarded as functional connections. *In* Feelings and Emotions: The Moosehart Symposium. McGraw-Hill, Inc. New York, N.Y.

27. MENZEL, E. W. Communication of object-locations in a group of young chimpanzees. *In* Behavior of the Great Apes. D. Hamburg and J. Goodall, Eds. Holt, Rinehart and Winston. New York, N.Y. In press.

28. MENZEL, E. W. 1974. A group of young chimpanzees in a one-acre field. *In* Behavior of Nonhuman Primates. Vol. 5. A. M. Schrier and F. Stollnitz, Eds. Academic Press. New York, N.Y.

29. KUMMER, H. 1968. Social Organization of Hamadryas Baboons. S. Karger. Basel, Switzerland.

30. LANGER, S. K. 1942. Philosophy in a New Key. Harvard University Press. Cambridge, Mass.

CROSS-MODAL PERCEPTION IN APES*

Richard K. Davenport

Georgia Institute of Technology and
The Yerkes Regional Primate Research Center
of Emory University, Atlanta, Georgia 30322

I should like to describe some experiments in cross-modal perception with apes and monkeys and to attempt to relate this phenomenon to the origins of speech and language.

The sensory modalities of most human adults operate in concert as an integrated system of systems. Information received via one modality is coordinated in some manner with information from other modalities, and much of adaptive behavior, including language, presumably depends to a large extent on this intermodality integration. The existence of cross-modal perception and the unity of the senses in humans was graphically testified to by von Hornbostel when he said, "It matters little through which sense I realize that in the dark I have blundered into a pigsty."[1] In routine activities, we are seldom aware of the marked discrepancies in information originating in the several sensory modalities. The extent to which this capacity is shared with psychologically and neurologically unusual humans, infants, and other animals is not entirely clear.

The interrelatedness of the senses, variously termed intermodal or cross-modal transfer, intermodal integration or generalization, cross-modal perception, and the like has a long philosophical history, extending at least as far back as the early 1700s with Locke and Berkeley, but a relatively brief clinical and experimental history. Neurological case studies of the late 1800s provided some interesting data, and von Senden's observations published in 1932 on early-blinded people whose sight was restored in adulthood were more directly relevant. Experimental work with humans, including the blind, deaf, neurologically damaged, very young children, and normal adults, has accelerated in the past few years (see reviews by Freides[2] and Gibson[3]). Experimental investigations with nonhuman animals aimed directly at cross-modal perception are recent and still rather few in number.

There are a number of fundamental issues regarding cross-modal perception which require clarification:

1. What are the roles of maturation and experience in its expression?

2. What are the neurological requisites for the phenomenon and in what manner do neuroanatomical characteristics facilitate cross-modal perception (in part a phylogenetic issue)?

3. What is the nature of the information processing that permits integration of information among the several modalities?

4. To what extent do other behavioral capacities such as language mediate or facilitate perceptual integration?

5. To what extent do cross-modal capabilities contribute to adaptive behavior in general, and cognitive processes and language in particular?

6. In what manner and to what extent do intramodality characteristics or limitations in and of themselves contribute to cross-modal functioning?

*Preparation of this paper and some of the reported research was funded in part by grants from The National Science Foundation and by U. S. Public Health Service grant RR 00165, Division of Research Resources, National Institutes of Health. Reprints may be requested from the author, School of Psychology, Georgia Institute of Technology, Atlanta, Georgia 30332.

Some of these issues are discussed below, but it should be said in advance that cross-modal perception is in general poorly understood.

The assumption that cross-modal integration is related to language comes from several sources: first, from the repeated failures of investigators to demonstrate clear cross-modal perception in nonhuman primates until recently,[4-8] although it has been frequently shown in normal human adults; second, neuroanatomical differences between man and nonhuman primates, the relative independence of the auditory, visual, and somasthetic association areas in the latter,[9-12] which were assumed to severely limit cross-modal perception and possibly preclude language; third, the apparent ontogenetic improvement in cross-modal perception accompanying the development of language in human children; and fourth, the frequently observed language limitations in humans congenitally deprived of a sensory modality, especially audition.

The failures to demonstrate cross-modal perception without specific training in monkeys and its assumed dependence on language development in young children led to the assumption that it was a uniquely human capacity and was necessarily mediated by language.

A half-dozen behavioral experiments in the last five or six years have challenged these views, at least in the modalities of vision and touch. Subsequently in this paper, the term "haptic" will be used in place of "touch" to denote more specifically active manual exploration. Since 1970, our own research[13-16] has shown that apes have the capacity for haptic-visual cross-modal perception of multidimensional objects and representations of those objects without specific previous associational experience with specific test objects. At last, monkeys have been shown to have similar abilities.[17] Preverbal human infants (below one year of age) also have been found to have visual-haptic cross-modal perception without specific training.[18]

Psychologists have become sometimes painfully aware over the years that the inabilities of their animal subjects to behave in a desirable manner are likely to result from the inabilities of the investigators to arrange the appropriate situation or give the proper "instructions" to the animal. Demonstrations of cross-modal perception seem to fall in this category. Of course, basing theories on negative results can be hazardous.

A related problem applies to the assessment of the abilities of children. In the majority of cross-modal studies with children, the task is described by verbal instruction and/or given by demonstration. When there is failure to perform correctly, however, the experimenter cannot determine the basis for the failure; i.e., whether the subject is indeed incapable of the task or whether he did not comprehend and/or remember what he was supposed to do—a failure of instruction.

There are two main procedures for the study of intermodal functioning: a transfer of training design and a matching-to-sample design. In the transfer of training method, the subject is required to learn a discrimination in a single modality and then perform (or learn) the same discrimination in another modality. For example, a subject learns to discriminate a cube from a sphere visually and then haptically. If learning occurs more rapidly in the second modality than in the first, cross-modal transfer of a learned discrimination is said to have occurred and cross-modal perception is assumed. The effects are usually measured by a savings in learning score in the second modality. Since subjects are exposed to an extended series of discrimination tasks, their performance may be improved by rule learning, learning sets, or general facilitation. Thus, before cross-modal transfer can be assumed, proper control groups must be used. Additionally, when performance in the second modality is not facilitated by experience in the first, it may be because the subject is treating the two tasks as unrelated discriminations, since the subject has not been trained to relate the two.

The matching-to-sample procedure permits more direct and unambiguous study of cross-modal perception. Cross-modal matching requires the subject to match an object presented in one modality with an identical object presented in another modality. Usually, problems are presented repeatedly and the discriminanda become familiar. As in transfer experiments, rapid learning of a conditional discrimination may facilitate performance when stimuli and problems are repeated. This effect is ruled out if only a single trial on each separate problem with unfamiliar objects is given. No strategy other than the perception of stimulus equivalence can be used to achieve greater than chance matching accuracy. (The same end can be achieved in the transfer design if analysis is limited only to the first trial in modality two.)

A delayed matching-to-sample paradigm further requires the subject to register the sample in some manner and respond after a delay on the basis of this remembered information.

Ettlinger[4,19] has argued for the conceptual difference in transfer and matching methods; however, we see them to be the same in principle. In the transfer situation, the subject must discover by trial and error in the original discrimination the critical stimulus (the correct object) that is explicit (the sample) in matching. A major difference is that in the transfer design the "instruction" or training is less explicit. Basically, as far as cross-modal perception is concerned, there is little to indicate that the methods assess different abilities, as has been suggested by Ettlinger.[4,19]

An important methodological consideration should be mentioned here. Bryant[20] has pointed out that failures in cross-modal experiments can be caused either by a failure in cross-modal operation or problems in intramodality functioning. Using Bryant's suggested controls, the addition of within modality assessment, Milner and Bryant[21] showed that some presumed cross-modal deficiencies could be attributed to failures of intramodal discrimination. Failure to include this obvious control in many developmental studies with children led to the conclusion that there is a strong ontogenetic trend in cross-modal improvement, relatively independent of intramodal functioning. Before one can make statements about intermodality abilities (except to say they are present), it is necessary to know how these abilities compare to intramodal functioning of each of the separate involved modalities. Changes that may appear to be due to intermodality functioning may, indeed, be attributable to intramodality improvement.

We have been engaged in cross-modal research with apes since 1969 and have demonstrated several cross-modal phenomena, using a matching-to-sample design:

1. Visual to haptic cross-modal perception with complex stereometric objects.[13] The phrasing "visual to haptic" means that the sample was presented visually and the subject selected its match on the basis of haptic cues. Haptic to visual is the reverse. The method for this study and those following is sketched here. On any one trial, the subject received three multidimensional objects, one of which, the sample, could be seen but not touched, and two other objects, one a match for the sample and one different, which could be touched but not seen. A tug on the matching object produced a reward; a tug on the nonmatch went unrewarded. Repeated trials (the sample being randomly changed) were given on this set until the subject chose correctly on a reasonable number of trials. Other sets were similarly presented for training until we were fairly confident that the subject was either: 1) matching on the basis of cross-modal equivalence, or 2) was performing on the basis of simple associational learning. To test these alternatives, subjects were given 40–60 "unique" matching-to-sample problems composed of new objects never seen or felt before. Only a single trial was given on each problem, thus eliminating specific learning and transfer. Apes did match significantly often on these first exposures, which could be done only on the basis of perception of cross-modal equivalence.

2. Haptic to visual cross-modal perception with complex stereometric objects.[15]

Here the sample was presented haptically and the choice objects behind windows for examination and selection. To indicate a choice, the subject simply touched the covering window. Otherwise, the experiment followed the procedure described above and confirmed the bidirectionality of the phenomenon. Within the limits of our experiment, i.e., a small number of subjects, objects of unknown discriminability, and a relatively few unique test problems, the task was equally easy in both directions.

3. Haptic-visual perceptual equivalence when the visually presented discriminanda are photographs of an object.[14,15] Several investigators have suggested that chimpanzees do recognize photographs;[22,23] however, it was not clear in their reports that recognition occurred on first exposure and was not based on specific associational training. In our replication of previously described experiments but using life-size photographs as discriminanda, chimpanzees demonstrated cross-modal perception. This laid the foundation for other studies of the chimpanzee's ability to respond on the basis of a "representation" of an object. We further degraded the visual stimulus properties of the discriminanda by using half-size photographs, poor quality line drawings, and high-contrast photographs.[16] In high-contrast photographs, textural and dept. cues are eliminated. By photographic manipulation, the object is a solid black figure on a homogeneous white background. The apes were still successful in the equivalence testing, even without specific training. This was of some special interest, since it has been contended that primitive (photographically naive) people may be unable to recognize the representational character of snapshots of even familiar objects without specific learning.[24,25]

4. Delayed cross-modal matching-to-sample was our first experiment focused directly on memory as a variable. Here, a delay was imposed between the sampling response and the presentation of the choice objects. Interestingly, accuracy was about the same as in the previously used simultaneous procedures.

5. Haptic to visual cross-modal perception in a transfer of training design. In this experiment, after discrimination tasks had been learned in one modality (that is, after the "sample" had been identified, according to the aforementioned rationale), the same discriminanda were given for a single trial in the other modality. Apes were successful in this.

Our subjects performed with about 70-80% accuracy. The question has been raised that if the animals had learned the cross-modal task, why was their performance not better?[18,19] First, the tasks were difficult, requiring close attention in both modalities. Second, the chimpanzee hand seems to be less sensitive than that of the human, and, on close observation of their search pattern, there was a tendency to touch only a portion of the object; thus, haptic information may have been impoverished. To the human observer, the task was rather boring and the animals were under weak extrinsic motivation. In addition, object preferences, transient position tendencies, and distractions no doubt accounted for less than perfect performance.[15,16] Even the asymptotic performance of highly motivated, sophisticated chimpanzees in two choice object-quality discrimination learning sets falls far short of perfection.[26]

6. Auditory-visual cross-modal perception with apes and monkeys in our laboratories, even after prolonged training in the matching design, has so far been a failure. The aim of the procedure is to present Morse Code-like pulse trains, auditorially or visually, which are to be matched to an identical train in the other modality on discrete trials. These experiments are continuing.

7. Haptic/visual cross-modal perception in monkeys using essentially the same procedures and apparatus that had been successful with apes, was a failure. We

believe the apparatus and procedures were not appropriate for these animals, and general inattention, carelessness in palpating objects, a tendency to develop position habits, and other strategies contributed to the failure. We abandoned our own work on this after publication of the ingenuous experiment by Cowey and Weiskrantz,[17] in which haptic-visual cross-modal perception was found with use of a radically different and more appropriate procedure. They presented monkeys overnight in the dark with stereometric shapes, some of which were edible and some inedible. After several such exposures, during which the objects were explored by touch (and the edible ones consumed), the subjects were given discrete choice trials, each composed of an edible and an inedible object. The monkeys routinely chose the edible objects using vision alone, thus demonstrating haptic-visual cross-modal perceptual equivalence.

Several studies have shown that human children can recognize the equivalence of what is seen and touched,[21,27] but verbal mediation as the key mechanism was not ruled out until an experiment by Bryant et al.,[18] in which preverbal children (below one year of age) successfully showed equivalence in vision and touch without specific learning.

Significant cross-modal transfer of an intensity or pulse-pattern discrimination has been found in a prosimian,[29] rats,[30] and rabbits,[31] but no studies of visual-haptic object equivalence have been reported in animals simpler than the monkey. To make sensible comparisons of taxa, methods, modalities, and stimulus properties, clearly much more research is needed. Intuitively, it seems that cross-modal transfer of intensity and pulse pattern is a fundamentally different and simpler phenomenon than the perception of cross-modal equivalence of complex discriminanda. Cross-modal integration of these elementary stimuli might well be handled by common neural mechanisms,[32] including multimodal cells.[33-35] Bental et al. concluded that, ". . . the theory about modality specificity cannot be upheld . . . ," and that ". . . there exists an interaction between the auditory and visual pathways giving rise to convergence of flash and sound stimuli at the single-cell level in the primary visual cortex." Such a process could lay the foundation for cross-modal function where elementary visual and auditory stimulation is involved.

Ettlinger[19] has suggested the possibility of higher order cortical systems in apes and man (and presumably some monkeys) which enable cross-modal perception, whereas prosimians and nonprimates may possess a lower subcortical mediational system for cross-modal integration.

Unfortunately, we know very little about the phylogenesis of cross-modal perception, since so few taxa have been studied in so few situations. It cannot be assumed, for example, that because cross-modal perception for some stimulus features or percepts is found in a particular organism that the organism will have equal or equivalent abilities for other stimulus features. Indeed, it is not clear under what circumstances in humans and other animals perception based on multimodal cues is an advantage over perception based on more limited input. Exploration of this has just begun.

Of what relevance is cross-modal perception to the origin and evolution of speech and language? First, it appears that multimodal information extraction of environmental information is likely to result in more veridical perception, and may facilitate cognitive functioning. Second, in my view, cross-modal perception requires the derivation of modality-free information, a "representation." That an organism can have the same representations, concepts or percepts, regardless of the method of peripheral reception, confers great advantage on that animal in coping with the demands of living. This would hold true for general adaptation, for individuals in unusual environments where one modality is operating suboptimally or, for example, when quick response may be required on the basis of partial information, and in circumstances where cognitive manipulation is required.

To the extent that an organism has a "tag" for the representation, be it sound, gesture, or combination, the process would be greatly facilitated. What evolutionary occurrence could have accounted for this is not yet known. (One suggestion [9,10] is that in man, the angular gyrus is the neurological elaboration which is critical for the attachment of a "name" to the cross-modal percept.)

Considering the efficiency of human phonological information processing, there would be enormous advantage to a similarly equipped animal in having a "name" for a perceptual "representation" for use in memory, problem-solving, and other cognitive functions, and ultimately for interanimal communication of complex information.

ACKNOWLEDGMENTS

The author gratefully wishes to recognize the collaboration of C. M. Rogers, Department of Psychology, Auburn University, Auburn, Alabama, and I. S. Russell, M.R.C. Neural Mechanisms of Behaviour Research Unit, University College, London, England, in much of the original work cited here.

REFERENCES

1. ELLIS, W. D. 1938. A Source Book of Gestalt Psychology. Harcourt, Brace. New York, N.Y.
2. FREIDES, D. 1974. Human information processing in sensory modality: Cross-modal functions, information complexity, memory, and deficit. Psychol. Bull. 81(5): 284–310.
3. GIBSON, E. J. 1969. Principles of Perceptual Learning and Development. Appleton-Century-Crofts. New York, N.Y.
4. ETTLINGER, G. 1967. Analysis of cross-modal effects and their relationship to language. In Brain Mechanisms Underlying Speech and Language. C. G. Millikan and F. L. Darley, Eds. Grune and Stratton. New York, N.Y.
5. ETTLINGER, G. & C. B. BLAKEMORE. 1967. Cross-modal matching in the monkey. Neuropsychologia 5: 147–154.
6. ETTLINGER, G. & C. B. BLAKEMORE. 1969. Cross-modal transfer set in the monkey. Neuropsychologia 7: 41–47.
7. WILSON, W. A. & O. C. SHAFFER. 1963. Intermodality transfer of specific discrimination in the monkey. Nature, Lond. 197: 107.
8. WEGENER, J. G. 1965. Cross modal transfer in monkeys. J. Comp. Physiol. Psychol. 59: 450–452.
9. GESCHWIND, N. 1965. Disconnection syndromes in animals and man. Brain 88: 237–294 & 585–644.
10. LANCASTER, J. B. 1968. Primate communication systems and the emergence of human language. In Primates: Studies in Adaptation and Variability. P. C. Jay, Ed. Holt, Rinehart and Winston.
11. JENSEN, A. R. 1971. The role of verbal mediation in mental development. J. Genet. Psychol. 118: 39–70.
12. HEWES, G. W. 1973. Primate communication and the gestural origin of language. Curr. Anthropol. 14(1–2): 5–24.
13. DAVENPORT, R. K. & C. M. ROGERS. 1970. Intermodal equivalence of stimuli in apes. Science 168: 279–280.
14. DAVENPORT, R. K. & C. M. ROGERS. 1971. Perception of photographs by apes. Behaviour 39: 2–4.

15. DAVENPORT, R. K., C. M. ROGERS & I. S. RUSSELL. 1973. Cross-modal perception in apes. Neuropsychologia **11:** 21–28.
16. DAVENPORT, R. K., C. M. ROGERS & I. S. RUSSELL. 1975. Cross-modal perception in apes: Altered visual cues and delay. Neuropsychologia **13:** 229–235.
17. COWEY, A. & L. WEISKRANTZ. 1975. Demonstration of cross-modal matching in rhesus monkeys, *Macaca mulatta*. Neuropsychologia **13:** 117–120.
18. BRYANT, P. E., P. JONES, V. CLAXTON & G. M. PERKINS. 1972. Recognition of shapes across modalities by infants. Nature **240:** 303–304.
19. ETTLINGER, G. 1973. The transfer of information between sense-modalities: A neuropsychological review. *In* Memory and Transfer of Information. H. P. Zippel, Ed. Plenum. New York, N.Y.
20. BRYANT, P. E. 1968. Comments on the design of developmental studies of cross-modal matching and cross-modal transfer. Cortex **4:** 127–137.
21. MILNER, A. D. & P. E. BRYANT. 1970. Cross-modal matching by young children. J. Comp. Physiol. Psychol. **71:** 453–458.
22. KÖHLER, W. 1925. The Mentality of Apes—translated from the 2nd Revised Edition by E. Winter. Harcourt, Brace & Co., Inc. London.
23. HAYES, C. 1951. The Ape in Our House. Harper & Brothers. New York, N.Y.
24. SEGAL, M., D. T. CAMPBELL & M. J. HERSKOVITS. 1966. The Influence of Culture on Visual Perception. Bobbs-Merrill. Indianapolis, Ind.
25. DEREGOWSKI, J. B. 1972. Pictorial perception and culture. Sci. Amer. (Nov.): 82–88.
26. DAVENPORT, R. K., C. M. ROGERS & E. W. MENZEL. 1969. Intellectual performance of differentially reared chimpanzees: II. Discrimination-learning set. Amer. J. Ment. Defic. **73:** 963–969.
27. BLANK, M. & W. H. BRIDGER. 1964. Cross-modal transfer in nursery-school children. J. Comp. Physiol. Psychol. **58:** 277–282.
28. FRAMPTON, G. G., A. D. MILNER & G. ETTLINGR. 1973. Cross-modal transfer between vision and touch of go, no-go discrimination learning in the monkey. Neuropsychologia **11:** 231–233.
29. WARD, J. P., A. L. YEHLE & R. S. DOERFLEIN. 1970. Cross-modal transfer of a specific discrimination in the bushbaby (*Galago senegalensis*). J. Comp. Physiol. Psychol. **73:** 74–77.
30. OVER, R. & N. J. MACKINTOSH. 1969. Cross-modal transfer of intensity discrimination by rats. Nature, Lond. **224:** 918–919.
31. YEHLE, A. L. & J. P. WARD. 1969. Cross-modal transfer of a specific discrimination in the rabbit. Psychon. Sci. **16:** 269–270.
32. SUTHERLAND, N. S. 1959. *In* Proc. Symp. on Mechanization of Thought Processes, Vol. 2: 575. HMSO. London.
33. SPINNELLI, D. N., A. STARR & T. W. BARRETT. 1968. Auditory specificity recordings from cats' visual cortex. Exp. Neurol. **22:** 75–84.
34. HORN, G. 1965. The effect of somaesthetic and photic stimuli on the activity of units in the striate cortex of unanesthetized, unrestrained cats. J. Physiol. **179:** 263–277.
35. BENTAL, E., N. DAFNY & S. FELDMAN. 1968. Convergence of auditory and visual stimuli on single cells in the primary visual cortex of unanesthetized, unrestrained cats. Exp. Neurol. **20:** 341–351.

LANGUAGE AND SKILLED ACTIVITY

Peter C. Reynolds

Department of Anthropology
Research School of Pacific Studies
Australian National University
Canberra, A.C.T. 2600, Australia

It is well known that language can be mediated by a variety of channels—vocal-auditory, gestural-visual, and visual and tactile writing systems—but in spite of this variety, the relationship between language and channel is not arbitrary. There is the privileged relationship between language and speech pointed by by Liberman,[12] and there is also a more general privileged relationship between language and skilled behavior. That is to say, if the behavior of an effector cannot be programmed as a skill, it cannot be used as a language channel. The capacity for skillful programming of effectors is not a general property of neuromuscular tissue. For example, Paul Weiss[23] showed that, in salamanders, removing a limb and grafting it onto the wrong side of the body had no effect on the behavior of the limb during walking. It would continue to flex and extend itself at the *times that would be appropriate if it had remained in its original location.* That is, the central nervous system (CNS) continues to treat, say, a transplanted left limb as if it were still on the left side of the body, although it is on the right side and connected to the CNS by right-side nerves. Further, the central program is not dependent upon feedback from the periphery. It continues to address the muscles in their normal order whether or not the sensory pathways from the limbs have been severed. Nor does it ever correct the situation, although it is behaviorally inappropriate. These facts force us to distinguish between the peripheral organization of behavior and a central controlling program. In this case, however, the central program functions autonomously. It is innate, as Coghill[6] showed for *Amblystoma*, and it is resistant to environmental modification. There are other neuromusclar systems that function as *chains.* These are widespread in insect behavior.[24] For example, the hunting behavior of the wasp, *Philanthus triangulum*, originally described by Tinbergen,[21,22] is a behavior sequence in which the next unit of the sequence is triggered off by the consummatory stimulus of the previous act in the sequence. This chain is also innate.

Skilled activity shares properties with the types of neuromuscular activity just mentioned, but it also has some properties peculiar to itself.[2-4,5,7,14,20] First, skilled activity is a *central program* and not simply regularity in actions at the periphery. As Lashley[11] pointed out, some skilled activities, such as piano playing, take place too rapidly for the behavioral units to be related to each other as chained kinesthetic feedback from the periphery. Second, there are sequence errors, like letter reversals in typing, that are more easily interpreted in terms of a central model than a chain model. Third, the possible sequences can be so variable that it is more parsimonious to assume a central productive program than a number of independent representations. Moreover, the central programs of skilled action differ from those that Weiss described for the salamander in being *environmentally programmable.* However, the example of chaining also has its counterpart in skilled behavior. A fully integrated skill may not require peripheral feedback for its successful execution, but a developing skill probably does. Since the normal use of skilled activity is to induce certain environmental effects, the presence or absence of such effects can influence the subsequent behavioral sequence. For example, error-correcting actions may be interposed in a sequence to produce the required environmental effect before the rest of the program unfolds. Such events are inexplicable without a concept of sensory feedback. However, once behavior becomes so well-adapted to its environment that correct effects of prior action can be assumed, the central program can unfold with the rapidity that we associate with skillful action.

Since skilled activity is characterized by the capacity to insert error-correcting procedures into a behavioral string and to produce alternate and novel strings, we must view it not only as centrally programmed but *productively* programmed as well (FIGURES 1 & 3). As an example of skilled behavior that is nonlinguistic, consider the use of spades by children in sandpit activity. TABLE 1 defines some of the behavioral units that can be reliably distinguished in spade-use activity, and TABLE 2 lists the sequences of actions performed by one child in the course of one filmed session of 3 minutes and 56 seconds duration. The actions are arranged in chronological order and follow each other continuously, unless otherwise noted.

The use of a spade in skilled activity is much more complicated than it might first appear. The first complication is that we do not use a spade *per se*: we use a configuration composed of a *tonic* (or sustained) grasp pattern of our hand (or hands) plus a spade plus movements of this entire complex. To speak of object-use or tool-use is misleading because it places emphasis on the physical object and instrumentality at the expense of other constituents. The phylogenetic and ontogenetic precursor of object *use* is a configuration that I call a *conjunctor*, which is a physical object plus a tonic holding behavior plus a body part performing the action. Great apes will often play together while holding objects in their hand, foot, or mouth. The conjunctor is there but the instrumentality often is not (FIGURE 2).*

A central program that generates particular sequences of behavior is termed a *routine*. It is similar to what Piaget[17] would call a "schema," and it is functionally equivalent to the use of "routine" in computer science. Routines, like the "acts" discussed by Pribram,[18] are recognized by what they do; that is, by their effects. The effect of digging is to break up dirt and transport it from one place to another. Thus the dig routine, written $^R/DIG/$, can be assumed to be in operation whenever the same environmental effects are being produced, although the behavioral manifestations will vary considerably. We would want to distinguish digging with a spade from digging with a bucket from digging with just the hands. In our terminology $^R/DIG/$ could occur with different conjunctors, such as $^C/HAND + BUCKET/$, $^C/HAND + SPADE/$ and $^C/HAND + \emptyset]$. Further, additional complexity is introduced by the fact that the same conjunctor can function with different routines, as when we pour or throw sand out of a bucket. Also, routines can occur alone or in conjunction with other routines. For example, when sand is raised off the ground in digging, it can be either poured or thrown. $^R/POUR/$ and $^R/THROW/$ must be considered routines in their own right because they occur in other behavioral environments. Moreover, there may be *subroutines* in a routine, such as the $^R/DIG/$ usually having a component that loads sand onto the spade. The co-occurrence of routines indicates that we must regard skilled activity as *stratified* as well as combinatory. For example, the sequence

$$^R/TRANSPORT/ + ^R/POUR/$$
$$\text{sand} \qquad\qquad \text{sand}$$

when performed with $^C/BUCKET/$ will differ in the configuration of the hands than when performed with the $^C/SPADE/$. Sand is usually poured off a spade by a

---

*In representing conjunctors in notational form, the tonic grasp behavior may be left out for reasons of economy: $^C/HAND + HOLD + SPADE/$ becomes $^C/HAND + SPADE/$. If the meaning is clear, $^C/HAND + SPADE/$ may become $^C/SPADE/$.

FIGURE 1. Variants (conjunctorons) of the conjunctor C/HAND + SPADE / and different uses of these variants. RH = Right hand, LH = Left hand, hl = handle, sh = shaft, U = upper, L = lower. (A) *Chop* behavior pattern + ^{CN}((RH + Ush) + (LH + Lsh)) as used in "play". (B) *side-neutral position* + ^{CN}*(RH + Sh)*. (C) *Chop-scrape* behavior pattern + ^{CN}((RH + Sh) + (LH + hl)). (D) *Chop* behavior pattern + ^{CN}(RH + hl) as used in ^{R}/HIT/, aggressively motivated. (E) *Downswing* + ^{CN}((RH + Sh) + (LH + hl)) + ^{R}/DIG/. (F) *Waist-high neutral* position + ^{CN}((RH + Sh) + (LH + hl)). (G) *Upswing-diagonal* behavior pattern + ^{R}/THROW/ + ^{R}/DIG/ + ^{CN}((RH + Ush) + (LH + Lsh)).

rotation of the blade along the longitudinal axis. This can be done without changing the position of the hands on the shaft. Buckets are usually carried by holding the rim with two hands or the handle with either one or two hands. In either case, the transition from transport to pour requires a placement of one hand under the bucket to tip it. While this is obvious enough now—though it probably was not once—it is formally complex. It requires that certain sequential changes on the routine stratum be accompanied by changes on the conjunctor stratum. That is, there are alternative realizations for each conjunctor and these have functional significance (FIGURE 1). In

FIGURE 2. Gorilla hitting one stone with another: ^{CN}(LH + STONE A) HITS ^{CN}(RH + STONE B).

FIGURE 3. Alternate realizations of the ^{R}/POUR/ routine with different conjunctors. (A) POUR from a ^{C}/HAND + SPADE/ by raising the arm at the shoulder; target is ^{C}/HAND + SPADE/ of another child. (B) POUR from a ^{C}/HAND + PITCHER/ by flexion at the wrist; target is a ^{Mat}/BOTTLE/. (C) Simulative execution of a ^{R}/POUR/ with a ^{C}/HAND + BUCKET/; no materia in the BUCKET; no visible target; flexion at the wrist. (D) POUR in which ^{C}/HAND + SAND/ is released to give the POUR; extension of the fingers; target unknown.

the ^{C}/HAND + SPADE/, for example, two-hand contact predominates in ^{R}/DIG/ activity, whereas one-hand contact is more characteristic of an off-line ^{C}/SPADE/. Moreover, the *point of contact* made by the hands is important, since it must be relevant to the center of gravity, which in a spade is on the shaft just behind the blade. In overhead *chop* behavior patterns, it is best to hold the spade near the handle, but in digging it is best to have one hand near the center of gravity and the other nearer to the handle. As might be expected by this point, there are also *alloconjunctors* that appear to be idiosyncratic functional equivalents. Some of the variants of the ^{R}/POUR/ routine are shown in Figure 3, using the notation of stratificational grammar.[10,13] Lastly, each variant of a routine is expressed ultimately in *behavioral components* that occur in sequences specified by the routine logic. These components are the smallest observable unitary action patterns, and they are written as underlined or italicized words. In Figure 4 is shown a "Lambgram" or "spaghetti notation" diagram of the ^{R}/DIG/+^{C}/SPADE/ using behavioral components.[10,13] The components are defined in Table 1.

To describe the logical structure of skill is one thing, to describe the empirical realizations quite another. If the logical structure is best described by the methods of linguistics, the recording of skilled behavior is best done mechanically, through some iconic device like videotape. To recode this iconic record into categories is a formidable undertaking. This is of practical concern to me, because I have been trying to recode my videotape data into computer-compatible form. Since the four minutes of activity shown in Table 2 have about 140 separate behavioral items for the hands alone, not counting conversation, expression, and other body movements, and since there are 286 minutes of such data, the need for computerization will be appreciated. The kinds of information that are relevant to a categorical description of skilled activity are listed in Table 3. It is possible to digitize the behavioral stream in

TABLE 1

BEHAVIORAL COMPONENTS OF THE DIG ROUTINE, AS EXPRESSED WITH THE SPADE CONJUNCTOR

1. *Waist-high neutral point.* Point at which spade is normally held prior to *downswing.*
2. *Downswing-diagonal* (DSdi). Blade transcribes an arc roughly from *waist-high neutral* to ground, with blade pointing toward ground and concave surface of the blade facing up, and with movement diagonal to plane of ground.
3. *Downtilt* (DT). With blade in a fixed position, relative to handle, spade is moved toward ground on a plane perpendicular to the ground.
4. *Upswing-diagonal* (USdi). The reverse of DSdi. It usually occurs simultaneously with DT's to balance dirt on blade.
5. *Rotate-long-axis* (Rla). The blade is rotated on the long axis of the shaft. A 90° rotation is sufficient to convert *upswing-diagonal* into a POUR dirt action.
6. *Thrust* (Th). With blade pointing toward ground, spade is moved groundward on a plane parallel to the long axis of the shaft. In repeated *thrusts* the action is reversed before the next *thrust.*
7. *Foot Thrust* (FTh). One foot is placed on the top edge of the blade before a *thrust* is executed.
8. *Chop.* Blade is rotated on long axis of shaft (Rla) until the broad surface of the blade is facing perpendicular to the plane of the ground. Then a *downswing-perpendicular* from *waist-high neutral* or *higher* is executed.
9. *Downswing-perpendicular* (DSper). Same as DSdi (item 2), except that motion is on a plane perpendicular to the plane of the ground.
10. *Contact ground* (CG). The spade makes contact with the ground: the test condition for a *thrust.*
11. *Sudden Acceleration* (Acl). Done at the top of the *upswing-diagonal* to convert the upswing into ^{R}/THROW/.
12. *Scrape* (Scr). A *Thrust* in which the spade is pushed along the surface of the ground.
13. *Uptilt* (UT). Reverse of a *downtilt.*
14. POUR. A routine. See item 5.
15. *Smooth.* Moving the flat of the palm across a surface.
16. *Materia* (Mat). Any physical object or matter incorporated into a routine.

TABLE 2

SEQUENCES OF ACTIVITY WITH A SPADE BY A FOUR-YEAR-OLD CHILD IN THE COURSE OF 3 MINUTES, 56 SECONDS*

---

(1) *+DSper + Th + UT + Th + * + USdi

(2) DSdi + Th + USdi + (altercation with another child; * Rt. hand holds spade by side) * + DSdi + Th + USdi + POUR

(3) DSdi + (hits bucket accidentally; * Left hand moves bucket) * + USdi + POUR

(4) DSdi + Th + USdi + * + POUR

(5) DSdi + Th + Th + * + USdi + POUR

(6) DSdi + * + * + * + Th + Th + USdi + POUR

(7) DSdi + Th + USdi + (* Left hand steadies bucket) + POUR

(8) DSdi + Th + (PAUSE; stands up leaving spade point in ground) + USdi + POUR

(9) * + DSper + Th + (Bends then stands) + * + USdi + POUR

(10) * + DSper + Th + (Bends then stands) + USdi + POUR

(11) DSper + Th + (Bends then stands) + USdi + * + TRANSPORT + * + POUR

(12) (* Right hand holds spade at side) + * + Th + Th + Th + Th + Th + Th + USDI + TRANSPORT + * + POUR

(13) * + USdi + (Hold spade at waist-high neutral with Right hand while giving sand on spade 7 smoothing motions with left hand) + DSper + POUR + (1 chop on bucket with spade + PAUSE + 4 chops with spade on bucket + * + *)

(14) DSdi + Th + Scr + USdi + POUR

(15) * DSdi + (Bend over) + Th + Scr + Scr + Scr + (stand) + USdi + POUR

(16) DSdi + Th + USdi + POUR

(17) DSdi + Th + Th + Usdi + POUR

(18) DSdi + Th + USdi + * + * + (Right hand holds spade at waist-high neutral position while left hand makes 9 smoothing motions of sand on spade) + POUR

(19) * + DSdi + Th + USdi + POUR

(20) DSdi + Scr + Scr + Scr + Scr + USdi + POUR + *

(21) (11 second pause with spade blade resting on ground) + * + DSdi + Th + USdi + POUR

(22) DSdi + Th + USdi + POUR

(23) DSdi + Th + USdi + POUR

(24) DSdi + Th + USdi + POUR

(25) (Bends down and taps bucket 3 times with spade held in the right hand; then smooths sand in bucket with left hand; then * drops spade and manipulates sand with hands)

---

*Behavioral components are defined in TABLE I. Asterisks indicate a shift to a different point-of-contact variant of the conjunctor /SPADE + HANDS/. Note error-correction embeddings in (3) and (7) and the embedding of different routines within the DIG routine, as in (13) and (18).

purely arbitrary ways, but the coded record is only readable to a computer. The most *understandable* way to recode the information dimensions of TABLE 3 in categorical form is by natural language. Is this just because we are used to language and not used to, say, 15 simultaneous channels of alphanumeric codes? Experience probably does not have much to do with it, for natural language works just as well as a description of skilled behavior of alien species. Consider the following two descriptions.

The protagonists in this first drama are two apes: C, a chimpanzee, and, O, an orang-utan.

English description: O play-bites C's foot while C grapples O with his arms and play-bites O's neck. Then C rolls onto his own back, with his head directed away from O, while O continues to play-bite his foot. Then both C and O grapple each other with their arms while play-biting each other's heads while facing each other.

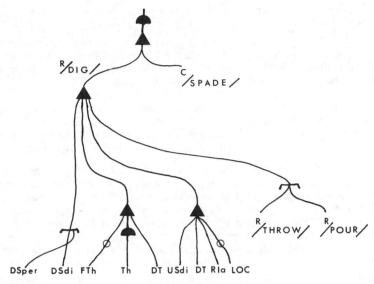

FIGURE 4. Lambgram of the ^{R}/DIG/ routine as realized with the conjunctor ^{C}/HAND + SPADE/. LOC stands for "locomotion," the output of a ^{SR}/TRANSPORT/. Behavioral components are defined in TABLE 1. *Scrape*, which sometimes replaces *thrust* empirically, is considered to be a modified *thrust*.

TABLE 3

CATEGORIES OF INFORMATION RELEVANT TO THE DESCRIPTION OF SKILLED ACTIVITY*

1. The thing to which action is directed, if observable (*objectum*).
2. The *classes* of *actions* based upon their form, such as running versus jumping.
3. The thing which performs the action (*agent*).
4. The thing which supports the agent and objectum in a gravitational field (*support*).
5. The place at which action occurs, if relevant to past action (*locus*)
6. The direction of an action relative to an objectum, such as running towards or away (*directionality*)
7. The *distance* between agent and objectum.
8. *Body orientation* of agent relative to its *support*.
9. *Body orientation* of agent relative to *objectum*.
10. The distinction between a *leading agent* and a *following agent*, e.g. the hand would be a following agent relative to arm movements, though both hand and arm would be agents because both would move. Leading and following agents are physically connected.
11. The *temporal* relationships of actions *relative to each other* (*tempus*).
12. The *energy* or *intensity* of an action measured as force applied.
13. The *duration* of an action.
14. The length of the arc traversed by an action relative to others of the same type, e.g. a wide sweep of the arms (*sweep*).
15. The *speed* of action.

* *Thing* means an observable entity that can be the exemplar of an object-concept, such as persons, balls, stones, toy trucks, and so forth. *Action* is any observable behavior of a thing, such as falling, running, hitting, shattering, etc. This list is not necessarily exhaustive.

Then both stop as suddenly as they began. The play bout lasted one and one-half minutes.

In Scene II, the protagonists are macaque monkeys, OA and E. A rope hangs from the roof of the cage, its free end resting on the ground. OA climbs the rope from the ground to the top, then climbs back down headfirst, jumping to the ground as she nears the bottom. At this point E walks toward the free end of the rope, then sits down and mouths the rope and pulls on it with her hands, while sitting. . . . OA climbs to the roof via the wall and hangs upside down by her hind feet from the roof, pulling the rope away from E, hand over hand, by the tied end. E climbs to a log and then jumps to the roof toward OA, who walk-climbs away from E while upside down. E bites the tied end of the rope, then climbs down it headfirst.

These descriptions are economical and accurate. If "play-bite" and "grapple" were defined photographically, as they can be, it would be possible for the director of *Planet of the Apes* to use these vignettes as screenplays for portions of another film. The descriptions do not include all the information listed in TABLE 3, but they encode the story line and they encode it very economically. What do we mean by the story line? We mean events that have cause-and-effect relationships to each other, and these can be physical causes or social causes. Social causes have observable physical effects, but there is no necessary *physical causal* relationship between the effect and its antecedent: the antecedent has the effect it does because of species-specific circuits in the brain of the perceiver. Threat vocalizations are a case in point. It is suggested here that language matches skilled behavior in two ways. First, it is itself skilled behavior and shares most of its properties with skilled activities that no one would call linguistic. Second, the semantic categories of language make it especially well suited for representing skilled activity. The reason why language does describe skilled activity so well is that skill in general is concerned with encoding cause-and-effect relationships in behavioral form.

I suggest that the basic units for the representation of skilled action and the basic units for the causal analysis of events are in fact formally isomorphic. The basic unit of skilled action is a unit composed of an agent, an action, and an *objectum*. (The term "objectum" is used to avoid confusion with physical "objects.") Virtually all of the components of the activity listed in TABLE 2 can be decomposed into one or more units of this kind. *Downswing* is ^{C}/SPADE/*moving* toward *ground*; the ^{SR}/ LOAD is ^{C}/SPADE/*loads sand*; ^{R}/POUR/ is realized by ^{C}/SPADE/*pours sand + sand falls* (to) *bucket*; and so on. FIGURE 5A gives the *Agent-action unit*, as I term it, in Lamb notation, and FIGURE 5B the joining of two Agent-action units (AAU) to form a higher order unit with two AAU constituents. If in expressions like 5B the objectum of the first unit is the agent of the second and the first unit precedes the second in time, then we have the formal equivalent of the *causal frame*: "X Acts$_1$ y/y Acts$_2$" is equivalent to "*X has the effect Act$_2$ on y*"; alternately, "*X Act$_1$ y causes y Act$_2$*". A unit with 2 AAU's in which the agents are both leading agents is termed a *two-move* sequence (cf. TABLE 2 for *definition* of *leading agent*).

Using the Agent-action unit, we can define the levels of behavioral complexity already distinguished. Thus,

1. [Ag + Act] is undirected action,
   e.g. [Hand + grasp].
2. [Ag + Act + objectum] is directed action,
   e.g. [Hand + grasp + spade]
3. [[Ag + objectum + tonic action] + Act] is undirected conjunctor action,
   e.g. [^{C}/SPADE/ + downswing]

4. [[Ag + objectum + tonic action] + Act + objectum] is directed conjunctor action,

e.g. [^{C}/SPADE/ + downswing + ground]

5. [[[Ag + objectum + tonic action] + [Ag + objectum + tonic action]] + Act + objectum],

e.g. [2 Hand ^{C}/SPADE/ + downswing + ground].

More complex structures are also possible, such as one child pouring sand from his own spade onto the spade held out by another (FIGURE 3A). In such a case, one objectum is itself a conjunctor formed by another leading agent. Moreover, routines are also definable as the logical structures which generate variable sequences of Agent-action unit hierarchies in real-time. The integration of skillful action requires that elementary cause-and-effect relationships become routinized into higher-order constitutents which then become units vis-à-vis further levels of integration.

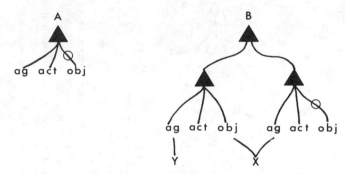

FIGURE 5. (A) An AAU, composed of agent, action, and optional objectum related through a simultaneous AND node. (B) A *two-move sequence*, defined as two AAU's related through a sequential AND node, in which the objectum of the first AAU is the leading agent of the second AAU.

In addition, using the construct of the two-move sequence, which is an action sequence directed toward another individual who then responds, it is possible to define social interactions. FIGURE 6 shows the real-time distribution of rhesus monkey play encounters on a typical day. Note that they fall into easily delimitable units based upon the individuals in them or by a pause in the interactions or both. Each encounter consists of a series of behavioral exchanges. These exchanges are recorded in a vocabulary of rhesus behavior, as devised by primatologists,[1] and utilize the *move* construct, which is behavior that is responded to by another or directed to another in the course of an interaction. The behavior patterns and move sequences for some sample dyadic encounters are shown in TABLE 4. The normal way for these monkeys to end encounters is to move away from the other monkey. This is called a Loc⁻ constituent, for "locomotion directed away," and about 89% of encounters end this way. Out of the 263 dyadic encounters in our sample, however, 53 had Loc⁻ constituents in both medial and final positions. This suggested that perhaps long continuous move sequences between the same pair of animals were concatenations of shorter sequences, called *rounds*, with each round terminating in a Loc⁻ constituent. As it turned out, *all* of the long encounters (the longest being 19 moves) had medial Loc⁻ constituents. The parsing of an encounter into rounds is shown in examples 1 and 6 in TABLE 4, and it yields two classes of encounters,

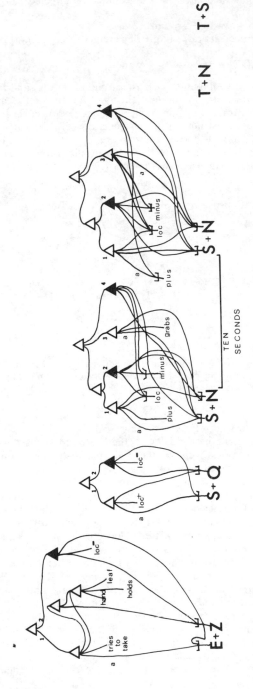

FIGURE 6. Typical sequence of dyadic encounters during a 3-minute observation period of young rhesus monkeys. The large letters at the bottom are the names of the monkeys in each encounter. The move sequence for the first 4 encounters is shown above in Lamb notation. The moves in each encounter are numbered consecutively. The agent of the first move in each move pair is indicated by an "a" next to the name line. Where the same pair of animals interacts more than once, the duration of the interval between interactions is noted. As an example, the first encounter is to be read as: "E tries to take away a leaf held by Z, who locomotes away from E." The third encounter is "S locomotes toward N as N simultaneously locomotes away from S; then S grabs N, who locomotes away from S." All action here is continuous in time.

TABLE 4

EXAMPLES OF RHESUS MONKEY DYADIC ENCOUNTERS EXPRESSED AS ROUNDS, MOVES, AND
BEHAVIORAL COMPONENTS *

1. t Turns head and eyes$^+$, Walks$^+$ d/d Walks bipedally$^+$ t/t Backs$^-$ d;d Jumps$^+$ t/t Backs$^-$ d;d
   Jumps$^+$ t/t Backs$^-$ d.
   [3 rounds, 7 moves]
2. d Touches e/ (d Grapples, Playbites and Stands up e/e does same to d)/
   (d shifts to hanging from hind feet while grappling and playbiting /e does same to d)/d
   Walks$^-$ e.
   [1 round, 6 moves]
3. z Presents d/d Ignores, Walks$^-$ z.
   [1 round, 2 moves]
4. b Walks$^+$ z/z Walks$^-$ b.
   [1 round, 2 moves]
5. t Touches b/b Touches t/ (b Play face t/t Play face b)/t Touches b/b Touches t/t Touches
   b/b Walks$^-$ t.
   [1 round, 8 moves]
6. d Walks$^+$, Touches e/e Backs$^-$ d; d Walks$^+$ e/e Grabs d/d Turns eyes and head$^+$, Lunges$^+$
   e/e Runs$^-$ d; d walks$^+$, then stops e/e stops running, Walks$^+$ d/d Walks$^+$ e [Adult
   intervenes].
   [3 rounds, 9 moves]
7. d Walks$^+$ z/z Presents d/d Touches z/z Touches d/d Walks$^-$ z.
   [1 round, 5 moves]

* Letters (t, d, etc.) are the names of monkeys. The symbols "+" or "−" means *toward* or *away*
respectively. The symbol "/ " means a move boundary, and ";" means a round boundary.
Expressions enclosed in parentheses are simulataneous. Simultaneous moves are counted as 2
moves. Encounters are divided into rounds on the basis of a terminator pattern (Locomotion$^-$)
in medial position.

uniround and multiround. Rounds are never more than nine moves long, and if an
encounter is longer than nine moves it always has more than one round (FIGURE 7). It
suggests, at the least, that monkeys may be more structurally inclined than they are
often thought to be.

These facts led us to postulate two types of structure in rhesus interactions: a
move-round level that serves as a frame and a *social routine* content that is plugged
into it.[19] The social routines express such behavioral differences as play, aggression,
grooming, and so on. It is of interest that Garvey[8] has made exactly the same
distinction in her study of playful *verbal* exchanges in children: they exchange
variable linguistic utterances within a move-round framework. The constraints on
rhesus interaction are not uninteresting, and they are expressed in Lamb notation in
FIGURE 8. It can be seen that there is a routine content plugged into a move-round
frame, in which a move is our old friend, the agent-action-objectum bundle. In this
grammar, it is not assumed that the agent has to be represented to himself: he needs
only a distinction between *him* vs. *me* to perform in these interactions. To parse
behavior from the viewpoint of an external observer, however, the agent
representation is needed. George Herbert Mead,[15] in his analysis of human social
behavior, noted that it was based on the capacity to "see ourselves as others see us."
That is, it requires the capacity to represent ourselves in both the agent and objectum
roles of the interactive routines in which we participate. What is probably only
implicit in monkeys would have to become explicitly represented in the brain of man.
Thus the AAU has wide application, not only in asocial skills but in social ones as
well.

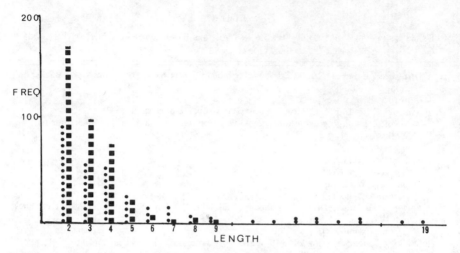

FIGURE 7. Frequency of encounters and rounds of different lengths as measured in moves. Squares indicate the frequency of rounds of N moves, circles the frequency of encounters of N moves. Note that no rounds have more than 9 moves, though encounters can be up to 19 moves.

To put these observations in context, it must be stressed that Agent-action units are neither sensory nor motor units, but both. They are a relationship between an agent, an action, and (usually) an environmental component. One of the most interesting things about skilled behavior from a linguistic perspective is that it already incorporates a structure in which motor representations interact with sensory representations to form externalizable sequences of behavior.

The view taken here is that language is a phylogenetic derivative of the skilled motor system. It is a system of communication that requires the skilled motor system not only for its acquisition but for its ordinary expression. That is, to repeat, any effector that cannot be incorporated into skilled behavior cannot be used as a language channel. The skilled motor system has a phyletic distribution wider than the human species, although man has carried this type of behavioral organization further than any other species. Maturation time is a good measure of the degree of externable programming of the brain, and the data of the Napiers[16] show that maturation time is a progressive characteristic in primates, increasing from prosimians through monkeys through apes to man. Moreoever, maturation in these other species is characterized by the same progression we find in man from playful execution of poorly integrated routines in infancy to very rapid goal-oriented execution in adulthood, suggesting a role for the skill system.

The skill system, as the term has been used here, is not an anatomical division of the nervous system but a functional division. There is no skill center. Instead, there is probably a unique type of interaction among such anatomical systems as the cerebellum, motor cortex, gamma efferent system, pyramidal tract, and other brain components, leading to a particular type of relationship between sensory and motor activity. This relationship, as I suggest, is not unique to the human species, although some of its features may be. One property of the human skill system that would have to be singled out as a progressive feature is the human capacity for observational learning. Like skill itself, it shows a progressive development in the order Primates. If we define *observational learning* as the acquisition of a motor routine through the observation of others performing the actions, macaque monkeys, at least, have very little capacity for it. Monkeys can bring the components of their behavioral repertory under stimulus control through observational learning,[9] but they do not seem to acquire sequences of behavior in this way. Apes can acquire novel behavior patterns through observation, but their capacity to acquire routines is certainly inferior to man's. If the argument presented here is correct, then the primate ability to acquire behavior through observation depends upon the ability to parse sensory representations of behavior with a causal frame. That is, as Bruner[5] points

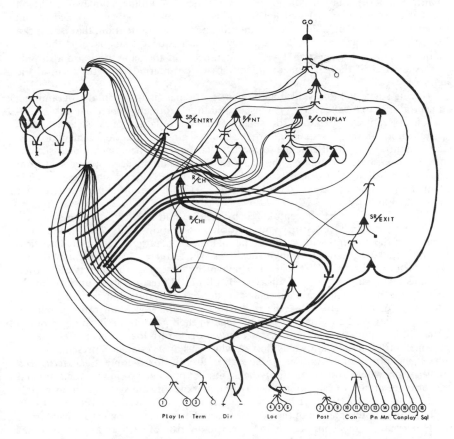

FIGURE 8. Provisional grammar of dyadic social play encounters in young rhesus monkeys. Symbols: The notation is standard stratificational grammar notation with the exception of the small black square, which CLEARS (or disables) any enablers that were turned on by the node to which both enabler and CLEAR are joined. Triangles are AND nodes, open circles on the middle of a line are OPTIONALITY markers, open circles at the end of a line are ZERO REALIZATION markers, large half circles are RECURSIVE circuit nodes, horizontal bars are OR nodes, and small closed circles touching a line are ENABLER nods. The numbers in circles at the bottom of the diagram are behavior patterns, and X and Y (top left) are dummy monkeys. SR = subroutine, R = routine, PNT = present-mount, CONPLAY = contact play, CH = chase, CHI = chase initiate, Play-in = Play-initiate, Term = terminator, Dir = directionality marker, Loc = locomotion, Post = postural, Con = contact behavior, Pn = present, Mn = mount, and Sql = squeal.

out, the intention to create a perceived environmental effect antedates the ability to induce it skillfully. In visual-motor skills, as in language, competence precedes performance.

Intentionality can also be defined in the Agent-action unit framework. When the second move of the causal frame is represented in the brain of the performer prior to his own first move, the behavior can be called *intentional*. The human proclivity to assume intentionality in the behavior of others (the *intentionality axiom*) and the human capacity to infer the intention of others from their action (the *intentionality capacity*) underlies human skill acquisition in general and human linguistic ability in particular. Thus the property of *semanticity* is also already implicit in skilled action: an action is understandable if we can infer the performer's intention; that is, if it can be assimilated to a causal frame and its sensory consequences simulated in the brain of the perceiver. I suggest that verbal utterances, in the same way, are also only understandable if the performer's intention can be inferred from the form of the action.

Having suggested that skilled activity in general has environmental programming of central hierarchical control systems, embedding, productivity, recursion, a cause-and-effect frame, aggregation of smaller units into larger ones, stratificational organization as well as sequential organization, segmental and nonsegmental units, and semanticity (as well as some properties that have not been mentioned, such as affective information riding on the same channel), it might be supposed that I am equating skilled activity with language. I am not, for the evidence suggests that while language is externalized as skilled activity, it is not simply skilled activity but *meta*skilled activity.

This concept can be conceptualized by the diagram in Figure·9. Here the skill system, Box B, can have sensory and motor representations as its content, and it can operate on the contents with various types of logical operations, such as hypothetical test runs that we might gloss linguistically as "If . . . then . . ." statements: "If I hit Billy, then he will. . . ." There is good behavioral evidence that the activity of children contains very many test runs of this type. Box B would presumably be able to employ such operators as the logical quantifiers: "If this ball rolls downhill, then *all* balls roll downhill." And so forth. While the skill system contains logical operations, and can produce behavioral outputs that require logic in their generation, it cannot produce behavioral outputs that contain *representations* of its own logic. This is presumed to be a metaskill function, shown as Box A, which has as its content representations of Box B, including representations of the logic of Box B. Box A content, *if externalized as behavior*, would contain not only behavioral expressions of internal sensory and motor representations but explicit behavioral markers of skill system logic as well. It is still a large step from drawing such boxes to explaining the development of a higher-order representation of the skill system and explaining how a shared system of such externalizations could come about; but the virtue of such an approach is that makes possible the use of nonlinguistic models for the investigation of the origin of language.

The concept of a skill system and a metaskill system also suggests an origin of some transformation rules. As can be seen from the protocols presented in Table 2 (items 13 and 18), it is commonplace for the skill system to embed one routine in the middle of an execution of a prior routine. In item 18, for example, the spade is loaded with sand and brought to *waist-high neutral position* by both hands. Then the left hand is disengaged from the spade and put to work smoothing the sand on the spade blade. Now from a formal point of view, there are two objecta here, the sand that is maintained on the blade by the TRANSPORT subroutine and the sand that is smoothed by the SMOOTH routine. Empirically, however, they are realized by the same sand. If we assume that the metaskill system represents only the empirical realizations of skill system categories, then the metaskill system will see this as only one sand for two objecta. An externalization of the metaskill representation will look, to an external observer with an AAU parsing frame, as if one objectum had been deleted. The metaskill system in its representation of other skilled activities could conceivably lead to discrepancies between the skill and metaskill externalizations, which would appear to an observer as transformations of the skill system content.

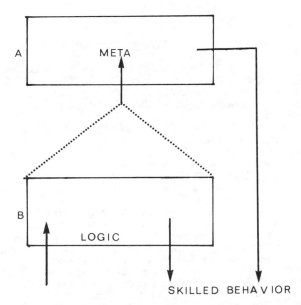

FIGURE 9. Schematic of the relationship of language to the skill system. The prelinguistic skill system is represented as Box B. Input to B is a representation of sensory and motor information which can be operated on by deduction, induction, quantification, and other logical operators to yield novel and generalized outputs of the skill system. Box A is a representation of *both* the contents and logic of Box B to yield skilled behavior containing externalizations of both Box A logic and content.

ACKNOWLEDGMENTS

I wish to thank the Director and Staff of the University Child Care Centre at the Australian National University for the opportunity to film children at play, and Dr. Geoffrey Bourne, Director of The Yerkes Regional Primate Research Center, for the opportunity to observe and film play in young anthropoid apes. The Yerkes observations were partially financed by a Sigma Xi grant-in-aid-of-research.

REFERENCES

1. ALTMANN, S. A. 1962. A field study of the sociobiology of rhesus monkeys, *Macaca mulatta*. Ann. N.Y. Acad. Sci. **102**(2): 338–435.

2. BEKOFF, M. 1972. The development of social interaction, play, and metacommunication in mammals: an ethological perspective. Q. Rev. Biol. **47**: 412–434.
3. BERNSTEIN, N. 1967. The Co-ordination and Regulation of Movements. Pergamon Press. New York, N.Y.
4. BRUNER, J. S. 1972. Nature and uses of immaturity. Am. Psychol. **27**: 1–23.
5. BRUNER, J. 1973. Organization of early skilled action, Child Development **44**: 1–11.
6. COGHILL, G. E. 1929. Anatomy and the Problem of Behavior. Cambridge University Press. Cambridge, England.
7. DOLHINOW, P. J. & N. BISHOP. 1970. The development of motor skills and social relationships among primates through play. Minn. Symp. Child Psychol. **4**: 141–198.
8. GARVEY, C. Some properties of social play. Merrill-Palmer Quarterly. In press.
9. HALL, K. R. L. 1963. Observational learning in monkeys and apes. Br. J. Psychol. **54**: 201–226.
10. LAMB, S. M. 1966. Outline of Stratificational Grammar. Georgetown University Press. Washington, D.C.
11. LASHLEY, K. S. 1951. The problem of serial order in behavior. *In* Cerebral Mechanisms in Behavior. L. A. Jefress, Ed. John Wiley & Sons, Inc. New York, N.Y.
12. LIBERMAN, A. M. 1974. The specialization of the language hemisphere. *In* The Neurosciences: A Third Study Program. Schmitt and Worden, Eds.: 43–56. MIT Press. Cambridge, Mass.
13. LOCKWOOD, D. G. 1972. Introduction to stratificational linguistics. Harcourt Brace Jovanovich. New York, N.Y.
14. McBRIDE, G. 1968. On the evolution of human language. Soc. Sci. Information **7**: 81–85.
15. MEAD, G. H. 1967. Mind, Self and Society: From the Standpoint of a Social Behaviorist. University of Chicago Press. Phoenix Books. Chicago, Ill. (First edit. 1934.)
16. NAPIER, J. R. & P. H. NAPIER. 1967. A Handbook of Living Primates: 40. Academic Press. New York, N.Y.
17. PIAGET, J. 1962. Play, Dreams and Imitation in Childhood. Norton. New York, N.Y.
18. PRIBRAM, K. H. 1971. Languages of the brain. Prentice-Hall. Englewood Cliffs, N.J.
19. REYNOLDS, P. C. & K. H. PRIBRAM. The structure of social encounters in young rhesus monkeys. Submitted for publication.
20. SECHENOV, I. 1968. Selected Works. Bonset. Amsterdam, The Netherlands.
21. TINBERGEN, N. 1950. The hierarchical organization of the nervous mechanisms underlying instinctive behavior. *In* Physiological Mechanisms in Animal Behavior. Symp. Soc. Exp. Biol. no. 4. Academic Press. New York, N.Y.
22. TINBERGEN, N. 1953. Social Behavior in Animals. Methuen. London, England.
23. WEISS, P. 1952. Central versus peripheral factors in the development of coordination. Res. Pub. Assoc. Res. Nerv. Ment. Dis. **30**: 3–23.
24. WIGGLESWORTH, V. B. 1964. The Life of Insects. Weidenfeld and Nicolson. London, England.

DISCUSSION

Sam Glucksberg, *Moderator*
Department of Psychology
Princeton University
Princeton, New Jersey 08540

DR. DONALD DAVIDSON: What I'd like to do is raise a general question concerning the significance of the facts that we've just been hearing about. This question is about our ability to make use of information concerning children and animals in trying to learn something about the origin of language.

Of course, I'm not in doubt about the facts themselves; nor am I, for that matter, in doubt about their being relevant to our understanding origins of languages. The question is, how to make the best use of the facts?

Prof. Menzel emphasized, very well I thought, the complicated interrelations between cognition, perception, and the use of language, and particularly the importance, when interpreting what people say, of knowing a great deal about what they believe, what they perceive, how they see their own behavior, how they're placed in the environment.

A speaker makes heavy use of what he knows or thinks he knows about his hearers. The interpreter, on the other hand, makes heavy use of what he knows, or thinks he knows, about the speaker's beliefs, intentions, desires, and the like. If a parent says to his child, "In this house we don't eat peas with a knife," he assumes that the child knows that he isn't making a statement that is intended to be true. In fact, under the circumstances it's one that's very apt to be false, and the fact that the speaker knows that the hearer knows that is essential to getting the right effect.

Prof. Fillmore this morning made a point when he talked about the importance of Frames in the interpretation of language. But now if this is true, if there really is this extremely heavy dependence of interpretation of speech on knowledge of the speaker's beliefs, intentions, perceptions, and so on, then doesn't this throw doubt on our ability to make clear sense of what it is that animals are signaling when they do something like make signs to one another, and for that matter also throw doubt upon our ability to know what it is that they believe, or what they perceive, or what they intend? If these things are interrelated in this way, and it seems to me quite clear that they are, then it becomes harder, not easier, to see what the relevance of animal behavior is to the understanding of the origins of language.

DR. IRA WEISS (*Children's Hospital, Washington D.C.*): Dr. Menzel, it seems to me that the conceptualization of language in this session is quite different from what it was this morning. The emphasis seems to have shifted from the morphology of language per se to something much more general. If one defines language in terms of perception and cognition, and animals' reactions to that perception, one can argue, I think, that animals use language or even "speak," if you wish; but under the same circumstances you would probably have to say the same thing for a tree. As a matter of fact, at one point in your talk you went so far as to make a comparison between a child's ability to speak "up" or "down" to his listeners and the fact that the bright colors of a flower reflect the perceptual capabilities of bees.

I wonder if you would like to comment on this. Hasn't the concept of language been changed to the point where it is no longer interesting to know whether or not animals can use it?

DR. MENZEL: The topics of this session are indeed different from those of this morning; they are not language per se (whatever that is), but certain broader

167

problems that the conference organizers and the various authors feel are "substrates" of that more specific but fuzzy problem, or somehow useful for an accurate comparative perspective. Dr. Johnson and I, incidentally, made no attempt to define language per se or to impute it to flowers or even to chimpanzees. As our title indicates, our topic was the broader problem of communication and cognitive organization.

Two other ways in which our paper differs from those of most linguists is that we approached our topic from a functional point of view (rather than, say, a structural or morphological one), and we were more interested in examining similarities and continuities between species than in emphasizing the differences. To compare species or to point out the similarities we did is not to deny that species differ.

In our opinion (and presumably in the opinion of those who invited the various speakers to this conference), neither a purely functionalistic approach nor a purely structural-linguistic approach affords a complete picture of the general topic of this conference. Had Dr. Johnson and I intended to be offering a completely rounded biological comparison of human and animal communication systems, we would, of course, have had to try to answer all of the "standard" questions that biologists would ask about a phenomenon, such as, "What is its structure? How does it function? How did it develop? How did it evolve?" and so on. In this sense our account is obviously incomplete. In the same sense I am puzzled when a linguist such as Chomsky (this volume) claims that he studies language in the same way that biologists study the liver or some other physical organ—unless the biologists to whom he refers are all human anatomists who believe that physiology, ecology, and other branches of biology, especially comparative anatomy, are unnecessary.

Finally, I have to agree that from my point of view it is not very interesting to know whether or not animals "have language." I would, in fact, be happy if we settled such all-or-none questions with a toss of a coin (or turned them over to lawyers), and then asked ourselves, So what? If as a scientist I can't think of any more to say about the nature and evolution of human and nonhuman communication systems, I didn't have anything to say in the first place. In other words, the real question in our paper was not *whether* people and animals communicate (an issue we tried to settle by dictum in the first page), but *what* they communicate, *how* they do it, how they came to do it, and so on, with emphasis upon certain similarities.

JOHN PFEIFFER, *New Hope, Pa.:* Dr. Menzel, when you say that animals know, "If another animal looks like me it can probably do what I do," do you imply that animals know what they look like? and if so, how does an animal get an image of itself?

E. W. MENZEL: For the purposes of our paper it is not necessary to assume that animals have a self concept in any very precise sense (cf. Terrace and Bever, this volume). If you prefer a more cautious or neutral statement, you can change the pronouns in that quote from first person singular to third person.

There is, however, good evidence for self concept in the strict sense in anthropoid apes. For example, Gordon Gallup exposed chimpanzees and rhesus monkeys to a mirror for several hours and then he anesthetized them and put an odorless dye on one ear. After they came out of anesthetic he gave them the mirror again and on looking into it the chimps immediately reached up to feel the ear that had been dyed. The monkeys showed no similar behavior and Gallup suggests that they (and probably most nonanthropoids) do not have self concepts.

Non-anthropoids do, however, show many types of discriminatory behavior which suggest that they have a fairly accurate picture (albeit possibly an indirect one) of themselves and their own capabilities. Consider, for example, the simple ability to discriminate a member of one's own species from a member of another species, or the fact that most play and fighting occurs between animals of the same sex and approximately the same size and strength and age. If you put strange monkeys or even chickens together for the first time, dominance relationships are often established with no fighting at all (if, that is, the animals differ in sex and size). In these cases it is of course possible that instead of directly comparing the stranger to himself the animal is comparing the stranger to some other standard which just so happens to be similar to himself. This distinction is important if one is interested in self concept in a very strict sense but I don't think it is crucial in the context of our paper.

I don't really know how an animal gets an image of itself or learns what it is like, so I will speculate. Certainly for many species I would expect that imprinting and prior social experience are crucial, and for most species in the wild, experience with reflecting surfaces is a trivial factor. In other words, the self concept, such as it is, is probably built up less by looking at oneself directly than by indirect means such as looking at one's caretakers and playmates and becoming attached to them and seeing how they react to one. Isn't this true even of humans? I would bet that if you asked people—even those who have had extensive experience with mirrors and with pictures of themselves—whether or not they look like an ape their reaction would be more predictable from what their parents and peers have told them or otherwise impressed upon them than from any other variable, including physical looks and intelligence. The Hayes's chimpanzee, Viki, was probably operating on the same principle when she was sorting photos of people and apes into two different piles and put a photo of herself in with the "people" pile.

DISCUSSION PAPER:
CHILD LANGUAGE AND THE
ORIGINS OF LANGUAGE

Lois Bloom

Teachers College
Columbia University
New York, New York 10027

Information about children learning language in the twentieth century may be instructive in reflecting on the question of how language originated with prehistoric man. The information about child language that I will discuss comes from longitudinal studies of four children who learned American English as their first language in the 1960s and 1970s in New York City. We observed the children in their homes: three of the children were observed for eight hours every six weeks, and the fourth child was observed for five hours every three weeks. The children were about 19 months old at the beginning of the investigation and 36 months old when the observations ended. We described the children's language behavior and paid particular attention to how their speech related to the objects, events, and relations in the contexts in which they spoke. We know (1) the kinds of things the children talked about, (2) the kinds of words and grammatical structure that they learned to use, and (3) how their speech related to the speech that they heard from others in the context.

The observations of the children were tape-recorded and transcribed, and the data for analysis consisted of what was said by the child and by others in relation to the description of what was happening in the context. The data were examined in the course of repeated passes through each annotated transcription in order to determine the regularities and variation among behaviors. Descriptions were quantitative: the more frequently a behavior such as a semantic-syntactic structure or a discourse contingency occurred, the more important it was considered to be for inferring something about what the children knew or were learning about the relationship between events in the world, and the language that represents information about events in the world.

The results of these studies have been reported in detail and at length elsewhere,[1-7] and the following generalizations about the emergence of language in the children we have observed are strongly supported by those studies. First, children talk about the ways in which objects relate to one another; they do not simply tell other people what objects are or the names for objects. The relational information that children talk about has to do with the existence, disappearance, nonexistence, or recurrence of an object (the relation of an object to itself); the actions of persons that affect objects; the locations and changes in location of objects and persons; the objects that are possessions or otherwise within the domains of other persons. Children talk about what they do to objects and what they do with objects, but they do not mention objects as instruments of actions on other objects (the importance of tool-making in the evolution of the species notwithstanding). (See Ref. 3, and see Ref. 7 for comment regarding the conspicuous lack of the instrumental relation of nouns to verbs in sentences in child language.)

Movement is critically important in early child language—among the first names of objects that children learn are the names of objects that move (e.g. persons, pets, balls, etc.),[8-10] and semantic-syntactic structures are used to encode action events before they are used to encode stative events. With respect to movement, children talk overwhelmingly of their own intentions to act, e.g. "eat cookie" as the child reaches for the cookie, or their desire for another to act, e.g. "Mommy open" as the child gives Mommy a box to open. Children talk far less frequently about what they have already done or what they have just seen others do.

None of these results is, in retrospect, surprising. It is well known that during their first two years, children learn about the nature of objects and the ways in which objects move and relate to themselves and to one another.[11] One might expect, then, that these are the kinds of things that children first learn to talk about. It is entirely reasonable to speculate that each of these generalizations about early child language has its analog in the origins of language in the human species: talking and understanding about movement, intentions to act, and the relations among objects. It is relevant that observations of the creation of "new" languages—pidgins and Creoles—have revealed the dominance of encoding dynamic aspects involving movement in events over the static aspects of events in the origins of such languages.[12]

One can look for support for such speculation in the behaviors of phylogenetically more primitive species. In this regard, it is perhaps more appropriate to look at the behaviors of other species in much the same way as we look at the behaviors of children—where animal behavior is described in the context of its own indigenous environment (as, for example, in the studies of laughing gulls by Colin Beer reported on in this conference)—than to look at the behaviors of a species that has been taken out of its indigenous context (as, for example, in the current studies that teach communication to chimpanzees). Beer has described the considerable importance of contextual variation on the communication behavior of laughing gulls, and the importance of movement (away from the nest, approach, etc).[13] The importance of context, movement, location, and individual possession or rights looms particularly large in Beer's studies of laughing gulls and our studies of children.

Children actively seek out what they want to know about language from the language that they hear. In studies of children's imitation and discourse with adults, it appeared that the children responded to the speech that they heard for social reasons and in order to maintain the topic of conversation, but predominantly, in order to learn those aspects of the language that they were ready to learn or that they were in the process of learning. As a result, adults in the environment modify their speech to children in order to adjust the target language according to the child's needs and expectations. Phylogenetically, it might be argued, there was no such model or target language. When, however, one considers that languages evolved, not over generations or centuries but over thousands of centuries, then the lack of a standard, target, or model language becomes less of an issue. In this regard, the finding by Beer,[13] that parent gulls modify their calls to their young as the young mature and gull chicks differentially respond to those changes in the calls of parent gulls over the space of a few weeks, is particularly instructive. There is an accommodation, then, between parent and young in different species; the child instructs the parent as to what he is ready to learn and what he needs to learn, at the same time that the adult instructs the child regarding what is available for learning. The mutual influence of each over the other enhances capacities and enlarges the communication repertoire. The effect of such accommodations between child and adult language on the structure of the target language has been recognized.[14]

It is perhaps neither fanciful nor adventurous to speculate that such resonation between the communication behaviors of children and birds is the reverberation of the earliest communications that began in prehistoric time. Birds are very different from persons; chimpanzees are less different from persons; but such species differences are far greater today than they were long ago. Finding such resonations may be of some heuristic value for the study of the origins of language in the evolution of humans.

REFERENCES

1. BLOOM, L. 1970. Language Development: Form and Function in Emerging Grammars. MIT Press. Cambridge, Mass.
2. BLOOM, L., L. HOOD & P. LIGHTBOWN. 1974. Imitation in language development; if, when and why. Cog. Psychol. **6**: 380–420.
3. BLOOM, L., P. LIGHTBOWN & L. HOOD. 1975. Structure and Variation in Child Language. Monogr. Soc. Res. Child Devel.
4. BLOOM, L., P. MILLER & L. HOOD. 1975. Variation and reduction as aspects of competence in child language. *In* Minnesota Symposium in Child Psychology. Vol. 9. A. Pick, Ed. Univ. Minnesota Press. Minneapolis, Minn.
5. BLOOM, L., L. ROCISSANO & L. HOOD. 1976. Child-adult discourse: developmental interaction between information processing and linguistic knowledge. Cog. Psychol. **6**. In press.
6. BOWERMAN, O. 1973. Early Syntactic Development: a Cross-Linguistic Study with Special Reference to Finnish. Cambridge Univ. Press. New York, N.Y.
7. BROWN, R. 1973. A First Language, the Early Stages. Harvard Univ. Press. Cambridge, Mass.
8. LEOPOLD, W. 1939. Language Development of a Bilingual Child. Vol. 1. Northwestern Univ. Press. Evanston, Ill.
9. HUTTENLOCHER, J. 1974. The origins of language comprehension. *In* Theories in Cognitive Psychology. R. L. Solso, Ed. Lawrence Erlbaum Assoc. New York, N.Y.
10. NELSON, K. 1973. Structure and Strategy in Learning to Talk. Monogr. Soc. Res. Child Develop.
11. PIAGET, J. 1960. Psychology of Intelligence. Littlefield and Adams. Paterson, N.J.
12. TRAUGOTT, E. Explorations in linguistic elaboration: language change, language acquisition and the genesis of spatio-temporal terms. *In* Proc. First. Int. Conf. Histor. Linguistics. J. Anderson & C. Jones, Eds. In press.
13. BEER, C. 1973. A view of birds. *In* Minnesota Symposium in Child Psychol. Vol. 7. Univ. Minnesota Press. Minneapolis, Minn.
14. JAKOBSON, R. 1941. Kindersprache, aphasie und allgemeine lautgesetze. Uppsala. English translation, 1968. Mouton and Co. The Hague, The Netherlands.
15. BEVER, T. 1970. The cognitive basis for linguistic structures. *In* Cognition and the Development of Language. John Wiley & Sons. New York, N.Y.

THE ONTOGENY OF PRIMATE INTELLIGENCE AND ITS IMPLICATIONS FOR COMMUNICATIVE POTENTIAL: A PRELIMINARY REPORT

Suzanne Chevalier-Skolnikoff*

Department of Anthropology
Stanford University
Stanford, California 94305

G. W. Hooper Foundation
University of California, San Francisco
San Francisco, California 94143

INTRODUCTION

The communicative potential of a species is intimately related to its intellectual capacities. This paper is a preliminary report on a study still in progress, focusing on the relationships between cognitive abilities, communicative potential, and species differences in primates. Comparative methods derived from Piaget's model of human intellectual development are used as a framework for making such comparisons.

Previous researchers have attempted to correlate intellectual capacity as viewed from a Piagetian perspective with the development of early child language from the appearance of the first word at about one year, or from the appearance of two-word utterances that occurs at about 18 months.[1-4] There has, however, been little attempt to apply a Piagetian model to prelanguage communicative development, from birth to 18 months, the period to which the application of sensory-motor abilities is most relevant. Furthermore, little previous work has focused on comparative primate intelligence and its relationship to communicative ability. The primary reason for this has been the lack of methodological techniques for making such comparisons. Piaget's model of human intellectual development during the Sensory-Motor Period (from birth to two years) provides a systematic objective framework for comparative studies. This model defines a series of qualitatively different behavioral stages incorporating increasing voluntary control, and increasing complexity and flexibility. Each stage in the series is characterized by a new level of functioning based on new behavioral parameters,[5] or abilities, that become incorporated into the behavior. Behaviors are characterized by increasing voluntary control, increasing complexity (additional motor patterns and more contextual variables), and increasing flexibility (motor patterns become nonstereotyped and contexts more varied) in successive stages.

METHODS

This study is based on a Piagetian perspective and uses comparative data on infant and adult behavior in three primate species: humans, stumptail macaques (*Macaca arctoides*), and lowland gorillas (*Gorilla gorilla gorilla*). Two developmental series from Piaget's Sensory-Motor Period are considered: the Sensory-Motor Intelligence Series and the Imitation Series. Human infants pass through six

---

*Address reprint requests to Dr. S. Chevalier-Skolnikoff, c/o The Editor, G.W. Hooper Foundation, University of California, San Francisco, Calif. 94143.

TABLE 1

CHARACTERISTICS OF THE SENSORY-MOTOR INTELLIGENCE SERIES* AS MANIFESTED BY HUMAN INFANTS

Stage	Age (mos.)	Description	Major Distinguishing Behavioral Parameters	Example
1 Reflex	0–1	Involuntary responses to nonspecific stimuli	Involuntary	Roots and sucks
2 Primary circular reaction	1–4	Infant's action is centered about his *own body* (thus "primary"); he learns to repeat actions ("circular") in order to reinstate the event; first acquired adaptations occur	Repetitive coordinations of own body; acquired adaptations; recognition of various objects and contexts	Repeats hand-hand clasping; exhibits conditioned reflexes
3 Secondary circular reaction	4–8	Repeated ("circular") attempts to reproduce *environmental* ("secondary") events initially discovered by chance	Environment-oriented behaviors; establishment of object/action relationships; semi-intentional (initial act is not intentional, but subsequent repetitions are); active attempts to effect changes in environment; simple orientations toward a single object or person	Swings object and attends to the swinging spectacle, or to the resulting sound; repeats
4 Coordination of secondary behaviors	8–12	Two or more independent behavioral acts become intercoordinated, one serving as instrument to another	Intentional; goal is established from the outset; establishment of relationships between two objects; coordination of sev-	Sets aside an obstacle in order to obtain an object behind it

Stage	Months			
			...eral behaviors toward an object or person; objects explored as well as acted upon; familiar behaviors applied to new situations; infant begins to attribute cause of environmental change to others	
5 Tertiary circular reaction	12–18	Child becomes curious about an object's possible *functions* and about object-object relationships ("tertiary"); he repeats his behavior ("circular") with variation as he explores the potentials of objects through trial and error experimentation	Behavior becomes variable and nonstereotyped, as the child invents new behavior patterns; repetitive trial and error experimentation begins; interest in novelty for its own sake; coordination of object-object, person-object, object-space and object-force relationships; considers others entirely autonomous	Experimentally discovers that one object, such as a stick, can be used to obtain another object
6 Invention of new means through mental combinations	18+	The solution is arrived at mentally, not through experimentation	The child can symbolically represent objects and events not present	Mentally figures out how one object can be used to obtain another object

*Abstracted from Piaget with modifications from Sugarman Bell. In press.

developmental stages in each series. The general characteristics of the stages, the ages at which they appear in human infants, examples of behaviors from the two series, and some of the parameters that delineate them are presented in TABLES 1 and 2.

The data on stumptail macaques are derived from the studies on intellectual development by Parker[5,6] and on my previous study on communicative development.[7-9] Parker's 137 hours of observation focused on the intellectual development of one infant from birth to five months. The infant was living in a small social group with his mother and an older infant. My study, consisting of 500 hours of observation, focused on the development of communication in three infants, from birth to six months, living in a social group consisting of seven additional adult and subadult animals. Information on their communicative behavior was also collected.

The data on gorillas are derived from current observations on intellectual and communicative abilities in five infant and five adult gorillas. The gorilla subjects range in age from birth through adult, though not all age periods are represented (see TABLE 3). Two of the infant gorillas, Mkumbwa and Sunshine, from the San Francisco group, are being group-reared with their mothers and two other adults. Binti is being reared with her mother, Dolly. Jim has been hand-reared from birth. Koko was reared in the San Francisco group during her first six months, and has been hand-reared since. From one year of age, Koko has been learning sign language in a study under the direction of Penny Patterson.

TABLE 2

CHARACTERISTICS OF THE IMITATION SERIES* AS MANIFESTED BY HUMAN INFANTS

Stage	Age (mos.)	Description
1 Reflexive contagious imitation	0–1	Reflexive behavior (e.g., crying) is stimulated by the behavior in a model
2 Sporadic "self-imitation"	1–4	Imitation by the model of the infant's own motor patterns (self-imitation) stimulates diffuse vocal activity in the infant. It is unclear whether the infant distinguishes the model's behavior from his own
3 Purposeful "self-imitation" (social facilitation)	4–8	Self-imitation in which matching becomes more precise. For visual imitation, the infant's acting body part must be visible to him
4 Imitation using body parts the infant cannot see	8–12	Imitation using unseen body parts. Infant attempts to imitate new behavioral acts, but often fails to precisely match the model. Infant now has some notion of number and of sound qualities
5 Imitation of new behavior patterns	12–18	Imitation of new motor acts, precisely accommodating behavior to that of the model through repeated attempts at matching
6 Deferred imitation	18+	Child precisely imitates new motor acts, without preliminary attempts at matching, through symbolic representation. Child manifests deferred imitation

*Abstracted from Piaget.

TABLE 3

GORILLA SUBJECTS

Subjects	Sex	Age Observed	Institution
Mkumbwa*	M	birth–4 months	San Francisco Zoological Society
Binti†	F	7 months 8 months	San Diego Zoological Society
Sunshine*	M	13–20 months	San Francisco Zoological Society
Jim‡	M	18 months 20 months	San Diego Zoological Society
Koko‡	F	4 years	San Francisco Zoological Society and Stanford University (being taught sign language by Penny Patterson)
Dolly (Binti's mother)	F	adult	San Diego Zoological Society
Missus (Sunshine's mother)	F	adult	San Francisco Zoological Society
Jacqueline (Koko and Mkumbwa's mother)	F	adult	San Francisco Zoological Society
Bwana	M	adult	San Francisco Zoological Society
Pogo	F	adult	San Francisco Zoological Society

*Reared with mother in social group.
†Mother-reared.
‡Nursery-reared.

Several methods are being employed in gathering the data on gorillas. Both cross-sectional and longitudinal methods are being used (see TABLE 3). Animals living with conspecifics are being observed as they behave spontaneously in their captive environments. Objects are also being introduced to the animals living in groups in order to give them better opportunity to demonstrate their intellectual capacities. Hand-reared animals are being formally tested, presented with problems (e.g., how to obtain an out-of-reach object with a tool), or tested for imitative ability as well as being presented with objects that they may freely manipulate. Although Koko can use signs, no sign language is used during testing in this study.

Observational data are recorded in running narrative either by hand or on a tape recorder. Test data are recorded on check sheets. The testing procedures and check sheets are derived from those of Uzgiris and Hunt,[10] modified for use on gorillas. Behavior is also being recorded on film: three hours of film have been collected to date. The data on gorillas presented here are based on a total of 100 hours of observation collected over a period of eight months.

Information on human infants is derived primarily from the literature, especially from the work of Piaget.[11-13] Some of the human behavioral examples are derived from unsystematic observations of my own two children.

Analysis of gorilla data consisted of abstracting all recorded behaviors that could be distinguished as relevant to the Sensory-Motor Intelligence Series and the Imitation Series. These behaviors were then categorized under one of the six stages of each series according to the behavioral parameters (see *The Stage Concept* below for a discussion of the validity of stage classification). Piaget's framework was used as a model, but, following the methods of Parker,[5,6] was modified to accommodate the behavioral parameters of monkeys or apes when they were different from those of humans. The ages at which the first behavior characteristic of each stage in each series appeared was noted. Behaviors were then categorized according to sensory modality. Stage behaviors, and ages at onset of a stage, were then compared for the different sensory modalities in the three species. Communicative behavior in the three species was analyzed in a similar manner. Cognitive and communicative capacities of the three species were then compared.

RESULTS

Cognitive Abilities

An examination of the intellectual abilities of stumptail macaques, according to sensory mode and body part, shows that while these monkeys complete all six stages of the Sensory-Motor Intelligence Series in the tactile/kinesthetic mode and in the visual/body mode,† they complete only the first stage in the visual/facial and vocal modes, and they do not manifest any of the six stages in the visual/gestural (manual behaviors received visually) or auditory modes. In addition, stumptail macaques manifest behaviors that differ from those of humans, in that they are nonrepetitive, but satisfy some of the requirements of stages 2 and 3 in the visual/facial and vocal modes. Behaviors incorporating some of the behavioral parameters characteristic of stage 2 (see TABLES 1 and 4) may incorporate acquired or learned adaptations to the environment as it impinges upon the infant—recognition of objects and contexts and body coordinations. But these behaviors are not repetitive. Actions incorporating some stage 3 behavioral parameters may include environmental orientation and semi-intentionality; the monkey becomes environmentally "intrusive" as he initiates environmentally-oriented activities (such as visual, manual, and oral investigation). But these behaviors are not repetitive, nor do they establish *relationships between objects and actions*; they do not involve *attempts to initiate* changes in the environment. Parker has called these behaviors "linear," because they do not incorporate repetition, whereas the "circular" human stage 2 and 3 behaviors do. Visual and vocal emotional expressions are prominent among the linear reactions, especially in stage 3. These behaviors are limbic and are mediated by the lower subcortical areas of the forebrain, with some participation of the cortex;[14] they thereby contrast with stage 3 circular reactions, which are undoubtedly cortically-mediated. Since human infants also manifest behaviors that could be classified as "linear," human behavioral development could have been classified under the two (circular and linear) Sensory-Motor Intelligence Series, but in this study I have followed the more traditional single-series Piagetian classification for humans. The completion of stage 3 and later stages in the tactile/kinesthetic and visual/body modes means that stumptail macaques are capable of learning to voluntarily affect the behavior of others through behavior in these sensory modes (as in sexual interactions and in play). However, the complete lack of environmentally directed *repetitive* behavior patterns in all but the body modes means that these macaques do not learn to voluntarily effect environmental changes, either in objects or in the behavior of conspecifics through facial expression, gesture, vocal or auditory behavior. Consequently they evidently cannot

†This interpretation differs from that of Parker,[5,6] which did not analyze stumptail abilities according to sensory mode and body part.

make a facial expression they do not emotionally feel, they cannot make a hand gesture,‡ and they cannot make a nonemotional vocalization or a sound § in order to obtain a goal from a conspecific. In addition, not having learned self-initiated cause and effect relationships in the visual/gestural channel as human infants do during stage 3, they cannot proceed to stages 4 and 5, and they cannot learn to relate objects to each other, as in tool-making (see TABLE 4). Furthermore, in the vocal modality, they do not coo (stage 2) or babble (stages 3 and 4), and therefore do not learn to voluntarily effect changes in the vocal behavior of others through their own vocalizations, as human infants do in their stage 3 babbling "games."

In the Imitation Series, macaques achieve only stage 3 in the visual/ body mode, stages 2 and 3 in the visual/facial mode, and stage 3 in the vocal mode. Consequently they only show imitation of familiar motor patterns in these modes. In the visual/ gestural and auditory modes, they show no imitation at all (see TABLE 5).

Great apes, like macaques, also complete the entire Sensory-Motor Intelligence Series in the tactile/kinesthetic and visual/body modes. But unlike the macaques, and like human infants, they complete all the higher stages in the visual/gestural modality. Consequently, they manifest "secondary" and "tertiary" circular reactions in these modes, and through gestures they are able to initiate and effect changes in their environments, and can experimentally, or mentally invent new means to accomplish such changes. Apes also complete the higher stages of the visual/facial mode. In the vocal mode, however, the apes are similar to macaques and radically different from humans, completing only stage 3 in the linear series, and probably stage 1 in the Piagetian series; thus they fail to manifest repetitive self-vocalizations (cooing) or repetitive vocal attempts to effect changes in the environment (babbling, or vocal "games"). In the auditory mode, apes are intermediate between monkeys and humans, showing stage 3 and stage 4 behaviors, as they make noises by repeatedly banging objects in their environments (stage 3) and incorporating these repetitive noises into their displays (see stage 4, TABLE 6).

In the Imitation Series, also, gorillas manifest abilities in the highest stages except in the auditory mode in which they show only stage 3 and stage 4 behaviors, and the vocal mode, in which they manifest only stage 3 behavior. In the vocal modality, gorillas, like macaques, are capable only of "socially facilitated" imitation. In the auditory modality, apes, unlike macaques, are able to imitate nonvocal noisemaking, and to incorporate it into their displays. In the visual channel, great apes are capable of imitating new motor patterns using parts of their bodies they cannot see, with exact matching on the first attempt (stage 6) in all body areas (see TABLE 7).

Human infants complete the whole Sensory-Motor Intelligence Series and the whole Imitation Series in all modes (see TABLES 8 and 9).

Correlations Between Cognitive Capacities and Communicative Abilities

Correlated with their intellectual capacities, macaque communication systems consist of voluntary, nonstereotyped behaviors and circular behaviors (stages 3, 4, 5,

---

‡A few manual behaviors have been observed in stumptail macaques that could possibly be interpreted as visual hand gestures, such as "present hand," "grab at," and "hit at."[7,9] These behaviors usually result in contact, however, and when contact does not occur they appear to represent abortive tactile behaviors.

§Branch-shaking in macaques may produce a noise as well as a visual display, and could, perhaps, be classified as an auditory secondary circular reaction, though it is derived from a tactile/kinesthetic and visual/body reaction.

TABLE 4

The Sensory-Motor Intelligence Series as Manifested by Stumptail Macaque Infants

Stage	Age	Example					
		Tactile/ Kinesthetic	Visual/Body	Visual/Facial	Visual/ Gestural	Vocal	Auditory
1 Reflex	0–2 wks.	Rooting; sucking; clinging;* jerking†	Jerk; startle reflex†	Rooting; sucking; rhythmic tongue protrusion*	—	Negative reflexive vocalizations: squeak, gecker, scream†	—
2 Primary linear (non-circular) reactions	ca. 2 wks.– 3 mos.	Nonrepetitive hand-mouth coordination;‡ tactile investigation of own body;‡ "baby" walking;‡ voluntary clinging;† response to touch-contact signals†	—	Visual following of own hand;‡ pucker lip† lip smack*		Positive emotional vocalizations: trilled whistle, girn†	—
Primary circular reactions		Repeated climbing on and off mother;‡ repeated climbing on and off objects‡					
3 Secondary linear reactions	1–3 mos.	Grabbing objects;‡ pushing and pulling objects;‡ poking objects;‡ climbing down fence feet first;‡ jumping onto objects;‡ responding	Present;* crouch;‡ hopping and scampering‡	Facial expressions of emotion: lip smacking, open-mouth eyelids-down (play); open mouth threat*	Reaches out for objects in the environment.‡	Emotional vocalizations: chirl threat, staccato grunt*	

Stage			
Secondary circular reactions	to visual cling signals;† mounting†		Branch-shaking†
4 Coordination of secondary linear reactions — 2 mos. +	Interanimal mouthing;† branch-shaking†	Present-sexual; hand-to-hand transfer;‡ pushing another animal away while holding an object;‡ foot-storage‡	—
Coordination of secondary circular reactions	Rough and tumble contact play† serial application of different body reactions to same object or surface—e.g., alternate forelimb-hindlimb hanging†		Visual adjustments for rough and tumble play†
5 Tertiary circular reactions — 4 mos. +	Trial and error approach-avoidance play;‡ present for grooming†		Trial and error approach-avoidance play;† present for grooming†
6 Invention of new means (tertiary) through mental combinations — ?	Mentally figuring out tactics for approach-avoidance play†		Mentally figuring out tactics for approach-avoidance play†

*Observed by both Parker and Chevalier-Skolnikoff.
†Chevalier-Skolnikoff, Refs. 7 and 9 and personal observation.
‡Parker[5,6]

TABLE 5

THE IMITATION SERIES AS MANIFESTED BY STUMPTAIL MACAQUE INFANTS

Stage	Age	Example			
		Visual/Body	Visual/Facial	Visual/Gestural	Vocal
1 (No imitation)		—	—	—	—
2 Sporadic "self-imitation"	3 wks.	—	Lipsmack†	—	—
3 Purposeful "self-imitation"	4 wks.	Climbing fence upon seeing another doing same;* sitting on mother's hand upon seeing another doing same;* Presenting upon seeing another doing same;* manipulating object upon seeing another doing same*	Facial expressions of emotion elicited by others doing same: lipsmack;† open mouth-eyelids down (play) face;† open mouth stare (threat);† eating upon seeing another doing same†	Eats a particular food upon seeing another doing same.	Emotional vocalizations elicited by others doing same: threat;† fear‡

*Parker.[5,6]
†Observed by both Parker and Chevalier-Skolnikoff.
‡Chevalier-Skolnikoff.[7,9]

TABLE 6

THE SENSORY-MOTOR INTELLIGENCE SERIES AS MANIFESTED BY GORILLAS

Stage	Age (mos.)	Example					
		Tactile/ Kinesthetic	Visual/ Body	Visual/ Facial	Visual/ Gestural	Vocal	Auditory
1 Reflex	0–1	Roots; sucks; clings	Moro reflex; startle reflex	—	—	Reflex crying (not observed)	—
2 Primary linear reactions	1–3	Conditioned reflexes: learns to recognize and seize nipple visually; learns touch-cling signals	—	—	—	—	—
Primary circular reactions		Repetitive hand-to-mouth contact; repetitive hand-to-foot contact.					
3 Secondary linear reactions	3–<7	Grabs objects	Presents	Facial expressions of emotion: open mouth (play); pout; whimper	Reaches out to objects in the environment.	Emotional vocalizations whimper; laugh	—
Secondary circular reactions		Rubs hand repeatedly on substrate; bangs hand repeatedly on substrate	—	Repeatedly charges and runs into rocking clown toy to reactivate it; display running	Repeatedly waves branch and watches	—	Repetitive object-banging

TABLE 6 (Continued)

Stage	Age (mos.)	Example					
		Tactile/ Kinesthetic	Visual/ Body	Visual/ Facial	Visual/ Gestural	Vocal	Auditory
4 Coordination of secondary linear reactions	<7–14½	Hand-to-hand transfer of objects; foot-storage	—	—	—	—	—
Coordination of secondary circular reactions		Picks up branch, rubs it on substrate, or slides along ground on branch; brings branch over head and around shoulders to behind rump, sits on it (nesting)	Holds branch in mouth, beats chest, swaggers and runs (display); runs at object, banging or kicking it (display)		Repeatedly holds branch out to another, then withdraws it (a game); holds branch in mouth, beats chest (display)	—	Self- and object-banging incorporated into displays
5 Tertiary circular reactions	14½–>20	Experimentation with body-force and body-space relationships; plays "keep away"*	Experimentation with body-force and body-space relationships; plays "keep away"*	Trial and error; making faces	Gravity/space: water play (watches drips; submersion); piles objects; tosses objects in air and catches them; puts one object into another; object/space, object/person; uses one object (stick) to ob-	—	—

6 Invention of new tertiary means through mental combinations	<18	Mentally figures out body-force and body-space adjustments; figures out tactics for "keep away"	Mentally figures out body-force and body-space adjustments; figures out tactics for "keep away"	Makes pout face (friendly expression) to human observer, then aggressively smashes observer's hand against cage when attempt is made to pet ape (lying)	(food); uses stick to hit another ape during an attack; feeds leaf to mother; palm up, extended hand brought *toward* body ("give me"); hand *extended* palm up in sweeping gesture ("let's go")	Gravity/space: anticipates new gravity-space relationships; mentally figures out new object-object relationships; signs (ASL) paired in new combinations;* young ape hugs human, looks into eyes and surreptitiously steals watch (lying); offers food to an attacking ape to placate him;* trades one object for another*

*Observed in older subject.

TABLE 7

THE IMITATION SERIES AS MANIFESTED BY GORILLAS

Stage	Age	Example				
		Visual/ Body	Visual/ Facial	Visual/ Gesture	Vocal	Auditory
1 Reflexive contagious imitation	0–	—	—	—	—	—
2 Sporadic self-imitation	0–	—	—	—	—	—
3 Purposeful self-imitation	3–8 mos. or earlier	Climbs on box upon seeing other ape climb on box	Makes hoot face upon seeing other ape doing same;† imitates human model making familiar facial expressions (e.g., pout)	Pats on surface after seeing ape model doing same; shakes rag after seeing human model do same;* beats on mother after seeing other infant ape beat chest	Makes cough-grunt after hearing human model attempt same; makes hoot after other ape hoots*	Bangs on gong upon seeing and hearing human model do so

4 Imitation employing invisible body parts	8 mos. or earlier	Mother lies on back, infant lies on back next to mother	Imitates human model; pointing to different parts of face*	Imitates human model pointing to different parts of face;* imitates human or ape model putting cloth over head; attempts to imitate ape model's hand gesture by watching and attempting to match	Koko makes kissing noise after hearing human model kiss over telephone
5 Imitation of new behavior patterns	before 4 y	Imitates somersaults	Imitates human model making a new facial expression: tongue stuck out, lower lip protruded†	Imitates human model stringing beads;* draws parallel lines after seeing human model do so;† imitates ape model's begging gesture	—
6 Deferred imitation	before 4 yr	Somersaults after model has stopped doing same	Makes new expression a few minutes after model has stopped*	Chips stones months after seeing human model do so*	—

*Observed in older animals.
†Patterson, personal communication.

TABLE 8

THE SENSORY-MOTOR INTELLIGENCE SERIES[13] AS MANIFESTED BY HUMAN INFANTS

Stage	Age (mos.)	Example					
		Tactile/ Kinesthetic	Visual/ Body	Visual/ Facial	Visual/ Gestural	Vocal	Auditory
1 Reflex	0–1	Roots; sucks[12]	Moro reflex; startle reflex*	Reflex smile	—	Reflexive vocalization (crying)[17]	—
2 Primary circular reaction	1–4	Repetitive finger-sucking; repetitive hand-hand clasping[12]	—	Smile in response to human face[51,52]	—	Repetitive self-vocalization (cooing)[21,53,55]	—
3 Secondary circular reaction	4–8	Repeatedly strikes object;[12] repeatedly rubs object on substrate;[12] repeatedly pushes-pulls object[12]	Repeatedly wiggles body to shake object and watches;[12] kicks legs in response to smiling adult*	Facial expressions of emotion (noncircular): laughing, crying; smile used in circular reaction with smiling adult	Repeatedly swings object and watches[12]	Emotional (noncircular) vocalizations: laughing, crying, back-and-forth vocalizing "games"; repeatedly vocalizes to another in order to obtain a like response[50] (babbling)[21,53-55]	Repeatedly shakes, strikes or rubs noise-making object[12]
4 Coordination of secondary behaviors; their application to new situations	8–12	Pushes adult's hand to make him resume previous activity[12]	Rises on tiptoes and raises arms to be picked up*	Looks, smiles at adult to obtain social contact[50]	Removes one object in order to obtain another[12]; reaches up to adult's face to obtain social contact[50]	Begins to combine sounds (babbling);[54] attempts to imitate new sounds and words (echolalia);[21] vocalizes to adult to obtain social contact[50]	Pushes adult's hand toward bell so he will ring it[13]

5 12–18 Tertiary circular reaction, and the discovery of new means by active experimentation	Gravity/space: postures the body to accommodate to gravity-space relationships: catches a ball; pushes box under object that is out of reach Trial & error approach-avoidance play*	Plays "keep-away"*	Trial & error face-making in mirror*; facial expressions used to obtain a goal—looks at adult then at desired object[50]	Gravity/space: water play (watches drips, submersion); piles objects; tosses object in air and catches it; puts one object into another	Object/object Uses one object (stick) to obtain another (toy); feeds mother;* reaches hand toward desired object that is out of reach and looks at adult*	First words,[21,54] Vocalizations, including single words used to obtain desired end; vocalizes to adult and reaches toward chair (adult places child in chair)[50]	Object-banging to attain desired end, e.g., bangs on high chair tray to be put down* Trial & error rhythmical and musical combinations*
6 18+ Invention of new means through mental combinations	Mentally figures out body-force and body-space relationships; mentally figures out tactics for "keep-away"*	Mentally figures out body-force and body-space relationships; mentally figures out tactics for "keep-away"*	Mentally figures out desired facial expressions often to attain a goal (as in lying)	Gravity/space: anticipates gravity-space relationships; mentally figures out new object-object relationships		Babbling ceases; 2-word utterances[4] often to attain a goal	Mentally figures out rhythmical musical combinations*

*Chevalier-Skolnikoff, personal observations.

TABLE 9

THE IMITATION SERIES AS MANIFESTED BY HUMAN INFANTS

Stage	Age (mos.)	Example				
		Visual Body	Visual/ Facial	Visual/ Gestural	Vocal	Auditory
1 Reflexive contagious imitation	0–1	—	—	—	Sporadic contagious crying*	—
2 Sporadic self-imitation	1–4	Moves head from side to side after model does same*	—	Clasps hands after model does same*	Repetition of own sounds when made by self or by a model (cooing);† model says "aa" baby vaguely imitates	—
3 Purposeful self-imitation	4–8	Imitates model performing familiar body motions, e.g., kicking foot‡	Smiles or laughs when adult does so‡	Imitates model performing secondary circular reactions (e.g., swinging a hanging object);§ imitates model wiggling his thumb§	Imitates own sounds when made by model, matching more precise than in stage 2 (babbling)	Imitates model performing secondary circular reactions (e.g., banging on resounding surface)‡
4 Imitation employing	8–12	Attempts to imitate jumping model by hanging onto sup-	Imitates various facial expressions already in reper-	Imitates unseen gestures;* putting finger in mouth;§	Attempts to imitate new syllables* model says "pa"	Attempts to imitate auditory sequences (e.g.,

	Age					
body parts the infant cannot see		port and jumping up and down without lifting feet (matching not entirely successful)‡	toire: sticking tongue out;§ attempts to imitate new facial expressions, but often fails to match model	attempts to imitate new motor pattern: model bends fingers, baby opens and closes hand*	and baby says "pa;" model says "papapapapa," baby may say "papapapa"§ (babbling, echolalia)	one beat, or a series of beats)‡
5 Imitation of new behavior patterns	12–18	Successfully imitates model performing new motor patterns through repeated attempts at matching: sitting in an adult chair‡	Successfully imitates new facial expressions through repeated attempts at matching: moves tongue to side of mouth§	Imitates new motor patterns involving object-object relationships: drawing with a pencil on paper§	Imitates new words§	Precisely imitates simple auditory sequence‡
6 Deferred imitation	18+	Reinacts previous events involving new motor patterns: sitting in an adult chair‡	Successfully imitates new facial expressions without trial & error matching: imitating gaping expressions;§ deferred imitation of new facial expressions	Reinacts previously observed behaviors involving new motor patterns: crossing and uncrossing arms and hitting shoulders with hands§	Deferred imitation of new words§	Deferred imitation of simple auditory sequences‡

*Piaget.[11]
†Both Chevalier-Skolnikoff, personal observations, and Piaget.[11]
‡Chevalier-Skolnikoff, personal observations.
§Piaget.[12]

and 6) in the tactile/kinesthetic and visual/body modalities. These variable tactile/kinesthetic and visual/body communicative patterns are most prominently seen in sexual interactions (Chevalier-Skolnikoff),[15] and in play; they occur for example, during chasing and hiding "games" in which animals experiment and mentally figure out how to catch or how to escape from one another. A number of tactile/kinesthetic and visual/body communicative patterns have also been distinguished in interactions between mothers and infants in the context of initiating and terminating clinging;[8,9] these communicative behaviors are based on stage 2 and 3 linear abilities. The earliest contact signal to be learned by infant stumptails is the touch-cling signal. Mothers normally hug their newborn infants to their ventrums as they begin to get up and locomote, or as they shift position. By one month of age, infants respond to a light touch on the back (even when the mother does not actually hug the infant to her ventrum) by clinging. These stage 2 infants have learned to associate a touch on the back with forthcoming maternal movement, and have learned to adapt to the mother's signal. This kind of learning is similar to "molding" (active teaching involving repeated physical placement of the animal's hands or body in a particular position, in a specific context), a method used to teach sign language to chimpanzees,[16] except that the monkey mother is not voluntarily *teaching* the signal to her infant. Stumptail infants were not observed beginning to *initiate* contact signals, that is, sending them to their mothers, until they were over one month of age, when they had entered stage 3 and the first environment-oriented behaviors had appeared. Nine different kinds of cling signals have been distinguished. They are evidently idiosyncratic behaviors, since only particular signals are used between particular mother-infant, or adult-infant pairs. These communicative behaviors are based on stage 2 and 3 linear abilities.

Unlike their nonstereotyped tactile/kinesthetic and visual/body behaviors, the facial and vocal communicative abilities of stumptail macaques are limited to visual and vocal emotional displays (stage 1, 2, and 3 linear behaviors), over which the animals have only limited voluntary control. They can inhibit these displays or direct them, but they evidently cannot make them out of emotional context (they cannot lie) nor can they learn or invent new expressions, gestures, or vocalizations (see FIGURES 1 and 2, which graphically demonstrate the comparative cognitive abilities of monkeys, great apes, and humans, in the Sensory-Motor Intelligence Series and the Imitation Series, and FIGURE 3, a–f, which shows the correlations between cognitive and communicative capacities in the three species).

The cognitive abilities of great apes correlate with their communicative abilities; they are capable of incorporating voluntary, nonstereotyped behavior in the tactile/kinesthetic, visual/body, visual/facial, and visual/gestural modes into their communications. (See Hess, 1973, and Hess, film on variable tactile/kinesthetic behavior during sexual interactions in gorillas.[17,18]) Stage 5 and 6 communicative behaviors have been distinguished in communications between conspecifics in all of these modes except the visual/facial. Despite experimental evidence that gorillas can imitate new facial expressions (stage 5, see FIGURE 4, a & b), and in spite of my own observations of both a stage 5 gorilla infant and an adult sitting alone and making faces to themselves (they had no mirror and could not have seen their expressions), I have not yet seen gorillas use voluntary nonstereotyped facial expressions in interactions with conspecifics. Stage 4, 5, and 6 gestural communications occur quite frequently in interactions between conspecifics in the captive group. Untrained group-living apes have been observed making trial and error hand gestures, carefully looking at their hands as they experiment with them. Animals will imitate new hand gestures that are used communicatively (see FIGURES 5 & 6). They often use objects in threat (see FIGURE 7) or as weapons. They roll tires at one another as well as teasing,

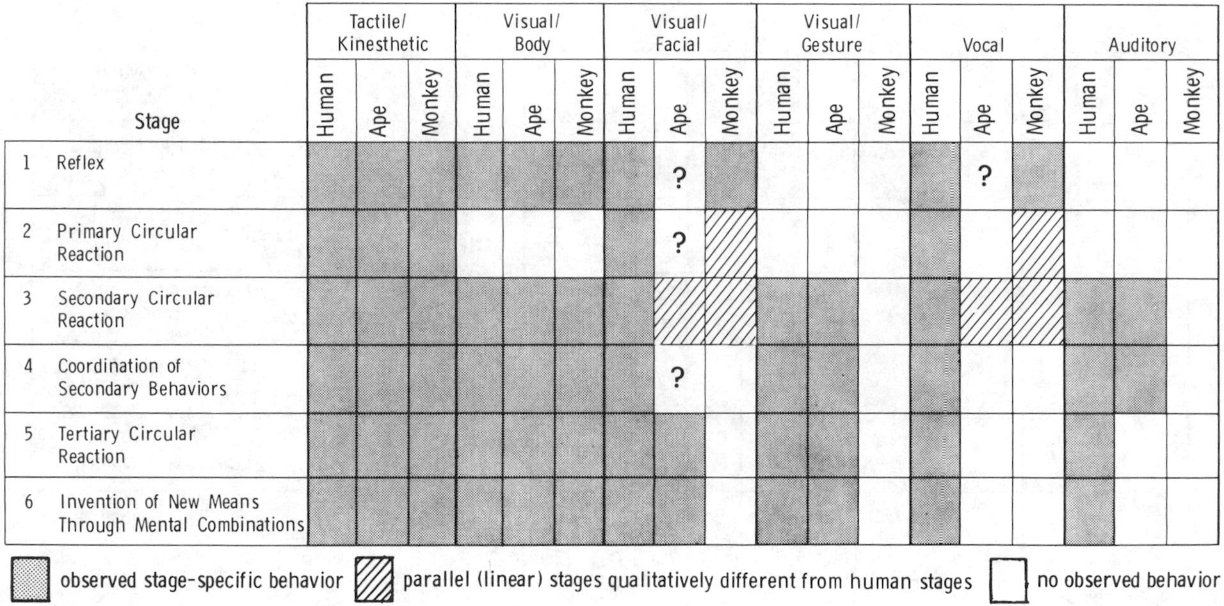

FIGURE 1. The Sensory-Motor Intelligence Series as manifested by three primate species. Question marks indicate that abilities are suspected but have not been observed.

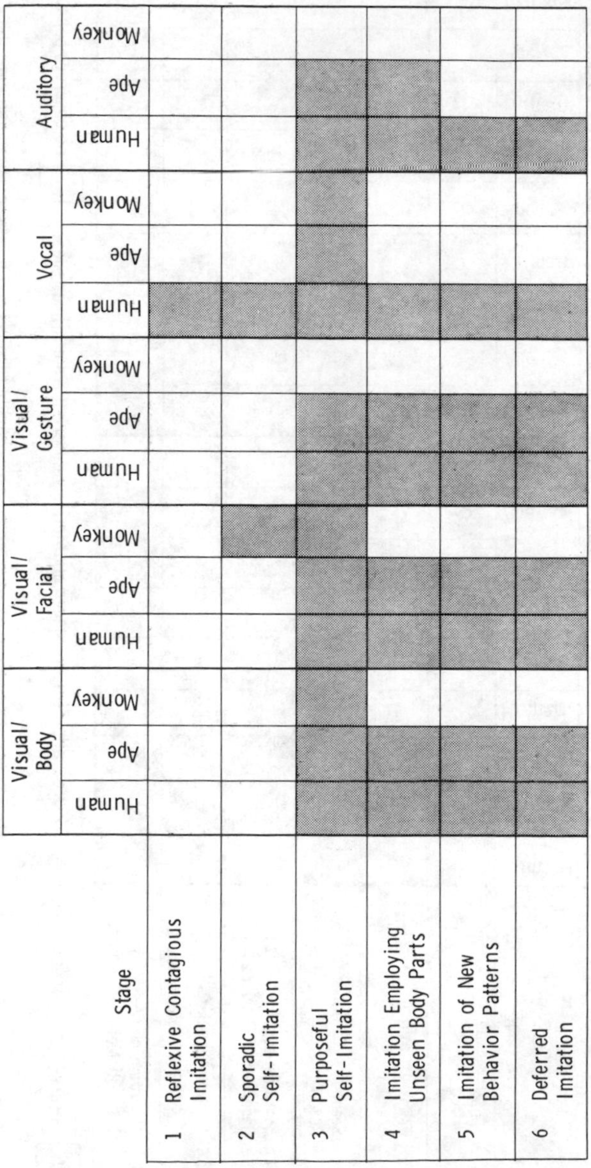

FIGURE 2. The Imitation Series as manifested by three primate species.

taunting and attacking each other with boughs. They also offer each other food as a means of obtaining a goal. It is these stage 5 and 6 gestural abilities that provide the great apes with the capacity for sign language.

Stage 4 auditory communications are particularly prominent in gorillas, as they incorporate them into their displays, coordinating object-beating with display running and hooting. However, despite their ability to voluntarily move their mouth musculature, gorilla voiced¶ vocal communications, like those of the macaques, consist of emotional vocalizations that the animals evidently are able only to inhibit or direct.

Human infants complete both the Sensory-Motor Intelligence Series and the Imitation Series in all modalities, and these intellectual capacities provide them with a basis for incorporating voluntary nonstereotyped behavior from all these modes into their communication systems. Thus they can acquire the advanced stages of body language, they can make facial expressions signifying emotions they do not feel, and they can learn, use, and invent sign language, vocal language, Morse code, and music.

In summary, from the data available on stumptail macaques, gorillas, and human infants, there appears to be a complete correlation between cognitive capacities and communicative abilities in all sensory modalities (refer to FIGURE 3, a–f). Thus, the mode-specific cognitive capacities of a primate at any stage of development are evidently intimately related to the animal's communicative potential. This correlation suggests that one system may be an adaptation for another; possibly advanced cognitive abilities are at least in part adaptations for social communication.

DISCUSSION

This study suggests a number of hypotheses, and also raises a number of theoretical issues.

The Stage Concept

In one sense, development is a continuous process. Nevertheless, using Piaget's model, behavioral development can be described as a series of stages, since the behavior changes qualitatively as different levels of functioning (stages) appear. Stage transitions can be precisely dated since the first behavior possessing all the parameters of a particular stage (the criterion used in this study) appears at one specific time. During the stage, the behavior increases from a frequency of zero to a relatively high frequency, generally followed by a decline. Meanwhile, the behavioral parameters of the next stage will have appeared and marked the end of that stage and the beginning of the subsequent stage (see FIGURE 8).

Not all sensory modes attain a particular stage at precisely the same time, however, and not all the behavioral parameters of a particular stage always appear at once. For example, in the visual/gestural mode in stage 3 in gorillas, *environmental orientation* appears before *repetition*, and repetition before *intentionality* and the *relationships between objects and actions*. Therefore one could say that a particular level of functioning (stage) actually develops in a series of substages, or that it

¶Gorillas are able to voluntarily make a few unvoiced sounds, such as very loud kissing sounds that they make with their lips. Koko imitated such a sound made by the observer over the telephone, a situation in which the auditory channel comprised the total input.

Tactile/Kinesthetic **a**

Stage #	Human	Ape	Monkey
1	Rooting and sucking	Rooting and sucking	Rooting and sucking
2	Voluntary rooting, sucking	Voluntary rooting, sucking	Voluntary rooting, sucking
3	Repeatedly touches mother's face (a game)	Repeatedly hits mother	Interanimal mounting
4	Pushes adult's hand to make him resume previous activity	Rough and tumble play	Rough and tumble play
5	Trial and error approach-avoidance play	Trial and error approach-avoidance play	Trial and error approach-avoidance play
6	Mentally figuring out tactics for approach-avoidance play	Mentally figuring out tactics for approach-avoidance play	Mentally figuring out tactics for approach-avoidance play

Visual/Body **b**

Stage #	Human	Ape	Monkey
1	Startle reflex	Startle reflex	Startle reflex
2	Imitates side-to-side head movement		
3	Kicks legs in response to smiling adult	Display running	Branch-shaking
4	Raising on tiptoes and raising arms to be picked up	Swaggering and running displays incorporating objects	Visual adjustments to rough and tumble play
5	Trial and error approach-avoidance play	Trial and error approach-avoidance play	Trial and error approach-avoidance play
6	Mentally figuring out tactics for approach-avoidance play	Mentally figuring out tactics for approach-avoidance play	Mentally figuring out tactics for approach-avoidance play

Visual/Facial **c**

Stage #	Human	Ape	Monkey
1	Reflex smile	?	Reflex rhythmic mouth movements
2	Smile in response to human face	?	Lipsmack to monkey face
3	Smile used in circular reactions with smiling adult	Facial expressions of emotion	Facial expressions of emotion
4	Facial expressions used to obtain social contact	Attempts to imitate model making new facial expressions	
5	Facial expressions used to obtain an object or goal	Imitates model making a new facial expression	
6	Mentally figuring out facial expressions, often to obtain an end (as in lying)	Deferred imitation of new facial expression	

Visual/Gestural **d**

Stage #	Human	Ape	Monkey
1			
2	Imitates model clasping hands		
3	Imitates model swinging an object	Imitates model swinging a branch	
4	Reaches up to an adult's face to obtain social contact	Imitates human model touching different parts of face	
5	Smiles at adult and reaches for object in adult's hand	Communicative hand gestures to attain a goal: begging gesture	
6	Mentally figuring out gestures to attain an end (as in lying)	Mentally figuring out gestures to attain an end (as in lying)	

FIGURE 3. Correlations between intellectual ability and communicative ability in three primate species a. tactile/kinesthetic; b. visual/body; c. visual/facial; d. visual/gestural; e. vocal; f. auditory. (See p. 198 for e & f.)

Shaded areas represent categories in which Piagetian intellectual abilities are manifested. Hatched areas represent categories in which linear intellectual abilities are manifested. Communicative examples are entered in categories in which communicative abilities are manifested. Blank areas represent absence of intellectual or communicative abilities. Question marks indicate that abilities are suspected but have not been observed.

Vocal **e**

Stage #	Human	Ape	Monkey
1	Crying	?	Reflective vocalizations
2	Cooing		Positive emotional vocalizations
3	Babbling	Emotional vocalizations	Emotional vocalizations
4	Vocalizes to adult to obtain social contact		
5	Vocalizations, including single words to obtain desired ends		
6	2-word utterances		

Auditory **f**

Stage #	Human	Ape	Monkey
1			
2			
3	Imitates model banging on resounding object	Imitates model patting on substrate	
4	Pushes adult's hand toward bell, so he will ring it	?	
5	Object-banging to obtain a goal		
6	Deferred imitation of rhythmic sequences		

FIGURE 3 (*continued*)

FIGURE 4. Without being instructed, Koko imitates a new facial expression, not in the gorilla repertoire of emotional facial expressions (Imitation Series, stage 5). a. Koko looks at the model and sticks out her tongue. b. She matches her body position to that of the model.

develops "gradually." It is not yet clear to me whether this "gradual" development really represents a series of discrete substages (which I could definitely identify) or whether it represents a continuum of even more subtle behavioral changes that I have not yet been able to identify. In any event, Piaget's six sensory-motor stages represent a series of objectively-definable behavioral levels, or categories, that are useful for behavioral analysis, even if they actually represent an abstraction of the actual developmental sequence.

Stage-to-Stage Progression

The data from this study indicate that there is a general stage-to-stage developmental progression, one stage following the next in a particular sequence. However, there are some exceptions that can be seen at a glance in FIGURES 2 and 3. There are a

FIGURE 5. Without being instructed, Koko imitates Penny Patterson by touching a part of her body she cannot see (Imitation Series, stage 4). In this photograph, she puts a finger on her eye.

couple of possible reasons for the absence of a stage 1 and 2 behaviors in some of the modalities. One possibility is that additional observation is needed to distinguish them. This is probably true for the stages marked with question marks. Additionally, some stages in some modes may be theoretically untenable. For example, most potential nonvocal sounds would be made in interaction with the environment (e.g., object-banging), but during stages 1 and 2, environmentally oriented behaviors are absent. However, in the Sensory-Motor Intelligence Series, early stages in which behaviors do not seem to occur in some sensory modes (because the stage is evidently theoretically impossible), higher stages apparently develop out of lower stage abilities in other, somewhat related, sensory modes. While some sensory modes appear to be

FIGURE 6. Bwana, an adult male, makes a begging gesture (Sensory-Motor Intelligence Series, stage 5). Sunshine imitated this gesture (Imitation Series, stage 5) at 18 months of age. Photograph by William Townsend.

FIGURE 7. Sunshine coordinates several behavior patterns as he incorporates objects into a threat display (Sensory-Motor Intelligence Series, stage 4). He runs bipedally, beating his chest, holding a small stick in his mouth, and dragging a branch. Photograph by William Townsend.

absolutely distinct from one another (e.g., the tactile and vocal modes), others are interrelated to at least some degree (e.g., kinesthetic with visual/body and visual/facial; and tactile/kinesthetic with visual/gestural). Consequently, it is possible that the more advanced abilities in the sensory modes that have no predecessors have grown out of earlier abilities in other modes. For example, in human infants, stage 3 sensory-motor abilities in the visual/body and visual/gestural modes probably have grown out of stage 2 abilities in the tactile/kinesthetic mode (see FIGURE 2). Similarly, in human infants and in apes, stage 3 behavior in the auditory mode (secondary circular reactions such as object-banging) seems to develop out of transitional substage 2 and 3 tactile silent object-patting; and in apes, stage 5 behavior in the visual/facial mode may develop from stage 5 kinesthetic behavior, since visual feedback is often or always absent, as when apes make faces to themselves without a mirror. Thus, while the data are not conclusive, in the Sensory-Motor Intelligence Series, development appears to progress in an ordered stage-by-stage sequence, although an ability in one mode may grow out of an earlier ability in a related mode.

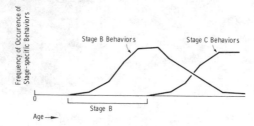

FIGURE 8. The development of a hypothetical stage (stage B) in terms of frequency of stage-specific behaviors.

Based on the Piagetian analysis of communicative and cognitive capacities presented in this paper, it appears that the communicative capacities of adult humans are based on early cognitive potentials in the infant, that mature through a stage-by-stage developmental sequence in which the development of one stage is dependent upon mastery of the previous stage. This appears to be the case, since the stage-to-stage sequential development has been repeatedly observed.[11-13] There are also theoretical reasons for this sequence, since, in the Sensory-Motor Intelligence Series particularly, it is difficult to understand how higher levels of functioning could develop without the lower levels as a basis. For example, it is difficult to imagine how coordinations of several secondary circular reactions (stage 4) could occur before secondary circular reactions themselves (stage 3) had developed. Similarly, it does not seem possible that variable trial-and-error experimentation with the functions of objects, object-object relationships, and object-force relationships (stage 5) could occur before the (stage 3) establishment of relationships between objects and actions, or before coordinations of these simpler behaviors (stage 4) had occurred. Consequently, in the vocal channel it appears that a baby must coo (a secondary circular reaction) before he can babble (a tertiary circular reaction) and that he must babble before he can speak.** Similarly, an ape must presumably possess all the early stage-specific gestural cognitive potentials before he can sign.

Speculations on the Development of Sign Language in Infant Gorillas

Using a Piagetian model, I will venture to predict the ages and specific stage-related abilities and learning mechanisms that gorillas will manifest when taught sign language from an early age—from one month of age or earlier.

An infant gorilla could theoretically begin to learn its first signs through molding during stage 2, between one and three months of age. These early signs would be learned through associations developed through classical conditioning, and would be based on stage 2 capacities for acquired adaptations. However, these signs would occur only in *response* to environmental changes that impinged upon the infant (see TABLE 10).

Between approximately three and seven months of age, based on stage 3 imitative abilities, infants should begin to learn signs through imitation of behaviors already in their repertoires. They should also begin to develop contextual associations for signs already learned by means of modeling or stage 3 imitation through operant conditioning. Learning through operant conditioning would be based on stage 3 sensory-motor abilities to *initiate* semiintentional environmentally oriented behavior combined with stage 2 potential for conditioned learning. Consequently, infants of this age would be expected to *initiate* signing interactions. Furthermore, early manual-gestural "babbling" with signs, based on stage 3 abilities to repeatedly make semi-intentional attempts to effect changes in the environment might begin to appear. For example, they might initiate gestural "games," such as repeatedly making the same gesture or sign that might be responded to in kind by the teacher, thereby making it a game. This early stage 3 babbling would presumably be different from the later stage 4 and 5 babbling that would involve combinations of signs (stage 4) and experimental gestural variability (stage 5).

Between about 7 and 14 months of age, based on stage 4 imitative abilities, infant gorillas should begin to attempt to imitate new motor patterns, though their success may be poor. Based on stage 4 sensory-motor abilities, they may also begin to use familiar signs in new appropriate contexts, such as using a sign to accomplish a predetermined goal, and coordinating goals, contexts, objects, persons and signs. Based on these sensory-motor abilities, they might also begin to occasionally coordinate two signs. During this period, gestural babbling should continue, and should begin to involve combinations of gestures.

Between approximately 14 months and 20 months or more, based on stage 5 imitative abilities, gorillas should begin to successfully imitate signs involving new

---

**Lenneberg,[19-21] states that there is an orderly progression from crying to cooing to babbling in normal infants before they begin to speak. However, Lenneberg, 1968, suggests that children with abnormal trachea, who learn language late, may not pass through these stages. Ervin (Discussion in Lenneberg,[20]) states that Lenneberg found that children suffering from aphasia do recapitulate the normal stages of prelanguage vocalizations as they relearn to speak. There are insufficient data, and the reports are inconclusive. However, observations from this study suggest that it is the *cognitive* aspects that must develop in sequence, not necessarily the articulation; therefore the nature of the sounds in late-developing speech may not resemble cooing, babbling, etc., but *functionally* they may incorporate secondary circular reactions, then coordinations, and then tertiary circular reactions.

TABLE 10

SPECULATIONS ON THE DEVELOPMENT OF SIGN LANGUAGE IN GORILLAS

Stage	Age	Ability	Behavioral Parameters Underlying Specific Abilities
1	0–1 month		
2	1–3 mos.	Signs taught by molding	SMIS* acquired adaptation
		Associations develop through classical Pavlovian conditioning	SMIS acquired adaptation
3	3–<7 mos.	Signs based on own repertoire learned by imitation	IS† purposeful self-imitation
		Associations develop through operant conditioning	SMIS semi-intentional; environmental orientation; acquired adaptation
		Repetitive gestural "babbling" with signs	SMIS semi-intentional; repetitive environmental orientation
		Gestural "games"	SMIS establishes relationships between actions and objects; active attempts to effect environmental changes (in persons)
4	<7–14½ mos.	Attempts to imitate signs involving new motor patterns—matching often poor	IS attempted imitation of new motor patterns
		Uses single familiar signs in new appropriate contexts	SMIS intentional; goal established from the outset; coordination: establishment of relationships between objects (signs and environment)

		Voluntarily initiates environmental changes (behavior of others) using signs	SMIS attributes to others the power to cause change
		Understands the signs of others	SMIS attributes to others the power to cause change
5	14½->20 mos.	Gestural "babbling" continues, with attempts at two-sign combinations	SMIS intentional; goal established from outset; coordinations (relationships and signs)
		Successfully imitates signs involving new motor patterns after repeated attempts	IS imitation of new motor patterns through repeated attempts at matching
		Attempts using signs to effect complex person-person, person-object changes	SMIS intentional; environmental orientation; goal established from outset; behavior variable; repetitive trial & error experimentation; coordination of relationships between persons, objects and signs; understanding of the autonomy of others
		"Babbling" incorporates experimental combinations	SMIS intentional; behavior variable; repetitive trial & error experimentation
6	<18 mos.	Imitates signs involving new motor patterns on first try	IS symbolic imitation of new motor patterns, without matching
		Deferred imitation of new signs	IS deferred imitation
		Mentally figures out new two-sign combinations and uses them in new appropriate contexts on first try	SMIS symbolic invention of new means through mental combinations
		"Babbling" ceases	SMIS symbolic thought becomes prevalent

*SMIS = Sensory-Motor Intelligence Series.
†IS = Imitation Series.

motor patterns, after repeated attempts at matching. Based on stage 5 sensory-motor abilities, they should begin experimenting with signs, producing new two-sign combinations, often to attain goals. They should also begin to communicate *about* object-object, person-person, object-space and object-force relationships. Experimental babbling combinations should also occur, becoming more complex and more innovative as the stage progresses, and regressing as stage 6 is entered.

After about 18 months of age, gorilla infants should begin successfully imitating new signs involving new motor patterns on the first try. Based on stage 6 sensory-motor abilities to symbolize, they should be able to use two-sign combinations in appropriate contexts on the first try.

The sparse data available on the acquisition of sign language in chimpanzees and gorillas support some of these speculations. The Gardners' infant chimpanzees, Moja and Pili, whose sign language training began at birth, learned their first signs at about three months of age, presumably during stage 2,[22] and Fouts reported that another chimpanzee infant, Salome, learned her first sign at about four months.[23] In addition, Fouts[24] and Patterson[25] have found that early sign language acquisition in chimpanzees and gorillas occurs through molding (a stage 2 ability), and not through imitation (which first occurs in stage 3). The Gardners' chimpanzee, Moja, was first recorded as combining two signs at six months of age,[26] and Koko produced her first two-word sign combination when she was 14 months old.[27] Both animals presumably made their first two-sign combinations during stage 4; Moja, whose sign language training began at birth, early in stage 4, and Koko, whose training started at one year, late in stage 4. The Gardners' chimpanzee, Washoe, whose sign language training started at about two years, was observed to use signs learned by delayed imitation (stage 6) by about three years of age.[28]

Sensory Modality and the Organization of Intelligence

The analysis of intelligence in terms of sensory modes indicates that intelligence is not necessarily a global capacity. An organism does not necessarily possess equal intellectual abilities in all sensory modes. Intelligence appears to be mode-specific (though some modes are interrelated), and mode-specific intellectual capacities evidently have different evolutionary histories. In addition, cognitive capacity has different relationships to different anatomical body areas. Stage-specific intellectual capacities that may be expressed through or "understood" in terms of one acting anatomical area need not necessarily be expressed or transferable to another. In other words, an animal may not necessarily be able to demonstrate a cognitive capacity with its voice that it can express with its hands. However, even though the cognitive potentials of at least some of the modalities have evolved independently, it is not clear whether they are still independent in *Homo sapiens*. It is possible that human beings have evolved a capacity for cross-modal transfer resulting in a truly global organization of intelligence, as has been suggested by Geschwind[29] and Lancaster.[30] Further study will be needed to clarify this issue.

The Evolution of Communicative Abilities in Different Sensory Modes

Primatologists often emphasize the multimodality of nonhuman primate communications, as contrasted with a strong reliance on vocal communication, or speech, in *Homo sapiens*. Actually the evolution of communicative capacity is characterized by the evolution of increasing communicative abilities in all sensory modalities. Apes possess greater potential for facial, gestural, and auditory communication than macaques. Unlike macaques, they can make auditory displays, lie with their faces, and use sign language. Humans, in addition to possessing all these advanced abilities of apes, can play music, sing, and speak. Therefore it is misleading to conclude that nonhuman primates have exceptional multimodel communicative abilities, while in humans communicative abilities are mainly vocal. In actuality, nonhuman primates vary in their communicative abilities and should not be lumped, and *Homo sapiens* excels in virtually all communicative modes (except olfaction, which has not been considered in this paper), with vocal abilities in humans being particularly remarkable.

The Generality of These Findings

Despite the small sample of apes upon which this report is based, the kinds of stage-specific behaviors, their sequence of appearance, and the general ages of appearance will probably be replicated in further studies on gorillas. Knoblock and Pasamanick's study on the development of "adaptive" behavior in a hand-reared gorilla from 18 days to 24 months[31] offers some supporting evidence. Behaviors classifiable as stage 3 (one hand approach and grasp and shakes rattle definitely) first appeared at the same age as observed in this study.

Similarly, Goma, hand-reared by Lang from birth to 18 months,[32] demonstrated stage 2 behavior in the Sensory-Motor Intelligence Series (putting her fingers in her mouth) at about six weeks of age, stage 3 behavior (swinging a cloth and watching it; rattling beads) at about three months, stage 4 behavior (coordination of two behaviors—beating a basket and chewing on it; recognizing signs in others—standing up signifying leaving) at about three-and-a-half to four months. Goma also manifested stage 3 imitation (imitating pulling weeds) at eight months of age, and stage 4 imitation (imitating putting a chain around her neck) at nine months.

However, Knoblock and Pasamanick did not note any behaviors classifiable as tertiary circular reaction up to 24 months of age. Yerkes, 1927,[33] also reported little evidence of behavior as classifiable as tertiary circular reactions in the gorilla, Congo, at five years of age, although he subsequently[34] presents numerous examples of tertiary circular reactions in Congo at six years of age. Nor have field workers reported much evidence of gorillas manifesting tertiary circular reactions in the wild.[35] The only references to such behavior being those of Pitman, 1931,[36] and Philipps, 1950,[37] who observed gorillas using sticks to obtain food that was out of reach. This scarcity of data probably occurs because implementation is evidently a late-developing category of tertiary circular reaction, developing some time between two and four years (and possibly later in some subjects), because free-ranging gorillas may only rarely exhibit implementation, since their food is generally immediately available, and because the earlier-developing tertiary circular reactions such as experimentation with object-force and object-space relationships (which free-ranging and captive animals all may display) are less obvious to researchers not working with a Piagetian model. In addition, gorillas have not been as extensively studied as chimpanzees and macaques. Further work should clarify precise ages of appearance and ranges of individual variability. In addition, further observations on the ontogenetic development of behaviors, the development of which has not been observed in this study, could alter the stage classification of some specific behaviors, as the information is gathered on the behavioral parameters of developing behaviors.

These data on gorillas may also pertain to other great apes, chimpanzees (*Pan troglodytes*, and *P. paniscus*) and orangutans (*Pongo pygmaeus*), as 14 animals of these species are also under observation. Though I have fewer data on these other ape species, the stages that have been observed have appeared in the same order, and at roughly the same times as those of gorillas, although I suspect future work will show that the precise ages of appearance of the stages will differ slightly in the different species.

However, while I am confident of the positive data, one must always entertain the possibility that negative data are a product of insufficient observation or inadequate methods. It is possible that future studies of apes will reveal additional abilities.

Negative data from the macaques must again be accepted with reservation, especially since the study on intelligence in stumptail macaques was based on a small sample (three animals). Nevertheless, it is impressive that Parker never saw a secondary or tertiary circular reaction in the visual/gestural mode in 137 hours of observation, and though I was not focusing on intelligence, I never saw one in 500 hours of observation. In contrast, these categories of behavior were frequent among the apes. For example, when Sunshine was well into stage 5, in his nineteenth month, he manifested behaviors incorporating the method of the tertiary circular reaction at an average frequency of 50/hour (with a range of 26–62 per hour). Furthermore, there are few recorded observations in the literature of any behaviors displayed by macaques that could possibly be interpreted as secondary or tertiary circular reactions. The best candidates for such interpretation are the potato-washing and wheat-sifting behaviors reported in Japanese macaques (*Macaca fuscata*),[38-44] the leaf-rubbing behavior reported in wild crab-eating macaques (*M. fascicularis*),[45] by Chiang, and the use of a rake to obtain food by trained captive rhesus macaques (*M. mulatta*) reported by Warden, Koch, and Fjeld.[46] The absence of evidence for macaques using stage 5 trial-and-error experimentation suggests that potato-washing, leaf-sifting, and leaf-rubbing probably originated by chance, through stage 3 linear exploration, rather than through stage 5 experimentation, and the successful associations were probably learned through operant conditioning—a stage 3 linear ability. Evidently, the behaviors were then transmitted through stage 3 imitative mechanisms, since no new motor patterns were learned. The rhesus monkeys who learned to rake in food were probably taught the motor patterns through molding—a stage 2 mechanism—and as training proceeded, the associations may have been facilitated through operant conditioning.[47] Should future studies show that macaques do have some limited ability to perform secondary or even tertiary circular reactions, I suspect the rarity of their occurrence will still stand in striking contrast to the abilities of the great apes; for while apes have repeatedly been reported to perform these kinds of behaviors, both in captivity and in the wild (for a review see Van Lawick-Goodall, 1970),[48] macaques can be observed for hundreds of hours without the observer seeing a single incidence of a secondary or tertiary circular reaction.

While the data presented here on stumptail macaques can probably be generalized to other macaques, since all the macaques are genetically closely related, further research is needed to determine the intellectual capacities of other Old World monkey species, though the scarcity of reports suggesting higher intellectual capacities in these species[49] suggests that they, like stumptail macaques, have little propensity for manifesting higher (stages 3–6) intellectual abilities.

CONCLUSION

Species differences in communicative ability correlate with differences in intellectual capacity. Macaques do not complete any of the stages of the Sensory-Motor

Intelligence Series or the Imitation Series in the gestural and auditory modes, and only some of the first stages of these series in the visual/facial and vocal modes; their communication systems consist primarily of emotional facial expressions and vocalizations. Apes complete the whole Sensory-Motor Intelligence Series and Imitation Series in the gestural modality, but not in the vocal modality; their communication systems include voluntary nonstereotyped gestures, and they are capable of learning sign language—but they cannot learn to speak.

Human infants complete the whole Sensory-Motor Intelligence Series and Imitation Series in the gestural and vocal modalities. These intellectual accomplishments during the Sensory-Motor Period (birth to two years) provide them with the basis for learning the first stages of language and speech, as well as gestural communications and sign language.

ACKNOWLEDGMENTS

I wish to thank the San Francisco Zoological Society, William Mottram, Robert McMorris; the San Diego Zoological Society, Clyde Hill, and James Dolan; Stanford University, and Penny Patterson for providing access to the animals as subjects. I would also like to thank Penny Patterson, John Alcaraz, Richard Cuzoni, and Sue Shrader for the time and effort they so graciously gave to this project.

I thank Sue Parker for her collaboration and for many intellectually stimulating conversations on primate intelligence, which greatly influenced the conception of the study, and for collecting a portion of the data on which this study is based.

I wish to extend thanks to Sherwood Washburn, John Watson, Harriet Oster, Dan Slobin, Susan Sugarman Bell, Jacques Chevalier, and Penny Patterson, who read and made helpful comments on a previous draft of this manuscript.

I thank William Townsend for taking some of the photographs and Harriett Lukes for typing the manuscript.

This research was supported by two grants from the Academic Senate Committee on Research, University of California, San Francisco, and by a grant from the Endowment Fund of the Hooper Foundation, University of California, San Francisco.

REFERENCES

1. BROWN, R. 1973. A First Language. Harvard University Press, Cambridge, Mass.
2. MACNAMARA, J. 1972. Cognitive basis of language learning in infants. Psychol. Rev. **79:** 1–13.
3. SINCLAIR, H. 1971. Sensorimotor action patterns as a condition for the acquisition of syntax. In Language Acquisition: Models and Methods. Proceedings of a C.A.S.D.S. Study Group on "Mechanisms of Language Development" held jointly with the Ciba Foundation, London, May, 1968, being the third study group in a C.A.S.D.S. program on "The Origins of Human Behavior." R. Huxley & E. Ingram, Eds.:121–135. Academic Press. London, England
4. SLOBIN, D. I. 1971. Psycholinguistics. Scott, Foresman and Company. Glenview, Ill.
5. PARKER, S. 1973. Piaget's sensorimotor series in an infant macaque; the organization of nonstereotyped behavior. Unpublished Ph.D. Dissertation, Department of Anthropology, University of California, Berkeley.
6. PARKER, S. Piaget's sensorimotor series in an infant macaque: A model for comparing nonstereotyped behavior and intelligence in human and nonhuman primates. In Bio-Social Development among Primates. S. Chevalier-Skolnikoff & F. E. Poirier, Eds. Garland. New York, N.Y. In press.

7. CHEVALIER-SKOLNIKOFF, S. 1971. The ontogeny of communication in *Macaca speciosa*. Ph.D. Dissertation, University of California, Berkeley.
8. CHEVALIER-SKOLNIKOFF, S. 1973. Visual and tactile communication in *Macaca arctoides* and its ontogenetic development. Am. J. Phys. Anthrop. **38:** 515–518.
9. CHEVALIER-SKOLNIKOFF, S. 1974. Contributions to Primatology: The Ontogeny of Communication in the Stumptail Macaque (*Macaca arctoides*). Vol. 2. S. Karger. Basel, Switzerland.
10. UZGIRIS, I. C. & J. McV. HUNT. 1966. An instrument for assessing infant cognitive development. Unpublished manuscript.
11. PIAGET, J. 1951. Play, Dreams and Imitation in Childhood. Translated by C. Gattegno & F. M. Hodgson. W. W. Norton & Company, Inc. New York, N.Y.
12. PIAGET, J. 1952. The Origins of Intelligence in Children. Translated by Margaret Cook. International Universities Press, Inc. New York, N.Y.
13. PIAGET, J. 1954. The Construction of Reality in the Child. Translated by Margaret Cook. Ballantine Books. New York, N.Y.
14. CHEVALIER-SKOLNIKOFF, S. 1973. Facial expression of emotion in nonhuman primates. *In* Darwin and Facial Expression. P. Ekman, Ed.:11–89. Academic Press. New York, N.Y.
15. CHEVALIER-SKOLNIKOFF, S. 1974. Male-female, female-female, and male-male sexual behavior in the stumptail monkey, with special attention to the female orgasm. Arch. Sex. Behav. **3:** 95–116.
16. FOUTS, R. S. 1972. Use of guidance in teaching sign language to a chimpanzee (*Pan troglodytes*). J. Comp. Physiol. Psychol. **80:** 515–522.
17. HESS, J. P. 1973. Some observations on the sexual behaviour of captive Lowland gorillas, *Gorilla g. gorilla* (Savage and Wyman). *In* Comparative Ecology and Behaviour of Primates. R. P. Michael & J. H. Crook, Eds.:508–580. Academic Press. London, England.
18. HESS, J. P. 1973. 16 mm black and white film, light-sound, duration 30 minutes, available through Swiss Scientific Film Association, Kapellenstrasse 33, 4000 Basel, Switzerland.
19. LENNEBERG, E. H. 1964. Speech as a motor skill with special reference to nonaphasic disorders. Monogr. Soc. Res. Child Dev. **29:** 115–127.
20. LENNEBERG, E. H. 1966. Speech development: Its anatomical and physiological concomitants. *In* Brain Function. Proceedings of the Third Conference, November 1963, on Speech, Language, and Communication. E. C. Carterette, Ed. Vol. III: 37–66. University of California Press, Berkeley and Los Angeles, Ca.
21. LENNEBERG, E. H. 1967. Biological Foundations of Language. John Wiley & Sons, Inc. New York, N.Y.
22. GARDNER, R. A. & B. T. GARDNER. 1975. Early signs of language in child and chimpanzee. Science **187:** 752–753.
23. FOUTS, R. S. 1973. Talking with chimpanzees. *In* Science Year: World Book Science Annual, 1974.:34. Field Enterprises Educational Corporation. Chicago, Ill.
24. FOUTS, R. S. 1975. Personal communication.
25. PATTERSON, P. 1975. Personal communication.
26. ARTICLE. September, 1973. Signs for our time. Cited in P. Patterson.[27]
27. PATTERSON, P. The gestures of a gorilla. *In* Perspectives in Human Evolution. D. Hamburg, J. Goodall & E. McCown, Eds. Benjamine, Inc. Menlo Park, Ca. In press.
28. GARDNER, R. A. & B. T. GARDNER. 1969. Teaching sign language to a chimpanzee: A standardized system of gestures provides a means of two-way communication with a chimpanzee. Science **165:** 664–672.
29. GESCHWIND, N. 1964. The development of the brain and the evolution of language. Monogr. Ser. Lang. Ling. **17:** 155–169.
30. LANCASTER, J. B. 1968. Primate communication systems and the emergence of human language. *In* Primates: Studies in Adaptation and Variability. P. C. Jay, Ed.:439–457. Holt, Rinehart and Winston. New York, N.Y.
31. KNOBLOCK, H. & B. PASAMANICK. 1959. The development of adaptive behavior in an infant gorilla. J. Comp. Physiol. Psychol. **52:** 699–704.
32. LANG, E. M. 1963. Goma, the Gorilla Baby. Doubleday & Company, Inc. Garden City, N.Y.
33. YERKES, R. M. 1927. The mind of a gorilla. Part I. Genetic Psychol. Monogr. **2:** 1–191.

34. YERKES, R. M. 1927. The mind of a gorilla. Part II. Genetic Psychol. Monogr. **2:** 377–551.
35. SCHALLER, G. B. 1963. The Mountain Gorilla. The University of Chicago Press. Chicago, Ill.
36. PITMAN, C. R. S. 1931. A game warden among his charges. London, England. Cited in G. B. Schaller.[35]
37. PHILIPPS, T. 1950. Letter concerning: Man's relation to the apes. Man **272:** 168.
38. FRISCH, J. E. 1968. Individual behavior and intertroop variability in Japanese macaques. *In* Primates: Studies in Adaptation and Variability. P. C. Jay, Ed.:243–252. Holt, Rinehart and Winston. New York, N.Y.
39. ITANI, J. 1958. On the acquisition and propagation of a new food habit in the troop of Japanese monkeys at Takasakiyama. Primates **1:** 84–98. [Eng. transl., *In* Japanese Monkeys, Collection of Translations. K. Imanishi & S. A. Altmann, Eds.:52–65. University of Alberta Press. Edmonton, Canada, 1965.]
40. ITANI, J. & A. NISHIMURA. 1973. The study of infrahuman culture in Japan. Symp. IVth Int. Congr. Primate 1: Precultural Primate Behavior.:26–50. S. Karger. Basel, Switzerland.
41. KAWAI, M. 1965. Newly acquired pre-cultural behavior of a natural troop of Japanese monkeys on Koshima Island. Primates **6:** 1–30.
42. KAWAMURA, S. 1959. The process of sub-culture propagation among Japanese macaques. Primates **2:** 43–60.
43. TSUMORI, A. 1967. Newly acquired behavior and social interactions of Japanese monkeys. *In* Social Communication Among Primates. S. A. Altmann. The University of Chicago Press. Chicago, Ill.
44. YAMADA, M. (KAWABE). 1957. A case of acculturation in the subhuman society of Japanese monkeys. Primates **1:** 30–46.
45. CHIANG, M. 1967. Use of tools by wild macaque monkeys in Singapore. Nature **214:** 1258–1259.
46. WARDEN, C. J., A. M. KOCH & H. A. FJELD. 1940. Instrumentation in cebus and rhesus monkeys. J. Genet. Psychol. **56:** 297–310.
47. CHEVALIER-SKOLNIKOFF, S. 1975. An analysis of primate "protoculture" in terms of the comparative intellectual abilities of macaques, great apes and human beings. Paper read at 74th Annual Meeting of American Anthropological Association, December, 1975, San Francisco, Ca.
48. VAN LAWICK-GOODALL, J. 1970. Tool-using in primates and other vertebrates. *In* Advances in the Study of Behaviour. D. S. Lehrman, R. A. Hinde & E. E. Shaw, Eds. Vol. 3: 195–249. Academic Press. New York, N.Y.
49. BECK, B. B. 1974. Baboons, chimpanzees, and tools. J. Hum. Evolut. **3:** 509–516.
50. SUGARMAN BELL, S. In press. Some organizational aspects of preverbal communication. *In* Language in Social Context. I. Markova, Ed. Wiley International Publishers, Ltd. London, England.
51. SPITZ, R. A. (In collaboration with W. Godfrey Cobliner) 1965. The First Year of Life: A Psychoanalytic Study of Normal and Deviant Development of Object Relations. International Universities Press, Inc. New York, N.Y.
52. WOLFF, P. 1963. The natural history of a family. *In* Determinants of Infant Behaviour II. Proceedings of the Second Tavistock Seminar on Mother-infant Interaction Held Under the Auspices of the Ciba Foundation at the House of the Royal Society of Medicine, London, September, 1961. B. M. Foss, Ed.:139–167. Methuen & Co., Ltd. London, England.
53. HURLOCK, E. B. 1950. Child Development. McGraw-Hill Book Company, Inc. New York, N.Y.
54. McELROY, C. W. 1972. Speech and Language Development of the Preschool Child. Charles C Thomas. Springfield, Ill.
55. ERVIN-TRIPP, S. 1966. Language development. *In* Review of Child Development Research. L. W. Hoffman & M. L. Hoffman, Eds. Vol. 2:55–105. Russell Sage Foundation. New York, N.Y.

THE DEVELOPMENT OF LANGUAGE AS PURPOSIVE BEHAVIOR

Ernst von Glasersfeld

Department of Psychology
University of Georgia
Athens, Georgia 30602

Yerkes Regional Primate Research Center
Atlanta, Georgia 30322

We have come to this meeting to discuss Origins and Evolution of Language and Speech. The two conjunctions in the title indicate that we are dealing with a composite subject. The items in each pair are certainly related, but they are also different. At the risk of being considered a nit-picker, I shall pursue these differences for a moment. Formulating them has helped me a great deal to clear my head and will, I hope, justify some of the things I am going to say later.

To begin, we may say that there could hardly have been an evolution of speech, or language, if there had not been an origin. We can even generalize and say that there is no evolution without an origin. When we think in terms of the *theory* of evolution, we tend to focus on the way it functions, and then it seems quite natural that it must have been operative from the very beginning. Yet, it is fairly clear that for something to evolve, something must be there—and this something would be called the source, or the *origin*, of everything that evolved from it. I am not making this point in order to stir a metaphysical wasp's nest. I am making it because I believe it has to be made if we are to understand one another. "The origin of speech" refers to an item, an event, or a state of affairs, which we consider to have been the starting point for the "evolution of speech." When we say "speech," we inevitably have in mind vocal sounds that have a certain function—not just incidental vocal noises that are produced in a haphazard way. Yet, to have an *evolution* of speech, a species must have been producing haphazard vocal noises, the raw material, as it were, that could then acquire the function of speech. This raw material is at the origin, and the subsequent changes, transformations, and additions that eventually brought it to what we now call "speech," is its evolution. We could, of course, also investigate how that species came to produce haphazard vocal noises; but if we included that study under the heading "evolution of speech," we should have to include the study of how that species came to have the physiological structures that happen to produce noise, and so on, I'm afraid, right back to a study of how anything came to be alive. A theorist, as Hebb once suggested,[1] is in one way like a bricklayer: if he wants to get on with his building, he has to accept bricks as bricks. If he becomes interested in the structure of bricks and how they are made, he ceases to be a bricklayer. So much for the distinction between origin and evolution.

With the two terms of the second pair in our title, things may not go so smoothly. For a considerable time, linguists have implicitly and even explicitly equated "language" with "speech." They did so quite naturally because "language" had always implied human language, and human language was presumed to have manifested itself in speech long before it found other channels, such as hieroglyphs and alphabets. But there is another, less ingenuous reason. The bulk of linguistic research, having chosen to follow Bloomfield—rather than Sapir, his teacher—developed a militant disregard for the *function* of the phenomenon it was studying.

Interest was focused on those manifestations that could be called directly observable or physical. Phonology thrived, and semantics, the study of meaning, which is at the core of the communicatory function of language, was thwarted.[2] Maybe it was necessary to follow that narrow path almost to its dead end, before one could begin to take to heart Sapir's admonition that a speech-sound, "even when associated with the particular movements of the 'speech organs' that are required to produce it, is very far from being an element of language. It must be further associated with some element or group of elements of experience, say a visual image or a class of visual images or a feeling of relation, before it has even rudimentary linguistic significance."[3] Today we have a rather well-developed theory of communication that should help us to keep apart *signals*, such as speech-sounds and other transmittable and perceivable items, from the messages or meanings to which they are linked by a given code. From this point of view, then, *speech* would be a collective term for the vocal signals humans use *to transmit messages*; the messages, on the other hand, are the meaning or content that is semantically tied to the signals, and it is only when we consider this whole complex of signals, semantic nexus, and meaning, that we should use the term *language*. As a system of communication, language is not at all restricted to vocal signals but can be implemented by visual or tactual signals (e.g. American Sign Language, braille, etc.).

Although many of you may not be inclined to accept so radical a division, some such division has to be made, if we want to investigate the *evolution* of language. For if we maintained that language is no more than the production of certain sounds, we should inevitably get into the embarrassing position of having to concede that a parrot or a minah bird that has a repertoire of a dozen sentences differs from us only quantitatively, in that he can make fewer speech-sounds or combinations of sounds than we can. Though that is probably true enough, we could not help feeling that there is some qualitative difference as well. The difference, I suggest, is that, no matter what the bird *says*, he is not *telling* us anything; which is to say, he is not sending a message.[4] That is why, whatever the bird says, our response is likely to be "Amazing!" or "How clever!" We ourselves, on the other hand, would be concerned, to say the least, if under normal circumstances (i.e., excepting foreign-language lessons and certain cocktail parties) all our utterances elicited that kind of response and no other.[5] Our concern would be similar in kind (but not in degree) to the concern we feel when we turn the steering wheel of our car and the car continues to move in a straight line; i.e., when an activity we have learned to consider instrumental in achieving a certain result suddenly fails to achieve that result. It is in this sense that communication must be considered "instrumental," "goal-directed," and therefore "purposive."[6]

In a later section of this paper I shall try to show that the semantic connection between signals and their meanings, though a necessary condition, is in itself not a sufficient condition for the application of the term "language." For the moment, the point I want to make is that, just as we cannot have evolution without a raw material that can evolve, we cannot have speech without the development of language, and we could not have language unless there was something to be communicated and a motive for communicating it.[7] And since we are speaking of evolution in terms of an established theory, we must also assume that the ability to communicate did in some way enhance the survival of organisms that developed it. If these two assumptions are to have any theoretical (let alone practical) value, we shall have to show that there is a way of thinking about prelinguistic organisms that strips any miraculous aspect from the appearance of language and explains it as just one more step in the natural evolution of complex survival mechanisms.

Purpose and Negative Feedback

I have deliberately introduced the term "communication" in the context of the modern *theory* of communication,[8] because if we do not carefully restrict its meaning there will be no end to our misunderstanding. The literature of animal communication, for instance, is a blatant example of how human communication breaks down when the central term in a discussion remains, as Sebeok has recently said, "an undefined prime."[9] One of the reasons why "communication" was either left thoroughly opaque, or defined with such generality as to include *any* kind of organismic interaction,[10] is that the concept of "purpose" had been declared out-of-bounds for scientific explanation. The reaction to Aristotelian teleology had been so vigorous and sweeping that many of the arbiters who decided what was to be "scientific" and what not, failed to notice that some scientists were creating a new approach to teleology and that purposiveness of which we are all subjectively aware.

In 1943, Rosenblueth, Wiener, and Bigelow published their pioneering paper that provided not only a hard definition of "purpose" but also an extremely successful model for the actual construction of "goal-seeking" devices.[11] Three years later, in a conference sponsored by the same Academy that has called our meeting, Wiener explained the function of "negative feedback" with an example of a grasping motion: "I regulate my motion by the amount by which my task is not yet accomplished. This makes it possible to accomplish the same task regardless of my initial position and the object to be picked up."[12] A remembered "image" or "representation" of the picked-up object is the goal in this example. A comparison between it and the sensory signals that indicate the actual situation gives rise to negative feedback, i.e., an error-signal, by means of which the motion of the hand can be adjusted. The gist of Wiener's contribution is this formulation of the feedback loop, which demonstrated that purposive behavior could come about without infringing the principle that says no organism "can call on the future to influence the past."[13]

It was precisely the lack of a functional model, such as a feedback system, that had compelled Hofstadter, a few years earlier, to ascribe only descriptive but not explanatory power to his brilliant analysis of "objective teleology."[14] The subsequent development of control theory and the application of the feedback model in the study of cognitive behavior give Hofstadter's logical exposition an almost prophetic quality. He sums up his description of objectively observable teleology: "Thus *the unitary attribute of the teleological actor is not the possession of end alone, or sensitivity alone, or technique alone, but of all three in inseparable combination*." (Hofstadter's italics.) He goes on to say that "although they can not be separated in the unitary attribute, they may nevertheless be analyzed out independently by the use of a plurality of acts of the same agent."[15] If we substitute the modern cyberneticist's terms for the three components, we have *reference value* (for "end"), *sensory function* (for "sensitivity"), and *effector function* (for "technique"). That is to say, we have the three components of the basic feedback loop which, we know, can never be constituted by anything less than these three components, because the operation of the loop depends on their circular arrangement in which there is no one point that we can isolate as initial cause, nor one that we can isolate as terminal effect. It is a unitary arrangement in the way it *functions* and not only in the way in which we describe it; and since it has been implemented in functioning mechanisms, we can hardly deny its explanatory power.

An activity, thus, will be called "purposive" if it serves to reduce or eliminate the discrepancy (negative feedback) between the value of a sensory signal and the reference value in such a "teleological" unit. Clearly this is a way of looking at behavior that is in one important point very different from the traditional behaviorist view. While S-R theories (with or without mediating links) posit a linear connection between sensory stimulus and behavioral output, in a feedback system it is never the sensory input itself that determines the output of a behavior, but its difference from the relevant reference value. (Which, if that should be necessary, explains why food is not much of a "reinforcer" for a well-fed animal.)

The simple feedback loop, of course, can serve as a model only for the simplest kinds of behavior, such as avoidance, seeking, and pursuit of conditions that are characterized by a single one-dimensional reference value each. Several such loops, with different sensory functions, may be found in one organism, but that does not raise the functionally primitive level of that organism's behavior. Two important features have to be added if feedback theory is to provide models for more complex behaviors. The first is an hierarchical arrangement of feedback loops, such that the reference value of one loop can be set and changed by the effector function of another. Systems of that kind have been described by DuBrul,[17] Ashby,[18] MacKay,[19] and recently, in great detail, by Powers.[16] The technical intricacies do not concern us here. The important point is that a system of that kind, if it is equipped with some sort of memory that records "disturbances" (sensory signals that do *not* match the reference value), "activities" (effector functions), and such "perceptual" changes (sensory functions) as occur within a specified space of time *after* an activity, then it can begin to optimize reactions to disturbances on the basis of what-has-followed-what in the past. At that stage, the system, in fact, has already the basic components that are required for "learning" or, as Maturana would say, to operate as an *inductive* system.[20] For induction, whether it is conscious in the form of a conclusion we draw, or unconscious in the form of a behavior that becomes established because of its success, springs always from the same root: a more or less regular recurrence in past experience.

A human observer of such a "learning organism," who experiences the organism and its environment as separate entities, can say that the organism is adapting its behavior to the environment. From the point of view of the kind of system we have described, however, there is no possibility of discriminating an environment, because all the system can so far do is associate or correlate neural signals.

Though it might be tempting to see what epistemological conclusions we could draw from this cybernetic model about the "reality" of what we perceive as *our* environment,[21] we had better pursue the evolution such a model would have to undergo to achieve the capability of communication. Rather than attempt to spell out that evolution step by step—which seems quite impossible, given the present state of the art—let us ask what further capabilities an organism would have to have in order to develop behaviors that we, the observers, would call "communicatory."

LEARNING AND REPRESENTATION

Using its "inductive" method of exploiting regularities of the past in order to employ, in the case of a specific disturbance, the particular activity that has most often eliminated that disturbance, presupposes the capability of coordinating "data" that originate in different channels. The simplest discrimination tasks require such a capability, for whenever we say that an organism has *learned* a certain response, it implies that the organism has associated a given stimulus (event in a sensory channel) with a behavior (event in an effector channel or, to be more precise, a "reafferent" channel). We know very well that relatively primitive organisms can do that. We also know that the stimuli to which these organisms react (especially in the wild) are frequently not single perceptual signals but compounds of several features, such as color, sound, smell, and so on. That means that the organism is already able to coordinate neural signals from different *sensory* channels. Besides, it must be able to record or in some way maintain these patterns of coordination, for there is no doubt that it can learn to recognize them when they crop up again. In fact, most of an organism's learning and individual adaptation to its environment would seem to be dependent on such a capability.

From the observer's point of view, the organism can now not only discriminate but also recognize objects. This recognition of objects (which is not to be confounded with Piaget's more demanding paradigm of "object permanence") manifests itself in the fact that the organism has learned to respond with specific behaviors to specific objects and does so in a reasonably reliable way whenever it perceives them. Objects, and the behavioral responses that have become associated with them, will fall into several different classes: objects that are usually eaten, objects that are actively avoided, objects that are climbed on, and so on. For the observer, all these objects are clearly in the organism's environment. For the organism, however, there cannot be any such thing as an "environment." It operates with clusters of sensory signals that have been coordinated because they were in some way relevant to the reduction or elimination of a disturbance in some feedback loop. They have no "existence" in their own right. They are part and parcel of a cluster of activities that have been compounded because, in the past, they effectively counteracted a disturbance. In other words, what the observer calls an "object" is for the organism an inseparable component of an activity cluster. Nevertheless, at this point the stage is set for a momentous step that opens the way to a new kind of operation. No doubt, this step, like every other in the process of evolution, is fostered by the selective pressure of the environment; but for the functioning of the organism, it constitutes a discrete novelty like the opening of a new pathway in its processor.

An object, a cluster of sensory signals, now becomes a reference item in its own right. It sets up its own feedback loop, and this feedback loop, in the same "inductive" manner as the established ones, begins to select activities that are effective in transforming a somewhat different cluster of *actual* sensory signals (i.e., a "percept") until it matches the reference item. In order to become a reference item, the object has to be cut loose from its original context, where it was a more or less relevant *sensory* adjunct to an activity cluster, and it must become something very like a "representation." This is the same development that every normal child goes through on his way to acquiring the concept of "object permanence," when he begins to "externalize" his perceptual constructs.[22] Operationally this transfer is perhaps not so astonishing. The learning process already required that the organism be able to retrieve a recorded action program and to implement it in an effector channel as an actual activity. The transfer of a recorded cluster of sensory signals to a channel other than the one in which the cluster originated is no different in principle. The revolutionary aspect is that this cluster of sensory signals is now placed in the position of a reference value and that the feedback loop which it controls becomes a phase in the activity cycle of an already operating feedback loop. To use a fashionable word, it becomes "embedded" in another loop, and, whenever it is called into action, its specific reference item temporarily supersedes the reference value of that other loop.

DuBrul has expressed the same idea in somewhat different terms: "Information from a new monitoring feedback circuit has captured the final common path."[17] He proposes a neurological hypothesis as to how such a development might come about. I am in no way competent to evaluate its plausibility. Instead, I shall cite a well-known example to show that some such development must have taken place: the termite-fishing chimpanzees that Jane van Lawick-Goodall has filmed.[23] The remarkable thing, there, is not that a chimpanzee, at some time, incorporated the use of a twig into the presumably already established activity chain (or program) of termite-finding and -eating. Such incorporation of items, modifying or extending an organism's repertoire, must obviously happen very frequently. But when the chimpanzee "chooses" a twig, breaks it from the shrub, strips off the leaves, and takes it to the termite heap, where it is going to be used for "fishing," then a totally new feedback loop controlling the *modification* of the twig has been embedded in the larger loop that controls the finding and eating of termites. It does not matter much if the activities that are now put into the service of the subsidiary feedback loop had already been coordinated and recorded as program in some other operational chain. What does matter is that they are now detached from that original chain (say, tearing leaves off a branch in order to eat them) and inserted into an activity chain where they reduce feedback that is negative in relation to a different reference value (tearing off leaves in order to transform a twig into a stick-like tool).[24] The reference item of this embedded loop is also qualitatively different from those of the primary loops, in that it is constituted by an individually coordinated cluster of perceptual signals and not by one of the original homeostatic values that control the organism's biological functions. In this sense we could, indeed, call this new reference item and the cycle it controls "artificial."

I do not intend to suggest that in the course of evolution, tool-making is necessarily the first complex activity that requires the embedding process and a representational capability as part of an organism's operational repertoire. There may well be others, but in tool-making examples, such as the "fishing twig," the requirement is particularly clear because the chimp's manifest assessment of shape, length, and flexibility of the twig is not guided by a perceptually present model.

THE COMMUNICATION SITUATION

What I have called a "momentous step," then, consists of the acquisition of two operational possibilities. One, the embedding of one feedback loop in another; and, two, the creation of a reference item that is, in fact, a representation, i.e., a cluster of recorded signals which, though originally composed of perceptual material, is no longer dependent on signals in the channels of sensory perception.

Both these capabilities are certainly necessary for communicatory behavior. But even if we can show that an organism has acquired them, their mere presence does not explain the emergence of communication. This can become plausible only if we can envisage situations in which development of the new capability would constitute a significant advantage. In addition, the envisaged situations must be plausible in the light of what can actually be observed.

Before trying to conjure up such a plausible situation, let me put into exact focus the activity whose emergence we are looking for. Fifty years ago, Malinowski said: "Speech is the necessary means of communion; it is the one indispensable instrument for creating the ties of the moment without which unified social action is impossible."[25] Cherry, in his classic work, adopted this point when he defined the term "communication": "The establishment of a social unit from individuals, by the use of language or signs. The sharing of common sets of rules, for various goal-seeking activities."[26] He adds that there are many "shades of opinion," but even so, one might assume that the many authors who have cited him as an authority on communication would not altogether disagree with his definition. Since I have the impression that this is not so, I quote another passage from Malinowski that expresses the point I want to make even more clearly: "In its primitive uses, language functions as a link in concerted human activity, as a piece of human behavior. It is a mode of action and not an instrument of reflection."[27] Malinowski, as a rule, makes no distinction between "language" and "speech" and rarely uses the term "communication." In the present context, that does not matter, because what he says of language goes for communication as well. I should also like to stress that, although once "language" *has* developed, it will quickly acquire its function as an "instrument of reflection" and an almost indispensable tool of thought, this function can hardly be held responsible for its evolutionary inception.

According to this view, communicatory behavior is a *mode of action*, its function is to link concerted activity, and it is indispensable, because without these links there could be no *unified social action*. Thus it is an *instrument*, which is to say, a *tool*. Malinowski also gives a number of examples. The natives of the Trobriand Islands, whom he studied, go fishing, and they use large nets that have to be spread by a number of men in several canoes. Their action has to be coordinated and synchronized. The men's hands are busy, so they have no choice but to communicate by vocal signals. It seems clear that this kind of concerted activity could not have been developed *without* a communication capability. The example, of course, in no way demonstrates the origin of communication, but it does show the kind of situation in which the ability to communicate makes possible activities that enhance survival and that, under certain circumstances, might even become crucial for survival. On the strength of that, we might tentatively say that communicatory behavior *could* develop in situations where cooperation requires not merely the additive activity of several individuals but some form of sequencing, or organization, in the sense of a division of tasks. The communication experiment of Mason and Hollis shows that this is indeed possible and does happen.[28] Rhesus monkeys developed their own signals to inform a partner monkey of the location of food which the first monkey could see but not reach, while the partner could reach but not see it. Although the experiment is an elegant demonstration of the monkeys' communicatory potential, we cannot derive anything beyond that for an evolutionary hypothesis. The necessity of cooperation was contrived and utterly unlike any need for cooperation that might arise in a natural setting.

I do not know whether there is any real evidence for the spontaneous inception of collaborative behavior among relatively sophisticated organisms. There are, of course, anecdotes, but they amount to nothing compared to the wealth of documentation we have on aggressive, agonistic, and competitive behavior. Yet, from the point of view of the feedback model, there would seem to be only a small operational difference between the development of cooperation and that of antagonism.

A Possible Beginning of Cooperation

Having described an organism as a hierarchical system of feedback loops, in each of which certain activities have been "inductively" selected as effective, it is not too difficult to envisage situations where the accidental addition of a new element could lead to a novel function. Whenever a number of individuals of the same species share, for instance, a hunting area, the following episode, as seen by an observer, may not be unlikely: an individual pursuing a prey does not get to making the kill, because another individual has come upon the scene and successfully killed the prey. If no already acquired behavior patterns prevent them from sharing the prey, both individuals will feed on it. If we translate this sequence of events into the terms of the feedback model, we get somewhat different operational sequences for the two individuals. For the *second* one, a "normal" well-established cycle has run off: an internal disturbance, "hunger," has led to certain activities and they have been effective once more, in that they resulted in eating behavior which successfully eliminated the original disturbance. For the *first* individual, however, there is an anomaly. The episode also begins with "hunger" as originating disturbance, which leads to the well-established sequence of activities, but the "normal" course of the sequence is impeded, some of the activities are frustrated. Yet their result—eating behavior that eliminates the original disturbance—is nevertheless achieved. Since it is a basic feature of a learning feedback system that it records its activities and consequent changes of disturbances, the anomalous activity chain will be recorded as a thoroughly effective one. In the place of the impeded activities, however, the record will contain some elements that have never before been associated with the activity chain that is controlled by the "hunger" disturbance. These novel elements, for instance (in observer language), "approaching and making contact with a conspecific individual," may already have been coordinated as components of some other activity chain. If the episode recurs and repeatedly leads to the elimination of the "hunger" disturbance, it must become an operational alternative to the original activity chain controlled by the nutritional feedback loop. Preying in pairs and groups will be the result, and with this, the necessary conditions for the development of cooperative preying will have been created. On the other hand, if in that same episode, the first individual is prevented not only from making the kill, but also from feeding on the prey, the sequence of activities will be recorded as a "failure." In this case the novel elements, i.e., the activities involving the conspecific, are associated with the failure and will lead to avoidance or to competitive behavior in the future.

In both cases, what has happened is similar to the transfer of the twig-stripping activity of the chimpanzee's ordinary feeding cycle to his "termite-fishing" cycle. The transfer in our hypothetical case would be more probable, if anything, because the perceptual item involved (i.e., another organism of the species) would certainly have been coordinated into a recognizable object very early in the organism's ontogenic development, and is perhaps already well established as an object in its own right. By this I mean that a cluster of sensory signals, first coordinated as a recurrent pattern in the context of a specific activity, has been recognized in the context of other activity cycles and has thus come much closer to becoming an externalized "permanent object."

Similar episodes will happen in defense against predators. Whenever one individual acts and, by his activity, reduces not only his own disturbance but also the disturbance of other individuals, this will inevitably lead to the formation of relatively cohesive groups, because the reduction of disturbance in these very simple situations will be reciprocal for some time. Organism A today happens to be instrumental for B, and tomorrow B is instrumental for A. Once this begins to take place, it is highly probable that particularly efficient individuals are more often the actor who reduces the common disturbance and thus become the focus of the group's cohesion—with all the implications for the gradual development of dominance and patterns of social equilibration.[29]

At the same time, however, the situation of reciprocal instrumentality has the potential of developing into collaboration. Its realization on a scale greater than the accidental synchronization and integration of the actions of two individuals may well require a drastic change in the environment that suddenly creates a serious and persistent disturbance in many or all of the individuals. Among humans, crises that dramatically increase collaborative efforts are a commonplace. Theoretically, it would seem extremely probable that, if environmental pressure rises for a species that has already evolved the operational mechanisms I have outlined, the cooperative situations will become more frequent and they will quickly come to involve more than two individuals. And once that stage has been reached, it will not take long before some form of communication will arise.[30] It would be communication by means of *ad hoc* signs, similar, perhaps, to the idiosyncratic signs invented by the monkeys in the Mason and Hollis experiment. In the natural environment it is, however, likely that such *ad hoc* signs will be extremely difficult to discriminate and recognize for the human observer.[31] But whatever their individual form and mode of transmission, they would be genuine communicatory signs, because operationally they have the same purposive instrumental function and status as the "termite-fishing" tool of the chimpanzee.

SIGNS, SYMBOLS, AND LANGUAGE

Communicatory signs are, of course, still very far from language. The distance between the two tends to be obscured by the widespread gratuitous application of the term "language" to a variety of behavioral manifestations that should be classified as signaling systems because they show none of the characteristics that we normally expect in a language. If we are to investigate the development of language it will be indispensable that we assess that distance and specify what intermediary points are necessary to bridge it. Before we can do this, however, we shall have to adjust some of the concepts that have been used in attempts to describe language *without* reference to its purposive instrumental function.

Charles Hockett's "design features" (DF) are probably the most elaborate scheme to specify the characteristics of human language, and since they have been widely discussed in the literature, I shall use them as points of departure. They originated as a set of 13 descriptive criteria that were to help an observer to recognize "language" when he found it.[32] Since they were first shaped in an attempt to characterize *spoken* human language, they explicitly exclude all communication systems that are not implemented in a VOCAL-AUDITORY CHANNEL (DF 1). Other design features (DF's 2, 3, 4, 5, 9) concerning the purely technical aspects of signals, transmission, and reception, strengthen this somewhat anthropocentric restriction. The remaining 7 DF's, however, focus on characteristics of communication systems in general, and they constitute a very valuable approximation to the criteria we should want to use in order to distinguish communication from interaction, and language from signaling systems. The first of these, DF6, is SPECIALIZATION, by which Hockett intends that a sign is constituted, not by the mere energy change that is transmitted (i.e., the *physical* signal) but by the informational or semiotic content the physical signal carries. This point, first formulated by Wiener and later applied to animal communication by Haldane,[33] has been accepted, as far as I know, by everyone who has come to investigate communication. It is an indispensable point because it rules out any form of direct mechanical interaction in which the receiver's reaction (or consequent state) can be thermodynamically accounted for in terms of the amount of energy received. Hockett's formulation, however, does not help us to discriminate communicatory signs from others that are no more than a perceptual event from which an observer draws an inductive inference (e.g., the sight of smoke, from which he infers the presence of a fire; or a thundering sound, from which he infers a stampeding herd and that he had better get out of the way). If such inductive inference is not excluded, "communication" becomes a vacuous term. There have been many attempts to patch the leak with subsidiary criteria, but none has proved satisfactory.[34] It does not seem possible as long as one refuses to consider the basic purposive nature of communicatory signs. Susanne Langer analyzed this problem long ago,[35] and the definitions she provided for "natural" and "artificial" signs are applicable to animal communication with only a very minor change.[36]

The fact that communicatory signs must be related to their meaning, not by an inferred connection (causal, correlational, part-whole, etc.), but by an altogether different kind of link, is partially implied by Hockett's DF 7 and DF 8, SEMANTICITY and ARBITRARINESS. But the discussion in which he states that English words such as "unicorn" or "and" *lack* obvious semantic ties, shows that his SEMANTICITY is derived from the traditional theory of reference, which requires "real" objects as referents. The semanticity of signs is, indeed, an essential condition for communication, but the only limitation on the semantic ties and the items which they link to signs is that they must be the same for all users of the sign; i.e., their use must be *conventional*. This is inevitably so for all artificial signs, if they satisfy the condition of ARBITRARINESS (DF 8), which prescribes that the meaning of a sign must *not* be derived from some perceptual analogy, or "iconic" relation, to the item it signifies (such that it could be inferred from the physical characteristics of the sign). This condition entails that a prospective communicator has no way of acquiring the proper use of a sign, except by agreement with the other users (when the sign is being newly created) or by learning it from them through CULTURAL TRANSMISSION (DF 12). I can see no reason why specific signs and their semantic content should not be passed on by *genetic* transmission. This seems particularly plausible in the case of signs that originated as "incipient movements,"[37] i.e., as a part of a chain of movements that comes to signify the whole sequence (e.g., a resting dominant male's raising its head *as though* it were about to get up and charge). Once such an incipient behavior is performed, not as the first step of the sequence to which it belonged, but as a means of obtaining the result of the *whole* chain (e.g., to restore the desired distance when another individual has come too close), it is on the way to becoming an "artificial" sign. In Hockett's terminology it would, of course, be an iconic sign, but from the point of view of communication theory it is irrelevant whether the semantic link between sign and meaning is iconic or arbitrary—what matters is that this relation is a conventional one and thus, by definition, the same for sender and receiver.

Hockett's DF 10, DISPLACEMENT, is one of the two most relevant for the characterization of *linguistic* communication. He explicates it by saying: "We can talk about things that are remote in time, space, or both from the site of the communicative transaction."[38] Once more we agree, but the statement covers only half of what a viable criterion of "language" would have to contain. It is the remnant of the stimulus-response dogma that cripples this DF: the implication that a linguistic expression or sign cannot be used unless it refers to a specific occurrence (instance) of its "referent." Though at one time Hockett says that DISPLACEMENT implies "the ability to discuss today what happened yesterday or what may come to pass tomorrow," he then explains it it in terms of information storage, and states: "Any delay between the reception of a stimulus and the appearance of the response means that the former has been coded into a stable spatial array, which endures at least until it is read off in the response."[39] If we can read off today (response) what will be encoded tomorrow (stimulus), then the future would, indeed, be determining the present. Not for a moment would I suggest that this is what Hockett intended. But I *would* suggest that it comes out that way because he was bent on avoiding terms such as "concept" or "representation." They would have smacked of mentalism or, worse, teleology—and that was taboo.

Language allows us to talk, not only about things that are remote in time and/or space, but also about things that are nowhere and never happen at all. DISPLACE-

MENT has to become "symbolicity." To turn into a symbol, the sign's one-to-one relation to a perceptual "referent" must be severed.[40] That is to say, the sign must be semantically tied to a representation that is independent of the perceptual signals available at any time (not only at the time and place of the sign's use). Thus, the semanticity of a *linguistic* sign is constituted, not by a tie that links it to a "thing," but by one that links it to a representation or concept.[35] The fact that a sign, be it verbal or nonverbal, has acquired symbolicity, does of course not preclude that it still be used as a perception-bound sign whenever there is a perceptual input that corresponds to the representation it designates; nor does it preclude that it be used by the sender to trigger a conventional active response in the receiver (as in the case of an "imperative"). But what gives a sign the status of symbol is that it *can* be used without such a "stimulus" and without triggering the active response. The sign for tiger, for instance, will be a symbol when it can be used without reference to a present, past, or future perceptual instance of a tiger and without the receiver taking such steps as he would if he did perceive a tiger.

The difference between symbolicity and displacement comes out clearly if we look at the "language of the bees."[41] In Hockett's terms, the bees' signs ("dancing") *always* manifest DISPLACEMENT, because their messages concern distant locations.[42] In my terms, the bees do not qualify for symbolicity, because they have never been observed to communicate about distances, directions, food sources, etc., without actually coming from, or going to, a specific location.

The last feature (DF 11) that is essential for the characterization of "language" is OPENNESS (or "productivity"). "New linguistic messages are coined freely and easily, and, in context, are usually understood." The technical particular that provides for OPENNESS is DUALITY OF PATTERNING (DF 13), i.e., the fact that the sign system shows "patterning in terms of arbitrary but stable meaningless signal-elements and also patterning in terms of minimum meaningful arrangements of these elements."[38] The first of these two patternings concerns the composition of *signals*, i.e., the physical sign-vehicles. Hockett would call "language" only those communication systems that use a compositional code in which signals are assembled out of smaller recurrent units (phonemes, cenemes, etc.). This characteristic clearly is of enormous importance if we consider the economy of a coding system. From the evolutionary point of view it constitutes a spectacular advance. It involves the acquisition of special signal-composition mechanisms and, consequently, an increase of operational complexity and memory space. As a criterion, it would exclude semiotic systems that have no alphabet and use only ideograms. From the communication point of view, this seems an unnecessary restriction.

The second type of patterning covered by DUALITY, however, is indispensable as a criterion to distinguish linguistic systems from other sign systems. To be considered a "language," a system must "provide certain patterns by which these elementary significant units (morphemes or meaningful signals) can be combined into larger sequences, and conventions governing what sort of meanings emerge from the arrangements. These patterns and conventions are the *grammar* of the language."[39] Though linguists have tended to consider "syntax" merely a set of rules that govern the combinability of words (i.e., signals), Hockett makes clear that the crucial point is that *new meanings* emerge from the combining of signs. Thus, in addition to the conventions that establish and fix the meaning of individual signs (lexical semantics), there must be a second set of conventions (grammar) that establishes and fixes the semantic function of sign combinations (syntactic or relational semantics). Since the single meaningful signs that are available to the user at a given time are always a closed set (lexicon), OPENNESS can be achieved only by the rule-governed meaningful combination of the available signs.

To sum up this discussion of linguistic communication, I would suggest three criteria to distinguish "language," all of which are necessary but individually insufficient:

1) There must be a set (lexicon) of communicatory signs, i.e., perceptual items whose meaningfulness (SEMANTICITY) is constituted by a conventional tie (semantic nexus) and not by an inferential one.
2) These signs must be symbols, i.e., linked to representations (SYMBOLICITY); therefore they *can* be sent without reference to perceptual instances of the items they designate, and received without "triggering" a behavioral response in the receiver. As symbols they merely activate the connected representation.
3) There must be a set of rules (GRAMMAR) governing the combination of signs into strings, such that certain combinations produce a new semantic content in addition to the individual content of the component signs.

Conclusion

In the preceding sections I have presented some ideas and definitions which, I believe, are essential for an investigation of the evolution of language from a communication-theoretical point of view. To conclude this sketch, I should like to sum up the salient points and, in doing so, show very briefly how they might be fitted into a more or less coherent hypothesis.

To discuss "Origins and Evolution of Speech and Language" it has to be made clear that evolution requires a raw material at its origin and that "speech" and "language" refer to different parts of a communication process. Restricting "speech" to designate the specific signal-system that uses an acoustic channel and human vocal-auditory transmission and reception apparatus, I defined "language" as a semiotic system with three criterial characteristics: A *lexicon* of signs, *symbolicity*, and a *grammar* that governs semantically productive combination. Linguistic communication, thus, is a more sophisticated system than communication by simple signs, regardless of the mode of transmission and the physical aspects of the signals. For speech to evolve, there had to be organisms producing incidental sounds at the origin. For language to evolve, there had to be organisms with a certain information-processing capability and, above all, with something to communicate.

The organism is seen as an hierarchical organization of feedback loops, the "primitive" and oldest of which control chains of activities that have been "inductively" selected for their effectiveness in eliminating disturbances relative to reference values that control the organism's basic biological functions.

An analysis of tool-making shows that it requires the operational capability, in the active organism, to isolate recorded clusters of sensory signals and to detach them from the original chain in order to set them up as reference values of a new feedback loop that becomes embedded in an existing one. This detaching of recorded sensory coordinations constitutes the formation of a *representation* and is the cybernetic equivalent of Piaget's analysis of the ontogeny of the "permanent object" concept.

If the meaning of linguistic signs is always a representation, it is clear that the semantic nexus that links signs to their meaning cannot be established until the organism has the operational potential of forming representations. Also, the sending of communicatory signs is considered an instrumental activity serving (like all other activity) the elimination of disturbance. This suggests that the acquisition of communicatory signs requires much the same stage of operational evolution as does tool-making.

Incentive to communicate may arise in situations where several organisms are led to cooperative efforts by the occurrence of reciprocal elimination of their disturbances. Such situations are likely to happen in predation and in defense against predators (when A beats off a predator, the disturbance is eliminated also for B, C, etc.). I suggest that the recurrence of such situations will lead to cooperative activity and, eventually, to cooperation that requires degrees of organization and synchronization attainable only by means of communication.

Since there is at present no evidence concerning the natural evolution of a communicatory signaling system toward the symbolic and combinatorial system of human language, it is, I believe, premature to advance a detailed hypothesis as to how this feat was achieved. The work of the Gardners, Premack, Fouts, and our group at the Yerkes Center[43] has shown that chimpanzees have the operational mechanisms to handle both combinatorial and symbolic processes. That chimps have not been observed to use these capabilities in the wild may be due to the fact that, in the absence of a language *common* to observer and observed, these capabilities are difficult to discover without experimental testing. On the other hand, it may simply be that the great apes have so far managed to survive quite well without the linguistic tool of social and cognitive organization. Our human species has certainly demonstrated the power of that tool. But evolution, presumably, has not yet come to an end—and if, today, we look at what we have done with the help of that splendid tool, one may begin to wonder whether, at some future time, it will still seem so obvious that language has enhanced the survival of life on this planet.

ACKNOWLEDGMENTS

I should like to thank Charles Smock and Stuart Katz for their helpful comments on a draft of this paper, and to express my lasting gratitude to the late Ray Carpenter, who first introduced me to the world of nonhuman primates.

NOTES AND REFERENCES

1. HEBB, D. O. 1958. Alice in Wonderland or psychology among the biological sciences. *In* Biological and Biochemical Bases of Behavior. H. F. Harlow and C. N. Woolsey, Eds: 451–467. University of Wisconsin Press. Madison, Wis.
2. e.g., GREENBERG, J. H. 1954. Concerning inferences from linguistic to non-linguistic data. *In* Language in Culture. H. Hoijer, Ed.: 3–19. University of Chicago Press. Chicago, Ill.; and HOCKETT, C. F. 1954. Chinese versus English: An exploration of the Whorfian hypothesis. *In* Language in Culture: 106–123.
3. SAPIR, E. 1921. Language. Harcourt, Brace & World. New York, N.Y.
4. LEWIS, B. N. & J. A. COOK. 1969. Toward a theory of telling. Internat. J. of Man-Machine Studies 1: 129–176.
5. This frustration, if speech-sounds are not interpreted as a *message*, is already observable in children at the stage of language acquisition, whenever the adult receiver fails to interpret their signals correctly because they do not conform to the adult code. In these cases it also becomes very obvious that a smile, a pat on the back, or saying "good," is not much of a "reinforcement" compared to the addressee's *understanding* the message and reacting according to the sender's expectation.
6. For a full exposition cf. MACKAY, D. M. 1972. Formal analysis of communication processes. *In* Non-Verbal Communication. R. A. Hinde, Ed.: 3–26; and THORPE, W. H. 1972. *In* Non-verbal Communication: 27–47.
7. PLOOG, D. 1974. Die Sprache der Affen: 76. Kindler. Munich, Germany.

8. It is important to keep apart the *Theory of Communication*, based on the work of HARTLEY, WIENER, and SHANNON, and *Information Theory*, which was developed by GABOR AND MACKAY; cf. CHERRY, C. 1957. On Human Communication. MIT Press. Cambridge, Mass.; and for a lucid, nonmathematical explication, MACKAY, D. M. 1953/55. Operational aspects of some fundamental concepts of human communication. Synthese. 9(3-5): 182-198.

9. SEBEOK, T. A. 1975. The semiotic web: A chronicle of prejudices. Semiotica. In press.

10. e.g. ALEXANDER, R. D. 1960. Sound communication in orthoptera and cicadidae. *In* Animal Sounds and Communication. W. E. Lanyon and W. N. Tavolga, Eds. American Institute of Biological Sciences. Publ. 4: 38-92. Washington, D.C.

11. ROSENBLUETH, A., N. WIENER, & J. BIGELOW. 1943. Behavior, purpose and teleology. Philosophy of Science. 10: 18-24.

12. WIENER, N. 1948. Time, communication, and the nervous system. Ann. N.Y. Acad. Sci. 50(4): 197-219.

13. See Ref. 12, p. 203. It was the assumption that "purpose" necessarily involves a temporal inversion of the cause-effect sequence that mars the otherwise excellent analysis of purposive behavior by the early behaviorist philosopher R. B. PERRY. 1921. A behaviorist view of purpose. J. Philos. 28(4): 85-105.

14. HOFSTADTER, A. 1941. Objective teleology. J. Philos. 38(2): 29-39.

15. See Ref. 14, p. 34-35. I am indebted to Thomas Sebeok for having drawn my attention to Hofstadter's essay. It clearly was unknown to the biologists who, more recently, have struggled to introduce "teleonomy" in the scientific analysis of goal-directed organisms or processes. E.g. PITTENDRIGH, C. S. 1958. Adaptation, natural selection, and behavior. *In* Behavior and Evolution. A. Roe and G. G. Simpson, Eds.: 390-416. Yale University Press. New Haven, Conn. MAYR, E. 1965. Cause and effect in biology. *In* Cause and Effect. D. Lerner, Ed.: 33-50. Free Press. New York, N.Y. MONOD, J. 1970. Le hasard et la nécessité. Editions du Seuil. Paris, France. To my knowledge, only Francisco AYALA (1970 Teleological explanations in evolutionary biology. Philosophy of Science. 37(1): 1-15) comes anywhere near the precision and usefulness of Hofstadter's definition.

16. POWERS, W. T. 1973. Behavior: The Control of Perception. Aldine. Chicago, Ill.

17. DUBRUL, L. E. 1960. Structural evidence in the brain for a theory of the evolution of behavior. Perspect. Biol. Med. 4(1): 40-57.

18. ASHBY, W. R. 1970. Symposium on Artificial Intelligence. Univ. of Tennessee. Tullahoma, Tenn.

19. MACKAY, D. M. 1966. Cerebral organization and the conscious control of action. *In* Brain and Conscious Experience. J. C. Eccles, Ed.: 422-445. Springer. New York, N.Y.; and 1967. Ways of looking at perception. *In* Models for the Perception of Speech and Visual Form. W. Wathen-Dunn, Ed.: 25-43. MIT Press. Boston, Mass.·

20. MATURANA, H. R. 1970. Biology of Cognition. Report 9.0 Biol. Computer Lab., Univ. Illinois. Urbana, Ill.

21. VON GLASERSFELD, E. 1975. Radical constructivism and Piaget's concept of knowledge. 5th Annual Symp. J. Piaget Soc. Philadelphia, Pa.

22. PIAGET, J. 1967. Six Psychological Studies. Random House. New York, N.Y.; and 1972. Problèmes de psychologie génétique. Editions Denoel. Paris, France.

23. Reported also in VANLAWICK-GOODALL, J. 1968. Animal Behavior Monogr. 1: 161-301.

24. HOLLOWAY, R. L. 1969. Culture: A human domain. Curr. Anthropol. 10(4): 395-412. This author minimizes the issue by introducing the term "iconic" for the relation between the raw twig and the stripped one. This obscures the fact that the chimp must "see" the fishing tool in a twig that grows on a shrub and has hitherto been seen as an adjunct to leaf-eating only.

25. MALINOWSKI, B. 1923. The problem of meaning in primitive languages. *In* The Meaning of Meaning. C. K. Ogden and I. A. Richards, Eds.: 310. Harcourt, Brace & Co. 8th edit. New York, N.Y.

26. CHERRY, C. 1957. See Ref. 8, p. 305.

27. MALINOWSKI, B. 1923. See Ref. 25, p. 312.

28. MASON, W. A. & J. H. HOLLIS. 1962. Communication between young rhesus monkeys. Anim. Behav. 10(3-4): 211-221.

29. BARTH, Fredrick, 1972, provides the conceptual schema for the analysis of this development in: Analytical dimensions in the comparison of social organizations. Am. Anthropol. **74:** 207–220.

30. A detailed, copiously documented explication of this hypothesis is given by HAMILTON, JAMES (1974. J. Human Evolution. **3:** 417–424); cf. also HILL, J. H. 1974. Possible continuity theories of language. Language **50**(1): 134–150.

31. Even in a seminaturalistic setting where communication could be demonstrated, isolation of specific signals was difficult; cf. MENZEL, E. W. 1971. Communication about the environment in a group of young chimpanzees. Folia Primat. **15:** 220–232; and 1973. Leadership and communication in young chimpanzees. Proc. 4th Internat. Congr. Primatol. **1:** 192–225. Karger. Basel, Switzerland.

32. HOCKETT, C. F. 1960. Logical considerations in the study of animal communication. *In* Animal Sounds and Communication. W. E. Lanyon and W. N. Tavolga, Eds.: 392–430. Amer. Inst. Biol. Sciences. Washington, D.C.

33. See Ref. 11, p. 18; and HALDANE, J. B. S. 1955. Animal communication and the origin of human language. Sci. Prog. **43:** 383–401.

34. Hocket was well aware of the problem, cf. Ref. 32, p. 408. In his integration of "design features" into "descriptive frames," an attempt was made to be more specific and less proscriptive, cf. HOCKETT, C. F. & S. A. ALTMANN. 1969. A note on design features. *In* Animal Communications. T. A. Sebeck, Ed. Indiana Univ. Press. Bloomington, Ind. BURGHARDT, G. M. 1970. (Defining "communication." *In* Communication by Chemical Signals. J. W. Johnston, D. G. Moulton, and A. Turk, Eds.: 5–18. Appleton-Century-Crofts, New York, N.Y.) provides an extensive survey of the contradictions and insufficiencies of subsidiary criteria.

35. LANGER, S. K. 1942. Philosophy in a New Key. Harvard University Press. Cambridge, Mass.

36. VON GLASERSFELD, E. 1974. Signs, communication, and language. J. Human Evolution. **3:** 465–474.

37. TINBERGEN, N. 1952. 'Derived' activities: Their causation, biological significance, origin, and emancipation during evolution. Quart. Rev. Biol. **27**(1): 1–32.

38. HOCKETT, C. F. & S. A. ALTMANN. 1969. A note on design features. *In* Animal Communication. T. A. Sebeok, Ed.: 61–72. Indiana University Press. Bloomington, Ind.

39. HOCKETT, C. F. See Ref. 32, p. 117.

40. cf. MOUNIN, G. 1974. Review of Hinde's Non-Verbal Communication. J. Linguistics. **10:** 201–206.

41. VON FRISCH, K. 1974. Decoding the language of the bee. Science **185:** 663–668.

42. HOCKETT, C. F. 1960. The origin of speech. Scientific American **203**(3): 88–96.

43. GARDNER, B. T. & R. A. GARDNER. 1971. Two-way communication with an infant chimpanzee. *In* Behavior of Nonhuman Primates. A. M. Schrier and F. Stollnitz, Eds. Vol. 4: 117–184. Academic Press. New York, N.Y. PREMACK, D. 1971. *In* Behavior of Nonhuman Primates: 185–228. FOUTS, R. 1973. Acquisition and testing of gestural signs in four young chimpanzees. Science **180:** 978–980. RUMBAUGH, D. M., E. VON GLASERSFELD, H. WARNER, P. P. PISANI, & T. V. GILL. 1974. Lana (chimpanzee) learning language: A progress report. Brain and Language **1:** 205–212.

SYNTAX AND SEMANTICS OF
CHILDREN'S LANGUAGE

Patrick Suppes

Institute for Mathematical Studies in the Social Sciences
Stanford University
Stanford, California 94305

In this article I take a retrospective look at work in which I have been engaged with younger colleagues for a number of years. We now have at hand several large corpora of spoken English, one of French, and a smaller one of Mandarin Chinese. All of the speech is by young children, in the age range from 22 months to approximately 50 months, and by persons with them at the time, usually their parents. Previous reports of the work are to be found in Smith,[1] Suppes,[2,3] Suppes, Léveillé, and Smith,[4] and Suppes, Smith, and Léveillé.[5,6]

The first part describes the steps taken in the analysis, ending with the test of different developmental models of grammar. In the second part, I discuss various questions and issues that have currency in the continuing controversies about the nature of language acquisition. The matters addressed in the second part are related to the concrete details of the work outlined in the first part.

STEPS OF ANALYSIS

I have broken the process of analyzing the syntax and semantics of a child's speech into six steps, but there is nothing magical about the number six and it would be easy to subdivide further or even to coalesce certain steps for some purposes. The six steps I have used are record, transcribe, write grammar, test probabilistic fit of grammar, construct semantics, and test developmental models.

Recording

The first step is to select a child and some part of his environment and to record his speech and that of the other persons around him for a selected number of hours. In our largest corpus, that of the speech of a young girl, Nina, recordings were made periodically from the time she was 23 months until she was 39 months; the resulting corpus of her speech alone consists of 102,230 tokens. In the case of Philippe's spoken French, running from the age of 25 months to 39 months, there are 56,982 tokens. A great deal of work in linguistics, psycholinguistics, and the philosophy of language does not depend in any way on the collection of a corpus; it seems to me, however, that the empirical study of children's speech must depend, at least partially, on the collection of data, and especially for the study of developmental models, a corpus collected over an extended period of time seems desirable.

Transcribing

After recordings have been made there remains the massive problem of transcribing the speech. The exact method of transcription will depend upon the interest of the investigator. For example, if the interest is primarily syntactical or semantical, a detailed transcription emphasizing either phonetic or prosodic features will probably not be made, in order to reduce somewhat the amount of effort required to obtain a workable transcription. This is the procedure we followed, and we have used normal word boundaries where possible. Thus, our transcriptions are not satisfactory for studies of the development of phonology or prosody. On the other hand, we have directly entered the transcriptions into the files of the Institute's PDP-10 computer system, and we are able to investigate the edited transcriptions in great systematic detail; the superb assortment of sophisticated programs written by Dr. Robert L. Smith for this purpose has been especially helpful.

Writing the Grammar

The objective of this step is to write a generative grammar for the entire corpus of the child's speech. By and large we have attempted to write context-free grammars with transformations entering only where absolutely required. The level of complexity of children's speech in the age range mentioned above is sufficiently low that most of the spoken speech fits rather naturally into a context-free grammar, but we have no ideological position against transformations and believe they should be used whenever simplification of the grammar results.

The initial measure of success is the percentage of the utterances of the corpus that are parsed by the grammar, but already the use of such an evaluation measure has to be treated with care. It would, for example, be trivial in every case to write a universal grammar in terms of the vocabulary such that any concatenation of the child's vocabulary would be a well-formed utterance and thus the grammar would properly parse any utterance whatsoever. What is to be regarded as a natural restriction on the grammar in the case of a young child's speech is not obvious, although in practice what is done by a great many investigators is to write a grammar that deviates from the standard adult usage only when necessary. Of course, with this approach the grammar is simpler than one concerned with adult usage but corresponds rather closely to a fragment of adult usage with certain notable exceptions. In broad terms, this is the strategy adopted by Suppes, Smith, and Léveillé[6] for the spoken French of Philippe.

Excellent examples of the construction of such grammars are to be found in the books and articles of Roger Brown and his collaborators.[7,8]

Testing the Probabilistic Fit of the Grammar

For persons with a background in mathematical models in the social sciences, especially probabilistic models, a natural further step to take to tighten the criteria for goodness of fit of the grammar is to introduce probabilistic parameters for each production rule and to estimate these parameters from the data. On the basis of the estimated parameters, a straightforward goodness-of-fit test in standard statistical terms can be applied to the grammar. Psycholinguists who are not familiar with parametric models or linguists who abhor statistical linguistics find this step from writing a grammar to testing its probabilistic fit a difficult one to accept. I have engaged in polemics on this matter several times in the past,[9,10] and so I shall not engage in a further defense here. I can say from experience that the attempt to fit a grammar probabilistically can lead to insightful and important changes in the details of the grammar. What it especially affects is the level at which various production rules are introduced. A common effect of fitting a probabilistic grammar is to raise in the hierarchy of rules the position of those that generate holophrastic utterances, that is, single-word utterances that seem to have the semantic content of complete utterances but not the grammatical form.

Constructing Semantics

The next step is to put a semantic hand into the syntactical glove and show that it fits snugly. The approach in this case is to assign to each production rule of the grammar a semantic function and to build in an appropriate way a model-theoretic semantics for the child's speech. This approach is outlined in Suppes,[2] and a detailed working out for the corpus of Erica is to be found in Smith.[1] If the grammar is fully written before the semantics is begun, in all likelihood the working out of the semantics will cause a revision in the grammar. If space permitted I would illustrate this point with examples of grammatical production rules that are often suggested by linguists but that cannot lead to a reasonable semantics. Examples of this character and a detailed discussion of such matters as the semantics of propositional attitudes in children's speech are discussed in Suppes.[3]

I shall have something more to say about model-theoretic semantics below and so I shall not attempt a further explication at this point. I do, however, want to make the point that model-theoretic semantics for children's speech and for natural language in general is a natural outgrowth of the long tradition of semantics in logic and philosophy, a tradition that has been too much ignored, at least until recently, by most linguists and psycholinguists.

Testing of Developmental Models

With a systematic syntactical and semantical apparatus at hand it is then possible to test specific developmental models of children's language. The overview of development does not have to be restricted to consideration of a few salient instances of speech, but can be examined in a more systematic and global way. From the standpoint of development of grammar it is a virtue of the probabilistic approach that it provides a natural tool for studying grammatical development. In Suppes, Léveillé, and Smith,[4] specific alternative models of an incremental or discrete-stage sort are tested, and I shall have something later to say about what I term the myth of stages.

Roughly speaking, the methodology is this. The grammar, and if desired the semantics as well, can be written to cover the entire range of the corpus, but then probabilistic parameters can be estimated for each block of time. The changes in the parameters directly reflect changes in the uses of grammatical rules, some of the more complex rules, for example, having probability zero in the early period. Alternative models then deal with the conceptual way in which the changes in usage of rules take place. The two natural and simple polar opposites are a continuous incremental model versus an all-or-none stage model. In the data we have analyzed thus far, the continuous incremental model is supported more by the data, although, as is not surprising, neither model, given its simplicity, has as good a fit as one would like.

These ideas about developmental models may be illustrated by drawing on the data and analysis given in Suppes, Léveillé, and Smith.[4] The basic assumptions of the all-or-none stage model are two. First, development is discontinuous and may be represented by a relatively small number of stages. Second, within each stage there is a constant probability of a rule being used. The specific assumption appropriate to this situation is that the probabilities of rules being used within a given stage constitute a multinomial distribution, and thus satisfy assumptions of independence and stationarity. In the data reported in Suppes, Léveillé, and Smith,[4] six distinct time sections were analyzed. Thus, by having six stages, a perfect fit to the data would be obtained. In order to have a reasonable test and also because of the relatively restricted time span, a two-stage model was tested against a linear incremental model. From rather natural qualitative assumptions the following equation is derived for the incremental model in the report.[4] The exponential distribution occurring in the model is a natural generalization for the continuous-time assumption of the usual geometric distribution characteristic of discrete time processes. The equation is:

$$p(t,r) = \pi_r - (\pi_r - p_r)e^{-\alpha(t-t_1)}$$

where t is the time parameter, r is a given grammatical rule, π_r is the asymptotic probability of r's being used, p_r is the initial probability of the rule being used at the beginning of the time t_1 in which observations were made of Philippe's beginning French, and α is the learning parameter estimated from the data.

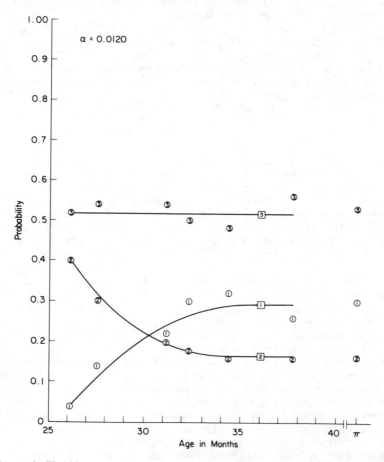

FIGURE 1. Fit of incremental model for production rules at the highest level.

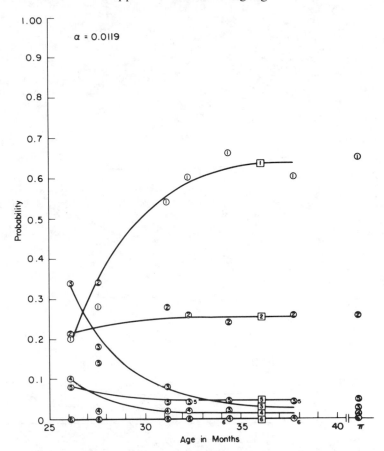

FIGURE 2. Fit of incremental model for high level production rules generating incomplete utterances.

As remarked, the fit of the incremental model was considerably better. I exhibit in several figures the sense of that fit. In these figures, Philippe's age in months is plotted on the abscissa, and the ordinate shows the probability of use of the rules. The rules are divided into subgroups, and thus the probabilities are conditional probabilities of use within a given subgroup. The curves, labeled in square boxes, show the theoretical functions predicted by the incremental model. The data points of the individual rules are numbered; for example, the numeral 1 in a circle indicates a data point for rule 1 of the group, etc.

FIGURE 1 shows data for the highest level rules in the grammar, for example, production rules for sentences. The production rules, beginning with the start symbol S of the grammar, divide the types of utterances into: first, short utterances consisting primarily of adverbs, locutions, interjections, and numerals; second, utterances consisting of noun phrases and adjective phrases that stand as utterances without a verb; and, finally, utterances in which a verb is present or questions that occur with or without a verb.

FIGURE 2 shows the data and theoretical curves of top-level rules that produce incomplete utterances. FIGURE 3 shows the data and theoretical curves for the rules

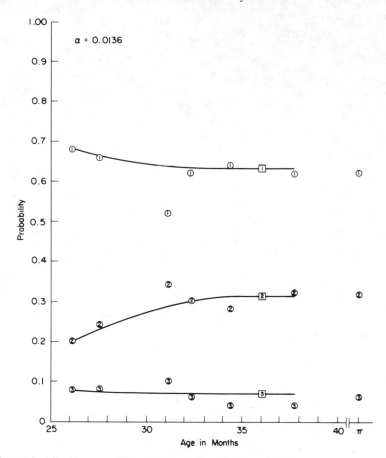

FIGURE 3. Fit of incremental model for production rules generating object noun phrases.

that generate object noun phrases, that is, noun phrases that occur as objects and not as subjects of verbs. The rules for incomplete utterances mainly generate terminal nodes directly to which it is then only necessary to apply lexical rules. The rules for producing object noun phrases have the form one would expect, but they also have some special features that will not be examined here for noun phrases in object position.

FIGURE 4 shows data and theoretical curves for rules that produce verb phrase structures. The 15 rules of this group have been generated into seven subgroups in order to consolidate the data. The first subgroup consists of the single main rule represented by Curve 1, which generates simple verb phrases. (What I mean by *simple* will be clear from the description of the other subgroups.) Subgroup 2 generates verb phrases that begin with a preposition or a personal pronoun. Subgroup 3 introduces auxiliaries, and Subgroup 4 generates several sorts of verb phrases that include an auxiliary or a modal. Subgroup 5 generates verb phrases with a modal followed by a verb phrase that begins with a preposition or a personal pronoun. Subgroup 6 generates verb phrases with a modal followed by a simple verb phrase, that is, one governed by Subgroup 1. Finally, Subgroup 7 generates verb phrases with a personal pronoun before the modal or the auxiliary. As can be seen and as would be expected, the simple verb phrases generated by Subgroup 1 dominate Philippe's usage of verb phrase structures. The fit of theory to data is especially good for FIGURE 4.

It is to be emphasized that what I have given is a very brief description of a considerably more complicated analysis in Suppes, Léveillé, and Smith.[4]

Size of Grammar

I have in the past characterized the present stage of our knowledge of how to construct grammars of children's speech as the pre-Ptolemaic stage. What I have in mind is that we do not yet seem to have even the degree of fundamental insight characteristic of Greek astronomy with respect to the subtle and complicated data it

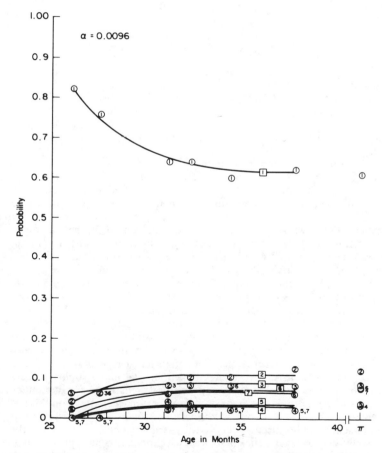

FIGURE 4. Fit of incremental model for production rules generating verb phrase structures.

faced. One way of expressing this concern is by considering the large size of all of the grammars I know of that have attempted to encompass a corpus in complete detail. The grammar, for example, that we have written for Philippe[4] is already extremely large, consisting of more than 300 rules, and yet the grammar does not reflect all of the requirements of inflection nor does it fit more than about 75 percent of the utterances in the corpus. This might be thought to be a part of the irregularity and spontaneity of a young child's first speech, but something like the same situation obtains when we turn to what should be one of the most regimented domains one can think of: written language of elementary mathematics. The dissertation of Nancy Smith[11] was directed at the problem of writing a grammar for the written language of elementary-school mathematics. This seems like a simple, relatively artificial fragment of English, but in fact it turns out to be as full of difficult and subtle problems as the corpus of any of the children's speech we have discussed. It is awe inspiring to contemplate what must be the full set of rules required to describe the speech of a young child from the age of 24 months to 48 months. I suspect we are not approaching the problem in the correct way, but what I do not have is a good insight as to how to change the approach and I see no reasonable alternatives available to us in the work of others.

Nature of Semantics

It is a commonplace that constructive production of speech as meaningful commentary in a given perceptual and social context could scarcely proceed simply on the basis of model-theoretic semantics as a complete theory of meaning. There are many ways of stating the difficulty. One way is that it will not do to talk about the set of red objects as the extension of the concept *red* in the world as it is. Other more constructive methods of computing along intensional lines are surely required. The model-theoretic semantics we have used in our analyses is meant to provide an analysis of semantics and correspondingly to provide a theory of meaning of children's speech at the level of abstraction characteristic of set theory in general.

I have come to recognize what I feel is the root of misunderstanding on the part of many psycholinguists and some linguists about the nature of model-theoretic semantics. It is characteristic of a great deal of empirical work in psycholinguistics that it is concerned with the acquisition of the meaning of individual words. The problem of how children acquire the meaning of individual words is an important and central one, but it is only one part of an adequate theory of meaning. What has been the primary concern in logic and philosophy has been the development of a theory to account for the meaning of a complex utterance as built up from the meaning of its parts. This is the problem that Frege recognized as central to a theory of meaning, and it was first given a constructive and concrete formulation in Tarski's famous monograph on truth.[12] Model-theoretic semantics is addressed to the problem of giving an account of how the meaning of the whole is built up from the meaning of its parts—I here use *meaning* in a way that includes the theory of reference and the theory of truth or satisfaction. What goes on in the child's head will need more detailed constructive characterization. The many sophisticated efforts currently under way to characterize procedural semantics for computer programming languages provide perhaps one of the best lines of attack on this problem. I do want to emphasize that out of the tradition of psycholinguistics proper, or linguistics itself, there has been as yet no really serious competitor to model-theoretic semantics and there is no evidence that either psycholinguists or linguists will offer on their own a serious theory of meaning. The chances do seem good that within the framework of computer science the proper constructive extension of model-theoretic semantics is being put together and will be ready for appropriate mutation as a theory of the semantics of natural language. Development of procedural semantics for children's language is, in my judgment, the most important next step in the theory of children's language.

Myth of Stages

The developmental models described earlier, in which we tested the two alternative hypotheses of incremental change or all-or-none change by stages, decisively supported the incremental change, even though the detailed fit of neither model was as good as could be expected. The talk about stages has affected the conceptual apparatus of psycholinguistics to such an extent that the myth of the reality of stages will not be easily eradicated. On another occasion[13] I have criticized the myth of stages in Piagetian theory. The ubiquitous use of the concept of stages by Piaget has encouraged a similar use in psycholinguistics. In view of the lack of serious tests in almost all cases of alternative hypotheses, the presumed existence of stages has exactly the epistemological status reserved for myths. From the evidence I know about, language development at the level ordinarily discussed by psychologists proceeds by continuous change and not by stages. The case for stages is to be found in the microlevel of the learning of individual items of great simplicity. At this microlevel, evidence for stages can be found, as was demonstrated amply in the early 1960s in the enormous literature on this subject in mathematical learning theory. There is, in contrast, no serious evidence in support of stages on the scale of a child's language performance between the ages of 18 months and 36 months, if we have in mind grouping his development within five or six stages, and not at the level of calling the learning of each new word a stage.

On the other hand, it is clearly an open research problem for the future to characterize in a more precise and satisfactory manner the actual development of children's language. The models and theories we have at hand at present are clearly too simplistic and too simple to do an adequate job.

Nativism and Rationalism

The strongly empirical tone I have adopted might lead to the conclusion that I advocate some simple empiricism as the appropriate framework for a detailed theory of children's acquisition of language. This is not the case. A simple *tabula rasa* theory seems to me as much out of place as a correspondingly simple rationalistic theory. Platitudes about these matters are easy. A child obviously comes to the age of language learning with an enormously flexible apparatus for perception and learning, much of it clearly fine tuned to what he will hear. We have, it seems to me, as yet too little theoretical definiteness about the way in which children acquire language to parcel out the variance between genetic endowment and environmental influences. The extensive empirical work we have done on children's language over the past seven years seems to weigh very little on either side of the issues, except perhaps to discourage premature closure on any simple theoretical position.

There is one amusing point of numerical comparison that I sometimes like to use when engaged in dialogue with nativists. Elementary computations on the corpora we have collected indicate that a child between the ages of 24 months and 36 months will produce about half a million utterances and will hear from his parents and other persons almost a million utterances. This is just in the one-year span. In contrast, a child who is learning elementary-school mathematics will ordinarily work at most about 4,000 exercises a year for a total of 24,000. In gross terms, these data suggest that the more developed innate potential really present in children is arithmetic and not linguistic. All children do not learn arithmetic simply because they do not get the few thousand trials needed to activate the rationalist potential. Given similarly limited exposure to language, certainly the same would be true. Perhaps arithmetic should replace language as the new nativist stronghold.

Theses about Expressive Power

In other papers in this volume there has been considerable dispute about the relative expressive power of various natural languages. Keenan, for example, has defended the thesis that natural languages vary greatly in their expressive power. Katz, on the other hand, has essentially advocated the thesis that all natural languages have the same expressive power. To make the discussion interesting, additional distinctions are needed. There is, for example, a large literature in logic coming at the problem of expressive power from a number of different directions, and a variety of interesting results has been established. I am not suggesting for a moment that the results in logic can be interpreted in any direct way as bearing on the issue of what is the expressive power of a given natural language. What that tradition does suggest, however, is that it is important to think in terms of appropriate kinds of distinctions and to settle the issue not once and for all but in terms of a particular aspect of the general and vague concept of expressive power. For example, the many interesting results established by Tarski[14] for the interpretability of one theory expressible in first-order logic in terms of another introduces a number of concepts that seem applicable with appropriate changes to the current controversy. I restrict myself to one other example, a more recent one. In general discussions of elementary logic it is standard dogma to make the point that definitions play no essential role if they are proper, that is, if they satisfy the standard criteria of eliminability and noncreativity. Working practice in logic and mathematics shows very well that this is far from the case. Any substantial mathematical theory requires the introduction of a succession of definitions to be manageable, to have, in other words, the right expressive power. One thesis lurking in the background in discussing the expressive power of natural languages is that one can always define new concepts by the resources available in the language. Thus, if we take a primitive language, the claim would be we could bring it up to the standards of modern science by appropriate introduction of new terms by definition. The plain man would, of course, regard this much-extended language as a new language, and so claims about the expressive power of the thus extended language would not amount to the same thing as claims about the original language. The rationalist who believes in the quality of the expressive power of all natural languages might want to report that he can in principle dispense with the new terms by using their definitions and by expanding any scientific language back into the original language. I do not believe that any rationalist precisely holds that such explicit expansion into the original natural language of all scientific terminology is possible, but approximations to this thesis seem to be present and sufficiently close to make the point I want to make. The point is that the expressive power of languages with or without explicit definitions is of quite a different character. This can be shown in several ways, but let me just cite one interesting recent example. Statman[15] has shown that if we consider mathematical argument or proofs as an example of expressive power, and if we use the genus of the graph of a proof as the measure of its complexity, then there is no upper bound on the genus of proofs that result from eliminating the use of explicit definitions. In other words, if the genus of a proof that uses explicit definitions is n, then a proof of unbounded complexity is in some cases required of the same theorem once explicit definitions are eliminated. Clearly the case of mathematical proofs is rather special, but it is exactly around issues of complexity that the more detailed discussion of expressive power should center; and it would be my conjecture that as the discussion becomes more definite and specific, examples can be constructed of conceptual importance that support Keenan's thesis.

In contrast, in examining the grammar and semantics of English, French, and Chinese that we have constructed for the children's speech available to us, we have found no significant differences in expressive power; or if they do exist in the corpora we are not sensitive to them. On the basis of what evidence I have seen, fragmentary though it may be, I could imagine myself believing a thesis of approximately uniform expressive power for most natural languages as used by very young children, but being skeptical that such a uniformity thesis can be maintained as we move up the scale to older and more sophisticated speakers and listeners.

References

1. SMITH, R. L. 1972. The syntax and semantics of ERICA. Tech. Rep. 185, Institute for Mathematical Studies in the Social Sciences. Stanford University. Stanford, Calif.
2. SUPPES, P. 1971. On the grammar and model-theoretic semantics of children's noun phrases. Tech. Rep. 181, Institute for Mathematical Studies in the Social Sciences. Stanford University. Stanford, Calif. Published in: Problèmes Actuels en Psycholinguistique **206**: 49–60 (1974).
3. SUPPES, P. 1974. The semantics of children's language. Am. Psychologist **29**: 103–114.
4. SUPPES, P., M. LÉVEILLÉ & R. L. SMITH. 1974. Developmental models of a child's French syntax. Tech. Rep. 243, Institute for Mathematical Studies in the Social Sciences. Stanford University. Stanford, Calif.
5. SUPPES, P., R. SMITH & M. LÉVEILLÉ. 1972. The French syntax and semantics of PHILIPPE, Part 1: Noun phrases. Tech. Rep. 195, Institute for Mathematical Studies in the Social Sciences. Stanford University. Stanford, Calif.
6. SUPPES, P., R. SMITH & M. LÉVEILLÉ. 1973. The French syntax of a child's noun phrases. Arch. Psychol. **42**: 207–269.
7. BROWN, R. 1970. Psycholinguistics: Selected Papers. Free Press. New York, N.Y.
8. BROWN, R. 1973. A First Language. Harvard University Press. Cambridge, Mass.
9. SUPPES, P. 1972. Probabilistic grammars for natural languages. Synthese **22**: 95–116.
10. SUPPES, P. 1973. Semantics of context-free fragments of natural languages. In Approaches to Natural Language. K. J. J. Hintikka, J. M. E. Moravcsik & P. Suppes, Eds.: 370–394. D. Reidel Publishing Co. Dordrecht, The Netherlands.
11. SMITH, N. 1974. A question-answering system for elementary mathematics. Tech. Rep. 227, Institute for Mathematical Studies in Studies in the Social Sciences. Stanford University. Stanford, Calif.
12. TARSKI, A. 1935. Der Wahrheitsbegriff in den formalisierten Sprachen. Studia Philosophica **1**: 261–405. Translation: The Concept of Truth in Formalized Languages. In Logic, Semantics, Metamathematics. A. Tarski, Ed. (J. H. Woodger, Trans.): 152–278. Oxford University Press. Oxford, England (1956).
13. SUPPES, P. 1973. Facts and fantasies of education. In Changing Education: Alternatives from Educational Research. M. C. Wittrock, Ed.: 6–45. Prentice-Hall. Englewood Cliffs, N.J.
14. TARSKI, A. 1953. Undecidable Theories. North-Holland Publishing Co. Amsterdam, The Netherlands.
15. STATMAN, R. 1974. Structural complexity of proofs. Ph.D. Dissertation. Stanford University. Stanford, Calif.

DISCUSSION

Lois Bloom, *Moderator*

Department of Psychology
Teachers College
Columbia University
New York, New York 10027

UNIDENTIFIED SPEAKER: Much has been said about behavior. I'd like to address a question chiefly to Prof. von Glasersfeld. You said that it may be preferable, for certain purposes at least, to say that behavior controls perception, rather than that perception controls behavior. In this connection, I'd like to ask you and perhaps the other speakers whether you'd care to sharpen your definition of behavior. I'm often bothered by the meaning of the term. Obviously you couldn't have meant it in the broad sense in which one says that "psychology" is the "science of behavior." In the sense in which organisms can be said to behave, there's no such thing as nonbehavior. What is the behavior that controls perception?

PROF. VON GLASERSFELD: I think there are two parts to your question. The first part concerns a criterion for *behavior*. We need several, but I'll just mention the most important. It was first used by Haldane to define communication, but I believe it is applicable also to behavior. There must be an interaction of two entities that is not mechanical but informational; that is a way of saying that "behavior" requires some form of interaction that is not thermodynamically explicable. Something happens, there is a change of energy and a reaction, but it is not calculable in terms of energy equations, because another commodity is involved, which we call "information."

The second point that matters is that I view behavior as a self-regulating maneuver. It is anything an organism does in order to maintain certain values, reference values, if you like. It is not always easy to establish what the reference value is, but recently several methods have been developed by means of which one can, in fact, establish with good approximation what kind of value an organism is trying to maintain; or, if you turn that around, to what kind of disturbances an organism will react in order to maintain its reference value. It is in this sense that Powers formulated the phrase that "behavior controls perception," because the disturbance is always something perceived and measured against a reference value. Now if you think about that from the organism's point of view, you get a situation which, in traditional terms, is very like *solipsism*, because all the organism has to work on are its own sensory signals. On the one side there are signals from the so-called receptors. On the other side, are the signals which really should be called reafferent, from effector action, and it is between these two groups of signals that the organism establishes connections and learns to use them in order to keep certain values constant. Any manifestation of that I would call "behavior," and I think anyone can demonstrate that it is very different from the "behavior" of billiard balls or other things that are not self-regulating, but merely reactive.

JOHN DAVIES: Prof. Glasersfeld, in the context of your remarks, Langer's view concerning the intentional use of signs and Powers' view that behavior controls perception, when children watch television or movies as intentional sequences of signs, they may be doing so as if they were watching communication. It seems to me that they are watching as language, and are therefore learning a visual language. Do you agree with that?

PROF. VON GLASERSFELD: I would not agree with that, because I think there's a great difference between communication in general and language. Now, you can make various sets of criteria for discriminating language from signaling systems. You can make criteria for discriminating signaling systems from inductive information-gathering or information-processing. TV watching involves all that and more. Ultimately it depends on which definition or set of definitions works best for what you want to do. I hold no belief that any one definition or explanation is truer than another. What matters is that it enables me to set up a relatively coherent, consistent, noncontradictory explanation of as wide an experiential field as possible.

DR. JERISON: Concerning intelligence and speech: are these two things going to be differentiated? Well, the IQ test you know is a good *ad hoc* sample of behavior developed over the years; it's gotten a lot of knocks in recent years, but it seems to work in all sorts of ways. If you've done IQ testing, you know that you can give the vocabulary test and get about the same amount of information as you would with full-scale IQ, for many purposes.

On the point of body: the fact is, a body can grow, and as the body grows, the brain gets bigger, and the connection between these is a very intimate one. Furthermore, across species, there's an intimate relation between body and brain; with respect to "species intelligence," you can almost partial out a fraction of the brain not related to the body which can provide a reasonable anatomical correlate of what you might call "biological intelligence."

Part V. Artificial Intelligence

BRAIN ARCHITECTURE AND MECHANISMS THAT UNDERLIE LANGUAGE: AN INFORMATION-PROCESSING ANALYSIS

Robert J. Baron

Department of Computer Science
The University of Iowa
Iowa City, Iowa 52242

INTRODUCTION

This paper describes a neural network model for certain elementary kinds of natural language processing. The model suggests how visually perceived objects and their attributes might be named, and how simple sentences that relate to visual processing might be understood. When people hear sentences such as "What is that?", "What is above the house?", "Is the car near the tree?", and so forth, they understand the meaning of the sentence immediately. The words are processed in real time, and the sentences are understood without any conscious grammatical analysis. Moreover, if a person hears a construction such as "What is blue the above?", or "What is house?", he knows just as quickly that it is syntactically incorrect. The model that will be presented here provides for the analysis of such simple sentences in terms of underlying neural mechanisms. The model is specifically concerned with sentences relating to visual information processing, but there are no assumptions made that restrict the model in any way to visual input. The model describes low-level linguistic processing only, and no attempt is made to describe how the brain might analyze questions more complex than the above examples.

Before describing the model, I would like to give a brief historical review of machine translation (MT), question-answering (QA) systems, and neural modeling research in order to place into better perspective the relationship between this research and related areas of artificial intelligence (AI).

QA and MT Research

The earliest computer-based research on natural language started soon after the advent of the digital computer and involved attempts by several research groups at writing computer programs to translate language. These early attempts at MT involved simple syntactic analysis of sentences, word or phrase substitution, thesaurus look-up, and other relatively simple transformations. For the most part the translations were considered unsuccessful because of their poor quality, and the only positive results of the early research were several important programming techniques involving string and list processing. In 1960, Bar-Hillel[1] wrote a critical analysis of the automatic machine translation projects and concluded that high-quality language translation by computer would not be possible until techniques were developed to enable the computer to "understand" the meaning of the passage to be translated. This, he suggested, would mean that the computer must have stored not only all the knowledge about the world that is common to both the reader and writer, but deductive procedures for obtaining facts that are not directly stored as data.

In the years following Bar-Hillel's critique, several researchers developed computer-oriented theories of "understanding." One of the earliest was proposed by

240

Quillian[2] with his "Teachable Language Comprehender," a computer program in which the idea of a semantic network was first introduced. A semantic network is an information structure in which words, concepts, and meanings form a graph that can be used by the computer to determine the meaning of other statements or questions presented for analysis. When given an input sentence to analyze, the computer can trace through the semantic network and relate the words and structure of the input sentence to the words and structures in the semantic network. This enables the computer to obtain the meaning of the input sentence. The initial success of Quillian's model, albeit in a restricted domain, motivated other researchers to develop more elaborate and comprehensive models in which semantic networks encode very detailed and complex information. These networks not only encode the meanings of words and phrases but also facts and theories about the world in general. Like the earliest programs, most modern programs also include routines for syntactic analysis of the input sentences, thesaurus and dictionary look-up, and general procedures for tracing through the semantic networks to obtain the meaning of the input sentence. Many programs include deductive routines for determining facts neither given as input nor stored in the data base. One of the most comprehensive models of this type was recently presented by Rieger.[3]

Taking a somewhat different approach to language understanding, Winograd[4] wrote a very elaborate program in which knowledge is represented in the computer as a collection of procedures (programs). The ability of the computer to understand and process sentences is based on the fact that the procedures could be invoked to determine whether or not certain facts were true within the context of the sentence being analyzed. His program was restricted to questions and statements about a scene comprised of blocks, the so-called "blocks world," and understanding was demonstrated by the system's ability to answer questions about the scene. For example, if several blocks are piled up, one on top of another, the program could deduce that the top block is above the bottom block in the pile, a fact not directly stored in the data base.

The trend today is toward developing more complete systems for representing facts and theories about the world, and most systems use either semantic networks, procedures, or both as the building blocks.

For those who wish to acquaint themselves with the literature of this field, there are several good review articles and collections of research papers that describe MT and QA research to date. Minsky,[5] Rustin,[6] and Schank and Colby[7] edited books containing papers about semantic information processing, and Simmons[8,9] has written two survey articles on QA research. A book by Winograd[4] describes his own work in detail. Papers by Rieger[3] and Charniak[10] are also of interest and describe recent results. There are several critiques and analyses of QA and MT research including those by Bar-Hillel,[1] Josselson,[11] and Wilks.[12]

All the work discussed so far concerns language processing by computer. Although researchers in this area naturally take account of linguistic theories and psychological evidence relating to natural language, they make no attempt to describe the brain mechanisms underlying language. The QA and MT programs represent abstract or psychological theories of language and memory, not physiological theories.

Neural Modeling

At the same time that the QA and MT research got under way, other researchers were attempting to model various aspects of the nervous system. Most of the models fall into one of two categories: (1) models of specific properties of neurons or neural activity, and (2) models of some visual, psychological, or linguistic process in terms of neural activity. Within the first category are models of nerve impulse transmission, retinal activity, single-cell electrophysiology, spike-train statistics, cerebellar activity, and so on. These models are explicit theories of biological processes and can (potentially) be verified or contradicted by an experimental investigation.

The second category consists of models of learning, memory, visual information processing, linguistic processing, and so forth. These models attempt to simulate a psychological process rather than model a biological phenomenon. In general, these models use abstract or mathematical "neurons" as basic computational elements, and their structure is defined by formal mathematical systems. Terms such as "neuron," "coupling coefficient, "firing rate," and so on are sometimes used in descriptions of mathematical properties of the models to indicate a correspondence between the mathematical construct and its intended biological counterpart. But this vocabulary is more often than not intended merely to aid the reader in understanding the model, not to imply anything about the biology of the brain. I shall use such terms in this way myself.

One of the earliest models of this type was proposed by McCulloch and Pitts[13] and was based on a "neuron" that approximated the logical computations performed by biological neurons as they were understood at the time. Using the McCulloch-Pitts neuron, Rosenblatt[14] proposed his perceptron model of memory and learning. Although these early models were inadequate for many reasons, they paved the way for more sophisticated models that followed. Models of information storage, for example, have since been proposed by Beurle,[15] Westlake,[16] Longuet-Higgins,[17] Grossberg,[18,19] Baron,[20] Cavanagh,[21] Kohonen et al.,[22] any many others. These models vary a great deal in their mathematical structure, but they have in common the fact that they are an attempt to describe some aspect of human memory or learning in terms of its underlying neural mechanism. Most frequently, the details of neuronal activity are not critical to the behavior of the model and so for convenience are highly simplified. For this class of models, what is important is a mathematical account of a psychological process rather than a precise description at the cellular level.

Relating Neural Network Models to QA and MT Systems

Although at first there does not appear to be much of a relationship between neural network models and QA or MT systems, a more careful look reveals that these classes of models belong to a natural hierarchy of descriptive levels for cellular mechanisms and psychological processes. The lowest relevant level of description is that of cellular mechanisms and concerns the metabolic and information-processing activity of single cells or very small groups of cells. This level of abstraction is appropriate for modeling single neuron behavior but is inappropriate for describing the behavior of large groups of cells. As a result, a more abstract level of description is required, that of the flow and transformation of information in neural networks. At this level, information is usually specified in terms of axonal firing rates of the cells of the network, and the model then describes how the activity in one group of cells affects that in a second group. Groups of cells are represented as matrices, and connections between cells are defined in terms of matrix transformations or their equivalent. This level of abstraction is adequate for modeling relatively simple neural networks but is inappropriate for describing the complex networks that may be assumed to mediate psychological processes. As a result, symbolic systems and models are used. Symbolic systems include formal grammars, semantic network models, computer simulation models, QA and MT systems—in general, the types of model that have arisen in the fields of artificial intelligence, psycholinguistics, and psychology, particularly perceptual psychology and memory. (See for example Norman,[23] Tulving & Donaldson,[24] Anderson & Bower,[25] and Melton & Martin.[26]) At the present time there is a significant gap between the neural model level of description and that of symbolic systems. In time, however, this gap should narrow, and neural network models may be expected to account for the processes that underlie the behavior of symbolic systems.

The model I will describe in this paper lies at the interface between neural networks and symbolic systems. My principal interest is in the mechanisms of neural information processing, and it is probably this bias which most distinguishes my own work from other AI models. My earliest work was a model for cortical memory, a neural network model for an associative memory store which gave a more or less plausible account of how information could be stored, recognized, and recalled by the cerebral cortex. Although it was successful in describing information storage and recall, the model did not attempt to account for any complex psychological processes. The question arose then as to what additional networks would be needed, and how they might be connected together in order to explain more complex psychological processes. My second model used the cortical memory model as a storage network and proposed a mechanism for the processing and encoding of visual information within the brain. This model used several memory stores, information-transformation networks, and a rather complicated control strategy to account for various perceptual processes, including how visual experiences are encoded in memory, how visually perceived objects are recognized, and how current experiences enable past experiences to be recalled. The model I will describe here includes these visual processing networks but is extended to explain how visually perceived objects and their attributes can be named and how very simple sentences relating to visual processing can be understood. It is my intention that each of the networks used in the model be taken to correspond to one or more physical networks in the brain. However, the exact way in which the networks do their jobs is not (with the exception of the memory stores) spelled out, and it is for this reason that the model is not strictly a neural network model but falls into the realm of AI. I do not believe that enough is known, at present, to permit fruitful neural network modeling of, for example, the control processes proposed in my model; there are still too many possible alternatives.

GENERAL PRINCIPLES

Some guiding principles for the modeler of human information-processing networks emerge from a study of brain function. First, the various networks, and often parts of networks, may function independently, in that damage to one part need not render the entire network inoperable. The retina of the eye is a good example. Second, networks may function semiautonomously. Control inputs may specify what process is to be performed, but the process itself occurs entirely within the network. Finally, there is a high degree of parallelism in the networks of the brain, and it is therefore natural to assume that there is a great deal of replication of basic computational units. In the cerebral cortex, for example, small columnar groups of cells appear to be the basic processing unit, and these units are replicated many millions of times (Mountcastle,[27] Hubel & Wiesel,[28,29] Kabrisky.[30]) Semiautonomous functioning, parallel neural circuitry, and replication of simple processing units appear to be general principles of neural architecture.

Types of Visual Information

There are many types of visual information and many ways in which it can be analyzed. (For a recent review, see Bishop & Henry.[31]) Visual information originates either at the retina or else internally, from within the networks of the visual system. Information originating at the retina can be analyzed to identify objects, determine their size, color, texture, brightness, and so on. Many of these properties appear to be independently analyzed. We can recognize certain spatial properties of objects even without extensive "semantic" processing: we can recognize when one object is above another; we can determine the size of an object even if we do not recognize the object, and we can estimate the speed at which an object is moving. The reason that we can recognize these properties is in part due to the fact that we process the signals that position the eyes, head, and body, and signals that select for our attention certain regions of the visual field. The signals generated within the system are as important to normal activity as is sensory information and are an integral part of our experience. The same is true in other sensory modalities.

The General Notion of Association

Whenever information of two different types is to be associated, there must be a convergence of signals of the two types within the brain. For example, if a person is able to name an object when seeing a picture, there must be some location within the brain where a neural representation of the image of the object converges with a neural representation of the name of the object. Furthermore, if the person is able to respond with the name of the object, then there must be a convergence between either the encodings of the image or name of the object and the motor encoding—the signals which, when transmitted to the vocalization system, produce the spoken word.

There are at least two ways in which information of different types can converge. First, both types may be stored in the same memory location of an associative memory store. If this happens, then one type of information may gain access to the memory location and recall will also cause the second type of information to be recalled, thus completing the association. A second possibility is that the control signals to two or more memory stores converge so that memory locations in several different stores are controlled by the same regulatory signals. If information patterns of two different types are stored in memory locations that are thus functionally tied together, recall of one type of information will simultaneously cause recall of the second type of information. This completes the association. Both associative mechanisms may be present.

INTRODUCTION TO THE MODEL

In the remainder of this paper I will summarize the structure and operation of a model of visual naming and simple sentence understanding. (For a complete description, see Baron.[32,33]) I will first give an information-processing description of a neural network model for storage, recognition, and recall of information. The storage network is called a "cortical memory model" (Baron;[20] Pribram *et al.*[34]) and is a major component of the system being presented. It is important to understand this storage network, and particularly its control structure, in order to understand the remainder of the model. I will next describe those networks of the model that are necessary for naming. Finally, I will extend the model to include sentence under-standing.

A Summary of a Model for Cortical Memory

The Architecture of Memory Stores

The architecture of the model for cortical memory was motivated by the architecture of the cerebral cortex. Memory locations are distributed across an essentially flat, layered network. The input neurons arrive at the memory store perpendicular to its surface, and they distribute across the memory store to individual memory locations. The memory locations are columnar, the columns standing perpendicular to the sheet of the memory store. Information moves vertically through the columns. Individual memory locations are essentially inde-pendent processing units sharing only input and output circuitry. The control signals also arrive, and are transmitted, perpendicular to the plane of the memory store. This is shown in FIGURE 1.

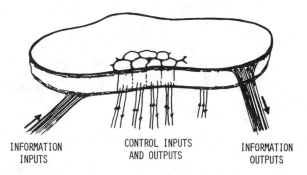

INFORMATION
INPUTS

CONTROL INPUTS
AND OUTPUTS

INFORMATION
OUTPUTS

FIGURE 1. The architecture of a memory store. Control inputs and outputs from each memory location are: (1) input signals to initiate storage; (2) input signals to initiate recall; and (3) recognition signals.

What Is Stored

The information to be stored by a given memory store is the firing pattern in a specified collection of input cells to that memory store. Storage is the process of modifying cellular parameters so that recall of the firing pattern at an arbitrary later time is possible. Recall is the process of generating in a specific collection of output cells a copy of the firing pattern that occurred in the input cells during storage. Although there is not necessarily an output cell for every input cell (there may be fewer outputs than inputs), during recall the firing rate of each output cell reproduces in time the firing rate of its corresponding input cell. Storage is the conversion of a dynamic firing pattern in the input cells into a spatial distribution of cellular parameters, and recall is the process of generating a copy of the firing pattern that occurred during storage. Putting it another way, storage is the conversion of information from the temporal to the spatial domain, and recall is the conversion of information from the spatial back to the temporal domain.

The modality of a memory store is the modality of the inputs to the memory store. A memory store that has inputs from several sources is a mixed-modality memory store. If a memory store has inputs of two modalities, its outputs are of the same two modalities. Associative access to stored information requires only that the inputs of one modality be similar to the stored information of the same modality.

Within a given memory store, information is organized into "packets" which contain the input information that arrived during a specified interval of time. If one packet contains stored information which lasts for five seconds, then recall of that packet can last for at most five seconds. A memory location is the physical storage unit, a small localized group of cells, which holds a packet of information. Depending on different network parameters, memory stores are capable of storing packets of different length, some a fraction of a second long, others several seconds or perhaps longer. (Motivation for the assumption that information is stored in packets comes in part from Penfield & Perot.[35])

Access to Stored Information is Associative

In order to recall a packet of information, a recent input to the memory store must be similar to some of the information contained in that packet. If, for example, an encoding of the sequence of letters "ABCDEF" ("A" followed in time by "B" followed in time by "C," etc.) is stored in a packet, then an input of the sequence "ABC" might enable recall of the entire packet "ABCDEF." Two recognition parameters of an associative memory store are the degree of similarity necessary to enable access to a packet, and the length of time during which the input must maintain this degree of similarity. Recognition is the decision to enable access to a packet of stored information.

The Analyzer Concept of Memory

Each memory store is an associative memory that continuously analyzes its inputs. Each memory location is a computational unit that evaluates the similarity between its stored pattern and the current input pattern to the memory store. The recognition signal from a memory location is high (fast firing rate) when the input to the memory store is similar to the information stored in that memory location, and the recognition signal is low (slow firing) when the input is not similar to the stored information. Recognition signals may be transmitted from a memory store to other networks for processing and analysis, and as such they are a representation (transformation) of the input information to the memory store. In addition, the recognition signals are used by the memory store to determine which packets of information will be made available for recall, but recognition signals *do not* initiate recall. External signals must do that.

Stores of Experience

The recognition signals from a memory store are an encoding of the information received by the memory store. For example, suppose that a memory store contains the records of visual experience, and further suppose that the experiences are organized in the memory stores according to the time of their occurrence. When a current event is similar to a past event, the pattern of recognition signals will be an encoding of exactly when in the past other, similar events occurred. The memory store is a "temporal analyzer" which converts the sensory encoding of the current event into an encoding which denotes when similar experiences occurred.

Naming Stores

By way of contrast, suppose a memory store contains the encodings of images of objects that can be named when seen. That is, the memory store contains not only the visual encodings, but also verbal encodings (the names) of the objects. I will call this type of associative memory store a "naming store." Further, suppose that the information in this naming store is organized according to the pictorial similarity of the stored images. For example, images of winged things—moths, butterflies, birds, airplanes, and so on—are all stored in nearby memory locations. In that case, when the input is the encoding of a winged thing, that region of the naming store containing engrams of similar-looking things would respond with high-recognition signals. The name of the thing seen as well as the names of visually similar things become available for recall. This type of memory store is a "conceptual analyzer" which converts the sensory encodings of visually perceived objects into activity which denotes the conceptual class of the image. (A conceptual class, here, is the set of all things that are pictorially similar.) (Motivation for this type of organization comes in part from Penfield & Roberts,[36] Chapter X.)

It is easy to form a conceptual analyzer using an associative memory store. When information is presented to an associative memory store for storage, recognition signals are generated by all memory locations in the store. The current input information is simply stored in an unused memory location in that region of the store which gives the largest recognition signals. Since the recognition signals are a measure of similarity between current input and stored information, the current input becomes stored in a region containing the engrams of other pictorially similar images. The result of storing engrams in this way is the formation of a conceptual analyzer.

THE MODEL

Now that we have a picture of the general properties of memory stores and some feeling for how information may be associated and accessed, we are in a position to see how several different networks and memory stores might be connected together to enable the naming of visually perceived objects and the understanding of simple sentences. What follows is a description of the model shown in FIGURES 2 and 3. I will begin with a discussion of the visual preprocessing networks and continue with a more complete description of the naming store. I will then propose one additional memory store called a "sentence store" which is to be responsible for the recognition and understanding of certain simple classes of sentences.

Visual Preprocessing

The sensory information stores and the stores of visual experience are all part of the visual preprocessing networks and are described in detail elsewhere (Baron[37]). What is important for this analysis is the fact that the pictorial and control patterns that are presented to the naming store are recognizable by the naming store. In order

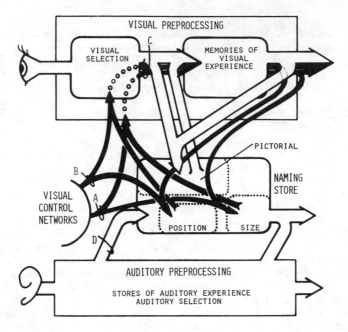

FIGURE 2. Networks for naming objects and attributes of objects. Some pathways are: (A) signals that specify the size of the selected region of the visual field; (B) signals that relate to eye-head-body movement; (C) encodings of visual experience; and (D) encodings of sounds.

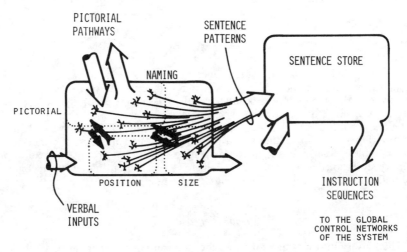

FIGURE 3. The architecture of the naming and sentence stores showing the origin of the sentence patterns. See FIGURE 2 for additional details.

to achieve this goal, the information-processing networks can select regions of the visual field for analysis, transform the images obtained from those regions into a form appropriate for analysis, and filter out extraneous information before delivering the encodings of the visual images to the memory stores. In addition, the memory stores of visual experience are part of the visual processing networks. All visual inputs that occupy the focus of visual attention are stored in this memory store, and all current inputs are correlated against the encodings of images stored there. The information can be recalled and used by the visual processing networks as necessary while searching the visual field.

Inputs to the naming store come either from the visual system or from the verbal (auditory) system. Inputs from the verbal system are encoded as strings of tokens, each representing a word. Inputs from the visual system are of three types. The first type delivers an encoding of the image which is projected on the retina and is the "pictorial" input to the naming store. Pictorial inputs are encoded as two-dimensional digitalized images. The second type delivers signals that relate to eye-head-body movement and therefore encode the locations of objects in the visual field. These input patterns arrive at the region of the memory store which names positional attributes. The third type delivers the control signals that specify to the visual selection networks the size of the region of the visual field that is selected for analysis. These input patterns arrive at the region of the memory store which names size attributes and are encoded as numbers which specify the vertical and horizontal size of the selected region of the visual field.

A General Naming Store

The simple naming store described above needs to be modified for this model. Inputs to and outputs from the naming store are both verbal (e.g. those which carry the encodings of words), and nonverbal (e.g. those which convey the encodings of the objects, attributes, or processes). The verbal inputs distribute across the entire naming store and make inputs to all memory locations in the naming store. Other types of inputs distribute locally, reaching some, but not all, of the memory locations in the naming store. As shown in FIGURE 2, one region of the naming store receives pictorial inputs, another region receives the control signals that determine the size of the region selected for visual analysis, and another region gets signals that are related to eye-head-body movement. Accordingly, that region which gets the pictorial components is used for naming visually perceived objects; that region which gets the size information is used to name the size and relative size of objects; and that region that gets the signals related to eye-head-body movement is used to name the position and relative position of objects. Regions that get only verbal inputs are not used for naming, but they play an important role in sentence recognition.

Processing Simple Sentences

Throughout verbal and visual processing, recognition signals are continually being generated by the naming store. For example, suppose the input question is: "What is the small object above the book?" Recognition signals are generated by the naming store from each memory location containing the representation of a word occurring in the question. The word "small" is recognized by the size region of the naming store and is associated with a control pattern that selects a small region of the visual field for analysis. The word "above" is recognized by the positional region of the naming store and is associated with the signals that are related to the control signals that move the eyes from one position to a higher position, and the word "book" is recognized by the pictorial region of the naming store and is associated with visual encodings (possibly hundreds) of books. The remaining words are recognized in purely verbal regions of the naming store. Thus, even before trying to answer the question the system has access to a great deal of information pertaining to the question.

The information that is made available when the sentence is analyzed can be used while scanning the visual field. For example, the system can recall and use the control pattern that is associated with the word "small" to select a small region of the visual field for analysis, and it can recall and use the control pattern that is associated with the word "above" to move the eyes from their current position to a higher position (and therefore look for a higher object). The way that the specific control patterns associated with "small" and "above" would be used is determined by the control networks of the visual system, a process that is beyond the scope of this paper.

Understanding Simple Sentences

The question that I wish to pursue here is: how are the signals analyzed which are generated while processing a sentence, and how does this result in "understanding" the meaning of the sentence? What I would like to suggest is that understanding the meaning of a sentence must result from an analysis of some pattern of activity by a memory store. We may now ask: what is the pattern of activity that is generated when the sentence is understood, in which memory store does the analysis take place, and what is the result of the analysis? One thing we may assume is that the system need not recognize specific sentences, but it should "understand" the meaning of *classes* of sentences. (Recognition of specific sentences depends on the records of experience, not on linguistic analysis.) For example, there are numerous sentences of the form: "Is that a cat?", 'Is that a dog?", 'Is that a horse?", etc. The system should recognize the form "Is that a $<$object$>$?" and "understand" thereby that it must look in the visual field and identify something, namely $<$object$>$. Similarly, "Is the door above the patio?" and "Is the boy below the tree?" are alike in form. In these questions, the structure is: "Is the $<$object 1$>$ $<$relation$>$ the $<$object 2$>$?", where $<$object 1$>$ and $<$object 2$>$ refer to objects, and $<$relation$>$ refers to a spatial relationship between the objects. Understanding in this case means that the system should look for the two objects indicated by $<$object 1$>$ and $<$object 2$>$, determine whether or not they stand in the geometric relation $<$relation$>$, and respond accordingly.

Understanding a sentence of this type can be broken down into two parts: (1) determining the procedural meaning of the sentence; i.e., what process to invoke in order to obtain information necessary to answer the question, and (2) analysis of the tokens within the sentence ($<$object 1$>$, $<$object 2$>$, $<$relation$>$, etc.) that identify specific attributes or things to look for or determine.

Now let us look at the activity of the naming store during the processing of the example sentences given above. The question "Is that a $<$object$>$?" would make sense only if the response invoked at the naming store by the word $<$object$>$ occurred in a region of the naming store that is associated with physical objects. For example, the sentences "Is that a blue?" and "Is that a below?" would not make sense. Similarly, the question "Is the $<$object 1$>$ $<$relation$>$ the $<$object 2$>$?" makes sense only when $<$object 1$>$ and $<$object 2$>$ refer to physical objects and $<$relation$>$ is a positional relationship. These observations suggest that one pattern that may be analyzed in determining the meaning of a sentence is the pattern of recognition signals that are generated by the naming store as it processes a sentence. It is this idea that I will now pursue.

The pattern of neural activity that is generated by the naming store and is analyzed for semantic content is a "sentence pattern." A sentence pattern is a pattern obtained by averaging the recognition signals from small regions of the naming store containing several memory locations, and it is this pattern that is delivered to the "sentence store" for analysis. See FIGURE 3. A sentence pattern is an encoding of the sequence of types or categories of words (object, position, size, etc.) as they appear in the sentence and is therefore an encoding of the structure of the sentence. The sentence patterns show a major departure from all other patterns described so far in that they depend both on the *specific information* that is stored in the naming store and on *where it is located*. Hence they are not a simple encoding of a sensory stimulus but depend very much on the history of inputs to the system; sentence patterns do not resemble the sensory encodings of sentences.

The "sentence store" is an associative memory store in which there is associated with each sentence pattern an "instruction sequence" or "program," which is a specification of *what to do* in order to respond properly to sentences matching that

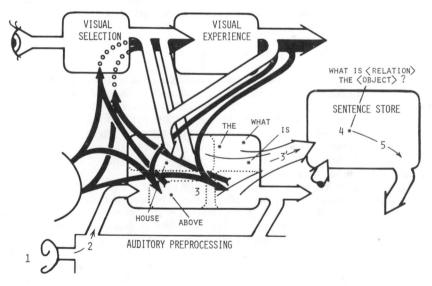

FIGURE 4. Initial processing of the sentence "What is above the house?" See text for explanation.

pattern. The origin of the instruction sequences is not specified in the model. Their destination, when recalled from the sentence store, is the global control network of the entire system. An instruction sequence is used to regulate the activity of the system as it responds to the sentence being analyzed, and it is by this process that the system "understands" the meaning of the sentence.

Consider the question "What is <above> the <house>?" (Triangular brackets indicate that the specific word is a token that may be replaced by any token of the same general type.) Refer to FIGURE 4 for this discussion. As the sentence is heard (1), auditory encodings (2) of words are delivered to and analyzed by the naming store (3). The stars (*) in FIGURE 4 are used to identify memory locations that contain the words in the input sentence. Information in these memory locations is made available for recall. At the same time, the sentence pattern (3') is generated by the naming store and delivered to the sentence store to be analyzed. Recognition of the sentence pattern (4) enables access to a memory location in the sentence store, and recall from that memory location (5) gives an instruction sequence that may be followed in answering the question. At this point the meaning of the sentence is understood. A possible instruction sequence for this type of sentence is: (a) locate a <house> in the visual field; if there is none, then respond with "I DON'T SEE A <house>."; (b) look <above> the <house>; (c) if an object is recognized by the naming store, then respond with the name of the object; if an object is located which is not recognized by the naming store, then respond "I DON'T KNOW WHAT IS <above> THE <house>."; if an object is not located, then respond with "I DON'T SEE ANYTHING <above> the <house>." The specific responses given here are intended only to illustrate how the system might use the token information in the input sentence to generate a verbal response. In actuality, the instruction sequences contain only encodings of "respond negatively," "respond positively" and so on, depending on the outcome of the processing, and an entirely different part of the verbal system, not given in this model, would be used to generate the response.

Pathology of the Model

One way to determine whether or not a model is in good correspondence with the brain is to compare syndromes induced by "damage" to the model with observed pathological syndromes of the brain. If there is a close correspondence between the pathologies of the model and of the brain, then our faith in the model is strengthened. On the other hand, failures of correspondence may call attention to inadequacies of the model and point the way to its improvement. (For an excellent treatise on clinical syndromes of the brain, see Luria.[38] For an analysis of disconnection syndromes in animals and man, see Geschwind.[39,40])

"Pure" pathological syndromes of the model can be generated by damage to a single part of a network or of a connecting pathway between networks. If a pathway is severed, the result is a disconnection syndrome. If a memory store is damaged locally, then the information that was stored in the damaged memory locations would be lost and, more importantly, the analysis performed by that region of the memory store would no longer occur. Finally, temporary blockage of small regions of the memory stores would correspond to brain syndromes induced by electrical stimulation to the surface of the brain (assuming the model is in good correspondence with the brain). Refer to FIGURE 5 for the following discussion.

Disconnection syndromes are the simplest to describe. The following are typical of the model: If the auditory input pathway to the naming store is severed (A), auditory encodings of words and sentences would not be analyzed by the naming store. This would result in the inability to understand or perceive spoken language (auditory aphasia). The ability to make new records of auditory experience and remember old ones would remain intact. If the visual input pathway to the naming store is severed (B), the result would be an inability to name visually sensed objects (agnosia, anomic aphasia). If the pathway between the naming store and the sentence store (C) is severed, the result would be an inability to understand spoken language. Individual words might be recognized and understood, but the meaning of sentences would be lost. (Because the naming store is large, the neural pathway between it and the sentence store would be more distributed than the other pathways described.

Damage to part of the pathway would result in the inability to use certain sentence constructions while leaving others intact. Thus, this syndrome would not be as clearly defined as the previous ones mentioned so far.) Other disconnection syndromes include: (D) inability to describe prior visual experience; (E) inability to recall prior events based on verbal descriptions; (F) inability to understand or use spatial relationships; and (G) inability to understand and use size relationships.

Regional damage to the naming store would result in various syndromes, depending on the region damaged and the extent of the damage. For example, damage to an area of the pictorial region of the naming store (H) might result in the inability to name certain objects or class of objects. Damage to the region of the naming store that names size relationships (I) would result in an inability to specify

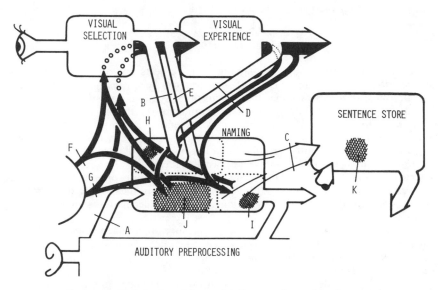

FIGURE 5. Pathologies of the model. See text for explanation.

the size of an object, and damage to the region of the naming store that names positional attributes (J) would result in an inability to name and use positional relationships. If the damage is local, then re-storage of the words and images in other memory locations of the same region of the naming store could result in partial or complete recovery of the lost function. If an entire functional region of the naming store is permanently destroyed, the ability to use the specific aspect of language for which that region of the store was responsible would never be recovered. For example, if the entire region of the naming store that receives the control patterns which relate to eye-head-body movement (J) is permanently damaged, then the ability to use or name spatial relationships that are based on eye-head-body movements would be lost. The words may be stored in other parts of the naming store, but since they could never be associated with eye-movement control patterns that specify the position of objects in the visual field, understanding and use of corresponding positional relationships would be permanently lost. If, on the other hand, only part of that region of the naming store is damaged, then recovery of the function might be possible.

Regional damage to the sentence store (K) would result in the lack of understanding of the types of sentence whose sentence patterns are stored there. This type of loss would, I expect, be very difficult to detect.

There are two processes involved in recovering from damage to the naming store. First, the encodings of items to be named must be restored along with their names. This can occur provided that some memory locations in the appropriate regions of the naming store are still intact. After the new naming engrams are made, the sentence patterns generated by the naming store would not be the same as before. That is so because the sentence patterns depend on the location of words in the naming store, and some of the locations have now been changed. The second step in the recovery of lost function is, therefore, to store the modified sentence patterns along with their associated instruction sequences. This re-storing process would indeed take longer than simply relearning the lost words.

Summary

A neural network model for naming visual objects and their attributes, and understanding certain simple types of sentences has been presented. The model is based on neural processes rather than linguistic or symbolic constructs.

The following are the major structural features of the model:

1. Memory stores are associative networks that perform an analysis of their inputs in real time. This analysis converts the input pattern into a "recognition pattern" that depends on the specific stored information and its location in the store.

2. The naming store is an analyzer network that converts the sensory encoding of a sentence into a "sentence pattern." The sentence pattern is obtained by averaging the recognition signals from several memory locations in the naming store. Because of the organization of words in the naming store, sentence patterns are an encoding of the structure of the sentences.

3. The sentence store is an associative memory store that recognizes sentence patterns and associates with each one an "instruction sequence" or "program" that specifies how the system should respond to the sentence. It is the enabling of access to this "program" that constitutes "understanding."

Sentences are understood in real time, without the explicit grammatical analysis that is usual in sentence-understanding systems. Understanding a sentence involves two functionally distinct processes: (1) associating with its sentence pattern an instruction sequence that specifies *what to do* in order to generate an appropriate response to the sentence matching that pattern: for example, to look in the visual field for an object, determine its location, and so on, and (2) analysis of the tokens in the sentence that indicate specific attributes or entities to look for or determine.

Acknowledgment

I wish to express my sincere thanks to Steven Epstein, who gave me considerable help in the final preparation of this paper.

References

1. BAR-HILLEL, Y. 1960. The present status in automatic translation of languages. *In* Advances In Computers. F. L. Alt, Ed. Vol. **1**: 91–163. Academic Press, New York, N.Y.

2. QUILLIAN, M. R. 1969. The teachable language comprehender: a simulation program and theory of language. Comm. ACM. **12:** 459–476.
3. RIEGER, C. J. III. 1974. Conceptual memory: A theory and computer program for processing the meaning content of natural language utterances. Stanford Artificial Intelligence Lab. Memo AIM-233.
4. WINOGRAD, T. 1972. Understanding Natural Language. Academic Press. New York, N.Y.
5. MINSKY, M. Ed. 1968. Semantic Information Processing. MIT Press. Cambridge, Mass.
6. RUSTIN, R. Ed. 1973. Natural Language Processing. Algorithmics Press, Inc. New York, N.Y.
7. SCHANK, R. C. & K. M. COLBY, Eds. 1973. Computer Models of Thought and Language. W. H. Freeman and Company. San Francisco, Calif.
8. SIMMONS, R. F. 1965. Answering English questions by computer: a survey. Comm. ACM. **8:** 53–70.
9. SIMMONS, R. F. 1970. Natural language question answering systems: 1969. Comm. ACM. **13:** 15–30.
10. CHARNIAK, E. 1972. Towards a model of children's story comprehension. Massachusetts Institute of Technology. Artificial Intelligence Lab. Tech. report AI TR-266.
11. JOSSELSON, H. H. 1971. Automatic translation of languages since 1960: a linguist's view. *In* Advances in Computers. F. L. Alt, Ed. Vol. **2:** 1–58. Academic Press. New York, N.Y.
12. WILKS, Y. 1974. Natural language understanding systems within the AI paradigm. Stanford Artificial Intelligence Lab. Memo AIM-237.
13. McCULLOCH, W. S. & W. PITTS. 1943. A logical calculus of the ideas immanent in nervous activity. Bull. Math. Biophys. **5:** 115–133.
14. ROSENBLATT. F. 1962. Principles of Neurodynamics. Spartan Books. Washington, D.C.
15. BEURLE, R. L. 1956. Properties of a mass of cells capable of regenerating pulses. Phil. Trans. R. Soc. Lond. [Biol. Sci.] **240:** 55–94.
16. WESTLAKE, P. R. 1968. Towards a theory of brain functioning: A detailed investigation of the possibilities of neural holographic processes. Ph.D. thesis. Univ. California at Los Angeles. Los Angeles, Calif.
17. LONGUET-HIGGINS, H. C. 1968. The non-local storage of temporal information. Proc. R. Soc. London [Biol.] **171:** 327–334.
18. GROSSBERG, S. 1969. Some networks that can learn, remember, and reproduce any number of complicated space-time patterns, I. J. Math. Mechanics **19:** 53–91.
19. GROSSBERG, S. 1970. Some networks that can learn, remember, and reproduce any number of complicated space-time patterns, II. Studies in Appl. Math. **49:** 135–166.
20. BARON, R. J. 1970. A model for cortical memory. J. Math. Psych. **7:** 37–59.
21. CAVANAGH, J. P. 1972. Holographic processes realizable in the neural realm: prediction of short term memory performance. Tech. rep. Université de Montreal. Montreal, Canada.
22. KOHONEN, T., P. LEHTIÖ & J. ROVAMO. 1974. Modelling of neural associative memory. Ann. Acad. Sci. Fenn. [Med.] **167:** 1–18.
23. NORMAN, D. A., Ed. 1970. Models of Human Memory. Academic Press. New York, N.Y.
24. TULVING, E. & W. DONALDSON, Eds. 1972. Organization of Memory. Academic Press. New York, N.Y.
25. ANDERSON, J. R. & G. H. BOWER, 1973. Human Associative Memory. V. H. Winston & Sons. Washington, D.C.
26. MELTON, A. W. & E. MARTIN, Eds. 1972. Coding Processes in Human Memory. V. H. Winston & Sons. Washington, D.C.
27. MOUNTCASTLE, V. B. 1957. Modality and topographic properties of single neurons of cat's somatic sensory cortex. J. Neurophysiol. **20:** 408–434.
28. HUBEL, D. H. & T. N. WIESEL. 1962. Receptive fields, binocular interaction and functional architecture in the cat's visual cortex. J. Physiol. **160:** 106–154.
29. HUBEL, D. H. & T. N. WIESEL. 1968. Receptive fields and functional architecture of monkey striate cortex. J. Physiol. **195:** 215–243.
30. KABRISKY, M. 1966. A Proposed Model for Visual Information Processing in the Human Brain. Univ. Illinois Press. Urbana, Ill.
31. BISHOP, P. O. & G. H. HENRY. 1971. Spatial Vision. Ann. Rev. Psych. **22:** 119–159.
32. BARON, R. J. 1974. A theory for the neural basis of language. Part 1: A neural network model. Int. J. Man-Machine Studies **6:** 13–48.

33. BARON, R. J. 1974. A theory for the neural basis of language. Part 2: Simulation studies of the model. Int. J. Man-Machine Studies **6:** 155–204.

34. PRIBRAM, K. H., M. NUWER & R. J. BARON. 1974. The holographic hypothesis of memory structure in brain function and perception. *In* Contemporary Developments In Mathematical Psychology. D. H. Krantz, R. C. Atkinson, R. D. Luce & P. Suppes, Eds. Vol. **II:** 416–457. W. H. Freeman and Co. San Francisco, Calif.

35. PENFIELD, W. & P. PEROT. 1963. The brain's record of auditory and visual experience. Brain **86:** 595–696.

36. PENFIELD, W. & L. ROBERTS. 1959. Speech and Brain Mechanisms. Princeton University Press. Princeton, N.J.

37. BARON, R. J. 1970. A model for the elementary visual networks of the human brain. Int. J. Man-Machine Studies, **2:** 267–290.

38. LURIA, A. R. 1966. Higher Cortical Functions in Man. Basic Books, Inc. New York, N.Y.

39. GESCHWIND, N. 1965. Disconnexion syndromes in animals and man: Part 1. Brain **88:** 237–294.

40. GESCHWIND, N. 1965. Disconnexion syndromes in animals and man: Part 2. Brain **88:** 585–644.

PROBLEM-SOLVING APPROACH TO FIRST-LANGUAGE ACQUISITION

L. Siklóssy

Computer Sciences Department
University of Texas
Austin, Texas 78712

INTRODUCTION

Although no satisfactorily complete grammar has yet been built for any natural language, human beings continue to learn natural languages, starting at an early age. The acquisition of a first language by a human being has been studied extensively. We know well the rates of acquisition, the various stages of learning the language, and so on. But we still do not understand well the *processes* used by a child that make the learning of the language possible. Our approach toward solving the mystery regarding which processes the child uses would be to argue that language acquisition possesses many similarities to problem-solving techniques used by humans and computer programs.

Our arguments would be considerably stronger if we could exhibit a computer program that could learn a language given such problem-solving capabilities as matching, generalization, special case handling, and others. No such program exists today, nor is one feasible in the immediate future. We shall describe a programmed experiment to implement a very incomplete language-learning system. We shall argue that the limitations of the program lie not so much with the information processing techniques used, but rather with the great difficulties that we experience in trying to represent large amounts of dynamic information about the world, coupled with the difficulties we have in manipulating this information. A twelve-to-eighteen-month-old child already has a highly sophisticated representation of his environment. Our present computer representations of similar environments are far less sophisticated than the infant's representation.

LANGUAGES EXPRESS SITUATIONS

The language-learning program Zbie[1,2] (no acronym) is concerned with learning natural language expressions of situations. Zbie does not try to build a grammar in the conventional sense. Instead, it attempts to build internal structures and various kinds of information about situations so that it can express these situations in the natural language that it is trying to learn. The language is language *about* something; namely, situations. A situation can include selected objects, persons, desired goals, feelings, time dynamics, *et cetera*. As learning progresses, complex relations between situations and their natural language expressions are built.

The design of Zbie has been influenced by the Language-through-Pictures booklets by Richards *et al.*[3] In the booklets, simple situations are described by pictures. Persons in the pictures are represented as stick figures. Certain conventions, such as dotted lines and arrows, are used to represent dynamically varying situations, and to introduce notions of time. With every picture is associated a set of utterances in the natural language. In simple situations, there is a close equivalence between the picture, which, for example, may represent a foot, and the written utterance: "This is a foot."

To learn a language with the Language-through-Picture booklets, the pairs "picture representation—language expression" are to be compared. Slowly, the student learns to express more and more situations. The knowledge acquired is subsequently used to partially understand new situations.

The program Zbie follows a learning paradigm similar to that which should be followed by the student of the Language-through-Pictures booklets. Since the behavior of Zbie has been described extensively elsewhere,[1,2] we shall only sketch it here.

Initially, Zbie has no knowledge about the natural language. But it has some knowledge of situations: it can recognize that two situations are similar, that one is a more detailed description of another, and so forth. From first presentation of two similar situations, and their associated language expressions, Zbie builds a pattern of situations, and learns rules as to how the class of situations described by this pattern are to be expressed in the natural language. The patterns are built with the help of sets in context, and, recursively, also patterns.

Subsequently, when a new situation is presented, Zbie searches its store of patterns to find one pattern that includes or is close to the new situation. (The situation is partially or totally matched to a previous pattern.) When the situation can be expressed correctly, there is no problem. When it cannot, Zbie tries to express as much of it as possible, while also trying to understand the language expression. If all goes well, a previous pattern may be expanded, or a new pattern created, to understand the new situation. Generalizations are made possible by the recursive form of the patterns and the transfer of sets from one pattern to another.

As Zbie learns to express more and more situations, some of the structures it builds begin to acquire classical grammatical properties. For example, a set may consist mostly of masculine nouns in the genitive (Zbie mainly tried to learn Russian).

LIMITATIONS OF THE LEARNING PROGRAM

The limiations of the program are instructive. We should expect many limitations, since the program is small, smaller, for example, than a Monopoly playing program.

Representational Inadequacies

As in the Language-through-Pictures booklets, we assumed in Zbie that the learner could understand situations. Hence, we had to represent the situations in an understandable way. The booklets assume that every learner will understand the pictures and stick figures. Even now, the capabilities of picture-processing programs are inadequate for the understanding of the pictures found in the booklets. Therefore, instead of giving Zbie pictures, we represented a situation using a tree, in a representation similar to a functional calculus. The functional representation has the advantage of being uniform, structured, and easily manipulable by programs.

But the difficulties are not over. In the booklets, a picture is taken in the context of a person's knowledge about the world. We can have a picture representing a half-sun, and a person in bed. The natural language text might say something similar to: "This is Ann. She is in bed. The sun is rising. It is day. Ann will get up. She does not like to get up. She likes to stay in bed." With sufficient knowledge about simple objects (sun, bed, Ann, etc.), actions and relations (to like, to get up, to stay, etc.), and the picture that provides a context and numerous clues, the little story can be understood easily. Unfortunately, a program cannot come close, at present, to a person's understanding of the little story. Considerable efforts are expanded on representational techniques that describe a person's vast knowledge of the world. A number of schemes, variously called scripts, frames, slides, processes, and other names, have been proposed to represent the world.

None of the schemes has yet passed the test of being used successfully in the implementation of a sizeable chunk of dynamic knowledge.

In fact, the knowledge about the world that we can give a computer is minuscule when compared to the knowledge of the world possessed by a child of twelve to eighteen months, when it begins to learn a natural language. The simple expression "I want a cookie" exhibits considerable knowledge of the world. The child expressing the desire "I want a cookie" knows about cookies, their crunchiness, and their yummy taste. He remembers eating cookies, and has pleasurable sensations associated with this activity. He also knows that his father is a possible agent for procuring a cookie. Finally, he has learned that the utterance is a possible means for achieving the desired situation of possessing, and subsequently eating, a cookie. The knowledge about cookies and related agents, pleasures, experiences, and so on, is too complex to be represented adequately in the computer by presently known techniques. The machine has not yet achieved the visual or gustative capabilities of a two-year-old. The extended conceptual knowledge associated with the word "cookie" itself could be represented now in an unsatisfactory and ad-hoc manner at best.

The Selection of Contextual Information

Returning to the bedroom scene, we see that the language expressions interact with our world knowledge by selecting certain aspects of our considerable extended knowledge that can be reached when thinking about "bedroom, sleep, getting up," and so on. It is remarkable that the selection of knowledge can take place so quickly. Computer programs, such as problem solvers and theorem provers, that must select relevant information among much irrelevant information, have not been very successful. They have been more successful when only relevant information has been provided, and they can then go deep in a chain of deductions. By contrast, the information-processing behavior of human beings, especially at the linguistic level, seems to be characterized by good selection of relevant information followed, perhaps, by some very shallow deduction. Human beings also can adequately process a large variety of details and exceptions, whereas programs often are not designed to be able to do this.

Language Influence on World Representation

An even greater challenge to a language-learning program is given by the interaction of the language with the representation of the world. Most Americans have ten fingers and ten toes, but Russians have twenty finger/toes, since the same noun is used both for finger and toe. In English, we can talk of the flight of a bird and the flight of a plane. In French, the satirical weekly *Le Canard Enchaîné* headlined several years ago: "Les Russes ratent tous leurs vols" (The Russians miss all their flights/thefts), where "vol" referred both to the unsuccessful flight of an airplane (a supersonic Tupolev exploded in flight) and the unsuccessful shoplifting attempt of a Russian athlete in Paris. The particular idiosyncrasies of a natural language will color the interpretation given to situations and the forms taken by the representation of the world. A language-learning program must therefore, almost from the start, structure its world knowledge in ways that agree with the particularities of the language. The initial representation of the world, which was necessary for the learning process to begin, will be changed. Present computer programs have much difficulty in restructuring their knowledge, especially on a continuous basis.

Implications for Subsequent Language Learning

Hence, as a language is learned, the original world representation is influenced by and changed to resemble the view of the world of the natural language being learned. After a certain time, perhaps several years, we can expect that the modified world representation becomes the principal working representation. If our scenario is correct, it would explain the difficulties experienced by human beings in their attempts to learn a new language at a later age. When the second language is learned late, the world representation incorporates too many idiosyncrasies that conflict with the idiosyncrasies of the second language. If the second language is learned at an early age, the idiosyncrasies of the first natural language would not have had time to become fixated yet. Similarly, if someone has learned several languages, we can assume that none of the conflicting language idiosyncrasies could dominate to produce a world-representation sclerosis which would hinder the acquisition of a new language. Similarly, intelligent programs often cannot process information that has a unique representation. Often, translations to other representations must be made.

Language as Object of Linguistic Discourse

In the crib, and later, children practice their languages and correct themselves. Soon, language takes on a reality of its own and becomes an object of the world that can participate as an element of situations, and hence can be talked about. Many concepts of common usage have only a linguistic existence. In informatics, we are barely beginning to develop some sophistication with programs that understand, modify, or create other programs, possibly including themselves.

CONCLUSIONS

Starting from an experimental incomplete language-learning program, we have speculated on the information-processing features that a language-learning program would possess. We have argued that the limitations of our present world representational techniques must be overcome before much progress can be made. Additional hurdles to be surmounted include the bootstrapping of linguistic knowledge about itself and its continuous restructuring. The information-processing capabilities needed by an adequate language-learning program are all too often not yet available, although their development is being pursued.

REFERENCES

1. SIKLOSSY, L. 1971. A language-learning heuristic program. Cognitive Psych. **2:** 479–495.
2. SIKLOSSY, L. 1972. Natural language learning by computer. *In* Representation and

Meaning: Experiments with Information Processing Systems. H. A. Simon & L. Siklóssy, Eds.: 288–328. Prentice-Hall. Englewood Cliffs, N.J.

3. RICHARDS, I. A. *et al.* 1961. Russian through Pictures. Book 1. Washington Square Press. New York, N.Y. (There are similar books for English, French, German, Hebrew, Italian, and Spanish.)

DISCUSSION

Roland Puccetti

Department of Philosophy
Dalhousie University
Halifax, Nova Scotia, Canada B3H 3J5

In an age when neuroscientists increasingly use the language of computer technology to describe central neural processes, there is nothing surprising about computer scientists contributing to a conference on the origins and evolution of language and speech. We can be grateful to Dr. Baron and Dr. Siklóssy for these reports on their work at the interface of man and machine viewed as information-processing entities.

It is, however, by no means obvious that mathematical models of neural networks will aid us in understanding how the human brain achieves complex psychological processes, nor that a theoretically similar behavioral output by machine and man would show that the same means are used to get the same result.

Take, for example, the connection between visual recognition and naming, dealt with at length in Dr. Baron's paper. What is striking about the human brain is that it is bilaterally organized and, more important, that there is a functional asymmetry between the cognitive information processing of the two hemispheres. Visual recognition, particularly of complex forms like human faces, is done primarily, or at least with superior speed and precision, in the right hemisphere. So much was suspected for a long time from the fact that visual agnosia in general and prosopagnosia in particular result almost exclusively from lesions to the right parietal lobe.[1,2] Support for this finding has also come from recent split-brain studies, where in the same human subjects a decided right-hemisphere superiority was demonstrated for recognition, after brief exposure, of chimeric figures and unfamiliar faces.[3] Apparently, in the normal, cerebrally intact human, the right hemisphere recognizes the object and sends this information across the splenium to the dominant (left) hemisphere's angular gyrus, where it is integrated with the speech area for naming. (Exactly how it does this, of course, awaits further research.)

Now, this could have important implications for mechanical recognition programs. For the right hemisphere does not seem to process information analytically, linearly, step-by-step. Rather, it synthesizes what it receives holistically, in an all-at-once or *Gestalt* manner. This would appear to explain why it is so difficult to provide an accurate verbal description of someone's face in the absence of unusual conspicuous features. (It is interesting that in the most thorough facial recognition program I know of, key details of the face, like curvature of the nose and thickness of the lips, had to be judged by humans before they could be incorporated into the program.[4]) But if digital computers really model left-hemisphere information processing, and if indeed all computers necessarily operate on analytic principles, does this not suggest that we are on the wrong track in trying to simulate visual recognition mechanically? I have discussed this elsewhere at length,[5] and will here add only a word or two. It has been suggested[6] to me that the trouble is not that computers necessarily operate on analytic principles, but that so far we have been able to give them only left hemisphere algorithms. If we could give them right hemisphere-type algorithms, then the same machines might be able to do what our right hemisphere does when, for example, it recognizes a face. Unfortunately for this suggestion, it is just the inaccessibility of right-hemisphere cognitive processes to left hemisphere understanding—even in our own brains—that seems to prevent our left hemisphere's writing such algorithms.

But to return to Dr. Baron's paper, in its last section he discusses pathological syndromes that could be induced by damage to the model and invites us to compare these with known neuropathological syndromes arising from brain damage. A close correspondence between these, he suggests, would strengthen faith in the model. Now, I do not want to deny that one can find analogous pathologies in the literature. But what is important to neuropathology is being able to predict the lesion site in the brain itself; i.e., mapping control units and linking pathways on the brain so as to add to our knowledge of its functional neuroanatomy. Dr. Baron's model would have medical use, for example, to clinical neurologists, only if from it one could predict hitherto unsuspected damage and confirm this at autopsy or by other means. Yet there does not seem much chance, at least in this stage of its development, that the model will have such predictive consequences, precisely because investigation of brain function is the most painstakingly empirical science we have. To see this we need only ask ourselves if early Nineteenth Century neurologists, armed with Dr. Baron's model, could have used it to discover the critical importance of what we now call Brodmann's area 17 to visual perception, or of the superior colliculus in the brainstem to visual orientation.

I come now to Dr. Siklóssy's interesting communication. If I understand him correctly, he is suggesting as a result of his success with the Zbie program that first-language acquisition in humans is a problem-solving task like many others, and hence that we need not postulate separate language-acquisition devices in the human brain.

This is a bold and ingenious suggestion, but where humans are concerned, many considerations appear to weight against it. First, while all human life beyond the first postnatal months involves problem-solving activities of many kinds, language learning seems to be a developmental milestone gone through at a critical stage in preadolescent maturation. In those fortunately rare cases of normal children reared in an artificially language-deprived environment to age ten or twelve, they are usually unable to learn language thereafter.[7] But if language acquisition is just another problem-solving task, they should be able to learn more quickly when older and placed in a language-rich environment, because their problem-solving abilities increase with age and experience.

Second, if first-language acquisition does not require separate devices (i.e., specialized cerebral structures), then an otherwise normal adult with severe Broca's aphasia resulting from lesions at the foot of the third frontal convolution (Brodmann's areas 44 and 45) on the left side should be able to *relearn* full language functions. After all, we are talking about perhaps only 7 grams of tissue in a problem-solving mass of tissue 200 times that weight. Yet in many cases, relearning does not take place with twenty or so years of effort.

Finally, if Siklóssy were right, there ought to be a gradation of language-learning ability across species close to man, just as there is a gradation of other problem-solving abilities. It is true that the great apes show cognitive abilities preadaptive for acquisition of symbolic language, but they do not develop this in natural conditions and, as some reports in this conference clearly show, can be taught to acquire this under human tutelage only with arduous training and limited success. There does, when all is said and done, appear to be something special about human language-learning and the neural mechanisms that subserve it. Perhaps we should be wary of language-learning programs using conventional problem-solving techniques; their success may mask the difference between them and organic information-processing entities like ourselves.

REFERENCES

1. McFie, J., M. F. Piercey & O. L. Zangwill. 1950. Visual spatial agnosia associated with lesions of the right cerebral hemisphere. Brain 73: 167–190.
2. Hecaen, H. & R. Angelergues. 1962. Agnosia for faces (prosopagnosia). Arch. Neurol. 7: 92–100.
3. Levy, J., Trevarthen, C. & R. W. Sperry. 1972. Perception of bilateral chimeric figures following hemispheric deconnexion. Brain 95: 61–78.
4. Harmon, L. D. 1973. The recognition of faces. Sci. Am. 229: 71–82.
5. Puccetti, R. 1974. Pattern recognition in computers and the human brain: with special application to chess playing machines. Brit. J. Phil. Sci. 25: 137–154.
6. Butler, S. 1974. Personal communication.
7. Dennis, W. 1951. A further analysis of reports of wild children. Child Dev. 22: 153–158.

COMMENTS ON COMMENTS

Dr. Siklossy: Before coming to Dr. Puccetti's criticism of my paper, I should like to mention, for the sake of clarification, that Harmons's work (Ref. 3) uses the computer only as a statistical helper. In Harmon's system, features of a face have been selected by a human, and also measured by a human. The computer only applies some statistics to the measurements. Therefore, Harmon's work hardly uses the computer beyond a big calculating machine. Other face recognition programs use the computer in more sophisticated ways.

The principal criticisms of my paper are as follows:

1. Language learning occurs with well-defined milestones.
2. Older children should learn languages more easily, since their problem-solving capabilities are enhanced.
3. Lesions in Brodmann's areas 44 and 45 (only some seven grams of tissue) limit language-relearning capabilities.
4. Since there is a gradation of problem-solving capabilities across species, there should be a gradation of language-learning capabilities.

We should like to answer these criticisms very briefly. A full development would require considerable further work.

1. Problem-solving abilities, and in particular, advances in representation, also occur with well-defined milestones. Piaget's work has amply demonstrated the above.
2. We have argued that the process of language learning involves a bootstrapping of linguistic knowledge into the representation of the world. Older children who have not acquired language would have a representation of the world that has become too fixated for the bootstrapping to occur. I tried to argue along similar lines to explain the difficulties in second language-learning by someone who is no longer young.
3. There is considerable redundancy in the human brain's capabilities. The fact that lesions in some areas prevent language relearning does not mean that the processes embodied in that region are unique. We could imagine that some problem-solving processes (or monitoring processes) are implemented in that region, as well as in others, but that they are used only in the region under question for language. The analogy with a computer program in memory should make matters easier. Suppose that I have a program, stored in memory, and that I cut out (turn off) some of the memory. Some of the functions of the program will no longer work, but that does not mean that the cut-out piece of memory had intrinsically special properties. It may even be that some of the remaining parts of memory are essentially identical to the

cut-out part (up to address translation, etc.) but the program still will not work if it cannot reorganize itself to transfer the load of the cut-out part to the still active identical (or similar) part of the memory.

Hence, nothing about the findings about the lesions would negate the problem-solving approach to language learning.

4. There are, in fact, in many other species, more or less sophisticated means for communication; i.e., languages. That apes have difficulties learning human means of communication is not surprising. Human beings have not yet mastered the full repertoire of grunts and gestures used by apes, and could master it "only with arduous training and limited success" (the quote is taken from Puccetti's comments, and just used in the other direction!) We should not forget that human beings are far superior problem solvers than apes, or other species. It is not surprising that their language capabilities are also superior. In our approach to language learning, we mentioned that problems of representation and language bootstrapping were extremely serious. In particular, *we* human beings have enormous difficulties in understanding them in computer programs. It would not be surprising if other species' limited problem-solving capabilities could not solve these problems, thereby resulting in limited language capabilities.

Part VI. Paleobiological Approaches

TOOLMAKING, HUNTING, AND THE
ORIGIN OF LANGUAGE

Ashley Montagu

Princeton, New Jersey 08540

To the inarticulateness of nature man has added a new dimension—speech. He is the only creature who talks, in the sense of using a shared set of abstract rules for creating and communicating ideas about the world. Hence, it has more than once been suggested that, instead of being called by that oafishly arrogant, prematurely self-bestowed name *Homo sapiens*, he would be more accurately described as *Homo loquens*.

In this paper, which is in two parts, I shall be concerned first with a brief inquiry into some of the factors that may have contributed to the origin and development of speech, and second, with a discussion of the importance of the study of prehistoric tools as a means of learning something about the behavior of early man.

Let me begin, then, by saying that there exists a widespread belief among those of us who should know better that the tools of the early Oldowans were of the simplest kind, typically represented by the unifacial and bifacial choppers that one sees almost exclusively illustrated in books—mine, I regret to say, among them—on prehistoric man. Indeed, for a long time this is the only type of tool I believed had been found at the oldest Olduvai levels. Illustrations should present assemblages of the tools found, *not* figures of a single allegedly "typical" implement. Otherwise, it is easy to fall victim to the imprinting of the "typical pebble tool" solecism. It is easy enough to point to the mistakes of others; what is more difficult is for us to digest the unpalatable truth that such mistakes are equaled only by those we ourselves commit. In that spirit may I then, as uncaptiously as possible, note that in the proceedings of a recently published conference on the origin and evolution of language and speech we find one of the contributors stating that "The first tools, which are associated with the australopithecines and *Homo habilis*, are either unshaped stones or stones that have a flake or two taken off them."[1] Curiously, in his references the author lists Mary Leakey's superb description of the tools and other artifacts found in Beds I and II at Olduvai.[2] That work shows the early Oldowans used quite a variety of skillfully made tools, not only of stone but also some of bone. There was evidence also of several other interesting artifacts.

The tools from Bed I (site DK 1A) are typical Oldowan and are made from two kinds of lava, also from chert and tuff, and consist of five types of choppers, polyhedrons, discoids, light duty scrapers, and burins, as well as other varieties of heavy duty tools. In addition, artificially flaked and abraded bone tools were also recovered. It was at this level also that the remains were found of a loosely piled circle of stones suggestive of an artificial structure. No primate fossil remains have been found at this level, but the tools suggest use in cutting, pounding, scraping, and the butchering of small animals.

Whoever made these tools must not only have been able to select the appropriate materials—bone, various kinds of stone, and possibly wood—but also to shape them for a particular purpose, and to teach the techniques of making them to others.

It is suggested that the kind of cognitive processes involved in the making and the transmission of the art of making the Oldowan-type tools mentioned, implies the existence of some form of speech, however rudimentary. We know that it is possible to think without speech; deaf-mutes do it. It is not, however, possible to speak without thinking. A creature that learns to make tools to a complex preexisting pattern, calculated to serve a series of complex future purposes, among them the making of other tools, must have the kind of abstracting mind that would be of high selective value in facilitating the development of the ability to communicate such skills by the necessary verbal acts.

It is further suggested that it was toolmaking in interactive relationship with small-game hunting that supplied the other necessary factor that constituted the sufficient conditions which led to speech.

It has on several occasions been suggested that big-game hunting was probably a principal condition in the origination of speech. I am suggesting here that speech originated earlier than that.

At a stage probably somewhat earlier than the Oldowan, small-game hunting led to the development of tools for the more efficient butchering of the kill. We know that small-game hunting in itself would not lead to speech, since chimpanzees and some baboons engage in that activity.[3] Furthermore, small-game hunting is usually pursued in silence. Food-gathering, the securing of skins, tendons, bones, and possibly other useful parts of the bodies of animals, seem to have been among the main reasons for the gradual invention and development of a variety of tools designed to secure those ends.

It hardly need be said that speech did not spring full-blown from early man's head, but that it must have been at first quite rudimentary and practical, restricted to simple names for things and words for processes, relating principally to toolmaking and usage, as well as to the hunt.

At Olduvai, site FLK North, there were five fossil-bearing levels, four of these being living floors and the fifth a butchering site where the skeleton of an elephant was found imbedded in clay associated with tools and flakes. All levels contained large quantities of microfauna, including reptiles, rodents, insectivores, small birds, and so on. Mary Leakey says that the repeated discovery of the skeletal remains of large animals embedded in clay, antelope (*Paramularius altidens*), goats *Pelorovis oldowayensis*), a *Deinotherium*, and an elephant, associated with numbers of stone tools, looks as if these animals may have been deliberately driven into swamps by early hominids. Depressed fractures above the orbits on the antelope skulls suggest that these animals were killed by means of an accurately placed blow (Ref. 2, p. 61).

If elephant (*Elephas* and *Deinotherium*) were, in fact, driven into swamps and either killed or allowed to die there, then we can see how the beginnings of big-game hunting may have come about. In Bed II at site SHK and Bed IVa the remains of two herds of antelopes similarly embedded in clay have been found. The suggestion is that they were driven into the swamps by early Oldowans.

In addition, other evidence of the mental development of the early Oldowans is the curiously grooved and pecked phonolite cobble found at level I in Upper Bed I at FLK North. This stone, which has been artificially shaped, and seems unlikely to have served as a tool for any practical purpose, bears a striking resemblance to the head of a baboon. A similar quartzite cobble, which appears to have been naturally produced, has been described by Dart from Makapansgat.[4] As Mary Leakey says, "The occurrence of such stones at hominid sites in such remote periods is of considerable interest (Ref. 2, p. 269).

Also at level I in Upper Bed I FLK North, symmetrical stone balls first make their appearance. Such spheroids are relatively rare at this level, but become markedly more numerous in Middle and Upper Bed II, where they are never less than 20% of the tools and where they range in size more extensively than in earlier assemblages (Ref. 2, p. 266). Mary Leakey thinks they may have served as the essential parts of bolas. The different sizes of the stones suggest that, if they were used as bolas, animals of different sizes were the targets. Bolas are missiles that can bring animals down by entangling their legs both on the ground and in the air. Richard Leakey has shown that a pair of such spheroids, each attached to a cord about a yard long, entangle more effectively around upright posts than a group of three (Ref. 2, p. 266). Such spheroids have been found in association with *Homo erectus* and Neanderthal man, facts which tend to strengthen the belief that these stones may well have been used as parts of an ingenious hunting implement.

The probability that such a sophisticated hunting implement was made and used by the early Oldowans, taken together with the other evidence of their economic activities, renders it very difficult to believe that they had not customarily employed some form of speech.

Everyone agrees that the development of big-game hunting (and we follow Teleki here in accepting any animal weighing 10 kg or more as big game[3]) was closely related to the elaboration of speech. It seems to me, however, that the evidence indicates that speech originated prior to the development of big-game hunting, and that rather than being the result of such hunting, the latter was one, at least, of the effects of speech; that speech, in fact, made big-game hunting possible or at least contributed to making it possible.

Much more is involved at many complex levels in big- than in small-game hunting. Most important would have been the planning and attention to logistics and strategy, as well as roles. Crude as all this may have been, it would undoubtedly have been most economically achieved by verbal means, just as communication during the hunt would have been.

The influence of toolmaking upon the development of intelligence must have been considerable. The intimate relation between the skillful hand and the intelligent mind has been many times the subject of comment. It is not surprising that the hand should have formed the subject of one of the earliest and greatest contributors to our understanding of the nervous system, Charles Bell, in his Bridgewater treatise of 1833.[5] Nor did the relationship between hand, brain, and the erect posture escape the acute mind of Frederick Engels, in 1896, in his *Dialectics of Nature*.[6] In his *Creative Evolution*, published in 1902,[7] Bergson discussed at considerable length the relationship between the invention of tools and the development of intelligence, and another philosopher with anthropological interest, Lucien Lévy-Bruhl, in one of his books, observed that "The progress of the mind is due to the co-operation between the mind and the hand." The idea is implicit throughout Frederic Wood Jones' notable book on the hand,[8] and in many references to the subject since. It is to be noted that the area of the brain devoted to the hand is remarkably large. In this connection it has more than once been observed that the size of the cerebral and cerebellar areas devoted to any function is related not so much to the size of the structure or part of the body involved as to the skill in using it.[9] It is also not without significance that the areas of the cerebral cortex for hand, tongue, and speech situated within the left hemisphere, as well as the area for hand gestures during speech, are all closely associated with the areas for logical analytical operations on perceptual material and temporal sequential ordering.

Toolmaking greatly contributed to skill in the use of the hands and to mental development, in a feedback interactive relationship that led to a continuing reinforcement in the skills of both; that is, mental and manual skills.

Man's ideas, his words, are conceptual tools, mental analogs of material tools. Man has to learn how to "handle" these conceptual tools, just as he does other implements. Prehension, meaning "to grasp," "to lay hold of," is a function both of the hand and of the mind. In their book *Biogenetic Structuralism* Laughlin and d'Aquili define prehension as "the inputting of data through any of the sensory receptors into the brain plus the simultaneous association of those data with other data and associations of data stored in memory within the brain." [10] Mind and hand work interoperatively together. Thought constitutes man's principal adaptive response to the challenges of the environment. Laughlin and d'Aquili take a similar view when they write of prehension being cognitively extended, enabling protohominids to predict the utility of a hand-held tool beyond the period of immediate use (p. 93), beyond immediately prehended relationships to more expansive ones in time and space. In short, with the domination of inert matter and the ability to mold it to one's needs for some future purpose must have gone the ability to conjure with the "not-here" and the "not-now." Language molded on matter and on man's action on matter resulting in an instrument free from matter, a device to triumph over mechanism.

Bergson [7] postulated that "Intelligence in its initial form may be considered to be the ability to produce artificial objects, particularly tools, and to continue making them by a variety of methods." And he goes on to suggest that if we would ignore pride and allow ourselves to be guided by history and prehistory, we would call ourselves not *Homo sapiens* but *Homo faber*. The toolmaking kind of intelligence Bergson calls "creative intelligence" (the "practical intelligence" of later writers), believing that the evidence of prehistory and history shows that creative intelligence preceded rational intelligence.

By creative or practical intelligence is meant, unlike conceptual or logical intelligence, not the application of abstractions to facts, but the purposeful use of movements and actions for dealing with the shape of objects and with external events. [11]

The Bergsonian distinction between creative or practical intelligence and rational intelligence has a certain validity, as Piaget's [12] and other studies of children have shown, and it is not unreasonable to suppose that the earliest toolmaking, well antedating the toolmaking of the early Oldowans, was the product of the practical intelligence.

It seems probable that success in small-game hunting, assisted by the making of a variety of implements useful in securing quarry and by the manufacture of other tools useful in butchering, sharing, and utilizing various parts of the remains, would have served to improve the general conditions of life and contributed to social development. The growing mastery over the environment would have produced a novel form of interactivity between the members of the group in which speech facilitated the communication of ideas, practical ideas, relating to the manufacture of tools to serve various purposes in response to the challenges presented by the variety of animal food. In this way, in a quite complex feedback interrelationship, small-game hunting, toolmaking, and speech would have reciprocally served to provoke each other to further advances. In this manner speech itself would develop as a special kind of tool designed to operate on man himself (Ref. 11, p. 20).

It has been observed by more than one writer on the subject that any description of the processes involved in language or speech could also be employed to describe the processes of toolmaking, that there exists, in short, a grammar of toolmaking in much the same sense that there exists a grammar of language and of speech.

Speech is designed to communicate meaning to others, to put oneself "in touch" with others. This is accomplished by the use of certain formal rules relating to the modification, transformation, and positioning of certain stylized chopped-up segments of sound. The techniques of producing these sounds must be learned according to a particular pattern and transmitted by those who are familiar with it to those who are not. Briefly summarized, these are exactly the kind of processes that occur in toolmaking. At a more detailed level of analysis the parallel between language and toolmaking becomes even more striking, but although several writers on the subject have seen this [1],[13,14] no one, so far as I know, seems to have made a detailed study of toolmaking as a clue to the cognitive processes of early men and the origin and evolution of language and speech. What is needed is a scientific study of tools, a science, as it may be called, of *hoplonology* (Gr. *Oplon*, a tool, implement). The hope is that by giving such a science-to-be a name, it may be conjured into existence. Such a scientific study of tools could go a long way toward the reconstruction of something of the character and evolution of the behavioral characteristics of early man. As Sollas put it many years ago, "The works of man's hands are his embodied thought." [15]

But to return to the grammar of toolmaking. Every technical skill is an intellectual achievement. In toolmaking it is the hand and mind in a continuous feedback of learned muscular acts, involving touch, pressure, and temperature senses, that is responsible for the hand's activities. For the making of each tool, it is clear a quite specific sequence of acts is required, each one of which must follow upon the other in a strictly ordered manner. It is suggested that a certain isomorphism exists between the grammar of toolmaking and the grammar of speech.

The grammatical precision of toolmaking at a level as old as Bed I at Olduvai strongly suggests that speech was already well established among the makers of those tools, so that for the origins of language and speech we shall have to look to earlier horizons, and perhaps to even earlier forms of man. It seems to me, however, that in broad outline the conditions to which I have referred were probably responsible for the origination of language and speech based possibly on a repertory of vocalizations long practiced by man's immediate ancestors.

When one studies in detail the manufacture of stone tools, one soon discovers that a very clear and purposive idea lies behind every motion that has been employed to create them.[16] I can best illustrate this with the aid of some Acheulian tools from the Lower and Middle gravels of Swanscombe, in Kent, England. From the study of these implements it is possible to determine not only how they were held, and hence what they were most likely used for, but it is also possible to discern what went on in the minds of the individuals who made them. And this is what we find:

First, that each tool was probably made to fit the hand of the individual who intended to use it. This means that although many tools could have been used by everyone, there were others that were specially made for the use of a particular individual. The smaller handaxes may have been made for the use of women, and the really small ones, about three inches in length, beautifully finished, may well have been made for children—which does not exclude their possible use by adults. The really large hand-axes, about nine and ten inches and more in length, were probably manufactured for exclusive use by males, for they are very heavy and must have required the employment of both hands when in use.

Second, to accommodate every part of the palmar surface of the hand, a specific area was shaped on the stone. Thus (FIGURE 1) for the palm the original rough surface was left untouched in order to afford a firmer grip. Immediately above this a large flake was removed, leaving a concave surface (E) for the reception of the thenar eminence. Extending from this an area was prepared, also by flaking, for the reception of the thumb. On the reverse side, portions of the stone were prepared in such a way that the tip of each finger would find a firm resting place. In the example illustrated here, the ingenious prehistoric fabricator has prepared the areas for the reception of the tip and ball of the index and especially the middle finger in the form of double-indented triangular fossae (D, 2A & a). This, so far as anyone knows, is unique among Acheulian implements, but quite clearly what the inventor—for such he may well have been—had in mind was the establishment of as firm a grip as possible upon this implement. Toward that end he made certain that his fingers would never slip to the slightest degree. The result is an implement that can be held so firmly in the hand that under the greatest application of pushing or pulling forces, it remains steady and immoveable.

Third, the position in which this tool was held in the hand indicates that it was indeed used as a hand-axe, but mainly for digging up thickly rooted plants and tubers of various sorts.

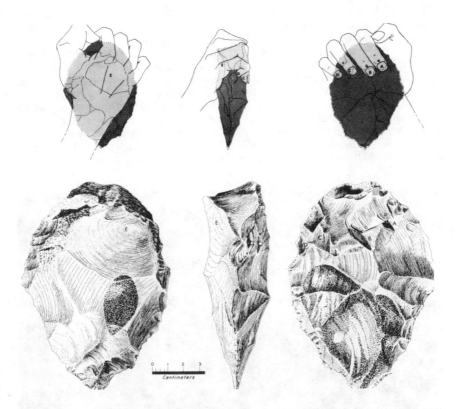

FIGURE 1. Acheulian hand-axe from the Middle Gravels of Swanscombe, Kent, England. E = Thenar fossa; D = Flaked depression for little finger; C = depression for tip of ring finger; c = depression for ball of ring finger; B = depression for tip of middle finger; b = depression for ball of middle finger; A = depression for tip of index finger; a = depression for ball of index finger. To the side of the latter on the untreated rough surface of the flint there is a rest position for the thumb.

Fourth, it is clear that each flake has been removed in order to produce the cutting edges and point of the tool with the minimum number of strokes; for if one examines this tool carefully, one may readily perceive that no more flakes have been removed than were minimally necessary to produce the desired result.

Turning to another hand-axe from Swanscombe (FIGURE 2) this time from the Lower gravels, and hence early Acheulian, one can immediately see that the maker had much the same end in view as the maker of the Middle Acheulian hand-axe, except that the earlier Acheulian tool is rather more crudely made. All the elements of the Middle Acheulian implement are present, but they are far less economically and skillfully executed. The thenar concavity is evident and so are the prepared areas for the tips of the fingers and the thumb. If my interpretation of these areas is correct, then this particular tool was probably made and used by a left-handed individual, for the artificially prepared surfaces fit far better in the left hand than they do in the right, with more of the tool left with which to work.

Finally, I wish to draw attention to a Middle Acheulian tool, also from Swanscombe, which was clearly devised for the cutting of animal skins (FIGURE 3). Among the remarkable things about this tool is the fact that it almost exactly resembles the modern furrier's knife—except that the Acheulian tool is far more versatile. The Acheulian knife is serrulated, and in one place notched, along its lower edge, and also along the anterior half of its upper edge, which, like a modern cutting knife, curves downward to meet the lower edge in a point. The upper cutting edge is designed to be rotated downward so that it becomes a lower cutting edge, used for cutting requiring greater precision and the cutting of small areas of skin. It is a very remarkable instrument indeed. Its surfaces are prepared in such a way as to render the instrument stable in the hand whatever the cutting edge to which one has rotated it. The individual making such a tool must have been characterized by a very high

FIGURE 2. Acheulian hand-axe from the Lower Gravels of Swanscombe, Kent, England. Left = Palmar surface showing thenar fossa. Right = finger surface. The flaked areas for the reception of index finger and thumb are, unfortunately, in shadow. The tip of the tool was broken away not long after it was made.

FIGURE 3. Acheulian furrier's knife from the Middle Gravels of Swanscombe, Kent, England. The stone knife shown together with a modern furrier's knife (the cutting blade has not been inserted in the beaked area of the latter). The lower back portion of the stone knife was broken away some time after its manufacture. The earlier 20th century furrier's steel knife even more closely resembled the Acheulian tool than the latest version shown here.

order of intelligence, and I think there can be little doubt that he was capable of speech of a quite complex order.

The tools I have described were made by men who lived considerably after the earliest hominids. I have discussed these tools, first, because they happen to be the only ones available to me, and second, because they serve as simple illustrations of the kind of inferences that can be drawn concerning the behavior of early men at every level, from the congealed behavior, as it were, by which they were represented in their tools.

REFERENCES

1. LIEBERMAN, P. 1975. The evolution of speech and language. In The Role of Speech in Language. James F. Kavanaugh and James E. Cutting, Eds.: 102. The MIT Press. Cambridge, Mass.
2. LEAKEY, M. D. 1971. Olduvai Gorge: Excavations in Beds I and II 1960–1963. Cambridge University Press. New York, N.Y.
3. TELEKI, G. 1975. Primate subsistence patterns: collector-predators and gatherer-hunters. J. Hum. Evol. **4:** 125–184.
4. DART, R. A. 1959. How human were the South African man-apes? South African Panorama. Nov.: 18–211.
5. BELL, C. 1833. The Hand: Its Mechanism and Vital Endowments as Evincing Design. Pickering. London, England.

6. ENGELS, F. 1896. Dialectics of Nature. International Pub. New York, N.Y.
7. BERGSON, H. 1902. Creative Evolution. Macmillan. London, England.
8. WOOD JONES, F. 1920. 1942. The Principles of Anatomy as Seen in the Hand. 2nd edit. Ballière, Tindall & Cox. London, England. Williams & Wilkins Co. Baltimore, Md.
9. GERARD, R. 1959. Brains and behavior. *In* The Evolution of Mans Capacity For Culture. J. N. Spuhler, Ed.: 14–20. Wayne State University Press. Detroit, Mich.
10. LAUGHLIN, C. D., JR. & E. G. D'AQUILI. 1974. Biogenetic Structuralism: 76. Columbia University Press. New York, N.Y.
11. VIAUD, G. 1960. Intelligence: Its Evolution and Forms.: 20. Harper & Bros. New York, N.Y.
12. PIAGET, J. 1952. The Origins of Intelligence in Children. International Universities Press. New York, N.Y.
13. LIEBERMAN, P. 1975. On the Origins of Language. Macmillan. New York, N.Y.
14. HOLLOWAY, R. 1969. Culture: A human domain. Curr. Anthropol. **10:** 395–412.
15. SOLLAS, W. J. 1924. Ancient Hunters.: 63. 3rd edit. Macmillan. New York, N.Y.
16. SEMENOV, S. A. 1964. Prehistoric Technology. Barnes & Noble. New York, N.Y.

STAGES OF CULTURAL ELABORATION IN THE PLEISTOCENE: POSSIBLE ARCHAEOLOGICAL INDICATORS OF THE DEVELOPMENT OF LANGUAGE CAPABILITIES

Glynn L. Isaac

Department of Anthropology
University of California
Berkeley, California 94720

Asking an archaeologist to discuss language is rather like asking a mole to describe life in the treetops. The earthy materials with which archaeologists deal contain no direct traces of the phenomena that figure so largely in a technical consideration of the nature of language. There are no petrified phonemes and no fossil grammars. The oldest actual relics of language that archaeologists can put their hands on are no older than the first invention of writing systems some five or six thousand years ago. And yet the intricate physiological basis of language makes it perfectly clear that this human ability has deep roots, roots that may extend as far as, or farther back in time than, the documented beginnings of tool-making some two and a half million years ago.

However, to return to the simile: if the forest has been cut down and all that remains are the roots, then the mole may not be such an inappropriate consultant. So it is with the history of language development. Comparative studies can indicate phylogenetic patterns, while detailed understanding of the structure and physiology of modern human linguistic capabilities can suggest possible successive stages of prehuman development; however, beyond a certain point, historical understanding demands dated evidence for successive developmental stages. This record, if it is to be obtained at all, must be sought from paleontologists and archaeologists. It is probable that the search is not quite as hopeless as it may look at first glance, but it is equally certain that there are no very simple answers.

In my mind there stand out two possible lines of approach to the problem. The *first* involves scrutiny of the record of developing protohuman material culture systems and consideration of its potential relevance to the problem in hand. Stone artefacts are the best and most persistant long-term markers, but during the last five percent of the time span, we can also deal with more fancy evidence such as burials, ornaments, art, notations, cult objects, structures, and so forth.

The *second* approach involves taking archaeological evidence which is indicative of the economic behavior and the adaptive patterns of early hominids and then considering the potential effects of varying intensities of information exchange on the functioning of the systems. This second approach should contribute to an understanding of the selection pressures that have moulded the evolution of language abilities. PART I of this paper follows the first approach, and PART II the second.

PART I. THE EVOLUTIONARY IMPLICATION OF THE RECORD OF DEVELOPMENT IN MATERIAL CULTURE*

In recent years our understanding of the early development of human culture has undergone several important changes: the known and measured time span of cultural

---

*This section incorporates material from an unpublished review that I prepared for presentation in a symposium on Form and Formative in the Symbolic Process, organized by Mary LeCron Foster and Peter Claus, at the 73rd annual meeting of the American Anthropological Association, Mexico City, November 1974.

traces has been extended by potassium argon dating and by new finds in East Africa from a grudging half-million years to at least 2½ or 3 million years. This extension not only stretches the record; it affects our understanding of the evolutionary processes involved. We see now that the early stages of material culture were by our standards incredibly long-lasting and static. This has helped to jolt prehistorians out of the propensity to treat the whole archaeological record as a series of chapters in a conventional history, a narrative of events in which the human nature of the actors is tacitly assumed throughout. The long time scale makes us realize that we are dealing with nonhuman antecedents, rather than with quaint, archaic "early men." We have to grapple with the reconstruction of behavioral patterns that no longer have any living counterparts.

It is artefacts that normally function as the distinctive markers of human or protohuman behavior in the geological record, and the earliest artefacts known at the present time have been found in East Africa at sites such as Olduvai, Omo, and East Rudolf, where they can be geophysically dated to between 1½ and 2½ million years. Ancient as they are, they document definite purposive tool-making activity: the formation of sharp edges by the organized and insightful banging of rocks together. The forms, however, are essentially opportunistic, involving empirical appreciation only of the fact that a suitable blow produces two potentially useful results: a sharp-edged flake of variable form, and a jagged-edged scar on the parent block. Either or both items could be, and seem to have been, used as tools. Modern humans can acquire an appreciation of the possibilities of Oldowan techniques in a few moments, and can produce examples of most of the forms with very little practice indeed. There was a minimum of design and control.

By a million years ago, some stone tool makers were producing objects that impress us as much more refined. They involve more definite design and control. Balanced, symmetrical objects such as a handaxe are much harder to manufacture; they require a stronger sense of purpose, more example and instruction, and more practice. By 100,000 years ago, some stone tool assemblages really begin to look elaborate, even to our technologically conscious eyes, and to learn to make them properly, takes years of practice. By 30,000 or 40,000 years ago, a kaleidoscopic diversity of forms and techniques were being utilized, and changes began to be breathtakingly rapid by the standards of the early periods. Explicit traces of symbolizing and ritual become evident: burials with offerings, personal ornaments, engraved lines, representational painting, and sculpture. By about 30,000 years ago, the archaeological record looked like a segment of ethnography. Presumably most of what happened since then has been the cumulative exploitation of the potential that had previously come into being. Another indication of rising levels of effective adaptability is provided by the expansion of hominid ecological range. Existing evidence suggests that hominids were confined to the tropics and warm, temperate zones until about 500,000–700,000 years ago; that is, for two thirds of the time span of the total record.[1,2]

The immediate question is: Can we find in the archaeological record elements that will help us understand the genesis of human faculties other than technological ones? Do artefacts offer evidence that can help us discern changing levels of capability with symbols, rules, and codes? I will report on the large-scale features of the archaeological record on the assumption that hominid capacity for conceiving and executing increasingly elaborate material culture designs has been connected with rising capacity for manipulating symbols, naming, and speaking. I hope that this conference will stimulate active discussion of these interrelationships.

Gauging Complexity

If we are to use the complexity of artefacts as an indicator, then we have to ask the technical question: What constitutes elaboration and complexity among artefacts? How is it to be measured? These are questions on which we all have intuitive sense, but I am not aware of much systematic work among either archaeologists or ethnographers. For the present purposes, I propose to use the following variables as yardsticks:

1. The number of distinct artefact classes, each with its own distinguishable set of rules. This has a connected but separate aspect.
2. The degree of latitude; that is, the amount of variation among representatives of a distinct class.
3. The number of operations involved in the production of an artefact. This may lead eventually to another quantum jump.
4. Compound artefacts; for example, stone-tipped spears, harpoons.
5. The extent of nonrandom differentiation in space and time; that is, the division of material culture into regional industries with successive distinct episodes or phases.

Paleolithic prehistorians have hitherto made few explicit attempts to measure these qualities and to plot the trajectory of change through time.

There is one qualifying warning to which attention must be drawn at once: I am trying to deal with hominid capacity for, and capability with, the conception and execution of craft designs. In assessing this, positive features of the record, rather than negative ones, must be interpreted. Few, if any, of the assemblages have ever approached in complexity the limits of capability of their makers. Even the complex material culture of modern times has not presumably reached the extremes of which mankind is capable. Thus, lack of elaboration does not prove lack of capability; however, evidence for a particular level of complexity must reflect at least a minimum level of ability. If we look at ethnographic information on the artefacts of recent nonagricultural peoples, we find great differences in the degree of elaboration as measured in various ways,[3] in spite of the fact that inherent capabilities are not known to differ. This view of the situation leaves me with the tentative model of change through time that is presented in FIGURE 1.

I would argue that an assymptote in the minimum level was probably reached long ago. This involves such basic tool forms as digging sticks, spears, containers, cutting tools, and chopping tools. The recorded equipment of the Tasmanians seems to have been quite close to this minimum. The maximum attainment of elaboration appears in the record to have gone creeping up through the whole span of prehistory. It was certainly not a linear growth pattern, but whether it was a simple geometric growth curve or one with a series of episodic surges remains to be ascertained.

The diagrams in FIGURES 2 and 3 provide rough guides to what little data I have been able to put together regarding the growing complexity of material culture through time. FIGURE 2 presents a tentative timetable for the incorporation of increasing numbers of elements. Simple artefacts such as digging sticks are included on a speculative basis. They are preserved so rarely in the record that the oldest known examples almost certainly provide no real indication of the date when their use began. However, they are such basic agents of the adaptive strategy of tropical hunter-gatherers that I feel quite confident in guessing that their antiquity extends back at least as far as that of stone tools. Containers such as bags and baskets are essential ingredients of human behavioral organization, since without them, recipro-

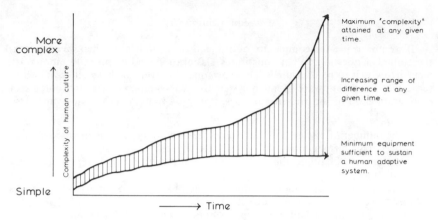

FIGURE 1. A diagrammatic representation of the trajectory of change in the maximum (upper) and the minimum (lower) levels of complexity in material culture, during the course of human evolution.

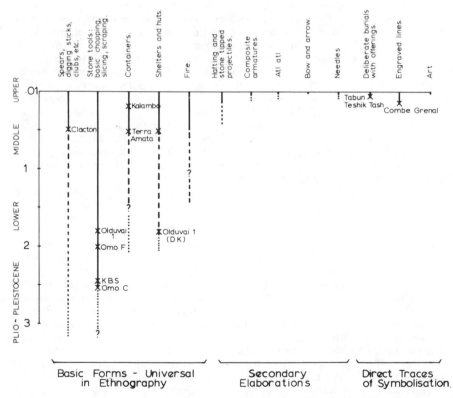

FIGURE 2. A time-table showing the oldest known archaeological evidence for a series of important items of equipment. Dotted lines show conjectured time ranges. (See text.)

cal sharing of meat and vegetable foods is difficult, if not impossible. We do not know when they first came into use, but it could be argued that the presence on even the earliest sites of numerous small stone artefacts that were probably not made there, implies the use of at least simple pouches or bundles. Certainly by 1½ million years ago, the volume of artefacts at sites such as those of Upper Bed II Olduvai and of the Upper Member of the Koobi Fora Formation is so great that one feels certain that containers must have been in use. Mary Foster (personal communication) has suggested that appreciation of the properties of containers represents an important and formative step in hominid cognition and symbolizing abilities.

FIGURE 3 shows a tentative timetable for important conceptual steps in the development of methods of making stone tools.[1-3]

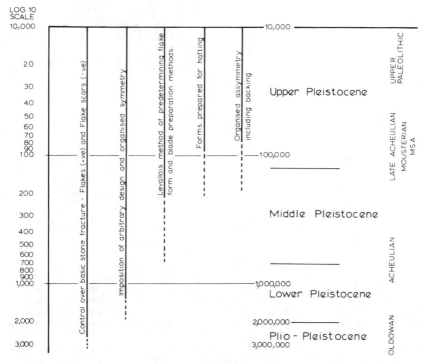

FIGURE 3. A time-table showing the known time range of significant concepts and techniques used in material culture, especially as evident from stone tools. (See text.)

Differentiation

Stone tools, for all their limitations, constitute the best long-term record of changes in cultural systems that we have, and I think there are interesting features, as yet dimly perceived, that may be relevant to the problem in hand. One of these is a rise through time in the degree of differentiation shown by the most elaborate industry of any given period. Two factors are involved in the phenomenon as I perceive it: 1) The degree to which there were distinct target forms in the minds of the craftsmen, as determined by cultural experience and neurophysiological capacity for design conception: a mental template; and 2) the degree to which the craftsman can control his productions so that an orderly series of replicating forms results.

The two combine to make up what can be termed a "rule system"; that is, an empirical code governing artefact form. In practice, of course, archaeologists study samples of artefacts and must try to recognize from them replicating patterns and hence infer the tool-making habits, rules, and targets of an extinct population.

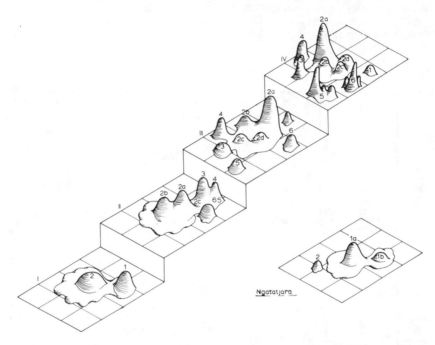

FIGURE 4. A diagrammatic representation illustrating increasing degrees of stone-artefact elaboration and differentiation. The number of topographic humps denotes the number of distinguishable modalities; the height and pointedness of the peaks denote the degree of standardization within the modality. The recent Australian Data (Ngatatjara) is based on the account of Gould et al.[29]

I, eg Oldowan: 1 = core-choppers, 2 = casual scrapers; II, eg Acheulian (Olorgesailie): 2a = scrapers, 2b = nosed scrapers, 2c = large scrapers, 3 = handaxes, 4 = cleavers, 5 = picks, 6 = discoids; III, eg Mousterian: 2a = racloir, 2b = grattoir, 2c = r. convergent, 3 = percoir, 4 = point, 5 = burin, 6 = biface; IV, Upper Paleolithic: 2a = grattoir, 2b = nosed scraper, 2c = raclette, etc., 3 = percoir, 4 = point, 5 = burins, 6 = backed blades, etc.

Ngatjara: 1a = hafted adzes (purpunpa), 1b = scrapers (purpunpa), 2 = bec. (pitjuru pitjuru).

Differentiation, as I am using the word, is not the same as diversity. The fragments that are taken from a stone-crusher for use as road metal are diverse, but the wide range of forms are not patterned in a way that can be said to show intentional differentiation. In this respect, early stone artefact assemblages are much more like road metal than are many more recent stone artefact assemblages. FIGURE 4 presents a diagrammatic expression of how I imagine increasing differentiation may have come about through a series of successive phases. At each stage, the maximum intensity of differentiation extended beyond that of previous phases. The convention of the diagram is such that in each frame, a topographic surface is depicted so as to represent the pattern of differentiation. Location on the horizontal surface denotes morphology, whereas the vertical scale denotes relative frequency. Each topographic hump represents what I regard as an intrinsic modality. Pinnacles represent very distinct replicative series; low mounds represent series sharing some features, but showing low overall morphological coherence. Very often these unstandardized forms have the air of opportunistic and casual tools. Properly, the volume of each feature should be scaled in proportion to relative abundance. Ultimately we should seek to map differentiation in some such way as this, but paleolithic archaeologists are as yet only groping toward such a conceptualization.

The earliest industries show only two or three distinguishable modalities, and within each there was little detailed rigor of design, either because the targets were vague or because the execution was imprecise and opportunistic, or both. To state this differently, the early assemblages seem to contain few really distinct artefact classes, and the degree of latitude in design was wide. By the end of the Pleistocene, many stone industries, particularly those outside tropical areas, showed extensive design differentiation and considerable fastidiousness in the execution and replication of particularities. Some industries of intermediate age show convincing intermediate states of differentiation. Notice that the last three frames involve progressively less time differences than the first ones: the process was speeding up dramatically toward the end. Note that the diagram also attempts to express the fact that the total range of forms does not change extensively through time. From the very beginning, there were razor-sharp edges, beveled edges, angular spurs, pointed projections, etc.; however, they occur in anarchic combinations with other variables of object form. In some later industries, particular forms were picked out by custom and were carefully produced as a replicating series. Because the change is not so much in available forms as in the exactitude of the rules governing demand and production, the functional consequences cannot be regarded in a simple-minded fashion. It is not necessarily true that the increase in complexity reflects an increase in the number of tasks performed with stone tools, nor are the fancy tools necessarily more efficient in an engineering sense. This is a point that has seldom been recognized, and I will return to discuss it further.

Another aspect of differentiation is the propensity for all later Pleistocene industries to show marked regional idiosyncrasy, in a manner that one cannot help comparing with language and dialect. As we go back in time, variation among industries becomes less and less clearly patterned in relation to geography. There are problems in the resolving power of available samples, but I think that this aspect of changing cultural systems is real and important. The less internal differentiation there was, the less opportunity there was for arbitrary stylistic divergences. Perhaps the increase in differentiation reflects changing patterns of cultural transmission and increasing specificity of language variants.

Because I have discussed elsewhere the technical problems of measuring increasing intra- and interassemblage differentiation and have given tentative diagrammatic representations of such poor data as we have, I will avoid pursuing these issues here.[4,5]

That more and more exacting designs were imposed on materials is also apparent from the record. First, some 1½ million years ago, we see the definite creation of symmetry, as in handaxes; then, about ½ million years ago, into the repertoire there entered deliberate and highly organized techniques of core preparation, such as the Levallois method, and, later, prismatic blades.

One can see as a culmination of this increase in conceptualization and control, the preparation of compound forms: stone-tipped spears, hafted scrapers, and borers. The oldest examples known to me of stone forms showing deliberate modifications that I think indicate hafting are of late Middle or early Upper Pleistocene date, perhaps 100,000–200,000 years ago. However, recent peoples of Australia and New Guinea haft suitable unprepared stone fragments, so the practice may be much older than the first recognizable traces.

The fitting together of parts may well have important interconnections with cognition as a whole. At about the same time, pieces such as backed knives that show deliberate and organized assymmetry were differentiated, although they do not become very common until later.

Elaboration and Adaptation

There is good evidence that a carefree stone knapper can generate a stock of chopping, slicing, scraping, and piercing edges that are fully adequate to perform all the basic adaptive functions of a hunter-gatherer. Why, then, the increasing involvement with such qualities as symmetry and balance? Why the concern to produce series of objects that replicate each other in accordance to what must have been definite rule systems?

My intuition in this matter is that we see in the stone tools the reflection of changes that were affecting culture as a whole, and whose functional significance can only be understood in this light. Probably more and more of all behavior, often but not always including tool-making behavior, involved complex rule systems. In the realm of communications, this presumably consisted more and more of elaborate syntax and extended vocabulary; in the realm of social relations, perhaps increasing numbers of defined categories, obligations, and prescriptions; in the realm of subsistence, increasing bodies of communicable know-how. The elaborated systems as a whole may have conferred adaptive advantages on the practitioners, even when specific individual components such as fancy tools were not directly adaptive. Thus I envisage that once the capability existed, the elaboration of rules and categories could, in some societies, simply extend into various realms of material culture, whether differentiation was functionally important or not. Perhaps there is an underlying pattern of determinants such as that perceived by Mary Douglas in the relationships between social configurations, religion, and the elaboration of explicit ritual.[26] Certainly there seems to me to be a tendency to greater elaborations of Pleistocene rule systems in the cold and temperate zones than in the tropics. Meg Fritz[6] has suggested that this may, in part, relate to social marking under conditions of stress.

Stages of Development

In summary, then, I see in the record a rise in complexity and in capacity for design rules that comprises a continuum divisible into the following segments.†

Step 1: (2½–1½ Million Years ago). Simple tools, the form of which was determined by the mechanical properties of natural materials. The imposition of design was minimal. These tools are core-choppers and flakes, plus spears and

†Steps 1–4 coincide fairly closely with Modes 1–4 as defined by Grahame Clark.[14]

digging sticks, at a guess. Apes can make and use simple tools, the forms of which are determined more by the material than by the ape.[7-9] It seems probable to me that the designing and symbolizing capabilities of Plio-Pleistocene hominids was not necessarily vastly beyond that of contemporary pongids.

Step 2: Middle Pleistocene (1½–.2 Million Years Ago). Some but not all tools involve the imposition of arbitrary design rules and a new concern with symmetry and regularity—for instance, the handaxe. The repertoire of definite, arbitrary designs was always very small: one or two, to three or four. Technical systems show increasing insight and ingenuity, as in the Levallois preformation method. There was little tendency to systematic, stable, geographic differentiation in material culture rules. I would surmise that containers came into use early in Step 2, if not before. This must be seen as the main formative phase for the more elaborate faculties of mankind. During this period changes in brain size resulted in a doubling of cranial capacity, whatever that means. Although there were few dramatic changes, the maximum expression of qualities such as differentiation and refinement, had increased very conspicuously by the end of the phase.

Step 3: Late Acheulian, Mousterian, Middle Stone Age, etc. (.2–.04 Million Years Ago). In hindsight, this phase appears as transitional between subhuman and fully human capabilities. The first burials, grave offerings, and traces of cult come in during this span, and the first engraved artistic squiggles.[10] The first forms that are explicitly designed for hafting appear in this span, although this practice may have begun earlier. The maximum degree of differentiation of design increased sharply. Regional differentiation of rule systems became pronounced, but both are still at markedly lower levels than in Step 4.

Step 4: (.04 Million Years Ago, Upwards). The maximum level of design complexity and of differentiation again rose sharply. Explicit traces of representational and abstract art appeared in areas as far apart as Europe and Australia, and then became common. Traces of ritual and overt symbolism became more and more frequent, and the maximum scale of these increased. Regional differentiation of rule systems became increasingly conspicuous, and the turnover in design norms or style became increasingly rapid.

Step 4 material culture has long given archaeologists a feel of being organized on much more elaborate principles than Step 3, and there is still heated debate over whether the change from 3 to 4 involved the spread of genes determining superior capabilities.[11-13] Alternative hypotheses more recently advanced suggest the spread of cultural and/or linguistic innovations that put behavior across a crucial organizational threshold, perhaps a cognitive and communications equivalent of the agricultural revolution.

The comparative richness of Upper Paleolithic material culture, particularly in Europe, has stimulated a voluminous and varied body of literature. Most archaeologists familiar with the field seem to be convinced that they are dealing with the products of human societies in possession of the full biological capabilities of our species as it exists today. In other words, the archaeology of this period can be treated as a segment of ethnography. It appears that variety among cultures that have existed during the last 30,000 years is to be regarded as due to the differential accumulation and modification of traditions disseminated in a reticulate communications web, involving varying degrees of specific adaptation and partial isolation. Grahame Clark[14] has discussed the humanistic significance of the dawn of self-consciousness and the growth of symbolic activity that the bodily adornment, burial practices, and art of the period would seem to indicate. Alexander Marshack's work has also stimulated renewed awareness of these aspects of the Upper Paleolithic.[27,28] I find it hard to evaluate in detail the claims that some of the engraved bones of this period represent systematic notations of lunar cycles, and so forth. However, his work has shown clearly that the markings are organized in a much more complex fasion than had previously been realized. If prehistorians are correct in their supposition that the Upper Paleolithic societies had modern levels of ability in cognition and organization, then Marshack's findings are perfectly credible. They affect the date that we put on the achievement of present levels of linguistic capabilities rather than the question of the stages and processes by which they originated. Many other workers are also pursuing careful analytical studies of social organization, style, symbolism, and cultural marking for this time range, so that a much more detailed understanding must emerge in a few years time.

PART II. ARCHAEOLOGICAL RECONSTRUCTION OF THE BEHAVIOR OF
EARLY HOMINIDS: THE ROLE OF LANGUAGE

Another approach that has value for our present inquiries is to ask what we know about the way of life of early hominids. What were the influences that encouraged the development of language capabilities? Two lines of evidence can contribute: one is the morphology of fossil hominid bones which provide indications of changing appearance and physical capabilities; the other, which is probably more important for our purposes here, is the archaeological record of activities. It should be stressed that artefact studies of the kind to which the attention of Part I was devoted constitute only a small part of modern Pleistocene archaeology. In addition to serving as repositories of fossilized information, the stone implements serve as indicators for the location of hominid activities. Through association with artefacts, archaeologists can identify traces of diet, butchered carcasses, and camp sites. Further, the location of the traces in a reconstructed paleoenvironment gives important additional clues to the ecology and land-use patterns. It is to the interpretation of economy and activities that much of the attention of current research is devoted.

Details of the evidence are clearly beyond the scope of this essay (see References 15–17), but I can offer a brief summary. Researches, mainly along the Rift Valley in East Africa at localities such as Olduvai, the Omo, East Rudolf, Chesowanja, and Hadar show that by two to three million years ago, the adaptation of at least some hominids involved the following ingredients:

Bipedal Locomotion. The forelimbs were free of supportive and propulsive functions. This is clearly documented by postcranial fossils from South and East Africa.

Tool-Making. The purposive transportation of materials over at least several miles is most clearly documented by the quantities of flaked stone at archaeological sites that are often remote from sources of rock. Presumably sticks, fibers, and skin were being shaped and carried, as well as stone.

Meat Eating. The hominids were consuming quantities of meat including flesh from carcasses of animals much larger than themselves. Examples include proboscideans at Olduvai[15] and a hippo at East Rudolf.[16,17] This aspect of diet and activity is evident from recurrent associations of artefacts at butchered carcasses, and the repeated presence of scatters of broken-up bone where discarded stone artefacts also occur.[16,18] Until now we have found it difficult to distinguish between bone refuse from hunted as opposed to scavenged carcasses, although Elizabeth Vrba, working in the Transvaal, has recently found some promising criteria.[19] It is clear that the early hominids were more strongly carnivorous than any other living primate, and one suspects that, like other large carnivores,[20] they got their meat from an opportunistic combination of hunting and scavenging.

Gathering (?). As yet, we lack direct evidence regarding the consumption of plant foods by very early hominids, but everything we know about primates and about nonfarming peoples in the tropics suggests that plant foods would have been of crucial importance, presumably at least 70% or 80% of the diet. We do not know when the shift occurred away from the feed-as-you-go mode characteristic of primates to the common human pattern of gathering followed by preparation and quasicollective consumption. As we have seen in Part I, the quantities of stone may imply the existence of bags or baskets. I will return to comment on the probable importance of gathering in early socioeconomic systems.

Home Bases. The existence of dense patches of discarded artefacts at specific localities in the paleolandscape is clear evidence that early hominid activities were at times spatially focused. The coincidence of food refuse at these sites seems to imply that in some degree the human institution of camps or home bases had come into existence. From such a focus, different members of a social group could have gone out and engaged in separate pursuits, returning later, confident of rejoining the band.

Food Sharing. The presence of scatters of broken-up bone in coincidence with scatters of discarded artefacts implies that meat was being eaten. When, however, as at Olduvai and Koobi Fora the bones derive from several different cracasses which are unlikely all to have been freshly killed at the same spot, then the evidence also implies that foodstuffs were being carried back to the home base. Perhaps it was transported to feed infants, but it seems very likely that the archaeological evidence attests to the beginnings of a crucial evolutionary shift into food sharing and partial division of labor. We have direct evidence only of transport and sharing of meat foods, but if the sharing involved reciprocity between segments of the group, then gathered plant foods, which may well have been the staples, would have been as important, or more so.

Considered individually, these behaviors that archaeology shows were established by 1½–2 million years ago, are not exclusively human traits, but all of them have been developed to a much higher intensity and level of importance in man than in any other primate. If we look at them we see that they are a functionally interrelated set, such that each component reinforces the utility of the others; many of the traits are not possible in isolation. Thus bipedalism allows for the transport of equipment and of food for sharing; stone tools enable a primate to cut up a large carcass as effectively as a carnivore; digging sticks give access to additional underground food sources; bags and trays allow gathered foods to be carried, and so on. In addition, gathering and food sharing served as an insurance policy that made it possible to engage in the quest for meat, even though that was an enterprise which might succeed only once in three attempts.[21] Thus it can fairly be said that bipedalism, the transport of materials, and the manufacture and use of equipment, together with food sharing, constitute an adaptive complex of great importance in the differentiation of men from apes. The archaeological evidence is consistent with the notion that these behavioral modifications and the bodily changes that made them possible are the foundations on which the superstructure of human evolution has depended.

But what has all this to do with the origin of language? It is entirely conceivable that this kind of adaptive strategy could be operated by creatures with apelike social behavior patterns, but it is also clear that the adaptive value of food sharing and division of labor would be greatly enhanced by improvements in communication; specifically, the passage of information other than that relating to the emotions, becomes highly adaptive. This has proved to be the case also in other zoological phyla that have made the acquisition of food a collective responsibility, as is shown, for instance, by the development of the so-called language of bees and other social insects. Thus I would argue that archaeological researches on relicts from the time range before one million years ago contributes in a crucial way to our understanding of the milieu in which capabilities for language were first important.

We can now look at the way in which the separate approaches of Part I and Part II of this paper fit together. I can best do this by offering an archaeologist's view of the stages in development.

Phase I. The establishment of the first protohuman adaptive complex (bipedalism, transport, tool-making, food sharing). We do not know when this evolutionary shift began, but its effects were sufficient for them to be archaeologically detectable by about two million years ago. However, hominids of those times may well not have been human at all, in our sense.

Phase II. The establishment of this adaptive system put selection pressure on the enhancement of communication and information exchange systems, which presumably began to develop even during Phase I, but which went on to mature during Phase II. Archaeologically, this finds expression in the long oscillating record of such Lower Paleolithic entities as the Acheulian, which span the time from around 1½ million years ago to 0.1 m.y. (i.e., 100,000 years ago). As we have seen, there were developments in the level of technique and design complexities, but by our standards they are not large in relation to the vast span of time involved. In spite of the somewhat monotonous character of this phase, it must have been the main formative period for human cultural and communications capabilities. On the basis of present evidence, I imagine that if we could observe the hominids of 1½-2 million years ago, we would first of all be struck more by differences from our sense of what is human than by similarities; by the end of Phase II, a host of indicators imply a basically human grade of organization.

Much has been made of the evolutionary influence of big-game hunting on human development in this phase.[22,23] Hunting may have been influential to a degree, and doubtless the success of intensive hunting patterns such as those in evidence at Olduvai BK, Olorgesailie DE/89, or at Torralba did exert their own evolutionary influence.[16] However, I would surmise that selection pressure has in fact favored all those qualities that facilitate varied and flexible way of making a living, of which hunting was one when the need and the chance arose. Our evolutionary niche is probably best described as opportunism, and language is surely the foremost of the skills that make us such effective opportunists.

Phase III. The maturation of cultural and presumably linguistic capabilities during the Middle Pleistocene seems to have opened up new potentials. Between about 50,000 and 100,000 years ago the archaeological record documents a quickening of the tempo of change.[4,14] Finally, about 30,000-40,000 years ago, the record gives the appearance that a threshold was crossed with the emergence of much more complex and more style-ridden systems of material culture. From this same period, as we have seen, come the first surviving manifestations of art and of bodily adornment. At present we really cannot say whether the change of tempo and the apparent crossing of a threshold is due to some kind of discrete innovation that created a surge of change that looks like a discontinuity, or whether we are seeing simply the trace of a critical bend in a geometric or hypergeometric growth curve. As far as I am aware, Kenneth Oakley was one of the first to suggest that crucial developments in language may provide the best explanation of the Upper Paleolithic cultural spurt.[24] This remains an untested, but, in my view, very plausible hypothesis.

The interpretations of Lieberman and Crelin[25] can be viewed as potentially related, but I feel that there will have to be a careful appraisal of their results by anatomists and speech physiologists before archaeologists should incorporate them in their arguments.

Much of what has been set out in both PART I and PART II of this paper is necessarily speculative. It is certain, however, that the evolutionary enlargement of human language capabilities did take place as a concomitant of the technological and socioeconomic developments to which the attention of archaeology is usually confined. I have sketched two aspects of the perception of human evolution that an archaeologist gains from evidence in the ground. I hope that this mole's-eye view can be brought into a profitable relationship with other patterns that are described by anthropologists, ethologists, and linguists, each viewing the problem from a different stance.

ACKNOWLEDGMENTS

The ideas in this essay have been developed over the years, especially in discussion with Sherwood Washburn, J. Desmond Clark, and Barbara Isaac, who also did the drawings. The research into early hominid life on which Part II depends is an enterprise I share with the East Rudolf Research group and other close colleagues in Africa. In recent years my interest in the relationship between artefacts and the origins of language has been stimulated by conversations with Mary LeCron Foster.

REFERENCES

1. BORDES, F. 1968. The Old Stone Age. McGraw-Hill Book Co. New York, N.Y.
2. OAKLEY, K. P. 1966. Frameworks for Dating Fossil Man. Aldine. Chicago, Ill.
3. LEAKEY, L. S. B. 1934. Adam's Ancestors. Methuen. London, England.
4. ISAAC, G. L. 1972. Chronology and the tempo of cultural change during the Pleistocene. In Calibration of Hominoid Evolution. W. W. Bishop & J. A. Miller, Eds.: 381–430. Scottish Academic Press. Edinburgh, Scotland.
5. ISAAC, G. L. 1972. Early phases of human behaviour: models in Lower Palaeolithic archaeology. In Models in Archaeology. D. L. Clarke. Ed.: 167–199. Methuen. London, England.
6. FRITZ, M. Paper presented to the 73rd Annual Meeting of the American Anthropology Association. Mexico City. November 1974.
7. KOEHLER, W. 1927. The mentality of apes. Translated from 2nd Revised Edit. International Library of Psychological, Philosophical and Scientific Method. London, England.
8. GOODALL, J. M. 1964. Tool-using and aimed throwing in a community of free-living chimpanzees. Nature 201: 1264–66.
9. WRIGHT, R. V. 1972. Imitative learning of a flaked stone technology—the case of an orangutan. Mankind 8: 296–306.
10. BORDES, F. 1972. A Tale of Two Caves. Harper and Row. New York, N.Y.
11. BREUIL, H. 1912. Les sub-divisions du Paléolithique supérieur. Congrès International d'Anthropologie. Geneva, Switzerland.
12. GARROD, D. A. E. 1938. The Upper Palaeolithic in the light of recent discovery. Proc. Prehistoric Soc. 4: 1–26.
13. BORDES, F. Ed. 1972. The Origin of Homo sapiens. UNESCO, INQUA. Paris, France.
14. CLARK, G. 1970. Aspects of Prehistory. Univ. California Press. Berkeley, Calif.
15. LEAKEY, M. D. 1971. Olduvai Gorge Vol. 3. Excavations in Beds I and II, 1960–1963. University Press. Cambridge, England.
16. ISAAC, G. L. 1971. The diet of early man: aspects of archaeological evidence from Lower and Middle Pleistocene sites in Africa. World Archaeology 2: 278–298.

17. ISAAC, G. L. Early hominids in action: a commentary on the contribution of archaeology to the understanding of the fossil record in East Africa. *In* The Yearbook of Physical Anthropology for 1975. J. Buettner-Janusch, Ed. In press.
18. ISAAC, G. L. Archaeological evidence for the activities of early African hominids. *In* Human Evolution: Louis Leakey and the East African Evidence. G. L. Isaac & E. R. McCown, Eds.: 483–514. W. A. Benjamin. Menlo Park, Calif.
19. VRBA, E. S. 1975. Some evidence of chronology and palaeoecology of Sterkfontein, Swartkrans and Kromdraai from the fossil *Bovidae*. Nature **254**: 301–304.
20. SCHALLER, G. B. & G. P. LOWTHER. 1969. The relevance of carnivore behavior to the study of early hominids. Southwestern J. Anthropol. **25**: 307–40.
21. LEE, R. B. What hunters do for a living, or, how to make out on scarce resources. *In* Man the Hunter. R. B. Lee & I. DeVore, Eds. 30–48. Aldine, Chicago, Ill.
22. PFEIFFER, F. E. 1969. The Emergence of Man. Harper and Row. New York, N.Y.
23. CAMPBELL, B. 1974. Human Evolution: an Introduction to Man's Adaptations. 2nd. edit. Aldine. Chicago, Ill.
24. OAKLEY, K. P. 1951. A definition of man. Science News.
25. LIEBERMAN, P. 1975. On the Origins of Language—an Introduction to the Evolution of Human Speech. MacMillan. New York, N.Y.
26. DOUGLAS, M. 1970. Natural Symbols. Barrie & Rockcliffe. London, England.
27. MARSHACK, A. 1972. Upper Paleolithic notation and symbol. Science **178**: 817–828.
28. MARSHACK, A. 1972. The Roots of Civilization. McGraw Hill. New York, N.Y.
29. GOULD, R. A., D. A. KOSTER & A. H. L. SONTZ. 1971. The Lithic assemblage of the Western Desert Aborigines of Australia. Amer. Antiquity **36**: 149–169.

SOME IMPLICATIONS OF THE PALEOLITHIC SYMBOLIC EVIDENCE FOR THE ORIGIN OF LANGUAGE*

Alexander Marshack

Peabody Museum of Archaeology and Ethnology
Harvard University
Cambridge, Massachusetts 02138

In this introductory paper I shall present some new analytic data and a few theoretical considerations and interpretations based on the data that may be relevant to an understanding of the evolved human capacity for symbol-making and language.

Based largely on the tool industries and on the occasional human skeletal material excavated during the last century, the European Paleolithic of the last 400,000–500,000 years has been divided into three stages or periods: an early or Acheulian with indications of the presence of nearly modern man (Swanscombe), a middle or Mousterian during which Neanderthal man lived, and a late or Upper Paleolithic when Neanderthal was gone and a number of fully modern *Homo sapiens* types appeared.

I shall present symbolic materials from each of the periods with an analysis of the cognitive and linguistic problems they pose.

In 1931 a collection of animal statuettes and one crude anthropomorphic figure were found at the small cave site of Vogelherd in southern Germany.[1] They represent the most important group of symbolic artifacts made by early Cro-Magnon man. The Middle Aurignacian level at Vogelherd, in which one set of these statuettes was found, has been carbon-dated recently at 30,000 B.C., which puts it exceedingly close to the Mousterian ending at c. 35,000 B.C. In the 45 years since these statuettes had been excavated and published, they had been locked in a bank and had been unavailable for study. The following descriptions are based on the first analyses of these figures that have been permitted.

FIGURE 1 is a 2½-inch carved horse of mammoth ivory, making it at 30,000 B.C. one of the earliest examples of "art"—that is, of a manufactured "representational" image—known. Yet it is an extraordinarily sophisticated image, in its way as sophisticated as any image from the terminal Upper Paleolithic 20,000 years later, usually considered as the high point of Ice Age art. Analysis of this horse and the other animal statuettes from Vogelherd indicates that they are out of place in all the standard chronologies of styles of rendering animal images which begin with an assumption that the first animal images were crude outlines.

In looking at the statuette, FIGURE 1, *we* see an animal and a horse. Because of this obvious recognition, animal images of the Upper Paleolithic were long termed aspects of "hunting magic." The concept was supported by the heavily weighted nature of the Paleolithic archeological evidence consisting of tools and animal bones and by generalizations about "primitive" human behavior in anthropological theories of the first half of this century.

*This paper was prepared while the author was a Fellow of the Harry F. Guggenheim Foundation. The archaeological field work was funded by the National Geographic, the Samuel H. Kress Foundation, and the National Endowment for the Humanities. © Copyright Alexander Marshack, 1976.

289

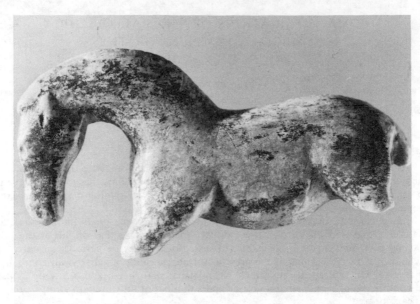

FIGURE 1. Carved horse of mammoth ivory from the site of Vogelherd, Germany, the Aurignacian culture of the Upper Paleolithic, c. 30,000 B.C. The statue shows the wear and polish of long use, suggesting it was a symbol in persistent use. The Vogelherd statues are the earliest representational images known. Size: 2½ inches. © Alexander Marshack, 1972.

Let us approach the image analytically, *not* as the "horse" *we* recognize but merely as a human artifact, a symbolic product that had a manufacture and use at the very beginning of the modern period.

Microscopic examination of the statuette revealed that eye, ear, nose, mouth, and mane had been carefully carved, but that these had been worn down by long handling and perhaps by carrying in a pouch. The length of time required for such wear on ivory might be a number of years. The microscope also revealed that at one point in the use of the horse an angle that was still fresh had been cut into the shoulder representing a late use of the horse, perhaps as part of a symbolic "killing," though for what purpose is not known. The horse had obviously not been made to be killed for success in a hunt, but had been kept and used and then at some point had a differentiated, specialized use. Every one of the Vogelherd images, including the crude human figure, had evidence either of long-term use or of an applied symbolic marking.

FIGURES 2a and 2b comprise the anthropomorphic image, crudely and hastily carved, perhaps feminine, with two rough breast marks. It contains three sets of marks on the body, made by different tools marking different types of strokes. This quite clearly represents a *use* of the image, but whether for a killing, a curing, a birth, or as an act of participation or application is not clear.

From an Aurignacian level at La Ferrassie in France comes sets of carved vulvas with the same type of overmaking. The technique of *using* images by symbolic overmarking persists for 22,000 years to the end of the Upper Paleolithic.

A decade of research has shown that Upper Paleolithic images were often used and reused, and that any image could be used in a number of different ways and contexts.[2] Among such uses was the association of a primary image with a library of subsidiary motifs and symbols. The animal or human images we recognize were, therefore, almost never merely representational or reportorial; they were symbols made for use in a variety of cultural contexts.

FIGURE 2a. Crude anthropomorphic figure from Vogelherd, Germany, c. 30,000 B.C., with three sets of marks made by different tools and types of stroke, suggesting a periodic symbolic marking.

FIGURE 2b. Detail of the marks on the Vogelherd anthropomorph indicating the different engraving points and types of stroke. Animal statues from Vogelherd were similarly "used" by being periodically marked.

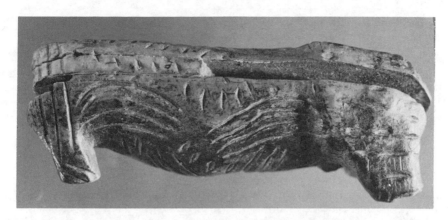

FIGURE 3a. Fragment of an animal figure from Vogelherd, Germany, marked symbolically with a motif of multiple arcs and zigzags. The motif indicates that this was not an animal made to be killed in hunting magic, but represented a symbol in the culture.

Another Vogelherd statuette will clarify the problem. Figures 3a, 3b, & 3c illustrate the fragment of a horse or reindeer marked "unrealistically" with a motif of multiple zigzags, multiple arcs, and many small strokes. The statuette is dated at about 29,000 B.C. and is slightly later than the horse of FIGURE 1, making it the earliest known "decorated" animal image of *Homo sapiens*. Clearly the overengraved motif is not a trap, a hut, or a male or female sex sign, to mention some of the traditional interpretations of the many motifs that are associated with animals. Geometric patterns associated with animals are found throughout the full Upper Paleolithic and have posed persistent problems for interpretation. They are currently under intensive investigation. The multiple zigzag and the multiple arc show up later both east and west of Vogelherd as decorative motifs, first in the East European

FIGURE 3b. The underbelly of the Vogelherd statuette indicating the multiple zigzag motif.

Upper Paleolithic and then in the French Magdalenian. I am not at this point interested in their meaning or dispersion but rather in their use with a recognizable image as an aspect of the earliest *Homo sapiens* symbolism. One class of symbol is used with another class as part of a complex, interrelated tradition of usage. This, of course, is the way in which diverse symbol systems are used today.

In 1891, at the site of Cro-Magnon in Les Eyzies, France, where the first Cro-Magnon skeletons were found, there was excavated a reindeer rib with a crudely engraved anthropomorph overmarked with a zigzag motif (FIGURE 4). Significantly, it was published *without* the zigzag overmarking, since this was considered distracting and meaningless.[3] The zigzags, however, represent a significant aspect of the image's use, again one class of symbol used with another.

I have already published evidence for the presence of a system of sequential, cumulative notation in this period, the Aurignacian of the early Upper Paleolithic.[4-8] In addition, the Aurignacian burials provide a well-known evidence for a use of amulets, pendants, and beads, forms of *personal* decoration that have been considered hallmarks of Upper Paleolithic symbolism.

Remember, we are here but a single step—about four or five thousand years—from the Mousterian. The questions, then, are obvious: how long would it have taken for diverse symbolic traditions of this complexity to have developed? Could they have evolved rapidly in a few thousand years? What level of language competence would have been required to support such interrelated systems, images, and usages? At what point would that level of linguistic competence have been manifested, since the traditions illustrated here must have developed later? There seems no choice but to look at the Mousterian and at the still earlier near-*Homo sapiens* of the Acheulian period.

The literature on Mousterian symbolism published during the last century was concerned with certain gross aspects of Neanderthal ritual or ceremonial behavior. This was because the available evidence was composed primarily of Neanderthal burials, animal bones arranged intentionally in a burial or cave, and bits of red ocher occasionally found in habitation sites.

FIGURE 3c. Schematic rendition of the marking on the Vogelherd animal statue. This is the earliest known "decorative" motif associated with an animal image.

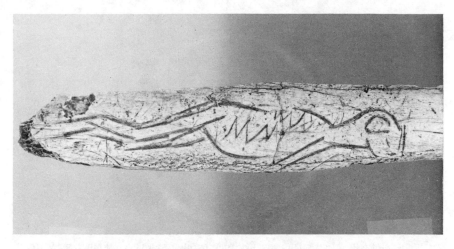

FIGURE 4. Anthropomorphic figure from the site of Cro-Magnon, France, the Aurignacian culture. The image is overmarked with a zigzag motif, indicating that it had been used symbolically.

It seemed from these artifacts that Neanderthal man used the natural materials around him symbolically—skulls, horns and antlers, mineral colors, stone slabs—but that true art and symbol expressed in the manufacture or alteration of forms had to be assigned to the following Upper Paleolithic cultures and to fully modern man. Discussions of Neanderthal symbolism referred vaguely to the "first" awakening of the religious spirit and to the supposedly "new" Neanderthal awareness of death and the passage of life and time.[9] The recent research of Lieberman may have constituted an effort to explain this apparent inadequacy in the Neanderthal record.[10] A recent study by S. Binford compared Neanderthal burials with those of the Upper Paleolithic and found a comparative poverty in Mousterian grave goods, suggesting a lesser social capacity and stratification.[11] Solecki published the report of a Mousterian burial on a bed of flowers at Shanidar, leading him to dub his Neanderthalers "the first flower people."[12-13a] † The sense one gets from these data and interpretations is of a struggling, seminal, almost mute awareness of death and a kind of incipient protosymbolism.

There is, however, accumulating evidence of a different type. H. Martin, in a classic report on the Mousterian site of La Quina in France, published in 1910 the illustrations (FIGURES 5a & 5b) of a pendant made from a reindeer phalange (5.0 cm) and another from the canine of a young fox (3.3 cm) which had been fractured in the

---

†After delivery of the present paper Leroi-Gourhan published an analysis of the pollens in the soil of the Shanidar burial, identifying at least seven species of flower that had been laid around the corpse, many of which, according to Solecki, have been used in folk medicine within recent or historic times. Whether these flowers were used "medicinally" or whether plants were used as hallucinogens in Mousterian times cannot, of course, be ascertained. But that flowers were used symbolically in contexts which were related to human processes opens the intriguing possibility that species of flowers or plants may quite early have been used in essentially symbolic curative efforts, with random success occasionally uncovering a potential potency or biological effect.

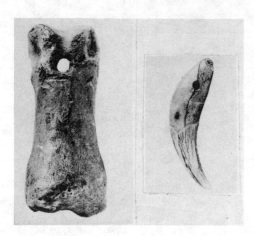

FIGURE 5, a & b. Mousterian pendants from the site of La Quina, France, made from a reindeer phalange (*left*) and the canine of a young fox (*right*). (Natural size. After Martin.[14])

process of boring the tiny hole and had, therefore, according to Martin, been discarded.[14] He also illustrated a bovide shoulder blade engraved by a Neanderthaler with exceedingly fine, long parallel lines, forming a composition of a type that is found later in the Upper Paleolithic. In 1909 D. Peyrony found a small bone in a Neanderthal burial at La Ferrassie in France (FIGURE 6) of which he wrote, it "contains a series of fine intentionally incised marks recalling the notched bones of the Aurignacian. Perhaps it had some meaning and was placed intentionally by the side of the corpse."[15]

These artifacts were never again mentioned in the professional archaeological literature, since they were unique and seemed aberrant or experimental efforts and since there was no other known evidence for a Neanderthal tradition of personal decoration or of manufactured symbolism.

In the early 1970s J. Kozlowski found a nonutilitarian fragment of bone in the Mousterian site of Bacho Kiro, Bulgaria, that had been engraved with zigzag motif in a most unusual manner (FIGURES 7a, 7b, & 7c). The microscope revealed that when the maker came to the end of an engraved line in the zigzag at left in FIGURE 7b, he did not lift his tool to make a joining line in the other direction, but left it on the bone and turned or twisted it, leaving the print of the turning in the corner of each of the

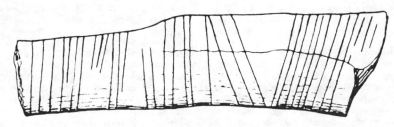

FIGURE 6. Finely engraved, nonutilitarian Mousterian bone from a Neanderthal grave at the site of La Ferrassie, France. (After Peyrony[2])

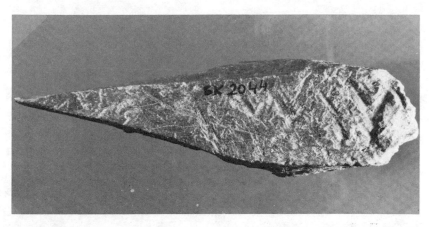

FIGURE 7a. Nonutilitarian fragment of bone from the Mousterian period engraved with a zigzag motif. Bacho Kiro, Bulgaria.

angles. It was clear that these were not work or cutting marks but the creation of an intentional zigzag image.

In the later Upper Paleolithic, the zigzag appears as a ubiquitous motif on nonutilitarian fragments, as decoration on tools and "batons de commandement," and in association with animals painted or engraved on cave walls. FIGURE 8 is a typical Magdalenian zigazg motif from the end of the Upper Paleolithic. It was first engraved on a fragment of bone and then symbolically ochered red.

FIGURE 7b. Detail of the zigzag motif on the Mousterian bone from Bacho Kiro indicating the circular marks of turning in the angles of the zigzag at left.

FIGURE 7c. Schematic rendition reconstructing the sets of zigzags on the Bacho Kiro fragment.

In studying the above artifacts, the researcher is faced with analytic problems which, supposedly, belong only to the study of the artifacts of *Homo sapiens*. In the manufacture of a tiny pendant, for instance, clearly one hand did the boring while the other, somehow, held the object steady. But having made the pendant, the Neanderthal artisan now had to provide a string, perhaps of skin, fine enough, about 1 mm wide, to thread the tooth or phalange, a craft skill that would require a two-handed manipulative discrimination, including a visual acuity and a control in the working of a pliant material, that was perhaps finer and more delicate than that required to bore the hole. If, as seems possible, the pendants were part of a cultural tradition, they pose a problem. They were not tools made for practical use or in order to make other

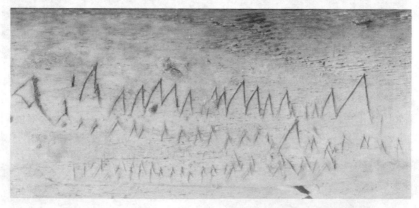

FIGURE 8. Symbolic zigzag motif on a fragment of bone from the Magdalenian period, the Grotte de Goyet, Belgium, c. 12,000 B.C. After engraving the motif, the bone was ochered red, indicating its symbolic nature. The motif appears through the full Upper Paleolithic.

tools, but were instead part of a sequence and strategy that was "nonadaptive" except in a cultural context. The engraved artifacts pose an even more intriguing problem, since they suggest the presence of a tradition of nonrepresentational symbolic marking that may have required some form of "linguistic" explanation.

There is a growing body of Mousterian engraving and carving that will probably alter the nature of the discussion of early symbol use and language. The most important document for our purposes was found by Laszlo Vertés at the Mousterian site of Tata in Hungary more than a decade ago.[16] It is the carved and shaped section of a mammoth molar about 4½ inches (10.8 cm) long, ovaloid, and big enough to be held comfortably in the hand (FIGURES 9a & 9b). It has been carbon-dated at about 50,000 B.C., which would place it in the Middle Mousterian. In the original Hungarian publication it was poorly illustrated as a grey blob. Actually, the surface is the brilliant white of polished enamel or cementum, making it the most sensuous of all Paleolithic mobiliary artifacts, both to the touch and eye. Vertés published it as a "churinga" of the type usually made of wood and used ritually in Australia and comparable also to a class of nonutilitarian symbolic plaques made of bone and ivory found in the Upper Paleolithic. At one point in the use of the plaque—and perhaps more than once—it had been ochered red. Such ochering occurs on both the Australian churingas and the Upper Paleolithic plaques. The microscope revealed other interesting data.

The lamelle or section came from a mammoth molar, a large, heavy, composite tooth weighing a number of pounds (FIGURE 10). There is clearly a rough cognitive-visual connection between flakes that are struck from a pebble core and plates sectioned from the tooth. But there is a profound qualitative difference. The materials are different and require other working strategies and sequences. But, more important, in working Paleolithic stone one plans for a functional edge. Here the artisan *planned* for a "nonutilitarian," symbolic object.

As you can see, the section of tooth was cut and carved and the rear was then beveled back, making a nearly perfect oval (FIGURE 11). Work of this type and quality had not previously been documented for the Mousterian. The microscope also shows that the thin edge of the highly polished face was rounded as though from long handling, with no evidence of the original cutting or scraping. Here, then, is evidence for the manufacture of symbolic artifacts intended for *long-term*, probably periodic use within the Mousterian, 20,000–30,000 years before the appearance of the Aurignacian images, which had a comparable cultural usage.

I should note that the Mousterian skills and strategies involved in making the churinga and pendants and in marking the sets and zigzags are similar to those found in the later Upper Paleolithic bone industries. It is possible, therefore, that the small number of symbolic artifacts in the Mousterian record is due, in part, to a use of other materials. If one were to attempt to reconstruct the symbolic complexity of the hunting-gathering cultures of the historic period from what remains in the archeological record, one would find the task impossible. Australian symbolic artifacts are largely a perishable "software," composed of wood, feathers, blood, ocher powders, incisions, circumcisions, sand drawings, songs, dances, myths, and so on. Only the rock faces would retain the painted and engraved evidence for a strange symbolism. In like manner, the evidence for American Indian and Eskimo shamanism or periodic group ritual and ceremony would be largely dissolved in any long burial. The fact is, sparse though it may be, there is now evidence for a number of contemporaneous symbol systems in the Mousterian. How far back does such evidence go?

I present one rare and, therefore, still tentative example from the period before the Mousterian.

FIGURE 9a. Carved symbolic plaque or "churinga" made from a section of a mammoth molar excavated at the Mousterian site of Tata, Hungary. The edge is rounded and polished from long handling. The plaque had been symbolically ochered red.

FIGURE 9b. Reverse face of the Tata plaque, indicating the beveling and shaping of the tooth.

FIGURE 10. A compound mammoth molar indicating the sections; one such section was used to form the Tata churinga.

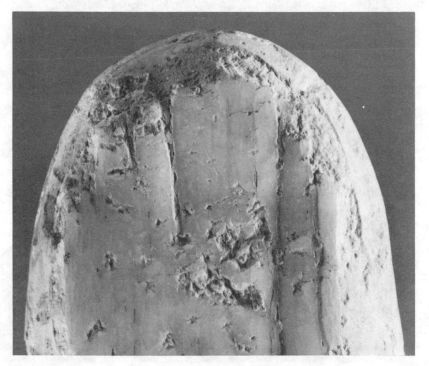

FIGURE 11. Detail of the beveled edge of the Tata plaque, indicating the near-perfect shaping of the mammoth tooth. This is the only example of such skilled, careful workmanship of bone from the Mousterian.

In 1969 Francois Bordes, a leading authority on the Mousterian cultures, published a report on an engraved ox rib he had excavated at the site of Pech de l'Azé, France, in a level that was approximately 300,000 years old, that is, from the Acheulian period of *Homo erectus*, who was already verging toward being *sapiens* (FIGURE 12a).[17] The man of this period was already building huts.[18] Bordes described the rib as the earliest intentional engraving yet excavated.[19] A full description of my analysis of the bone and the tradition of which it is a part is now in press.[20] The microscope showed that the image had been made sequentially as a series of connected, festooned double arcs, beginning at left and ending at right with a multiple marking (FIGURES 12b & 12c). Precisely this tradition of engraving festooned or serpentine images on nonutilitarian objects and on cave walls appears later throughout the full 25,000 years of the Upper Paleolithic. It is perhaps the most prevalent motif of the Upper Paleolithic, yet it has not until now been systematically studied. From the Italian cave site of Romanelli, at the very end of the Paleolithic, c. 8,500 B.C., there comes an engraving of the serpentine meander on a piece of limestone, made by attaching one section to another in the manner of the Pech de l'Azé engraving (FIGURES 13a & 13b). Meander or serpentine marking in this tradition has been found as far as Australia, in the cave of Koonalda, dated at about 20,000 B.C.[21]

FIGURE 12a. Engraved rib from an Acheulian level at the site of Pech de l'Azé, France, c. 300,000 B.C.

I have refrained from any interpretations of the above images or traditions since I am, at the moment, interested in them only as products of the human capacity for symboling and in their possible relation to the origins of language.

Briefly, I indicate these points:

1. We have evidence that in the Mousterian, at least, there was a variety of symbol systems. Items such as the pendants and the churinga probably served as markers and referrants in culturally structured intragroup relations involving age, sex, rank, and role differentiation, and in symbolic group activities such as rituals and ceremonies. These are the ways in which such artifacts have been used in historic times. In addition, images such as the zigzag and the meander may have had a phenomenological reference, documenting awareness of the natural world. Such

FIGURE 12b. Detail of the central engraved portion of the engraved rib from Pech de l'Azé, indicating the festooned serpentine image.

images, however, were probably *used* symbolically, instead of being mere abstracted representations.[20] The marking or accumulation of sets form still other systems. Finally, the skill in using tools and in working bone evidenced in the carving of the churinga suggests that it was made by an adult male familiar with some specialized aspect of Mousterian symbolism and was perhaps intended for shamanistic or group use.

No such assumptions of complex, "artificial," cultural structures have been made before for Mousterian daily life. Add to the above artifacts the evidence of ritual burial and the ceremonial arrangements of bones and skulls, and one has a picture of a symbolized cultural complexity that was fully *sapiens*.

If there was language, it would have been involved in marking these intragroup relations and activities. Language, in fact, may have been as useful, or more useful, in this cultural realm than in the comparatively self-evident strategies utilized in hunting, butchering, and gathering.

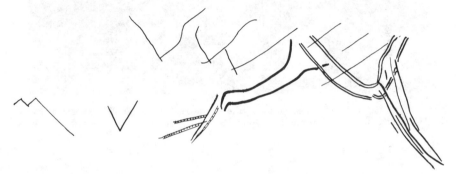

FIGURE 12c. Schematic rendition of the primary engraved image on the Pech de l'Azé rib with the subsidiary marking of angles and parallel lines.

2. The symbolic artifacts document a cognitive capacity and competence for abstraction, modeling, and manufacture of a different order than that which can be deduced from the subsistence tool industries. Although this competence involved a use of hands and tools, it is probably allied to linguistic competence rather than to tool-making, in both an evolutionary sense and in contemporaneous Mousterian usage.

It is significant in this regard that where symbolic artifacts are known in the Paleolithic record, they always document aspects of adult tool or material use that are different from those involved in subsistence activities. The complex nature of this difference needs to be explained, since it is apparently intimately related to linguistic competence.

3. In tool manufacture or in subsistence activities such as digging, gathering, hunting, butchering, or hut building, the strategy sequences are performed visibly and move toward verifiable ends. One gets a cutting edge, a tuber, a shank of meat, a shelter. The skills may require learning and a certain cognitive capacity, but they do not necessarily require a complex use of language. Symbolic artifacts, on the other hand, are not validated or explained by their utility in the natural or phenomenological world, even when they are derived from the real world or are directed at it. They are viable only within "artificial" or *cultural* contexts.

FIGURE 13a. Nonutilitarian limestone pebble with engraved, symbolic meander or serpentine image, from the site of Romanelli, Italy, the late Upper Paleolithic, c. 8,500 B.C.

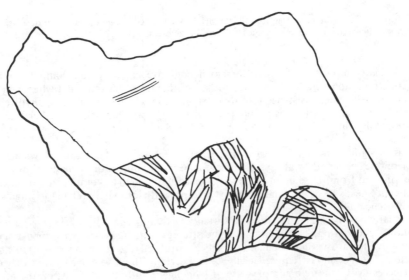

FIGURE 13b. Line rendition of the meander image on the Romanelli limestone, indicating that it was made intentionally, section by section, in a tradition that was maintained through the full Upper Paleolithic.

In the field of paleoarcheology there has not been, to date, a substantive discussion of the nature of such cultural contexts and certainly not as they may have functioned in hominid evolution. "Culture" has most often been described as those subsistence activities involved in tool-making, hunting, and adaptive problem-solving in the phenomenological world with some discussion of protocultural changes in interpersonal relations due to biological changes concerned with sex and maturation.[22,23] The data I am presenting suggest that the capacities evolving in man were far more complex.

4. In the manufacture of a Mousterian symbolic image, one hand (presumably the right, in most cases) held the cutting tool and shaped the image. The other hand held the material being worked, adjusting it for orientation and judging weight, size, hardness, pressure, and so on. The right hand was forming a particular class of image in what might be termed a "specifying" activity which, though nonlinguistic, was related to "naming."

It was not merely the manipulative capacity of the hominid hand as tool-user that was involved [24] but a two-handed competence with a highly evolved right-handed, vision-oriented specialization for symbol forming, aided by a left hand supplying a different input. This, of course, has relevance for lateralization, cerebral dominance, cross-modal association, and so on, but involved also are such "modes" or aspects as motivation, planning, cognitive modeling, symbolic sequencing, and an exceedingly fine acuity in the kinesthetic, somesthetic, and visual inputs. Above and behind these testable skills there is the more generalized capacity to create and to function within long-term, artificial (or cultural) "equations of relevance." In the Mousterian each of these modes is totally human and far more evolved than is evidenced in a chimpanzee's use of symbol or tool. Some comparisons, however, may be useful.

CROSS-MODAL LANGUAGE ORIGINS

If one assumes that in the Acheulian and Mousterian the use of symbolic images required some form of spoken language to maintain and explain the tradition, one must explore the possibility that visually oriented "two-handedness" of the human type, with all of its cross-modal neurological correlates, evolved in conjunction with an increasingly lateralized, corticalized capacity for vocal communication. A brief model for such a possible evolutionary development follows.

Most biological systems have a certain range of potential variability. In scientific research and under laboratory conditions, it is often this range that is tested, rather than the system of behavior that is functional under biologically "natural" conditions. In part, it is some aspect of this capacity for potentially variable behavior that will function adaptively for an organism under new environmental conditions and then be selected for genetically. The behavioral systems of the anthropoids exhibit the widest range of what I heuristically term the "potential variable capacity." It is an aspect of this capacity that is currently being tested under artificial conditions in chimpanzee research on language acquisition. The range of the "potential variable capacity" inherent in the eye-hand-brain system of the early hominids is, at most, roughly suggested by the chimpanzees' capacity for tool, gesture, and symbol use in the wild and in the "cultural" conditions of the laboratory.

One assumes some degree of evolved difference in the behavioral capacity of the hominids, associated with such factors as upright posture, full bipedalism, freed hands, and the brain-structuring that would accompany such anatomic changes. Still, the chimpanzee capacity does suggest aspects of the evolving potential, and these require study for their relevance to spoken language.

In the wild, chimpanzee hands are used in a number of ways: 1) relationally to gesture, groom, and hold; 2) practically to gather food, make and use simple tools, and solve simple manual problems in time and space; and 3) agonistically to display, threaten, throw, or hit. They already function, therefore, *cross-modally* in different contexts.

Unfortunately, although chimpanzee cognition and handedness (including the use of the hand in vision-based "language" systems) have been studied in the laboratory and wild, the primate call system has *not* been explored to ascertain whether it has any inherent potential variability within the species capacity. Early research to test if the chimpanzee could vocalize human phonemes was perhaps asking the species to perform at biological levels for which it was not suited, much as though it had been asked to perform two-handed tasks involving complex, separate cognitive strategies and sequences for each hand like those involved in skinning an animal or playing the piano.

Primate call systems are used to differentiate and institute affect reactions. Instead of trying to teach the chimpanzee to vocalize human language, it is possible that a human could learn the chimpanzee call system and its relational and affect usage and then be able to modulate or modify both the calls and their usage in order to "affect mark" aspects of structured cultural relations and situations, including elements of a hand-gesture system or a symbol-sign system.

It is at this level of possible potential variable capacity in the eye-hand and the affect-call systems that the evolution of spoken speech may have begun. Whether the results of such tests with the chimpanzees were positive or negative, the data would be of significance for the continuing study of speech and language origins.

Theoretically, of course, there should be *some* degree of potentially variable capacity in the chimpanzee call system, even without hominid laryngeal development. Still, by the time of the hominid differentiation, it was probably the increased potential variability in the capacity of both systems, the eye-hand and the vocal-auditory, that contributed toward the development of speech and language.

At the point in time during which the hominids were making and using the multipurpose Oldowan chopper, the hands, according to the industry and faunal evidence, were already functioning as variable doers, specifiers, and differentiators. They were involved in rather complex strategies and sequences requiring specialized locating, securing, processing, forming, and object discrimination. The hominid omnivores were not only making stone tools and killing animals, but they were also apparently involved in a "cultural" differentiation of classes, according to their presence in different realms, areas, and periods: wood usable or not, insect edible or not, serpent dangerous or not, amphibian reachable or not, carnivore threatening or not, roots ready or not, stone practical or not, fruit ripe or not, nesting bird present or not, and so on.

Any regular or structured relation to such diverse objects and species from different realms, areas, and periods would have involved the hand-eye system of an omnivore in cognitive and spatiotemporal strategies of the so-called "logical" class, including evaluations and judgments as to size, weight, hardness, distance, speed, and so on. But it would also have included some form of cultural terrain "modeling" with the indications of place and direction perhaps performed by pointing. Many of these capacities are already evidenced in simple, nonlinguistic form in the chimpanzee.[25] In the hominid context the complexity probably would have involved some activity specialization and dispersal by age, sex, and perhaps rank. Relational and subsistence activities were both becoming "cultural."

The hands involved in these complex, specialized, often "cultural" or learned skills would already be involved in a system with potential for internally relevant, iconic signing. Before the development of a formalized gestural syntax, a concomitant capacity for modulation of the call system would have made it possible to lend affect to the hand-signing process.

Since affect vocalization serves in various ways to affirm or negate, that is, to warn, calm, approve, demand, comfort, indicate state, and mark events or situations via the limbic system, modulated vocalization could have served in what might be termed "adverbing" and "affect-negation/affirmation."

A hand can gesture "snake" and indicate size and direction, but concurrent modulation of the danger or fear call could indicate whether it was dangerous. The hand, then, would be involved in what might be termed description or modeling with a tendency toward "nouning," some "adjectival" marking, and "verbing" or indication of action or process.

The two systems overlap, with a degree of redundancy. To the extent that objects, species, areas, or actions had strong affect, a specifying, modulated vocalization *within a hand-signing context* would itself have "naming" content. The specific vocalization accompanying a signing for serpent, for instance, could itself become a sign for the class. Once instituted as a functional mode, such specifying affect vocalization could function at a distance in time and space from the object. It would thus become an abstracted, noniconic symbol and, though originally of limbic derivation, it could now serve, protolinguistically, in a gestural, symbolically structured situation with lessened affect.

Being *volitional*, such modulated vocalization would *require* association with the hand-eye signing system. In fact, it could function only with reference to the inputs or the iconography of the visual system. Modulated affect vocalization without such cross-modal reference to the visual system would have little communication value.

The question is whether such vocalization entailed a use of the "potential variable capacity" of the hominids and subsequent selection for an increase in that adaptive capacity under increasingly "artificial" cultural conditions or whether it awaited some mutation with subsequent selection for an increase in a newly instituted capacity.

The primate hand can also indicate state, affect, negation and demand. It is significant that these two evolving systems, the hand-eye cognitive and the vocal-auditory marking, as they became increasingly lateralized, specialized, separate and cross-modally associated, did *not* lose their original limbic-motor connections and modes. They still exist in man. Instead, they became overlain by superseding neocortical functions and capacities.

Such a model has the advantage of operating at each point in evolutionary development within the biological capacity of the species and its evolving subsystems, as well as within the adaptive needs of the developing hominid cultures.

In such a model it is the culture complex and not tool-making or hunting that provides the environmental matrix and the selective pressures. In fact, tool-making and hunting remained profoundly conservative for some two million or more years. With an increasing complexity in hominid cultures there would be need for an increased capacity for variable marking both in the visual and the vocal modes. This would be due in part to the increasing variability and the concurrent culturalization of objects, processes, actions and relations. The formalized "structures" that result from production within both modes under these conditions will be discussed in another paper.

The problem of language and speech origins is clarified from another direction by the ontogenetic nature of the language capacity. If, at any point in the evolutionary process "language" or protolanguage was to be learned, it would not have been in the context of the hunt. It would have been learned young, and before the individual was economically productive. It would have been learned in the context of the maturing, generalized cognitive capacity and within a child's widening, increasingly complex relational competence. Language and symbolization are always learned as an aspect of the marking of cultural and relational "equations of relevance."

The nonlimbic, voluntary modulation of a danger call, for instance, could call a child back to a hominid windbreak or shelter even if there was no immediate danger. But such a voluntary call could be uttered only if the adult knew of potential dangers. Call modulation could also express approval of an effort or a developing skill in the child, or the utility or capacity of a stick, stone, or bone. Such affect-related marking would be possible and useful only in the context of other, already known and learned equations. It could serve as protolanguage, once again, only in a cultural context.

This, of course, poses a profound theoretical problem. Language production always marks or describes less than is known, for both speaker and hearer. It marks or describes an aspect of what is "known," and what is known is largely nonlinguistic. This is true at any point in the evolution or the ontogeny of language. What are some of these nonlinguistic aspects of "knowing"?

A chimpanzee learning a man-made "language" in a man-made context is learning some of what man knows but he is also using the primate potential capacity for learning, not simply a use of hands or a use of symbol, but also certain forms of nonlinguistic "equations of relevance." These are fundamentally relational and only partly "cognitive." The language mode itself is such an equation of relevance.

This form of knowledge is apparent in those human aphasias where production of language is damaged but in which the equations for which language is sought remain undamaged. The effort toward speech, itself an equation, may be likewise undamaged. The outsider can often supply the word or phrase, and the equation or concept is affirmed. These equations are often purely cultural formulations, culture-specific, culture-bound, and without phenomenological reference. They are often not "logical" in the psychologist's use of the term, or "cognitive" or primarily linguistic.

By contrast, in certain aphasias the patient can lose the capacity for formulating or specifying equations or sequences of relevance, yet maintain a capacity for the production of nonsensical phonemic language. The "deepest" structures of language, in this sense, are equational and nonlinguistic.

To return to our primary data, the symbolic images of the Mousterian and Upper Paleolithic could probably be "named" and the meaning and use of any one image could perhaps be explained. But the use of such artificial images was itself a mode and an "equation of relevance," one that had to be learned and yet could not be linguistically explained. Human languages, like human image systems, function only in devised contexts. The search for language origins, therefore, should be directed toward the complex nature of the evolving, generalizing hominid capacity for artificial, cultural modeling and symbolic structuring in all modes.

REFERENCES

1. RIEK, G. 1932–33. Altsteinzeitkulturen am Vogelherd bei Stetten ob Lontal (Württemberg). Ipek 8: 1–26.
2. MARSHACK, A. 1969. Polesini: a reexamination of the engraved Upper Paleolithic mobiliary materials of Italy by a new methodology. Rivista di Scienze Preistoriche 24(2): 219–281.
3. RIVIÉRE, E. 1897. Nouvelles recherches à Cro-Magnon. Bull. de la Société d'Anthropologie de Paris 8: 507 (Figure 2).
4. MARSHACK, A. 1970. Notation dans les Gravures du Paléolithique Supérieur: Nouvelles Méthodes d'Analyse. Publications de l'Institut de Préhistoire de l'Université de Bordeaux No 8. Bordeaux, France.

5. MARSHACK, A. 1972. The Roots of Civilization. McGraw-Hill Book Co. New York, N.Y.
6. MARSHACK, A. 1972. Upper Paleolithic notation and symbol. Science 178: 817–828.
7. MARSHACK, A. 1972. Cognitive aspects of Upper Paleolithic engraving. Current Anthropol. 13(3–4): 445–477.
8. MARSHACK, A. 1974. Reply to letter. Current Anthropol. 15(3): 328–332.
9. BLANC, A. C. 1961. Some evidence for the ideologies of early man. In Social Life of Early Man. S. Washburn, Ed.: 119–136. Aldine Publishing Co. Chicago, Ill.
10. LIEBERMAN, P. & E. S. CRELIN. 1971. On the speech of Neanderthal man. Linguistic Inquiry 2(2): 203–222.
11. BINFORD, S. R. 1968. A structural comparison of disposal of the dead in the Mousterian and the Upper Paleolithic. Southwestern J. Anthropol. 24(2): 139–154.
12. SOLECKI, R. S. 1971. Shanidar: The First Flower People. Alfred A. Knopf. New York, N.Y.
13. LEROI-GOURHAN, A. 1975. The Flowers Found with Shanidar IV, A Neanderthal Burial in Iraq. Science 190: 562–564.
13a. SOLECKI, R. 1975. Shanidar IV, a Neanderthal Burial in Northern Iraq. Science 190: 880–881.
14. MARTIN, H. 1907–1910. Récherche sur l'Evolution du Mousterien dans le Gisement de la Quina. Vol. 1: Industrie Osseuse. Schleicher Frères. Paris, France.
15. CAPITAN, L. & D. PEYRONY. 1921. Les origines de l'art a l'Aurignacien moyen: La Ferrassie. Revue Archéologique 31: 92–112.
16. VERTÉS, L. 1964. Tata: Eine Mittelpaläolithische Travertin Siedlung in Ungarn. Series Nova XLIII. Akademai Kiado. Verlag der Ungarischen Akademie der Wissenschaften. Budapest, Hungary.
17. BORDES, F. 1969. Os percé Mousterien et os gravé Acheuleén du Pech de l'Azé II. Quaternaria XI: 1–6.
18. DE LUMLEY, H. 1969. A Paleolithic camp at Nice. Sci. Amer. 220: 42–50.
19. BORDES, F. 1972. A Tale of Two Caves. Harper & Row. New York, N.Y.
20. MARSHACK, A. The meander as a system: the analysis and recognition of iconographic units in Upper Paleolithic compositions. In Biennial Conference, Australian Inst. Aboriginal Studies. 16 May–2 June, 1974. P. Ucko, Ed. Canberra, Australia. In press.
21. EDWARDS, R. & L. MAYNARD. 1971. Wall markings. In Archaeology of the Gallus Site, Koonalda Cave. R. V. S. Wright, Ed.: 61–80. Australian Institute of Aboriginal Studies. Canberra, Australia.
22. LAUGHLIN, C. D. & E. G. d'Aguili. 1974. Biogenetic Structuralism. Columbia Univ. Press. New York and London.
23. ISAAC, G. LL. 1972. Chronology and the tempo of cultural change during the Pleistocene. In Calibration Of Hominoid Evolution. W. W. Bishop & J. A. Miller, Eds. Scottish Academic Press, for The Wenner-Gren Foundation.
24. NAPIER, J. 1962. The evolution of the hand. Sci. Amer. 207: 56–62.
25. TELEKI, G. 1974. Chimpanzee subsistence technology: materials and skills. J. Human Evolution 3: 575–594.

THE EVOLUTION OF LANGUAGE
IN THE LATE PLEISTOCENE

Julian Jaynes

Department of Psychology
Princeton University
Princeton, New Jersey 08540

In this paper I shall first address the question of when language evolved, basing my answer on three assumptions. I shall then attempt the question of how language evolved, appealing to a principle of intensity differentiation of call endings and describing how this may have resulted in first modifiers, then commands, and then nouns and names. I shall then insist that this development is roughly correlated with the hastening sequence of archeological artifacts from the Acheulean to Neolithic times. Finally, since such a view demands an exceedingly swift evolution, I shall close with several possibilities of how this "leveraged" evolution, as I shall call it, could have occurred.

WHEN LANGUAGE BEGAN

To answer the question of when language evolved, I would like to introduce below three reasonable constraints upon a possible solution.

Survival Value

In thinking about the evolution of language, we naively assume that language is always beneficial. But this is questionable. If some subhuman primate could be taught vocal speech or if those who have already learned sign language could be fired up with some missionary zeal to return to the wilds to teach their conspecifics, it is not at all certain that it would have the slightest survival value whatever. In fact, if a species is fully adapted to its ecological niche, it could perhaps be shown that the sudden ability to communicate syntactically would be disastrous. At the very least, the sounds might attract predators; or if the communication is gestural it might position its users in more vulnerable open situations. More importantly, however, the communication itself might detract from the innate signaling systems that already have organized the successful social grouping of that species. Also, the genetically based spacing mechanisms would be altered and an outbreak of intraspecific aggression might result. Too much communication is a bad thing.

It follows from such considerations that human language developed only during an era in which some portion of the human population was being persistantly forced into new ecological niches to which it was not fully adapted. For any trait that is as universal in a species and that has as precise a neurological substrate as language in man must have developed during an age when it had a great and persisting survival value. And it is certainly a requirement of any theory of language evolution that this survival value be specified with some precision.

312

Behavioral Sequelae

Words are of such huge moment in the life of men that the acquisition of them and the ability to organize them into sentences that convey meaning must have resulted in very real behavioral changes; and these changes must be reflected in the artifacts left behind. This constriction will not be so readily consented to, but let me remind you of a fundamental principle of vertebrate learning: that acquiring different consistent responses to different things makes them more discriminable, and makes it easier to acquire new responses to those things.[13] This is exactly what language does. A differential lingual response to an object is a training of attention upon it. To look at an object and to name it at the same time allows a concentration upon it that otherwise would be absent. Without names for things, we cannot readily get our own or others' attentions to the right places or keep them there very long. Speechless children, such as the wild boy studied by Itard,[11] or even normal children before the advent of speech, have difficulty in maintaining attention for very long. Language is an organ of perception, not merely a means of communication.

But the effect of language on behavior goes much further and deeper than orientation and attention. Stimuli when labeled are actually easier to remember. Children who can name colors better can remember and recognize them better.[16] And what is remembered, is shaped by the terms that express it.[7] Moreover, stimulus differences when labeled can be responded to in a much more encompassing way: behavior can be reactions to relational concepts rather than to the actual stimuli themselves, something impossible without words.[17] Language thus allows us to code and compare attributes of objects verbally, thereby freeing us from the momentary perceptual impact of one attribute or another. Many workers feel this is the very essence of cognitive development.[5] There are also many studies, both in Russia[25] and America,[26] which show that the teaching of verbal descriptions of various response alternatives allow children to bridge situational changes or extensive time gaps by verbal mediation, which would be impossible without language.

And so it was with mankind when speech first developed. Just as the psychobehavioral development of a child leaps forward with speech, so a similar leap must, I think, have occurred when man as a species first developed language. The position can be taken therefore with some assurance that the development of language produced a qualitatively different level of mentality that resulted in behavioral sequelae whose artifacts we may find archeologically.

Brain Structure

Any theory of the development of language must at least where possible make some sense of what we know of brain development over these time periods. The reason for this is that the three cortical areas involved in language, the supplementary motor cortex and Broca's area in the frontal lobe, and Wernicke's area around the fissure of Sylvius where the temporal lobe joins the parietal are in a probalistic way[2] present in all contemporary speakers, and may thus be assumed to have been necessary for the complete development of language as we speak it today.

Glaciation and Language

Now let us apply these constraints to the problem of when language developed. We have inferred that so dramatic a development as language had to coincide with significant ecological changes during which man's life and habits underwent significant change. This inference obviously points to the great periods of glaciation, when ice accumulated in polar zones and slid southward to cover most of the North temperate regions four separate times just as man evolved from *Homo habilis* through *Homo erectus* and *Homo sapiens neanderthalensis* to *Homo sapiens*. Each glaciation lasted roughly 70,000 years. The approximate dates of the middle or coldest part of each of these periods are 600,000, 400,000, 150,000 and 35,000 B.C. The warm interglacial periods are without sufficient ecological challenge to provide language with the survival value that we have insisted it must have had, and may thus be ruled out as the loci of its development.

The three constraints I have mentioned taken together eliminate all but the fourth glaciation. During the first two glacial periods, man was largely an African animal and far removed from their serious effects. The third glaciation occurring in the middle Pleistocene is certainly a period when the more northern living hominids were put under intense ecological pressures. That race of *H. erectus* called Peking man is now known to have been a hunter of large game animals of considerable variety during the third glaciation. And he did this with a tool kit almost as crude as those of his ancestors in Africa.[8] But it is just because of the crudity of their tools and the primitiveness of their subsistence that makes it doubtful that language developed at this time; nor had the brain of Peking man evolved to the size and structure that we have assumed to be necessary at least for the complete development of language.

At this point, some objections could possibly be raised. How was it possible for proto-man to function, to live in caves, to hunt, to use fire, to make pebble choppers or hand axes if he could not speak? The answer is that he communicated just like all the other primates, with an abundance of visual, vocal, and tactile signals very far removed from the syntactical language that we practice today. Nor is language necessary for the transmission for such rudimentary skills as simple tool using and making from one generation to another. Indeed language might even have hindered. It is almost impossible to describe the method for chipping flints to make simple choppers and hand axes with language. This art was transmitted solely by imitation in exactly the same way in which chimpanzees transmit the trick of inserting vine stems into ant hills to get ants, or Japanese macaques the method of using leaf-sponges and other nutrient-handling tasks that have then diffused without vocal language. In our own culture, it is doubtful if language is at all necessary in the transmission of such skills as swimming, riding, or other motor skills.

Characteristics of the Late Pleistocene

All indications, then, point to the fourth glaciation during the late Pleistocene as the period during which speech evolved and developed. This period began about 70,000 B.C., and was one in which the climate north of the equator became gradually colder, causing dramatic changes in the flora and fauna. Its coldest part came about 35,000 B.C. The glaciation then slowly receded and temperatures became normal about 8,000 B.C. The temperature changes through these periods were not steady or gradual, but were characterized by wide variations corresponding to variations in the advance and retreat of glacial conditions, all of these factors causing huge migrations of both animals and men.

While *H. erectus* had been venturing quite far outside Africa since perhaps the second glaciation, it is only during the fourth glaciation that the human population in significant numbers expanded out into the Eurasian subartic, and then into Australia and a little later into the Americas. Population density around the Mediterranean reached a new high and this area became the leader in cultural innovation, transferring man's cultural and biological focus from the tropics to the middle latitudes. His fires and furs were a kind of transportable microclimate that allowed these migrations to take place. We are used to referring to these people as late Neanderthalers. They were not a separate species of man as was thought at the beginning of this century, but were part of the general human line, which had great variation, a variation that allowed for an increasing pace of evolution as man spread into these new ecological niches. It is important here to stress both the variation and the nomadic quality of life that was spreading over such wide distances. Some tribes, certainly, were following the herds of reindeer, mammoths, horse, and bison into the forest-tundra during the winter, and returning with them onto the broad expanse of herbaceous tundra in summer. Others most likely were going in a lateral direction, from campsite to campsite wherever food might be had.

These conditions then fulfill the three constraints we have placed upon the solution. Such climatic changes as occurred during the fourth glaciation certainly provide a theater of sufficient selective pressures such that a communication system such as language would, as I shall later show, have considerable survival value. The artifacts of the cultures, beginning with an explosion of new and different tools about 40,000 B.C., fulfills the second requirement, the record of artifacts showing that changes in man's way of living were occurring at an increasing tempo. And thirdly, through evolution, the brain, particularly with the increase in the frontal lobes with Broca's area, was reaching its contemporary proportions.[19]

We have inadvertently in our discussion suggested the place in which language most likely developed. Again applying the three constraints, it would be an area in which there were sufficient selective pressures, where excavated artifacts reveal the most change and where skulls show the increase we have referred to. This area is indeed the north temperature zone in a band from France and Spain all across Europe, North Africa, the near East and Asia, and from there spreading southward. It is interesting to consider whether or not it is possible that this Northern locus of the origination of language had any effect on just how languages were formed, or left any traces of their age in present languages.

HOW LANGUAGE BEGAN

In the discussion I am about to attempt I would like it to be continually understood that I am painting in the broadest strokes possible. All stage theory, be it in the development of a child, an idea, or a nation, requires this qualification: stages are never really discrete and differ in different instances. They are true only in general. And this is particularly so of anything as hazardous as the present undertaking. I am describing an ideal model of which the actualities are probably variants. After all, Neanderthal man was widely distributed over Africa, Europe, and Asia at this time. It is very likely that language developed somewhat differently and at a different pace in different ecologies and races. The problem of persistant migration and diffusion is a hugely complicating factor, demanding almost a new kind of social psychology for Neanderthal tribes. What follows therefore is not meant as any exceptionless succession. It is rather a broad working model intended to provoke a new kind of thinking about the development of language and speech.

Stage I: Intentionalization of Vocalization

First of all, let me here glance sideways at a view very much in evidence at this conference. This is the interesting idea of the gestural origin of language,[9,27] an older theory recently invigorated by the teaching of sign language of various sorts to chimpanzees. I myself am skeptical of how far early hominid facial, gestural, and postural communication approached modern sign languages. But whatever the comparison, there is little doubt that at least some system of visual signals did exist as it does in most primates, that it was complex, and that it was largely composed of intentional signals rather than merely incidental signals.

This is an important distinction. An *incidental* signal is simply a concomitant of some ongoing behavior. It may or may not evoke a response in another animal, and may even be emitted when the animal is alone. An *intentional* signal, on the other hand, is only emitted in a social context, and tends to be repeated until it is turned off by the behavior of the animal to which it is addressed. Territorial bird songs are incidental signals. But the distress cries of nidifugeous hatchlings are intentional, ceasing or changing to contentment sounds at the approach of an imprinted object.[14] Threat postures and the like in primates are intentional signals, tending to continue until some change in behavior in a conspecific occurs. Intentional signals are thus a more complicated sort. I am using the term descriptively in a completely behavioristic way, and do not imply any consciousness or cognitive purposiveness in its emission.

Many monkey or ape visual signals are intentional, but almost all their vocal signals are simply incidental. They merely accompany the visual signals. Vocal signals given alone apart from the total multisensory gestalt of posture, facial expression, gesture, movement, and often touch have little significance. I suggest this was also true among early hominids such as *h. habilis* back around 400,000 B.C., who had perhaps an incidental call system of perhaps 15 or 20 cries as in a present-day anthropoid.[20] The first and important step toward speech is the generalization of the intentional signaling system from the visual channel to the auditory channel.

Neurologically, this change is tantamount to the encephalization of vocalization. It is an absolute prerequisite for speech. The incidental vocal signals of present-day subhuman primates are incidental because they are controlled by the limbic system. They are emotional expressions accompanying other behavior. The entire vocal repertoires in rhesus monkeys[24] and squirrel monkeys,[23] for example, can be elicited by electrical stimulation of points throughout the limbic circuit. Although such information is not really conclusive on this point, it nevertheless suggests that this limbic control of vocal calls was true of early hominids. The transfer to cortical control occurred, I suggest, by the evolution of additional frontal cortex in the region ventral to the cortical substrate of the already intentionally gesturing hand, thus selectively suppressing and releasing the limbic centers for vocalization beneath it.

Under what ecological pressures could this have happened? As populations of Middle Pleistocene man with their Acheulean culture migrated out of African savannas and alluvial flats into northern climates, visual signals were less effective for a variety of reasons. Such a migrant to the north during the third glaciation lived more and more in dark caves or smoky shelters, perhaps hunting diurnal animals by night in situations where visual, facial and gestural signals could not be seen as readily. Moreover, his bipedalism and tools in themselves created new selective pressures, making it important to free the hands and body for his increasingly complicated activities. It is therefore plausible that incidental vocal signals under these persisting pressures took on the intentional function that was formerly the property of visual signals only. This was a momentous step, and probably had a long evolution that was not complete until the end of the Middle Pleistocene and the approach of the fourth glaciation.

Stage II: Age of Modifiers

The first real elements of speech, were I suggest, the endings of intentional cries first varying simply by intensity, and then being differentiated further. This Principle of Intensity Differentiation is central to my view of language development. An example will help us here. Let us say that man has evolved an intentional warning cry of *wah! wah! wah!* We can perhaps imagine a caveman, gesturing wildly and often impotently, rushing back to his dark cave screaming this cry at the approach of any danger. It is an innate dynamism that the intensity of such a warning signal corresponds to the intensity of the danger whether the signal be gesture or vocalization. Indeed, the same dynamism could be applied to the gestural theory as a way segmentation began. In vocalization, such intensity differentiation would be reflected little by little and perhaps more and more in the way the cry was uttered, particularly perhaps in its ending phoneme. And after a period of development, we could imagine that a dangerous approaching tiger or bear might result in *wahee!*, while a tiger or bear far off and going in another direction might result in a cry of much less intensity and develop a different ending such as a more relaxed *wahoo*. It is these endings, then, that become the first modifiers meaning near and far. And the next huge step toward syntactic language was taken when these endings could be separated from the particular cry with the same indication and attached to some other cry.

What is of crucial importance here is to appreciate that the differentiation of verbal qualifiers had to precede the invention of the nouns that they modified, rather than the reverse as is assumed by most of this audience. And what is more, this state of speech had to remain for a long period until such modifiers became stable. This slow development is also necessary so that the same basic repetoire of alarm vocalizations is kept intact to perform their intentional functions. Thus we might expect that a small lexicon of modifiers like near, far, at the river, behind the hill, etc. was developed in this way long before the specific referents themselves could be differentially indicated.

This "age of modifiers" perhaps included most of what in Europe is known as the Mousterian period and lasted perhaps up to 46,000 B.C. Neanderthal skulls of this time show a frontal angle of 65 degrees (our's is nearer 90 degrees) denoting undeveloped frontal lobes. Casts of some of the better skulls show that the lower frontal lobe where Broca's speech area is located is not fully developed, and the Fissure of Silvius is extremely wide, showing an undeveloped Wernicke's speech association area.[19] It is over the next stages late in Pleistocene times that the human brain fully evolves its characteristic speech areas. For those who find it impossible to think of evolution of these areas going on in so short a period, it is good to stress again the immense migrant variety on which this natural selection for modifier development had to work under the intense selective pressures of the coldest part of the glacial period.

Stage III: Age of Commands

Modifiers once separated from the cries they modified become commands. Just as these endings once modified cries, now they modify men's actions themselves. Thus as in the above example, a new cry of *ee!* shouted to a recipient could mean nearer, while *o!* could mean further. The advantage of such commands in such an endeavor as group hunting of the huge new mammals that abounded everywhere at that time is quite obvious. Particularly as man relied more and more on hunting in the chilled climate, the selective pressure for such a group of hunters controlled by vocal commands must have been immense. But the use of such modifiers in other skills is equally important. We may imagine that the industry of flint and bone tools was passed down by imitation, but the invention of a modifier meaning sharper as an instructed command or self-repeated command would be of extreme importance. I would suggest that this period corresponded to the Aurignacian period in Europe, with its much sharper blades and other tools, which lasted perhaps to 25,000 B.C. All speech up to this period has been holophrastic.

Two further developments possibly occurred during this long period, I have called the stage of commands. The first is interrogation; and here, I think, we can invoke a Principle of Buccolaryngeal Response Generalization. Just as in careful manipulatory skills we often twist the tongue and mouth in a corresponding way (more often in children), so in early man, postural and gestural intentional signals, particularly when done carefully because they were less effective, generalized to the mouth and larynx, altering vocalization in a corresponding fashion. In interrogation the originating postural signal would have been the quick upward movement of the brows and look of expectant waiting common in many primate dyadic social situations. Thus, the leader of a hunting group, while raising his brows and looking expectantly, might command *nearer!* with an expectant intensity ending that raised its pitch slightly, carrying it over the distance to the hunter on the other side of the prey. And the recipient of the message might then repeat the command *nearer* over and over to himself as he accomplished this act, the intensity ending being much diminished, since it was to his own ears that he was speaking. Using our punctuation, it would be *nearer?*, with the 'reply,' *nearer*. And out of this kind of repetition it is a simple matter to derive inflectional questioning. This may also have resulted in chanting of various sorts and the beginning of primordial ritual. It should be particularly noted that placing the development of inflectional questioning as early as the age of commands, indicates a very strong genetic basis.

The second development is that of negation. It is probably of a different order. I suspect that its origin is prelingual possibly as a disgust cry. Again, a part of its development may have been a buccolaryngeal generalization from a facial, gestural, or postural signal of rejection. It then may have developed into an intentional cry as from a parent to a child to stop it in what it was doing. Toilet training, which with the progressive prematurity of birth and cave living probably now became a problem, may have been the carrier. The survival value of its use as a command in group hunting is obvious.

Stage IV: Life Nouns

Once a tribe has a repertoire of modifiers and commands, the necessity of keeping the integrity of the old primitive cries can be relaxed for the first time so that they can indicate the referents of the modifiers or commands. Thus from the original *wah* and *wahee!* we might have *wakee!* for an approaching tiger or *wabee!* for an approaching bear, the consonant differentiation being again a buccolaryngeal generalization of imitated tiger or bear behavior. And these would be the first sentences with a noun subject and a predicative modifier. This may have corresponded in Europe to the Gravetian and Solutrean cultures, which existed between 25,000 B.C. and 15,000 B.C. The pace of language development is increasing.

Some of you may be exasperated at this point and wish to exclaim, how arbitrary! But the succession from modifiers to commands, and only when these become stable, to nouns, is no arbitrary succession. Nor is the dating entirely arbitrary. Just as the stage of modifiers coincided with the making of much superior tools, so the stage of nouns for animals coincides with the beginning of drawing animals on the walls of caves or on horns and tools carved from horns. Once animals—particularly those that were hunted—had nouns that could designate them, they had a kind of extra being, one indeed that could be taken far back into the caves and drawn upon its walls. And from this time on the first animal silhouettes develop into the well known cave paintings of bison and reindeer, which I suggest, could only occur after the beginning of life nouns. The fact that such paintings rarely include men drawn with the same life-like similitude may suggest a lack of words for different men.

Stage V: Thing Nouns

This is really a carry-over from the preceding stage. Just as life nouns began animal drawings, so nouns for things beget new things: the invention of pottery, of pendants, and ornaments, bone carvings, harpoons, and most important the invention of the barb for harpoons and spearheads. It corresponds perhaps in parts of Europe to the Magdalenian culture. By this time, the brain has the modern language areas.

Stage VI: Names

We are now in the Mesolithic period, about 10,000 B.C. to 8,000 B.C. It is the period of man's adaptation to the modern postglacial environment, keying in to specific environmental situations, to grassland hunting, to life in the forest, to shellfish collecting, or to the exploitation of marine resources combined with terrestrial hunting. Such living is characterized by a much greater stability of population, rather than the mobility of the hunting groups with their large mortality which preceded them. And thus with these more fixed populations, with more fixed relationships, and probably larger numbers in the group, we have the carry-over of nouns into names for individual persons. While noun-names may have occurred for troop leaders or special individuals much earlier, it appears to me that it is the Mesolithic period in which names become universal. Once a tribe member has a proper name, he can in a sense be recreated in his absence, thought about. While rare, individual, ceremonial graves date from much earlier, this is the first age in which they become common and elaborate. But just as a noun for an animal makes that relationship a much more intense one, so too does a name. And when the person dies, the name still goes on, and hence the relationship as in life, and hence an elaboration of burial practices and mourning. The Mesolithic midden-dwellers of Morbihan, for example, buried their dead in skincloaks fastened by bonepins and sometimes crowned them with stagantlers and protected them with stone slabs. Other graves from the period show burials with little crowns, or various ornaments, or possibly flowers in carefully excavated places, all, I suggest, the result of the invention of names.

Again, I would like to emphasize that the above sequence of stages may in no particular tribe or region have been actual throughout the enormous time spans we are speaking of. Migrations and therefore behavioral and cultural diffusion were on a level far beyond anything that had happened earlier in man's protohistory. Such diffusion as applied to aspects of speech in different regions and times and evolutionary development is profoundly complex. Hence any series of stages as I have propounded should perhaps be regarded as a logical analysis to which a kind of commonality of the historical realities might approximate.

Other Developments

It is to be noted in the above discussion that our own sense of what is necessary for primitive communication has not demanded of us a separate stage of verbs. Words denoting actions were common among the first modifiers and commands. A modifier meaning 'running' to follow a danger call is not in a different class than other modifiers. But when turned into a command it would have an obvious greater value. Similarly, most commands have verb qualities. And after the stage of nouns, we may imagine that intensity differentiations operated upon them as well to produce the first verb declensions. It is not far from a sentence such as *mammoth nearer* to *mammoth nearers!* as the animal begins to run, letting the added *s* here stand for some primordial sound produced by increased intensity.

Prepositions perhaps came about by intensity differentiation of the beginnings of place modifiers. A modifier meaning *in cave* as in *tiger in cave!* might separate into *in cave* and *out cave* on the basis perhaps of the initial intensity of the intentional communication. It might even be possible to order an historical sequence of prepositional meanings on the basis of their ease of dichotomization.

As for syntax, there is a kind of ordering that is inherent in the development I have presented. And this ordering is dependent upon the process I have called intensity differentiation and whether it occurs at the beginning of the communication as in prepositional differentiation or at the end as in the original modifier differentiation. Most primordial syntax can be derived from this in obvious ways. I hope it is apparent here that the vowel and consonant sounds naturally produced by any primate at high intensity or low would make an extremely important study.

As for the other parts of speech, pronouns being redundant with names, would develop very late, and even in some older languages never get much beyond verb endings first differentiated on the basis of intensity. Articles and conjunctions, also because they are redundant with the paralingual or expressive behavior of language are also perhaps one of the final additions to the parts of speech.

LEVERAGED EVOLUTION

In what sense is it correct to say that language evolved through these various stages? The question points to the somewhat hazy problem as to the relationship between the innate and the learned developments necessary for language. This haziness can be clarified by a consideration of what is known as the Baldwin Effect in evolutionary theory: when some new ecological pressure or species demand forces individuals to learn a particular thing to survive, and this is repeated generation after generation, there will be a continuous selection for those biologically best able to learn that particular thing. Thus what was purely learned in one millennium can become partly innate in the next. We have already pointed out the tremendous biological advantage in learning the linguistic components in the several stages I have outlined. And thus we may assume that Baldwinian evolution was continually operating, and that successive generations were building in step-by-step the innate capacity to learn a language. Indeed this is, of course, what is evolved, not the articulated language itself—a quite obvious point that is not always remembered.

But how was it possible to have the evolution of such a thing as speech over a mere 70,000 years? We know that the evolution from the skull of *H. erectus* to the Cro-Magnon type did take place during this short time. To account for this I suggest that we should speak of evolution being leveraged in this particular instance. There are several reasons for the assumption of this leveraged evolution in relation to language.

Retarded Fetal Development

If one plots the brain volume of fossil skulls over time, there is evident a tremendous leap from *H. erectus* with an averaged brain capacity of 1000 cc. to Neanderthal skulls as large as 1650 cc. only 60,000 years later. As the skull of the fetus enlarged, maternal mortality would select for slower fetal development or birth at an earlier and earlier functional age. The evolution of this slower gestation development was also hastened by the narrowing of the mother's pelvic outlet that was a consequence of erect posture, although this was partly compensated for by the evolution of more flexible skull bones in the fetus and of a relaxation of the pelvic ligaments to enlarge the outlet during parturition.

There are several very important results of this:

(1) it increased the death rate, since successively more and more premature infants would be less likely to survive.

(2) This increase in infant mortality increased the birth rate since the cessation of suckling and therefore lactation would allow more frequent ovulation. (The first estrus after parturition occurs in primates only after nursing has stopped—a kind of built-in birth control). Both increased birth rate and death rate speed up the evolution of anything that the ecological pressures at the time select for. One of these may have been intentional vocalization.

(3) Another important result of this slower fetal development is the much longer period of dependency upon the mother. Newborn primates of other species can move about on the mother or on the ground around the mother by themselves. But the premature human infant must communicate its needs by its cries and obtain the mother's help in everything. In such a situation, the tremendous advantages of increased communication between mother and infant are obvious. And during this long infancy with a high infant mortality, one can see how children who responded to the mother with vocalizations would be more carefully cared for on the one side and on the other side, that the mothers who could vocally communicate and obtain vocal responses from their infants, being better mothers, would pass on their own genetic constitution through their children to the future more readily.

Child Education

With the increased infancy caused by retarded development in the gestation period, there is also a lengthening out of human childhood with its greater need for parental guidance. The importance of language in directing children what to do or in stopping them from doing something harmful is obvious. Neanderthal children who could not understand parental commands would be much less likely to reach an age where they could reproduce. It is indeed quite plausible to think of tribes during the Fourth Glaciation simply disposing of speechless children in the exigencies of their strenuous seminomadic life. This is not natural selection but human selective breeding that could have leveraged language evolution even by itself.

Social Organization

Language certainly changed the kind of hierarchical social organization within the tribe. The dominant male in a tribe of *H. erectus* was probably the strongest. But in the first semispeaking Neanderthal tribes, the dominant male might be the best speaker, the best able to give commands as the men surrounded prey during a hunt or in apportioning its results. It is common in social organizations of primates that the dominant male does more of the mating than is his numerical share. In some instances, as in the baboons, he does most of it. If such an organization existed in Neanderthal tribes, if the best speaker did most of the mating, it would leverage the evolution of language considerably.

I have already referred to the immensely complicated problem of the diffusion of speech. But as it did diffuse, what were the consequences of this most profoundly important change in human behavior? While it must have enormously increased the human population of the world, I do not think it increased the basic size of the hunter-gatherer troop. This probably remained fairly stable at from 20 to 30 as it had for the last 100,000 years.[12] The reason is that the group was defined by a certain hierarchical structural, and the limitation of its size was due to the requirement that the members of the community remain within sensory contact particularly with its alpha male. Language simply changed the sensory channel of this communication and made it infinitely more efficient. It did not expand those channels to include significantly more individuals.

But the spacing of the individuals and the way they live together, partly because of the technological expansion, but also because of language itself must have been considerable. There may have been changes in postural adjustments, changes in how the head was held so as to be able to hear language more keenly. The distancing between individuals in a campsite may have been much closer to hear what was said. And we do not have words to even describe the change in the intensity of relationships between the individuals that came with the kind of communication between individuals that language can encompass, let alone the intenseness of relationship already mentioned that was introduced by proper names. All the words that one might wish to use are really metaphors with consciousness, and consciousness, as I have tried to show in another work,[15] is a much later addition to the behavioral functioning of *H. sapiens sapiens*.

The advent of language also provided the paradigm known in behavioral therapy as desensitization. Speaking the noun of a feared thing, or even possibly giving it a proper name and repeating that, could little by little decrease the fear by associating that now part of it which is its word with undangerous situations. Thus the naming of animals and the consequent cave art of drawing them in places safe from them perhaps made men more courageous hunters along the banks of the Vezere and elsewhere.

Water may be another example. Almost all subhuman primates fear water, nor do any of them swim. A stream that cannot be leaped acts as a natural barrier to the movement of many anthropoid troops. Similarly the location of premesolithic campsites seems to indicate that early man shared this fear of water with other primates.[28] But in the mesolithic era, all this changes. And I suggest this change may have been due to the desensitization training of repeating the word for water with no danger present. And it is thus at this time that the first boats are invented thereby opening up huge new ecologies all the way to the Arctic with a new kind of fishing, and permitting such settlements as the well-known lake-dwellers of Neuchatel in Switzerland.

By now it is evident that I am making language not merely one among several of the remarkable evolutionary achievements of the late Pleistocene, but the very pioneer and promoter of the rest. Chiefly this is a matter of attention, of the holding power of language upon a thing or an action, both in the direction of the attentions and actions of others and of oneself. And it will be thus no surprise to the reader when I suggest that language was also the aegis of agriculture as well. Without a word for seed, for earth, for growth, waiting, and for the ripened grain, man would not put seed in the ground and wait for the harvest. If man had had words for these matters a million years earlier, I think it would have been inevitable that agriculture would have begun then instead of only around 8000 B.C.

The chief objection to the model I have presented is its timing. The earliest languages that we know, the languages of the most primitive peoples and the most civilized, seem to have about the same complexity. And the attempts to reconstruct such languages as Indo-European of perhaps 2000 B.C., seem to be just as complex. If there has been so little change in linguistic complexity over the last 4000 years, how could there be such a huge change in only 10 times that time span?

There are several considerations which at least dilute the strength of this objection. First, the kind of reconstructions of Indo-European on which this objection is based may rest on assumptions that exaggerate the similarity of its linguistic complexity to that of present day languages. It would be interesting to examine critically such reconstructions from this point of view. Second, given diffusion and migration, it must be agreed that linguistic change cannot be quantified, and that therefore to trace a trajectory back to prehistoric times is a questionable procedure. Thirdly, even if such a theory is forthcoming, the chances that it will be even near a linear accumulation of complexity are very small. Once the rules of language are evolved into brain structure, it is far more likely that we would have—as we do in the developing child—an explosion almost to asymptote, filling semantic space over a few millennia. And this is what I suggest took place even as man's first stable agricultural communities suddenly swelled into cities of thousands.

CONCLUSION: A COMPARISON WITH Previous Theories

The main features of the model that I have presented are in contrast to previous proposals about the origin of language. Most have placed it historically much further back, perhaps a million years ago, and its place of origin as Africa. I instead have placed it in Southern Europe, the Near East, and Asia in the midst of a hastening sequence of technological advances during the period of the fourth glaciation. Previous models all emphasize nouns as coming first. But a central feature here is that modifiers not only preceded everything else but necessarily had to do so until they were stabilized into commands before the call system itself could be relaxed into nouns.

Most importantly for a science of archelinguistics, is its feature that each step towards language brings with it some new technology or skill. It is certainly to be hoped that closer analyses than I have been able to present here may result in a much tighter tying together of the Würm interstadial episodes, the artifacts of their cultures, and the formation of parts of speech. Indeed, it may in some plausible future be possible to read off the development of language in any area from its archeology.

One final question. While the outdated Biogenetic Law of the nineteenth century that ontogeny recapitulates phylogeny is now merely a way of entering a much more complex issue, it is nevertheless perfectly proper to ask whether or not the sequence of language development in the child in any way resembles its sequence in the species as a whole. Other models have little to say on the matter. The call-blendings of the Hockett-Ascher model[10] do not seem to be pertinent to the data on children. But looking at the present theory in its largest contour, it is at least reminiscent of Braine's distinction between pivot and open classes of words in child language.[4,21] The age of modifiers and then the age of modifying commands may specifically have evolved the neural basis of the pivot class during those eras, while the three successive noun stages that followed evolved the neurological structure for the open class and its relationship and differences from the pivot class. If this is so, and if verbs are not primary evolved elements as I have indicated, it could mean that the evolved neurological structure that makes language possible is not so involved with the distinction between noun phrases and verb phrases as contemporary traditions of parsing might indicate.

REFERENCES

1. BELLUGI, U. 1976. Sign language of the deaf as a clue to the "roots" of language. This volume.
2. BOGAN, J. E. 1976. Werwicke's area: Where is it? This volume.
3. BLANK, M. & W. H. BRIDGES. 1964. Cross-modal transfer in nursery school children, J. Comp. Physiol. Psychol. 58: 277–282.
4. BRAINE, M. D. S. 1963. The ontogeny of English phrase structure: the first phase. Language 39: 1–13.
5. BRUNER, J. S., R. R. OLVER, P. M. GREENFIELD, et al. 1966. Studies in Cognitive Growth. Wiley. New York, N.Y.
6. BUTZER, K. W. 1964. Environment and Archeology: an Introduction to Pleistocene, Geography. Aldine. Chicago, Ill.
7. CARMICHAEL, L., H. P. HOGAN & A. A. WALTER. 1932. An experimental study of the effect of language on the representation of visually perceived form. J. Exp. Psychol. 15: 73–86.
8. CLARK, G. & S. PIGGOTT. 1965. Prehistoric Societies. Hutchinson. London.
9. HEWES, G. W. 1976. The current status of gestural origin theory. This volume.
10. HOCKETT, C. F. & R. ASCHER. 1964. The human revolution. Current Anthropology 5: 135–68.
11. HUMPHREY, G. 1932. The Wild Boy of Aveyron. Century. New York, N.Y.
12. ISAAC, G. L. 1968. Traces of Pleistocene hunters: an East African example. In Man the Hunter. R. B. Lee & I. DeVore, Eds. Aldine. Chicago, Ill.
13. JAYNES, J. 1950. Learning a second response to a cue as a function of the magnitude of the first. J. Comp. Physiol. Psychol. 43: 398–408.
14. JAYNES, J. 1956. Imprinting: the interaction of learned and innate behavior: I. development and generalization. J. Comp. Physiol. Psychol. 49: 201–206.
15. JAYNES, J. 1976. The Origin of Consciousness in the Breakdown of the Bicameral Mind. Houghton Mifflin. Boston, Mass.
16. KIMBALL, M. & P. S. DALE. 1972. The relationship between color naming and color recognition abilities in preschoolers. Child Development 43: 972–980.
17. KUENNE, M. 1945. Experimental investigation of the relation of language to transposition behavior in young children. J. Exp. Psychol. 36: 471–490.
18. LAWRENCE, D. H. 1949. Acquired distinctiveness of cues: I. Transfer between discriminations on the basis of formulants with the stimulus. J. Exp. Psychol. 39: 770–84.
19. LE GROS CLARK, W. 1964. The Fossil Evidence for Human Evolution, 2nd edition. U. of Chicago Press. Chicago.
20. MARLER, P. 1965. Communication in monkeys and apes. In Primate Behavior. J. DeVore, Ed. Holt Rinehart and Winston. New York, N.Y.
21. MCNEIL, D. 1970. The Acquisition of Language. Harper and Row. New York, N.Y.
22. MONTAGU, A. 1971. Touching. Columbia U. Press. New York, N.Y.
23. PLOOG, D. 1967. The behavior of squirrel monkeys as revealed by sociometry, biocoustics and brain stimulation. In Social Communication among Primates. S. A. Altmann, Ed. U. of Chicago Press. Chicago, Ill.
24. ROBINSON, B. W. 1967. Vocalization evoked from the forebrain in Macaca Mulatta. Physiology and Behavior 2: 345–54.
25. SLOBIN, D. I. 1966. Soviet psycholinguistics. In Present Day Russian Psychology. N. O'Connor, Ed.: 109–151. Pergamon Press. Oxford.

26. SPIKER, C. C. 1963. Verbal factors in the discrimination learning of children. Monographs of the Society for Research in Child Development **28:** 53–68.
27. STEKLIS, H. & S. HARNAD. 1976. From hand to mouth: some critical stages in the evolution of language. This volume.
28. WASHBURN, S. L. & C. S. LANCASTER. 1968. The evolution of hunting. *In* Man the Hunter. R. B. Lee & I. DeVore, Eds. Aldine. Chicago, Ill.

DISCUSSION

Horst D. Steklis, *Moderator*
Department of Anthropology
Livingston College
Rutgers University
New Brunswick, New Jersey 08903

Dr. John Pfeiffer (*New Hope, Pa.*): Before commenting briefly on individual papers, I want to indicate what this session, what the entire conference, represents. Above all, I think it shows investigators getting down to business, closing in on problems central to the origins and evolution of language. Not long ago we had lots of good ideas, but not much else. Now there is a real effort to look at things more intensively, in greater detail, and with more imagination. As a result, of course, we are seeing things we never saw before.

Ashley Montagu, after a new and closer examination of a Swanscombe handaxe, reports finding a thumb-hole and other features which were previously missed and which provide clues to the purposes and ingenuity of the handaxe maker. He also stresses Mary Leakey's recent analysis of tools found at the lowest level in the Olduvai Gorge, an analysis indicating that nearly 2,000,000 years ago people were making a surprisingly sophisticated range of tools, not just crude choppers and bashers as had been previously believed.

There are also symbols of a sort at Olduvai, or at least protosymbols. Richard Hay of the University of California has found pieces of pink quartz at living sites, pieces that had not been worked and that had been brought in from a distance, presumably because they were pretty. And there are spheroids big as basketballs, far too large to hurl. Giant handaxes come from other sites, some of them more than two feet long and weighing about twenty-five pounds. I think these items are rather good examples of symbols, tools carefully shaped and far too big to use.

Alexander Marshack is looking at prehistoric art and prehistoric patterns in the same way, in the same spirit, that Mary Leakey looked at early Olduvai tools—and he is also seeing things that no one had seen before. In some cases, particularly cases involving items dating back before the Upper Paleolithic, I think he is pushing too hard and seeing things that aren't there.

But that is only in part a criticism. He is searching for facts, for information, and is actively engaged in the business of extracting every possible bit of data from the material at hand. Binet once said something to the following effect: "Tell me what a man is looking for, and I'll tell you what he'll find." The main point is that he should be looking for something, and describing it with sufficient precision so that if others look, they will also see.

Yesterday I told Julian Jaynes that I disagreed completely with major portions of his theory and his timetable for the origins and development of language. I also told him that my reaction happens to be irrelevant to the value of what he is doing. He has been constructively specific, suggesting specific stages of development, and even having the courage to put rough dates on those stages.

It is too early to say whether or not his notions are valid, or even valuable. We will not know that for some time, until they have been disproved—and, of course, we need a great many more notions that can be disproved, because the other sort are of no use at all. For example, Jaynes suggests that there was a time when language included modifiers but no commands, and a later time when it included both modifiers and commands.

326

The next step must be to try to figure out how that difference might show up archaeologically. Would people with only modifiers behave any differently from people with modifiers plus commands? If so, how? And would the differences show up in the archaeological record, in patterns of artifacts excavated from appropriate sites? Unless we can figure out what might be found and go digging and find it, we are simply playing, not doing science. I am only afraid that Jaynes will be bewitched by the plausibility of some of his arguments, and begin believing instead of hypothesizing.

It is encouraging that investigators are becoming increasingly aware of such problems. They are spelling things out in detail and committing themselves to experiments and new observations and ideas that can indeed be checked. I think we are getting somewhere, and that this is an exciting meeting and period.

DR. HARRY JERISON (*University of California/Los Angeles, Los Angeles, Calif.*): This session presented the most marvelous and outrageous collection of ideas, at least half of which are wrong—in my opinion. But of course Dr. Marshack's stuff is completely undisagreeable with-able. Just beautiful. That horse of Marshack's. Who could argue with that horse? I will make just a couple of points for Dr. Montagu and Dr. Jaynes.

"Ideas as tools." In a sense, you are talking here about the prediction of action that results from ideas generated prior to the action. An important fact to keep in mind is that there are many predictive actions in the normal repertoire of behavior of many animal species. When a cat moves there is a mass of anticipatory activity in the cat's brain. It's like a wildfire going through the brain and can even be recorded in something as gross as the electroencephalogram measured with surface electrodes. Does tool-using require a more complex brain than the brain that keeps a cat moving toward whatever it decides, or keeps a cat's head and eyes rotated and pointed toward things the cat wants to look at? Does the production of a tool really require a nervous system more fine, more excellent as a predictor system, than a nervous system that directs a cat's head and eyes to turn toward a moving object or that controls the fine muscle movements and is activated in anticipation of gross movements of the body? I suggest that, from the point of view of the brain's work, making and using a tool is no more difficult than controlling the elaborate musculature of limbs and eyes in motion.

"A small point on linguistic fundamentals." Dr. Jaynes suggested that negatives always begin with a nasal sound. I have a counterexample here that many will recognize. The Hebrew word for "no" is pronounced "low," as in a nonnasal low-bridge.

Finally, on the "dating of the beginnings of Neanderthal language" Dr. Jaynes' suggestion of about 50,000 years ago. Julian, why don't you put the whole thing back an extra million years or so? And then let language develop from that base. The point is that the brain started to evolve to a bigger size in the hominids at least two million years ago. Why did it start getting bigger and keep on getting bigger? The answer could have something to do with language. . . . I would guess quite a bit. I am most comfortable with a dating from the time that the brain was ready to do the job.

DR. JAYNES: The question was, why don't I shift all my intensity-differentiating mechanisms back a million years, where I could be safely vague and free from contradiction. The important reason is what I have tried to stress in my talk, that I simply cannot imagine a species with words for actions, qualities, and things leaving so few and only such primitive artifacts around for us to pick up now. What words do to us and to our behavior and what we can do is a very, very explosive thing. My answer is very direct: I think the development of language is correlated with the development of artifacts.

Let me add here a certain qualification about dating: When any of us are talking about the origin of language, for simplicity's sake we are speaking about a central tendency of our species in a very general way. Behind this manner of talking lies the very real geographical diversity of Neanderthal tribes and the tremendously complicated problem of migration and the diffusion of speech. I do not doubt that some regions were much more advanced in speech than others, or that some aspects of speech could develop in a region at one time and then just decay. This means that my dates are approximations to a central tendency. But I cannot conceive of speech as long ago as a million years, because words do things to people's culture, and we should find the evidence in their remains.

DR. JERISON: As far as I know, the gestation period for human beings and that for other primates are either comparable, or the human gestation period is longer.

DR. MONTAGU: The gestation period for the apes is roughly about the same, plus or minus a few weeks. It has recently been determined that the Australopithecines had a gestation period of about 266 days on the average, which is virtually identical with *Homo*.

DR. WASHBURN: Robert Merton has an interesting statement, where he says that generally it's a good idea to know what you're doing and why you are doing it. He calls it the "principle of limited sloppiness," that if you have premature closure in a subject matter, then you're in trouble, and I think it's clear that we've had an excellent illustration here of this principle in the extreme form.

Now I think if we're going to consider languages more than three million years old or down to 70,000 years old, something of that order, we have to develop some rules, and I'm going to suggest one only as something that we can think about as this goes on, and then I'll get an illustration. This rule is that *you may not make deductions about fossils that you cannot even make if you know the whole anatomy of the contemporary form.*

In other words, if you have the complete anatomy of a gorilla, you cannot predict its gestation period. If you had the complete anatomy of a monkey, you don't know the gestation period, unless you raise monkeys and determine the gestation period. Therefore I think the stated figure of 266 days is absolutely wrong, because there's no way to check it. You couldn't do it even if you had the whole skeleton of the animal. And to emphasize this point, I'd just like to make a good baboon noise.

DR. PHIL LIEBERMAN: It is possible to formally analyze the "grammar" of tool-making. The cat probably could make tools; they'd just be simpler tools. Blue jays use tools. (See Reynolds, this annal.)

DR. MONTAGU: May I interrupt for a moment. First of all, man is not defined as a tool-making animal. He's defined as an animal that makes tools with which to make other tools on which he becomes continuously dependent. All these three are requirements of this definition of man. It's not merely tool-making.

DR. LIEBERMAN: I doubt if you're going to find any definition that's an either/or thing, because there's going to be a grade and just precisely where you define when you have machine tools will be very, very fuzzy in limiting conditions. What's more interesting is to look for continuity of development in tool-making, and in that the grammar will give you an important insight.

Now, to Professor Jaynes: you've proposed a theory; theories are good because you can refute them, and I'd like to cite several pieces of data. Frog calls are intentional. I don't think we have to look to *Homo sapiens* for the first intentional calls.

Second, there have been numerous attempts to *instruct* people to make tools; you end up needing a language to do this, and that technique goes back, I think, at least 300,000 years.

My last point is that you have hominids that were in the chain of human evolution at least 100,000 years ago. They were quite distinct, let's say, from the Neanderthal types that were dated at least 300,000 years ago.

DR. JAYNES: As to the first question, there are indeed instances of intentional calls in primitive species. But not generally in subhuman primates. I think we will agree that in most subhuman primates today, calls are incidental and under limbic rather than cortical control. Others before me, such as Steklis and Harnad (this volume) have emphasized the importance in evolution of freeing these vocalizations from limbic control as a first step toward speech.

As to the second question, the necessity of speech for teaching tool-making is perhaps the central issue of this particular session. Prof. Lieberman's point of the difficulty of learning such tool-making today without the help of speech is well taken. This could mean, however, that we today have a learned dependence on speech in such situations which we can not readily shake off. And on the other side of the argument, I would remind you of the exceedingly complex motor skills which present-day chimpanzees learn observationally from each other and from us. Even the intricacies of sign language are primarily learned without language. And this is in a species with much smaller brains than early hominids.

It is therefore not beyond at least my own imagination, which I guess most of you think is fairly large at this time, to imagine early man being able to transfer tool-making of a considerable sort without the use of our syntactic language.

PALEONEUROLOGICAL EVIDENCE FOR LANGUAGE ORIGINS

Ralph L. Holloway

Department of Anthropology
Columbia University
New York, New York 10027

INTRODUCTION

If there is any hallmark that might be said to be unique to the human animal, it is surely the ability to speculate about the origin of language. I have too much respect and regard for the intellective capacities of chimpanzees to imagine them prone to such exercises in egoistic futility. Thus I approach the topic with a mild case of schizophrenic serenity, in which I simultaneously share an agreement with the very rational Frenchmen of the Nineteenth Century who banned such discussions from their learned society, and yet share a delight that the topic is available for organized discussion from so many viewpoints, disciplines, and scientific experimentation as represented by the interactants of these conferences. For me, at least, the very fact that this Conference has been organized, and that human animals are ready to engage in a great "garrulity" over the merits and demerits of essentially unprovable hypotheses, is an exciting testimony to the gap between human and other animals, whether continuous or not in nature.

My assigned task is to assess the paleoneurological evidence for language resulting from our rather meager fossil hominid record. This is, at least on one level, an exceedingly simple task, since there is *no* good paleoneurological evidence as yet from the fossil hominid record that either proves or disproves when this or that hominid acquired the capacity for language. At the level of precise unambiguity, the endocasts leave much to be desired, as I have repeatedly emphasized.[1-8] Still, these are the most proximal evidencial links we have, and when combined with the other indirect lines of evidence from the fossil record, such as stone tools made to standardized patterns of arbitrary shape, or the rest of the musculoskeletal evidence, or the remaining archaeological record of different functioning sites, the combination raises significantly, I believe, the probability that this uniquely human activity came relatively early in hominid evolution, perhaps two to three million years ago.[7-9] I have tried in most of my publications to suggest that "reorganization of the brain," i.e., the study of the quantitative changes in the various neural systems of the brain and their integrated interactions, coupled with our ever-increasing knowledge of neurofunctioning, is a profitable way of approaching the problem of human (indeed any taxa) brain evolution. Most of those earlier publications were a reaction to the views most popular during the 40s to the early 60s, in which brain mass, taken alone, by and of itself, was regarded as *the* level at which human behavioral specificities would be eventually understood. Consequently, I purposely played down the role of brain size alone in the case of human evolution. Perhaps I went too far, judging by the reactions of some of my critics.[10-13] Still, I never claimed that brain size was totally meaningless; only that it was insufficient as a lone datum level from which human behavioral evolution, or even a truly comparative neurobiology, could be understood.[14-16] In the last few years this position is being met with serious rebuke by other scientists,[10-13] who have raised a number of issues with greater clarity than existed before. In this paper, I will address myself to certain of these criticisms as they particularly relate to the question of language origins, attempt to clarify my position, and, it is hoped, suggest some different approaches to the question of paleoneurological evidence and its interpretation.

PROBLEMS OF EVIDENCE FOR ASYMMETRY IN HOMINID ENDOCASTS

Except for the *possible* case of the Neandertal fossil, La Chapelle-aux-Saints,[17] I know of no other hominid brain endocast studied so far that can unambiguously demonstrate the presence of an easily measured natural (undistorted) asymmetry between left and right hemispheres in regions currently regarded as involved in language ability, either motoric, receptive, or integrative. I must also admit my skepticism that this fossil endocast shows the critical gyral and sulcal configurations as LeMay[17] and LeMay and Culebras[18] have suggested. When I examine the original endocast in Paris, or good copies available at the AMNH, or in my laboratory, rather than the illustrations from Boule and Anthony[19] dating from 1911, I cannot be certain where the Sylvian sulcus ends on either right or left sides, let alone identify posterior ascending or anterior limbs of the Sylvian or lateral fissure.

Lest my present pessimism be taken as a total denial of any value to paleoneurological studies, I stress that so far I have been talking about *unambiguous* demonstration of surface features relating to language function from fossil hominid endocasts that might be hopefully quantified in some manner. It has, after all, been only within the last decade that reasonably unambiguous demonstration of gross anatomical asymmetries between right and left hemispheres in modern *Homo sapiens* have been made on anything that might be called a "sample," [18,20,21] or in the case of neurophysiology and behavioral observation, the works of McAdam and Whitaker, Morrell and Salamy, Kinsbourne, Kimura.[22-25] In fact, I *am* optimistic that more careful morphometric analysis of reasonably complete hominid endocasts, as particularly represented by most of the Indonesian *Homo erectus* specimens, will offer suggestions, if not conclusive proof, of cerebral asymmetries in particular areas *related* to language function such as the inferior parietal lobe (Wernicke's area), or the third inferior frontal convolution (Broca's area), without resorting to what Jerison[11] derisively refers to as "Phrenology Rediscovered" (p. 41):

> The study of reorganization of the brain in fossil hominids is a kind of new phrenology using lumps on an endocast rather than the traditional bumps on the skull; the scientific basis for this phrenology is somewhat more substantial than Gall's. . . .

Jerison is here referring specifically to my articles[6,8] on the SK1585 robust australopithecine endocast, and the article in Scientific American claiming that the Taung endocast in particular shows reorganizational changes in diminution of lateral extent of visual striate cortex and a corresponding increase in temperoparietal "association" or eulaminate cortex.

Since I will defend my position about this at more length somewhat later in this article, I am concerned here only with indicating that other approaches might be profitable in demonstrating *human* reorganizational patterns on certain hominid endocasts. Because these are currently under investigation in my laboratory, the results to date are not yet complete enough to report.

Essentially two projects are in progress in addition to the other involved with reconstructing the early East African endocasts: (1) Fourier and stepwise discriminant analysis of contour changes along selected arcs of the dorsal endocast surface, with use of a craniometric stereoplotter suggested by Dr. Alan Walker at Harvard;

(2) simultaneous measurements with a three-dimensional cartesian coordinate vernier caliper system with an accuracy of 0.1 mm on endocasts with good bilateral representation that are undistorted, such as on the *Homo erectus* endocasts from Indonesia.

In the first set of methods, the endocasts are positioned so that frontal and occipital poles lie within the same horizontal plane, and are equidistantly placed between two pointers. By varying the angle of a separate dip pointer in two planes every 10°, some 300+ data points can be recorded in polar coordinates on the dorsal surface alone, to an accuracy of 1.0 mm, and a variety of morphometric analyses attempted using multivariate statistical techniques. This work has just begun, so sample sizes for comparative purposes involving techniques such as trend surface analysis, contour mapping, or Fourier and discriminate analysis are as yet too small for profitable discussion and reproduction here. Needless to say, I believe 300+ data points will be a form of mathematical overkill, and without any meaningful functional significance if taken altogether, except possibly for classificatory purposes. The data do allow a choice of transects in certain functionally key areas, where a minimum of 18 points can be treated as a trend or matrix, and, with complete endocasts, could provide a quantifiable method of demonstrating both asymmetries and functional differences between or among lineages.

In the second method, the endocast is clamped into a position where the midsagittal plane is placed as accurately as possible in the vertical plane, and points on both lateral surfaces read either simultaneously or independently. Obviously, visual inspection and choice of plane are on the capricious side, but a wide sampling of points from all regions, including the frontal and cerebellar lobes, should indicate a lateral bias to one side which can then be used as a correction factor when comparing slope velocity changes in more functionally key areas. One of the problems with both methods is that they are exceedingly time-consuming and tedious. Another problem is that only relatively undistorted endocasts with both hemispheres (or sides) intact can be so measured in the second method, a constraint, alas, that eliminates all of the hominid endocast specimens earlier than the Indonesian *Homo erectus* specimens. It is a great pity that the Australopithecines apparently decided to die on either their right or left sides, rather than sitting vertically on their heads or lying either perfectly prone or supine!

QUESTION OF REORGANIZATION AND THE TAUNG AND SK1585 ENDOCASTS

Jerison[11] has claimed that my position regarding a decrease in primary visual cortex in the australopithecine endocasts (Taung and SK1585) and a concomitant increase in temperoparietal association cortex is somehow physically impossible. Jerison contends that such a decrease to humanlike proportions would have so distorted the medial surface around the calcarine fissure that it could not ". . . possibly be classified as hominid." (p. 43) To support this unusual contention, Jerison cites the "quantitative analysis" by Passingham and Ettlinger,[12] which shows that the absolute volume of visual cortex shows incremental increases going from rhesus macaque to chimpanzee to human. Since most of the increase must be packed around the calcarine fissure on the medial surface, ". . . one would find it necessary to expand and distort the medial cortical surface so radically that even a major feature like the corpus callosum would be unrecognizable in its posterior area." (p. 43)

Just what the medial surface of the brain of any of our fossil hominids was like is a phrenological jump that not even Gall would have considered, let alone myself.

"Quantitative analysis," however, indicates a curious perceptual selectivity on Jerison's part in this controversy. First of all, "quantitative analysis" of *both absolute and relative* volume and surface area of striate cortex was given long before Passingham and Ettlinger's [12] paper: Brodmann [26] published in 1912 on the question, von Economo and Koskinas [27] in 1925, Solnitsky and Harmon [28] in 1946, and von Bonin [29] in 1945 on Filimonoff's 1933 work. [30] I reviewed these data in my 1968 review. As most have pointed out, yes, the absolute volume and surface area of visual striate cortex does increase from monkey to man. They *also* pointed out that the *relative* amount *decreased* (See TABLE 1), as can be seen on pps. 147–149 of my 1968 review. In point of fact, Passigham and Ettlinger [12] had this to say about the striate cortex (p. 241):

"Striate cortex . . . increases in the prosimians, but within simians there is little trend . . . and man's striate cortex is the size predicted for a primate of his body weight . . . the striate cortex forms proportionately less of the total neocortex in higher than lower primates . . . Figure 2 shows that the striate cortex of man is 2.4 times as small in proportion to the total neocortex as would be predicted for a primate with his size of neocortex. This implies that other areas of neocortex have grown more than would be predicted."

TABLE 1

SOME PUBLISHED QUANTITATIVE DATA ON ABSOLUTE AND RELATIVE SIZE OF STRIATE CORTEX*

Species	Absolute Area (mm^2)	Percentage Total Cortex		Vol. of Striate Cortex %
Lemurs		15		(26)
Apes		10		(26)
Man		2.0–2.5		(27)
Man	2613	3.0		(29,30)
Orang.	1876	8.5		(29,30)
Cercopithecus	933	10.3		(29,30)
Galago	58	15.1		(29,30)
Felis		67.3	Percentage	(28)
Galago		66.0	of Area 17	(28)
Cercopithecus		41.1	to whole	(28)
Orang.		39.6	Occipital	(28)
Homo		25.4	Lobe	(28)

*Adapted from Holloway,[3] 147–149.

Some selected quantitative data showing relative reduction on surface area and volume of both the occipital lobe, and area 17 striate cortex in *Homo*, suggestive of reorganization, involving an increase in temperoparietal association cortex. If Shariff's [69] data on volumes of agranular (area 6), Eulaminate, and koniocortex (sensory cortex, visual and postcentral) are used in Hebb's [70] A/S ratio, (ignoring agranular cortex), the ratios of association to sensory cortex are as follows: *Homo* = 27.8, chimpanzee = 20.4, and Malaca = 4.8. As the curve in the Passingham and Ettlinger [12] article makes clear, these % differences cannot be explained purely by allometry.

Indeed, their Figure 2 on p. 242 shows that the point plotted for *Homo* on a straight-line log-log regression is *substantially below the line*, whereas the neocortical volume is considerably to the right of the line, suggesting a very poor fit between the two measures in relation to the overall regression line. I wonder how the authors reconcile this with the first part of the quote given above. Jerison himself claims that through the "additive hypothesis," reorganization did take place, including addition of association cortex, but in his 1973 book,[10] the whole matter of "reorganization" is seen as simply trivial, which must sound somewhat strange to those here reporting their latest researches on laterality, cerebral dominance, asymmetry, and so on. The trouble, for me at least, is that his type of analysis, based on brain-body weight regressions, encephalization, and "extra neurons," will not tell us *where* the "additions" took place.* If we don't know "where" the additions took place, how will we ever be able to relate selection pressures for behavioral repertoires somewhat more specific than "intelligence" or "information processing," as Jerison repeatedly claims? If association cortex does increase, as too many neuroscientists to mention here have shown, and as both Jerison and I agree, *what* decreases, relatively speaking?

No, it is not the "new phrenology" which is questionable, but rather Jerison's interpretation of it. This can be supported by examining Jerison's[11] argument regarding the cebus monkey's cortical "tail area," which is enlarged compared to that of the macaque, even though the convolutions are very much alike. I have explicitly cautioned about the lack of any endocast evidence in either pre- or postrolandic gyri in most of my publications. I can think of no stronger argument for reorganization than this (see also my 1969 paper[15]). The difference between the tail "region" really has nothing to do with the level of analysis presented in my papers on evidence for reorganization, which were directed toward showing that indeed the Taung and SK1585 show a diminution of lateral extent of striate cortex compared to any ape, and that the temperoparietal association cortex increased relatively, and surely absolutely. I do not recall ever claiming that australopithecines had a larger "hand area," "foot area," "mouth area," or even "tail area" than the pongids.†

I apologize if airing this controversy has bored the reader, but I am afraid it has been necessary, given Jerison's vehemence in denying validity to both the concept of reorganization and the palaeoneurological evidence from the endocasts. As I have pointed out before,[7] it is the *combination* of morphological features on the endocasts which together form a *Gestalt* that enables one to distinguish between pongid and hominid endocasts, regardless of how the *Gestalten* compare to the sorts of primitive measurements and indices one can make with tapes and calipers on either the endocasts or good scale diagrams or photographs of them. As one can see from the measurements given in earlier publications,[6,7,9] there is a very considerable range of overlap between pongids and hominids on the endocasts, which can be appreciated by comparing FIGURES 1 through 8. By and large, however, the height of the cortex

---

*As the figures in TABLE 1 should suggest, the lateral extent of *striate cortex* is clearly not of pongid proportions in the endocasts discussed in text. The reader should appreciate that there is no way to judge the precise extent of truly striate cortex from the endocasts. The endocasts give only an indication that the *occipital cortex* was reduced in lateral extent. If Jerison regards "additions" as a part of reorganization, and seems willing to admit that such additions did take place involving association cortex in the temperoparietal area, why should the medial cortex along the calcarine be jammed to the point of distortion? Even if the point for *Homo* in Passingham and Ettlinger's Figure 2 (the regression line between log neocortex and log striate cortex) were to fall exactly on the line, why would this necessarily indicate a distortion on australopithecine endocasts, which *are* encephalized above the pongid level? I have not claimed that the striate cortex, or even occipital cortex on these hominids was precisely like that of modern man, only that they approach the pattern.

†I particularly invite the reader to peruse my 1969 paper[15] carefully, in Ann. N.Y. Acad. Sci., where I explicitly discussed the "tail" area, the difference in behavior patterns between old and new world monkeys for "penile displays," and the unknown underlying neural differences that have yet to be demonstrated, but which we must accept on logical grounds alone.

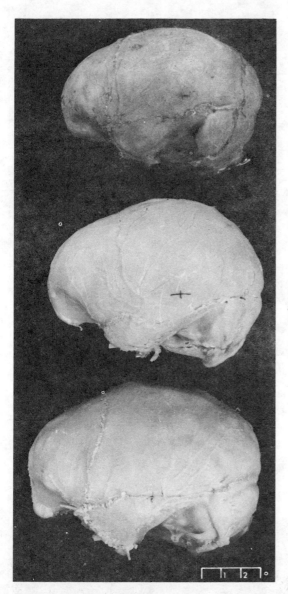

FIGURE 1. Lateral views of rubber latex endocasts prepared by the author from specimens kindly lent by the AMNH. Top to bottom: *Pan paniscus, Pan troglodytes*, and *Gorilla gorilla.* (Courtesy Amer. Mus. Nat. Hist.[7])

above the cerebellar lobes does tend to be higher in the *earliest* hominids, but certainly not the *Homo erectus* Indonesian endocasts, where platycephaly appears to more extreme and the rule. TABLE 2 shows some of these crude indices in a few of the hominids and a small sample of pongid endocasts prepared by the author. Expanding the *Pan paniscus* is currently in progress, and when the sample is finished (N = 40), the results will be published. Extending the sample obviously extends the range, but

TABLE 2

SOME CRUDE INDICES ON HOMINOID ENDOCASTS*

Specimen	Vol. (ml)	Darc/Larc	Darc/L	H^3/V
Taung	404	1.13	1.48	1.41
SK 1585	530	1.73	1.42	1.37
STS 5	485	1.08	1.39	1.27
STS 60	428	1.00	1.35	1.29
OH 5	530	1.47	1.37	1.20
Homoerectus I	943	1.10	1.33	1.02
Homoerectus II	815	1.06	1.35	1.08
ER 1470	770	1.04	1.37	1.30
Modern Homo	1442	1.10	1.43	1.25 (aver. of 4)
Range	1324–1586	1.04–1.14	1.39–1.46	1.11–1.42
Pan paniscus (N = 8)				
Average	325	0.99	1.33	1.04
Range	284–363	0.97–1.01	1.28–1.37	0.86–1.21
Pan troglodytes (N = 29)				
Average	394	0.96	1.28	1.09
Range	334–474	0.88–1.01	1.20–1.34	0.95–1.23
Gorilla gorilla (N = 36)				
Average	498	0.98	1.26	1.04
Range	383–625	0.94–1.04	1.19–1.33	0.84–1.24

*Symbols: D arc, L arc are dorsal and lateral arc measurements between frontal and occipital poles made with a tape; L = chord length between frontal and occipital poles; H = chord length from vertex to lowest plane of temporal lobe; V = volume. While there is clearly some overlapping between pongid and hominid endocasts in these indices, it should be apparent that the hominids show a distinct tendency toward higher cerebral heights. See Holloway[7] for further details and other specimens of *Homo erectus* and earlier African hominids.

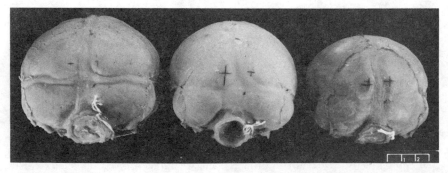

FIGURE 2. Occipital view of same specimens as in FIGURE 1. *Gorilla gorilla* on left; *Pan paniscus* on the right. (Courtesy of Amer. Mus. of Nat. Hist.[7])

by and large, certainly Taung and SK1585 endocasts tend to be very high in most indices reflecting greater cerebral height.

Second, the anterior tips of the temporal lobes are larger and more rounded in the hominids than in the pongids, but this is such a complex region, where the relationships between the neural portions, the dural sheath, and sphenoid bone, that endocasts cannot give a precise picture of the region in pongids. Fresh brains, however, of pongids, are in accord with this observation. Third, the orbital surface of the frontal lobe has a more pronounced and pointed beak in pongids, and is more sharply angled upwards. Fourth, the inferior border of the temporal lobe shows enlargement by the smaller, more acute angle of the petrosal cleft.

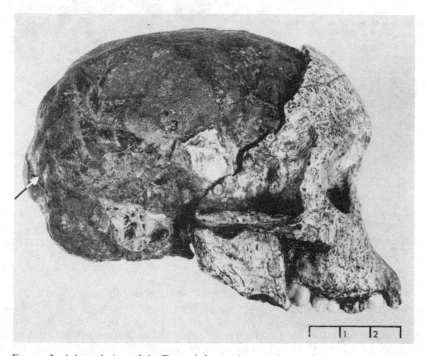

FIGURE 3. A lateral view of the Taung infant endocast with the facial portion. The arrow points to the lambdoid suture, which is very probably the most anterior limit to the "lunate" sulcus. (Courtesy Amer. Mus. Nat. Hist.[7])

Fifth and most important is the matter of the famous "lunate" or "simian" sulcus, which tends to divide the primary visual (striate, or area 17) cortex from the adjacent parietal and temporal "association" cortex. In all pongid brains I have seen, or that have been figured in the literature (i.e., References 31, 32), this landmark is fairly anterior in position (but less so in monkeys) compared to modern *Homo sapiens*, if indeed it shows itself at all, the highest percentage being about 10 or 11%.[33] As FIGURES 1–4 show, the position of this sulcus must definitely be accorded a posterior position. It is this pattern which is, I believe, the strongest evidence for cortical reorganization to a human-like pattern. As I have pointed out before (e.g.,

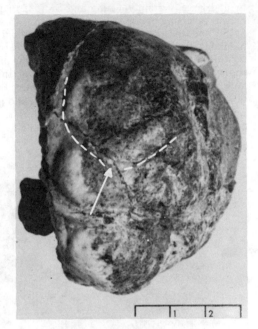

FIGURE 4. The Taung endocast in occipital view, showing the very distinct lambdoid suture, and a conformation of gyral curvature both superior and anterior to the lambdoid suture proving that a more anterior position of the "lunate" would be highly unlikely. (Courtesy Amer. Mus. Nat. Hist.[7])

References 1, 3, 5, 7, 8, 34), this observation was suggested by Dart in 1925,[35] Schepers,[36] and more or less agreed upon by LeGros Clark,[37] although Keith[38] did not believe the placement could be so posterior. Finally, the gyri and sulci, in number and extent, and the 3rd inferior frontal convolution (Broca's region) give the impression of more advanced development, but this is only impressionistic, and should be ignored until verified quantitatively.‡

It should be pointed out that these *Gestalten* are best seen on the South African australopithecine endocasts rather than on the unquestionably less controversial hominid endocasts so far available from East Africa (that is, in terms of absolute dating, and assignment to the genus *Homo*). Unfortunately, none of the East African endocasts, and E.R. 1470 in particular, show the surface details as well as the S. African specimens because of erosion to the inner table of cranial bone from which the endocasts are made. Unfortunately, endocasts are just plain "conspiratorial" in denying scientists ready access to their surface configurations, but that is hardly sufficient reason to ignore them, however frustrating their study becomes.

Obviously, such observations and suggestions as have been made so far regarding this aspect of reorganization cannot prove the hominids capable of language ability, using arbitrary symbols. Nor can the pessimistic but very empirical observations of vocal tract anatomy by Lieberman and his colleagues[39-41] be accepted as proven, considering the recent work by Falk[42] which shows that the former authors might be wrong in their reconstructions. My point is, and remains, that the endocasts of early hominids show a combination of features suggestive of a pattern of organization that

‡These landmarks are definitely larger on the E.R. 1470 *Homo* (sp. indet) endocast than on the australopithecines.

is not pongid but human-like, and thus is evidence of reorganization, neurally, which if involving the cortex, must also have involved subcortical structures, particularly the pulvinar of the thalamus. I will return to the way I view these points somewhat later. For the present, I will continue with the evidence for reorganization as I see it.

THE MATTER OF RELATIVE BRAIN SIZE AND ENCEPHALIZATION

An additional argument I have advanced toward suggesting that early hominid brains were reorganized toward a human rather than pongid pattern is that *relative* brain size, i.e., the ratio between brain and body weights, was increased even in the early australopithecines. In doing so, I have been very aware of the difficulties in any accurate assessment of body weights from the scrappy postcranial bony evidence at hand, and have made such warnings explicit.[5,43,7,9,8]

Recently, thanks to the research efforts of Dr. Henry McHenry, of the University of California at Davis, some newer estimates of body weights for the gracile and robust australopithecines, based on the 12th thoracic and 5th lumbar vertebrae for STS14 and SK3985, have been made.[44,45] Using material from the Terry collection (n = 43), McHenry found a correlation of .69 between body weight and a

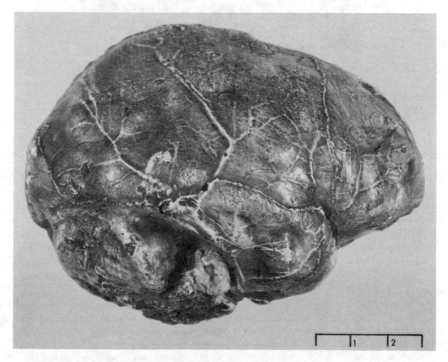

FIGURE 5. The SK 1585 endocast shown here is a plaster replica of the original. A small portion of the frontal lobe is missing. Notice the large anterior portion of the temporal lobe, and the very posterior position of the lambdoid suture, which obliterate the "lunate." (Courtesy Amer. Mus. Nat. Hist.[7])

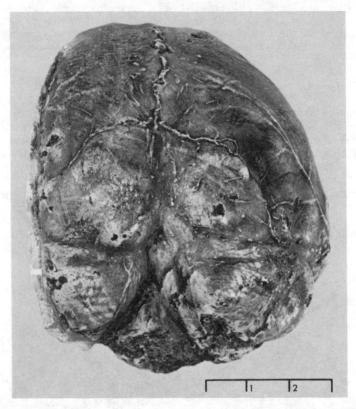

FIGURE 6. An occipital view of SK 1585. Notice the remarkable relief on the left cerebellar lobe. This view does not show the posterior position of the "lunate" well, but compare it to FIGURE 1. (Courtesy Amer. Mus. Nat. Hist.[7])

Homo, but *lower* than the range for human values given by Stephan. In my papers, I preferred the use of the "progression index, or PrG" of Stephan because it related the combination of vertebral diameters on the two mentioned vertebrae. This led to the regression formula,

$$\text{body wgt(kg)} = 12.16(\text{vertebra})^{0.603}$$

giving body weights for STS14 and SK1585 of 27.6 kg and 36.1 kg, respectively. These weights are certainly heavier than I used, based on Lovejoy and Heiple's[46] analysis (ca. 20 kg for the gracile form). When McHenry's newer estimates are put into either Jerison's[10] or Stephan's[47] encephalization formulas, the relative brain weight and encephalization indices for the australopithecines fall between *Pan* and encephalization to a broad basal insectivore brain-body weight sample, rather than all modern mammals as in Jerison,[10] which is, of course, larger, but not as relevant in evolutionary terms to the primates as are the basal insectivores used by Stephan. I also used Stephan's index because it was the only data showing the *range* of modern human values, which vary between 18 and 53, with an average PrG of 28. Using a range of body weights of 18–27 kg for the gracile *Australopithecus* and an average brain volume of 442 ml, the PrG index varied between 16.9 and 21.4, the higher value (lower body weight) within the low range of modern *Homo*, but still above *Pan* at about 12.0 according to Stephan (p. 161). (McHenry's value for Pan is 10.8.)

Two important points need to be made. (1) Even accepting McHenry's estimates, the encephalization indices for the australopithecines by whatever methods (e.g., Jerison or Stephan) are still above the pongid values, indicating that selection pressures for brain-body relationships had taken place early in hominid evolution, ignoring for the moment the whole thorny issue of where the S. African forms and the ER 1470 *Homo* (sp. indet.) fit, either in time or lineage. *That* was the major point of my articles, *not* that the fossil encephalization was necessarily within the modern *Homo* range. (2) Using McHenry's data, which he has so kindly given me, a straightforward stepwise multiple regression using all eight vertebral measurements gives a correlation of around .72, which results in an estimated body weight of about 24 kg and a PrG index of 17.9. In fact, by combining the raw measurements and ratios between thoracic and lumbar dimensions, the coefficient can be raised to 0.77, using multiple regression techniques, but it does make the calculation of body

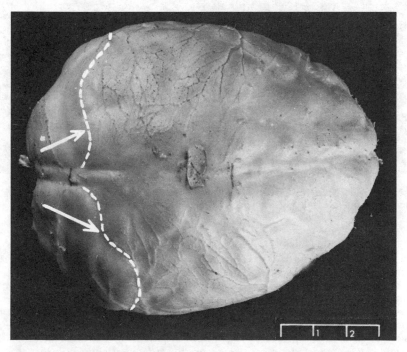

FIGURE 7. Dorsal view of an endocast (latex) of *Pan troglodytes*. Note that the anterior limits of the "lunate" are well forward of the lambdoid suture. (Courtesy Amer. Mus. Nat. Hist.)

weights cumbersome, without radically differing the weight outcome. Obviously, as welcome as McHenry's newer estimates are as more objective sources for predicting body weight, considerable caution must be exercised regarding the statistical techniques used, as well as the implicit assumption that australopithecine bipedality and functional anatomy are best based on modern human material. (See for example Oxnard.[48])

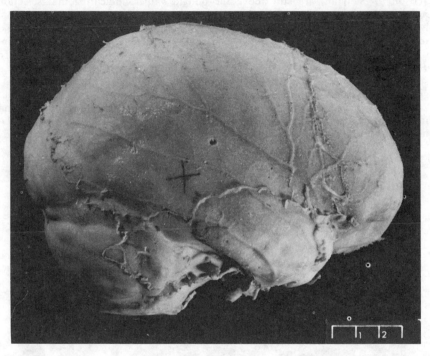

FIGURE 8. Endocast of modern *Homo sapiens* from a specimen belonging to Columbia University. Compare with previous figures. (Courtesy Amer. Mus. Nat. Hist.[7])

In sum, regarding relative brain weight, the australopithecines' brain volumes, for which we have good endocast evidence, show an encephalization different from that of the pongids, and very close to, if not within, the modern human range of variation. *This says nothing, nor can it, with regard to the question of language, except to indicate that selection pressures of brain weights, at least, were already in operation several million years ago during early hominid evolution, and as encephalization must reflect patterns of postnatal growth timing between the brain and body, suggests that selection pressures for prolonged growth of the hominid brain was already in effect, which has great significance toward understanding the role of social behavior and "intelligence" in hominid evolution.*[5,7] It is a picture that is fully concordant with our present understanding of the essentially social nature of language and speech, whether regarding language in the banal form of "object naming" having adaptive value,[49] or its less well-appreciated relationship to social interaction, social control, imposition of arbitrary form upon the environment,[50,51] role in extending figure-ground relationships, and its imbeddedness in perceptual selectivity, visuospatial integration, and thus stone-tool-making and hunting behavior.

THE PLACE OF "REORGANIZATION" IN HUMAN BRAIN EVOLUTION

Since this is a conference about the origins of language, which so far is a human attribute only, although certain apes may convince some of us otherwise, or disprove it, one might ask what importance the concept of neural reorganization has to understanding (1) the neural and social bases for language, and (2) the focal points for natural selection during hominid evolution. It is frankly curious to see the considerable difference between Jerison's 1973[10] book and his more recent (1975)[11] paper regarding this concept. In the 1973 book, Jerison discounted the reorganization concept as essentially trivial, since all animals' brains are neurally reorganized differently to allow for species-specific behavior and adaptations. If I were particularly interested in proposing a general theory about brain mass and behavior in the whole Vertebrate Phylum, I would probably regard the reorganization concept trivial as well. It seems odd to me that it is necessary to point out that I have been quite specifically oriented in my writings and research toward understanding *human evolution* and the role of the brain in that evolution. I have never said that brain mass or allometric relationships were of no consequence in human brain evolution. After all, the demonstrated facts of such relationships, particularly allometric growth and a lawful relationship of varying lability between brain and body size have been appreciated § since the latter part of the nineteenth century!![52] My point has been that these two facets are not sufficient by themselves to explain human behavioral repertoires, a position shared by the late Professor Lenneberg[53] as well as many others. Indeed, I would be willing to argue the converse of Jerison's position (p. 67–81): since all vertebrates, at least, show a roughly 0.66 exponential relationship between their body and brain weights, it is the general law that is trivial and the *residuals* that are critical for understanding species-specific behavior (that is, as a "first approximation"). *How will we accomplish this if we don't know where the residuals occur in the brains?* I think that Noback[54,55] is completely correct when he characterizes Jerison's treatment of neural reorganization as that of a "black box" approach. Trying to reintroduce the concept of reorganization as an instance of the "additive hypothesis," being additions of neural mass here and there, is hardly a

---

§The analysis of allometric relationships is not without controversy, although it would be outside the limits of this Conference to discuss them in any detail, as can be found, for example, in Sholl, D. 1948. Proc. R. Soc. Lond. [Biol.] **135:** 243–258, or Count, E. W. 1947, Ann. N.Y. Acad. Sci. **46:** 993–1122, or for that matter, in Jerison.[10] First of all, most examples used to explain away reorganization as an instance of allometry use the logs of a very small quantity against the. log of a usually much larger quantity of which the former is often a part. This introduces the problem of "closure." A second but more important point that is not well appreciated is that the points seldom lie exactly on the line. A trend around a lawful constraint is something different than perfect adherance to the constraint, which is, after all, only a mathematical abstraction resulting from a least squares fit between two variables. The residuals remain, and explaining tham away as only so much statistical error is obviously *ad hoc* or *post hoc*, depending on where one enters the argument. Finally, why, exactly, should the laws of allometry hold only between taxa and not within?

conceptual tool capable of either advancing our understanding of *where* or the functional integration of the *where* with the *how*, and can never lead us to an understanding of the "*why*." Only a careful examination of the exact quantitative shifts, in particular neural nuclei, pathways, and cortical organization, can provide a framework that can be synthesized with more molecular levels, such as differential hypertrophy and hyperplasia of neural nuclei and pathways as controlled through epigenetic development, which in turn can be synthesized *both* with functional activity (behavior) and the broader foci for natural selection pressures in an environment or series of environments. Furthermore, this kind of approach is the only one that can be hoped to gain any further understanding about the relationships between neural and behavioral variability within different levels of taxa, but particularly within the species level. The "additive hypothesis" of Jerison is not specific enough for such tasks, at least as presently formulated, which does not necessarily detract from its application to comparisons and explanations involving higher taxonomic levels.

Obviously, the paleoneurological approach I have taken in trying to demonstrate evidence for reorganization (cortical, at least) is and must be very limited. We will know nothing of relative ratios between fornix fibers and mammillary bodies, or the size of the geniculate bodies from the endocasts, or neurochemical differences between various nuclei. That is the reason why I have tried in my publications to suggest we are not limited exclusively to the direct palaeontological evidence afforded by endocasts. 1) First of all, there is comparative psychology, ethology, and primatology, which together provide an impressive litany of behavioral differences and similarities between human and other animals. Unless these are to be viewed as Platonic essences without neurophysiological bases, it should be apparent that the human brain, indeed any mammal brain, has been modified during its evolutionary development. 2) Unlike most other fossils, hominids *did* leave behind traces of their cognitive abilities, e.g. stone tools made to standardized patterns of varying degrees of arbitrary form, stone workshop and butchering sites, home bases, shelters, and so on. It really is not that much of a speculative leap to infer that their cognitive abilities depended on their brains, whether by the addition of neurons (where?) and/or by reorganization of neural subsystems. The "hunting way of life," so often conjectured by Washburn[56-58] and his colleagues, has unfortunately never really been broken down into its specific components to a degree sufficient for making syntheses between behavior, structure, and adaptation, that offer testable hypotheses about structure and behavior at a genetic level. For this we should turn to the suggestions offered by Laughlin,[59] which looked at hunting behavior in terms of elements that offer a richer harvest for integration with neuroanatomical variables, a task I attempted in 1970,[16] and which led to the suggestion that many if not all levels of the brain could have been focal points for selection pressures during hominid evolution.

I am fully aware that these asides do not bring us closer to joining the question of language origins and paleoneurology together, except to point out hopefully that language and speech origins should not be divorced from the total range of adaptive considerations that the paleoanthropologist must consider, of which paleoneurology is but a part.

3) There is additional evidence from the rest of hominid fossil anatomy aside from the endocasts. Hands, feet, pelvi, the trunk, jaws, etc., all were used somewhat differently than in other primates, even chimpanzees, and their morphometric properties are also different. How did the attached muscles differ? How did they contract and elongate in form and size? What perceptual and conceptual patterns "drove" them? In what adaptive enterprises were they used? All of this is *indirect* evidence of neural reorganization, involving surely a plurality of brain regions, or

subsystem structures, not just the cortex or part of it. Such patterns of specific adaptation cannot be fully explained by pseudoscientific reliance on such mystical and nebulous concepts as "intelligence," "information processing," "consciousness and imagery," "cognitive maps," "hunting way of life," "cognitive extension of prehension," "object naming," etc.

I can agree with Jerison[11] that considerations such as enumerated above are trivial if one is not concerned specifically with human and other primate evolution. As a model, however, they are the same considerations which must in general be given in any evolutionary account of a *particular* line of animals, whether dogs, cats, sheep and goats, cattle, finches, bottom-feeding teleosts, snakes, or camels (e.g. Radinsky's[60-62] beautiful palaeoneurological work on otters, the felids and canids, and the earliest primates).

Finally, whether human language and other attending behavioral aspects such as babbling, echoing, and the epigenesis of conceptual worlds through human growth are to be related *purely* to allometry, "extra neurons," or reorganization of neural elements already present in most mammals, and surely all primates, is very unlikely. Both have surely been important, but in terms of language, I still believe reorganization must be given its due, and that its development lay more in the realm of social behavior and its control, than in expanding imagery, object-naming, or manipulating the environment. The human animal is still alone in its ability to *depict invariance* through arbitrary, socially sanctioned, and learned conventions, which we call symbolization.

LATERALITY, CEREBRAL DOMINANCE, PALEOANTHROPOLOGY, AND SOME SPECULATION

It cannot be my task here to summarize all of the more recent exciting findings concerning laterality and cerebral dominance, since they will be more than adequately covered by others more specialized in these areas during this Conference. I want to pursue the topic somewhat, however, because I believe that the fossil hominid record and the attending evolutionary dynamics can be better understood when joined with the more recently acquired evidence from such current studies as those of Levy, Bever, Warren, Kinsbourne, Kimura, Whitaker, and Sperry and Gazzaninga.

Two particular activities stand out from all of the archaeological evidence thus accumulated by the archaeologists and palaeoanthropologists working in Africa.[63-64] These are: (1) Standardized tool-making, requiring manual dexterity and, I believe, forms of social concensus too complex to be explained through observation-learning, "object-naming," or any gestural theories of communication; (2) a growing dependence, and one must assume sophistication, on the utilization of other animal protein, involving very complex spatiovisual integration. Levy[65] has offered the suggestion that the laterality known for the human animal between left and right hemispheres, and language behavior and visuospatial and temporal integration, respectively, developed to prevent interference between the hemispheres, or "noise"; that is, verbal and nonverbal functions evolved in different sides to keep interference between them to a minimum. As I pointed out before,[9] both apes and humans are capable of underarm and overhead throwing of objects, but it is the human animal alone that is capable of delivering the total combination of great power, accuracy, and distance, a point that Washburn and Strum[56] failed to emphasize. As far as I know, only the human brain is capable of the necessary complex computations and coordinations allowing powerful and accurate utilization of stone and wood objects as missiles. The complexity of spatial tasks does not rest just with weaponry, predation, and defense against predators. The materials used for some of the stone tools described by the archaeologists must have come from fairly displaced locations from those where they were made or used. The associated faunal elements discovered with the early hominids indicate a growing utilization of larger and more far-wandering mobile game, all of which suggests that natural selection would have strongly favored those capable of complex spatiovisual integration.

It is surely no accident that the regions for hand and mouth control on the pre- and postrolandic gyri are so close together, and both Kinsbourne's[24] and Kimura's[25] work clearly implicates a conjoint functional pattern between language integration tasks and manual gestures. Both the stone tool evidence and that of the faunal remains suggests an ongoing evolutionary development of complexity, requiring more integration of elements having smaller units in their make-up, and synthesis within wider ranging behavioral patterns. That is, as the tools become complex and sophisticated, they are made up of a larger number of more atomistic units (i.e., blanking, chipping, rotation, edge and platform preparation, etc.) and hunting of larger animals further removed in both time and space from any "home base." I am not unaware of the recent superb field observations of my colleague Geze Teleki,[66-68] showing the beginnings of such patterns in certain free-ranging chimpanzee groups in the Gombe Reserve in Tanzania. These observations add to the argument rather than detract from it, given the more advanced disposition of the hominid brain and the archaeological evidence from the African sites. I still remain firmly convinced that there are very great similarities between the cognitive operations involved in language production and stone tool-making, which I elaborated upon in an earlier publication.[50] I doubt if the paleoneurological evidence from early hominid endocasts will ever be sufficient to show lateralization of function, unambiguously demonstrated by quantitative methods, although I believe it is worth the effort.

CONCLUSION

My main point, however, to sum up the arguments presented thus far, is that the endocasts of the early hominids already display evidence of reorganization toward a human pattern, particularly as regards the added development of the temperoparietal regions on the lateral surface. If this shows on the australopithecine brain casts, it surely must be present on the East African hominid remains assigned to the genus *Homo*, and is strongly suggestive that even two to three million years ago natural selection was operating on econiche adaptation, and that cognitive and social behavior was surely the main focus. However, I see these evolutionary forces within the contexts of social behavior, not as isolated manual skills. As I put it in the James Arthur Lecture:[7]

> It would be a great oversimplification, if not a mistake, to relate cranial capacity in any linear or causal sense to the increasing complexity of stone tools during the Pleistocene. Early hominids accomplished more than simply making stone tools for future archaeologists' digs. Their tools were used in a variety of different environments, and their cooperative social behavior was an important part of adaptation to a hunting and gathering existence. Hunting and associated activities require a complex organization involving not only perceptual and motor skills, but an understanding of animals and their habits, plants, terrain, spoor and tracks, anatomy, butchering techniques, and perhaps storage. It is the total range of cultural adaptations that relates to brain increase; the making of stone tools is only one example, and of course, the most permanently recorded one. (p. 36)

I contend that it is this evidential complexity from multiple sources that can be best integrated with the growth and reorganization of the hominid brain, as reflected by the palaeoneurological evidence of endocasts. Of particular importance to any such theory will be the crucial aspect of prolonged dependency and growth of offspring, requiring a social nexus of a more differentiated and cooperative nature than recent primate studies have shown, and that language will be a key ingredient in this scheme, not so much for "object-naming," but for purposes of social control and allocation of labor and talents. The palaeoneurological evidence suggested in these pages fits into such a schema but cannot be taken in isolation from the total matrix of evidence of which it is but a part. Hopefully, a more objective and sophisticated set of methods can be applied to the "new phrenology," which will unambiguously demonstrate the arguments I have advanced. Surely, a reasonable beginning has been made.

REFERENCES

1. HOLLOWAY, R. L. 1966. Amer. Anthropol. **68:** 103–121.
2. HOLLOWAY, R. L. 1967. General Systems **XII:** 3–19.
3. HOLLOWAY, R. L. 1968. Brain Res. **7:** 121–172.
4. HOLLOWAY, R. L. 1968. *In* Culture, Man's Adaptive Dimension. M. D. Montague, Ed.: 170–196. Oxford Univ. Press. Oxford, England.
5. HOLLOWAY, R. L. 1972. *In* Functional and Evolutionary Biology of Primates. R. Tuttle, Ed.: 185–204. Aldine Press. Chicago, Ill.
6. HOLLOWAY, R. L. 1972. Amer. J. Phys. Anthropol. **37:** 173–186.
7. HOLLOWAY, R. L. 1975. The Role of Human Social Behavior in the Evolution of the Brain. 43rd James Arthur Lecture (1973), Amer. Mus. Nat. Hist.
8. HOLLOWAY, R. L. 1974. Sci. Amer. **231:** 105–115.
9. HOLLOWAY, R. L. 1975. VIIIth Internat. Cong. Anthrop. Ethnol. Sci. *In* Primate Functional Morphology and Evolution. R. Tuttle, Ed.: 396–416. Mouton. The Hague, The Netherlands.
10. JERISON, H. J. 1973. Evolution of the Brain and Intelligence. Academic Press. New York, N.Y.
11. JERISON, H. J. 1975. Ann. Rev. Anthropol. **4:** 27–58.
12. PASSINGHAM, R. E. & G. ETTLINGER. 1974. Int. Rev. Neurobiol. **16:** 233–299.
13. SACHER, G. 1970. *In* The Primate Brain. C. R. Noback and W. Montagna, Eds.: 245–288. Appleton-Century-Crofts. New York, N.Y.
14. HOLLOWAY, R. L. 1966. Amer. J. Phys. Anthropol. **25:** 305–314.
15. HOLLOWAY, R. L. 1969. Ann. N.Y. Acad. Sci. **167:** 332–340.
16. HOLLOWAY, R. L. 1970. *In* The Primate Brain. C. R. Noback and W. Montagna, Eds.: 299–309. Appleton-Century-Crofts. New York, N.Y.
17. LeMAY, M. 1975. Amer. J. Phys. Anthropol. **42:** 9–14.
18. LeMAY, M. & A. CULEBRAS. 1972. N. Eng. J. Med. **287:** 168–170.
19. BOULE, M. & R. ANTHONY. 1911. L'Anthrop. **22:** 129–196.
20. GESCHWIND, N. & W. LEVITSKY. 1968. Science **161:** 186–187.
21. ASTAKHOVA, A. T. & A. A. KARACHEVA. 1970. Trans. Krasnoyarsk Med. Inst. 9(5): 9–12.
22. McADAM, D. W. & H. A. WHITAKER. 1971. Science **172:** 199–502.
23. MORRELL, L. K. & J. G. SALAMY. 1971. Science **174:** 164–166.
24. KINSBOURNE, M. 1972. Science **176:** 539–541.
25. KIMURA, D. 1973. Sci. Amer. **228**(3): 70–78.
26. BRODMANN, F. 1912. Anat. Anz.: 211.
27. VON ECONOMO, C. & G. N. KOSKINAS. 1925. Die Cytoarchitektonik der Hirnrinde des Erwachsenen Menschen. Springer. Berlin, Germany.
28. SOLNITSKY, O. & P. J. HARMON. 1946. J. Comp. Neurol. **108:** 173–224.
29. VON BONIN, G. 1945. The Cortex of Galago. Univ. Chicago Press. Urbana, Ill.
30. FILIMONOFF, I. N. 1933. J. Psychol. Neurol. (LPX) **45:** 69–137.

31. CUNNINGHAM, D. J. 1892. Contributions to the Surface Anatomy of the Cerebral Hemispheres. Cunningham Memoirs, No. VII. Ray. Acad. Dublin, Ireland.
32. CONNOLLY, C. J. 1950. External Morphology of the Primate Brain. Charles C. Thomas. Springfield, Ill.
33. LEVIN, G. 1936. Amer. J. Phys. Anthropol. **22:** 345–380.
34. HOLLOWAY, R. L. 1964. Ph.D. Thesis. Univ. California at Berkeley. Berkeley, Calif.
35. DART, R. 1925. Nature **115:** 195–199.
36. SCHEPERS, G. W. H. 1946. Transvaal Mus. Mem. **2:** 155–272.
37. CLARK, W. E. LEGROS. 1947. J. Anat. **81:** 300–334.
38. KEITH, A. 1931. New Discoveries Relating to the Antiquity of Man. Williams and Norgate, Ltd. London, England.
39. LIEBERMAN, P. 1975. On the Origins of Language. Macmillan. New York, N.Y.
40. LIEBERMAN, P. & E. S. CRELIN. 1971. Ling. Inq. **2:** 203–222.
41. LIEBERMAN, P. et al. 1972. Amer. Anthropol. **74:** 287–307.
42. FALK, D. 1975. Amer. J. Phys. Anthropol. **43:** 123–132.
43. HOLLOWAY, R. L. 1973. J. Hum. Evol. 449–459.
44. MCHENRY, H. M. 1975. Nature **254:** 686–688.
45. MCHENRY, H. M. 1974. Amer. J. Phys. Anthropol. **40:** 329–340.
46. LOVEJOY, C. O. & K. G. HEIPLE. 1970. Amer. J. Phys. Anthropol. **32:** 33–40.
47. STEPHAN, H. 1972. In The Functional and Evolutionary Biology of Primates. R. Tuttle, Ed.: 155–174. Aldine. Chicago, Ill.
48. OXNARD, C. F. 1975. Uniqueness and Diversity in Human Evolution. Univ. Chicago Press. Chicago, Ill.
49. LANCASTER, J. 1968. In Primates. P. Jay, Ed.: 139. Holt, Rinehart, Winston. New York, N.Y.
50. HOLLOWAY, R. L. 1969. Current Anthropol. **10:** 395–412.
51. HOLLOWAY, R. L. 1968. pp. 28–48. In War: The Anthropology of Armed Conflict and Aggression. M. Harris, M. Fried, and R. Murphy, Eds.: 28–48. N.Y. Nat. Hist. Press. New York, N.Y.
52. DUBOIS, E. 1897. Arch. Anthropol. **25:** 1–28.
53. LENNEBERG, E. H. 1967. The Biological Foundation of Language. Wiley & Sons, New York, N.Y.
54. NOBACK, C. R. 1975. Amer. J. Phys. Anthropol. **43:** 156–157.
55. NOBACK, C. R. 1975. Current Anthropol. **16:** 411.
56. WASHBURN, W. L. & S. C. STRUM. 1972. In Perspectives in Human Evolution. Vol. II: 469–491. S. L. Washburn & P. Dolhinow, Eds. Holt, Rinehart, Winston. New York, N.Y.
57. WASHBURN, S. L. & D. A. HAMBERG. 1965. In Primate Behavior. I. DeVore, Ed.: 1–15. Holt, Rinehart, Winston. New York, N.Y.
58. WASHBURN, S. L. & C. S. LANCASTER. 1968. In Man the Hunter. R. B. Lee & I. DeVore. Eds.: 293–303. Aldine. Chicago, Ill.
59. LAUGHLIN, W. 1968. In Man the Hunter. R. B. Lee & I. DeVore, Eds.: 304–320. Aldine. Chicago, Ill.
60. RADINSKY, L. 1970. In The Primate Brain. C. R. Noback & W. Montagna, Eds.: 209–224. Appleton-Century-Crofts. New York, N.Y.
61. RADINSKY, L. 1968. J. Comp. Neurol. **134:** 495–505.
62. RADINSKY, L. 1969. Ann. N.Y. Acad. Sci. **167:** 277–288.
63. LEAKEY, M. D. 1971. Olduvai Gorge. Vol. III. Cambridge Univ. Press. Cambridge, England.
64. ISAAC, G. 1974. Current Anthropol. **15:** 508–514.
65. LEVY, J. 1969. Nature **224:** 614–615.
66. TELEKI, G. 1973. The Predatory Behavior of Wild Chimpanzees. Bucknell Univ. Press. Lewisburg, Me.
67. TELEKI, G. 1974. J. Human Evol. **3:** 575–594.
68. TELEKI, G. 1975. J. Human Evol. **4:** 125–184.

MORPHOLOGICAL CEREBRAL ASYMMETRIES
OF MODERN MAN, FOSSIL MAN, AND
NONHUMAN PRIMATE

Marjorie LeMay

Departments of Radiology
Harvard Medical School and
Massachusetts General Hospital
Boston, Massachusetts 02114

Nearly fifty years ago, Dr. Weil of Montefiore Hospital in New York pubished a paper on comparative studies of the endocranial casts of man, prehistoric men, and anthropoid apes.[1] His studies led him to believe there were no marked asymmetries of the cerebral hemispheres. Modern technology has added new dimensions for this present echo of Dr. Weil's study, and it is now apparent that there are gross asymmetries.

MODERN MAN

Little difference has been noted in the weights of the cerebral hemispheres of modern man. Boyd, in 1861, reported the left hemisphere to be slightly heavier than the right,[2] but studies since then have found the right hemisphere to be more often heavier than the left.[3-7] Braune and Wilde noted that the right hemisphere weighed slightly more than the left, but that the left cerebellar hemisphere weighed slightly more than the right. In 12 cases in which Braune found the right cerebellum to weigh more than the left, there was no history of left handedness. Melley,[8] in a study of 450 brains, found an inverse relationship between the weights of the hemispheres and the size of the ventricles.

Differences in length of the hemispheres of adult brains are also small. The topology of the brain follows closely the internal configuration of the vault,[9] and most estimates of the lengths of the hemispheres have been by measurement of the skull. Hrdlicka,[10] and Hadziselimovic and Cus[9] found the left hemisphere to average slightly longer than the right, but right preponderance was found in a series of East African skulls by Gundara and Zivanovic[11] and in 75.5% of 721 Egyptian skulls by Hoadley.[12] Measuring fixed brains, Cunningham found the left hemisphere to be longer in 50% and the right hemisphere longer in 31.7%.[13] Connolly also found the left hemisphere to measure slightly longer in a series of male brains, but in a smaller series of female brains the right hemisphere averaged 1 mm longer than the left.[14]

In fetal and children's brains, the left hemisphere is commonly longer than the right. In 11 brains from newborns and children, Connolly found the left hemisphere to be longer in 7, and the right longer in 3.[14] On photographs of 49 fetal and newborn brains from the Yakovlev collection at the Armed Forces Institute of Pathology in Washington, D.C., and from the Eunice Shriver Kennedy Center in Waltham, Massachusetts, the brains were found to be of equal length in 17, the left longer in 24 and the right longer in only 8.[15]

Ventricular Asymmetries

Scientists have pointed out in the past that in studying evolutional development the structural organization of the brain is of greater importance than its size or

349

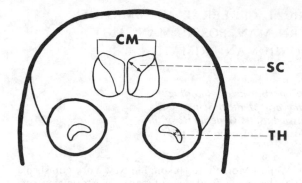

FIGURE 1. Measurement of the lateral ventricles on pneumoencephalograms. C M: cella media—width of roof of lateral ventricles; S C: septal-caudate—width of distance from superior margin of septum pellucidum to narrowest point along the margin of the caudate nucleus; T H: temporal horn.

density.[16,17] Variations in size and shape of localized areas of the brain are common. The size and shape of the lateral ventricles of the brain correlate to some extent with the size and shape of the skull,[18-20] and it is possible that the asymmetry seen in the size of the lateral ventricles points to hemispheral asymmetries that we are ignoring.

Volumetric measurements of the lateral ventricles by Knudsen[5] note the left ventricle to be larger than the right in 48% of his cases and the right ventricle larger in only 15%. Ventricular cast studies in 23 brains by Last and Thompsett[21] also show left ventricular volumes greater than the right. Numerous studies have shown the body of the left lateral ventricle to be wider than that of the right.[5,21-26] Ventricular asymmetries have usually been measured radiographically on studies performed with gas in the ventricles. On films taken with the patients head brow-up, the width of the bodies of the lateral ventricles is usually measured across their superior margins, referred to as the "ventricular span" or "cella media" measurement, or from the superior margin of the septum pellucidum to the nearest point along the caudate nucleus, "septal-caudate line" (FIGURE 1). The width of the anterior tips of the temporal horns can also be measured on brow-up films.

TABLE 1 shows comparative widths of the bodies of the lateral ventricles and the tips of the temporal horns in 185 pneumoencephalograms of patients without evidence of localized intracranial disease. The body of the left lateral ventricle was wider than the body of the right in 76% of the cases. The tips of the left temporal horns measured wider than those of the right in 60%. Lodin noted in studies on children that there is a physiological increase in width of the lateral ventricles, particularly anteriorly, during the first year and that ventricular asymmetries are noticeable after the first year.[27]

Although no striking differences have been found in the overall lengths of the cerebral hemispheres, Bruijn in pneumoencephalographic studies found the left lateral ventricle to be longer than the right in 125 (77%) and the right to be longer in only 36 studies (22%).[22]

Some relationships between length of the occipital horns and cerebral dominance was noted by McRae and associates.[28] In 100 consecutive pneumoencephalograhic studies, 87 were of right-handed individuals; in 60% the left occipital horn was longer and in 10% the right occipital horn was longer. In the 13 ambidextrous or left-handed individuals the left occipital horns were longer in 38% and the right longer in 31%. These same authors noted that in air studies on 140 seizure patients, 75 (54%) were left-handed or ambidextrous. In the individuals with seizures, the occipital horns in the right-handers were of equal length in 60.3% of the cases and in those who were left-handed or ambidextrous the occipital horns were of equal length in 58.3%, suggesting an altered development of the brain in either pre- or postnatal life.

Local Hemispheral Asymmetries

Anatomists and anthropologists in the past have called attention to local protuberances of the brain, which often result in local impression on the inner table of the vault.[9,11,12,20,29] Local impressions on the inner table of the vault by the hemispheres have been referred to as occipito-petalia, fronto-petalia, etc. Extensive work in this field has been done by Hadziselimovic and his colleagues.[9,20] They noted the occipital poles to be symmetrical in 44% of 250 skulls, left occipito-petalia in 36.8% and right occipito-petalia in 19.2%. The contour most frequently found in skulls (28%) was a left occipito-petalia associated with right temporo-parieto-petalia and right fronto-petalia. The most frequent local asymmetries accompanying right occipito-petalia was left fronto-petalia and left temporal parieto-petalia. These same workers also showed a relationship between position of intracerebral structures and the shape of the vault.

Measuring coronal sections of 200 fixed brains, Inglessis[30] noted frontal areas asymmetries in 10.5%, with the left frontal lobe larger in 11 brains and the right larger in 8. He found asymmetry of the occipital regions in 90.5%, with the left being larger in 161 brains and the right in only 16. He noted less left occipital enlargement in women than in men.[31]

Using x-ray computerized tomography (CT) it is now possible to view the inner table of the vault and the cerebral hemispheres, including the ventricles, in living persons without injection of contrast materials.[32] At the present time in routine CT studies of the head, usually 6 to 8 narrow sectional studies are made (FIGURE 2).

The visualization of the inner table of the vault on the CT scans gives an indication of what would be seen on an endocranial cast of the skull. In scans of the brains of individuals with some brain atrophy it is often possible to see a space between the hemispheres, which allows correlation of the width of the hemispheres. An iodinated compound is frequently given intravenously during CT studies to

TABLE 1

COMPARATIVE WIDTHS OF THE BODIES OF THE LATERAL VENTRICLES AND TIPS OF THE TEMPORAL
HORNS IN 185 PNEUMOENCEPHALOGRAMS*

	Cella Media			Septal-Caudate			Temporal Horns		
				Right		Left	Right		Left
AGE	<40	41–50	>51	Longer	Equal	Longer	Wider	Equal	Wider
0–10	9	9		4	2	5	3	2	5
11–20	14	4		6	1	10	1	7	10
21–30	19	8	3	5	6	16	3	5	21
31–40	18	5	1	2	2	17	4	5	14
41–50	4	11	2	1	3	13	3	4	9
51–60	10	10	5	2	4	19	7	5	13
60	15	24	21	5	7	45	11	12	40
Total	89	64	32	25	25	125	32	40	112

*All pneumoencephalograms (PEG) are of patients without evidence of localized brain disease.

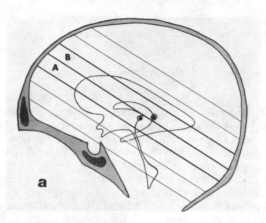

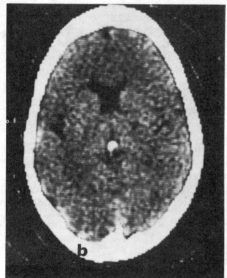

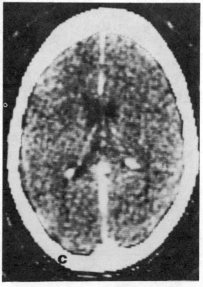

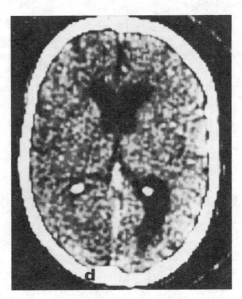

FIGURE 2. *a.* Diagram of sections taken through the brain during a routine examination by x-ray computerized axial tomography (CT). *b.* A CT scan through section *a*. The frontal horns and body of the lateral ventricles are shown as well as part of a thin third ventricle. The white midline spot at the posterior end of the third ventricle is the calcified pineal; its center lies slightly to the left of the midline. *c.* A CT scan through section *b*. The falx is shown as a midline white band. The 2 white spots on either side of the falx are the calcified glomi of the lateral ventricles. The dense spot between the calcified glomi, superimposed over the falx is a vein. It is midline. The patient had been given an iodinated compound intravenously prior to the study that enhanced visualization of the falx and the choroid plexuses, which are shown as narrow white bands in the lateral ventricles angling forward and medially from the calcified glomi. There is a left occipito-petalia and the glomus of the left lateral ventricle lies posterior to that of the right. *d.* A CT scan through section *b* in an individual with right occipito-petalia and left fronto-petalia.

enhance any tumor tissue that may be present, and this also usually causes visualization of the falx lying between the hemispheres, thereby allowing identification of the medial limits of the hemispheres and enabling correlation of hemispheral widths. Because a limited number of sections through the head are studied on routine CT examinations, some areas of local asymmetries in the brain and on the inner surface of the vault will be missed; but striking statistically significant cerebral asymmetries are seen, nevertheless.

Measurements of the width of the forward and occipital portions of the hemispheres were made in 277 right-handed and 63 left-handed individuals above the age of 10 years (TABLE 2). The frontal measurements were made in the lowest section going through the frontal horns of the lateral ventricles in which the interhemispheric fissure could be clearly determined. The occipital measurements were made through the occipital lobe region in the section cutting through the trigone and/or occipital horns of the lateral ventricles. Impressions on the inner tables of the vault are less common in children and so measurements are not included on CT scans made of children 10 years or younger in age. All measurements could not be made with

TABLE 2

COMPARISON OF THE WIDTH OF THE FRONTAL AND OCCIPITAL PORTIONS OF THE BRAINS AND ALSO OF THE EXTENSION ANTERIORLY AND POSTERIORLY OF ONE HEMISPHERE IN RELATION TO THE OTHER*

| | Width of Hemispheres | | | | | | Impression of the Hemispheres on Frontal and Occipital Bones | | | | | |
| | Frontal | | | Occipital | | | Frontal-Petalia | | | Occipital-petalia | | |
	Left Wider	Equal	Right Wider	Left Wider	Equal	Right Wider	Left Anterior	Equal	Right Anterior	Left Posterior	Equal	Right Posterior
Right-handers												
M	11	17	54	50	17	12	9	53	37	90	33	10
F	4	20	68	51	14	14	5	77	25	95	27	14
	15	37	122	101	31	26	14	130	62	185	60	24
Left-handers												
M	5	11	14	7	8	14	8	19	6	22	7	6
F	5	9	5	4	8	9	4	16	5	13	8	6
	10	20	19	11	16	23	12	35	11	35	15	12

* On x-ray computerized tomographic scans.

certainty in all scans. The available measurements show that in right-handers the anterior portion of the right hemisphere measures wider than the left in 70% of 174 brains, while the left is wider in 8.6%. The left occipital area was wider in 63% and the right in 16.5% of 158 brains. The right frontal lobe extended anterior to the left in 30% and the left was found forward in only 7% of 206 brains. Left occipitalia was found in 69% and right occipitalia in 9% of 269 brains. Asymmetries were less striking in left-handers; the right occipital lobe was more often wider than the left, which is the opposite of that found in right-handers.

On the present routine CT studies it is not possible to be certain of the true shape of the ventricles, particularly their lengths. Hadziselimovic and his colleagues[9,10] called attention to the common association of a long occipital horn with an occipito-petalia of the same side (FIGURE 2d), and demonstrated that in brains with a fronto-petalia, the anterior horn of the ventricle on the side of the fronto-petalia often extends anterior to that of the opposite hemisphere (FIGURE 3). They also noted that when the brain shows a right occipito-petalia there is often a left fronto-petalia and the left lateral ventricle lies slightly forward to the right.

The association of a more posterior location of the lateral ventricle on the side showing an occipito-petalia is suggested in CT studies by the frequent backward location of the glomus of the choroid plexus of the lateral ventricle in the hemisphere with occipito-petalia (FIGURE 2c). Examination of the horizontal and half-axial brain slices through the region of the glomi usually show the thalamus on the side of the occipito-petalia to lie slightly posterior to that on the opposite side.[15] TABLE 3 shows the position of the calcified glomi of the choroid plexuses in 120 scans from patients without focal disease, in whom the choroid plexuses contained calcium and could therefore be identified, and the close correlation of their position with occipito-petalia.

Another asymmetry notable on the CT scans is the frequent location of the pineal slightly to the left of the midline, which is associated with a right hemisphere centrally wider than the left. Routine CT scans of 50 males and 50 females who had no evidence of localized intracerebral disease showed the center of the pineal calcification to be in the midline in 38; in 53 patients it lay slightly to the left of the midline whereas it lay slightly to the right in only 9 patients. There was no sex difference in pineal position. The frequent location of the pineal slightly to the left of the midline is in harmony with the frequent asymmetry Hadziselimovic and his co-workers[9] found in brains of right temporo-parieto-petalia in association with both symmetry of the occipital lobes and left occipito-petalia.

Gyral Asymmetries

Frontal Area

Although the right frontal lobe measured wider than the left on the CT scans in 70% of 174 right-handed patients, the anatomical variants to account for these differences are not readily apparent. As mentioned earlier, Inglessis measured asymmetries in 200 coronally sectioned brains and noted asymmetry in 33%, which he felt was probably due to pathology.[30] In specimens, the differences in width of the frontal lobes are seen best on whole brains or on horizontal or half-axial cuts, but even then the hemispheres do not as often show the right frontal widening that is seen on the CT scans.

Because of the great variation in size and number of the cerebral sulci and some variation in their position due to various shapes of the brain, it is difficult to define

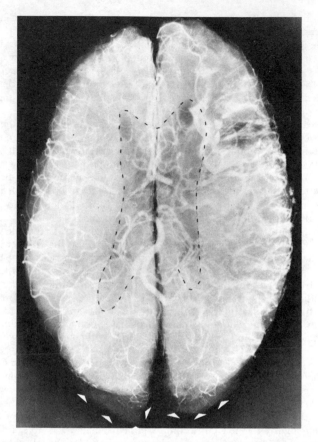

FIGURE 3. X-ray of a brain in which the blood vessels were injected with an opaque substance post mortem. The tips of the occipital lobes are shown by white arrow heads. The ventricular outlines are shown by interrupted dark lines. Note the left occipito-petalia and right fronto-petalia. The frontal and central portions of the right hemisphere are wider than the left.

TABLE 3

RELATION OF CALCIFIED GLOMI OF CHOROID PLEXUSES OF THE LATERAL VENTRICLES TO EACH OTHER AND TO THE POSTERIOR EXTENSION OF THE OCCIPITAL POLES

Occipital Pole	Postion of Glomus of Choroid Plexus of Lateral Ventricle		
	Left Posterior	Equal	Right Posterior
Left petalia	59	21	2
Symmetrical	6	22	2
Right petalia	—	2	6

significant asymmetries in them. In a study of the cytoarchitectonic structure of the frontal lobes, Konovova[33] noted that although the surface areas of the frontal lobes were nearly equal the variability of the gyral pattern was much greater on the left and particularly in the lower frontal and opercular area. Wada and colleagues[34] measured the opercular portion of the third frontal gyrus on photography of 100 adult and 85 infant brains and found the right side to be more often larger than the left in both adult and infant brains. The left opercular area was noted to be larger in approximately 10% of the cases. In this same region, Cunningham[13] noted that a single anterior ramus of the Sylvian fissure is seen more frequently on the right; but more commonly, particularly in the male and in the left hemisphere, two separate rami are present. Two rami arise from a common stem in some brains and Cunningham found this latter pattern more often in the left hemisphere and in females.

Parietal Area

Hemispheral asymmetries are commonly apparent in the parietal region. During the development of the brain, a small area on the lateral surface of each hemisphere, known later as the insula, does not grow as rapidly as the adjacent portions of the brain. It becomes covered by the parietal operculum from above and the temporal operculum from below. The meeting of the two opercula forms the sylvian fissure. The sylvian fissure was reported to be longer on the left than the right by Ebenstaller[35] and by Cunningham[13] in the last century. Cunningham also noted that the angle formed by a line through the sylvian fissure and a line perpendicular to the greatest length of the hemisphere at the anterior end of the fissure, was less on the right than the left. This is so because the distal end of the sylvian fissure, the sylvian point, is usually higher on the right than the left (FIGURE 4). The difference in height of the sylvian points is seen most clearly on coronal sections of the brain. In a series of 18 brains of individuals dying without gross neurological disease the sylvian point was higher on the right in 14.[38] Associated with a lower sylvian point, the left postcentral gyrus, especially its lower portion, is wider than on the right and there is a greater degree of fissuration on the left between the central sulcus and the posterior end of the sylvian fissure.[13,14] In left-handers the posterior ends of the sylvian fissures are more often nearly equal in height.[38] A comparative estimation of the levels of the sylvian points can be made on cerebral angiography.[36] TABLE 4 shows a comparison of the sylvian points in 106 right-handed and 28 left-handed persons. Plato believed that handedness was due to the "folly of nurses and mothers."[37] In 10 fetal brains, one of them of a 16-week gestional period, the sylvian point was noted to be higher on the right than the left in all 10.[38] This finding and the differences noted in lengths of the hemispheres present in fetal brains suggest that the template for cerebral dominence is present before birth.

In archiotechtonic studies, Stankevich[39] found the cortex of the inferior parietal gyri to show very active growth during the first two years of life. Growth rate was greater on the left than the right in 5 of 7 brains. In similar studies, Gurevich and Knachaturian[40] noted the cortical area of the superior parietal region to be greater on the left than the right in 4 brains. In two patients, one known to be left-handed, the superior parietal lobule was larger on the right.

Temporal Lobe

Asymmetries of the temporal lobes are associated with the asymmetries of the sylvian fissures and parietal lobes. The superior temporal gyrus is more often wider

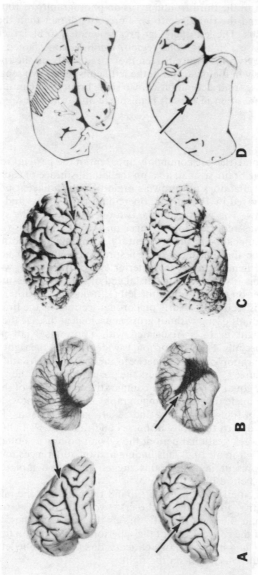

FIGURE 4. Lateral views of the right and left hemispheres of: A. Orangutan; B. 16-week human fetus; C. Adult male; D. Drawing from the endocranial cast of the La Chapelle-aux-Saints skull.[54] Arrows note the posterior ends of the sylvian fissures, which are higher on the right than on the left.

on the right,[41] and breaks are more frequent in the left superior temporal sulcus than the right.[14] Heschl's gyrus lies in the central portion of the temporal operculum, which covers the lower portion of the insula. The surface of the operculum lying behind Heschl's gyrus is known as the planum temporale. Pfeifer[42] noted in 1936 that the planum was larger on the left, but he gave no statistical data. Geschwind and Livitsky,[43] in 1968, found the left planum temporale to be larger than the right in 65 of 100 adult brains. In only 11 brains was the right planum larger. These findings were confirmed by Wada and colleagues[34] and Witelson and Pallie,[44] who also found the same asymmetries in newborn and fetal brains. This difference in size of the planum temporale is no doubt associated with the difference in height of the posterior ends of the sylvian fissures.

TABLE 4

RELATIVE POSITIONS OF THE POSTERIOR ENDS OF THE SYLVIAN FISSURES*

	Right Higher	Equal	Left Higher
Right-handers	71	27	8
Left-handers	6	20	2

* As determined on carotid angiograms of 135 patients without evidence of localized brain disease.

Occipital Lobes

Although the left occipital pole is significantly wider and frequently extends further posteriorly than the right, striking gyral asymmetries have not been noted. Wen[45] pointed out that a hook of the calcarine fissure is more frequently present on the left than on the right side.

Venous Channels

One of the most predictable cerebral asymmetries is the curving to the right of the posterior end of the sagittal sinus. The main flow of the sagittal sinus into the right transverse sinus was noted in 61% of 111 carotid angiograms by Hochberg and LeMay.[36] In only 12.6% was the main flow to the left. In 102 arteriograms of right-handers, the right transverse sinus was higher than the left in 55 (54%). In 16 arteriograms of left-handers the transverse sinuses were of equal height or the left was higher in 11 (69%). A main flow of the superior venous channels, "plexus sagittalis," into the right transverse sinus was shown by Streeter[46] to be apparent in the 20 mm fetus.

As the sagittal sinus turns to enter the transverse sinus a deep groove is present in the medial posterior margin of the occipital lobe, known to early anatomists as "Bastian's groove,"[47] which of course is more often present, and deeper, on the right than the left. The position of the sagittal, and usually the right and occasionally the left transverse sinus, can be identified on most occiput-down half-axial skull films and also on many endocranial casts.

Medulla Oblongata and Spinal Cord

The pyramidal (cortico-spinal) tracts descending from the cerebral cortex of each hemisphere through the internal capsules, cerebral peduncles and bulbar pyramids to both sides of the spinal cord are distributed on the two sides of the spinal cord asymmetrically.[48-50] It has been found in both fetal[48] and adult brains[49,50] that in 80% of normal individuals both the crossed corticospinal tracts from the left (contralateral) hemisphere and the direct corticospinal tracts from the right (ipsilateral) hemisphere are larger on the right side of the spinal cord. In only 20% of the fetal and adult brains and spinal cords was this asymmetry of the pyramidal tracts from both hemispheres found "skewed" to the left side of the spinal cord. Professor Yakovlev refers to this common asymmetry as a "developmental torque." The difference in the bias of the torque cannot at this time be related to right- or left-handedness. In a few brains that were from individuals who were allegedly left-handed, the torque in the decussation and distribution of the pyramidal tracts from both hemispheres to the two sides of the spinal cord was still to the right. Insufficient studies have been done on the brains of left-handers to determine if there are any statistically significant differences in the torque between right- and left-handers.

Fossil Man

A modern perspective of the evolution of the brain has been presented by such well known scientists as Holloway,[17] Jerison,[50] Radinsky,[69] and Tobias,[16] but they have rarely commented upon the cerebral asymmetries of early man. Local variations of contour present in the brains of fossil man can be studied to some extent on endocranial casts of the better preserved skulls. Unfortunately, most of the fossil skulls are damaged and fragmentary; however, the endocranial casts of them have usually been made with painstaking work by scientists knowledgeable in the field.* The following discussion is based mainly on photographs and/or drawings of the endocranial casts presented in the literature by scientists who have studied the individual casts.

The detail presented on the endocranial casts depends on the pressure of the brain on the inner table of the vault during the life of the individual. Evidence of pressure on the vault of modern man is seen on x-ray films, and the impressions are greater in individuals who have increased intracranial pressure, i.e., in individuals with obstructive hydrocephalus or premature synostosis of the sutures. The growth rate of the brain is also important in the formation of impressions on the vault and on radiography they are found to be most marked during adolescence.[52] The impressions are less often prominent in older individuals. Connolly, in a study of endocranial casts of individuals from adolescence to 51 years of age noted the fissural detail to be maximal between the ages of 12 to 17 years.[14] The base of the brain and the occipital and frontol pole gyri are more often shown, however faintly, than those of the parietal region.

Hirschler[53] prepared casts of human and simian skulls, and from his own study and from the literature he concluded that distinct reproduction of cerebral fissures was rare. The sylvian fissures are deep and are usually the most easily identifiable

*I wish to thank Professor R. Holloway, Department of Anthropology, Columbia University, New York, for exposing me to his large collection of endocranial casts of fossil man and beast and for warning me of the difficulties of interpretation of minor variations in the casts.

fissures of the hemispheres. Connolly, during his studies of endocranial casts, noted that although the sylvian fissures were not always clearly identifiable, their posterior ends usually were. The sylvian fissures appear to show on a drawing of the endocranial cast of the La Chapelle-aux-Saints skull by Boule and Anthony.[54] As in the brains of most modern right-handed persons, the posterior end of the sylvian fissure is higher on the right than the left. An endocranial cast of *Sinanthropus pekinensis*[55] also hints of upward curvature of the posterior end of the sylvian fissure on the right, and the posterior end of the right sylvian fissure of a cast from a Swartkraus skull, SK1585, appears to curve upward.[70]

Asymmetries of the frontal and occipital portions of the endocranial casts of fossil man are common. The cast of the first found Neanderthal skull[54] shows left occipito-petalia and right fronto-petalia, the common finding in modern man. The La Chapelle-aux-Saints endocranial cast appears to have a slight right occipito-petalia.[54] The cast of Pithecanthropus I[56]† appears to have a slight right occipitopetalia, whereas that of Pithecanthropus II[16] may have a slight left occipito-petalia. There is no striking asymmetry of the occipital poles on the endocranial casts of the Rhodesian[57] or La Quinna skulls.[58]

We cannot speculate intelligently upon the functional significance of the asymmetries found in ancient man until we know more about their significance in modern man. G. E. Smith in the early part of this century suggested that occipital asymmetries were associated with handedness,[59] and he later suggested that Pithecanthropus I and the individual belonging to the 'London skull' were left-handed because the right occipital pole predominated over the left.[29] In 1910, Keith suggested that "Gibralter man" was right-handed because the left occipital pole was larger than the right.[60] Our computerized axial tomographic studies of modern man suggest that the width of the occipital poles is more closely related to handedness than length of the poles.

NONHUMAN PRIMATES

Cerebral asymmetries are also present in the brains of higher apes.[61] TABLE 5 shows asymmetries found by measurements made on photographs to scale of preserved brains of 69 subhuman primates from the Smithsonian Institution in Washington and the National Institute of Health. As in brains of modern man, differences in lengths of the hemispheres are small, except the right hemisphere of the gorilla was found to be longer in 5 of 7 brains. In the great apes, right occipito-petalia was more often present than left. Differences in the width of the occipital poles were noted in the chimpanzee; in 6 of 9 brains the left was wider than the right, as is common in man. In none was the right occipital pole wider. The heights of the sylvain points were measured by superimposing tracings, from photographs to scale, of the outer borders and sylvian fissures of the brains. Asymmetries were found in 17 brains of the great apes, and in only one was the posterior end of the left sylvian fissure higher than the right whereas the right was higher in 16. The most striking differences were noted in the orangutan.

Measuring the outside of the frontal portion of the skulls, including the facial areas, of some mountain gorillas the left side was found to be greater, and Groves and Humphrey questioned if this was associated with lateralization of brain func-

---

† Endocranial casts at Peabody Museum, Harvard University. I thank E. Trinkaus for his courtesy in showing me the casts.

TABLE 5

HEMISPHERAL DIFFERENCES IN THE CEREBRAL HEMISPHERES OF NONHUMAN PRIMATES*

	No. of Brains	Length		Occipito-petalia		Occipital Pole		Height of Sylvian Point	
		Left Longer	Right Longer	Left Posterior	Right Posterior	Left Wider	Right Wider	Left Higher	Right Higher
New World monkeys									
Cebus (capuchin)	3	2	1	1	1				
Alouatta (howler monkey)	1								
Ateles (spider monkey)	5	3		2					1
Old World monkeys									
Papio (baboon)	8	1	1		1	3			
Macaca	3		1			1	2		
Cynopithecus (black ape)	1						1		1
Presbytis (leaf monkey)	4	1		1		1			1
Nasalis (proboscis monkey)	5	2	1	2	1	1			
Lesser apes									
Hylobates (gibbon)	10	1	2			4	1		
Symphalangus (Siamang)	1								
Great apes									
Pongo (orangutan)	12	4	4		3	2	2		10
Pan (chimpanzee)	9	1	5		3	6	1	1	4
Gorilla (gorilla)	7	1	5	2	5	3	3		2

* Differences in length of hemispheres and extent of protrusion of one occipital pole (occipito-petalia) denote a difference of 1 mm or greater. The widths of the occipital poles were measured 1 cm from the posterior end in the great ape brains and 5 mm in the other primate brains.

tion.[62] Even though the external surface of the skull continues to grow after cessation of increase in size of the endocranium[63] it would seem possible that the "developmental torque" of the brain could, when marked, effect a change in the external skull. The forehead of the individual whose CT scan shows the most marked "clock-wise torque" that I have seen (striking left fronto-petalia and right occipito-petalia) protrudes more on the left than the right. She has no abnormal neurological findings and she is right-handed.

Handedness is more difficult to determine in subhuman primates than in man. Striking differences have not been noted in the chimpanzee.[64] Schaller[65] studied chest beating displays in 8 mountain gorillas and noted that all of them showed a right hand preference in starting the chest beating. Le Gros Clark[66] described the brain of John Daniels II, a gorilla who died at about 5 years of age and who was described as being obviously right-handed. As commonly found in right-handed modern man, Clark's gorilla's brain showed left occipito-petalia, the posterior portion of the left hemisphere was wider than the right, the sagittal sinus turned to the right and the posterior end of the right sylvian fissure was higher than the left. Handedness in the orangutan has not been reported, but would be of interest since their sylvian point differences have been found to be more striking than those of other great apes. It is of interest that some of the early evolutionists considered the orangutan, in particular to be a human ancestor.[67]

Summary

Cerebral asymmetries are common in modern and fossil man and the great apes. Those occurring most often are listed here:

1. The left sylvian fissure in man is longer than the right and in both fetal and adult brains the posterior end of the right sylvian fissure is commonly higher than the left. Associated with these findings, the left planum temporale is usually longer than the right.

2. The left occipital pole is often wider and usually protrudes more posteriorly than the right.

3. The left lateral ventricle, and especially the occipital horn, is usually larger than the right.

4. If one frontal pole extends beyond the other it is usually the right.

5. On x-ray computerized axial tomograms (CT) of the brain the right frontal lobe and the central portion of the right hemisphere more often measure wider than the left.

6. The CT studies commonly show a Yakovlevian anticlockwise torque (taking the nose as 12 o'clock), with the left occipital pole longer and often extending across the midline toward the right and a wider right hemisphere in its central and frontal portions and frequent forward protrusion of the right frontal pole. This is found also in newborns.

7. The posterior end of the sagittal sinus usually lies to the right of the midline and the sinus flows more directly into the right transverse sinus than into the left.

8. The right transverse sinus is usually higher than the left.

9. In left-handed and ambidextrous individuals the posterior ends of the sylvian fissures are more often nearly equal in height and the occipital regions are more often equal in width or the right may be wider.

10. The torque of the pyramidal tract and the hemispheral torque cannot at present be related to right- or left-handedness. Statistics concerning left-handedness are somewhat confounded, because it is likely that not a few individuals are left-

handed because of an early injury of the left hemisphere in a normally right-handed individual.[68]

11. Cerebral asymmetries are found in fossil man similar to those in modern man.

12. Asymmetries of the sylvian fissures similar to those of modern man have been found in the great apes and are particularly common in the orangutan.

13. The most striking and consistently present cerebral asymmetries found in adult and fetal brains are in the region of the posterior end of the sylvian fissures— the areas generally regarded as of major importance in language function.

REFERENCES

1. WEIL, A. 1929. Measurements of cerebral and cerebellar surfaces, comparative studies of the surfaces of endocranial casts of man, prehistoric men, and anthropoid apes. Amer. J. Phys. Anthrop. **13:** 69–90.
2. BOYD, R. 1861. Tables of the weights of the human body and internal organs in the sane and insane of both sexes at various ages arranged from 2114 post-mortem examinations. Phil. Trans. **151:** 241–262.
3. BRAUNE, C. W. 1891. Die Gewichts verhältnisse der rechten zur linken Hirnhälfte beim Menschen. Arch. Anat. Physiol. Anat. (abstr.): 253–270.
4. BROCA, P. 1885. Data reported by P. Topinard, Elements d'Anthropologie Generale,: 591. A. Delabraye et E. Lecrosnier. Paris.
5. KNUDSON, P. A. 1958. Ventriklernes Storrelsesforhold i Anatomisk Normale Hjerner fra Voksne. Copenhagen Theses. Andelsbogtrykkeriet. Odense, Denmark.
6. WAGNER, N. 1864. Massbestimmungen der Oberfläche des grossen Gehirns. Cassel, Trummer, and Deitrich (Georg-August Universitat, Gottingen).
7. WILDE, J. 1926. Über das Gewichts verhaltnisse der Hirnhalften beim Menschen, Litvijas Univ. raksti **14:** 271–288.
8. MELLEY, A. 1944. Application d'une methode de correlation à la capacite ventriculaire dans différentes affections neuro-psychiatriques. Conf. Neurol. **6:** 57–64.
9. HADŽISELIMOVIĆ, H. & M. CUŚ. 1966. The appearance of the internal structures of the brain in relation to the configuration of the human skull. Acta Anat. **63:** 289–299.
10. HRDLICKA, A. 1907. Measurements of the cranial fossa. Proc. U.S. Nat. Mus. **32:** 117–232.
11. GUNDARA, N. & B. ZIVANOVIC. 1968. Asymmetry in East African Skulls. Amer. J. Phys. Anthrop. **28:** 331–338.
12. HOADLEY, N. F. 1929. On measurement of the internal diameters of the skull in relation: (I) to the prediction of its capacity, (II) to the "pre-eminence" of the left hemisphere. Biometrik **21:** 85–123.
13. CUNNINGHAM, D. J. 1892. Contribution to the Surface Anatomy of the Cerebral Hemispheres. Royal Irish Academy. Dublin.
14. CONNOLLY, C. J. 1950. External Morphology of the Primate Brain. Charles C Thomas. Springfield, Ill.
15. Personal data.
16. TOBIAS, P. V. 1971. The Brain in Hominid Evolution. Columbia University Press. New York & London.
17. HOLLOWAY, R. L. 1968. The evolution of the primate brain: Some aspects of quantitative relations. Brain Res. **7:** 121–172.
18. BAILEY, P. 1970. Variations in the shape of the lateral ventricles due to differences in the shape of the head. Arch. Neurol. Psychiat. **35:** 932.
19. BERG, K. J. & E. A. LÖNNUN. 1966. Ventricular size in relation to cranial size. Acta Radiologica 4 (New Series Diagnosis) : 65–78.
20. HADŽISELIMOVIĆ, H. & N. RUŽDIĆ. 1966. Appearance of the base of the brain in relation to the configuration of human skull. Acta Anat. **65:** 146–156.
21. LAST, R. J. & D. H. THOMPSETT. 1953. Casts of cerebral ventricles. Brit. J. Surg. **40:** 525–542.

22. Bruijn, G. W. 1959. Pneumoencephalography in the Diagnosis of Cerebral Atrophy. Drukkerij, H. J. Smits Oudergracht. Utrecht, The Netherlands.

23. Burhenne, H. J. & W. Davies. 1968. The ventricular span in cerebral pneumography. Amer. J. Roentgen. **90:** 1176–1184.

24. Kohler, M. 1957. Encephalographische Befunde bei Kindern mit besonderer Berucksichtigung der Mikroventrikulie und der Peripheren Liquorraumen. Kinderarztl. Prax. **25:** 87–97.

25. Reitmann, F. 1951. Evaluation of air studies. Dis. Nerv. Syst. **12:** 44–46.

26. Fortig, H. 1922. Eine Neue Theorie über die materielle grundlage der funktionellen Superioretat der linken Hemisphare. Dtsch. Med. Wschr. **48:** 312–313.

27. Lodin, H. 1968. Size and development of cerebral ventricular system in childhood. Acta Radiol. **71:** 385–392.

28. Mc Rae, D. L., C. L. Branch & B. Milner. 1968. The occipital horns and cerebral dominance. Neurology **18:** 95–98.

29. Smith, G. E. 1925. Right-and-left handedness in primative men. Brit. Med. J.: 1107–1108.

30. Inglessis, M. 1919. Einiges über Seitenventrikel und Hirnschwellung. Arch. f. Psychiat. **74:** 159–168.

31. Inglessis, M. 1925. Untersuchungen uber Symmetrie und Asymmetrie der Menschlichen Grosshirnhemispharen. Ztschr. f.d.ges. Neurol. Psychiat. **95/96:** 464–474.

32. Hounsfield, G., J. Ambrose & C. Bridges. 1973. Computerized transverse axial scanning. Brit. J. Radiol. **46:** 1016–1051.

33. Konovova, G. P. 1960. (1938) reported by P. I. Yakovlev, p.17, *In* Mental Retardation. W. Bowman & H. V. Mautner, Eds. Grune & Stratton. New York.

34. Wada, J. A., R. Clarke & A. Hamm. 1975. Cerebral hemispheric asymmetry in humans. Arch. Neurol. **32:** 239–246.

35. Eberstaller reported by D. J. Cunningham. 1884. Contribution to the Surface Anatomy of the Cerebral Hemispheres. Royal Irish Academy. Dublin.

36. Hochberg, F. H. & M. LeMay. 1974. Arteriographic correlates of handedness. Neurology **25:** 218–222.

37. Hamilton, E. & H. Cairns, Eds. 1963. Plato, The Collected Dialogues of Plato. Bollinger Series **71:** 366. Pantheon Books. New York.

38. LeMay, M. & A. Culebras. 1972. Human brain morphologic differences in the hemispheres demonstrable by carotid angiography. New Engl. J. Med. **287:** 168–170.

39. Stankevich, I. N. 1960. (1938) reported by P. I. Yakovlev, p. 17. *In* Mental Retardation. P. W. Bowman & H. V. Mautner, Eds. Grune & Stratton. New York.

40. Gurevich, M. O. & A. A. Knachaturian. 1960. (1936) reported by P. I. Yakovlev, p. 17, *In* Mental Retardation. P. W. Bowman & H. V. Mautner, Eds. Grune & Stratton. New York.

41. Hyde, J. B., E. J. Akesson & E. Berinstein. 1973. Growth of the superior temporal gyri in man. Experientia **29:** 1131.

42. Pfeifer, R. A. 1936. Pathologie der Horstrahlung und der Corticalen Horsphare, Handbuch der Neurologie **6:** 533–626. by Bumke & Foerster, Eds. Springer Verlag. Berlin.

43. Geschwind, N. & W. Levitsky. 1968. Human brain: Left-right asymmetries in temporal speech region. Science **161:** 186–187.

44. Witelson, S. F. & W. Pallie. 1973. Left hemisphere specialization for language in the newborn: Neuroanatomical evidence of asymmetry. Brain **96:** 641–646.

45. Wen, I. C. 1933. A study of the occipital region of the Chinese fetal brain. J. Comp. Neurol. **57:** 477–506.

46. Streeter, G. L. 1915. The development of the venous sinuses of the dura mater in the human embryo. Amer. J. Anat. **18:** 145–178.

47. Horsley, V. 1892. On the topographical relations of the cranium and surface of the cerebrum. *In* Contribution to the Surface Anatomy of the Cerebral Hemispheres by D. J. Cunningham. Royal Irish Academy. Dublin.

48. Yakovlev, P. I. & P. Rakic. 1966. Patterns of decussation of bulbar pyramids and distribution of pyramidal tracts on two sides of the spinal cord. Trans. Amer. Neurol. Assoc. **91:** 366–367.

49. KERTESZ, A. & N. GESCHWIND. 1971. Patterns of pyramidal decussation and their relationship to handedness. Arch. Neurol. **24:** 326–332.
50. YAKOVLEV, P. I. 1972. A proposed definition of the limbic system. *In* Limbic system Mechanisms and Automatic Function. C. H. Hockman, Ed. Charles C Thomas. Springfield, Ill.
51. JERISON, H. J. 1973. Evolution of the Brain and Intelligence. Academic Press. New York & London.
52. DuBOULAY, G. 1956. The significance of digital impressions in children's skulls. Acta Radiol. **46:** 112–122.
53. HIRSCHLER, P. 1942. Anthropoid and Human Endocranial Casts. N. V. Noord-Hollandsche, Uitgevers Maatschappij. Amsterdam.
54. BOULE, M. & R. ANTHONY. 1911. L'encephale de l'homme fossile de la Chapelle-aux-Saints. L'Anthrop. **22:** 129–196.
55. SHELLSHEER, J. L. & G. E. SMITH. 1934. A comparative study of the endocranial casts of Sinamthropus. Philos. Trans. Royal Soc. London. Ser. B. **223:** 469–487.
56. McGREGOR, J. H. 1925. Studies on the skull and brain of Pithecanthropus. Nat. History **25:** 544–559.
57. PYCRAFT, W. P., G. E. SMITH, M. YEARSLEY, J. T. CARTER, R. A. SMITH, A. T. HOPWOOD, D. M. A. BALE & W. E. SURNTON. 1928. Rhodesian man and associated remains. Brit. Mus. (Nat. History) London.
58. ANTHONY, R. 1913. L'encephale de l' homine fossile de La Quina. Bull. et Mem. de la Soc. d'Anthrop. de Pais **42:** 117–195.
59. SMITH, G. E. 1908. Right-handedness. Brit. Med. J. :596–597.
60. KEITH, A. 1910. The Gibralter Skull. Nature **89:** 88–89.
61. LeMAY, M. & N. GESCHWIND. 1975. Hemispheric differences in the brains of great apes. Brain Behav. Evol. **11:** 48–52.
62. GROVES, C. P. & N. K. HUMPHREY. 1973. Asymmetry in gorilla skulls: Evidence of lateralized brain functions? Nature **244:** 53–54.
63. BAER, M. J. & J. II. HARRIS. 1969. A commentary on the growth of the human brain and skull. Amer. J. Phys. Anthrop. **30:** 39–44.
64. JACKSON, W. J., M. H. REITE & D. F. BUXTON. 1969. The Chimpanzee Central Nervous System. Primates in Medicine, Vol. **4:** 1–51. Karger Publ. Basal/New York.
65. SCHALLER, G. B. 1963. The Mountain Gorilla. Chicago University Press.
66. CLARK, W. E. LE GROS. 1927. Description of cerebral hemispheres of the brain of the gorilla. J. Anat. **61:** 467–475.
67. BLACKMORE, R. 1714. The Lay-Monk. S. Keiner, Publ. London.
68. ROBERTS, L. 1955. Handedness and cerebral dominance. Trans. Amer. Neurol. Assoc. **80:** 143–148.
69. RADINSKY, L. B. 1974. The fossil evidence of anthropoid brain evolution. Amer. J. Phys. Anthrop. **41:** 15–28.
70. HOLLOWAY, R. L. 1972. New Australopithecine endocast, SK1585, from Swartkraus, South Africa. Amer. J. Phys. Anthrop. **37:** 173–185.

DISCUSSION PAPER:
LANGUAGE, NEURAL ORGANIZATION, AND THE
FOSSIL RECORD

Simeon Locke

Neurological Unit, Boston State Hospital
Boston, Massachusetts 02124

In an analysis of the origins and evolution of language and speech, the best the fossil record can offer is information about morphology. Reconstructions of the vocal tract or of the gross topography of the brain allow only the most tentative inferences about speech and language. The few conclusions that can be drawn are probably more warranted for speech than for language, and the distinction between the two must be kept strict. However language is defined, it cannot be understood only in terms of morphology of the brain. Perhaps the most rigorous definitions available are the ones offered by linguists for the product of neurological function. Implicit in the division of the grammar into its aspects is an acknowledgement of the distinction between speech and language—a distinction that would be true even if phonology were replaced by some other signaling system with a specific set of distinctive features. That the ontogenic development of phonological features occurs in advance of semantic acquisition should not allow the inference that language grew out of speech or that there is a mandatory relationship between language and its modes of expression.

One way of viewing the distinction—perhaps a neurological way—is to conceive of language as an internal state that constitutes a comparatively stimulus-independent representation of reality, and of speech as a system for projecting that representation back on the environment. Language, then, is a strategy for dealing with the most abstract aspects of the environment. The abstraction deals with the "meaning" of stimuli in their relation to the organism. Some preconceptions underlie this formulation. One is that language is a product of the nervous system and is somehow "represented" there. It seems reasonable to assume that the rules which govern language, the product, have some analog in neurological organization. This product is not represented in the nervous system as "language," nor are the rules that govern linguistic organization isomorphically represented. It should be evident that because neurological lesions in a specified area of the brain interfere with "language"—whether this be performance, or competence, or both—no conclusion necessarily follows as to what (if anything) is represented in these regions. That is, the "what" of representation may not be an entity such as language but may simple be an essential aspect of a process.

This view assumes also that there is some relationship between the neural processes that underlie language and the neural mechanisms that serve other functions. That is, the rules of organization of a specific cortical function should not be conceived as qualitatively different from, rather than an elaboration of, those rules that govern the organization of other parts of the neuraxis. This is not to suggest there is no difference between cortical function and function of other regions. It is also not to suggest that the principles of cortical organization of specific areas do not differ from principles of organization of other areas. Rather, it means that a cortical region operates in the context of operations of other cortical areas and of noncortical neurological processes. It means that the way a given cortical region functions is contingent, in part, on input from elsewhere—from cortical as well as from lower levels of the nervous system. Differences in areal cortical function perhaps represent differences in organization of cell assemblies as a manifestation of the imposition of "rules" by experience, in the sense that the innate orientation specificity of simple visual cortical cells can be modified by early life visual exposure. Although there seems to be no way at this time of determining the relationship between functions of single cells or of cell assemblies on the one hand and of phenomena such as perception or language on the other, it seems a safe assumption that somewhere in the nervous system, perception, conceptualization, and cognition occur in some relation to what is happening at the cellular level.

One unresolved issue of importance is just how necessary language is for these phenomena. There is reason to believe that conceptualization can occur in advance of language. There is no doubt that the acquisition of language increases the capability enormously, and that the categorization imposed by language, like any other tool man has devised, can be used to shape the real world as well as its perception. What is not clear is that language is necessary for this.

One way to get at the question is to raise the issue of semantics. The semantic load of a word presumably reflects, in some nonarbitrary way, the "semantic load" of the object to which it refers. It is reasonable that there is a relation between the meanings of words and the meanings of things the words represent, although these meanings are not quite the same. In biological terms a given thing may evoke a given response from a given organism at a given time. It serves as an adequate stimulus presumably because it has biological "meaning." The lexical representation of that thing may or may not serve to evoke the same response. If it does, it is probable that all parameters of the processes in the two instances are not the same. For the semantic load of a lexical item to serve as an adequate surrogate stimulus, the assumptions, preconceptions, frame of reference, and context of the responding organism must be different. It is even more complicated than that, for a given "thing" is not an adequate stimulus in an inflexible sense. Its adequacy depends on a number of factors that include the physiological state and neurological integrity of the responding organism. The patient "paralyzed" as a consequence of a cerebral lesion may not raise his arm when asked to do so; if thrown off balance the "paralyzed arm" lifts automatically to interrupt the fall. Customarily we explain this in terms of the response mechanism, invoking notions of "voluntary" and "involuntary," but really what is changed is the stimulus adequacy. What is represented in the nervous system is not a word as a word or a group of muscles as a group of muscles. What is represented is a way of viewing the world so that those "semantic" aspects which have the greatest meaning for the biological integrity of the organism have the widest representation and the greatest stimulus adequacy. They are not represented the same way at every level of the neuraxis, nor is the quality of the response the same at each level. But the preponderant effect of the relation between trigger and output, no matter at which level of neuraxis, is to achieve a goal in terms of the biological "meaning" of the stimulus, or of the integrity of the organism. This is often evident with respect to the "semantic" aspects of the perceptual environment, presumably mediated in some relation to the primary projection areas, and seen best in the reduced nervous system. It is uncertain, however, whether *nonperceptual* nonlinguistic "semantics" can occur; that is, whether levels of prelinguistic conceptualization exist. If they do, the processes responsible presumably have as morphological counterpart the "association areas" of cortex. The cascading influx of input to cerebral polysensory convergent zones constitutes the substrate of a semantic system further and further removed from the reality it represents in terms of biological urgency; that these zones receive cross modal input is of interest, but may not be crucial. These areas may also mediate abstract aspects of meaning, and so can be viewed as the morphological foundation for the emergence of language. Dominance, in this view, is the unilateral representation in brain of the "meaning" of both halves of the environment, demonstrable by the bilateral effect of a unilateral cerebral lesion. The median divider we impose on the world is not an attribute of the real environment. Objects, actions, and meaning at this level of neurological analysis are independent of field of reference while remaining to some degree field-dependent. It should not be surprising that morphological asymmetries parallel these functional asymmetries and therefore that the morphological asymmetries manifest in the fossil record can provide inferential information about the emergence of language.

DISCUSSION PAPER: THE PALEONEUROLOGY
OF LANGUAGE*

Harry J. Jerison

Department of Psychiatry
University of California/Los Angeles
Los Angeles, California 90024

This is actually an essay on why the human brain is so big. Language is clearly part of the answer, and it may be the whole answer—that the hypertrophy of the primate brain in the hominid lineage was due to the evolution of language, and of language-like cognitive capacities. Most of this report is a quantitative exercise to consider encephalization in hominids, the evolution of the enlarged brain, as it would be interpreted if all or most of it were attributable to the evolution of the capacity for human language. In the process, a number of anatomical and physiological questions are raised, and a particular point of view on both how to ask and how to answer the questions is developed. To put the issue in perspective, I will also say something about language as a faculty of mind.

More speculative than the essentially quantitative analysis of encephalization, the view on the nature of language is fundamentally conservative in its account of the evolution of a novel trait. It is the view that the selective advantage inherent in the *beginnings* of language was not in the enhanced capacity for communication that so clearly characterizes this trait in living humans. Rather, the advantage is attributed to an enhanced capacity for imagery in perception and memory, which enabled early hominids to create and retain cognitive maps of the vastly extended ranges required by their environmental niche. The reason for suggesting such a history is that comparable histories can be suggested for encephalization in other groups of mammals; the causes for the corticalized control of language are analogous to the causes that have been assumed for encephalization in the earliest mammals relative to their reptilian ancestors and the further encephalization in later mammalian lineages.[1]

In the first parts of this essay the hominid brain is examined to indicate the enlargement that would be required to accommodate the "language areas" of a living human brain. Presenting a style of thinking that circumvents the almost impossible problem of identifying localized language areas in fossil endocasts, this approach also reassesses the role of Rubicon models and shows how these can be used to establish criteria for judgments about the evolution of language. The concluding section, THE NATURE OF LANGUAGE, presents a point of view that can be accepted by evolutionists who seek the roots of novel traits in "conservative" requirements for adaptations to existing niches.

---

*This article was prepared to fulfill my assignment as discussant. The very similarly titled paper by Holloway[11] elsewhere in this annal was to have provided a basis for discussion, but since so much of it is a critique of my work[1,4], rather than an analysis of the general topic, the best approach to a discussant's role seemed to me to provide an example of the approach that is being criticized. There is, thus, something of a reversal in roles in the two articles, and Holloway's may be read as a discussion of the present article. Our disagreement on methodology is fundamental; it would not be constructive to debate that here, and I restrict myself to a few comments in a footnote at the conclusion of this article.

HOMINID ENCEPHALIZATION

The actual history of the evolution of encephalization in the hominids is outlined in FIGURE 1. All of the available presapient endocast data are included, and these are compared with data on living chimpanzee and human brains (rather than endocasts). The data on living brains fall within the range of endocast mean and variance for chimpanzee and human populations as reported by Ashton and Spence,[2] so that all of the information presented in FIGURE 1 can be treated as representing comparable measurements on different hominoid species.

FIGURE 1 presents not only a set of data but an analysis of the set. The cumulative distributions are scaled to linearize a probability function, and the extent to which straight lines fit the data measures the appropriatness of the hypothesis that the distributions are "normal," or Gaussian. Here it is important not to be misled by apparent departures from linearity. None of the samples illustrated in FIGURE 1 is "significantly" nonnormal according to conventional statistical[3] tests (p > 0.05). A second important point is that there is an *increase* in variability in cranial capacity with increased mean cranial capacity if the data are presented on linear scales of cranial capacity. This inhomogeneity of variance is not apparent in the graph because it is "corrected" by the logarithmic scale used for cranial capacity. The parallel orientation of the lines on the probability logarithmic coordinate system of FIGURE 1 indicates that variability was proportional to mean cranial capacity in the evolution of the hominid brain.[1,4] The more usual way of graphing the straight lines is by graphing the first derivatives, and these are presented in the upper half of FIGURE 1 as the set of bell-shaped, normal, curves.

From FIGURE 1 we can read the means and standard deviations for each distribution. In round numbers, the mean cranial capacities are 500 ml for the australopithecines, 650 ml for the habilines, and 900 ml for the pithecanthropines. Median brain size was 350 g for the chimpanzees and 1250 g for female *Homo sapiens* (who are generally acknowledged as language-competent hominids). The standard deviation in each case is of the order of 10% of the mean. I treat 400 ml and 1200 ml as representing the pongid and sapient grades.

In approaching data as presented in FIGURE 1, it should be appreciated that curve-fitting procedures always depend on a choice of an ideal mathematical function that generates a particular curve, and in this case the normal, or Gaussian, probability distribution provides the ideal curve. This does not mean that a particular set of assumptions used to derive the normal curve (e.g., as the limit of a binomial distribution related to genetic models) has to be accepted in a theory to explain normality. In fact, a complete and rigorous acceptance of the normal curve for fundamental theory of brain size is impossible, since the tails of the curve have no limits, and there would exist probabilities (albeit low ones) even for negative values of cranial capacity. To make a fine point, the normal curve can be a "model" rather than a "theory" for the system under analysis; if it is the basis of theory, it is not on brain size but on decision-making about brain size. In the latter case the use of the normal curve and the very good fit of data to the curve enable one to use rigorous decision-theory methods.[5] It is with such methods that one can use Rubicon models correctly in the analysis of the evolution of encephalization.

By describing the information on cranial capacity in FIGURE 1 as data on encephalization, I am emphasizing the fact that the several hominoid groups that are represented are about equal in body size. The best guess is that they differed by no more than a factor of 2, and if we exclude the gracile australopithecines, the difference is considerably less—all could be characterized as having weighed about 50 kg. When one has an increase in absolute brain size in an evolutionary sequence

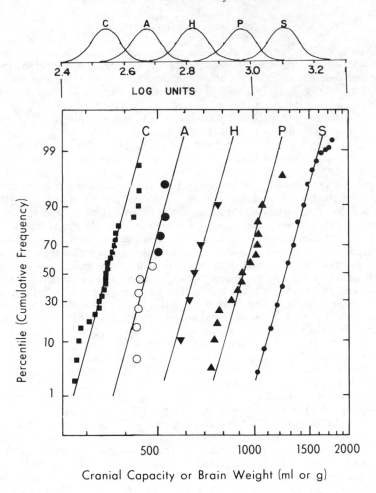

FIGURE 1. Cumulative frequency distributions of brain size in chimpanzees (C) and living humans (S), and of all available data on cranial capacity in three groups of fossil hominids, the australopithecines (A), the habilines (*Homo habilis*, H), and the pithecanthropines (*Homo erectus*, P). Chimpanzee data are from Bauchot and Stephan;[21] other data described in Jerison[4] and Holloway[10,11] and summarized by Tobias.[22] When graphed on a "probability" coordinate system in which rank-ordered data of a population are given percentile-ranks, a Gaussian ("normal") distribution results in straight-line fits with the slope proportional to the standard deviation of the population. The normal curves at the top of this graph are derived from those straight-line fits. The lines are parallel when cranial capacity is measured on a logarithmic scale. This indicates that the variances are proportional to the means (coefficients of variations are approximately equal). The normal curves at the top are exactly equal in variance and area, and their metric is in log-units, which are the logarithms of the units shown at bottom (e.g., Log 1,000 = 3.0; Log 250 = 2.4).

without clear changes in body size, or greater than that predictable from body size, the increase is "encephalization" by definition, hence the use of this term here.

QUANTITATIVE MODELS

The approach now will be to use the pondid and sapient grades as points of departure for assessing the effects of adding or subtracting the "proper mass" of brain tissue for human language. These will then be used to suggest various Rubicons, or decision criteria, for judging the likelihood of a sapient grade of language competence in the several nonsapient fossil hominid samples in FIGURE 1. This approach has the Neanderthals at the sapient grade; their degree of encephalization is indistinguishable from living humans.[1] In applying such a model I will indicate probabilities of errors in the decisions. Since the proper mass of language areas in living humans had to evolve through prior grades that were intermediate between a pongid and sapient grade of language-competence, the approach does not exclude protohominid language beyond a pongid grade.

How large are the language areas? If these are defined by language deficits following traumatic brain damage,[23] a fairly straightforward answer can be suggested, as in FIGURE 2. Assumptions implicit in the use of FIGURE 2 are reviewed, briefly, in the legend.

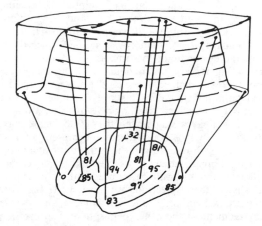

FIGURE 2. Approach to estimation of "proper mass" of human language areas. ("Proper mass" defined as amount of brain tissue required to control a particular system of functions in a species, in this case the language functions in the human species.) Numbers on sketch of brain are Luria's[23] report of the percentage of patients with brain damage localized in that region who showed temporary or permanent posttraumatic language disorders. Using these data to define the proper mass for language implies a nonexclusive definition of a functional area of the brain. It is not necessary for this view that every neuron in an area be devoted to the processing of language—as long as some neural elements are sufficiently central to the processing that their damage (whether temporary or permanent) disrupts behavior sufficiently to be detectable in a relatively crude clinical examination. The "hat-box" and "hat" in the upper part of the illustration estimate the volume of the language area (the "hat") as about 50% of the total volume of the cortex in one hemisphere (the "hat-box"). Heights of the "hat" are proportional to the probability of presence of language-area; the probability is estimated by the frequency of brain damage.

The frequencies of language deficits following damage in various regions, treated as probabilities of representation of language, generate the distribution projected on the surface above the sketch of the brain. A slab of unit-height on that surface represents the volume of cerebral neocortex on the convexity of one hemisphere, and the probabilities are the ordinates of a plane that divides the slab into language and nonlanguage fractions. This procedure results in an estimate of about 50% of the neocortex of a human hemisphere for the proper mass of language.

From other evidence[1,6] we can estimate the total surface (S) and volume (V) of neocortex (cgs-units) from the gross brain weight (E):[1]

$$S = 3 \; E^{0.93} \tag{1}$$

and

$$V = 0.4 \; E \tag{2}$$

Taking 1200 g as typical human brain weight (a somewhat smaller than average figure, but common for living human females and certainly a weight representing a "language-competent" human brain), (1) leads to a total cortical surface of 2200 cm². Taking 2 mm as the average cortical thickness,[7] this leads to an estimate of 440 ml for cortical volume and 110 ml for the proper mass of the language areas. The direct estimate with (2) leads to approximately the same values: 480 ml for neocortical volume and 120 ml for the proper mass of language in the human brain.

These computations, despite their inherent simplifications, provide a sense of the order of magnitude of the mass. Normal weights of human brains from single populations range from about 1 to almost 2 kg, and using different values of E in (1) and (2) would obviously produce different results. The estimate of 50% of a hemisphere as "language area" is equally simplified, since the circuits for language probably involve the entire brain in some sense. (To illustrate, the pattern of eye movements in reading is very much determined by the linguistic content of the material and any narrowly defined "language" areas must make connections with the elaborate neural circuitry that controls eye movements.) Much more restricted amounts of brain may be defined for language by criteria other than brain damage. Without adding further caveats, however, the 50% estimate may, if anything, be too low rather than too high. It is heuristic for the present analysis.

The next step is to ask how enlarged the entire brain at a pongid grade would be if the proper mass for human language were added to its cerebral cortex. Similarly, how much would the human brain be reduced if the proper mass for language were subtracted? To answer these questions we must, first, deal with the asymmetry of language as represented in only one hemisphere and decide how to treat the homologous enlargement of the other hemisphere. Uniformitarianism as an evolutionary principle[8] directs us toward the assumption that present adaptations are representative of past ones and that the line of evolution that led to asymmetric lateralization[9] is an ancient one, presumably true for much of the evolutionary history of human language as a function of the brain. Further this requires the evolution of the homologous areas in the "minor" hemisphere as part of the evolution of language. The entire cortical volume for language-related cognitive processes, bilaterally, would then be twice that for narrowly-defined language: 220 or 240 ml.

The answers for the preceding questions are summarized in TABLE 1. To construct this table, I began with estimates of brain size of 400 and 1200 ml for a language-incompetent pongid grade and language-competent sapient grade. I then used (2) to estimate cortical volumes for those sizes, added (to the "pongid") or subtracted (from the "sapient"), a proper mass of 240 ml and redetermined the brain sizes. Equations 1 and 2 give about the same results, and (2) which is simpler for this didactic exercise, was used to generate the data of TABLE 1.

The results are instructive. Under these assumptions, to advance to a normal language-competent grade from a pongid grade the brain must increase from 400 ml to 1,000 ml in volume; to go in the opposite direction it must be diminished from 1200 ml to 600 ml. This results in a range of 600–1000 ml for uncertainty about the decision. Hominid species with characteristic brain sizes greater than 1,000 ml are within the language-competent range and those below 600 ml are below that range. The intermediates would be left in a linguistic limbo. The Rubicons might change, and the width of limbo could be reduced by determining the proper mass of the language system of the brain more exactly.

Related to FIGURE 1, this analysis would have the australopithecines as language-incompetent and *Homo sapiens* as language-competent. Since some *H. erectus* populations (the sinanthropines) average more than 1,000-ml endocasts, one would be disinclined to reject the pithecanthropine grade as a language-competent grade, although acceptance or rejection would not carry much weight. It is a borderline decision with weak criteria. The habilines are in limbo for decisions on their sapiency with respect to language.

TABLE 1

RUBICONS FOR LANGUAGE (VOLUMES IN ML)*

| | "Pongid Grade" | | "Sapient Grade" | |
	Brain	Cortex	Brain	Cortex
Language-Competent	1000	400	1200	480
Language-Incompetent	400	160	600	240

*Data generated by assuming a 400-ml primate brain as language-incompetent and a 1200-ml one as language-competent, applying Equation 2 to obtain cortical volumes and adding or subtracting a "proper mass" of 240 ml to the cortex to raise it to a "competent" grade or diminish it to an "incompetent" grade; brain size was then recomputed with Equation 2. Essentially the same results are obtained with (1) assuming a cortical thickness of 2 mm.

To illustrate further the style of thinking, the decision on the pithecanthropines can be examined more carefully. All available data on pithecanthropines (15 values) led to a graphic estimate of a mean cranial capacity of 2.96 log-units (920 ml) and a standard deviation of .04 log-units. The language-competent "Rubicon" for this computation is at 3.0 log units (1,000 ml) on the log-scale. The Rubicon represents a point on a decision-axis that is the mean of a distribution, and it is reasonable to assign to it the same standard deviation of 0.04 log-units. If we assume that there is error in the Rubicon's placement, and if we treat the distribution of the Rubicon as representing errors in placement of its mean, we can estimate the errors associated with placing the pithecanthropines above or below the Rubicon of 3.0 ± .04 log-units on the basis of their mean of 2.96 log units.

The decision should be to place them below the Rubicon into linguistic limbo, and the probability that this is a wrong decision is .16. (The "limbo" is ours as decision-makers, not of our ancestors as the users of some kind of human or other "language.") Conventional "statisticians" would reject the limbo-hypothesis as not "significant" at the 0.05 level. But there is more trouble with the null-hypothesis of "no difference" between the sapients and pithecanthropines, because if one accepts the null hypothesis the probability of error is 0.84, which is (I suppose) even less significant at the 0.05 level. Given the model of TABLE 1 the odds are about 5:1 in favor of the limbo hypothesis. In other words, the odds are in favor of concluding that we don't know.

It is useful to indicate the odds on the limbo-hypothesis versus the language-incompetent hypothesis for the australopithecines and the habilines. This lower "Rubicon" is 2.8 ± .04 log units (600 ml) and the mean of the australopithecine grade is about 2.7 log units (500 ml). This is 2.5 standard deviations below criterion (Rubicon), and the odds are 166:1 in favor of the incompetent hypothesis over the limbo hypothesis.

The habiline cranial capacity is less well determined than the others, with KNM-ER 1470 estimated at 775-800 ml and the other four specimens at a value of about 650 ml. In view of the much better condition of the largest endocast, one is inclined to accept a higher figure such as 2.84 log-units (700) ml as typical for the species." The model of TABLE 1 would put the odds on the habilines being in limbo at 5:1 over their being language-incompetent and at about 33,000:1 against their being language-competent.

A final example is on dwarfism and cerebral pathology in living humans and on ontogenetic effects in very young children, in which brain sizes of the order of 800 ml or less occur in individuals capable of human language. Although these are within-species questions that are specifically excluded from this analysis, they suggest potential sources of error if a pathological or immature fossil happens to be collected. If the only evidence on the fossil is the endocast, then the error is unavoidable, and one must include it in estimating the risk of errors of wrong decisions. The likelihood of such an error is extremely small, as witnessed by the identification of one australopithecine (the Taung specimen) as a juvenile. If enough information is available to suggest the species or genus there is no problem for a correct "Rubicon model." The model is, after all, for decisions about species, and there is considerable room for individual differences within a species—in fact, one could even include nanocephalics in a population, though they should really be treated as representing a separate group outside of normal evolutionary analysis.[1] If included within the population the very label (for example, *Homo sapiens*) would force the decision that they were language-competent, since the decision is made with respect to the mean of the population. In a word, the decisions made with Rubicon models are at the species level, not at the individual level.

The preceding should be enough to suggest the approach and how significant questions are stated and resolved with it. Much more precision is possible, even now, but it would require a longer exposition to develop it. The precision requires better statements of the proper mass of the language areas as well as more accurate quantitative determinations of the relations between gross structure and microstructure in various primate brains. The decisions were guided by TABLE 1, and it is obviously the case that minor alterations in the assumptions for TABLE 1 could have altered the conclusions, although it would actually have taken major changes to make much difference. With most sets of reasonably tenable assumptions about the pongid and sapient grade and the proper mass of the language areas we would conclude that the australopithecenes were language-incompetent, that the habilines were in limbo, and that the pithecanthropines were borderline-competent.

LOCALIZATION AND UNIFORMITARIANISM

The conventional alternative to this quantitative approach is based on the uniformitarian hypothesis applied to the analysis of fissural patterns to localize "language areas" by attempting to identify landmarks of these areas and other structural patterns on the endocast. Holloway[10] has followed this strategy, which I have recently reviewed critically.[4] To comment on the lengthy example of its application in this volume,[11] I reiterate my skepticism. I am not persuaded by Holloway's argument on the lunate sulcus. Aside from morphological questions that it raises for the organization of other parts of the brain, there is a question of identifying almost any sulcus in primate endocasts. The lunate is the human "homologue" for the *Affenspalte*, one of the most pronounced sulci in the brain of monkeys. There is usually equivocal evidence of an *Affenspalte* on monkey endocasts despite the fact that it is a major and unequivocally identifiable landmark on the monkey brain. It is still less clear in endocasts of great apes. The lunate sulcus is rarely identified even on the brains of humans. To argue that a particular depression in a natural endocast in a fossil hominid represents a posteriorly shifted lunate and, therefore, enlarged language areas anterior to the lunate seems to me futile and probably false.

These criticisms notwithstanding, it is legitimate to ask where in the brains of fossil hominids the language areas evolved. Here the uniformitarian hypothesis guides us surely and unequivocally to the regions around the angular gyrus that concern Holloway. These are identifiable because they surround the posterior portion of the sylvian fissure, which is usually visible on an endocast. It is certainly in that part of the brain that some of the expansion—encephalization—must have occurred. This is a valid inference from living brains and a necessary consequence of uniformitarianism. Is there further evidence in the endocasts themselves for localized expansion of the language areas? In my view, aside from the evidence of asymmetry[12,13] the answer is no.

Since there is evidence for encephalization in the australopithecines beyond the pongid grade, it is appropriate to ask about the source of that encephalization and to speculate about the neural structures involved in the enlargement of the brain. From the later history of the hominids, and from the fact that almost all of the difference in cranial capacity between language-competent and language-incompetent species could be associated with language (see TABLE 1) I am inclined to consider the evolution of language and language-related cognitive capacities as the source of essentially all of the advance from the pongid to the sapient hominid grade. This suggests that the intermediate advances in grade of encephalization in the hominids, including the earliest stages, can be consider as evidence of the evolution of at least a protohominid grade of language-competence. The next questions are, therefore, on factors determining the first advance in grade and how they could have led to language as we now know it.

THE NATURE OF LANGUAGE

Unlike linguists, anthropologists, psychologists, and neurologists, evolutionists should not be satisfied with the idea that hominid language evolved as a response to selection pressures for improved communication. Ethological data suggest that most mammalian species communicate with the help of neurohumoral fixed-action-patterns, and that even vocal communication in the form of grunts and warning cries tends to be organized subcortically rather than cortically.[14,15] The evolution of an elaborate communication system in early hominids should have been an elaboration of such systems to be consistent with primate or other mammalian patterns. The most probable picture that an evolutionist should draw (without the benefit of the knowledge of what actually happened) would be one in which a rigidly fixed language was fairly completely genetically coded. We would all then "speak" the same language, with a limited vocabulary and set of sentences, and it would develop with much less variability in the final code, certainly nothing as radical as the creation of languages as different as English and French. It is not difficult to imagine a rather extensive set of signs available in an elaborated communication system that follows normal mammalian patterns of neural and genetic control.

The plasticity in living languages is atypical for a mammalian communication system and has many features of cortically controlled sensorimotor systems of mammals. It would be the equivalent of the systems involved in locomotion and the varied stratagems and actions of prey and predators during the hunt and during escape, in which flexibility of action is the key. Many of these behavior patterns are learned, sometimes early and sometimes late in life, but often in association with maternal or paternal care during, for example, the first few years of life of social carnivores.[16]

The rapidity of hominid encephalization, which is unique at least in its recency (no other Plio-Pleistocene mammalian species showed evidence of encephalization during the past few million years), suggests that a niche uncharacteristic of primates had been invaded and that unusual adaptations were evolving. The generally suggested niche is that of social predators;[17] some aspects of that niche would challenge primates in unusual ways, which suggest a different picture of the why of early language. If we also accept the kind of analysis used to explain encephalization in other vertebrate groups and appreciate the relative rarity of encephalization as an adaptation, we will try to identify selection pressures in the niche of social predators that put unusual demands on the nervous system. These should be pressures satisfied by behaviors for which large amounts of neural tissue would be required. The requirement for superior communication does not fit in that category, since it could be effected with relatively little tissue, even if vocal signals were used and auditory analyzers evolved on the perceptual end. We know that this is the case from the evidence of some species of birds, which are encephalized to about the same degree as average mammals and significantly below monkeys and apes, yet can produce marvelously variable sounds, respond with some selectivity to many specific songs, and show considerable plasticity in developing environmentally induced "racial" variants on their calls.[18]

The kind of conservative explanation used in the analysis of encephalization is one that identifies a selection pressure to which the normal biological response is not available and some neurobehavioral innovation is required to produce an equivalent response. The unusual aspect of the niche of social predators, such as wolves, is their great daily range and the requirement for accurate navigation of the range. Wolves, and many other predators, handle this problem by developments in the olfactory system and of scent-marking systems. Primates are unusually nonolfactory animals, with much reduced olfactory bulbs, and one reasonable conjecture is that the early hominids, faced with the problem of "mapping" a range broader than that with which a primate brain can normally cope, evolved the vocal-acoustic ("language") system as a substitute for the olfactory system.

The main characteristic of this new system in its early forms would have been its contribution to nonvisual as well as visual cognitive imagery.[1] It should be thought of as contributing especially to the temporal dimension of all images and enhancing capacities for time-binding (integrating events perceived over relatively long time intervals into single events, an extension of the kind of capacity that binds sequences of tones into rhythmic melodic structures), and in the form of coordinating vocal labels with auditory experience—i.e., naming objects in space and time. It also may be the basis of labeling "time" as an experience[1]. The corticalization of this system would be expected if it is one of the sensoriperceptual systems of the brain. This explains the corticalization of the normally subcortical vocal control system[14,15] but does not account for the lateralization of the language system. One might argue that lateralization was not characteristic of the beginnings of language. It may have been that the system was at first relatively undifferentiated or bilaterally symmetrical and that asymmetry evolved only when the language functions became more specialized, and syntactic structures were differentiated from more *gestalt*-like aspects of language. This is actually implied by the model of TABLE 1 and the data of FIGURE 1. The advance in cranial capacity from the pongid to the australopithecine grade was about 100 ml, the order of the "proper mass of language" according to the model. Such a mass could have been added only if it were distributed between the hemispheres and not lateralized asymmetrically.

The enormous amount of tissue required by language function in living humans was not required by the australopithecines, who, according to the analysis earlier in this article, would not be classified as language-competent. Nevertheless, there is evidence that encephalization was already beyond the pongid grade in the australopithecines, and it is this group of early hominids who are presumed to include wide-ranging predatory species. The reason for such enormous amounts of tissue being required eventually (and noticeable amounts being required from the beginning) may be associated with some of the peculiar features of human language. One of these is the complexity of the motor control system that has to be developed to produce the complex sounds of human speech.[19] When this system was evolving as a motor system, the neural control mechanisms would have had to be as fine as any cortically controlled motor system, with the capacity to integrate events over 100 msec or more into single units of action, a further strain on the neural control system. Although the control system for fine movement, e.g., of hands and feet and the whole body, also requires considerable temporal integration in the nervous system (and also uses considerable amounts of tissue for this control), there is, perhaps, no motor system that requires finer controls than that of the voice box and its associated organs, and in which the context of motions involves so many interactions—when a vowel sound apparently identical in two words is, in fact, altered by the consonants that surround it. It is appropriate to recall here the importance of motor systems for consciousness[20].

The development of such an acousticovocal system as a system that interacts with other sensorimotor systems in the creation of a cognitive map of an extended range would have an almost immediate potential for use in communication. In evolutionary terms it would be "pre-adaptive" as a communication system. This arises from the vocal component and from the likelihood that producing the vocal portion of an image to which the "language" system contributes should conjure up the entire image with visual, tactile, auditory, and even olfactory dimensions. The vocalizations of one member of the species should elicit appropriate images from other members, and we see here the beginning of one of the most unusual features of language. Through the medium of language, shared consciousness (images) among different individuals is truly possible.

SUMMARY AND CONCLUSIONS

The data of paleoneurology can be used as the basis of quantitative decisions about the evolution of language in the hominids if they are combined with information about the proper mass of the language areas in living humans. From the available evidence it is reasonable to conjecture that the neural mass required to control a human grade of language competence was not achieved until the evolution of *Homo sapiens*, although relatively minor changes in one's data or assumptions would place *Homo erectus* at the same grade. It is impossible to reach a decision about the habilines. The australopithecines seem to have been clearly below a language-competent grade, although the evidence of their encephalization beyond the pongid level encourages speculations about pre-adaptations for human language in these early hominids. These pre-adaptations would involve auditory-vocal contributions to a cognitive map of an extended range through which the australopithecines are assumed to have moved as social predators. The role of the auditory-vocal system is considered as analogous to that of the olfactory system of carnivores in comparable niches. Evolutionary considerations point to the localization of language areas in the brain as being in the same general area in all of the hominids, and although this is very likely a valid conjecture according to concepts of uniformitarianism and the conservation of adaptation, it is impossible to use evidence of fossil endocasts as part of the argument in its favor.*

---

*Holloway and I probably disagree on the final sentence of this summary, although the disagreement may be in the degree of confidence with which the assertion is defended or argued against. We almost certainly disagree on the first sentence, since Holloway has argued strongly against the use of "Rubicon models" in paleoanthropology. These disagreements have both personal and general relevance; I will try to avoid the personal tone that enters so easily into a discussion of disagreements. For the nonspecialist, a personal tone sometimes leads to the feeling that the data as well as the analysis are the subject of controversy. Here it is appropriate to assert that the data of fossil endocasts are the most direct evidence of the evolution of the brain, and it is to Holloway's credit that he has contributed so many data. The controversy is on how best to analyze the data and how far one may develop the implications of various evolutionary and neurobiological models in the analysis. Controversy is sometimes a result of misunderstandings that follow differences in style of thinking; I have chosen to respond to two points in Holloway's criticisms of my work, because these are clearly related to matters of style rather than substance, but may mislead a general reader on the issues.

There is enough truth in Holloway's statement that I analyzed the morphology of the (invisible) medial surface of a hemisphere of an australopithecine endocast to win debating points if one is arguing for the fun of it. The scientific issue here is worth more serious argument. My analysis was part of a "thought problem" of the kind often used in science, and the issues are not easily avoided. The problem was: how would the gross morphology of the posterior medial surface of a cerebral hemisphere be affected if a considerable amount of additional neural tissue had to be packed into it? The problem arises if one accepts Holloway's localization of the lunate sulcus in australopithecines as being in a position comparable to that of living humans, and the australopithecine brain as a linearly scaled-down equivalent of the human brain. As is evident from FIGURE 1 of this article, the australopithecine brain was only slightly larger than that of the chimpanzee, and the required placement of the lunate would force one to package almost all visual cortex at the medial surface. One must imagine oneself in the role of a design engineer, seeing to it that things fit where one plans to put them. In chimpanzees about one-third of the visual cortex is on the lateral surface, and this is the amount that would have to be added to the medial surface. If one works on the problem as a bit of design engineering it turns out to require moving structures into unusual positions, including the rostral displacement and distortion of the splenium of the corpus callosum. This major landmark of the medial surface of the cerebral hemisphere would then be unrecognizable as a brain structure in a placental mammal.

The second point is on how to make quantitative comparisons, specifically on the question of how to compare striate cortex in different species. If this is done as "percent of total cortex" it is not clear whether the percentage changes because total cortex remains the same and visual "proper mass" changes, or visual proper mass stays the same and total cortex changes. Data on the human and chimpanzee brain as reported by Holloway (his Table 1) correctly show approximately the same (proper) mass for striate (visual) cortex in the two species, indicating similar amounts of visual information processing of the type carried out in that part of the

REFERENCES

1. JERISON, H. J. 1973. Evolution of the Brain and Intelligence. Academic Press. New York, N.Y.
2. ASHTON, E. H. & T. F. SPENCE. 1958. Age changes in the cranial capacity and foramen magnum of hominoids. Proc. Zool. Soc.: **130:** 169–181 London, England.
3. SHAPIRO, S. S. & M. B. WILK. 1965. An analysis of variance test for normality (complete samples). Biometrika **52:** 591–611.
4. JERISON, H. J. 1975. Fossil evidence of the evolution of the human brain. Ann. Rev. Anthropol. **4:** 27–58.
5. CHERNOFF, H. & L. E. MOSES. 1959. Elementary Decision Theory. Wiley. New York, N.Y.
6. ELIAS, H. & D. SCHWARTZ. 1971. Cerebro-cortical surface areas, volumes, lengths of gyri and their interdependence in mammals, including man. Z. *Säugetierkunde.* **36:** 147–163
7. HARMAN, P. J. 1957. Paleoneurologic, neoneurologic, and ontogenetic aspects of brain phylogeny. James Arthur Lecture on the Evolution of the Human Brain. Amer. Mus. Nat. Hist. New York, N.Y.
8. SIMPSON, G. G. 1970. Uniformitarianism. An inquiry into principle, theory, and method in geohistory and biohistory. *In* Essays in Evolution and Genetics in Honor of Theodosius Dobzhansky. M. K. Hecht and W. C. Steere, Eds.: 43–96. North-Holland Publishing Co. Amsterdam, The Netherlands.
9. TEUBER, H.-L. 1974. Why two brains? *In* The Neurosciences: Third Study Program. F. O. Schmitt and F. G. Worden, Eds. 71–74. MIT Press. Cambridge, Mass.
10. HOLLOWAY, R. L. 1975. The role of human social behavior in the evolution of the brain. James Arthur Lecture on the Evolution of the Human Brain. Amer. Mus. Nat. Hist. New York, N.Y.
11. HOLLOWAY, R. L. This annal.
12. LeMAY, M. 1975. The language capabilities of Neanderthal man. Am. J. Phys. Anthropol. **42:** 9–14
13. LeMAY, M. This annal.
14. PLOOG, D. AND T. MELNECHUK, Eds. 1969. Primate communication. Neurosciences Research Program Bulletin 7: 419–510.
15. MYERS, R. This annal.
16. WILSON, E. O. 1975. Sociobiology. Harvard Univ. Press. Cambridge, Mass.
17. WASHBURN, S. L. & R. S. HARDING. 1970. Evolution of primate behavior. *In* The Neurosciences: Second Study Program. F. O. Schmitt, *et al.*, Eds. 39–47. Rockefeller Univ. Press. New York, N.Y.
18. HINDE, R. A., 1969. Bird Vocalizations: Essays Presented to W. A. Thorpe. Cambridge Univ. Press. London, England.
19. LIBERMAN, A. M. 1974. The specialization of the language hemisphere. *In* F. O. Schmitt &

brain. The reason for the reduction in the percentage of striate cortex in humans is that we are more encephalized, in toto, than chimpanzees; there is more tissue in the rest of our brains. The use of percentages, like the use of simple ratios, is justifiable only when transformations in evolution were linear (or isometric) with respect to relative size. To state that "the *relative* amount [of visual cortex] *decreased*" is essentially meaningless for the problem of visual functions controlled by that cortex. If the absolute amount stayed the same, the functional significance of that part of the cortex as an information-processing system may be assumed to be the same.

Although I do not comment further on Holloway's criticisms, this should not imply that I find them acceptable. They are largely irrelevant for the theme of these proceedings, however, and can probably only be understood in the context of the criticized work. Here I should point out that my position is not entirely conventional from the point of view of the neurosciences, and that some of Holloway's views are shared by many neuroscientists. If I think these wrongheaded, it is partly a personal reaction, although I have reviewed some of my reasons in the references cited by Holloway and in the "Reply" statement that I contributed to the multiple reviews of my book in Current Anthropology (1975, **16:** 403–426).

F. G. Worden, Eds.: The Neurosciences: Third Study Program 43–56. MIT Press. Cambridge, Mass.

20. SPERRY, R. A. 1952. Neurology and the mind-brain problem. Amer. Sci. **40:** 291–312
21. BAUCHOT, R. & H. STEPHAN. 1969. Encéphalisation et niveau evolutif chez les Simiens. Mammalia **33:** 225–275.
22. TOBIAS, P. V. 1975. Brain evolution in the Hominoidea. In Antecedents of Man and After. R. H. Tuttle ed. Mouton. The Hague, The Netherlands.
23. LURIA, A. R. 1970. Traumatic Aphasia: Its Syndromes Psychology and Treatment. Mouton. The Hague, The Netherlands.

DISCUSSION

Leonard Radinsky, *Moderator*
Department of Anatomy
University of Chicago
Chicago, Illinois 60637

DR. RADINSKY: The task of this session was to review the evidence from fossil endocranial casts for the origin of language. My assessment of the data presented is that they point more to questions that must be answered by future research than allow conclusions to be drawn regarding the question at hand. Fossil hominid endocasts are now sufficiently well known to provide some evidence of hominid neuroanatomy during the past two to three million years. The functioinal significance, however, of the observed distinguishing features of hominid endocasts, with respect to acquisition of language or other behavioral abilities, remains to be demonstrated.

LeMay's review of morphological cerebral asymmetries in modern humans and apes provides a needed background for interpreting asymmetry in fossil hominid endocasts. Of particular interest is her demonstration of asymmetry in the brains of great apes, particularly orangutans, since asymmetry was a feature long thought to distinguish human brains from those of apes. LeMay infers cerebral asymmetry from some fossil hominid endocasts, but Holloway questions some of the interpretations, owing to the difficulties of accurately delimiting some key landmarks, such as the posterior end of the sylvian sulcus. Surely this is a question that can be easily resolved by comparing modern human ape brains with their respective endocasts. LeMay's work suggests two directions for future research. One is to survey more thoroughly and to determine more precisely the extent of morphological asymmetry in human and other primate brains. The second is to determine the functional significance of the observed cerebral asymmetries in humans and other primates.

Holloway has provided the most accurate estimates of fossil hominid endocranial volumes yet assembled, plus the most rigorously compiled list of features that distinguish the endocasts of early hominids from those of apes. He considers those features, most of which involve differences in size and proportions of various cortical lobes, to be suggestive of a pattern of organization that is human-like rather than pongid. However, I think that conclusion is unwarranted, because we do not know the functional significance of the features involved (such as more bulky temporal lobes). One can see comparable or even greater differences in shape and proportions between brains of closely related forms, such as small and large domestic dogs, or some species of wild felids, where the underlying factor seems to be merely a difference in relative brain size. As Holloway points out, we must determine more precisely where the changes have occurred that distinguish the brains of hominids from those of pongids. Owing to the nature of hominid endocasts, such determinations will have to be based largely on comparisons between brains of living primates. Further, once those differences are accurately determined (and it is surprising to see how little is known at present about the ways in which human brains differ from those of other primates), then their functional significance must be determined before we can speculate about form/function implications of the changes that have occurred in human brain evolution.

One of the most suggestive features that Holloway (and others) note is the apparent caudal position of the lunate sulcus on the one australopithecine endocast where it is visible. That feature distinguishes modern human from ape brains, and suggests expansion of the parietal association cortex in australopithecines. Jerison contests that interpretation of the position of the lunate sulcus in australopithecines, asserting that the medial surface of their occipital lobes was too small to accomodate the area of striate cortex predicted for primate brains the size of theirs. To demonstrate that assertion, however, Jerison would have to provide estimates of the available medial surface area of australopithecine occipital lobes, including the banks of the inferred calcarine sulcal complex (surface area could be augmented by increasing the degree of cortical folding). Until such estimates are made, and are shown to be clearly inadequate to accommodate the inferred area of striate cortex, I consider Holloway's interpretation of the position of the lunate sulcus in *Australopithecus*, based on surface details of the endocast, to be the most likely. (Jerison also questions the possibility of identifying almost any sulcus on primate endocasts. I have prepared endocasts of about 60 species of primates, representing almost all of the living genera, and find that, with the exception of the great apes and humans, almost all of the sulci present on the outer surface of the brain are reproduced on the endocast. Sulcal details may be blurred on large monkey endocasts, but even in large baboons, individual skulls can be selected that preserve clear imprints of all of the cerebral gyri. Knowledge of sulcal patterns of living primate brains allows identification of sulcal imprints on endocasts.)

Jerison attempts to estimate minimal brain volumes necessary for human language as an approach to determine whether early hominids were capable of language. However, in my opinion he makes a series of unwarranted assumptions that invalidate his conclusions. First, because lesions over wide areas of human neocortex result in some kind of language deficit, he assumes that at least 50% of the human neocortex, or about 240 ml of tissue, is the necessary mass of neocortex required for language. That assumption ignores circuitry and the possibility that some lesions are cutting tracts rather than destroying directly neurons involved in language. Second, even if that amount of neocortex is involved, in various ways, in modern human language, why should we believe that it is the minimum amount necessary for language, in humans or other species? Third, even if one could estimate a minimum amount of brain tissue necessary for language, there is no reason to assume that that amount would have to be added to a chimp's brain to provide language competence, since part of the existing chimp brain could be involved in language. Model-making can be enlightening, but only when based on reasonable assumptions. I consider Jerison's exercise more harmful than helpful, because readers who fail to examine critically the assumptions of his model will consider it proven that australopithecines, with brains under 600 ml in volume, must have been incapable of language.

In summary, fossil endocranial casts provide some information (particularly regarding size and gross external morphology), about the evolution of the human brain. More, however, must be learned about the functional significance of observed changes in brain size and shape before reliable inferences can be made from the endocasts about changing behavioral abilities, including language capability. Given the nature of hominid endocasts, I believe that the archeological record and other aspects of the paleontological record will ultimately allow more inferences about behavior than will the endocasts.

DR. PRIBRAM: I have a question for Dr. LeMay. It seems to me that you showed that the right Sylvian fissure went up more than the left. Wernicke's area is supposed to be below the Sylvian fissure in the temporal lobe, so it seems to me that you have showed that Wernicke's area is really larger on the *right* side than the left side in right-handed people, all of which makes absolutely no sense at all. Is that right?

DR. LeMAY: Comparing the lateral surface configurations of the left and right hemispheres in right-handed individuals, one commonly finds that the posterior end of the Sylvian fissure is higher and the posterior portion of the temporal lobe larger on the right than on the left side of the brain. One cannot draw from this alone the conclusion that the size of the so-called Wernicke's "speech-area" in the temporal bank of the Sylvian cleft is larger or smaller on the left or on the right side of the brain, because other dimensions must be taken into account; for example, the left Sylvian fissure is generally longer than the right (Cunningham, 1892; Connolly, 1950*), the planum temporale is longer in the left hemisphere (Geschwind & Levitsky, 1968), and, most of all, one must take into account the relative surface areas and structure variables of the cytoarchitectonic fields of the temporal cortex on the two sides of the brain. To my knowledge, the precise limits of Wernicke's field have not as yet been defined (see Bogen, this volume).

In my experience, the Sylvian fissures in left-handed individuals are often both low and therefore more nearly symmetrical in position on the two sides of the brain. A lesion of either hemisphere in "left-handers" often results in aphasia, but their aphasia clears more rapidly than in "right-handers."

Aphasia develops most commonly in right handers with lesions in the left cerebral hemisphere. I have seen, however, arteriographic studies in right-handers whose Sylvian fissures were both fairly low and symmetrical in position, resembling in this the left handers; these developed aphasia as a result of a lesion in the *right* hemisphere. I have also seen right-handed individuals with arteriograms showing the Sylvian fissures to be equal in height who developed aphasia following large left-sided cerebral lesions, yet in whom the aphasia cleared as quickly as cases of aphasia in left handers. I believe that correlation of the position of the Sylvian fissures and other cerebral asymmetries, some of which were discussed today, may be of value in the studies of localization of the specifically human cortical functions such as language.

DR. JERISON: When there's more parietal operculum you drop the Sylvian.

DR. PRIBRAM: Some time ago on a monkey we demonstrated that auditory area III is in the parietal operculum; maybe that's the important thing here. We'll be hearing from Bogen on this later (this volume).

DR. JERISON: I did a Ph.D. thesis in which we removed that area on both sides of the brain and discovered that the monkeys lost the perception of tonal patterns.

DR. JASON BROWN (*New York University, New York, N. Y.*): I think one of the reasons why we have so much disagreement as to what Wernicke's area is and where it is is that there's really no agreement on what Wernicke's *aphasia* is, and of course Wernicke's area is inferred from localization studies of Wernicke's aphasics. Wernicke's aphasics can be patients who have severe comprehension impairment, patients with semantic jargon, patients with neologistic jargon, etc. Patients with various different types of language disorder are grouped together as Wernicke's aphasics. So naturally, without a clearer qualitative delineation of different aphasic types localization studies really don't mean anything. We can very easily be dealing with a very wide area (I would prefer to think of it as a field rather than an area), in which we may see *gradients* with different types of aphasias associated with different involvements within a wider zone.

I think the other thing that we have to take into consideration is that there is good evidence now that in left handers not only do we have incomplete lateralization but they are also more diffusely organized *intra*hemispherically than right-handers. You get very similar types of aphasias with more widely scattered lesions in left handers than you do in right handers.

*For complete references, see LeMay, this volume.

AN ETHOLOGICAL THEORY OF THE ORIGIN OF VOCAL LEARNING*

Peter Marler

The Rockefeller University
New York, New York 10021

In striving to reconstruct the events that led to the emergence of human speech and language, one difficulty has been the multiplicity of processes involved. I have chosen to focus on one aspect, namely emergence of the ability for vocal learning. The capacity to modify vocal production as a result of auditory experience and to produce sounds with a novel morphology by the imitation of external models is fundamental to the normal employment of speech in language. This ability is restricted to vertebrate animals, and is adequately documented thus far only in birds and man. I shall present comparative evidence on mechanisms of vocal learning, including both the avian and the human cases, with a view to deriving testable hypotheses about the origin of speech learning in pre-human primate evolution.

I shall begin with a particular *interpretation* of the vocal learning process, and then try to reconstruct the steps that must have been taken in the evolution of our own capacity for learned speech. I shall argue that the vocal learning process is subject to genetic constraints, constraints that tend to favor development in certain directions. To the extent that speech is designed for communication within groups of individuals, the intrusion of learning into its development is subject to some unusual conditions. While there is a premium on the capacity to learn new words for novel objects, new operations, and new concepts, the need to *share* features of signal structure and organization with other members of the communicative group imposes restrictions. The template-matching hypothesis of vocal learning that I shall present suggests how a compromise may be struck between the need for a degree of common rule-sharing in members of a species and the advantages of learned diversification of signal structure and use. I shall present evidence that speech and birdsong are subject to similar basic principles in this regard.

The interpretation of speech learning I lean towards is similar to that of Fry, who proposed in 1966 that "a word that is recognized means an auditory pattern stored in the child's memory. When the child utters a word, he links this auditory memory with a very complex pattern of activity. The muscles receive their operating instructions from the brain and course of their activity is controlled through the kinesthetic and auditory feedback loops."[1]

The evidence on vocal learning in birds suggests a similar interpretation, but with the addition of innate but modifiable auditory templates as a key factor in avian vocal learning and perhaps in the human case as well. My approach relates to the classical ethological concept of the "innate release mechanism" formed by Lorenz some 40 years ago to conceptualize the inherited responsiveness of organisms to particular patterns of external stimulation without their necessarily having had prior exposure to such stimuli from the environment. The evolution of such mechanisms depends on the assumption in phylogenetic history by certain external stimuli of particular valence for survival of the species. Although a predisposition to be especially responsive to such stimuli is physiologically preordained, responsiveness is

*Research reported here was supported by grants from the National Science Foundation (GB33102) and The National Institute of Mental Health (MH 14651).

also viewed as being modifiable as a consequence of experience, as happens in imprinting for example.[2,3] The sequence visualized here in vocal learning resembles that in imprinting in that an organism begins with inherited responsiveness to patterns of external stimulation. In the course of responding to them, it acquires more selective responsiveness to a particular subset of more specific attributes, characterizing the particular stimulus situation that the individual has experienced. As a final step these "sensory templates" are invoked in the development of motor behavior (TABLE 1). As motor activity is performed, sensory feedback is generated, and as long as the appropriate sensory channels are intact, the organism proceeds to match feedback to dictates of the sensory template, either in its innate form, or as modified as a consequence of experience. Such a process is believed to lie at the heart of the acquisition of learned song in certain birds.

TABLE 1

SENSORY TEMPLATES AND LORENZIAN INNATE RELEASE MECHANISMS

Emphasis in original concept retained	Selective filtering of external stimuli
Initial selectivity develops without prior experience of a model	Modifiability of selectivity by external stimulation
Development of concept required	Incorporation in motor development

A male white-crowned sparrow usually begins full song at 100–200 days of age. The song is highly species-specific in certain properties, but also exhibits well marked local dialects.[4] Konishi demonstrated that if such a bird is deafened between 40 and 100 days of age, before singing has started, it subsequently develops a highly abnormal song, a scratchy buzz, amorphous and variable in structure, in complete contrast with the highly controlled, tonal morphology of the normal song.[5] Related species, whose normal songs are different in many respects, converge on a very similar amorphous raspy song after deafening early in life.

Audition obviously plays a role in *development* of the species-specific characteristics of the song. Further studies reveal two rather different roles. Hearing permits the young male to listen to his own voice and to hear conspecific song from other birds as models for imitation. It is here that the Kaspar Hauser experiment is illuminating. A young male white-crowned sparrow, taken from the nest prior to fledging, and raised by hand with hearing intact, but out of hearing of his own species, develops a song which, although abnormal, is less so than that of an early deafened bird. The song has a definite, patterned morphology, made up of relatively pure and sustained tones. Thus the song of such a Kaspar Hauser sparrow shares some normal characteristics with wild, white-crown sparrow singing, although several significant normal song properties are lacking.[6,7] If you compare the three versions of white-crowned sparrow song, the normal wild type, that of a hearing bird reared in isolation, and that of an early deafened male, they represent a series with progressive loss of species-specificity.

A songbird, like a child, must learn from others if it is to vocalize normally. Patterned acoustical stimulation from other individuals may have several effects on song development, including the process of direct imitation. If a young male white-crown is trained with normal song playback before he is 50 days of age, his song will subsequently develop normally. It will be a copy of the model to which he was exposed, including the dialect it presents.

A vital point here is that this song learning ability, manifest during a sensitive period early in life, is also selective. If a male white-crown is given playback of both conspecific song and that of another species it will learn only the conspecific song. Exposed to the alien song alone, it will ignore it and develop a song like that of an untrained Kaspar Hauser. When you think of the many sounds that impinge on a young male in nature, it is not surprising that an ability for selective learning has evolved, specifying which models are most acceptable. There is every reason to think that the song patterns of close relatives are within the vocal compass of a white-crowned sparrow, so that motor constraints don't provide an adequate explanation; and instead we must look to sensory mechanisms, the auditory templates. These are conceptualized as involving the neural pathways for auditory processing in such a way as to sensitize the organism to certain patterns of sound stimulation. As such, they embody information about the structure of vocal sounds, with a capacity to guide motor development.[8]

The progression we hear from subsong through plastic song to full song, which is so typical of a developing songbird, is viewed as a reflection of the gradual acquisition of skill in using the motor equipment for sound production and the process of bringing it under full auditory control. The auditory template of a Kaspar Hauser, with its genetic specifications, is adequate to produce only an approximation of normal song, though it is still sufficiently specific to focus the young bird's attention upon conspecific models if they are presented, thus providing an explanation for the selectivity of the learning process.

TABLE 2

ESSENTIAL FEATURES OF VOCAL LEARNING ACCORDING TO "AUDITORY TEMPLATE" THEORY

1. Inherited responsiveness to species-specific vocal features serves to select appropriate models for vocal learning and to guide in extraction of critical features.

2. Learned modification of auditory templates precedes development of vocalizations destined for morphological shaping through experience.

3. Learned vocal development proceeds by matching auditory feedback to auditory template specifications.

The key points then in this interpretation are the following: first, selective responsiveness by the young organism to particular patterns of acoustical stimulation; second, the ability to modify responsiveness as a result of exposure to sounds within the acceptable set; third, the inclination to vocalize; and finally the tendency to match vocal output by auditory feedback to the customary memory or engram of previously learned acceptable sounds (TABLE 2). Auditory templates explain the selectivity and provide a bridge between sounds heard and sounds produced. Recent research suggests that a similar model is applicable to the human case. If you will forgive a nonspecialist's oversimplifications, I would like to interpret some of the data for you.

Descriptive studies of speech development reveal changes with age that are consistent with gradually improved skill in using the motor equipment and matching the specifications of auditory templates. Eguchi and Hirsh[9] have shown how the variability of critical temporal features of speech sounds such as the voice onset times in [b], [p], and [t] decreases with age to stabilize at "an adultlike minimum value at 7 or 8 years." Kewley-Port and Preston[10] have documented the gradual changes in the distributions of voice onset times in the phonemic categories [d] and [t] between the ages of 6 months and 4½ years, randomly distributed at first, then becoming orderly as one might expect if a child is gradually acquiring skill in matching vocal output to the dictates of auditory templates.

The significant difference between two adjacent speech sounds such as [pa] and [ba] lies in the elapsed time between the first plosive sound from the lips and the beginning of laryngeal voicing, long in [pa] and short or nonexistent in [ba]. Long series of experiments with synthetic speech by Liberman et al. at Haskins Labs, in which the voice onset time is consistently varied, reveal how sharp the perceived boundary is between these two phonemic categories.[11-13] All sounds with voice onset time longer than about 30 msec are classified as [pa] and those shorter as [ba]. Still more intriguing from a comparative viewpoint is the relative insensitivity of adult subjects to within-category variations in voice onset time, even though variations of a similar degree in the boundary zone are readily perceived. This "categorical" feature of our perception of certain speech sounds is what one might expect if *special* physiological mechanisms were involved.

Other lines of evidence also point to perceptual mechanisms with properties different from those employed in processing other classes of sounds. Dichotic listening studies in which competing sounds are presented to two ears reveal that certain speech sounds are more readily perceived when the sounds arrive at the right ear than at the left, whereas there is dichotic equivalence or left ear dominance for nonspeech sounds.[14-16] Electrophysiological studies, using averaged evoked potentials as a measure of responsiveness to speech and nonspeech sounds, also indicate a tendency for separation of the processing of speech and nonspeech in the two hemispheres, a further indication of special processing.[17,18]

In itself the demonstration of especial sensitivity to variation in speech sounds close to critical boundaries is hardly unexpected, and perhaps of more concern to psychologists than to biologists. However, two further findings draw the phenomenon firmly into the biological realm. One is the demonstration by Abramson and Lisker at Haskins that some of the critical boundary features, such as voice onset times, seem to be universals in all languages studied thus far, so that one may think of them as species-specific characteristics.[19-22]

The other concerns the work of Eimas and his colleagues,[23-25] which demonstrates that similar segmental processing of speech sounds, with equivalent boundary values, occurs in infants as young as 4 or even one month of age. This ability is manifest before they have begun to speak or to babble. The method hinges on habituation of a sucking response linked to playback of speech sounds, using revival of the response by a new stimulus as an index of the degree to which pre- and posthabituation stimuli contrast with one another. Using synthetic speech sound continua varying in such properties as voice onset time, infants prove to be sensitive to variations in the same boundary zone to which adults are so responsive, suggesting that they are prone to appropriate categorical processing without the need for prior exposure to models. Eimas feels it appropriate to infer from these results the existence of special detectors for certain speech sounds.

Finally several investigators have detected an ability to discriminate between speech sounds as a class and sounds of other types at a very young age, in some cases within a few days of birth.[26-29] While further work is needed to exclude the possibilities of intrauterine and rapid postnatal learning, it begins to seem feasible that the initial ability to discriminate between speech and nonspeech sounds does not depend upon prior experience of speech sounds. Certainly the ability of a human infant to recognize speech sounds as a class prior to the development of speaking is well established.

If we invoke innate but modifiable templates for certain speech sounds, it seems that they could serve a prespeech child in two ways. Firstly, they would focus the infant's attention on a class of external stimuli appropriate for social responsiveness. Secondly, auditory templates for certain speech sounds could serve as an orderly frame of reference for the infant's developing responsiveness to speech patterns of the culture in which it's growing up.

Given the myriad of complex and highly variable properties of normal speech there is value in drawing the naive infant's attention to a particular subset, with some universal significance. While auditory templates for speech sounds would become highly modified and multiplied in the process of learning a language, some guidance while taking the initial steps in the perceptual analysis of speech would favor the abstraction of similar rules for speech perception in all users of the language, thus insuring a common communicative base.

It is puzzling that no hint of similar processes has yet been discovered in any primate other than man. Thus the problem of the origin of speech learning as I construe it is to understand how innate but modifiable auditory templates for the perception of conspecific vocal sounds became incorporated in vocal development in the course of higher primate evolution. This is the subject of my final remarks. For the sake of discussion I shall present four speculative propositions or postulates to identify some of the key issues (TABLE 3).

Postulate 1. *The existence of discrete vocal signalling implies that categorical auditory processing of conspecific vocal stimuli is common in primates.* The notion of categorical processing is probably implicit in the ethological concept of innate release mechanisms, although it has never been directly tested so far as I know. I would speculate that discretely separate signals imply categorical processing. Discrete vocal patterns, organized in nonadjacent categories with no grading intermediates between, have been recorded in several primates, including a number of forest Cercopithecines and prosimians.[30-32] I infer that categorical auditory processing of vocal stimuli is probably widespread. Tests should be conducted on primates possessing discretely distinct vocal signals to see whether and where stimulus boundaries are in fact drawn.

Postulate 2. *The distinctive emergence of continuously graded vocal structure in some primates implies a shift to continuous auditory processing of their vocalizations.* Descriptive studies of highly social animals have now documented an unusual emphasis on graded vocalizations. This trend is especially emphatic in higher primates, including the gorilla, the chimpanzee and several macaques, species among the most advanced in intelligence, social organization and phylogenetic status.[33-38] I find this unusual emphasis on continuously varying sound signals hard to interpret unless one assumes a parallel shift in the mode of perception, from categorical to continuous perceptual processing.

We urgently need direct evidence on this question. One approach is to condition subjects to respond differently to pairs of sounds in their own vocal repertoire and then to present them with a series of intermediates to see where they delineate a boundary. Following the example of speech research, such experiments are best done with synthetic rather than natural stimuli. If there is anything equivalent to the categorical boundaries for speech in nonhuman primates, attempts to move boundaries by changing the training stimuli in one direction or the other along stimulus continuum should meet with resistance.

Another approach combines study of averaged evoked brain potentials triggered by playback of sound stimuli, together with an habituation technique. This has been used in several studies with human subjects to demonstrate categorical processing of speech sounds, confirming boundaries established by behavioral techniques.[17,39]

Preparations are being made to test this possibility with macaques. The method has the added advantage of revealing lateralization of cerebral processing of the speech sounds of man.[40,41] It thus opens a possibility of uncovering asymmetries in nonhuman primates, a later topic in this conference. The consistent bilateral asymmetry in skulls of the mountain gorilla hints at some intriguing possibilities here,[42] and the discovery of lateralization in cerebral control of birdsong by Nottebohm adds another important dimension.[43-47]

TABLE 3

PRIMATE ORIGINS OF VOCAL LEARNING

Postulate 1.	The existence of discrete vocal signalling implies that categorical auditory processing of conspecific vocal stimuli is common in primates.
Postulate 2.	The distinctive emergence of continuously graded vocal structure in some primates implies a shift to continuous auditory processing of their vocalizations.
Postulate 3.	An early stage in the evolution of human speech behavior was the introduction of modifiable categorical processing of predominantly graded vocal stimuli.
Postulate 4.	The introduction of auditory template matching into the control of motor development permitted: a. At least a partial reversion to a more discrete signal morphology, as in modern speech and, b. The introduction of learned modification of vocal morphology by matching auditory feedback to multiple, modifiable, categorical, auditory templates for elementary speech sounds.

One could even imagine that the earliest steps in primate lateralization might have been taken not in the service of categorical processing by the speech hemisphere, but rather in the nonspeech hemisphere, for the *continuous* perceptual processing of these graded sound signals. The intermingling of categorical and noncategorical processing might have called for some radical changes in the physiology of perception. Thus a shift of human perceptual speech processing from the continuous to the categorical mode, may in a sense have been a reversion to an earlier condition, but with a novel application, namely to the processing of sounds that were not discrete, but at least to some extent organized in a continuously graded fashion. Meanwhile, the simultaneous retention of continuous processing for nonspeech sounds and some features of speech and singing, a perceptual mode we think of as primitive for man but perhaps an advanced one for other primates, may have created physiological problems that were to an extent resolved by the assignment of prime responsibility of these different perceptual modes to different cerebral hemispheres. The method of averaged evoked brain potentials promises a direct test of this speculation.

Postulate 3. *An early stage in the evolution of human speech behavior was the introduction of modifiable categorical processing of predominately graded vocal stimuli.* Descriptive acoustical studies of the sounds used in natural adult speech reveal that many phonemic components are not discretely different from one another, but grade together, with significant numbers of continuous intermediates. In this sense adult speech has more in common with those nonhuman primate repertoires that are highly graded than with those that are more discretely organized.

Yet the perceptual processing of at least some graded speech sounds is categorical. I have postulated that the perception of graded nonhuman primate sounds is more likely to be continuous. Thus a re-emphasis on categorical processing must be postulated at some stage in the emergence of human speech behavior. This step might have been earlier or synchronous with the next change postulated. Provisionally one may suppose that while genetically shaped categorical perceptual filters were involved in this step they were also modifiable and multipliable by experience and tutelage.

Postulate 4. *The introduction of auditory template matching into the control of motor development permitted (a) at least a partial reversion to a more discrete signal morphology, as in modern speech and (b) the introduction of learned modification of vocal morphology by matching auditory feedback to multiple modifiable categorical auditory templates for elementary speech sounds.* The apparent generality of the template-matching interpretation of vocal learning in both birds and man suggests to me that the advent of control of vocal development by auditory feedback was a critical step in the evolution of human speech learning. It becomes important to establish the role of auditory feedback in the vocal ontogeny of other primates. Present information is limited so far as I know to one species, the squirrel monkey, where both early and late deafening seems to have little effect on the morphology of the vocal repertoire that develops.[48] However, the vocal repertoire of the squirrel monkey is predominantly discrete in organization.[49] The impact of early deafening on the vocal behavior of a more advanced old-world primate with highly graded vocalizations, such as a chimpanzee or a macaque, must be studied.

Evidence for learned modification of vocal morphology in nonhuman primates is still sporadic and inconclusive. Green has found local dialects in one vocal pattern of Japanese macaques, which may hint at a role for learning in development, though other interpretations are possible.[50] The duetting behavior of gibbons, in which male and female develop highly coordinated complementary antiphonal vocal patterns, seems to imply a role for learning in development.[38,51] The potential of higher nonhuman primates for intraspecific vocal learning must be approached by direct ontogenetic experimentation.

According to the view presented here, the frame of reference for auditory feedback would be provided by templates, probably already in ancestral use for the categorical perceptual processing of graded sounds. For efficient social application, these templates would already have been modifiable as a result of auditory experience of sounds of other conspecific individuals, allowing the developing animal to acquire responsiveness to points on a vocal stimulus continuum associated with behaviorally significant contexts. By the mechanism proposed, the assumption of auditory feedback control would have immediately opened up the possibility of learned modification of vocal behavior to match sounds heard from conspecific animals earlier in ontogeny. Whether any living nonhuman primate develops vocal behavior in this way we do not know. Perhaps the perceptual requirements are satisfied but not the motor aspects. Again these questions are subject to investigation.

My justification for this line of theorizing is that it points up those lacunae in our knowledge of primate vocal perception and ontogeny that must be filled if we are to advance understanding of the evolution of speech. Above all, the apparent dichotomy between categorical and continuous perceptual processing, of great theoretical interest to ethologists and physiologists, merits comparative study. It may also throw further light on what I believe is emerging as a general theory of vocal learning to which any species is likely to conform if it is to exploit the advantages of learned, traditionally transmitted social signals while minimizing the hazard of individual idiosyncrasies, which, if no one else can understand them, fail to achieve the primary function of speech.

ACKNOWLEDGMENTS

The author is indebted to Fernando Nottebohm, Robert Dooling, and Stephen Zoloth for discussion and criticism of the manuscript.

REFERENCES

1. FRY, D. B. 1966. The development of the phonological system in the normal and the deaf child. *In* The Genesis of Language. F. Smith and G. A. Miller, Eds. M.I.T. Press. Cambridge, Mass.
2. LORENZ, K. 1932. Betrachtungen über das Erkennen der arteigenen Triebhandlungen der Vögel. J. Ornithol. **80:** 50–98. Republished in English translation *In* Studies in Animal and Human Behaviour. Vol. 1. Harvard University Press. Cambridge, Mass. 1970.
3. LORENZ, K. 1935. Der Kumpan in der Umwelt des Vogels. J. Ornithol. **83:** 137–213, 289–413. Republished in English translation *In* Studies in Animal and Human Behaviour. Vol. 1. Harvard University Press. Cambridge, Mass. 1970.
4. MARLER, P. & M. TAMURA. 1962. Song dialects in three populations of White-crowned sparrows. Condor **64:** 368–377.
5. KONISHI, M. 1965. The role of auditory feedback in the control of vocalization in the white-crowned sparrow. Z. Tierpsychol. **22:** 770–783.
6. MARLER, P. & M. TAMURA. 1964. Culturally transmitted patterns of vocal behavior in sparrows. Science **146:** 1483–1486.
7. MARLER, P. 1970. A comparative approach to vocal development: Song learning in the white-crowned sparrow. J. Comp. Physiol. Psychol. **71:** 1–25.
8. MARLER, P. Sensory templates and species-specific behavior. *In* Simpler Networks: An Approach to Patterned Behavior and its Foundations. J. Fentress, Ed. Sinauer Associates. New York, N.Y. In press.
9. EGUCHI, S. & I. J. HIRSH. 1969. Development of speech sounds in children. Acta otolaryng. Suppl. **257:** 1–51.
10. KEWLEY-PORT, D. & M. S. PRESTON. 1974. Early apical stop production: A voice onset time analysis. J. Phonetics **2:** 195–210.
11. LIBERMAN, A. M., K. S. HARRIS, H. S. HOFFMAN & B. C. GRIFFITH. 1957. The discrimination of speech sounds within and across phoneme boundaries. J. Exp. Psychol. **54:** 358–368.
12. LIBERMAN, A. M., K. S. HARRIS, J. KINNEY & H. LANE. 1961. The discrimination of relative onset time of the components of certain speech and nonspeech patterns. J. Exp. Psychol. **61:** 379–388.
13. LIBERMAN, A. M., F. S. COOPER, D. S. SHANKWEILER & M. STUDDERT-KENNEDY. 1967. Perception of the speech code. Psychol. Rev. **74:** 431–461.
14. KIMURA, D. 1961. Cerebral dominance and the perception of verbal stimuli. Canad. J. Psychol. **15:** 166–171.
15. KIMURA, D. 1964. Left-right differences in the perception of melodies. Q.J. Exp. Psychol. **16:** 355–358.
16. STUDDERT-KENNEDY, M. and D. P. SHANKWEILER. 1970. Hemispheric specialization for speech perception. J. Acoust. Soc. Amer. **48:** 579–594.
17. WOOD, C. C., W. R. GOFF & R. S. DAY. 1971. Auditory evoked potentials during speech perception. Science **173:** 1248–1251.
18. MOLFESE, D. L. 1972. Cerebral asymmetry in infants, children and adults: Auditory evoked responses to speech and noise stimuli. Unpublished doctoral dissertation. Pennsylvania State University. College Park, Pa.
19. ABRAMSON, A. S. & L. LISKER. 1965. Voice onset time in stop consonants: Acoustic analysis and synthesis. *In* Proceedings of the Fifth International Congress on Acoustics, A51. Liege, Belgium.
20. ABRAMSON, A. S. & L. LISKER. 1970. Discriminability along the voicing continuum: Cross-language tests. *In* Proceedings of the Sixth International Congress of Phonetic Sciences, Prague, 1967. Academia 1970: 569–573.

21. LISKER, L. & A. S. ABRAMSON. 1964. A cross-language study of voicing of initial stops: Acoustical measurements. Word **20:** 384–422.
22. LISKER, L. & A. S. ABRAMSON. 1970. The voicing dimension: Some experiments in comparative phonetics. *In* Proceedings of the Sixth International Congress of Phonetic Sciences, Prague, 1967.
23. EIMAS, P. D., E. R. SIQUELAND, P. JUSCZYK & J. M. VIGORITO. 1971. Speech perception in infants. Science **171:** 303–306.
24. EIMAS, P. D. in press. Speech perception in early infancy. *In* Infant Perception. L. B. Cohen & P. Salapatek, Eds. Academic Press. New York, N.Y.
25. CUTTING, E. J. & P. D. EIMAS. 1975. Phonetic feature analyzers and the processing of speech in infants. *In* The Role of Speech in Language. J. F. Kavanagh & J. E. Cutting, Eds. M.I.T. Press. Cambridge, Mass.
26. MOFFITT, A. R. 1971. Consonant cue perception by twenty- to twenty-four-week-old infants. Child Development **42:** 717–731.
27. MORSE, P. A. 1972. The discrimination of speech and nonspeech stimuli in early infancy. J. Exp. Child Psychol. **14:** 477–492.
28. TREHUB, S. E. 1973. Infant's sensitivity to vowel and tonal contrasts. Developmental Psychology **9:** 91–96.
29. PALERMO, D. S. 1975. Developmental aspects of speech perception: problems for a motor theory. *In* The Role of Speech in Language. J. F. Kavanagh & J. E. Cutting, Eds. M.I.T. Press. Cambridge, Mass.
30. STRUHSAKER, T. 1967. Auditory communication among vervet monkeys (*Cercopithecus aethiops*). *In* Social Communication among Primates, S. A. Altmann, Ed.: 281–324. Chicago University Press. Chicago, Ill.
31. MARLER, P. 1973. A comparison of vocalizations of red-tailed monkeys and blue monkeys, *Cercopithecus ascanius* and *C. mitis*, in Uganda. Z. Tierpsychol. **33:** 223–247.
33. JOLLY, A. 1966. Lemur behavior. Chicago University Press. Chicago.
33. ROWELL, T. E. 1962. Agonistic noises of the rhesus monkey. Symposium of the Zoological Society of London **8:** 91–96.
34. ROWELL, T. E. & HINDE, R. A. 1962. Vocal communication by the rhesus monkey (*Macaca mulatta*). Proceedings of the Zoological Society of London **138:** 279–294.
35. GAUTIER, J. P. 1974. Field and laboratory studies of the vocalizations of talapoin monkeys (*Miopithecus talapoin*). Behaviour **60:** 209–273.
36. GREEN, S. 1975. Communication by a graded vocal system in Japanese monkeys. *In* Primate Behavior. L. A. Rosenblum, Ed. Vol. **4:** 1–102. Academic Press. New York, N.Y.
37. MARLER, P. 1975. On the origin of speech from animal sounds. *In* The Role of Speech in Language. J. F. Kavanagh & J. E. Cutting, Eds. M.I.T. Press. Cambridge, Mass.
38. MARLER, P. & R. TENAZA. Signalling behavior of wild apes with special reference to vocalization. *In* Animal Communication. T. Sebeok, Ed. Indiana University Press. Bloomington, Ind. In press.
39. DORMAN, M. F. 1974. Auditory evoked potential correlates of speech sound discrimination. Perceptions and Psychophysics. **15:** 215–220.
40. MOLFESE, D. L. 1972. Cerebral asymmetry in infants, children and adults. Acta oto-laryng. Suppl. **257:** 1–51.
41. MATSUMIYA, Y., V. TAGLIASCO, C. T. LOMBROSO & H. GOODGLASS. 1972. Auditory evoked responses: Meaningfulness of stimuli and interhemispheric asymmetry. Science **175:** 790–792.
42. GROVES, C. P. & N. K. HUMPHREY. 1973. Asymmetry in gorilla skulls: evidence of lateralized brain function? Nature **244:** 53–54.
43. NOTTEBOHM, F. 1971. Neural lateralization of vocal control in a passerine bird. I. Song. J. Exp. Zool. **177:** 229–261.
44. NOTTEBOHM, F. 1972. Neural lateralization of vocal control in a passerine bird. II. Subsong, calls, and a theory of vocal learning. J. Exp. Zool. **179:** 35–49.
45. NOTTEBOHM, F. Neural asymmetries in the vocal control of the canary. *In* Lateralization in the Nervous System. S. R. Harnad and R. W. Doty, Eds. Academic Press. New York, N.Y. In press.

46. NOTTEBOHM, F. & M. NOTTEBOHM. Left hypoglossal dominance in the control of canary and white-crowned sparrow song. J. Comp. Physiol. Series A. Submitted for publication.

47. LEMON, R. E. 1973. Nervous control of the syrinx in white-throated sparrows (*Zonotrichia albicollis*). J. Zool. Lond. **171:** 131–140.

48. TALMAGE-RIGGS, G., P. WINTER, D. PLOOG & W. MAYER. 1972. Effect of deafening on the vocal behavior of the squirrel monkey (*Saimiri sciureus*). Folia Primat. **17:** 404–420.

49. WINTER, P., D. PLOOG & J. LATTA. 1966. Vocal repertoire of the squirrel monkey (*Saimiri sciureus*). Its analysis and significance Exp. Brain Res. **1:** 359–384.

50. GREEN, S. 1975. Dialects in Japanese monkeys, vocal learning and cultural transmission of locale-specific vocal behavior. Z. Tierpsychol. **38:** 304–314.

51. LAMPRECHT, J. 1970. Duettgesang beim Siamang, *Symphalangus syndactylus* (*Hominoidea, Hylobatinae*). Z. Tierpsychol. **27:** 186–204.

RELATIONS BETWEEN THE ONTOGENY AND PHYLOGENY OF LANGUAGE: A NEO-RECAPITULATIONIST VIEW

John T. Lamendella

Linguistics Program
San Jose State University
San Jose, California 95192

Of all the evidential domains considered in recent attempts to understand the origins of language, one of the most neglected has been *child language acquisition*. Over the past 20 years or so, psycholinguists have gathered a good deal of information on the manner in which children acquire language (see, e.g., Ferguson and Slobin [16]). There is a reasonably good consensus on the properties of the observable stages of communicative behavior, including the sequence in which these stages appear and the relative times during which they are operable. Data on the progressive development of the child's communicative competence are relevant to understanding the evolutionary development of communication systems by ancestral hominid species, not merely because they illustrates a growth from simple to complex communication systems, but also because there is, as we shall see, every likelihood that ontogeny manifests a repetition of several phylogenetic stages in the evolution of the neurofunctional systems that allow human infants to learn language. The goal of this paper will be to demonstrate the value of examining ontogenetic maturational stages of language development in order to shed light on stages in the evolution of human communication. To do this, it will be necessary to reformulate the incorrect *Biogenetic Law* of Haeckel, and explore the extent to which it is reasonable to expect ontogenetic stages of communication in our hominid ancestors to still be reflected in the ontogeny of the modern child. The purpose will not be to make claims about particular stages, but to demonstrate the validity of such an endeavor.

"Recapitulation" wasn't always a dirty word. Probably because our understanding of embryological development increased concurrently with our understanding of evolution, there was an early recognition of a profound relationship between ontogenesis, phylogenesis, and the contemporary "scale of beings." In its strawman form, the recapitulation hypothesis of Haeckel was taken to mean that each stage of the individual embryo approximates one of the complete series of adult ancestors.* Haeckel viewed evolutionary modifications as being directly tacked onto the adult form of the ancestor, hence he saw the process of ontogeny as the abbreviated unfolding of the cumulative history of the species. With further evolution, ancestral forms were thought to become retracted deeper and deeper into the "germinal expression."

During the twentieth century, the strict recapitulationist view fell on hard times, with few proponents and many scholars eager to point out instances where the sequence or nature of embryological development for many species violates known evolutionary history.[12] It was not only counterexamples that caused the downfall of the view that phylogeny causes ontogeny, however. One important factor was the rise

---

*Haeckel[22] himself admitted that there would be gaps in the sequence, and, because of the brief span of ontogeny, that one could not expect the full sequence of ancestors to be manifested. He also allowed for the interposition of nonrecapitulative (*caenogenetic*) stages as an adaptation to environmental conditions of the immature organism.

of an empiricism that preferred to look outside the organism to the environment for an explanation of the nature of postnatal ontogeny. Twentieth century positivists chose to ignore the internal structure of organisms because it was unobservable by their methods of scientific inquiry. In making a strict dichotomy between the concerns of biology and psychology, behaviorists allotted to biologists the task of describing genetically determined prenatal anatomical and physiological characteristics. They reserved for themselves the job of describing learned behavior during the postnatal period and discovering how stimulus-response associations determine the nature of the individual's personability and intelligence. For methodological reasons, recapitulative developments after birth were condemned to the same limbo as innate cognitive structures and mental processes in general.

Embryologists, on the other hand, have never been able to share the convenient myopia of behaviorists. There is a large body of incontrovertible evidence that many ancestral traits are retained in the ontogeny of descendants.[12] Among biologists, arguments over the extent and nature of recapitulation present in a given species has not cast doubt on the importance of phylogenetic evolution as a determiner of ontogenetic development. Even while condemning the recapitulation hypothesis, DeBeer recognized that the basic flaw in Haeckel's position was only the false belief that it is the adult form of the ancestor that is repeated during ontogeny. The recapitulation that does occur is an approximation not to adult ancestors, but to homologous stages in the development of *immature* phylogenetic precursors. An embryo of a reptile, bird, or mammal never possesses the functional gills of an adult fish, but rather the immature structures of a fish embryo at an equivalent stage of development (as had already been noted by von Baer[3]). Furthermore, the original version of the recapitulation hypothesis mistakenly attempted to look globally at the embryo and identify complete correspondence with some one ancestor. In fact, questions regarding the extent of recapitulation in a species must be raised for particular physiological functional systems arising from different evolutionary sources and manifesting independently varying developmental schedules. *When these two modifications are made in the recapitulationist position, the majority of the objections raised against it no longer apply: some traits repeat ancestral ontogeny and others do not.*

Most scholars have no problem in accepting the notion of phylogenetic repetitions for basic anatomical and physiological systems in the embryo, but there seems to be a general distaste for entertaining the idea that postnatal stages of human cognitive or linguistic information processing might also be a repetition of our species' history. Even many of those who posit innate cognitive structures rarely wonder how those structures got there, and in general seem to treat the whole idea of recapitulation as merely one of those cute foibles of unenlightened nineteenth century thought. However, whether postnatal recapitulative sequences exist is an empirical question that must be asked and answered for each developmental domain. Whatever the difficulties in obtaining clear evidence, phylogenetic recapitulation plays such a strong role in the ontogeny of so many functional systems that it would be unwise to ignore its possible role in the cognitive and linguistic domains simply because the time of birth has passed. The birth process changes only the quality of the infant's environment and not the nature of ontogenetic maturation. Much of human neural development takes place only after the infant has left the carefully controlled uterine environment. In fact, a general characteristic of primate evolution has been an extension of neural maturation well beyond the time of birth in a way allowing postnatal experience and learning to shape developing functional systems in specified ways.[38,39] The interactions between the primate infant and other members of the social group release the child from total reliance on wired-in, stereotyped behavior patterns. Maturation concomitant with individual experience directing organizational growth in appropriate directions not only relieves the genetic code of a heavy burden of detailed specificity, but allows *learning* to assume a prime role in the adaptation of both the individual and the species. Immaturity of neural systems that are nevertheless operational provides the developing infant with flexibility and the chance to adapt successfully as an individual to an ecological niche in a highly variable environment that may not be predictable in advance.

The notion that the developing child manifests a recapitulation of the stages of human cultural and mental evolution was first postulated by J. J. Rousseau and elaborated by G. Stanley Hall. The hypothesis has been offhandedly pooh-poohed by behaviorists, cultural relativists, and humanists. However, their rejection was often based merely on the incorrect assumption that no aspects of culture or cognition could in principle be genetically specified, or the mistaken idea that biological evolution all but ceased for our species when cultural evolution began (cf. Nesturkh[37]). Although unique in many ways, cognitive information processing is still based on anatomical and physiological specializations of neural systems. Even if we don't know much about these specializations, cognitive and linguistic functions have been just as subject to selective pressures as more basic physiological systems. It strains credulity to pretend that language as we know it suddenly sprang up intact as a cultural invention in the absence of extensive cognitive and communicative preadaptations. It is almost as misguided to pick out a single feature of human communication such as *naming* and think that acquisition of this isolated behavior could explain how linguistic systems evolved beyond hominoid call systems (cf. Lancaster,[32] 1968; Jaynes, this volume). More plausible is the belief that language has a long history within hominid evolution and that its invention within some culture depended on the prior attainment of less complex, but similar verbal systems. It is highly probable that cognitive, sociocultural, and communicative evolution occurred together in a series of mutually supportive stages.[9,19]

Some conservative species have remained virtually unchanged over hundreds of millions of years, while the evolution of other species (ours for instance) has involved many progressive, hierarchically additive modifications of functional systems. Successive stages in the evolution of some traits could have become frozen into the genetically controlled developmental schedule for a number of reasons, the basic one being what amounts to a piling up of additional information in the genotype during the evolution of the species. Ancestral traits may not be compressed further and further back as Haeckel believed, but there has been a lengthening of the maturational process and an increase in the number of prematurational stages. This happens because new information encoded into the genotype tends to become active in regulating ontogenetic maturation only during later stages. It is not clear whether the major physical basis for the change is a new order of genes in a chromosome, sequence changes in the proteins synthesized, or new organizational relations among the functional components of regulatory gene systems. Given the uncomfortably high degree of similarity between the genetic material of humans and chimpanzees, it is more likely to be based on modifications in the mechanisms that control the expression of genes than on new structural genes per se.[28,29] Whatever their biochemical basis, new gene systems have arisen that are able to direct the differentiation of novel structures with novel functions on a precise time table. These new functional capabilities allow the offspring of individuals with the new genotype to respond to the environment of development in a new way.

More recently encoded genetic information generally tends to unfold later in ontogeny so as to preserve the temporal sequence in which the new components of the genetic information code were laid down. With further evolutionary specializations, however, at least three things can happen to genetically determined maturational stages during the ontogeny of descendants: *a. Some stages of ancestral ontogeny are retained in the ontogeny of descendants.* For example, the various sensory modalities develop in the same order in all mammal infants. Even totally nonfunctional traits such as the extensive body hair (lanugo) of the human fetus may be retained. *b. Certain quantitative or reorganizational modifications arise in the ontogeny of descendants.* In primates, the prenatal maturational schedule of sensory systems is accelerated over that of motor systems. *c. Certain qualitative novelties arise during the ontogeny of descendants.* In hominids new systems developed for bipedal locomotion and upright stance. When external factors select and preserve genotypes manifesting changes of the second and third types, and when these traits become characteristic of a sizable genetic population, we say that *evolution* has taken place. By definition, the retention of ancestral traits in the ontogeny of descendants is recapitulative.† We might say that *vestigial recapitulation* exists when older functional systems are superseded by more recently evolved systems, but are still maintained in the ontogenetic schedule of descendants in either their original or in a modified form. Between one evolutionary stage and the next, functional systems can change from being the prevailing basis for adult behavior to a vestigal status whenever some more recent system arises in ontogeny and takes over their functional role.

The trick, of course, is to be able to tell from the modern condition which combinations of the three cases described above obtains for a given development. The problem is compounded after birth, because one must then also sort out those responses of the individual to postnatal environmental experience that are genetically specified to a high degree (i.e., innate) versus those that are less fully constrained genetically (i.e., learned). The problems of identifying recapitulative aspects of cognitive or communicative development are complicated further by the small degree to which comparative data from other modern species are applicable. Our closest living primate relatives are extremely limited in the levels of cognitive information processing and communicative interactions they can attain (claims to the contrary notwithstanding, cf. footnote ¶). Positive comparative neurological evidence is lacking since by definition species-specific human neural specializations such as the lateralization of cerebral systems for speech are not shared homologously by other primates. Similarly, direct fossil evidence on the neurological organization of hominid precursors and their communicative capabilities is meager in spite of the many revealing facts that can be determined (e.g., see Holloway,[26a] Holloway, this volume). The best domain of evidence for recapitulative stages in the evolution of human communication remains child development itself, corroborated where possible by what other evidence does exist.

The picture is not as grim as might appear at first glance. There are only a limited number of reasons why an otherwise orderly recapitulative developmental schedule can be interfered with over and above the effects of further evolution. TABLE 1 gives an informal summary of some of the factors that interact during ontogeny to produce a patchwork of recapitulative and partially recapitulative traits in the child. Often, the groundwork for later stages must be prepared by the development of nonfunctional preadaptations during earlier stages. Such preparations are particularly prone

---

†I think the word "recapitulation" has become general enough in meaning to survive Haeckel's connotations of being an abbreviated and exact repetition of whole stages in the evolution of ancestral adults. As a matter of terminology, one could follow DeBeer in replacing it with the unoffensive term "retention" to express the reformulated notion.

to change the *sequence* in which traits develop (*heterochrony*), while leaving the functional systems themselves more or less intact. So, for example, in the history of vertebrates the teeth evolved before the tongue, but in mammalian ontogeny teeth develop after the tongue. One derivative of the principle of *Functionality* is what Anoukhin[1] has called *systemogenesis:* the constraint that those neural systems whose operation is essential for the survival of the young of any species in its particular environmental circumstances develop first and must be functional at birth. Thus, in mammals, the development of neuromotor systems for locomotion occurs prenatally (only) when dictated by the life habits of a given species. For primates, it is sufficient in this regard to develop reflex connections allowing the neonate to cling to its mother. Newborn human infants have a temporary ability to support their own weight when suspended by the hands (via the *palmar grasp reflex*) and feet (via the *plantar grasp reflex*) as a vestigal recapitulation of an ancestral stage when prehominid infants clung to their mother's fur immediately after birth.[40]

TABLE 1

SUMMARY OF FACTORS PRODUCING A NONRECAPITULATIVE ONTOGENY

The following general principles result in the introduction of quantitative, reorganizational, and qualitative, nonrecapitulative novelties into the developmental sequence of descendants and the modification or elimination of recapitulative traits:

(1) *Principle of Functionality.* At all stages of development from egg to adult, the individual must be a complete and functional organism adapted to the particular environmental circumstances of that stage.

(2) *Principle of Systemic Integration.* At every stage of development, all of the many different physiological functional systems of the individual interact and exert mutual influences to shape ontogenetic development in ways that modify recapitulative traits.

(3) *Principle of Differential Phenotypic Response.* Systems that evolved specifically to facilitate the adaptation of the individual to one sort of environment may produce different phenotypic results when that environment is no longer present for descendants.

(4) *Principle of Systemic Annexation.* Recapitulative systems carrying out superseded functions may be assimilated into other functional systems and take on new roles and perhaps new structure as well in later stages of ontogeny.

(5) *Fudge Principle of Random Parsimony.* Recapitulative developmental traits not forming part of some essential ontogenetic sequence may or may not be retained in the ontogeny of descendants. As a result of various poorly understood phenomena (e.g., genetic drift), they may be altered, reduced, eliminated, accelerated, or rearranged.

Some functional systems operate during embryonic development as the necessary means for the survival of the embryo in that environment at that time, and then disappear at a later time. Other systems persist into adulthood after abandoning their original functions to take on new functions and perhaps new structure as well. Still others neither take on a new form nor a new function, but nevertheless survive as vestigal traits of adults. The existence of over 100 vestigal organs in modern adult *Homo sapiens*[2] attests to the conservative nature of the evolutionary process and the ease with which ancestral backwash remains in the gene pool. Of course, ontogenetic development is too complex a process to be viewed merely as a recapitulation of past history, but by the same token it is too complex to be viewed merely as a straight-line progression toward the goal of the adult form. Each developmental stage must be evaluated first in its own terms and only then against the background of prior developments and future potentials. This is particularly important to bear in mind when considering the long postnatal developmental sequences that produce the high level functional systems responsible for language.

While psycholinguists generally agree on the observable properties of the stages in the child's communication development, there is little agreement on the theoretical interpretation of stages of overt behavior or the internal organization of the neural systems that produce them. Disagreement remains on the extent to which there is genetic specification of neurophysiological functional systems specialized for communication. The field is just beginning to overcome several unproductive biases, including a tendency to view the child only from the adult perspective and an overemphasis on the vocal-auditory channel to the point of totally ignoring nonverbal communication. One of the problems in psycholinguistics has been a failure to realize that up to some point in ontogeny the child communicates using vocal and nonvocal systems that are qualitatively different from language. "Human language" is a linguistic communication system of a definite type, characterized by a quite specific syntactic, morphological, and phonological organization. A reduction of this system to an abstract set of essential "design features" à la Hockett and Ascher[26] may in some strange sense capture the "essence" of language, but attainment of some or all of these features by a child or chimpanzee in no way guarantees possession of a unified internal language system underlying communicative interactions. Even where the child's prelanguage communication uses elements derived from adult lexical items or phonological structures, it is clear that some of the nonlanguage systems used by the child could not possibly be learned from models in the environment. These systems arise universally out of an innate development schedule at specifiable ages and stages in all children from all cultures.

A 15-month-old child in the so-called *holophrastic* or *one-word* stage does not have the "beginnings" of language, but instead possesses a multimodal system of communication with its own organizational character.[7,42] It doesn't matter that some of the sounds produced by the child in this stage are *morphemes* and *words* from the adult perspective, what matters is what they are for the child. Holophrastic utterances and their accompanying symbolic gestures are no more "rudimentary language" than crawling is rudimentary running. Both crawling and running are forms of locomotion and employ the same operators, but they are based on different kinds of internal systems and serve in different functional contexts. The place of crawling before running in the developmental schedule does not imply that crawling forms part of some logical hierarchy of skills leading to running, but only that this is the manner in which the maturation of human locomotor systems occurs. (Crawling is in fact a modified recapitulation of an ancestral ontogenetic stage of cross-coordinated quadrupedal locomotion before the evolution of bipedal locomotion.[40]) Similarly, the stages of communication development do not merely represent a gradual accretion of bits and pieces of language that suddenly fall into place as a linguistic system. At each stage the child is operating with a nonlanguage system of a definite type, a system adequate to satisfy the child's needs at that time in that environment. These systems exist for a while and then give way to new levels of communication systems. There are several explanations possible for such a progression of systems, one of the most likely being a vestigal retention of prematurational stages of ancestral communication.

It would be possible to describe human evolution in terms of the interlocking series of different species of hominid precursors that lead up to modern *Homo sapiens*. We might represent the series (in an oversimplified fashion) by listing the precursors as: *Hs −1, Hs −2, Hs −3, . . . , Hs −n*, where *Hs −n* stands for the first hominid species and *Hs 0* would represent our species at the present time. The communication systems used by adults in the sociocultural interactions of *Hs −n* were by definition the earliest systems in use by hominids after their taxonomic split from other hominoids. Somewhere along the series of hominid species leading to *Hs 0* there occurred the development and evolution of higher level communication systems resulting in the type of linguistic system characteristic of our modern species. In *Hs 0*, new individuals learn the particular language used by people in their environment, along the way manifesting the universal series of prelanguage stages summarized in FIGURE 1.[30,31] To make a recapitulation claim for any one of these seven types of systems, it would be necessary to demonstrate that the stage is a repetition of an innate stage in the ontogeny of at least one hominid precursor, say *Hs -i*. This claim in itself does not entail the further claim that a system of this sort was actually used by adults of *Hs -i*, but only that *Hs -i* infants developed this system as the result of specific genetic encoding. Neither does it follow necessarily that some precursor to *Hs -i*, say *Hs -j*, employed a system of this type in *their* culture. The question of vestigial stages must be kept separate from the issue of whether or not a given stage is a re-creation of a learned system once used by adults of some ancestral species. It is probably worthwhile to employ two terms such as *vestigial retention* and *vestigial facsimile* to distinguish the two conditions. A claim that a stage is a vestigal facsimile would be based on the assumption that the learned adult system of an ancestral species became incorporated into the genetic material of succeeding generations as some diachronically homologous transformation of the original system. The plausi-bility of such a belief depends on how reasonable it is to expect such a change to have taken place given what we know about the evolutionary process and the history of primates.

One needn't believe in the hereditary transmission of acquired characteristics to believe that the learned communication system used by adults in a group of hominids could later become incorporated into the genetic material of future generations. Nor is it necessary to invoke the old standby explanation of serendipitous *mutations* to explain away apparent cases of Larmarkian inheritance. At any given time in a species' history, individual members of the species manifest a differential capacity to acquire and use certain types of adaptive behavior patterns. A clear example of this principle in operation across taxonomic boundaries can be seen in the drastically varying abilities of primates to make cross-modal nonlimbic associations of sensory stimuli. An adult human being can tactually identify an object after seeing it only once, but a chimpanzee needs 500 trials to learn to recognize an object by touch after its visual presentation.[10] Monkeys require up to 1000 trials to achieve cross-modal identifications with 70–80% accuracy[8,11,15] The original claim of Geschwind[20] that there has been a specialization in human evolution of parietotemporal cortex to make cross-modal associations is not vitiated by these experimentally demonstrated abilities of other primates. In such tasks, there obviously exists a drastic difference in the degree of help provided various primate species by the genetic material. Neural specializations of individuals of the same species similarly show great disparity in the facility particular individuals have for learning to adequately perform information processing tasks (cf. Waddington[47]). The poor performance of human infants in such tasks[6] supports the view that the capacity to make cross-modal associations arose during hominid evolution based on the development of specialized neocortical systems.

If the genetic material of all (or some segment)‡ of the members of our species has specialized to determine the development of the same linguistically relevant neural

---

‡Ontogenetic traits do not have to be manifested in each and every individual of a species in order to be innate within some subgroup. Because all individuals except monozygotic twins are genetically unique, even wide differences in the nature or sequence of ontogenetic stages of

systems, this can only be the evolutionary result of the selection and preservation of adaptive genotypic idiosyncracies of some ancestral individual or groups of individuals. Within a hominid culture possessing a learned communication system of a given type, certain children would have a distinct advantage in acquiring the system more readily with less formal training.§ Such advantages could exist in the realm of neural organization as well as in vocal tract anatomy. (Cf. the general claims in Lieberman[35] regarding specializations of the human vocal apparatus.) To the extent that a greater aptitude for acquiring the communication system of the culture would give individuals a selective edge over their slower-learning comrades, these individuals would tend to propagate their kind. The eventual result would be a concentration of genotypes producing this trait in the gene pool of the species. At the point when a sufficient number of individuals had this same advantage in acquiring the system of adults, an adequate base would exist for the cultural development of a new order of communication system that had selective value because it better satisfied the needs of sociocultural organization at that time. Hominid groups with a high percentage of individuals possessing these specializations might tend to expand at the expense of groups using less adequate communication systems.

The nature of a new communication system would always be constrained by the neural equipment a given generation of children could bring to bear in acquiring it.¶ It just would not have been feasible for early hominid adults to spend thousands of hours over several years in rigorous training sessions with each child. Only when a child is neurally predisposed to process information in exactly the right way can language learning be successful with as little attention as modern parents (of all cultures) give the process. When a new communication system did arise in the culture of a particular group of hominids, once again certain immature individuals would have had a greater aptitude for acquiring this second system more easily. The maturational stage reflecting the operation of the first set of neural specializations would have been likely to remain in the ontogenetic schedule of descendants whenever the second set was built up out of the first. The second order specializations would produce a second prematurational stage of development as regulated by the

---

communication would not constitute disproof of a specific genetic basis. It is entirely possible that a universal development could exist innately in one segment of the population, and result from learning in another (cf. discussion below). Thus, universality would neither be a sufficient nor a necessary condition for claiming innate status for any ontogenetic trait.

§ A differential capacity to learn the communication system of the environment may be one of the reasons why certain modern children do not acquire the regular language system as fast or as well as normal children. In severe cases some individuals require rigorous training and specialized help to attain normal language competence (See, e.g., Lerner[34]; Schiefelbusch and Lloyd.[44] The cause in many of these cases may not be "minimal brain dysfunction," but genotypic idiosyncracies that fail to provide as much built-in help as for the majority of children.

¶This statement holds true for the communication abilities of other modern primates as well. The belief of some psychologists that the cognitive and communicative abilities of a species is limited only by the quality of their environmental experience is obviously false. In spite of their sweeping claims, the Gardners and their colleagues have not succeeded in training chimpanzees to use American Sign Language or any system on a par with normal language (Gardner and Gardner[18]; also Fouts[17]; cf. Premack[41]; and Hewes.[23]) It is demonstrably true that neither the child at the gestural or lexical stages nor any chimp thus far possesses a linguistic system with the syntactic, morphological, and phonological (or equivalent) properties possessed by every human language. The production of isolated overt behavior sequences that are interpretable as being based on design features also present in language, or as being actual 'pieces' of a language system, cannot validly be claimed to ipso facto be proof of the possession of an internal linguistic system in either child or chimpanzee.

Hominid Precursor *Hs -j*

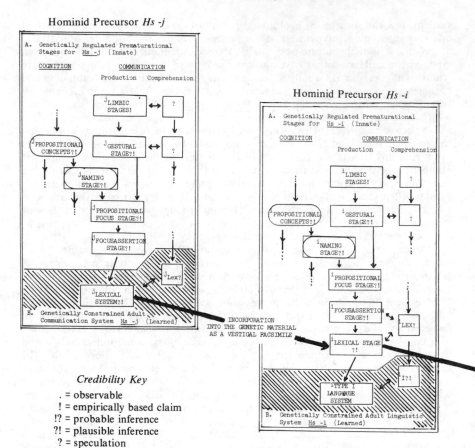

Hominid Precursor *Hs -i*

Credibility Key

. = observable
! = empirically based claim
!? = probable inference
?! = plausible inference
? = speculation

FIGURE 1.

The example above posits two specific hominid ancestors in order to illustrate the general claim that as more complex symbolic communication systems became adaptive for hominid subspecies, selection for appropriate sorts of genotypes led to the additive incorporation of new prematurational stages in the acquisition of communication systems into the ontogenetic development of descendants. This in turn provided the basis for the phenotypic learning of a qualitatively new order of communication system and, in cyclic fashion, to the eventual incorporation of a reflex of this system into the genetic material of the evolving species. For the descendants, the new stage in the acquisition of the adult communication system would, in all likelihood, not be identical to the ancestral system, but would be some homologous diachronic transformation of the system it recapitulates. Needless to say, each specific claim for the status of a communication stage in the modern child as a vestigial repetition or vestigial facsimile is subject to independent empirical verification.

Homo sapiens sapiens Hs o

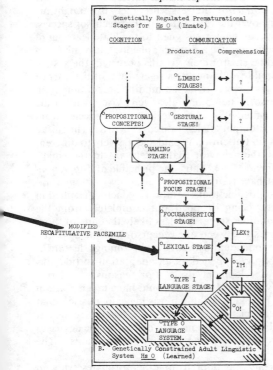

A. Genetically Regulated Prematurational Stages for Hs 0 (Innate)

COGNITION   COMMUNICATION
Production   Comprehension

B. Genetically Constrained Adult Linguistic System Hs 0 (Learned)

Even in the absence of any applicable comparative data from other modern primates, or direct neurological evidence from fossil remains, it would be possible to formulate probabilistic reconstructions of stages in the phylogenetic evolution of human linguistic communication systems by projecting backwards from the innate, universal stages observable in the acquisition of language by children. It is hypothesized that some of these stages exist only as modified repetitions of the prematurational ontogenetic stages in the development of communication systems by some hominid precursors.

genetic material. Progressively higher levels of communication could be achieved in a precursor-descendant series by: *a.* the development of a communication system within a particular group of hominids; *b.* the incorporation of this system into the genetic material in the form of neural systems organized to facilitate its acquisition; and *c.* the creation of a population base with the new genotype, allowing the development of a higher level communication system. It is this sort of bootstrap evolution that probably lies behind the development of language systems by our species.** The result of such a process would be precisely such a series of prematurational stages of communication as is observable in the ontogeny of modern *Homo sapiens.*

To claim that a communication stage of the child is a vestigal facsimile, a reflex of a learned adult ancestral communication system, one would have to show how the five factors listed in TABLE 1 *could not* or *did not* interfere with otherwise straightforward realizations of vestigal repetitions over the relevant series of precursor species. For example, it is possible that neural equipment designed to facilitate learning of one type of communication system could produce a different phenotypic result when that system was no longer present in the environment. If this occurred, the system underlying the overt behavior of the child would not be a re-creation of the learned system used by an ancestor, even though it might remain a modified repetition of an immature stage for some other precursor. The communicative environment of the child includes all of the modes of social interaction characteristic of our species, from limbic sign and signal behavior to the output of lateralized neocortical linguistic systems. Observing the child, it seems that attention is paid successively to different aspects of adult behavior, specifically the behavior that is relevant to the child's current stage of development (see Lamendella[31]). Thus, the principle of *Differential Phenotypic Response* may or may not have resulted in modifications of prematurational communication stages. It is also possible that evolutionary factors resulted in some nonessential recapitulative stage being dropped out completely from the ontogenetic schedule or merged with another stage. It is less likely that any of those stages that do exist popped up capriciously between one precursor and the next. If a new stage did develop in the immature individual without ever becoming a feature of adult behavior (caenogenesis), it probably happened as an adaptation to (identifiable) factors within communication development itself. For reasons of internal consistency, it doesn't seem that many sequence changes could have taken place in the progression of stages discussed in FIGURE 1, although it is logically possible that *naming* and *holophrasis* in particular may have evolved in reverse sequence. Obviously a great deal of effort would have to be expended to determine the degree to which specific claims concerning the extent of nonrecapitulative modifications can be supported by the available evidence.

Comparative neurological and behavioral data from other primates who do possess limbically regulated sign and signal systems make it highly probable that both the preconceptual limbic stages of the child and the limbic communication of adults are homologous repetitions of systems present over the entire series of hominid ancestors (Jürgens and Ploog[27]; Robinson[43]; Bastian[4]; Lancaster[32]; Eibl-Eibesfeldt.[14])

On the other hand, the status of the conceptually based prelanguage and language stages must remain a matter of conjecture until some brave soul musters the evidence to support a claim of vestigial retention or vestigial facsimile of a particular stage in

---

**That is, the type of evolution F. Müller[36] labeled "over-stepping" (also called *hypermorphosis*) in contrast to "progressive deviation" in which descendants diverge more and more from the ontogenetic stages of the ancestor.

the ontogeny of a particular ancestor. FIGURE 2 gives an (empirically unsupported) example of the general form such a claim might take. The example is based on the *lexical stage* of prelanguage development, operable in the child between 18 and 24 months of age (See II. E., FIGURE 1). Notice that what is being asserted for the sake of this illustration is that the three systems underlying

> *a.* [i]LEXICAL SYSTEM: The learned communication system of an adult community of ancestral hominids;
> *b.* [j]LEXICAL STAGE: An innate prematurational stage in the ontogeny of some later hominid; and
> *c.* [o]LEXICAL STAGE: The "telegraphic" stage of prelanguage in the ontogeny of modern *Homo sapiens*

are systems of the same general type and level, based on the activity of homologous neural systems. This example further hypothesizes that the [j]LEXICAL SYSTEM of *Hs −j* is the basic cause for the existence of the neural systems that produce [i]LEXICAL STAGE in *Hs −i*, and that a reflex of [i]LEXICAL STAGE continues to reside in the human gene pool in the form of [o]LEXICAL STAGE. There is no reason to assume that the specific organizational character of the three systems would be identical. The lexical systems of various modern children in this stage exhibit wide differences of detail, and one could expect an even wider range of differences to exist between diachronically homologous stages of children separated by thousands, hundreds of thousands, or even millions of years.

It is worth pointing out that the speech production of many severe Broca's aphasics embodies a lexical system of essentially the same type as the child's lexical stage. Utterances consist of "agrammatical" strings of lexical items, with minimal syntactic or morphological specification of the conceptual content of the message, or the functional relations between lexical items.[21,5] Along with language development of the normal child, *language disorders* in children and adults represent an underexploited realm of evidence for the evolutionary stages of human communication. As neurolinguistics develops a better understanding of how linguistic information is processed by neural systems (cf. Ref. 13), more and more data bearing on the evolution of language systems should come to light.

At about 21 months, when the child finally does begin to acquire a communication system that qualifies as *language*, speech production abilities progress not merely as a function of the linguistic system found in the environment, but in accordance with a set of universal constraints. As described by Slobin,[46] the rate and order in which the child learns to produce syntactic and morphological contrasts depends on the degree to which the language of the environment is in conformity with certain strategies that all children bring to the language-learning task. Slobin argues convincingly that these cross-cultural features of language acquisition arise because of a built-in set of "operating principles" in terms of which the child confronts the native language.†† These innate principles exist as aspects of genetically specified functional systems that, whatever else they do, structure the order in which the child attends to the grammatical expression of conceptual distinctions. While some involve cognitive information-processing activities that are general in scope, others seem

---

†† An example is Slobin's *Operating Principle A:* Pay attention to the ends of words (Ref. 46, p. 191). This heuristic strategy is reflected in the following observed developmental universal: *Universal A1:* For any given semantic notion, grammatical realizations in the form of suffixes or postpositions will be acquired earlier than realizations in the form of prefixes or prepositions (Ref. 46, p. 192).

I. PRECONCEPTUAL LIMBIC STAGES

From about two weeks postnatally, the infant exhibits a fixed set of multimodal sign complexes that allow a receiver to infer a closed set of graded messages. The perception of specified internal or external conditions results in the automatic implementation of a set of differentiated responses produced by action schemata of subcortical components of the limbic system. From about 6 mo., higher level paleocortical limbic components integrate with the neocortical motor systems that control voluntary motor activity to allow the intentional production of existing limbic responses as a conscious means of communicating motivational states to those in the environment. The infant becomes more responsive to the affective and conative content of adult behavior and, from about 9 mo., prosodic features such as intonation contours become part of limbic signal complexes. Certain universal limbic 'words' (e.g., mam "food"), while retaining roughly the same phonetic form, make the transition from involuntary sign to intentional signal.

II. PRELANGUAGE COMMUNICATION SYSTEMS

A. Gestural Stages: Multimodal gesture complexes output by secondary neocortical movement schemata are systematically and willfully used in particular contexts to communicate the substantive and relational content of an open set of propositional conceptualizations. As various components of gesture complexes become non-representational and conventionalized, the transition is made from signal to symbol. Vocalizations have no special high status as against the other components of a given schema such as facial expression, visual orientation, body orientation, body configuration, rhythmic and patterned movements.

B. Phonological Labeling Stages (Naming Stage): Phonologically structured names act as labels on object-level and propositional concepts in such a way that hearing a given phonological form can lead to the retrieval of a concept from long-term memory. Perceptions that lead to the conceptual recognition or recall of a given generic or token concept may result in the overt vocal production of the child's label for that concept. Such articulatory output is organized by lateralized neocortical movement schemata based in Broca's convolution. Though apparently not used to communicate propositional messages, labeling vocalizations are used in social interactions to identify objects and as vocatives.

C. Propositional Focus Stages (Holophrastic Stage): Neocortically based communication systems insert phonologically structured labels into previously existing gesture complexes. One function of the verbal component of a gesture complex is to draw an addressee's attention to the information focus of a given propositional message. The conceptual content of one word utterances becomes increasingly differentiated over and above that of the gestural substratum. For the most part, both the messages the child encodes and those decoded from adult speech are still approached in terms of an immediate action strategy.

D. Propositional Focus-Assertion Stages (Pivot-Open Stage, Two-Word Stage) Two word utterances accompany gestural complexes, functioning to identify the information focus and also to make an assertion or predication regarding this focus. While relational concepts are still expressed almost exclusively by gestures, or by relying on the contextual situation, the child increasingly opts for the auditory-vocal communication channel. Vocalizations more and more begin to independently communicate substantive concepts that are part of the message.

E. Lexical Stages (Telegraphic Stage): The mean length of utterances goes up as the child outputs strings of lexical items capable of assuming a major burden in communicating the substantive content of messages including some relational notions. No syntactic structure exists, although word order may be fixed. Even though lexical strings remain subject to misinterpretation, the limbic and gestural systems are of diminished importance in the child's overall communicative repertoire.

III. LINGUISTIC STAGES

Lateralized neocortical systems produce sentences that communicate both relations and substantives by means of syntactic devices and grammatical morphemes used with lexical items. In general, the conceptual grasp of a given distinction precedes its linguistic expression. The mastery of linguistic forms is subject to certain universal constraints. Sentences become increasingly independent of accompanying gestures and situational context.

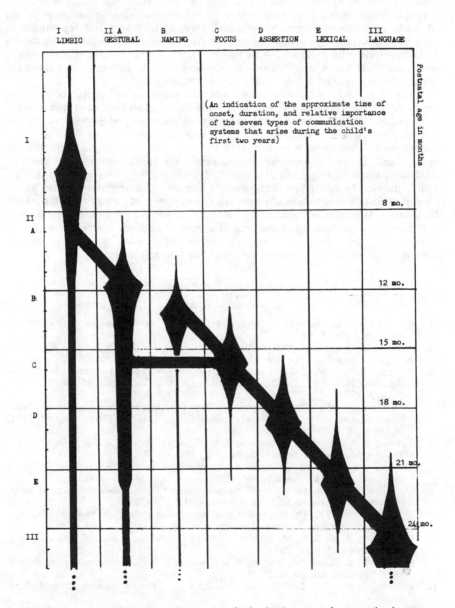

FIGURE 2. Outline of the maturational stages in the development of communication systems by the child.

quite specific to language learning. As for why they should exist, the reader will probably not be surprised when I suggest the possibility that some of Slobin's principles might reflect a repetition of the specialized information processing systems of some immature phylogenetic precursor. Over and above preconceptual limbic systems and prelanguage verbal systems, language learning itself may involve the use of skills acquired by some long-gone hominid species. It is possible that the way in which the child learns language systems can help us to understand more about the origin and structure of the languages our ancestors spoke.

In spite of the current bad reputation of the recapitulation hypothesis, there can be no doubt that repetition of ancestral traits exists as an important factor in the relationship of mutual causality existing between ontogeny and phylogeny. There is nothing about postnatal communication development that would exempt it from this general rule. Those who have proposed a *limbic* origin for language (implicit in Hockett and Ascher[26]) a preverbal *gestural* origin (e.g. Hewes,[24] Hewes, this volume), a referential *naming* origin (e.g., Geschwind[20]; Lancaster[33]), or a *syntactic* origin (cf. Hill[25]) may all be right! The acquisition of human communication systems by the child manifests a progression of stages reflecting systems of each of these types (and then some). Moreover, in the course of acquiring a language, the child discloses how it is possible to progress from one type of system to another. I hope this paper has demonstrated the validity of asking whether this progression occurs as an ontogenetic recapitulation of ontogenetic stages of our hominid ancestors.

REFERENCES

1. ANOUKHIN, P. K. 1964. Systemogenesis as a general regulator of brain development. Progr. Brai Res. **9:** 54–86.
2. AREY, L. B. 1970. Developmental Anatomy, 7th edit. Saunders. New York, N.Y.
3. BAER, K. E. VON. 1828. Über die Entwicklungsgeschicte der Tiere. Vol. **1:** 224.
4. BASTIAN, J. R. 1965. Primate signalling systems and human languages. *In* Primate Behavior: Field Studies of Monkeys and Apes. I. DeVore, Ed.: 585–606 Holt. New York, N.Y.
5. BERKO-GLEASON, J. 1974. Comprehension and production in Broca's aphasia. Paper presented to the Bay Area Neurolinguistics Group, Stanford Univ., Stanford, Calif. March 1974.
6. BRYANT, P. E., P. JONES, V. CLAXTON & G. M. PERKINS. 1972. Recognition of shapes across modalities by infants. Nature (Lond.) **240:** 303–304.
7. CARTER, A. L. 1974. The Development of Communication in the Sensorimotor Period: A case study. Unpubl. PhD. dissertation, University of California, Berkeley.
8. COWEY, A. & L. WEISKRANTZ. 1975. Demonstration of cross-modal matching in rhesus monkeys, Macaca mulatta. Neuropsychologia **13:** 117–120.
9. D'AQUILL, E. G. 1972. The biopsychological determinants of culture. McCaleb module in Anthropology **13:** 1–29. Addison-Wesley. Reading, Mass.
10. DAVENPORT, R. K. & C. M. ROGERS. 1970. Intermodal equivalence of stimuli in apes. Science **168** (3928): 279–280.
11. DAVENPORT, K. R., C. M. ROGERS, & I. A. RUSSELL. 1973. Cross-modal perception in apes. Neuropsychologia **11:** 21–28.
12. DEBEER, G. R. 1951. Embryos and Ancestors (rev. edit.) Clarendon Press. Oxford, England.
13. DINGWALL, W. O. & H. A. WHITAKER. 1974. Neurolinguistics. Ann. Rev. Anthropol. **3:** 323–356.
14. EIBL-EIBESFELDT, I. 1975. Ethology: The Biology of Behavior, 2nd edit. Holt. New York.
15. ETTLINGER, G. & C. B. BLAKEMORE. 1967. Cross-modal matching in the monkey. Neuropsychologia **5:** 147–154.

16. FERGUSON, C. A. &. D. I. SLOBIN, Eds. 1973. Studies of Child Language Development. Holt. New York, N.Y.
17. FOUTS, R. S. 1974. Language: Origins, definitions, and language. J. Human Evolution 3: (6): 475–482.
18. GARNDER, R. A. & B. T. GARDNER. 1969. Teaching sign language to a chimpanzee. Science 165: 664–672.
19. GEERTZ, C. 1962. The growth of culture and the evolution of mind. In Theories of Mind. J. Scher, Ed.: 475–482.
20. GESCHWIND, N. 1964. Development of the brain and evolution of language. Georgetown Monograph Series on Language and Linguistics 17. Georgetown Univ. Press. Washington, D.C.
21. GOODGLASS, H. & J. BERKO(-GLEASON). 1960. Agrammatism and inflectional morphology in English. Journal of Speech and Hearing Research 3: 257–67.
22. HAECKEL, E. 1874. Die Gastraea-Theorie, die phylogenetiche classification des Thierreichs und die Homologie der Keimblätter. Jenaische Zeit. Naturwissenschaft 9(402).
23. HEWES, G. W. 1973a. Pongid capacity for language acquisition: An evaluation of recent studies. In Symposia IVth Int. Congr. Primatology. Karger. Basel, Switzerland.
24. HEWES, G. W. 1973b. Primate communication and the gestural origin of language. Cur. Anthropol. 14(1–2): 5–12.
25. HILL, J. H. 1972. On the evolutionary foundations of language. Am. Anthropologist 74(3): 308–317.
26. HOCKETT, C. F. & R. ASCHER. 1964. The human revolution. Cur. Anthropol. 5(3): 135–168.
26a. HOLLAWAY, R. L. 1974. The casts of fossil hominid brains. Sci. Amer. 231(1): 106–115.
27. JURGENS, U. & D. PLOOG. 1970. Cerebral representation of vocalizations in the squirrel moneky. Exp. Brain Res. 10: 532–554.
28. KING, M-C. & A. C. WILSON. 1975. Evolution at two levels in humans and chimpanzees. Science 188 (4181): 107–116.
29. KOHNE, D. E., J. A. CHISCON & B. H. HOYER. 1972. Evolution of primate DNA: A summary. In Perspectives on Human Evolution. S. L. Washburn & P. Dolhinow, Eds.: 166–168. Holt. New York, N.Y.
30. LAMENDELLA, J. T. 1975. Maturational stages in the development of communication systems by the child. Paper presented to the California linguistics Association Conference, May.
31. LAMENDELLA, J. T. The Early Growth of Language and Cognition: A Neuropsychological Approach. In preparation.
32. LANCASTER, J. B. 1968. Primate communication systems and the emergence of human language. In Primates: Studies in Adaptation and Variability. P. C. Jay, Ed. Holt. New York, N.Y.
33. LANCASTER, J. B. 1975. Primate Behavior and the Emergence of Human Culture. Holt. New York.
34. LERNER, J. W. 1971. Children with Learning Disabilities. Houghton Mifflin. Boston.
35. LIEBERMAN, P. 1975. On the Origins of Language: an Introduction to the Evolution of Human Speech. Macmillan. New York, N.Y.
36. MÜLLER, F. 1864. Für Darwin. Leipzig.
37. NESTURKH, M. F. 1958. The Origins of Man (in Russian). USSR Academy of Science, Moscow.
38. NOBACK, C. R. & M. MOSCOWITZ. 1963. The primate nervous system: functional and structural aspects in phylogeny. In Evolutionary and Genetic Biology of Primates. J. Buettner-Janusch, Eds. Vol. 1. Academic Press. New York, N.Y.
39. NOBECK, C. R. & W. MONTAGNA, Eds. 1970. The Primate Brain. Appleton. New York.
40. PEIPER, A. 1963. Cerebral Function in Infancy and Childhood (in Trans.) Consultants Bureau. New York.
41. PREMACK, D. 1971. Language in chimpanzee? Science 172: 808–822.
42. REED, J. W. 1972. A Grammar of the Holophrastic Phrase. Unpubl. PhD. dissertation, Southern Illinois Univ. Carbondale, Ill.
43. ROBINSON, B. W. 1972. Anatomical and physiological contrasts between human and other

primate vocalizations. *In* Perspectives on Human Evolution. S. L. Washburn & P. Dolhinow, Eds. Holt. New York, N.Y.

44. SCHIEFELBUSH, R. L. & L. L. LLOYD, Eds. 1974. Language Perspectives: Acquisition, Retardation, and Intervention. University Park Press. Baltimore, Md.

45. SCOVEL, T. 1972. Does language ontogeny recapitulate language phylogeny? *In* Proc. XIth Int. Congr. Linguists Societa editrice il Mulino. Bologna, Italy.

46. SLOBIN, D. I. 1973. Cognitive prerequisites for the development of grammar. *In* Ferguson and Slobin, Eds.: 175–208.

47. WADDINGTON, C. H. 1957. Strategy of Genes. London.

48. WEIZKRANTZ, L. & A. COWEY 1975. Cross-modal matching in the Rhesus monkey using a single pair of stimuli. Neuropsychologia **13:** 257–261.

SOME COMPLEXITIES IN THE COMMUNICATION BEHAVIOR OF GULLS*

Colin Beer

Institute of Animal Behavior
Rutgers University
Newark, New Jersey 07102

This article returns to a theme that I tried to develop once before[1]: the place of preconceptions in the study of animal behavior. Here, however, I shall focus the discussion more narrowly, concentrating on aspects of my own work on the communication behavior of laughing gulls (*Larus atricilla*).

But first, some general preliminaries. According to Chomsky[2]:

> Each known animal communication system either consists of a fixed number of signals, each associated with a specific range of eliciting conditions or internal states, or a fixed number of "linguistic dimensions," each associated with a nonlinguistic dimension in the sense that selection of a point along one indicates a corresponding point along the other. In neither case is there any significant similarity to human language.

At least until recently, this statement was consistent with the published research on animal communication. Nevertheless the ideas that informed this research and governed its interpretation have changed as the facts have accumulated, and the changes have been in the direction of recognizing greater and greater complexity in animal communication.

If we begin with the work of the ethologists in the period when instinct was their ruling concept we find animal communication treated as though it consisted of sets of lock and key combinations. The signals—postural displays, vocalizations, and so forth—were described as social releasers because they were thought to engage, on a one-to-one basis, "innate releasing mechanisms" in the recipient individual, thus opening the way to the flow of accumulated instinctive excitation into pathways governing a specific social response, thereby causing its performance. Being parts of instinctive systems, the releasers and innate releasing mechanisms had to correspond to one another as species characteristics; hence little or no consideration was given to the possibility of individual differences or individual recognition in animal social interactions. Even in the study of imprinting the matter was viewed as the means by which an animal gets tuned to the features of its kind, rather than as the means by which one individual gets socially attached to other individuals.

Observation showed the social interactions of animals to be less predictable than they should be according to instinct theory. The instinct theory allowed for variation in intensity of response, as a consequence of variation in intensity or completeness of the releaser and variation in level of internal excitation. But the observations also showed variation in kind of response, and this was not according to theory, except for the special case of what was called "displacement activities." So the journal

*Research reported in this paper was supported by Grants GM 12774 and MH 16727 from the United States Public Health Service. The United States Fish and Wildlife Service granted permission for the work to be carried out in the Brigantine National Wildlife Refuge, and made available a building in the Refuge for the use of the project. The cooperation and hospitality of the Refuge Manager and his staff are also gratefully acknowledged. This is publication #226 from the Institute of Animal Behavior, Rutgers University.

articles became populated with flow diagrams representing sequence patterns and their relative frequencies by curving arrows of differing thicknesses. Instead of being obligatory, the sequence combinations were seen to be probabilistic, and the analysis of social interactions became statistical. We became used to having the behavior dispersed in transition matrices and described in terms of stochastic processes and quantities of information or uncertainty. To more simple-minded persons, like myself, however, it was not always clear what all the numbers meant or where they were leading. We seemed to be getting sophisticated quantitative descriptions of the "what" of animal communication, but not much understanding of the "how" and "why."

Some help came with the discovery of the significance of context in animal communication. W. John Smith[3,4] saw how context could make sense of some of the complexity in the interaction sequences of the tyrranid flycatchers he had been studying. Independently and at about the same time, the same point was perceived by G. H. Manley in a study of black-headed gulls (*Larus ridibundus*) in England, but his work remains unpublished. The point is that signals are not self-contained transmissions; they arrive in a setting or frame, which can include the state or status of the receiver, and this contextual accompaniment can affect what a signal signifies to the receiver. For instance, the song of a territory-holding male songbird signifies threat to another male but sexual invitation to an unmated female; and the call that sounds alarm when given by a laughing gull inside the gullery announces discovery of food when given outside the gullery. Smith used the semiotic scheme of Charles Morris[5] to develop his conception of communication, as qualified by context, into a comprehensive approach to social communication in general. What is encoded in a signal by its sender he called the "message" of the signal; this he considered to be an internal state conducive to some particular action or actions, the state probably being the same for all transmissions of the signal. The response to the signal he called the signal's "meaning," which is determined jointly by the signal itself and the context. Since the context can vary, so too can the meaning of a signal, even though the message of the signal may be the same in all contexts.

Manley's version of the role of context in animal communication was slightly different from Smith's. He wrote of "context interpretations" when referring to the variations in response to a signal that Smith had described as differences of meaning. But he also argued that there is "context determination" by which he meant that the same signal could be used to encode different information on different occasions by being assembled with different contextual accompaniments. The contextual accompaniments to which Manley paid most attention were the details of such features as posture and orientation with which a signal was given, and the other behavior performed by the signaler before and after the signal. Thus, according to Manley, the so-called "upright" posture of the black-headed gull expresses a conflict state between tendencies to attack and to flee when performed with head-on orientation in an agonistic context in which attacking and fleeing are the actions most likely to occur in sequence with it; but when performed in a sequence that goes "oblique-and-long-call, forward, upright, head-flagging," with parallel orientation to a female, it expresses the motivation of pair-formation. So, in Smith's terms, Manley would say that the same signal can be used to encode different messages by varying the context in which it is presented, whereas Smith would say that the same signal probably always encodes the same message irrespective of context.

The difference here could perhaps be resolved by removing some of the vagueness about what is to count as a signal. If signals were demarcated on the basis of message-carrying function, the isolated upright of the gulls could be considered as one kind of signal and the whole sequence "oblique-and-long-call, etc." as another and different kind of signal, for example. This would preserve uniqueness of signal-message couplings, as Smith would have it, at the same time as allowing Manley's point that morphologically the same bits of behavior can be put to different expressive uses. However, this move runs into the difficulty that we often have to make our judgments about what the distinct displays, vocalizations, and so forth are, on the basis of what strikes our eyes and ears as distinct and consistent patterns, long before we have any understanding of the message or meaning content that attaches to them. There is also the drawback that the possibility of compound signals, and hence compound messages, is, if not ruled out, at least made unlikely to occur to the thinking that would make the lines round signals coincide with the lines round messages. To one less committed to a belief in the uniqueness of signal-message coupling, the possibility of compound messages does not seem unlikely, indeed is given substance by example. To take perhaps the simplest, there are cases in which it appears that what is expressed by a certain signal in one context is negatively expressed in another context by presentation of the signal in concert with qualifying behavior. For instance, the upright of the gulls expresses hostility in agonistic contexts, and may carry the same message in a courtship context where, however, its being followed immediately by the posture called "facing-away" appears to negate the message of hostility. Constancy of message for a signal in different contexts is thus not incompatible with the idea of compound messages; indeed, as in this case of the upright of gulls, it may be necessary for some kinds of compound message. In other cases, however, there appears to be considerable semantic flexibility in the use of signals by animals, instances of which I shall come to shortly.

In the meantime I return to the theme of preconceptions. Why should the complexity of animal communication behavior, including the possibility of semantic flexibility of the kinds I think we now have to consider, have gone so long without getting attention from ethological investigators? Part of the answer is that research has to wait on advances in technology in some areas, and some of the complexity with which we now have to deal in animal communication studies has only recently become apparent through the use of machinery that was not available earlier. But at least equally important influences have been the bogey of anthropomorphism and Lloyd Morgan's solution to it, as well as the more general constraints imposed by deterministic and reductionistic ways of thinking on what is regarded as admissible as explanation in science. The prevalent conception of the animal is still the Cartesian one of a causally determined machine in which the human attributes of intention, reason, and so forth are excluded. With the invention of machines like guided missiles we can now talk comfortably about animals as goal-directed in their behavior; and computer technology has opened up reaches of analogical possibility the exploration of which has only begun. Nevertheless, I suspect that many of us still suffer a twinge of scientific conscience when we catch ourselves attributing intention or subjectivity to the actions of an animal.

To think of an animal as a machine is usually to see its behavior as emitted movement or elicited response. In either case, causal mechanisms will be assumed and sought, as they have been in physiology and ethology, and the conception of the animal as an active agent using action in the pursuit of ends will probably not even come to mind. The idea of use here entails the notion of intention, and this is too mentalistic a notion for most behaviorists, even though, as Charles Taylor[6] has pointed out, they sometimes unwittingly imply it in the forms of their descriptions. Hence the suggestion that an animal might use the same signal to express different messages, by varying what accompanies or occurs in sequence with it, has a heretical taint and so will not occur to the minds of the pure in science, or will be shunned as a threat to salvation in causality. Moreover, the suggestion has a suspicious resemblance to a description of language, and the serious will agree that anyone who thinks animals can talk is lost in a Disneyland of whimsies.

It seems to me, however, that neither causal nor stochastic conceptions have come to close grips with the complexity that now appears to exist in the communication behavior of some species. In the short run at least, other sets of preconceptions may be more likely to prove heuristic. In what follows I shall illustrate some of the forms of complexity with examples from the laughing gulls, and shall suggest that some analogies from language might be useful in making at least preliminary sense of them.

MARGINS OF MEANING

The vocal repertoire of a mature laughing gull contains about twelve distinguishable calls—distinguishable, that is, on the basis of how they sound to our ears and how they appear to function in the social behavior of the gulls. Some of the calls grade into one another; most of them are quite distinct from one another.

Sonagrams of these calls show them to be made up of notes of a small number of types, distinguishable on the basis of duration and "shape," some of which occur in more than one type of call. If one were to take scissors and cut out a note from sonagrams of the short-note part of a long-call, a gackering call, a copulation call, an alarm call, and a food-finding call, the similarity of form would be found to be such that reassigning the notes to the kinds of call from which they came would turn out to be a game of chance, especially if all the calls had been recorded from the same bird (FIGURE 1). This is one illustration of Manley's point that morphologically the same bits of behavior can be put to different expressive uses by being strung together in different ways.

It can be objected that sonagrams abstract only certain features of a sound, and hence that distinguishing features in the notes selected might have escaped representation in my guessing game. It is well known that there is often considerable disparity between how similar or different two voices sound to our ears and how similar or different the sonagrams of these voices look to our eyes. However, the sounds uttered by gulls appear to be much simpler in form than are the sounds uttered by people, and consequently the sonagrams show much cleaner patterns of frequency modulation, frequency spectra, and temporal partitioning. These together with amplitude modulation are the only obvious parameters for comparison.

I claim, then, that one can draw a distinction, in the vocal productions of laughing gulls, between the minimum units of sound used and the minimum units of sense, in something like the way in which one distinguishes between phonemes and morphemes in language. The minimum units of sound are notes, of which there are perhaps six recognisably distinct kinds. Some of these, such as the disyllabbic "ke-hah" note and the "head-toss note," are also minimum units of sense. That is to say, they serve as signals even when uttered by themselves, singly. But most notes contribute to communication by being strung together, either in repetitions of the same kind of note, as in the copulation call (FIGURE 1), or in combination of more than one kind of note, as in the long-call (See FIGURES 1, 3, 4, 5). Where different call types have the same note type the difference between the call types is in the number of repetitions of the note—for example alarm calls consist of only two or three short notes of the type that occurs in indefinitely long strings in gackering and the copulation call—or in temporal patterning of repetition or the amplitude contours, as distinguish the copulation call, in which notes of equal duration and loudness are repeated at a constant rate, from gackering, in which the notes vary in duration and loudness and are unevenly spaced.

The communication behavior of laughing gulls consists of more than calls, however; the birds also use posture and movement in displays, most of which accompany a call of one or more types. The distinction between units of form and units of sense can also be applied in analysis of the displays. For example, lifting the carpel joints of the wings away from the sides of the body is a component of most of the display types. It does not occur by itself—that is without being accompanied by any of the other component types—and would presumably be meaningless as a signal if it did. The head-toss movement, accompanied by the head-toss call, does occur by itself as a signal, as well as being the terminal component of most long-calls. The communication system of laughing gulls can thus be viewed as a limited number of basic vocal and postural elements, which can be assembled in combinations and sequences to form message carrying patterns or signals.

This hierarchical scheme should not be too hard to entertain. It is, after all, the sort of scheme we take to apply to motor patterning in general. On the bottom tier are the basic movement possibilities, consisting of all the flexions, extensions, adductions, abductions and so forth that the body has available to it. Then there are the combinations of these into functional patterns of movement, such as running, punching, kicking and so forth. Thirdly, there is the combining of movements into actions, such as attacking, fleeing, avoiding, searching, and so forth. And finally, if we go along with Miller, Galanter and Pribram,[7] there are the combinations of actions in the realizations of plans, as in building, courting, cooking, and so forth. I have not yet come to complexity in my gulls that cannot be accommodated within the bottom two levels of this scheme. The long-call may necessitate adding a third level to the communication hierarchy however, for it appears to serve for the composing of compound messages.

A FRAME FOR MEANING

The long-call of the laughing gull is what gives the bird its name. It consists of a string of notes, short and quick at the beginning, and then longer and slower, which it is not hard to hear as rather derisive laughter. The call is also the most complicated in the laughing gull repertoire, both in its structure and in its use.

Structurally the long-call can be divided into at least three sections, which I refer to as the short-note section, the long-note section and the head-toss section. The short-note section consists of between 2 and 15 brief and rapidly uttered notes; the long-note section consists of between 1 and 12 notes that are about twice as long as those of the short-note section and spaced farther apart; and the head-toss section, which may be omitted, consists of between 1 and 8 notes slightly shorter than the long-notes and variably spaced. Sonagrams of typical examples of laughing gull long-calls are illustrated in FIGURES 1, 3, 4, and 5. Strings of long-notes and head-toss notes can occur without preceding short-notes, and in isolation from one another. Frequently a string of long-notes precedes as well as follows the short-notes. And even further variation is added with the varieties of posture in which the notes are uttered.

Long-calls are given on the wing, while swimming or floating, and while sitting, but I shall more or less restrict my comments to what is perhaps the commonest case: a bird standing on the ground. Such a bird gives the short-note section in the full "oblique" posture: body more or less horizontal, neck fully extended at an angle of

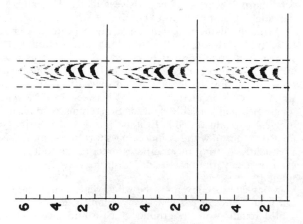

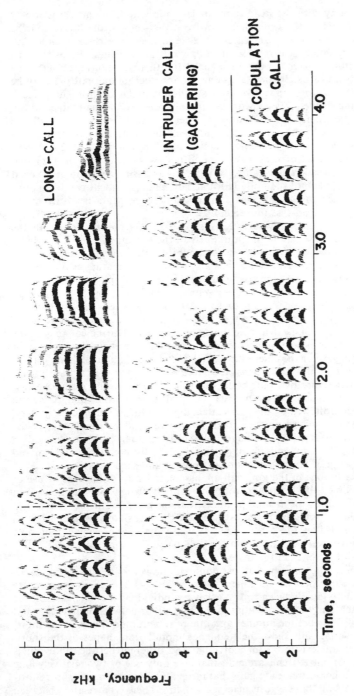

FIGURE 1. Sonagrams (wide band) of Laughing Gull calls, illustrating similarity of notes in three types of call.

about 45° to the body with the head more or less horizontal; the mouth is widely open, the carpel joints of the wings held out from the sides of the body, and the contour feathers are "sleeked"—pressed down close to the skin surface (FIGURE 2a). In some situations the body axis may be tilted upwards at the front, even as much as 45°, the head pointing upwards at the same angle. In other situations the bill may be pointed slightly downwards. In the long-note section the oblique posture may be maintained with little change, apart from some reduction in the extension of the neck and degree of lifting of the carpels. More commonly, the neck is maintained at full stretch and the angle changed so as to lower the head towards being in line with the body. Typically the head is lowered a little with each long-note. Consequently, long long-note sections end up with head, neck and body all in line (FIGURE 2b). Head-toss notes are accompanied by head-tosses: rapid backward flexing of the neck and upward jerking of the head, which can be so vigorous as to bring the top of the head into contact with the back of the body (FIGURE 2c). The movement can be kept to little more than a flick of the bill, however, and one even hears head-toss notes unaccompanied by any head-toss movement.

The range of situations in which the long-call occurs covers almost all the distinguishable classes of social interaction. Early in the breeding season it is used by males in much the same way in which male songbirds use song: to threaten other males that might challenge territorial claims and to advertise mating availability to unmated females. During courtship, the long-call is the first display in the sequence of displays referred to as the "greeting ceremony," which both birds of a pair go through side by side and more or less in unison. After laying, when the birds of a pair take turns at incubating the eggs, long-calls may be exchanged at nest relief. Incubating gulls will also long-call at neighbors and strangers. During hatching of the eggs, gulls sometimes look as though they are long-calling to their pipping eggs or newly hatched young. After the chicks have reached the age of about eight days post-hatching it is quite definitely the case that the parents direct long-calls at their chicks, particularly just after returning to the home site if the chicks are some distance away. A gull will also long-call at chicks other than its own, both at home and away, and this calling is usually followed by the gull's attacking the chicks. Outside the gullery, long-calls are given by roosting gulls to others flying overhead, by a gull that has just displaced another from its perch, by what usually turns out to be the dominant gull in scrambles over food, and by gulls flying in flocks. This list could be added to and refined by the drawing of finer distinctions of context and sequence.

Some of the variations in the long-call are associated with differences of use or context. For example, the long-calls with the longest strings of long-notes and marked holding of the low horizontal posture are those given during courtship by a bird landing beside its potential mate, especially if the birds have been apart for a spell. Incubating gulls, on the other hand, typically have abbreviated long-note sections and do not lower the head from the oblique position, at least if the call is being given to a bird other than the mate.

Other variation in the calls cuts across contexts, however. If one spends a few hours a day in the same part of the gullery for several days one learns to recognize some of the gulls individually by ear, most easily by individual characteristics of the long-calls. The pitch and timbre qualities of the calls differ between individuals, but even more distinguishing are the number and rate of repetition of notes in the short-note section. The sonagrams show the frequency modulation shapes of the short-notes also to be characteristic for an individual and different between individuals (FIGURES 3 and 4). At one extreme are gulls that give only one or two relatively long short-notes; at the other extreme are gulls that rattle off fifteen or so very short short-notes in rapid succession that suggests machine-gun fire. There is correlation between

FIGURE 2. Long-call postures of the Laughing Gull: *a*. Full oblique, in which short notes are given; *b*. Low horizontal posture at the end of a long long-note section; and *c*. Head-toss.

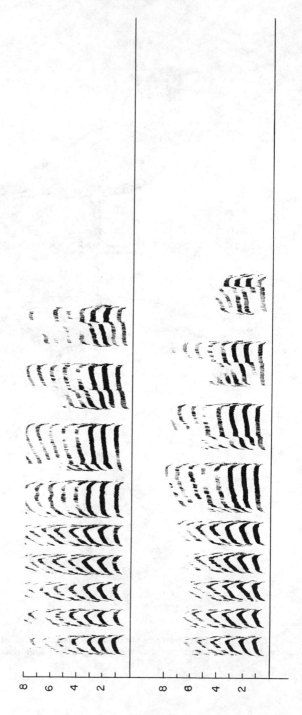

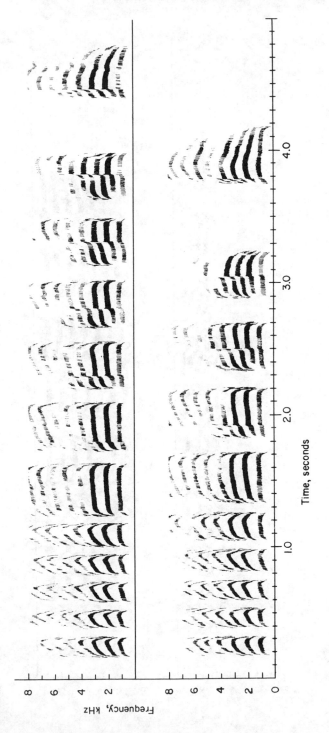

FIGURE 3. Sonagrams (wide band) of four long-calls by the same gull.

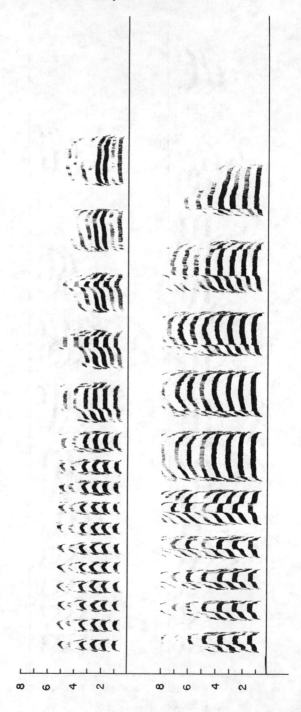

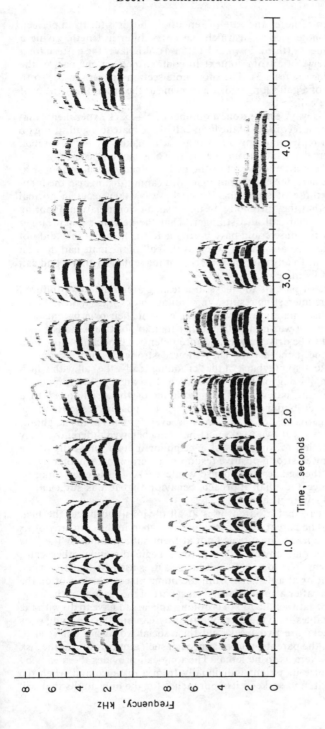

FIGURE 4. Sonagrams (wide band) of long-calls by four different gulls.

number of notes, duration of note, and rate of repetition, but it is far from perfect. Some gulls have a short-note section in which the notes differ in length, giving a broken rhythm to the sequence (third down in FIGURE 4). Whatever the pattern for a particular gull it varies very little from context to context or from one part of the breeding season to another (FIGURE 3). The short-note section appears to be, so to speak, the signature tune of a gull's long-call, announcing at the outset the identity of the individual making the call.

Do the gulls hear it this way? I have done a number of playback experiments that show that they do. Playing a recording of the long-call of the mate to a gull sitting on its nest elicited calling in reply, standing up as though to make way for nest relief, and, in some cases, even departure from the nest. To a similar recording of a neighbor gull, or a gull from a remote part of the gullery, there was no response at all.[8] The lack of response here does not mean that gulls cannot distinguish the long-calls of neighbors from those of strangers. From the ways they react in normal circumstances it appears that they probably do make such discrimination, ignoring the neighbor when they would call at a stranger. That the neighbor and stranger playback calls elicited no response could have been due to the fact that they did not occur in a context that required any action, whereas the call of the mate had the nest relief context waiting for it. In any case the experiment made it clear that a gull can recognize the long-call of its mate.

Playback of long-calls of parents to chicks in a testing arena indoors produced what to me were even more interesting results. Very young chicks—less than 48 hours post-hatching—showed discrimination between long-calls of their own parents and long-calls of a neighbor, but it was in negative rather than in positive response: they tended to be silenced and to be driven away and into defensive crouching more by a neighbor's call than by the parent's call. They showed strong positive response—approach, vocalization, etc.—to playback of the "crooning" call—the call with which parents accompany their offering of food to their chicks—and no discrimination between the crooning of the parent and the crooning of the neighbor.[8,9] In a recording containing both crooning calls and long-calls, the positive response to the crooning overrode the negative response to long-calls, even for calls of the neighbor. Chicks tested in the same ways at two weeks post-hatching behaved differently. They still showed negative reaction to long-calls of a neighbor, but to long-calls of the parent they almost all showed strong positive response. To crooning, whether by the parent or by a neighbor, they made no response whatever. At this age crooning by itself can no longer induce the filial approach behavior that it was sufficient to command when the chicks were nestlings.

Crooning is the only call that a parent uses at all obviously to direct the filial behavior of its nestlings. The parent does give long-calls when in the company of its nestlings, but these calls appear to be directed not at them but at adults. By the time the chicks are two weeks old, however, the parents begin directing other calls, including long-calls at them. The long-call, as I have said, is used particularly when the chicks are out of sight or at a distance from the home place, which is often the case when a parent returns after a spell away. At least part of the reason for the long-call's taking over part of what was the job of crooning appears to have to do with the fact that the long-call enables individual recognition by ear but the crooning does not. By the time the chicks are two weeks old their social world has enlarged to include adults other than the parents, and to approach such adults is to run the risk of abuse that can be so severe as to be lethal. The long-call provides the means by which a chick can recognize its parent individually from a distance and when the parent may be out of sight, and so keep its approaches for the only adults that will treat it with parental care.

But a laughing gull chick, two weeks old and more, does not approach in response to every long-call by one of its parents. This fact was brought home to me unexpectedly in a series of tests in which response to playback of the parent's long-call was very strongly positive for all the chicks except two, and these two were in such marked contrast to the rest that I looked for something special in the circumstances of their testing. They turned out to be the only ones for which I had used recordings made when they were nestlings, the other chicks having been tested with recordings made on the day of testing or the day before. I then deliberately tested two-week-old chicks with recordings of their parents' long-calls made when they were nestlings and made at the time of testing. These chicks also showed little or no response to the earlier calls, but responded strongly and positively to the later calls. Nevertheless there were indications that the chicks recognized the earlier as those of their parents, for they did not show the negative response to them that they showed to some of the long-calls of neighbors that were played to them. There are several possible explanations for the discrimination between the earlier and later calls, but the one that I favored was that a parent gull uses a version of the long-call when addressing its chicks that is different from the version or versions it uses when addressing adults. As I have already mentioned, a gull with nestlings appears not to direct long-calls towards them, but a gull with two-week-old chicks does direct some of its long-calls at its chicks, the rest being directed at adults or foreign chicks. In selecting recordings to use in the tests of older chicks I had probably unwittingly chosen mostly calls directed at chicks, for these are more likely to be clear of interference from other calls being uttered at the same time than are calls directed at adults. In any case, I ran another series of tests in which I compared the responses of older chicks to playback of long-calls that the parents had directed at them in the field, and to playback of long-calls that the parents had directed at adults, both sets of recordings having been made at the time of testing. Again the chicks showed discrimination: their responses to the calls that had been directed at them were stronger than their responses to the calls that had not.[9]

How did these chicks know which call was which? My initial supposition was that the message-carrying part of the long-call is in its last two sections, the short-note section being merely the individually identifying introduction. I failed to find any consistent difference between the two classes of call in the long-note and head-toss note sections, however. Contrary to my expectations, the differentiating characteristic turned up in the amplitude modulation of the short-note section; in the chick-directed calls the first one or two notes were louder than those following, whereas in the adult directed calls the first one or two notes were softer than those following, or there was a steady increase in loudness from note to note in the string (FIGURE 5). I had difficulty believing in this result until I returned to the gullery and listened for the difference. Then it stood out so distinctly that I marveled at how blind perception can be.

I am far from a full understanding of how the laughing gulls use their long-calls. Already, however, two points are clear. Firstly, utterance of a long-call conveys more than one kind of information: the caller identifies itself and it transmits a message which is of the nature of a warning, a command, an invitation or an advertisement. Secondly this message can be varied on different occasions of use of the long-call, through variation of features internal to the call. The identification can thus be coupled with a variety of other information; in this sense the long-call can be considered as conveying compound messages. Again, however, we have the question of what should count as a distinct signal or display; in this case should it be the utterance form that we refer to as the long-call or the distinguishable message-carrying versions of it. At present we are unable to say how many different message carrying versions there are or what distinguishes them. In any case, it is convenient, especially for comparative purposes, to go on speaking of the long-call as the display entity. But from the evidence of multiplicity in the ways in which it is used, its semantic versatility, I think it is more accurate to think of it as something like a syntactic form or framework, rather than as a display in the sense that it is fixed in either of the ways described by Chomsky in the statement I quoted at the beginning.

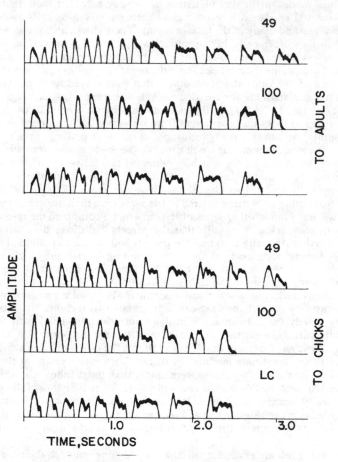

FIGURE 5. Amplitude-time sonagrams (wide band) of long-calls of three gulls, illustrating the difference between calls to adults (above) and calls to chicks (below).

It is very likely that variation of external features, in addition to variation of internal features, contributes to the variety of message that can be encoded in long-calls or for which long-calls can be used to encode. This raises the possibility of compound messages of more complex types than those that can be contained within the long-call; but an even more promising display for realizing this possibility is facing-away.

FIGURE 6. "White" facing-away.

MEANING IN MASKING

Facing-away, or "head-flagging" as it was originally called,[10] is a display, or component of displays, shown by gulls, in which the bird turns its head to look in the direction away from the other towards which it is displaying. In so doing it removes its bill, eyes and, in those species possessing one, the mask or hood from the view of the other bird. It is most typically performed in the posture known as the upright in which the neck is extended vertically upwards, with the head more or less horizontal and the carpel joints lifted; but, at least in the laughing gull, facing-away can also be superimposed on most of the other display postures as well. I shall restrict my comments to facing-away in the upright. In the laughing gull this display occurs in two forms. In one the dark hood is completely hidden from behind, the margin of the hood being pulled into a more or less vertical line and the feathers behind it being raised to form a shielding ruff (FIGURE 6). In the other form, part of the hood is still visible from behind, the margin being kept more or less horizontal and the feathers being flattened so that even the white tufts just above and below the eyes are kept on show (FIGURE 7). There are intermediates between these two extremes, and a bird can

FIGURE 7. "Black" facing-away.

shift from one to the other during performance of the display; but the transitions are usually rapid, occupying considerably less time than is spent holding in either of the contrasting forms, which I refer to as "white" facing-away and "black" facing-away.

Three alternative functions have been suggested for facing-away in gulls: 1. appeasement of a hostile opponent; 2. allaying of fear in a mate or potential mate; and 3. "cut-off" of visual stimulation liable to cause the displaying bird to attack or flee, in situations in which either action would be against the displayer's interests.[11] The first two suggestions assume that the frontal aspect of the head presents a provoking or threatening appearance, the turning away of which reduces the probability of either attacking or fleeing by the other bird. Cut-off is supposed to work in the same way for the displaying bird.

My first guess at why there should be two forms of facing-away in laughing gulls was that the black form provides a way of effecting cut-off at the same time as keeping part of the hood visible to convey threat, while the white form provides cut-off and the canceling of threat. From this it should follow that black facing-away belongs in agonistic contexts—those in which the aim is to drive the other bird away—and that white facing-away belongs in contexts in which the aim is to keep the other bird from leaving, as in courtship. Laughing gulls show facing-away in both agonistic and courtship contexts, so, as a first test of my interpretation, I compared numbers of occurrences of the two kinds of facing-away in these two kinds of situation. The agonistic encounters were according to expectation: most of the occurrences of facing-away were of the black sort. Courtship encounters did not conform, however: occurrences of facing-away were about equally divided between the two forms. I then looked at the behavior of the displaying bird immediately after facing-away. Again the two contexts showed differences that were different from expectation. In the agonistic sequences, a bird facing-away in the black form was likely either to attack or to flee immediately afterwards. The few showing the white form in this situation, with some exceptions that I shall come to directly, fled when attacked but did not themselves attack, the hostility coming from birds to which the displaying bird faced-away while approaching its nest. The evidence from agonistic encounters suggests that in this context a gull uses black facing-away for cut-off combined with threat, and white facing away as appeasement. In courtship sequences attack was infrequent; when it did occur following facing-away it was most often from the white form (in contrast to what was the case in the agonistic encounters). Black facing-away was most often transitional to leaving, usually by flight. After white facing-away the two birds of a courting pair usually went on performing courtship behavior or stood quietly side by side preening. The evidence from the courtship encounters suggests that in this context both forms of the display signify lack of hostility, black facing-away indicating a tendency to leave, thus warning the other bird not to press its suit too vigorously, and white facing-away indicating that the bird will stay and is strongly attracted to the other. In the incubation period facing-away occurs at nest-relief, when abbreviated versions of the courtship ritual are often performed. Then the relieving bird, the one that will stay, typically does white facing-away, and the relieved bird typically does black facing-away just before flying. Thus the two birds continue with a difference the pattern of the courtship period.

Courting gulls frequently become involved agonistically with a third. A common sequence in this mixed situation consists of one of the courting birds, usually the male, launching an attack on the outsider and facing-away to its partner as it does so. Invariably this facing-away is in the white form, and is thus apparently an exception to the rule that white facing-away in agonistic encounters signifies lack of hostility. But in this situation the display is not directed at the opponent, but at the courtship partner, and appears to have the function of indicating to the partner that the manifest hostility is directed elsewhere. As in the pure agonistic situation, therefore, the white facing-away signifies lack of hostility to the bird towards which it is directed; but the total motivation of the displaying bird is obviously different in the two situations, being low in attack tendency in the one case and overtly expressing attack tendency in the other.

There are "family resemblances" between the uses of facing-away in the different contexts in which the display occurs in the social behavior of laughing gulls, but it does not appear to be the case that the underlying motivational states can be the same across all these contexts. But if the same display can express different motivational states in different contexts is there not the possibility that the bird displayed to will be confused or misled, particularly if the contexts grade into one another or overlap, as do agonistic and courtship contexts? Mistakes do occur in the social interactions of laughing gulls, but their probability is apparently kept low by the fact that when facing-away occurs in courtship it is very often in sequence with specific other displays, the order of which is quite stereotyped. This is the sequence I referred to earlier as the greeting ceremony. Such regular sequential patterning is lacking in the occurrences of facing-away in agonistic interactions. As Manley observed, the context that can qualify the meaning of a display can include the other displays in sequence with which it occurs and so provides the displayer with a way of using the same display to express different messages. And even when the message of the display might be the same across contexts, as in the use of white facing-away in the pure and mixed agonistic situations, the accompanying behavior makes it possible for the display to be used to express different compound messages. Again, of course, one could argue about where to draw distinctions between functional categories in the communication system, and what the most appropriate terms for these categories might be. But however we divide and describe in this matter of the communication behavior of gulls I think we have to do with a complexity that the instinctivist, behaviorist or stochastic conceptions of animal behavior overlook and do not provide for, and which does not conform to either of the systems described in the quotation from Chomsky.

CONCLUSION

I suspect that the relevance of my gull studies to the theme of this conference, the origins and evolution of language, is, if anything, only of a rather negative, indirect and unspecific sort. Perhaps the most general point that my work illustrates is that the more that animal communications behavior is studied the more complex it tends to turn out to be. So when animal work is used to make comparative points in discussions of language I should advise being tentative about it, lest tomorrow's discoveries make today's conclusions look silly.

In part, the recognition of the greater complexity has resulted from, and in turn caused, changes in preconceived views about animal communication, including the models in terms of which animal communication has been thought about. At least in my own case, linguistic analogies have, to some extent, taken the places previously occupied by causal and statistical models. At least for the time being I do not think, as I have no doubt some others do, that this is a retrograde step. On the contrary, the study of language is so far ahead of the study of animal communication that it should not be surprising if linguistics has more to offer the animal studies than vice versa. Not that the analogies are very tight. I realize that when I talk of the syntax of gull communication I have to be understood as using the word in a sense that excludes much of what it connotes in its linguistic context. We cannot, for example, parse a sequence of gull signals in any precise sense, at least not yet. But I doubt whether I should be looking in that direction at all if I had kept to the views seen through the lenses of social releasers and transition probabilities.

REFERENCES

1. BEER, C. G. 1971. Diversity in the study of the development of social behavior. *In* The Biopsychology of Development. E. Tobach, L. R. Aronson & E. Shaw, Eds. Academic Press. New York, New York.
2. CHOMSKY, N. 1966. Cartesian Linguistics. Harper. New York, New York.
3. SMITH, W. J. 1963. Vocal communication of information in birds. Amer. Natur. **97:** 117–125.
4. SMITH, W. J. 1968. Message-meaning analysis. *In* Animal Communication. T. A. Sebeok, Ed. Indiana University Press. Bloomington, Indiana.
5. MORRIS, C. W. 1938. Foundations of the theory of signs. Encyclopedia of Unified Science. Vol. 1, No. 2. University of Chicago Press. Chicago, Illinois.
6. TAYLOR, C. 1964. The Explanation of Behaviour. Humanities Press. New York, New York.
7. MILLER, G. A., E. GALANTER & K. H. PRIBRAM. 1960. Plans and the Structure of Behavior. Holt. New York, New York.
8. BEER, C. G. 1970. On the responses of laughing gull chicks to the calls of adults. II. Age changes and responses to different types of call. Animal Behav. **18:** 661–677.
9. BEER, C. G. 1973. A view of birds. *In* Minnesota Symposia on Child Psychology. A. Pick, Ed. Vol. **7:** 47–86. University of Minnesota Press. Minneapolis, Minnesota.
10. NOBLE, G. K. & M. WURM. 1943. The social behavior of the laughing gull. Ann. N.Y. Acad. Sci. **45:** 179–220.
11. CHANCE, M. R. A. 1962. An interpretation of some agonistic postures: the role of "cut-off" acts and postures. Symp. Zool. Soc. Lond. **8:** 71–89.

DISCUSSION PAPER: THE EVOLUTION OF DISTANCE COMMUNICATION IN BEES

Howard M. Reid*

Department of Psychology
University of Maine
Orono, Maine 04473

At a conference dealing with the origins and evolution of language and speech, a researcher might be asked which characteristics would be desirable in a perfect subject for study. Two properties would certainly be included in his answer. First, use of an extensive communication system that is comparatively easy to study, and second, variation in the complexity of this language both across and within species. The language of bees fits these attributes quite well, for it is probably the most extensive communication system in the animal kingdom after that of man[1] and a variety of racial and across species "dialects" have been reported.[2,3]

One form of communication in honey bees (*Apis mellifera*) involves the performance of a series of "dances," the type and rate of which are related to the distance between the hive and the food source (reviewed in Refs. 4, 5). The "tail-wagging" dance has been the most extensively studied of these communication dances. Frisch and Krathy[6] have reported equations for the relationship between the rate of the "tail-wagging" dance and the distance flown from the food source to the hive. The present paper presents an alternative mathematical description, a description of the same general type that has also been found to fit human psychophysical data. FIGURE 1 shows three graphs of the data from two of the most extensive studies that have related distance flown and resulting dance tempo (reviewed in Frisch[3]). The top graph is a linear-linear plot of these data. Each curve is of a similar concave downward form. The middle graph is a log-log plot of the same data. Except for one deviant point (see arrow), the data fall along straight lines. The data, therefore, fit a power function relationship of the form $R = kD^n$, where R = the sensation magnitude (dance rate), D = the stimulus magnitude (distance to feeding station), and k and n are constants.[7] In the field of psychophysics, this equation is known as Stevens' Power Law, which states that "equal stimulus ratios produce equal subjective ratios" (Ref. 7, p. 16). The data do not fit a Weber-Fechner Log Relationship, the other major psychophysical function that relates stimulus intensity and perception (note curves in the linear-log plot of the data, bottom graph).

Similar but less extensive data are available for several other species of bees.[2] When these data and additional data comparing the races of *Apis mellifera* are plotted on linear-linear coordinates, concave downward curves are again found (FIGURE 2, top graph, species other than *Apis mellifera*; FIGURE 3, top graph, races of *Apis mellifera*). When the same data are plotted on log-log coordinates, straight lines are obtained except for most points corresponding to flights of under 100 meters (see arrows; FIGURE 2, bottom graph, species other than *Apis mellifera;* FIGURE 3, bottom graph, races of *Apis mellifera*). Simple power functions, therefore, fit the body of the data well. Thus, for each species of bee examined, a change of a specific fraction of the distance from the food source to the hive results in a constant fractional change in the "tail-wagging" dance speed. It should be noted, further, that the lines in FIGURE 1, middle graph, FIGURE 2, bottom graph, and FIGURE 3, bottom graph, are approxi-

*Present address: The Jackson Laboratory, Bar Harbor, Maine 04609.

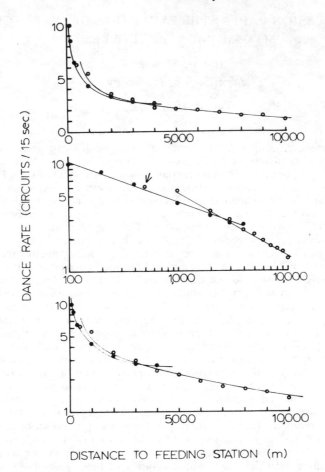

FIGURE 1. Tail-wagging dance rate as a function of distance between the hive and a food source in *Apis mellifera carnica*. Open and closed circles represent two studies. Top graph: data plotted on linear-linear coordinates (from Ref. 3, somewhat simplified). Middle graph: same data plotted on log-log coordinates. Bottom graph: same data plotted on linear-log coordinates.

mately parallel. This consistancy means that all of the races and species of bee studied have approximately the same power function relating distance flown to dance speed; it is primarily the constant, k, in the equation $R = kD^n$ that has changed. More specifically, those species of bee with the smallest constants, k, (those which dance the slowest for a particular flight distance) tend to be physically the smallest, whereas those species of bee with the largest constants, k, tend to be physically the largest and have the greatest maximum flight ranges (see also Frisch[3]).

The view expressed thus far does not, of course, explain the occurrence of the deviant points (see arrows; FIGURE 2, bottom graph and FIGURE 3, bottom graph) that correspond to flights of less than 100 meters. There appear to be at least two possible explanations. First, the discrepancies may be due to an emphasis upon the wrong variable. Frisch and Jander[8] have reported that it is the duration of the straight run segment of the "tail-wagging" dance, not the overall rate of the dance, that is the best index of distance. Although both of these measures are highly correlated, a graph of only the duration of the straight run segment of the "tail-wagging" dance might fit a power function over the entire range measured. Wenner,[9] however, has published data that refute such an interpretation. FIGURE 4, top graph, is a linear-linear plot of the data from this study relating flight distance to the overall dance rate. A concave downward curve is found, similar to those seen previously. FIGURE 4, bottom graph, is a log-log plot of the same data. As before, the data fall along a straight line except for points corresponding to flights of less than 100 meters (see arrows). FIGURE 5, top graph, and FIGURE 6, top graph, are linear-linear plots of two variables that have been suggested as better indices of distance than the overall dance rate; the duration of only the straight-run segment of the "tail-wagging" dance,

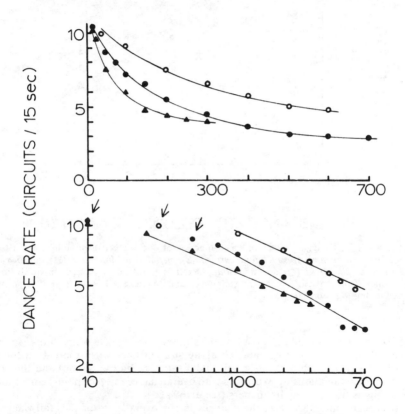

DISTANCE TO FEEDING STATION (m)

FIGURE 2. Tail-wagging dance rate as a function of distance between the hive and a food source for three species: *Apis florea* (▲), *Apis indica* (●) and *Apis dorsata* (○). Top graph: data plotted on linear-linear coordinates (from Frisch,[3] somewhat simplified, and Michener[5]), Bottom graph: same data plotted on log-log coordinates.

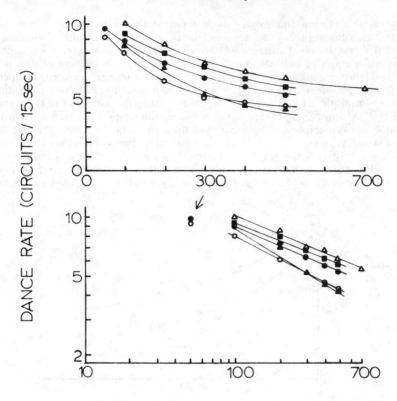

DISTANCE TO FEEDING STATION (m)

FIGURE 3. Tail-wagging dance rate as a function of distance between the hive and a food source for seven races of *Apis mellifera: carnica* (△), *mellifera* and *intermissa* (■), *ligustica* and *caucasica* (●), *lamarcki* (O) and *adansonii* (▲). Top graph: data plotted on linear-linear coordinates (from Frisch,[3] somewhat simplified, and Michener.[5] Bottom graph: same data plotted on log-log coordinates.

and the number of sound pulses during the straight-run segment of the "tail-wagging" dance. Both of these sets of data fall along straight lines when plotted on log-log coordinates (FIGURE 5, bottom graph and FIGURE 6, bottom graph) and thus fit a power function relationship except, as with overall dance rate, for points corresponding to flights of less than 100 meters (see arrows).

It appears, therefore, that the changes in the overall rate of the "tail-wagging" dance are an accurate indicator of the ability of bees to communicate distance information over the entire range for which the "tail-wagging" dance is employed. Consequently, overall "tail-wagging" dance rates that result in a region of little or no slope when graphed on log-log coordinates indicate informationally equivalent messages (see arrows; FIGURE 2, bottom graph, FIGURE 3, bottom graph, and FIGURE 4, bottom graph). It appears, therefore, that the "tail-wagging" dance does not indicate distances below 60–70 meters in any of the races of *Apis mellifera* or in *Apis dorsata*, or below 20–30 meters in *Apis indica* or *Apis florea*, even though it is employed for communication concerning shorter flight distances.

Lindauer[2] presents data that suggest a progression in the communication abilities of bees, with *Apis florea* the most primitive, then *Apis dorsata*, and finally *Apis indica* and *Apis mellifera*. From the previous discussion, however, it is *Apis florea* rather than one of the advanced species that appears to have the most accurate distance communication system. In part, this conclusion is a consequence of the limited range of distances examined. *Apis florea* is physically a small bee and has a much shorter maximum flight range than *Apis dorsata* or *Apis mellifera*. It is perhaps not surprising, therefore, that *Apis florea* may be more accurately able to communicate information about food located relatively close to the hive than more advanced but also wider-ranging species. This implies a trade-off between precision and generality which could have been achieved in only a limited number of ways without extensive modification of the entire communication system.

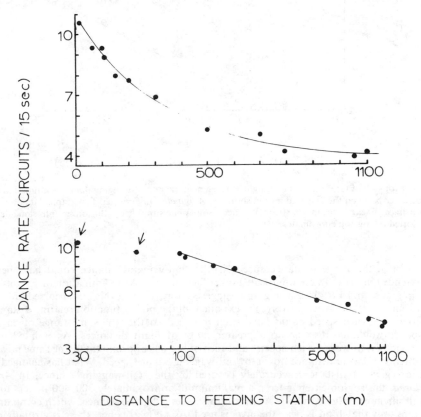

DISTANCE TO FEEDING STATION (m)

FIGURE 4. Tail-wagging dance rate as a function of distance between the hive and a food source in *Apis mellifera ligustica*. Top graph: data plotted on linear-linear coordinates (from Wenner,[9] somewhat simplified). Bottom graph: same data plotted on log-log coordinates.

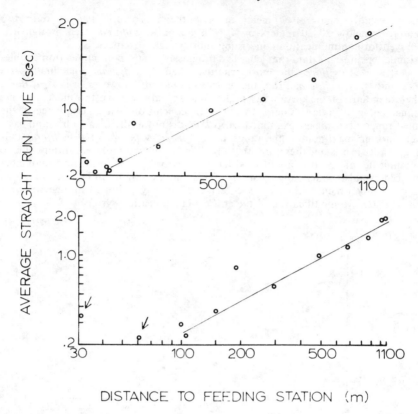

FIGURE 5. Duration of the straight-run segment of the tail-wagging dance as a function of distance between the hive and a food source in *Apis mellifera ligustica.* Top graph: data plotted on linear-linear coordinates (from Wenner,[9] somewhat simplified). Bottom graph: same data plotted on log-log coordinates.

First, the range of dance speeds in the "tail-wagging" dance could have been extended in order to communicate longer flight ranges. An examination of FIGURE 1, top graph, and FIGURE 2, top graph, suggests, however, that this has occurred only to a limited extent. Alternatively, the exponent of the power function relating distance flown to dance speed could have been modified so that the same range of dance speeds would correspond to a greater range of flight distances. As pointed out previously, however, each species and race of bee has approximately the same power function relating distance flown to "tail-wagging" dance speed. What has changed is the region of distances accurately covered by the "tail-wagging" dance. In *Apis florea*, this region extends from a maximum of approximately 300–400 meters to a minimum of only 20 meters. At shorter distances a "round" dance, which communicates only that food is near the hive, is used. As a consequence, there is virtually no region without effective distance information. In longer ranging species, such as *Apis dorsata* or *Apis mellifera*, the effective communication region of the "tail-wagging" dance has been shifted outward to cover a region extending to at least 4000 meters under normal conditions. A consequence of this shift, however, is poor distance information from the "tail-wagging" dance for distances of less than 100 meters (FIGURE 7). With the limitations previously stated, there are only two possibilities for improving distance communication in this region; extend the use of the "round" dance at the cost of sacrificing the directional information of the "tail-wagging" dance or "inventing" a new word to expand the range of the language. *Apis dorsata* does not show either option, and consequently is hypothesized to have an extensive region below approximately 100 meters with only limited distance information. In *Apis mellifera*, however, the use of the "round" dance has been extended (FIGURE 8). Further, in precisely that region where there is hypothesized to be limited distance information in the language of *Apis dorsata,* a new transitional dance form, the "sickle" or other closely related type, is found in *Apis mellifera* (FIGURE 8). A human

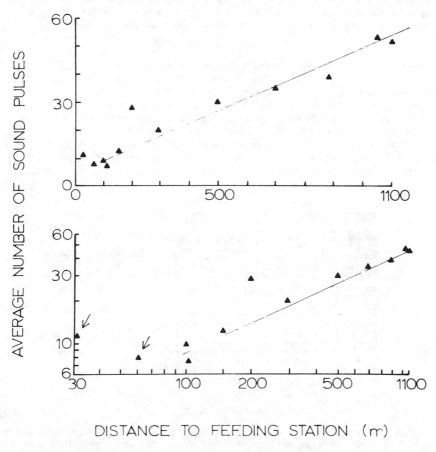

DISTANCE TO FEEDING STATION (m)

FIGURE 6. Number of sound pulses during the straight-run segment of the tail-wagging dance as a function of distance between the hive and a food source in *Apis mellifera ligustica*. Top graph: data plotted on linear-linear coordinates (from Wenner,[9] somewhat simplifed). Bottom graph, same data plotted on log-log coordinates.

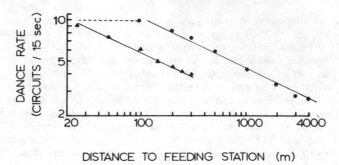

FIGURE 7. Comparison between tail-wagging dance rates as a function of distance between the hive and a food source in *Apis florea* (▲) and *Apis mellifera carnica* (●). Dashed line represents the approximate region for which it is hypothesized that no distance information could be communicated by the tail-wagging dance in *Apis mellifera carnica*.

observer can obtain both distance and direction information from this transition region. What is not at present clear, however, is whether bees are communicating distance information to each other in this region. If they are, though, it would be a clear instance of the natural origin of a new communication form.

It is obvious from the previous discussion that certain aspects of the language of bees have remained relatively fixed across species, while others have varied considerably. Thus, the power to which Stevens' Power Function must be raised (slope of the line on log-log coordinates) to fit the "tail-wagging" dance data has remained remarkably constant considering the great procedural differences between studies.

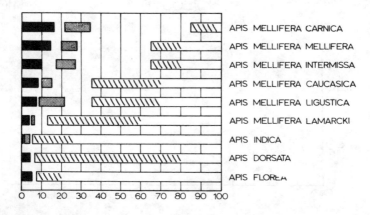

FIGURE 8. Comparison between the type of dance as a function of distance between the hive and a food source in four species of *Apis* including six races of *Apis mellifera*. Black rectangles represent the region of the round dance, gray rectangles represent the region of the sickle or closely related dance, and white rectangles represent the region of the tail-wagging dance. Areas between rectangles represent transition dance forms (from Frisch,[3] and Michener[5]). Slash lines in white rectangles indicate the approximate region of the tail-wagging dance for which it is hypothesized that no distance information is communicated.

Furthermore, there is at least as much variability within species or races as between them (compare FIGURE 1, middle graph; FIGURE 2, bottom graph; and FIGURE 3, bottom graph), which points away from there being a general evolutionary trend. One study[3] suggests, however, that additional research on the long distance commucation of bees may be of value for quite different reasons. FIGURE 9, top graph, is a linear-linear plot of the data from this study relating flight distance to overall dance rate. A concave downward curve is found, similar to that seen previously. When plotted on log-log coordinates, however (FIGURE 9, bottom graph), different segments of the data appear to have different slopes. If one compares these slopes with

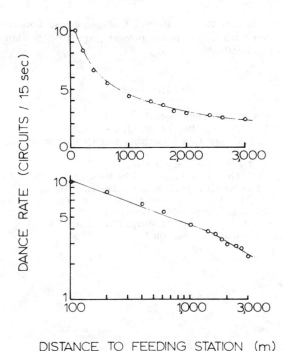

DISTANCE TO FEEDING STATION (m)

FIGURE 9. Tail-wagging dance rate as a function of distance between the hive and a food source in *Apis mellifera carnica*. Top graph: data plotted on linear-linear coordinates (from Frisch,[3] somewhat simplified). Bottom graph: same data plotted on log-log coordinates. See text for further explanation.

slopes from different studies but using the same type of bee, *Apis mellifera carnica*, the similarity is apparent (FIGURE 1, middle graph). These data suggest, therefore, that the language of bees is more dynamic than might otherwise have been expected in that certain aspects of the communication system may change to fit fluctuating environmental conditions.

In conclusion, Stevens' Power Law was found to fit the data relating the "tail-wagging" dance rate to the distance flown between a food source and the hive in several species of bee. The present analysis suggests, therefore, that organisms very distantly related phylogenetically nevertheless perceive changes in their respective environments in the same general way and, further, is the first datum showing an across-species comparison of the Power Law. Finally, the present analysis predicts that the "tail-wagging" dance communicates little information at precisely those distances for which it might be felt to be of most value and, in addition, offers an explanation for the paradox that the most advanced species of bee make less use of the "information rich" "tail-wagging" dance at short distances than the more primitive species.

ACKNOWLEDGMENTS

I am deeply grateful to Dr. Robert Collins, whose constant support and stimulating questions made this paper possible, and to Dr. Alan Stubbs, whose critical analysis was invaluable.

REFERENCES

1. GOULD, J. L. 1975. Science **189:** 685–693.
2. LINDAUER, M. 1956. Z. Vergl. Physiol. **38:** 521–557.
3. FRISCH, K. VON. 1967. The Dance Language and Orientation of Bees. Belknap Press. Cambridge, Mass.
4. FRISCH, K. VON. 1974. Science **185:** 663–668.
5. MICHENER, C. 1974. The Social Behavior of the Bees. Belknap Press. Cambridge, Mass.
6. FRISCH, K. VON & O. KRATKY. 1962. Naturwissenschaften **49:** 409–417.
7. STEVENS, S. 1975. Psychophysics: Introduction to Its Perceptual Neural and Social Prospects. John Wiley and Sons, Inc. New York, N.Y.
8. FRISCH, K. VON & R. JANDER. 1957. Z. Vergl. Physiol. **40:** 239–263.
9. WENNER, A. 1962. Animal Behavior **10:** 79–95.

DISCUSSION

Jane Lancaster, *Moderator*

Delta Regional Primate Center
Covington, Louisiana 70433

WAYNE COWARD (*Queens College, Flushing, N.Y.*): I'd like to address a question to Dr. Marler. In connection with the auditory templates that you mentioned, have you given any thought to the parameters by which they might be specified? In particular, what sort of constrast would you expect between the templates as they might be found in birds and in human beings?

DR. MARLER: I don't think there's anything necessarily mysterious in the kind of neurophysiological processes that might sensitize an organism to particular patterns of sound. The interesting thing about the case of the voice-onset-time-threshold studied by Eimas and his colleagues in human infants is that a number of people have presented animals with the same kind of stimulus continuum. It appears that animals as diverse as rhesus monkeys and even chinchillas are predisposed to recognize a boundary somewhere around 30 milliseconds. This has been interpreted by some as evidence that the voice-onset-time boundary was not especially evolved for the perceptual analysis of speech, (see Liberman, this volume).

I would speculate that if an organism such as man was evolving devices for the perceptual analysis of its own vocal sounds and it happened that there already existed in its sensory equipment predispositions to demarcate certain boundaries along a stimulus continuum, these would naturally be exploited. There may be some elementary explanations for the responsiveness to this particular stimulus boundary, which we share with other mammals. If there is such sharing, it suggests that such physiological devices do not necessarily have to be highly sophisticated, though some may be. Of course they would often have different design features in different organisms.

To the extent that we can acquire selective responsiveness, by learning, to almost any stimulus pattern, there has to be a physiological basis for this ability. I don't find any particular difficulty in imagining the same kind of physiological machinery being generated either through learned modification of neural function or through genetic instructions.

DR. SUPPES: Prof. Marler, looking at your Postulate One, I'd like to ask the following question: Given the different size of the vocal tracts in the male and female of the species, when you talk about categorical data, do you really want to hold to *absolutely* categorical data, or rather *relationally* categorical data in which invariants may be *contrasts* in, for example, frequency, pitch, or intensity, rather than the absolute values. What do you mean by categorical data or the use of categorical information?

DR. MARLER: Some of us are currently engaged in a project to present macaques with synthetic vocal sounds that mimic continua known to exist in their natural vocal behavior. We are going to ask them whether they treat these vocal continua as if they are segmented. It is conceivable that some of the continua are segmentalized on the basis of features that can only be characterized by the pattern, rather than by some absolute parameter such as frequency range. There are hints that this may be so from the descriptive study which is the starting point for this work on Japanese macaques

443

by Steven Green, conducted in Japan.* He made exhaustive analyses of vocalizations produced by these animals in a variety of circumstances resulting in the first mapping of a graded vocal system, relating subdivisions within this graded system to different contexts. He found the correlations to be close, with quite different contexts for categories of sound separated by subtle criteria—often criteria of pattern. For example, tonal sounds may be inflected and the circumstances of production may be different if the inflection is early in the tone or late. The essence of categorical perception was defined in the paper by Studdert-Kennedy *et al.* in 1970.† One feature is the manifestation of boundaries and the other is desensitization to within-category variations. The idea that ten-millisecond variations in voice-onset-time are extremely difficult even to detect within a category such as [pa] or [ba], but are obvious when close to the boundary is fascinating to me as a biologist. The fascination is increased by the finding by Pisoni and Tash that response-time latencies for within-category pairs of different sounds presented to subjects for discrimination are different from those for identical pairs.‡ This suggests that we can detect within-category variations even though our conscious judgment is that they are not there. Perhaps this is a human equivalent of the ethologist's "innate release mechanism"?

UNIDENTIFIED SPEAKER: There's a great deal of work on humans and nonhumans like chinchillas that directly addresses the questions that have been raised in the last few minutes. The feature detectors for, say, formant transitions in humans clearly operate after a *normalizing* device. First some sort of preprocessor adjusts for the fact that the person speaking is a male with a 17-centimeter-long vocal tract, or a female with a 15-centimeter-long vocal tract, or a child with a 12-centimeter-long vocal tract. After this operation takes place, you then have categorical perception in terms of absolute detection of, for example, various vowel or consonant boundaries. If you deliberately shift ranges you hear something is wrong. Now this same process has been demonstrated very recently in the chinchilla. Verdick and Miller, in a paper published in the July 1975 issue of the Journal of the Acoustical Society, trained chinchillas to press bars on presentation of the vowels e, a, u, as spoken by four speakers. Chinchillas were able to generalize to 27 speakers who had very different formant frequencies.

Second, as Peter stated, the mechanisms that are responsible for voice onset distinctions in humans clearly come from the same mechanisms that are involved in telling the minimal difference between two different acoustic events. What this demonstrates is the continuity of evolution. The same mechanisms that are perhaps involved in telling the difference between two temporal events, such as whether or not a rock is falling, have become adapted and used for language. This suggests that language isn't that distinct from other forms of behavior.

---

*S. Green 1975. Communication by a graded vocal system in Japanese macaques. *In* Primate Behavior. L. A. Rosenblum Ed. 4: 1–102. Academic Press. New York, N.Y.

†Studdert-Kennedy, M., A. M. Liberman, K. S. Harris & F. S. Cooper. 1970. Motor theory of speech perception: a reply to Lane's critical review. Psychol. Rev. 77: 234–249.

‡Pisoni, D. B. & J. Tash. 1974. Reaction times to comparisons within and across phonetic categories. Percept. Psychophys. 15: 285–290.

FROM HAND TO MOUTH: SOME CRITICAL STAGES
IN THE EVOLUTION OF LANGUAGE

Horst D. Steklis

Department of Anthropology,
Livingston College, Rutgers University
New Brunswick, New Jersey 08903

Stevan R. Harnad

Department of Psychiatry
CMDNJ-Rutgers Medical School
Piscataway, New Jersey 08854

THE TRANSLATABILITY THESIS

In the evolution of linguistic behavior, as in the evolution of other traits, the actual sequence of events often proceeds by accretion and overlay upon prior developments such that a purely synchronic consideration of the end product can be considerably misleading as to its lineage; i.e., how it got that way. Although the actual optimal route taken in evolution may sometimes seem somewhat circuitous with respect to the final stage if the latter is considered in isolation, it need not appear that way if antecedent conditions are taken into account.

An indisputable fact about language is that it is currently a phenomenon intimately and almost inextricably linked to the medium of speech. Almost all language is spoken language. Most orthographies are derived from phonology, or are at least one-to-one with the words of a spoken language, and even in the brain, linguistic functions seem to be closely bound with, if not identical to, speech functions. In fact, it is virtually impossible to find a medium-neutral general term for the function in question, because "language," "linguistic," "glossogony," and so on, are all etymologically linked to (the) "tongue." However, capitalizing upon a general diachronic trend in the "evolution" of word meanings—namely, a gradual change away from "iconicity" toward "arbitrariness"[43]—we will use the term *language*, ignoring its etymological speech-origins, to denote *a general system for encoding and communicating propositional information by arbitrary, syntactically-concatenated symbols which* (and this is the most important definiendum) *can provide a translation* (not necessarily one-to-one) *of anything that anyone can say in a natural language* (with "natural language" here standing for our intuitions as to what we are all capable of saying or writing). A *proposition* is an intentional claim or a prediction about what is the case; i.e., a description or an explanation of something.

The purpose of the "translatability" criterion, which is certainly a particularly strong one, is to settle unequivocally questions of the type "does organism X have language" or "is Y a language." Should such a question arise, the critical test would be whether, given enough time and attention, a translation of, say, Plato's *Cratylus*, could be accomplished by or for X in Y. It is a linguistic truism that there is no such thing as a "primitive" language. Any existing natural language can do anything any other one can. We simply extend this as a conjecture about all possible languages.*

---

*We suspect that our translatability criterion is equivalent to Katz' "effability hypothesis" as expressed in this volume.[55] It is particularly interesting that attempts to provide counterexamples to the translatability criterion are doomed by their very effability! A revealing illustration is

SERIAL MOTOR PRAXIS

Our strategy in the present attempt to reconstruct language phylogeny will be to focus upon certain critical transitions that may already be familiar but that either have not yet been linked with language evolution explicitly or have not been fully appreciated in that specific context. For example, we feel that it is neither irrelevant nor a coincidence that both speech and motor dominance are co-lateralized in the same, left, hemisphere, or that tool-fashioning and use, which many authors have attempted to link somehow with speech, partake of this same asymmetry. It is likewise significant that gestural signaling with the emancipated forelimbs of hominoids would provide the most direct link between these two species of complex lateralized praxis.

Any human language must take the form of serial motor activity. First of all, we have no way of generating complex outputs in "parallel." Most behavior is serial in time, one chunk at a time.[22] Nor are we efficient parallel processors, especially with respect to propositional information. What a computer can direct an output device to throw on a whole page at once, we (and indeed the computer too) must "read" sequentially, item by item.[29] So, as input/output devices, and also as central processors, we are constrained to temporal-sequential activity. In this connection, Lashley[22] predicted that "analysis of the nervous mechanisms underlying order in the

---

provided by Kiparsky's attempt in the discussion section following Keenan's paper in this volume.[58]

In English the comparative "he is smarter than she is" allows an option not present in all languages. The default provides an implicit "than she is **smart**" in this case, but one could also have said "he is smarter than she is beautiful." The argument is that in some languages this option is not available, and the comparative is constrained to a single dimension. One could not even say "the building is wider than it is tall" in such languages.

But of course a powerful and rather illuminating rebuttal is possible. There are, in fact, two ways of translating the English message into a language which has the constrained comparative. Let us call one translation "internal" and the other "external." Each provides a profound explication of the power of effability and the scope of translatability.

The "internal" translation would run something like this: "The degree to which the house is wide is greater than the degree to which the house is tall." This involves no problem for the dimensional constraint (degree/degree) and it also shows how plastic the internal resources of a language really are, in terms of what is readily effable. Faced with a situation in which we would use our "heterodimensional" comparative, speakers of a language with a "homodimensional" comparative would, of course, immediately and quite naturally use the kind of circumlocution just mentioned. Did anyone seriously think that they would be stopped mute in their tracks, or, more absurd still, that they would display some sort of Whorfian agnosia for the real world state of affairs corresponding to a heterodimensional comparison? "How can buildings be taller than they are wide?" or some nonsense like that!

The "external" means is still more enlightening, for it is the very means to which Kiparsky or Keenan must resort in intimating to *us* the putative limitation of a language. The critical point is that, in the case of natural languages, "meta-linguistic" statements are every bit as *linguistic* as are "object-linguistic" ones. So one could just as easily go to the native speakers with the homodimensional comparative and tell them (much as Kiparsky and Keenan tell us), "Listen, you have a kinky sort of comparative here; it can only do so-and-so, while in other languages it can do so-and-so." Would the native stare with bewildered receptive aphasia for such intimations? Of course not. He would understand at once. Nor would a sudden new dimension of cognitive experience be opened up for him upon the realization of the new syntactic horizons vouchsafed by languages other than his own. He would simply nod and acknowledge that others say what he says and knows in a different way. But know it he does, and say it he can. Q.E.D.

more primitive acts may contribute ultimately to the solution even of the physiology of logic." Thus, in many respects the story of the evolution of language must begin with the evolution of serial motor activity and its nervous control.

A quick inventory of the principal organs of serial motor activity in primates yields the following: [1] The muscles of the eyes and head; these have their work pretty much cut out for them, as they have crucial responsibility in orienting toward incoming visual, auditory, and olfactory information, as well as performing their parts in species-typical behaviors such as feeding and aggression. [2] The muscles of the limbs; in quadrupedal primates, these are primarily dedicated to locomotion as well as components of species-typical behavior. [3] The vocal apparatus; this is involved in species-typical vocalizations, principally of an emotive sort. [4] The facial musculature; this, too, is involved in species-typical emotional expression.

Of the above motor candidates for taking on a linguistic function, [3] the vocal apparatus is certainly the least "busy" in terms of being occupied by other duties. Furthermore, vocalization is much more versatile than the other semi-employed contender, facial expression, especially in the relatively "deadpan" prosimians. Vocalization, however, has one critical shortcoming: it hasn't any relevant experience: its normal function is far-removed from what would be demanded of a motor organ that was to take on the role of producing language.

ENCEPHALIZATION

Of course, at this point we are no longer discussing the motor end organs themselves, but the brain which controls them. What does it mean to say that the vocal apparatus "lacks experience" relevant to language? It means that the neural control of the vocal activity of nonhuman primates is somehow not adapted to the kind of activity involved in language. These vocalizations are controlled by evolutionarily primitive regions of the brain which are involved in stereotyped species-typical communicative behaviors and emotion.[32,38] They lack the requisite independence from affect to assume other duties. Furthermore, they are not particularly disposed toward learning. Although there is evidence for some minimal conditionability of monkey vocalization under certain conditions,[32] previous attempts to shape chimpanzee vocalizations have been unsuccessful overall.[13] Primate calls are a relatively restricted and predictable set for a particular species, and even if they depend upon experience for acquisition,[35] the amount of variation in the final product is negligible compared to the variety of learned complex behaviors of which the limbs, the most qualified candidates of all, are capable. In short, the neural control of vocalization lacks the requisite plasticity, both in terms of available repertoire, prior experience, and modifiability by experience.

In contrast, the limbs are relatively better qualified. They are adapted to operating on the environment and being guided by feedback from it. They have, and display, a much wider range of variability in their activities than does vocalization, or any of the other candidates. Their only drawback is that they are already fully employed. In quadrupedal primates they can hardly be spared for outside work unless some of them, at least, are released from their full-time duties. Furthermore, in these lower primates the limbs are not totally independent agents. They are primarily under the control of those previously mentioned areas of the brain which are involved in stereotyped behavior and affect. These limbic and associated brain-stem nuclei govern the programming of holistic, patterned species-typical behaviors.[27] They cannot subserve the kind of fine tuning of complex motor activity that only neocortical mediation can provide.

The process of increasing control of function by the neocortex is called *encephalization*, and fully quadrupedal limbs, besides being otherwise occupied, are not very advanced in this respect. Much better qualified are the forelimbs of hominoids, with their specialization for prehensile and manipulative functions.[1,33] Extrapyramidal control, characteristic of lower primates, is now supplemented by neocortical, pyramidal mediation for skilled precision movements.[36] This permits increased flexibility in voluntary sequencing, fine control of the digits, manipulative proficiency, and a plasticity to experience, all characteristic of increased motor encephalization.

MOTOR DOMINANCE

Relieved from doing double duty with the hindlimbs in locomotion, the emancipated hominoid forelimbs still exhibit a basic duplication of function, in that there are two of them, and for many reasons these must be prepared to be equipotential.[18,61] There is no evidence for anything like "cerebral dominance" in these organisms, nor extant primates, who are equally skilled in manipulation with either arm even in their most skilled acts.[48] There is a tendency (probably not a genetic one) for an individual monkey or ape to display relatively stable hand preferences under unbiased circumstances.[3,6,20,30] However, these preferences are easily reversed by experience,[49] and vary randomly in being left or right for individuals in a population; so they are probably idiosyncratic, rather than genetically transmitted.

The first evidence for a "nonrandom" distribution of handedness comes with tool- and weapon-use by Pleistocene *Australopithecus*.[5] Middle paleolithic tools associated with *Homo erectus* from Choukoutien, China, show that the majority were chipped by right-handers.[37] A similar conclusion has been reached[37] on the basis of the few arm and hand bones known of Neanderthal man. The latter's skull displays further evidence of cerebral asymmetry, as does that of *Homo erectus*.[24] Precise origins of these first asymmetries can only be conjectured, but it would seem most parsimonious to assume that they were related to the evidence itself, namely that functions requiring sophisticated asymmetric *use* of the forelimbs,[37] such as the power and the precision grip,[34] particularly in skilled sequential acts requiring bimanual coordination, must encephalize asymmetrically. This means that the tool- and weapon-use of contemporary chimpanzees,[19,47] who do not seem to display consistent laterality, is not the kind that demands asymmetric encephalization.

Gross movements of the forelimbs can be initiated by either side of the brain in monkeys, and only fine movements of the digits are under exclusive contralateral control.[21] Apparently, unlike in man,[8] nothing that contemporary nonhuman primates do with their hands, gross or fine, demands any differentiation between the motor control regions on the two sides. Concerning the origins of laterality, then, it seems reasonable to suppose that it was the degree of elaboration of learned asymmetric movement sequences that tilted the balance, and it was early man's critical reliance on these new behaviors as a means of survival that consolidated the gain.

COUPLING

Next something must be said about "coupling" in the nervous system. We have suggested that it is unlikely that the pressures for asymmetry issued simply from unimanual weapon use; however, it seems reasonable to expect that a population that already favors the right in the context of skilled bimanual use would favor it also in the simpler unimanual function. In general, unless some antagonism can be demonstrated, it seems reasonable to suppose that there was some kind of coupling between the two tendencies. By coupling is meant either a partially shared substrate or a synergy between two functions. One of the most striking examples of the latter kind of coupling in the nervous system is that of "turning tendencies."[17] Local activity on one side of the brain has, besides its specific function, the effect of turning the organism's attention, responsiveness, and sometimes even his body toward the side opposite the activated region. Local activity and contraversive turning are coupled.

From the existence of coupling one might be led to expect a mutual facilitation if the coupled functions are compatible. For example, if local activity in the brain occurred at a time when there was need for attention to contralateral space, then one would expect the latter performance to be improved. Experiment, in fact, supports this.[18] Conversely, there may be situations in which coupling produces interference, and there is evidence for this too.[10]

In the studies just cited it happens that the coupled functions investigated were verbalization, hand use and contralateral turning. Verbalization and the processing of verbal materials induce a detectable rightward turning tendency in man. They are also compatible with concurrent, sequential arm-tapping and dowel-balancing with the left hand, but interfere with these tasks on the right. The mediating factor is, of course, the fact that language functions are predominantly lateralized in various regions of the left cerebral hemisphere in man. Facilitation occurs when the coupled functions are compatible with the task, such as the detection of verbal materials in the right field, but interference occurs when they are incompatible, such as in the attempt to concentrate on tapping or dowel-balancing with the right hand at the same time as speaking. These tasks are performed better when divided between hemispheres through the use of the left hand.

To return now to early hominids with their newly developed asymmetric hand use, we claim that the pressures for asymmetric use resulted not only in increased elaboration in the left hemisphere for right-hand skills, but that the control of coordination and sequencing of all skilled *bimanual* performance also lateralized to the hemisphere controlling the more specialized hand. There is evidence that this is the case in contemporary man,[16,26] whose left hemisphere is specialized for organizing the performance of patterned limb-movements while the isolated right hemisphere is proficient only in directing axial movement.[8] Unimanual specialization became coupled with dominance for bimanual coordination, and finally the dominant hemisphere came to assume the programming of all forms of complex serial praxis.

THE ALLEGORY OF THE ROOMS

We now come to a stage in language evolution with respect to which this paper does not purport to suggest hypotheses, namely, the stage of language-specific environmental pressures. We do not know what these pressures were, although we venture to doubt certain attempted explications. Concerning the relation between tool-use and language, there have been three kinds of suggestion, of which we espouse only the last, which is the weakest.

1. The first kind of suggestion has been that language is somehow a prerequisite for tool-making and hunting. It is not at all apparent to us why this should be so. Tool-making and hunting are certainly not themselves verbal activities, although it is undeniable that they, like virtually all other human skills, have profited, both in terms of their exercise and their transmission, from the existence of language.

However, australopithecines did not do the kind of sophisticated big-game hunting for which some have claimed language to be essential[51] (cf. Ref. 23). Furthermore contemporary artisans are celebrated as the principal exponents of the so-called "nonverbal" functions.[25] So it seems improbable that the critical pressures for language were in the service of either of these activities (cf. Refs. 17, 67, 68).

2. The second kind of suggestion has been that there is an important analogy between tool-fashioning-and-use and language; that they somehow have a common cognitive mechanism. In this view, language is simply an elaboration of the tool-function. We do not see this analogy, except for the fact that both seem to be planned, skilled motor-sequential activity. The latter fact is certainly important, and we will make use of it below to explain motor continuities, but it is surely not sufficient to account for the specific origins of language, nor to account for those critical cognitive characteristics in which language differs from all other forms of planned sequential behavior (cf. Ref. 69).

It seems to us that the source for insights as to language-origins is more likely to be in the dialogue between man and man than between man and tool, and to this end we propose a simple paradigm for the state of affairs which does telescope the kind of cognitive capacity which we feel is unique to language. One is to imagine two organisms out of sight from one another in two rooms with identical contents, identically located, consisting of more-or-less familiar objects. A third party enters one of the rooms and displaces one of the subjects. The task of the observing organism is to signal to his counterpart in the other room what has been done, so that the counterpart can do the same. The critical properties of this scenario are that the objects and the act of displacement can be *any whatsoever* with which the organism is familiar (i.e., can and has perceptually discriminated) and the information to be conveyed to his counterpart must not be conveyed iconically (i.e., by imitation). We feel that this paradigm comes closer to mirroring the competence that language uniquely confers, and we see nothing in the skills of tool-use or hunting that resembles it in any significant way (cf. Ref. 70).

3. The third and weakest suggestion seems more plausible, although it leaves a good deal still to be accounted for; namely, that it is difficult to imagine a hominid with the cognitive capacity to fashion tools and artifacts of the kind that have been found[11,67] who did not also have the capacity for linguistic communication. This is not to imply that he would need language to do what he does, or that language is in any important sense *like* what he does, but simply that one would expect language too to go hand in hand with such cognitive sophistication. The compellingness of this last suggestion is increased by what is known about the cognitive and communicative capacities of contemporary apes,[28,46] and particularly by the recent experiments on the acquisition of gestural and other symbolic communication systems by chimpanzees.[40,41,45]

GESTURES AND PROPOSITIONS

None of the factors cited, however, seem to constitute necessary and sufficient conditions for language-origins, so that will have to remain an acknowledged gap in this sequence as we are tracing it. Some minor links, however, do suggest themselves. First, the motor state of affairs we have sketched makes it seem highly unlikely that language would have begun in the vocal mode. For one thing, vocalization is at this stage still largely under the control of the limbic system, and there is no reason it should not be. The advanced encephalized end-organ of choice at this juncture is surely the forelimb. Furthermore, to return for a heuristic moment to our allegory of the rooms, it seems reasonable to expect that an immediate *imitational* solution to such a problem would have preceded the linguistic one. Therefore, all one need do is remove the partition between the rooms, and the task is easily accomplished.

Now, to proceed from this simplified version by a series of approximations to the full-blown paradigm of the rooms, one may suppose that the imitative act could by degrees become less iconic as it came more into use. Whole acts could become progressively as short-circuited as circumstances and experience would allow.[53] Pointing, and more and more approximate and arbitrary icons, could replace the full-blown pantomime; and as these arbitrary sequences came increasingly to be relied upon as communicating information in their own right (rather than by obvious immediate iconic correspondence with their immanent referents), a gesturer may well be held *accountable* for what he has signaled. That is, his signal could be construed as a *claim*, and not just a direct interaction with objects which it would make no sense to deny or disbelieve. In this way, a proposition could be born.

This is not to say that "deception" is the origin of propositionality. There is certainly deception in nonpropositional intentional contexts, such as hiding or withholding food, and so on. Furthermore, in the room allegory it is not the act itself which is the proposition. Initially, a gestural act may just be a short-circuited iconic sequence, which it would make no sense to deny as long as it continues to retain some isomorphism with its referent and the referent is present for verification. What makes an act a proposition is the possibility of misleading, of claiming something false. Once a communicative act can give intentionally misleading information, it is a proposition.

So as soon (in the allegory of the rooms) as the gestures are divorced from their immediate referents and are intended and relied upon to transmit information about those referents, *propositionality* is involved. But let this not be taken to mean that *language*, in the sense we have earlier defined it in this paper, is necessarily involved yet. A gestural propositional system may still not be able to sustain a translation of everything which can be said in a natural language. It may be restricted to certain contexts and simply never used in others. Its users may simply not be inclined to exploit its full potential. Yet there seems to be something very arbitrary about restrictions of this sort. One feels, as with the sophisticated tool-maker, that if he can do that much, then he ought to have the brains to go all the way. And perhaps that is in fact the reason for the rapid explosion of artifacts that occurred in that putative period in the Upper Pleistocene when language is believed to have flourished.[11] Once begun, it is hard to imagine the function staying within bounds. At that point, only motivation had to be selected for; i.e., motivation to communicate propositional information, and the rest could be transmitted—one would like to say by "word of mouth," but at this stage it is only by "sight of hand."

Now what of those hands which were doing this gestural signaling? There were two of them; were they both gesturing? On the basis of contemporary evidence from sign language of the deaf,[44,53] one can conclude that both were indeed used, and perhaps asymmetrically. However, the "leading hand," in the sense not merely of setting the pace, but of governing the planning and sequencing of the gestures, was surely the right, or more appropriately, the control regions for complex serial praxis in the left hemisphere.[59] There is evidence, also from contemporary deaf signers, that left-hemisphere damage causes sign-language aphasia, just as it causes aphasia for speech.[42] So we suggest that the programming of gestural language came to be assumed by the hemisphere already dominant for praxis.

THE ADVENT OF SPEECH

Now we come to the limitations of sign-language. There is still the problem of the partition between the rooms in our allegory. This is not just an arbitrary stipulation. It is meant to allow for the absence of the referent, particularly if it is in the past or the future, as well as for what one may conceivably wish to express while the all-important eyes and hands are otherwise occupied. So certain intrinsic limitations of a gestural language immediately suggest themselves. Not only are gestures of no use in the dark, or across partitions, or when the hands or eyes are otherwise busy, but they are slow and inefficient. So we propose that as the dramatic potentialities of language became manifest, and it became more and more critically relied upon, gesture-specific shortcomings began to intrude: at night, across distances, when several people were communicating, when crucial information had to be communicated rapidly, or when the hands were not free. One can almost hear the grunts of frustration!

And there, too, was the obvious solution. Language was already present, and increasingly exploited and depended upon. Now was the time for a relatively unoccupied fellow traveler to get into the act, and language became coupled with vocalization. Since gestures were already quite arbitrary by this time, there was no reason why they should not be supplemented by vocalization to further differentiate and extend them. This coupling may first have been only an incidental suprasegmental intensity marker for gesture [12] due to limbic intrusions into communicative acts,[54] but as it became increasingly relied upon for differentiating meaning and remedying the shortcomings of gesture, control of vocalization underwent encephalization, and, in accordance with the pattern of coupling and accretion described so far, the most natural locus for the neocortical control of speech was again the left side, co-lateralized with its linguistic and praxic precursors.†

Furthermore, this allowed for a very felicitous division of labor, because the more limbic emotive and iconic vocalizations, which could potentially interfere with that necessarily affect-free medium,‡ speech,[2] could be segregated to the minor hemisphere for continued participation in emotional expression,[7] music,[9] and other nonverbal activities.[62] The elaboration of speech-specific mechanisms on the left then proceeded, not only with the development of neocortical control of rapid voluntary articulatory sequencing, but also with specialization of speech-specific central auditory mechanisms.[50,31,65,66] Cognitive bifurcations in the service of verbal ideation also appeared and were duly lateralized.[62,25]

From there it was only a matter of time until it became apparent that it was in fact gesture which was now the excess baggage, and that last relic of iconicity could drop out, to leave only the vestigial coupling between speech and gesture which we still display today.[15,4,14]

---

†Lateralization is not an evolutionarily unprecedented solution for the neural control of complex learned vocalization, as Nottebohm has shown in passerine songbirds.[56] In man there is the added advantage that the corresponding receptive sensory system, audition, is not very busy either, both peripherally and centrally,[57] compared to vision. And there may already exist in primates a tendency toward lateralization of auditory function[63] as well as anatomical asymmetries in auditory regions.[64,24]

‡Neither the contemporary preoccupation with so-called "nonverbal communication," or "total communication" (cf. Tanner, Ref. 60), nor the otherwise valid concern for the iconic aspects of communication[43,53] are pertinent here. The uniqueness of *linguistic* communication (refer to our definition of "language" above) is quite distinct from these, and even if it is often complemented by them, the evolutionary question is how it is that we came to rely so heavily upon *linguistic* communication as a species.

REFERENCES

1. BISHOP, A. 1964. Use of the hand in lower primates. *In* Evolutionary and Genetic Biology of Primates. J. Buettner-Janusch, Eds. Vol. **2**: 133–225. Academic Press. New York, N.Y.
2. BRONOWSKI, J. S. 1969. Human and animal languages. *In* To Honor Roman Jakobson. Vol. **1**: 374–394. Mouton. The Hague, The Netherlands.
3. COLE, J. 1957. Laterality in the use of the hand, foot, and eye in monkeys. J. Comp. Physiol. Psychol. **50**: 296–299.
4. CONDON, W. S. & L. W. SANDER. 1974. Neonate movement is synchronized with adult speech: interactional participation and language acquisition. Science **183**: 99–101.
5. DART, R. A. 1949. The predatory implemental technique of Australopithecus. Amer. J. Phys. Anthropol. **7**: 1–38.
6. FINCH, G. 1941. Chimpanzee handedness. Science **94**: 117–118.
7. FLOR-HENRY, P. This annal.
8. GESCHWIND, N. 1975. The apraxias: Neural mechanisms of disorders of learned movement. American Scientist **63**: 188–195.
9. GORDON, H. W. 1974. Auditory specialization of the right and left hemispheres. *In* Hemispheric Disconnection And Cerebral Function. M. Kinsbourne & W. L. Smith, Eds. Charles C Thomas. Springfield, Ill.
10. HICKS, R. E. 1975. Intrahemispheric response competition between vocal and unimanual performance in normal adult human males. J. Comp. Physiol. Psychol. **89**(1): 50–60.
11. ISAAC, G. L. This annal.
12. JAYNES, J. This annal.
13. KELLOGG, W. N. 1968. Communication and language in the home-raised chimpanzee. Science **162**: 423–427.
14. KENDON, A. 1970. Movement coordination in social interaction: Some examples described. Acta Psychologia **32**: 100–125.
15. KIMURA, D. 1973. Manual activity during speaking. 1. Right-handers. 2. Left-handers. Neuropsychologia **11**: 45–50 & 51–55.
16. KIMURA, D. & Y. ARCHIBALD. 1974. Motor functions of the left hemisphere. Brain **97**: 337–350.
17. KINSBOURNE, M. 1970. The cerebral basis of lateral asymmetries in attention. Acta Psychologia **33**: 193–201.
18. KINSBOURNE, M. This annal.
19. VON KORTLANDT, A. 1968. Handgebrauch bei freilebenden schimpansen. *In* Handgebrauch und Verständigung bei Affen und Frühmenschen. B. Rensch, Ed. Verlag Hans Huber. Bern and Stuttgart.
20. KRUPER, D. C., B. E. BOYLE & R. A. PATTON. 1966. Eye and hand preference in rhesus monkeys (*Macaca mulatta*): Psychonom. Sci. **5**(7): 277–278.
21. KUYPERS, H. G. J. M. 1973. The anatomical organization of the descending pathways and their contributions to motor control especially in primates. *In* New Developments in EMG and Clinical Neurophysiology. J. E. Desmedt, Ed. Vol. **3**: 38–68.
22. LASHLEY, K. S. 1951. The problem of serial order in behavior. *In* Cerebral Mechanisms In Behavior. L. A. Jeffress, Ed. John Wiley & Sons. New York, N.Y.
23. LAUGHLIN, W. S. 1968. Hunting: An integrating biobehavior system and its evolutionary importance. *In* Man The Hunter. R. B. Lee & I. De Vore, Eds. Aldine. Chicago, Ill.
24. LE MAY, M. This annal.
25. LEVY, J. This annal.
26. LOMAS, J. & D. KIMURA. 1975. Intrahemispheric interaction between speaking and sequential manual activity. University of Western Ontario Res. Bull. 314. January.
27. MACLEAN, P. D. 1973. A triune concept of the brain and behavior. *In* The Clarence M. Hincks Memorial Lectures, 1969. T. J. Boag & D. Campbell, Eds. Part **1**: 6–66. University of Toronto Press. Toronto, Canada.
28. MENZEL, E. & M. JOHNSON. This annal.
29. MILLER, G. A. 1956. The magical numbers seven, plus or minus two: Some limits on our capacity for processing information. Psych. Rev. **63**(2): 81–97.
30. MILNER, A. D. 1969. Distribution of hand preferences in monkeys. Neuropsychologia **7**: 375–377.

31. MORSE, P. This annal.
32. MYERS, R. This annal.
33. NAPIER, J. R. 1960. Studies of the hands of living primates. Proc. Zool. Soc. London. **134:** 647–657.
34. NAPIER, J. R. 1962. The evolution of the hand. Scientific American **207**(6): 56–62.
35. NEWMAN, J. D. & D. SYMMES. 1974. Vocal pathology in socially deprived monkeys. Developmental Psychobiol. **7**(4): 351–358.
36. NOBACK, C. R. & N. MOSKOWITZ. 1963. The primate nervous system: Functional and structural aspects in phylogeny. *In* Evolutionary and Genetic Biology of Primates. J. Buettner-Janusch, Ed. Vol. **1:** 131–177. Academic Press. New York, N.Y.
37. OAKLEY, K. P. 1972. Skill as a human possession. *In* Perspectives on Human Evolution. S. L. Washburn & P. Dolhinow, Eds. Vol. **2:** 14–50. Holt Rinehart & Winston, Inc. New York, N.Y.
38. PETERS, M. & D. PLOOG. 1973. Communication among primates. Ann. Rev. Physiol. **35:** 221–242.
39. PHILLIPS, C. G. 1971. Evolution of the corticospinal tract in primates with special reference to the hand. Proc. 3rd Int. Cong. Primatol. **2:** 2–23. Karger. Basel, Switzerland.
40. PREMACK, D. This annal.
41. RUMBAUGH, D. This annal.
42. SARNO, J. E., L. PECK SWISHER & M. TAYLOR SARNO. 1969. Aphasia in a congenitally deaf man. Cortex **5**(4): 398–414.
43. SEBEOK, T. A. This annal.
44. STOKOE, W. This annal.
45. TERRACE, H. This annal.
46. VAN LAWICK-GOODALL, J. 1968. A preliminary report on expressive movements and communication in the Gombe Stream chimpanzees. *In* Primates: Studies in adaptation and variability. P. C. Jay, Ed.: 313–382. Holt Rinehart & Winston, Inc. N.Y.
47. VAN LAWICK-GOODALL, J. 1970. Tool-using in primates and other vertebrates. *In* Advances in the Study of Behavior. R. A. Hinde, Ed.: 195–249. Academic Press. New York, N.Y.
48. WARREN, J. M. 1976. Handedness and cerebral dominance in monkeys. *In* Lateralization in the Nervous System. S. R. Harnad, R. W. Doty, L. Goldstein, J. Jaynes & G. Krauthamer, Eds. Academic Press. New York, N.Y.
49. WARREN, J. M. & A. NONNEMANN. This annal.
50. WARREN, R. This annal.
51. WASHBURN, S. L. & J. S. LANCASTER. 1968. The evolution of hunting. *In* Man the Hunter. R. B. Lee & I. De Vore, Eds.: 293–303. Aldine. Chicago, Ill.
52. WYKE, M. 1971. The effects of brain lesions on the learning performance of a bimanual coordination task. Cortex **7:** 59–72.
53. BELLUGI, U. This annal.
54. ROBINSON, B. This annal.
55. KATZ, J. J. 1976. This annal.
56. NOTTEBOHM, F. 1976. Asymmetrics in neural control of vocalization in the canary. *In* Lateralization in the Nervous System. S. R. Harnad, R. W. Doty, L. Goldstein, J. Jaynes, and G. Krauthamer, Eds. Academic Press. New York, N.Y.
57. MARIN, O. This annal.
58. KEENAN, E. This annal.
59. KIMURA, D. and Y. ARCHIBALD. 1974. Motor functions of the left hemisphere. Brain **97:** 371–384.
60. TANNER, N. Discussion paper. This annal.
61. CORBALLIS, M. C. 1974. The left-right problem in psychology. The Canadian Psychologist. **15**(1): 16–33.
62. HARNAD, S. R. 1973. Interhemispheric division of labour. Presented at: Bucke Soc. Conf. on Transformations of Consciousness. Montreal. Ms.
63. DEWSON, J. H. 1976. Preliminary evidence of hemispheric asymmetry of auditory function in monkeys. *In* Lateralization in the Nervous System. S. R. Harnad, R. W. Doty, L. Goldstein, J. Jaynes, and G. Krauthamer, Eds. Academic Press. New York, N.Y.

64. YENI-KOMSHIAN, G. H. & BENSON, D. A. 1976. Anatomical study of cerebral asymmetry in the temporal lobe of humans, chimpanzees and rhesus monkeys. Submitted for publication.
65. LIBERMAN, A. This volume.
66. MARLER, P. This volume.
67. MARSHACK, A. This volume. Science **192:** 387–389.
68. MONTAGU, A. This volume.
69. REYNOLDS, P. This volume.
70. MASON, W. A. & HOLLIS, J. H. 1962. Communication between young rhesus monkeys. Anim. Behav. **10**(3–4): 211–221.

LANGUAGES OF ORGANISM: REQUISITE FABRIC FOR AN EVOLUTION OF THE SPEECH FUNCTION: SOME THEORETICAL CONSIDERATIONS*

Earl W. Count†

Department of Anthropology
Hamilton College
Clinton, New York 13323

The anthropologist, at a Conference on the Origins and Evolution of Language and Speech, must find himself stimulated and embarassed—stimulated, in that there are so many disciplines other than his own, that have concentrated their fire upon this most crucial topic of humanness; embarrassing, in that his discipline lies but peripherally to it, whenas it should be a cardinal one. With Paul Broca among our founders, you might expect that we would be leading the research of brainmind,‡ but a Ralph Holloway remains a *rara avis* among us. Except for the testimony of fossil endocasts (whatever that may be worth), anthropology has almost nothing of its own to say about the essential subject of this Conference. Yes indeed—anthropologists often have a great deal to discourse anent The Difference It Makes that we possess so much brainmind; but clearly this is an entirely different matter.

I take it that the title of our Conference owes its vague expanse to its intention of being as eclectic as possible; leaving thus to each of us his own opportunity of interpreting it. It has to mean different things to the linguist and to the bioanthropologist. Speech—speaking—is exclusively a human endowment. Language is a category universal to animals. It is communicative coding, whatever be the vehicle that externalizes it. The code is always shared by a conspecific. Speech, in man, is never exercised without a concomitant mobilization of the rest of the body. Theoretical as well as empirical considerations can show why and how it is that what are sometimes misleadingly termed "paralinguistic" factors are the basics, within which vocalized verbalism is embedded. This at once converts speaking into an *ad hoc* segment of behavior—and translocates it within the sciences of behavior, including, decidedly, that of ethology.

This, however, shall not be the topic of the present paper. To us, the "origin and evolution" concern the phylogenesis of a *function* occurring within brain mechanisms; which, in previous studies of the vertebrate biogram and of its peculiarly human expression, I have called "phasia"; and so, hereinafter.

Therefore, we are arguing, within evolutionary frame, an anticipatory function which "terminally" contributed to the definition of man. For all the substance of this defining, we anthropologists must beg or borrow from you neurologists and psychologists; but the problem itself belongs to us. Not, let me add quickly, as a monopoly; but insofar as our discipline is a man-science, we are obligated to come to grips with it. It follows that we must have something *sui generis* to contribute.

*Particular thanks is due that remarkably charismatic man, Dr. Karl Pribram, for the semipirated title of this paper. He has been exploited further, both for his happy distillations of the thoughts of others, and, still more, for his own imaginative insights.

†Professor Emeritus. Present Address: 2616 Saklan Indian Drive, Walnut Creek, Calif. 94595.

‡One word. This paper shrugs the problem of the psychophysical dichotomy that has dogged Occidental thought for two millennia.

What may that be?

Many years ago, Kroeber likened anthropology to a holding-company. We may never match the expertise of the economist, say, in the economics of China, or of the geographer in its geography. Yet we may see relationships between the two when neither of the authorities does or is willing to engage . . . to say nothing about some universals of human socioculture that are wider and profounder than either and both.

Merely for the sake of orientation—this paper would contribute to the theory of a vertebrate-to-human biogram. This will be the last time that the "biogram" shall be mentioned; briefly, it states that there exists a behavioral configuration that participates ineluctably in the morphology of any vertebrate taxon or individual thereof; and so has evolved *pari passu*, generating homologies; however, behavior is but the external symptomatology of central nervous system (CNS) processes; symptoms being without an existence on their own recognizance, they do not evolve. But CNS processes do; and our problem becomes one of translating processes into symptoms.

ORGANISM AS A "SELF-ORGANIZING" SYSTEM

Now to our task. Herewith some preliminary statements of organism-as-system; but no proof is appended; it could be supplied, were the occasion appropriate.

1. A living *system* is negatively entropic, and self-organizing, within cybernetic meaning.

2. It is arguable as being a system of communication: internal, first; external thereupon, by extension of the same dynamics of process. This is actually but an expanded paraphrase of point 1.

3. Living systems have evolved in terms of hierarchial levels of order. It really is not a "secondary" process but a "prime"; i.e., it is intrinsic in the definition of the order concepted in points 1 and 2. In Schrödinger's phrasing—it states "order from order." There is development of development itself. To expand these expressions— each succeeding development of a level of organization follows the constraints set by the preceding level; each new level acquires further degrees of freedom of choice. As a system of communication, each new level effects some new coding, some new logic module. At the interfaces, there must occur transformations, of a kind that summons investigation; somehow, an antecedent coding maps into a consequent one.

4. For our consideration, the most important diagnostic of a living vs. a nonliving "computer" is, that in the former the "fabric" of it participates: whence the "goals" and the "interests" of a living self-organizing system, which the nonliving cannot have.

5. It is unhelpful to bring in "natural selection" as an *explicatio*, whenas it really is an *explicandum*. We learn nothing about the evolution of organic mechanisms by an inappropriate misuse of it—as so frequently is done. In the jargon of communication theory, this is "noise." For, what we are asking is: What relations within this system are its working constitution? If then they be such-and-such—what developmental transpirings effected them, over a phylogenetic course? All this we ask, even if we are researching the alterations of a DNA. Next—once a system exists, how does it replicate? This assembles a new set of questions, ontogenetic ones, related, to be sure, to phylogenetic ones, yet distinguishable from them.

The metascientific point is clear. We are appealing to the organism-as-system to supply its own explication, even when we are remembering that organism-in-environment is wider and ultimately the minimum-adequate universe of discourse. We are arguing steady states, but beyond them the problem of the parameters that disturb those steady states; in some cases temporarily, in others permanently. We are deeply involved in the nature and the properties of code; and the mathematical bioscientists already are constructing sophisticated models that sooner or later the rest of us will draw upon. But for the nonce, we pause at the stadium where organism-as-system is autochthonous; i.e., self-organizing. At all events, we shall, I believe, get farther by appreciating the degree of truth that this represents, than by accommodating to the tyranny of environment as first and final prescription for an explanation. Let us realize that, if we pursue "natural selection" to its logical ultimate, every organism that has ever existed has been "successful" sheerly by virtue of ever having come into existence at all. The difference between an aborted embryo and a Perissodactyl lineage is, that the latter's far longer duration has produced many more features of interest. But these assertions are not being cast as points for debate in present context; they represent statements of position in this paper.

6. A final metascientific point. It was the theoretical-physicist Boltzmann who originally formulated information as exactly the negative of entropy; it was the laureate physicist Schrödinger who cast the aphorism that "life feeds on negative entropy" ("negentropy"). A mechanistic biology, striving for a reduction to a physics and chemistry that conforms but to the second law of thermodynamics, ignored or was unprepared for the tremendous consequences of Schrödinger's restatement of Boltzmann; it has a hard time with a Weaver, a Wiener, an Ashby, a Quastler. Well, what we are concerned with is not the adaptivity of orthogradation, or the greater adaptive efficiency of the *Pliohippus* limb over that of *Eohippus*, or placentation over the marsupial mode of gestation, or man's pedal arch and pelvis, but with the evolution of nervous control. And so, let us note that positive entropy, as it proceeds in the universe, *converges* upon a zero of order, while negative entropy, by a like token, *diverges* indeterminately; so that each succeeding level of order has more degrees of freedom than its antecedent level has. The evolution of nervous control, consequently, has been that of a divergent trend coming to terms with the convergent trend of a physics-chemistry that argues the second law of thermodynamics. The mechanics of physical morphology is arguable according to the latter; the *development × development* of information processing which is argued by the nervous system is an argument of negative entropy. Once we grasp this, it ceases to be anomalous that, in both Insecta and Vertebrata, high bodily evolution and high evolution of intelligence do not necessarily go together.

There is a corollary. Evolution of nervous control does not stop with whatever makes a physical morphology adequate for coping with the second law of thermodynamics, in whatever form it encounters it ("adaptation to environment"). Were that the case, it is doubtful if said control would ever have experienced anything above the most primitive metazoa. Mere physical adaptations for survival (as some would have it—successful efficiency in the quest for energy to metabolize) are, after all, not so far apart in frog and man. The progressively richer psychic life of animals (demonstrably, a frog behaves more intelligently than a cyclostome) shows up as "creativity"; i.e., "intelligence" manifests more or less wide margins of choice in coping with novelty—and, yes, of making "novelty" come about.

PREREQUISITES FOR A SPEECH-FUNCTION: THE EVOLUTION OF NERVOUS CONTROL

We come to the vertebrate nervous system itself.

Bishop[3] has remarked that the vertebrate nervous system owes its success not so much to its basic morphology as to its capacity for "almost infinite elaboration of its details" (p. 395). It is the capacity for error that makes learning possible: our brain is a very inaccurate computer—which is a saving grace. It secures a viable programming by matching errors and concluding a tolerable probability. It is the author of all the constraints that have channeled the evolutionary elaborations ("Weiterbildingen"). It is the seat of the stability and the monitoring that go with the system. It is worth noting, in passing, that the vertebrate CNS uniquely has "invented" the introduction of the circulatory system into the very intimacy of its neurohistology; which enables its extraordinary growth in bulk and neuronal proliferation. The core function of a nervous system is to gather and process information of an extrinsic nature, from which the brain itself takes no profit. Of course, one is left free to argue that this is what any organ of the body does, be it heart or liver or stomach. I shall not enter into this. Suffice it that a liver transacts chemically on behalf of the body economy, the brain transacts informationally on the same behalf. So—if you double the size of the liver, you may get something of the order of twice the chemical product; double the size of the brain, and you get the difference between an ape's and a pithecanthropine way of thought. . . .

CODING AGAIN: SOME NEUROPSYCHOLOGICAL REMARKS

Thoughout the gathering complexity which shall take us to phasia, neurons persist in talking graded responses, fields induced by cumulative slow potentials at synaptic junctions of neuron populations, the digital all-or-none behavior at those junctions, facilitation, inhibition, afferent terminal differentiation, and so on. (cf. Bishop[3] p. 396). And here we encounter, I think, our first difficulty of principle. As we ascend through the hierarchies of order, of complexity, we can see that our problem is one of how we map an earlier and lowlier level into a later, higher, more complex one. But when we reach the culminative level where at last linguistics may operate, there is no way for us to turn around and recover from these, retropolatively, the course of the syntheses.

Does not all this begin to suggest that an origin and evolution of language must wait upon an origin and evolution of phasia? And for the shaping of phasia we are not yet ready to hunt for clues; we must hunt first for the metaclues that direct our search for the clues.

There are corroborative considerations. The human infant, as he learns to speak, in no way recapitulates the phylogenesis of phasia, for the simple reason that he is merely slogging down through the epigenesis or the program of templates already written into his DNA schedule; whereas the phylogenesis of phasia had to be that of constructing all those DNA emendations in the first place. Furthermore, the course of the degenerative aphasias seldom if ever dissects, retropolatively, along the ontogenetic lines of speech acquisition and, of course, along those of phylogenesis— which really are unknown, in the first place. Finally, the linguists' metalanguages, e.g. the time-honored heurism of phoneme, morpheme, syntax, or the Chomskyan deep analysis or transformations, or any other you may name, do not furnish evolutionary categories. The reason therefor should be obvious as it is simple. Logical categories do not evolve, and it is such that linguistic analyses supply us. The evolution of phasia has been one of transformations in biopsychological processes. How logical categories relate to biopsychological processes is at least as much yours to tell me as vice versa.

We have arrived at where we can begin to argue neuropsychological processes themselves. In the understanding of these there has been a progress no less than explosive, over the recent three decades or so. Let me jot down some changes of understanding.

1. The long-established "connectivism" of neural tracts and circuitry is being supplemented by models of holography and/or correlography; the obvious implication being, that (disregarding even the neurochemistry of it—which we really have no business doing) wiring-models have been found wanting. This has been necessitated by new realizations such as interdendritic potentials essential to maintaining the steady states upon which axonal impulses perform, may I say, as parameters. That long-elusive search for the engram seems to have become slightly less elusive: long-term memories, for instance. Images seem retrievable from distributed information systems if the appropriate "filter" be applied; the engram includes a "filter" among its components. Perhaps it will help if we think of the ordinary photograph as a mosaic of "atomographs" as against the "holograph," wherein the entire image registers in any part of the field, while you vary the size of that field as you please. What this means for us, I think, is, that we shall have to reconstruct a phylogenesis of the neurology of phasia in terms other or more than a connectivism.

A Speaking Brain

2. The conventional conception—at least, I fancy, among us laymen—of "associational" neocortex is rather a vague one, and confined to assumptions of an intracortical traffic, to the neglect of any subcortical; and somehow, therewith, somatosensory, associative, and motor cortexes behave differently, since injuries to them produce characteristically different behaviors. Let us overhaul such an idea. The cortex functions cybernetically, i.e., both afferently and efferently throughout the entire continuum from perception to externalization of a program. Essentially, it monitors even what it shall perceive. Theoretically, information is a measure of the reduction of uncertainty, and a nervous system exploits redundancy in the processing. Consistently with the holographic principle, Pribram[13] analogizes "association" with the searching one can do with a zoom lens: Extend it, and the brain monitors a wider input from the external environment; retract it, and the monitoring narrows down upon internal configurations. By this, token, the so-called "motor cortex" becomes rather a "sensory cortex for action" (Ref. 13, p. 248), but we think of "action" rather in terms of the now-familiar TOTE model, which certainly is cybernetic. This does not, I believe, do away with the utility to the clinician of his symptomic distinction between a Wernicke's and a Broca's aphasia, but it is better theoretical biology.

Histoarchitectonics

We speak with the entire brain. It behooves us to comprehend this neuropsychological fundamental. I can only suggest its intricate schema selectively; some notes, therefore, on the reticular formations, the limbic system, the cerebral cortex; the first, precisely because it is present in all vertebrate brains, and is as primitive in the human as in any other mammal§; the second, because it certainly is active in the symbolic processes; the third for reasons that are not quite so obvious as they are frequently assumed to be.

§The mammalian formation is, fundamentally, about as primitive as in other vertebrates; however, it has added a mantle that seems correlated with the additional evolution of the cerebral hemispheres.

The Reticular System

Yakovlev[14] (p. 293) once ventured that "it is from this primordial neuronal swamp that human thought arose like a sinful orchid." I have been frustrated in all attempts to discover whether he ever expatiated upon this tantalizing bit of poetry; but I cannot tear myself from it. But the vital significance of the reticular formation to *thinking* has been recognized by others (e.g., Hebb;[6] and see Kilmer *et al*[7]).

It traffics significantly even with the cerebral cortex. While its histoarchitecture in the mammals—and this undoubtedly is of telltale significance in the case of man—has added a cortical layer atop the more primitive basic formation, it holds that the reticular neurons, although of varying sizes, are small, their axons are short and branching. The formation builds up some of those celebrated junctional slow potentials, it arouses or deactivates states, according to aminergic or cholinergic stimulations, it effects "mood." But, just because it receives instructions from the cerebral cortex, we must understand "amount" of arousal as no merely quantitative excitability; rather, as an "alteration in the configuration of expectancies" when an input invades the brain state (cf. Pribram,[13] p. 206). Roughly, the formation tells the cortex to pay attention to something that is informative, but leaves it to the cortex to secure that information. This is a way of spelling out the meaning of "orientation." Recalling the functions of the cortex—we have the problem of what the cortex is capable of imparting, joined with what the reticular formation is capable of receiving; and this cortical "whatness" differs in rat and man. But we have gained the very crucial insight that phasia must engage interrelations between quite conservative and very advanced subsystems of the brain; further, that even here man and his fellow mammals are much more alike than different; so that we are dealing with what the theoretical physicist David Bohm[5] (pp. 19 ff) has called "similar differences and different similarities."

The Limbic System

The amygdala and the hippocampus evaluate immediate behavior, as they register short-term memories. Let us say, picturesquely, that the frontal lobes decide what shall be done with the registers and evaluations done by the amygdala and the hippocampus. This, Pribram puts at the base of his idea of symbol-making. We may note, parenthetically, that the human and the monkey amygdala and hippocampus are cytoarchitectonically about on a par; also, that the monkey frontal lobes are proportionately about as large to the rest of the brain as the human lobes are. (In present context and at the present level of discourse, "monkey" requires no sharper specification.) For whatever worth there may be to crude volumetrics, the monkey should be as capable of handling judgmentally whatever the rest of its brain submits, as in the human case.

Speaking is a behavior; behavior is a program; the TOTE executes a programming. Speaking is not just a cortical programming. Speaking is also a mobilization of the self-image. The clinical cerebrologist encounters this dramatically in disturbances of body-scheme. About this we have known at least as early as Hughlings Jackson; and also about the devastations of the speech function that may accompany them. Kubie,[8] in a remarkable series of studies, concluded that it is precisely where the limbic lobe engages the basal part of the nonlimbic temporal lobe that the I-not-I polarity resolves itself during ontogenesis and persists throughout life; here is where the external and internal environments, the past and present, are integrated; the parameters of the physical world of space and time are converted to psychological space and time. Here (still following Kubie) is where the "symbol," in its psychological sense, has its bipolar resolution; and he suggests for MacLean's "visceral brain" the label "psychosomatic organ" (Ref. 8, p. 32). Significantly, MacLean[9] has speculated that the hippocampus is capable of "foolish" symbolisms because it is incapable of the further, fine resolutions of the neocortex; also, that but for the limbic system, we should be as "disembodied spirits" (p. 619). I don't know, of course, what "foolish symbolisms" monkeys with our "quality" of limbic system but an inferior neocortex can engage in; but the laboratory evidence is pretty clear, I think, that they too can be converted, by experimental ablations into "disembodied spirits" of a MacLean variety. The point at this juncture is that speaking is an *ad hoc* mobilization of the *human* self-image in confrontation with the not-I.

The mammalian cerebral cortex being, in a computative way, the most complicated mechanism known to us in the entire universe, it is not hard to see why its machinations have permitted a variety of models that answer to no more than an *ad hoc* aspect of the phenomenon engaged. And it suggests to me that we are in a greater need, not of schemes, but of an appropriate theory of schemes.

I have only a slight notion of what use neurophysiologists or neuropsychologists have found for Pitts and McCulloch's[12] models of manifolds that can scan inputs so that "universals" are recognized; undoubtedly, it will be superfluous to invite the attention of some of this audience to the studies of Michael Arbib;[1] quite as certainly, others will appreciate the reference, if they consult it. The logical calculus of the ideas that are immanent in nervous activity, which Pitts and McCulloch adduced in 1947, is beyond my powers of application; but no matter. They seem to have mounted the entire question in terms only of a binary, a digital logic; and of course they were modeling the processing of present inputs only. The Image as an archived hologram still lay in the future. How do we program an uttered proposition, if the tracts and circuitry of sign and symbol (the respective tracts and circuitry are not the same) must be engaged with a holography?

Still, we have gained one truth out of the creative ingenuity which all this mounting complexity hints at. The cat knows universals by means of exactly the same kind of scanning manifold as we do. If *we* go on to use it for our speech programming, it is because we have a "better" specimen of the same gadget. Of course, you have the perfect right to ask, What is "better"? I'll leave that to the successors of Pitts and McCulloch. A legitimate question—and, I am sure, an answerable one.

Some Features of Neocortex

After these remarks, there should follow some on how thalamus and cerebral hemispheres interrelate. Please indulge my timidity; I shall avoid them; the next remarks, about cortical cytoarchitectonics, are "safe" enough.

The mammals have devised, out of very primitive and rudimentary anlagen of the reptilian brain roof, this evolutionary *nova* that simply has no precedent or analogy anywhere. Of the six histologic laminae of the mammalian cortex, lamina IV is the extrinsic one, and represents, evolutionarily, the fiber extension from the thalamus as the cerebral hemispheres commenced their upgrowth from the telencephalon— presumably, in the theromorphs. Surficial and deep to it lie intrinsic laminae; respectively, I–II III and V–VI. Both of these sets receive and export corticocortical fibers, and all of the cortex possesses the six laminae; but their several proportions of thickness to the total differ and are recognizable with respect to areas in which they occur; so that they must have local stylistic dialects about their scannings. Lamina

IV, for instance, is thinnest in the "motor" cortex, thickest in the "sensory" or "sensory-associational." The quotation-marks are intentional, for these adjectives are not perfectly apt, yet they have to be used still, *faute de mieux*.

But how did this histomorphology arise? What psychic enrichment did it initiate in the theromorphs, and how did it proceed to a further *Weiterbildung*? No one yet knows. Well, while the roots of Yakovlev's sinful orchid continued to abide in the primordial neuronal swamp, a very unpromising bloom was taking its unlovely shape upon a ground that was not yet soil.

AND SOME FURTHER FEATURES: TRANSMODALITIES

Are any alloprimates capable of modal transfer in cognition? Transcortical, subcortical? Partially so—say, audiovisual yet not tactile-auditory or tactile-visual? In some limited degree only? Whatever the answers, the overriding present question is, In how far is transmodality a requisite for the emergence of phasia? We can agree that transmodal capability in *Homo sapiens* has been an advantage; but this is quite another matter, and not really as simple as it has been portrayed in writings.

A field observer of alloprimate behavior must often remain uncomfortably unconvinced when the psychology laboratory fails to discover modal transfers in monkeys; he cannot help wondering whether the trouble may not lie with the experiment as conceived, that is, may have outsmarted itself. But I would not have mentioned it, except that laboratory experiments on man have indicated that he, too, has difficulty with some kinds of modal transfer—so that certainly the origin of phasia was not dependent on those particular kinds.

The inverse of this question is whether, with all possible intermodal transfer in cognition, there need come about any verbalization of it. Such questions are indeed being asked; can they be legitimately asked, before the theoretical premises on which their inductions must be based, are perfectly clear?

Meanwhile, when Washoe heard a dog bark and signed "dog" for the animal she was in the habit of so designating on sight, she rather confounded a few doubtings about an ape's modal transfers in cognition. Notice, too, that it is hard not to presume that she really signed, not a "name" but a holophrastic proposition: there was an assertion within a context, and a summoning of long-term memory from an archive, unreinforced from an immediate visual perception. This, it seems to me, is all that we should require of a phasial beginning, on its cognitive side—which raises unavoidably the question of "naming," although we need not go into it deeply. The notion has persisted among the impedimenta of an earlier period in our thinking; it is, I believe, an arm-chair philosophical speculation sometimes given a scientific dress. That it disappears in certain aphasic disturbances tells us nothing, of course, about its phylogenesis. Nor is it the initiant of speech in ontogenesis. Undoubtedly, a "holophrase" is mistaken more often than not, for a first naming by the infant; but for our theoretical purposes, even this term is not fully satisfactory, since its semantic boundaries are so indeterminate. On the strength of all that has gone before, in this argument, I suggest that we are not ready to define it for a neuropsychology; it is more at home, I think, in a psycholinguistics. When, then, did "naming" come into the evolution of phasia? When, at last, phasia had arrived at that level where it could "name."

If the foregoing argument be sound, then the inadequacy of a purely connectivistic explication of the definitive origin of phasia lies in its too-narrow assignment of a neurological causality: a local developmental specialty of tracts or neuronal populations, e.g., some extra development in Wernicke's area (in the more restricted identification of that surface). It would not matter (I don't think this is an incautious speculation) how much of an angular gyrus a chimpanzee might develop; phasia would not be his, sheerly because his cortical neurons are smaller, more compact, less capable of an indeterminate dendrification, and of both the junctional slow potential fields and commensurate axonal impulses needed. Related to this is the notion that a gestural messaging, such as, let's say, Washoe's, might have been transferred to vocalizing. I have indicated the difficulties underlying this notion; they seem far greater than those who adopt this guess have any inkling about. It will help us here, however, if we reconsider Pribram's appraisal of the "motor" cortex as a "sensory cortex for action": there occurs "an external representation of a psychological set or Plan" (Ref. 13, p. 241). This is no mere expulsion of an output. It enlists the entire TOTE over the cortical activity. The cybernetist Pask[11] once remarked: "The organism views a universe of discourse rather than the flux of physical events to which its receptors are sensitive" (p. 4). The "sensory cortex for action" does not escape this universe of discourse. And from the postrolandic syntheses to the prerolandic gyrus, properly seen, we have but another case of transmodality. Again the plea is for the discovery of metaclues before seeking clues in inductions whose premises first need scrutinizing.

"Hemispheral Dominance."

Perhaps the most widespread and entrenched notion about the functional asymmetry in the human cerebral hemispheres is that, since in the majority of cases the left hemisphere is "dominant for speech" and is responsible for right-handedness, these two properties must be genuinely and functionally related. Apparently, the fact that this conclusion is founded on nothing really more substantial than statistical coincidence, is overlooked. The other fact, that even in Hughlings Jackson's time, there were occasional but significantly numerous cases of the other three matrix possibilities, is likewise disregarded. But most seriously, this sins against the scientific canon that one exception to a stated rule vitiates the authority of the other 999. It is not necessary to review this argument, beyond brief statements. The infant learns to speak several years before its hemispheres have established their functional asymmetry; for a significant length of time, phasial disaster to the incipiently dominant hemisphere may be remedied by the other's takeover. Handedness, however, behaves along a different pattern. It may be inverted without affecting phasial dominance, even in adulthood; what skills may have been learned by one hand may be practised, although clumsily at first, by the other.

An antomist may well wonder how any functional intimacy between the two phenomena ever came to be surmised in the first place. The motor representations of hand and buccopharynx on the precentral cortex are near each other, but not adjoined. This is no serious objection; what is more anomalous for the notion that the behaviors are somehow related, is the fact that it is precisely representations of the vocalizing and articulating mechanisms that are functionally coequal: there is no cerebral dominance-subordinance. I speak with both sides of my face and pharynx.

At the same time—the statistical incidence for speech and for handedness is quite consistent with the hypothesis that their high frequency-in-common is a case of independent origins that have so persisted. A brief and informal explication will do. Assume that the protohuman brain was confronting the unbiased choice of settling, respectively, a speech dominance and a handedness in either hemisphere. The choice being 50-50 for each trait, clearly there will be four equal possibilities of combination. Both functions "chose" to locate in the left hemisphere, on the whole, but not 100%.

In a statistical biology, perhaps such distributions occur more frequently than not. (I doubt if anyone can find any selective value in the actually predominant frequency.)

There is something more positive to say about it, however, from the standpoint of evolving self-organizing systems.

Interhemispheral relations, particularly the role of the corpus callosum, are currently so much under research that one cannot be sure but that anything he says today will be obsolete tomorrow. Any one of us, I daresay, could ask some unanswerable questions about this gigantic paradox, and for the nonce we may expect it to grow even bigger as knowledge increases. But our commitment to our topic will not permit us to dodge it.

Cytoarchitecturally and physiologically, the two hemispheres are so closely identical, that they "ought to" produce identically. Moreover—quite certainly the "minor" hemisphere is not phasially idiotic, whatever else we may say about it. The human corpus callosum is the largest of all commissures (though I know nothing about that of the whale); should one not expect a tremendous, double-barreled, mutual reinforcement? Is it not paradoxical that we are not more intelligent than we really are? These are naive questions that actually have been asked, in earlier days; their trouble lies in that they are miscast.

A homogeneous self-organizing system, if it is growing even more complex, eventually reaches a state where it logically and necessarily segregates within itself heterogeneities, without ceasing, so to say, being itself. This is a general principle, be it noted. Moreover—with respect to nervous activity, it is being realized that the *inhibitory* role has been neglected—it having been assumed that the function of a neuron is to transmit impulses, if it can. But an organized action represents an orchestration; it is a configuration of constraints. This is not just a figure of speech; but let us treat it for the moment as a metaphor. The occasional silences of certain orchestral instruments is a *positive* part of the score, not just a functional deletion. And the score was written by *one* composer, and the playing is done under *one* baton. I don't know where the homunculus who monitors the orchestration of an utterance is seated within the brain, but the two hemispheres seem to know. Let us try to think in terms of neurophysiological states, with impulses occurring as parameters invading those states. The orchestrations of the hemispheres may happen, if the respective hemispheres do not duplicate their states, so that the impulses cannot duplicate, either. Moreover, it is feasible, at the most elementary level of consideration, to think of communication in terms of bits transmitted under constraints; but at the most complex level, where thought is programmed and given exit, *constrained nontransmission* is also part of the act of communication. (Any linguist can illustrate this, within his universe of discourse.) The corpus callosum seems to know this full well, having been told so by the hemispheres. Now it should be clear why I am unenthusiastic about "dominance-subordinance," "major-minor"—until and unless they can be so leached as to become merely neutral labels.

Shall we think of the two hemispheres, plus their tremendous commissure, as a system of relationships *before* we take them apart to find out what each does? This procedure would conform to holistic theory, wherein the information of the whole is much more than the sum of the information of its parts, and is not recoverable from that information.

To return for a moment to the universals of Pitts and McCulloch—they have said that the brain does not and need not use the language we use toward each other. Obviously, coded transformations must occur, somewhere, repeatedly, recurrently. We recall that every time an antecedent neuronal aggregate transmits to a consequent aggregate, this is a neurologic *proposition*. Moreover, the antecedent is a constraining environment to the consequent. All speech also is a proposition—but, *fide* Pitts and McCulloch, in a language other than brain language. We recognize that the one cannot occur without the other, but this gives no comfort at all to proponents of any kind of psychophysical parallelism. I am suggesting only that the transform processes that do the translating belong within the *metaclues* we are seeking, before we run astray among false clues.

Now by way of an epilogue. There exists the very dubious assumption that alloprimate brains possess no such functional asymmetries. But really, we simply do not know whether they do or not, nor have we yet devised ways for finding out. Surely such discovery does not lie in referring the alloprimate brain to the manifest uniquenesses of human functional asymmetries. For that matter, as yet we know but little about other, less dramatic asymmetries in the human brain; although the spectacular work being done in southern California by means of the split-brain tactic comes to mind immediately, and (to me) that of Dr. Joseph Bogen in particular.[4] And may I suggest (while we are in this speculative mood) that when at last we have learned to ask the right questions, we may discover that functional asymmetry in the mammalian cerebral hemsipheres is their general and common characteristic. Quite obviously, this would stand the whole argument about human laterality on its head. The right questions and the right answers will first be *metaclues*; only subsequently and consequently will the clues show up.

REFERENCES

1. ARBIB, M. A. 1971. How We Know Universals. Retrospect and prospect. Math. Bioscience **11**: 95–107.
2. ASHBY, W. R. 1962. Principles of the Self-Organizing System. *In* Principles of Self-Organization. H. V. Foerster and G. W. Zopf, Eds. Pergamon. New York, N.Y.
3. BISHOP, G. H. 1958. Natural History of the Nerve Impulse. Physiol. Rev. **36**: 376–399.
4. BOGEN, J. E. 1969. The Other Side of the Brain. Bull. Los Angeles Neurol. Soc. **34**: 73–104, 135–162, 191–220. See further, with H. W. Gordon. 1974. Hemispheric Lateralization of Singing after Intracarotid Sodium Amylobarbitone. J. Neurol. Neurosurg. Psychiatry **37**: 727–738.
5. BOHM, D. 1969. Some remarks on the notion of order. *In* Towards a Theoretical Biology. C. H. Waddington, Ed.: vol. **II**: 18–60; also, 90–92. Aldine. Chicago, Ill.
6. HEBB, D. O. 1959. Intelligence, Brain Function and the Theory of Mind. Brain **82**: 260–275.
7. KILMER, W. L., W. S. McCULLOCH & J. BLUM. 1968. Towards a theory of the reticular formation. *In* The Mind: Biological Approaches to Its Functions. W. C. Corning and M. Balaban, Eds. Interscience Publishers. New York, N.Y.
8. KUBIE, L. S. 1953. Some implications for psychoanalysis of modern concepts of the organization of the brain. Pscyhoanal. Quart. **22**: 21–68.
9. MACLEAN, P. D. 1958. Contrasting functions of limbic and neocortical systems of the brain and their relevance to psychophysiological aspects of medicine. Amer. J. Med. **25**: 611–626.
10. McCULLOCH, W. S. & W. PITTS. 1943. A logical calculus of the ideas immanent in nervous activity. Bull. Math. Biophys. **5**: 115–133.
11. PASK, G. 1966. A Cybernetic Model for Some Types of Learning and Mentation. Mimeo. Richmond, Surrey, England.
12. PITTS, W. & W. S. McCULLOCH. 1947. How We Know Universals. Bull. Math. Biophys. **9**: 127–147.
13. PRIBRAM, K. H. 1971. Languages of the Brain. Prentice Hall. Englewood Cliffs, N.J.
14. YAKOVLEV, P. I. 1959. Remarks in First Conference on the Central Nervous System and Behavior. M. A. B. Brazier, Ed. Josiah Macy, Jr. Fdn., New York, N.Y.

DISCUSSION PAPER: THE EVOLUTION OF HUMAN COMMUNICATION: WHAT CAN PRIMATES TELL US?*

Nancy Tanner

Merrill College
University of California, Santa Cruz
Santa Cruz, California 95064

Adrienne Zihlman

Oakes College
University of California, Santa Cruz
Santa Cruz, California 95064

FRAMING THE QUESTION

The seeming discontinuity between nonhuman primate and human communication poses a dilemma: if humans can speak, but monkeys and apes cannot, if humans communicate via an ordered system of arbitrary symbols called language but other primates do not, then how was this "great divide" between "man and beast" bridged? To compare human language in its narrower sense with an overly simple account of nonhuman primate communication—i.e., seen as strictly limited to the expression of motivational states—can highlight what has been added during the course of human evolution. Such a dichotomous formulation, however, makes it difficult to conceptualize *how* human communicatory behavior and the underlying anatomical structures could have developed from precursors. Speech is an important component of human communication, but does not in itself constitute the whole system. The relevant comparison is between human communication in its entirety and primate communication in its full complexity and sophistication. We approach the task of tracing out continuity by suggesting a framework, and use the chimpanzee as a model to identify the features which early humans may have shared with the ancestral population. We conclude by raising questions to delineate further the continuity between nonhuman primate and human communication.

COMMUNICATION: A CONFIGURATION OF MULTIPLE MODES

Mammalian communicatory systems utilize all of the senses—visual, olfactory, auditory, tactile—but the overall configuration differs from one species to the next. The kinds of information received and transmitted vary according to the species' sensory-motor modes and relate to its way of life: whether active by day or night, whether social or solitary, whether living in trees or open areas. The organs used in communication—an elephant's trunk, a monkey's hand or tail, or the human face and vocal apparatus—rely on sensory-motor elaborations and specializations of the nervous system.

Even though certain senses and expressive and manipulatory modes may predominate for different species, communication usually takes place through a patterned

*The Ford Foundation (grant no. 739-003-200 to N.T.), the Wenner-Gren Foundation for Anthropological Research (grants to A.Z.) and the Faculty Research Committee, University of California, Santa Cruz (N.T. and A.Z.) partly supported research from which these ideas developed.

467

combination of modalities. In most situations, communication between animals is a complex of visual, auditory, tactile and sometimes olfactory signals.[50] The significance of any one signal is affected by the matrix of signals into which it is incorporated.

In monkeys and apes, and to some extent, humans, the visual sense predominates. Orientation, position, and movement of body, tail, face and limbs—including facial expressions and gestures—communicate to others at close range. Vocalizations often accompany the visual information.[50] Among prosimians, by contrast, the visual mode is less well developed, whereas chemical communication and the sense of smell are essential. For monkeys and apes there is also considerable reliance on tactile communication through many forms of body contact—grooming, touching, sitting next to another animal or, for the young, clinging to and being embraced by the mother.

Complexity of communication systems among mammals, including primates, is relative. When all types of signals sent and the senses utilized to receive these signals are considered, the complexity of the repertoire (number of modalities) is surprisingly comparable from one group to another, even for species as different as shrews and spider monkeys.[17] Complexity, in itself, is not an issue. We focus on nonhuman primate, specifically chimpanzee, communication not because it is more complex but because the anatomical and sensory-motor bases are similar to our own.

Human communication typically integrates the monkey/ape system of tactile and visually based cues with an almost infinite combination of vocalizations, including both speech, a symbolic vocal code, and paralinguistic vocal behavior. Like chimpanzees and other mammals, humans utilize all the senses in communication to some extent. Yet, because of our conceptual and symbol-using abilities, spoken language, with its anatomical correlates in the brain and vocal apparatus, makes possible transmission of a broad range of information, provides a way to express past and future, and expands the range of social interactions. Humans also have the ability to devise many types of codes: written language, Morse code, computer languages, musical scores, American sign language, and ritual. This, of course, gives the human communication system a different configuration from that of other mammals; even so, the systems share a great deal. It is the finely tuned integration of modalities in human and in other mammalian systems that expresses meaning. The senses—vision, hearing, touch—receive these signals, and the brain decodes and interprets the overall message. The human communication system overlaps that of apes, monkeys, and other mammals to varying degrees, but has its own characteristic configuration.

CHIMPANZEES AS A MODEL OF THE ANCESTRAL POPULATION

If the question is "how did the specific configuration of the human communicatory system evolve?" rather than the origin of language or speech *per se*, then nonhuman primate and especially chimpanzee behavior becomes a rich source of ideas concerning the basis for the development of the human communication system. Nonhuman primates have long been regarded as the logical starting point for hypothesizing evolutionary continuity with the behavior of the human primate. As data have accumulated in the past decade, the case for looking closely at chimpanzees in particular has become compelling. In anatomy, behavior, and genetics, humans and chimpanzees are very similar.[43,87,88,95] The emerging picture from biochemistry suggests that in genetic terms chimpanzees are little removed from humans. It is probable that chimpanzees are much like the population that gave rise to living chimpanzees, gorillas, and humans, a radiation that occurred perhaps only five million years ago.[75] This means that many traits that we share with living chimpanzees probably existed in the common ancestor. It is no accident that data on chimpanzee communication and mental capacities are immensely suggestive for questions concerning human communication.

The traditional studies showing human and ape similarities in anatomy and behavior, by Darwin[12] and Huxley[39] and later expanded by Köhler,[45] Yerkes,[94] and others are now supplemented by extensive field and experimental behavioral research. Experimental studies identify and compare cognitive and sensory-motor capacities and the way chimpanzees, humans, and other species utilize space and objects. Field studies show the complexity and flexibility of chimpanzee social organization, their large and ecologically diverse home ranges, and their extensive object manipulation. For example, they use a wide variety of materials as tools with many functions—for probing when termiting and ant-dipping, for pounding nuts, opening fruits, prying, sponging, wiping, and throwing.[85]

Chimpanzees possess a range of behaviors, even if in elemental form, very similar to our own. Field and experimental data provide reason to believe that the population immediately ancestral to the human line already possessed, as do living chimpanzees, some of the underlying mental capacities necessary for further communicatory development, particularly with regard to the referential function. This is crucial; in evolution no capacity or anatomical structure appears without a behavioral precursor. An integrated communicatory system with a configuration that included elements essential to the fully human system was probably beginning to evolve as early as the transitional hominid population.

Chimpanzee Social Interaction and Communication

Regional populations or "communities" of chimpanzees number some 30–80 individuals that associate in temporary groups of shifting composition, seldom larger than 20–30 animals.[41,42,62,64,77,80] Individuals meet in the course of their travels around their home range. Presumably all these individuals recognize each other, but interaction among them is not random. Adults of the same sex who associate may be sisters, mother and daughter, or brothers; those of the opposite sex, sister and brother, mother and son.[27,30] Individual preferences, personality traits, or sexual attraction may also be bases for association. Social interactions between the sexes and among individuals of different ages and social positions are frequent and less rigidly patterned than for baboons and other species of monkeys.

In the context of the temporary nature of chimpanzee groups and their loose social structure, patterns of communication in fact define relations between and among individuals and reinforce and maintain social bonds. Friendly behaviors, such as kissing, embracing, and for males, touching genitals, seem unusually elaborate in chimpanzees.[29,63] Gestures appear to reflect situational factors and individual expression, and do not represent merely a measure of dominance/subordinate relations, as is thought to be the case for other primate species. The chimpanzee communication system provides the mechanisms and abilities for coordinating and facilitating social relations within their flexible, multipatterned social organization.

Chimpanzees' rich nonverbal repertoire shows that many social interactions can be mediated without the use of language, or even of vocal communication. These social communications are more elaborate, complex, and more specifically *interanimal* in nature (i.e., truly communicatory) than would be expected if they were strictly expressions of somatic or motivational states such as fear, anxiety, anger or excitement. Expressions of "reassurance" such as patting, hugging, and kissing involve physical contact and may occur when animals have been frightened, attacked, or excited.[29] One chimpanzee may "comfort" another by putting an arm around that individual, or an adult may pat a young animal on the head or another adult on the back. Similarly, an animal's selection among "conciliatory" gestures, such as presenting, bowing, bobbing, crouching, kissing, and grinning as an appropriate reaction to another's agonistic behavior exemplifies an awareness and weighing of the intensity of the other animals' intent. A smaller animal may solicit reassurance from a larger one that aggression will not occur.

The range of postures, gestures, and facial expressions help explain the relatively low frequency of aggression observed in free-ranging, unprovisioned chimpanzees.[72,78,79] Such signals may avert actual fighting, so that avoidance is unnecessary. Their fluid social organization, where individuals are not restricted to continual association with the same animals, means that they can and do avoid fighting by avoiding each other. Because, however, their communicatory repertoire offers many alternatives to aggressive behavior, avoidance between animals is not always necessary, and their sociability is thereby reinforced.

Although this communication is "expressive," chimpanzees evince an awareness of what is being communicated. A gesture, the outstretching of a hand, for example, may be made and responded to in a variety of ways, which change with context. When one animal has food that another wants, one will "beg" from the other by an outstretched hand, palm up, combined with looking intently into the face of the individual with the preferred object. The animal begged from may give some to the begging animal, threaten, pull away, or turn its back on the other individual and by implication on the request itself.[28,83] In another context, an animal that is hurt, frightened, or excited, may seek reassurance from another animal with an outstretched hand.

Their social interaction and communication appear to reflect an incipient concept of "other." What is meant by this is not, of course, a complex philosophical construct but the fact that chimpanzees recognize and greet a number of other chimpanzees, prefer the company of certain ones, show awareness of another's emotional state, and have an appropriate behavioral response. Experimental studies (see below) indicate that a complementary awareness of "self" also exists. Chimpanzees interpret what they observe in their social environment. Their social interactions are communicatory in nature, and conversely, much of their communication is social.

Experimental Studies and Mental Abilities

Recent experimental studies on chimpanzees have gone beyond Köhler's earlier studies[45] showing their "cleverness" with objects, and reveal more about the underlying mental capacities. We will discuss four kinds of experiments: on sensory modalities; on self-recognition; on use of space and "cognitive mapping"; and those in which chimpanzees are taught to communicate with signs designed by humans through gestures or inanimate objects.

Chimpanzees and to a more limited extent monkeys[11,91] do abstract and exchange information between different sensory modalities, specifically between vision and touch.[13-15] This capacity, known as cross-modal perception, previously was thought to be an exclusively human trait. These abilities have been expressed experimentally by chimpanzees viewing squares, circles, and triangles and then in a blind situation identifying the correct shapes by feeling wooden cutouts. Other experiments give chimpanzees the opportunity to feel a variety of objects and later to see and identify them.[14] Cross-modal transfers are a necessary, although not sufficient, basis for language as we know it because the ability to name objects, a fundamental element of human language, depends upon the capacity to make these transfers.[25]

Gallup[21] has shown that chimpanzees, but not monkeys, have a concept of self-recognition. After chimpanzees were exposed to mirrors, behavior directed toward the self in the form of self-grooming to parts of the body otherwise virtually inaccessible without the mirror increased, whereas social responses directed to the mirror image (as if it were another chimpanzee) decreased. As further experimental evidence, an eyebrow ridge and top of the opposite ear were marked with red dye on four chimpanzees. Mark-directed responses dramatically increased as they visually inspected the dyed areas in the mirror. By contrast, six macaque monkeys were exposed to mirrors, but even after three weeks continued to respond to the mirror as if it were another monkey. The capacity of chimpanzees for self-recognition and self-directed behavior again illustrates their high level of cognitive ability.

In experiments in an acre enclosure Menzel[51,53,57] demonstrated that chimpanzees use space differently from monkeys. Chimpanzees are more aware of their environment, spend more time in the center of an area, cover an area more systematically and notice and investigate more kinds of objects. Most activity in the one-acre enclosure was centered about objects of some kind. This further confirms that chimpanzees are exceptionally object-oriented, as is also evident in field studies.

Chimpanzees can find and eat food selectively.[55] Preferred foods (fruits) and other food (vegetables) were hidden randomly around the enclosure; a chimpanzee was carried and shown where each piece of food was hidden. When released, the animal found and ate the preferred food first, obtained by a least-distance strategy, then located and ate the other food. Such behavior indicates a "cognitive mapping" ability, i.e., that chimpanzees can organize information about the environment and utilize it selectively.[55]

A series of studies aimed at teaching chimpanzees to communicate using human modalities—i.e., gestural signs from a standard sign language, ASL[19,20,22-24] and plastic chips with arbitrary meanings[68-70]—further explicate the extent of chimpanzee cognitive abilities. The Gardners taught Washoe, a young female chimpanzee, simplified ASL in a stimulus-rich environment. Of particular interest was the two-way nature of the ASL communication. An example of appropriate contextual response and spontaneous use of ASL signs was Washoe's making the sign combinations "Key open food," in front of the locked refrigerator. Typical dialogues included (1) *Washoe*: "Please."; *Person*: "What you want?"; *Washoe*: "Out." (2) *Washoe*: "More"; *Person*: "More what?"; *Washoe*: "Tickle." Some of Washoe's "mistakes" were as revealing as her correct usage. For example, she confused the signs for "comb" and "brush," showing that an association of function occurred.

The problem of determining whether a given gesture is or is not a certain ASL sign has been bypassed by the Premacks.[70] Plastic chips of different colors and shapes, each of which had been arbitrarily assigned the meaning of an English noun, verb, or grammatical category such as the interrogative or conditional, were used as the medium in these experimentally rigorous attempts to "teach language" to Sarah, a young chimpanzee. Sarah, working and interacting with human researchers (e.g., in a "social context," though more structured than Washoe's interaction with the Gardners), learned to recognize and respond to about 130 of these plastic chips with 75-80% reliability. She learned to understand their use to express relatively complex matters and could respond well enough to receive the reward. For example, she learned the meaning of the sign $\supset$, which marked the conditional, and thus was able to respond to "Sarah take banana $\supset$ Mary no give Sarah chocolate." Sarah learned not to eat the banana, which she liked, so that she might get chocolate, which she liked better.

These studies demonstrate a range of chimpanzee cognitive abilities: they do think and they possess potentialities essential for symbol-using communication. Although chimpanzees have only the expressive, somatic modalities with which to communicate, they possess a considerable capacity to take in, process, and act on information. Given a vehicle—ASL gestures or plastic chips—chimpanzees can learn to express their wants and communicate with humans by means of codes devised by humans.

Equally if not more important than chimpanzee-human communication is interanimal communication in their natural setting. Most chimpanzee communication takes place at close range: the visual mode is important. Chimpanzees observe even minor changes in facial expressions, body posture, and orientation. Menzel's research on eight young chimpanzees living together illuminates *what* they can communicate to each other and *how* they can do so.[52,54,56,58] In several experiments chimpanzees rapidly learned and systematized information about the environment and then communicated it to each other, using subtle behavioral cues. Experimenters carried and showed novel objects to a chimpanzee that was released afterward along with the others.[52,58] The responses of "follower" chimpanzees differed, depending on the nature of the object in the enclosure and the personality of the "leader." If it was a fear object such as a snake, they followed far behind; if a preferred food, they rushed ahead, and tried to find and so reach the food first. But they seldom bothered to follow one chimpanzee who rarely shared. The rate at which a chimpanzee approached a hidden distant object varied with social conditions and the nature of the object; rate and direction of movement provided cues to the group. Other cues are probably still to be identified.

Particularly fascinating were chimpanzees' attempts to conceal information.[54] When a particularly desired object was shown to the "leader" chimpanzee, occasionally it initially moved away from the object to throw others off the track, then doubled back. Some awareness of—and an attempt to control—what information was being communicated to the others obviously occurred.

Whatever signals the group members were "reading," the information provided by the "leader" was sufficient for them to behave differentially, depending on the object shown to the "leader."[58] The movements, gestures, facial expressions, and vocalizations long regarded as "expressions of motivational states" evidently have both interanimal communicatory functions and also transmit information about the environment. The cognitive ability evinced in how chimpanzees utilize space, their preoccupation with objects and their ability to communicate to each other about objects in the experimental context are doubtless integral to their dietary adaptations in the wild.

REEVALUATING PRIMATE COMMUNICATION: THE LIMITATION OF DICHOTOMIES

Until quite recently it was possible to state that "it is the communication of thought, rather than the thought itself, that is unique to man, makes human culture possible, and that is the primary factor in separating man from beast."[90] Today we must acknowledge that humans are no more unique in this respect, as compared with chimpanzees, than in tool-using and -making. As experimental studies show, chimpanzees do more than express mood or emotional states; they apparently have the ability to transfer information external to themselves to other animals, and to withhold information as well. The earlier dichotomy between animal tool-using and human tool-making no longer stands; it is now known that chimpanzees regularly select materials and modify objects for future use. Similarly, the communication of chimpanzee thoughts, in an elemental way, takes place.

Discussions have centered on the question of whether a gestural language may have preceded the development of vocal language. Proponents of an early gestural language note that considerable nonvocal communication occurs among apes,[37,38] and experiments indicate that chimpanzees can be taught human sign language and elemental grammar, but not to speak.[36] Further, as Steklis and Harnad point out, "both speech and motor dominance are co-lateralized in the same, left hemisphere" and "tool-fashioning and use . . . partakes of the same asymmetry." They suggest this is not coincidental and that "gestural signaling . . . would provide the most direct link between these two species of complex lateralized praxis."[76] On the other hand, Washburn has stressed that human language is a unique vocally based system whereby, through the recombination of a limited number of arbitrary elements (phonemes) it is possible to produce vocal signs for a potentially endless variety of meanings.[89,90] At one stage it was important to set up a dichotomy, as Washburn has done, so that it is possible to define issues. Today, with more data available and a perspective that emphasizes continuity, we can begin to formulate the intervening steps.

Lancaster, as Washburn, earlier claimed that primate communication systems "are not major steps toward language," and focused her attention on the "major gap which separates language from nonhuman communication."[47] At the same time, Lancaster correctly points out that investigators have overstressed vocalizations in nonhuman primate communication and that primates communicate by utilizing a complex constellation of many modes—postural, gestural, vocal, facial expression, movement—within a social context. But the gestures, postures, facial and bodily movements so much a part of primate communication are integral to human communication as well.[2,5,26,34]

Social context, body movements, facial expression, stylized gestures, and paralinguistic vocal qualities such as breathlessness, tone of voice, and rapidity of speech, are all exceedingly important in human communication and are essential to our evaluation of linguistic utterance and to the decoding of meaning: Is the person telling the truth? How important is the information? What is left unsaid? The meaning we read from an utterance, and the action we therefore take or do not take, frequently has more to do with nonverbal aspects than with the words themselves. This is why it is possible to have misunderstandings between cultural groups even though they speak the same "words," or alternatively, for people to communicate to some degree even when speaking different languages. Just as students of primate communication formerly overemphasized vocalization, so also in the past students of human communication focused too exclusively on formal language, e.g. grammatical and semantic categories.

Early anthropologists were fascinated with relationships of "language and culture," of symbol system to symbol system,[3,4,18,40,73,74,92] a theme subsequently elaborated in "cognitive anthropology."[8,31,86] Later, the importance of studying symbols in action was stressed and a new subdiscipline developed that dealt with the use of speech in society.[32,33,71,81] With studies on "kinesics," "paralanguage," and "nonverbal communication," the full range of elements that enter into human communication (and so social interaction) is becoming apparent.[2,5,34] For example, work on both verbal and nonverbal communication illustrates how the communication system of Black Americans differs from that of members of the white subculture.[1,44,46,60] "Language and culture" has been too limiting a framework; similarly, "speech and society." If origins of human communication are to be fathomed, paralinguistic, kinesic, and other nonverbal aspects must be integrated with speech in its social context and language as a symbol system.

Dichotomous formulations have inhibited explorations of the evolution of human communication. Most discussion has been phrased in terms of 1) language and speech rather than communication and 2) gestural versus vocal language. A more useful question is: How did the somatic expressive communication system already present in an ancestral ape-like population of perhaps five million years ago mediate the development of the more arbitrary, symbolic, and referential aspects of the fully human communicatory system?

HUMAN COMMUNICATION: AN EVOLUTIONARY PERSPECTIVE

For virtually all of human evolution, from the australopithecines of three or more million years ago, through *Homo erectus* and even for *Homo sapiens*, almost up until the beginning of recorded history a few thousand years ago, humans have associated in small face-to-face communities that were rarely more than 100 and ordinarily less than 50 or even 30 individuals. Think of the evolution of human communication in that context: known individuals, regularly associating, traveling together or resting in camps where there were no walls between an individual and others. Every gesture, every gleam of an eye, each nod or outstretched hand, a smile or a grimace, a face pallid or flushed, was readily observable. However speech developed, it clearly evolved in a matrix of extensive nonverbal communication.

For *Australopithecus* and *Homo erectus*, face-to-face interaction probably became more intense from that of the chimpanzee-like ancestor. With the move on to the savanna, individuals were more visible to each other than in the forest habitat; and the existence of campsites suggest that many individuals were in more regular and closer association than seems to be true for forest-living chimpanzees. Draper's research[16] on contemporary Bushman gatherer-hunters of the Kalahari desert documents close interaction in campsites, the kind of physical and social association that may have characterized early hominids. Although Bushman groups disperse during the day to gather fruits and vegetables and to hunt animals, at the end of the day they come together and concentrate in camps of 30–40 people with average space of only 188 square feet per person. The regular face-to-face contact which very likely occurred throughout human evolution had important implications for the configuration of the developing communication system.

With such face-to-face contact, control of "expressive" nonverbal communication probably increased. With growing awareness of self, others, and communication itself, plus the development of expressive control, selective "sending" and even prevarication became possible. As Hewes has aptly stated, "The ability to lie is not so much a matter of language use or abuse, but of demeanor ... Lying is often expressed in language; but its essence seems to be in the ability to conceal emotional cues, to suppress signs of one's intentions, or to fail to provide information useful to others."[38] At an early stage in evolution there is still no need to hypothesize speech or any other form of linguistic interchange for selective "sending" to occur. Recall Menzel's chimpanzees and their ability to mislead.

For humans, aspects of nonverbal communication are, at least to some degree, under conscious control and play an important role in social interaction and organization.[26] Human prevarication and partial conscious control of demeanor suggest that the first step in the development of a distinctly human communication system lay in increased links between the "emotional" and "cognitive," in greater control over somatic, expressive forms of communication.

As mental capacities expanded, and evolving hominids were taking in, processing, interpreting, and acting on more and more information gleaned from the natural and social environments, some means of selectively organizing and transmitting such information became necessary. Similarly, as hominids became more and more enchanted and troubled by memories of dream images, a need for symbols to define and order meaning emerged. Such symbols then could be used to communicate not only remembrances of dreams but to share memories of what was seen or done during the day with others after returning to camp.

Another explanation, that communication using arbitrary signs arose in the context of subsistence, appears less likely. Most human, like nonhuman primate manual behaviors—those requiring hand-eye coordination—and therefore most subsistence activities, are learned through observation and practice. Among Eskimos, for example, in learning hunting skills there is more emphasis on practical "on the job" training and less on verbal instruction of youths by older men.[61] Chimpanzee foraging, food collecting, and predation[28,83] further dissuade us that speech would be necessary (or even advantageous) for early gatherer-hunters. While gathering plants, speech would add little, although do no harm; during predation or hunting, anything as noisy as speech would likely frighten away the prey.

Similarly, theories postulating prior development of a gestural language—although attractive in that these theories take cognizance of gestural sensory-motor potentials shared by humans and apes[6]—are also unlikely if too tightly tied to pragmatic concerns. The hands are not free during either gathering or hunting. Visualize a gatherer carrying a digging stick, gathered food, and possibly an infant. Hands carrying a butchering tool and animal flesh were no less occupied. Quite possibly the context for communicatory control and the development of arbitrary symbols for expressing meaning is to be sought in leisure or in food-processing activities back in camp where many individuals were associated, rather than in seeking food away from camp.

We suggest that for *Australopithecus* and early *Homo erectus*, expressive control—of facial expressions, vocalizations, gestures; that is, control of what is "sent" and "not sent"—in the context of face-to-face interaction with known individuals at camp was an initial step toward language: this was an elaboration of abilities already present and shared with the chimpanzee-like ancestor. Stylized gestures may have developed to some extent; the similar gestural sensory-motor capacities of apes and humans make it difficult to ignore this possibility totally. The expressive face and vocalizations, however, were also coming under increasing conscious control, and their importance for communication in camp was enhanced when hands were busy. To the extent that communication continued past dusk, control of vocalization in communication would be particularly advantageous.

With developing minds came the possibility for mental "aloneness" even when in physical proximity. Speech could maintain or increase sociability (and decrease "loneliness") by acting as a means for sharing thoughts, especially disturbing ones. Chimpanzees, for example, upon observing the accidental death of another known chimpanzee, engaged in somewhat "frenzied" activity and interaction.[84] Language could substitute for such behavior by providing an alternative means of expression and social contact. As speech developed, perhaps it was less essential for teaching motor skills associated with food-getting or for organizing action during gathering, predation, or, later, hunting[92] than for constructing beliefs and ritual to deal with separation and death, for telling stories and relating dreams, musing about the past, and proposing tomorrow's activities.[95]

COMMUNICATION AS AN EVOLVING BEHAVIORAL SYSTEM: RELEVANT QUESTIONS

We see two research areas as particularly promising for understanding the evolution of human communication: (1) detailed comparisons of the configurations of human, ape, and monkey communication systems and (2) continuing exploration

.natomical bases, particularly the brain's role. How is the brain organized?
does it function to integrate and orchestrate the various sensory-motor
.lities so that meaningful exchanges can occur?

During human evolution the configuration of communicatory patterns shifted—
 hough most, if not all, the elements may be present in a rudimentary sense in
chimpanzees and perhaps in the others apes, or even monkeys, as well. How can the
essential elements be identified and the similarities and differences in the configurations of nonhuman primate and human communication systems be described?
Suzanne Chevalier-Skolnikoff's comparisons of sensory-motor developmental sequences (using categories adapted from Piaget) among young humans, gorillas, and
macaque monkeys[6] exemplifies one way that this task can be approached. Identification of similarities and differences in nonhuman primate and human patterns will
enable more refined comparisons. As questions improve and additional fine-grained
data accumulate, it will become possible better to hypothesize the intermediate steps
that may have existed prior to the development of the fully human communication
system which includes speech as an integral part.

Changes in the brain are clearly a key to understanding how speech became an
aspect of human communication.[59,66] Chimpanzees' ability to communicate with
human codes when trained suggests that once brains have the capacity to decode
expressive behavior in order to obtain information about the social and physical
environment, and to send information via "expressive" modalities, those brains *also*
have the ability to use symbolic codes if available. This is not the same as inventing
the codes, and we still do not know when or how the first language was invented.

What are the anatomical bases for the human communication system? Asymmetry of the brain has been linked with language and speech and was once considered a
distinguishing feature of the human neocortex.[65] But recent research[48] shows that
there is possible asymmetry in the cortex of great apes (orangutan and chimpanzees).
Hemispheric asymmetry implies specialization of function; coordination and integration therefore become critical. The size of the corpus callosum, a bundle of nerve-
fibers connecting the right and left hemispheres, is consistent with the possibility of
some hemispheric asymmetry for the great apes. This structure is relatively (and
absolutely) large in humans, next in apes, then in monkeys; its volume (compared to
the medulla) is 1.2 to 1 for monkeys, 1.8 to 1 for chimpanzees and 3 to 1 for
humans.[90] In addition to investigating the anatomical bases, viewing communication
in a social context with brain-behavior interrelationships[67] is an approach that will
assist in integrating many types of data.

Count has offered a powerful imagery of brain orchestration.[10] What is important
about his conception of the human brain is his emphasis that it is an interacting
system.[9] Count claims, "We speak with the whole brain."[10] More to the point, we
communicate with the whole brain—by an orchestration of several modalities:
speech, paralinguistic qualities, facial expressions, gestures, and other kinesic
behavior. What has been the nature of the interrelation of anatomy and function, of
brain and communication, in evolution? Perhaps what was critical initially was the
encephalization of "expressive" features: making these features accessible to symbolization, first in "decoding" as chimpanzees do, then in encoding them as well, as in
the human communication system. More extensive linkages between the "emotive"
and the "cognitive" in the brain may also provide a key to vocalizations becoming
"cerebral," and therefore to vocal behavior becoming a potentially available mode
for symbolic expression and leading eventually to the development of spoken
language as one aspect of human communication.

Over the past decade, research in a number of disciplines illuminates the
continuity in cognitive abilities between human, ape, and monkey. Investigating

animal and even nonhuman primate communication as a means to learn about human language has been questioned.[49] This, however was before biochemical comparisons (which indicate that a recent divergence of humans and African apes is highly probable)[43,75,93] and the extensive research on chimpanzees, such as field work by Goodall and associates,[27-30] and by Japanese field researchers;[41,42,62-64,77-80] Menzel's experiments on several chimpanzees in a large enclosure;[51-58] Davenport, Rogers, and Russell's documentation of cross-modal transfers in apes;[13-15] and research by the Gardners[22-24] and Premacks.[68-70] Further, continuity in cognition between monkey and ape is suggested by studies on the ability of monkeys to make cross-modal transfers, and on possible cerebral dominance.[11,35,91] These many recent studies make a persuasive case for using primates, particularly chimpanzees, to help understand roots of human behavior and for reframing the exploration of human communication origins.

We have attempted to integrate and interpret some of the recent research on apes and to provide a framework from which to generate questions. In this way we believe diverse data can be brought together and clues can be found that eventually will make it possible to forge a viable theory of the evolution of human communication.

ACKNOWLEDGMENTS

E. W. Menzel's data was a basis for the germination of some of our ideas; Clifford Geertz encouraged our thinking along these lines; and S. L. Washburn gave us the evolutionary perspective.

REFERENCES

1. ABRAHAMS, R. D. & J. F. SZWED. 1975. A comprehensive annotated bibliography of American Black English. Amer. Anthrop. 77 (2): 329–335.
2. BIRDWHISTELL, R. L. 1970. Kinesics and Context. Essays on Body Motion Communication. Univ. Penn. Press. Philadelphia, Pa.
3. BOAS, F. 1911. Introduction. Handbook of American Indian languages. Bur. of Am. Ethnol. Bull. 40 (1): 1–83. Smithsonian Inst. Washington, D.C.
4. BOAS, F. 1934. Geographical names of the Kwakiutl Indians. Contrib. to Anthrop. No. 20. Columbia Univ. Press. New York, N.Y.
5. CHAPPLE, E. D. 1970. Culture and Biological Man. Explorations in Behavioral Anthropology. Holt Rinehart and Winston, Inc. New York, N.Y.
6. CHEVALIER-SKOLNIKOFF, S. This annal.
7. CONDON, W. S. & L. W. SANDER. 1974. Neonate movement is synchronized with adult speech: interactional participation and language acquisition. Science 183: 99–101.
8. CONKLIN, H. C. 1956. Hanunóo color categories. Southwest. J. Anthrop. 11: 339–344.
9. COUNT, E. W. 1973. Being and Becoming Human. Essays on the Biogram. Van Nostrand Reinhold Co. New York, N.Y.
10. COUNT, E. W. This annal.
11. COWEY, A. & L. WEISKRANTZ. 1975. Demonstration of cross-modal matching in rhesus monkeys, *Macaca mulatta*. Neuropsych. 13 (1): 117–120.
12. DARWIN, C. 1871. The Descent of Man and Selection in Relation to Sex. Random House, Modern Library. New York, N.Y.
13. DAVENPORT, R. K. & C. M. ROGERS. 1970. Intermodal equivalence of stimuli in apes. Science 168: 279–280.
14. DAVENPORT, R. K., C. M. ROGERS & I. S. RUSSELL. 1973. Cross-modal perception in apes. Neuropsychol. 11: 21–28.
15. DAVENPORT, R. K., C. M. ROGERS & I. S. RUSSELL. 1975. Cross-modal perception in apes: altered visual cues and delay. Neuropsychol. 13 (2): 229–235.

16. DRAPER, P. 1973. Crowding among hunter gatherers: the !Kung. Science **182** (4109): 301–303.
17. EISENBERG, J. F. 1973. Mammalian social systems: are primate social systems unique? Symp. 4th Int. Congr. Primat. Vol. 1: 232–249. Karger. Basel, Switzerland.
18. FISHMAN, J. A. 1960. A systemization of the Whorfian hypothesis. Behav. Sci. **5**: 323–339.
19. FOUTS, R. S. 1973. Acquisition and testing of gestural signs in four young chimpanzees. Science **180**: 978–980.
20. FOUTS, R. S. 1974. Language: origins, definitions and chimpanzees. J. Hum. Evol. **3**: 475–482.
21. GALLUP, G. G. 1970. Chimpanzees: self-recognition. Science **167**: 86–89.
22. GARDNER, B. T. & R. A. GARDNER. 1971. Two-way communication with an infant chimpanzee. In Behavior of Nonhuman Primates. A. Schrier & F. Stollnitz, Eds. Vol. 4: 117–184. Academic Press. New York, N.Y.
23. GARDNER, R. A. & B. T. GARDNER. 1969. Teaching sign language to a chimpanzee. Science **165**: 664–672.
24. GARDNER, R. A. & B. T. GARDNER. 1975. Early signs of language in child and chimpanzee. Science **187**: 752–753.
25. GESCHWIND, N. 1964. The development of the brain and the origin of language. Monog. Series on Language and Linguistics **17**: 155–169.
26. GOFFMAN, E. 1963. Behavior in Public Places. Free Press. New York, N.Y.
27. GOODALL, J. 1967. Mother-offspring relationship in free-ranging chimpanzees. In Primate Ethology. D. Morris, Ed.: 287–346. Weidenfeld & Nicholson. London, England.
28. GOODALL, J. 1968. The behavior of free-living chimpanzees in the Gombe Stream Reserve. Anim. Behav. Mongr. **1**: 161–312.
29. GOODALL, J. 1968. Expressive movements and communication in free-ranging chimpanzees. In Primates: Studies in Adaptation and Variability. P. Jay, Ed.: 313–374. Holt Rinehart and Winston, Inc. New York, N.Y.
30. GOODALL, J. 1971. In the Shadow of Man. Houghton Mifflin. Boston, Mass.
31. GOODENOUGH, W. H. 1951. Property, Kin and Community on Truk. Yale Univ. Publ. in Anthrop. No. 46. Yale Univ. Press. New Haven, Conn.
32. GUMPERZ, J. J. & D. HYMES. 1964. The Ethnography of Communication. Amer. Anthrop. Special Publ. Vol. 66 (6). Part 2.
33. GUMPERZ, J. J. & D. HYMES. 1972. Directions in Sociolinguistics. Holt Rinehart and Winston, Inc. New York, N.Y.
34. HALL, E. T. 1959. The Silent Language. Doubleday & Co., Inc. New York, N.Y.
35. HAMILTON, C. R., S. F. TIEMAN & W. S. FARRELL. 1974. Cerebral dominance in monkeys? Neuropsychol. **12** (2): 193–197.
36. HAYES, K. J. & C. HAYES. 1951. The intellectual development of a home-raised chimpanzee. Proc. Amer. Phil. Soc. **95** (2): 105–109.
37. HEWES, G. W. 1973. Primate communication and the gestural origin of language. Cur. Anthrop. **14** (1–2): 5–24.
38. HEWES, G. W. 1973. Pongid capacity for language acquisition. Symp. 4th Int. Congr. Primat. Vol. 1: 124–143. Karger. Basel, Switzerland.
39. HUXLEY, T. H. 1863. Evidence as to Man's Place in Nature. Univ. of Michigan Press. Ann Arbor, Mich.
40. HYMES, D. 1964. Language in Culture and Society. A Reader in Linguistics and Anthropology. Harper & Row. New York, N.Y.
41. ITANI, J. & A. SUZUKI. 1967. The social unit of chimpanzees. Primates **8**: 355–381.
42. IZAWA, K. 1970. Unit group of chimpanzees and their nomadism in the savanna woodland. Primates **11**: 1–46.
43. KING, M. & A. C. WILSON. 1975. Evolution at two levels in humans and chimpanzees. Science **188**: 107–116.
44. KOCHMAN, T. 1972. Rappin' and Stylin' Out. Univ. Ill. Press. Urbana, Ill.
45. KOHLER, W. 1925. The Mentality of Apes. Routledge & Kegan Paul, Ltd. London, England.
46. LABOV, W. 1972. Language in the Inner City: Studies in the Black English Vernacular. Univ. of Penn. Press. Philadelphia, Penn.

47. LANCASTER, J. B. 1968. Primate communication systems and the emergence of human language. *In* Primates: Studies in Adaptation and Variability. P. Jay, Ed.: 439–457. Holt Rinehart and Winston, Inc. New York, N.Y.
48. LE MAY, M. & N. GESCHWIND. 1975. Hemispheric differences in the brains of great apes. Brain, Behav. Evol. **11** (1): 48–52.
49. LENNEBERG, E. H. 1967. Biological Foundations of Language. John Wiley & Sons, Inc. New York, N.Y.
50. MARLER, P. 1965. Communication in monkeys and apes. *In* Primate Behavior. I. DeVore, Ed.: 544–584. Holt Rinehart & Winston. New York, N.Y.
51. MENZEL, E. W. 1969. Chimpanzee utilization of space and responsiveness to objects. Proc. 2nd Int. Congr. Primat. Atlanta, Ga. 1968. Vol. 1: 72–80. Karger, Basel, Switzerland.
52. MENZEL, E. W. 1971. Communication about the environment in a group of young chimpanzees. Folia Primatol. (Basel) **15**: 220–230.
53. MENZEL, E. W. 1971. Group behavior in young chimpanzees: responsiveness to cumulative novel changes in a large outdoor enclosure. J. Comp. Physiol. Psych. **74** (1): 46–51.
54. MENZEL, E. W. 1973. Leadership and communication in young chimpanzees. *In* Precultural Primate Behavior. E. M Menzel, Ed. Vol. **1**: 192–225. Karger. Basel, Switzerland.
55. MENZEL, E. W. 1973. Chimpanzee spatial memory. Science **182**: 943–945.
56. MENZEL, E. W. 1974. A group of young chimpanzees in a one-acre field. *In* Behavior of Nonhuman Primates. A. M. Schrier and F. Stollnitz, Eds. Vol. 5: 83–153. Academic Press. New York, N.Y.
57. MENZEL, E. W., R. K. DAVENPORT & C. M. ROGERS. 1972. Protocultural aspects of chimpanzees' responsiveness to novel objects. Folia primatol. (Basel) **17** (3): 161–170.
58. MENZEL, E. W. & S. HALPERIN. 1975. Purposive behavior as a basis for objective communication between chimpanzees. Science **189**: 652–654.
59. MILLIKAN, C. H. & F. L. DARLEY. 1967. Brain Mechanisms Underlying Speech and Language. Grune and Stratton. New York, N.Y.
60. MITCHELL-KERNAN, C. 1970. Language Behavior in a Black Urban Community. Lang. Behav. Res. Lab. no. 2. Berkeley, Calif.
61. NELSON, R. F. 1969. Hunters of the Northern Ice. Univ. Chicago Press. Chicago, Ill.
62. NISHIDA, T. 1968. The social group of wild chimpanzees in the Mahali Mountains. Primates **9**: 167–224.
63. NISHIDA, T. 1970. Social behavior and relationship among wild chimpanzees of the Mahali Mountains. Primates **11**: 47–87.
64. NISHIDA, T. & K. KAWANAKA. 1972. Inter-unit-group relationships among wild champanzees of the Mahali Mountains. Kyoto University African Studies. Vol. **8**: 131–169.
65. PASSINGHAM, R. E. 1973. Anatomical differences between the neocortex of man and other primates. Brain, Behav. Evol. **7**: 337–359.
66. PENFIELD, W. & L. ROBERTS. 1959. Speech and Brain-Mechanisms. Princeton Univ. Press. Princeton, N.J.
67. PLOOG, D. 1971. Neurological aspects in social behavior. *In* Man and Beast: Comparative Social Behavior. J. F. Eisenberg and W. S. Dillion, Eds.: 93–125. Smithsonian Institution Press. Washington, D.C.
68. PREMACK, D. 1971. Language in chimpanzee? Science **172**: 808–822.
69. PREMACK, D. 1971. On the assessment of language competence in the chimpanzee. *In* Behavior of Nonhuman Primates. A. Schrier & F. Stollnitz, Eds. Vol. 4: 184–228.
70. PREMACK, A. J. & D. PREMACK. 1972. Teaching language to an ape. Sci. Amer. **227**(4): 92–99.
71. PRIDE, J. B. & J. HOLMES. 1972. Sociolinguistics. Penguin Books. Harmondsworth, Middlesex, England.
72. REYNOLDS, V. & F. REYNOLDS. 1965. Chimpanzees of the Budongo Forest. *In* Primate Behavior. I. DeVore, Ed.: 425–473. Holt Rinehart and Winston, Inc. New York, N.Y.
73. SAPIR, E. 1921. Language. Harcourt, Brace. New York, N.Y.
74. SAPIR, E. 1931. Conceptual categories in primitive languages. Science **74**: 578.
75. SARICH, V. & J. CRONIN. 1975. Molecular systematics of the primates. *In* Progress in Molecular Anthropology. Burg Wartenstein Symp. 65. Wenner-Gren Foundation for Anthropological Research. New York, N.Y.

76. STEKLIS, H. D. & S. R. HARNAD. This annal.
77. SUGIYAMA, Y. 1968. Social organization of chimpanzees in the Budongo Forest, Uganda. Primates **9:** 225–258.
78. SUGIYAMA, Y. 1969. Social behavior of chimpanzees in the Budongo Forest, Uganda. Primates **10:** 197–225.
79. SUGIYAMA, K. 1973. The social structure of wild chimpanzees. *In* Comparative Ecology and Behavior of Primates. R. P. Michael and J. H. Crook, Eds.: 376–410. Academic Press. New York, N.Y.
80. SUZUKI, A. 1969. An ecological study of chimpanzees in a savanna woodland. Primates **10:** 103–148.
81. TANNER, N. 1967. Speech and society among the Indonesian elite: a case study of a multilingual community. Anthrop. Ling. **9(III):** 15–40.
82. TANNER, N. & A. ZIHLMAN. 1976. Women in Evolution. Part I. Innovation and Selection in Human Origins. Signs: J. of Women in Culture and Society. Vol. **1** (3, pt. 1): 585–608.
83. TELEKI, G. 1973. The Predatory Behavior of Wild Chimpanzees. Bucknell Univ. Press. Lewisburg, Pa.
84. TELEKI, G. 1973. Group response to the accidental death of a chimpanzee in Gombe National Park, Tanzania. Folia Primatol. (Basel) **20(2–3):** 81–94.
85. TELEKI, G. 1974. Chimpanzee subsistence technology: materials and skills. J. Hum. Evol. **3:** 575–594.
86. TYLER, S. A. 1969. Cognitive Anthropology. Holt Rinehart and Winston, Inc. New York, N.Y.
87. WASHBURN, S. L. 1951. The analysis of primate evolution with particular reference to the origin of man. Cold Spring Harbor Symp. Quant. Biol. Vol. **15:** 67–78.
88. WASHBURN, S. L. 1963. Behavior and human evolution. *In* Classification and Human Evolution. S. L. Washburn, Ed.: 190–203. Aldine, Inc. Chicago, Ill.
89. WASHBURN, S. L. 1973. Comments on "Primate communication and the gestural origin of language." Curr. Anthrop. **14(1 2):** 18.
90. WASHBURN, S. L. & S. L. STRUM. 1972. Concluding comments. *In* Perspectives on Human Evolution. S. L. Washburn and P. Dohlinow, Eds. Vol. 2: 469–491. Holt Rinehart and Winston. New York, N.Y.
91. WEISKRANTZ, L. & A. COWEY. 1975. Cross-modal matching in the rhesus monkey using a single pair of stimuli. Neuropsychol. **13(3):** 257–261.
92. WHORF, B. L. 1956. Language, Thought and Reality. Selected Writings of Benjamin Lee Whorf, J. B. Carroll, Ed. John Wiley & Sons. New York, N.Y.
93. WILSON, A. C. & V. M. SARICH. 1969. A molecular time scale for human evolution. Proc. Nat. Acad. Sci. USA **63:** 1088–1093.
94. YERKES, R. M. & A. W. YERKES. 1929. The Great Apes. Yale University Press. New Haven, Conn.
95. ZIHLMAN, A. & N. TANNER. Women in Evolution. Part II. Subsistence and Social Organization Among Early Hominids. Signs: J. Women in Culture and Society. In preparation.

DISCUSSION

Thomas A. Sebeok; *Moderator*
Indiana University
Bloomington, Indiana 47401

PROF. STOKOE: To a point in Steklis and Harnad's paper. As our chairman pointed out last night, the image of a creature's shadow or a reflection in water requires luminosity. But it's a mistake to assume that the sign languages of the deaf require luminosity. It's perfectly possible to communicate with deaf-blind persons using a gestural system, and deaf mothers of deaf children communicate very well in the dark. This is a system that is not dissociated simply in the visual mode, but has a tactile as well as a neuromotor base.

DR. PUCCETTI: My remark is to Steklis and Harnad concerning the neocortical areas taking over refined motor function in the evolution of primates: the recent work of Evarts, for example, indicates that there are some cortical neuron pools that are activated *prior* to the motor area in the cortex in intentional movement. Also, effective control of epileptic seizures can sometimes be instituted by artificial stimulation of the cerebellar cortex. That would seem to indicate that there are subcortical structures involved in refined movements in man.

DR. STEKLIS: We didn't mean to imply that only the motor strip on the neocortex is involved in the mediation of complex movement here. Obviously, evolution occurred throughout the brain, and along with the motor systems of the neocortex we have evolution of the neocerebellum and other associated subcortical nuclei to which various fibers project. We are aware of the work by Evarts and his colleagues; that work on evoked potentials preceding movement is in some ways not irrelevant here, since it does tell us something about the kind of patterning which already exists in the form of a *program*. But I certainly would agree with you that we are talking about evolution at several levels.

Part IX. Gestural Origin Theories

THE CURRENT STATUS OF THE GESTURAL
THEORY OF LANGUAGE ORIGIN

Gordon W. Hewes

Department of Anthropology
University of Colorado
Boulder, Colorado 80302

One of the most plausible glottogonic models assumes that the initial form of language was gestural, in the sense that the propositional, predicative, or reporting functions were based on gestural signs, with vocal sounds serving much as they do nonhuman mammals, for the social communication of affect. The gestural theory was actively debated in the 18th century,[40] although reference to gesticulation in connection with early language goes back another two millennia. In its older and simpler forms, the gestural theory shared with other glottogonic theories an ignorance of biological evolution and geochronology. Weak and strong versions can be distinguished. In the former, gesture is regarded as a very important or coequal aspect of early language, as in Kendon's recent statement.[53] (1975:4): "Gestural language systems may be at least as fundamental as is speech, . . . at the very least, reportive communication in gestural form emerged concurrently." The stronger version holds that for a long time gestural signs constituted the main body of language, with vocalization subordinate, although no reasonable advocates of the gestural theory claim that man was mute during the postulated gestural phase of language evolution. The hominids from the beginning of their separate evolutionary career must have been using vocal calls for social communication.

In a modern, updated formulation of the gestural theory, the behavioral emergent, propositional language, is seen to have followed the line of least biological resistance, such that its initial appearance and early development did not require new anatomical structures or behavior patterns previously impossible. That modern chimpanzees can acquire modest gesture-language competence without undergoing further biological evolution is therefore powerful evidence for the plausibility of the gestural pathway to language in the early hominids;[39] however, a good case can be made for the gestural theory on the basis of much other evidence.

In Plato's *Cratylus*, Socrates observes that sign-language could be used if man lacked speech.[80] Augustine, in his *Confessions* (ca. A.D. 400),[2] discussing language acquisition in young children, notes that adults point at things, directing attention toward them, at the same time uttering words which the child then associates with these ostensive definitions. "I saw and remembered what they called what they would point . . . that they meant this thing and no other was plain from the motion of their body, the natural language, as it were, of all nations, expressed by the countenance, glances of the eyes, gestures of the limbs, and tones of the voice, indicating the affections of the mind, as it pursues, possesses, rejects, or shuns." That deictic gesture is the natural path to propositionality is an old idea, so that it is not strange that when the Biblical account of Adam's acquisition of language came to be questioned, the possibility of gesture as a primordial form of language was considered. By the sixteenth century, literary and philosophical references to sign-language were numerous, including the use of gesture-language among the deaf and in certain monasteries. Rabelais satirizes sign-language in *Pantagruel* (1567),[83] and Bacon discusses such signing in *The Advancement of Learning* (1605).[3] The revival of drama and the study of rhetoric led to a re-examination of Greek and Roman writings about gestural communication.[8,48,74] Knowlson[56] has reviewed seventeenth and eighteenth century notions that gesture constitutes a kind of universal, natural language, more direct and spontaneous than speech, as suggested by Bonifacio in 1616. Cresollius, in 1620, quoted the brother of St. Basil, who declared that "the hands were what made vocal language possible" (Ref. 65, p. 282). John Bulwer's *Chirologia; or the Naturall Language of the Hand* (1644) also represents this genre. Practical use of gestural and pantomimic communication arose repeatedly in this era of European voyages and explorations, about which I have collected numerous accounts.[38] Dalgarno (1661) supposed that "the communicative power of gesture was greater for a long time than in voice, so that oral language remained for a long time more rudimentary than gesture which was able to develop into an art" (Ref. 65, p. 284). Wilkins[122] (1694) distinguished between gestures "ex congruo," where sign and referent had a natural resemblance, and "ex placito," where the connection was only conventional, or arbitrary. Cordemoy (1668)[10] calls gestures "the first of all languages", universal, understood everywhere, although there were some limited to particular nations, and others not even known to a whole local community. The Abbé Jean-Baptiste Dubos in 1719 said that visual signs were inherently more communicative than speech, and possibly more primitive (Ref. 91 and Ref. 72, p. 110).

Mandeville's *Fable of the bees*[66] (1728) contains an explicit description of how a language could originate in gesture, in the hypothetical circumstances of an isolated pair of children (cf. Megill,[72] pp. 114–110). Warburton, in 1741, supposed that gesture had been a very prominent part of early language, on the basis of various Old Testament references. Although Vico in *Scienza Nouva* (1725, 1730, 1744) accepted the Biblical account of the divine origin of Adam's language, he thought that after the Flood, man, having reverted to a state of savagery, had to reinvent language, and that one of the post-Deluge languages used gestures and physical objects. Later language became vocal through onomatopoeia and interjections (Ref. 72; ch. 6).

The Abbé de Condillac[9] (1775, 1947) went further in presenting a gestural origin model (Josephs,[48] p. 24), although neither he nor any eighteenth century writer provided a really detailed explanation of how a gesture-language could have been transformed into a mainly spoken one. Condillac said that, in principle, man could create language on his own, without divine inspiration. Following Mandeville, he supposed that two abandoned infants might survive and develop a "language of action" (that is, gestures), more expressive than vocal cries. Such gestures would not be merely instinctive, but would arise from association of ideas or analogy, and would eventually permit reference to past or distant matters. What would now be termed feedback would enhance the reasoning powers of the users of such a language. When sounds were first added to such a gestural language, a series of spoken words might be needed to represent what had been expressed by a single, comprehensive gesture. This would create, according to Condillac, the misleading notion that ideas exist in the mind in sentence-like strings. Rather like Vico, he thought that some infants, after the Deluge, might have created languages in this fashion, unconnected with the older Adamic language. Influences of the gesture-language explained the markedly figurative and metaphorical character of early spoken language. (Cf. Condillac,[9] Chouillet,[6] Josephs,[48] Megill,[72] Grimsley.[29])

In the mid-1740s, Condillac used to meet with Rousseau and Diderot for dinner in Paris, so that it is hardly strange that all three expressed ideas about glottogenesis. Diderot, in his letter on the deaf and dumb (1751) observed that the natural order of ideas would be best revealed by studying the sign-language of the deaf. Although he set forth no language origin theory, he explained how a person deaf from birth might invent signs, such as for drinking, but that temporal relationships might be difficult to render gesturally (Ref. 5, p. 112).

Maupertuis wrote in 1756 that gestures and cries developed into language before the rise of articulate speech, but that no nation retained gesture alone, owing to various advantages of speech[72,71] "If one could go back," he said, "to the time when man did not have any sort of language, they would have sought to express their most pressing needs first, and certain gestures and cries would have sufficed for that. This was the first language of mankind, and it is still the one which all peoples understand, but it cannot render more than a very small number of ideas. It was not for a long time afterward that they thought of other ways to express themselves. One could make this first language more extensive by adding to its natural gestures and cries, cries and gestures by convention, which would supplement what the first could not render, and it is that which they apparently first did." (Ref. 71, pp. 437-8.) Later, articulate speech would have been formed, which would "provide a great number of articulations, combinably to infinity," causing gesture-language to decline, except where it was necessary to express the emotions.

Du Marsais, in his article in the Encyclopédie on grammatical constructions, makes the same point that gesture, along with cries, sighs, and so on, now serves for the language of the emotions more than for the intellect. Vico, Condillac, and Maupertuis saw the beginnings of language in gestures, but Rousseau saw gesture and voice operating together from the start, although he too felt that for a long time the voice was mainly expressive rather than propositional (Ref. 64, p. 482). But language arose according to Rousseau from needs and emotions rather than for practical communication. When the ancients said things most vividly, they did not speak, but used signs (Ref. 6, p. 56). Physical needs could be handled by gesture alone, and a society not too different from our own could exist with gesture-language instead of articulate speech (Ref. 72, p. 270). In his essay on the origin of language (1772), gesture language was said to be prior to speech; its replacement by the voice occurred in "northern regions" because of the greater challenges to human society under rigorous climatic conditions (Ref. 79, p. 83). Establishment of conventional meanings for spoken words requires a more firmly organized society than for a more natural, primitive gesture-language (Ref. 72, p. 269). In Émile, Rousseau writes that "in neglecting the language of signs, which speak to the imagination, one loses the most energetic languages" (Josephs,[48] 206). Men could hunt, Rousseau notes, without speaking. On hunting, Salvemini di Castiglione, in his criticism of the Rousseau's Essay on the origin of human inequality, while denying the possibility of the human creation of a spoken language, concedes that primitive hunters might use gestures and onomatopoeia to communicate about game animals (Megill,[72] p. 279). Helvétius, another philosophe, said in 1758 that man's superiority over other creatures came from the hand, but was troubled by the fact that monkeys, similarly equipped, did not therefore equal man (Ref. 30, p. 123).

Three contestants in the Berlin Academy's 1757 competition on the relationships of language to human knowledge, mention glottogenesis (Megill,[72], 290-294). One argued that language arose from pressing human needs, and that the first spoken signs were arrived at by agreement communicated gesturally. Another, agreeing that gesture and emotional cries were the natural human modes of communication, said that isolated children using them would nevertheless fail to create a single conventional sign. In 1764, Lambert remarked that if man lacked speech, he would employ gestures, to indicate numbers, shapes, and movement, but that gestures could not designate colors, smells, et cetera, in contrast to the powers of speech in this regard (Megill,[72] 306-307).

Voltaire was disinterested in the great eighteenth century language origin debate, but does say in his Philosophie de l'Histoire (1765) that man, always a sociable being, communicated gesturally before he spoke, when society was limited to small familial groups. Larger societies required speech, which originated in interjection and onomatopoeia, over a long period. Süssmilch, who upheld the divine origin of language against the *philosophes*, admitted in an argument with Jacob Carpov that hypothetical "Lucretian men" could have communicated in limited fashion by gestures, although this would not lead to speech. Süssmilch said in 1766 that human emotional cries could not have been transformed into speech, since they were of an entirely different nature from voluntarily produced articulate sounds. An anonymous reviewer of Süssmilch in 1769 rejected this on the ground that a born-deaf person known to him had developed his own sign-language, showing that a primitive system of gestures and cries could attain the complexities found in spoken languages (Ref. 72, p. 346).

Several entrants in the famous Berlin Academy essay contest of 1772 (set in 1769) refer to gesture-language. One essayist, said to have been a born-deaf Breslau baron, denied that isolated, hearing children would ever develop speech. Essay No. 2 contended that language originated from gestures and natural cries with no further explanation. Copineau, one of the identified contestants, argued that isolated children could develop four kinds of languages, one of which would consist of gesture and body movements, resembling the sign-language of the deaf. The winner, Herder, dealt with the origin of language in the vocal mode, ignoring Condillac's speculations about the "language of action"; Herder mentions gesture as being "embedded in the senses"[48] A decade later, the Scottish judge, Monboddo, began his six-volume treatise on the origin and progress of language, but by now could add little to the points raised in the Continental debate. Although acknowledging that primitive man communicated not only vocally, but gesturally, he derived language from "inarticulate emotional cries." The Russian savant, Lomonosov (1711–1765) thought gesture had been exaggerated as a factor in language origin, holding that speech was the oldest form of human communication, and that gesture would have been useless in the dark.

Julien Onffray de la Mettrie, although he did not deal with the origin of language as such, proposed in 1747 his *l'Homme machine*[59] that an anthropoid ape be taught to speak, and that the instructor should be someone familiar with teaching the deaf. His suggestion curiously foreshadows the successes of the Gardners, *et al.*, in developing language or language-like behavior in chimpanzees, although he was probably wrong in supposing that apes could master a vocally-based language.

Hervás y Panduro,[34] in 1789, saw gesture as man's first language in infancy: "As the infant grows in age and understanding, he speaks to us and gives us proofs of his rationality with looks, gestures, and actions. This mode of speaking is his first language, and it is superseded by the vocal, which we call speech [lengua] because it is with the tongue that we pronounce most of our words" (vol. 1, p. 231).

The thought of Condillac was revived around the end of the eighteenth century in Paris, by the circle known as the *Idéologues* (cf Seigel[98]). This group included the Abbé Sicard, teacher of the deaf and successor at the Institut des sourds et muets of the famous Abbè de l'Epée, Itard, the mentor of the supposed wild boy, Victor of Aveyron, Dégerando who was deeply interested in sign-languages, and Jauffret, who proposed that the Société des Observateurs de l'Homme, which had been formed by the idéologues, should replicate the Psammetichus experiment to obtain evidence about man's language-forming capacities. The Société also planned fieldwork on gesture-languages around the world, and the compilation of a world dictionary of signs. Laromiguère, another member, thought that a sign-language could serve as an international system, on the ground that it already exists, created by nature.[12,35,56]

The Société collapsed about 1804, without achieving its ambitious program. That the study of the sign-language of the deaf might provide insights on language origin was also expressed in a book by D. C. Ries, 1806.[88]

A new factor now shifted intellectual interest in language away not only from gesture theories, but from the entire topic of glottogenesis. This was the rapid rise of comparative philology, providing a vast field for empirical work, as well as a different theoretical climate. From about 1810 until 1850, relatively little was written about language origins, save in the framework of discussions about the possible origins of Indo-European "roots" (cf. F. Max Müller[73]). Murray (d. 1813) was the author of a work that appeared in 1823, claiming that speech had originated from precisely nine primordial syllables, the meanings of which had been established by gestural communication. He also noted the diminutive symbolism of the sound [i]. Madvig, in Denmark, alluded to a gestural antecedent (1842) for spoken language, and in 1850, Barrois tried to recover evidence for a gesture language from representations on ancient monuments. The Austrian playwright Grillparzer is also reported to have suggested that the earliest language was gestural, with the first spoken words onomatopoeic. Ernest Renan, who was a major figure in reopening the questions of glottogenesis (in 1848 and 1858) does not deal significantly with the gestural hypothesis.

Darwin's *Origin of Species* (1859) barely mentioned the possibility of human biological evolution, much less the application of the principle of natural selection to language, but philologists soon began to wonder if language might not be a field for evolutionary speculation (e.g., Schleicher, in an open letter to Haeckel in 1863.)[96] G. P. Marsh refers to the possible priority of gesture in a work on the English language in 1862. E. B. Tylor's interest in so-called "beast-children" in 1863[110] was followed almost immediately by F. Max Müller on the language behavior of feral children (1864). Communications on language evolution evidently became so annoying that the Paris Société de Linguistique enacted it famous ban against such papers in 1866. In that year Yves-Léonard Rémi Valade,[113] a teacher at the Paris Institute for the Deaf, wrote a detailed exposition of the gestural theory, in which he said that the born-deaf constitute a "daily instance" of the conditions of the Psammetichus experiment (p. 8) reproducing the language of the earliest humans. Valade's essay reflects his considerable knowledge of sign-language in a functioning institutional community, and merits more attention than I can give it here. Other contributors to the gestural hypothesis around this time were G. Jäger (1867–1870) and Lazarus Geiger (1868, 1869), who claimed that except for use of the voice for emotional expression, gestures were prior to speech, and that gesticulation in ancient times served to make vocal signs meaningful. By 1868, E. B. Tylor was writing about glottogenesis, and in books published in 1870, 1871,[111] and 1881,[112] he paid closest attention to the gestural origin theory, and in pursuit of first-hand evidence, visited institutions for the deaf in England and Germany. His 1881 book suggests the "mouth-gesture" path from manual to vocal signs, and in a review of it, Alfred Russel Wallace made the theory quite explicit, elaborating it in an 1895 article and his own book published in 1900. Meanwhile, inspired by Darwinism,[119] William Dwight Whitney set forth an evolutionary view of language development, as a product of man's developing social behavior (1867).[118,120] In 1885, in the *Britannica*,[121] Whitney discussed the advantages of speech over a possibly primordial language of gestures. Whitney's notion of the "linguistic community" was quite modern (McLeish and Martin, Ref. 70, p. 5.)

The possible gestural origin of language continued to be debated in the 'eighties. Rudolf Kleinpaul published a major work on "language without words" in 1888. Rambosson's *Origine de la parole*[84] (1880) discussed the gestural theory at length (pp.

380–386), suggesting that if the Darwinists were right, and man had appeared first in a primitive form, the first language would have been gestural. In his conclusions, he draws back from such a view, using the argument that even the most primitive surviving peoples possess highly complex spoken language, and that according to the most learned authorities, such as Virchow, no fossil remains of truly primitive mankind have come to light (pp. 390). A. H. Sayce (1880) [94] has language originating in gesture, onomatopoeia, and, to a more limited extent, in emotional cries, with the voice at first secondary and nonessential. Garrick Mallery,[65] ih his studies of North American Indian sign language, follows Sayce in this (pp. 282–285), though he states that man was never in a condition in which the voice was not used for communication. Gesture would have carried most of the burden of conveying meanings and predication, and further, has probably left traces in all spoken languages. Mallery did not think the primordial gesture-language would have closely resembled the developed sign-language of the Plains Indians. Joly (1887)[47] held that primitive man used "profuse gesticulation," but spoke in monosyllables (p. 320). He rejected Haeckel's notion of a stage in human evolution in which man was without speech. (Haeckel's "Pithecanthropus alalus"). In 1895, A. H. Keane [52] supposed that the primitive gestural form of language survived in stronger measure among living "primitive races," but also in some of the "more emotional higher races." At the end of the century, Herbert Spencer alluded briefly to gesture-language[101] as did T. Ziehen, a psychologist.

Serious and extensive attention to the gestural theory characterized Wilhelm Wundt's work on language, who displays considerable familiarity with the previous literature, including Mallery's study of the Plains Indian sign language. Wundt's ideas on the primordial language of gesture form part of his magnum opus, *Völkerpsychologie*, which went through several editions between 1900 and 1922, and a part of which has recently been reissued (Wundt, 1973).[124] Gestural communication arose from expressive movements, although Wundt knew that such movements were not similar to those in lower animals, not even, as he said, in the "most talented apes" (p. 127). Connotative gestures were derived from deixis, leading to a final stage of "symbolic signing" (Ref. 124, p. 130). The American, George Herbert Mead, was deeply impressed by Wundt's work on the "significant symbol."

However, as had happened a century earlier, linguistic scholarship separated itself from such problems, now strengthened by the doctrine of the arbitrariness of the linguistic sign promulgated by Ferdinand de Saussure. Glottogenesis became a topic mainly for psychologists,[40] among whom the gestural theory was espoused by Wilhelm Jerusalem (1907), Harold Höffding (1912), and Vladimir Bekhterev (1813). Max Meyer (1912, p. 332) suggested a mouth-gesture connection between fingerpointing and tongue-tip articulations. Floyd Allport discussed gesture, but said that while gestures and speech can both perform signing functions, this does not explain how there could have been a changeover from manual to vocal language. John Dewey briefly mentions the possibility of the transformation of "organic gestures and cries" into significant names, leading to language (1925, p. 175).

Elaborate theories about glottogenesis, involving mouth-gestures, were advanced starting about 1925 by Marcel Jousse,[49] and in more bizarre fashion by the Soviet linguist, N. Ya. Marr (1865–1934), who founded a once very influential "Marxist" school of linguistics, later thoroughly repudiated by none other than J. V. Stalin in 1951.[107] Marr supposed that the first language was manual gesture [ruchnoĭ yazyk], later turned into a spoken language derived from just four morphemes by magicians or shamans, for purposes of professional secrecy. Marr's glottogonic ideas were much more complex than this, to be sure (cf. West, 1937, and especially L. Thomas.[107] Meanwhile, R. A. S. Paget[76-78] in England, and Alexander Jóhannesson,[44-46] in Iceland were independently reviving a form of the mouth-gesture theory, resulting in a fairly long list of publications on the topic by end of World War II. If to these one adds the work of van Ginneken, who combined mouth-gesture with ideas about the glottogonic significance of click-consonants (cf. also work by R. Stopa, [102-104] and others) there is a surprisingly large body of material specifically dealing with this form of the gestural hypothesis, which could be brushed aside only after very careful analysis.

The most widely read and reviewed work on language origins in this period, however, by Géza Révész[86] (1942, 1946, and subsequent editions) rejects the gestural model; Kainz, in his monumental work on the psychology of language, gives it much attention, but remains unconvinced [50] (1962-1965, cf. vol. 2, 579-633). More recently, Suzanne K. Langer dismisses it, in a work which displays a formidable knowledge or modern biology and at the same time, an almost orthodoxly Cartesian rejection of cognitive contunuity between man and beast.[60]

This summary of gestural glottonic speculation should indicate that there is not much room for completely original views of the topic. By the beginning of the 1960s, it seemed that everything, pro or con, had already been said, many times over.

The greatest obstacle in any glottogonic theory is not that vocal sounds, or manual gestures, or whatever, could not be used as linguistic signs, but how any system based on seemingly arbitrary signs could have got started, and could have reached a condition in which sets or strings of such signs could be combined to form propositions or reasonably complex reports about the environment. It will not do simply to assert that species-specific calls, postures, or displays, commonly found in higher nonhuman animals, became language in response to novel social, subsistence, or other needs of early mankind. Language, as we find it in our species now, is institutional or cultural, even though its commonest form seems to rest on genetically programmed, specialized adaptations for both speech production and speech decoding. As other papers in this Conference make clear, spoken language has been in existence long enough in our slow-breeding species to become dependent on biologically built-in arrangements, even though it is also clear that only sociocultural continuity of a highly "artificial" kind enables language to survive from generation to generation. An imaginary Psammetichus experiment, affecting all infant members of our species (and eliminating their elders, while still permitting the infants to survive and grow up) would obviously set hominids back to square one, in spite of the superb cortical and vocal tract adaptations our ancestors have evolved for us. I shall bring in, later, an additional bit of evolutionary evidence for language, not related directly to speech, which you may not find convincing, but which I believe supports the gestural origin hypothesis.

Jerison,[42,43] in a comprehensive study of the evolution of the brain in vertebrates, views the importance of audition in the early mammals as a sensory channel for information of distant events as a transformation from the earlier reptilian use of vision for this function. He suggests further that audition is peculiarly suited for time-based perceptual integration, and that human language is primarily auditory; this represents an evolutionary continuity. He makes this point in spite of his own extensive discussion of the immense importance in some mammalian lines, notably the primates, of vision, which has apparently undergone a remarkable cerebral "internalization," away from the retina, which handled most of its perceptual integration in the lower vertebrates. I think one can find enough right in Jerison's book to refute his notion that the vocal-auditory basis of spoken language is the direct outcome of nocturnal dependence on hearing among the early mammals.

We may call those who support a straight-line derivation of language from vocal-auditory functions in prehuman ancestors "Vocalists," and those who envisage a sign-language detour on the road to speech, "Gesturalists," while recognizing many subvarieties in both schools. Part of the Vocalist argument is simply arguing from the status quo: nearly all human beings use speech, spoken languages are highly complex phenomena, indicative of a long development, and there is good evidence that between the pongids and ourselves, natural selection has built in several new systems or subsystems to cope with spoken language. The Vocalist position seems to have the advantage of parsimonious explanation. Postulating a prehistoric phase of gesture-language is thus seen as an unnecessary multiplication of entities. The pro-Vocalist arguments are familiar. Human infants who are not deaf tend to acquire speech-sounds in predictable sequences, and there is further universality in their mastery of syntax, taking into account the worldwide varieties thereof in natural spoken languages. Where sign languages exist, they are subordinate or secondary, used by special groups (such as the deaf), or by hearing individuals operating in unusual environments (such as construction workers on very noisy jobs, scuba-divers working underwater, etc.). Some highly developed sign-languages, such as ASL (Ameslan) exhibit numerous carry-overs from speech and writing of speech, as in finger-spelling. Linguists have neglected or ignored sign-languages for several good reasons. Most of the recognized language universals are *speech-universals*. And so on. Impressed by the apparent arbitrariness of most spoken language, it has been asserted that such arbitrariness is an essential criterion for language, or that a high degree of iconicity would interfere with understanding. The sign languages of the deaf, or the less well studied other sign-languages, are dismissed as crude, rudimentary, and if their users are unable to communicate except in such languages, they display various serious cognitive handicaps. To be sure, in thus asserting the crude or primitive character of sign language, the Vocalists may be unwittingly contributing to the *Gesturalist* case, to the extent that for very early hominids, gesture-language might have been much easier to acquire.

Speech possesses several advantages or supposed advantages, including its usability in darkness (although modern deaf signers manage to communicate, albeit more slowly, in the dark), its capacity to overcome obstacles in a line of sight, and the fact that in speaking, one does not have to interrupt useful manual work to communicate. Vocal sounds probably require less energy than manual gestures, although I do not think anyone has measured the caloric differences. On the other hand, for signaling over longer distances, loud yelling may lead more quickly to fatigue than might gesticulation. Gesture is often more effective for giving directions or locating things, and for teaching various technical skills. For the learner, manual gestures are all externally visible, and the teacher may shape the movements directly, whereas speech, produced within the vocal tract, has only a partial visual component, and presents formidable problems both to speech therapists and foreign-language instructors. The incompatibility between manual signing and other manual tasks, while real, does not appear to inconvenience deaf workers seriously, and minimizing conversation among skilled manual workers may improve their output. Work-songs or chants are probably controlled by the nonlanguage hemisphere.

Bipedal locomotion in the hominids may have facilitated both gesture-language and speech, by freeing the hands and arms from a direct role in body movement, and by eventual modifications in the head and neck region affecting the shape of the vocal tract air-ways. Less obviously, the occupation of new ecological niches made possible by man's easy striding bipedal gait may have entailed cognitive and conceptual changes with more of a bearing on the development of language than the locomotor or other mechanical changes resulting from regular bipedalism.

A strong part of the case against the Vocalists is that primate calls and cries are handled by parts of the cortex, bilaterally, some distance away from the lateralized "speech areas." The natural calls or cries of monkeys can be elicited by electric probes, whereas human speech cannot be so stimulated (the same kind of electric probing results in speech inhibition). The old limbic controls for involuntary human cries still exist, even though such cries can be voluntarily simulated to some extent. It is interesting that the only carry-over from articulate speech into this older vocal function consists of profanity or coprolalia, which may survive brain damage to the lateralized speech areas, or emerge during anaesthesia, and so on. If spoken language had evolved directly out of the primate call system, one would not expect it to have become localized in an entirely different portion of the cortex. Monkeys and apes are able to learn, by visual observation, various manual manipulations or gestures, both from conspecifics and human mentors. Without going into the thorny questions that always surround the topic of "imitative behavior," it is clear that nonhuman primates are singularly inattentive to nonthreatening environmental sounds, and show no propensity to "imitate them" (unlike some bird species). There is a discontinuity here between human and nonhuman responsiveness to sounds, suggesting that communication by means of learned vocal signals is a hominid emergent. An important dimension of propositional language is its capacity to be produced with minimal affect; language messages may contain information relating to flight, fear, aggression, submission, or nurturant behavior, delivered without significant emotional overtones. This has been termed *decontextualization*. The message "the house is on fire" can, if need be, be conveyed with no more excitement than the information that Paris is a city in France. Hattiangadi,[31] (p. 87) has observed that conceptual language must have been derived from "communication already freed from its social obligations." If this is so, manual gestural language might have been initially more suitable than vocal communication with its long-established evolutionary history of contextualization. The facial musculature (and the oculomotor system) must not be forgotten in connection with social communication on the visual channel, with both evaluative and locative powers superior to what can be achieved with vocal calls. Internalized language, "talking to one's self," is a very important function of language, whether it achieved such internalization in the speech mode or as a gestural code. In any case, an important aspect of such internal, private use of language, is that its external manifestations can be mostly suppressed. When control over private language breaks down, and it becomes audible to others, it is a familiar symptom of psychosis or strong emotion.

Efforts to teach apes to speak have been futile so far, beyond the few very poorly articulated "words" reported by Furness in 1916,[22] and K. and C. Hayes in 1950 and 1951.[32,33] No strings of such "words" were produced. Pongid speech deficiencies are not simply attributable to relatively smaller brain size; Lenneberg[62] and others have reported cases of human microcephals with brains smaller than those of the fossil Australopithecines and modern apes who could speak, and even engage in small talk characteristic of the severely mentally retarded. Some domestic animals, such as dogs, appear to have some receptive understanding of limited amounts of speech, and Fouts has recently reported this capability in the chimpanzee. Given what is now known of the complexities underlying the receptive speech processing capacity of man, it is obvious that we have a good deal more to learn about how dogs might be decoding some of our utterances to them. In any case, effective language requires two-way communication, and hominid protolanguage must have had, from the start, a system providing for both production and transmission using the same code. The primary auditory capabilities of nonhuman primates are not involved; they perceive sounds as we do, and there is even some very recent data that macaques may have categorical perception of some human consonants. Lieberman, Crelin, *et al.* have investigated certain speech-productive deficiencies in monkeys, apes, newborn human infants, and certain fossil hominids, and these requisites for spoken language will receive due attention elsewhere in this Conference. We may summarize this line of evidence by stating that it looks as if the special hominid capabilites underlying spoken language arose in the course of later hominid evolution, and not among the earliest known bipedal, stone-tool making, and part-time hunter or scavenger hominids.

Marler suggests (Ref. 67, p. 43) that ground-dwelling primates living in large social groups depend more on visual signaling, using graded vocalizations more than discrete calls to attract the visual attention of others. Their subsequent behavior, Marler adds, is as much "modulated by what they see as what they hear." What they see, however, is not gestural signals of the kind found in sign-languages, but rather body postures and movements, head-turnings, facial expressons (including tooth displays), and eye-movement or staring. Even in chimpanzees, hand and arm "gestures" are exceedingly few, consisting chiefly of the so-called begging gesture (which may involve touching the face of another individual), and perhaps some foot-displays serving as a "halt!" signal on the trail, according to Kortlandt. On the other hand, it could be that the very limited observation of chimpanzee gesturing arises from the same problem affecting observations of chimpanzee tool-making and tool-using in the wild. If, as Teleki shows,[106] chimpanzee tool behavior is traditional and not genetically programmed, it will exhibit a spotty geographical distribution, with marked local differences in usage (quite different ways of employing sticks or twigs have been reported across the breadth of Africa, from Gombe Stream to Río Muni: cf. Sabater Pí, 1974)[92] If gestural signing had arisen in the form of local "subcultural" traditions in various groups of chimpanzees, as has tool-behavior, the absence of observed gestural signing in Pan thus far may be simply due to insufficient observation. This would be a very feeble argument, except that the behaviors in question relate to voluntary manual activity, and that chimpanzees in human captivity can acquire both a wide range of tool-using skills, and manual sign-language.

Harry T. Jerison (Ref. 42; cf. also the extensive review in *Current Anthropology*, September, 1975)[43] is rather skeptical of the findings of Lieberman and Crelin with respect to the speech-limitations of early hominids, but feels strongly that the critical advances to true hominization occurred in the *Homo erectus* grade, which he thinks has been neglected as a result of the far more numerous and far more ancient discoveries of australopithecine hominids. I gather from Jerison's remarks that articulate speech might not have developed among the australopithecines, which is also the view of Lieberman, but might have begun among the much more culturally advanced hand-axe making, fire-using *Homo erectus* populations starting a million years or so ago, down to about 300,000 B.C. On the other hand, distinguished human paleontologists like Washburn, and prehistorians like Desmond Clark,[7] are now mentioning the possibility of "modern type language" no more than about 40,000–50,000 years ago; that is, coming in with *Homo sapiens sapiens*. Clearly there is some room, then, for a long evolution of language to have taken place. It would be absurd to argue that either because of their endocranial capacities, or manual manipulatory limitations, the australopithecine hominids would have been incapable of gesture-language.

Australopithecine implemental skills indicate entirely sufficient manual and arm capacities for sign-language communication, and there is less direct but fairly good evidence of adequate cognitive capacity to cope with the conceptual side of such a language system. The latter includes Leakey's notion of "manuports"—stone tool material carried in to living floors from a distance, the working of stones, and their probable use in butchering of game carcasses. Australopithecine evidence for hunting and/or scavenging of large mammals implies terrain knowledge or mental mapping, patterns of social coöperation,[36] and programmed butchery surpassing anything Teleki has reported about chimpanzee hunting behavior. Read-Martin and Read[85] have carefully reviewed the data suggestive of systematic scavenging. In previous articles, I have noted similarities between syntax and tool-making and tool-using.[37] I should now add that there are also important parallels between grammar and successful butchery of large carcasses, and that advances in butchering techniques were probably very important in making hunting a significant part of the early hominid subsistence system, along with tool-based vegetal food-processing.

The marked lateralization of human brain functions is often regarded as mainly the outcome of language, and of speech in particular, although it may be more plausible to view hemispheric specialization as the product of a division of cortical labor having to do with other perceptual and cognitive tasks, in part involving preferential handedness for manipulatory programs involved in tool-making and tool-using, spatial mapping of terrain (now evidently handled in the nonlanguage hemisphere), and sequential programs arising from skilled butchery and tool-mediated processing of plant foods. Laughlin and d'Aquili provide a convenient tabulation of current knowledge about cerebral lateralization,[61] which suggests that something besides language was probably implicated in the phenomenon of hemispheric specializations. The fact that lateralization for song-controls occurs in some song-bird species, as shown by Nottebohm[75] and that the first neurological evidence of cerebral lateralization in man, demonstrated by Broca in 1861, had to do with an aspect of aphasia, should not blind us to the possibility that factors not directly related to externalized social communication instigated hominid brain asymmetry. It would be interesting to determine, by the way, where the various chimpanzee signers and other language-learners are localizing their controls for this behavior, whether bilaterally or unilaterally, and if so, why? Although the few reports of sign-language using deaf persons who have suffered aphasic damage indicate that this form of visual language (as with writing) is lateralized more or less like speech in its various aspects, the unexpected discovery that aphasias in Japanese subjects whose script consists of Chinese "ideographic" characters and a phonetically based syllabary exhibit differential dyslexic deficit suggests that we may be oversimplifying if we assume neurolinguistic identity of manual sign-language and spoken language cortical representation.

B. K. Sladen[100] suggests (p. 45) that lateral dominance for language may be somehow associated with "hand gesturing." Doreen Kimura[54] (pp. 337–350, 349) writes, "our speaking is strongly tied to certain movements of the hand contralateral to the hemisphere involved in speech . . . these manual movements resemble those employed in the manual communication of the deaf. The left hemisphere has control over certain motor functions which *happen* (her emphasis) to lend themselves readily to communication." If we accept Jerison's view that in evolution, new functions tend to be built on older, established functions, in the brain as elsewhere, then we might view a formation of a manual-gesture language as an outgrowth of earlier programmed and sequenced manual manipulatory functions, and speech, much later, as a similar engraftment on to the sign-language template.[42] However, the new functions would not fit perfectly, or take over everything from the earlier systems, which would help to explain the great variety in aphasic disturbances, as in the case of Japanese *kanji* and *kana* reading skills.

In connection with hemispheric asymmetry, there seem to be anatomical and dermatoglyphic asymmetries in the hands, suggesting that the strong human tendency for right-handedness has led to some systematic morphological differences reflective of the lopsided dextrality in their functions. Jerre Levy has pointed to possible environmental-behavioral factors in the early hominids that might further help to explain the small but significant sex differences in spatial and language data-processing in the human brain (pers. commun., April 15, 1975). For Levy, language lateralization, usually in the left hemisphere, may have been an adaptation preserving high-level spatial reasoning in the right hemisphere, since a single system could not have optimally served both functions.

R. J. Duffy and K. L. Duffy comment:[14] "There is a common symbolic competence underlying gestural and verbal communication, and . . . aphasia is an impairment in this competence, which is reflected in impaired visual and gestural performance." They suggest that the voluminous aphasia research has been concentrated too narrowly on speech and written language deficits, to the neglect of nonverbal communication functions. Nelson Goodman,[28] (p. 25) asks, "Don't you think . . . that before anyone acquires language, he has had an abundance of practice in developing and using rudimentary prelinguistic symbolic systems in which gestures and sensory and perceptual occurrences of all sorts function as signs?"

Human infants, born with or without hearing, appear to start their symbolic or signing behavior in the gestural rather than the vocal mode. The Gardners have found that their infant chimpanzees are remarkably precocious with respect to sign acquisition,[23,24] compared to the age at which normal-hearing human infants begin to develop articulate vocal communication. Babbling, moreover, seems to be correlated with body and limb movements. Some attention is now being directed toward prevocal gestural communication in normal infants (Winkelstein[123]), although Lucretius, writing in the first century B.C., noted that infants communicate by pointing, and Augustine traced his own acquisition of language to watching the gestures of his mother and other adults. Winkelstein,[123] quoting an unpublished report by I. Uzgiris and J. McV. Hunt, says that the gestures which prespeech infants make on their own are also the ones they "imitate" when they are made by others. Human infant gestural precocity could be an indication of its phylogenetic priority over speech, misleading as the "biogenetic law" can be at times.

Profoundly deaf individuals, if they grow up in language-using human groups, may develop their own sign-language systems, as has been shown in recent studies of such systems in a Yorkshire village and on Rennell Island, south of New Guinea.[57] In complete linguistic isolation, however, this does not occur, as far as we can tell. I must amend Adam Kendon's statement[53] (p. 4) which is that "human beings will fashion a language out of whatever behavioral materials there are to hand, and that this will be done gesturally if no spoken language or the capacity to produce or receive one is available," to read, "as long as the individual lives in some kind of language-using community." The girl Genie, prevented from acquiring speech for 13½ years, was language-less when rescued.[11,21] Lack of opportunity to grow up in a community where language is used results in language agenesis, and contradicts the speculations of Mandeville and Condillac. Cases in which semi-isolated children have created "private languages" for themselves are not relevant. Even with our now formidable cortical and vocal tract specializations for (spoken) language, I doubt if the progeny of a hypothetical pair or group of present-day *Homo sapiens sapiens,* protected from any contact with an ongoing language system, would reinvent speech in less than many thousand generations, and the attainment of a gestural system might require most of that time. The girl Genie did employ several manual gestures in the period soon after her rescue, after she was placed in a hospital environment, and there are videotaped records of them. However, it is apparently impossible to determine whether she possessed these gestures during her long isolation, or quickly learned them from the people who worked with her. It is worth noting that although she has gradually learned to speak (as the result of intensive training) it was recently decided to teach her ASL (Ameslan) in an effort to improve her understanding of syntax (Victoria Fromkin, personal communication, 1975).

Gestural communication, if not in the form of developed sign language, is prevalent among the severely mentally retarded in institutions, and for a significant percentage of them, is said to be their only quasilinguistic means of communication. There has been very little study of such gestural communication (cf. Ref. 95, for a recent survey of language in mental retardation). In a few instances, there have been deliberate programs to use sign-language with the severely retarded,[17] in one case with the sign-language devised by R. A. S. Paget, the proponent of the mouth-gesture theory of glottogenesis.[78] Such experiments may not prove anything with respect to gesture as a primordial pathway to spoken language, but they lie in the appropriate direction.

Of the various forms of gesture, simple pointing or deixis seems the most basic, and the earliest to appear in human infants, although it does not show up in baby apes, spontaneously or in the wild, as far as we know. Although some anthropologists have claimed that such pointing is not culturally universal, what they are referring to is a rule of etiquette in which finger or arm pointing is taboo, and may be substituted for by lip-pointing (cf. Joel Sherzer's report on the Cuna Indians[99]). Many other cultures, including our own, have rules against pointing at certain kinds of things or persons. A common pointing taboo among North American Indians involved rainbows. On the other hand, explorers have found that pointing is evidentally understood, even if bad form, everywhere.[38] Even Leonard Bloomfield, in his 1914 book when he was still a follower of Wundt rather than of strict Behaviorism, asserted that pointing gesture was understood because of its "universal psychophysiological characteristics" (cf. Ref. 89, p. 370).

The most comprehensive treatment of pointing gesture as the starting point for language (no pun intended!) is a book by the Vietnamese philosopher, Trân Duc Thao in a work on language origins strongly Marxian in orientation.[108] Trân is aware that apes do not point, but observes that they may guide others to objects or other individuals. Gesture is therefore seen as a kind of "guidance at a distance," functioning initially as an appeal or request to direct attention or action on something at a distance (the distance may be very short). Trân ingeniously shows how from a single curved pointing movement, a lexicon can be generated, and eventually, a entire sign-language system. Unfortunately, Trân lacked personal experience with deaf users of sign-language, or the later stages of his scenario for language-generation might have been more satisfactory. He does consider the internalization of such a gestural sign-system, quoting Kant's *Critique of Pure Reason* (p. 49) to the effect that we cannot even think of a line without drawing it in thought. Another philosopher, F. Waisman,[114] examines gesture, picking up an idea of Ludwig Wittgenstein's on the possibility of a language, all the meanings of which had come from deictic definitions. Waisman, (Ref. 114, p. 95) shows how numerals and negatives could be derived from gestures, and concludes his discussion with the remark that while all languages probably contain terms based or basable on ostensive definitions, it would be possible to conceive of a language not formed on this basis. Eve V. Clark refers to ostensive definitions as part of the basis for infant language acquisition.

After a good start, Trân leaves us with gesture-language in being, and the beginning of speech, but he does not provide any plausible explanatin for the vocal stage of language, nor for that matter with survivals of gesticultory behavior as an accompaniment of speech. For this we must turn to Adam Kendon,[53] who, agreeing with my view that gesture has not withered away in the face of vocal language, goes much further than I did in a 1973 paper, and holds that gesture "may encode the most central and abstract ideas also being encoded in speech" (p. 21). Kendon regards manual gesture accompanying speech (also being investigated by Paul Ekman and

Wallace Friesen)[16] as no mere embellishment, but as a major communicative channel, distinguished by Ekman and Friesen as "illustrators," underscoring the semantic structure of the whole message. Significantly, Kendon can show, from frame-by-frame analyses of films, that the gestures either precede or are made at the same time as the relevant vocal signs, but never follow them. Normally, they anticipate the spoken words by several milliseconds. This priority is not what we might expect were the manual movements merely some kind of subconscious spillover or leakage from the primary vocal message; moreover, if the voice is interrupted, the gesticulatory sequence usually is not distrubed. Here, as in the case of the apparent gestural communicative priority in infants, we seem to have a suggestion that gesture is more fundamental, and thus perhaps may be phylogenetically antecedent as well. Professional sign-language interpreters for the deaf, who are hearing individuals, characteristically speak while signing, even though word order and syntax of the two languages (e.g., ASL and English) may differ significantly. This suggests a capacity to communicate simultaneously in two languages, and unlike the situation of a "simultaneous translator" from one spoken language to another (as at the United Nations), productively in both, rather than receptively in one and productively in the other. Such an accomplishment could have been the standard form of language during the hypothetical stage of its transformation from gesture to speech. That gesture and speech can be combined in still other unusual ways is exemplified by the case of a laryngectomized speaker of (Mandarin) Chinese, who learned to mark the vocal tones he could no longer produce in his larynx with four hand gestures,[25] which he was able to use in conversation with his Chinese friends who did not find it too difficult to switch to a visual code for the normal phonemic tones in their language.

It has been repeatedly stated that high iconicity is detrimental in language, and that languages like ASL, or early highly pictorial scripts must be less efficient than their much more arbitrary or conventionalized counterparts in speech or alphabetic systems. It seems clear that conventionalization or arbitrariness conserves the energy of the message transmitter, even as modern shorthands are faster to write than standard script. What is not so obvious is whether iconicity is such a disadvantage in decoding, or even memory-storage. In an undeservedly neglected monograph, Stanley Gerr[26] once strongly defended the efficiency of scientific and technical Japanese written mainly in *Kanji* (i.e., Chinese characters) over languages having alphabetic writing. After years of using written signs on highways and other public places, there has been a recent movement to install signs of a highly iconic or pictoral character (in part to accomodate foreigners, but also because study has shown such signs to be more unambiguous, except for the problem of devising a pictured differentiation between *push* and *pull* for doors!). To the objection that pictorialism is incapable of dealing with more complex or abstract ideas, it should be noted that Catholic missionaries in sixteenth century Mexico devised some highly ingenious pictorial catechisms, and the like, which survive as the so-called Testerian manuscripts.[27] David and A. J. Premack have wondered if visual representations can be found for every verbal distinction, whether in speech or sign-language (Ref. 81, p. 366). They discuss this under the heading "problems arising from the absence of the perceptual counterparts of language." It should be observed that spoken languages are not free of such defects; as Berlin and Kay have shown,[4] there are many languages in the world grievously lacking in color terms, which simply reverses the question raised by the Premacks.

Pictures appear to be processed for certain purposes considerably more rapidly than their verbal signs, spoken or written.[80a] The only trouble with pictures as language signs is that it takes too much time or skill to make them, although photography and television have solved part of that problem. If there was primordial gesture-language, it may have had a strongly pictorial or pantomimic character.

I have already mentioned in my historical survey that the mouth-gesture theory is available, along with onomatopoeia, to help explain how a visual-gestural language could have been transformed into a mainly vocal-auditory system (cf. Refs. 1, 109.). Unfortunately, we cannot find anything resembling either mouth-gesture or onomatopoeia among existing nonhuman primates, and must conclude that the vocal shift occurred well along in the course of separate hominid evolution. It seems unlikely that human abilities to make fair vocal approximations of the calls of other animals, or other noises, arose from the same ecological or ethological conditions which led to the sound-imitative capacities of various bird species. On the other hand, it is not utterly far-fetched to regard distinctive bird-calls as the source of the human vocal tags with which so many birds, in all languages, are named. Incorporation of vocal signs based on human interjections I regard as a special case of onomatopoeia; i.e., they are skilled but imperfect imitations or approximations only. I discovered in the reports of Captain Cook's voyages in the Pacific, a nice instance of the combination of manual gesture and onomatopoeia to indicate that the explorers were interested in trading some of their goods for chickens.[38]

Time is insufficient to develop all the points that might be made in connection with sound-symbolism, the serious and mostly psychological study of which is now the subject of a large literature (cf. Heinz Werner, and B. Kaplan, 1955; Sapir, 1929; Allott, 1975). Sound-symbolism is not the same thing as onomatopoeia, and is connected instead with the mouth-gesture and motor theory of speech perception research. A special ramification of the mouth-gesture and sound-symbolism line of investigation leads into the studies of click-languages such as Bushman and Hottentot, and the extent to which a case can be made that the earliest spoken languages may have been rich in click-consonants (cf. van Ginneken, 1939; also Refs. 102, 103, 82.) Although the point does not belong here, except that the postulated switchover to speech may have been taking place at a phase of hominization where big-game hunting was becoming highly skilled and successful, as indicated archaeologically, I should like to call attention to the visual or graphic character of the hoofprints of game animals, which are "read" by human hunters in somewhat the way ideograms might be read. Ordinary carnivores, if they track their prey, simply sniff at the tracks, and apparently do not "decode" them visually, determining the species, age or size, and speed of animal they are tracking by a visual sign that does not resemble the animal as a whole. Primitive trackers may sniff at dung, but to tell how long it has lain on the trail; they read the species from its shape and color.

Nineteenth-century philologists made much of the primordial character of the "roots" they reconstructed through their comparative studies, and F. Max Müller, who completely rejected the gestural theory for glottogenesis, nevertheless held that early human thought was embedded in the concepts to which the roots supposedly referred. (Müller, 1887,[73] esp. Vol. 2). Much later, Paget and Jóhannesson proposed that many if not most of these roots, in language families from all around the world, were derived from mouth-gestures, and had basic meanings that could readily be represented in manual gestures for common motor activities—cutting, breaking, stretching, scraping, pulling, and so on. Marcel Jousse came to similar conclusions in the Semitic languages, as did Roman Stopa for Bushman and Hottentot.[49] Modern linguists presumably find all such notions bizarre and hopelessly speculative, although the late Morris Swadesh,[105] and now Mary LeCron Foster,[18-20] find the worldwide coincidences of sound and meaning too much to account for by coincidence. Linguistics has been developing in directions away from such problems for almost a century, but it may be time to reexamine the evidence.

Since the 1960s, linguists have been engaged in a great return to the subject of syntax, seen in the perspective of universal grammar and of child language acquisition. It could be that thinking about language in its early phylogenetic development may be encumbered by the idea that its fundamental or deep structure is syntactic (cf. Premack, Rev. 81, p. 244) rather than semantic. The switchover to mainly spoken language, however, could have enhanced the importance of syntax. That a primordial, primitive language, of necessity, had to have a rigorous rule-ordered basis, "forbidding certain forms of utterances while permitting others," and so on, seems unlikely. Perhaps Premack, with Sarah and his later subjects, as well as Rumbaugh, et al., with Lana, have forced their chimpanzee language students into unnecessarily formal modes of communication. Klima[55] discusses the sentence or word-string, "the animals, the hunters, the kill," and observes that ambiguous though it may be, it conveys some low-grade meaning. Peter Reynolds (Ref. 87, p. 40) also feels that both for young children today, and phylogenetically, signal properties can be much less autonomized. Primordial language, gestural or spoken, would have been far more dependent than formal, modern speech or written language on the immediate social and environmental context for its decoding. Social class differences in the use of languages like English also indicate greater context dependency in the informal discourse of the less formally educated. It would be odd if hypothetical reconstructions of primordial language should have to be constrained by a kind of backward projection of the sort of normative grammar which we are, simultaneously, told should be eliminated from our schools. The curious syntactical looseness reported by I. M. Schlesinger[97] for deaf Israeli sign-language users (1970) may come closer to the condition of speech or gesture-language in Paleolithic times, than Seeing Essential English, with its effort to achieve syntactic and lexical correspondence of American sign language and the spoken vernacular.

The emergence of speech also raises the question of whether there might not have had to be a minimal set of phonetically distinctive sounds before "take off," so to speak. If so, if it turns out that a spoken language system could not function with, say, less than ten "phonemes," then gestures might have been utilitzed to eke out meanings and overcome ambiguities, much as in the case of the Chinese without a larynx, who learned to use manual signs to make up for his lack of tones. It should be unnecessary to remind you that although our apelike ancestors probably possessed a set of one or two dozen distinctive vocal *calls*, I do not think that speech simply took off making use of such calls at all. Morse Code utilizes only two distinctive sounds, along with the silence spaces between them, but is notoriously slower than speech, for decoding if not for transmission (by about a factor of ten). The speech of young children, with its characteristic failure to make enough standard phonetic distinctions, is usually decodable with confidence only by the parents of the child, and then only with much help from the familiar context in which the child communicates. If all adults were stuck with the kinds of speech deficiencies normal enough in early childhood, we would probably still be using a well-developed sign-language.

This topic leads us into the matter of the probable acceleration of language transmission and reception, to present-day rates (where, significantly, as readers we seem to have exceeded by many times the speed of even the fastest understandable speech). I suspect that the prime mover or major selective pressure on language, once it had emerged in rudimentary propositional form, was to bring it up to the normal speeds of nonverbal thinking, in which man does not seem to differ significantly from other mammals, even though we may be able to cope with much more intricate problems. For a language to be produced and received at speeds far slower than ordinary thinking results in mind-wandering deviations by the receiver, with a high risk of misunderstanding the message. If we are not trained in shorthand, we have probably experienced this in trying to take notes in longhand, or even on a typewriter. The social difficulties of stutterers, groping for words, may produce impatience even in the best-intentioned listener, and to hear one's familiar tongue slowly and painfully dragged out by a foreign speaker with considerably less than native fluency may produce a peculiar kind of fatigue. The sign-language of the deaf, in the hands of its native users, is evidently about as rapid as speech, although lessened redundancy may be a slight drawback. Without effective duality of patterning, an incipient spoken language may have been considerably slower to decode, or even to produce. The reduplications in many forms of baby-talk, and the frequently slower delivery of mothers talking to their young children, may suggest some of the problems besetting the earliest employment of speech.

Przyluski[82] supposed that because of these kinds of difficulties, gesture and voice were combined in a "mixed prephonemic system" (pp. 32–33), and Duncan (Ref. 3, p. 15), discussing the possible speech deficiencies of the Neanderthalers, also suggests that "gesture and speech could have supported each other until brain development and muscle control made vocal communication vastly superior to gesture." Lackner and Levine[58] remind us that human speech articulation entails motor activity at speeds surpassing those of oculomotor saccadic movements to peripheral visual targets, previously supposed to have held the record. Lieberman and others in this Conference have more to say about these matters than I do.

My last bit of possible evidence for a long gestural stage of glottogonic evolution may strike you as strange, since it has to do with skin pigmentation, not ordinarily regarded as a possible factor in language communication. As far as I know, the idea is original, so that I cannot cite previous investigations in support of it.[41] True, H. A. Rose, in 1919,[90] casually observed that the darker skin on the backs of the hands of South Indian dancers might affect hand visibility and thus perhaps explain some of the differences between their gestures and those of lighter-skinned dancers. The volar (skin of the palms and hands) surfaces, along with the fingernails, are pinkish in all human populations, however dark or light the rest of their skin, with little melanin, and no propensity to tan. Investigation of a large number of both Old and New World primates, from Prosimians to pongids, shows that in nonhuman primates volar skin is pigmented, usually darkly, in adulthood if not in early life, and that the nails of adult nonhuman primates are uniformly fairly dark, or even black. However, several primates have specialized areas of depigmentation, such as eyelids, or the sexual rump skin of females (as in chimpanzees), or the male genitalia (which may also display striking colors). These patches of depigmentation, or special coloration, function in social communication. Many primates undergo marked pigmentation changes with age, affecting both skin and hair, also with social communicative functions.

The characteristically pan-human depigmentation of the palmar skin, fingertips, and fingernails, enables us to monitor the position or movement of the hand and its digits in others, and in ourselves, even if the rest of the skin of the body is very darkly pigmented, or under conditions of low illumination. I propose that this uniquely human feature, found in no other primate, arose through natural selection during a long era of gestural communication, to maximize the efficiency of visual language, although palmar and fingernail depigmentation would also have served to make clear what the hands and fingers were doing in various manual technical processes, from stone-tool making to tying knots. Depigmentation of special parts of the primate body has occurred, evidently in connection with social communication, in a number of other species, and I can see no reason why it would not have arisen in conjunction with manual gesture language.

It may be asked why, since the feet and toes play no obvious role in communication, and only a minor role in tool-using, they too exhibit volar depigmentation. The answer is, I think, that genetically coded enzyme messengers, dictating the nonformation of melanocytes, do not distinguish between the ridged skin of the hands and feet. If such skin is surgically transplanted to a normally melanized portion of the body, it would still resist darkening. There is no disadvantage in having depigmented soles of the feet, or depigmented toenails, and in any case, barefoot hunter-gatherers have dusty or muddy feet most of the time anyhow, with very thick callus formation. I should make it very clear that volar depigmentation, whether or not it has anything to do with a hypothetical epoch of manual gesture language, is a pan-human feature, and not something limited to darkly pigmented populations.

Existing data are insufficient to pinpoint the time, in a gestural-origin scenario, of the first appearance of the first deictic gesture, possibly among the australopithecine hominids. Nor are they sufficient to indicate when speech began to develop, leading, as I suppose, to a considerable era of coexistent gesture and vocal language. It is interesting that a few linguists and prehistorians share the notion that language "of modern type" did not emerge until the beginning of the Upper Paleolithic, and the skeletally attested spread of modern mankind, *Homo sapiens sapiens*. Thus, J. Desmond Clark (Ref. 7, p. 194) says, "The rapid cultural diversification associated with the spread of modern man during the later Pleistocene cannot have been possible except through the medium of speech and it now seems probable that it was the possession of language proper that lay behind the phenomenally rapid success of Homo sapiens sapiens." By "language proper," Clark seems to mean articulate spoken languages, exhibiting duality of patterning, and perhaps fairly elaborate syntax along with large lexicons, closely resembling extant languages. The time of these later Pleistocene cultural diversifications and fully modern man in the morphological sense was about 40,000 years ago. This approximate date corresponds quite well to the linguistic "vanishing point" arrived at by means of statistical methods, admittedly not in universal repute among linguists. That a striking upsurge in prehistoric behavior indicative of enhanced cognitive capacities started about 40,000 years ago is undeniable,[63,68,69] although the role of language remains obscure.

For several decades, linguists have insisted on the absence of any useful evidence, in the whole huge corpus of their data, indicating the evolution of language in any consistent direction, save in the broad sense that techniques such as writing, printing, and recently, electronic and photochemical media, have enlarged human communicative capacities. In part this was a justifiable correction of nineteenth century and earlier views that the languages of so-called primitive peoples were crude and simple, consisting of only a few hundred lexical items, incapable of handling abstractions, and the like. The modern position also reflected the realization that even the societies with the longest histories of literacy and urbanization did not possess languages differing fundamentally from languages of peoples without such amenities. It thus became possible to ignore the possibility that languages in some parts of the world may have been effectively isolated for a great many millennia, and that in some respects, at least, they might contribute to our understanding of how language functioned at a more archaic sociotechnological level.

If, however, we seek to go still farther back, to build a picture of a "mixed prephonemic" system, or a still more hypothetical earlier mainly gestural language, we shall have to look for data on a much broader front—on chimpanzees, on the mentally retarded, from paleoneurology, reconstructions of fossil vocal tracts, inferences from stone tools, and a great many more rather unsatisfactory sources.

REFERENCES

1. ALLOTT, R. M. 1975. The Physical Foundation of Language: Exploration of a Hypothesis. 2 Vols. ELB Printers. Seaford, England.
2. AUGUSTINE. 1952. Confessions. Translated by E. B. Pusey, Vol. 18. Great Books of the Western World. Encyclopaedia Britannica. Chicago, Ill.
3. BACON, F. 1952. Advancement of learning. Vol. 30. Great Books of the Western World. Encyclopaedia Britannica. Chicago, Ill.
4. BERLIN, B. & P. KAY. 1969. Basic Color Terms: Their Universality and Evolution. University of California Press, Berkeley, Calif.
5. CALDWELL, R. L. 1971. Structure de la Lettre sur les Sourds et Muets. Stud. on Voltaire & the 18th Century. **84:** 109–122.
6. CHOUILLET, J. 1972. Descartes et le problème de l'origine des langues au 18e siècle. Dix-huitième Siècle (Revue Annuelle): 39–60.
7. CLARK, J. D. 1975. Africa in prehistory: peripheral or paramount ? Man **10**(2): 175–198.
8. COGER, L. I. & S. PELHAM. 1975. Kinesics applied to interpreters theatre. The Speech Teacher **24**(2): 91–99.
9. CONDILLAC, É. B. DE. 1947. Essai sur l'origine des connaissances humaines. *In* Oeuvres. Georges Le Roy, Ed. Paris, France.
10. CORDEMOY, G. DE. 1668. Discours Physique de la parole. English trans., Anon., A philosophicall discourse concerning speech, conformable to the Cartesian principles. Scholars' Facsimiles & Reprints, Inc., Delmar, N.Y.
11. CURTISS, S., V. FROMKIN, S. KRASHEN, D. RIGLER & M. RIGLER. 1974. The linguistic development of Genie. Language **50**(3): 528–554.
12. DEGÉRANDO, J. M. 1969. The observation of savage peoples. Translated by F. C. T. Moore. Univ. California Press. Berkeley, Calif.
13. DEGÉRANDO, J. N. 1827. De l'éducation des sourds-muets de naissance. 2 Vols. Paris, France.
14. DUFFY, R. J. & J. R. DUFFY. 1975. Pantomime recognition in aphasics. J. Speech Hearing Res. **18**(1): 115–132.
15. DUNCAN, R. M. 1975. Letter (with reply by P. Lieberman). The Sciences. May/June: 3.
16. EKMAN, P. & W. FRIESEN. 1972. Hand movements. J. Communic. **22:** 353–374.
17. FENN, G. & J. A. ROWE. 1975. An attempt in manual communication. Brit. J. Dis. Communic. 310(1): 3–16.
18. FOSTER, M. L. 1969. Ten postulates for primordial language reconstruction. Paper Amer. Anthropol. Assoc. Annual Mtg. New Orleans, La.
19. FOSTER, M. L. 1970. Explorations of semantic phylogeny. Paper, Amer. Anthropol. Assoc. Annual Mtg. San Diego, CA.
20. FOSTER, M. L. 1975. The symbolic structure of primordial language. *In* Perspectives in Human Evolution. S. L. Washburn & E. R. McCown, Eds. Vol. 4. Holt Rinehart & Winston, Inc. New York, N.Y. In press.
21. FROMKIN, V., S. KRASHEN, S. CURTISS, D. RIGLER & M. RIGLER. 1974. The development of language in Genie: a case of language acquisition beyond the "critical period." Brain & Language **1:** 81–107.
22. FURNESS, W. H. 1916. Observations on the intelligence of chimpanzees and orangutans. Proc. Amer. Philos. Soc. **55:** 281–290.
23. GARDNER, B. T. & R. A. GARDNER. Evidence for sentence constituents in the early utterances of child and chimpanzee. J. of Exp. Psych. In press.
24. GARDNER, B. T. 1975. Signs of language in child and chimpanzee. Amer. Psych. Assoc. Annual Mtg. Chicago, Ill.
25. GATELY, G. 1975. A technique for assisting speakers of Chinese to speak Chinese esophageal speech. J. Speech Hearing Dis. **40**(2): 274.
26. GEER, S. 1944. Scientific and Technical Japanese. New York, N.Y.
26a. VAN GINNEKEN, J. Les clics, les consonnés et les voyelles dans l'histoire de l'humanité. Proc. Third Internat. Cong. Phonetic Sciences. Ghent, Belgium.
27. GLASS, J. B. 1975. A census of Middle American Testerian manuscripts. *In* Handbook of Middle American Indians. R. Wauchope, Ed. Vol. 14. Univ. Tex Press. Austin, Tex.

27a. GLENN, E. n.d. Speculations on the origin of language. Communications Spectrum 7: 3–18.
28. GOODMAN, N. 1967. The epistemological argument. Synthese 17: 23–28.
29. GRIMSLEY, R. 1967. Some aspects of 'nature' and 'language' in the French Enlightenment. Stud. on Voltaire & the 18th Century. 66: 659–677.
30. HASTINGS, H. 1936. Man and beast in French thought of the Eighteenth Century. Johns Hopkins Stud. in Romance Lit. & Lang. Vol. 27.
31. HATTIANGADI, J. 1973. Mind and the origin of language. Philosophy Forum 14: 81–98.
32. HAYES, K. J. & C. HAYES. 1951. The intellectual development of a home-raised chimpanzee. Proc. Am. Philos. Soc. 95: 105–109.
33. HAYES, K. J. 1950. Vocalization and speech in chimpanzees. Am. Psychol. 5: 275–276.
34. HERVÁS Y PANDURO, L. 1789. Historia de la Vida del Hombre. Imprenta de Aznár. Madrid, Spain.
35. HERVÉ, G. 1909. Le premier programme de l'anthropologie. Soc. d'Anthrop. de Paris. Bull. & Mém. Sér. 5: 473–487.
36. HEWES, G. W. 1973. Primate communication and the gestural origin of language. Curr. Anthropol. 14: 5–24.
37. HEWES, G. W. 1973. An explicit formulation of the relation between tool-using and early human language emergence. Visible Language 7(2): 101–127.
38. HEWES, G. W. 1974. Gesture language in culture contact. Sign Language Stud. 4: 1–34.
39. HEWES, G. W. 1975. The evolutionary significance of Pongid sign language acquisition. Paper, Amer. Psych. Assoc. Ann. Mtg. Chicago, Ill.
40. HEWES, G. W. 1975. Language origins: a bibliography. 2nd Ed. Rev. 2 Vols. Mouton. The Hague, The Netherlands.
41. HEWES, G. W. 1975. Comments on Mattingly's paper and on Levallois tools. In The Role of Speech in Language. J. Kavanagh & J. Cutting, Eds. the MIT Press. Cambridge, Mass.
42. JERISON, H. T. 1973. Evolution of the brain and intelligence. Academic Press. New York, N.Y.
43. JERISON, H. T. et al. 1975. A current anthropology book review: evolution of the brain and intelligence. Curr. Anthrop. 16(3): 403–426.
44. JÓHANNESSON, A. 1946. Origin of language. Nature 157: 847–848.
45. JÓHANNESSON, A. 1950. The gestural origin of language. Nature 166: 60–61.
46. JÓHANNESSON, A. 1952. Gestural Origin of Language. Leiftur. Reykjavík Iceland; B. H. Blackwell. Oxford, Eng.
47. JOLY, N. 1897. Man Before Metals. D. Appleton & Co. New York, N.Y.
48. JOSEPHS, H. 1969. Diderot's Dialogue of Language and Gesture: le Neveu de Rameau. Ohio State Univ. Press. Columbus, Ohio.
49. JOUSSE, M. 1936. Le mimisme humain et l'anthropologie du langage. Rev. Anthropologique 46(7/9): 201–215.
50. KAINZ, F. 1962–65. Psychologie der Sprache. 3rd Ed. 5 Vols. F. Enke. Stuttgart, Germany.
51. KAVANAGH, J. & J. CUTTING, EDS. The Role of Speech in Language. The MIT Press. Cambridge, Mass.
52. KEANE, A. H. 1895. Ethnology. Cambridge Univ. Press. London, England.
53. KENDON, A. 1975. Gesticulation, speech and the gesture theory of language origins. In Biology & Language. S. K. Ghosh, Ed. In press.
54. KIMURA, D. 1974. Motor functions of the left hemisphere. Brain 97(2): 337–350.
55. KLIMA, E. 1975. Sound and its absence in the linguistic sumbol. In The role of speech in language. J. Kavanagh and J. Cutting, Eds. The MIT Press. Cambridge, Mass.
56. KNOWLSON, J. R. 1965. The idea of gesture as a universal language in the XVIIth and XVIIIth centuries. J. Hist. Ideas 26(4): 495–508.
57. KUSCHEL, R. 1973. The silent inventor: the creation of a sign language by the only deaf-mute on a Polynesian island. Sign Lang. Stud. 3: 1–27.
58. LACKNER, J. R. & K. B. LEVINE. 1975. Speech production: evidence of syntactically and phonologically determined units. Percep. Psychophys. 17(1): 107–113.
59. LA METTRIE, J. O. DE. 1912. Man a Machine. L'Homme Machine. Open Court. Chicago, Ill.

60. LANGER, S. K. 1972. Mind: an Essay on Human Feelings. Vol. 2. The Johns Hopkins Press. Baltimore, Md.
61. LAUGHLIN, C. D. JR. & E. G. D'AQUILI. 1974. Biogenetic Structuralism. Columbia University Press. New York, N.Y.
62. LENNEBERG, E. H. 1967. Biological Foundations of Language. John Wiley, New York, N.Y.
63. LEROI-GOURHAN, A. 1964–65. Le geste et la parole. 2 Vols. Albin Marcel. Paris, France.
64. LOI, I. 1971. Note all Essai sur l'origine des langues di J. J. Rousseau. Lingua e Stile 6(3): 479–486.
65. MALLERY, G. 1881. Sign language among North American Indians, compared with that among other peoples and deaf-mutes. Bur. Am. Ethnol. Ann. Rept. 1. Washington, D.C.
66. MANDEVILLE, BERNARD. 1924. (1728). Fable of the bees. Clarendon Press. Oxford, England.
67. MARLER, P. 1975. On the origin of speech from animal sounds. In The Role of Speech in Language. J. Kavanagh & J. Cutting, Eds. The MIT Press. Cambridge, Mass.
68. MARSHACK, A. 1971. The roots of civilization. McGraw-Hill. New York, N.Y.
69. MARSHACK, A. 1972. Cognitive aspects of Upper Paleolithic Engraving. Curr. Anthropol. 13(3.4): 445–477.
70. MCLEISH, J. & J. MARTIN. 1975. Verbal behavior: a review and experimental analysis. J. Gen. Psychol. 93: 3–66.
71. MAUPERTUIS, 1965. Dissertation sur les différens moyens dont les hommes se sont servis pour exprimer leurs idées. In Oeuvres. Vol. 2. Georg Olms Verlagsbuchhandlung. Hildesheim, Germany.
72. MEGILL, A. D. 1974. The Enlightenment debate on the origin of language. Ph.D. dissertation. Columbia University. New York, N.Y. 480 pp.
73. MÜLLER, F. M. 1887. The Science of thought. 2 Vols. Charles Scribner's Sons. New York, N.Y.
74. NORMAN, N. L. 1974. Gesticulation as a theoretical construct in speech communication. Ph.D. dissertation. Univ. Denver. Denver, Colo.
75. NOTTEBOHM, F. 1970. Ontogeny of bird song. Science 167: 950–956.
76. PAGET, R. A. S. 1927. The origin of speech. Nature 120: 47–48.
77. PAGET, R. A. S. 1956. The origins of language, with special reference to the paleolithic age. J. World Hist. 1: 399–414.
78. PAGET, R. A. S. 1963. Human Speech: some Observations, Experiments and Conclusions as to the Nature, Origin, Purpose and Possible Improvement of Human Speech. Routledge & Kegan Paul. London, England.
79. PERKINS, M. L. 1969. Rousseau on history, liberty and national survival. Stud. on Voltaire & the 18th century. 53: 79–169.
80. PLATO. 1921. Cratylus. H. N. Fowler, trans. & Ed. Loeb Classical Library & Harvard Univ. Press. Cambridge, Mass.
80a. POTTER, M. & B. FAULCONER. 1975. Time to understand pictures and words. Nature 253: 437–438.
81. PREMACK, D. & A. J. PREMACK. Teaching visual language to apes and language-deficient persons. In Language perspective—Acquisition, Retardation, and Intervention. R. Schiefelbusch & L. L. Lloyd, Eds. University Park Press. Baltimore, Md.
82. PRZYLUSKI, J. 1941. Le langage, la langue et la parole. J. de Psych., norm. et path. 37/38: 29–38.
83. RABELAIS, F. 1955. The histories of Gargantua and Pantagruel. Trans. by J. M. Cohen. Penguin Books. Harmondsworth, Eng.
84. RAMBOSSON, J. P. 1880–81. Origine de la parole et du langage parlé. Comptes Rendus de l'Acad. des Sciences Morales & Politiques 114: 757–758; 115: 106–132; 374–400.
85. READ-MARTIN, C. E. & D. W. R. 1975. Australopithecine scavenging and human evolution: an approach from faunal analysis. Curr. Anthropol. 16(3): 359–368.
86. RÉVÉSZ, G. 1946. Ursprung and Vorgeschichte der Sprache. Francke. Bern, Switzerland.
87. REYNOLDS, P. C. Comments on Marler's paper. In The role of speech in language. J. Kavanagh & J. Cutting, Eds. the MIT Press. Cambridge, Mass.
88. RIES, D. C. 1806. Versuche Vereinigung zweier entgegengesetzen Meinungen über den

Ursprung der Sprache, auf Erfahrungen und Beobachtungen an Taubstummen gegründet. Andreá. Frankfurt am Main, Germany.

89. ROBACK, A. A. 1954. Destiny and motivation in language. Studies in psycholinguistics and glossodynamics. Sci-Art Publishers. Cambridge, Mass.

90. ROSE, H. A. 1919. The language of gestures. Folklore 30: 312–315.

91. RUDOWSKI, V. A. 1974. The theory of signs in the eighteenth century. J. Hist. Ideas 35: 683–690.

92. SABATER PÍ, J. 1974. An elementary industry of the chimpanzees in the Okorobiko Mountains, Rio Muni (Republic of Equatorial Guinea), West Africa. Primates 15(4): 351–364.

93. SAPIR, E. 1929. A study in phonetic symbolism. J. Exp. Psychol. 12: 225–239.

94. SAYCE, A. H. 1880. Introduction to the Science of Language. Kegan Paul. London, Eng.

95. SCHIEFELBUSCH, R. L. & L. L. LLOYD, Eds. 1974. Language perspective—Acquition, Retardation, and Intervention. University Park Press. Baltimore, Md.

96. SCHLEICHER, A. 1863. Die Darwinische Theorie und der Sprachwissenschaft. Offenes Sendschreiben an Herrn Dr. Ernst Häckl. Weimar, Germany.

97. SCHLESINGER, I. M. 1970. The grammar of sign language and the problem of language universals. In Biological and Social Factors in Psycholinguistics. J. Morton, Ed. Logos Press. London, England.

98. SEIGEL, J. P. 1969. The Enlightenment and the evolution of a language of signs in France and England. J. Hist. Ideas 30: 96–115.

99. SHERZER, J. Verbal and nonverbal deixis: the pointed lip gesture among the San Blas Cuna. Lang. in Society 2: 117–131.

100. SLADEN, B. K. The evolution of the human capacity for language. Bull. Orton Soc. 24: 37–47.

101. SPENCER, H. 1899. Principles of Psychology. 4th edit. London, England.

102. STOPA, R. 1935. Die Schnalze, ihre Natur, Entwicklung and Ursprung. Polska Akad. Umiejetności Prace, Kom. Jçzykowej 23: xi–198.

103. STOPA, R. 1965. Die Entwicklung der Sprachlaute. Phonetica 13: 95–98.

104. STOPA, R. 1968. Kann man eine Brücke schlagen zwischen der Kommunikation der Primaten und derjenigen der Urmensch ? Homo, Ztschr. für die vergleichende Forschung am Menschen 19(3/4): 129–151.

105. SWADESH, M. 1971. The origin and diversification of language. J. Sherzer, Ed. Aldine-Atherton. Chicago, Ill.

106. TELEKI, G. 1974. Chimpanzee subsistence technology: materials and skills. J. Hum. Evol. 3: 575–594.

107. THOMAS, L. L. 1957. The linguistic theories of N. Ja. Marr. Univ. Calif. Publ. in Ling. 14: 1–176.

108. TRẦN DUC THAO. 1973. Recherches sur l'origine du langage et de la conscience. Editions Sociales. Paris, France.

109. TROJAN, F. 1957. Zeichen, Silbe und Laut in entwicklungsgeschichtlicher Sicht. Phonetica 1: 63–81.

110. TYLOR, E. B. 1863. Wild men and beast children. Anthropol. Rev. 1: 22.

111. TYLOR, E. B. 1871. Primitive Culture. London, Englånd.

112. TYLOR, E. B. 1881. Anthropology: an introduction to the study of man and civilization. London. 1904 Edit. J. A. Hill & Co. New York, N.Y.

113. VALADE, Y-L. R. 1866. De l'origine du langage et de l'influence que les signes naturels ont exercée sur sa formation . . . Discours prononcé à la distribution solenelle des prix de l'Institution Impériale des Sourds-Meuts de Paris. Imprimerie de Boucquin. Paris, France.

114. WAISMAN, F. 1965. The principles of linguistic philosophy. R. Harre, Ed. Macmillan. London, England.

114a. WERNER, H. & B. KAPLAN. 1955. On expressive language. Papers presented at the Clark Univ. Conf. on Expressive Language Behavior. Worcester, Mass. Clark University Monographs in Psychology and Related Disciplines, no. 1.

115. WERNER, H. & B. KAPLAN. 1957. Symbolic mediation and organization of thought: an experimental approach by means of the line schematization technique. J. Psychol. 43: 3–25.

116. WERNER, H. 1948. Comparative psychology of mental development. Follett. Chicago, Ill.
117. WERNER, H. & B. KAPLAN. 1963, Symbol Formation: an Organismic-Developmental Approach to Language and the Expression of Thought. John Wiley. New York, N.Y.
118. WHITNEY, W. D. 1867. Language and the study of language. Charles Scribner's Sons. New York, N.Y.
119. WHITNEY, W. D. 1873. Oriental and linguistic studies. Charles Scribner's Sons. New York, N.Y.
120. WHITNEY, W. D. 1875. The life and growth of language. The International Scientific Series. Vol. 16.
121. WHITNEY, W. D. 1885. See "Philology." Vol. 18. Encyclopaedia Britannica, 9th Edit.
122. WILKINS, J. 1694. Mercury, or the secret and swift messenger. The Mathematical and Philosophical Works of John Wilkins. London. 1707, 1802.
123. WINKELSTEIN, E. 1974. The development of a systematic method by which day care staff can select gestural imitation curriculum procedures for individual infants. Child Study J. 4: 169–178.

SIGN LANGUAGE AUTONOMY*

William C. Stokoe

Linguistics Research Laboratory
Gallaudet College
Washington, D.C. 20002

A major difficulty in tracing the origin of speech to animal sounds, the difference in nature between signal and linguistic symbol, Marler states thus:

> In animals the tendency is ... to pack as much information as possible into single, indivisible signals. Thus a bird alarm call is at once a symbol for a predator and a directive to escape. The "rough grunting" of chimpanzees announces the discovery of food and also invites others to come and share. This incorporation of noun and verb function in the same indivisible signal greatly limits the possibilities of syntactical rearrangement of signals to create new messages.[1]

Of course the vibration of laryngeal folds and the use of oral cavities to concentrate sound energy in two or three harmonics link man and other primates back to the anuran order of amphibia.[2] The problem is not to find how animal vocal sound production envolved into human but to explain how speech and hearing as language encoding-decoding processes can have evolved from apelike ancestors.

When this problem is improperly conceptualized, as Sarles notes,[3] the unwary accept the opinion of many linguists and animal callists that the seeker for evidence of speech evolution will find nothing. I agree with Sarles' opinion that if we look at the whole "gestural and vocal communication of all the social species, including Man,"[3] the search may be rewarding. Moreover, I share the opinion of Hewes, that language evolved not in a straight line from anuran to mammalian to human vocal and auditory function, but instead made a detour through the gestural and visual behavior of bipedal manipulating primates.[4] Hewes has parsimoniously explained a wealth of data and reduced problems by supposing that when Australopithecus, or a contemporary, began to fashion and use tools creatively, he also began to fashion and use a few gestural signs in partial language function.[5] If something of the kind did take place, language, as a system linking intellect to sense-perceptible expression, and speech, as a particular mode of that expression, need not have followed (for the two million years since Olduvai Gorge Bed I) a simultaneous and indivisible evolution.

The particular mode of language expression I have been investigating since 1955, the signs used by deaf persons, may not at first appear pertinent to asking if hominid language capability and function began with gSigns[6]—defined as bodily actions serving as signs in a semiotic system though without the connotation of *gesture*.[7] Sign languages used by contemporary deaf groups in all parts of the world (see *Sign Language Studies*, 1972) could be the product, as Kendon comments, of

> the resourcefulness and ingenuity of the human being when faced with a difficult situation [hearing deprivation]; a resourcefulness and ingenuity that has come about as a *consequence* of his language capacity, a capacity that emerged only when his ability to employ speech emerged.[8]

*The research for this paper was supported by the National Science Foundation, grant no. SOC 7414724.

Kendon continues:

> If, on the other hand, the spontaneous *linguistic* use of kinesis can be demonstrated to be widespread—that it is indeed a normal and integral part of *behaving as a speaker*—then this possible counter argument [against a gSign origin for language] would seem to carry much less weight.[8]

Studies and observations Kendon then cites not only attest to widespread linguistic use of kinesis but also suggest that the identical message is often signaled by speakers first in gSigns and then in speech: "a single *utterance*, with two outputs."[8]

Nevertheless, the line of argument I wish to take in support of the gestural origin theory of Hewes does not depend primarily on this occasional linguistic use of gSigns by speakers, nor on the constant and regular use of gSigns in highly encoded ways by deaf persons.[9] Instead, my argument depends on the autonomy of sign language.

A number of studies in the last fifteen years have shown, 1) that rules govern American Sign Language (ASL), 2) that ASL rules resemble *in form* the rules of other languages, and 3) the nature of some of these rules of ASL. Now, to emphasize the formal similarity of ASL to other languages adds to linguistic knowledge and may serve useful social functions: e.g. ignorance of ASL has led to denials that a sign language can have a grammar and thence to the forced formal teaching of inaudible spoken English to deaf children who should instead be getting a chance to acquire a language naturally.[10]

But in this conference on the origins and evolution of language and speech, a quite different aspect or interpretation of the same sign language phenomena ought to be central—not the similarity of ASL to other languages, but just those ways in which sign languages are unlike speech-mediated language.

Some justification for discussing sign language autonomy comes from the almost automatic assumption that speech or spoken language is an autonomous system; e.g. Halliday proposes:

> The human child from the earliest age uses his vocal resources to act on the people around him, and through them, both to act on and to learn about his environment. In this way the essential patterns of the culture are made available to him—not through instruction, but through the ordinary everyday use of language, in and around the house. We can gain some idea of the origins of language by watching this process take place.[11]

Halliday's first sentence is true but incomplete. It would cover more truth if it read ". . . *uses all his interactional resources . . .*" The second sentence would gain validity from this change, but it could be made much more explicit, thus: ". . . *use of language, paralanguage, kinesis, proxemics, eye contacts, etc.*" Then, we could "gain some idea of the origins of language by watching this "*total communication*" process take place.

Infant vocal resources are no more autonomous than adult speech. According to Fraiberg, "a sighted child, at six months, can communicate through visual contact the following feelings: longing or wanting, attention and interest, curiosity, doubt, coyness, and boredom."[12] Of course, some expression of these feelings may also be communicated through vocal output. Speaking about sign language autonomy is not intended as a claim that a visible system that encodes human feelings and thoughts for transmission is a law unto itself; rather, that sign language is as capable as speech of performing the complicated hook-up called grammar between either vocal or gSign transmission system and a message source, whether a human, a hominid, or a chimpanzee brain function. Then it becomes possible to examine ways in which gSigns as semiotic primes contain strong evidence, or suggestions, of earlier appearance than doubly articulated sound symbolism.

But to return to Halliday's proposal that we concentrate on the child's vocal resources, I intend to insist that if ideas relevant to the origin of language are sought in the human child's development, it makes no better sense to ignore sight than to exclude sound.

The linguistic argument against autonomy in a sign language can be stated thus: If true language originated when an overloaded hominoid vocal call system developed duality—its minimal meaningful signal elements becoming true movable morphemes,[13] then the existence of so-called sign *language* depends on fully evolved language function, and its rules, without autonomy, must be simple substitution rules of a gSign for one or more elements of spoken language.

Several flaws in this argument have already been noted: ASL rules differ from the rules of other languages as those rule sets differ from each other;[14] infants use eyes and actions as well as ears and voices (when they can); adults may give a single utterance two outputs, and the first may be the nonvocal.[8] Moreover, there is abundant evidence that in the development of intact human infants, limbic and gestural output (Lamendalla) and vision are fashioned into an interpersonal two-way communication system that works very effectively, whereas vocal-auditory communication is grossly one-sided; i.e., the child or infant may be responding to features[15] or to semantic units[16] of adult speech but still be months away from intelligible speech production. Add to this the widely reported testimony that deaf and hearing children of deaf signing parents begin to utter two-sign sentences six to ten months earlier than the first two-word spoken sentences, [17-19] and the argument that sign language depends on speech and spoken language falls.

One of the principles of spoken language, ordering, applies even in the first, two-word stage of child language.[20] The child may exhibit uncertainty for a time (if, e.g. *Milk all gone* and *All gone milk* really are synonymous), but soon casts two-word sentences into the pattern of order that will remain stable and in congruity with the adult usage of its community. One of the most often-observed differences between a sign language, however, and the language of the one making the observation concerns this same principle of ordering. In 1865, Lambert, writing about the difference between written French and French Sign Language, comments:

> The sign language phrase puts its elements, not in the order in which they come out in writing, but in the natural order of events themselves and of the ideas to which these correspond, proceeding always from the known to the unknown.[21]

Despite this, American observers of ASL have attributed the noun-adjective phrase structure occasionally to be seen in older signers to the contact signing had with French before its importation by T. H. Gallaudet in 1816.[22] And I. M. Schlesinger, in 1970, confesses to failure to find in Israeli Sign Language any order that unequivocally signals syntax or indicates the case relations to a verb of giving of its agent, object, and recipient.[23]

The conflicting testimony about word order in sign-language phrases negatively confirms Fischer's conclusion, that order in ASL is virtually free.[24] In an utterance of any length, signers must put some things ahead of others, but it is the nature of sign language to escape the constraints on linear temporal order that are most binding on the generation and expression of spoken utterances. Real or abstract time governs the phonology, morphophonemic patterns, phrase structures, and transformations of all language, according to strict linguistic theory. But in sign language, space has an equally important, though not necessarily symmetrical, role. And it is worth considering that *change from an immediately perceptible ordering of elements in space to an invisible, abstract kind of ordering in time seems a likelier evolutionary direction than the reverse.*

Neither space/time difference nor spoken/signed language difference is simple, and to examine some of the pertinent strands in the complexity, it may help to use an illustration. The scene is a laboratory. A student who has seen part of an experiment, asked by another, "What am I supposed to put into line 5 of my lab manual?" may say:

The rat ran from here to there.

About this utterance we can be sure of at least three points: 1) *Here* is closer to the speaker than is *there*. 2) The speaker has used at least two gSigns to help the syllables of *here* and *there* make clear their denotation. 3) The speaker is aware that the listener has seen the same event, and that both are aware that the experimental animal has been mentioned before—on an earlier line of the lab manual—as *a rat*.

If, in slightly changed circumstances, a deaf signer is telling another (i.e., not an authority figure) about the same event, we can be sure of several quite different points: 1) That part of the report corresponding with "from here to there" has nothing to do with which place is closer to the signer. 2) This same locative part of the signed utterance will look to a nonsigning observer more like one continuous action than like four easily separable units (though from one point of view the easy separability of words is an illusion peculiar to native speakers of the language the words belong to). 3) The utterance may not contain any discrete sign meaning "run," because the part of the utterance under discussion has already rendered the action sufficiently. 4) Past tense will not be signaled anywhere in the relation of an immediately past event jointly witnessed by signer and addressee. (Although surrounded by speakers of Indo-European tongues which must mark time in verbs, ASL signers need not and cannot make their time signs and verb signs into amalgams.) 5) The ASL sign glossed "rat" may not appear in the utterance either. If it is quite clear to the signer that the sign addressee saw the same nominal and verbal appearances (as Chafe designates parts of the event[25]), then telling the addressee that the rat was a rat constitutes barbarous redundancy or an insult to the addressee's intelligence.

Generally, in cases where both the situation and the use of gSigns are needed to make a spoken utterance clear, the generation and production of the utterance are governed by more than a set of narrowly linguistic rules. What is uttered is not a function only of what is seen and of grammatical and phonological rules but depends on a whole set of conventions or communication rules that characterize a language community and interpenetrate its whole set of cultural patterns. What is uttered, like what is done, in a given situation belongs to the continuously evolving social conventions of all social species. Some of these conventions are subtly, some radically different for members of a community who sign language instead of speaking it. Most radical perhaps is the use of space as a transform of time.

But the last statement seems to be an unwarranted reversal of natural order. The event in the hypothetical laboratory took place in time, but its salient fact to all but the most sophisticated observer is the rat's motion in space. The actual utterances of different speakers and different signers differ, but if the latter are using ASL and not English with its words coded in signs and alphabetical configurations of the hand, a signed utterance will include some sort of space-using re-presentation of the event. The scale and perspective of the signed presentation may vary, but indicated place, direction, motion, and speed will form part of the utterance. No one who has studied sign language can fail to see—as Sebeok pointed out here—that there is power in the icon, moreover that the event is the source and target of the representation and the potential in sign language for representing the visual world and actions in it is huge and largely unsuspected by "Man the Talker." [26] If the signed linguistic representation derives from the event, then the spoken linguistic representation can either have derived from the event independently in some as yet unexplained way or derived from a much earlier, hominid gestural representation of events not at first divided into nominal and verbal components.

A gSign which moves, starting from one place and stopping at another, not only furnishes the matrix from which verb and two locative nouns can be cut but also provides the clearly visible evidence of its own composite nature. I have written elsewhere of the lability of primates' pointing gestures, [6] and Trân Dûc Thâo has also treated the elaboration of basic deictic gestures into language-like signs. [27]

Transitive verb signs in contemporary, highly encoded sign languages may be interesting linguistic fossils, if, like rocks put to modern uses, they contain traces of ancient processes. Grasping an object, as an action or observed event, presents both a verbal and a nominal appearance. When a hand holding nothing re-presents in mimicry its own real action of grasping, the gSign immediately produced (for any observer including the maker who perceives a resemblance[28]) still works in contemporary sign languages either as verb or as verb plus inanimate noun—the absent or displaced object. It seems likely that the latter use, of sign for the whole event, antedates the former, which shows the verb part abstracted from the, at first undivided but in fact divisible, gSign signal.

Whenever the abstractive function occurred—even though as Hewes reminds us the "whenever" may stand for countless repetitions over thousands of years—[4] this act of abstraction was a giant step into language. What creature performed it is still undecided, but to see the chimpanzee Washoe[29] opening things, watching things opened, making a reasonable gSign representation of one kind of opening after being molded into that behavior, using the same gSign repeatedly when faced with many things *we* might call closed—this is to entertain the thought that the long process of abstracting and generalizing from experience, aided by gestural representation, may have begun with creatures not much different from chimpanzees and still vocally inarticulate.

If our suppositious reconstruction proceeds from the visible event (naturally of survival importance to organism and species) to the visible re-presentation of the event, then it is possible to find that the process reconstructed was for refining the raw material of mostly visual experience into the rudiments of syntax, without the need for vocal intervention.

Transitive sign verbs with two associated human nouns, or (as Chafe calls them for their semantic-syntactic valence[30]) verbs that are *processes* and *actions* with persons as both *agent* and *patient*, contain fossil remains perhaps of a different and equally important early syntactic form. Such events as *Alley hit ooP* (or *called, told, saw, blamed, questioned, sent away,* or *gave something to*) have in common an ASL representation that involves gSign movement from *Alley* and toward *ooP*. Moreover, the direction of the movement is a function both of the agent and patient and of the identity of the signer as one or neither. The expression (1) $A \rightarrow P$ schematically captures the verb, both of the personal nouns, and the case relations of both nouns to the verb. Furthermore,

$$(2)\ P \leftarrow A, \quad (3)\ P, \quad (4)\ A, \quad (5)\ P, \quad \text{and}\ (6)\ A$$
$$\qquad\qquad\quad \uparrow \qquad \downarrow \qquad \nearrow \qquad\quad \nearrow$$
$$\qquad\qquad\quad A \qquad P \qquad A \qquad\quad P$$

are all spatial transforms of the original expression that preserve both syntax and meaning. These, however, are more than variations on a graphic abstraction of a linguistic structure. If one were to view, from above, a signer and an addressee and a third person on the signer's right, one would see the action of the verb sign congruent in sense and direction with all six arrows. Using different verbs to illustrate, the six expressions above present the basic structure of, respectively:

(1) You teased her.   (4) You asked me.
(2) She hit you.   (5) I'll call her.
(3) I warned you.   (6) She'll blame me.

The unmistakable and automatic encoding of case relations may be regarded as a problem variously solved in the grammars of various languages. Formal inflection, intonation, semantic distinction, and linear ordering, singly or in combination, are the usual solutions. All four of these may have, as it were, embryonic presence in the solution sign language makes of the problem. Viewed as configuration and orientation of the active hand or hands, the form of a sign does change (i.e., inflect) as it occurs in the six frames just presented. Intonation is harder to generalize from acoustic to motoric performance, but differences in the initial and the terminal portions of a verb sign's action and in its physical performance can be treated as the gSign counterparts of intonation with interesting results.[31] It is also possible to consider that the part of signing activity concentrated in hands and their motion is analogous to vowel and consonant segments and the part played by head, face, and eyes is analogous to intonation. Either way, there is seen in the whole unanalyzed activity of signing a complexity of functioning that differs from the complexity of speaking chiefly in visibility.

Semantic distinction is no respecter of modes. That people eat food and food does not eat people is understood by children in the two-word utterance stage and by adults, by children born deaf, and by adults who have never heard speech. It seems to be understood also by experimental animals, but that is hard to confirm.

Recently, linguistic attention has elevated linear or abstract ordering to dominant position in the solution of syntactic problems; i.e., the surface order of elements in an utterance may be transformationally different from underlying order. But if the sign-language solution of the problem is given serious consideration, then it appears that surface and depth more nearly coincide. As we have seen, the coincidence is more spatial than temporal; yet one may recall Lambert's dictum that order in a sign-language phrase coincides with "the natural order of events,"[21] which is restating in different terminology our finding that an event and its gSign representation are visibly similar. The underlying order in situation-event may be spatial-temporal even though the deepest order in spoken language structure is temporal-abstract. If it is possible to identify the grammatical formula SVO with the ASL expression $A \rightarrow P$, it may also be possible to view sign language autonomy as a function of visually reality made possible by the progressive abstraction facilitated by gSign representations.

Another problem in syntax may have been originally solved by signed structures similar to those just examined using the process-action verb and its associated nouns. Underlying the pronoun forms and the rules for their use in all languages is a single "term-set," as Henderson calls it.[32] Its first order elements are (1) *speaker*, (2) *listener* (sc signer, addressee), (1 2) *both* these, and (3) *another*. The next order of elements (plural) admits further combination of these first three with one or more others (3); i.e. 1 3, 1 2 3, 2 3, 3 3. The sex (gender) of the elements makes real and linguistic difference as well, but this can be relegated to another dimension of the matrix.

So described the term-set numbers eight. The *word-class* that in English represents the term-set has five members; in French, six. But the *sign-class*, i.e., word-class, in ASL has eight members. There is for the signer no neutralization or overlap, as the tabular presentation shows. Inclusive, exclusive, and differential "we" as well as singular and plural "you"—all the terms of the set have clear, unequivocal forms in ASL.

The explanation for differences between term-set and word-class can usually be found in histories of specific languages and the peoples speaking them; e.g. when *thou/thee* was current in English, the language had a six-word class, and in some places 2 3 is distinguished as *you-all*. But whatever the phonological and social causes of change, it is the word-class which changes, and not the term-set. Thus *the eight-word class of a sign language can much more easily be derived from the underlying*

TABLE 1

TERM-SET (AFTER HENDERSON[32]) AND WORD-CLASSES IN FRENCH, ENGLISH, AND SIGN FOR PERSONAL PRONOUN SYSTEM

Term-Set:	1	2	12	3	1 $\dot{3}$	1 2 $\dot{3}$	2 $\dot{3}$	3 $\dot{3}$
Word-Class ASL:*	$G^{\intercal}$	$G^{\perp}$	$K^{\mathcal{I}}$	$G^{\curlyvee}$	$K^{\natural}$	3^{ϑ}	K^{ζ}	G^{ζ}
French:	je	tu	nous	(il/ elle)	nous	nous	vous	(ils/ elles)
English:	I	you	we	(he/ she)	we	we	you	they

*Key: G = index finger extended

   K = index finger extended, middle finger extended and supported by tip of thumb at its second joint

   3 = thumb, index, and middle fingers extended

   $\intercal$ = motion toward signer

   $\perp$ = motion away from signer

   $\mathcal{I}$ = motion to and from signer

   $\curlyvee$ = motion obliquely away

   $\curlyvee$ = motion obliquely away and back

   $\mathcal{z}$ = motion side to side

   ϑ = circular motion

term-set than from some other language's smaller word-class. Moreover, having the whole term-set at hand in gSign representations would prove advantageous when resymbolizing the system in vocal signs came to be done. There is no advantage in working the other way round. Just so, children can be seen (once they have learned about the polysemy of names for self and parents) getting the hang of the *you/me* switching system of reference *by looking and pointing*. I trust that no one has yet observed a child learning to look and point by using an already mastered spoken-language pronoun system.

   In conclusion, I would call attention again to the necessity of keeping levels clearly separated. On the levels of social use, linguistic encoding, and cognitive capacity, contemporary sign languages of relatively self-determining groups of deaf people are fully developed systems showing the same order of utilization of human language capacity as many other language. But on the level of sign-to-denotatum relationship, there are features of signs and sign combinations that suggest that gSigns not only preceded spoken words as the name for things and as ways of designating persons but also may have provided the matrix from which those things we have come to call "abstract syntactic relations" were differentially separated.

References

1. MARLER, P. 1975. On the origin of speech from animal sounds. *In* The Role of Speech in Language. J. Kavanagh & J. Cutting, Eds.: 33f. MIT Press. Cambridge, Mass.

2. LEIBERMAN, P. 1975. The evolution of speech and language. *In* On The Origins of Language: 156f. Macmillan. New York, N.Y.

3. SARLES, H. 1974. A sense of language—in the context of human ethology. *In* Language Origins. R. Wescott, Ed.: 69–82. Linstok Press. Silver Spring, Md.

4. HEWES, G. 1974. Language in early hominids. *In* Language Origins. R. Wescott, Ed.: 1–34; and 1975. *In* The Role of Speech In Language. J. Kavanagh & J. Cutting, Eds.: 76–82.

5. HEWES, G. 1973. Primate communication and the gestural origin of language. Current Anthropology 14(1–2): 5–24.

6. STOKOE, W. 1974. Motor signs as the first form of language. *In* Language Origins. R. Wescott, Ed.: 35–50. (Also *In* Semiotica 10(2): 117–130).

7. SEBEOK, T. 1976. The semiotic web: a chronicle of prejudices. Bull. Literary Semiotics 2: 1–63.

8. KENDON, A. *In* Language Origins. R. Wescott, Ed.: 182.

9. ABBOTT, C. 1975. Encodedness and sign language. Sign Language Studies 7(June): 109–120.

10. STEVENS, R. 1975. The educational implications of learning a first language in school. Paper presented at Convention of American Instructors of the Deaf. Greensboro, N.C.

11. HALLIDAY, M. In press.

12. FRAIBERG, S. 1974. Blind infants and their mothers. *In* The Effects of the Infant on its Caregivers, Lewis & Rosenblum, Eds. John Wiley. New York, N.Y. (Quoted in Stevens.[10])

13. HOCKETT, C. & R. ASCHER. 1964. The human revolution. Current Anthropology 5(3): 135–168.

14. BATTISON, R. M. 1974. Phonological deletion in ASL. Sign Language Studies 5: 1–19.

15. EIMAS, P. D. In press. Speech perception in early infancy. *In* Infant Perception, Cohen & Salapotek, Eds. Academic Press. New York, N.Y.

16. HUTTENLOCHER, J. 1974. The origins of language comprehension. *In* Theories in Cognitive Psychology. Solso, Ed. Earlbaum Assoc. New York, N.Y.

17. WILLIAMS, J. S. 1968. Bilingual experiences of a deaf child CAL-ERIC, ERDS # ED 030 092.

18. SCHLESINGER, H. & K. MEADOW. 1973. Sound and Sign. Univ. California Press. Berkeley, Calif.

19. Deaf parents with deaf children report first use of 2-sign utterances at about 14 months.

20. BROWN, R. A First Language: The Early Stages. Harvard Press. Cambridge, Mass.

21. LAMBERT, L. M. 1865. Le Langage de la Physionomie & du Geste. Lecoffre. Paris, France.

22. HODGSON, K. W. 1953. The Deaf and Their Problems. Heinemann. London, England.

23. SCHLESINGER, I. M. *In* Psycholinguistics. Morton, Ed. Univ. Ill. Press. Urbana, Ill.

24. FISCHER, S. 1973. Sign language and linguistic universals. Paper presented at Collogue Franco-Allemand sur la Grammaire Transformationelle du Francais.

25. CHAFE, W. L. 1972. The linguistic expression of experience, quoted in STOKOE. 1974. Appearances, words, and signs. *In* Language Origins. R. Wescott, Ed.: 51–68.

26. FARB, P. 1974. Word Play: What Happens When People Talk. Bantam. New York, N.Y.

27. TRAN DUC THAO. 1973. Récherches sur l'Origine du Langage et de la Conscience. Editions Sociales. Paris, France.

28. STOKOE, W.C. 1975. Review of GREENLEE. 1974. Pierce's Concept of Signs. Mouton. The Hague, The Netherlands. Sign Language Studies **6**: 104–108.
29. GARDNER & GARDNER. 1973. Teaching Sign Language to the Chimpanzee Washoe (Film). The Psychological Cinema Register, Univ. Park, Pa. PCR No. 2249.
30. CHAFE, W. L. 1970. Meaning and the Structure of Language. Univ. Chicago Press. Chicago, Ill.
31. COVINGTON, V. C. 1973. Juncture in ASL, and Features of stress in ASL. Sign Language Studies **2**: 29–38, 39–50.
32. HENDERSON, T. S. T. 1974. Personal pronouns and reference. MS.

TWO FACES OF SIGN: ICONIC AND ABSTRACT*

Ursula Bellugi

The Salk Institute for Biological Studies
San Diego, California 92112

Edward S. Klima

University of California at San Diego
La Jolla, California 92093

INTRODUCTION

What would be the nature of a language which has developed in the absence of auditory input? There are numerous possible channels in which a language may develop. In the human species, we might expect that language—in the absence of hearing—would develop using the most important of the remaining senses: vision. The language that has been the object of our research at The Salk Institute for Biological Studies† has in fact developed as a *visual* language—using the *hands*, rather than the vocal apparatus, as articulators. This visual-gestural language is called American Sign Language (ASL) or Ameslan. It is the language developed in large part by deaf people themselves and passed down from one generation to the next in deaf families. American Sign Language is entirely distinct from English and from other spoken languages. It is a language in its own right with its own set of lexical items; its own way of incorporating semantic information into those items; and its own grammatical rules. That is, American Sign Language (ASL) is not a form of English rendered visually on the hands.

When we first began our studies in the nature of the language used by deaf people of deaf parents, there were hardly any *linguistic* studies of sign language in this country (aside from the important and sophisticated contributions made by William Stokoe,[1] and Stokoe *et al.*[2] Reading through the scanty literature about signs and signing, we found that what earlier observers invariably stressed was their impression of the language as being "pictorial," "pantomimic," "concrete," "iconic"—"a loose collection of pictorial gestures," as one observer put it.[3] These impressions would make American Sign Language appear essentially different from spoken language, for there is a long tradition in linguistics that characterizes the lexical items of language as *essentially* arbitrary: the form of a morpheme having no part-for-part relationship to the form of what it denotes.

FROM MIMETIC REPRESENTATION TO SIGN

Not only does pantomimic representation seem a likely candidate as the historical source for many ASL signs, it also plays a very important role in the total range of

*This research was supported in part by National Institutes of Health grant no. NS-09811 and National Science Foundation grant no. GSOC-7401780 to The Salk Institute for Biological Studies.

†Members of our current research group include Bonnie Gough, Scott Liddell, Don Newkirk, Carlene Pedersen, and Ted Supalla. Others who have been with our research group, whose work is mentioned in this paper, include Geoffrey Coulter and Dr. Susan Fischer, Dr. Nancy Frishberg, and Dr. Patricia Siple.

devices currently used when the deaf communicate among themselves; that is, signing is interspersed with other gestures, including pantomime.

When we analyze a typical conversation or narrative among deaf signers, we find that nearly all of the manual gestures that are made are ASL signs. Actual ASL signs are a rich set of conventional symbols that conform to a specific set of systematic formational constraints that distinguish American Sign Language, from other sign languages and from gestures in general.[2,4-8] Those gestures in deaf communication which are *not* actual ASL signs will be the focus of the first part of this paper.

We shall call a certain set of nonsigning gestures that occur in deaf communication "mimetic representation." The amount of such mimetic representation varies, of course, from individual to individual and from situation to situation. It is significant that in deaf communication, the sign-symbolic (i.e., the "linguistic") and the mimetic are in the same channel. Deaf signers, however, have a very strong sense of the difference between the extremes: between what counts as an ASL sign and what is clearly pantomime.

"cinnamon roll"   "sand crab"   "milk shake"

FIGURE 1. Nonce signs invented by young deaf children.

We can make some distinctions among varieties of mimetic representation; gestures that are not actual ASL signs. Full *pantomime* means reenactment where one assumes the role of the agent in the event portrayed and acts in realistic fashion. *Gestural delineation*, usually with the hands, is describing the shape or other salient characteristics of an object, e.g. the moon, or designing the sail to represent a boat. (A more detailed classification of similar phenomena may be found in Schlesinger, *et al.*, in press.) Yet another category of mimetic representation consists of creations which, while not actual ASL signs, nonetheless conform to the systematic formational constraints of actual signs: these are *nonce signs* and *neologisms* and may well be a rich source of new signs in the language.

In deaf communication, mimetic aspects are very much alive, and the "signs," for example, that children create are clearly mimetic in form. We have observed many cases of the creation of nonce signs among the young deaf children of deaf parents learning ASL as a native language in our longitudinal study of the acquisition of sign language. We note that some of these invented signs are not only mimetic, they also share in the restricted parameters of the language; that is, they conform to the systematic formational constraints of the adult language. For example, one three-year-old deaf child invented a nonce sign for "cinnamon roll" which she made with a cupped hand representing the roll, and an active pointing hand indicating the swirls of cinnamon sugar on top of the roll (FIGURE 1). This invented neologism has a base hand like the regular ASL sign for GROW or SEAT; an active hand like the ASL sign for WHAT or PAY; a movement like the ASL sign for TEA or WHO.‡ In our studies of the acquisition of ASL, we have seen other signs invented by deaf children which have this same kind of dual aspect: they are clearly mimetic representations while at the same time sharing in the specific properties of ASL signs. For the purposes of illustration we have selected two additional nonce-signs created by young deaf children: a sign for "sand crabs" and a sign for "milk shake". (See FIGURE 1).

Among deaf adults, mimetic aspects are also very much alive as a source for new signs in the language. One example is provided by deaf researchers within our laboratory. There was no regular sign in ASL for "video taperecorder." In referring to the machine, our deaf researchers first used the index fingers of both hands moving clockwise to indicate the tape moving from one reel to another. The reels themselves, of course, also both move in a clockwise direction. We noticed, however, that in a short period of time, some of the realism of the representation was lost. Now the neologism is made with the index fingers describing circles that both move inward; not the way the reels of a video taperecorder actually move, but in a way that is easier to perform and, in fact, more sign-like. (See FIGURE 2).

"video taperecorder"   "VIDEO-TAPERECORDER"

FIGURE 2. A recent neologism in ASL.

It is important to note that in addition to using mimetic representation in the creation of new signs, adult signers may also subject actual ASL signs to mimetic elaboration, thus extending the modulations on a sign beyond the boundaries of regular grammatical processes and into the realm of depiction. (Some of the regular grammatical processes are described later in this paper.) For example, one signer made the sign BUTTERFLY in a narrative, and then made the hands flutter around as a butterfly would move, but still using as a basis the particular handshape and other formational characteristics of the ASL sign for BUTTERFLY.[9]

‡We have adopted some notational conventions for the purposes of this paper. Whenever a regular ASL sign is referred to, the sign is represented by an English gloss presented in capital letters: EGG. The form of the sign need not, of course, have any relationship to the form of the English word used to represent it. Whenever two words are required to translate a single ASL sign, the two words are joined with a hyphen, as in VIDEO-TAPERECORDER or TOTAL-COMMUNICATION. When two signs are joined in a compound relation, the glosses for the two signs are connected with ⌢, as in EAT⌢NOON, meaning "lunch."

We now turn to some examples of pure mimetic representation in deaf communication and the distinctions between such gestures and regular ASL signs.

Mimetic Representation in the Absence of an ASL Sign

In order to study the distinction between mimetic representation and ASL signs, we have used signed narratives from a study of paraphrase in ASL. Deaf signers were asked to sign a story by James Thurber called "The Unicorn in the Garden." In the course of the narrative we found that occasional pantomimic representations were interspersed into the flow of regular ASL signs. We discovered, for example, that there is no commonly accepted sign for "strait-jacket" or for "unicorn." Since these concepts figure in the story several times, this gave us an opportunity to study the invention of nonsign representation by different signers and enabled us to observe the changes in the representation of these concepts as the narrative progressed. We shall consider here the representations of "strait-jacket": we noted that each signer produced a different pantomime, focusing on different aspects of a strait-jacket and/or the act of getting into one, and most renditions involved several steps (a series of different actions).

These pantomimes for strait-jacket involved activities like putting the arms into the two sleeves, fastening the cords, crossing the arms, tying different kinds of knots in various ways, pulling tight, constraining the wrists, depicting a jacket, clothing, sleeves, straps from shoulders, and so on. For each signer, it was the initial introduction of his representation of "strait-jacket" into the narrative that was the most elaborate, involving as many as five activities in sequence. At later points in the story, individual representations could reduce to two or even one activity. Extracting from different performances, one deaf researcher gave her interpretation of the step-by-step progression from highly pantomimic rendition to abbreviated, more sign-like rendition, finally having the restricted form of a possible sign. (See FIGURE 3).

The signer first pantomimed putting her arms straight out, one after the other, as if they were being forced into the sleeves of an outstretched jacket. The arms were wrapped, again one after the other, across her body, each ending on the other side of the opposite elbow. She held her arms in this awkward position for a brief interval; then her hands relaxed. Then, as if becoming the hands of someone else, her own hands went through an elaborate tying motion at the center line of the body, knotting and pulling tight in a realistic if convoluted fashion. The impression one has in watching the rendition is that the signer has been put into the jacket, the action occurring to her arms and body as a passive agent; and then switching roles, the signer violently ties the straps that hold the jacket in place in an elaborate knot, which involves curves and twists of motion, and considerable physical effort (FIGURE 3).

At the other extreme, the simplified final sign-like version was reduced to two steps and was highly abbreviated, with no trace remaining of the original physical effort depicted. The final two parts of the representation had been reduced and simplified to something that had characteristics of a single ASL compound sign.§ In the reduced sign-like version, the arms no longer wrapped around the body but instead contacted the torso one above the other without crossing; immediately following this, and very close in space (as is typical of the parts of a compound in

---

§The form of compound signs in American Sign Language is discussed in the section GRAMMATICAL PROCESSES AND THE SUPPRESSION OF ICONICITY.

Pantomime of "strait-jacket"

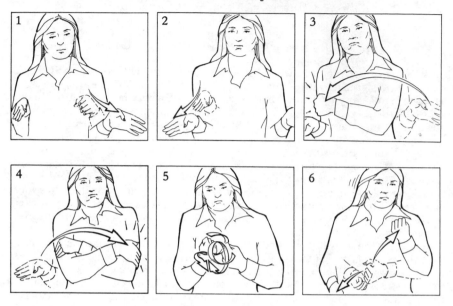

Sign-like Reduction of "strait jacket"

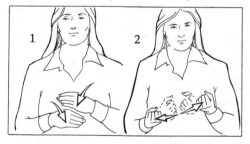

FIGURE 3. From pantomime to invented sign.

ASL) was an abbreviated straightened version of what originally represented the elaborate "tying," which now simply involved moving the hands apart a short distance. The preliminary activities were not now even represented in the reduced sign-like version. What was created was a nonce sign. Although sign-like in form, note, however, that the final shortened representation is still iconic; i.e., aspects of its form are directly related to what is represented. Thus this example presents a typical change from highly pantomimic (elaborate, many steps, actual "acting out") to highly sign-like (condensed, shortened, stylized), in a mimetic representation occurring where there is no corresponding sign. (See FIGURE 3).

Comparison of Pantomime and ASL Sign

In the case of "strait-jacket" we studied the invention of a pantomimic representation of something for which there is no regular ASL sign. As another way of examining differences between mimetic representation and sign, we asked ten nonsigners to convey in gestures the meanings of the individual English words for which actual ASL signs exist. One of the words was "egg," and this was rendered in many different ways. In most cases the pantomime involved a number of steps; and there were "thematic" elements common to many of the renditions. The common elements included the following: picking up a small oval-shaped object; hitting it against the edge of a real or imaginary surface; breaking it open and emptying the contents of the shell; putting the two halves of the shell into one hand and throwing them away. But the way these general thematic elements were realized varied enormously from subject to subject. For all intents and purposes, the details of each rendition were absolutely different (FIGURE 4).

By contrast, let us consider what is involved in signing EGG in American Sign Language. As FIGURE 4 indicates, the ASL sign EGG is clearly related to one step within the complex pantomimed sequence of actions: namely, the breaking open of the eggshell so that the contents run out. But the relation between the sign itself and the action is a highly stylized, conventionalized one. The movement proper to the ASL sign involves a repetition; the "corresponding" motion of emptying the shell was, of course, never repeated in the pantomime. The sign is stylized in that the two fingers of one hand cross the same two fingers of the other hand in a way that would not occur if one were actually holding an egg; in pantomime, holding an egg is depicted realistically. Thus, while the sign is iconic and suggestive of an aspect of the pantomime, the two performances—pantomime and ASL sign—are distinctly different. (See FIGURE 4).

Although the pantomimes portraying "egg" varied enormously from one person to the next, the various renditions of the ASL sign for EGG are recognizably the same across signers. Note, for example, that the ASL sign for EGG requires a particular handshape and that handshape only. We have seen a deaf mother correct her deaf child's signing when the sign was made in the same way but the hands were

Pantomime of "egg"   ASL Sign EGG

FIGURE 4. Comparison of pantomime and ASL sign—(1).

held with four fingers outstretched instead of two. That there is a recognizably appropriate way to form the sign EGG—that there are, in fact, conditions of well-formedness in ASL—is indicated by the mother's correction of the child's "mispronunciation." In the pantomime, it matters not at all how the hands are shaped in holding an imaginary egg, nor how many fingers are straight or curved: what counts in the pantomime rendition is that the hands are held *as if* surrounding or holding an egg-shaped object. In the final analysis, the distinction is between well-formedness in the sign and effectiveness in the pantomime.

In order to study more carefully some of the diagnostic characteristics of ASL sign and pantomime (when presented in *citation form*), we chose a set of signs that retain a high degree of iconicity; that is, ASL signs that were close in form to some plausible pantomimic representation (like ZIPPER, BED, BOOK, DIG, STEAL.) Bernard Bragg, a deaf actor and mime artist from The National Theater of the Deaf, produced for us on video tape some pairs of representations: pantomimes and corresponding ASL signs. We asked him to keep the renditions similar to one another but yet each natural to its own mode of communication, in order to illuminate the diagnostic characteristics of pantomime as opposed to ASL sign. In general, we found, as before, that there were a varied number of thematic images in the pantomime and only one in the regular ASL sign, and that the pantomimes were much longer and more varied in duration. The individual pantomimes ranged from 3 to 12 seconds; the individual ASL signs were all far shorter and more uniform in duration, most of them around one second. In the discussion which follows, it should be kept in mind that these are signs in their citation form, presented individually and carefully; signs are much shorter in duration in connected discourse. D. Newkirk from our laboratory has made a detailed comparison of the set of pantomimes and signs.[10]

Each sign always had a well-defined beginning and end. Since the signs were presented as separate individual signs, i.e., not in a sequence, the initial position (or beginning) of a sign was always characterized in the following way: the hands always started from a resting position and a relaxed, nonspecific shape; then there was a transitional movement to the start of the sign, by which time the hand had taken on the specific handshape of the sign to be made. Thus one could recognize the beginning of a sign by the brief temporal holding—observable in slow-motion playback—of the specific handshape in an initial position. In pantomime, no such hold was required; the hand could move directly from the rest position through the series of motions into the pantomime itself.

We chose one pair of representations for illustration in this paper to reveal some of the fine distinctions between pantomime and sign—distinctions that also reveal criterial attributes of ASL signs. This is the pantomime and sign for "steal," as performed by Bragg (see FIGURE 5). Actual tracings from the video tape were made at selected intervals.¶ We intentionally chose a pantomime that was simple in terms of the activities represented, in order to have a more direct basis for comparison. In this particular pantomime (FIGURE 5), the first five drawings (fields 1 through 227) constitute a preamble representing a person furtively looking to one side and then reaching over in preparation of the actual "swiping" of an object. The last seven drawings (fields 228–338) represent the act of stealing—and here, the thematic image is the same as in the sign. Bragg's total pantomime sequence takes 338 fields (over 5½ seconds); his ASL version of the sign STEAL requires only 34 fields (about ½

¶ Individual fields on the video tape (60 fields per second) were numbered with the aid of a Video Numbers Generator (Data Systems Design, Model no. 44-2) for ease of counting.

second). Even if we omit the preamble sequence and count only the shared thematic image, the pantomime is three times as long as the sign.

The eyes provide one differentiating clue to separate sign from pantomime. In producing signs in citation form, Bragg makes direct eye contact with the camera (or addressee) throughout the sign. When he is producing the corresponding panto-

Bernard Bragg's Pantomime of "steal"

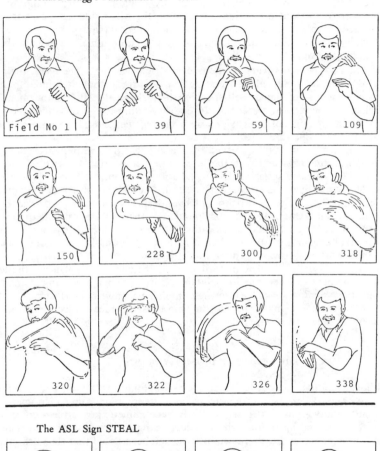

The ASL Sign STEAL

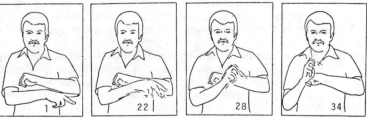

FIGURE 5. Comparison of pantomime and ASL sign—(2).

mimes, his eyes instead participate in the action, sometimes anticipating, sometimes following the hands. In this pantomime for "steal," the hands are not held in one of the specific handshapes of ASL, whereas the sign starts with a specific well-defined ASL handshape; two fingers spread as in "V for victory." The pantomime involves reaching all the way across the body to the contralateral side beyond the elbow, and then making a large sweeping motion back to the other side; the movement of the sign is short, precise, and well specified, the two fingers bending as the hand moves upward and to the right. The movement of the two hands differs in the pantomime; only one hand moves in the sign. One hand moves in a large sweeping motion from one side, across in front of the face, around to the other side, in the pantomime; whereas the movement in the sign is along a single vertical plane parallel to the torso. The shoulders, body, and head moved during the pantomime, whereas in the sign only the hand moved.

To sum up: the signs were condensed, restricted in the space used, the action transferred to the hands alone. The action occurred along a limited plane of movement, with a restricted well-specified handshape, location, movement. The pantomimes, by contrast, were realistic in time, duration, size, and direction of movement; in signing, all dimensions were altered: condensed, compressed, reoriented, and conventionalized.

The progressions we have observed from complicated pantomime to simple sign-like units that are consistent with the formational constraints of ASL are far from unique to the particular situations discussed above. In fact, it has been demonstrated that similar tendencies have characterized the actual historical development of American Sign Language. N. Frishberg has undertaken a study of historical change in American Sign Language and has found that there is a consistent direction to observed changes in the form of signs within the past 100 years. The general direction of historical change in the form of signs is from what was in the past more iconic and more representational to what is now more arbitary and more constrained, conforming to a tighter system.[11,12] The historical trend includes: concentrating the lexical content in the hands rather than in facial or bodily movements, moving from outside to within the "signing space," centering, simplifying movement. The result of this change in the form of signs is not that they have lost all traces of iconicity, only that their iconicity is less transparent.

The Degree of Iconicity of ASL Signs

Although, as pointed out above, there is a definite distinction between regular ASL signs and the sort of spontaneous mimetic representation characteristic of pantomime, many regular ASL signs clearly have mimetic properties—constrained, to be sure, more and more through historical change by the systematic-formational system of the language. Furthermore, it has often been noted that the vocabulary of American Sign Language—and, to our knowledge, of other primary sign languages as well—undeniably is a great deal more iconic than are the morphemes of spoken languages.

Of course, to claim that there is an iconic relationship—that aspects of the form of a sign are related to aspects of the form of what is denoted—does not determine to any degree the actual details of the form of that sign. As an example, consider the sign for TREE in American Sign Language. It is made with the forearm upright, the hand spread wide, and a twisting of the wrist and forearm. As FIGURE 6 shows, it can be said that the upright forearm represents the trunk of a tree, the outstretched hand represents the branches, and the twisting motion represents the movement of the wind through the branches of a tree. The sign for TREE in Danish Sign Language is also iconic, and yet it differs in all details from the ASL sign: the two hands symmetrically outline the rounded shape of the outer perimeter of a tree and then outline the shape of the trunk. The sign for TREE in Chinese Sign Language is yet again different, but still iconic: the two hands symmetrically encompass the shape of

FIGURE 6. Sign for TREE in three different sign languages.

the trunk of a tree and indicate its extent. (FIGURE 6 represents the sign TREE in American Sign Language, Danish Sign Language, and Chinese Sign Language. The drawings to the right indicate the relation of each sign to some representation of a tree.) Thus, the sign TREE in each of three different sign languages is iconic, and yet the three signs are entirely distinct, both in what they represent and in the way in which this is expressed in forming the sign.

Incidentally, it should be noted that deaf people are especially aware of the potential of the iconic aspect of signs when teaching signs to hearing adults. In this situation, deaf people very often assign some iconic interpretation for mnemonic purposes. Handbooks of signs often contain information on how to form the sign, and then specify some representational aspects of signs: "YEAR; the earth revolving around the sun," or "WEEK; one row of dates on the calendar." Disregarding the problem of which and how many of these are "true" etymologies, it is a fact that a great many signs of American Sign Language and probably other primary sign languages invite iconic interpretation.

As a first step toward assessing the degree of general iconicity of ASL signs, we designed two pilot studies which approach this problem from different angles. One study asks the question: how obvious is the basis for the relationship between a sign and its meaning? That is, given a sign and its meaning, to what extent do nonsigners agree on the basis for the relationship between the two? The other study asks: how transparent or self-evident are ASL signs? That is, given a sign, to what extent can a nonsigner—in the absence of any prior knowledge—guess its meaning? It is important to note that in these first approaches to the degree of iconicity of signs, we ask how *non signers* can make the connections between the form of the sign and what it denotes. Of course, a more important question from the point of view of the structure of the language—and one to which we shall address our attention later in this paper—is the significance of the iconicity of signs for deaf people whose native language is sign language.

The Relationship of the Form of a Sign and Its Meaning

To a group of ten hearing people who had no prior knowledge of sign language, we presented a collection of ASL signs along with the English translation-equivalent of each sign. In the instructions for the task, we told subjects that ASL signs are often said to be representational and we gave an example of an iconic sign that was not on the list, presenting the ASL sign CAR paired with its meaning and suggesting as a possible response that it represents "turning the steering wheel of a car." Subjects were thus instructed to describe what they considered to be the basis for the relationship between the form of each sign and its meaning in terms of the corresponding English word. We used as stimuli a set of 90 different signs that had been previously chosen for use in a memory experiment—chosen because they were commonly known among the deaf and had fairly direct translations into English nouns. Each sign was presented on video tape (by a native signer) followed by a spoken presentation of its meaning. The signs were made in citation form and with a neutral facial expression. The subjects were told to provide some written response for each sign-meaning pair. The 90 signs included items like APPLE, BIRD, BOY, CANDY, EARTH, FRIDAY, GRAVY, IDEA, MEAT, SCIENCE, SENTENCE, TREE, WEEK, and so on—i.e., both abstract and concrete nouns, including a few proper nouns.

A corresponding task for a spoken language might be to ask English-speaking subjects who know no German what it is about the sound of the German word pronounced [h ʊ n t] (i.e., *Hund*) that suggests a dog, or about the sound of the German word [b a y n] (i.e., *Bein*) that suggests a leg. With most common German words, there would, of course, be no obvious answer to the question. On the other hand, this small informal study supports the notion that for many ASL signs there is a representational aspect.

For more than half of the 90 signs presented, the responses of the subjects showed overall agreement on the basis for the connection between the shape of a sign and its meaning. For example, when the sign produced was the one we gloss here as VOTE and the subjects were told that it means "vote," there was general agreement among the responses. Subjects wrote: "putting a ballot in a ballot box," "placing vote in a ballot box," "motion of placing ballot in container," "ballot in a box," and other equivalent responses. For the sign WOOD, they responded: "sawing a board," "motion of sawing as in sawing pieces of wood," "sawing motion on board," "sawing action," "sawing a log," and other equivalent responses. Extracting from the responses on which there was agreement of a similar nature, we find the following:

Sign Presented	Agreed-upon Relationship of Sign and Meaning
WOOD	Sawing
TRAFFIC	Cars passing each other
TENT	The poles of a tent
QUEEN	Sash worn across the shoulder
GRAVY	Drippings from a piece of meat
GIRL	The soft cheek of a girl
TREE	Trunk and branches of a tree
WEEK	One line across the calendar
TICKET	Punching a ticket
MELON	Thumping for ripeness
LETTER	Placing a stamp

The results of this small study support the notion that many ASL signs have a representational aspect. Specifically, such signs are what we call *translucent*; i.e., nonsigners tend to see essentially the same basis for the relationship between the sign and its meaning. This need not, of course, mean that the agreed basis corresponds to historical fact. The ASL sign GIRL, for example, did not in fact originate from a representation of "the soft cheek of a girl" as our nonsigning subjects said, but rather, according to historical sources, the sign GIRL originally represented either the bonnet strings of hats worn by young girls or the curls that lay along girls' cheeks.

For some of the signs, there was not overall agreement in responses; in these the basis described ranged widely from subject to subject. For example, for the sign CANADA, subjects responded "close neighbor," "fine woolens," "someone proud of what he is," "sounds like collar," "you need a coat because winters are colder than in the U.S.," *et cetera*. Other signs for which there was a wide variety of responses included AMERICA, APPLE, COLOR, EARTH, FATHER, HOME, SCIENCE. Nonetheless, the subjects did agree on specifying the relationship between form and meaning in what was to us a surprising number of instances—certainly *far* higher than we would predict if the items presented were spoken words in an unknown language.

The Transparency of Signs

We decided next to investigate the degree of iconicity of signs in a more demanding way: given an ASL sign, and no other information, could a nonsigner correctly ascertain its meaning? To the extent that this is possible, a sign would be considered *transparent*. If we were presenting successful pantomime, which has the aim of being self-evident from its form alone, we would expect that uninitiated subjects would be able correctly to interpret the pantomime; i.e., successful pantomime is by definition transparent. The comparable question concerning sign language is: to what extent is the meaning of a sign self-evident from its form alone? We used the same set of 90 signs as in the previous study and asked another group of hearing people with no knowledge of sign language to view each of the signs and to guess—under conditions of free choice—the meaning of that sign in American Sign Language. Except in the case of a mere handful of signs (9 out of the 90), not a single subject was able to guess the meaning of the signs presented. The few signs from our list that were transparent to any one of the hearing subjects in this special sense were: BED, BUTTON, EAR, EYES, MARBLE, MILK, OPERATION, PIE, SURPRISE. But for each of these there were also many responses that were *not* acceptable translations as well. For the other 81 signs, the subjects made only incorrect, and highly varied, guesses. Thus it is obvious that according to this criteria, the ASL signs are not at all transparent; that is, their meaning is not self-evident from their form.

We then constructed a multiple-choice test in which the correct English translation and four other possible meanings were listed for each ASL sign. The alternatives were selected from the responses given to the sign by the subjects in the free-choice test, with some filler items added in. Thus some of the alternatives were "likely," though incorrect, meanings. This gave us a five-item multiple choice test that we could use with hearing nonsigners to determine a more limited degree of transparency of signs. As an example, for the sign glossed as HOME, the choices listed were:

———— kiss ———— home ———— math ———— comprehend ———— orange

On the multiple choice test, a new group of ten hearing subjects—again with no knowledge of sign language—viewed the signs and marked the response that corresponded to what they thought the sign meant in American Sign Language. These subjects did no better than chance at choosing the correct meaning for a sign— there were 18.2% correct responses on the five-item, multiple-choice test. Thus, given a situation in which one must select the correct meaning of a sign from among five choices, our subjects were not successful. The ASL signs were *opaque*, according to this narrow criterion of iconicity.

For only a few of the signs (12 out of 90) did a majority of subjects select the correct meanings. The twelve non-opaque signs were BED, BLOSSOM, BODY, BOTH, BUTTON, DAY, EAR, EYES, ODOR, OPERATION, SURPRISE, and YEAR. Note that six of these were the same signs that had generated at least one correct response on the free-choice test. For a large number of signs on the multiple-choice test (36 of the 90), not one of the subjects selected a correct meaning. Among the opaque signs whose meaning was *never* correctly selected from the five choices provided were: APPLE, BOY, CANADA, COLOR, EARTH, GIRL, GRAVY, HOME, IDEA, SCIENCE, SUGAR, SUMMER, and WEEK.

For a few of the signs (nine) most subjects (eight or more) agreed in their selection of a particular *incorrect* response. For example, for the sign HOME, all ten subjects chose the meaning "comprehend." For these nine signs, the response chosen was always a "likely" alternative provided by subjects in the free-choice situation, and apparently was a compelling alternative. Thus, while such signs are not transparent— i.e., their actual meaning in ASL is not self-evident from their form—nonetheless, their form is highly suggestive of "meaning".** The incorrect meanings selected in common by most of the subjects for the nine signs are noted below.

**For similar results and a further discussion of transparency of ASL Signs, see Ref. 13.

Sign Presented	Incorrect Meaning Guessed on Test
HOME	comprehend
COLOR	conversation
SENTENCE	unravel
EARTH	hinge
WEDDING	gather
TREE	unsteady
PIE	divide
SWEETHEART	imitate
PENNY	think

So far, we have shown that aspects of the form of many signs in ASL may have a direct relation to aspects of their meaning, although the signs are not in themselves so unambiguously representational that a nonsigner can guess the correct meaning—not even when that meaning is presented as one of several possible meanings.

However, the more relevant and important question is not how transparent are signs for a nonsigner; it is, rather, what is the role of the iconicity of signs for deaf people who are native users of the language. As we mentioned before, we have found that deaf people are definitely aware of the representational aspects of signs, and bring these out (or sometimes fabricate them) in teaching signs to hearing people who are nonsigners.

That the deaf are aware of the undertones and overtones of iconicity can also be shown in other more significant ways. In communicating among themselves, or in narrative, we find considerable mimetic extension, enhancing or exaggerating the mimetic character of individual signs. We have made a collection of plays on signs, studying the properties that deaf people use to create new or additional meanings in "colorful" signing.[14] One facet of playing with signs may involve exaggerations of their mimetic character. We have collected numerous instances of such exaggerations, two of which we will illustrate here. In a film made in 1913 of an elderly deaf signer with an eloquent signing style we found the following finale: the deaf man signed that he hoped it would not be "long before we meet again." The ASL sign LONG is made with the index finger of one hand moving along the back of the wrist of the other hand, part way up the forearm. As shown in FIGURE 7, the signer expressed himself instead in an exaggerated rendition of the sign, elongating it from his left toe up across the body and ending above his right shoulder. The ASL sign LONG became as *long* as it could possibly be made on the human body!

The other example we have chosen illustrates two aspects of playing on signs: blending of one sign into another, and in addition, an exaggeration of iconic aspects of the signs. There is an ASL sign TOTAL-COMMUNICATION, which is the term educators use for signing and speaking at the same time, thus providing deaf students with information from the lips and from signs. According to one story current among the deaf, a visitor to a deaf school asked why all the students looked so happy. A deaf student responded by making the sign TOTAL-COMMUNICATION, a nontransparent sign which has a back and forth movement (See FIGURE 8). He continued making the sign, moving his hands alternately back and forth, but each time coming closer to his mouth, until the sign TOTAL-COMMUNICATION had become (i.e., been reanalyzed as) the alternating highly iconic signs DRINKING and SMOKING. The original sign had blended into two other signs, giving the response a double meaning. Furthermore, the latter two signs were enhanced by playing on their iconic aspects: inhaling as if enjoying a smoke and throwing the head back as if emptying a glass. Thus, the response indicated that the students were happy because of the total

The ASL sign LONG is normally made on the back of the wrist and forearm. In this sign-play, it has been greatly elongated.

FIGURE 7. The iconic elaboration of an ASL sign.

communication used at the school, but at the same time, their joy was evident in the pleasures of drinking and smoking.

We also find an exaggeration of iconic aspects of signs and their meaning in poetic or art-sign presentations: the ASL sign SLOW in one poem about the creeping pace of summer was made with such exaggerated slowness that it took twice as long as any other sign in the verse. Or the sign SUMMER ("wiping perspiration from the brow") in the same verse was made in such an intensified manner that it brought out the sense of the heat and perspiration of summer, at the same time that it indicated the particular season of the year. (For further examples, see Ref. 15.)

So far, these examples of the role of iconicity in the signing of deaf people refer to the extent to which mimetic or iconic aspects of signs are brought out in special

TOTAL-COMMUNICATION   SMOKING   DRINKING

The ASL sign TOTAL-COMMUNICATION has been blended into iconically exaggerated forms of "smoking and drinking."

FIGURE 8. Iconicity in a play on signs.

linguistic activities such as plays on signs, poetic signing, or in teaching signs to hearing people. These are, of course, quite special activities, and may not reflect what happens in normal, everyday communication. We now want to turn to a completely different question: what is the role of iconicity in the rapid processing that takes place when deaf people are engaged in everyday conversation?

Let us begin by suggesting something about the rate at which such processing must take place. In one of our early studies, we examined some aspects of the rate of producing signs, and observed that signs in a narrative were produced at around 2½ signs per second by three native signers.[4]†† In processing (i.e., encoding) signs at such a rate, what is the role of the iconic or representational aspect of signs? Of course we have no direct way of measuring this, but we can ask a related question: how are signs coded in short-term memory? We will presume that the encoding of signs in short-term memory bears some relationship to what goes on in processing signs in conversation.

The Insignificance of Iconicity in Memory Processing

We have completed a series of experiments in short-term memory processing of ASL signs by fluent deaf signers. We presented random strings of signs in list lengths from three items to nine items; we compared ordered recall and free recall; we compared recall in signs with recall in the written English translation-equivalents of the signs; we compared memory for random lists with memory for partially structured and highly structured lists of signs. In all these studies, one result emerges strikingly across all conditions of presentation and all conditions of ordered recall. The multiply occurring intrusion errors‡‡ made by deaf signers are consistent in a special respect, and these errors reveal something significant about the way in which fluent deaf signers process signs in short-term memory.[16,8]

Because signs are so much more iconic in general than words, it would not be unreasonable to expect that deaf people might encode them differently from the way in which hearing people encode the highly abstract, arbitrary words of spoken language. We might expect that signs would somehow be encoded basically in terms of their iconic or representational qualities—in terms of, let us say, some more general pictorial images. Let us try to imagine what kind of evidence would support some sort of basic iconic encoding. Consider the example of the sign for BIRD, which by the opening and closing of the thumb and index finger at the lips "represents a bird opening and closing its beak." If the errors which were made for the sign BIRD included "feathers," "wing," "claws," "song," "cage," "beak," or even "pecking," we might posit some sort of iconic storage of the sign. But the errors that were made to signs were not of that sort at all; nor, of course were they errors based on the visual or phonetic properties of the English words corresponding to the ASL signs.

We found, in fact, that the multiply occurring errors were predominately and consistently signs that were close in *systematic-formational* aspects—rather than in

††In the Bellugi and Fischer study,[4] we compiled the mean rates of narrative signing for three native signers, eliminating pauses whenever possible. The rate of about 2½ signs per second represents the rate of signing in connected discourse, and thus is considerably faster than the rate cited earlier for single signs which are presented in citation form.

‡‡ By intrusion error, we mean any response given in a particular serial position that was an incorrect response and at the same time was not a repetition of an item in that list or an item from the immediately prior list.

semantic or iconic aspects—to the sign presented on the test. Typically, the errors were similar in form to the sign presented in all but one respect. For example, a common error for BIRD was NEWSPAPER; and the signs representing BIRD and NEWSPAPER are exactly alike in form in all respects except for the place of articulation. A common error for CANDY was JEALOUS; the signs representing CANDY and JEALOUS are alike in all respects except for the configuration of the hand. A common error for the sign EGG was NAME; the signs representing EGG and NAME are alike in all respects except for movement. The examples given here are representative of the predominant type of intrusion error made in short-term memory, and these errors were similar in form according to specific recurring formational parameters of American Sign Language. (For further details, see Ref. 8.) In fact, the parameters are essentially those originally suggested by Stokoe in his seminal early work on the linguistic description of signs: place of articulation, configuration of the hand, and movement.[1,2]

Thus we see that the evidence from memory experiments supports the theory that deaf people do not *encode* signs in terms of their iconic representational properties. Even the iconic aspects of signs that are "alive" to deaf people are entirely disregarded when deaf signers encode signs in our experiments. What counts, instead, are certain systematic-formational properties of the signs (analogous to the phonological properties of words).

It is important to point out that these recurring systematic-formational properties themselves are—like the phonemes of spoken language—in general arbitrary in terms of meaning (even in signs which are themselves iconic). If one knows that a sign has the particular hand configuration proper to the ASL sign EGG, this would predict little or nothing about the meaning of that sign. The same hand configuration occurs not only in EGG but also in many other ASL signs, some of which have representational aspects and some of which do not. The particular distinctive *handshape* of EGG also occurs in the ASL signs NAME, UNCLE, TRAIN, SHORT, WEIGH, STAMP, BUILDING, FUN, HORSE, SUGAR, NATION, BUTTER, CATHOLIC, CHAIR, as well as many others. For some of the signs listed—when considered as a whole—representational aspects have been suggested: the form of the sign HORSE as representing the ears of a horse; the form of the sign BUILDING as representing piling bricks one on top of another; the form of the sign BUTTER as representing spreading butter on bread, and so forth. The vast majority of ASL signs that have the same handshape as EGG, we note, have little or nothing in common except for the formational fact of that shared handshape.

This is not to say that there is nothing parallel to sound symbolism in American Sign Language; indeed there are such phenomena, in which "families" of signs are related at the same time in both formational and semantic aspects. In fact, according to our observations, the ASL analogue to "sound symbolism" is undoubtedly more widespread in sign language than that process is in spoken language (see Ref. 17).

Nonetheless, the general point remains. No matter whether the signs presented on the memory test were transparent, translucent, or opaque—i.e., whether they had representational aspects or not—there was no difference in the nature of the intrusion errors that occurred. In fact, in terms of general principles of encoding, none of our results indicate that signs are encoded differently from words, despite the fact that signs are, in general, surely more iconic than words.

GRAMMATICAL PROCESSES AND THE SUPPRESSION OF ICONICITY

Until now we have been discussing the basic form of the sign, analogous to what Jespersen calls "the naked word"—the kernel without any formatives either before or after—the free morpheme abstracted from its combinations with other morphemes in derivational and inflectional morphology. But how is modulation of meaning accomplished in a visual language like American Sign Language? In spoken language, such modifications of meaning of the naked word are typically (but by no means exclusively) expressed by the addition of affixes before, within, or after the sequence of segments constituting the word, although some spoken languages also modulate meaning through certain nonsegmental modifications such as tone or stress.

In American Sign Language, there is *no* tendency to modify the basic units of the language—the signs—with the addition of segmental prefixes or suffixes; in fact, there seems to be a great resistance to segmental affixation. (There are only two segmental suffixes that appear in handbooks of American Sign Language, and these are clearly borrowed from the English comparative and agentive; and we find that in colloquial ASL even these are not used.)

On the other hand, our observations indicate that American Sign Language has other kinds of processes that operate on signs to change their form class or to modulate their meaning. These processes basically are modulations of some aspect of the inherent *movement* of the sign; i.e., instead of adding a segment before or after the sign, typically some special type of movement is *superimposed* onto the basic movement of the sign. In fact, the parameter of movement seems to be the parameter most frequently affected in such modulations.

In our studies of ASL, we are now at the point where we know what kinds of dimensions to look for in the modulation of meaning of signs, although our analysis is far from complete. (Incidentally, while it may be relatively easy for hearing people to learn the unembellished form of signs, it is certainly very difficult for the inexperienced eye and hand to learn the fine distinctions in movement that mark modulations of meaning.) American Sign Language is a language in which a slight but specific elongation of movement, a slight but specific difference in tempo, a minor but specific variation in the form of a repetition, may signal a critical but regular difference in meaning. In *function*, indeed the dimensions that are marked by such superimposed variations in the ASL sign are similar to those marked by other languages. But the *form* of the modifications on signs—superimposed changes in movement—is radically different from segmental suffixation in speech, and in our opinion, also differs basically from the ablaut, umlaut, stress, and tonal variation in spoken languages, in that classes of modulations in ASL involve formational properties not characteristic of base forms of lexical items.

One of the most striking effects caused by grammatical operations on signs is the distortion of the signs to such an extent that the original iconism of the base form is overridden and submerged. This is an important point for the general theme of our argument: grammatical processes—which may themselves incidentally have some degree of iconic associations—operate on the basic form of signs. Often the result is an obfuscation of the representational aspects of the original sign.

The modulations we will discuss here are those which operate on the basic form of the sign to change its meaning. In our laboratory, we have only begun to unravel the mutations on the form of signs that give clues to the underlying regularities of the language: S. Fischer and B. Gough have described a set of operations on verbs of American Sign Language,[18] and T. Supalla is currently working on modulations of meaning affecting nouns, as well as the derivation of nouns from verbs.[19,20]

Let us consider what happens to the form of a sign when it undergoes certain regular modulations. Consider first the sign WEEK (FIGURE 9a), which, according to one handbook of signs (and according to hearing subjects in one of our studies on transparency described earlier), indicates "one row of dates on the calendar." The basic unembellished movement characteristic of the sign WEEK is made once only, with the active hand brushing along the palm. If the sign is made with the movement repeating several times quickly, the meaning is changed to "every week" or "weekly." If, instead, the movement is changed so that the brushing is lost and is replaced by a contact at the base of the palm, a slow arc forward, and another contact at the fingertips, the meaning is changed to "all week long." If the sign is made with slow repetition—a slow brushing movement that extends beyond the palm of the hand, a

a. The ASL Sign WEEK

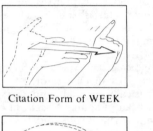

Citation Form of WEEK

Modulation: "weekly"

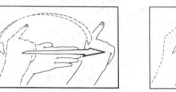

Modulation: "for weeks and weeks"   Modulation: "all week long"

b. The ASL Sign YEAR

Citation Form of YEAR   Modulation: "yearly"   Modulation: "for years and years"

FIGURE 9. The submerging of iconicity through grammatical operations—(1).

slow arc-like movement back to the original position, another brushing movement, but so that the movement is continuous—the meaning is changed to "for weeks and weeks." There are many other modulations that can occur superimposed on the basic sign WEEK, but we will limit our discussion to this small set for now. (See FIGURE 9a).

These same general types of repetitions—a fast repetition in the same place of articulation, a slow movement between two end contact points, a slow repeated movement in which there is an arc-like return—operate on "time" signs in general, but are by no means limited to that narrow category of signs. The sign YEAR, according to our handbook and our hearing subjects "indicates the earth revolving around the sun." One hand in a fist remains stationary; the other hand contacts it, makes a full revolution around it, and returns to contact again (FIGURE 9b). For a meaning equivalent to "all year long," the first contact is lost and one hand moves around the other in a slightly modulated circle. To modulate the sign for the meaning "for years and years" or the meaning "yearly," it is no longer the case that one hand moves around the other. For the continuous meaning, the active hand moves above the base hand in a circle and contacts only at the top of the hand; for the habitual meaning, the active hand moves along the top of the base hand in a brushing forward motion which is repeated quickly. In both cases, the original iconic value of "the earth revolving around the sun" is completely lost, since one hand no longer revolves around the other. (See FIGURE 9b.)

This is a way of illustrating our general point. The form of modulations in themselves may have some iconic basis: to indicate that an event (or state or action) occurs regularly, habitually, one can superimpose a rapid repetition of movement on the basic movement of the sign. To indicate that an event (or state or action) continues for a long period of time, one adds a slow drawn-out repetition to the motion of the sign, which usually entails a slow circular or arc-like motion (since not only is the movement of the sign affected, but the transition between movements is also involved). In many cases, the superimposition of movement or type of repetition suppresses the representational aspects of the basic sign.

The sign QUIET is made with two hands on the mouth, which then separate as they move downward (as one informant said, "it indicates a smoothing down, or a calming"), (see FIGURE 10). If the sign is repeated slowly with a circular or elliptical motion superimposed, the meaning changes to "quiet for a long time." If the sign is repeated quickly, the meaning changes to "habitually quiet" or "quiet by nature." With the rapid, repeated movement superimposed on the basic single movement of the sign, any sense of smoothing, quiet, or calming in the *form* of the sign is suppressed completely. Again, an iconically based modulation on a sign—which itself has representational aspects—can obscure or totally submerge the iconicity of the original sign (see FIGURE 10).

One can observe the lessening of iconicity also under the grammatical processes by which nouns can be derived from verbs, or predicates from nouns. T. Supalla, from our laboratory, has shown that there is a regular process by which nouns can be derived from many action verbs in American Sign Language. If the verb has a single nonrepeated movement, the derived noun will have a small repeated movement. The sign SIT (FIGURE 11) is made with two fingers of one hand (representing legs) moving down once onto the two fingers of the other hand, as if "sitting." The sign CHAIR is just the same in form except that it has a small repeated movement; this entails some loss of iconicity—unless one wanted to argue that a chair is something you sit on, get up again, and sit on again. The same relation holds (single movement in the verb, repeated movement in the noun) for a large number of noun-verb pairs, and represents a productive pattern.

Still another process changes a noun sign to a predicate sign, with the special meaning of "to act like an X" or "X-ish." The ASL sign BABY clearly derives from the pantomimic act of holding a baby; the arms are crossed and sway back and forth with some remnant of the act of rocking a baby (FIGURE 12). But to sign "act like a baby" or "baby-ish," a different type of movement is superimposed. The sideways

The ASL Sign QUIET

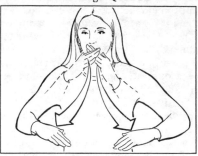

Citation Form of QUIET

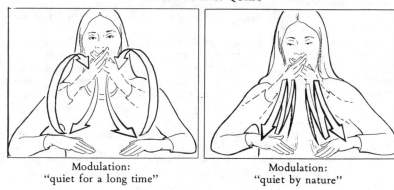

Modulation: Modulation:
"quiet for a long time"   "quiet by nature"

FIGURE 10. The submerging of iconicity through grammatical operations—(2).

rocking motion disappears, the hands are moved closer together, and the motion is changed: it is an intense movement, the overlapped hands jerk downward repeatedly in a way that would be most inappropriate for the meaning of the original sign. The modulation, again has completely submerged the iconicity of the base form of the underlying sign BABY. (FIGURE 12 shows the progression from a pantomime to a citation form sign BABY and from the latter to the modulated sign meaning "babyish".)

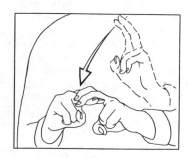 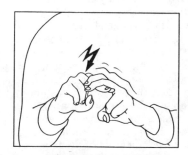

The ASL Verb SIT   The ASL Noun CHAIR

FIGURE 11. The derivation of noun from verb in ASL.

The mutations presented here are only a very small part of what constitutes a rich system of modulations on signs of American Sign Language. In our view, the form of these modulations is one of the most distinctive aspects of American Sign Language as a human language.

Finally, let us consider one other historical process in American Sign Language. Creating a sign for a new concept in ASL, as in other languages, is sometimes accomplished by compounding: two signs that exist as independent units in the language are combined to create a new lexical unit which can then itself undergo

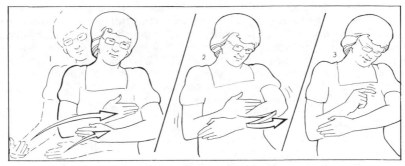

Pantomime of "baby"

The ASL Sign BABY   Modulated Form of ASL Sign:
                                     "to act like a baby"

FIGURE 12. The submerging of iconicity through grammatical operations—(3).

grammatical modulations. In this respect American Sign Language utilizes an essentially *sequential* process; however, we have found that historically the two once-separate signs tend to become merged in various ways into the form of a single sign.

We have studied several hundred ASL compounds, and discovered their special properties. In the process of combining two lexical items in a single unit, we find that there is a special rhythm to compounds: the two signs are made closer together and reduced in temporal length so that their combined duration is only slightly longer than that of a single sign. In particular, the first member of a compound is drastically shortened, thus affecting its formational properties—in particular, its movement. In terms of the historical development of American Sign Language, compound signs tend to reduce over time until in fact they have the properties of single signs; that is, they tend to merge into single signs. Under this kind of temporal reduction and merging, the iconic properties of the original signs may again be totally submerged.

A classical case of this is illustrated in the current ASL sign HOME (FIGURE 13). The current form of the sign HOME turns out to be *opaque* in both of our studies of iconicity discussed in the paper. Hearing nonsigners when presented with the sign HOME guessed "comprehend," "orange," "whisper," and other meanings, but never "home" or any related meaning. Even when the meaning was given along with the sign, there was no agreement on the basis for the relationship between the two: our subjects responded with "familiar," "touch base," "close to a person," "feminine and masculine," "moves backwards like going home," "where I speak the most," *et cetera*. Not one of our subjects guessed that the sign HOME is directly related to eating and sleeping. But in fact, the current opaque sign HOME is historically a merged compound, deriving from the two highly transparent ASL signs EAT and SLEEP: the ASL sign EAT represents bringing something to the mouth; the ASL sign SLEEP involves one hand at the side of the head as if laying the head on the cheek. Over time, there were distinct changes in the form of the compound signs EAT and SLEEP: the same handshape prevailed throughout the sign; then the contact points were brought closer together so that instead of one contact on the mouth and one on the cheek, there are now two touches on the cheek alone (See FIGURE 13). As a consequence of these changes, there is a complete loss of the iconicity of the original two signs, and the sign HOME has now become one of the more opaque signs of ASL.

Through the historical process of merging, many other compound signs of American Sign Language have undergone similar mutations of form and loss of iconicity. Thus both current grammatical processes operating in the language and historical processes result in diminished iconicity.

SUMMARY

In this paper, we show that the total range of the communication system of the deaf is considerably enriched but at the same time rendered more difficult to analyze, because pantomime and other spontaneous nonsign representations occur in the same mode as regular ASL signs in deaf discourse. We note that the rarification of what was originally nonsign depiction is clearly an important source of regular ASL signs. We show that criteria can be established that would distinguish the clear cases of pantomime from the regular ASL signs. Nonetheless, there remain a sizable number of regular ASL signs which, although they are neither pantomimic nor otherwise freely mimetic, still appear to retain an iconic cast. We show that very few ASL signs are actually transparent; that is, a nonsigner cannot guess the meaning of a sign in the absence of further information. On the other hand, many signs are iconic in the sense that nonsigners, when given the sign and its meaning, show considerable agreement in how the two are related.

More important in terms of language and its users is the significance of iconicity for deaf signers themselves. This paper shows that while in special circumstances the deaf do play on iconic elements of certain signs for special effects, iconicity plays no observable role in the coding of signs in short-term memory. The abstract forma-

Separate "Transparent" ASL Signs

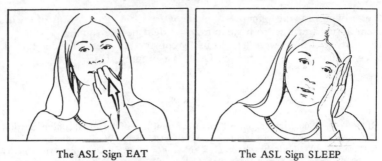

The ASL Sign EAT   The ASL Sign SLEEP

Formal ASL Compound Sign

EAT͡ SLEEP

Informal "Opaque" ASL Sign

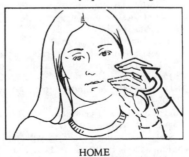

HOME

FIGURE 13. The submerging of iconicity through compounding.

tional parameters definitely dominate. We further note that it is the abstract system and not purely iconic aspects that have determined observed historical change in the form of ASL signs. We interpret this as indicating the deeper structural significance of the abstract formational level. Finally, we show that very widespread and productive grammatical processes, especially suited for a visual-gestural language, override the iconic aspects of signs also at the synchronic structural level.

Acknowledgments

The drawings for this paper were made by Frank A. Paul. Many of the drawings represent actual tracings from video tapes of deaf people signing.

The historical films were lent to us by courtesy of the Gallaudet Film Library Archives, Gallaudet College for the Deaf, Washington, D.C.

References

1. Stokoe, W. 1960. Sign language structure: An outline of the visual communication system of the deaf. Studies in Linguistics. Gallaudet College. Washington, D.C.
2. Stokoe, W., D. Casterline, & C. Croneberg, 1965. A Dictionary of American Sign Language on Linguistic Principles. Gallaudet College Press. Washington, D.C.
3. Lewis, M. M. 1968. Language and Personality of a Deaf Child. National Foundation for Educational Research in England and Wales. Occasional Publication Series XX: 38.
4. Bellugi, U. & S. Fischer. 1972. A comparison of sign language and spoken language: rate and grammatical mechanisms. Cognition: Int. J. Cognitive Psychol. 1: 173–200.
5. Bellugi, U. & E. S. Klima. 1975. Aspects of sign language and its structure. In The Role of Speech in Language. J. Kavanagh and J. Cutting, Eds.: 171–205. M.I.T. Press. Cambridge, Mass.
6. Klima, E. S. 1975. Sound and its absence in the linguistic symbol. In The Role of Speech in Language. J. Kavanagh and J. Cutting, Eds.: 249–270. M.I.T. Press. Cambridge, Mass.
7. Klima, E. S. & U. Bellugi. Perception and production in a visually based language. Ann. N.Y. Acad. Sci. 263: 225–235.
8. Bellugi, U., E. S. Klima & P. A. Siple. 1975. Remembering in signs. Cognition: Int. J. Cognitive Psychol. 3(2): 93–125.
9. Coulter, G. 1975. American Sign Language Pantomime. Manuscript. The Salk Institute. San Diego, Calif.
10. Newkirk, D. 1975. Some Phonological Distinctions between Citation-Form Signing and Free Pantomime. Manuscript. The Salk Institute. San Diego, Calif.
11. Frishberg, N. 1975. Arbitrariness and iconicity: historical change in American Sign Language. Language 51: 696–719.
12. Frishberg, N. 1976. Some Aspects of Historical Change in American Sign Language. Unpublished doctoral dissertation. Univ. California, San Diego, Calif.
13. Hoemann, H. W. 1975. The transparency of meaning of sign language gestures. Sign Language Studies 7: 151–161.
14. Klima, E. S. & U. Bellugi. 1975. Wit and poetry in American Sign Language. Sign Language Studies 8: 203–224.
15. Klima, E. S. & U. Bellugi. 1976. Poetry and song in a language without sound. Cognition: Int. J. Cognitive Psychol. 4: 45–97.
16. Bellugi, U. & P. A. Siple. 1974. Remembering with and without words. In Current Problems in Psycholinguistics. F. Bresson, Ed.: 215–236. Centre National de la Recherche Scientifique. Paris, France.
17. Frishberg, N. & B. Gough. 1973. Morphology in American Sign Language. Manuscript. The Salk Institute. San Diego, Calif.
18. Fischer, S. & B. Gough. Verbs in American sign language. In The Signs of Language. E. S. Klima and U. Bellugi, Eds. Harvard University Press. Cambridge, Mass. To be published.
19. Supalla, T. How Many Seats in a Chair? The Derivation of Nouns from Verbs in American Sign Language. The Salk Institute. San Diego, Calif. In preparation.
20. Supalla, T. The Derivation of Nouns from Verbs in American Sign Language. The Salk Institute. San Diego, Calif. In preparation.
21. Schlesinger, I. M., B. Presser, E. Cohen & T. Peled. Transfer of Meaning in Sign Language. Working Paper No. 12. The Hebrew University of Jerusalem. Jerusalem, Israel.

DISCUSSION PAPER: HUMAN LANGUAGE AND PRIMATE COMMUNICATION*

Michael J. Raleigh

*University of California at Berkeley and
Behavioral Sciences Foundation
Berkeley, California 93720*

Frank R. Ervin

*Behavioral Sciences Foundation and
University of California at Los Angeles
Los Angeles, California 90024*

Hewes,[1] Stokoe,[2] and Bellugi's[3] presentations are significant contributions to the discussion of the origin and evolution of speech and language. Their arguments may be supplemented by considering the implications of the form and functions of nonhuman primate communication.

The details of nonhuman primate communication have been thoroughly reviewed by Marler,[4] Lancaster,[5] and Peters and Ploog.[6] From these reviews, it is obvious that monkeys and apes utilize gestures and postures and tactile and chemical signals as well as vocalizations in communicating. Sight and touch seem to be the dominant modalities for communication in nonhuman primates. For instance, more than 80% of the coalitions formed in a captive vervet group observed by us were created without any obvious vocal signals being exchanged between the participants. Although these modalities appear to dominate information exchange, it is obvious to the naturalistic observer that no single input or output channel functions in isolation in most normal circumstances, no matter what its power may be in laboratory situations. For instance, preliminary analysis of data from the vervet population mentioned above indicates that in less than 50% of the threats (n = 793) was there only one signaling system obvious to the observer. In these cases it was most frequently a complex visual display (e.g., facial threats).[7]

Consistent with this emphasis on nonvocal communication is the observation of Malmi[8] that in free-ranging baboons visual cues are employed much more frequently than vocal and that information is commonly transmitted through the simultaneous use of several modalities. These points do not minimize the significance of vocalizations in nonhuman primate social behavior. Lost call, alarm barks, and territorial vocalizations appear in many species in a variety of ecological circumstances and for the animal isolated from visual contact may function independent of all other modalities. Although this important distance communicating function of vocalization confers some special adaptive advantages, it is not productive to describe either vocalization or facial expression (or for that matter chemical outputs) as though they represented entirely independent systems of interindividual communication.[9]

Nonhuman primates communicate information relating to the immediate environmental and social situation and to the individual's internal states. This information is sufficient to permit the effective functioning of nonhuman primate societies. Within these societies individuals are well known to each other and much information can be acquired by observational learning. For instance, much of what baboons,[10] and chimpanzees[11] eat and hunt [12,13] is the result of observational

*Partly supported by NIH training grant GM-1224 and the H. F. Guggenheim Foundation.

learning. Menzel's[14] and Menzel and Johnson's[15] elegant experimental evidence demonstrates that chimpanzees can pattern their behavior after each other and that the location, quality, and relative quantity of concealed objects can be communicated. Nonetheless, the contrast between this complex communication and the human extreme should not be minimized. Humans are capable of conveying a wider variety of more precisely denoted information than other primates, are not bound to the immediate context, and can readily create novel expressions.[9]

The multimodal nature of nonhuman and human primate communication and the tremendous difference between human and animals with regard to the type and amount of information conveyed have two implications for the study of language evolution. First, it is crucial to determine if there are extant forms that can be used as models for the intermediate evolutionary situation. Without such intermediate examples it is difficult to document the stages involved in the shift to the human situation; an analysis comparable to Bellugi's demonstration of the shift from the use of iconic to arbitrary signs is precluded. In the absence of transitional forms, accounts purporting to document the phases in the evolution of language should be regarded as exceedingly speculative, and all of the proposed "stages" in language evolution should be given probability statements.

At this time the neural correlates of naturalistic chimpanzee communication should be determined experimentally. As Myers,[16] Robinson,[17] and Steklis and Harnad[18] pointed out, there is apparently a dichotomy between the neural correlates of human language and those underlying nonhuman communication. Should the neural system of chimpanzees be intermediate between monkeys and man, chimpanzees could be used as models of intermediate forms. Should, however, the chimpanzees' situation approximate that found in monkeys, they cannot serve as transitional models. Another area where intermediates might be found is the linguistic-like behavior of trained chimpanzees. By monitoring EEG's, evaluating evoked potentials, and performing Wada tests, this information could be acquired in a nontraumatic fashion. If chimpanzee linguistic-like behavior is mediated by structures analogous to those implicated in human language, the gestural origin theory would be supported. On the other hand, should there be no difference between the correlates of this behavior and those underlying complex memory tasks (such as that described by Menzel,[19]), the chimpanzees cannot be viewed as an intermediate form. Determining the neural foundations of both naturalistic chimpanzee communication and of the language-like behavior, Premack,[20] Fouts,[21] Rumbaugh,[22] the Gardners,[23] and others have taught them, can readily be done and would provide valuable data bearing on the status of the gestural origins theory.

A second implication arising from the form and function of nonhuman primate communication is that a gestural origin of human language is questionable. If hominids employed a system in which information was transmitted primarily or entirely by gesture, the shift from gestural to vocal modalities represents a major biological problem in the evolution of speech and language. The nonhuman primate systems are effective and from slow cultural change during the early phases of human evolution Isaac[24] suggests that the early hominid communicative systems were not strikingly more effective. It is conceivable that the basic multimodal system became increasingly complex with all means of communicating gestures, facial expressions, and vocalizations becoming encephalized at about the same time. The shift to the human state may have involved the liberation of all modalities from "limbic control" at nearly the same time. Had an effective gestural system existed, its replacement by a primarily vocal system is difficult to envision; it seems equally probable that such a system would have been retained and refined. However, if both gestures and vocalizations were employed, the limitations of sign language (as noted by Steklis and Harnad,[18]) make it easy to envision speech becoming the primary means of expressing language.

This alternative view is compatible with the observation that extensive components of the human brain mediate speech and that these neural systems appear to be closely associated with (perhaps identical to) those mediating language. Presumably these neural systems are the result of long periods of evolution. It might be speculated that had language been expressed primarily by gestures for a considerable time period, the representation of speech and language should be more readily dissociated.

ACKNOWLEDGMENTS

The cooperation of the government of St. Kitts-Nevis-Anguilla is gratefully acknowledged.

REFERENCES

1. HEWES, G. W. This annal.
2. STOKOE, W. This annal.
3. BELLUGI, U. This annal.
4. MARLER, P. this annal.
5. LANCASTER, J. B. 1975. Primate Behavior and the Emergence of Human Culture. Holt Rinehart and Winston, Inc. New York, N.Y.
6. PETERS, M. & D. PLOOG. 1973. Communication among primates. Ann. Rev. Physiol. 35: 221–242.
7. RALEIGH, M. J. In preparation.
8. MALMI, W. 1975. Ph.D. dissertation. Univ. California at Berkeley. Berkeley, Calif.
9. WASHBURN, S. L. 1975. The Origin of Language. In press.
10. GOODALL, J. VAN-LAWICK. 1973. The behavior of chimpanzees in their natural habitat. Am. J. Psychiatry 130: 1–12.
11. McGREW, W. C. 1975. Preprint.
12. STRUM, S. C. 1975. Primate predation: Interim report on the development of a tradition in a troop of olive baboons. Science 187: 755–757.
13. TELEKI, G. 1973. The Predatory Behavior of Wild Chimpanzees. Bucknell Univ. Press. Lewisburg, Pa.
14. MENZEL, E. 1971. Communication about the environment in a group of young chimpanzees. Folia primatal. 15: 220–232.
15. MENZEL, E. and MARCIA K. JOHNSON. This annal.
16. MYERS, R. E. This annal.
17. ROBINSON, B.W. This annal.
18. STEKLIS, H. D. & S. HARNAD. This annal.
19. MENZEL, E. 1973. Chimpanzee spatial memory organization. Science 182: 943–946.
20. PREMACK, D. 1971. Language in chimpanzee? Science 172: 808–822.
21. FOUTS, R. S. 1973. Acquisition and testing of gestural signs in four young chimpanzees. Science 180: 978–980.
22. RUMBAUGH, D. This annal.
23. GARDNER, B. T. & R. A. GARDNER. 1971. Two way communication with an infant chimpanzee. In Behavior of Nonhuman Primates. A. M. Schrier and F. Stollnitz, Eds. Academic Press. New York, N.Y.
24. ISAAC, G. L. This annal.

DISCUSSION

Jean Kitahara-Frisch, *Moderator*

Chiyoda-Ku, Kioicho
Sophia University
Japan

UNIDENTIFIED SPEAKER: Dr. Bellugi, it's the first time I've seen a demonstration of American sign language, and it seemed to me that one hand is dominant for most arbitrary signs. I wonder if well-lateralized left-handers have to use the right hand for most signs, or if they can use the other?

DR. BELLUGI: Having catalogued the signs in Professor Stokoe's dictionary, we noticed that for over two-thirds of the signs one hand is dominant. One can be either right- or left-handed in sign. Among our staff of three, we have someone who is very left-handed by all the tests that we've given her, and she's consistently using her left hand as dominant in signing. Also, it is a sign language universal that a sign never signals a difference in meaning from its mirror-image.

DR. KITAHARA-FRISCH: May I make a comment very relevant to the question raised? I've been working with the deaf for about 11 years now, mostly with the emotionally disturbed deaf. Sign language can be divided broadly, as all of you know, into the finger-spelling part and the actual sign language. Sometimes when discussing emotional matters the deaf will resent insistance on continual finger-spelling or grammatical presentation (which is more left-hemispheric) because that takes away from the emotional aspect which is expressed better in body movement, gesture, and pantomime (which may be in these patients more right-hemispheric).

DR. FINK (*Univ. of Washington, Seattle, Wash.*): I would like to ask a question of Dr. Stokoe and also perhaps Dr. Bellugi, relating to thinking. Thinking in silence, that is. When speaking people think silently (which is characterized by some "silent speech") they produce micromovements of the muscles which they would use if they were talking aloud. I would like to know if there is any information on what is happening to the muscles for people who are using American sign language when they're thinking by themselves.

DR. STOKOE: I don't know of any systematic treatment of that. We have a good deal of casual evidence of persons spelling things to themselves, paying attention to a speaker or letting their attention wander. Some deaf people have even been observed moving their hands in their sleep.

DR. ROBBIN BATTISON (*Gallaudet College, Washington, D.C.*): I'd like to say a little bit about what I've observed about lateralization and sign language. And I'd like to make a response to the gentlemen over here who says he's worked eleven years with the deaf, that it's a bit of a trap to think of oral language as being completely under the aegis of the left hemisphere, and sign language being basically "spatial" must therefore be on the right; a "kick it over to the other side" kind of thing. Sign language, as Ursula Bellugi and Dr. Stokoe have shown, *does* involve many spatial dynamics and interaction; much of the articulation is based on spatial rather than temporal or linear organization.

But, it also *does* involve linearity, temporality, coordination in time, rapid movements, changing in hand postures and finger movements, and rapid movements from one location of the body to the other.

When you look at the evidence for where sign language is lateralized in the brain, first of all you find that not many normal lateralization studies have been done with deaf subjects. You don't know how they process certain kinds of verbal information. Those things are being done now.

But looking at the aphasic evidence you *do* find people who make errors in sign language consequent upon left hemispheric lesions. I think this says something about sign language *not* being over there on the right.

And with regard to the deaf resenting finger spelling: it's not a resentment of performing a left-hemisphere function. It's a resentment of being forced to use a *foreign language*, much as Puerto Ricans would resent being interviewed by their social worker in English, that kind of thing.

One other thing is that I've seen lots of signers who alternate dominant hands in normal conversation. I think this is just one more log in the fire.

STEVAN HARNAD: I appreciate Mike Raleigh's comments about the multimodal aspect of communication; they were not unlike Nancy Tanner's earlier comment about "total communication." But if I don't misinterpret Ursula Bellugi's message, the whole point is that these other aspects—you might call them *iconic* or otherwise—of communication, are not really the *linguistic* ones. And the people who emphasize gestures as the first carrier of the *linguistic* information are making precisely that point. They're not trying to devalue any of the other modalities, but simply claim that the gesture itself carried the linguistic message. And in fact, in keeping with the trend to minimize iconicity, you would expect that such nonlinguistic, suprasegmental modes must in fact have been *minimized* in the beginning; until vocalization took over.

DR. CHEVALIER-SKOLNIKOFF: I wanted to underscore Dr. Raleigh's comments about multimodality. Despite Dr. Harnad's comments about it not being perhaps so relevant to speech and language in itself, if you want to look at the evolution of communication, not only are nonhuman primate communications multimodal, but what is so striking is that *human* communications are even *more* multimodal. In the Old World monkeys, (or at least the macaque) the only communicative system which has a lot of variability is the body visual and tactile systems. With the apes, you have variability and voluntary control of the hands, too, as well as a little bit in terms of sound-making. But it's with humans that you get voluntary control and mobility in the face as well as sound production. Only people can lie with their faces and only people can make music.

DR. CHARLES LAUGHLIN (*Univ. of Pennsylvania*): In accounting for the principle problem in the gestural theory, that is that evolutionary decussation between a gestural mode and an auditory one, you, Dr. Hewes, have argued in the past that the gestural mode was inherently slow; Steklis and Harnad have argued the same. Now, haven't we just had empirical proof in opposition to that point of view?

DR. HEWES: The existing sign languages as used by the deaf do not appear to be particularly slow, but we have no idea what their predecessors were like.

DR. HARNAD: Let me add two points: (1) We also have no idea what is being *lost* in a rapid translation into contemporary sign language such as we have been witnessing here. (2) Even if contemporary sign language is relatively fast and efficient, let us not forget that it has benefited from the fact that language is now well entrenched, genetically and neurologically. The primordial form, when language was still a tentative, inchoate faculty whose survival value was undergoing its critical testing and shaping, was surely not as fully optimized as our present legacy. Moreover, slowness was only one of many disadvantages of the gestural mode (see Steklis and Harnad, this volume), some of which even the most militant protagonists of sign language—a medium which, as has been demonstrated again here, to but see is to love, and we have not been immune to this—will admit have not been overcome even today.

MECHANISMS OF INTELLIGENCE: PRECONDITIONS FOR LANGUAGE*

David Premack

*Department of Psychology
University of Pennsylvania
Philadelphia, Pennsylvania 19104*

Introduction

Language is so deeply enmeshed in intelligence that a discussion of the psychological prerequisites for language is at the same time a discussion of (some of) the mechanisms of intelligence. In this summary of the learning and cognition section I will review the following mechanisms: causal inference, representational capacity, memory, second-order relations, conditionability and voluntary control of the motor systems, categorical discrimination of speech sounds, and intermodal association—in each case, attempting to decide, often on the basis of meager evidence, in which species the mechanisms are likely to be found.

Causal Inference

In acquiring language one acquires labels for existing concepts; this proposal can be tested with admirable directness in many cases. Can the subject discriminate between conditions that exemplify same and different? all and none? red and black? etc. If so, according to the proposal, it should be possible to teach the subject names for same-different, the quantifiers, and the like. Not all concepts are as simple as those in the examples, however, and some of them must be approached differently. For instance, in the case of if-then or the conditional relation, we approach by observing that the conditional sentence is a way of expressing a causal relation. "If you drop that, it will break." "If you smile at Mary, she will smile back." "If you touch that, you'll get burned." These sentences and the infinitely many like them that are possible express a causal relation between the antecedent and the consequent. Only a species that made a causal analysis of its experience would use sentences of this form productively. Hence, in the case of the conditional relation, we designed the test to answer the question: Does the subject make a causal analysis of its experience?

A simple visual test can be used to answer this question.[1] The subject was given an intact object, a blank space, and the same object in a changed or terminal state, along with various alternatives, and was encouraged to complete the sequence by placing one of the alternatives in the blank space. For example, the subject was given such items as an intact apple and a cut apple; a dry sponge and a wet sponge; a clear piece of paper and one that had writing on it. In these cases, the three alternatives given the subject consisted of a knife, a bowl of water, and a writing instrument.

Three of the four chimpanzees tested in this way required no more than general adaptation to the test format before responding correctly, not only to training items but to an extensive set of transfer items. Their ability to place the knife between the

*Based in part on research supported by NIMH grant 7 R01 MH-28077-01, and NSF grant BMS-75-19748.

intact and severed apple, the water between the dry and wet sponge, and the pencil between the unmarked and pencil-marked paper showed that they correctly identified the instrument or operator needed to change each object from its initial to its terminal state. Moreover, their ability to respond in this fashion was not limited to familiar object-implement pairs. They performed equally well on pairs they had never experienced, some of which were anomalous or nonsensical, such as apples that had been written on, sponges that had been cut, and writing paper that had been dunked in water.

Simple as this outcome is it can be given a stronger interpretation than may first meet the eye. The visual sequences are infinitely ambiguous: each can be coded in indefinitely many ways, such as red-blank-red, one-blank-two, round-blank-flat, large-blank-small, and so on. The three alternatives are no less subject to indeterminately many codings. For instance, knife need not be coded as knife (instrument that cuts) but can be read as sharp, metal, long, shiny, and so on, and the same holds for the other alternatives. Nevertheless, the subjects did not code the sequences or alternatives in these ways but consistently chose alternatives compatible with only one coding; namely, How do you get from the intact to the terminal stage? With what instrument do you produce the change? Thus the subjects read the sequences in a specific and consistent way. The fact that they found the same question in each of the sequences indicates that they have a schema, a structure that assigns an interpretation to an otherwise infinitely ambiguous sequence.

It is noteworthy, also, that the visual sequences were by no means iconic representations of the actions tested. Cutting, wetting, and marking are analogue processes in which an agent brings about a continuous change in an object. In cutting, for example, an agent applies a knife to an apple, exerting pressure until the apple divides. The test items did not portray the gradual division of the apple, but presented only the digital highlights of the analogue process, and did not present the agent at all. Nevertheless, the chimpanzees evidently recognized the test sequences as representations of the actions. If the tests had failed, it would have been reasonable to consider motion pictures or other iconic forms of representation; but the animals succeeded despite the abstract form of the representation. Thus chimpanzees not only have a schema for cause-effect relations but one that can be activated by noniconic representations.

Because the present tests dealt only with the physical domain, they leave open whether or not the chimpanzee can recognize cause-effect relations in the psychological or social domain. We have been held back from making such tests by the lack of appropriate stimuli, although it is easy enough to describe the form such tests would take. For example, in on such test, frame one shows Elizabeth begging food from Peony, frame two is blank and is to be filled-in by the subject, and frame three shows Elizabeth and Peony playing, engaging in mutual grooming, or hugging one another. The alternatives given the subject include Peony ignoring Elizabeth's request, Peony sharing with Elizabeth, Elizabeth stealing Peony's food, and the like. Of these alternatives, only Peony sharing with Elizabeth is compatible with the harmonious outcome shown in frame three, and the chimpanzee's appropriate choice in this and comparable tests would indicate that it can recognize representations of social as well as of physical actions. Notice, incidentally, that the test is designed so that selection of the missing frame cannot be based simply on a knowledge of physical action. If both animals were shown eating in the third frame, one could conclude on physical grounds that Peony must have shared with Elizabeth. But since, in fact, neither animal is shown eating in the third frame, the content of the second frame can only be inferred from the social character of the behavior in the third frame.

Once we obtain the stimuli, we will make these tests, but let us assume for the sake of discussion that the chimpanzees pass the social tests as they have the physical ones—which does not seem too risky an assumption. If the chimpanzees can recognize representations of both physical and social actions, perhaps they can also recognize higher order structures that are built up out of physical and social actions. Stories, novels, tales, indeed, all basic prose narratives are formed by appropriate combinations of social and physical actions. Therefore, if a species can recognize the basic elements of which stories are formed, perhaps it can also recognize stories themselves.

Consider the following as an example of a story that is both simple and germane to the life of the present chimpanzees. Amy leashes Peony and takes her for a walk in the countryside. Peony breaks the leash and runs off. She is surprised by a pack of German shepherds who surround her and threaten to attack. She escapes by climbing a tree. But the dogs remain below, keeping her trapped in the tree. She spends a cold night in the tree. In the morning she is rescued by Amy and others from the lab, who drive off the dogs. Next time Peony goes for a walk, even though Amy drops the leash, Peony does not run off.

The theme of this story can be described as breeched union followed by reunion— which is more than coincidence; quest for union or reunion is among the most popular themes in children's and probably all human stories (for background on story comprehension, see Kintsch[2]).

The above story can be represented by from six to eight pictures, depending on how elliptically the verbal story is translated into a visual one, and may be simple enough for the chimpanzee to comprehend. We are presently testing the chimpanzee's comprehension of picture stories in two ways. First, we have given both Peony and Sarah storybooks; in some the pictures are in the appropriate order and in others they are out of order. It is possible that the animals will show a preference for the books in which the pictures are in appropriate order. Second, we have given Sarah four serial learning tasks, each of which requires that she arrange five pictures in a designated order. In two cases the designated order is the normal order in which the pictures occur in a story book, and in two cases it is not. If Sarah's serial learning is sensitive to the sequence of the story, so that she learns the former faster than the latter, this too can be taken as evidence of her ability to comprehend picture stories. These measures, preference and serial learning, are substitutes for the more direct measures which it is possible to use with the verbally competent subject, and which Walter Kintsch, his students, and I are now using in studying picture-story comprehension with children. Four-year-old children can be instructed to describe the pictures and, after the pictures have been removed, to recall their descriptions. The recall measure has proved to be exceptionally sensitive. When the pictures were shown the children in the normal story order, they were far better able to recall their descriptions than when the pictures were shown them in a scrambled order. Although this revealing verbal measure could actually be used with Sarah, her present language competence painfully limits the kind of stories that can be used with her. For the time being, we are relying on the indirect measures.

REPRESENTATIONAL CAPACITY

The representational capacity of the chimpanzee is such that the experimenter can, for example, place a red card on a green one and ask the chimpanzee "? red on green" (Is red on green?). Similarly, the chimpanzee can be asked not the *yes-no* form, but the *wh*-form, of the question, "? on green" (What is on green?). In correctly answering such questions, the chimpanzee shows that it can recognize the relation between an item, red on green, and a representation of the item, "red on green." Furthermore, in answering similar questions in the *absence* of the red and green cards, tests that we have carried out more recently, the chimpanzee shows that it can also recognize the relation between its knowledge of an item and a representation of its knowledge.

This representational capacity can be appreciated by contrasting it with the probable parallel incapacity of the bee. The bee has a code—a correlation between items inside and outside of its body—but not necessarily a language in the sense that a language is a code that can be used in specific ways. The most critical of these ways depends on the capacity in question, on being able to recognize representations of one's self—body, behavior, and knowledge.

Suppose a forager bee were allowed to gather information about the direction and distance of a food source from its hive. The bee can encode this information in its dance (and a second bee decode the dance), but if it were shown a dance, could it judge whether or not the dance accurately represented the direction and distance of the food source? That is, could the bee recognize the dance as a representation of its own knowledge? It is precisely this kind of judgment that the chimpanzee can make, and it is the capacity for this judgment, more than any other, perhaps, that qualifies the chimpanzee for language. When shown one or another condition, such as an apple in a pail, a red card on a green one, even an act of one kind or another carried out by some trainer, the chimpanzee can be asked to judge the agreement between the condition it has observed and a representation of the condition. The chimpanzee can be interrogated, as the bee (presumably) cannot, and as a consequence it can make what amount to true-false judgments, as to my knowledge the bee cannot.

Map Reading

The representational capacity involved in language is of a nonspatial kind. A second kind of representational capacity is spatial and is involved, for example, in the reading of maps. There are two reasons, in addition to the chimpanzee's nonspatial representational capacity, to suppose that it may be able to read maps. First, the chimpanzee can negotiate the two formal transformations involved in a map: dimension and size. For instance, the ape can match pictures to objects and vice versa,[3,4] as well as match objects reduced in size. Furthermore, since the pictures used in these studies were not the same size as the objects they represented, the chimpanzee can evidently negotiate the transformations even when they are applied together, as they are in a map.

Second, when chimpanzees were shown the location of a number of items hidden in a one-acre compound, they subsequently retrieved the items in a direct way, rather than searching circuitously as they did when hunting similar items the locations of which were not known to them.[5] Tinklepaugh[6] reported similar data for chimpanzees and, to a lesser extent, even monkeys. Performance of this kind led Menzel to infer that the chimpanzee had stored a "cognitive map." Although the use of Tolman's expression here is a metaphor, and one does not know the form in which the information is stored in the ape's head, a maplike representation must be included among the possibilities (cf. Shepard[7] for elegant defense of this form of storage in man). For these several reasons, Menzel and I are now testing the chimpanzee's ability to learn to use maps.

In human infants, sucking and visual orientation can be reinforced with still and motion pictures (cf. Salapetek[8]). Yet we cannot conclude from this that the infant recognizes the relation between the pictures and the items they represent. Suppose the infant were given a number of pictures from the same class, such as smiling faces or people (in keeping with the pigeon experiments) until it habituated, whereupon it was shown another picture that either did or did not belong to the class. If the infant showed greater recovery from habituation for the picture that did not belong to the class, this would show that it could distinguish between members and nonmembers of the class. Would it also show that the infant recognized the relation between the class of pictures and the objects they represent?

No, for one must show in addition that procedures affecting the infant's response to a class of pictures would have a corresponding effect on the items represented by the pictures. For instance, if the infant were habituated to pictures of people, its responsiveness to actual people should be reduced, more so at least than if its habituation were to pictures of some other class. For the same reasons, the data showing the pigeon's ability to discriminate between pictures of man and nonman do not establish that the pigeon recognizes the relation between the pictures and the items they represent. Here, too, it must be shown that the response established for the pictures will transfer to the items they represent. For instance, birds taught to peck at pictures of people, should be more inclined to peck at actual people than birds taught to peck at pictures of nonpeople.

Furthermore, even the demand that there be transfer from pictures to items represented by pictures is by itself insufficient to sustain the representational claim. If the subject responded in the same way to both, it would appear to regard them as equivalent and thus not to know the essential difference between them. This would be the case for a pigeon that, after being fed by people, sought food from a picture of people as readily as from people, or for an infant who smiled at a picture of its mother no less than at its mother.

To maintain that the subject recognizes a picture as a representation of an item, the subject must show transfer between them, but it must also show that it can distinguish between occasions on which it is and is not appropriate to respond in the same way to items and to pictures of the items. That is, the subject must be able to distinguish between functions for which a picture can be substituted for the item it represents, and other functions for which the substitution is unwarranted. The subject who could not make this distinction would equate the picture and the item represented by the picture, drawing no more distinction between them than it would between two of the pictures or between two of the items.

In the chimpanzees, in contrast to the birds and infants, all these desiderata were realized. Sarah and the other subjects chose the same alternatives in match to sample tests when the sample was a blue triangle (meaning apple) as when the sample was an actual apple—which is a necessary but not a sufficient condition for the representational claim. In addition, the chimpanzees showed that, even as there were functions for which they were prepared to exchange apple and "apple," there were other functions for which they would not accept the exchange. After a certain point in training, the apes did not apply pieces of apple or other fruit to the board, or conversely put the word apple or other words into their mouths. They neither wrote with nonlinguistic items nor made any attempt to eat the linguistic ones. Furthermore, when told to put the cracker in the pail on one occasion, and the name of the cracker on another, Sarah responded appropriately.

Notice how these tests profit from the present language system. With a vocal language or one based on sign, it would be a struggle to find acts that could be applied equally to words and to referents, very likely a futile struggle. Yet, except as there were acts that could be applied equally to both words and their referents, the fact that the subject did not apply them equally could not provide the desired evidence.

One could go on to describe still stronger evidence. The subject's ability to write an essay on representation could allay any further doubts one might entertain on the basis of the evidence described. Yet I think the twofold evidence described above is both necessary and sufficient for the claim, although I am always in favor of allaying residual doubts.

Why is it that the chimpanzee can recognize representations of various items including its own knowledge, whereas other species presumably cannot? It cannot be because nonprimates do not have knowledge of any kind. One of the most demonstrable forms of knowledge is that of spatial relations and not only primates but rats[9] and even insects can be shown to have information of this kind. For instance, the homing of insects[10] shows that these species have a maplike knowledge of their home terrain, and the inference is supported as well in their case as in the case of the ape. Although it is not possible to say for any species how the information is actually stored in the head, the simplest assumption in all cases is that of either an image or a cognitive map.

Since not only primates but even insects have a knowledge of spatial relations, the question can be repeated in a more explicit form: Why is a cognitive map not itself a sufficient condition for the use of an actual map? Perhaps I am mistaken in assuming that nonprimates could not be taught to use maps, but if I am not, then we must explain why a species could have a maplike representation of its home terrain in its head and yet not recognize the relation between its cognitive map and an actual map.

Perhaps either the quality or abstractness of the image or cognitive map must attain a certain level before representations of it could be recognizable. But that seems an unprofitable line of inquiry, for neither the measurement of quality nor the definition of abstractness is simple. A more interesting—and ultimately testable—hypothesis is that the ability of a species to use either maps or language depends in the first place on the species having at least two different forms of representation or information storage. If the species can store information not only in a pictorial form, to which insects may conceivably be restricted, by also in a propositional form, which is demonstrably the case for at least man and chimpanzees, then it seems certain that on occasion the same information will be stored in both forms. Cases of this kind would provide the opportunity for species to recognize (not the right word but I cannot find a more suitable one) the equivalent between the two internal representations. And experience of this kind may help a subject recognize the relation between an item and a representation of the item, for in principle that relation is not different from the one between two equivalent internal representations.†

Certain kinds of information may naturally lend itself to an image or maplike form, and other kinds to a propositional form (and these extremes may never be represented in both ways), but other kinds may be intermediate with respect to form and may be represented in both forms either more or less automatically or on different occasions. For instance, the kind of information Tinklepaugh[6] used in his memory tests with apes and monkeys could be fairly easily modulated so as to potentiate an image form of storage on one occasion, a propositional form on another, and possibly both forms on still another occasion.

Tinklepaugh tested the apes by arranging 16 pairs of containers in a circle (diameter, 20 feet), baited one container of each pair while the ape observed from the center of the circle, and then after varying delays released the ape to find the baited containers. The 16 containers consisted of painted and unpainted wood boxes, tin cans and cups, and one pair of cigar boxes that were as dissimilar as possible.

†This idea arose in discussion with my colleague Randy Gallistel, and is more his than mine.

Tinklepaugh did not change the order of the containers from trial to trial, but the original order was not systematic and the baiting was essentially random.

For Tinklepaugh's arrangement and baiting system, an image seems the most revealing form of storage. The circular arrangement he used would make the coordinate system on which maps are based less suitable; half of the pairs of containers would have the same value on the abscissa and the other half the same value on the ordinate, which must reduce their identifiability (if the containers had been arranged on a line this would not be the case, and then a map and an image would be equally suitable). A propositional form of storage would also seem unsuited. It could be used, as it always can be, but the lack of systematic relations between the type of container and the baiting system would deny the propositional format those advantages this form of storage can have once the information is patterned or systematic.

For example, if for all tin containers the left member of each pair were baited, whereas for all wood containers the right member of each pair was baited, this information could obviously be stored economically in a propositional format. Moreover, the propositional format would not seem to involve any predicates not included in the conceptual structure of the chimpanzee. Sarah was successfully taught the quantifiers, the use of modifiers comparable to wood and tin in "wood and tin containers," and though not taught "right-left," taught to label other distinctions, e.g., "top-bottom," of seemingly comparable difficulty.

In principle, it would seem possible to titrate the subject's form of storage—image, map, or propositional—by modulating several parameters: the pattern or lack of pattern in the information, the shape of the geometrical arrangement, and whether or not the experimenter changed the position of the containers after baiting them (such changes should have no effect on the subject's performance if it used a propositional format, but should seriously impair it if it used either an image or a map). At intermediate values of these parameters, subjects who are capable of more than one form of storage may be inclined to use both forms, thereby setting up an equivalence between two different internal representations, which, I suggest, is the kind of experience that may be helpful in leading a subject to recognize the relation between an item and an external representation of the item. Although at the moment I do not see how to test this hypothesis with a satisfying degree of directness, indirect or circumstantial tests have already suggested themselves, and it may be hoped that they will suggest more direct tests.

MNEMONIC CAPACITY

Of all the prerequisites for language, none is more vital, or more easily overlooked, than memory, yet language is possible in the first place only because of memory. It is not objects, actions, or properties as such that are associated with words, but rather the representations of these items which the subject has stored in memory. If the stored representation of an item is complete, then, barring some form of "leakage," the information associated with the name of the item should be commensurately complete.

A representation might be incomplete for either of two reasons. First, a young organism or an inexperienced old one might know little about the item in question. Children know far less about the world than do adults, and when asked about the world, reveal their ignorance by the inaccuracy of their answers. However, normal children need only adequate experience in order to form well-defined representations. Second, despite extensive experience with the items in question, certain species may never form well-defined representations. An organism may see an item clearly or accurately and yet be unable to form an accurate representation of what it has seen. We do not yet know whether, in fact, species differ in the quality or power of the information they can store. But if they do, this would set a limit on the effectiveness of the language they could acquire; for the name of an item cannot be more informative than the stored representation of the item with which the name is associated.

A common expression speaks of the "power of the word," although this refers, of course, to human words. Can we talk about chimpanzee words in a similar vein, or are the pieces of plastic,[11] keys,[12] and manual signs[13,14] that chimps have been taught a lesser device that only appear to be like words but differ from them in critical respects? To answer this question we must first decide what is meant by "power of the word." I suspect that what the phrase celebrates is the extraordinary extent to which the word can be substituted for its referent. This substitution is made possible by the subject's ability to use the word as an information retrieval device. Thus, the phrase implies that, in the human case, the name of an object can be virtually as informative as the object itself.

To assess the chimpanzee's memory of objects on the one hand and the information it had associated with names of the objects on the other, we used fruit and the names taught for the fruit. We decomposed the fruit into a number of pieces, gave the apes one piece of the fruit and then asked them to identify other pieces that belonged to the same fruit. The logic of this measurement is based on the assumption that if one knows a great deal about an object, one should need only a small sample to identify the object from which the sample was taken. For instance, if given only a stem or a seed or a taste, the knowledgeable subject should be able to identify the fruit from which the component was taken.

Consider the difference between what a subject can perceive about an object and what it can reconstruct from memory. When the subject is required to match redness to an apple, both the sample and correct alternative instance the matching criterion, giving a measure of perception. If, however, the sample remains red but the apple is now painted white, the sample and correct alternative will no longer instance the matching criterion. Instead, they will match on the basis of information associated with but not directly represented by the correct alternative, and the subject must reconstruct the missing information from memory. However, tests that require reconstructing information from memory do not depend specifically on distorted alternatives. The relation between stem and peel, stem and seed, seed and peel, and so on, color and shape, shape and size, et cetera, and color and stem, shape and seed, and so forth, are all cases of this kind. Items in these pairs do not share common features but are related simply through being attributes of the same object.

In making the present tests, fruit were divided into four canonical components and two features: wedge, stem, peel, and seed; plus color and shape. Taste was added as the one nonvisual attribute. Eight fruits were decomposed in this manner—banana, orange, apple, lemon, peach, pear, grape, and cherry. The subject was given one or another of the components or features as a sample, along with two other components or features as alternatives, and was required to select the alternative that came from the same fruit as the sample. For instance, the subject was given an apple seed as the sample and two stems as alternatives—one apple, the other lemon—and required in this case to choose the apple stem.

After completing the test series of approximately 24 individual tests with each of the four subjects, it was possible to rank-order the components and features according to their informativeness. Not surprisingly, the whole fruit was the most informative cue. Color and peel were next, followed closely by taste, after which there was essentially a tie between shape, wedge, and stem, and lastly there was seed, the least informative cue of all. Sarah, impressively, was able to use all cues correctly; but the other three subjects that showed differences were most able to identify the source of the attribute of a fruit from its color or peel, and least able from its seed.

In the next test series, actual parts of the fruit were no longer given as alternatives. They were still given as samples, but now the alternatives were plastic words that named the fruits. The results of these tests were unusually clear-cut. When the informativeness of the plastic words was compared with that of the actual parts of the fruit, the words were found to be more informative than any part except the whole fruit itself. In brief, words could be substituted for their referents in match-to-sample tests without loss of accuracy. In another test series, we used names of colors rather than of objects and obtained identical results. For instance, the word "red" could be substituted for an actual instance of red in the matching tests without loss of accuracy. In the ape, too, the word substituted vigorously for its referent. For these reasons it seems proper to speak of the "power of the word" for the chimpanzee and not only for man.

The ability of fruit and color names to substitute for their referents without loss of accuracy shows that a major consequence of giving arbitrary objects, such as pieces of plastic, linguistic prerogatives is to transfer to the arbitrary object some or all of the information contained in the associated referent. Under what circumstances does this transfer of information take place? Perhaps it occurs only after the piece of plastic has been used in a wordlike way, to request or describe the referent some number of times. That would be the only tenable hypothesis if the only way to produce names was by associating them with their referents in one linguistic context or another. However, we already know that this procedure can be short-circuited. Names can be generated more directly by instructions of the form "X is the name of Y," where X is a so far unused piece of plastic and Y a so far unnamed object. Following instruction of this kind, Sarah used X in all the ways she used names introduced in the more standard way. Thus, the effect of such instructions as "X is the name of Y" must be to transfer to X some or all of the information the subject has stored in memory about Y. This fact clarifies some of the power of language, and at the same time suggests the kind of intelligence a species must have in order to acquire it.

To qualify for language a species must be capable of storing a rich representation of Y; if not, the information transferred to X would be weak and the name would be a poor substitute for the referent. That is, if the mnemonic capacity of the species were limited, then information associated with names would be commensurately limited; and names could not then be substituted for their referents in match-to-sample tests without loss of accuracy as, in fact, they can be in the chimpanzee. In addition, instructions of the form "X is the name of Y" must have the force of transferring to X some—ideally all—of the information that the subject has stored about Y. These are not the only capacities a species must have in order to qualify for language, but they are two that seem to be basic.

Sarah was capable of displacement, of comprehending statements about "things that are not there." When given the instruction "brown color of chocolate" as a means of introducing "brown" and subsequently told "take brown," she performed correctly, choosing the brown disk from the four that were offered. The chimpanzee's ability to comprehend statements about "things that are not there" derives from its demonstrated ability to store adequate representations of items and to use words to retrieve the information it has stored. In substituting, say, the word "apple" without loss of accuracy for an actual apple in all of the matching tests, it gave direct proof of this ability. Displacement is not a uniquely linguistic phenomenon but the consequence of a certain quality of memory.

SECOND-ORDER RELATIONS

Even the simplest sentence contains both relational and absolute terms. Consider such sentences as "Daddy home," "Mommy purse," "Bill hit Mary," and "Mommy take flower." In the last two cases, the relational terms—"hit" and "take"—are explicit, whereas in the first two strings the relations are not explicitly marked, and strings of this kind are interpreted as sentences by inferring the relations. In the first case, we may infer a locative type of relation between daddy and home, e.g., "Daddy is home," and in the second, convert the two-word string into a sentence by interpreting the string as a genetive relation, e.g., "Mommy's purse." These examples suggest that a sentence could be defined, in the weakest possible sense, as a string of words in which there is an implicit or explicit dependence among the words of a kind that can be represented by the relation between a predicate and its arguments. The point of this definition is to stress that a sentence is inconceivable without a relational term, either explicit or implicit. A species that could not learn a relational term and thus could not fulfill even this weak condition could not possibly fulfill the inordinately stronger conditions imposed by adult sentence structures.

Second, it is not sufficient that the species be capable of responding to relations; to acquire language it must be able to respond to relations between relations. This can be seen even in such simple predicates as "same-different," which are nonetheless representative of more complex predicates such as "name of," "color of," "if-then," and the like. For instance, when pigeons are given two red particles on some trials, a red and a grey particle on other trials, and are required to peck on the left when given the former and on the right when given the latter, they ultimately learn to do so; i.e., to respond differentially to A-A and A-B. However, when given B-B, or comparable cases instanced by new elements, e.g., C-C, C-A, and the like, they respond at chance. Correct responding requires that the subject be able to observe not only that the relation between, say, red and red is same, as that between say, grey and grey is likewise same, but also that the relation between red and red is the same as that between grey and grey. Calling the first relation same$_1$ and the second one same$_2$, the subject must recognize that same$_1$ is the same as same$_2$—a recognition involving a second-order relation, or the ability to respond to a relation between relations. Identical requirements apply to all other language predicates. For instance, to use "name of" productively, the subject must recognize that the relation between, say, "apple" and apple ("apple" name of apple) is the same as that between, say, "banana" and banana; i.e., that name of$_1$ is the same as name of$_2$.

If the subject belonged to a species that lacked a capacity for second-order relations, each time a predicate occurred with a new argument, the subject would have to be retaught the predicate. The tendency to diminish this phenomenon by calling it (nothing but) generalization, does not evade the fact that, even if we view the phenomenon in this light, it is evidently not a kind of generalization that is open to all species.

The evidence for second-order relations in nonprimates is slight. That the rat may be capable of acquiring second-order relations in the case of brightness is indicated in an ingenious study by Lawrence and DeRivera,[15] a study that in view of its importance seriously needs to be replicated. There is a bit of evidence for the dog in the case of same-different judgments,[11] a finding that needs to be amplified as well as repeated; and recent, more substantial evidence for this same capacity in the Dolphin.[16] Although we can say that a capacity to learn second-order relations is a necessary condition for language, we cannot yet say in which species the capacity is found. Neither can we say whether if a species evidences the capacity for one predicate, it will do so for all other predicates. Although in man capacities tend to be general, this is apparently less so in other species. Conceivably, the rat could learn second-order relations in the case of brightness but not for other distinctions.

CONDITIONABILITY AND VOLUNTARY CONTROL OF THE MOTOR SYSTEM

Beginning from remarkably different data bases, Myers[17] and Chevalier-Skolnikoff[18] have reached strikingly similar conclusions. In man, all sensory-motor systems are encephalized, subject to voluntary control and conditionable; in short, they are all equally capable of expressing intelligence. This is not true in the ape, however, and it is even less true in the monkey. Chevalier-Skolnikoff reached this conclusion through observing infants. Using Piaget's sensory-motor intelligence and imitation series, she coded the behavior of human, gorilla, and monkey (Macaque) infants, examining not only the stage each species attained, but also the sensory-motor mode in which the stage was realized. The human infant completed the sensory-motor series in all modes; the ape in the tactile/kinesthetic, visual/body, visual/facial, and visual/gesture modes, but not in the vocal and auditory modes; and the monkey in only the tactive/kinesthetic and visual/body modes. Results for the imitation series are largely comparable. Chevalier-Skolnikoff summarized her findings with such phrases as ". . . intelligence is not necessarily a global capacity . . . an animal may not be able to demonstrate a cognitive capacity with its voice that it can express with its hand."

What detracts from Chevalier-Skolnikoff's otherwise interesting conclusions is that the categories with which she coded the infants' behavior are themselves ambiguous. Some acts are coded as intentional, whereas others are dismissed as reflexive, although there are no clear rules for distinguishing between them. The most critical category, diagnostic of the highest sensory-motor intelligence, involving "invention of new means through mental combinations," is reported without comment as to the difficulty of identifying such cases; a difficulty recognized by, for example, the historical controversy between Köhler[19] and Thorndike[20] concerning whether learning occurs by insight or by trial and error. There is a further lack of appreciation for von Schiller's[21] data which showed that the likelihood a response sequence would contribute an insightful solution to a problem depended on whether or not elements in the sequence had previously occurred in the chimpanzee's play.

Relying on neuroanatomical and conditioning studies, rather than infant behavior, Myers concluded that facial expression and vocalization are not volitional or conditionable in infrahuman primates in the degree they are in man. Ablation of "speech" areas in monkey cortex—areas corresponding to speech areas in man— produced little deficit in vocalization,[22-25] whereas ablation of appropriate limbic areas produced marked deficits.[24,26] In addition, most attempts to condition vocalization in monkeys, including Myer's own, have been only partly successful, at best. Contrasting these failures with the ready conditioning of forelimb responses in the same species, he concluded along with Lancaster,[27] Premack and Schwartz,[28] and others that vocalization in infrahuman primates is largely emotional, limbic, and species-specific. Therefore, vocalization in apes and monkeys should be contrasted with speech—which is cortical, volitional and learned—and not seen as the source of it.

Conditionability is not a unitary factor but concerns the modifiability of three factors: response form, rate of occurrence, and the stimulus occasions on which the response occurs. On the sensory side it may also concern the subject's ability to discriminate responses—facial expression, vocalization, forelimb movements—and to associate them as stimulus events with other responses. Most of the emphasis in the present discussion has concerned the first factor, modifying the form of the response; therefore I will concentrate on that factor.

Since there has been no genuine comparative study of the conditionability of the different motor systems either within or between species, it is not possible to say one system is more conditionable than the other. There have been scattered reports of failures to condition vocalization in monkey, along with some reports of success, and of course it is true that most operant conditioning is based on forelimb and pecking responses. These sociological facts do not necessarily converge on a biological conclusion, however, for they may reflect technical difficulty, such as the fact that it is more difficult to arrange contingencies with vocalization and facial expression than with bar presses and key pecks.

Although reports of modest success [29,30] have been countered by reports of failure to condition vocalizations in monkey,[31] Green [32] has recently found not only indirect evidence for conditioning of vocalization but also evidence for imitation of vocalization in monkeys. He observed differences in the fine structure of the food call of three adjacent Japanese Macaque troops, and argues convincingly that these "dialects" are related to learned factors. The calls occur during food provisioning, a practice first begun when some of the monkeys on the islands were older and not inclined to imitate; these same monkeys are the only members of the group that do not show the dialects or variation in the fine structure of their food calls. This field observation emphasizes our classical difficulty in interpreting negative outcomes, a difficulty further complicated by the recent emphasis of biological constraints on learning.

One determinant of conditionability is the magnitude of variation to be found in the unconditioned state of the response. It is difficult to modify a system that has little or no variability in the first place; what appears to be differential susceptibility to conditioning may thus depend on an unconditioned factor, one that may indirectly affect conditionability. For instance, the change in heart rate, body temperature, and the like can be produced by exploiting the variation that exists in these responses. Because 98.6 degrees is an average temperature, with a distribution of both higher and lower values, by rewarding the higher values, it is possible to produce higher than normal average temperatures. If the subject is rewarded in those intervals when its temperature is, say, 98.8, and the reward is successful, there will be an upward shift in the distribution, after which the criterion can be increased again, with further upward shifts in the distribution. (Whether values higher than those found in the original distribution can be produced in this manner is not yet known.) Marler[33] and Nottebohm[34] propose that vocal learning, which is a precondition for speech, requires openness or unconditioned variability in the species' calls, a view entirely compatible with my own.

Conditionability also concerns the rate at which a response occurs or the occasions on which it occurs. Modification of rate and occasion are less dependent on unconditioned variability than on whether or not the response has a well-defined or discriminable feedback. Operant conditioners implicitly exploit feedback by arranging that the operation of the lever or disc be accompanied by a cue, such as a relay click, which signals the end of the operation. Though this factor has been more exploited than studied, it is probably important for sequential learning. Some years ago Jacobson, Rugh, and I tried to condition rats to perform a series of responses that did not coincide with a natural sequence but was arbitrarily considered a unit by an artificial sensing device. Whenever the rat occupied some portion of the cage for a minimum period of time and simultaneously kept a part of its body above a vertical line, the sensing equipment registered a response. We were not able to modify the frequency of this arbitrary sequence by reinforcing it. Similarly, human observers who observed the rats were largely unable to describe the rat behavior that caused the device to signal. There was little consensus among observers, individual observers were inconsistent over trials, and only four of twelve subjects were able to give a correct definition of the responses that would actually cause the sensing device to produce a signal.

A simple clinical test has enabled neurologists successfully to distinguish between emotional and intentional facial expressions and vocalizations, according to Myers. On one occasion, they ask patients to smile (or scream) and, on another, expose them to a joke (that may produce a smile) or a kick (that may produce a scream). They sometimes find patients with deficits in emotional but not in volitional smiles or screams, and vice versa, these corresponding to lesions that are in predominantly limbic or cortical areas. Veterinarians would have difficulty with the neurologists' test, although with nonverbal animals it may be possible to substitute play for verbal instruction. Does an animal bare teeth, scream, snarl, only when fighting? Do pelvic thrusts and neck biting occur only during copulation? Are these responses not frequently seen in play? The more often a response occurs in play, the more likely is it to be subject to voluntary control (although I am not certain that play has been shown to be associated with cortical control).

Despite the classical difficulty of distinguishing between voluntary and reflexive, invention with and without prior motor behavior, and the like, the basic conclusion of Chevalier-Skolnikoff and Myers is redeemed by the simple difference in frequency with which acts of certain kinds occur in the sensory-motor systems of the several primate species. Provided the intent is not to argue from negative evidence as to what species can and cannot do, or to distinguish categorically between limbic and cortical control, it is probably both safe and revealing to consider that the sheer frequency of certain acts—and thus the underlying indigenous disposition to express the acts— closely measures how well formed the capacity is in the species. An especially well-developed capacity will be expressed often, in all possible sensory-motor modes, and will attain complex forms of expression indicative of the highest level of cognitive availability. For example, children acquire reference relations with scant training, and correspondingly engage in frequent symbolic play, using one item to stand for another both in language and in play. Chimpanzees, by contrast, can be taught reference relations only with struggle, and correspondingly are seldom observed to engage spontaneously in nonverbal symbolic play (see Premack[35] for a few exceptions). Insensitive readings of ape behavior in the wild may underestimate the ape's untutored use of symbols, but I do not expect the most sensitive readings to close the gap between ape and man. In keeping with this simple difference in frequency of manifestation of symbolic acts, I do not anticipate reading essays on symbolization written by chimpanzees. The capacity to symbolize is undeniably present in the chimpanzee; it will meet the most rigorous operational standards, but this does not conceal the fact that the capacity in the ape is frail compared to the one in man.

ASSOCIATIVE MODELS AND THE LEARNING OF WORDS

What associative model best describes the procedure(s) used to teach words to the apes? The answer seems clearly instrumental or operant conditioning, in contrast to either classical conditioning or autoshaping, for in the beginning at least the procedure entailed a clear correlation between the performance of the subject and that of the trainer. Only if the subject put the word, say, "apple" on the board in the presence of the piece of apple did the trainer give the subject the piece of apple, and this requirement held in all cases. Later, however, words were introduced in other ways, either by explicit instruction such as "'peach' name of peach," "brown color of chocolate," and the like, or by the informal though no less effective procedure of simply holding a new piece of plastic beside a so-far unnamed object. In these cases there was no correlation between the subject's response and what the trainer gave the subject: the subject did nothing other than look at or attend to the stimuli, and the trainer did not give the subject anything except perhaps an approving glance. These cases are less easy to ascribe to one associative model or the other. If we treat them as classical conditioning, it is far more because of the absence of an instrumental correlation than because of an explicit resemblance between the training and classical conditioning.

In deciding which of the traditional associative models describes the acquisition of words most aptly, we are diverted from a more important question. Ultimately, the basic question is not procedural, not a question of what the trainer did, but a question of what the subject learned as a result of the procedure. Even if apes and pigeons were exposed to the identical procedure, it is quite possible that what they learned would not be identical. The representations these and other species form of the stimuli and/or responses that are to be associated may not be the same. Higher species may form more determinate representations, organize the information more hierarchically, rely more (or less) on prototypes, adjust the kind of representation they use in different situations more flexibly. Furthermore, a greater proportion of the information contained in the representations may enter into the associations in higher species—that the full content of a representation is invariably conditioned does not seem to have been established—and that proportion may be both more subject to adjustment and sensitive to situational demands. These questions are not easily answered, and unfortunately, they receive little help from the response measures used in traditional learning experiments. For example, two species may both respond discriminatively to the same stimulus, as well as show the same response pattern to the reinforcement schedule, and yet differ in the information they can retrieve with the discriminative stimulus. One species may be able to use the stimulus to retrieve a powerful description of the reward associated with the stimulus, whereas the nature of the other species may be such that for it the question of what can be retrieved with the stimulus is virtually unanswerable. If match-to-sample procedures are not applicable to a species so that it cannot engage in features analyses, there is no alternative but to systematically alter possibly relevant aspects of the stimulus situation, feature by feature, or in some other manner, and then relate these changes to traditional response measures. This approach is so arduous that I would expect to see little answer to representational questions for any species that is accessible only by this approach.

Although many critics of this line of research are well justified in their criticism, others seem to have missed the point. How profoundly they have missed it is sometimes shown in the accusation with which they would open a discussion. "Those are not words," they say, pointing to the pieces of plastic. "They are nothing but conditioned stimuli." This accusation implies that human words were not also learned by an associative procedure, or that children when first learning words did not do so by associating words and referents. The accusation errs further in assuming that the true nature of a conditioned stimulus has been definitively established. If the critic has in mind, as he most likely does, the account of conditioning given in most introductory psychology tests, then he is quite correct in maintaining that the human word is not a conditioned stimulus. By the same argument, however, he should also maintain that the chimpanzee word is not a conditioned stimulus. All language learning begins inescapably with an associative procedure of some kind. The question of import is, What was learned as a result of the association?

CATEGORICAL DISCRIMINATION OF SPEECH SOUNDS

"Because there has been great difficulty accounting for the perception of speech sounds in terms of invariant acoustic properties, theorists have proposed that speech sounds are recognized by 'special processing' . . . ,"[36,37] either phonetic feature detectors[38] or speech-sound decoders compatible with the "motor theory" of speech perception. Both forms have been thought to be unique to man. This general view was encouraged by the recent finding of categorical speech sound detection in human infants: month-old infants discriminate speech sounds in the categorical manner characteristic of adult speakers.[38] However, the relevance of the infant data for the assumption of species-specific speech-processing devices has been called into question by additional data of two kinds. First, nonhuman species have been found to discriminate certain speech sounds in a categorical manner. Rhesus monkeys[40] and chinchillas,[39,41] whose auditory capabilities are similar to man's, discriminate the voiced-voiceless distinction in the contrast between /t/ and /d/ in essentially the same categorical manner as the adult human speaker. Second, categorical discrimination, once taken to be unique to discrimination of speech sounds, has since been found for nonspeech sounds. Adult human listeners discriminate between a bowed and plucked instrument in a categorical manner.[42] Given, on the one hand, that speech sounds are discriminated categorically by nonhuman species and, on the other, that nonspeech sounds are also discriminated categorically, the discrimination of speech sounds may not depend on devices that are unique either as an auditory device or as a device specific to species. The acoustic properties of certain sounds, for reasons that remain to be formalized, may make them especially discriminable, and these kinds of sounds may form the physical basis of speech. The neuroanatomical properties underlying categorical perception, be it of speech or nonspeech sounds, may be quite primitive. Consider that monkeys have relatively little voluntary control of vocalization and yet discriminate speech sounds categorically. Speech-sound discrimination may thus depend on properties of the auditory system laid down before brain lateralization and even before encephalization of the auditory-vocal system. This could suggest that the productive and receptive structures for speech had separate evolutionary histories, the receptive occurring well before the productive. From this we might infer that lateralization had more to do with the production than with the comprehension of speech sounds. All of this is recognizably speculative.

INTERMODAL ASSOCIATION

Differences in the angular gyrus area in primates led Geschwind[43] to propose that the capacity for forming intermodal associations would be proportional to the neuroanatomical parameter. He suggested, for example, that since words are intermodal associations, primarily visual-auditory, speech would be possible only in man. Those interested in language as opposed to speech sidestepped the problem by using sign and other visual forms of language, although sidesteps may not have been entirely necessary. Apes have been shown to be capable of intermodal association, including visual-haptic, haptic-visual[44] and gustatory-visual.[11] More recently, haptic-visual association has also been shown in monkeys.[45] However, the case of greatest interest to language, visual-auditory, has remained recalcitrant. Davenport[44] and his group reported a recent failure with chimpanzees. Their studies required apes to match long and short pulses of sound to long and short flashes of light, respectively. The failure must be regarded as inconclusive, rather than final, for duration may or may not be a salient factor for apes. They may do well matching soft and loud tones to dim and bright lights, or few and many bleeps to few and many flashes. In addition, the form of the test, independent of the intensity and numerosity dimensions used, is more demanding than necessary for demonstrating simple intermodal association.

With a less demanding test, we found not only auditory-visual associations but in addition, a series of associations evidently formed on an incidental basis.[1] When chimpanzees were learning plastic words, trainers frequently accompanied the words and their referents with spoken English, as in the early stages of training, a trainer might teach the animal the plastic words "TAKE APPLE," while saying "Take apple." Approximately two years after their language training had been discontinued, we tested two of the apes, Sarah and Peony, for evidence of auditory-visual associations by giving them instructions only in spoken English with no plastic words present at all. For example, while offering an apple, banana, and orange, the trainer told the animals to "Take apple." Both Sarah and Peony performed significantly above chance, although the plastic words were absent, indicating that they could choose the correct visual item on the basis of auditory instruction alone.

In our test, the subject had only to associate a stimulus in one modality with an arbitrary second stimulus in another modality, whereas in the Davenport tests, the animal had to associate the same item experienced in two different modalities.[44] This requirement is substantially more demanding and undoubtably presupposes mechanisms not involved in our study. Certainly there are species that could pass the one test but not the other. To pass the Davenport *et al.* tests, an animal must have a capacity to map two kinds of information; for example, it must be able to translate the sounds an object makes in rolling along a surface into the shape of the object. Words do not require a mapping ability of this complexity. The animal has only to associate arbitrary stimuli from different modalities—the requirement of the simple test.

Ultimately, intermodal association is significant both because it underlies speech, and because it makes an abstract kind of representation possible. In species capable of intermodal association, an item can be represented in memory in a unified way despite the different modalities in which the species may have experienced the item. Rain, for instance, which can be experienced as sound, a fresh smell, a drop, or by wetness, could be represented by a single item. If a species could not make intermodal associations, each of these experiences would be isolated from the other; so from the sound of rain in the distant trees, such a species, on entering the forest would never be prepared, in spite of the patter of the rain, for the drenching it inevitably received.

This ethological example might raise some doubt as to whether there are any mammalian species that are incapable of simple intermodal association. The earlier assumption that monkeys lacked this capacity, which has since been infirmed, may have prevented investigators from testing still lower species. But it is time to restudy nonprimates on this problem, keeping in mind while doing so the distinction between demonstrations of intermodal association that do and do not require mapping information from one modality into another. The issue of intermodal association illustrates a general problem of reductionism. Translating neuroanatomical differences into behavioral ones, while a desirable enterprise, is at the same time a risky one.

This survey did not lead to the discovery of qualitative differences between man and other species. Those who find satisfaction in this failure will insist that this is the simple truth of the matter: There is both mental and anatomical continuity from one species to another; all differences are quantitative. It is also possible, however, that the inability to find more radical differences is revelatory not of the genuine lack of such differences but of simple ignorance. I do not think the latter view can be dismissed at this time, and in this sense I may be in closer accord with the humanist than the biologist. In one sense, however, I am surely not in accord with the humanist. Even on those occasions when my intuitions outbid my logic, and "I" insist that man is unique, I cannot accept the arrogance that believes it knows in what the uniqueness consists.

References

1. PREMACK, D. 1976. Intelligence in Ape and Man. Lawrence Erlbaum Assoc. Hillsdale, N.J. In press.
2. KINTSCH, W. 1975. Representation of Meaning in Memory. Lawrence Erlbaum Assoc. Hillsdale, N.J.
3. HAYES, K. J. & C. H. NISSEN. 1971. Higher mental functions of a home-raised chimpanzee. *In* Behavior of Nonhuman Primates. Vol. 4. A. M. Schrier and F. Stollnitz, Eds. Academic Press. New York, N.Y.
4. DAVENPORT, R. K. & C. M. ROGERS. 1971. Perception of photographs by apes. Behaviour 39: 2-4.
5. MENZEL, E. W. 1973. Chimpanzee spatial memory organization. Science 182: 943-945.
6. TINKELPAUGH, O. L. 1932. Multiple delayed reactions with chimpanzees and monkeys. J. Comp. Psychol. 13: 207-243.
7. SHEPARD, R. N. 1975. Form, formation, and transformation of internal representations. *In* Information Processing and Cognition: The Loyola Symposium. R. Solso, Ed. Lawrence Erlbaum Assoc. Hillsdale, N.J.
8. SALAPATEK, P. 1975. Pattern perception in early infancy. Infant Perception: From Sensation to Cognition. In L. B. Cohen and P. Salapatek, Eds. Vol. 1. Academic Press. New York, N.Y.
9. OLTON, D. S. & R. J. SAMUELSON. 1976. Remembrance of places passed: spatial memory in rats. J. Exper. Psychol.: An. Behav. Proc. 2: 97-116.
10. VAN IERSEL, J. A. A. & J. VAN DEN ASSAM. 1969. Aspects of orientation in the diggerwasp *Bembix rostrata*. Animal Behaviour (Suppl.) 1: 145-162.
11. PREMACK, D. 1971. Language in chimpanzee? Science 172: 808-822.
12. RUMBAUGH, D. M. & T. V. GILL. This volume.
13. GARDNER, R. A. & B. GARDNER. 1969. Teaching sign language to a chimpanzee. Science 165: 664-672.
14. FOUTS, R. 1972. The use of guidance in teaching sign language to a chimpanzee. J. Comp. Psychol. 80: 515-522.
15. LAWRENCE, D. H. & J. DeRIVERA. 1954. Evidence for relational transposition. J. Comp. Physiol. Psychol. 47: 465-471.
16. HERMAN, L. M. & J. A. GORDON. 1974. Auditory delayed matching in the bottlenose dolphin. J. Exp. Anal. Behav. 21: 19-26.
17. MYERS, R. E. This volume.
18. CHEVALIER-SKOLNIKOFF, S. This volume.
19. KÖHLER, W. 1951. Mentality of Apes. The Humanities Press, Inc. New York, N.Y.
20. THORNDIKE, E. 1911. Animal Intelligence. MacMillan. New York, N.Y.
21. VON SCHILLER, P. H. 1952. Innate constituents of complex responses in primates. Psychol. Rev. 59: 177-191.

22. MYERS, R. E. 1969. Neurology of social communication in primates. Proc. 2nd Int. Congr. Primatol. **3:** 1–9. Karger. Basel, Switzerland.
23. YAMAGUCHI, S. & R. E. MYERS. Cortical mechanisms underlying vocalization in rhesus monkey: prefrontal-orbitofrontal, anterior temporal, and cingulate cortex. Neuropsychologia. In press.
24. YAMAGUCHI, S. & R. E. MYERS. Effects of "speech" area lesions on vocalization in monkey. Brain Res. In press.
25. SUTTON, D., C. LARSON & R. C. LINDEMAN. 1974. Neocortical and limbic lesion effects on primate phonation. Brain Res. **71:** 61–75.
26. ERVIN, F. R., M. RALEIGH & H. D. STEKLIS. 1975. The orbital frontal center and monkey social behavior. 5th Annual Mtg., Soc. Neurosci.: 554. New York, N.Y.
27. LANCASTER, J. B. 1968. Primate communication systems and the emergence of human language. *In* Primates. J. C. Jay, Ed.: New York: Holt, Rinehart & Winston, 439–457.
28. PREMACK, D. & A. SCHWARTZ. 1966. Preparations for discussing behaviorism with chimpanzee. *In* The Genesis of Language. F. L. Smith and G. A. Miller, Eds. M.I.T. Press. Cambridge, Mass.
29. MYERS, S. A., J. A. HOREL & H. S. PENNYBACKER. 1965. Operant control of vocal behavior in the monkey *Cebus albifrons. Psychonomic Sci.* **3:** 389–390.
30. SUTTON, D., C. LARSON, E. M. TAYLOR & R. C. LINDEMAN. 1973. Vocalization in rhesus monkey: conditionability. Brain Res. **52:** 225–231.
31. YAMAGUCHI, S. & R. E. MYERS. 1972. Failure of discriminative vocal conditioning in rhesus monkey. Brain Res. **37:** 109–114.
32. GREEN, S. 1975. Dialects in Japanese monkeys: vocal learning and cultural transmission of locale-specific vocal behavior? Z. Tierpsychol. **38:** 304–314.
33. MARLER, P. 1975. On the origin of speech from animal sounds. *In* The Role of Speech in Language. J. F. Kavanagh and J. E. Cutting, Eds.: 11–37. M.I.T. Press. Cambridge, Mass.
34. NOTTEBOHM, F. 1975. A zoologist's view of some language phenomena with particular emphasis on vocal learning. *In* Foundations of Language Development. E. H. Lenneberg and E. Lenneberg, Eds.: 61–97. Academic Press. New York, N.Y.
35. PREMACK, D. 1975. Putting a face together. Science **188:** 228–236.
36. LIBERMAN, A. M. 1970. The grammars of speech and language. *Cognitive Psychol.* **1:** 301–323.
37. STEVENS, K. N. & A. S. HOUSE. 1972. Speech perception. *In* Foundations of Modern Auditory Theory. J. V. Tobias, Ed. Academic Press. New York, N.Y.
38. EIMAS, P. D. & J. D. CORBIT. 1973. Selective adaptation of linguistic feature detectors. Cognitive Psychol. **4:** 99–109.
39. KUHL, P. K. & J. D. MILLER. 1975. Speech perception by the chinchilla: voiced-voiceless distinction in alveolar plosive consonants. Science **190:** 69–72.
40. MORSE, P. A. & C. T. SNOWDON. 1975. An investigation of categorical speech discrimination by rhesus monkeys. Percept. Psychophys. **17:** 9–16.
41. BURDICK, C. K. & J. D. MILLER. 1975. Speech perception by the chinchilla: discrimination of sustained /a/ and /i/. J. Acoust. Soc. Am. **58:** 415–427.
42. CUTTING, J. E. & B. ROSNER. 1974. Categories and boundaries in speech and music. Perceptions and Psychophysics **16:** 564–570.
43. GESCHWIND, N. 1964. The development of the brain and the evolution of language. *In* Monograph Series on Language and Linguistics. C. I. J. M. Stuart, Ed.: 155–169. Georgetown University Press. Washington, D.C.
44. DAVENPORT, R. K. Cross-modal perceptions in apes. This volume.
45. COWEY, A. & L. WEISKRANTZ. 1975. Demonstration of cross-modal matching in rhesus monkeys, *Macaca mulatta.* Neuropsychologia **13:** 117–120.
46. CHOMSKY, N. 1965. Aspects of the Theory of Syntax. M.I.T. Press. Cambridge, Mass.
47. SKINNER, B. F. 1957. Verbal Behavior. Appleton-Century-Crofts, Inc. New York, N.Y.
48. TELEKI, G. 1974. The omnivorous chimpanzee. *In* Biological Anthropology. S. H. Katz, Ed. W. H. Freeman & Co. San Francisco, Calif.

THE MASTERY OF LANGUAGE-TYPE SKILLS
BY THE CHIMPANZEE (*PAN*)*

Duane M. Rumbaugh and Timothy V. Gill

Georgia State University
Atlanta, Georgia 30303
and
Yerkes Regional Primate Research Center
Emory University
Atlanta, Georgia 30322

Studies of chimpanzee language-relevant skills stimulated by Project Washoe[1] are having a major impact upon scientific thought regarding the nature of language, ape, and man. The purpose of this paper is (1) to examine certain basic assumptions, methods, and findings of these studies, (2) to examine implications for the definitions of communication and language, (3) to consider short- and long-term directions of chimpanzee language research and its possible applications, and finally, (4) to survey the results of the Lana Language Project.

BASIC ASSUMPTIONS

Although initially the Gardners' research[1] was presented primarily in the context of "two-way communication" and Premack's[2] in terms of "intelligence" and the partitioning of language into basic functional units, both parties now are more immediately concerned with the properties of language, the acquisition of specific language skills, and with comparisons between the linguistic performances of the chimpanzee and human child from a developmental/comparative perspective.[3,4] These same issues have concerned the interdisciplinary team of the Lana Language Project.[5,6] A fundamental assumption of all of these projects, then, has been that language—whatever its requisites, processes, and functions might be—may not be a uniquely human attribute: certain rudiments of language may be discernible in life forms other than man.

A second major assumption has been that near relatives of man—the great apes (Pongidae)—are the most promising subjects for this line of inquiry. Although other animal forms might master certain linguistic-type skills, the apes, with their relatively well-developed brains, should be more competent. Of the apes, chimpanzees have been the favorite subjects, although not because they are the most intellectually endowed of the pongids. In fact, empirical evidence supports the conclusion that either there is no major difference among the three great ape genera (*Gorilla, Pan, Pongo*) for the presumed higher-order cognitive processes measured by the Transfer Index,[7] a learning set[8] technique designed for comparative assessments, or that if there is a difference, the edge is held by either *Pongo* or *Gorilla*, and not *Pan*. Quite apart from that assessment, it is probably true that the captive chimpanzee interacts more naturally with man than does either the gorilla or the orangutan, an important consideration, since all of the language projects have entailed close working relationships between man and ape. As the Gardners selected the American Sign Language

*This research was supported by National Institutes of Health grants HD-06016 and RR-00165.

for the Deaf (Ameslan)[9] for their research, it was critical that their subject have a well-developed, hominian hand. All the great apes are thus qualified; however, the chimpanzee promised a certain advantage because of the evidence that it commonly uses its hands for gestural communication in the field.[10]

A third assumption has been that language is not contingent upon speech, or, in a broader sense, the vocal-auditory channel. The essential failure of earlier efforts[11] to teach chimpanzees to speak directed the attention of the Gardners to a "speechless" language, Ameslan. For Premack,[12] it directed efforts toward the innovation of a language in which plastic units served as words, and for the Lana Project[5] it spurred the development of a computer-based language-training system in which distinctive keys on a console functioned as words. All three of these approaches are consonant with Hewes' thesis that the origin of language might have been nonvocal, e.g. gestural.[13]

Views regarding when the ape subject should be introduced to language training and what the environment should be warrant special attention. The Gardners[3] have concluded that the ape subjects should be steeped in a rich linguistic context and should be started in formal training as soon as possible after birth; only then might the full capabilities of the ape be realized in its mature years. By contrast, Premack's initial work was with a young juvenile chimpanzee, Sarah, and his reports reflect impressive accomplishments despite the fact that she was about six years old when training commenced, that she was maintained in a cage of standard proportions for primate laboratories, and that she was worked with during a relatively small portion of each day. To continue, and still by contrast, Lana Chimpanzee was slightly over two years of age when training commenced in the basic confines of a primate laboratory; apart from formal sessions, the day's events (including outings and social interactions with her attendants) were contingent upon her mastery and execution of language-type skills at her keyboard.

Although the Gardners make a convincing case for starting their subjects in Ameslan as soon after birth as feasible, the results of the Lana Language Project indicate that the critical age might not be quite so young. In fact, it is our impression that Lana's rapid progress would have been no greater and possibly not so great had she been started at an earlier age. There is a considerable difference, however, between methods that require subjects to produce lexical units through manual/limb movements (Ameslan) and those that ask subjects to manipulate plastic units or keys on the console of a computer-controlled system. Consequently, the ideal age for commencing training might differ with the method employed.

It is important that the necessary studies be conducted to determine whether the optimal course of language-type skill training with apes parallels the course of language acquisition for the human child. To the degree that the two are similar, homologous (as opposed to analogous) processes supporting their functions would be suggested. And to the degree that homology is evidenced, the more likely it is that new perspectives of man's language and attendant abilities can be gained through comparative studies of the apes.

TRAINING VS. TESTING

All three of the basic approaches—the teaching of Ameslan,[1] the use of a plastic-word language,[12] and the computer-controlled system approach[5]—entail a one-on-one training procedure and, consequently, intense human involvement.

The presence of the human has been a cause for concern; there is the possibility that the ape subjects might be cued, allowing them to perform at levels speciously beyond whatever linguistic competence they might have. This concern, though warranted, is not new to behavioral studies; controls must always be carefully designed and implemented to preclude cueing of performances from all sources, including the experimenter and extraneous aspects of equipment function (relay operations, etc.)

There has been a special problem of employing controls in ape-language *training*, however: frequently it has been impossible to utilize a tightly controlled procedure, such as a discrete-trial method, for initially there has been little to indicate what kind of training will be effective. Consequently, training frequently has been of a pilot or exploratory nature—informal, with modifications implemented and guided judgmentally. (This is but *one* limitation when N = 1.) But once *training* methods have been perfected, tightly controlled *testing* sessions can be (and have been) interjected so as to *test* the subject's proficiency level in a unequivocal fashion. During test sessions it should not be too disconcerting if the subject performs at a level slightly below that during training. Apes are particularly stressed by alterations of a social nature; because the experimenter and animal are isolated during tests, a performance decrement can result without its necessarily being the case that the performance level during training was speciously supported by cueing from the experimenter.

For the foregoing reasons, reports should clearly identify linguistic performance recorded in informal training as opposed to formal test sessions. Understandably, it is difficult to assess *all* linguistic functions (as when man and ape converse) under conditions of tight experimental control, for language acquisition as a form of *cognitive socialization*[14] calls for interaction between animates. Nonetheless, direct social contact with the apes must be denied from time to time so that tests of proficiency can be conducted objectively. Apart from the scheduled tests, there are occasional fortuitous instances in which the ape subject, on its own initiative and in solitude, behaves linguistically in a convincing manner, its performance recorded by video tape, film,[15] or a secluded observer. In a sense, these are "self-controlled" demonstrations of competence; however, they are weak to the degree that the antecedents are obscure, hence not accessible for experimental manipulation.

COMMON FINDINGS

Apes are rather facile in the acquisition of vocabulary, regardless of the three methods (above) employed. The limit of their vocabulary acquisition is clearly beyond 200 words, "words" in the sense that upon perception of an exemplar a correct response of identification (sign, key depression, etc.) is reliably given. But the important question is—"How do we know when the ape subject *understands* words in a conceptual sense?" After all, it is not difficult to conceive of an ape giving 500 conditioned responses to 500 discriminative stimuli in the same manner as a good dog can learn to respond differentially to a large number of vocal and hand signals for work in the field. Is there a difference between *responding correctly* and *knowing*, and if there is, how might that difference be detected?

We hold that vocabulary *qua* vocabulary, though necessary for other linguistic functions, is not convincing evidence of linguistic competence. Only when the subject productively uses a word in novel interaction with other words (syntactically) is there evidence that it has a conceptual meaning, hence "knows" the word. For Lana to have asked, as she did, for an orange (fruit) as though it were an apple[6] might have been a simple instance of stimulus generalization, the name "apple" being given in response to an apple-like object, the orange, for which she had no name. But for her to ask for the orange as the "apple which-is orange (colored)" reflects conceptual recognition of certain similarities of apples and oranges as things to eat and/or things that are round and, further, the recognition of at least one difference between them— their color. That she reliably asked for the orange as the "apple which-is orange" from that point on, suggests that complex cognitive processes were operating in the initial formulation of the novel term.

Apes also go beyond basic vocabulary usage quite readily. Washoe started to chain signs into strings very early in training, even when she had mastered only ten or twelve. Why this is so is not clear, but there seems to be a readiness for apes to advance, on their own initiative, beyond the lowest common denominator of their trained competence.

The evidence is also clear that apes generalize or transfer word usage appropriately from original training contexts to novel, first-time-encountered problem contexts. Many instances can be recounted; for the purpose of this paper, the following instances must suffice: (1) Washoe transferred the use of the sign for "open"—learned in response to doors of her house—to all doors, to the lids of briefcases, boxes, and jars, and eventually to ask that a water faucet be turned on;[1] and she rejected the word "duck," terming the fowl instead, "water birds";[16] (2) Lana transferred her use of names and colors from her training set to a wide variety of novel objects and pictures; asked for an orange-colored (Fanta) soft drink as the "coke which-is orange" and an overly ripe banana as the "banana which-is black"; and spontaneously asked for the name of a container baited with candies and then immediately used the name (box) to request that it be given to her.[17]

There are numerous other findings specific to the various language projects; however, the above listed ones—facile vocabulary acquisition, word chaining, and transfer of word usage—are, we believe, the main "universal" phenomena reported to date.

IMPLICATIONS FOR THE DEFINITIONS OF COMMUNICATION AND LANGUAGE

The problem of defining terms in this realm are exacerbated by the fact that we must use language to define both terms—language itself and communication—and their relationship.† We agree that communication subsumes language,[17] and we hold that language is differentiated from other forms of communication primarily by its openness and plasticity which allows for the exchange of novel messages. The openness of language is achieved mainly through the addition of new lexical units and through their interactional (syntactic) use which allows for the modulation of meanings.

Elsewhere,[17] we have argued that to the degree an organism has hominian intelligence, it has the private, covert, processes of symbolism and attendant concept formation; and that whatever the nature of these processes are, they *are* linguistic. We hold that language is inherent in the covert cognitive operations that provide for the comprehension of relationships, the formulation of strategies for problem solving, and other expressions of creativity. These operations also direct the search for the encoding of information in attempts to communicate via public, overt language-*type* communication. Successful communication clearly entails competent encoding and transmission by the communicator and competent reception and decoding of the communication by the receiver via reference to his own linguistic processes.

† Pointed out to the authors by Mr. Thomas G. Snider.

A requisite for this type of communication is that the communicator and the receiver must have basic agreements regarding the symbolic referents/meanings of the lexical units/signs/words employed in the public transmission. Only man's intelligence is sufficient for agreements to be approximated regarding the meanings/symbolic-referents of the lexical units. It would appear that the necessary intelligence levels must be higher than those of the anthropoid apes; otherwise they would have developed a public, language-type of communication in the field, if it is true that, as generally held, such communication has significant survival value. Man's intelligence is clearly sufficient to that end, and the success of the language projects with ape subjects serves as *prima facie* evidence that man's intelligence is also sufficiently keen to bridge the gap between his own and that of the anthropoid ape through the use of Ameslan and artificial language systems. Communication of man with apes has been possible, however, only because *both* parties, ape as well as man, have the covert cognitive processes of language.

DIRECTIONS OF CHIMPANZEE LANGUAGE RESEARCH AND POSSIBLE APPLICATIONS

There are obvious risks in predicting research trends; they will surely be in error. However, in the interests of gaining a reasonable perspective of where chimpanzee language research projects are and where they might well be directed for maximum contribution to science, we are willing to take at least minumum risk to proffer certain views and recommendations.

It seems clear that to date the chimpanzee language projects have served primarily to stimulate thought regarding the nature of man in relation to the great apes. The past decade has witnessed the accumulation of substantive biological evidence[18] that indicates a closer-than-expected similarity between man and ape, notably the chimpanzee. Although the animal-learning literature of the past 50 years contains numerous reports of concept mastery,[7] particularly by primates, the information has had negligible impact compared with that of the current language projects. The reasons for this observation are at least twofold: (1) it is generally accepted that while the majority of animal forms learn, none has learned anything which challenges that which man learns, and (2) apart from a relatively small number of comparative psychologists, there has been relatively little interest in the animal learning literature expressed by the scientific community. However, with demonstrations that chimpanzees can learn skills that suggest certain rudiments of man's advanced language-type communication system, reconsideration of (1) the chimpanzee's psychological and cognitive capabilities in relation to man's and (2) the essence of man's communication system have been of prime interest. Because the chimpanzee language projects have grown out of the field of comparative animal learning, we predict a renewed interest in animal learning studies, for eventually the data of the language projects must be synthesized with the other data and theory of that field.

Without question, the results of the ape language projects are in accord with the evolutionary perspective of comparative psychology. Although new abilities, such as language, might emerge as seemingly unique, mutant attributes of species, it is more probable that they emerge because of quantum evolutionary developments in processes selected for their adaptation value in dealing with other problems and functions in more primitive life forms. To us, it is the dimension of cognitive evolution that has laid the critical foundation for the emergence of language and the advanced creativity it provides in man; however, the cognitive skills which, in conjunction with other neurological and anatomic factors, allow for man's public language are extant and functional for other kinds of adaptations in man's nearest relatives which comprise the order Primates. Regardless of one's definition of language, man, or ape, the data from the ape language projects serve only to narrow the "cognitive gap" which separates man from ape and other animals.

With reference to the definition of the all-important term, *language,* it follows that totally anthropocentric definitions should be supplanted with one which takes into account clear implications of the evolutionary and comparative psychological perspective. In our estimation, the definition should be in terms of *processes* rather than performance attributes. To clarify, the psychological processes which allow for the execution of a public-type of linguistic communication should be of primary focus. To do otherwise, to define language in terms of the characteristics of natural language systems, denies any reasonable integration of the data from the ape language projects with man's linguistics. To define language in terms of competency with a specific set/variety of linguistic skills will not suffice either; the consequence will be only the unending escalation of the "language threshold" through amendment designed to keep the apes out of the linguistic domain. Our position is similar to Hymes',[19] in which he proposed to restrict the term *language* to refer to underlying structures and the use of the term *verbal behavior* to refer to everything else. Clearly, the use of the term *verbal behavior* would exclude all syntheses of data from ape-language projects, so we would not recommend its use. In its stead we recommend the term *language-type communication,* or, alternatively, Hymes' suggestion of language $_1$ and language $_2$ for reference, respectively, to underlying structures and to public linguistic communications.

Regarding the short- and long-term directions of ape language research, we believe that it will be characterized primarily by efforts (1) to demonstrate an increasing variety of linguistic-relevant skills, (2) to assess the relative efficacies of various training methods, (3) to define the psychological/cognitive requisites for the mastery of various linguistic skills, (4) to relate language development in children with the mastery of linguistically relevant skills by apes, and (5) to assess the feasibility of utilizing the chimpanzee as an animal model for linguistic-type research that must not be conducted with human children because of ethical constraints. With regard to the last projection, we envisage that future experiments will utilize groups of young chimpanzees, differentially maintained or stimulated at various levels of development in order to determine which cognitive requisites are crucial to the formulation of a readiness for the mastery of initial language skills. We believe that young apes might be of unique value in research programs directed to the definition of the requisites of first-language skills in the human child. Ideally, young apes would be used to pretest alternative rearing/treatment/educational programs to the benefit of the language-deficient child. Some efforts have already been made to this end; others are underway.

Lastly, we are hopeful that Norman and Rumelhart[20] are correct in their conjecture that a new field, *cognitive science,* might be emerging from the research in the related disciplines of linguistics, artificial intelligence, and psychology. Their perspective is that ". . . complex cognitive acts accompany the processes of language understanding and of recognizing perceptual events. Information in memory consists of all of our knowledge of the world. The process of understanding involves a large variety of cognitive processes, all working together to integrate new information into the structures that already exist in a person's mind." We would only change the word "person's" to "primates" and trust that continued comparative learning research and ape language studies will make important contributions to the field which Norman and Rumelhart see emerging.

THE LANA LANGUAGE PROJECT

The Lana Language Project began on February 1, 1972. Discussions between the senior author and Professor Harold Warner, a biomedical engineer of the Yerkes Laboratories, had led to the conclusion that it might be possible to develop a computer-controlled language-training situation so as (1) to objectify inquiry into the skills reported by the Gardners from Project Washoe, (2) to facilitate inquiry through use of modern technology that might reduce the investment of human effort, (3) to collect and record the linguistic-relevant behaviors in a fashion that would permit computerized summary and analysis, (4) to develop a technology that would support studies of replication and systematic variation of selected independent variables, and (5) to perfect training methods that might be applied to the benefit of language-deficient children. By doing so, we were confident that we would gain a better understanding of language and the requisites/parameters of its acquisition. We formed an interdisciplinary team, including a psycholinguist, Ernst von Glasersfeld, and a computer specialist, Pier Pisani, from the University of Georgia; Timothy V. Gill, an author of this paper, as a behavior specialist; Josephine V. Brown, of Georgia State University, as an infancy consultant; and Charles Bell, an electronics technician, which addressed itself to the myriad of questions and decisions inherent in the design and construction of a computer-controlled language-training system.

As the details of the sytem,[5] the language (*Yerkish*),[21] and the initial training methods and observations have been reported elsewhere,[17] only a brief summary will be given to prepare the reader for a review of basic findings and their interpretation. It is important to note that we viewed the project as a pilot study, a feasibility study for a novel approach to the language-relevant behaviors reported by the Gardners and by Premack. The Lana Language Project is a beginning point, not an end. (After all, among other limitations, when N = 1, the constraints are numerous.)

We wanted a system that would be operational 24 hours each day and that would put the majority of control over the events of each day into the linguistic competence of the ape subject. To this end, we designed one in which the subject and the researcher were equipped with banks of keys. The two keyboards were equivalent in function; however, the ape's had keys which were coded by the embossment of geometric configurations, *lexigrams*, on their surfaces. The researcher's board consisted of simple push buttons with the English functionally equivalent meanings abbreviated on tags. A PDP8-E computer served to monitor and to classify all linguistic exchanges in terms of grammaticality, to honor certain requests for food and drink and entertainment from the ape, and to activate a teleprinter so as to record the events in printed copy and punched paper tape.

Linguistic expressions were accomplished through the selection and depression of visually distinctive keys, which functioned as words, in accordance with the basic grammar of the artificial language devised for the project. An important notation is that the keyboards were designed so that the locations of the keys on the subject's console could be scrambled in order to make their positions and their linguistic functions only randomly associated. By scrambling the keys, we taught our subject, Lana, to select keys on the basis of geometric lexical designations, and not their locations on the console (FIGURE 1).

As the language was visual, it was also silent. The depression of keys resulted, in turn, in the production of facsimiles of the lexigrams upon projectors in a row positioned above the two keyboards, respectively. Hence, both ape and man were able to refer to the sentences being transmitted and received so as to exchange communications.

One of our concerns was that our subject might encounter great difficulty in learning to attend to and to discriminate the facsimiles produced in the row of projecters (concurrent with the depression of the keys) and to "read" their meanings in accordance with their syntactic relationships. To our surprise, Lana learned to do so without special training. We believe that an important factor in her doing so was that coinciding with the depression of each given key, there was always a flash of light and the appearance of a new projected image (lexigram) on the next projector in the row above her board. The flashes of light likely served to attract her attention to the

FIGURE 1. Lana (at age 4½) at the keyboard. Each key of her console has a distinctive lexigram, representing a word, on its surface. Depression of the keys results in the production of facsimiles of the lexigrams, of their surfaces, on the projectors above her console. The positions of the keys are scrambled frequently in order to make their locations unreliable cues to their linguistic functions.

projectors, but that she *equated* the projected images with the lexigrams on the keys' surfaces carries important implications concerning the perceptual and cognitive competence of the chimpanzee, despite (or because of?) immaturity. Within the first six months of formal training, Lana demonstrated the keen ability (about 90% accuracy) to differentiate between correct and error choices in the formulation of her sentences (she came to erase her errors promptly through use of the "period" key) and to complete and to reject, respectively, valid and invalid sentence beginnings provided to her by the experimenter through use of his separate keyboard.[22]

Initially, Lana was taught a number of stock sentences, so-called because they reliably served to actuate the various vending and event devices (for movie, projected slides, music, the opening of a window to allow an out-of-doors view) regardless of the presence of human attendants. These stock sentences were taught through use of standard operant conditioning procedures; consequently, their initial acquisition should not be viewed as linguistic in any sense of the word. But it was through the use of those sentences that Lana did come to differentiate reliably between correct and incorrect sentence structures, be they made by herself or by the experimenter through the course of experiments to assess her skills in so doing.

YES AND NO

In at least a limited sense, Lana came to answer either YES or NO in response to questions regarding the states of the door to her room and the movable blind which covered her window. Specifically, in response to questions as to whether the door and the window (blind) were "open" or "shut," Lana would respond YES or NO after visual inspection of them. It was interesting to us that from this training Lana extended the meaning of NO as a negation to that of protest. She first protested with NO when a technician was drinking a coke and she had none. Protestations of this type were reliably made in systematic tests where the technicians ate/drank when she could not and when they would take food from the vending devices from which she obtained her rations through use of stock sentences. Lana's extended use of NO, the redefinition of its use from a response of negation to one of protestation without formal training, is, retrospectively, the first evidence that supports the inference that she had learned something about the arbitrary meanings assigned to words (lexigrams); to us it suggested that semantically, certain word meanings might be rather closely mapped/related in cognition.

THE LEARNING OF NAMES

Names of objects and events are clearly fundamental to linguistic communication. Names allow for reference of objects/events remote in time and space; their initial mastery possibly provides the germinal bed from which a variety of semantic differentiations stem. Consequently, we set about teaching Lana not just the names of things, but that things have names.[23] We did this by initially presenting her either an M & M candy or a slice of banana on a plastic tray immediately after the question posed through the computer, "? What name-of this." After several hundreds of trials, Lana learned to respond correctly (better than 90% on controlled tests) either "M & M name-of this," or "Banana name-of this." Subsequent transfer tests were conducted with other exemplars which, too, were familiar in the sense that she had worked to obtain them by requesting the "machine" for them through the use of stock sentences. With tests on the first set of five exemplars (ball, slices of apple, pieces of monkey chow, bread, and a glass of juice), she correctly named *ball* on the first trial and within the last five of ten trials of the items randomly sequenced, she was 80% correct. Subsequently, she was correct on the first trials when a glass of milk and her blanket served as exemplars. From this we concluded that she had learned which words of the stock sentences were, in fact, the names of that dispensed and, more generally, that things have names by which references to them can be made. Learning names for objects and people has been relatively simple for Lana subsequent to the training just described, where from an arduously mastered initial discrimination between two exemplars, a readiness to learn the names of other familiar things came forth. It is difficult to avoid the conclusion that Lana did, in fact, learn considerably more than what could be accounted for simply by the discrimination training that we gave her in this type of skill. Her cognitive processes, her intelligence took her well beyond that for which our training procedures would, at face value, provide (TABLE 1).

USE OF STOCK SENTENCES IN A NOVEL SETTING

Lana extended her use of stock sentences from their initial purposes to other problem situations.[17] This feat was first observed in her use of the sentence,"? Beverly move behind room." This request was mastered and used (when Beverly was present) to have her move literally around and behind Lana's room so as to be positioned for viewing when the blind to the window was lowered through use of another stock sentence, "Please machine make window open." (Initially, the view of the out-of-doors was not sufficient incentive for Lana to ask for the window to be opened, but to view a person positioned behind the window blind apparently was.) Lana's first use of the request for Beverly to move behind the room, for other than getting her positioned as a target for viewing through the window, occurred when Beverly was about to leave the test area for the day after having loaded pieces of bread for Lana's consumption in one of the vending devices. Due to an equipment malfunction, Lana's requests through use of the stock sentence, "Please machine give piece of bread," went unfulfilled. In brief, after a few other expressions, Lana came forth with repeated requests that Beverly "move behind (the) room." As Beverly approached the area where the vending devices were positioned, Lana moved near the one that contained bread; Beverly then noted that no bread had been delivered. With the malfunction remedied, Lana again asked repeatedly (now successfully) for pieces of bread. In subsequent tests over the course of the next week, when equipment "failures" were preplanned, it was observed that Lana very reliably asked for the one present, by name, to move behind the room. We believe that this indicates either (1) that the request for Beverly to do so, if fortuitous, was, nonetheless, learned to perfection in a single episode, or (2) that the initial request to Beverly stemmed from Lana's concluding a relationship between where the problem was, i.e., "behind the room," and that Beverly, if moved behind the room, would be in a position to do something about it. In support of the latter possibility, it is clear that Lana has a rather thorough appreciation of her training system. For example, on her own initiative she came to ask for the activation of whatever unit (projector, tape deck, etc.) a technician happened to be adjusting or working with, and subsequently she would ask appropriately for their activation whenever a technician would simply point to a unit: pointing to the tape deck would lead Lana to request, with the stock sentence, "Please machine make music,"—one example.

CONVERSATIONS

Language is frequently used to transmit a single message to a specific person, but more commonly it is used for the exchange of messages between individuals, i.e., conversations. Our working definition of *conversation* in the Lana Project has been: 1) there must be a linguistic-type of exchange between the ape subject and us; 2) there must be novelty in at least one of the messages transmitted by each party; and 3) the topic of the exchange must be relatively coherent and stable across the time of its duration. At the risk of oversimplification, through conversation humans attempt to exchange information, including what is and is not understood about some topic, to a point in time when some communicative goal is either achieved or abandoned.

TABLE 1

WORDS USED IN NOVEL "PRODUCTIVE" SENTENCES BY LANA (AUGUST 15, 1975)

Things

   Autonomous Actors
- machine
- Beverly
- Susan
- Lana
- Shelley
- Tim
- roach

   Ingestibles

      Edibles
- apple
- banana
- bread
- chow
- M&M
- cabbage

      Drinkables
- "coke"
- coffee
- juice
- milk
- water

   Transferable Items
- ball
- blanket
- bowl
- box
- can
- shoe
- cup
- feces

   Fixtures
- door
- room
- cage
- piano
- window

   Body Parts
- eye
- ear
- nose

   Pronouns
- you
- this

   Semantic Indicator
- name-of

Activities
- drink
- eat
- groom
- give
- make
- move
- swing
- tickle
- want
- put

Prepositions
- behind
- in
- into
- of
- on
- out-of
- to
- under

Color/States
- black
- blue
- green
- orange
- purple
- red
- yellow
- white
- shut
- open

Conceptual Category
- color

Markers
A. Identity-difference
- same-as
- different

B. Attributive
- which-is

C. Sentential
- please
- "?"
- no
- yes
- "." (period)

Comparative Determiner
- more

Ambiental Conditions
- movie
- slide (projected)
- music

In our initial plans for the Lana Project, we hoped one day to engage Lana in conversation to learn about a variety of things from the perspective of an ape, if you will. We are still far from the point of being able to engage her in conversations about topics at random; however, we can and have engaged Lana in a number of conversations regarding the procurement of food and drink, incentives that have enduring and limitless appeal, it would seem.

Of significance is the fact that without specific training to do so, Lana was the one who initiated the first conversation.[6] It transpired on March 6, 1974, 15 months into training. As Lana viewed Tim casually drinking a coke in the late afternoon, she came forth with the novel request, composed of phrases from other sentences but nonetheless totally appropriate to the context of the moment, "? Lana drink this out-of room." The interpretation was that Lana wanted to come out of her room and drink "this" with Tim. The request was honored, and the scenario was repeated twice to determine if her initial statement had been other than a fortuitously "correct" sentence. (It was not; Lana repeated her original request.) As we reflected upon the fact that Lana knew the word *coke* in that she asked for it from the machine by that word, Tim returned to the room with another coke to determine if it was, in fact, the referent for the word "this," which she had used. He did so, and rather promptly she came forth with the request as cast earlier, "? Lana drink this out-of room," whereupon Tim questioned, "? Drink what." Lana's prompt response was, "? Lana drink *coke* out-of room." There seemed little room to question that coke was, indeed, the referent for the pronoun, "this." Even in her first conversation, Lana correctly interpreted a novel message from Tim (? Drink what) *and* responded with the exact information requested.

Elsewhere[17] we have presented examples in which Lana posed questions to herself and then answered and complied. For instance, from the seclusion of the corridor outside of Lana's test room, beyond her view, the second author has seen her pose the question, through use of her keyboard, "? Lana groom," to which the answer was, "Yes," with the ensuing activity being self-grooming. We have also reported her use of stylistic variations, use of the pronominal, her spontaneous introduction of her own name as the indirect object, use of the word "this" to denote a specific incentive, and her composition of the request that a technician move food from one point to another in space, a requisite to its being loaded into the vending devices, even though she had had no specific training to do so. From having learned how to ask technicians (by name) to move "behind the room," she apparently inferred that she could ask them to move "things"—food—to where the vending devices were located. After various approximations to that kind of request, she came forth with the incomplete statement, "? Tim move milk behind—." Tim responded with a request for additional information, "? Behind what." Lana responded, "? Tim move milk behind *room*." As before, she produced the information requested.

To us, the most important conversational phenomenon that Lana has generated was when she asked us for the name of something for which she had no name (a box, baited with M & M candies), and then used the name forthwith to ask that it be given to her; she had had no specific training to do so. Initially she asked for the box by use of names "can" and "bowl" (objects from the set of materials used to extend her skills in naming). When use of those names resulted only in her being given an empty can or an empty bowl, in turn, she came forth with the request, "? Tim give Lana name-of this," to which Tim responded, "Box name-of this." After a one-word response, "Yes"—something the *technicians typically say* to her whenever she responds correctly on a trial or question—she asked, "? Tim give Lana this box." Tim complied, Lana got her box and candy, and the conversation stopped.

Lana has also generated names for things, as when she asked for the orange (fruit) as the "apple which-is orange (in color)." On other occasions she has asked for the fruit as the "ball which-is orange," and in terms of its location (in bowl). These and other conversations have been reported and analyzed in detail elsewhere.[17] For the purposes of this paper it must suffice to point out (1) that Lana initiated the first conversation, (2) that in conversation, Lana has been innovative in the generation of novel sentences (TABLE 2) appropriate to the theme of the moment—how to gain access to a food/drink incentive not conventionally accessible, (3) that conversation with her has spanned more than 20 consecutive minutes, on certain occasions, and (4) that Lana's persistence in conversation has been strictly pragmatic—once the desired incentive has been achieved, the conversation *ends*!! (TABLE 3) It should be noted also that Lana has never initiated conversations to "broaden her horizons," if you will. She has never asked for the names of things unless they held some food or drink that she apparently wanted; she has never "discussed" spontaneously the attributes of things in her world nor really ever capitalized upon conversation to extend her access to information about things. It might be that these limitations are artifacts of her training to date; perhaps she will do so someday, but at this time we are doubtful if chimpanzees will ever be noted for their exploiting linguistic-type skills to request additional information that might enhance their broad understanding of their world and how things in it work. We believe that this is an important point that might reliably differentiate language utilization by the child from the ape—perhaps the ape will use its language-type skills to the most pragmatic ends (as to obtain things),

TABLE 2

LANA'S REQUESTS FOR COFFEE†

	? BRODY MOVE COFFEE TO LANA.
	? LANA DRINK COFFEE.
	LANA DRINK COFFEE.
	LANA WANT DRINK COFFEE.
	PLEASE MACHINE GIVE COFFEE.
	PLEASE MACHINE GIVE COFFEE TO LANA.
	PLEASE MACHINE GIVE COFFEE TO ME.
	PLEASE YOU GIVE COFFEE TO ME.
	? SHELLEY GIVE COFFEE.
*	? SHELLEY GIVE LANA COFFEE.
*	? TIM GIVE COFFEE CUP.
	? TIM GIVE COFFEE TO LANA.
*	? TIM GIVE CUP COFFEE.
	? TIM GIVE CUP OF COFFEE.
*	? TIM GIVE LANA COFFEE.
*	? YOU GIVE LANA CUP OF COFFEE.
*	? YOU GIVE COFFEE OUT-OF ROOM
	? YOU GIVE COFFEE TO LANA.
	? YOU GIVE COFFEE TO ME.
	? YOU GIVE COFFEE TO ME.
	? YOU GIVE CUP OF THIS.
*	? YOU GIVE LANA COFFEE.
	? YOU GIVE THIS COFFEE.
	? YOU GIVE THIS WHICH-IS BLACK.

† All examples represent instances of transfer from training with other materials. With the exception of those indicated (*), they are grammatically correct in *Yerkish*. (Technicians named are altered according to which one is present.)

TABLE 3

CONVERSATION BETWEEN TIM GILL AND LANA (JUNE 11, 1975)

Conditions: *Formal Test.*

Tim had entered the anteroom with a bowl of monkey chow. Lana had asked that it be loaded into the machine; however, the conditions of the test called for Tim *not* to comply, to load cabbage for vending instead, and to declare that chow (which she had requested) was in the machine. Although Lana might have asked the machine to vend "chow," she did not— appropriate to the fact that cabbage, and not monkey chow, was in the vendor. She said:

Lana:	Please machine give piece of cabbage.	16:53
	? you (Tim) put chow in machine. (5 times)	16:54–16:55
Tim:	(lying) Chow in machine. (In response to each of the 5 requests.)	
Lana:	? Chow in machine.	16:57
Tim:	(still lying) Yes.	16:57
Lana:	No chow in machine. (which was true)	16:57
Tim:	? What in machine. (repeat once)	16:57 & 16:58
Lana:	Cabbage in machine. (which was true)	16:59
Tim:	Yes cabbage in machine.	16:59
Lana:	? You move cabbage out-of machine.	17:00
Tim:	Yes. (Whereupon he removed the cabbage and put in the monkey chow.)	17:01
Lana:	Please machine give piece of chow. (Repeatedly until all was obtained.)	17:01

Conclusion. Lana discerned what had, in fact, been loaded in the machine, did not concur with Tim's assertion that it was "chow," asked that he remove it, and then asked for "chow" when it was loaded for vending.

whereas the child readily goes beyond that use of language to learn about the nature of things, how they work; in short, the nature of its everyday world.

REFERENCE TO OBJECTS BY NAME OR COLOR

To expedite Lana's acquisition of names of selected objects and colors, a set of 36 items was devised: blue, purple, red, black, yellow, and orange shoes, bowls, balls, boxes, cans, and cups. Initially Lana learned to give the names of objects regardless of color and then the color regardless of the objects' names. Through the course of study, she eventually was able to give either the name or the color upon request (randomly sequenced) in response to projected pictures of the 36 objects, sequenced randomly in formal tests. Still additional work resulted in Lana being able to give either the name or the color of any one of six different objects (of the set of training objects, each one of a distinctive color) as referenced by either of two questions randomly sequenced across trials—"? What name-of this which-is (color, e.g., blue)," or "? What color of this (object name, e.g., cup.")." In short, Lana gave either the *name* of an object referred to by color, or the *color* of an object referred to by name, with six distinctively colored different objects present. Her performance in formal test conditions was about 90% correct,[24] good evidence that she differentially decoded questions, selected the object for which additional information was requested either by its name or attribute (color), and encoded the information requested for transmission via the computerized keyboard.

CROSS-MODAL PERFORMANCE

Under controlled conditions it was demonstrated that Lana very readily eliminated essentially all errors in judging pairs of objects from her set of training materials (described above) for sameness and difference, with one member presented visually and the other haptically. We believe that it was Lana's linguistic-type skills that facilitated both the training of her in the task to be executed and in the rapid attainment of high level of proficiency in her judgments.[17] In addition, formal tests with unnamed objects demonstrated that familiarity with the objects (prior) to cross-modal tests) facilitated sameness-difference judgments and obtained qualified evidence that names, apart from familiarity as such with the objects, facilitated judgments. We believe that the evidence supports the interpretation that Lana's skills functioned linguistically for her in the cross-modal tasks, for she was considerably better in them than other apes have been reported to be.[25]

DISCUSSION

The Lana Language Project has demonstrated the feasibility of employing a computer-controlled language system in research addressed to the determination of the linguistic-type behaviors reported initially from Project Washoe. The advantages attendant to the use of such a system have been described earlier in this report. Lana's learning rate has been rapid and has exceeded our initial expectations. Her acquisition of vocabulary has been relatively nonproblematic; however, Lana's "definitions" of the lexical units are not necessarily identical to ours. Nonetheless, the meanings of the lexical units to Lana are sufficiently common to ours so that is has been possible for rather complex tasks to be mastered and for rather informative conversations to be conducted with her.

To us it seems reasonably clear that Lana's success has been contingent upon her having hominian intelligence, as chimpanzees in general have, due to their close biological and psychological relationship to man. (The level of that intelligence, incidentally, is likely greater than we had anticipated, for we have no reason to believe that Lana is a particularly intellectually gifted specimen.)

As man and ape share, within limits, a common sensory and perceptual world, it has been possible to build a linguistic-type bridge through the employment of the systems and methods conceived.[1,2,5] Without question, it has been the ape's readiness to learn and predilection to extend skills beyond the bounds of specific training which has allowed the projects to succeed, as we believe that they have.

We conclude that the findings of the ape-language studies serve to encourage the redefinition of language in terms of an evolutionary comparative perspective which emphasizes the psychological processes which underly the public transmissions of a language-type of communication. Thought and research in this kind of framework[1,2,17,26] will, it is hoped, expedite our understanding of language, its etiology, the parameters of its acquisition and use even by the normal child. We are also hopeful that it will lead to the development of the ape as an animal model for the conduct of basic research projects of a linguistic-type which, by virtue of ethical constraints, must not be conducted with the child. The conduct of such projects, we trust, should assist us in devising systems and methods that will facilitate the special educational efforts of the language-deficient child. We proceed with such research, confident that results cannot be interpreted in terms of simple-response chains and that either they are, at best, part and parcel of man's linguistic functions or, at the very least, important analogues of man's linguistic functions which should be fully researched for the above reasons.

We recommend continued research with chimpanzees (*as* chimpanzees) in language-type studies and, also, conservatism on the part of all so far as drawing conclusions as to (1) what their data mean and (2) what the limitations of the chimpanzee might be for the acquisition of language-type skills.

REFERENCES

1. GARDNER, B. T. & R. A. GARDNER. 1971. Two-way communication with an infant chimpanzee. *In* Behavior of Nonhuman Primates. A. M. Schrier & F. Stollnitz, Eds. Vol. 1: 117–184. Academic Press. New York, N.Y.
2. PREMACK, D. 1971. Language in chimpanzee? Science 172: 808–822.
3. GARDNER, R. A. & B. T. GARDNER. 1975. Early signs of language in child and chimpanzee. Science 187: 752–753.
4. PREMACK, D. & A. J. PREMACK. 1974. Teaching visual language to apes and language-deficient persons. *In* Language Perspectives—Acquisition, Retardation, and Intervention. R. L. Schiefelbusch & L. L. Lloyd, Eds.: 347–376. University Park Press. Baltimore, Md.
5. RUMBAUGH, D. M., E. C. VON GLASERFELD, H. WARNER, P. PISANI, T. V. GILL, J. V. BROWN & C. L. BELL. 1973. A computer-controlled language training system for investigating the language skills of young apes. Behav. Res. Meth. Instrumentation. 5(5): 385–392.
6. RUMBAUGH, D. M. & T. V. GILL. 1975. Language, apes, and the apple which-is orange please. Proc. Symposia Fifth Congr. Inter. Primatol. Soc.: 247–257. Japan Science Press. Tokyo.
7. RUMBAUGH, D. M. 1970. Learning Skills of Anthropoids. *In* Primate Behavior: Developments in Field and Laboratory Research. L. A. Rosenblum, Ed.: 1–70. Academic Press. New York, N.Y.
8. HARLOW, H. F. 1949. The formation of learning sets. Psychol. Rev. 56: 51–65.
9. STOKOE, W. C., D. CASTERLINE & C. G. CRONEBERG. 1965. A dictionary of American Sign Language. Gallaudet College Press. Washington, D.C.
10. VAN LAWICK-GOODALL, J. 1968. The behavior of free-living chimpanzees in the Gombe Stream reserve. Animal Behavior Monographs.
11. HAYES, K. J. & C. H. NISSEN. 1971. Higher mental functions of a home-raised chimpanzee. *In* Behavior of Nonhuman Primates. A. M. Schrier & F. Stollnitz, Eds. Vol. 4: 60–116. Academic Press. New York, N.Y.
12. PREMACK, D. 1971. On the assessment of language competence of the chimpanzee. *In* Behavior of Nonhuman Primates: Modern Research Trends. A. M. Schrier & F. Stollnitz, Eds. Vol. 4: 185–228. Academic Press. New York, N.Y.
13. HEWES, G. W. 1973. Primate communication and the gestural origin of language. Current Anthropol. 14(1–2): 5–24.
14. BROWN, R. W. 1956. Language and categories. *In* A Study of Thinking. J. S. Bruner, J. J. Goodnow & G. A. Austin. Appendix: 247–312. John Wiley & Sons, Inc. New York, N.Y.
15. GARDNER, R. A. & B. T. GARDNER. 1973. Teaching sign language to the chimpanzee. Films in the Behavioral Sciences. Pennsylvania State Univ. University Park, Pa.
16. FOUTS, R. 1974. Language: origins, definitions and chimpanzees. J. Human Evolution 3: 475–482.
17. RUMBAUGH, D. M. & T. V. GILL. 1976. Language and the acquisition of language-type skills by a chimpanzee. Ann. N.Y. Acad. Sci. 270: 90–135.

18. KING, M. C. & A. C. WILSON. 1975. Evolution at two levels in humans and chimpanzees. Science 188: 107–116.

19. HYMES, D. 1971. Competence and performance in linguistic theory. *In* Language Acquisition: Models and Methods. R. Huxley & E. Ingram, Eds.: 3–28, 73. Academic Press. New York, N.Y.

20. NORMAN, D. A. & D. E. RUMELHART. 1975. Explorations in Cognition. W. H. Freeman. San Francisco, Calif.

21. VON GLASERSFELD, E. C. 1975. The Yerkish language for nonhuman primates. Am. J. Computational Linguistics. Microfiche 12.

22. RUMBAUGH, D. M., T. V. GILL, & E. C. VON GLASERSFELD. 1973. Reading and sentence completion by a chimpanzee (*Pan*). Science 182: 731–733.

23. GILL, T. V. & D. M. RUMBAUGH. 1974. Mastery of naming skills by a chimpanzee. J. Human Evolution 3: 483–492.

24. GILL, T. V., S. ESSOCK & D. M. RUMBAUGH. 1975. Color and object naming skills of a chimpanzee. Paper presented at Soc. Res. Child Development. Denver, Colo.

25. DAVENPORT, R. K. & C. M. ROGERS. 1970. Intermodal equivalence of stimuli in apes. Science 168: 279–280.

26. RUDER, K. F. & M. D. SMITH. 1974. Issues in language training. *In* Language Perspectives—Acquisition, Retardation, and Intervention. R. L. Schiefelbusch & L. L. Lloyd, Eds.: 565–607. University Park Press. Baltimore, Md.

WHAT MIGHT BE LEARNED FROM STUDYING LANGUAGE IN THE CHIMPANZEE? THE IMPORTANCE OF SYMBOLIZING ONESELF

H. S. Terrace and T. G. Bever

Department of Psychology
Columbia University
New York, New York 10027

What do you see when you turn out the light?
I can't tell you, but I know it's mine.

—Lennon and McCartney
A Little Help From My Friends

Ten years ago, there was little reason to believe that much could be learned from studying language in the chimpanzee. Earlier reports (e.g. Ref. 1, 2) of a chimpanzee's inability to use language seemed to demonstrate that biological factors limited the extent to which the chimpanzee could learn to use abstract symbols. Thanks to the work of the Gardners,[3,4] Premack,[7,8] Fouts,[9,10] and Rumbaugh and Von Glaserfeld,[11] we now know that a chimpanzee has a much larger linguistic potential than was ever imagined. Once allowance was made for the vocal limitations of a chimpanzee (Lieberman, 1968; Lieberman *et al.*, 1972), it became possible to teach it to use arbitrary gestures, plastic tokens, or the lexigrams of a computer console in a manner that parallels the human use of single symbols. Most provocative have been demonstrations that chimpanzees can use *sequences* of symbols. This suggests a syntactic potential as well as a symbolic one.

In the eagerness to establish whether a chimpanzee can acquire syntactic competence, certain more basic functions of language appear to have been bypassed. Our main purpose in this paper is not only to assess the syntactic accomplishments of Washoe, Sarah, and Lana, but also to delineate other functions of human language that can be studied in the chimpanzee—functions that do not require syntactic competence.

Before considering nonsyntactic functions of human language, it is of interest to digress briefly to compare studies of language in a chimpanzee with studies of language in another currently popular subject, the computer. At present, there is nothing to suggest that computers can simulate the *acquisition* of language. However, language acquisition by another being may illuminate parallel processes in humans. As compared with the computer, the chimpanzee has many obvious advantages. First, because of its biological and social similarity to man, a chimpanzee is a much more likely source of useful contrastive information on human language. Second, a computer can do nothing more than execute the instructions of its programmer. We cannot be sure *what* a chimpanzee will do with symbols once it has learned their meanings.

Human language has two important functions: (1) it facilitates communication (particularly about events and objects displaced in time and/or space) and (2) it structures how we perceive ourselves and the world. The child's tendency to symbolize interpersonal relations between himself and others is obviously a fundamental ingredient of personality development in all human societies—in particular, the concept of *self* bounded on one side by desires and on the other by social patterns. A child's ability to refer to itself, its desires, and the social pressures of its environment requires little, if any, syntactic ability. Yet this basic function of language has profound effects. We suggest that the mastery of language to express feelings and to encode socially desirable and undesirable behaviors to oneself, may provide sources of motivation for advancing to more elaborate usages of language—usages that do require syntax. A necessary condition of human language may prove to be the ability to symbolize *oneself*. In our own research, we hope to see if this condition is sufficient for an already socialized chimpanzee by teaching it the concept and use of "self."

The assumptions from which our hypothesis derives can be formulated in comparative terms. *All the ingredients for human language are present in other species—they do not become language until an animal learns that it can refer to itself symbolically.* Many animals learn to respond to *symbols*, and to remember them (as in discrimination learning or delayed-response tasks). Many animals also exhibit *hierarchically organized behavior* patterns (e.g. as in Hullian "habit families" or in Tinbergen's analysis of stickleback courtship), and *transformations*, (e.g. shifting from one mode of locomotion to another in maneuvering through a maze, or "displacement reactions" of various animals). Many animals can also perceive and act on *relations* between themselves and other members of their species (e.g. dominance patterns, and courtship interactions). Finally, at least a chimpanzee (and perhaps other species as well) demonstrate a concept of "self" by their ability to deal with their own mirror image.[12]

Our hypothesis is that the potential to attach a symbol to "oneself" is an important factor in the recruitment of preexisting potentials for using symbols, hierarchies, and transformations into "language." The motive for this is clear: once we can think about ourselves symbolically, we can think abstractly about our relations to others and to the world. A basic function of syntax is to express the internal relations between different symbols. This, in turn, facilitates the representation and exploration of relations in the outside world. Accordingly, in the present discussion, we consider how language can be used to demonstrate a concept of symbolized self in a chimpanzee before evaluating the extent to which its utterances have a syntactic structure.

One indicator of a symbolic self in a symbol-learning chimpanzee would be specific reference to its own emotions and feelings. As a creatrure prone to emotional expression of fear, anger, happiness, frustration, like, dislike, sadness, and so on, it may prove possible to teach a chimpanzee to name those states. As far as we can tell, neither Premack nor Rumbaugh has attempted specifically to teach their chimpanzees words describing emotional states. While the Gardners reported that words such as *funny* and *sorry* were part of Washoe's vocabulary, it is not clear that either of these words was used to refer to internal as opposed to external stimuli.

For example, in the Gardners' glossary of Washoe's vocabulary, *sorry* was defined as an "apology, appeasement and comforting; usually the response to *Ask pardon*" (Ref. 4, p. 266). Although Nim, the chimpanzee we are teaching to communicate via sign language, has yet to learn the sign *sorry*, it is clear that he has learned to seek reassurance after having done something wrong (such as touching a forbidden object, or biting too hard). On some occasions, Nim will sign *hug* in order to obtain reassurance. From the Gardners' description of Washoe's usage of *sorry*, and from our own experience with Nim's attempts to make up by signing *hug*, it appears as if these signs may function as requests for reassurance rather than as descriptions of an emotional state.

As the psychological literature on attribution clearly shows, description of emotional states often entails reference to external and internal states.[13-16] It is plausible that chimpanzees can learn to identify emotional expression, as might be portrayed in pictures. It has been shown that monkeys can learn to discriminate between the expression of different emotional states, as shown on video displays.[17] The Gardners[18] and Fouts[10] have demonstrated that a chimpanzee takes well to the task of naming various pictures with appropriate signs. Thus, learning to label emotional displays may not prove difficult for chimpanzees.

Symbolic discrimination of emotional expressions exhibited by others is easier to demonstrate than reference to one's own emotions. While we have no basis at present for asserting that a chimpanzee could engage in the kind of introspection that is entailed in a description of its own feelings, or emotions, we find this possibility intriguing. Introspection of any kind requires a symbolic consciousness of self that has yet to be clearly demonstrated in chimpanzees.

Language plays a vital role in a child's incorporation of the concepts and values of its environment. Although this may seem obvious, its significance does not appear to have been perceived in previous studies of language in a chimpanzee. An unrecognized obstacle in the path of fully simulating the syntactic features of human language in a chimpanzee may be the absence of the motivation experienced by a child who learns language both to please its parents and to represent its world. Chimpanzees such as Washoe, Sarah, and Lana have obviously been motivated to learn *something*. The question remains, however, whether their motivation and learning have been intrinsically linked to socialization itself.

How human children and chimpanzees learn the names of objects provides an interesting basis for comparing the motivation in each case. Consider, for example, Lana's communication to the computer *what name of this?* when she wanted to learn the name of a box in order to obtain the box, which contained candy. Quite obviously this is an impressive example of a chimpanzee's having learned that things have names. In the case of children, it is commonplace that they ask for the names of objects in their environments. But in the only example we know of in which a chimpanzee asked for the name of something it is clear that learning the name of the box was in the service of obtaining the box and its contents. On the other hand, a child willl persist in asking *what that?* simply to learn the names of objects without any obvious extrinsic consequences. The child seems to be acquiring the names of things to use in social discourse, or in the mastery of its world—a motive fundamentally different from that of obtaining the object in question itself.

With these considerations in mind, it is instructive to consider the three major recent studies of language in the chimpanzee. One purpose is to evaluate the extent to which syntactic competence has been demonstrated in the chimpanzee; it is also necessary to evaluate each chimpanzee's socialization and its motivation for using language. We consider first the cage-reared chimpanzees, Sarah and Lana.

PROJECT SARAH

The initial strategy Premack followed in teaching Sarah to use a symbol system, in which words were represented by plastic chips of different shapes and colors, was to utilize behavioral techniques for demonstrating a list of so-called "exemplars" of human language. These included (1) words, (2) sentences, (3) questions, (4) metalinguistics (using symbols to talk about symbols), (5) class concepts such as *color, shape,* and *size,* (6) the copula ("is"), (7) quantifiers such as *all, none, one,* and *several,* and (8) the logical connectors *if* and *then.* As Premack notes, "This list is in no sense exhaustive, nor are the items of comparable logical order" (Ref. 7, pp. 808–809). In demonstrating a particular exemplar, simple training procedures were used that presumably mapped linguistic knowledge onto discriminations that Sarah had already mastered. For example, the word *apple* was trained by requiring Sarah to offer the word for apple (a blue plastic triangle) in exchange for an actual apple. The "interrogative" was trained by placing the interrogative symbol between objects that are either the same or different. In this case Sarah is required to replace the interrogative symbol with the appropriate symbol, one that means *same* or one that means *different*.

Most of Sarah's behavior appears to have been motivated initially by food reward. Premack (Ref. 8, p. 200) does indicate that "on one occasion, . . . she stole the test material before the lesson, as she has done from time to time, and went on both to produce many of the questions we had taught her, as well as to answer them." Furthermore, after many months of intensive training, Sarah could learn a new symbol-object relationship simply by observing an experimenter pair them together. In these instances, Sarah appears to have been manipulating the materials without the support of an extrinsic incentive. But, as far as can be gleaned from Premack's description of his experimental procedures, initial training was motivated by food reward, as were actual testing sessions.

The solution of the problems presented to Sarah usually required the simple substitution of one symbol for another. Within a particular training set, most of the problems required that Sarah choose only between two alternatives. For example, if she was tested on her ability to identify objects that were the same or different through her use of the sumbols *same* and *different*, these were her only choices. In other problems, requiring the naming of colors, symbols for numerous colors were provided. However, it was still the case that the only alternatives from which Sarah could choose were symbols designating different colors, i.e., of the same class of answers.

During a typical day, Sarah was given as many as four brief sessions, each containing about 20 problems. All of the problems in a given session were of the same type. Thus, one session might concentrate on same-different problems, another on color-of problems, another on shape-of problems, and so on. Accordingly, it is an open question whether Sarah's usage of these exemplars constitutes a simulation of human language. Training procedures that allow for only one type of problem could establish a "set" for that type of problem and accordingly, may not elicit a "natural" use of language. A related limitation of the results is that during any session the set of symbols that define the answers to that problem (often just two) were all of the same linguistic category. This also is not representative of a human language.

Of course, the most important question is whether Sarah shows evidence of having mastered structural rules governing sequences. The strongest argument that Sarah is sensitive to the structure of sentences comes from the demonstration that she could respond appropriately to a sentence such as *Sarah insert banana pail apple dish*. In this situation, Sarah was required to place an apple and a banana in the appropriate container. In order to demonstrate Sarah's understanding of this sentence, she was provided with a choice of fruit and a choice of containers. Premack argues (Ref. 8, p. 215) that the organization of the sentence can be shown to be hierarchical. "*Banana* and *pail* go together, likewise *apple* and *dish* . . . *insert* not only applies to *banana* and *pail* but to both cases, and finally, . . . it is Sarah who is to carry out the whole actions." Thus, on this interpretation the response could not occur as a result of simple response-chaining.

This interpretation is uncertain for a number of reasons. Typically, Sarah was tested on only one kind of problem for an entire session. Thus the first two symbols (*Sarah* and *insert*) are redundant. Unless *insert* is contrasted with some other verb, it is not clear how one could demonstrate its hierarchical status in the "sentence." Even though Sarah responded appropriately when *withdraw* was contrasted with *insert*, one wonders whether Sarah needs to understand the symbol *insert* in order to solve the problem. If the pail and dish were empty before the problem was given, then she need only pay attention to the extralinguistic cue provided by the condition of the container in front of her.

At the very least, we must see many more variations of the sentence *Sarah insert apple pail banana dish*, along with appropriate behaviors, before concluding that Sarah understood the hierarchical structure of a sentence.

For example:

Sarah withdraw apple banana pail insert peach can apple box.

Sarah wash apple red dish insert banana round dish.

Sarah achieved impressive abilities to deal with symbols as such. She clearly "learned to learn" new symbols—i.e., she discovered that things can have a "name." Premack has also shown that Sarah has the cognitive ability to solve problems requiring the use of symbols in a metalinguistic manner. For example, Sarah could respond correctly to questions concerning the shape or the color of an apple when all she was shown was the symbol for an apple—a blue triangle. She could *also* answer questions about the plastic symbol itself. However, she did not show unequivocal evidence of the use of sentence structure, nor did her other usages of symbols occur in the varied contexts that characterize human language.

PROJECT LANA

However we interpret Sarah's achievements in relation to human language, they demonstrate convincingly the chimpanzee's symbolic potential. However, a frequent criticism of Project Sarah is that Premack and his trainers were transmitting nonlinguistic cues during the training procedure that shaped her responses (cf. Ref. 16). Of course, it is just the personal interchanges required by Premack's technique which gives it a naturalistic relation to human-language learning. In order to test for this so-called "Clever Hans" (or Clever Gretel) phenomenon, Premack employed a naive tester who was unfamiliar with the meaning of the symbols used in Sarah's training. Here was a deficit in the level of Sarah's performance. It was, however, still significantly greater than chance. Furthermore, such a performance drop with a strange tester has many interpretations: we might expect to find a similar decrement in a human child's performance in a similar situation. It is reasonable to argue that personal cues in Sarah's interactions may only have strengthened her understanding of the linguistic situation, as it would a child's. Nobody *tricked* Sarah into learning what a symbol is, which we find to be her most impressive skill.

Of course there might be a trivial "Clever Hans" effect in which Sarah was responding each time to an unconscious covert personal cue that was functionally the same for each trainer and tester. Unlikely as this seems, Rumbaugh and his colleagues[11] are employing a computer as an interactive device to avoid the possibility of linguistically irrelevant cues. This not only minimizes the possibility that the subject could benefit from cues in the physical proximity of the trainer; it also provides the possibility of a complete record of all symbolic transactions. Instead of plastic symbols, Rumbaugh's experiment with a chimpanzee, Lana, employs lexigrams, each of which appears on the keyboard of a computer console. The functions of these lexigrams are similar to that of the plastic chips used by Premack.

One major difference between Lana's lexigrams and Sarah's plastic chips is that the lexigrams and the computer are available just about all the time. Thus, Lana has continuous access to a much larger set of alternative symbols than did Sarah. At the same time, many of Lana's performances have been trained and practiced in long sessions devoted to just one type of problem. As we indicated earlier, this raises problems of "set" and is a basic departure from what happens in the case of a natural language. Indeed, a general cost of using the computer is the reduction of the social interactions that ordinarily provide the context for the use of symbols.

Rumbaugh's initial report on Lana referred to her ability to "read and write" in "sentence completion" tasks[11] that employed the computer's "language." If this was all that Lana had accomplished, it would seem gratuitous to refer to this as "linguistic" behavior. (Indeed, Rumbaugh and his colleagues are appropriately cautious about this—see Glasersfeld, in this volume.) For example, the sequence they gloss as *Please machine give Lana M & M* or *Please machine give Lana piece of raisin* or *Please machine show Lana movie* can be analyzed as a complex X-R chain. In these sentences, the sentence beginning *Please machine* is completely redundant and obviously requires no understanding of what the term allegedly stands for. What Lana has to learn is simply to associate the symbol *give* with the lexigram (secondary reinforcer?) for such inventives as an M & M, raisin or apple, and to associate the symbol *show* with the lexigram for such incentives as movie or slide shows. At best, Lana's ability to discriminate between valid and invalid "sentence" beginnings and to supply appropriate endings for valid sentence beginnings appears to be a weak demonstration of a finite state of grammar, in which possible successive elements of a sentence are determined completely by the immediately prior response. Such two-step chained associations are not hard to demonstrate in many animals. Indeed, this behavior is the formal and pragmatic equivalent of that of a rat in a double T maze.

An important potential of Rumbaugh's approach is inherent to the continuous record it provides of all transactions between Lana and her trainers. It should be possible to have a complete corpus of all of Lana's utterances as well as of all the questions that have been put to her. This advantage should, however, be weighed against a certain unnaturalness of the procedures used to train Lana. This includes the fact that the language is artificial, there is minimal socialization, and the fact that all Lana's training requires the constant support of primary reinforcement. It is also not entirely clear that the expensive utilization of the computer has entirely circumvented the Clever Hans possibility, at least when the computer is used as the basis for "conversing" with trainers. The trainers can vary the time, rate, and choice of presentation, which leaves open the possibility that Lana's performance is still being shaped by uncontrolled factors (which often appear to be unrecorded), e.g., Lana's cage position, her drive state, the trainer's current assessment of her position and state, and so on. Since many of her most striking "utterances" occur with a trainer present, this uncertainty is particularly poignant. However, like Sarah, Lana appears to have mastered the notion that objects can be "named," and that she can ask for the name of a new object if she wants it.

As far as we can tell, a complete corpus of Lana's symbolic sequences has yet to be published. Thus, there is no way of evaluating the novelty of particular sequences (which one would assume are drawn from the best examples). Even in the "showcase" examples, it was apparent that Lana can err in generating a sequence. Until one knows the nature and frequency of her errors, the significance of her "sentences," novel or otherwise, remains unknown.

Despite these limitations, Lana's achievements are considerable, and the potential suggested by the computer technique is substantial. Like Sarah, Lana has clearly learned that objects have names. Indeed, Lana appears to have gone one step further in that she has been observed to ask for the "name" (i.e., lexigram) of new objects (at least when she desires them).

PROJECT WASHOE

Unlike Sarah and Lana, Washoe was reared in a highly socialized environment—an environment that contained many of the features of the social environment of a human child. The same procedures are being used in the Gardners' current study of two infant chimpanzees, Moja and Pili.[5] As in Project Washoe, the medium of communication in these studies is Ameslan, a language used by the deaf. The obvious social advantage of this natural language is that both the chimpanzee and its human companions can sign to each other spontaneously, without the support of extraneous devices such as plastic chips, or computer lexigrams. The obvious comparative advantage is that sign is a "natural" human language, perhaps with a semantics as rich and a grammar as complex as in any spoken language (see Refs. 18, 19). In our opinion, socialization and the use of a natural language make the approach of the Gardners conducive to the development of language skills in a chimpanzee that are most comparable to those of a human child.

For this reason, our project uses procedures similar to those used by the Gardners. In some respects, our procedures for socializing our chimpanzee Nim are more intensive than those used by the Gardners. Unlike Washoe, Moja and Pili, Nim lives together with his caretakers and eats at least one meal a day with them. It is our feeling that a high degree of socialization is not only important in that it provides many opportunities for signing, but also in that it may increase Nim's self-control. Additionally, a high degree of socialization should also prove helpful in establishing a linguistic concept of self, if such is possible.

It is too early to report decisive linguistic consequences of our efforts to socialize Nim as one might a child. At 22 months, Nim has an active vocabulary of about 30 signs; his passive vocabulary is somewhere between 50 and 60 signs. Early this year, Nim made his first combination of two signs, and at the end of the summer he was observed to make combinations of three and four signs. We have yet to perform tests to determine whether Nim's multisign combinations show evidence of syntactic structure. In order to do so, we feel that analyses more stringent than those provided by the Gardners will be necessary.

It is mainly on this point that we part company with the Gardners. It is not sufficient simply to compare the performance of a child to that of a chimpanzee. For example, in a recent paper the Gardners note that "the failure of linguists and psycholinguists to devise a behavioral definition of language is an obstacle that we try to avoid by obtaining observations of the acquisition of sign language by young chimpanzees that can be compared with observations of the acquisition of spoken language and sign languages by human children. Any theoretical criteria that can be applied to the early utterances of children can also be applied to the early utterances of chimpanzees. If children can be said to have acquired language on the basis of their performance, then chimpanzees can be said to have acquired language to the extent that their performance matches that of children" (Ref. 6, p. 244).

To date, the Gardners have shown that semantic interpretations of two-sign utterances (irrespective of order) match those that have been found in children. In a recent publication, they also argue that Washoe responded to *wh* questions in a manner similar to that of a Stage III child. In neither of these demonstrations, however, do the descriptions of performance derive from a model of the linguistic structure necessary to capture the complexity of all the children's utterances (cf. References 18–20)—a complexity that requires structural analysis, not merely behavioral criteria. To use an analogy, the fact that a horse can walk on its hind legs does not prove that it has the walking capacity of a two-year-old child.

CONCLUSION

To summarize, chimpanzees have proved themselves to be an important source of information regarding the development of language. To date, there is no demonstration that the chimpanzees have learned to generate strictly ordered syntactic sequences. Rather, they appear to "speak" by combining semantically related symbols, in most cases, according to preset schemata. The difficulty in proving that they use syntax lies partly in the training procedures used to produce evidence of syntax. If one wants to maximize the chances of producing an approximation of human language, it will not suffice to drill a chimpanzee in separate tasks that represent certain features of human language. It is also necessary to show that these features of language occur under conditions similar to those that obtain for humans. At minimum, linguistic ability should not be specific to particular training situations and the use of language should not be solely in the service of acquiring an external object. We should also like to emphasize that a concept of self whereby a chimpanzee is able to conceptualize its feelings, intentions, and so on, in relation to other individuals in its environment, may be a crucial step in motivating the chimpanzee to acquire the syntactic competence characteristic of human language. As far as we can tell, neither Sarah nor Lana developed a linguistic concept of self; the evidence in Washoe is at best equivocal.

Just as there is no clear answer to when a child "knows" language in a syntactic sense, there is no clear answer to this question in the case of a chimpanzee. Indeed, our willingness to attribute syntactic competence to a young child is often based upon little more than an extrapolation backwards from the anticipated state of adult affairs. Unfortunately for the chimpanzee, this type of extrapolation is not yet possible. Accordingly, evidence that a chimpanzee can generate and understand sentences, as humans do, will necessitate comprehensive demonstrations that a chimpanzee cannot only string symbols together, but that such sequences reveal syntactic structures and that they function as they do in human languages. A single demonstration would fall short of the mark just as it would in the case of human children. A convincing case that a chimpanzee uses language in a human manner will require numerous demonstrations that lengthy sequences are used systematically in order to enable the chimpanzee to describe something about itself in relation to others, to deceive others, to contrast ownership of objects, to describe relations in space and time, and so on. In short, if you want to teach a chimpanzee to use language as humans do, make sure it socializes with humans, and make sure that it uses language to refer systematically to itself in relation to its human companions.

Of course, this leaves open the possibility that any training procedures with chimpanzees will elicit only a "natural" *chimpanzee* language that differs from human language because of intrinsic differences in chimpanzee cognition. To test for this possibility it is also true that a great variety of constructions and symbols will be required to delineate any difference between "human" and such a potential "chimpanzee" language.

It is worth elaborating the notion of "species—specific natural language" at this point. In this view, the capacity for symbols cannot be *taught*, but can be trained if the species has the potential for them. It is entirely possible that every primate species has the capacity for some symbolic behavior, but that the effects of learning symbols differ according to the cognitive context of the species. There may be many kinds of language, just as there may be many covert representations and organizations of the world. This makes irrelevant the question of how similar to human language a primate symbol system is. Rather, the question becomes: what is the structure of the primate language itself, and how does it reveal how a primate manipulates symbols?

Whereas it is of interest to see to what extent a chimpanzee can use language as do humans, it is of equal interest to see whether they may seek to use language in their own manner.

This view might seem inconsistent with our emphasis on the acquisition of the linguistic concept of "self." After all, if an animal's cognition determines the kind of language it can have, how could an autonomous linguistic development have general effects? In our view, symbols provide an important mode of explicit internal representation of the world, a kind of "private scratchpad." Once such a facility is developed, it may *release* a variety of otherwise latent capacities, even if it does not *cause* them. Our contention is that the symbolization of "self" is such a releaser.

Of course, if we succeed in eliciting a true human language in a chimpanzee, we will face Kafka's question—*Have we taught a chimpanzee to talk or have we released a human being?*

REFERENCES

1. HAYES, J. H. 1951. The Ape in Our House. Harper & Brothers. New York, N.Y.
2. KELLOG, W. N. & L. A. KELLOG. 1933: The Ape and the Child: A Study of Environmental Influence Upon Early Behavior. McGraw-Hill, Inc. New York, N.Y.
3. GARDNER, R. A. & B. T. GARDNER. 1969. Teaching sign language to a chimpanzee. Science **165:** 664–672.
4. GARDNER, B. T. & R. A. GARDNER. 1971. Two-way communication with an infant chimpanzee. *In* Behavior of Nonhuman Primates. A. Schrier and F. Stollnitz, Eds. Vol. 4: 117–184. Academic Press. New York, N.Y.
5. GARDNER, R. A. & B. T. GARDNER. 1975. Early signs of language in child and chimpanzee. Science **187:** 752–753.
6. GARDNER, B. T. & R. A. GARDNER. 1975. Evidence for sentence constituents in the early utterances of child and chimpanzee. J. Exp. Psychol. **104**(3): 244–267.
7. PREMACK, D. 1970. A functional analysis of language. J. Exp. Analysis Behav. **14:** 107–125.
8. PREMACK, D. 1971. On the assessment of language competence in chimpanzees. *In* Cognitive Processes of Nonhuman Primates. A. M. Schrier and F. Stollnitz, Eds. Academic Press. New York, N.Y.
9. FOUTS, R. 1972. Use of guidance in teaching sign language to a chimpanzee (*Pan troglodytes*). J. Comp. Physiol. Psychol. **80:** 515–522.
10. FOUTS, R. 1975. Field report: The state of apes. Psychology Today 7(8): 31–54.
11. RUMBAUGH, D. M., E. C. VON GLASERSFELD & T. V. GILL. 1973. Reading and sentence completion by a chimpanzee. Science **182:** 731–733.
12. GALLUP, G. G. 1971. Chimpanzees: Self-Recognition. Science 167(3914), 86–87.
13. BEM, D. J. 1972. Self-perception theory. Adv. Exp. Social Psychol. Academic Press. New York, N.Y. **6:** 1–62.
14. HEIDER, F. 1958. The Psychology of Interpersonal Relations. John Wiley. New York, N.Y.
15. KELLEY, H. H. 1967. Attribution theory in social psychology. *In* Nebraska Symposium on Motivation D. Levine, Ed. **15:** Lincoln, Neb.: University of Nebraska Press. Lincoln, Neb.
16. SCHACHTER, S. & J. E. SINGER. 1962. Cognitive, social and physiological determinents of emotional state. Psychol. Rev. **69:** 379–399.
17. MILLER, R. E., J. H. BANKS, JR. & N. OGAWA. 1962. Communication of affect in "cooperative conditioning" of rhesus monkeys. J. Abnormal and Social Psychol. 1962, **64**(5), 343–348.
18. STOKOE, W. C., JR. 1960. Sign language structure: an outline of the visual communication system of the American deaf. Studies in Linguistics: Occasional Papers. No. 8. University of Buffalo. Buffalo, N.Y.
19. BELLUGI, U. & E. KLIMA. 1975. Ann. N.Y. Acad. Sci. **263:** 225–235.

20. MCNEILL, D. 1970. The acquisition of language: A study of developmental psycholinguistics. Harper and Row. New York, N.Y.
21. BRAINE, M. D. S. 1963. The ontogeny of English phrase structure: The first phase. Language. **39:** 1–14.
22. BLOOM, L. 1974. One Word at a Time: the Use of Single Word Utterances before Syntax. Mouton. The Hague, The Netherlands.
23. LIEBERMAN, P. 1975. On the Origins of Language. MacMillan Publishing Company. New York, N.Y.
24. BROWN, R. 1973. A First Language: The Early Stages. Harvard University Press. Cambridge, Mass.

DISCUSSION PAPER: COMPARISON OF SIGN LANGUAGE PROJECTS AND IMPLICATIONS FOR LANGUAGE ORIGINS

Roger S. Fouts

Department of Psychology
University of Oklahoma
Norman, Oklahoma 73069

At present there are several different research projects examining language-like behavior in chimpanzees. These studies have been reported in the literature in addition to several more that have been reported by the popular press. Although the projects being performed by established investigators are different from one another in their methodology, it is encouraging to note that in spite of the methodological differences many of the conclusions concerning the capacities of chimpanzees to engage in language-like behavior have been similar.

In addition to the similar findings by the different researchers, there have been different findings that may be because of the different methodologies used or particular questions the experimenters were examining. Their differences, however, are complimentary to one another in terms of understanding the chimpanzees' cognitive capacities.

In this paper I shall attempt to point out a few of the differences between two projects using American Sign Language; the project directed by R. Allen Gardner and B. T. Gardner in Nevada, and the sign language project of which I am in charge at the Institute of Primate Studies at the University of Oklahoma.

First, the Gardners' project[1] can be classified as a long-term longitudinal study, examining the *development* of Sign in chimpanzees. They have been using an immersion technique; i.e., immersing their chimpanzees in an environment of sign language and raising them in much the same fashion as a human child would be raised. At the same time, they were quantifying and recording the sign development by the chimpanzees.

In regard to this technique I have heard criticism from individuals who have seen films of the Gardners' first chimpanzee, Washoe. The criticisms concentrate on the fact that in the films Washoe was constantly being drilled and her environment was full of experimenter-imposed contingencies requiring Washoe to use sign language. This criticism comes from individuals who have not read the many published reports by the Gardners[1] or myself[3] concerning the project. The purpose of the Gardners films were to record what a chimpanzee looked like when producing signs. It was not intended to represent a day in Washoe's life. If it had been, then only a very small percentage of it would have been concerned with drilling, data collecting, and testing. The vast majority of time I spent with Washoe, perhaps over 90%, was spent signing to Washoe about such things as breakfast, lunch, tea, dinner, changing diapers, cleaning up potty mistakes, brushing teeth, cleaning the trailer, playing hide and seek, playing go-games, playing in the sand box, and so on. Relative to the signing occurring in the regular routine the time spent in establishing and recording sign reliability data was small indeed.

In regard to contingencies imposed on Washoe, these were, in my experience, not unlike those contingencies I place on my own children in regard to language. If my son points to and makes a grunting sound in regard to a glass of milk, even though the meaning of his actions is clear, I require him to ask for it in a correct and polite manner. On occasion, Washoe, as do most children, would make similar attempts. These attempts would be met with responses that are typical of parents whose children try the same method.

The Gardners are gathering invaluable data with this method, but conditions (mainly financial, personnel, and nature of facilities) do not always permit such time-demanding research. The research I am involved in takes quite a different approach because of the different existing conditions. I am more interested in examining the cognitive and conceptual capacities of the chimpanzee; and American Sign Language is a most useful tool with which to do so. The research I am engaged in is to a much lesser degree longitudinal and much more cross-sectional in that I am more interested in what the chimpanzees are capable of doing through the use of Sign. For example, my studies are pointed toward explaining the chimpanzee's conceptual capacities and analogs to human language. In this respect my research is similar to research done by David Premack[4] or the research done by Duane Rumbaugh et al.,[5] but I am using a different mode.

In addition, the skilled and well-thought-out studies such as those of Dr. Premack, Dr. Rumbaugh, Dr. Terrace and the Drs. Gardner, there are attempts being made by various untrained students who have a chimpanzee, who claim to be doing a Gardner-type of project. These are most ambitious projects when you consider that they generally do not have the proper funding or, more importantly, properly trained personnel who are skilled in the use of Sign. Even the Gardners[2] have pointed out the extreme importance of the latter point, having skilled people in the use of Sign. On Project Washoe, only a small percentage of the members used Sign as their first language. The Gardners have corrected this shortcoming of Project Washoe in their present project by hiring more native signers who are either deaf themselves or by hiring people of deaf parents.

This improvement of the Gardner's present project is a reaction to a simple yet well-taken point. A chimpanzee will acquire and use the dominant form of communication in its environment that it is capable of producing. As a result, if signs are used only occasionally or sporadically in the chimpanzee's environment and vocal language or nonverbal communication is used instead, then the chimpanzee will use nonverbal communication to communicate its needs and desires. Oftentimes, English-speaking people find it easier to use nonverbal communication than to spend the time learning the second language of American Sign Language.

Finally, I would like to address myself to the question of what are we studying, and what does it have to do with language origins. This would apply to all the projects examining chimpanzee language or communication behavior. In order for it to be used as evidence for a common origin of language in the two species it must be a homologous behavior. That is, it must be the result of certain common neurological structures in both species. To the best of my knowledge, the present state of the science of neurology does not allow us to determine the answer to this question.

The alternative is to conceive of chimpanzee language or communications as being an analog to human language or communication. Chimpanzees are most definitely a different species, and based on this simple observation it seems reasonable to conclude that chimpanzee language or communication is unique to chimpanzees. Likewise, human language or communication is unique to humans.

It is also much more comfortable for psychologists to study analogs, since that is what we have been trained to do. To clarify this point, I will use an often used example; an insect flies using wings that are made from an epidermal fold, and birds, of course, use a form of their upper extremity. By comparing these two methods of locomotion they are both flying, and by studying them we can observe that they both use the air-foil principle. Psychology is often the study of such analogies. For example, by studying the partial reinforcement effect in pigeon,. rats, dogs, humans, and so on, we are able to determine the range of applicability that this principle of learning has for the various species. The study of analogies ca1. be most illuminating, as has been shown by the various studies examining the analog of human language in the chimpanzee.

I am afraid that the study of behavior in a homologous sense must wait upon the neurological sciences for its final support. Presently, as Atz[6] has stated, there are enormous problems involved in applying the homologous model (which was developed to explain morphology) in an attempt to explain behavior. However, to conceive of any complex behavior as being totally separate and totally unique in any species is to show one's ignorance of the effect of biological evolution upon behavior.

REFERENCES

1. GARDNER, B. T. & R. A. GARDNER. 1971. Two-way communication with an infant chimpanzee. *In* Behavior of Nonhuman Primates. A. M. Schrier & F. Stollnitz, Eds. Vol. **4:** 117–184. Academic Press. New York, N.Y.
2. GARDNER, B. T. & R. A. GARDNER. 1975. Evidence for sentence constituents in the early utterances of child and chimpanzee. J. Exper. Psych.: General. **104**(3): 244–267.
3. FOUTS, R. S. 1975. Communication with chimpanzees. *In* Hominisation and Behavior. H. Kurth & I. Eibl-Eibesfeld, Eds. 137–158. Gustav Fischer Verlag. Stuttgart, Germany.
4. PREMACK, D. 1971. On the assessment of language competence in the chimpanzee. *In* Behavior of Nonhuman Primates. A. M. Schrier & F. Stollnitz, Eds. Vol. **4:** 185–228. Academic Press. New York, N.Y.
5. RUMBAUGH, D., T. V. GILL, & E. C. VON GLASERFELD. 1973. Reading and sentence completion by a chimpanzee (*Pan*). Science **182:** 731–733.
6. ATZ, J. W. 1970. The application of the idea of homology to behavior. *In* Development and Evolution of Behavior. L. R. Aronson, E. Tobach, D. S. Lehrman & J. S. Rosenblatt, Eds. 53–74. W. H. Freeman and Co. San Francisco, Calif.

DISCUSSION PAPER: THE COMMUNICATIVE COMPETENCE OF CHILD AND CHIMPANZEE

Lyn W. Miles

Department of Biocultural Anthropology
University of Connecticut
Storrs, Connecticut 06268

The use of sign language,[1,2] plastic symbols,[3] and computer keyboard[4] by apes is of growing interest to psychologists, linguists, and anthropologists interested in assessing the linguistic competence of apes and understanding the development and evolution of language in humans. I should like to discuss two areas of further research suggested by Rumbaugh and Gill in this volume: 1) the comparison of the linguistic competence of apes and human children, and 2) the examination of communication with apes through conversation.

Most studies of child language have concentrated on the development of abstract linguistic structures, especially grammar. This focus is also found in linguistic comparisons of children and chimpanzees by Brown,[5] B. Gardner and R. Gardner,[6,7] and R. Gardner and B. Gardner.[8,9] These and other studies have shown that a chimpanzee's cognitive linguistic ability allows it to construct a linguistic proposition to convey a conceptual content at approximately a human two-year-old level. Rumbaugh[4] and B. Gardner and R. Gardner[7] have shown that chimpanzees are aware of what constitutes a grammatical syntactic construction. Although it is not yet known if chimpanzees utilize syntactic encoding in their constructions, there is evidence that chimpanzees can form sentences, categorize in terms of semantic attributes, generalize the use of words, and invent new terms.[2,3]

But language acquisition involves more than grammar—it also involves communicative competence. A child acquiring speech or sign language and an ape acquiring sign or artificial language must also learn how to use it appropriately in actual situations. In addition to grammatical comparisons, it is important to compare the communicative competence of children and chimpanzees by analyzing the communicative intentions expressed by their linguistic constructions.

The analysis of communicative functions and the pragmatics of language use is a new approach in child language studies. In this approach, language is understood as an information-transmitting system for communicating social intentions as well as linguistic propositions. It proposes an integration of the relationship between the functional and grammatical aspects of communicative competence.[14]

A functional analysis begins with the speech act, suggested by Austin[10] and Searle[11] as the basic unit of linguistic communication. A speech act is composed of 1) a linguistic proposition that conveys the conceptual content of an utterance, *plus* 2) an illocutionary force which indicates whether the utterance is an assertion, promise, request, question, or other kind of act. The primary determinant of the illocutionary force of an utterance is the speaker's communicative intention.[13] Communicative intentions are expressed through illocutionary acts that convey how a speaker intends an utterance to be taken. Illocutionary acts are understood primarily in relation to the context and response of the recipient of the communication.

For example, the proposition, "Joe tickle Ally" can be expressed as a request, "Tickle Ally, Joe," which communicates the intention, ". . . to induce in a listener the recognition that the speaker intends the utterance to be taken as a solicitation,"[12] in this case, a solicitation for the performance of an action. The same proposition can also be expressed as other acts, e.g. a question, "Is Joe tickling Ally?" or a description of an event, "Joe is tickling Ally," with differing communicative intentions.

Dore [12,13] has examined the uses of language by children in the early stages of language acquistion. He systematically sampled the spontaneous conversation of children in relatively unrestrained natural settings, and classified their utterances according to a variety of illocutionary acts. He found that very young children using only single-word utterances produce "primitive speech acts" that function to convey their intentions before they acquire sentences.[19] By the time children use sentences their illocutionary acts include requests, questions, agreements and disagreements, statements, descriptions, qualifications, and other acts.[13]

The categories of illocutionary acts devised by Dore can also be applied to the use of the American Sign Language for the Deaf by chimpanzees. By using the same procedures developed by Dore for children, it is possible to determine the "communicative acts" of chimpanzee sign communications, *analogous* to the illocutionary acts of children. Whether or not the linguistic structures underlying these acts prove to be *homologous* will depend on neurological evidence that is not yet available.

A functional analysis of chimpanzee sign acts also permits the testing of hypotheses concerning chimpanzee communicative competence. For example, reports and films of chimpanzees using sign language have left the impression with some observers that chimpanzees do not use their linguistic skills productively, and engage solely in naming objects and making requests. Films of chimpanzees using signs, including my own, are often designed to illustrate the acquisition of vocabulary items and include as many examples as possible within a brief period. Although investigators R. Gardner and B. Gardner[1] and Fouts[15] have indicated otherwise, the notion that this is the extent of their usage has persisted.

A functional analysis permits a testing of this hypothesis by analyzing the communicative functions of the signed communications which occur spontaneously during natural conversation rather than during vocabularly drills or experimental settings. In conversation, unlike artificially structured situations, the chimpanzee is free to construct sign communications of its own to convey its communicative intentions.

In order to evaluate chimpanzee use of signs and test this and other hypotheses, I analyzed the communicative acts used by a chimpanzee and compared the results with studies of children. In this analysis three assumptions were made: 1) the theoretical and performance criteria that can be behaviorally applied to the use of language by deaf and hearing children can also be applied to the use of signs by chimpanzees; 2) relaxed social contexts foster the spontaneous use of sign language by chimpanzees and permit an examination of natural communication in a conversational setting, and 3) a functional analysis of the communicative intentions and communicative acts of the use of signs of chimpanzees illustrates their communicative competence.

Ally, a five-year-old male chimpanzee at the Institute for Primate Research at the University of Oklahoma, was videotaped while engaged in sign-language conversations with a human partner during relaxed play contexts. Based on guidelines established by Stokoe[16,17] and Hoffmeister,[18] Ally's use of signs during ten 15-minute conversations was transcribed from the videotapes and classified according to communicative act types adapted from Dore's studies.[12] These categories included various types of requests, descriptions, statements, and questions.

The classification of Ally's sign acts was based on four criteria: 1) the sign communication (the semantic content of the communication itself); 2) the behavioral accompaniments (the chimpanzee's behavior, including gestures, facial expressions, body movements, focus of attention, emotional state, and vocalizations); 3) the

TABLE 1

ALLY'S COMMUNICATIVE ACTS

Communicative Act	Number	Percentage
Action Request	226	46%
Naming	189	38%
Other Acts	79	16%
Total	494	100%

context (the social and physical situation, including activities, topic of conversation, games events, and objects or persons present); and 4) the response (the signed communications and behavioral accompaniments of the human partner receiving the communication).

In the distribution of Ally's communicative acts shown in TABLE 1, action requests and naming represent 84% of Ally's communicative acts. TABLE 1, however, does not distinguish unsolicited communicative acts initiated by Ally from those which were solicited by a WH-question from his conversational partner. distribution of these is shown in TABLE 2.

TABLE 2 indicates that one/third of Ally's communicative acts were solicited as a response to a WH-question. The vast majority of these (91%) were action requests and namings. This is because Ally's partner usually asked WH-questions such as "Who?," "What's this?," and "What do you want?," as a way to introduce new topics of conversation and induce Ally to converse. This inflated the number of action requests and namings produced by Ally, since these acts are the most appropriate responses to the partner's WH-questions. Brown reports that this phenomenon also occurs in child language studies, ". . . when over-anxious adults distort the conversational setting through determined efforts to elicit communications by asking names of things and producing strings in the respondent, rather than interacting in a natural way."[5]

TABLE 2 also shows that two/thirds of Ally's communications were unsolicited, that is, initiated by Ally. In addition, one/third of all Ally's communications were action requests, and one/fifth were namings, together constituting 54% of Ally's acts. Ally produced more than four times as many acts other than action requests and namings when allowed to initiate communications than when required to respond to his partner's solicitations. This suggests Ally's solicited responses are not really characteristic of his natural use of signs and should be considered an artifact of the method.

TABLE 2

SOLICITED AND UNSOLICITED COMMUNICATIVE ACTS

Communicative Act	Solicited		Unsolicited	
	Number	Percentage of Total	Number	Percentage of Total
Action Request	65	13%	161	33%
Naming	86	17%	103	21%
Other Acts	14	3%	65	13%
Total	165	33%	329	67%

The distribution of Ally's communicative acts when solicited naming and action requests are excluded is shown in TABLE 3. Solicited other acts were included because although they were responses to WH-questions, they were not really solicited. They represent communications that were made in addition to a naming response by Ally, and thus were double-coded.

TABLE 3 represents the most accurate distribution of communicative acts initiated by Ally. It shows that although action requests and naming constitute the bulk of Ally's communications, 23%, or almost one/fourth of his natural acts, express other kinds of communicative intentions. These other acts include attention devices, internal reports, questions, descriptions of events, descriptions of properties, statements of possession, and statements concerning the attributes of others.

Internal reports, property descriptions, and statements about the attributes of others are of particular interest in understanding Ally's conceptual processes. These acts express Ally's feelings and state of mind, his representations of observable characteristics of an object, and his beliefs about another individual's internal state.

For example, when Ally's badly injured foot became painful he reported, "shoe hurt." On another occasion he commented on the strong smell of his partner's pipe tobacco, and then noticing another trainer, George, standing nearby, signed, "George smell Roger." These acts illustrate Ally's expression of his own feelings and the sensations of other.

TABLE 3

COMMUNICATIVE ACTS EXLUDING SOLICITED ACTION REQUESTS AND NAMING

Communicative Act	Number	Percentage
Unsolicited Action Request	161	47%
Unsolicited Naming	103	30%
Other Acts	79	23%
Total	343	100%

During a conversation about a rubber boot which shared some properties with a large rubber box, Ally asked, "shoe that box?" When presented with a feather for the first time, Ally called it a "string," the most appropriate choice in his vocabulary. He described a brightly colored feather duster when held feathers-up like a bouquet, as a "flower string." When Ally was tickled with the duster held feathers-down, Ally described it as a "tickle string." Ally also described an orange peel as a "food smell," and a woven straw hat as a "string hat." These acts show he was able to describe aspects of his environment using novel combinations as a way to map his concepts.

Comparison of these results with the use of language by two-year-olds, probably the most appropriate group based on Ally's Mean Length of Utterance, is not yet possible. Dore, however, has described the early stages of language use by 1–1½ year-olds and three-year-olds. He reports the use of two "primitive speech act" styles in 1–1½ year olds, a "symbol-oriented" style (predominantly naming, repeating, and practicing words) and a "message-oriented" style (predominantly action requests and action-oriented communication).[19] Although Ally would occasionally sign to himself with no apparent intention to communicate, he initiated one and a half times as many action requests as namings, which would suggest his style is "message-oriented."

Dore also identified the illocutionary acts of seven three-year-olds.[13] As in Ally's use of signs, action requests and namings were the two largest categories. They represented 10% (action requests) and 7.9% (namings) of the three-year olds' communicative acts. Ally, however, performed only nine types of communicative acts, while Dore's three-year-olds performed 32 acts. Thus, the overall proportion of action requests and namings is larger in Allys' smaller repertoire of communicative acts, although it should not be concluded that this performance exhausts Ally's repertoire.

Dore also notes the striking "rationality" of the discourse of his three-year-olds, which contained few nonsequiturs.[20] Ally's discourse was similarly striking, and contained long conversational exchanges about various subjects including environmental referents such as birds flying overhead, and a cat stalking a frog. This confirms the importance of a conversational setting for acquiring a representative sample of a chimpanzee's communicative acts.

In conclusion, the evidence so far suggests Ally's use of signs to communicate his intentions is similar to the use of speech by children. It is hoped that information on the use of signs by deaf children, the most appropriate comparison, will be available in the future. Ally's use of signs extends beyond naming and action requests to include other communicative acts that consitute almost one/fourth of his initiated communications. This demonstrates that Ally uses signs not only for labeling and instrumental goals, but also for expressing notions about himself, others, and his environment.

Further research may reveal some differences between the use of signs by Ally, and the use of language by children. But the results so far suggest that any differences that do exist between the communicative competence of Ally and children in the early stages of language acquisition are probably ones of degree, not kind. The linguistic competence of apes is not sufficient to claim they have language, but it does raise the issue of whether or not this ability is expressed in their natural communication system, particularly in the gestural mode. It also provides a model for the initial linguistic competence of language-evolving hominids.

REFERENCES

1. GARDNER, R. B. GARDNER. 1969. Teaching sign language to a chimpanzee. Science **165**: 664–672.
2. FOUTS, R. 1973. Acquisition and testing of gestural signs in four young chimpanzees. Science **180**: 978–980.
3. PREMACK, D. 1972. Language in chimpanzee? Science **172**: 808–822.
4. RUMBAUGH, D. 1973. Reading and sentence completion by a chimpanzee. Science **182**: 731–733.
5. BROWN, R. 1973. A First Language: The Early Stages. Harvard University Press. Cambridge, Mass.
6. GARDNER, B. & R. GARDNER. 1974. Comparing the early utterances of child and chimpanzee. In Minnesota Symposium on Child Psychology. A. Pick, Ed. Vol. 8. University of Minnesota Press. Minneapolis, Minn.
7. GARDNER, B. & R. GARDNER. 1975. Evidence for sentence constituents in the early utterances of child and chimpanzee. Science **104**: 244–267.
8. GARDNER, R. & B. GARDNER. 1974. Review of R. Brown's A First Language: The Early Stages. Amer. J. Psychol. **87**: 729–736.
9. GARDNER, R. & B. GARDNER. 1975. Early signs of language in child and chimpanzee. Science **187**: 752–753.
10. AUSTIN, J. 1962. How To Do Things With Words. Oxford University Press. New York, N.Y.
11. SEARLE, J. 1969. Speech Acts. Cambridge University Press. Cambridge, England.

12. DORE, J. 1974. Communicative intentions and the pragmatics of language development. Unpublished manuscript.

13. DORE, J. 1975. Children's illocutionary acts. *In* Discourse Production and Comprehension. R. O. Freedle, Ed. Lawrence Erlbaum Assoc. Inc. Hillsdale, N.J.

14. DORE, J. 1975. Holophrases, speech acts and language universals. J. Child Language **2**: 21–40

15. FOUTS, R. 1975. Communication with chimpanzees. *In* Hominisation and Behavior. H. Kurth & I. Eibl-Eibesfeld, Eds.: 137–158. Gustav Fischer Verlag. Stuttgart, Germany.

16. STOKOE, W. 1965. A Dictionary of American Sign Language. Gallaudet College Press. Washington, D.C.

17. STOKOE, W. 1972. Semiotics and Human Sign Language. Mouton. The Hague, The Netherlands.

18. HOFFMEISTER, R. Some procedural guidelines for the study of the acquisition of sign language. Sign Language Studies. In press.

19. DORE, J. 1974. A pragmatic description of early language development. J. Psycholinguistic Research **3**: 343–350.

20. DORE, J. 1975. Communicative, conceptual and grammatical conditions on the acquistion of speech acts. Unpublished manuscript.

DISCUSSION PAPER:
CHIMPANZEES AND LANGUAGE EVOLUTION

William A. Malmi

Department of Anthropology
University of California/Berkeley
Berkeley, California 94720

Among the most remarkable developments of recent years has been the opening of a "dialogue" between human and chimpanzee.[1-4] The relevance of chimpanzee performance to human language evolution is controversial, but may be somewhat easier to assess if the debate is framed in explicitly evolutionary terms so that behavioral reconstruction may follow established biological principles. In this pursuit, several lines of research are implied that may refine, if not resolve, some of the questions being asked.

Whether or not *Washoe* (*Washoe* is used herein as representative of all the "linguistic" apes) is using "language" is not particularly useful in this context. The word is used so variously that any consensus is unlikely, a difficulty that is compounded if the dimension of time is introduced: given either a continuum of change or a succession of stages in the transition from chimp-like antecedent to speaking human, where is the linguistic Rubicon to be placed? Moreover, most definitions of language rely on the presence or absence of design features,[5,6] so that whether a particular output is linguistic is determined by whether or not it involves *syntax, displacement,*[7] *separation from affect,*[8] or some such trait. The result has been that features are proposed which are presumed unique and crucial to human language; these are taught to apes; new features are proposed. But design features are not useful for establishing evolutionary continuity.[9] Also, it is as unrealistic to expect chimpanzees to emulate all the features of human language as it had been previously to deny that they could learn some of them. The important issue is not whether or not they can learn all the "crucial" aspects of human language, or even what assemblage of traits is to be deemed sufficient criterion of language, but what is the relationship of the performance which has already been demonstrated to language evolution? Does *Washoe* evince language-like behavior because she is employing neural/cognitive systems similar to those underlying human language as a consequence of common origin, or are the structural similarities superficial and dependent largely on training procedures?

In biological terms, the issue is one of *homology* vs. *analogy.*[10,11] One of the reasons the design-feature approach is not useful in assessing homology is that traits of common origin may diverge markedly over a short time, whereas traits of different origins may converge so as to appear virtually identical: "homologous structures may be extensively similar or dissimilar. Therefore, similarity is to be considered something quite apart from considerations of homology." (Ref. 12, p. 101.)

Before examining ways of assessing homology, it is well to consider briefly some aspects of human and nonhuman cognition and communication in relation to homology. In the first place, presumed phylogenetic closeness is not sufficient to establish behavioral homology, especially when the behavior does not naturally occur in one of the species but is elicited only through extensive training. The point is worth making because, whereas the chimpanzee researchers have, especially more recently, recognized this to be the case (perhaps more so than most of their critics), they sometimes write as though it is not. Fouts, for example, after a good discussion

598

of homology, including the important suggestion that the neural basis of the behavior must ultimately be investigated, goes on to say that "the extreme physiological, behavioral and evolutionary closeness of Man to chimpanzee should actually lead one to conclude that a very similar biological mechanism is operating at the basis of language behavior in the respective species." (Ref. 13, p. 476.) Rumbaugh & Gill (this volume), although careful not to overstate the significance of Lana's performance, cite a recent article by King and Wilson[14] which indicates 99% genetic similarity between chimpanzee and human, and which to the lay reader may give a false impression of physiological closeness.

The most recent date postulated for the separation of human and ape lines is about 5 million years ago.[15] This date, based on biochemical comparisons, is extremely controversial, since most other researchers place the divergence at a minimum of 15–20 million years ago.[16] If correct, it would imply a much closer relationship between man and chimpanzee than previously supposed, but it should be remembered that evolutionary rates vary considerably, and that in mosaic evolution some traits are rather conservative, whereas others change rapidly. Human evolution has involved especially dramatic shifts in diet, locomotion, technology, social organization, communication, and the brain. This means that whether apes and humans are remarkably similar depends on what is being compared. In fact, the point of the King-Wilson article is to reconcile the observed genetic similarity with the known morphological and behavioral differences: "Most important for the future study of human evolution would be the demonstration of differences in the timing of gene expression during development, particularly during the development of adaptively crucial systems such as the brain." (Ref. 14, p. 114.) The 99% similarity in genotype thus reflects recent time of separation, whereas the 1% dissimilarity includes some phenotypically important mutations (the 1%, incidentally, represents at least 40 million base-pair differences).

It is important also to keep in mind that "cognition," like "intelligence," is not just a rather generalized means of coping that improves as we move up the phylogenetic scale; it consists of a number of capacities, some of which humans share with other species, others of which have been sufficiently modified in hominid evolution to be considered species-specific for humans. Language is undoubtedly based on both kinds of cognitive capacity. In emphasizing the similarities between chimpanzee and human linguistic capacities it must be realized that, unless the nature and origins of the differences can be ascertained, the process of reconstruction can hardly move forward from our chimp-like antecedents. In comparing the formal aspects of simian and human "language" there should be some attempt to distinguish between similarities resulting from training procedures, from features of mammalian cognition, and from capacities more directly relevant to the events of the last million years or so.

Humans are natural language-users, but chimpanzees are not. It has, of course, been suggested that chimps do use language in the wild, but that it is too subtle and too different from human speech to be recognized as such. There is, however, no evidence for this, despite close observation of vocalizations, facial expressions, postures, and gestures over thousands of hours by a number of trained observers. It may also be asked why such a system would be so different from our own if it is assumed that chimpanzees and humans are remarkably similar. The natural communication of chimpanzees[17-19] appears typical of nonhuman primate systems,[20,21] and is very different from human language. In fact, it is beginning to appear that nonhuman primate communication is characteristically mammalian[22,23] rather than a novel development, so that the ape, like the monkey, expresses itself in ways that have more in common with a dog or cat than a human language-user. The conservatism of mammalian signal systems is remarkable in the face of considerable morphological, socioecological, and cognitive diversity, and serves to underscore the uniqueness of human expression. Comparative neurological work suggests that both animal communication and human nonlinguistic expression are mediated largely by the primitive limbic structures of the brain,[24-26] whereas language derives largely from reorganization of neocortex.[26-28] Unfortunately, most of this work has been done on humans and a few species of monkey, and there is little information on the substrates of ape communication, although research on the gibbon[29] suggests that their call system is organized similarly to monkey vocalization.

On the other hand, it is not surprising that there is evidence (Menzel & Johnson, this volume; Davenport, this volume) that apes exhibit cognitive/intellectual capacities not shared with monkeys, and that in some respects these are more "humanoid" skills. It would be reasonable to assume that capacities like some of these, in the early hominids, changed in ways that ultimately led to language and speech. Can these aspects of cognition be isolated? What have they evolved for in chimpanzee behavior? After all, preadaptations for a behavior (in this case, language) will not be maintained in a population unless they confer some immediate benefit. If the normal chimpanzee behavior for which such skills have evolved could be demonstrated, it might provide a clue to the origins of human language: greeting? hunting? tool use? Perhaps something very different from what might be expected: "No biological phenomenon is without antecedents. The question is, 'How obvious are the antecedents of the human propensity for language?' It is my opinion that they are not in the least obvious." (Ref. 9, p. 234.)

To return to *Washoe* and the question of homology, it must be asked, "Are some of the skills underlying *Washoe*'s performance particularly relevant to an understanding of human language evolution? If so, what are they and what is their normal employment in free-ranging chimpanzee behavior?" Note that this is a very different question from whether or not *Washoe* is using language as determined by design features of the human and chimpanzee linguistic systems.

Homology is judged on the basis of any of the following, all of which have been represented in this volume:

1. Traits may be traced to their common origin by reference to the *fossil record*. Unfortunately, behavior does not fossilize, so that it must be inferred from morphological landmarks or the archeological record. Compounding the difficulty, the language-relevant soft tissue of vocal tract and brain are not preserved, but must be reconstructed from somewhat unreliable landmarks on the skull. Finally, the fossil record for humans and more particularly for apes is extremely fragmentary.

2. If traits share a *multiplicity of similarities*, homology is likely, especially if such similarities are not functionally related to one another. This approach underlies the practice of amassing a roster of design-feature similarities. Unfortunately, in *Washoe*'s case the similarities are largely related to one another not only because some design features are contingent on the presence of other design features, but also because nearly all of them result from training.

3. Behaviors that are similar because of retention of features derived from common origin tend to be *similar in ontogenesis*. Both the schedule and the modes of language acquisition are being compared between chimp and child.

4. Evolution is more conservative in micro- than in macrostructure. The bat is morphologically convergent with birds because of its aerial niche, the porpoise with fish because of its aquatic habitat. In each case, mammalian affinities are revealed by examination of blood, skeleton, eyes, brain, and other features less subject to environmental features than fins, wings, and snouts. Thus, traits should be examined

for *minuteness of similarities.* This concern, of course, lies beneath some of the argument over whether, say, *Washoe*'s productivity is really very much like linguistic productivity, or whether her acquisition strategies are genuinely similar to those of humans.

In dealing with behavioral as opposed to morphological comparisons, there is a corollary that may be added. That is, that the biological substrates underlying the performance must be examined. This is because behavior is much more plastic than its physiological basis. Among mammals, and especially the higher primates, learning plays an important role and behavior is very dependent on experience. Humans take advantage of this in training animals, so that apes have been taught to ride bicycles, have tea parties, smoke cigarettes, drink from a glass, and use "language." All but the last can have played no role in chimpanzee evolution, so that success in such activities stems from modification of skills that are present in the chimpanzee repertoire for other purposes. By examining the neural basis of *Washoe*'s behavior, it may be possible to determine whether those skills are relevant to human language or whether we are confronted with a situation of clever chimp, clever trainer.

Fouts,[13] in particular, has noted the importance of ascertaining the neural basis of behaviors being compared, but is perhaps unduly pessimistic because it is not presently possible to detail how such neurological organization works to produce the behavior. The neurological investigations of nonhuman primate communication have not explained just how such behavior is produced, but they have suggested a great deal about its organization. The work of Ploog and his associates,[24] and of Robinson (this volume) among others, has not only indicated the vast differences between the substrates of language and primate communication, but has suggested why primate signals take the forms they do and express the things they do. Unfortunately, such mapping is difficult, time-consuming, and expensive, and would be difficult to extend to the chimpanzee. Moreover, it requires chronic deep electrode implantation, and, usually, ultimate sacrifice of the subject. Despite the scientific benefits, it becomes increasingly difficult to justify such techniques for chimpanzees due to financial, conservational, and ethical considerations.

There are, fortunately, alternatives that are more feasible, although somewhat less refined than deep electrode implantations. One would be the selective use of drugs. The Wada test, for example, is used to determine language dominance in humans prior to brain surgery. This involves the injection of sodium amytal into the left or right carotid artery, and blocks speech functions in the speech-dominant hemisphere. Would it affect chimpanzee production or comprehension of "language"? If so, is there a lateralized effect? If the behavior is in some sense lateralized, is it consistently dominant on a particular side of the brain for all chimps? Does the Wada test also interfere with other kinds of activities?

Especially intriguing is the suggestion of Raleigh and Ervin (this volume) that EEG monitoring be employed. Application of such techniques to language behavior is not new;[9,31] in fact, Melnechuk has urged that there be electrophysiological investigation of human and nonhuman communication.[30] Analysis need not initially be very refined, but concerned with such parameters as cortical/subcortical, lateralized/nonlateralized, anterior/posterior, and so on. Particularly important is that brain activity be monitored through surface electrodes so that it may be studied in intact, free-ranging animals who have not been subjected to surgery. Assume several possibilities in the case of *Washoe*'s performance:

similar output—different neural basis (nonhomologous)
similar output—similar neural basis (homologous)
different output—similar neural basis (homologous)

The first two instances are the most frequently debated, and both are amenable to various kinds of analysis, but it is in the third case that EEG could prove especially useful. Without some kind of ongoing monitoring, it seems unlikely that homology would be suspected in behaviors that appear superficially quite different from one another. In any case, if homologies are suggested they may be telemetered in free-ranging chimpanzees. Moreover, developmental aspects of human and nonhuman acquisition can be compared. Human signers can be compared with chimpanzee signers with speakers with aphasics, and so on: the permutations of comparison are considerable. The potential advantages of EEG analysis outweigh the technical difficulties involved in interpreting the brain-wave patterns, and this avenue should be investigated.

In closing, it should be stressed that, while homologies need to be investigated, preferably by examination of neurological substrates, analogies and the design-feature approach are potentially valuable, if not used to argue evolutionary continuity. By comparing language and nonhuman primate communication in terms of environmental reference, displacement, and duality of patterning, for example, not only can the capacities of the systems be compared, but one may ask, for instance, how duality of patterning might arise, what advantages it would confer, whether it is already present in the cognitive but not expressive capacities of monkeys and apes, and so on. Similarly, there may be analogues in animal behavior that are useful. It has been observed[32] that there are remarkable parallels in the anatomy and acquisition of bird song to those of speech. These may be only coincidental, or related to aspects of bird behavior that will reveal little regarding speech, but such similarities are potentially instructive and should not be discarded merely because there is no possibility of homology with human speech. Marler (this volume) has indicated how aspects of speech and bird song acquisition may be related to the development of vocal learning.

Finally, it would be useful to have more extensive investigation of the communication of free-ranging primates. Although there is presently a large *corpus* of data, most of it has been derived either in the course of studying other aspects of socioecology or collected in such a way that signals are separated from the social matrix of which they are an essential part. The relationship of signal form to function, and to social system and ecological context, has been analyzed in only a few extant field studies, none of which involve the great apes.

REFERENCES

1. GARDNER, R. A. & B. T. GARDNER. 1969. Teaching sign langauge to a chimpanzee. Science **165:** 664–672.
2. RUMBAUGH, D. M., T. V. GILL & E. C. VON GLASERSFELD. 1973. Reading and sentence completion by a chimpanzee. Science **182:** 731–733.
3. PREMACK, A. J. & D. PREMACK. 1972. Teaching language to an ape. Sci. Amer, **227**(4): 92–99.
4. FOUTS, R. S. 1973. Acquisition and testing of gestural signs in four young chimpanzees. Science **180:** 978–980.
5. HOCKETT, C. F. & R. ASCHER. 1964. The human revolution. Current Anthropol. **5:** 135–168.
6. ALTMANN, S. A. 1967. The structure of primate social communication. *In* Social Communication Among Primates. S. A. Altmann, Ed.: 325–362. University of Chicago Press. Chicago, Ill.
7. BRONOWSKI, J. & U. BELLUGI. 1970. Language, name and concept. Science **168:** 669–673.
8. BROWN, R. 1970. The first sentences of child and chimpanzee. *In* Psycholinguistics: Selected Papers. R. Brown, Ed.: 208–231. Free Press. New York, N.Y.

9. LENNEBERG, E. H. 1967. Biological Foundations of Language. John Wiley & Sons, Inc. New York, N.Y.
10. SIMPSON, G. G. 1961. Principles of Animal Taxonomy. Columbia University Press. New York, N.Y.
11. MAYR, E. 1969. Principles of Systematic Zoology. McGraw-Hill, Inc. New York, N.Y.
12. CAMPBELL, C. B. G. & W. HODOS. 1970. The concept of homology and the evolution of the nervous system. Brain, Behavior and Evolution. 3: 353–367.
13. FOUTS, R. S. 1974. Language: origins, definitions and chimpanzees. J. Human Evolution. 3: 475–482.
14. KING, M. C. & A. C. WILSON. 1975. Evolution at two levels in humans and chimpanzees. Science 188: 107–116.
15. SARICH, V. M. 1968. The origin of the hominids: an immunological approach. In Perspectives on Human Evolution. S. L. Washburn & P. C. Jay, Eds. Vol. 1: 94–121. Holt Rinehart & Winston. New York, N.Y.
16. POIRIER, F. E. 1973. Fossil Man: An Evolutionary Journey. C. V. Mosby. St. Louis, Mo.
17. REYNOLDS, V. & F. REYNOLDS. 1965. Chimpanzees of the Budongo forest. In Primate Behavior: Field Studies of Monkeys and Apes. I. DeVore, Ed.: 368–424. Holt Rinehart & Winston. New York, N.Y.
18. GOODALL, J. 1965. Chimpanzees of the Gombe Stream Reserve. In Primate Behavior: Field Studies of Monkeys and Apes. I. DeVore, Ed.: 425–473. Holt Rinehart & Winston. New York, N.Y.
19. VAN LAWICK-GOODALL, J. 1968. A preliminary report on expressive movements and communication in the Gombe Stream chimpanzees. In Primates: Studies in Adaptation and Variability. P. Jay, Ed.: 313–374. Holt Rinehart & Winston. New York, N.Y.
20. MARLER, P. 1965. Communication in monkeys and apes. In Primate Behavior: Field Studies of Monkeys and Apes. I. DeVore, Ed.: 544–584. Holt Rinehart & Winston. New York, N.Y.
21. PLOOG, D. & T. MELNECHUK. 1969. Primate communication. Neurosci. Res. Prog. Bull. 7(5): 419–510.
22. MOYNIHAN, M. 1970. Control, suppression, decay, disappearance and replacement of displays. J. Theor. Biol. 29: 85–112.
23. EISENBERG, J. F. 1973. Mammalian social systems: Are primate social systems unique? Symposia IVth Inter. Congr. Primatol. Vol. 1: 232–249.
24. PLOOG, D. W. 1967. The behavior of squirrel monkeys (Saimiri sciureus) as revealed by sociometry, bioacoustics, and brain stimulation. In Social Communication Among Primates. S. Altmann, Ed.: 149–184.
25. PLOOG, D. & M. MAURUS. 1973. Social communication among squirrel monkeys: Analysis by sociometry, bioacoustics and cerebral radio-stimulation. In Comparative Ecology and Behavior of Primates. R. Michael & J. Crook, Eds.: 211–233. Academic Press. London, England.
26. LANCASTER, J. B. 1968. Primate communication systems and the emergence of human language. In Primates: Studies in Adaptation and Variability. P. Jay, Ed.: 439–457. Holt Rinehart & Winston. New York, N.Y.
27. GESCHWIND, N. 1965. Disconexxion syndromes in animals and man. Brain 88: 237–294, 585–644.
28. ROBINSON, B. W. 1972. Anatomical and physiological contrasts between human and other primate vocalizations. In Perspectives on Human Evolution. S. L. Washburn & P. C. Jay, Eds. Vol. 2: 438–443.
29. APFELBACH, R. 1972. Electrically elicited vocalizations in the gibbon Hylobates lar (Hylobatidae) and their behavioral significance. Zeitschrift für Tierpsychologie. 30: 420–430.
30. PLOOG, D. & T. MELNECHUK. 1971. Are apes capable of language? Neurosci. Res. Prog. Bull. 9(5): 600–700.
31. MCADAM, D. W. & H. A. WHITAKER. 1971. Language production: Electroencephalographic localization in the normal human brain. Science 172: 499–502.
32. NOTTEBOHM, F. 1972. Neural lateralization of vocal control in a passerine bird. J. Exp. Zool. 179: 35–50.

DISCUSSION

David Premack, *Moderator*

Department of Psychology
University of Pennsylvania
Philadelphia, Pennsylvania 19104

DR. PREMACK: In their paper, Terrace and Bever perpetuate some old errors concerning my work as well as introduce one or two new ones. My own failure to have emphasized certain aspects of the work may be at fault in some cases, although the errors are not so easily understood in other cases.

In contending that Sarah's performance was a case of Clever Hans, Terrace and Bever perpetuate an interpretation introduced by Roger Brown in 1973 (A First Language: The Early Stages. Harvard Univ. Press. Cambridge, Mass.). Sarah not only acquired a certain degree of syntax but acquired it in an order different from the one Brown says is inviolate in the case of the child. One way to deal with such data is to cast suspicion on them. Brown was given the opportunity to do so when, in the formal tests we made for the possible use of social cues, Sarah performed less well than she did normally.

The test for social cues was based on the use of a trainer who could only pretend to know the language, for, in fact, he did not know it. He was able to carry out the pretense through the use of a code—numbered pictures of the plastic words—and an auditory (microphone-earphone) connection with another trainer who was outside the test room in the hall. With the code, the dumb trainer was able to write out instructions for Sarah to comprehend, and also to translate the sentences she wrote into a sequence of numbers that he relayed to the trainer in the hall. After a moment, the dumb trainer heard either "yes" or "no" through his earphones and then, depending on the answer, either gave Sarah the item she had correctly requested along with a bit of praise, or withheld both the item and the praise.

On these tests Sarah performed about 10% below her normal level, approximately 75% correct on both comprehension and production, compared to her normal 85% correct. She also showed a certain amount of emotionality: she lined the words up in a more slovenly way than usual, and, more important, regressed to an earlier form of sentence production that she had abandoned some months earlier. Sarah had passed through two stages before finally arriving at the stage in which she wrote sentences in the correct order directly. Earlier she had put words on the board in an incorrect order and then rearranged them before settling on a final order; and with the dumb trainer she reverted to this earlier form of production.

Brown interpreted the decrement as suggesting that Sarah had never learned the language but had merely memorized the sentences she did know, having learned them on a trial-and-error basis in the first place. If the sentences Sarah received on the dumb trainer test were all old sentences, sentences Sarah had either produced or comprehended before, Brown felt this would be a definite possibility. There are numerous difficulties with Brown's proposal, but we need consider only two.

First, Sarah received about 60 different sentences on the dumb trainer tests. This may not be an unreasonable number of four-word strings for a chimpanzee to memorize. However, by the time the tests were given, Sarah had experienced approximately 3000 different sentences, and since she could not know which subset of these would appear on the test, to pass the test she would have had to memorize not 60 sentences, but about 3000.

604

Second, all the sentences given Sarah were not old or familiar to her. Over a quarter of them were new, and Sarah performed at approximately the same level of accuracy on both old and new sentences. This simple fact directly invalidates Brown's interpretation, and incidentally, it is a fact that Brown could have ascertained easily; as he pointed out, we were in the same department for a year and he had every opportunity to ask questions about her data.

Why did Sarah show a 10% decrement on the dumb trainer tests? Emotionality seems the best answer, and I suspect that a child tested in the same way would show a similar decrement. But we need not speculate about the interpretation in order to observe that the probability of choosing four words from a sample of eight and arranging them in the correct order is extremely small, one in 1680 times. Even though we would like to understand the deficit produced by the test—was it emotionality or some other factor?—we have no reason to doubt that the obtained 75% level was highly significant.

Terrace and Bever continue along with Brown in noting that Sarah failed to exceed about 85% correct in her normal use of the language. This is contrasted with the 100% correct which, it is implied, people characteristically attain in their use of language. Are people always 100% correct either in word choice or word order? It is difficult to find the ethnographic data that would permit calculating the accuracy level of everyday language use. More important, however, both Sarah and another more recent subject, Elizabeth, did have one use of language in which they were close to 100% correct. After Sarah had achieved a moderate degree of language competence, virtually every lesson included a period in which the words were passed to Sarah and she was allowed to use them as she chose. No longer required either to comprehend the trainer's instructions or to answer her questions, Sarah produced constructions of her own. Two things were notable about this section of the lesson, which we called creative writing.

First, once Sarah's lessons came to rely increasingly on comprehension—for she could be required to comprehend longer and more complex sentences than she was likely to produce—giving Sarah the words became a virtual necessity. It forestalled her seizing them and running off to the middle of the cage where she wrote on the floor, hunching over her constructions, making it difficult for us to read them. When given the words, she wrote on the language board and could be easily read and recorded.

Second, Sarah's accuracy in "creative writing" was close to 100%, about 15% higher than her accuracy for the same material when dealing with the trainer's assertions or questions. Elizabeth showed a similar difference in accuracy in describing herself, on the one hand, and describing trainers, on the other. The acts, words, and sentence forms she used in the two cases were the same, yet Elizabeth was almost 100% correct in describing herself, and 10–20% lower in describing the trainer. How can we explain this difference?

In Sarah's "creative writing" as well as in Elizabeth's self-description, the behavior was self-paced. Sarah did not answer questions at the trainer's discretion but only when she chose to ask herself a question in the first place. Similarly, her comments or assertions were not made in response to specific requests by the trainer but only when she chose to make them and then only in response to aspects of the situation that she selected, rather than to those the trainer selected for her. The same distinction applies to Elizabeth. When required to describe the trainer, Elizabeth was subject to the standard forced-response constraint that is typical of all tests. Each time the trainer acted, Elizabeth was required to describe the act. She could not choose which act to describe, or whether to describe any at all, but was required to describe all of them and was scored incorrect for any failure. Contrast this with self-description, where she was free to describe (or not describe) whichever of her acts she chose, described less than 25% of them, but was virtually 100% correct in doing so.

Consider now the similarity between people's everyday use of language and the use by Sarah and Elizabeth in the self-paced situations. In everyday use, a speaker speaks when he chooses, and a listener listens when he chooses. The agreement between the two parties is seldom perfect; because it is not, the listener may occasionally request repetition or have repetition forced on him (should the speaker observe his flagging attention) or bluff, wearing a facial expression feigning understanding while actually picking up the speaker's meaning downstream in the conversation. In successful conversation there is generally enough agreement between speaker and listener so that the listener can limit his replies to those occasions that are functionally equivalent to the easy trial; he has been listening, he is interested, he has understood and is therefore in an excellent position to reply. Moreover, if these optimizing conditions are not met, and the listener is nonetheless obliged to respond, there are standard strategems that virtually eliminate even the possibility of error. The inattentive listener may now say "What?" or "I don't think I follow you," or even "I don't know." In the chimpanzees' routine language use, none of these prerogatives were extended to the chimpanzees. They were never allowed to escape a hard trial by saying "I don't know" and, indeed, one never is in a test situation.

The difference between the apes' 85% level and the everyday human level is less likely a species difference than a difference between situations. In a test situation, when every question must be answered, the human subject does not always use language at the 100% level. Conversely, when the chimpanzees use language in a nonforced response situation, which in that factor at least approximates the human everyday use, they do not perform at the 85% level, but approach the customary human level.

DR. VON GLASERSFELD: I wish I had half an hour to deal with some of the confusions that Herbert Terrace has introduced into this discussion. I haven't, so I shall deal with only two: one very short one, and one that pervaded the whole paper.

The first one is the old cliché that computers can do no more than they are programmed to do. That is undoubtedly true, but it depends on what you mean by "do." If "do" is taking the decisions, evaluating new input that is not known at the time of programming, I suggest that it is very close to the activity of a living organism.

The second is the equally confusing introduction of the term "reinforcement." If I have understood anything of behaviorist literature, reinforcement means that after it has been administered, the preceding response becomes more frequent. I think that's a very useful term. But imagine for a moment that you're sitting at a dinner table, you're asking for the mustard, you get it immediately; what do you do—ask for it again? I think that brings out the difference between ordinary behavior and communicatory behavior; because in communication the characteristic thing is that we can ask for the things we want and we are not reinforced by anything else.

If Sarah or Lana or Washoe ask for a piece of apple, she or he wants a piece of apple. And to call that a primary reinforcer, I think is nonsense. Thank you.

DR. TERRACE: I'll just respond very briefly. I never said the computer could not do anything new in the sense that you were suggesting. I said there is a closer similarity to the biological preparation of a chimpanzee in understanding human language as compared with that of a computer. I still think that's quite true. How a computer simulates language may or may not have some biological overlap with what a chimpanzee or a man does.

As to the second point about the reinforcement, I was simply distinguishing between different categories of reinforcement. Some require no history of conditioning and some do. Clearly, Sarah is asking for something more than a primary reinforcer, but I think the distinguishing fact between a piece of apple and another human being or primate is quite apparent. I'm simply pointing out that there is a difference between social reinforcement and that provided by objects.

DR. RUMBAUGH: I would just interject that Lana sometimes, in our procedures, is given the option of asking for what type of "reinforcer" she wants for correct responses in linguistic training and testing. The "please" key is pushed by Tim and then Lana finishes the sentence to ask for whatever she wants. And it's not always for things to eat. Sometimes it's to be tickled, sometimes it's to be swung. She gets a lot of social interaction with people around her.

DR. JOSEPHINE HAMMERS *Center for Research on Bilingualism:* The evidence presented seems to show that chimps are capable of showing abilities to acquire linguistic structures; they also show the ability to use them for social communication. Is there any evidence so far that chimps also have abilities to use their linguistic structures for other functions; namely, cognitive processes?

DR. RUMBAUGH: I'll keep my comment brief. Lana has used her language-type skills in very adroit ways to solve problems that we had never intended that she even perceive: for example, to bring our attention to equipment malfunctions. And though I covered the subject very quickly in my presentation, we believe that we have good reason to conclude that Lana's excellent cross-modal competence reflects her use of language-type skills as mediating mechanisms in discrimination.

DR. BEVER: The question that you raise is, I think, very much at the core of what Dr. Terrace and I are concerned to find out; namely, the implications of acquiring the symbol system for cognition and areas of personality.

There are specific tests which we haven't carried out yet because the chimp we're working with isn't quite ready. But there exist tests drawn from the experimental literature with people, testing for the influence of a language or labeling system on problem-solving capacities. We've designed parallel experiments to be able specifically to show that the effect of having a label for a particular object determines the way in which the animal goes about solving an independently presented problem. So I think these are experimentally answerable questions.

DR. PREMACK: Just a brief comment on the same issue. The Whorfian hypothesis is attractive, but not because of the evidence that supports it. As a matter of fact, most of the evidence goes in the opposite direction, that linguistic skill depends very, very heavily upon a *preexisting* perceptual capacity.

I'll give you one example. In Fillmore's extremely interesting paper (this volume), he noted that in the human case words have several different kinds of meanings e.g. "breakfast." It may mean "first meal of the day" or "a meal of a certain content." So we're distinguishing between a functional and a physical definition, for example.

At lunch I described to him an experiment recently completed by Mike McClure in our lab which shows the perceptual analog of that in a chimp. He succeeded in getting Sarah to reassemble objects. Chimps are notorious for tearing things apart but little known for putting them back together. The animal was finally induced to reassemble coffee pots. So you have a nest that carries the coffee, the stem, and the lid—parts of the pot with which you're all familiar.

It was asked then to make judgments about the equivalence of various parts of two different coffee pots that were dissimilar, and did a very, very poor job, much to our surprise. When asked to make these judgments about parts of coffee pots that are identical, of course it's at nearly the 100% level. But when the coffee pots differ dimensionally, the animal performed very badly.

Then we gave the animal an opportunity to observe coffee being made. So now it learns about the functions of the nest, the stem, and the like. And when retested now about the equivalence of the various parts of the coffee pot, the animal now performed at almost 100% level. This seems to me a perfect perceptual analog of that case in which words have their meaning defined in one case on physical grounds and in the other case on functional grounds.

This is the reverse, however. This is not language adding to the perceptual capacity or the computational power of the species; this is the computational power or perceptual capacity of the species being *exhibited* and labeled according to how man has taught it. But the labels do not (*contra* Whorf: all the evidence runs against Whorf) add importantly to the computational power. Computational power is there, and then language is overlaid.

WESLEY PENUNZIO (*Southeastern Massachusetts Univ.*): I was particularly pleased with the comment Tom Bever just made concerning the role of consciousness or of self. Indeed, this morning while Dr. Steklis was making his presentation I had sought to ask a question which is pertinent to both of these papers.

Based upon personal observation of my own, I would ask whether or not there has been an attempt to distinguish *the self perceiving the self*, as opposed to *the self merely perceiving*? Or to state that better, "self perceiving" is the first phase and "self consciously perceiving the fact of its own perception" is the second level. I feel that these are distinct, and that the consciousness of the individual is distinct at these two levels.

DR. BEVER: I think that resonates with the point that Dr. Premack made about the nonhuman primate that can look in a mirror and deal with its mirror image in a way that we believe to be appropriate. That would seem to me to exhibit the first level of self that you refer to.

It remains an open question, I think, whether the chimpanzee goes on further to be conscious of its own self. And I think that's a distinction that's run through a number of the comments today. Again, to say it a different way: What we are concerned to find out is what the chimp that we're working with thinks about himself; what he thinks about his language, what he thinks about the uses to which language can be put, like lying as opposed to telling the truth.

At the center of our concern is the exploration of the effects that are brought out by the existence of language or his self-consciousness.

I also want to use this as an opportunity to reply to the points that Dr. Premack made a couple of times. We're not of the opinion that language causes certain structures to come into existence in the human being. Rather, it seems, in any conservative view, that language is in many instances crucial and in other cases simply an important facilitator of the emergence of whatever internal capacities human beings have.

The question will be: does it facilitate in the chimpanzee the emergence of parallel personality structures and attitudes towards social life?

PAUL KAY (*Univ. of California at Berkeley, Berkeley Calif.*): This question is addressed to Dr. Terrace and Dr. Bever. It's exactly on the same issue of linguistic concept of "self."

I believe you said, Dr. Terrace, that you felt that if the chimp got a linguistic concept of self, that would specifically promote syntactic development. That surprised me, just because I tried to make a connection between the general principles of syntax and concept of self, and I couldn't make the connection. I wonder if you have something in mind that you didn't say.

DR. TERRACE: What I said was that learning how to use language to refer to one's self so as to describe internal states and relationships with various individuals may be a positive thing for the organism, chimpanzee, or child. One function of syntax is to express relations between one's self and various other people. Having mastered this function of language, a child or chimpanzee may feel motivated to master other relational aspects of language. The ability to represent one's self symbolically doesn't require syntax in any powerful sense. But that experience may be a crucial way station in the development of other syntactical relationships.

DR. KAY: I would find that very acceptable if it didn't seem that chimps already have relational capabilities according to what has already been demonstrated. But it seems to me that we've seen chimps use proper names in relational contexts, and I don't see a concept of self building to relational concepts as such because we already have them.

DR. TERRACE: I guess it's a question of whether the proper names have been used in a relational sense as opposed to just a means toward obtaining something. The question is, what is the nature of the evidence that shows that chimpanzees can refer to themselves and other people in these various relational senses? I think the example of Rumbaugh—, *tickle Lana*? may be specific to that situation. And one simply doesn't know yet what other sequences that sequence contrasts with. I think that as you generate more and more sequences where, for example, you have a subject and object and so on, the ability to relate one's self to others becomes more obvious. As far as I know, the evidence obtained from chimpanzees is not very solid on this point.

DR. RUMBAUGH: On the last point I would just like to say that it is inaccurate and therefore untrue. It is the case that Lana will use the formal name of whichever person is present as long as she has his or her name. If she does not have a name, she will use the pronoun "you." And she will, for example, ask a question like "Lana groom Tim?" or whoever is there, as opposed to "question: Tim, or whoever is there, groom Lana?" She uses it in a relational and reciprocal way.

DR. TERRACE: My only point about that is: how do we know Lana hasn't learned two chains, one where the object is in the first position in both cases? The only way we can answer that question is to look at data on all instances of name and pronoun use.

DR. RUMBAUGH: I can give you many more. We have an experiment finished in which either Tim or Lana, on a randomly sequenced basis, takes a ball and puts it either in, on, or under either a bowl or a box. Lana's job at the end of each trial is always to go to the board and to recount whether she or Tim did put the ball in, on, or under the bowl or the box.

DR. TERRACE: This fits in exactly with my earlier comment that if you have a sequence of problems, all of the same variety, then you don't have to talk about the linguistic properties of the problem as opposed to the extralinguistic properties of the problem. There are three outcomes in that situation, and again we don't know just what functions of language are represented here.

DR. RUMBAUGH: Recompute. There are far more than three.

DR. PREMACK: Let me comment, too, because this reminds me of another egregious error: The charge that the animal is not doing anything remotely like natural language because it is always choosing from two alternatives. That's simply false. One starts out using two alternatives in our experimental paradigm because one wants to reduce the difficulty of the problem and see whether you get learning. After you've got learning with two alternatives you go to four alternatives. And then many, many alternatives.

Once Prof. Terrace makes contact with the data, he will see that that was a routine part of the procedure. After Sarah had been taught to distinguish between "name of" and "not name of," she was ultimately asked whether the relationship between two things was "name of," "not name of," "size of," "not size of," "color of," "not color of," and six to ten randomly chosen irrelevant alternatives.

Did every lesson deal monolithically with one point? It did not. There are about 20 lessons scattered throughout the record of several hundred where the topic was nonmonolithic.

Now, what's of interest here is the following point: several topics occurred in the same lesson without diminution in accuracy. There was a charge made by Brown, essentially just repeated in a less elaborate form by Terrace, that this is very unlike natural language because in natural language (when the human being uses it) the sentences that he might produce or comprehend are *infinite*, whereas in the chimp situation it has a "bounded" training program with a narrowly defined semantic topic and the like.

Now, the major factor this contrast overlooks is the extraordinary contribution of *contextual* factors to the human use of language. No human being would understand any sentence if, in fact, the momentarily functional pool from which that sentence was being drawn were *infinite*. The weight of contextual factors in human language comprehension and production is enormous.

Now the only contextual factor that the poor chimp gets is from the existence of a semantically bound lesson, because most of the questions that the chimp is being asked to answer are nonsense questions. They are not questions that are guided by the preceding portion of the conversation. And all of the abundant work showing that humans comprehend and process language through extraordinary dependence upon contextual factors, factors that momentarily are difficult to measure, is overlooked in dwelling on considerations such as the accusation that ours is a "well-defined semantic topic," while in natural language man chooses from "infinitely many sentences." That is simply an egregiously misleading contrast.

DR. BEVER: Dave, let me say just one thing about that. "The price of hemp in New Delhi has become extremely high." Now, you understood that sentence, if you heard it. And there is no context to determine its meaning.

DR. PREMACK: As a matter of fact, I guess the reason I have to answer, I didn't understand it, is because I didn't "hear" it, on your theory. What's the probability that I hear it, you see?

DR. TERRACE: Could I just make a very brief comment about the presumed inaccuracy. If my statement was inaccurate, I stand corrected. As far as I can tell from all of your published accounts, these kinds of tests have not been part of the public domain. If that's true I'm very happy to hear about it.

DR. PREMACK: They are, and they are not part of the public domain. But that's an inconsequential part. At any rate, the point is that often enough in introducing a term, the positive version was contrasted with the negative. Then the point was made: can you really argue that an animal knows the difference between say "name of" and "not name of" when there are only two alternatives—no. But would it increase your confidence if she were asked to choose between alternatives including "name of," "not name of," "red," "green," "brown," "banana"—not very much. Accordingly, you had to wait until you introduced some other alternatives the ability to discriminate among which is impressive, such as "size of," "not size of," "color of," "not color of," "shape of," "not shape of." Once those had been taught, then it was not only possible to introduce many alternatives, but alternatives among which it was impressive to choose correctly. Those data have been in the literature for five years.

DR. TERRACE: I guess it's a question of degree. I think there are still very few choices.

DR. KURT SALZINGER (*Biometric Research Unit & Polytechnic Institute of N.Y.*): It seems to me that we have here agreement among all the speakers that there is similarity between human and nonhuman primates. The difference seems to lie in the manner in which these similarities are studied. Premack and Rumbaugh, on the one hand, seem to start with the functional analysis of what language consists of and then try methodically to determine whether these functions may be learned by a chimpanzee.

On the other hand, Terrace and Bever seem to be approaching the same problem almost in an experimental anthropomorphic approach. That is, they begin with such notions as "natural language," "emotion," "self," which they know exist in human beings (but which some of us are still looking for data for) and now, after teaching Nim sign language awhile, they're apparently going to *inquire* "Is it true that you have a self?" "Do you like to lie?" And so on.

It seems to me that the hazard of imposing concepts which in our human literature still are vague and woozy on animals is rather great. The only hope I have is that since animals are not as easily talked into following instructions as human beings are, Nim will let you know about the self in natural language.

DR. TERRACE: Kurt, you argue that the concept of self and private events are extrascientific. I would simply refer you to one of your own heroes, Skinner, who wrote a very brilliant paper on how to analyze private events.

PHYLOGENY OF THE HUMAN VOCAL TRACT

Jan Wind

Department of Otorhinolaryngology and Institute of Human Genetics
Free University
Amsterdam, The Netherlands

INTRODUCTION*

The very existence of words like *phylogeny* and *vocal tract* illustrates man's ability and propensity for (largely unconsciously) recognizing clusters of similar characteristics within the multitude of phenomena that are perceived by our senses and that at first sight impress as being unrelated and even chaotic. Establishing biological classifications, as well, usually starts with and heavily relies on such cluster recognition. It is difficult, indeed, to give a water-tight definition of concepts like "vocal tract" or "airway," especially in comparative zoological discussions as rendered in this paper. Strictly speaking, therefore, such concepts are of heuristic value only. Nevertheless, an attempt may be worhtwhile to give a short discussion of the evolutionary history of the peripheral vocal organs of man.

In this paper I define (1) sounds as vibrations of air or water that can be perceived by the human ear, (2) vocalizations as sounds that establish communication between living individuals, (3) speech as the usual vocalizations of man, and (4) airway and respiratory tract as the set of organs through which air passes used for respiration.

It is not coincidental that the respiratory tract is usually considered as being identical with the vocal tract, and in most mammals there will be no disagreement as to what constitutes the airway and as to its synonymity with the vocal tract. When observing lower vertebrates, however, there is less overlap of these concepts; e.g., many fish species use their swim-bladder and specialized bones for generating sounds (probably for communication[1]), and the aquatic turtle *Podocnemys* obtains 90% of its oxygenation by cloacal respiration.[2]

The guideline I will follow is one indicated by morphology rather than by function. Many ancestral species have undoubtedly used sounds for communication, but these sounds, even when produced in the airways, have probably not all been produced by structures homologous to the ones used by man. This can be explained by convergent evolution and the selective advantage of sounds over other means of communication. Although, conversely, the ancestral structures homologous with the human vocal tract have not always been used for sound generation or for respiration, in this paper mainly these structures (and their functions) will be reviewed.

One of the basic properties of the Earth is its typical surface structure which has provided the possibilities for the origin of the self-propagating systems which we call living organisms; and the very interaction and evolution of the hydrosphere and the atmosphere have—together with the interaction between the evolving organisms and via the mechanisms of genetic variation and selection—largely shaped the human vocal tract.

The main tools for reconstructing the evolutionary history of the vocal tract are provided by paleontology and comparative zoology. The airway, however, mainly consists of soft tissues that are unlikely to provide the firm fossil evidence that is

---

*The data in the body of the text with no reference are described or referred to in Reference 3.

available for reconstructing, for example, the ancestral locomotor apparatus or cranial anatomy. Accordingly, we have to rely rather heavily on comparative observations. Now, in the usual phylogenetical discussions the choice of modern animals that represent ancestral ones often impress as being arbitrary and subject to preconceived ideas. Ideally, the modern animal species of such a sample should be similar to the ancestral ones. This is, however, clearly very difficult if not impossible to achieve, since most of the now-living organisms are themselves the end-product of a long evolution. The arbitrariness here lies in the choice of the parameters to be compared (for instance, size of the individual, relative or absolute size of comparable organs, and ecological factors), and in the assumption of comparable organs having similar functions and being homologous, i.e., being controlled by similar genes.[3]

An illustration of these problems is provided by *Latimeria*. This "living fossil" is generally assumed to bear a strong resemblance to the late Devonian fishes that were evolving into the first terrestrial vertebrates; this assumption is based on various osteological arguments. However, its "lungs" appear to consist of one solid, fatty[4] or ossified[5] organ that is completely unfit for the usual pulmonary gas exchange. The *Latimeria* "airway" thus is very unlikely to be representative of that of the first terrestrial vertebrates. Yet, when choosing, instead of *Latimeria*, for instance, a lungfish like *Protopterus*, whose lungs do function as gas-exchange organs, we have only a somewhat higher level of reliability. This increase of reliability is based on the similarity of ecological pressures (i.e., a semiterrestrial habitat with air-breathing) and of morphological characters.

Some additional approaches should be mentioned. (1) The basis of phylogenetical reconstructions should be, if possible, tracing the ecological selective pressures, because these can often be derived from physical sciences like geology, climatology, paleochemistry, and so on, that provide more hard evidence than comparative observations alone. (2) The recapitulation theory based on Haeckel's "Biogenetic Law" states that ontogeny (the development of the individual) recapitulates phylogeny. However, such an approach has turned out to be of only small help,[6] probably because the selective pressures having shaped the present-day ontogenetical development differ greatly from those having shaped form and function of adult ancestors; furthermore, the two processes are completely different and virtually imcomparable.[3,7,8] (3) Archeology is a useful tool but limited to assessing the presence of only one and a comparatively recent function of the vocal tract, i.e., speech. (4) The same applies to comparative linguistics, which is, when seen from a biological point of view, merely the study of intraspecific variation of one special behavior mode; unfortunately, it provides little evidence for vocalization behavior of ancestral species.

It is clear, therefore, that only a hypothetical reconstruction of the phylogenetical history of the human vocal tract can be given.

THE EARLY VERTEBRATES

Life started about 3×10^9 years ago, giving origin to unicellular organisms and subsequently to the multicellular organisms or Metazoa. The close cooperation between different cells, the division of tasks, and specialization† must have formed the basis for the origin of the later evolving airway. Obtaining and maintaining a

---

†It is to be hoped that the reader will not blame me for using these anthropomorphisms: they convey my intentions much better than more physically determined terms would do.

higher energy level than their environment implies that living cells interact chemically and physically with it. A basic property, then, is the diffusion of gases (mainly O_2 and CO_2) between living cells, and their environment. Because life started in water, this process started as simple diffusion from one watery solution toward another.

The evolutionary line from these early metazoans toward man runs via the earliest Chordata which originated in the Cambrium about 400 million years ago, and which bore resemblance to the modern Amphioxus, a small fish-like organism. It shows the ground-plan of all vertebrates, such as a primitive backbone, a metamerical longitudinal body and head organization, and a symmetrical architecture alongside the backbone. Observations of Amphioxus suggest that the first vertebrates were small, aquatic, free-swimming animals, whose head contained a ventrally placed food-gathering device composed of the metamerically organized branchial system, but no respiratory organs.

The ecological selective pressures that must have shaped this basic vertebrate ground-plan are not completely clear, but—somewhat hypothetically—the following reconstruction can be rendered. Gravity and oxygen-diffusion speed determined the architecture of the organs that were going to constitute the vertebrate airway. Gravity caused the small food particles to descend to the bottom of the early vertebrates' habitat, and hence must have determined the ventral localization of the mouth, and this, together with burrowing habits, determined the more dorsal position of the backbone. The small body size allowed oxygen to diffuse through the skin and endoderm of the pharynx into the blood vessels in sufficient quantities to allow some, but compared with modern vertebrates, little body movement. The dorsal position of the central nervous system was caused by the ventral position of the digestive tract and by the selective value of light sensitive cells. The sense organs became localized anteriorly because they had to gather information about the qualities of the environment the individual was moving into and of the food to be taken up. Accordingly, the olfactory organ became to be positioned dorsally and anteriorly.

An Amphioxus-like branchial feeding device can be considered as a preadaptation for an increased gas exchange, which, given the same metabolic cell properties, is associated with a larger body size and increased mobility such as is found in later vertebrates. For the food-filtering pharynx, with its relatively large surface and with large quantities of water passing through it, could via comparatively few mutations be changed into an organ that was able to exchange gases much more quickly than simple diffusion via nonspecialized cells.

The paleontological record shows that during the evolution from the earliest vertebrates to man the branchial system, with its associated structures, has progressively reduced the number of its elements, and that at the same time these elements became more specialized (a classical example of "Williston's law"[3,9]). For heuristic purposes this gradual change can be divided into six steps, as schematically pictured in FIGURE 1.

The first step can be exemplified by comparing the Amphioxus pharynx with that of one of the most primitive taxa of modern vertebrates, the jawless fishes, such as the lamprey. These Agnatha are somewhat similar to the Silurian Ostracoderms. The Agnathan branchial system consists of mouth, pharynx, and, depending on the species, of 7 to 14 pairs of gills that, next to the skin, function as gas-exchange organs. Because the Ostracoderms were covered by a bony armor, it is likely that their oxygenation took place mainly via the gills. Though these were probably still engaged in food collection as well, oxygenation, despite this double function, must have been sufficient for the sluggish Ostracoderms.[10]

The Ostracoderms possessed a single slit medially on top of the head leading to the so-called nostril; this opening, however, had nothing to do with respiration, but had a connection with the hypophysis. The Ostracoderms may have had a tongue-like organ, as suggested by the presence of such an organ in modern Agnatha in which it, however, has been adapted to the relatively recent parasitic feeding habits.

The second step occurred with the transition from the jawless vertebrates to the Placoderm fishes. In these the anterior branchial elements had evolved into jaws, probably due to intra-Agnathan feeding and/or predating selective pressures. At the same time, the number of gills diminished to five pairs. In view of their close morphological similarity to the gills of most modern fishes, it is likely that their function was similar as well. This means that the countercurrent flow of water and blood operant in the gills of modern aquatic vertebrates is likely to have existed already in the Placoderms. This system probably offers a very, if not the most, effective way of exchanging oxygen and carbon dioxide between an aquatic chordate and its environment, as suggested by its ubiquity and its sheer physical properties.

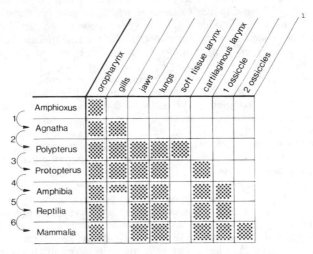

FIGURE 1. Schematic representation of the possible evolution of the main branchial derivatives as exemplified by some modern taxa. For heuristic purposes this evolution is divided into 6 steps. It shows a progressive differentiation into specialized organs. "1 ossicle" indicates the presence of the auditory columella; "2 ossicles" indicates the additional presence of the malleus and the incus.

It therefore seems somewhat puzzling that these Devonian fishes already possessed lungs, as is strongly suggested by the paleontological record.[10,11] Perhaps this can be explained by the lower atmospheric oxygen levels in the Devonian. One of the most primitive bony fishes that still exists, the Nile ganoid *Polypterus*, may be more or less representative of the Placoderms. Accordingly, it possesses gills and lungs, though the latter are hardly or not at all engaged in oxygenation. The lungs and their entrance in *Polypterus* and the Placoderms can be considered to constitute the most primitive, respectively the first, vertebrate airway. Yet, they cannot reasonably be considered to constitute the first, respectively the most primitive, vertebrate vocal tract because there are no sounds known to be produced by the *Polypterus* airway.

Since we have, unfortunately, little paleontological information about the finer details of the Placoderm airway, we have to turn to *Polypterus* to get some idea of the first airway and its function. When dissecting a specimen of the Nile ganoid a very small slit is visible medially in the floor of the mouth. This is the entrance of the lungs, and it can be considered as the most primitive larynx, consisting of slightly elevated edges, some sphincter and possibly some dilator muscle fibers. A very short "trachea" leads to the right lung, which has a connection with the left one.‡ The lungs are simple saccular structures that do not impress one as being very suitable for gas exchange as mammalian lungs for example are.

Like most bony fishes, *Polypterus* possesses a pair of nostrils that have no connection with the mouth, but only with the olfactory brain cells.[13]

THE EARLY TERRESTRIAL VERTEBRATES

Somewhere in Devonian times the Placoderms gave rise to the crossopterygians (or Choanichthyes). Probably due to climatic selective pressures, these fish species became able to survive dry periods and to move from one pool to another, and they are assumed to have been the immediate ancestors of the amphibians. To be sure, the only surviving crossopterygian, *Latimeria*, is of great interest for comparative observations, but it is not as far as its airway anatomy and physiology are concerned: as mentioned in the introduction, its single lung has degenerated into a fatty organ unsuitable for gas exchange. This may have been a result of *Latimeria* or its ancestors having been forced by competing sympatric would-be amphibian species into its present deep-sea niche. Here, selective pressures favoring aerial respiration are absent, and gas-filled hollow organs may even have a negative selective value.

Although the taxonomic relations are not yet fully clear, it is likely that the present-day lungfish species are closely related to the crossopterygians, and they do have functioning lungs. Dissection of, e.g., the African lungfish *Protopterus annectens* discloses that medially in the floor of its mouth there is equally a small slit: it leads toward the lungs, and its relative size is about the same as in *Polypterus*. Anatomically there are three differences, however; (1) there are clearly more muscle fibers around the laryngeal entrance, especially dilator ones, (2) there is a cartilaginous plate in front of the slit, and (3) the inner pulmonary surface is much larger because of the presence of primitive alveoli, the lungs being in fact very similar to amphibian ones.[14,15] Functionally, the respiration rate is much higher in *Protopterus*, and indeed it needs aerial respiration. Not all details are known about lungfish respiratory physiology, but the main points of interest here are: (1) the respiration

---

‡A remarkable feature of the *Polypterus* airway is its asymmetrical organization: apart from the previously mentioned connection between the left and the right lung, the latter is about twice as large as the left one. Even more interestingly, there are signs of a vestigial larynx to the left side of the above-mentioned one, visible as a very small depression covered with ciliary epithelium similar to that covering the "normal" larynx.[3,12] This asymmetrical arrangement has, to my knowledge, never been found in other vertebrates; it shows that in this primitive vertebrate genes do exist that control the growth of structures indicative for a double larynx. This suggests that originally the whole of the airway has been paired, just as, for that matter, all of the organs of the protovertebrates must have been (except for the chorda, the central nervous system and the digestive tract). The reason that in all other vertebrates the middle part of the airway is not paired is probably given by physical, i.e. aerodynamic, properties favoring a single connection in this part of the airway because of the smaller resistance. It can be speculated that these aerodynamical selective pressures, because of the absence or rarity of breathing movements, in *Polypterus* and its ancestors have been weaker than in all other vertebrates, and that the asymmetrical arrangement of the intrathoracic organs, and maybe even of the human cerebrum, is still an expression of the same genes.

rate is 1 to 20/h; (2) inspiration takes place by lowering the mouth bottom during surfacing and keeping the mouth open; (3) a "bolus" of air is probably swallowed into the lungs; (4) the cartilaginous plate does not have an obvious function; (5) the paired nostrils do not have a respiratory function, though they open into the mouth via choanae.

Sound production in the *Protopterus* airway does exist, but the only frequent sound is a very weak hissing one during each inspiration;[3] expiratory sounds are rare and they have never been demonstrated to have any communicatory function. The same applies to the other lungfish species. Hence, the lungfish airway cannot be called a vocal tract, although it may reflect ancestral conditions that gave rise to organs that can be called vocal ones.

Comparative observations of modern *amphibians* suggest that aerial respiration in the first land-dwelling vertebrates was accessory to gill and skin respiration. Yet, the central and most intriguing respiratory organ, i.e. the larynx, in amphibians shows a differentiation as compared with the lungfishes. In the Urodela, such as the salamanders, there are a number of so-called lateral cartilages, i.e., a paired arytenoid cartilage (or *pars arytaenoidea*) and some cricotracheal cartilages. In addition, the muscular system consists of dilators and constrictors and is relatively better developed than in the lungfishes. Functioning gills are present in the early ontogenetical stages of all amphibians and are retained in the adult stages in some species. In the anuran amphibians, like the frog, the larynx consists of a paired arytenoid cartilage and a single (circular) cricoid cartilage next to a well-developed muscular system. There is hardly a trachea in the amphibians, but in contrast to the lungfishes the nasal passages are used for respiration.[16] The choanae, which in the lungfish are located quite rostrally, in the amphibians have moved caudally, and they serve the double function of olfaction and respiration. There is, however, a considerable gap between the choanae and the laryngeal intrance, implying a relatively long common pathway of the respiratory and the digestive tract (FIGURE 2).

Most modern amphibians use their airways for the production of vocalizations, which suggests a similar behavior in the early amphibians. This is also suggested by the presence of a tympanum in the early fossil amphibians.[17] Though modern amphibian vocalizations are clearly generated in the larynx, the sequence of evolutionary events remains obscure: if the differentiation of the crossopterygian larynx into the amphibian one was a consequence of respiratory selective pressures, the amphibian airway can be considered as having been preadapted for the production of vocalizations. If, on the other hand, vocalization selective pressures were first or stronger, the amphibian airway must secondarily have acquired its present respiratory functions. Personally, I would favor the first possibility.

The breathing movements in the Urodela are essentially the same as in the lungfish; i.e., swallowing the air into the lungs; the respiratory rate is usually similarly low. In the anuran amphibians, breathing movements are more complicated, occurring in various phases and being effected, among others, by nostrils, tongue, and mouth bottom musculature.[16] In addition, their respiratory rate is higher. Accordingly, their vocalizations are much more differentiated.

Though the comparative embryological data are somewhat equivocal, it is likely that the mentioned Willistonian reduction of the branchial system during vertebrate evolution was apparent in the amphibians as the first visceral arch skeleton evolving into the lower jaw and the single auditory ossicle (the columella); the second one into the hyoid; the third to sixth one into the—partly rudimentary—gills; and the seventh one into the laryngeal cartilages.

Compared with fishes, most amphibians have a quite mobile tongue used for swallowing food and air, and in some also for catching prey.

REPTILES

Reptiles show roughly the same airway anatomy as do the anuran amphibians, but since in most reptiles oxygenation is secured entirely by the lungs, the respiration rate is generally somewhat higher. There are some differences, however, that are relevant for the evolutionary history of voice production. The thoracic cage in most reptiles is actively involved in respiration, the ribs being used for creating a negative intrathoracic pressure during inspiration. Consequently, the reptilian trachea is

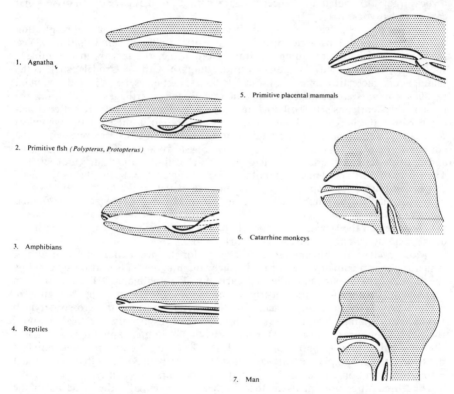

1. Agnatha

2. Primitive fish *(Polypterus, Protopterus)*

3. Amphibians

4. Reptiles

5. Primitive placental mammals

6. Catarrhine monkeys

7. Man

FIGURE 2. Schematic illustration of the possible evolution of the airway (thick lines) during human phylogeny as indicated by some modern species. In *Protopterus* the nostrils are not pictured because they are not homologous with those of higher vertebrates and because they have no function in breathing. (By permission of the publisher of Ref. 3.)

equipped with cartilaginous or osseous rings that prevent the walls from collapsing. In some reptilians like the crocodilians there is in addition a diaphragm-like structure between thorax and abdomen, adding to the above negative pressure.[18] This costal suction pump, in contrast to the amphibians, ensures a greater functional independency for the oropharyngeal structures, and it facilitates the inspiration of fresh air. By contrast, in the Anurans, though having the most elaborate breathing mechanism of amphibians, there always is considerable mixing of expired and inspired air before it enters into the lungs.[19] Reptilian lungs consist of sacs, somewhat similar to the amphibian ones, the walls of which are partly folded.

Compared with the amphibians, reptiles do rarely produce differentiated vocalizations, the gecko being an exception.[10] Crocodilians sometimes roar; the New Zealand tuatara *Sphenodon* sometimes croaks.[21] In most reptilians, however, vocalization is rare, and it is limited to simple hissing, as caused by the forceful passage of air through a nearly-closed larynx.[22] Accordingly, modulation of vocal signals is virtually limited to that of their frequency, duration, and amplitude. The number of messages per time unit that can be transmitted by vocalizations is therefore in reptiles smaller than in mammals, most of which are able to modulate their voices' pitch as well (see below). The effector organs that control voice modulation in reptiles are mainly the expiratory muscles and the laryngeal constrictors; in some, the muscles controlling opening the mouth may have some effect as well.

In view, however, of the absence of reliable modern representatives of the Therapsids, the extinct early reptiles that gave rise to the mammals, all such comparative evidence has only a limited value for our purpose. Fortunately, interesting information is provided by Therapsid paleontology. Typically, these mammal-like reptiles show a secondary palate, which means that their internal nostrils (or choanae) were placed more caudally, and this may have been an adaptation for preventing interference with breathing during mastication;[10,23] the airway and digestive tract did not share a common pathway any more, because the laryngeal entrance could get contact with the choanae.

Perhaps even stronger evidence for nonreptilian and more mammalian-like respiration in Therapsids is adduced by Bakker;[24] among other things, fossil predator/prey biomass ratios and microscopic bone structure suggest that these early mammal-like reptiles were already warm-blooded (or rather, endothermic). Because of the necessarily higher metabolism, their respiration rate is likely to have been higher than in present, cold-blooded (or ectothermic), reptiles, therefore to have been subject to a more subtle control, and consequently to have been preadapted for more frequent and more differentiated vocalizations.

Considering the typical reptilian skull anatomy present in the Therapsids, their branchial system derivatives were most probably organized as they are in the modern reptiles; i.e., a larynx consisting of a circular cricoid, a pair of arytenoids (variously shaped in various species), the hyoid anatomically and functionally closely being linked with the larynx (FIGURES 3a & 3b), and the middle ears containing a single columellar ossicle. Whether or not such a reptilian larynx could meet mammalian-like respiration and vocalization requirements remains to be proved. Therefore, laryngeal anatomy and physiology provide one explanation for the enigmatic long time, i.e. 150 M years,[10] it took for the mammal-like reptiles to evolve into true mammals. Other explanations are provided by lower atmospheric oxygen levels,[25] and by climatic changes that produced a monotonous geographic topography to which the small mammals could adapt themselves better than, the Dinosaurs,[24] for example.

An argument in favor of the first hypothesis is provided by avian biology: though birds are outside the lineages leading from the reptiles to the mammals they provide evidence because of similar selective pressures due to convergent evolution. The birds have a reptilian larynx, which they do not use for vocal purposes but only for respiratory ones. They developed a special vocal organ, the larynx-like syrinx, located in the caudal part of the trachea.[26] This suggests the impossibility for an endothermic vertebrate to use a reptilian larynx for vocal and respiratory purposes simultaneously.

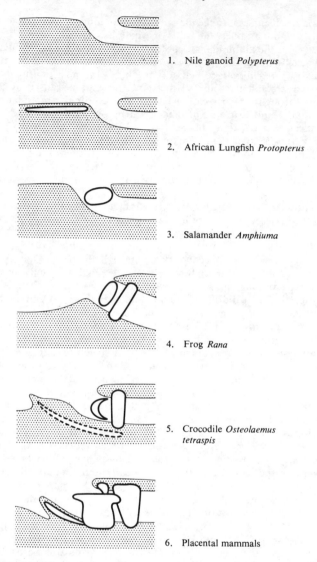

1. Nile ganoid *Polypterus*

2. African Lungfish *Protopterus*

3. Salamander *Amphiuma*

4. Frog *Rana*

5. Crocodile *Osteolaemus tetraspis*

6. Placental mammals

FIGURE 3a. Possible evolution of the laryngeal skeleton (thick lines) during human phylogeny, illustrated schematically by some modern species. The hyoid, though not belonging to the laryngeal skeleton, has been indicated in the crocodile by a dotted line because of its close anatomical, functional, and possibly embryological relationships to the larynx. Lateral view. (By permission of the publisher of Ref. 3.)

MAMMALS

The first true mammals, as diagnosed osteologically, evolved as small insectivores in the late Cretaceous, some 70 million years ago. One of their cranial characteristics was and still is a typical organization of their branchial derivatives: the first visceral arch gave rise to the lower jaw and two auditory ossicles (i.e., the malleus and the incus), the second a.o. to the lesser horn of the hyoid and the third ossicle (the stapes), the third to the hyoid's greater horn, the fourth and the fifth to the (typical mammalian) thyroid cartilage, the sixth possibly to the (typical mammalian) epiglottis, and the seventh possibly to the arytenoid and the cricoid cartilages (FIGURES 1 and 3).

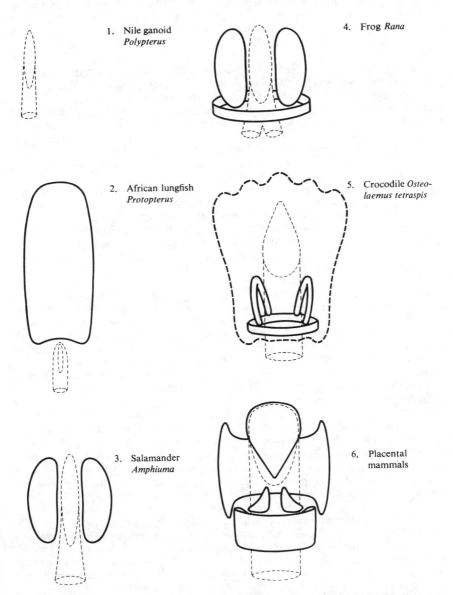

1. Nile ganoid
   Polypterus

4. Frog *Rana*

2. African lungfish
   Protopterus

5. Crocodile *Osteo-laemus tetraspis*

3. Salamander
   Amphiuma

6. Placental
   mammals

FIGURE 3b. See legend for FIGURE 3a. Dorsal view. The fine, dotted line indicates the laryngeal entrance and the airway. (By permission of the publisher of Ref. 3.)

Now, one might well ask: why did the mammals develop these two new laryngeal elements? Interpreting such a question not as a sign of teleological thinking but rather as that of curiosity about a possible evolutionary explanation, we have to look for the selective value of these two cartilages and their soft tissue appendages.

A similarly shaped *epiglottis* is present in all mammals and in most it establishes a connection between the laryngeal entrance and the choanae. Thereby it creates a connection between the lower and the upper airway which in most nonmammalian vertebrates are separated by the mouth or pharynx (FIGURE 2). Though such an approximation may have been present in the Therapsids already, as mentioned before, it must have been less effective because of the probable absence of an epiglottis.

How the Therapsids bridged the gap can possibly be inferred from the conditions present in other modern reptiles which show an oropharyngeal evolution convergent to that in the mammals; i.e., the crocodilians. In these not the respiratory selective pressures alone but those of an aquatic habitat as well bridged the gap between the lower and the upper airway. This is achieved by an epiglottis-like rostral flap of the hyoid projecting into the pharynx and being able to touch the palate. In an aquatic habitat this is of selective value, because it enables the crocodile to breathe with just its nostrils (and its eyes) above the surface, while at the same time its mouth can remain open. (Maybe, Therapsid hyoid structure could give some clues, though in crocodilians the larger part of the hyoid including the flap is cartilaginous rather than osseous). The flap, however, extends over the whole width of the mouth, and consequently in crocodilians either the respiratory or the digestive tract can be used at a time. Furthermore, the mobility of the flap is smaller than that of the mammalian epiglottis: the hyoid in crocodilians must serve a double function: that of giving origin to a number of muscles, mainly those of the tongue, and that of establishing a connection with the choanae.

Therefore, if the Therapsids did use their hyoid in a crocodilian way, they are likely not to have had the mammalian respiratory capabilities. These comprise the simultaneous use of both tracts by the epiglottis being present just in the middle part of the pharynx and the food passing alongside it via the so-called lateral food channels. These are established by the epiglottis and the aryepiglottic folds.[27] Such constant use of the airway is not only associated with a higher respiration rate but also with a constant olfactory check on the air inspired. This check is operant in predator/prey relations, in intraspecific social relations, and in the selection of food.

Whereas the epiglottis thus serves respiratory, olfactory, and deglutitive functions, the *thyroid cartilage* probably evolved primarily in relation with vocal and respiratory functions. Its evolution implied the achievement of folds, i.e., the thyroarytenoid folds, present alongside the airway the tension and the position of which can be controlled. This means that (1) vibrations can be generated by the air passing alongside them, (2) the frequency of these vibrations can be subtly varied (by varying their tension), and (3) the space in between them can be subtly varied by muscles controlling their position (Mm. interarytaenoideus, thyreoarytaenoidei, cricoarytaenoidei posteriores, arytaenoidei obliqui).

An additional function of the thyroarytenoid folds is their *valve* action. In the amphibians and reptilians the laryngeal entrance has some valvular action as well, but here it is limited to an inlet-valve action; the larynx is present in the pharynx as a protruding eminence, implying that a raised intraoral pressure automatically closes the laryngeal entrance, when it is not actively opened by the dilator muscles. In many mammals, including the primates, there is also some outlet-valve action of the larynx, as formed by the caudally directed upper thyroarytenoid folds.

Not only anatomically but also functionally the mammalian branchial specializations are closely linked. On the one hand, the laryngeal and respiratory differentiation of mammals enabled them to produce more frequent vocalizations that could be varied much more subtly in pitch and amplitude than the lower vertebrates could; on the other hand, *auditory sophistication* enabled more, and possibly more complicated, sounds to be perceived, analyzed, and decoded. Ethological observations suggest that mammalian vocalizations (like, for that matter, probably animal sounds in general) are mainly used for intraspecific communication, implying a proprioceptive, auditory, feedback. Therefore, auditory decoding capacities must have been shaped by selective pressures gearing it to vocalization capacities. In fact, I think that in most mammalian species the frequency range of the vocal tract (mainly determined by the larynx) largely coincides with that of the auditory system. This means that, if acoustic properties can be deduced from fossil middle ears, the vocalization frequencies of extinct species can be reconstructed as well.

Two other characteristics of mammals are related to vocalization; i.e., homeothermy and the very activity for which this Class is named: sucking. Apart from the consequences for the respiratory functions mentioned, a raised metabolism associated with *endothermy* must have implied (1) a more frequent taking in of food and a faster digestion of it, selecting for oropharyngeal adaptations; these include tooth specialization, greater tongue mobility, the development of facial and cheek muscles, and a rostrally located larynx enabling the animal to continue breathing and smelling while eating, and (2) a better insulation which must have been of selective value especially for the small-sized early mammals (because of the allometrical relationship between body size and body surface); this was achieved by skin adaptations like hairs that worked more efficiently when they could be erected. From these superficial muscles evolved those ensuring the subtle mobility of the whiskers (or vibrissae) and later the facial muscles so important for communication in the primates.[28,29]

The adaptations associated with *sucking* are partly the same as those for endothermy; i.e., oropharyngeal specializations enabling the buildup of a negative pressure and the possibility of simultaneously drinking and breathing, and the development of facial and cheek musculature.

Because the oropharyngeal and facial musculature plays an important part in human vocalizations, endothermy and sucking can be considered as preadaptations for speech, which originated, of course, much more recently.

The *upper* and *lower* parts of the airway are of less interest for reconstructing the evolutionary history of the human vocal tract. The nose, in the earliest vertebrates merely a smelling organ, came to be used in the amphibians and the later evolving vertebrates for respiration. Smelling acuity must have increased already by the evolution of choanae enabling the stream of water or air to pass right through the nose, instead of the slower diffusion of the osmic stimuli present in the early fish like the Placoderms. In the mammals the nose, next to its respiratory and olfactory function, came to be used for vocalizations. Because of the almost intranarial position of the laryngeal entrance, many mammals are able only to breathe and hence to vocalize through their noses. The function of the typically mammalian paranasal sinuses remains enigmatic; they have no clear function in the production of vocalizations (except for the frontal sinuses in man that may have some effect on the proprioceptive feed-back in professional singers[2,3]).

In mammals *trachea*, *bronchi*, and *lungs* are adapted for a quicker and more intensive gas exchange (relative to the reptilians). The closed and often bony tracheal rings of reptiles evolved into U-shaped cartilages, the space between the legs of the U being provided with muscular fibers. The latter, like similar fibers in the bronchi, serve to regulate lumen size. This regulation is part of a sensitive feed-back system regulating the amounts of air inspired and the intraairway pressure changes. Other valves in this control mechanism, more important in primates, are the nose—the resistance of which can be changed by means of the nostril musculature and the mucosal swelling—and the larynx, the resistance of which can be varied by the size of the glottis opening; i.e., by the position of the thyroarytenoid folds. The lung structure in mammals, as compared with reptiles, shows a considerable enlargement of the gas-exchanging surface due to the presence of a huge number of small alveoli. These ensure an intensive contact between the inhaled air and the blood. A subtle regulation of breathing movements is a necessity because, among other things, surface tension tends to make the small alveoli collapse, which, therefore, next to surfactant action, need some negative pressure to keep them open and functioning.[30]

PRIMATES

A large part of this conference's audience is probably interested in the characteristics of the primates that have ultimately led to the emergence of speech in this taxon. For these attendants it may sound somewhat disappointing, but as far as the peripheral vocal organs are concerned, the number of these characteristics is, in my opinion, astonishingly small. Most of the airway preadaptations for speech are present in most modern mammals and have been mentioned before. Unfortunately, the paleontological record of primates is rather poor, and consequently, we have to rely mainly on comparative observations: primate fossil material may allow some inferences concerning the thorax and nose, but it provides little or no information about the most interesting part of the airway, viz. the middle—soft tissue—part containing larynx, pharynx, and mouth structures. To be sure, interesting attempts have been made by Lieberman and Crelin,[31] materializing my suggestion[3] for assessing a fossil's larynx position by determining the direction of the styloid process, and subsequently deducing the associated vocal properties. I do not think however, that such an approach has hitherto yielded much reliable information about ancestral vocal tract properties.[32-36]

The airway of extant primates is largely identical with that of other mammals, at least of those usually assumed to represent the human ancestors. these "model" mammals comprise the insectivores and the so-called lower, respectively higher, primates.

The *lower airway* morphology is in all primates virtually identical, although with increasing taxonomical proximity to man there is a reduction in the number of tracheal muscle fibers, and there may be slight relative size differences due to allometry. The *upper airway* shows some differences in the various primate species. Most obvious is the size of the nose and the number of its turbinals; both are relatively larger in the lower species.[37] These characters, however, are adaptations for olfactory and masticatory functions rather than for vocalizations, and are therefore of minor interest here.

In mammals, including the primates, it is the larynx, pharynx, and mouth that determine the specific character of the vocalizations, and the larynx, the most intriguing and central vocal organ, appears to be largely similar in the model mammals.

The main differences in *laryngeal morphology, topography* and *function* are: (1) The most primitive insectivores, like the S.E. Asian *Hylomys suillus*, have only one, paired, thyroarytenoid fold instead of two—an upper and a lower one—in the primates. This duplication is probably an adaptation for arboreal locomotion; the inlet valve formed by the lower folds contributes to maintaining the negative intrathoracic pressure necessary for effective contraction of the pectoral muscles.[27]

(2) The "model" primates, as well as the primitive primate-like tree-shew *Tupaia glis* have air-sacs (connected with the laryngeal lumen); their function remains enigmatic; man has none. (3) Relative arytenoid size is in the lower primates somewhat larger than in the higher ones including man. (4) In the model mammals, except for the apes, the laryngeal position is, compared with man, quite rostral (as it is, for that matter, in most mammals). Hence, their epiglottis touches the palate either in an antevelar or in a retrovelar position. In apes there is a small gap between the epiglottis and the palate, and in adult man this gap is somewhat larger. The presence of such a gap facilitates a subtle distribution of the air expired, e.g. during vocalization, between the mouth and the nose. (5) The chimpanzee, as compared with man, has a more funnel-shaped cricoid,[3] more variations in the anatomy of the small cuneiform and corniculate cartilages (present in the aryepiglottic folds), a smaller hyoid-thyroid distance, and a more broadly based thyroarytenoid muscle origin with a somewhat more ventral insertion.[38] (6) Histologically, there may be some peculiarities of the human vocal muscles as compared with those of monkeys, i.e., more cholinesterase-positive receptors.[39]

Concerning the *other vocal organs*, the most obvious morphological differences between the various primates are: (1) in man, and to a lesser extent in apes, the mesopharynx has a somewhat larger relative size than in the other primates. This may facilitate the production of some vowels,[31] and it is a consequence of the mentioned caudal position of the human larynx. (2) The tongue in nonhuman primates is generally flatter and somewhat less mobile than in man. The latter character is probably related with the V-shape of the human mandibular and maxillary tooth-row in contrast to the U-shape in the other primates. (3) Facial, and especially perioral and periocular mobility, is about in proportion with the taxonomic proximity to man,[28,29] the Rhesus monkey, and the chimpanzee nearing man's level.

VOCAL TRACT AND SPEECH

Now, the intriguing question remains to be answered: to what extent do the nonhuman primates' vocal tract morphology and function provide clues for understanding the origin of speech? In various primate species recordings of vocalizations have been made such as in lemurs,[40,41] Old World monkeys,[42-50] and the apes[38,51-58] (more references in Ref. 3). However, when comparing them, there appears no clear relation between their likeness to speech and the taxonomic closeness to man. They do show that all primates use their airway for generating sounds that have a communicatory function (though used less frequently than by man), that in the smaller species these sounds are mainly high-pitched, and that in the chimpanzees and other apes they may be lower pitched as well. Baboon vocalization may even be quite human-like.[43,43] Furthermore, it has been shown that a chimpanzee is able to produce labial and guttural consonants: the home-raised Vicky could, after much energy having been spent on her training, say a few words like "mamma" and "cup" (and she did so in the right context).[57] Also, chimpanzees show lip-smacking as a means of communication[53,54] and they can produce some other, rudimentary, vowels and consonants.[54a]

In addition to these comparative observations, human pathology provides some indications. It appears, then, that the human peripheral vocal organs have a considerable functional redundancy. Thus, after removal of the larynx most people are able to acquire speech again, by swallowing some air into the esophagus and subsequently using this "burp" for generating vocalizations that are often difficult to discern from normal speech.[58] Similarly, after removal of the epiglottis, (parts of) the tongue, palate, teeth, or lips, and in many other pathological conditions of the vocal tract, man is usually still able to make himself understood by his vocalizations. Most cases of aphonia and aphasia are essentially central of origin, having been caused by diseases of the nervous system.

The above evidence therefore led me to assert that if surgery would reach the level where a chimpanzee larynx could successfully be grafted into an otherwise normal human being, such a person would be able to acquire a speech hardly discernible from the normal.[3] In view of the progress of immunology, medicine, and surgery such a possibility is indeed not complete science-fiction. Let us, however, just for heuristic purposes, extend our fantasy into the realm of pure science-fiction, and assume that a whole chimpanzee vocal tract would be transplanted into a human individual while its nervous control would remain human. The vocalizations made by such a person would, of course, be somewhat different from average speech, some phonemes, especially the vowels having a different "color." Yet, only the encoding speed would be slightly lower than in most other humans, but for the rest such speech would hardly differ from the normal. If a baboon vocal tract would be used, the encoding speed would again be somewhat lower, and the human individual might have slight social difficulties in making himself understood. Bypassing monkey and prosimian transplants, let us finally assume that a suitably sized insectivore vocal tract is grafted; the person concerned would be able to utter little variable hisses, squeaks, and twitters. Yet, he would certainly communicate with his fellow humans by means of such phonemes albeit with an encoding speed considerably lower than normal (but still higher than that of Morse code). If on the other hand, these fellow humans would have the same vocal tract properties, his encoding speed would probably be near that of normal speech.

The point is that, though encoding speed may be different, all these humans may be assumed to be using *language* by means of sound signals. What they all have in common is the central nervous system capacity and propensity for decoding and encoding signals from and for fellow humans and for processing them, thereby establishing the communication system that we call language (the characters of which need not to be discussed here being ably treated by others). Whether softly or loudly speaking, whether using a clear or a harsh voice, whether using more or fewer phonemes, whether having undergone tooth extraction or a laryngectomy, or so on, the average man is able to communicate by voice with other humans, the communication system being language. This system operates as well when other signals are used such as written or gestural ones. The only essential difference between these various communication modes is the encoding speed.

Now, even when we assume that the most recent prespeech and the earliest speaking primates still possessed an ape-like vocal tract, the possible encoding speed is likely to have been about the same as in modern man. Their actual encoding speed must have been determined entirely by the nervous system properties. In view of the evidence from evolutionary biology in general, it is likely that during the evolution from nonhuman primates to man there have been mutual feedback forces shaping the morphology of the vocal tract and the central nervous system. I think, however, that these forces have been relatively weak, because the vocal tract, like the auditory system, is likely to have been already preadapted for speech in our prehominid ancestors.

Though in recent years language-like abilities have been shown to be present in chimpanzees,[56-65] I think that they never attain the human level, among other reasons because their encoding speed and the number of possible messages is lower; they use mainly the brain⟶limbs/face channel instead of the brain⟶vocal tract channel.

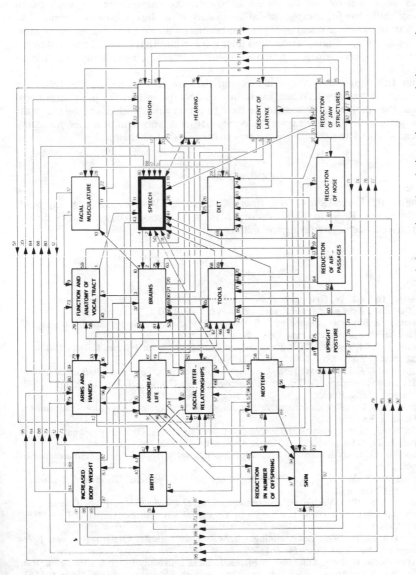

FIGURE 4. Schematic representation of the adaptations and their interactions that during primate evolution may have contributed to the emergence of speech. It shows that speech emergence must have been a complicated process in which not only the vocal tract properties have played a part. (Adapted from Wind [3]).

Comparative observations suggest that their leaving the vocal tract idle cannot be explained by its inadequacy but rather by a lack of internal, cerebral, wiring.

So, rather than vocal tract novelties, it seems to have been cerebral reorganization that has been decisive for the origin of speech-like communication, such as an increased ability to form cross-modal associations[66] and an increased memory. In addition to this and the vocal tract preadaptations discussed in this paper, there must have been many other adaptations and their interactions that have contributed to the emergence of speech during primate evolution,[3,67] as schematically pictured in FIGURE 4.

From this figure and the evidence put forward in this paper, the following conclusion can be drawn. When we want to assess the role of the peripheral vocal organs in the emergence of speech, we have to investigate which encoding speed fits into the picture that we are now able to reconstruct of ancestral primates, including their behavior and the selective pressures that have shaped them.

ACKNOWLEDGMENTS

I thank R. J. Andrew, L. de Boer, K. Deen, G. W. Hewes, G. J. Lijnzaad, Machteld Roede, R. Stein, C. H. Vroom, Mrs. B. M. Vroom-Dissen, and G. de Wit for their assistance in preparing the manuscript.

REFERENCES

1. DEMSKI, L. S., J. W. GERALD & A. N. POPPER. 1973. Central and peripheral mechanisms of teleost sound production. Amer. Zool. **13:** 1141–1167.
2. PETERSON & BELLAMY, quoted by J. B. STEEN. 1971. Comparative Physiology of Respiratory Mechanisms. Academic Press. New York, N.Y.
3. WIND, J. 1970. On the Phylogeny and the Ontogeny of the Human Larynx. Wolters-Noordhoff Publishing. Groningen, The Netherlands.
4. ANTHONY, J. & J. MILLOT. 1958. Crossoptérygiens actuels, *Latimeria chalumnae* dernier des crossoptérigiens. *In* Traitée de Zoologie. P. P. Grassé, Ed. Vol. **13-3:** 2553–2597. Masson. Paris, France.
5. HUGHES, G. M. 1963. Comparative Physiology of Vertebrate Respiration. Heinemann. London, England.
6. DE BEER, G. 1958. Embryos and ancestors. Clarendon Press. Oxford, England.
7. WIND, J. 1973. Biogenetic Law. Curr. Anthropol. **14:** 522.
8. WIND, J. 1975. Methoden zur Erforschung der Sprachursprung. Acta Teilhardiana. In press.
9. WILLISTON, S. W. 1914. Water reptiles of the past and present. University of Chicago Press. Chicago, Ill.
10. ROMER, A. S. 1966. Vertebrate Paleontology. University of Chicago Press. Chicago, Ill.
11. SCHMALHAUSEN, I. I. 1968. The Origin of Terrestrial Vertebrates. Academic Press. New York, N.Y.
12. BUMILLER, O. E. 1929. Beschreibung von Wachsmodellen der Glottisregion von *Polypterus bichir*. Anat. Anz. **66:** 361–369.
13. KLEEREKOPER, H. 1969. Olfaction in Fishes. Indiana University Press. Bloomington, Ind.
14. JOHANSEN, K. 1970. Air Breathing in fishes. *In* Fish Physiology. W. S. Hoar & D. J. Randall, Eds. Vol. **4:** 361–411. Academic Press. New York, N.Y.
15. STEEN, J. B. 1971. Comparative Physiology of Respiratory Mechanisms. Academic Press. New York, N.Y.
16. GANS, C. 1973. Sound production in the Salientia: mechanism and evolution of the emitter. Amer. Zool. **13:** 1179–1194.
17. NOBLE, G. K. 1954. The biology of the amphibia. Dover Publications. New York, N.Y.

18. BELLAIRS, A. 1969. The life of Reptiles. Vol. 1. Weidenfeld and Nicolson. London, England.
19. JONES, J. D. 1972. Comparative Physiology of Respiration. Edward Arnold. London, England.
20. PAULSEN, K. 1967. Das Prinzip der Stimmbildung in der Wirbeltierreihe und beim Menschen. Akademische Verlagsgesellschaft. Frankfort, Germany.
21. BOGERT, C. M. 1953. The Tuatara: Why is it a lonely survivor? Scientific Monthly 76: 163–170.
22. GANS, C. & P. F. MADERSON. 1973. Sound producing mechanisms in reptiles: review and comment. Amer. Zool. 13: 1195–1203.
23. GREGORY, W. K. 1929. Our face from fish to man. Reprinted by Hafner. New York, N.Y. 1963.
24. BAKKER, R. T. 1975. Dinosaur Renaissance. Sci. Amer. 232(4): 58–78.
25. WIND, J. 1975. Book Review of H. J. Jerison, Evolution of the Brain and Intelligence. Curr. Anthropol. 16: 412–413.
25a. WIND, J. 1976. Human drowning: phylogenetic origin. J. Hum. Evol. In press.
26. GAUNT, A. S. & M. K. WELLS. 1973. Models of Syringeal Mechanisms. Amer. Zool. 13: 1227–1247.
27. NEGUS, V. 1949. The Comparative Anatomy and Physiology of the Larynx. Heinemann. London, England.
28. CHEVALIER-SKOLNIKOFF, S. 1973. Facial Expression of Emotion in Nonhuman Primates. In Darwin and Facial Expression. P. Ekman, Ed.: 11–89. Academic Press. New York, N.Y.
29. WIND, J. 1976. The facial nerve and human evolution. In Advances in ORL 22. Karger. Basel, Switzerland. In press.
29a. FLACH, M., H. SCHWICKARDI & H. KÖHLER. 1973. Die Stirnhöhlenpneumatisation beim Sänger. Mschr. Ohr. hk. Wien 107: 543–549.
30. DE WIT, G. 1973. The function of the nose in the aerodynamics of respiration. Rhinology 11: 59–67.
31. LIEBERMAN, P. & E. S. CRELIN. 1971. On the speech of Neanderthal Man. Linguistic Inquiry 11: 203–222.
32. FALK, D. 1975. Comparative anatomy of the larynx in man and the chimpanzee: Implications for language in Neanderthal. Amer. J. Phys. Anthropol. 43: 123–132.
33. LEMAY, M. 1975. The language capability of Neanderthal man. Amer. J. Phys. Anthropol. 42: 9–14.
34. WIND, J. 1975. Neanderthal speech. ORL 37: 58.
35. WIND, J. 1976. Methods for tracing the origin of speech. In Biology, Language, and Human Behavior. S. K. Ghosh, Ed. University Park Press. Baltimore, Md. In press.
36. MORRIS, D. H. 1974. Neanderthal speech. Linguistic Inquiry 5: 144–150.
37. NEGUS, V. 1958. The comparative anatomy and physiology of the nose and paranasal sinuses. Livingstone. Edinburgh, Scotland.
38. JORDAN, J. 1971. Studies on the structure of the organ of voice and vocalization in the chimpanzees. Folia Morphologica (Warsz.) 30: 97–126, 222–248, 323–340.
39. ANZENBACHER, H. & W. ZENKER. 1962. Ueber die cholinesterase-aktiven Formelemente des M. thyreoarytaenoideus und ihre Beziehungen zur Struktur dieses Muskels. Z. Anat. Entw. Gesch. 123: 221–245.
40. PETTER, J. J. 1965. The Lemurs of Madagascar. In Primate Behavior. I. DeVore, Ed.: 292–319. Holt Rinehart and Winston, Inc. New York, N.Y.
41. JOLLY, A. 1966. Lemur behavior. University of Chicago Press. Chicago, Ill.
42. MARLER, P. 1965. Communication in monkeys and apes. In Primate Behavior, I. deVore, Ed.: 544–584. Holt Rinehart and Winston, Inc. New York, N.Y.
43. ANDREW, R. J. 1973. Comment on primate communication and the gestural origin of language. Curr. Anthropol. 14: 12.
43a. ANDREW, R. J. This volume.
44. ERWIN, J. & G. MITCHELL. 1973. Analysis of rhesus monkey vocalizations: maturation-related sex differences in clear-call frequency. Amer. J. Phys. Anthropol. 38: 463–468.
45. VOGEL, C. 1973. Acoustical communication among free-ranging common Indian langurs

(*Presbytis entellus*) in two different habitats of North India. Amer. J. Phys. Anthropol. **38:** 469–480.

46. BECK, B. B. & R. TUTTLE. 1972. The behavior of gray langurs at a Ceylonese waterhole. *In* The Functional and Evolutionary Biology of Primates. R. Tuttle, Ed.: 351–377. Aldine-Atherton. Chicago, Ill.

47. ROWELL, T. 1972. The Social Behaviour of Monkeys. Penguin Books. Harmondsworth, England.

48. PLOOG, D. 1972. Kommunikation in Affengesellschaften und deren Bedeutung für die Verständigungsweisen des Menschen. *In* Neue Anthropologie, H. G. Adamer & P. Vogler, Eds. Vol. 2/2: 98–178. Thieme Verlag. Stuttgart, Germany.

49. NISHIMURA, A. 1973. Age changes of the vocalizations in free-ranging Japanese monkeys. *In* Symp. IVth. Int. Congr. Primatol. W. Montagna, Ed. Vol. **1:** 76–87. Karger. Basel, Switzerland.

50. KERN, J. A. 1964. Observations on the habits of the proboscis monkey, *Nasalis larvatus* (Wurmb), made in the Brunei Bay area, Borneo. Zoologica (N.Y.) **49:** 183–192.

51. MARLER, P. 1969. Vocalizations of wild chimpanzees. *In* Proc. Second Inter. Congr. Primatol. C. R. Carpenter, Ed. Vol. **1:** 94–100, Karger. Basel, Switzerland.

52. REYNOLDS, V. & F. REYNOLDS. 1965. Chimpanzees of the Budongo Forest. *In* Primate Behavior. I. DeVore, Ed.: 368–424. Holt Rinehart and Winston, Inc. New York, N.Y.

53. LAWICK-GOODALL, J. VAN. 1973. In the Shadow of Man. Collins. London, England.

54. HOOFF, J. A. R. A. M. VAN. 1973. A structural analysis of the social behaviour of a semi-captive group of chimpanzees. *In* Social Communication and Movement. M. von Cranach and I. Vine, Eds.: 75–162. Academic Press. New York, N.Y.

54a. STOPA, R. 1976. Comment on: language, communication, chimpanzees. Curr. Anthrop. **17:** 16–17.

55. FOSSEY, D. 1972. Vocalizations of the Mountain Gorilla (*Gorilla gorilla beringei*). Anim. Behav. **20:** 36–53.

56. SCHALLER, G. B. 1963. The Mountain Gorilla. Ecology and Behavior. University of Chicago Press. Chicago, Ill.

57. HAYES, C. 1951. The Ape in Our House. Harper & Row. New York, N.Y.

58. DIEDRICH, W. M. & K. A. YOUNGSTROM. 1966. Alaryngeal Speech. Chas. C Thomas. Springfield, Ill.

59. GARDNER, R. A. & B. T. GARDNER. 1969. Teaching sign language to a chimpanzee. Science **165:** 664–672.

60. FOUTS, R. S. 1972. Use of guidance in teaching sign language to a chimpanzee (*Pan troglodytes*). J. Comp. Physiol. Psychol. **80:** 515–522.

61. FOUTS, R. S. 1973. Acquisition and testing of gestural signs in four young chimpanzees. Science **180:** 978–980.

62. PREMACK, A. J. & D. PREMACK. 1972. Teaching language to an ape. Sci. Amer. **227**(4): 92–99

63. RENSCH, B. Manipulierfähigkeit und Komplikation von Handlungsketten bei Menschen-haffen. *In* Handgebrauch und Verständigung bei Affen und Frühmenschen. B. Rensch, Ed.: 103–130. Hans Huber. Bern, Switzerland.

64. RUMBAUGH, D. M., T. V. GILL, & E. C. VON GLASERSFELD. 1973. Reading and sentence completion by a chimpanzee (*Pan*). Science **182:** 731–733.

65. MENZEL, E. W. & S. HALPERIN. 1975. Purposive behavior as a basis for objective communication between chimpanzees. Science **189:** 652–654.

66. GESCHWIND, N. 1964. The development of the brain and the evolution of language. *In* Report of the 15th R. T. M. on Linguistic and Language Studies. C. I. J. M. Stuart, Ed. Monogr. Ser. Languages and Linguistics.

67. WIND, J. Speech Emergence During Primate Evolution. Unpublished.

BIOMECHANICS OF SPEECH SOUNDS

E. Lloyd Du Brul

Department of Oral Anatomy
University of Illinois Medical Center
Chicago, Illinois 60680

"The physical event of speech is a pulse of discrete, vibrating, jointed segments of air. These segments are shaped by anatomical parts," consequently, "speech is first a morphological problem."[1] This conviction would make the soundest approach to the elusive problem of speech an identification first, of palpable, constant, peripheral constructs whose orchestrated deformations can produce the evanescent stream of sounds interpreted as speech. The acoustical specifications for the production of speech sounds can be met by the human vocal tract.[2,3] This is essentially a serially coupled, instantaneously adjustable, double-resonator system formed of pharyngeal and oral cavities. Speech output is molded as it flows up this tube of writhing walls from rima glottis to lips. The predominant need, then, is to define precisely what, and how, particular peripheral structural adaptations did arise in man to induce such a behavior. Based on such solid peripheral findings, the probability of penetrating believable "higher" mechanisms is increased by tracking the centripetal extensions of neural correlates of these primary structures.

MODEL OF THE MAMMALIAN OROPHARYNGEAL SYSTEM

In general, the oropharyngeal channel in mammals lies horizontally below the flat, elongate skull base. The oral segment is long and narrow; the entire tongue lies flat on the oral floor. The pharynx continues immediately behind as a short tube connecting the mouth with the esophagus. The larynx, as the antechamber to the lung, is fitted with special protective valvular folds. It rises from the floor of the pharynx to project up to and *through* the soft palate, thus dividing the foodway into two short parallel channels that join immediately behind at the esophagus (FIGURE 1). In this way the short pharynx has a continuous roof, interrupted only by a palatal aditus the muscular margins of which encircle completely and grip firmly the special, reciprocally grooved, raised walls of the larynx.[4] Thus the airway is kept continuous and intact in the vast majority of mammals. It has been amply demonstrated that this arrangement is admirably adapted to the functions of scent and strenuous breathing in attack and escape by predators and prey alike, such as the great cats and their widely diverse targets—deer, antelopes, horses, goats, sheep, tapirs, pigs, and so on.[5,6]

There are two critical points of interest here. First, since all mammals have a larynx fitted with "vocal" folds, what can this protective respiratory valve produce in the way of sound? Alone, practically nothing. Even in man, air blown through the narrowed slit of the rima glottis "is periodically varied in magnitude owing to the opening and closing action of the so-called vocal cords" but "the acoustic function of these cords or folds should not be regarded in analogy to vibrating membranes. Actually, they . . . do not generate sound oscillations of a significant magnitude by a direct conversion of mechanical vibrations of sound."[7]

The second is that, as has been shown in the general mammalian arrangement, exhaled air has little or no access to the oropharyngeal tract. However, the *potential* for breaking the integrity of the airway at the palatolaryngeal junction is universally

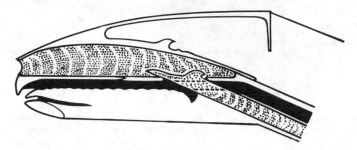

FIGURE 1. Model of mammalian oropharyngeal tract: airway stippled, foodway black. General layout of head and neck is horizontal. Larynx projects up through palatal aditus into posterior nasal space, sealed by palatopharyngeal sphincter. Airway is an uninterrupted channel. Oropharyngeal tract divides to pass on either side of larynx, indicated by dashed outlines.

present in mammals (except perhaps in whales). Such preadaptive potential is the essence of evolution and particularly pertinent in the present instance. It has been exploited in surprisingly diverse directions.

To bring the point home, we can demonstrate two adaptive extremes. The first is a striking example found in the panting behavior of a variety of animals (including birds). Clearly, the exhaled air must be made accessible to the oral channel. In dogs, just a simple first readjustment of the epiglottis to the soft palate seems to have instigated an adaptation. Here the epiglottis normally lies *below* the velum, although the rest of the larynx remains above, snugly within the palatal aditus. The relationship permits both a tight seal for a continuous airway, and a shunting of air through the mouth. Thus, vigorously expired air blows over the whole saliva-soaked surface of the mouth, which is completely open at the sides through the long oral slit. Extensive evaporation results. Profuse venous plexuses within the spongy coverings of the entire palate above and the elongated tongue below together "serve as a radiator through which blood percolates for cooling."[8] So, in the first instance, a simple beginning resulted in thermoregulation. In the second instance we find the airway also interrupted in man, but under extraordinarily different circumstances and in the service of entirely different functions.

EVOLUTION OF THE HUMAN OROPHARYNGEAL SYSTEM

In overzealous dedication to detail, the structure of the human head has too often in the past been explained as if it, or even its special parts, were isolated entities. That the skull is but an integral part of the total organism seems rarely to have been adequately emphasized. But, as in the history of all vertebrates, the hominid skull has continuously reflected adaptive adjustments both to general bodily changes and to local changes in its special organ complexes. It is now well established that three predominant influences have marked the evolution of human head form: the development of 1) erect bipedalism, 2) a big brain, and 3) a modified oral apparatus. All three have been essential contributors to the evolution of speech. Because the scope here is limited to peripheral structures, emphasis will focus on the extraordinary shift to completely erect, bipedal posture with its far-reaching effects on the oral complex and its immediate extensions.

Permanent 90° reorientation of an entire organism in the earth's gravitational field is a drastic occurrence. It has demanded severe readjustment of the hominid head. The essential alteration is a sharp bending of the originally elongate skull between its visceral and neural elements, giving much the effect of a bent taffy bar: domed on top, buckled on bottom. This satisfied two primary requirements. It retained the critical horizontal orientation of the special sense organs and feeding apparatus. It retained a relatively undisturbed, straight continuity between the brainstem and spinal cord. Obviously, this has necessitated considerable local integration. This is most commonly expressed as: 1) vaulting of the entire dorsum, 2) buckling up of the base at sella turcica, 3) downward and backward rotation and retrusion of the facial complex, 4) and downward and forward rotation of the nuchal plane, causing, 5) forward shift of the foramen magnum and its accompanying condyles. "By so doing, it introduces adaptation to balance and scanning rotation in a head posted on a vertical column."[9] But also by so doing, the base of the skull is severely squeezed and crowded, and the mouth parts are markedly shortened. In partial compensation, the oral space has been broadened and deepened, and its mandibular walls flared to accommodate the vital structures housed within and below.[10] The tongue, although distinctly shortened, has not been proportionately decreased in mass. As a consequence, it is now thick, deep, and specially bent at its base, due to the notable approximation of its opposite anchorages, the genial tubercles in front and the hyoid bone in back. Thus it becomes clear that balancing the skull on the vertical spine could have had the dangerous final effect of jamming the broad tongue base back into the larynx, vital protective valve of the airway. The final, crucial adaptation to this serious situation is seen in the extraordinary retreat of the larynx, far down the neck (FIGURE 2). It has left a wide gap between the palatal aditus and the aditus of the larynx. Because of this, man is the only animal capable of closing off the nasal outlet, completely and easily, from a widely patent oropharyngeal tract. The potential for this phenomenon appears to have been prevalent in

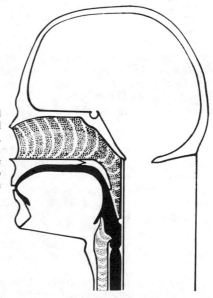

FIGURE 2. Model of human oropharyngeal tract: airway stippled, foodway black. General layout of head and neck is vertical, cranial base, airway and tract bent sharply to upright posture. Retruded jaws have jammed vertical tongue base back; larynx has retreated down neck leaving gap in airway. Palatal aditus indicated slanting down and back.

primates, so that a model suggesting the process can be easily pictured in an extant morphological sequence.[1]

The remarkable repercussions of extensive cranial renovations for vertical posture can be summarized simply. Forelimbs freed from locomotion were recruited to dominate in food prehension and preparation (which is not new, since it is common in crustaceans). The oral complex thus largely freed from these functions was opened to other tangents of adaptation. "Selection shifted at the timely release of this convenient apparatus and acted upon it for speech."[1]

GENERAL FEATURES OF THE RESONATOR SYSTEM

The human pharynx is a muscular funnel flattened from front to back by the backwardly thrust vertical plane of the tongue base and the forwardly thrust vertical plane of the cervical vertebral bodies. Its real upper limit is a sphincter defined by the complete margins of the soft palate, whose lateral arms, indicated by the steeply slanting, special upper rims of the palatopharyngeus muscles, meet low in the posterior pharyngeal midline.[11] In so doing, they embrace a "palatal aditus" which defines the actual posterior floor of the nasal space (FIGURE 2). Their sphincteric action in closing off the nose is clearly demonstrated in swallowing, as posterolateral rims move in to meet the velum.[12] The lower pharyngeal limit is defined by the cricopharyngeal sphincter, well below the level of the laryngeal aditus. This tube can be expanded anteroposteriorly by muscles that pull the hyoid bone and attached tongue and larynx away from the back wall of the pharynx, and can be expanded laterally by the lateral pull of stylopharyngeus muscles. It can be constricted in both dimensions by the encircling pharyngeal constrictors which form the continuous back walls of the tube. It can be shortened by the vertical pull of the stylopharyngeus muscles and lengthened by the sternohyoid-sternothyroid strap muscles which pull the thyroid and attached tract down toward the thorax.

The oral cavity is a channel flattened from top to bottom by the horizontal plane of the palate above and the horizontal plane of the anterior two thirds of the tongue below, completed laterally by the dental arches and cheeks. Its anterior limit is also a sphincter, defined by the margins of the lips surrounded by the orbicularis oris musculature. Its posterior limit is defined by a sphincteric system formed by special interlacing muscles connecting the soft palate above with the tongue below. The constricting action is reinforced by transverse bands of the styloglossus muscles, which swing medially to interlace with upper transverse intrinsic tongue muscles at the angle of the horizontal and vertical planes of the tongue. This cavity can also be expanded and contracted by the tongue, aided by jaw movements and facial muscles.

Both resonator cavities overlap functionally at the upper pharynx and soft palate. In this crucial area the two cavities can be made a widely continuous tube or can be narrowly separated by the precise operation of special musculature. The range of movements permitted this acoustical system is contained within the walls of the jaw and the envelope of its boundary movements, with the addition of leeway at its floor and front wall provided by the widely flared jaw. The extremes of this range are defined as the "vowel triangle" best demonstrated in the sounding of /i/, /a/, and /u/.

MANIPULATORS OF THE RESONATORS

Since the roof and rear wall of the vocal tract are rigidly backed by the bony palate and flat facade of the vertebral bodies, expansibility of the system is free only at the oral floor and front half of the neck. In these regions mobile walls are provided by the horizontal and vertical surfaces of the bent hominid tongue and side walls of the pharynx. But a gap disrupts the coupling of the resonators at the angle between roof and back wall. And in this region additional mobility is provided by the velopharyngeal hatch, which closes the gap and secures the coupling by opportune action.

Consider first the tongue complex. The mammalian tongue is said to be without a skeleton. Viewed in isolation, however, the tongue mass can be shown to behave like an entity with a hydrostatic skeleton. The functioning of such a system depends on two basic properties: the incompressibility of water with its capacity for transmitting pressure equally in all directions, and contractibility of the unit in three planes of space. Thus certain invertebrates manage locomotion essentially as a water-filled tube with circular and longitudinal musculature. Circular contraction (two planes of space) at one end yields a stable pressure base against the substrate from which pressure is transmitted along the tube to elongate it by timely release of the longitudinal muscles. The tongue is also a fluid-filled, enclosed mass packed with intrinsic muscles arranged in three planes of space and ample spongy connective tissue; vertical muscles flatten it out horizontally, transverse muscles bulge it up vertically, longitudinal muscles shorten it considerably. Transverse and vertical contraction elongate it when longitudinal fibers relax. In proper concert these muscles can perform extraordinary rhythms of tongue contouring with great virtuosity. But as a constituent integrated within the total oral complex, this peculiar mass is slung from the skull, directly and indirectly, by four pairs of strategically positioned muscles. The palatoglossi and styloglossi arise directly from the skull base; the genioglossi arise from the mandible, which is jointed to the skull base, and the hyoglossi arise from the hyoid bone, which is hung from the skull base by ligaments and muscles. And their concerted action, as a correlating link intercalated between tongue intrinsics and particular palatal musculature, is at the core of the coupled resonator mechanism.

The palatoglossus muscle arises from the undersurface of the tough, fibrous, palatine aponeurosis, which is but a mobile extension of the hard bony palate. Some of its bundles are continuous across the midline with the muscle of the opposite side. The muscle curves laterally, downward and forward, and again inward in a distinct, flat band. It forms the palatoglossal arch or anterior pillar of the fauces as the muscle penetrates the side of the tongue in the angle of its middle and posterior thirds. The fibers continue medially, mingling and twining with transverse intrinsic fibers, to meet fibers of its counterpart of the opposite side and produce a complete collar of muscle, or sphincter, between oral and pharyngeal spaces (FIGURES 3 & 4).

The styloglossus muscle arises from the lower third of the front and side of the styloid process and often from the adjacent stylomandibular and stylohyoid ligaments. It runs downward and forward as a wide, flat band to the level of the palatoglossal arch, where it diverges into three segments. The first segment swings sharply medially from its inner surface to penetrate the tongue and run with the combined palatoglossus and transverse intrinsic fibers in the area of the angle. The second, or major, segment continues forward along the outer rim of the tongue to the tip, where it curves medially to join its counterpart from the opposite side. It can be clearly seen that two slings resembling checkreins are thus formed, pulling back from the fixed styloid processes (FIGURES 3 & 4). The first retracts and raises the angle of the tongue, assisting the palatoglossal sphincter; the second controls and reins in the tongue tip. A third, lesser, segment continues downward and forward to weave into the fibers of the hyoglossus muscle.

The genioglossi together form a thick, sagittaly triangular, central partition of the tongue. They are separated only by the median fibrous septum which divides the

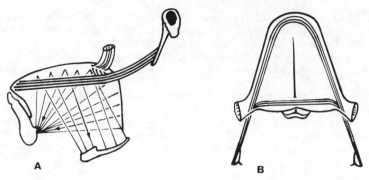

A   **B**

FIGURE 3. Model of tongue mechanics: A = lateral view. Muscle fibers are drawn to suggest direction (arrows) of force vectors. The sectioned chin is at left, styloid process and ear opening at right, and hyoid bone below and between. Genioglossus fibers splay out from tubercle behind chin; five vectors pull horizontal dorsum down toward tubercle, five vectors pull vertical base forward toward tubercle. Hyoglossal vectors pull horizontal dorsum down and back toward hyoid bone. Styloglossus, from styloid process above and behind, runs down and forward to tongue. Medial segment turns sharply medial into angle between middle and posterior thirds (posterior sling). Major segment continues to tip (anterior sling). Palatoglossus, from above, runs down to turn medially into tongue angle and join medial segment of styloglossus. B = superior view. Tongue slings. Posterior sling turns in at level of cut palatoglossal stumps. Anterior sling is continuous at tongue tip. Median septum and tip of epiglottis seen along tongue center and behind tongue base.

tongue in half to attach behind and below to the body of the hyoid bone. Each muscle arises by a short tendon from a genial tubercle projecting from its side of the inner surface of the jaw symphysis. Its anteriormost fibers run straight up to the underside of the dorsum some distance behind the tongue tip. From this front margin the muscle splays out posteriorly like a fan, its fibers inserting close below the dorsum along the entire length of the tongue parallel to the median septum. In this way the posteriormost fibers become horizontal to end in the fascia attached to the midpart of

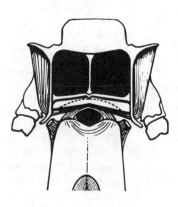

FIGURE 4. Coupling device: pharynx seen from behind. Black spaces above are openings into nose (choanae) separated by nasal septum. Black oval (blunted diamond) shaped opening below is faucial isthmus leading into mouth. Anterior wall of the pharynx (vertical surface of tongue base) descends to stippled tip of epiglottis below. Tensor palati muscles descend from skull base between nasal space and tooth row to hook around front of pterygoid hamuli and run transversely as the blackened palatine aponeurosis. The dashed arching line reaching posterior nasal spine indicates aponeurosis at rest; contraction of tensors pulls it down, lowering origin of palatoglossal sphincter. (Anteriorly aponeurosis is not flat, because of midline anchorage to nasal spine). Cut stumps of styloglossi are seen on either side; joint action of sphincter and styloglossi lift lateral tongue margins.

the body of the hyoid bone. Contraction of the various bundles controls the subtlest contouring of the tongue surface in joint action with the hyoglossus muscle (FIGURE 3).

The hyoglossus muscle is a relatively thin quadrilateral plate that arises from the front side of the body and entire length of the greater cornu of the hyoid bone. It overlays laterally the heavier triangular plate of the genioglossus muscle. The greater part of its fibers run upward and forward at fairly acute angles to most of the genioglossus fibers. They penetrate the tongue mass between the styloglossus laterally above and the inferior longitudinal intrinsic muscle medially below. The fibers end in the bulk of the warp and woof of the intrinsic tongue muscles near the dorsum. Some of the posterior fibers overlap the mass of the muscle to run more sharply anteriorly and join the styloglossus band. Contraction of this muscle pulls the tongue down and back when the hyoid is stabilized (FIGURE 3).

Consider now the palatal complex. Prevalent textbook descriptions of the soft palate, or "velum," are remarkably misleading. As has been shown, this so-called curtain is actually the strongly slanting roof of the downbent pharynx which continues along the side walls to end behind in the midline (FIGURE 2). At the same time it is the floor of the posterior nasal space which merges imperceptibly with the true pharyngeal space behind the velum when the soft palate is at rest. During swallowing, however, its contracting posterolateral muscular rims raise to meet the velum, which thus demarcates and separates the two spaces completely.

The pliable palatine aponeurosis is the base of soft-palate operation. This is a thick, dense, fibrous plate at its attachment on the oral surface of the bony palate from the palatine crest to, and including, the posterior edge of the palatine bone. It extends back about two thirds the length of the velum, gradually thinning out into a loose connective lacework. It is peculiar in that it functions as a hinge and is, at the same time, the terminal tendon of a unique pair of muscles, the tensor veli palati muscles.

The tensor palati is a broad, flat, triangular muscle narrowing as it runs down from the base of the skull. It arises from the scaphoid fossa at the root of the medial pterygoid plate and along the adjacent rim of the grooved sphenoid bone. Additional fibers are contributed from the membraneous strip of the auditory tube housed in the groove. The fibers converge below to end in a narrow tendon lying lateral to the base of the pterygoid hamulus. The tendon then turns sharply inward, running through the hamular notch well below the level of the hard palate. Immediately medial to the notch the tendon spreads out horizontally to fuse with (or form) the palatine aponeurosis by continuing with the flattened tendon from the opposite side (FIGURE 4). In the notch the tendon runs through a fluid-filled bursa that permits it to glide back and forth easily, like a cable around a pulley. Since the palatine aponeurosis is attached to the palatine bone at a higher level than the pulley, at rest it will lie in a slanting posture, higher in front. It can readily be seen that contraction of both tensors will pull the aponeurosis down sharply behind to a level with the hamular notch as well as tense it to form a stable origin for other palatal muscles (FIGURES 4 & 5, A).

The palatopharyngeus muscle is a combine of subsidiary special elements that promotes a division of pharyngeal labor. In its general aspect the muscle arises from the nasal surface of the palatine aponeurosis from which it sweeps laterally to spread down and around on the inner surface of the encircling constrictor muscles that constitute the pharyngeal walls proper. The upper elements of the palatopharyngeus are particularly pertinent here. At least two constant muscular bands are found, separated by the levator palati muscle as it penetrates the velum. The upper band arises from the upper anterolateral surface of the palatine aponeurosis. It swings laterally around the levator muscle, then down and back where its uppermost bundles meet the counterpart from the opposite side, as do many of the other palatopharyngeal fibers. When contracted, both muscles form a raised ridge running around the back of the pharynx (Passavant's Ridge), which is the posterior part of the sphincter of the "palatal aditus." The lower band follows a similar course at a lower level, where many of its fibers become vertical and end as longitudinal muscles in the wall of the pharynx.

The levator palati muscle is round in cross section in its origin and flattens at its termination. It arises in a short tendon from a circular area on the roughened petrous bone of the skull base between the carotid opening laterally behind and the auditory tube laterally in front. Fleshy fibers from the fascia of the carotid sheath and cartilaginous part of the auditory tube join the main fiber mass. The muscle runs downward, forward, and medially below the tube, to enter the pharynx over the upper concave rim of the superior constrictor muscle. It penetrates the soft palate behind the dwindling edge of the palatine aponeurosis to separate the two bands of the palatopharyngeus noted above. The fibers then cross the midline and mingle with

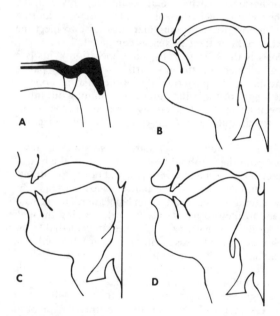

FIGURE 5. X-ray tracings of resonator contours: A = strong contraction of palatal sphincter in swallowing; soft palate indicated in black. The downward dip in front is effect of tensors on palatine aponeurosis (See FIGURE 4). Upward curve behind is effect of levators of palate. Pendulous thickened uvula at the right seals residual gap when rear wall of the pharynx is pulled forward. B = contouring for vowel /i/: constricted oral resonator, expanded pharyngeal resonator. C = contouring for vowel /a/: expanded oral resonator, constricted pharyngeal resonator. D = contouring for vowel /u/: both resonators expanded, coupling channel constricted. (From Sicher & Du Brul,[15] by permission of the C. V. Mosby Co.)

those of the opposite muscle, thus composing a continuous, suspended, muscular sling. The muscle pulls the posterior part of the soft palate up and back to complement the sphincter action of the palatopharyngeus as the posterior wall of the pharynx moves upward and forward to the same level (FIGURE 5, A).

CONTOURING FOR SOUNDS

The acoustical aspect of human speech is determined by the property of resonance of the supralaryngeal vocal tract. Vocal cord vibration sets the fundamental frequencies of air puffs pumped up through the tract. The particular resonant mode of the tract at the time shapes the formant frequencies we hear. Resonance is determined by area function, the relation between cross section and length of the resonator. This is exemplified by organ pipes. The sound of each pipe depends on length and shape. The human resonator system is an adjustable pipe. This may be best demonstrated by sounding the vowels /i/, /a/, /u/, since they are considered "language universal" and at the same time are produced by the extremes of vocal tract posturing.

The vowel /i/, as in teem, is formed by constricting the area function of the oral resonator and expanding that of the pharyngeal resonator (FIGURE 5, B). It is clear that in addition to pulling the hyoid bone forward by the geniohyoids, the lower five horizontal vectors representing the genioglossus muscle (FIGURE 3, A) will pull the vertical tongue base strongly forward, away from the rear pharyngeal wall, thus expanding the pharyngeal resonator. At the same time, the shortened tongue will be bunched so as to raise the dorsum toward the palate, assisted by contraction of the transverse intrinsics. This is augmented by relaxation of the vertical anterior five vectors of the genioglossi in conjunction with relaxation of the hyoglossi and the vertical intrinsics of the tongue (FIGURE 3, A). Appropriate adjustment of the oropharyngeal sphincter causing lifting of the lateral margins of the tongue in this area by palatoglossi and styloglossi (FIGURE 4) finally yields an unbroken resonating chamber narrowed anteriorly and broadened posteriorly (FIGURE 5, B).

The vowel /a/, as in top, is formed by the reverse of the above; the oral resonator is expanded and the pharyngeal resonator is constricted. Now the anterior five vectors of the genioglossi pulling downward and forward in coordination with the vectors of the hyoglossi pulling downard and backward yield a resultant pulling straight down (FIGURE 3, A). Thus the dorsum of the anterior two thirds of the tongue is depressed against the floor of the mouth with the assistance of the vertical intrinsics. Contraction of the posterior sling of the styloglossi (FIGURE 3, B) will lift and retract the angle of the tongue at its middle and posterior thirds. Relaxation of the lower five genioglossal vectors of the model allows the vertical tongue base to move back as a partial contraction of the pharyngeal constrictors completes the narrowing of the pharyngeal resonator (FIGURE 5, C).

The vowel /u/, as in tool, is formed by a combination of both of the above; both resonators are expanded, but coupled by a narrow connecting channel. The oral resonator is further expanded by increased depression of the tongue mass. Here the major effort seems to shift to the more vertically pulling hyoglossus. The oral floor is depressed by relaxation of the mylohyoid muscle and the oral resonator is lengthened by protrusion of the lips. The pharyngeal resonator is expanded as before, by geniohyoid and lower genioglossal contraction. The pharynx is further enlarged by the lateral component of the stylopharyngeus vector and by relaxation of the pharyngeal constrictors. The interesting feature constricting the coupling channel is seen in the exaggerated action of the tensor palati muscles. The palatine aponeurosis is lowered to its fullest extent, which brings the upper attachments of the palatopharyngeal sphincter down toward the angle of the tongue (FIGURE 4).

Completing this contouring, the posterior sling of the styloglossus lifts the lateral margins of the tongue higher in conjunction with the lateral segment of the palatoglossal sphincter. At this time it can be seen that an angle is formed in both the roof and floor of the channel forming a somewhat rounded diamond shape in cross section (FIGURE 4). The former is due to the fact that the midline of the palatine aponeurosis is attached to the posterior nasal spine, which is usually at a higher level than the lateral rear rims of the hard palate. The latter is due to the firm attachment of the median septum of the tongue to the lowered hyoid bone.

Certain unusual features of the neurology of the system are highly interesting from a biomechanical point of view. The muscles of the tongue are peculiar in that they do not operate in association with joint movements. Hence control of skillful movement cannot be guided by special neural information fed back from joint terminals, as it is elsewhere; the jaw joint, for instance. Despite the present uncertainty of precise neuromuscular spindle functions, their distinctive distribution in the tongue is highly suggestive of some function in information feedback control.

Spindles of the tongue respond to stretch in three planes of space[13] in harmony with the arrangement of its muscle fibers.[14] This is obviously not so in other muscle systems such as the limbs, where muscles do not weave crosswise. Because of this unusual feature, at least some information about the direction the tongue is moving must be fired centrally from the spindles. Take, for instance, the transverse intrinsic muscles; they arise from the median fibrous septum and insert in the submucosa of the tongue's edge. If fibers of one side only were to contract, the septum would deviate, and thus stretch signaling would emanate from spindles of the opposite side. Any pull on one side will cause signaling from the opposite side; the organ seems strangely like two appendages tied as one, by tugging on the median fibrous septum.

The distribution of spindles seems decidedly linked with the tongue mechanics, being strategically placed at areas of most movement. Spindles of intrinsic muscles are concentrated anteriorly at the junction between the freely movable tip and the bulk of the tongue mass, which is more solidly stabilized below by genioglossi and hyoglossi. Posteriorly, spindles are concentrated at the junction of the angle between middle and posterior thirds of the tongue where the palatoglossi and styloglossi enter at the center of the sphincter coupling action. Spindles of the extrinsic muscles are larger and are concentrated near the tongue base in two areas, anteriorly where the genioglossi penetrate the tongue mass and posteriorly at the entrance of the hyoglossi. A concentration of spindles on the lateral borders of the tongue is found about half way back "in that part that curves most in fine lateral movements,"[14] obviously by unilateral contraction of the styloglossus muscle. The problem of lack of position information from joint endings seems admirably replaced by "particularly sensitive exteroceptive systems,"[14] namely, the numerous touch and pressure receptors all over the tongue near the mucosal surface.

The purpose of this treatment of anatomy is not to describe all of the structures of the oropharyngeal system in detail. Hence, little has been said about such things as the encircling constrictor muscles, their attachments, overlappings, and so on. The objective is to explore and test the concept of a coupled resonator system that can magnify and filter vibration frequencies from the larynx to produce actual speech sounds. For the "acoustic theory of speech production"[7] to be valid, anatomical biomechanics must meet the rigorous specifications required for performing precise resonator area conformations. I believe this has now been demonstrated, which strongly supports the concept.

A NOTE ON EVOLUTION, AND THE RECONSTRUCTION OF FOSSIL RESONATORS

Recent reconstruction of the vocal tract of the La Chapelle-aux-Saints Neanderthal skull seems to be highly questionable.[2] The proposed position of the hyoid bone not only would obstruct the oropharyngeal system for usual feeding functions, but it is difficult to see how the creature could even open its jaw! Available casts of the fossil seem to indicate that the skull base is fragmented and warped up into the cranial cavity. I believe it is not nearly as flattened as the presently reconstructed skull cast suggests. But more to the point, the mechanics of jaw movements have not been taken into consideration at all. Opening movement of the mandible in modern man is accomplished by a force-couple action involving the lateral pterygoid and digastric muscles.

FIGURE 6. Opening the hominid jaw: Lateral view of the modern human skull superposed on the Frankfürt horizontal line. The upper dashed arrow pointing to the left indicates the resultant of the pull of the lateral pterygoid on the neck of the mandible. Below, the anterior and posterior bellies of the digastric are joined by a cable-like tendon sliding through a fibrous sling anchored to the stabilized hyoid bone. It is clear that if either belly contracts, or if both contract together, the resultant action on the chin would pull down and back as indicated by the lower dashed arrow. Both upper and lower vectors now form a force-couple which turns around an axis in the ramus to open the jaw.

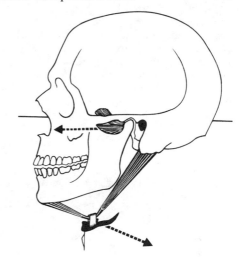

The movement is effected by an initial activity of the lateral pterygoids, which fix the condyles firmly against the posterior slope of the eminence. Immediately this is followed by contraction of the digastric muscles, and the sustained activity of both muscle pairs, acting as a force-couple, turns the mandible around a roving horizontal axis passing through the rami of the mandible.[15]

To do this the hyoid bone must normally lie well *below* the mandible. The vector of the anterior belly of the digastric is directed downward and backward (FIGURE 6), where the intermediate tendon slides through a connective-tissue sling on the still lower hyoid bone, to continue with the posterior belly of the muscle. Only by this

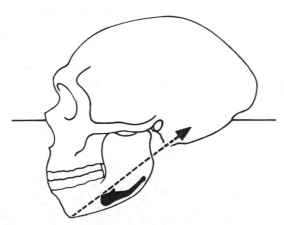

FIGURE 7. The problem of reconstruction in fossils: Lateral view of La Chapelle-aux-Saints, Neanderthal skull, traced from a photograph of the cast. Skull outline superposed on solid, Frankfürt Horizontal, line. Dashed line connects attachments of digastric muscle from center of digastric fossa in front to center of digastric notch behind. Blackened hyoid bone positioned so that the upper rim of body lies half way between the alveolar margin and lower border of jaw, as in proposed reconstruction,[2] intersecting dashed line. In this position digastrics can only pull jaw up and back into depth of glenoid fossa; force-couple action on jaw is impossible!

arrangement can the jaw be lowered. According to the reconstruction, the hyoid bone lies in a position such that both bellies must pull up and back in a straight line (FIGURE 7); only retrusion of the jaw is possible, pulling the condyle up into the depths of the fossa, which is known to be pathological.[15] The hyoid bone must have been positioned lower in Neanderthal. His vocal tract was intact and his ability to make highly effective speech sounds must have been considerable (though probably not exactly as ours), as evidenced by his highly complicated cultural achievements. Perhaps he merely spoke with a different "accent"?

REFERENCES

1. DU BRUL, E. L. 1958. Evolution of the Speech Apparatus. Monograph. Am. Lecture Series. no. 328. Charles C Thomas. Springfield, Ill.
2. LIEBERMAN, P. & E. S. CRELIN. 1971. On the speech of Neanderthal man. Linguist. Inquiry 2(2): 203–222.
3. LIEBERMAN, P., E. S. CRELIN & D. H. KLATT. 1972. Phonetic ability and related anatomy of the newborn and adult human, Neanderthal man, and the chimpanzee. Am. Anthropol. 74: 287–307.
4. WOOD-JONES, F. 1940. The nature of the soft palate. J. Anat. 74: 147–170.
5. NEGUS, V. E. 1929. The Mechanism of the Larynx. Messrs. Heinemann (Medical Books) Ltd. London, England.
6. NEGUS, V. E. 1949. Comparative Anatomy and Physiology of the Larynx. Grune & Stratton, Inc. New York, N.Y.
7. FANT, G. 1970. Acoustic Theory of Speech Production. Mouton & Co. The Hague, The Netherlands.
8. SCAPINO, R. P. 1967. Biomechanics of prehensile oral mucosa. J. Morphol. 122(2): 89–114.
9. DU BRUL, E. L. 1974. Origin and evolution of the oral apparatus. In Frontiers of Oral Physiology. Y. Kawamura, Ed. Vol. 1: 1–30. S. Karger. New York, N.Y.
10. DU BRUL, E. L. & S. SICHER. 1954. The Adaptive Chin. Monograph. Am. Lecture Series. No. 180. Charles C Thomas. Springfield, Ill.
11. WHILLIS, M. B. 1930. A note on the muscles of the palate and the superior constrictor. J. Anat. 65: 92–95.
12. ASTLEY, R. 1958. The movements of the lateral walls of the nasopharynx: a cineradiographic study. J. Laryngol. Otol. 72: 325–328.
13. BOWMAN, J. P. & C. M. COMBS. 1968. Discharge patterns of lingual spindle afferent fibers in the hypoglossal nerve of the rhesus monkey. Exp. Neurol. 21: 105–119.
14. COOPER, S. 1953. Muscle spindles in the intrinsic muscles of the human tongue. J. Physiol. 122: 193–202.
15. SICHER, H. & E. L. DU BRUL. 1975. Oral Anatomy. 6th edit. C. V. Mosby Company. St. Louis, Mo.

DISCUSSION PAPER:* VOCAL TRACT AND BRAIN: A SEARCH FOR EVOLUTIONARY BOTTLENECKS

Fernando Nottebohm

The Rockefeller University
New York, New York 10021

I should like to add two further remarks bearing on the phylogeny of the vocal tract in primates. One has to do with the occurrence of laryngeal air sacs, or extralaryngeal annexes, as they have also been called. Negus[1] was of the opinion that such sacs served mainly as extra air reservoirs that would permit a greater spacing of inspirations, with some alleged conservation of energy. But the most accepted explanation has been that the various kinds of air sacs associated with the larynx have to do with sound amplification (review in Gautier[2]). The correctness of the latter interpretation in *Cercopithecus nictitans* and *C. neglectus*, two West African forest monkeys, has been experimentally demonstrated by Gautier.[2] The same author also notes that high development of laryngeal air sacs occurs in forest dwellers such as *Pongo pygmeus, Gorilla gorilla, Alouatta paliata, Hylobates, Symphalangus,* and several *Cercopithecus* species which, with the exception of *Gorilla,* are also arboreal. The development of laryngeal resonating sacs in such species would be in line with Marler's[3] observation that forest primates tend to rely on loud, stereotyped vocalizations for the spacing of troups and avoidance of direct aggression (see also Waser[4]). More open country species, however, such as *Erythrocebus patas* and *Papio anubis* also have hypertrophied laryngeal sacs,[1,5] and a species such as the gorilla, with big sacs, is not particularly vocal. In the light of these somewhat ambiguous correlations, it is not clear that one should interpret the absence of laryngeal air sacs in man as evidence of a long-standing association with open, savannah habitats of the type anthropologists usually associate with man's australopithecine ancestors (e.g. Pilbeam[6]).

Loud calls used for spacing or contact purposes might not be adaptive in savannah habitats. Ground absorption, refraction due to thermal layering, and scatter induced by wind turbulence (e.g. Morton[7,8]) would severely limit the range of vocal airborn signals, or worse still, would draw the attention of potential prey and predators to the signaler. Perhaps the only inference to be made from the absence of laryngeal sacs and from the characteristics of sound transmission in open habitats is that man's vocal talents probably evolved for close-range communication. It is unlikely that we will ever have the fossil evidence to prove this, since soft, collapsible organs do not preserve well. Laryngeal air sacs could have been suppressed in man only in the relatively recent past, after part of the evolutionary sequence leading to present-day language was already well under way. I have dwelled on this issue of the laryngeal sacs because it typifies the kind of partial insight and ambiguous interpretation that seems to surround so much of our thinking on the phylogeny of the human vocal tract.

The second example I would like to discuss is the increased distance between larynx and soft palate in man. This feature of the human vocal tract has been much emphasized by earlier authors (Negus, 1949[1]; Lieberman *et al.*, 1969[9]) and has also

*Discussion of "Phylogeny of the Human Vocal Tract," by J. Wind, and "Biomechanics of Speech Sounds," by E. Lloyd Du Brul. Work discussed here was supported by National Science Foundation grant GB-16609, and by National Institute of Mental Health grant MH 18343.

been mentioned by Dr. Du Brul.[10] A tendency toward a lowering of the larynx with respect to the soft palate seems also to be present in anthropoid apes such as the chimpanzee, orang-utan and gorilla (Ref. 1, Figures 59, 35, and 159). Unfortunately, in the case of nonhuman primates, virtually nothing is known about distance and relations between the various components of the vocal tract during the act of phonation.

Dr. DuBrul noted, in the preceding paper, that a shift in laryngeal position can be related to the erect posture and to changes in the configuration and relations of the lower mandible (see also Refs. 10, 11). Though part of the descent of the larynx may well have added to the phonatory versatility of the vocal tract, as suggested by Lieberman et al.,[9] we do not really know if this was one of the selective pressures that brought about the anatomy of the vocal tract observed in modern man. An expanded bucopharyngeal and nasopharyngeal space would also amplify laryngeal sounds. An expanded nasopharyngeal surface and volume might affect thermal regulation, so that cold incoming air is better heated before it reaches the lungs, and expired air can better be used for purposes of evaporative cooling of a type that, unlike sweating, would not upset the body's salt balance. I make these suggestions reluctantly, since I am profoundly ignorant in this area. Medical doctors emphasize that the position of our larynx increases the chance of death by choking. The selective forces leading to this handicap may have been multiple, and it is not clear that they have all been identified or weighed properly, or that it is possible for this to be done.

When we try to make interesting statements about the evolution of speech or language, we should not focus on modern speech or language, but on a communicatory system of sounds that can be easily recognized and recombined so as to generate a diversity of words, with grammatical rules that permit organizing these words into an endless number of meaningful statements. I believe squirrel monkeys and humpback whales, chimpanzees and canaries, mynah birds and man, to mention a few species, have a sufficiently versatile vocal tract, as judged by the diversity of sounds they produce, to permit the evolution of such a communicatory system (e.g. Refs. 3, 12–18). If the vocal tract of such diverse species is not the variable precluding the evolution of a communicatory system akin to language, then we must find the limiting factors elsewhere, and I agree with Dr. Wind that "elsewhere" is the central nervous system.

Human language, as it occurs now, requires the following abilities: 1) Vocal learning, that is the acquisition of new sounds by reference to auditory information. 2) A relative degree of independence between emotional states or physiological needs and the sounds of speech. 3) Recombination of a limited set of sounds to generate a variety of words. 4) Encoding and decoding of grammatical relations. The first of these characteristics, vocal learning, is known to be broadly shared with other vertebrates. It is best represented among birds, where perhaps as many as one half of all living species have this talent.[19] Characteristic number 2, a degree of independence between speech and physiological needs or emotional state, may be inseparable, in an evolutionary sense, from vocal learning. Talented vocal mimics, such as the Indian hill mynah, Gracula religiosa, the grey African parrot, Psittacus erithacus, and many others, can imitate a most catholic array of sounds, including many used in human speech;[15,17] and unpublished observations); they mimic sounds while interacting with other individuals, avian or human, or as they leisurely work through their vocal repertoire. Birds that learn their vocalizations traverse during ontogeny a developmental stage known as "subsong," which has been likened to the babbling of a human child.[20,21] Subsong and babbling occur as vocal practice under neutral, relaxed conditions that are not part of an ongoing communicatory exchange. Indeed, the mastery of vocal learning may necessitate a developmental stage where, freed from the strictures of communication, vocal experimentation and play are possible. It is conceivable that during evolution, vocal learning was first circumscribed to vocalizations that, without a change in communicatory role, could be altered so as to change their stimulatory valence. Bird song might provide an example of this. The sex, species, territorial ownership, and reproductive condition of a male songster in spring are stated over and over again. Some species, such as nighthawks and owls, state this message in a very simple manner. Others, such as the mockingbird, *Mimus polyglottos*, and the brown thrasher, *Toxostoma rufum*, have an elaborate repertoire that includes hundreds of song motifs. Such baroque songs may have evolved to retain the attention of the audience and achieve sustained stimulation, even though the message they convey may have remained unaltered. The occurrence of characteristic 3, phoneme-like units, and 4, incidence of grammar, has not been sufficiently explored to rule out its possible occurrence in the natural communicatory system of some nonhuman vertebrates.

The interesting and supposedly unique properties of human language could have probably evolved in many other vertebrate forms, with little if any need to change their preexisting vocal tracts. Yet, there seems to be a real chasm separating human language from the much more limited vocal communication achieved by other extant vertebrates. The evolution of human speech was probably preceded by a mastery of vocal learning, a skill not requiring in itself an ad hoc explanation tailored just to man (see also Ref. 22). Students of the evolution of language would do well to focus less on the sounds of language and more on man's ability to imitate sounds. As far as primates are concerned, the switch from a genetically determined to an auditorily dependent vocal ontogeny may have been the initial and basic revolution, which in time led to language. If you stop to think about this, you might find it much harder to explain this first step, vocal learning, than the latter acquisition of language (see also Ref. 23). This first step is less amenable to the "easy" ad hoc explanations that have traditionally related the emergence of language to tools, hunting methods, and increasingly complex social relations. I suggest that we try to answer questions about the evolution of vocal learning in a broad, comparative manner. Explanations tailored to hominid evolution should be a last resort.

Reports presented at this conference suggest that the cognitive gap between man and chimpanzee is becoming narrower and narrower with each new set of experiments, and, as a result, the question of why man is the only living primate to have evolved language becomes all the more puzzling. The evolutionary reason for this uniqueness of man might be found in Gause's[24] principle of competitive exclusion (e.g. in Odum[25]). It states that two species exploiting resources in a similar way cannot coexist. One of the two will be better, outcompete the other, and force it to change or become extinct. Changes in vocal communication leading to vocal learning and language probably had to do with matters related in some way or other to exploitation of resources and reproductive fitness. Once man's ancestor modified its vocal ontogeny and started to evolve language, it filled an ecological niche. Other primates that might have evolved similar vocal adaptations would have been brought closer to early man and would have been forced into a competitive relation. From this we might predict that vocal learning in other primates will be found, if at all, restricted to highly specified contexts; i.e., not permeating the entire system of vocal communication, or among species whose distribution and foraging habits would preclude niche overlap with man.

As a parting comment, and to atone for the preceding speculations, let me illustrate the phonatory apparatus of an orange-winged Amazon parrot, *Amazona amazonica* (FIGURES 1 and 2). In this species, and probably in all birds, vocalizations are produced by the syrinx, not the larynx. A sample of some of the complex, learned

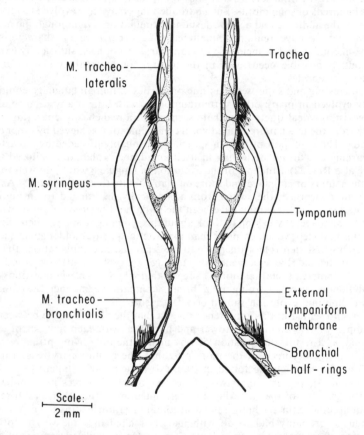

FIGURE 1. Longitudinal section of the syrinx of an adult orange-winged Amazon parrot. The syringeus and tracheobronchialis muscles control syringeal performance. The unstippled spaces in the tracheal and bronchial walls correspond to modified or unmodified tracheal rings and bronchial half-rings. (For greater details see Nottebohm.[26])

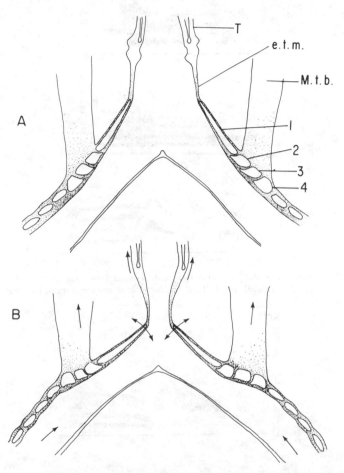

FIGURE 2. Schematic longitudinal section of the syrinx of *A. amazonica* at rest (A) and during phonation (B). Abbreviations: T-tympanum; e.t.m.-external tympaniform membrane; M.t.b.-musculus tracheobronchialis; 1, 2, 3, and 4-bronchial half-cartilages. Arrows inside bronchi indicate air movement during phonation; two-headed arrows through tip of first bronchial half-ring indicate its oscillatory movements as it pivots on its articulation with second bronchial half-ring. Cephalad pull by M.t.b. tips the first bronchial half-ring inwards. Simultaneously, the Bernouilli effect exerted by the expired air further draws the external tympaniform membranes into the syringeal lumen. Turbulent air-flow coupled to membrane oscillation are thought to give rise to vocal sounds. M. syringeus (not shown, but indicated by arrows) counters this effect by drawing the tip of the first bronchial half-ring cephalad and outwards. (From Nottebohm.[26])

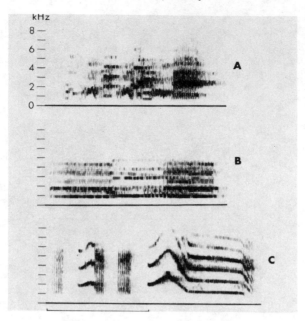

FIGURE 3. Bugling sounds of three different *A. amazonica* recorded in Trinidad, West Indies. Frequency is indicated in kiloHerz; the horizontal bar corresponds to one second.

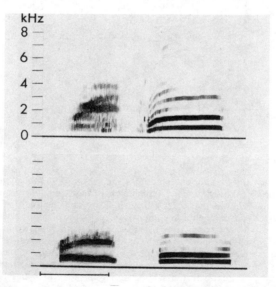

FIGURE 4. The lower sound spectrogram corresponds to the author's rendition of two words, "Praise God!" The upper soundspectrograph corresponds to the rendition of these words by a hand-reared *A. amazonica*. The human version of "Praise" includes two clear formants corresponding to the phonetic sound. The parrot version of this phoneme sounds similar to the human version, although its formant structure is different. The parrot formants are thought to be produced by the tracheal and nasopharyngeal spaces (for further discussion of this see Nottebohm[26]).

calls produced by free ranging orange-winged Amazon parrots is shown in FIGURE 3. FIGURE 4 shows sound spectrographs of two words, "praise God!", as produced by man and parrot. Clearly, once vocal learning is mastered, be it by man, bird, or some other creature, the potential for vocal change is enormous, so that size and variety of the vocal repertoire can increase in an explosive manner.

REFERENCES

1. NEGUS, V. E. 1949. The Comparative Anatomy and Physiology of the Larynx. Hafner. New York, N.Y.
2. GAUTIER, J. P. 1971. Etude morphologique et fonctionnelle des annexes extralaryngées des Cercopithecinae; liason avec les cris d'espacement. Biol. Gabonica 7: 229–267.
3. MARLER, P. 1969 Colobus guereza: territoriality and group composition. Science 163: 93–95.
4. WASER, P. M. 1975. Experimental playbacks show vocal mediation of intergroup avoidance in a forest monkey. Nature 255: 56–58.
5. HILL, O. W. C. 1966. Primate Comparative Anatomy and Taxonomy. VI. Catarrhini. Cercopithecoidea. Cercopithecinae. Univ. Press, Edinburgh, Scotland.
6. PILBEAM, D. 1970. The evolution of man. Funk & Wagnalls. New York, N.Y. 216 pp.
7. MORTON, E. S. 1970. Ecological sources of selection on avian sounds. Doctoral Dissertation. Yale University. New Haven, Conn.
8. MORTON, E. S. 1975. Ecological sources of selection on avian sounds. Amer. Nat. 108: 17–34.
9. LIEBERMAN, P. H., D. H. KLATT & W. H. WILSON. 1969. Vocal tract limitations on the vowel repertoires of Rhesus monkey and other nonhuman primates. Science 164: 1185–1187.
10. DuBRUL, E. L. 1958. Evolution of the Speech Apparatus. Charles C Thomas, Springfield, Ill.
11. FALK, D. 1975. Comparative anatomy of the larynx in man and the chimpanzee: implications for language in Neanderthal. Amer. J. Physical Anthropol. 43: 123–132.
12. WINTER, P., D. W. PLOOG AND J. LATTA. 1966. Vocal repertoire of the squirrel monkey (Saimiri sciureus), its analysis and significance. Exp. Brain Res. 1: 359–384.
13. PAYNE, R., & S. McVAY. 1971. Songs of humpback whales. Science 173: 585–597.
14. MARLER, P. 1969. Vocalizations of Wild Chimpanzees. Recent Advances in Primatology, 1: 94–100.
15. THORPE, W. H. 1959. Talking birds and the mode of action of the vocal apparatus of birds. Proc. Zool. Soc. (Lond.) 132: 441–455.
16. BERTRAM, B. 1970. The vocal behaviour of the Indian Hill Mynah, Gracula religiosa. Anim. Behav. 3. Monograph.
17. KLATT, D. H. & R. A. STEFANSKI. 1974. How does a mynah bird imitate human speech? J. Acoust. Soc. Am. 55: 822–832.
18. NOTTEBOHM, F. & M. E. NOTTEBOHM. 1976. Left hypoglossal dominance in the control of canary and white-crowned sparrow song. J. Comp. Physiol. Series A. 108: 171–192.
19. NOTTEBOHM, F. 1972. The origins of vocal learning. Am. Nat. 106: 116–140.
20. MARLER, P. 1970. A comparative approach to vocal learning: song development in white-crowned sparrows. J. Com. Physiol. Psychol. 71. Monograph.
21. NOTTEBOHM, F. 1970. Ontogeny of birdsong. Science 167: 950–956.
22. NOTTEBOHM, F. 1975. A zoologist's view of some language phenomena, with particular emphasis on vocal learning. In Foundations of Language Development. E. H. and E. Lenneberg, Eds. Academic Press. New York, N.Y.
23. MARLER, P. 1965. Communication in monkeys and apes. In Primate Behavior: Field Studies of Monkeys and Apes. I. DeVore, Ed. Holt Rinehart and Winston, Inc. New York, N.Y.
24. GAUSE, G. F. 1934. The Struggle for Existence. William & Wilkins, Baltimore, Md.
25. ODUM, E. P. 1959. Fundamentals of Ecology. Saunders. Philadelphia, Pa.
26. NOTTEBOHM, F. 1976. Phonation in the Orange-winged Amazon parrot, Amazona amazonica. J. Comp. Physiol., Series A. 108: 157–170.

DISCUSSION PAPER: EVOLUTION OF LARYNGEAL FOLDING*

B. R. Fink,† E. L. Frederickson,‡ C. Gans,§ and S. E. Huggins¶

†Department of Anesthesiology, University of Washington
Seattle, Washington 98195
‡Department of Anesthesiology, Emory University
Atlanta, Georgia 30322
§Department of Zoology, University of Michigan
Ann Arbor, Michigan 48104
¶Department of Biology, University of Houston
Houston, Texas 77004

EVOLUTION OF LARYNGEAL FOLDING

Conventionally, the larynx is thought to have evolved as a sphincteric valve operated by dilatator and constrictor muscular girdles.[1] It is believed that the primary design for protection was supplemented by modifications for olfaction (the epiglottis, supposedly degenerate in man), for respiration (optimal length of arytenoids, allegedly seven tenths of the diameter of the glottis; laryngeal air sacs), for deglutition (aryepiglottic folds; cuneiform cartilages), for regulation of intrathoracic pressure (inlet valve), for regulation of intraabdominal pressure (outlet valve), and for phonation (shortened arytenoid cartilages).

The conventional views, founded principally on comparative morphology, have become difficult to support in the light of dynamic studies.[2] From considerations outlined below it seems likely that the human larynx evolved as a folding mechanism. Taken in phylogenetic sequence, its components seem to have developed adaptively to augmented yet protected ventilatory exchange, and, in mammals, to phonation, in primates, to arboreoterrestrial habitat, and, in man to orthograde work efforts and tonal, amplitudinal, and formant variety in speech.

The motion picture we are exhibiting shows the behavior of the glottis during respiration in various land vertebrates. It was photographed with an Olympus fiberoptic laryngoscope and a super 8-mm Beaulieu camera at 18 feet per second. Unfortunately, a limited light source and the inverse square law make illumination uneven and inadequate for reproduction in print.

It is, of course, uncertain how closely any modern larynx resembles its taxal ancestors. In the frog, the laryngeal skeleton consists of a cricoid ring surmounted by half-dome-like arytenoids; a synovial articulation between the cricoid and the arytenoid is lacking. In a dead bullfrog the larynx remains closed (FIGURE 1). Furthermore, it closes spontaneously after an externally imposed opening force is released. One may conclude that this amphibian's larynx is endowed with springs that maintain the orad orifice shut. In the living animal the closed larynx is opened for respiration (FIGURE 2) by outward motion of the top of the half dome, hinged (unfolded) at the cricoarytenoid junction. Cartilaginous vocal shelves project medially from the arytenoids and remain roughly parallel during the open phase. The slit-like gap between them is the narrowest part of the open larynx and forms a primitive "glottis." The mechanism of opening constitutes a simple type of unfolding.

*Supported by grant HD08511, National Institute of Child Heath and Human Development United States Public Health Service.

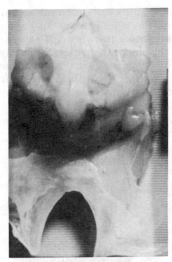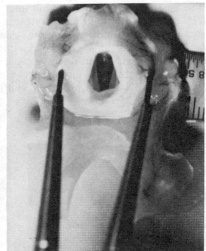

FIGURE 1. Excised bullfrog larynx. *Left*: closed. *Right*: opened artificially. *Lower scale*: millimeters.

In living unanesthetized reptiles exemplified by the boa constrictor, snapping turtle, Varanus lizard, and caiman, the buccal orifice of the larynx is predominantly closed and relatively briefly opened for ventilation, as first observed, in anesthetized *Alligator mississippiensis*, by Boelaert.[3] In the living caiman, the anterosuperior end of the aryte-oid is connected by a fold to the hyoid (hyoarytenoid fold). There is

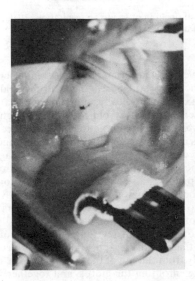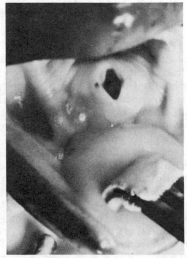

FIGURE 2. Living bullfrog. *Left:* larynx closed. *Right:* larynx open in respiration.

reported to be a synovial cricoarytenoid joint posteriorly and the larynx appears to be open by outward rotation of the arytenoid on this pivot (FIGURE 3). The action produces a quadrilateral entrance orifice, leading into a funnel-like passage, and a triangular exit or glottis. The apex and sides of the glottal triangle are formed by the arytenoids and the base by an interarytenoid fold that the animal can maintain at several different lengths. The photographs clearly suggest that the caiman's larynx makes increased provision for unfolding and increased provision for protection, as compared with the frog's.

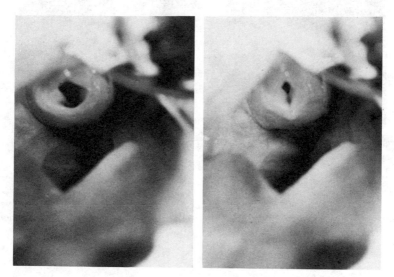

FIGURE 3. Living caiman. *Left*: early phase of opening of larynx in respiration. *Right*: late phase of opening of larynx: same magnification as FIGURE 1.

Monotreme and marsupial larynges have as yet not been photographed in action, and ideas about their mechanism are therefore still based on anatomy and on extrapolations from behavior in other taxa. Anatomically, a monotreme larynx (FIGURE 4) is notable for possessing the elements of a thyroid cartilage. Though the elements are unfused, they give attachment to a thyroarytenoid fold on each side. The addition of the thyroarytenoid folds results in a quadrangular glottic opening and an increase in glottic conductance, as compared with the triangular "glottic" passage in the caiman. The enlargement, however, increases the threat of invasion by foreign material, and explains the presence of an epiglottis, also a monotreme innovation, as a protective covering. It is often stated that the epiglottis primarily subserves the sense of smell, by enabling deglutition to be carried out even while respiration continues,[1] but no experimental support for this conjecture has yet emerged.

The marsupial larynx presents two major anatomical developments: fusion of the thyroid skeletal elements into a single cartilage and the appearance of corniculate cartilages projecting backward and medially from the top of the arytenoids. The one-piece thyroid cartilage is, in effect, a spring enfolding the glottis, and together with the corniculates maintains the glottis open except when the glottis is actively closed.

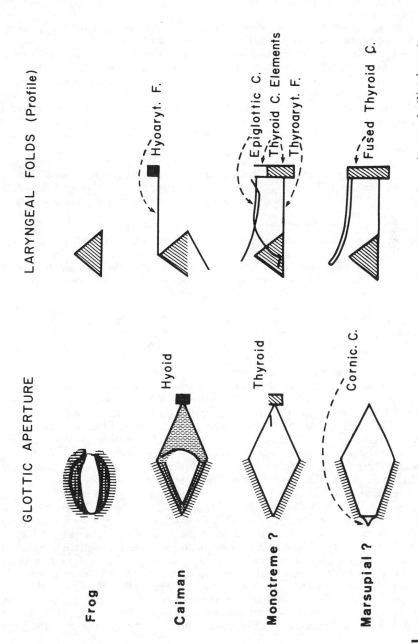

FIGURE 4. Diagrams of open glottis (transverse view) and laryngeal folds (profile) in preplacental tetrapods. (Not drawn to scale). F-fold; C-cartilage.

In so doing, these new developments bring about a further improvement in mean laryngeal conductance.

Laryngeal folding and unfolding ("plication") has evolved further in many placental mammals, though not to the same extent in all orders. In carnivora such as the dog and the cat the thyroarytenoid fold is found subdivided into cranial vestibular and caudal vocal portions (FIGURE 4), indistinctly separated by a ventricle. The upper fold is a specialization for protective closure, since it can be adducted and apposed to the epiglottis; it is ordinarily maintained in a far lateral, conductant position by a spring system based on the cuneiform cartilage, a cartilage encountered only in placental mammals. The lower fold, the vocal fold, is nearer the midline; it is specialized for phonation, and allows intermittent vibratory obstruction of the passage and the generation of sound.

The anthropoid primates manifest considerable additional evolution of laryngeal folding, notably of the epiglottic cartilage and the tissue anterior to its base (FIGURE 5). These structures form a veritable transverse median thyrohyoid fold in the anterior wall of the laryngeal entrance and can undergo several degrees of plication. In man, as one of us has shown,[2] the median thyrohyoid tissue tends to become unfolded, elongated, and attenuated during inspiratory descent of the larynx, thereby enlarging the entrance anteroposteriorly. Conversely, it becomes folded, shortened vertically, and thickened anteroposteriorly during ascent with expiration or effort closure, and its top folds down backward protectively in swallow closure. It has also been shown that in man the vertical movements of the larynx are mechanically coupled to the transverse movements of the arytenoids, and that descent of the larynx probably provides the principal force for transverse separation of the laryngeal folds during inspiration. Mechanical coupling is dependent on a particular shape and orientation of the cricoarytenoid facets, and since the shape and orientation of the facets in many present-day nonhuman anthropoidea[4] is known to be similar to those in man, it is reasonable to surmise that mechanical coupling of the vertical and transverse excursions occurs throughout the anthropoid suborder. Such coupling effects separation and approximation of the arytenoid vocal processes in parallel (somewhat like the folds in an accordion) instead of by rotation as in the cat, and converts the quadrilateral or narrowly pentagonal glottic aperture of other mammals into a widely pentagonal one. One may infer a related further reduction of respiratory flow resistance, or, reciprocally, a corresponding increase in laryngeal ventilatory conductance. The progressively lower station of the larynx in the series *Lemur, Macacus, Pan, Homo,* noted by Jordan,[5] implies increasing vertical mobility of the organ compatible with the operation of the mechanical coupling system.

Some of the anthropoidea present modifications of the median thyrohyoid fold that may be adaptive to their habitat. In Macacus a preepiglottic subhyoid air sac is present. According to a recently formulated hypothesis[2] the sac represents a spring that enables the larynx to close elastically in the execution of arboreal brachiation efforts. In the great apes and man the median air sac is absent, its place being taken by solid preepiglottic tissue bounded by elastic ligaments, and the epiglottic cartilage exhibits two distinct zones of folding: an upper pharyngeal part, the epiglottis, free standing and freely flexible, and a lower intralaryngeal or thyrohyoid portion, the epiglottic tubercle, whose flexibility is constrained by the preepiglottic median thyrohyoid tissue; the lower portion is nevertheless able to bend and unbend—to fold and unfold—in accommodation to changes in thyrohyoid approximation and separation.

In the apes the preepiglottic tissue may well function as a solid backing for check-valve action of the flap-like vestibular folds, such as has been hypothesized by various authors[3,6] to occur in man. Such action would facilitate the execution of brachial and

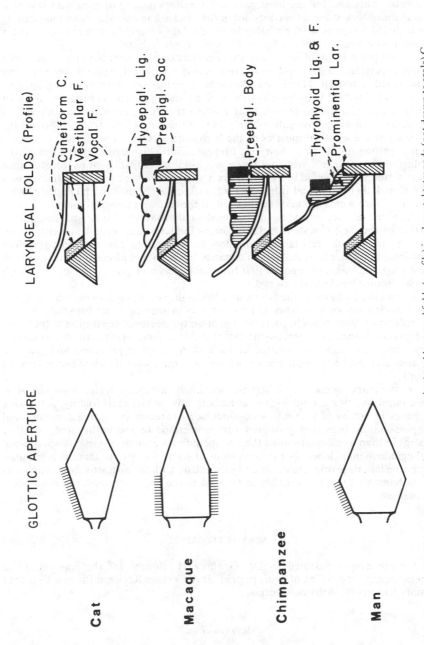

FIGURE 5. Diagrams of open glottis (transverse view) and laryngeal folds (profile) in placental tetrapods (not drawn to scale) C-cartilage; F-fold; LIG-ligament; LAR-laryngis.

other efforts while the animal is standing on the ground. In man, however, the vestibular folds are, for the most part, solid wedges instead of flaps, and it is now known that check-valve action does not occur.[7] Indeed, in man the entire plug closing the occluded larynx is solid, probably because solidity makes for firmer closure and is adaptive to intense physical effort in the orthograde habitus.

At this point I should like to ask the members of the audience to participate in a simple experiment. First, fold your arms across your chest. Second, keeping your arms folded, stand up. Thank you. Please be seated. In the effort of getting up most of you probably held your breath—that is, you closed your larynx because closure of the larynx enables one to pressurize and stiffen the trunk, in much the same way as pressurizing an air pillow stiffens the pillow. Stiffening of the trunk improves the efficiency of the attached muscles of the limbs and so facilitates effort by the limbs, such as getting up out of a chair. So, I repeat, effort closure of the larynx involving folding of the median thyrohyoid tissue is a usual accompaniment of forceful work effort. Orthograde manual work efforts are a highly important part of the human way of life, and their laryngeal infrastructure, including the all-solid laryngeal closing plug, therefore seems a crucial adaptation to the human ecological niche.

As noted above, unfolding of the median thyrohyoid tissue, with inspiratory descent of the larynx, widens and straightens the laryngeal vestibule anteroposteriorly and reduces the resistance to air flow in this region. This too must therefore contribute appreciably to the human capacity for sustained physical manual work in the orthograde stance, a capacity that historically has been one of the bases on which human culture has been developed.

In man the mobility of the larynx and foldability of the median thyrohyoid tissue are exploited not only in work efforts but also in shaping voice formants, for the production of formants is in part contingent on the degree of separation of the hyoid and thyroid. It therefore seems significant that this separation is relatively greater and hence more amenable to control in man than in other primates, and that the separation is markedly smaller in a newborn baby than when the child begins to learn to talk.

In summary, numerous otherwise seemingly arbitrary features of laryngeal mechanical function are intelligible as elaborations of laryngeal folding, subserving increases in laryngeal respiratory conductance, increases in voicing capacity, and proportionately increased provision for protection. In the anthropoid line they emerge in man as adaptations to the specific human ecological niche of speech and orthograde manual labor. For these reasons, it seems likely to us that the beginnings of spoken language originated contemporaneously with the distinctively human traits of the human larynx, and possibly as far back as the origin of completely orthograde locomotion.

ACKNOWLEDGMENT

We are deeply indebted to Dr. Geoffrey H. Bourne for the opportunity to cinematograph the larynx of living pongids at the Yerkes Regional Primate Center of Emory University, Atlanta, Georgia.

REFERENCES

1. NEGUS, V. E. 1962. The Comparative Anatomy and Physiology of the Larynx: 24. Hafner Publishing Company. New York, N.Y.

2. FINK, B. R. 1975. The Human Larynx: A Functional Study. New York, Raven Press. New York, N.Y. 193 pp.
3. BOELAERT, R. 1942. Sur la physiologie de la respiration de l'alligator mississippiensis. Arch. Int. Physiol. Biochem. **52:** 57–72.
4. LAMPERT, H. 1926. Zur Kenntnis des Platyrrhinenkehlkopfes. Morph. Jahrbuch **55:** 607–654.
5. JORDAN, J. 1960. Quelques remarques sur la situation du larynx chez les lémuriens et les singes. Acta Biol. Med. (Gdansk) **4:** 39–51.
6. MARSHALL, J. 1867. Outlines of Physiology, Vol. 1. p. 258. Longmans, Green. London, England.
7. LINDSAY, J. R. 1940. Laryngocele ventricularis. Ann. Otol. Rhinol. Laryngol. **49:** 661–673.

DISCUSSION

B. Raymond Fink, *Moderator*

Department of Anesthesiology
University of Washington School of Medicine
Seattle, Washington 98195

DR. LIEBERMAN: I shall begin with some comments on Dr. Nottebohm's discussion. First, work on artificial talking machines which has gone on for about 30 years demonstrates beyond reasonable doubt that the properties of human speech are essential for fast speech and encoding, so one cannot neglect these special properties.

Second, the reason you wish to emphasize the study of the peripheral organ is essentially that which Dr. DuBrul noted in a very succinct way. There is a match between the peripheral system and the neural system that goes back to frogs. There are neural mechanisms in frogs, for example, tuned to the formant structure of frogs.

The third comment is that although the production of speech by passerines has been studied in great detail, the work by Klatt and Stefanski on the Mynah bird demonstrates that the production mechanism is quite different acoustically in that species.

The next comments are directed to Dr. Wind. The larynx is really a relatively less critical component of human speech, except perhaps for its vertical mobility in changing formant structure. This view goes back to Von Kemplen at the end of the eighteenth century and to Johannes Müller about 1847.

The last comment relates to Dr. DuBrul, who very nicely amplified the comments that I, Dennis Klatt, and others have been making for years on the essential aspects of the supralaryngeal vocal track. In Chicago Dr. DuBrul advised me of this point about the jaw, this small minor point. But I think what you've got demonstrates that Neanderthal man did not open his jaw the way we do. I have here, by odd coincidence, a casting of the Lachapelle skull. I'll now pull back the position of the hyoid, and it will open. In fact I'll even pull back lower. Using the second law of motion, opposite force reaction gives a different sort of mandible and you can see you can still open it. It will open like a dog or chimp.

DR. NOTTEBOHM: That is not the way it opens. Why don't we handle questions one at a time? The comment I made was that you do not need language-typical sounds to generate speech or interesting ways of communicating, what I defined as the "interesting" aspects of speech. It doesn't matter where the larynx is as long as one can produce a variety of units which, upon recombination, can generate words, sentences, and grammatical structure.

DR. DUBRUL: Dr. Lieberman, you had a muscle attached to the inion. That means he couldn't have a backbone. Your muscle would be running right through the backbone. Since there cannot possibly be a muscle there, he can't open his jaw that way.

DR. BRUCE RICHMOND: I'd like to make some comments on the supralaryngeal characteristics of the pharynx and the oral cavity in relation to producing formants, at least in monkeys. I don't know about apes.

I've been making recordings of gelada monkeys from Ethiopia. On the basis of quite a large number of sonographs, there are movements of the formants that are associated with differences in the shape of the resonance capabilities of the supralaryngeal track.

Now, the point is that in order to make positive statements about what certain animals can't do, one must at least collect enough data on the actual sounds produced by monkeys. I've never seen any large variety of sounds produced by circopithican monkeys or apes as expected from Lieberman's work. And some of the particular sounds I've gotten have consisted of only a few examples over a period of five years.

Until we have actual x-ray motion pictures of nonhuman primates vocalizing in some sort of realistic situation, and until we have a wide enough variety of different acoustical data on actual sounds produced by nonhuman primates, I think it is much too premature to make positive statements about limitations of changing the shape of the vocal tract and changing the different kind of sounds that nonhuman primates can make, such as the importance of the oral cavity and the pharyngeal cavities in producing vowel triangle.

DR. DuBRUL: I tend to agree with Lieberman: Not with his reconstruction, but with his acoustics, because these sounds *can* be made with this double resonator system. Now, you may be able to get another system that will get close to these sounds. That's all right, although I'm not certain about that. But they *are* made, according to his acoustical studies, by this double resonator system which does exist in the human head. So I believe we do make our sounds in this way.

DR. FINK: I think there is a little more evidence on that subject that's due to be presented by Dr. Andrew this evening (this volume).

Part XI. Perception and Production of Speech (II)

INTERACTIVE MODELS FOR EVOLUTION: NEURAL
MECHANISMS, ANATOMY, AND BEHAVIOR

Philip Lieberman

Department of Linguistics
Brown University
Providence, Rhode Island 02912

Discussions of the evolution of language frequently involve several implicit assumptions. One premise that is very common is that language is an abrupt, all-or-nothing phenomenon. Thus "modern" humans have language, whereas all other animals do not. The inevitable question thus arises—when did language start? What grades of hominids had language, who didn't, and so on? This premise is apparent in some discussions of my work on the phonetic ability of Neanderthal hominids. Edmund Crelin and I in our 1971 paper [1] On the speech of Neanderthal man claimed that hominids of the class typified by the La Chapelle aux Saints fossil, which form a metrically well-defined class,[2,3] would lack the speech producing anatomy that is necessary for sounds like the vowels [i], [u], and [a], nasal versus nonnasal distinctions, and certain velar consonants. We did not claim that Neanderthal man could not "talk," nor did we claim that Neanderthal hominids lacked language. Our claim was that there were comparative phonetic deficiencies with respect to modern *Homo sapiens*.

These phonetic deficiencies, that followed from anatomical constraints, appeared to be significant, since comparative studies of vocal communication in various animals [4,5] show that neural mechanisms exist that are "innately" matched to facilitate the recognition of sounds that the organism can produce. The absence of certain sounds like the vowels [i] and [u] in Neanderthal hominids thus could be a sign of relatively less reliance on the vocal channel of communication in these hominids. Neanderthal hominids thus would represent an intermediate stage in the evolution of human language that places a heavy functional load on vocal communication. Present-day hominoids like chimpanzees do not appear to make much use of their vocal-auditory channel, whereas present-day humans rely almost exclusively on vocal communications for "linguistic" communications. The evidence of Neanderthal culture, which is apparent in their tools and their tool-making techniques, their rituals and their social order, which involved care for the infirm, all point to the presence of language [5] and in particular of a language that, like that of present day humans had a syntax that requires a transformational component.[2] In brief, the most significant result of our first Neanderthal study was that it demonstrated that hominids existed whose linguistic abilities differed slightly from those of present-day humans in the direction of more primitive living hominids. This established the continuity of evolution with respect to language.

Attacks on the alleged Lieberman-Crelin claim of no language in Neanderthal man thus are attacks on a straw man. However, it is important to understand why this straw man was constructed. Phonetic deficiencies would be correlated in an absolute sense with general linguistic deficiency if and only if there were a single, central biologic mechanism that determined linguistic ability. Unfortunately, many discussions of the evolution of language seem to involve this implicit premise, i.e., that there is a single neural mechanism that determines linguistic ability in a general sense. Lenneburg [8] and Washburn,[9] for example, seem to claim that a cortical mechanism exists that simultaneously regulates all aspects of linguistic ability. Thus chimpanzees do not manifest linguistic ability even though they use sign language, or push computer keys because they do not talk as humans do. Their argument rests on two assumptions: A, that hypothetical "unique" cortical structures exist in humans that are necessary for the control of the articulatory gestures that produce speech and B, that these same cortical mechanisms are necessary for other aspects of language. Reduced to its simplest terms, the argument is that chimpanzee communication is not linguistic because it does not make use of human speech. Thus it follows that Neanderthal hominids must have talked if they "had" language and conversely that the Lieberman-Crelin phonetic deficiency theory implies general linguistic incompetency.

It is tempting to make inferences concerning general linguistic ability from comparative phonetic deficiencies. I, in fact, must confess to a certain amount of "phonetic imperialism," insofar as I proposed that Neanderthal hominids probably had syntactic deficiencies because they had phonetic limitations.[10] I would now be more cautious, because genetic and behavioral studies show that animals are put together in bits and pieces. The neural mechanisms that are the biological bases of syntactic ability probably are better developed in a hominid like modern *Homo sapiens*, than they are in a chimpanzee or they were in *Australopithecus africanus*. Chimpanzees and *Australopithecus africanus* both manifest phonetic deficiencies with respect to modern *Homo sapiens*[6,10,11] but the correlation between phonetic and syntactic ability is probably the result of natural selection and an interactive process where there is positive feedback for more effective communication. Mutations that enhance phonetic ability are more likely to be retained if cognitive ability exists that makes linguistic communication more effective, or the reverse. In other words, I'm claiming that there are many independent biological mechanisms that underlie linguistic ability, that these mechanisms are usually under separate genetic control, that they can evolve or develop independently, and that the seeming coherence or "harmony" of human language is an artifact of the particular course of human evolution. Many forms of language existed and probably exist today besides that of present-day *Homo sapiens*. The only definition of a language that seems to make sense to me is one that takes the primary focus of language to be communication. A number of definitions of language have been proposed that essentially state that a communications system is not a language unless it has the full expressive power of contemporary human language; i.e., that a language is a language if and only if it has all the properties of "natural language," (where natural language reads all human languages). These definitions of language are similar to the following definition of an airplane, "An airplane is an airplane if and only if it's a 747." The definition that I like best is operationally defined[5] *A language is a communications system that is capable of transmitting new information.*

TESTING THIS THEORY: SUPRALARYNGEAL VOCAL TRACT ANATOMY

A theory is not really a scientific theory until it is presented in a testable form. A theory is also more useful and general if it is presented and tested in its strongest form. The strongest form of this theory that I can test is that the anatomical parts that go together to make up the supralaryngeal focal tract are under separate genetic control. The probable phonetic deficiencies of hominids like the Australopithecines and classic Neanderthal were deduced from Crelin's reconstructions of their supralaryngeal vocal tracts. These reconstructions indicate that they probably had what I shall call a "standard plan" supralaryngeal airway. Victor Negus, in his comprehensive and thorough comparative studies of the anatomy and physiology of the larynx, really introduced this concept, although he did not use the words "standard plan." Negus noted that there is a supralaryngeal vocal tract that typically occurs in terrestrial mammals.[12] The larynx is positioned high, close to the base of the skull, and the tongue lies almost entirely within the oral cavity. The pharynx lies behind the entrance to the larynx. This supralaryngeal vocal tract, which is, in a sense, the "standard plan" for the upper airways of the respiratory system, is typical of all normal nonhuman primates and newborn humans.

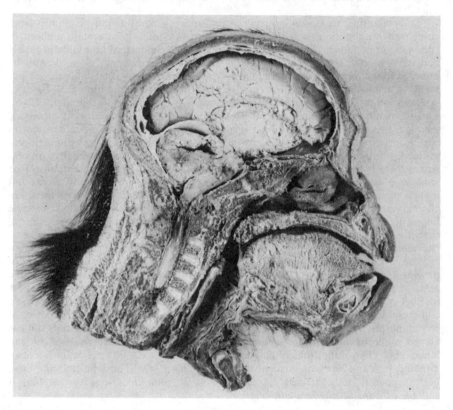

FIGURE 1. Head and neck of a young adult male chimpanzee sectioned in the midsagittal plane. Note the "standard plan" supralaryngeal airway. Note that the high position of the hyoid does not interfere with a chimpanzee's swallowing while feeding with his head upright, or in opening his mandible.

In FIGURE 1 we can see this "standard plan" supralaryngeal vocal tract in the midsagital section of a Chimpanzee. As Negus pointed out, this system is well adapted for swallowing, respiration, and olefaction. Despite Dr. DuBrul's (this conference) elegant logic, you can note that the high position of the hyoid bone relative to the insertion of the digastric muscles in the mandible does not prevent these animals from opening their jaws. DuBrul's claim that the high position of the hyoid bone in the Lieberman and Crelin's reconstruction[1] would prevent the

Neanderthal mandible from opening is not in accord with the behavior and anatomy of these animals. DuBrul's claim thus can be falsified, using these experiments of nature.

Note that the soft palate and epiglottis can seal off the oral cavity during inspiration and expose the olefactory sensors of the nose to the airflow. Respiration is also more efficient than is the case in the nonstandard bent human vocal tract.[14] Swallowing is also less risky, since the pathway to the esophagus through the pharynx is more isolated from the larynx than is the case for the adult human vocal tract.

It is appropriate to note that this standard-plan vocal tract, which is typical of nonhuman primates like the chimpanzee, does not interfere with swallowing while they are feeding in the upright position. Reynolds and Reynolds[15] report that chimpanzees in the Budongo Forest of Uganda ". . . spend between six and seven hours a day in active feeding. About 90% of their food is found growing in trees and they seldom feed intensively on the ground. . . . When satiated the chimpanzee frequently sits or reclines, sucking a large wad . . . for as long as 20 minutes." Van Lawick-Goodall[16] states: "When feeding in a tree, a chimpanzee will sit or stand on a branch (with one hand grasping an overhead bough . . .) and reach for food with its free hand." In addition to vegetable matter, chimpanzees also feed on termites and other insects, and on meat, which they frequently hunt. Specific feeding postures in regard to these activities are not discussed in the literature. However, Reynolds and Reynolds[15] provide photographs of chimpanzees working at termite nests. In all of these, chimpanzees are shown in sitting positions (Figures 12-8 through 12-11). In addition, all photographs in Teleki[17] show chimpanzees feeding in sitting positions (see particularly plates 13 and 14 on pp. 88-89). Finally, all photographs of chimpanzees feeding in Lawick-Goodall[16] show them in sitting positions, except for one photograph (plate 12e, p. 240), which shows a male chimpanzee lying on his back while eating a baboon head. Falk's[18] claim that Neanderthal hominids could not have had a high hyoid like chimpanzees is thus without substance, inasmuch as it is based on the erroneous supposition that these animals have difficulty in swallowing while they maintain an upright position.

RECONSTRUCTING FOSSIL SUPRALARYNGEAL VOCAL TRACTS

The basis for the reconstructions of the supralaryngeal vocal tracts of various fossil hominids[1,6,10] is the skeletal structure that always exists in *harmony* with this standard plan supralaryngeal airway. The harmonious skeletal structure involves a number of features. The high position of the larynx in human newborns and apes with the pharynx positioned behind the larynx is, for example, in harmony with the long distance between the anterior boundary of the foramen magnum and the posterior margin of the hard palate. There has to be room for the larynx and pharynx between the vertebrae and palate. The styloid processes are likewise inclined anteriorly and toward the horizontal plane, because the hyoid bone, which supports the larynx, is positioned close to the base of the skull in line with the opening into the nasal airway. The body of the mandible is long compared to the ramus height because the mandible must span the distance from its articulation with the skull to the anterior margin of the maxilla. These correlations between skeletal features and the soft tissue of the supralaryngeal vocal tract are more or less typical of all terrestial mammals.[12]

By contrast, the supralaryngeal vocal tract of normal adult-like *Homo sapiens* is quite different. We can see this in FIGURE 2. The pharynx forms part of the airway leading into the larynx, which is positioned low. The tongue's shape is quite different; it is thick and forms the anterior boundary of the pharynx, as well as the floor of the oral cavity. The skeletal features associated with the normal adult human supralaryngeal airways could not support the nonhuman supralaryngeal airways because there simply is not enough room between the foramen magnum and the hard palate for a larynx positioned close to the base of the skull with the pharynx behind it. The

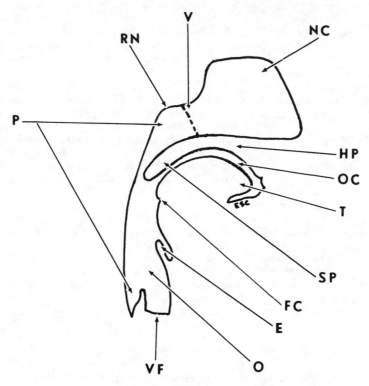

FIGURE 2. Schematic midsaggital view of adult human supralaryngeal vocal tract. NC-Nasal Cavity, V-Vomer Bone, RN-Roof of Nasopharynx, P-Pharynx, HP-Hard Palate, SP-Soft Palate, OC-Oral Cavity, T-Tip of Tongue, FC-Foramen Cecum of Tongue, E-Epiglottis, O-Opening of Larynx into Pharynx, VF-Level of Vocal Folds.

normal skeletal structure of the adult human skull is usually in "harmony" with the soft tissue of the adult supralaryngeal vocal tract. The styloid processes, for example, are usually inclined toward the vertical plane to furnish optimal support to the hyoid bone, which is positioned low. The styloid processes could be inclined as they are in a human newborn, but this would present greater shear forces to the bone of the styloid processes when the stylohyoid muscles contracted. The lower boundary of the interior surface of the symphysis of the mandible is likewise inclined to minimize shear forces on the geniohyoid and digastric muscles.[6,19]

    The harmony that exists between the skeletal features of the skull that support the soft larynx and the soft tissue of the supralaryngeal airways must be viewed as a consequence of natural selection that has retained independent mutations involving individual skeletal features and the soft tissue to yield a total system in which everything goes together reasonably well. The recurrence of the skeletal complex and airways of the "standard plan," nonhuman vocal tract throughout the order of Primates indicates that the adaptive value of these airways and the associated skeletal features is high. Thus, if the skeletal features of a fossil hominid are those usually associated with the "standard plan," nonhuman supralaryngeal vocal tract, it is most probable that the supralaryngeal vocal tract also was nonhuman.

Le May[20] shows that a number of the skeletal features that occur in newborn *Homo sapiens* and nonhuman primates, which we have noted occur in harmony with the typical "standard plan" supralaryngeal vocal tract, occur in pathologic adult and adolescent humans. Le May states that these individuals have "articulate" human speech (though she presents no acoustic data) and that by implication they have normal adult-like human supralaryngeal vocal tracts. She concludes that the reconstruction of the Neanderthal supralaryngeal vocal tract reported in Lieberman and Crelin[1] is "invalid." Le May's data are correct but they don't support her conclusion. Le May's data follow from the fact that humans, like other animals, are put together genetically in "bits and pieces." Developmental pathologies, which involve putting together bits and pieces that do not fit together, cannot tell us how the soft tissue of the supralaryngeal vocal tract would match the skeletal structure of a fossil hominid if the fossil hominid population were subject to the same selectional forces that are operant on all other primates. These selectional forces are operant on both phylogenetically simpler primates (monkeys and apes) than Neanderthal hominids, and the equivalent or somewhat more "advanced" primate modern *Homo sapiens*. In other words, the harmony between soft tissue and skeletal structure in the "normal" population of the order of primates is the result of natural selection; it is not built into the genetic regulatory mechanism in an absolute sense. Developmental pathologies that involve structural disharmony are not reliable guides for determining how fossil hominids probably were put together. Le May's argument implicitly seems to assume that the genetic mechanisms that govern human development are such that functional morphological complexes always develop as unified, harmonious systems. She seems to be taking the fact that an adult-like supralaryngeal vocal tract can occur with a pathologic skull that has many aspects of the skeletal morphology of a newborn as evidence that this combination is as likely a "solution" to the reconstruction problem for the normal population as that which actually occurs.

The study of structural disharmony is now new. Stockard[21] systematically explored structural disharmonies in dogs by crossing various breeds. He demonstrated that the genetic factors that govern the development of functionally related structures like the maxilla and mandible are complex and independent. As Stockard (Ref 21, p. 267), for example, notes, ". . . the upper jaw may develop on one pattern, and the associated lower jaw on quite another plan. . . ." This is also the case with regard to humans and the skeletal structure of the skull, mandible, and the larynx and soft tissue of the supralaryngeal airways. Some combinations are topologically impossible, but others can exist as disharmonious relationships. Pruzansky[22] has documented similar phenomena in humans. Many of these developmental anomolies result in speech pathologies.[23] It is a disservice to the patient to imply[20] that the speech of patients who have craniofacial anomolies always is "articulate." Though these patients are "articulate" in the sense that you can understand what they are trying to say, their speech is often not as intelligible as normal human speech.

Articulate Speech and Intelligibility

This is perhaps a good point in this paper to comment on the term "articulate speech" as it is used in relation to the evolution of language. The distinction between articulate speech and implied inarticulate speech is again one of the nonexistent all-or-nothing distinctions that obfuscate our understanding of the possible evolution of human speech and language. It implies that a hominid either possesses "articulate" speech that is equivalent to that of present humans or that the hominid cannot talk. In our discussions [1,6,10,11] of the phonetic deficiencies of Neanderthal hominids we noted that they couldn't produce sounds like the vowels [i], [u], or [a]. Does this make them articulate or inarticulate? The answer is that these terms are inappropriate qualitative descriptors.

It's quite straightforward to measure the intelligibility of speech signals to human listeners. This allows an assessment of the contribution of speech anatomy to intelligibility, since we have to measure the responses of human listeners who have whatever neural mechanisms are necessary for the perception of speech.

In FIGURE 3 the error rates of normal listeners whose native language is American English to 105 consonant-vowel-consonant syllables spoken by ten speakers of American-English is plotted according to the vowels present in these syllables.[24] The listeners were instructed in the use of phonetic notation, and appropriate controls were used to correct for dialect differences. Note that syllables with the vowels [i] and [u] were confused about two percent of the time, whereas other syllables, excepting those with vowels [a] and [o], were confused about seven percent of the time. The results are statistically significant at the .05 level. These results are in accord with earlier studies.[25,26] They demonstrate that there is a slight selective advantage for speech that contains tokens of the vowels [i] and [u].

The data that we have examined thus are consistent with the strong form of the theory that we tested. The parts of the human anatomy that support the supralaryngeal vocal tract are under separate genetic control, and we can quantitatively demonstrate a selective advantage. Speech intelligibility increases at least 5 percent when vowels like [i] and [u] occur.

How Did the Human Supralaryngeal Vocal Tract Evolve?

The next obvious question that follows from the test of a "strong version" of this theory is *how* the human supralaryngeal vocal tract evolved from the "standard plan" supralaryngeal airways that occur in other primates. The developmental data shows that the separate components of the supralaryngeal vocal tract are under independent genetic control. They therefore cannot have evolved in one step as the result of natural selection that operated on a single mutation that simultaneously changed the total skeletal and soft tissue morphology. Pathologic human cases [22,23] also show that a low larynx can occur with the skeletal morphology of a human newborn. The "new" supralaryngeal vocal tract, although it was not "harmonious" with the skeletal structure might have been retained because of the selective advantages yielded by enhanced vocal communication. The initial stage in the process of mutation and natural selection that yielded the human supralaryngeal vocal tract may have been the descent of the larynx. This, of course, means that the particular individual whose remains are now labeled the La Chapelle-aux-Saints fossil might have had a "disharmonious" skeletal and supralaryngeal structure, in other words, that he represented this first intermediate stage. This, however, is not a crucial or testable question, since he still would represent a mutation from ancestors who had the same skeletal structure, in harmony with the "standard plan" supralaryngeal vocal tract. A later stage in the development of the human supralaryngeal vocal tract might have been the reduction of the distance between the foramen magnum and the palate.

The controversy concerning Neanderthal speech can only involve the *stage* in hominid evolution at which phonetic ability comparable to that of modern *Homo sapiens* evolved. *Australopithecus africanus*, for example, has almost the same skull

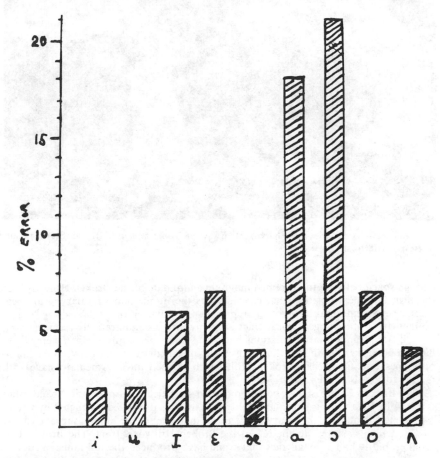

FIGURE 3. Percentage of error for consonant-vowel-consonant syllables identified by listeners who had to identify the utterances of ten speakers of American English. The syllables were presented in random order. Note that syllables with the vowels [i] and [u] are most intelligible.

base as present day apes and probably had a virtually identical supralaryngeal vocal tract.[6,11] Hominids *had* to evolve a specialized vocal tract that diverged from the "standard plan" supralaryngeal airways. Fossils like Broken Hill indicate that the process started at a point in time before the disappearance of Neanderthal fossils like La Chapelle-aux-Saints. We can be certain that this is the case because there is not

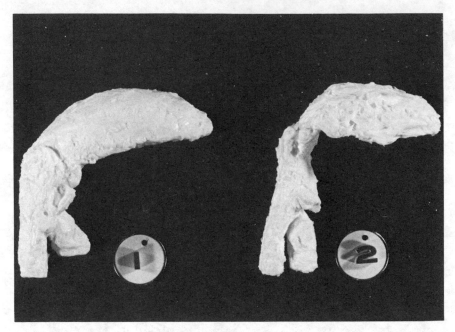

FIGURE 4. Casts of oral and pharyngeal airways of *Homo sapiens* (left) and reconstruction of Broken Hill fossil.

enough space between the foramen magnum and palate of the Broken Hill fossil for the high laryngeal position that characterizes the nonhuman supralaryngeal vocal tract. The Neanderthal lineage may represent a population that retained the "older" nonhuman supralaryngeal vocal tract anatomy into a comparatively recent period. Even if late Neanderthal populations had vocal tracts like adult humans there would have to be earlier hominids who represented intermediate stages between Australopithecines and forms like Broken Hill, which is itself an intermediate stage with respect to fossils like Es Skhul V.[6,11]

The Broken Hill fossil can be differentiated statistically from classic Neanderthal skulls.[2,3] In FIGURE 4 its supralaryngeal vocal tract as it was reconstructed by Crelin is presented. Note that the pharynx is shorter than that of the human supralaryngeal airway, which is shown to the left of the Broken Hill vocal tract. The Broken Hill fossil probably had a vocal tract that could have produced the full range of sounds typical of human speech. However, it may not have produced some of these sounds as effectively. The usefulness of sounds like the human vowels /i/, /u/, and /a/ derives, in part, from the fact that a normal human speaker can produce the acoustic signals that specify these sounds without being very precise as he maneuvers his tongue.[27] This quality, which can be appropriately termed the "acoustic stability" of these sounds,[6] follows from the bend formed at the approximate midpoint of the human supralaryngeal vocal tract. Typical vocal tract midsaggital views, cross-sectional area functions and spectra are shown for these human vowels in FIGURE 5. If the length of the pharyngeal cavity of a particular speaker is small relative to the length of the oral cavity, the acoustic stability of the speaker's /a/, /i/, and /u/ will not be as great as that of a normal human speaker.

INTERACTIVE EFFECTS: SPEECH AND HEAD BALANCE

The selective advantage of specific craniofacial skeletal mutations probably involved factors besides speech production and speech perception. In FIGURE 6 I have sketched the moments of inertia that are associated with the human and Neanderthal heads. The rough sketch shows that the moment of inertia of the Neanderthal head is greater than that of a normal human head. Greater muscular effort would be necessary to keep the Neanderthal head balanced in an upright position than is the case with the normal human head. The Neanderthal head is thus

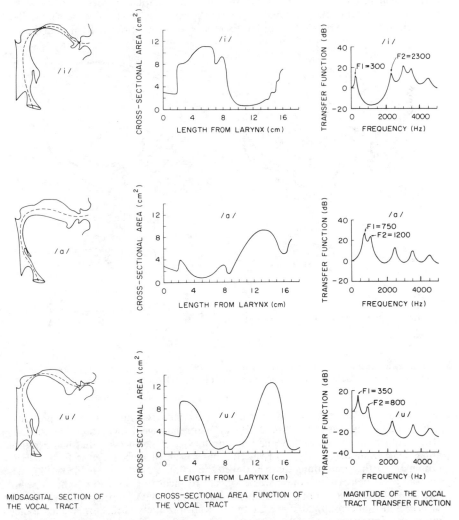

MIDSAGGITAL SECTION OF   CROSS-SECTIONAL AREA FUNCTION OF   MAGNITUDE OF THE VOCAL
THE VOCAL TRACT   THE VOCAL TRACT   TRACT TRANSFER FUNCTION

FIGURE 5. Typical midsaggital views and cross-sectional area functions of supralaryngeal oral and pharyngral cavities, and acoustic spectra for the human vowels [i], [u], and [a]. Note the discontinuities at the midpoint of the supralaryngeal airway, after Lieberman et al.[10]

not as well adapted for upright posture as the normal human head. It would be easy to determine the selective advantage of the normal human head and neck with regard to upright posture. Certain types of craniofacial anomolies[22] result in a head and neck anatomy similar to the "normal" Neanderthal configuration. Electromyographic techniques which measure the electrical activity of the muscles that support the head would provide a quantitative measure of the selectional advantage of the human head shape with respect to upright posture. Although it is possible to keep the head in an upright position with the anatomy of a nonhuman primate[15-17] it takes more muscular effort. The reduction of the space between the end of the hard palate and the anterior margin of the foramen magnum, the Staphylio-Basion distance that can be seen in the Broken Hill skull, thus has two adaptive values. It reduces the moment of inertia of the head making upright posture less costly since less muscular effort has to be expanded in order to keep the head upright. It also makes it

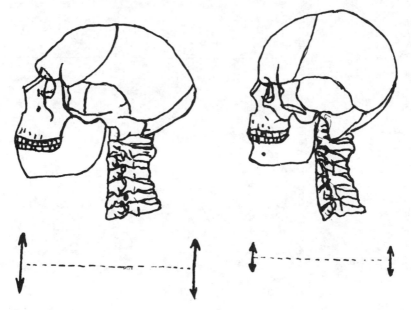

FIGURE 6. Moments of inertia associated with Neanderthal (left) and modern *Homo sapiens* heads. More muscular effort is necessary to keep the Neanderthal head in balance.

topologically impossible for the larynx to be positioned high, with the pharynx behind it as is the case in the "standard plan" supralaryngeal vocal tract. The Broken Hill fossil, therefore, must have had a supralaryngeal vocal tract that had a right-angle bend. Sounds like [i] and [u] could have been produced by the Broken Hill hominid. Further mutations that shortened the palate would have yielded still more efficient head balance and more stable vowel production. Fossils like Skhul V, who had a vocal tract that is not significantly different from that of normal modern *Homo sapiens* and modern humans, are the most recent products of this process involving interactive selectional coupling of speech and upright posture.

The question of what selectional force behavioral mode exerted the "stronger" is probably impossible to decide. The process of mutation must have involved small changes in the morphology of the skeletal and soft tissue complexes that we know are under separate genetic control. Particular mutations may have been selected for their adaptive value with respect to posture or speech in different social contexts. What's important and interesting is that the net change is of value for both language and keeping one's head erect.

I've discussed elsewhere the formal similarities between the Levalloisian tool-making techniques of Neanderthal hominids and the syntax of human languages. The cognitive grammars of tool-making and a transformational syntax are similar in a meaningful sense. The "same" neural mechanisms may underly both cognitive grammars. The study of the communications and cognitive processes of apes is thus a meaningful contribution to our knowledge of human language, since hominid evolution starts from animals who in many ways must have been closer to living apes than they are to us. The study of the evolution of phonetic ability both complements and emphasizes the importance of comparative studies of cognitive behavior in relation to communication. Neanderthal hominids represent an interesting case of very advanced hominids who, I think, probably had slight phonetic deficiencies and slight postural deficiencies. Much of the controversy attending the question of whether the La Chapelle-aux-Saints fossil could have spoken exactly as we do has missed the significant claims of the work that I have been associated with. These are: (1) that language does not evolve in a single path with the language of present day *Homo sapiens* being the end of a theological-linguistic "great chain of language." Other forms of language probably existed and may still exist in other living animals. (2) More efficient and intelligible speech offers a selective value and hominids, therefore, have retained mutations that made "better" vocal communication possible. (3) The selective value of mutations that enhanced linguistic ability also were relevant to "nonlinguistic" patterns of behavior. Head balancing and phonetic ability go together, as do tool-making and transformational grammar. The process of "auto-matization"[6,11] is useful for virtually all aspect of patterned behavior tool-making, hunting, skiing, swimming, and so on, as well as speech production.

The evolution of language thus is, in my view, an interactive process involving virtually all aspects of human and animal behavior and the biological mechanisms that underlie these behaviors. The search for the "uniqueness" of human language and the "unique" mechanisms that may underlie it are, so far as I can see, a search for the Holy Grail. Language is probably not unique, nor is it an isolated biological component.

REFERENCES

1. LIEBERMAN, P. & E. S. CRELIN. 1971. On the speech Neanderthal man. Linguistic Inquiry **2:** 203–222.
2. HOWELLS, W. W. 1970. Mount Carmel Man: Morphological Relationships. Proceedings, 8th Int'l. Cong. Anthropol. and Ethnol. Sci., Tokyo and Kyoto, Japan. 1968. Vol. 1, pp. 269–272.
3. HOWELLS, W. W. 1974. Neanderthals: Names, Hypotheses, and Scientific Method. Amer. Anthrop. **76:** 24–38.
4. CAPRANICA, R. R. 1965. The Evoked Vocal Response of the Bullfrog. M.I.T. Press. Cambridge, Mass.
5. WOLLBERG, Z. & J. D. NEWMAN. 1972. Auditory cortex of squirrel monkey: Response patterns of single cells to species-specific vocalizations. Science **175:** 212–214.
6. LIEBERMAN, P. 1975. On the Origins of Language: An Introduction to the Evolution of Human Speech. Macmillan. New York, N.Y.
7. CHOMSKY, N. 1957. Syntactic Structures. Mouton. The Hague, The Netherlands.

8. LENNEBERG, E. H. 1967. Biological Foundations of Language. John Wiley & Sons, Inc. New York, N.Y.

9. Washburn, S. Comments at this conference.

10. LIEBERMAN, P., E. S. CRELIN & D. H. KLATT. 1972. Phonetic ability and related anatomy of the newborn, adult human, Neanderthal man, and the chimpanzee. Amer. Anthropol. **74:** 287–307.

11. LIEBERMAN, P. 1973. On the evolution of human language: A unified view. Cognition **2:** 59–94.

12. NEGUS, V. E. 1949. The Comparative Anatomy and Physiology of the Larynx. Hafner. New York, N.Y.

13. DUBRUL, L. This annal.

14. KIRCHNER, J. A. 1970. Pressman and Kelemen's Physiology of the Larynx. rev. ed. Amer. Acad. Ophthalmol. and Otolaryngol.

15. REYNOLDS, V. & F. REYNOLDS. 1965. Chimpanzees of the Budongo Forest. Primate Behavior. Irven DeVore, Ed.: 368–424.

16. VAN LAWICK-GOODALL, J. 1968. The behavior of free-living chimpanzees in the Gombe Stream Reserve. Animal Behav. Monogr. **1:** 3.

17. TELEKI, G. 1973. The Predatory Behavior of Wild Chimpanzees. Bucknell Univ. Press. Lewisburg, Pa.

18. FALK, D. 1975. Comparative anatomy of the larynx in man and the chimpanzee: Implications for language in Neanderthal. Amer. J. Physical Anthropol. **43:** 123–132.

19. DUBRUL, E. L. 1958. Evolution of the Speech Apparatus. Charles C. Thomas. Springfield, Ill.

20. LE MAY, M. 1975. The Language capability of Neanderthal man. Am. J. Phys. Anthrop. **42:** 9–14.

21. STOCKARD, C. R. 1941. The Genetic and Endocrinic Basis for Differences in Form and Behavior. Wistar Instit. of Anatomy and Biology. Philadelphia, Pa.

22. PRUZANSKY, S. 1973. Clinical investigations of the experiments of nature. ASHA Report 8. Orofacial Anomolies: Clinical and Research Implications, Amer. Speech and Hearing Assoc.

23. PETERSON, S. 1973. Speech pathology in craniofacial malformations other than cleft lip and palate. ASHA Report 8. Orofacial Anomolies: Clinical and Research Implications, Amer. Speech and Hearing Assoc.

24. MOSLIN, B. & E. COWPER. 1975. Identification of CVC syllables in single and multispeaker ensembles. Working Paper, Linguistics Department. Brown University. Providence, R.I.

25. PETERSON, G. E. & H. L. BARNEY. 1952., Control methods used in a study of the vowels. J. Acoust. Soc. Am. **24:** 175–184.

26. FAIRBANKS, G. & P. GRUBB. 1961. A psychological investigation of vowel formants. J. Speech Hearing Res. **4:** 203–219.

27. STEVENS, K. N. 1972. Quantal nature of speech. *In* Human Communication: A Unified View. E. E. David, Jr. and P. B. Denes, Eds. McGraw-Hill. New York, N.Y.

USE OF FORMANTS IN THE GRUNTS OF BABOONS
AND OTHER NONHUMAN PRIMATES*

R. J. Andrew

Ethology and Neurophysiology Group
School of Biological Sciences
University of Sussex
Brighton, BN1 9QG
Sussex, England

Lieberman and his associates [26,28,27] have recently argued that the evolution of the ability to produce very distinct patterns of formants was a crucial step in the evolution of human language, and it seems likely that that the point at which this step occurred may potentially be identified by anatomical changes associated with laryngeal descent.

The possibility that other primates may be able to modulate glottal sound by changes in the resonances of the upper vocal tract (i.e. produce formants) is thus now a matter of immediate interest. It seems certain that formants must have become important in Hominid communication before the anatomical changes described by Lieberman could have acquired selective advantage, since these changes were directed toward improving communication by formants.

Apart from one short paper,[3] no systematic attention appears to have been paid to the presence of calls very like those of man in their tonal structure and resonances ("humanoid grunts": below) in nonhuman primates. It seems particularly important to examine the nature and distribution of such calls at this point in time, since Lieberman,[26] in his discussion of the subject, examined species (*Macaca mulatta*, *Pan*) which use such calls rarely or not at all, and analyzed calls (screams in distress, whines given in frustration, and what were probably distant contact calls), which are particularly unsuited to reveal resonances. Thus, although Lieberman has made it clear by computer simulation that macacque or chimpanzee vocal tracts *could* generate formants (although not over the full human range) if glottal sound with the right properties (below) were produced, readers are likely to be left with the impression that calls with formants are never actually given by subhuman primates.

In fact, as I will show, baboons use humanoid grunts very freely, and some other primates do so more rarely and in a more restricted range of situations. It thus seems possible that some of the factors leading to the evolution of humanoid grunts may be deducible from comparative study of modern primates.

PROPERTIES OF A "HUMANOID GRUNT"

The most essential feature of a call in which the resonances of the vocal tract are to be clearly revealed is a relatively complete and continuous coverage by sound energy of the range within which the resonances fall. Such broad coverage appears to be possible in three ways:

(1) Loud discordant screams and barks cover a great deal of the necessary range. They are usually performed, however, with a wide-open mouth, resulting in broaden-

*This study was supported by the National Science Foundation.

ing of the resonance zone, and with a wide glottis, which again broadens at least F_1.[12] The resonance structure is thus relatively obscured. Further, the coverage by glottally produced energy is very uneven: most of the energy is concentrated into zones centring round the preferred frequency of vibration of the glottis and its first overtone. (FIGURE 1).

(2) In man, whispers provide soft but continuous and complete coverage, apparently by the vibration of soft tissues with no one fundamental frequency. As far as I know, sounds of this sort are not used by other primates.

(3) The third possibility is glottally produced sound with a deep fundamental, and an associated structure of closely spaced overtones, through which the energy of the call is relatively evenly distributed. Andrew[3] termed such calls "humanoid grunts," and I will retain the term here. Human vowels and some of the calls of *Papio* and *Theropithecus* are typical humanoid grunts.

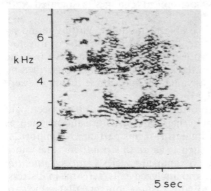

FIGURE 1. Scream of subadult *Papio anubis*. Note the way in which the high-pitched fundamental and first overtone of the first part of the call (at about 2.2 and 4.4 kHz respectively) broaden out into bands of noise, which might be mistakenly identified as the consequence of resonances of the upper vocal tract acting quite independently of glottal events. If resonances do affect such a call, coupling of glottis and vocal tract is presumably involved. It is particularly striking that the two bands retain their harmonic relation despite their breadth.

When trying to identify such calls in nonhuman primates, it is important to be sure that resonances are correctly identified. Concentrations of energy over a range of a kHz or more, which look rather like a resonance superimposed on a white noise source can often be seen in shrieks. These concentrations, however, can be shown to correspond to a high fundamental and first overtone of glottal sound. Thus the two bodies of sound always bear a harmonic relation to each other, and when a second overtone can be seen, this is true of it also. Further, at the beginning of some shrieks, the bodies of sounds can be seen to be narrow and rapidly ascending zones, which are quite clearly glottal harmonies (FIGURE 1). They then broaden out into zones of noise. The reasons for this broadening probably include, firstly, overblowing, with different parts of the glottis (and perhaps associated tissues) vibrating at slightly different frequencies, and, secondly, coupling between glottis and vocal tract resonances. The latter effect may affect the characteristics of glottally produced sound (just as the resonance of a trumpet affects the frequency of lip vibration of the player).

The problems of identification of true resonances are particularly acute in the case of calls in which high-pitched squeaks or trills readily develop out of grunts (e.g. *Cercopithecus*, below). Here, zones of emphasis of the overtones of the grunt sometimes can be seen to pass into fundamental and first overtone of the squeak. One guide is provided by the harmonic relationship of such zones of emphasis, but it is clearly essential to show that putative resonances are affected by changes in the vocal tract independent of glottal changes, before the existence of formants in primate calls can be held to be established.

STUDIES OF HUMANOID GRUNTS IN CAPTIVE BABOONS

All of the humanoid grunts that were used to provide data on which the results presented in this section are based were chosen as possessing a clear tonal structure with well-defined fundamental and overtones. Further, ones in which the fundamental changed frequency in such a way as to potentially confuse interpretation were also excluded; nearly all had a quite constant pitch. Narrow band spectrograms (Kay Sonagraph) were made of all calls in order to allow this check.

The main results to be presented were obtained from a young (probably second year) male *Papio hamadryas* obtained from Kenya but of unknown original provenance. Filming and recording were largely carried out over about three months, so that size and proportions of the vocal tract are likely to have changed only slightly during the study.

The sounds analyzed were identified on the optical sound track of the film (taken with an Auricon camera and zoom lens, through the newly cleaned plate glass front of the observation cage). They could, as a result, be synchronized with particular frames of the film.

The interpretation of the resonance changes that were found to coincide with various tongue and lip movements is based on the assumption that, in view of the long buccal cavity of *Papio*, the cavities within the upper vocal tract can be treated either as two resonators, separated by a narrowing due to the tongue, which is of variable position, or (when the mouth is opened) as a horn, with widening toward the mouth. Treatments of both approximations in the case of human vocalizations are given in Fant,[12] and will be followed here.

Hamadryas, like other baboons (superspecies *P. cynocephalus*, including *anubis*; *Theropithecus gelada*) may give humanoid grunts with a relatively immobile configuration of the upper vocal tract, or superimpose such grunts on the tongue and lip movements of grooming and incipient grooming, of mumbling food and of licking or exploring objects. All of these movements produce variants of the call, which can readily be distinguished by ear. The superimposition of the lip-smacking display, in which the tongue is moved rapidly in and out and the mandible is simultaneously lowered and raised, results in a particularly striking cyclic modulation. Andrew[3,4] discusses the potential importance of the resulting vocal component of this conspicuous display, which is derived from intention movements of grooming, and apparently serves much the same functions as mutual grooming, but can be performed at a distance.

In the *hamadryas* studied, the first and second formants (F_1 and F_2) proved to be inversely coupled in pitch, one rising as the other fell, in grunts recorded during lip-smacking and less ritualized incipient grooming movements (FIGURES 2 & 3).

Two changes occur in the vocal tract in association with these changes in F_1 and F_2 during lip-smacking: the mandible is lowered and the tongue comes forward; the reverse movements then follow. In intense lip-smacking the tongue tip can be seen to emerge between the lips at one extreme of the cycle, while the other can be timed by the sound of the teeth clicking together. The formant state in which F_1 is low and F_2 high can be shown to coincide with a vocal tract in which the tongue is forward, and the mandible at least somewhat lowered, with some degree of lip parting. The lines of evidence are as follows:

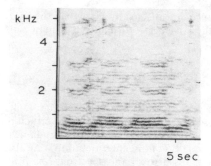

kHz

4 —

2 —

5 sec

FIGURE 2. Humanoid grunt of young male *Papio hamadryas*, showing modulation of formants by tongue and mandible movements during lip-smacking. The most obvious change is the brief fall in F_1 (which lies between 0 and 1kH$_2$) at three evenly spaced points. F_2 and F_3 (at about 2 and 3kH$_2$) rise at these three points. The clicks caused by the teeth coming together on the tongue tip is withdrawn and can be seen as narrow vertical bands of noise between 4 and 5 kH$_2$, which coincide with the beginning of each period in which F_1 occupies its higher position. F_1 is thus high with the tongue withdrawn.

(1) In films of lip-smacking, the face could be seen clearly enough in the case of four grunts to allow comparison of mandible movements (which were the easiest parameter to measure) and formant position. In all four it was possible to follow at least one formant cycle and show that the lowest pitch of F_1 coincided with the point of maximal lowering of the mandible.

(2) Two grunts were filmed as the tongue was retracted from licking the pane of glass through which filming was carried out. In both cases the grunt began at about the time when the tongue tip was about to disappear. F_1 rose over this period of time, when the tongue was certainly moving backwards in the mouth; F_2 showed an inverse change.

(3) In one grunt, F_1 fell as the lips were protruded. The grunt then ceased, so that further changes could not be followed. However, the lip protrusion ended in the emergence of the tongue and licking, so that it seems certain that the tongue was moving into an anterior position, while F_1 was rising.

(4) Tooth clicks can often be detected in spectrograms of grunts given during lip-smacking. The teeth clearly must come together during the phase in which the tongue is retracted, if the tongue is not to be bitten. The clicks can in fact be seen always to follow the periods of lowering of F_1 (FIGURE 3). These periods, which are usually shorter than the periods when F_1 is in its higher position, thus coincide with the periods of brief tongue protrusion; F_2 is at the same time raised.

(5) F_1 and F_2 can be seen to be inversely coupled in grunts given during chewing

FIGURE 3. The pitches of F_1 and F_2 at the extreme points of pitch changes are shown for values from humanoid grunts of a young male *Papio hamadryas*. Two grunts given during a lip-smacking display (hatched bars and black bar, respectively), and one that coincided with grooming movements of the tongue of a less ritualized nature, are shown. Two sets of values for a grunt in which no grooming movements of the tongue occurred are shown by zigzag lines. The values are ordered from left to right in sequence of increasing pitch of F_1. It will be seen that F_2 falls consistently as F_1 rises, and that the values for the grunt without grooming movements fall into the same sequence as those for the other grunts.

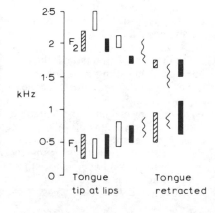

and mumbling movement (at least when higher formants are well developed). It seems likely that forward-and-back tongue movements occur at such times. (This and (4) have both been observed in several other individuals of *P. hamadryas*).

The behavior of F_3 deserves special comment. It was earlier claimed[5] to be a first overtone of F_2, in view of the fact that in a number of lip-smack grunts, it was exactly twice the pitch of F_2 and followed all its variations of pitch. This, however, is not always the case. In a number of grunts given during lip-smacking or grooming, F_3 lies at lower pitches than twice that of F_2, even though it shows the same pitch variations as does F_2. Further, these variations are not twice the amplitude of those of F_2, even though they are in the same direction.

It is possible at present only to speculate as to the more detailed causation of the changes in F_1, F_2, and F_3, which have just been described. F_1 and F_2 behave during forward movement of the tongue in *hamadryas* much as they do in twin-tube simulation of a vocal tract, in which the posterior tube broadens and the anterior tube narrows:[12] in human terms this corresponds (at least in direction of change) to a shift from the vowel "a" to the vowel "i." However, tongue movement cannot be the only important factor, since F_3 should fall as the tongue advances, whereas it falls. One possible explanation is that, with a long muzzle like that of *hamadryas*, lip parting accompanied by mandible lowering trends to shorten the buccal cavity from its anterior tip backwards, since the mouth corners extend progressively backwards (this is not true when there is simultaneous constriction of *orbicularis oris*, but this was not obvious during the grunts under discussion). An alternation between a condition with narrowed posterior chamber and one in which the anterior chamber is both narrowed (by the arrival of the tongue) and shortened would produce exactly the changes in F_1, F_2, and F_3, which are observed.[12]

A majority of grunts in *P. hamadryas* show little or no shift in formant pitch during their course. In the juvenile whose filmed grunts have been discussed, six such grunts with well-marked formants were chosen. Three were loud grunts given to a fellow at a distance, two were long grunts given during a period of alarm, and one had a fundamental rising in pitch in a way that often precedes higher intensity yips or shrieks. All had F_1 and F_2 values which fitted into the sequence shown in FIGURE 2. The factors that control formants during grooming movements of the tongue thus may well operate in other grunts as well.

Two other features of *hamadryas* grunts deserve note. First, in grunts during the course of which the mouth opens widely (e.g. two filmed during the development of a full play face), F_1 broadens considerably as the opening becomes wide. This probably corresponds to an increased damping of the resonance such as is discussed by Fant[12] for horn-shaped resonators, following widening of the mouth aperture. Second, nasal resonances would be expected in baboons, but cannot yet be identified with any safety: a weak resonance sometimes visible between F_1 and F_2 would lie at about the right pitch.

It is likely that other *Papio* species give similar grunts. Unfortunately, I do not have recordings of high enough quality of lip-smack grunts in species of the *cynocephalus* group to establish inverse coupling of F_1 and F_2. Recordings of humanoid grunts with the quality of long moans and sobs that were given by an infant *Papio cynocephalus* (probably of East African origin) illustrate two types of modulation of grunts that have not yet been mentioned. The infant was distressed by its isolation and was calling from a huddled posture, reminiscent of depressed phases of behavior in man and rhesus (Ref. 18, p. 208ff.).

The long moans (FIGURE 4) showed only F_1, perhaps because of complete mouth closure: a similar loss of upper formants occurs with firm lip closure in human vocalization.[12] Calls of this sort are present in *hamadryas*, although my recordings

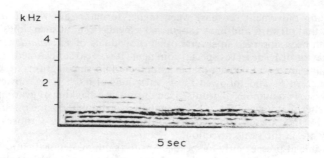

FIGURE 4. Long moans of an infant *Papio anubis*, showing what is almost certainly a marked F_1 with little or no development of higher formants (cf. calls of same individual given immediately subsequently: FIGURE 5). This condition may be associated with mouth closure.

are of poorer quality. I am not certain, on the other hand, whether sobs do occur in *hamadryas*. In the infant *cynocephalus* under discussion, they had the quality of those human vocalizations that are intermediate between sobs and laughter. They consisted of grunts broken into two or more segments by points at which sound energy began to disappear (FIGURE 5). In the grunts themselves, F_2 and F_3 could usually be seen, perhaps because the lips were loosely parted.

The remaining features of *Papio* calls which vary to produce differences that are obvious to the ear (length, pitch of fundamental, broadening of fundamental in a scream, amount of random noise) do not depend on changes in resonance structure and need not be discussed here.

The third species of baboon, *Theropithecus gelada*, is usually regarded (as shown by its separate generic status) to be somewhat removed phylogenetically from *Papio*

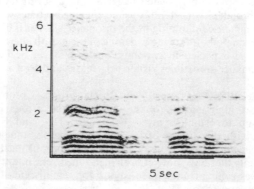

FIGURE 5. Sob of the same infant *Papio anubis* whose moan is shown in FIGURE 4. Note that F_2 and probably F_3 are also present in the first call, which was given with loosely parted lips. The breaks correspond to checks in expiration, and so of vigour of blowing at the glottis; they sound very like similar breaks in human sobbing.

spp. However, its humanoid grunts show much the same range of characteristics as those of *Papio. Gelada* grunts recorded from mature males show an even distribution of energy over a continuous system of overtones (with a fundamental at about 200–250 Hz), often to pitches as high as 8 kHz. Formants are marked, but show changes and patterns that appear to differ from those present in *Papio hamadryas*. F_1 rarely shows changes of pitch: in 11 recorded grunts with clear formants given by an adult male in greeting, often in close association with lip-smacking, there was only once a suggestion of pitch change in F_1. Since higher formants did show pitch changes, it seems possible that F_1 is generated in a different way in such grunts from the F_1 of *hamadryas:* a nasal origin is one obvious possibility. It should be noted, however, that F_1, F_2, and F_3 have broadly similar pitches in both species (F_1 0.5–1.0 kHz, F_2 1.5–2.0 kHz, F_3 in the general area 2.5–3.3 kHz in many *gelada* grunts: cf. Figure 2 and 3). Unfortunately, the interpretation of *gelada* grunts given during lip-smacking is complicated by the fact that extreme upper-lip retraction in a "smile"

FIGURE 6. Humanoid grunt of adult male *Theropithecus gelada* given during lipsmacking, probably in coincidence with upper lip and mouth corner retraction, which may explain the broadness of the formants. F_2 appears to rise but, as is common in *gelada*, there is no obvious change in F_1.

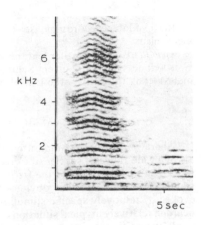

commonly develops during lip-smacking, and is likely considerably to increase the oral opening. Figure 6 shows a gelada humanoid grunt that was almost certainly coincident with lip-smacking of this sort, which may explain the rather broad formants that are shown. A fairly clear rise in F_2 can also be seen. Careful filming will be necessary to establish exactly what facial changes are responsible for such features.

Changes in formant pitch are clearer in two other recordings that were definitely not associated with upper-lip retraction. One, which was evoked by the sound of a human voice, and was not (apparently) associated with grooming movements of the tongue, shows a progressive rise in F_2, accompanied by a fall in F_3, and, more markedly, in F_4 (Figure 7). The same grunt illustrates perhaps the most characteristic change shown by *gelada* formants. This is a steep change in pitch of what is either F_5 or the upper part of a divided F_4: convergence of F_4 and F_5 or the joining together of the two parts of F_4 are obvious in the grunt shown in Figure 8, which was preceded and followed by unvoiced lip-smacks. The pitch change is substantial, being often over a kHz. No consistent pattern of associated change in F_2 and F_3 can be seen

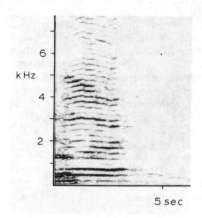

FIGURE 7. Humanoid grunt of adult male *Theropithecus gelada*, given to human voice and without obvious grooming movements of tongue or lips. Note the marked drop in pitch over the call in what is either F_4 or F_4 and F_5 (between 4 and 5 kH_2) and the accompanying rise in F_2 (1.5 to 2 kH_2). F_3 probably falls slightly.

in the available recordings, so that it is at present not possible to suggest a mechanism.

Gelada also shows other features present in *Papio* spp. Long moans in which only F_1 is well developed are given. Segmentation of grunts (e.g. in nervous but aggressive males) tends to result in the loss of higher formants at the points of segmentation.

USE OF HUMANOID GRUNTS BY BABOONS IN THE FIELD

Andrew[3] presented comparative data from captive and relatively tame individuals of a wide range of species of Cercopithecoidea. Although this approach allows at least rough comparison of the frequency with which different calls are given under standard conditions, it has obvious drawbacks. Calls which in the field are usually evoked by relatively specific stimuli (e.g. a particular type of predator) may be only heard in relatively atypical situations; others (e.g. territorial calls) may never be heard at all. In addition, by studying calls evoked by the withholding of reward,[2] it is likely that a rather misleading impression of a continuum of call types is obtained.

It is now possible to use data gathered in the field or under near natural

FIGURE 8. Humanoid grunt of adult male *Theropithecus gelada* which was preceded and followed by unvoiced lipsmacking. Note again the descent of F_4 (or F_5: over 60 to 4 kH_2). F_2 and F_3 do not change clearly in pitch.

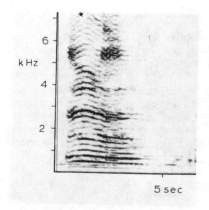

conditions to check the earlier conclusions drawn from captive animals about the use of grunts by different species.

Data gathered from captive animals indicated that *Papio anubis* (and probably the whole *cynocephalus* superspecies), *P. hamadryas*, and *Theropithecus gelada* all gave humanoid grunts in friendly greeting at a distance (female-infant, male-infant, adult-adult), during grooming including the lip-smacking display, during feeding, and in excited choruses when the grunts of one animal evoke grunts in others. The readiness with which grunts are answered suggested that they might be used in close contact.

In the case of *P. anubis*, grunts certainly occur in all of the above situations in the field and are used frequently and conspicuously (Andrew, unpublished, data from Kenyan populations): thus, to take two important examples, males grunt to black infants, and females grunt on meeting both at a little distance and while embracing. Aldrich-Blake *et al.*[1] confirm that *anubis* gives a continuous chorus of quiet grunts, audible to 20 m., while moving through dense cover. *P. hamadryas* certainly grunts in the field during grooming and similar bodily contact, and uses grunts as close contact calls.[24]

USE OF GRUNTS, INCLUDING HUMANOID GRUNTS, BY OTHER CERCOPITHECOIDS

In a number of other species humanoid grunts are certainly or probably given, although (with the possible exception of *Cercocebus*) very much less commonly than in baboons. Enough data exists for *Cercocebus*, *Cercopithecus*, and *Presbytis* spp. to allow brief discussion.

Cercocebus torquatus certainly gives humanoid grunts with clear formants; up to four may be visible above the F_1.[3] No data were obtained on mutual grooming and similar situations. Nearly all grunts were given during movement about the cage or to outside disturbances, very much as described by Chalmers[6] for *C. albigena* in the field, in which grunts were given in locomotion or to slight disturbances. They also occurred in the field during approach to conspecifics (when approaches were less likely than usual to result in agonistic behavior), and during chases and feeding. Both in Chalmers' study and in my captive animals it was common for nearly all energy to lie between 0 and 1 kHz (although grunts with energy running much higher and with indications of resonances were also recorded in the field). Grunts also sometimes departed from typical humanoid grunts in other ways: they were commonly broken up into short segments (whatever their energy distribution might be) and these were sometimes short enough for transients to tend to obscure any resonance structure. It was also my impression that *Cercocebus* grunts passed more readily into higher pitched calls than is true of baboon grunts. These correspond to the "chuckles" of Chalmers, given to predators and other sources of mild alarm. Chuckles are made up of about six short high pulses and are quite unsuitable to reveal resonances. Finally, although lip-smacking is common in *Cercocebus* (confirmed[7]), grunts were observed to alternate with such displays rather than coinciding with them; no great weight, however, can be placed on findings from such a restricted range of captive situations.

The calls of *Cercopithecus aethiops* have been extensively studied by Struhsaker.[42] Grunts ("woof" and "waa") are given by subordinates to the approach of a dominant, and by juveniles when approaching adults in order to groom ("rraugh"). "Waa" sometimes is clearly a humanoid grunt, with signs of resonances.

In addition, my own recordings of "gurgles" given by female *aethiops* during mutual grooming in large outdoor enclosures in Kenya (colony of Mrs. C. Booth) show what is probably a marked F_1, with faint higher formants. Such calls have not been recorded in the field, but they were so soft as to be readily missed at anything other than the closest range (cf. *Macaca mulatta*, below); it is likely that they are a usual part of the vocabulary of *Cercopithecus* spp.

Study of the original recordings of Struhsaker, however, to whom I am greatly indebted for the opportunity to examine this material, confirms the original conclusion[3] that *Cercopithecus* grunts (e.g. "waa") commonly rise suddenly to portions of very much higher pitch (e.g. 1 kHz fundamental). This introduces two complications. Firstly, in one recording of "waa" there was a transition from apparent resonances in the grunt portion to the fundamental and a harmonic in the high-pitched portion. It is clear, therefore, that much more detailed study will be needed before one can be confident that true resonances rather than a superimposed double pattern of glottal vibration are really commonly involved in *Cercopithecus* grunts. Secondly, even where it is probable that resonances are revealed, they may be confined to brief periods of the call (e.g. grunt portions at beginning and end in some "waa"), the remainder being too high pitched to reveal resonances readily.

In captive *C. neglectus* this was found also to be true of soft grunts given during friendly mutual grooming. In view of the close resemblance between the types of calls given by different *Cercopithecus* spp., it is probable that this is sometimes true also of *aethiops* grooming grunts.

In two other categories of *aethiops*, grunts (the progression grunt, used in close contact, and "woof") energy is commonly concentrated between 0 and 1 kHz. Sounds approximating to humanoid grunts are thus a limited subset of the grunts made by *aethiops* (and almost certainly the other *Cercopithecus* species such as *mitis* and *neglectus*, with which I am familiar in captivity). In addition, grunts of whatever kind (and calls in general) are almost certainly used much less commonly by *Cercopithecus* than by baboons in the situation in which baboons typically give humanoid grunts, although quantitative data are needed to establish this.

Finally, in females of both *C. neglectus* and *C. aethiops*, long tonal calls with relatively deep fundamentals ("moo"[3]) are evoked (at least in captive animals) when they see an infant *Cercopithecus* in the hands of a human being. These calls do not seem to coincide exactly with any of the alarm calls described by Struhsaker, but may represent a more intense variant of one of them. They show what are almost certainly resonances that vary somewhat in pitch within the course of the call. Thus, in calls that occur in a situation quite different from baboon humanoid grunts, *Cercopithecus* is probably capable of revealing vocal tract resonances.

Grunts certainly occur in some Colobids as well as in the Cercopithecids already discussed. Thus Poirier[35] found that *Presbytis johnii* gave deep guttural grunts when out of visual contact in dense foliage. The "hollow subordinate vocalization" that consisted of low-pitched expirations given in staccato bursts when approaching and sometimes embracing a dominant, is probably also a grunt. In *Presbytis entellus*[22] grunts are given in association with threat, but also in submissive situations (e.g. in the langur equivalent of the lip-smacking display, during embracing, presenting, and when avoiding a dominant). Grunts may also be given by a mother just before approaching her infant, when the group has been alerted. It is not yet clear whether true humanoid grunts are involved in any of these instances.

Equally important, if we are eventually to understand the evolution of humanoid grunts, are those Cercopithecoid species that are well enough known to allow us to conclude that they rarely or never give such calls.

The simplest case is that of *Erythrocebus patas*. This species, as judged from studies in both field and captivity,[14,15] is extremely silent in a variety of situations in which nearly all other Cercopithecoids would sometimes call: thus *patas* appears not to give calls during friendly interactions, nor in close contact. Distant contact calls probably exist (e.g. "moan") but are rare. The absence (or great rarity) of grunts may be thus merely one aspect of a general lack of calls.

Macaca mulatta is of much greater interest, as a highly vocal species that nevertheless almost or quite lacks grunts (field data;[29] data from captivity[38]). Firstly, grunts are not used in contact. Variants of a single call ("coo,"[29] clear call,[38] "woo,"[3]) are used over a range of separation where most species use two calls (e.g. *Papio anubis:* grunt in close contact, "wahoo" bark in distant contact.[1]) Short coos are used in dense cover, whereas at the other extreme, when an animal is lost, very long coos are given in rapid succession. Coos have a relatively high pitch (fundamental 0.5–1.0 kHz), and although they may be affected to some extent by resonance properties (e.g. the fundamental is often missing), they do not show any sign of separate formants, which they are ill-suited to reveal. Squeals and screeches are used in much the same way as in baboons and many other primates by animals frightened or attacked by a dominant, but calls given in friendly contexts are inconspicuous and/or rare. Thus females give "chortles" (very soft grunting sounds) to their own young infants, and also when they wish to touch an infant belonging to another mother.[29] The call is apparently very specific to this situation, and so must correspond in some way to the bark-like "explosive cough" described by Rowell & Hinde[38] as also specific to exactly the same situation; perhaps the two are low- and high-intensity variants. They show it as composed of a tonal noise with main energy between 0.8 and 1.5 kHz, and so quite unsuited to show resonances.

A second important category of calls are those given during grooming and embracing ("affectional calls"). "Girning" occurred in captive animals when joining another conspecific in order to huddle with it, during mutual grooming, and at similar times, often in association with lip-smacking; similar calls were not recorded in the field, but this was probably because they are very quiet. Girning has a definite tonal structure of deep pitch (c. 150 Hz); energy is present only or chiefly in harmonics between 0.5 and 1.5 kHz, perhaps as a consequence of a resonance of the whole upper vocal tract. In friendly social interactions over greater distance, *mulatta* is silent where baboons would often be grunting. Thus, in summary, *mulatta* is silent, or gives calls other than grunts or gives very soft grunt-like calls (which are probably not true humanoid grunts) in all the situations in which full humanoid grunts would be given by *Papio*. Other species of *Macaca* (e.g. *fuscata, maura*[3]) appear to be very like *mulatta*.

Chimpanzees do grunt, but much more rarely than baboons. In adults, soft grunts or very soft groans occur during resting and grooming, and also during traveling; louder grunts occur during feeding, although they often pass into loud barks and shrieks when the food is very desirable.[45] Fleischman[13] distinguishes between "glottal grunts" given in association with feeding and soft grunts in the other situations, and notes that soft grunts are most common in infancy in situations other than feeding, becoming rare (or perhaps absent in his captive but not caged animals) in adults, which only give glottal grunts to food.

In captive animals, I found that grunts to food had little or no energy above 0.5 kHz,[3] and so could not reveal resonances. True humanoid grunts, if present, are thus at least rarer than the above description of grunts in general would suggest. Further, it is clear that breathy calls are often given where baboons might grunt. Nishida[33] notes that "low panting calls" are given when chimpanzees meet, both as they approach and sit down, and as they approach their lips to the body of the other. Van Lawick-Goodall[45] noted similar soft pants in social grooming, and approaches to kiss, for example; such calls became louder in submissive behavior and in social play. Breathy calls may reveal resonances effectively, as do human whispers; it is equally possible (in the absence of good recordings) that they usually have zones of concentration of glottal energy which would mask resonances. Without much more data it is impossible to be sure. It is certain that such calls do not carry to a distance, as do humanoid grunts.

The other limitation on the use of grunts by chimpanzees is the readiness with which calls rise in pitch toward, on the one hand, barks and screams (in submission, tantrum, or excitement such as is associated with finding food) and, on the other, hoots (in distant contact or excitement). Thus Reynolds[37] describes "whoops" (i.e. hoot of van Lawick-Goodall,[45] and others) during group movements when groups meet or split up, on waking and in answer to similar calls at a distance. Hoots clearly function in part like the territorial calls of many other forest primates (e.g. *Cercocebus, Cercopithecus, Hylobates*; below) to advertise the position of the group, both to group members and to other groups. In the chimpanzee the latter function is probably reduced in importance, but Izawa[21] has argued for at least occasional vocal contacts of this sort between members of two major groupings that rarely or never coalesce, unlike the temporary subgroups, which are so variable within a major grouping. The first function seems to have been greatly increased, in that extraordinarily loud hoots, barks, and screams allow subgroups to detect over very long distances the discovery by others of sources of temporarily superabundant food,[43] and perhaps also allow concentration on a potential source of danger. Close-contact calls, on the other hand, appear to be of greatly reduced importance, presumably as one aspect of the readiness with which chimpanzee groupings other than mother and child break up and coalesce in new combinations.

DISCUSSION

Humanoid Grunts in Cercopithecoidea

It is now possible to attempt to summarize and discuss the various factors that may determine whether humanoid grunts are used extensively or not by a particular species.

Use of Grunts as Close-Contact Calls

Some species clearly lack close contact calls (i.e., calls given to keep contact while moving through dense cover) either because, like *Erythrocebus* and perhaps *Pan*, they do not attempt to sustain vocal contact under such conditions, or because, like *Macaca mulatta* they use a single call over a wide range of distances. It is possible that *mulatta* usually maintains contact only over greater distances, and has a call suited to this.

The advantages of calls of differing pitch for use in contact are difficult to assess without experiment. On the one hand, the longer the wavelength the less the loss by reflection. However, even at 1 kHz, reflection should be substantial only from quite large obstacles. Reflection begins to fall off steeply as the wavelength exceeds the approximate circumference of a spherical reflector;[39] at 1 kHz with a wavelength of about 34 cm this should be true of objects below about 10 cm across (i.e., most leaves and twigs). On the other hand, it seems likely that it is easier for a glottis to put more energy into high-pitched calls: for one thing, energy loss through damping due to repeated approximation of the glottal lips, such as occurs in grunts and can be seen in their pulsed structure in sonograms, can be minimized or avoided when the glottis is more tense.

Calls such as the *mulatta* coo may thus be best adapted to contact over some distance where much of the airpath is free of large obstacles. Deep grunts may be better suited to really close contact, where penetration to great distances is best avoided, or to contact in very dense cover, including large obstacles.

It will be noted that deep grunts rather than humanoid grunts are most obviously demanded by this latter argument, and indeed grunts with most of their energy below 1 kHz appear to be used in close contact by *Cercocebus* and *Cercopithecus*, for example.

It is relevant to this argument that gorillas use grunts in close contact[40] in a way in which chimpanzees do not. They also need to keep continuous contact in movement through dense foliage on the ground, since the group stays together.

Humanoid grunts may become of use in close contact when individual recognition is important, since they convey information about the size and proportion of the vocal tract that is likely to be to some extent characteristic of each individual. It is difficult to assess how effective such selection pressure might be. Chalmers[6] has pointed out that in *Cercocebus* deep grunts are broken up into component pulses, and that individuals differ in the spacing of such pulses: thus individual recognition through grunts need not involve resonances such as are revealed by humanoid grunts.

Further, in many cases it may be enough to be able to recognize and locate adult males by their distant contact calls. Distant contact calls seem sometimes to be used to initiate and guide group movements by leading males in *Papio anubis*;[1] the same may well be true of the various territorial or distant contact calls of *Cercocebus* and *Cercopithecus*.[42]

Individual recognition through close contact calls is likely to be of real importance in species in which individuals have particular alliances of interest, so that, for example, it is important to a female or juvenile (or even male) to know the location of a particular male who is likely to support or protect him or her; the matter is considered further below.

Use of Humanoid Grunts as Affectional Calls Audible over some Distance

The evidence from *Macaca* and *Pan* suggests that, when grunt-like calls are used very little, the one situation in which they are likely to occur is in affectional interactions involving grooming or cuddling. It is possible that the reason for this is that this is an ancient condition, derived from a common Cercopithecoid ancester. There are, however, also functional reasons that might explain such a finding. Firstly, such calls are intended to act over very short distances, and might be expected therefore to be of low intensity: low glottal tension may be particularly likely in very soft calls. Secondly, and more importantly, it may be useful to give information about tongue movements in such calls, as an indication when grooming is likely; where this is so, selection for a humanoid grunt structure would be expected.

One possible explanation for the very extensive use by baboons of humanoid grunts in exchanges that may be over some distance is that they have an unusual need for ready and explicit affectional transactions, that is, for interchanges which do not function simply to inhibit attack but which tend to establish a temporary or long-term bond which leads to mutual defense against predators and conspecifics, support like that afforded by a mother to her child. In baboons, humanoid grunts superimposed on grooming movements of the tongue (both unritualized and in lip-smacking) allow animals effectively to "groom" another at a distance, without coming close enough to evoke flight or attack. They could also be argued in a similar way to be able to substitute during communication for the embracing and cuddling with which they are commonly associated.

In my previous discussion of the evolution of humanoid grunts[3] I argued that it was essential for individual baboons, including subadult males, to remain members of their troop because it provided the only available refuge from predators while feeding out in the open. I contrasted this condition with that of "typical" macaques like *mulatta* and *fuscata*, in which individuals are readily able to leave the troop for long periods of time and survive successfully. It seemed appropriate, therefore, that baboons should have displays that tended to prevent the development of fighting, and that these should be of less importance in macaques.

To some extent, this contrast between baboons and macaques can still be drawn today. Fighting does appear to be frequent and intense in some *mulatta* troops: Lindburg[29] noted severe aggression with deaths of a male and female in his study area. Kummer,[24] in contrast, saw nothing worse than a few scratches as a result of sustained and vigorous fighting in *hamadryas* involving the whole of a large troop. Equally, baboons living alone for long periods, have still not been reported, as far as I know, while even leading males may leave the troop and become solitary in *fuscata*.[43]

The original argument, however, can now be seen to be inadequate. First, our much greater knowledge of baboon social behavior has made it plain that the idea of a closed troop that proceeds everywhere as a single unit is inadequate even for *cynocephalus* baboons. Thus Packer[34] has shown that young males commonly transfer to another troop of which they probably become permanent members. Second, it is necessary to consider the advantage of affectional transactions to both parties. A condition in which subadult males (for example) purchased the advantage of staying in the troop at the expense of the older males to which they displayed would be unlikely to be evolutionarily stable, since there is no reason why the older males should remain responsive to such displays.

The special feature of baboon social groupings that is relevant to the present argument can now be seen to be the need for powerful alliances of interest between particular individuals that are not based on the direct protection by a relative because he possesses genes which are also possessed by the protector. These alliances are required in order to provide defense against predation during foraging in the open; they may also provide access to knowledge of the distribution of resources possessed by some individuals but not others.[24] In *hamadryas* and *gelada*, small foraging groups are essential because of the scattered and scanty nature of food supplies.[10] The smallest group that can include a protecting male is clearly a one-male unit, which indeed is the basic social unit in both species.[8,24] Within such a unit, close permanent bonding between male and female resembling, and probably based on that between mother and infant,[24] is usual. Such a permanent bond should be of advantage to both partners, in that through it females purchase continuous protection during foraging, which is readily and easily available, even when they are not capable of evoking a sexual consortship. The male ensures through such a bond that his protection is efficiently used in that it benefits his own offspring, accompanying their mother; he also ensures that there are no gaps in protection, such as might result if females had varying relations with different males. *Anubis* appears to be able to fragment into relatively small groups in arid areas,[1] and this may explain selection for the potential occasionally to form intense male and female bonds noted by Ransom and Ransom[36] in *anubis*.

Male-juvenile bonding also occurs in baboons. In *hamadryas* this involves young females and allows the development of male-female units.[24] Bonding with infants (of either sex), which certainly sometimes occurs in *anubis*,[36] is more difficult to understand. *Anubis* males pick up and carry infants apparently in order to suppress aggressive behavior in other males (as do some macaques, e.g. *M. sylvana*,[9] but bonding appears not to be necessary for this to occur.[36] It is possible that in a species in which bonding is possible for other reasons that a longer term alliance with a particular infant becomes possible and proves advantageous for the reason just considered.

Male-male bonding is perhaps the most interesting. In *hamadryas*,[24] young males often associate with an older male (commonly one old enough to have apparently lost his females); here both partners obtain mutual protection during foraging. Similar alliances may well be involved in the all-male groups present in *gelada*[8] or in the juvenile male groupings of *hamadryas*.

Looser and more temporary alliances also would be facilitated by affectional displays. Thus two male *hamadryas* often associate during foraging[24] and coordinate their movements in a way that allows decisions to be taken in which both participate as to the next direction of movement. No doubt, comparable interactions occur in *anubis* and *gelada*. It is perhaps important in this context that close-contact calls (such as are given by the *hamadryas* males during their interactions on the march[24] in baboons are the same humanoid grunts that are also used in affectional displays: they would thus be suitable to promote at least temporary bonding as well as serving as close contact calls.

In *anubis*[11,16] mutual alliances between adult males are also important in interactions between troop members. Members of an alliance are better able to sustain high rank within the group. Here, too, affectional interchanges should be selected for.

Finally, the original argument concerning the minimization within the baboon social group of serious attack can probably be recast. Within a permanent social group of baboons, even when alliances or shared genetic material do not make it advantageous for one individual to prevent serious and protracted attacks on another, there remains a more general advantage in avoiding fighting spreading within the group. The loss of aggressive behavior within social groups cannot evolve, since there are genuine conflicts of interest between individuals. The performance of, and (crucially) the ready response to, affectional displays that would tend to prevent the development of serious aggression should thus be selected for.

Clearly, the above arguments require that alliances should be absent or of much less importance in species such as *Macaca mulatta* or *M. fuscata*. The support given by mothers to juvenile offspring is certainly important in these species (e.g. dominant mothers may give higher rank to their male offspring.[19] Lindburg[29] argues that this is the main sort of alliance in macacques, and adduces as evidence the fact that low-ranking female *mulatta* do not rise in status during consortship with a male in the way in which female *P. anubis* and common langurs do. A mother-offspring alliance differs clearly from the ones discussed above in that it does not require establishment between mother and juvenile, but rather survives from the period of infancy when strong bonding is inevitable and does not require displays effective over a distance. Further, it is not clear that the "alliance" is mutual. In opposition to this, Kawai[47] has shown in *fuscata* that females may rise in rank as a result of consortship, so that such effects are clearly possible in *Macaca*.

Further, Wilson[46] found that young male *mulatta* sometimes had the assistance in entering a new troop of a "sponsor," which was in certain cases known to be a brother who had made the transfer earlier. Kaufman[48] found that four-year-old males in one *mulatta* troop tended to act together as a group. Infant adoption by males occurs in a few *fuscata* troops.[20]

Some of the alliances shown by baboons are thus at least potentially present in *mulatta* or *fuscata*. The very long-term male/female associations of *hamadryas* and *gelada* clearly are not, but quantitative and directly comparable data are needed, particularly in the case of *cynocephalus*, to establish the postulated contrast with *Macaca mulatta* and *fuscata*.

The lesser use made of grunts by the chimpanzee than by baboons is of less relevance to the present argument, since the difference is difficult to interpret in view of the wider phyletic separation of chimpanzee and baboon. It is worth noting, however, that in the chimpanzee, also, sustained continuous association of adults other than at oestrus does seem to be excluded by all accounts of the variable and loose nature of subgroupings in this species.

The Ready Replacement of Grunts by Calls of Higher Pitch

It is impossible to establish unambiguously that chimpanzees pass more readily than baboons from grunts into higher pitched calls, as suggested by Andrew.[3] However, this does seem to be the case, both from the data already cited and from data from captive animals; thus Menzel[32] found that leading chimpanzees whimpered if not followed, rather than grunting. It has already been argued that this reflects the use by excited chimpanzees of a variety of very loud calls over long distances to promote aggregation at rich food sources.

Other primates that grunt also pass readily from grunts into higher calls. This is true of *Cercopithecus* spp. and perhaps of *Cercocebus* spp. (above) and of *Hylobates*.[3] Here the functional reasons are obscure. It is possible that it is preferable, other things being equal, to have calls varying along a continuum, which convey quantitative information about the animal's motivational state.[30] It may thus be the baboons which are unusual in having stabilized their humanoid grunts over a wider range of situations, thereby conveying equally detailed information, but indirectly as a result of making audible tongue and lip positions.

Territorial calls may perhaps also curtail the range of situations in which grunts are given. Certainly in captivity I have observed excited male *Cercocebus* pass into their species specific loud calls (e.g. whoop gobble[6]) in situations in which grunt choruses might have been expected in baboons.

CONCLUSIONS

It is clear that baboons can and do produce sounds that are well suited to reveal vocal tract resonances, and that they modulate these by tongue and lip movements. It is likely that such humanoid grunts are important in affectional exchanges, but direct experimental evidence is lacking.

The qualitative evidence that baboons are unusual among the Cercopithecoidea in the frequency with which they use full typical humanoid grunts is not satisfactory. Quantitative data gathered under comparable conditions and preferably by the same workers are needed. However, I believe that some differences are so marked (e.g. comparison of *Papio* and *Macaca*) that it is likely that they are genuine even on present evidence.

Only hypothetical arguments can be advanced to explain this special feature of baboon vocalization systems. One that seems worth testing is that alliances of interest are highly advantageous in species exposed to predation during terrestrial foraging. Such alliances have promoted the evolution of behavior that is effective in establishing affectional ties, since these make it more likely that animals will keep close to and continually monitor the position of individuals who will protect them and whom they should protect, and that in the face of a predator there will be vigorous mutual support and defense of a sort usually afforded to endangered infants in Cercopithecoids.

This hypothesis would be considerably weakened if a Cercopithecoid were found that gave humanoid grunts very freely in the same way as do baboons, and that yet was not exposed to the selection pressures of terrestrial foraging. A number of forest Cercopithecoids are likely to provide tests of just this sort.

Cercocebus remains an enigma. Species of this genus use humanoid grunts to some extent, although it is almost certain that they do so much less than do baboons; it is possible that such calls (as opposed to deep grunts) are actually rather rare in *Cercocebus*. Too little is known as yet of the organization of their relatively compact multimale groups[6] to allow useful speculation. Solitary males are recorded by Struhsaker.[42]

Equally, *Mandrillus sphinx*, which has multimale groupings, is known to give "two phase grunts," which probably serve in group cohesion.[42] In captivity (Andrew, unpublished) *sphinx* is certainly much more silent than *Papio* or *Theropithecus gelada*. It does give grunts in friendly contact with humans. These are commonly deep with energy concentrated below 1 kHz, but sometimes appear to be true humanoid grunts with strong indications of at least an F_1. Calls pass readily into high-pitched cackles (made up of short, noisy, repeated components) as food approaches. Overall, there is resemblance to the chimpanzee which is interesting in view of the relatively similar habitat of the two species. The scanty evidence from *sphinx* thus suggests a species, which is probably closely related to *Papio*, and possesses multimale groups, but which lacks both the selection pressures of foraging away from trees and also the free use of humanoid grunts.

DISCUSSION: HUMANOID GRUNTS IN AUSTRALOPITHECUS AND HOMO

Only brief speculation on this topic is justified. The justification for this paper is, of course, the possession by modern man of "humanoid grunts" which reveal conspicuous resonances of the vocal tract.

It should be noted that, given that a vocal language became of sufficient value to bring about its evolution in the human line, a wide variety of phonemes could easily have been achieved by, for example, the use of pitch changes of a high fundamental of the sort shown by *Cercopithecus* squeaks and trills. When one considers in addition tongue and teeth clicks and glottal transients, it is clear that human speech is by no means the only way in which a vocal language might have evolved.

An early prelanguage phase of human evolution, in which formants present in humanoid grunts were important in communication in the ways that have been postulated here for baboons, would make it more likely that formants would come to be important in speech when vocal language began to evolve (see further discussion in Ref. 4).

A baboon-like stage in the evolution of human vocalization is also suggested by a second line of evidence. The use of chuckles and laughter by present-day *sapiens* has many features in common with the use of baboon grunts in affectional interchanges. The sudden resolution of a potential dispute by shared laughter is particularly striking. The part played by "humanoid grunts" in such sudden changes deserves formal comparative study in both man and baboons. The cementing of friendly relations between adults by exchanges in which chuckles and laughter are common will be equally familiar to readers, as will the role of such vocalizations in adult-child relations: again comparison of quantitative data from man and baboons is badly needed. Clearly the possession of chuckles and laughter by present-day *sapiens* is no guarantee that similar calls were in use before the evolution of language, but their presence today does make it more likely that this was so.

Hewes[17] has argued that, since baboons have upper vocal tracts of unusual proportions because of their long muzzles, evidence from their calls is not relevant to the evolution of human vocalizations. This is, however, not the main point at issue. The humanoid grunts of baboons show that it is possible for nonhuman primates to evolve *glottally* produced calls that are entirely suitable to reveal resonances of the vocal tract (and do reveal such resonances). It is, of course, still possible (but difficult) to argue that primates without muzzles are incapable of modulating resonances by tongue and lip movements. Lieberman [26] concluded from computer simulation that such modulation would result from tongue movements in a rhesus oral cavity: clearly, direct evidence would be more satisfactory but the result is suggestive.

If it is accepted that a baboon-like stage in the evolution of Hominid vocalization is a possibility, then it becomes interesting to enquire whether humanoid grunts might have been evolved under the same selection pressures in both lines. The adaptations of *Australopithecus* for life on the ground are well known and fully established. The need for affectional interchanges to support alliances of interest during foraging away from the refuge of trees and cliffs is thus likely to have been important in *Australopithecus*, just as in present-day baboons.

One additional factor may have made permanent alliances of interest of even greater importance in the human line. This is the systematic provision of food for other individuals. The arguments that such behavior may have occurred early in the human line are unfortunately indirect and inconclusive. They rest on: (1) comparison with cooperative hunters of large prey such as hunting dogs and wolves,[31] in which males bring food to their mates and young. The correlation between such feeding and cooperative hunting is poor, however: in cooperative hunters such as the spotted hyena there is no cooperation at all between a female with young and a particular male (general review [23]). (2) The relative helplessness of the human infant may have tended to keep mothers with young near home bases, so that for them access to wider foraging areas would have depended on other adults. It is difficult to decide on available evidence how early and how powerfully in human evolution such an effect might have acted.

The comparison with baboons seems to me to remain the most useful and illuminating. Further study of the real value in communication of the resonances of the humanoid grunts of baboons should at least provide firm data from which to extrapolate to human evolution.

One important consideration with which I would like to close is that tongue and lip movements are used by primates to manipulate the environment and to control the behavior of social fellows. Hewes [17] has argued for a gestural origin of language on the score that limb movements and posture are under direct control in nonhuman primates in a way in which glottal events are not. Certainly in one important situation in which humans would use language (namely, the decision in which direction and to what spot the foraging group should proceed), exchange of information appears to depend on direction of movement, exchange of glances, and presentation of the rear in both chimpanzee [32] and *hamadryas* [24]; in the chimpanzee, beckoning and even pulling are also used.

Tongue and lip movements are much more likely than glottal coordinations to be accessible to direct control in nonhuman primates in the same way as such gestures. As a result, if they were being used to modulate grunts during the early stages of the origin of language, they would have allowed a continuing interaction between vocalization and gesture, making audible not only grooming and kissing movements, but feeding (potentially revealing the amount and consistency of the food) and the exploration of objects with lip and tongue. It would still be necessary to bring glottal events under more and more sophisticated control, but the changes involved could be relatively gradual.

Finally, it should be obvious that I am not attempting here to provide a comprehensive theory of the origin of vocal language, but merely to consider one stage that provides a plausible explanation for the earliest phases of its development. Other phases require explanation of a different sort: thus it may be worth reviving earlier comparisons between the factors leading to the learning of patterns of vocalization in birds and the possible causes of the evolution of such abilities in the Hominid line.[2]

Acknowledgments

I was greatly assisted in most of the work reported here by Mrs. Rosalie Stacey, to whom I am very grateful.

REFERENCES

1. ALDRICH-BLAKE, F. P. G., T. K. BUNN, R. I. M. DUNBAR, & P. M. HEALEY. 1971. Observations on baboons, *Papio anubis*, in an arid region in Ethiopia. Folia Primatol. **15:** 1–35.
2. ANDREW, R. J. 1962. Evolution of intelligence and vocal mimicking. Science **137:** 555–589.
3. ANDREW, R. J. 1963. Trends apparent in the evolution of vocalization in the Old World monkeys and apes. Symp. Zool. Soc. Lond. **10:** 89–107.
4. ANDREW, R. J. 1963. The origin and evolution of the calls and facial expressions of the primates. **20:** 1–109.
5. ANDREW, R. J. 1965. The origin of facial expression. Sci. Am. Oct.: 88–94.
6. CHALMERS, N. R. 1968. The visual and vocal communication of free living mangabeys in Uganda. Folia primatol. **9:** 258–280.
7. CHALMERS, N. R. 1971. Differences in behaviour between some arboreal and terrestrial species of African monkey. *In* Comparative Ecology and Behaviour of Primates: 69–100. R. P. Michael and J. H. Crook, Eds. Academic Press. London, England.
8. CROOK, J. H. 1966. Gelada baboon herd structure and movement: a comparative report. Symp. Zool. Soc. Lond. **18:** 237–258.
9. CROOK, J. H. 1970. The socio-ecology of primates. *In* Social Behaviour in Birds and Mammals. J. H. Crook Ed.: 102–168. Academic Press. London, England.
10. CROOK, J. H. & J. S. GARTLAN, 1966. Evolution of primate societies. Nature [New Biol.] **210:** 1200–1203.
11. DEVORE, I. 1962. The social behavior and organization of baboon troops. Ph.D. Thesis. University of Chicago. Chicago, Ill. Quoted in Ref. 25.
12. FANT, G. 1960. Acoustic theory of speech production. The Hague, The Netherlands.
13. FLEISCHMAN, M. L. 1968. Vocalisation of chimpanzees in non-caged captivity. Primates **9:** 273–282.
14. HALL, K. R. L. 1968. Behaviour and ecology of the wild Patas monkey, *Erythrocebus patas*, in Uganda. *In* Primates: Studies in Adaptation and Variability. P. C. Jay, Ed.: 32–119. University of Chicago Press. Chicago, Ill.
15. HALL, K. R. L., R. C. BOELKINS & M. J. GOSWELL. 1965. Behaviour of Patas monkeys, *Erythrocebus patas*, in captivity, with notes on the natural habitat. Folia primatol. **3:** 22–49.
16. HALL, K. R. L. & I. DEVORE. 1965. Baboon social behavior. *In* Primate behavior: field studies of monkeys and apes. I. DeVore, Ed.: 53–110. Holt Rinehart & Winston. New York, N.Y.
17. HEWES, G. W. 1973. Primate communication and the gestural origin of language. Current Anthropol. **14:** 5–24.

18. HINDE, R. A. 1974. Biological bases of human social behaviour. McGraw-Hill. London, England.
19. IMANISHI, K. 1960. Social organization of sub-human primates in their natural habitats. Current Anthropol. **1:** 393–407.
20. ITANI, J. 1959. Parental care in the wild Japanese monkey, *Macaca f. fuscata*. Primates **2:** 61–93.
21. IZAWA, K. 1970. Unit groups of chimpanzees and their nomadism in the Savanna woodland. Primates **11:** 1–46.
22. JAY, P. 1965. The common langur of North India. *In* Primate Behavior. I. DeVore, Ed.: 197–249. Holt, Rinehart & Winston. New York, N.Y.
23. KRUUK, H. 1972. The Spotted Hyena. University of Chicago Press. Chicago, Ill.
24. KUMMER, H. 1968. Social organization of Hamadryas baboons. University of Chicago Press. Chicago, Ill.
25. KUMMER, H. 1968. Two variations in the social organization of baboons. *In* Primates: Studies in Adaptation and Variability. P. C. Jay, Ed.: 293–312.
26. LIEBERMAN, P. 1968. Primate vocalizations and human linguistic ability. J. Acoustic Soc. Amer. **44:** 1574–1584.
27. LIEBERMAN, P., E. S. CRELIN & D. H. KLATT. 1972. Phonetic ability and related anatomy of the newborn and adult human, Neanderthal Man, and the chimpanzee. Amer. Anthropol. **74:** 287–307.
28. LIEBERMAN, P. 1973. On the evolution of language: a unified view. Cognition **2:** 59–94.
29. LINDBURG, D. G. 1971. The Rhesus monkey in North India: an ecological and behavioral study. *In* Primate Behavior: Developments in Field and Laboratory research. L. A. Rosenblum, Ed. Vol. **2:** 1–106. Academic Press. New York, N.Y.
30. MARLER, P. 1970. Vocalization of East African monkeys. 1. Red Colobus. Folia primatol. **13:** 81–91.
31. MECH, L. D. 1970. The Wolf. Natural History Press. New York, N.Y.
32. MENZELL, E. W. 1971. Communication about the environment in a group of young chimpanzees. Folia primatol. **15:** 220–232.
33. NISHIDA, T. 1970. Social behaviour and relationship among wild chimpanzees of the Mahali mountains. Primates **11:** 47–87.
34. PACKER, C. 1975. Male transfer in the olive baboon. Nature **255:** 219–226.
35. POIRIER, F. E. 1970. The communication matrix of the Nilgiri Langur, (*Presbytis johnii*) of South India. Folia primatol. **13:** 92–136.
36. RANSOM, T. W. & B. S. RANSOM. 1971. Adult male-infant relations among baboons (*Papio anubis*). Folia primatol. **16:** 179–195.
37. REYNOLDS, V. 1963. An outline of the behaviour and social organization of forest-living chimpanzees. Folia primatol. **1:** 95–102.
38. ROWELL, T. E. & R. A. HINDE. 1962. Vocal communication by the Rhesus monkey (*Macaca mulatta*). Proc. Zool. Soc. London. **138:** 290–294.
39. SALES, G. D. & J. D. PYE. 1974. Ultrasonic communication by animals. Chapman & Hall. London, England.
40. SCHALLER, G. B. 1965. The behavior of the Mountain Gorilla. *In* Primate Behavior. I. DeVore, Ed.: 324–367. Holt Rinehart & Winston. New York, N.Y.
41. STRUHSAKER, T. T. 1967. Auditory communication among vervet monkeys (*Cercopithecus aethiops*). *In* Social Communication among Primates. S. A. Altmann, Ed.: 281–374. University of Chicago Press. Chicago, Ill.
42. STRUHSAKER, T. T. 1969. Correlates of ecology and social organization among African cercopithecines. Folia primatol. **11:** 80–118.
43. SUGIYAMA, Y. 1960. On the division of a natural troop of Japanese monkeys at Takasakiyama. Primates **2:** 109–144.
44. SUGIYAMA, Y. 1969. Social behavior of chimpanzees in the Budongo Forest, Uganda. Primates **10:** 197–225.
45. VAN LAWICK-GOODALL, J. 1968. A preliminary report on expressive movements and communications in the Gombe Stream chimpanzees. *In* Primates: Studies in Adaptation and Variability. P. C. Jay, Ed.: 313–374. Holt Rinehart & Winston. New York, N.Y.

46. WILSON, A. P. 1968. Social behaviour of free-ranging rhesus monkeys with an emphasis on aggression. Ph.D. thesis. Princeton University, Princeton, N.J. Quoted in Ref. 9.

47. KAWAI, M. 1965. On the system of social ranks in a natural group of Japanese monkeys. 1. Basic rank and dependent rank. *In* Japanese Monkeys: a collection of translations. K. Imanishi and S. A. Altmann, Eds. Yerkes Regional Primate Center. Atlanta, Ga.

48. KAUFMAN, J. H. 1967. Social relations of adult males in a free-ranging band of rhesus monkeys. *In* Social Communication amongst Primates. S. A. Altmann, Ed. University of Chicago Press. Chicago, Ill.

SPEECH PERCEPTION IN THE HUMAN INFANT
AND RHESUS MONKEY*

Philip A. Morse

Department of Psychology
University of Wisconsin-Madison
Madison, Wisconsin 53706

According to Webster, the term "infant" means "without speech or voice." This developmental label, however, may have unfairly biased us in the past in our estimates of the speech capabilities of human infants. In traditional accounts of child development the period of "infancy" is generally restricted to the first year or so after birth. Although human children can hardly be considered avocal during this period, infants' abilities to *produce* human language are indeed rather limited at this age. By contrast, recent research on the *perception* of speech in infants has revealed that some important linguistic capabilities are already functional by the first few months of age. To explain the development of these early perceptual capabilities, we need not only an *ontogenetic* timetable for the perception of different speech sounds, but also an appreciation of the *phylogenetic* (evolutionary) factors that have contributed to these capabilities, as well as the *microgenetic* (e.g. memory) aspects of the infant's perception of speech in specific experimental situations. Although an ontogenetic timetable provides us with a valuable descriptive account of the development of infant speech perception, phylogenetic and microgenetic research enables us to explain how these perceptual capacities develop in the infant. The primary focus of the present paper will be on recent research on the phylogenetic and microgenetic aspects of the development of speech perception, although a brief summary of the relevant ontogenetic findings will also be included.

Before we can even begin, however, to determine an ontogenetic sequence for the development of infant speech perception, we need to know what speech perception questions to ask of infants and how to get reliable answers from these nonverbal, yet frequently vocal and uncooperative subjects. The majority of the studies on infant speech perception have employed either a heart-rate orienting response (OR) or a nonnutritive sucking paradigm in assessing the infant's ability to discriminate different speech sound contrasts. In the heart rate OR paradigm a particular speech sound (e.g., [ba]) is presented repeatedly for several trials and then followed by a few trials of a novel sound (e.g., [ga]). Typically, the infant attends to the initial presentation of the first sound as indexed by a heart-rate decelerative response (the cardiac component of the OR). With repeated trials of the same sound, the infant's attention (OR) to this "familiar" event decreases (habituates). Following habituation, if the infant exhibits recovery of the OR to a novel stimulus presentation, discrimination of the stimulus change may be inferred. The second paradigm, the operant, nonnutritive, high-amplitude sucking (HAS) paradigm, measures the infant's discrimination of a stimulus change in a slightly different manner. In the HAS procedure a particular speech stimulus (e.g., [ba]) is presented contingent upon HAS. As the infant learns that his/her HAS causes the speech sound to be presented,

* Preparation of this manuscript and the research reported herein was supported by USPHS grant RR00167 to the Wisconsin Regional Primate Research Center, by NICHD grant 5-01-HD 03352 to the Wisconsin Mental Retardation Center, and by NICHD grant 1-P01-HD-08240-01 to the author.

the infant typically increases his/her rate of HAS over the successive minutes of the experiment (acquisition). Eventually the infant begins to "habituate" (decrease) the rate of HAS, presumably as this first speech sound loses its reinforcing properties. If the infant's rate of HAS meets a predetermined habituation criterion, the sound is changed (e.g., to [ga]) and recovery of the infant's HAS to the novel stimulus (relative to a no-shift control condition) provides evidence for discrimination of the stimulus contrast.

Using these cardiac and sucking procedures, investigators have asked primarily two different types of questions of the infant's speech discriminative abilities. The first and most basic question is: Can infants even discriminate simple differences in speech sounds? For example, Moffitt[1] employed the heart rate OR habituation/dishabituation paradigm to demonstrate that infants five-to-six months of age *could* discriminate the difference between [ba] and [ga]. Although Moffitt's study demonstrates that the infant can *auditorily* discriminate this contrast, it does not reveal that the infant is responding to these stimuli as belonging to the adult speech categories [ba] and [ga]. Consequently, some investigators have asked a second question of the infant: To what extent are their discriminative abilities organized into adult phonetic categories?

The phenomenon in the adult speech perception literature known as "categorical perception" has provided one way of answering this phonetic question in human infants. Specifically, it is possible with the aid of a synthesizer to generate an acoustic continuum that varies in equal physical steps from [ba] to [da] to [ga]. The construction of the second-formant (F2) transition starting frequency continuum, which is sufficient for these distinctions in place of articulation, is illustrated in FIGURE 1. When stimuli were randomly selected from this continuum and presented to adult subjects for identification, Mattingly *et al.*[2] observed that listeners obligingly sorted the stimuli with the lowest starting F2 frequencies into the [b] category, those with the highest starting F2 frequencies into the [g] category, and the intermediate stimuli into the [d] category. When these same listeners were asked to discriminate pairs of these syllables from this continuum, discrimination was excellent if the two members of the pair were labeled as belonging to *different* phonetic categories (e.g., [ba] vs [da]). However, if a pair with an equivalent acoustic difference in F2 starting frequencies contained members from the *same* phonetic category (e.g., both [ba]), then discrimination of this contrast was near chance. In other words, discrimination *between* categories was excellent, whereas within-category discrimination was extremely poor. This phenomenon, in which discrimination is limited by subjects' abilities to differentially (phonetically) label stimuli, has been referred to as "categorical perception."

If adults categorically perceive speech stimuli along acoustic continua, such as that for the starting frequencies of F2 transitions, then one way of exploring the phonetic aspects of infant speech perception would be to investigate the discrimination of *categorical* differences in speech sounds using either the HAS or cardiac OR paradigm. Accordingly, Eimas[3] recently employed the nonnutritive sucking paradigm to determine if infants two-to-three months of age discriminate contrasts categorically along the same continuum of F2 transitions as shown in FIGURE 1. Eimas found that infants exhibited recovery of their HAS to a between-category change ([dae] vs [gae]), but not to a within-category or control shift. These results indicate that not only are infants able to *auditorily* discriminate differences in place of articulation, but that they do so phonetically, constrained by the adult phonetic categories for place of articulation. In addition, these results suggest that as we attempt to develop an ontogenetic timetable for the perception of various speech contrasts by infants, it is important to ask not only what speech sounds infants can discriminate at different ages, but when is this merely an *auditory* discrimination vs a *phonetic* discrimination.

ONTOGENETIC DEVELOPMENT

Although a reasonably sizeable body of data currently exists on infant speech perception, an attempt to organize these findings into an ontogenetic timetable is frustrated by the paucity of negative discrimination findings. With few exceptions, practically every speech contrast investigated to date has been shown to be discrimin-

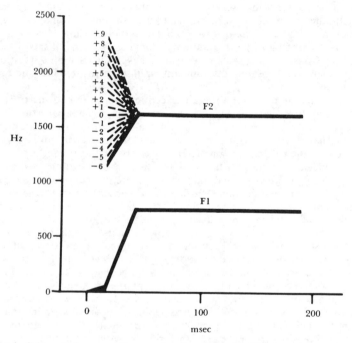

FIGURE 1. Schemata for generating a series of stop-vowel syllables varying in F2 transitions along the place of articulation continuum: (By permission of the publishers of Amer. Scientist.[45])

able within the first two to three months of age. This is not to imply that the infant does not develop any speech perception capabilities beyond the age of two to three months, but it is the case that virtually no developmental trends can be seen in the auditory and phonetic comparisons of the simple syllabic contrasts that have been studied to date.

The major contrasts that infants are able to discriminate at this early age include differences in stop consonants, fricatives, liquids, vowels, and intonation. Differences in place of articulation were found to be *auditorily* discriminable in infants five-to-six months of age,[1] as well as in six-week olds,[4] and to be *phonetically* discriminated in infants two-three months of age.[3] Similarly, contrasts in voicing (e.g., [ba] vs [pa]) have been found to be *auditorily* discriminated by infants 4–17 weeks of age[5] and discriminated *phonetically* by one-month-olds and four-month-olds.[6-8] In addition, Eimas[9] has recently observed that infants two-to-three months of age discriminate categorically the liquid contrast [r] vs [l]. Research on infant vowel discrimination has revealed that infants 4–17 weeks of age can *auditorily* distinguish [i] vs [a] and [i] vs [u].[10] Unlike, however, the categorical discrimination evidenced by infants for stop consonants and liquids, eight-week-olds discriminate the vowels [i] vs [I] continuously or noncategorically, with excellent between- *and* within-category discrimination.[11] This difference in the categorical/continuous discrimination of stops vs vowels is consistent with the adult data for these stimuli. Finally, a number of studies have demonstrated that young infants are capable of making other important auditory discriminations. For example, Morse[4] obtained evidence that six-week-olds were able to discriminate a falling vs rising intonation in the syllable [ba], Eilers and Minifie[12] observed that infants two-to-three months of age discriminated the fricative contrasts [va] vs [sa] and [sa] vs [ʃa], and Miller *et al.*[13] found that three-month-olds discriminated burst cues in the syllables [bu] and [gu].

In summary, these findings reveal that by one-to-three months of age, place of articulation, voicing, and liquids are already discriminated phonetically (i.e., categorically), vowels are continuously discriminated, and other speech contrasts (e.g., fricatives and intonation) are at least auditorily discriminated. Clearly, many important speech contrasts, both segmental and suprasegmental, have not yet been studied in this age range. Except however, for the failure to find discrimination for [sa] vs [za][12] and the absence of more categorical-like perception in vowels (which can be observed in adults under some conditions), no ontogenetic trends are as yet even suggested in the infant speech perception literature. In part, the absence of any major developmental trends in these data is due to the relative ease with which this age group can be tested with the cardiac and sucking paradigms and the particular ages selected for study by each investigator. Consequently, the development of these discriminative capabilities prior to one-to-three months has been largely unexplored. Furthermore, the cardiac and sucking paradigms have been primarily employed in investigating the discrimination of simple syllabic contrasts. *Adult* phonetic abilities, however, are not restricted to such simple contrasts or to the phenomenon of categorical perception. For example, the phonetic event [p] may be signaled by differences in voice-onset-time in [pad] vs [bad], in silence in [slit] vs [split], and in vowel duration in [tab] vs [tap]. Unfortunately, neither the cardiac nor the sucking paradigm is well-suited for studying the development of these more abstract phonetic classification abilities in infants. In contrast, a paradigm that permits two different responses from the infant enables us to study the infant's generalizations to a variety of speech stimuli. A recent study employing a head-turning procedure[14] has suggested one way in which these identification abilities might be examined. With this procedure, four-month-old infants found it easier to associate syllables (learn to turn their head to the same side, e.g., left) when they have the *same* initial consonants (e.g., [pi] and [pu]) rather than different ones (e.g., [pi] and [ka]). Perhaps as additioinal procedures such as this head-turning paradigm are developed, and different and more abstract phonetic questions are asked of infants using a wider variety of speech stimuli, stronger evidence of major ontogenetic trends will emerge during the period of infancy.

PHYLOGENETIC DEVELOPMENT

However, our present inability to construct an ontogenetic time-table of infant speech perception should not detract from the interesting developmental question of *how* these phonetic (i.e., categorical discrimination) abilities become functional by one-to-three months of age. Since data on the *production* of voicing and place of articulation contrasts indicate that these distinctions do not develop until much later in infant speech (e.g. Ref. 15), these phonetic discriminative abilities cannot depend on extensive experience with the articulation of these contrasts. Although no detailed data are available on the frequency with which infants are exposed to these contrasts in their environment prior to one-to-three months of age, recent cross-language studies[16,17,8] have suggested that infants are able to discriminate voicing contrasts that do not occur in the languages of their parents or community. These cross-language observations coupled with the data on the articulatory development of these phonetic contrasts suggest that the infant's auditory system may be equipped at birth to detect these phonetic categories.

Recent observations by Lieberman and his colleagues (e.g. Ref. 18) indicate that man has evolved a very special articulatory system for the production of human speech sounds. Thus, the infant's abilities to detect these phonetic contrasts at such an early age (if not at birth) may reflect the phylogenetic organization of an auditory system that corresponds to the phylogenetic structuring of a unique articulatory system. One way of investigating this phylogenetic explanation for the ontogenetic events described above would be to study the speech-perception abilities of nonhuman primates who lack the ability to produce the range of human speech sounds. Presumably, if the presence of phonetic categories in speech perception depends on a phylogenetic ability to produce human speech, then nonhuman primates should not be constrained in their discrimination of speech by phonetic boundaries. In other words, between-category and within-category discrimination should both be excellent (assuming a sufficiently sensitive auditory system) and *not* differ from each other. In contrast, the human infant should exhibit in a similar study, no within-category discrimination and impressive between-category discrimination.

In an initial test of these hypotheses, two studies of categorical discrimination were conducted, using the same paradigm: one with three-to-five-year-old monkeys[19] and the second with three-to-four-month-old human infants.[20] In view of some of the recent criticisms of the voice-onset-time stimuli employed in demonstrations of infant categorical discrimination,[21] stimuli from the place of articulation continuum for [bae-dae-gae] were selected for both studies. All stimuli were three-formant synthetic syllables which differed in their F2 and F3 transitions and were generated according to the acoustic parameters described in Pisoni.[22] Discrimination was assessed with use of a 20/20 cardiac OR paradigm. In this procedure, the subject is presented with 40 stimuli in a string. The first 20 are repetitions of the same syllable (e.g., [bae]), whereas the second 20 are tokens of a different syllable (e.g., [dae]). Each subject received a between-category, within-category, and control (no change) shift in counterbalanced order across subjects. The orienting response to initial stimulus onset (Stimulus 1) and to the stimulus change (Stimulus 21) was measured for each of the three conditions. In the human-infant study the stimuli were selected from the [dae-gae] portion of the continuum, whereas in the monkey study subjects were presented with stimuli from the categories [bae] and [dae]. In addition, the monkey subjects also received a [bae/gae] contrast. The infants in the human study were administered all three test trials in a single session, seated in an infant seat in a sound-attenuated chamber. In contrast, the rhesus monkey subjects were tested in Lehigh-Valley primate chairs in a sound-attenuated chamber and were tested for several days with a different condition on each day.

The cardiac responses to the stimulus changes for the rhesus subjects are shown in FIGURE 2. Analyses of variance performed on these data for trends over seconds revealed that the between-category condition exhibited reliably more orienting than

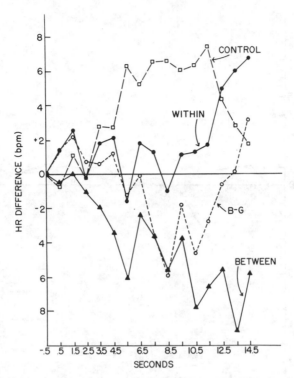

FIGURE 2. Rhesus monkey mean heart-rate difference scores to stimulus change as a function of shift condition. (From Ref. 19.)

the within-category condition *and* that the within-category condition differed reliably from the control condition. These results suggest that rhesus monkeys, despite their inability to produce the full range of human speech sounds, nevertheless discriminate a between-category change in place of articulation better than a within-category change. A detailed discussion of this unexpected finding will be postponed to the following section on Microgenetic Development.

The second aspect of the rhesus monkey data which also proved to be significant was the difference between the within-category condition and the no-change control condition. This finding of within-category discrimination for the same place of articulation contrast has also been recently reported in a reaction-time study with rhesus monkeys by Sinnott.[23] It is tempting to conclude from this result that the within-category discrimination of rhesus monkeys, unlike that of human infants,[3] is not constrained by phonetic categories, thereby permitting within-category discrimination to exceed that of a "chance" (control) level. However, some caution must be exercised in comparing the present rhesus monkey data with those previously collected on human infants.[3] First of all, studies of human *adult* speech perception have suggested that under certain experimental conditions, some within-category information about stop consonants is available to listeners.[24-26] Second, although the infant data on categorical discrimination of place contrasts evidenced no reliable difference between the within-category and control shifts,[3] it was collected using the operant sucking paradigm. Consequently, we cannot be certain that this apparent

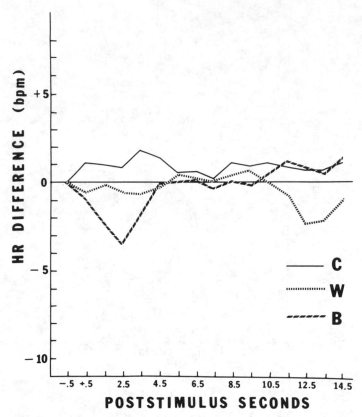

FIGURE 3. Human infant mean heart-rate difference scores to stimulus change (pooled over all three trials) as a function of shift condition. (From Ref. 20.)

superiority in the rhesus monkey's within-category performance is not due to a difference in the sensitivity or "voluntary" characteristics of the cardiac vs HAS paradigms.

In order to determine if human infants are more constrained by phonetic categories in their within-category discrimination than species that have not evolved a special articulatory apparatus for human speech, a similar study was conducted with 24 human infants aged three-to-four months. In the infant experiment, the same 20/20 paradigm was employed and each subject was presented with a between-category, within-category, and control shift. However, since it was also desirable to compare these heart-rate results with the HAS findings of Eimas[3] for place of articulation, the contrast [dae] vs [gae] was selected from the same acoustic continuum employed in the rhesus monkey study. The results for all three conditions averaged over the various orders of presentation are shown in FIGURE 3. Analyses of variance performed on these data (similar to those employed in the rhesus monkey study) revealed only a reliable between-category vs within-category difference and *no* evidence of a significant within-category vs control difference. Furthermore, when only the data for the first trial of the session were examined (n = 8), the same pattern of results emerged. These data are depicted in FIGURE 4. Again, categorical discrimination was substantiated in the trend analyses performed on these data, but no support was found for a reliable within-category vs control-shift difference. Thus, these 20/20 heart rate results not only replicate the Eimas[3] finding of categorical discrimination in infants, using a completely different paradigm, but they also permit a more direct comparison of infant place discrimination with the rhesus monkey findings. A comparison of these two 20/20 heart-rate studies reveals that indeed rhesus monkeys, unlike human infants, do *not* appear to be constrained in their within-category discrimination by phonetic categories. Both populations, however, seem to reflect an appreciation of phonetic categories for place of articulation in their between- vs within-category discrimination. If these phonetic categories are not necessarily a consequence of extensive ontogenetic articulatory or perceptual experience (in the human) or the phylogenetic development of a special articulatory apparatus, then how did categorical discrimination develop in these two primates? Furthermore, within this context, how can we interpret the relative within-category superiority of the rhesus monkey? Recent research on the *microgenetic* development of speech perception suggests some interesting explanations for these phylogenetic and ontogenetic findings that merit our attention.

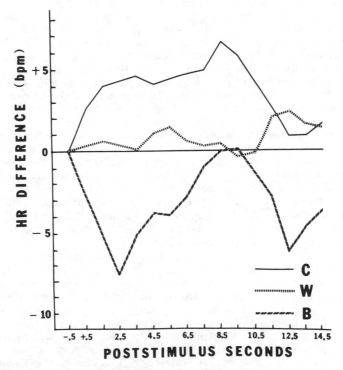

FIGURE 4. Human infant mean heart-rate difference scores to stimulus change (for first trial only) as a function of shift condition. (From Ref. 20.)

MICROGENETIC DEVELOPMENT

Microgenetic development for H. Werner (Langer[27]) referred to "short-term individual development" of the type involved in the development of a percept as an individual observes an object. In more recent times, we have come to refer to these short-term developmental aspects of perception and cognition as "stages of information processing." However, the term "microgenetic" will be retained in the present discussion because it reminds us of yet a third aspect of development (over experimental or situational time) that is critical for our understanding of the total "development" of speech perception in humans (also cf. Ref. 28 for a further discussion of its relevance to infant speech perception). Two aspects of the microgenetic development of speech perception, which are pertinent to our understanding of the rhesus monkey and human infant data on categorical discrimination, include research on (1) early stages of sensory processing of speech sounds, and (2) the role of memory factors in speech perception. In addition, both aspects of microgenetic development provide us with important new ways of viewing the ontogenetic findings presented earlier.

Research on the early stages of the sensory processing of speech sounds has recently suggested hypothetical neurophysiological mechanisms that may help to explain the categorical-like discrimination observed in human infants and rhesus monkeys. With the introduction into the adult speech perception literature of the selective adaptation paradigm,[29] a number of studies have implicated the existence of feature detector mechanisms analogous to those found in the visual and auditory systems of other species. These feature detectors or analyzers are presumed to be finely tuned to a variety of features in human speech (e.g., voiced/voiceless; bilabial/alveolar/velar). In the selective adaptation paradigm adult listeners are initially asked to identify stimuli randomly selected from an acoustic continuum (e.g., the voice-onset-time continuum underlying the [ba-pa] voicing distinction). In a subsequent session these same subjects are presented with several trials of one-minute repetitions of an adapting stimulus (e.g., [ba]) followed by four or five stimuli to be identified from the test (e.g., voicing) continuum. The typical outcome of this adaptation procedure is a *shift* in the phonetic boundary closest to the category of the adapting stimulus. For example, if the adapting stimulus is [ba], stimuli which were previously identified as [ba], but which are close to the [ba-pa] boundary, would now be categorized as [pa]. If the initial location of the phonetic boundary in listeners' identification responses is determined by the point along the underlying continuum where the feature detectors for both [ba] and [pa] respond with equal strength, then a shift in the boundary *toward* the adapting stimulus may reflect the fatiguing of the feature detector appropriate to the adapting stimulus and thus a shift in the point of equilibrium between the two feature detectors.

This indirect evidence for man's possession of feature detector mechanisms that respond to properties of human speech sounds suggests a possible explanation for the human infant and rhesus monkey categorical discrimination findings. If human adults possess these hypothetical neurophysiological detector mechanisms in their auditory systems, it is not unreasonable to presume that they are equipped with them from birth.[30] Furthermore, if the cardiac and sucking discrimination paradigms result in sufficient adaptation of the preshift stimulus, then categorical discrimination within these paradigms may be consequence of a within-category shift activating the *same* feature detector and a between-category shift activating a *different* feature detector. Eimas[8] has, in fact, recently proposed that the sucking paradigm does involve adaptation of the preshift stimulus and that the between- vs within-category difference observed in HAS studies of voicing and place of articulation may be attributed to the adaptation of feature detectors for these contrasts.

Although Eimas' proposal does provide an attractive explanation for the HAS sucking data on categorical discrimination in *early* infancy, considerably more research must be carried out on the adaptation paradigm before we can accept this interpretation of the infant data. For example, we do not yet know if *adaptation* of these feature detectors in the infant is necessary for the cardiac and sucking measures of categorical discrimination. Perhaps some direct tests of the adaptation procedure in conjunction with the variations of the cardiac or sucking paradigms using adult and/or infant subjects might shed more light on the importance of adaptation for these measures of speech discrimination. In addition, there is currently considerable debate in the adaptation literature whether feature detectors exist at auditory and/or phonetic levels of processing (cf. Ref. 31 for a more detailed discussion of this controversy). Evidence favoring *phonetic* feature detectors derives from the reliable boundary shifts observed for adapting stimuli which differ acoustically from the test continuum.[32,33] Evidence for *auditory* feature detector systems is based upon studies by Ades,[34] and Tarttar and Eimas,[35] which have shown that adaptation with *nonspeech* sounds containing various portions of the relevant acoustic information also yield significant shifts in phonetic boundaries. Indeed, it is quite likely that both auditory *and* phonetic levels of feature detectors are functional in man. This concern, however, over the levels of feature detectors should not detract from the relevant finding that adaptation procedures *do* result in reliable shifts in both the adult identification and discrimination boundaries for stimuli along the [bae-dae-gae] continuum.[36,37] The possibility that this effect may be in part attributable to the adaptation of auditory rather than phonetic feature detectors (e.g., Ref. 35) does not reduce the explanatory usefulness of feature detector mechanisms for the human infant and rhesus monkey results. In fact, the possibility that these adaptation effects may in part be due to auditory feature detectors increases the attractiveness of a feature-detector account for the rhesus monkey categorical-like discrimination data. One such account has recently been offered by Stevens.[38]

Stevens has proposed three types of feature detectors that might be sufficient to account for the categorization of [bae], [dae], and [gae]: (1) a detector responding to an upward shift in the frequency spectrum ([bae]), (2) a detector responding to a downward shift in the frequency spectrum ([dae]), and (3) a detector responsive to both an upward (F3) and a downward (F2) shift in the frequency spectrum ([gae]). According to such a model, discrimination may be expected to be relatively poor if two stimuli share the same acoustic features (e.g., an upward shift in the frequency spectrum), and better if they have different acoustic features (e.g., in between-category changes). Inspection of the F2 and F3 transition values employed in the rhesus moneky[19] and human infant[20] studies reveals that the within-category conditions of both studies would activate the *same* auditory feature detector pre- and postshift, whereas the between-category conditions would generally activate *different* auditory feature detectors.† In sum, an auditory feature detector model, such as that

---

† However, since it is necessary to make one assumption regarding the relative weighting of the F2 and F3 transitions for one of the stimuli employed in the rhesus monkey study, this account of the categorical discrimination observed in the rhesus monkeys needs to be replicated with other synthetic stimuli. Furthermore, since different contrasts along the same acoustic (place) continuum were employed in the rhesus monkey and human infant studies, the use of additional synthetic contrasts in studies of monkeys' speech perception would also extend the generality of these particular categorical-like findings (vis à vis the infants').

proposed by Stevens, might account for the categorical discrimination of the place of articulation contrasts [bae-dae-gae] in rhesus monkeys and human infants in terms of property detectors which may be characteristic of the primate auditory systems and *not* unique to humans. Inspection of rhesus monkey calls (e.g., Ref. 39) reveals instances of rapid shifts in the frequency spectrum for which such auditory feature analyzers might well be important in rhesus communication. In addition, recent research by Miller and his associates with chinchillas (e.g., Ref. 40) has suggested that under certain training conditions other nonhuman mammals besides the rhesus macaque are able to generalize their identifications of synthetic stop consonants in an adult-like categorical manner. Thus, *auditory* feature analyzers that permit the categorical discrimination of stop consonants may conceivably be a property of the mammalian auditory system, rather than unique to a species that has evolved the ability to produce the range of human speech.

Although feature analyzers that operate during the early stages of the sensory processing of speech sounds provide an attractive explanation for the categorical discrimination data observed in these two studies, how can we also account for the within-category discrimination differences exhibited in the monkey and infant? First of all, evidence that phonetic categories such as the [bae], [dae], and [gae] of the present studies may be coded in terms of complex auditory properties (e.g., rising or falling shifts in the energy spectrum) should not overshadow the vast amounts of evidence which demonstrate that human adults do make use of phonetic categories in *other* speech perception tasks.‡ Specifically, research on short-term memory (STM) for speech sounds (presumably a somewhat later stage than feature analysis in the microgenetic development of speech perception), has helped to clarify the role of phonetic categories in the categorical perception of adults. Fujisaki and Kawashima[41] and Pisoni[42,43] have proposed that listeners' categorical discrimination of vowel stimuli depends upon the relative availability of *auditory* vs *phonetic* STM in the experimental task. Accordingly, if the vowel stimuli are relatively long in duration and no long silent intervals intervene in the comparison task presented to the listener, thereby giving the listener relatively good access to auditory STM for vowels, then vowels such as [i] and [I] have been found to be less categorically discriminated. In contrast, shorter duration vowels separated by sizable silent interstimulus intervals force the listener to rely more on phonetic (categorized) STM, and thus these stimuli are more categorically discriminated. Unlike vowels, stop consonants do not generally yield within-category discrimination (availability of auditory STM) using these same variations in experimental conditions (e.g., Ref. 22). However, recent research by Pisoni and Tash[25] and Eimas and Miller[26] has suggested that under *some* experimental conditions within-category information (auditory STM) for consonants may be available to adult listeners. The within-category discrimination observed for rhesus monkeys in both the present study and in Sinnott's[23] experiment, *may* reflect the lack of phonetic STM in monkeys, thereby resulting in only an auditory STM of the preshift stimulus. In contrast, the human infants may rely on a phonetic STM for these consonants within the 20/20 paradigm, thereby resulting in no within-category discrimination.

‡It will be recalled that phonetic categorization has also been demonstrated in a few adaptation studies which have revealed significant adaptation effects for adapting stimuli that shared phonetic but not acoustic features with the test continuum. Thus, the possibility cannot be dismissed that some of the infant's feature detectors may also be tuned to phonetic as well as auditory features.

Although this interpretation is currently somewhat speculative, it does suggest that an understanding of the infant's *development* of speech perception must consider the roles of auditory and phonetic STM in categorical discrimination. More specifically, attention needs to be paid to the memory constraints of different infant discrimination paradigms and how the infant's discrimination of various speech contrasts (e.g., consonants vs vowels) is systematically affected by different paradigms. Two infant studies recently conducted in our laboratory illustrate the significance of these considerations. Evidence for the possible importance of the memory constraints of cardiac OR paradigms was suggested in a recent study by Miller *et al.*[13] on infant burst discrimination. In this study, infants three-to-four months of age did not discriminate a consonantal contrast ([bu] vs [gu]) signaled by a burst cue when tested with an habituation/dishabituation cardiac OR paradigm. Despite the significant habituation observed in the habituation/dishabituation paradigm, the long intertrial interval between the last preshift stimulus and the novel stimulus (26 seconds) may have been too long to sustain discrimination of this cue in infants at this age. However, burst discrimination of this contrast *was* evidenced when the long intertrial intervals were removed and infants were tested with the 20/20 paradigm employed in the rhesus monkey and human infant studies. Although this study did not examine the importance of these factors for cardiac measures of categorical discrimination, a second study recently completed in our laboratory[44] explored the possible roles of auditory vs phonetic STM in infant vowel discrimination as measured by the sucking paradigm. Since the eight-week-old infants in the Swoboda *et al.*[11] study discriminated 240 msec vowels continuously, Swoboda *et al.*[44] presented the infants of the same age, using the same HAS procedures, with shorter (60 msec) [i] and [I] vowels. In contrast to the results obtained for the long vowels, infants in this study discriminated a between-category change but *not* the within-category change in the vowels [i] vs [I]. However, since the difference between these two conditions did not prove to be reliable, these findings can be considered only suggestive of the relatively poor availability of auditory STM for short vowels. Perhaps older infants tested under these same conditions *will* exhibit relatively more reliance on their phonetic STM for these stimuli than eight-week-olds.

CONCLUDING REMARKS

In summary, a complete understanding of the *development* of infant speech perception requires not only research guided by efforts to construct an ontogenetic timetable of the infant's speech discriminative abilities, but investigations of the phylogenetic bases of these ontogenetic abilities, and much more concern for how the microgenetic development of speech perception affects our assessment of ontogenetic and phylogenetic development. The data presented in this paper on the categorical discrimination of place of articulation in rhesus monkeys and human infants illustrates the importance of considering phylogenetic and microgenetic aspects of development in explaining the origin of some of the infant's phonetic capabilities. In addition to continuing to explore the upper bounds of the infant's "phonetic" perceptual abilities, considerable research is now needed on the roles played by feature detectors, the adaptation of feature detectors, and short-term memory processes in the assessment of infant and non-human primate speech discrimination. Only then we will be able to appreciate fully the significance of a study demonstrating categorical discrimination in human infants.

ACKNOWLEDGMENTS

Special thanks are due to F. S. Cooper and A. M. Liberman for the generous use of the Haskins Laboratories' facilities and to D. B. Pisoni for making his synthetic stimuli available to us.

REFERENCES

1. MOFFITT, A. R. 1971. Consonant cue perception by twenty-to-twenty-four-week-old infants. Child Devel. **42:** 717–731.
2. MATTINGLY, I. G., A. M. LIBERMAN, A. K. SYRDAL & T. HALWES. 1971. Discrimination in speech and nonspeech modes. Cognitive Psychol. **2:** 131–157.
3. EIMAS, P. D. 1974. Auditory and linguistic processing of cues for place of articulation by infants. Perception & Psychophys.: **16:** 513–521.
4. MORSE, P. A. 1972. The discrimination of speech and nonspeech stimuli in early infancy. J. Exp. Child Psychol. **14:** 477–492.
5. TREHUB, S. E. & M. S. RABINOVITCH. 1972. Auditory-linguistic sensitivity in early infancy. Developmental Psychol. **6:** 74–77.
6. EIMAS, P. D., E. R. SIQUELAND, P. JUSZYCK & J. VIGORITO. 1971. Speech perception in infants. Science, **171:** 303–306.
7. MILLER, J. 1974. Phonetic determination of infant speech perception. Unpublished doctoral dissertation. Univ. of Minnesota. Minneapolis, Minn.
8. EIMAS, P. D. 1975. Developmental studies of speech perception. *In* Infant Perception: from Sensation to Cognition. Vol. II. L. B. Cohen and P. Salapatek, Eds.: 193–231. Academic Press. New York, N.Y.
9. EIMAS, P. D. 1975. Auditory and phonetic coding of the cues for speech discrimination of the [r l] distinction in young infants. Perception & Psychophys. **18:** 341–347.
10. TREHUB, S. E. 1973. Infant's sensitivity to vowel and tonal contrasts. Developmental Psychol. **9:** 91–96.
11. SWOBODA, P. J., P. A. MORSE & L. A. LEAVITT. 1976. Continuous vowel discrimination in normal and at risk infants. Child Devel. **47:** 459–465.
12. EILERS, R. & F. MINIFIE. Fricative discrimination in early infancy. J. Speech Hearing Res. **18:** 158–167.
13. MILLER, C. L., P. A. MORSE & M. F. DORMAN. 1975. Infant speech perception, memory, and the cardiac orienting response. Paper presented at Soc. for Research in Child Development, Denver, Colo. April, 1975.
14. FODOR, J. A., M. F. GARRETT & S. L. BRILL. 1975. Pi ka pu: The perception of speech sounds by prelinguistic infants. Perception & Psychophys.: **18:** 74–78.
15. KEWLEY-PORT, D. & M. S. PRESTON. 1974. Early apical stop production: A voice onset time analysis. J. Phonetics **2:** 195–210.
16. STREETER, L. 1976. Language perception of 2-month-old infants shows effects of both innate mechanisms and experience. *Nature* **259:** 39–41.
17. LASKY, R., A. SYRDAL-LASKY & R. KLEIN. 1975. VOT discrimination by four-to-six-month-old infants from Spanish environments. J. Exp. Child Psychol. **20:** 215–225.
18. LIEBERMAN, P. 1974. On the evolution of language: A unified view. Cognition **3:** 59–94.
19. MORSE, P. A. & C. T. SNOWDON. 1975. An investigation of categorical speech discrimination by rhesus monkeys. Perception & Psychophys. **17:** 9–16.
20. MILLER, C. L. & P. A. MORSE. The "heart" of categorical speech discrimination in young infants. J. Speech Hearing Res. In press.
21. STEVENS, K. & D. KLATT. 1974. The role of formant transitions in the voiced-voiceless distinction for stops. J. Acoustical Soc. Amer. **55:** 653–659.
22. PISONI, D. B. 1971. On the nature of categorical perception of speech sounds. Unpublished doctoral dissertation. Univ. of Michigan. Ann Arbor, Mich.
23. SINNOTT, J. M. 1974. A comparison of speech sound discrimination in humans and monkeys. Unpublished doctoral dissertation. Univ. of Michigan. Ann Arbor, Mich.

24. BARCLAY, J. R. Noncategorical perception of a voiced stop: a replication. Perception & Psychophys. **11:** 269–273.
25. PISONI, D. B. & J. Tash. 1974. Reaction times to comparisons within and across phonetic categories. Perception & Psychophys. **15:** 285–290.
26. EIMAS, P. D. & J. L. MILLER. 1975. Auditory memory and the processing of speech. P. D. Eimas Progress Report No. 3: 117–135. Developmental studies of speech perception. Department of Psychology. Brown University. Providence, R. I.
27. LANGER, J. 1970. Werner's comparative organismic theory. *In* Carmichael's Manual of Child Psychology. 3rd edit. Vol. I. P. Mussen, Ed.: 771–773. John Wiley & Sons. New York, N.Y.
28. MORSE, P. A. 1974. Infant speech perception: A preliminary model and review of the literature. *In* Language Perspectives: Acquisition, Retardation, and Intervention. R. Schiefelbusch and L. Lloyd, Eds.: 19–53. Univ. Park Press, Baltimore, Md.
29. EIMAS, P. D. & J. D. CORBIT. 1973. Selective adaptation of linguistic feature detectors. Cognitive Psychol. **4:** 109.
30. EIMAS, P. D. 1974. Linguistic processing of speech by young infants. *In* Language Perspectives: Acquisition, Retardation, and Intervention. R. Schiefelbusch and L. Lloyd, Eds.: 55–73. Univ. Park Press, Baltimore, Md.
31. COOPER, W. E. 1975. Selective adaptation to speech. In F. Restle, R. M. Shiffrin, N. J. Castellan, B. Landman, and D. B. Pisoni (Eds.), Cognitive Theory, Vol. I. Potomac, Md.: Erlbaum, pp. 23–54.
32. COOPER, W. E. 1974. Selective adaptation for acoustic cues of voicing in initial stops. J. Phonetics. **2:** 303–313.
33. DIEHL, R. H. The effect of selective adaptation on the identification of speech sounds. Perception & Psychophys. **17:** 48–52.
34. ADES, A. E. Some effects of adaptation on speech perception. MIT Res. Lab Electr. Quart. Progr. Rep., 1973, **111:** 121–129.
35. TARTTAR, V. C. & P. D. EIMAS. 1975. The role of auditory feature detectors in the perception of speech. Perception & Psychophys. **18:** 293–298.
36. COOPER, W. E. 1974. Adaptation of phonetic feature analyzers for place of articulation. J. Acoustical Soc. Amer. **56:** 617–628.
37. COOPER, W. E. & S. E. BLUMSTEIN. 1974. A labial feature analyzer in speech perception. Perception & Psychophys. **15:** 591–600.
38. STEVENS, K. 1973. Potential role of property detectors in the perception of consonants. M.I.T. Research Laboratory of Electronics Quarterly Progress Report **110:** 155–168.
39. ROWELL, T. & R. HINDE. 1962. Vocal communication by the rhesus monkey (*Macaca mulatta*). Proc. Zoological Soc. [London] **138:** 279–294.
40. KUHL, P. K. & J. D. MILLER. 1975. Speech perception by the chinchilla: voiced-voiceless distinction in alveolar plosive consonants. Science **190:** 69–72.
41. FUJISAKI, H. & T. KAWASHIMA. 1969. On the modes and mechanisms of speech perception. Annual Report Engineering Research Institute. Vol. 28: 67–73.
42. PISONI, D. B. 1973. Auditory and phonetic memory codes in the discrimination of consonants and vowels. Perception & Psychophys. **13:** 253–260.
43. PISONI, D. B. 1975. Auditory short-term memory and vowel perception. Memory and Cognition. **3:** 7–18.
44. SWOBODA, P. J., J. KASS, P. A. MORSE & L. A. LEAVITT. Memory factors in infant vowel discrimination. In preparation.
45. MATTINGLY, I. G. 1972. Speech cues and sign stimuli. Amer. Scientist **60:** 327–337.

AUDITORY PERCEPTION AND SPEECH EVOLUTION*

Richard M. Warren

Department of Psychology
University of Wisconsin-Milwaukee
Milwaukee, Wisconsin 53201

To what extent do auditory perceptual mechanisms used for processing speech reflect prelinguistic capacities shared with lower animals, and to what extent have basically new capacities developed capable of handling speech? First, consider the range of frequencies carrying the information necessary for speech comprehension. Frequencies from 200 to 5000 Hz suffice for excellent intelligibility. This range is well within the hearing capacity of other mammals and primates of today,[1] and presumably was within the range available to our prelinguistic primate ancestors as well.

Of course, speech does not consist of the simple sinusoidal tones used in audiometric determinations of frequency sensitivity, and it can be asked whether primates and other mammals can distinguish between the complex sounds used in speech. Dewson, *et al.*[2] have shown that rhesus monkeys could be taught to distinguish between /i/ and /u/, and were able to transfer this discrimination from a male voice with a fundamental frequency of 136 Hz to a female voice with a fundamental frequency of 212 Hz. The ability to distinguish between vowels is not limited to primates. Burdick and Miller[3] found that chinchillas could learn to distinguish between /a/ and /i/ not only for different vowel productions by the same talker, but could generalize this discrimination to vowel statements by different talkers, changes in pitch level, and changes in intensity.

Since extended speech sounds can be differentiated by animals that are themselves incapable of producing such sounds, it appears probable that our ancestors had the potential for discriminating speech sounds we now use before they could produce them. In addition to discriminating between relatively steady individual sounds, human speech comprehension requires discrimination between durations, types of transitions linking sounds, and permuted orders. As we shall see, other animals are quite capable of making each of these distinctions. Is there then any uniquely human ability in perception of auditory sequences? I will argue that some widely held views concerning sequence perception of humans are not valid, and that we possess two fundamentally different types of perceptual mechanisms for discrimination of sequences, whereas other animals possess only one of these types.

Let us first consider the nature of verbal sequences. The rate at which phonemes occur in discourse has been used as a measure of auditory resolving power for speech. Efron[4] gave a rate for normal English speech of 120–150 words/minute, which, according to his calculations, corresponds to an average of 12 or 13 phonemes/ second or 80 msec/phoneme. Lenneberg[5] analyzed the speech rate of three newscasters, who presumably spoke at a somewhat faster rate than in ordinary discourse, and derived an average of about 14 phonemes/second (although Lenneberg noted that with common phrases or clichés, rates of 20 phonemes/second or 50 msec/phoneme can be achieved). Of course, durations of individual phonemes vary considerably, and these figures are statistical averages.

*Preparation of this paper, and part of the research described, was supported by the National Science Foundation (grant BMS73–06786), the National Institutes of Health (grant HDO7855), and the University of Wisconsin-Milwaukee Graduate School.

These values agree with those offered by Joos for speech.[6] He suggested that intelligibility is lost at about 20 phonemes/second since a "time smear" of 50 msec prevents any greater resolution. This smear did not have a sharp upper limit, according to Joos, with some difficulty still encountered at 100 or even 150 msec/phoneme. He considered that metathesis is produced by this time smear, and that there is an especial tendency for sounds to be perceptually transposed when acoustically similar—such as "emnity" being heard as "enmity." However, it should be noted that average durations shorter than 50 msec can be achieved with compressed speech before intelligibility is lost.[7]

Roughly comparable calculations have been made for the complex sequences of music. Fraisse[8] noted that notes employed in melodic themes had durations down to 150 msec, and Winckel[9] stated that the rate of separate notes could be as high as 20/second or 50 msec/note before metathesis occurred.

When simple two-item sequences of unrelated sounds such as noise and tone were used, Hirsh[10] and Hirsh and Sherrick[11] found that reporting of order was possible down to about 20 msec/item, with other laboratories generally reporting somewhat higher values from about 30 to 60 msec (see Fay[12] for review).

The evidence discussed thus far for speech, music, and arbitrarily selected sounds seems fairly consistent. It has suggested to many investigators that we have a general ability to detect the order of auditory events, which (depending upon conditions) could operate on successive sounds with a lower limit of roughly 20–50 msec, and which is essential for intelligibility of speech. Observing that cortical lesions producing aphasia also interfered with detection of temporal order of pairs of tones, Efron[4] has suggested that time analysis, sequencing, and accurate speech perception were each functions dependent upon the same region of the cortex and its interconnections. Swisher and Hirsh[13] confirmed essential aspects from Efron's observations, and concluded that difficulties in temporal ordering of items in sequences and aphasia were parts of a common syndrome.

Some evidence, however, does not conform to this general scheme, representing, at the least, puzzling exceptions requiring special explanations.

One of these curious observations was reported by Ladefoged[14] and Ladefoged and Broadbent.[15] They found that brief extraneous sounds could not be localized in sentences, listeners sometimes missing the true position by a few words. A related observation has been reported for tonal sequences by Heise and Miller,[16] who noted that tones could each be perceived in an ordered pattern only as long as frequencies of neighboring items were close together; if one member of the series had a very different frequency, it would seem to pop out of the sequence and could not be localized relative to its neighbors. These difficulties in detection of temporal order have usually been attributed to special rules maintaining temporal coherence in speech and music.

Another curious observation concerning detection of temporal order was made by Warren,[17] using recycled sequences of nonrelated sounds, and it is this observation which is largely responsible for further experiments leading to the hypotheses concerning sequence perception in man and other animals to be developed in this paper. The initial observation was made with use of a tape loop formed by splicing together four 200 msec segments of recorded steady statements of separate sounds consisting of a tone, a hiss, a buzz, and a vowel. When played back, the four items were heard in a fixed order, which was repeated over and over. Subjects listened as long as they wished, and named the order starting with whichever sound they chose (there were six possible arrangements). The finding of interest was that even though each of the sounds could be identified clearly, the order could not be detected. It was not that any particular wrong order was perceived by the listener, but rather that a decision could not be reached concerning which sound preceded or followed another with any degree of confidence, even though the duration of each sound was considerably greater than the values that were generally accepted as permitting detection of temporal order.

However, a repeated sequence of four successive stimuli could be ordered correctly when each stimulus was a 200-msec word. As part of the initial study, a tape was prepared consisting of four spoken digits repeated over and over, each complete statement of the four items taking 800 msec. In order to avoid transitional cues to order, each digit was recorded separately, and the sequence spliced together. Although each of the digits is itself complex, requiring proper phonemic ordering within digits, correct identification was accomplished with ease by all listeners.

The last part of the initial study dealt with identification of temporal order for vowels. Sequences of four vowels were prepared by cutting 200 msec segments from longer steady statements of each vowel, and splicing the segments into a loop which repeated them without pauses. It was somewhat difficult for the untrained listeners to judge the order, even though performance of the group of 30 subjects was significantly above chance. It was easier when each vowel was reduced to 150 msec with 50 msec of silence between items, and it was easiest of all with single statements of each vowel with natural onset and decay characteristics for each statement, each vowel again lasting about 150 msec with 50 msec silences.[17] Subsequent work by Thomas *et al.*[18] with recycled sequences of four synthesized vowels led them to conclude that the ease of identifying temporal order was a possible way of measuring the speech-like quality of synthetic speech sounds.

Later studies in my laboratory investigated the influence of experimental procedure upon temporal limits for naming of order with recycled sequences containing three or four unrelated items.[19-21] In general, the threshold for identification of order remained well above 200 msec for such extended sequences with untrained subjects. As long as listeners received no information concerning the accuracy of their responses, practice did not help much.

It should be emphasized that these lower limits for the identification of order do not correspond to thresholds for temporal discrimination. Listeners can distinguish between patterns with permuted orders much more readily than they can name the order of items within these patterns. Wilcox *et al.*[22] and Warren[23-25] found that subjects could tell whether two sequences presented successively had their component items in the same or different order when the items in each sequence lasted between 100 and 200 msec.

It has been shown by other studies that thresholds for Same/Different judgments with permuted orders consisting of three recycled items, or consisting of two or three sounds each presented once, could be accomplished for item durations as low as 5 or 10 msec.[23,26,27] At durations below 5 or 10 msec the individual items are too brief to be identified as separate sounds, and discrimination between temporal arrangements can be considered as a problem in pitch or phase perception. Thus, Green[28] has used sounds having a constant energy spectrum but varying in phase spectrum (*Huffman sequences*), and has shown that differences in phase with these special stimuli can be discriminated down to one or two msec by trained listeners.

These experiments demonstrating recognition of permuted orders of nonrelated sounds at durations too brief to allow naming of order seem to have implications applicable to other types of auditory sequences, including speech. But before turning to speech, let us consider other aspects of sequence perception with nonrelated sounds.

I found that Same/Different discrimination of order with nonrelated sounds was not possible if the sequences to be compared differed somewhat in duration of items.[23,25] Such matching of pairs of four-item recycled sequences could be made by untrained subjects at levels significantly better than chance when the items in each sequence lasted 200 msec. But, when one sequence had each individual sound kept at 200 msec, and the other had durations decreased to 160 msec or increased to 415 msec, accurate Same/Different judgments of order could not be made. The limited temporal disparity permitting matching of auditory patterns is in contrast to the wide range of size differences and asymmetrical perspective transformations permitting matching of spatial patterns in vision.

A recent series of experiments was designed using a tentative hierarchical scheme for classifying discrimination of temporal order by humans.[23,27] The four ranks in this scheme are presented in order of increasing levels, with mastery at one task level considered to permit performance at all lower levels: (1) Same/Different judgments with sequences to be compared separated by a period of less than one second (so that the requisite time for information storage is well within the generally accepted limits for raw acoustic storage or *echoic* memory); (2) Same/Different judgments with sequences to be compared separated by intervals up to several seconds; (3) absolute judgments or identification using separate verbal labels for each of the sequential permutations (this level requires that a distinctive verbal label be attached to each sequence); (4) naming of order of component items within each of the sequential permutations (the naming of order can be considered a special type of absolute judgment in which the verbal label consists of ordered terms for each of the component items). Using recycled and nonrecycled sequences derived from a tone, a square-wave, and broad-band noise, it was found that subjects could be trained readily to achieve excellent performance at Levels (1), (2), and (3) with item durations from either 5 or 10 msec through 200 msec. (At item durations above roughly 200 msec, Level (4) can be reached without training.)

Performance at Level (3) (absolute judgments involving the use of learned verbal labels distinguishing between permuted orders of items) could be accomplished using any designated names for the sequences, but those actually provided to listeners were the names of the component sounds in their proper order.[23,27] Hence, operationally, they were performing at Level (4) with item durations as low as 5 msec, even though they could not name the order without special training, and were responding correctly only by rote when they recognized the overall pattern. As we shall see, there is reason to believe that many experiments in the literature designed to measure thresholds for naming of order (see Fay[12] for review) provided opportunities for some degree of unintended training, so that subjects were performing by rote at the reported thresholds and could not perceive directly the order of components. This suggestion is similar to that of Broadbent and Ladefoged,[29] who observed that detection of order within sequences at brief item durations seemed to be accomplished through *quality* differences which appeared following practice. A kind of self-training may occur when subjects, presented first with long item durations for which unaided naming of order is possible, are then presented with series of stimuli having decreasing item durations. Since permuted arrangements of sequences can be distinguished at item durations too brief for naming of order,[23,27] and since sequences differing slightly in item duration may also be compared for identity or difference in *quality* corresponding to order of components, a verbal label describing the order within the sequence having longer item durations may be identified with, and transferred to, the sequence with shorter item durations. By a series of successive generalizations to ever shorter items, a level can be reached which is well below the threshold possible without training. Using this procedure for threshold training in an unpublished study, I found it possible to obtain correct identification of order in recycled three-item sequences down to 10 msec item durations without communicating information concerning the order directly to the subject. For optimal training with this procedure, the steps employed for decreasing threshold mastery for naming order should be quite small. (Successive steps decreasing between 10% and 25% seem to be within the duration disparity permitting direct comparison of patterns by experienced listeners.) As we shall see, identification of phonemic components of speech in their proper order also appears to be accomplished indirectly through prior identification of familiar complex patterns, indicating that humans use the same perceptual strategy for identification of order of components with verbal and nonverbal sequences.

The holistic perceptual groupings recognized by listeners may be considered as *temporal compounds*; that is, an aggregation of auditory items into groupings having special holistic characteristics. Temporal compound formation in some ways is analogous to compound formation in chemistry. When elements are combined in certain lawful manners, a compound is formed having specific properties that do not reflect in an additive fashion those of the constituent elements. A particular compound may be distinguished from others, but it may not be possible (or generally desirable) for an observer to analyze these compounds into their elements directly. However, if the names of components and their arrangement have been learned earlier, than a two-stage process can be used if required: first, identification of the compound; second, recall of the preestablished analytical description. We have seen that temporal compounds can be formed readily in the laboratory with use of arbitrarily selected groups of sounds, and it seems that perception of speech and music may also involve the general ability to recognize holistically salient characteristics in the acoustic groupings of several sounds. While any two signals considered as examples of the same temporal compound are rarely exact repetitions, as noted earlier, a limited but measurable degree of durational flexibility is permitted for elements forming the temporal compound.[25] Also, environmental signals are almost inevitably mixed with irrelevant simultaneous sounds, and equivalent mechanisms seem to be used to minimize masking by such sounds both for speech and for nonspeech signals. One of these mechanisms, involving a detailed comparison of the simultaneous phase and intensity of spectral components delivered to the two ears, results in the well-studied "masking level difference," sometimes called "intelligibility level difference" for speech.[30] Another mechanism permits the use of context, together with a detailed spectral comparison of the actual noise with the anticipated signal, to restore sounds completely obscured by brief loud noises (this has been called auditory induction for the general case,[31] and phonemic restoration when speech is involved[32]).

The temporal compounds in speech perception may function in some ways as the perceptual units for speech. There is evidence from experiments with identification times that the size of these units can be considered for some purposes as syllabic or larger. Savin and Bever[33] and Warren[34] reported that identification time for phonemes is longer than for the entire syllables containing the phonemes. Thus, identification of a component phoneme takes longer than identification of a syllable containing the phoneme when the syllable is: (1) a member of a nonsense syllable list; (2) a member of a word list; or (3) a word in a sentence. It might be thought that phonemic identification and syllabic identification are parallel rather than serial processes, with the less familiar task of identifying component phonemes taking a bit longer. Warren,[34] however, varied the context of sentences so as to accelerate or retard the identification of a word, and found that the times required for identification of constituent phonemes were changed correspondingly. This study also measured identification time for letter targets in the spelling of auditory stimuli, and provided evidence that letter identification and phoneme identification are fundamentally different processes, each based on prior word identification.

The phonemic restoration effect provides additional evidence that phonemes are not perceived directly. When a speech sound is replaced by a louder noise, it is "heard" clearly, and the phoneme perceptually synthesized on the basis of context cannot be distinguished from those speech sounds physically present.[32,35,36] Thus, both types of phonemes (actual and restored) were perceptually equivalent in the judgment of listeners. This equivalence is consistent with the hypothesis that all phonemes are in a sense synthetic, being inferred following recognition and identification of the larger pattern. Since this model does not consider speech perception to proceed sound by sound, it would not be anticipated that noises within sentences could be localized accurately relative to phonemes. Accurate temporal ordering of brief sounds is to be expected only in cases of sounds forming part of the same temporal compound. In keeping with the model, listeners do not perceive the extraneous sound to be clearly at any particular location, but rather located within a sort of *temporal smear* coexisting with a portion of the sentence.

Then what is the role of individual phonemes, if they are not perceived as such during speech, and are derived following recognition of syllables and words? It would seem that while phonemes are constructs useful for transcribing and analyzing, they are without direct perceptual basis. Perhaps as suggested by some linguists (see Lüdtke[37]), phonemes are fictitious units based on alphabetic writing. It is reasonable and useful to base alphabets upon the limited number of discrete articulatory positions that speakers can identify when slowly and analytically producing fragments of speech. Of course, having once been established, spelling can diverge from pronunciation. While both phonetic symbols and graphemes are extremely useful for transcribing speech, neither appear to correspond to any organizational stage used in the perceptual processing leading to comprehension of speech. Many unnecessary difficulties for theories of speech perception seem to have resulted from confusing the units for transcribing with the units for perceiving speech. To take one example, a plosive such as the phoneme /p/ has articulatory significance but a protean acoustic signature, requiring a neighboring phoneme in order to exist and exhibit an appropriate acoustic form. Yet considerable speculation has been expended on the nature and behavior of "feature detectors" leading to perceptual identification of phonemes such as /p/.

If we consider that syllables and words behave like perceptual units or temporal compounds, it is clear that consideration must be given in perception to further linkage of these units into higher order groupings of phrases, sentences, and passages. To return to a chemical analogy, as an almost unlimited number of proteins can be formed by the arrangement of a limited number of organic units (amino acids) within chains, so an almost limitless number of sentences can be formed by the arrangement of a limited number of lexical units (words) within chains. The linkage of verbal units, of course, is based on syntactic and semantic rules. In order to perceptually resynthesize and comprehend the utterance of the speaker, the listener uses the same rules employed for generation—as illustrated by the ability to cancel the effect of masking of speech sounds by extraneous sounds and achieve appropriate phonemic restorations in the absence of acoustic cues to identity.[36]

If sounds in a sequence do not form temporal compounds, but rather unfamiliar strings of nonrelated sounds, it is possible to use another quite different perceptual strategy, and to discriminate between permuted sequences by naming the order of components if their durations are sufficiently long. If a recycled sequence of hisses, tones, and buzzes is heard with each sound lasting three seconds, it is hardly surprising that virtually everyone can identify the order correctly without practice. Listeners can, of course, name each sound aloud as it occurs, and then repeat this order if required after the sequence terminates. But why do listeners fail to make this identification at roughly 200 mseconds/item?[21] A clue to a possible answer is furnished by an experiment by Garner.[38]

It was found by Garner that accurate counting of the number of identical tone bursts in an extended series was not possible when the rate was six/second or more, corresponding to 167 msec/item or less. Both counting and the naming of order of items consist of the attaching of distinctive verbal labels to successive events. Warren[27] has suggested that it is the time required for verbal labeling of an ongoing stimulus that determines the limiting rate of item presentation both for counting and for naming of order within unfamiliar sequences. Successful performance of these tasks would require that verbal encoding of one item be completed before the onset of the next.

The durations required for naming of order while a sequence is continuing vary somewhat with practice, response procedure, and stimuli employed. For untrained subjects listening to recycled four-item sequences containing hisses, tones, and buzzes, thresholds were between 200 and 300 msec/item when the verbal descriptions for each of the sounds were on separate cards, which subjects tried to arrange in order of occurrence. However, when vocal responses were used by subjects, thresholds for the same stimuli were considerably higher—between 450 and 670 msec.[21] The use of card-ordering permits subjects to deal with the sequences in parts, making judgments involving only two of the names at a time. The vocal responses require description of the entire sequence at one time; and further, the possibility of the vocal description of one sound coinciding with the occurrence of another might be an additional source of difficulty.

Vowels form especially interesting recycled sequences. Rapid verbal encoding would be anticipated, since subjects are very familiar with the sounds; and perhaps more importantly, the names used are acoustic copies of the stimuli. Warren[17] found that recycled sequences consisting of steady state segments of four vowels could be ordered by unpracticed subjects using vocal responses at durations of 200 msec/item, and also that the proportion of correct responses at this duration became higher as the vowel segments approximated normal utterances (and vocal labels) more closely. In agreement with these observations, Thomas et al.[18] found that accurate naming of order of four recycled vowels was possible down to 125 msec/item.

To recapitulate, we have seen that there appears to be two categories of human auditory temporal discrimination. They have been called Type I and Type II.[27] In this paper, Types I and II will be given the more descriptive names "Identification of Components and their Order" (ICO) and "Holistic Pattern Recognition" (HPR), respectively.

ICO requires that listeners employ separate symbols for each sound, store these symbols, and retrieve them in appropriate order. Of course, humans use verbal symbols or names to identify sounds, and it appears that successful naming or ordering requires completion of verbal encoding of one component before the onset of the next in extended sequences. The lower limit for ICO depends upon the nature of the components and the response procedure, and generally requires items from 100 to 500 msec. There is virtually no upper duration limit for items.

HPR involves recognition of temporal patterns, and permits both Same/Different judgments, and (following appropriate training), absolute identification of overall patterns. HPR does not require prior familiarity and verbal categorization of component sounds, as does ICO. A succession of individual sounds, each lasting only a few msec and too brief to be identified as separate components, can combine perceptually to form the recognizable overall patterns called temporal compounds.[27] The upper limit of component sound durations permitting temporal compound formation appears to be two or three seconds/item. The temporal compounds of HRP seem to provide the basis for comprehension of speech and appreciation of music. Since new compounds can be formed quite readily in the laboratory with sequences of arbitrarily selected sounds such as tones, hisses, and buzzes, this category of sequence perception is not restricted to speech and music but appears to be quite general.

Now that this two-category model has been described for human sequence perception, let us consider other animals, including our prelinguistic ancestors.

ICO seems closed to nonhumans, probably because they cannot code, store, and retrieve symbols representing individual sounds. The inability of monkeys to achieve performance characteristic of ICO discrimination is demonstrated by an experiment by Dewson and Cowey.[39] Their three monkeys were able to discriminate accurately between two-item sequences, in which each of the items could be either a tone or a noise, when item durations were briefer than approximately 1.5 seconds (possibly through HPR, as will be discussed below). But when item durations were increased to more than three seconds, none of the monkeys could master the discrimination, apparently being unable to recall the first item after termination of the second (responses could not be made until termination of the entire sequence). Of course, for humans, ICO (permitting recall of a verbal representation of the stimulus rather than remembering the sounds directly) makes discrimination between such long sequences very easy indeed.

HPR between permuted orders of items appears to be used by many different species of animals. Birdsong consists of a series of notes arranged in particular orders, and it has been found that changing the order of components through cutting and splicing of a recorded song alters the responses of other birds of the same species.[40,41] Colavita et al.[42] trained cats to discriminate between sequences consisting of tonal intensity changes (loud-soft-loud vs. soft-loud-soft), each intensity level lasting 900 msec with 100 msec between levels. As a result of the nature of changes in performance and the ability to relearn following bilateral insular-temporal lesions, these investigators concluded that the cats' original sequence discrimination was holistic, and not based upon pairwise discrimination of the order of individual intensities.

Nonhuman animals can not only use holistic pattern recognition to distinguish between permuted orders of sounds, but can use HPR to discriminate fine temporal differences characterizing phonetic categories, such as in voice onset times differentiating voiced and unvoiced plosives. Work at the Central Institute for the Deaf by Kuhl and Miller[43] using synthetic speech has shown that chinchillas can distinguish between /ta/ and /da/; /ka/ and /ga/; and /pa/ and /ba/. In another study, using natural speech, Kuhl and Miller[44] found that following training, syllables containing either /t/'s or /d/'s can be discriminated by chinchillas despite variations in talkers, vowels following the plosives, and intensities. Recent work by Sinnott[45] with monkeys has shown that they are able to discriminate between acoustic correlates of the place of human articulation with /ba/ and /da/.

SUMMARY AND CONCLUSIONS

Human speech perception seems to involve the ability to recognize groupings of speech sounds rather than component phonemes, and to distinguish between permuted orders of items within sequences as holistic entities. Humans can use this

Holistic Pattern Recognition (HPR) not only with speech and music, but also with sequences of arbitrarily selected sounds after very little practice. Infrahuman primates, cats, chinchillas, and birds also seem to employ HPR with auditory sequences. Further, there is recent evidence that animals unable to produce speech sounds can nevertheless discriminate between closely related phonemes. Thus, it appears that human speech perception employs prelinguistic abilities shared with other animals to distinguish between phonemic groupings. Of course, use of speech for communication also requires establishment of phonemic groupings as symbols, and sequential arrangement of these symbols, by rule, to convey the desired message.

Identification of Components and their Order (ICO) for auditory sequences is limited to humans. ICO involves verbal categorization and storage of the names for successive auditory items as they appear, followed by retrieval of the names in the order stored. Thus, direct identification of the order of sounds within auditory sequences rests upon verbal ability, which provides an explanation for the difficulty that aphasics have in identifying order within nonverbal sequences. Much confusion in the literature on auditory sequence perception seems to have resulted from a failure to differentiate between HPR and ICO.

REFERENCES

1. KING, J. E. & J. L. FOBES. 1974. Evolutionary changes in primate sensory capacities. J. Human Evolution 3: 435–443.
2. DEWSON, J. H., K. H. PRIBRAM & J. C. LYNCH. 1969. Effects of ablations of temporal cortex upon speech sound discrimination in the monkey. Exp. Neurol. 24: 579–591.
3. BURDICK, C. K. & J. D. MILLER. 1975. Speech perception by the chinchilla: Discrimination of sustained /a/ and /i/. J. Acoustical Soc. Amer. 58: 415–427.
4. EFRON, R. 1963. Temporal perception, aphasia and déjà vu. Brain 86: 403–424.
5. LENNEBERG, E. H. 1967. Biological Foundations of Language. John Wiley & Sons. New York, N.Y.
6. JOOS, M. 1948. Acoustic phonetics. Supplement to Language 24: 1–136 [Language Monograph no. 23].
7. AARONSON, D. 1967. Temporal factors in perception and short-term memory. Psychol. Bull. 67: 130–144.
8. FRAISSE, P. 1963. The Psychology of Time. Harper & Row. New York, N.Y.
9. WINCKEL, F. 1967. Music, Sound and Sensation: A Modern Exposition. Dover, New York, N.Y.
10. HIRSH, I. J. 1959. Auditory perception of temporal order. J. Acoustical Soc. Amer. 31: 759–767.
11. HIRSH, I. J. & C. E. SHERRICK. 1961. Perceived order in different sense modalities. J. Exp. Psychol. 62: 423–432.
12. FAY, W. H. 1966. Temporal Sequence in the Perception of Speech. Mouton. The Hague, The Netherlands.
13. SWISHER, L. & I. J. HIRSH. 1972. Brain damage and the ordering of two temporally successive stimuli. Neuropsychologia 10: 137–152.
14. LADEFOGED, P. 1959. The perception of speech. In NPL Symposium no. 10, Mechanisation of Thought Processes. Vol. 1. Her Majesty's Stationery Office. London, England.
15. LADEFOGED, P. & D. E. BROADBENT. 1960. Perception of sequence in auditory events. Quart. J. Exp. Psychol. 12: 162–170.
16. HEISE, G. A. & G. A. MILLER. 1951. An experimental study of auditory patterns. Amer. J. Psychol. 64: 68–77.
17. WARREN, R. M. 1968. Relation of verbal transformations to other perceptual phenomena. In Conf. Publication no. 42, IEE/NPL Conf. on Pattern Recognition. Institution of Electrical Engineers. Teddington, England. (Suppl., 8 pp.)

18. THOMAS, I. B., P. B. HILL, F. S. CARROLL & B. GARCIA. 1970. Temporal order in the perception of vowels. J. Acoustical Soc. Amer. **48:** 1010–1013.
19. WARREN, R. M., C. J. OBUSEK, R. M. FARMER & R. P. WARREN. 1969. Auditory sequence: Confusion of patterns other than speech and music. Science **164:** 586–587.
20. WARREN, R. M. & R. P. WARREN. 1970. Auditory illusions and confusions. Sci. Amer. **223**(6): 30–36.
21. WARREN, R. M. & C. J. OBUSEK. 1972. Identification of temporal order within auditory sequences. Perception & Psychophys. **12:** 86–90.
22. WILCOX, G. W., U. NEISSER & J. ROBERTS. 1972. Recognition of auditory temporal order. Paper presented at the Eastern Psychological Association. Boston, Mass. April 28.
23. WARREN, R. M. 1972. Temporal resolution of auditory events. Paper presented at Amer. Psychological Ass. Honolulu, Hawaii. Sept 4.
24. WARREN, R. M. 1973. Temporal order discrimination: Recognition without identification by untrained subjects. J. Acoustical Soc. Amer. **53:** 316 (abstr.).
25. WARREN, R. M. 1974. Auditory pattern recognition by untrained listeners. Perception & Psychophys. **15:** 495–500.
26. WARREN, R. M. 1973. Temporal order discrimination: Identification and recognition by trained listeners. J. Acoustical Soc. Amer. **53:** 316 (abstr.).
27. WARREN, R. M. 1974. Auditory temporal discrimination by trained listeners. Cognitive Psychol. **6:** 237–256.
28. GREEN, D. M. 1971. Temporal auditory acuity. Psychol. Rev. **78:** 540–551.
29. BROADBENT, D. E. & P. LADEFOGED. 1959. Auditory perception of temporal order. J. Acoustical Society Amer. **31:** 1539.
30. TOBIAS, J. V. 1972. Curious binaural phenomena. In Foundations of Modern Auditory Theory. Vol. II J. V. Tobias, Ed. Academic Press. New York, N.Y.
31. WARREN, R. M., C. J. OBUSEK & J. M. ACKROFF. 1972. Auditory induction: Perceptual synthesis of absent sounds. Science **176:** 1149–1151.
32. WARREN, R. M. 1970. Perceptual restoration of missing speech sounds. Science **167:** 392–393.
33. SAVIN, H. B. & T. G. BEVER. 1970. The nonperceptual reality of the phoneme. J. Verbal Learning Verb. Behav. **9:** 295–302.
34. WARREN, R. M. 1971. Identification times for phonemic components of graded complexity and for spelling of speech. Perception & Psychophys. **9:** 345–349.
35. WARREN, R. M. & C. J. OBUSEK. 1971. Speech perception and phonemic restorations. Perception & Psychophys. **9:** 358–362.
36. WARREN, R. M. & G. L. SHERMAN. 1974. Phonemic restorations based on subsequent context. Perception & Psychophys. **16:** 150–156.
37. LÜDTKE, H. 1969. Die Alphabetschrift und das Problem der Lautsegmentierung. Phonetica **20:** 147–176.
38. GARNER, W. R. 1951. The accuracy of counting repeated short tones. J. Exp. Psychol. **41:** 310–316.
39. DEWSON, J. H. & A. COWEY. 1969. Discrimination of auditory sequences by monkeys. Nature **222:** 695–697.
40. FALLS, J. B. 1963. Properties of bird song eliciting responses from territorial males. Proceedings Int. Ornithological Congress **13:** 259–271.
41. FICKEN, M. S. & R. W. FICKEN. 1973. Effect of number, kind and order of song elements on playback responses of the golden-winged warbler. Behaviour **46:** 114-128.
42. COLAVITA, F. B., F. V. SZELIGO & S. D. ZIMMER. 1974. Temporal pattern discrimination in cats with insular-temporal lesions. Brain Res. **79:** 153–156.
43. KUHL, P. & J. D. MILLER. 1975. Speech perception by the chinchilla: Phonetic boundaries for synthetic VOT stimuli. J. Acoustical Soc. Amer. **57:** S49 (abstr.).
44. KUHL, P. K. & J. D. MILLER. 1974. Discrimination of speech sounds by the chinchilla: /t/ vs /d/ in CV syllables. J. Acoustical Soc. Amer. **56:** S52 (abstr.).
45. SINNOTT, J. M. 1974. A comparison of speech sound discrimination in humans and monkeys. Doctoral Dissertation. University of Michigan. Ann Arbor, Mich.

DISCUSSION PAPER

A. M. Liberman

Haskins Laboratories
New Haven, Connecticut 06510

The interesting papers we heard all dealt in one way or another with a question that is surely central to an inquiry into the biology of language: Are linguistic processes in some sense special, different from the processes that underlie nonlinguistic activities, and, perhaps, unique to man? To discuss that question, and the papers of the evening's session, I find it useful to distinguish two classes of specialized processes: auditory and phonetic.

Specialized auditory processes would serve, perhaps in the fashion of feature detectors, to extract those aspects of the acoustic signal that carry the important information. One is led to suppose that such devices might exist because it is true, and paradoxical, that some of the most important phonetic information is contained in parts of the speech sound that are not physically salient. Thus, a significant acoustic cue is in the formant transitions, though these are often of short duration and rapidly changing frequency. Perhaps there are devices devoted to detecting those transitions. If so, we should hold them up as examples of specializations in the auditory system. They would be important for the perception of language, but not properly part of its special processes.

If the acoustic signal were directly related to the phonetic message, then detection of the phonetically important cues would be sufficient for phonetic perception; no further processing would be necessary. But the relation between signal and message is peculiarly complex. (For summary accounts, see Refs. 1–5.) As a result, the specialized auditory detectors can only begin the job; the auditory display they produce must still be interpreted, because the phonetic message is there in such highly encoded form. If there are devices specialized to do that kind of interpreting, then I should consider them phonetic, not auditory. Since I will organize my comments on the papers of the evening in terms of that distinction, I should take a moment to illustrate what I mean.

Consider the formant transitions that are important cues for the perception of stop consonants in syllable-initial position, and call up in your mind's eye spectrographic representations (similar to those shown by Dr. Morse) of such transition cues as would be appropriate for [da] and [ba]. Now add a patch of fricative noise—the hiss of [s]—just before the [da]. If that patch is immediately in front of the [da], you will hear [sa], not [da]; the stop will have disappeared completely. But if the patch is moved away so as to leave about 50 msec of silence between the end of the hiss and the beginning of the formant transitions, then you will hear [sta]; that is, you will hear the stop once again. The generalization that captures those facts, and many others closely related to them, is that a necessary condition for the perception of syllable-initial stop consonants is a brief period of silence in front of the appropriate transition cues. But why should silence be necessary? Why should it be impossible to hear the stop when its acoustic cues follow closely on the fricative noise?

The simplest explanation, surely, is that we are here dealing with a characteristic of the generalized mammalian auditory system. That might seem reasonable if only because in putting the fricative noise in front of the transition cues we have

*Preparation of this paper was supported by a grant to Haskins Laboratories from the National Institute of Child Health and Human Development.

conformed to the paradigm for auditory forward masking. But a search of the literature on such masking uncovers no reason to suppose that it could, in fact, provide the account we seek; forward masking does occur, but it is not nearly so strong as to produce the total disappearance of the stop consonant in [sa]. (See, for example, Refs. 6 and 7.)

Consider, now, a second interpretation. Suppose there are transition detectors of the kind I speculated about, and suppose, further, that the fricative noise disables them, rendering them ineffective in extracting the transition cues for the stop consonant. In fact, there is very indirect evidence that such transition detectors may exist in man. Thus, work by Kay and Matthews[8] suggests that there may be detectors sensitive to frequency modulations, at least within a certain range. More, and perhaps more indirect, evidence comes from studies on the so-called adaptation-shift phenomenon, first found in speech by Eimas and Corbit[9] and since studied by a number of investigators. (For a review, see Cooper[10] and Darwin,[11] in press.) Among those studies is a recent one by Ganong[12] that I will describe, if only briefly, because its outcome has several implications for our concern with specialized processes: it suggests, as do several other such studies, that transition detectors may exist, but it also indicates that such detectors are in no way disabled by the fricative noise of our example.

Ganong's experiment went like this. Having first found the boundary between synthetic [da] and [ba], Ganong adapted his subjects with [da] and measured the resulting shift in the [da-ba] boundary. Then he put a patch of fricative noise in front of the [da] and adapted his subjects with the [sa] syllable that they all heard when the fricative-patch-plus [da] was sounded. The effect on the [da-ba] boundary was at least as great as when the adaptation was carried out with [da]. As a control against the possibility that [sa] had its effect because it worked on the same abstract phonetic-feature detector as [da] ([s] and [d] have the same place-of-production feature), Ganong adapted with a [sa] from which the formant transitions had been removed; in that condition the effect on the [da-ba] boundary was much smaller. Those results suggest that the adaptation shift in the [da-ba] boundary was caused by a change in the state of some device that responds to formant transitions; thus, they support the assumption that there are such things as transition detectors.

But Ganong's results also show, more generally, that the transition cues following the fricative noise were getting through in full strength, at least as auditory events. If those transition cues nevertheless failed to produce perception of a stop consonant, it was not because they were absent from the auditory display. (Other kinds of evidence for the same conclusion are reviewed in Liberman, in press.[12a])

We are led, then, to a third explanation for the disappearance of the stop consonant: silence is necessary for the perception of stop consonants, not because it provides time to evade normal auditory forward masking, and not because it prevents the disabling of specialized transition detectors, but because it provides information. The information is that the speaker did indeed make the total closure of the vocal tract necessary to the production of a stop consonant. Thus, given enough silence to indicate a sufficient closure of the vocal tract, a specialized phonetic device could interpret the transition cues as reflecting a linguistic event that included the stop-consonant segment [d]. Hence the perception [sta] when a silent interval of about 50 msec is placed between the end of the hiss and the beginning of the transitions. Without that silent interval the only reasonable phonetic interpretation is that the vocal tract did not close completely. Hence [sa].

So much, then, for the possibility that there are at least two different kinds of devices specialized for speech. Let me now comment on the papers of the evening with reference to that distinction.

In the presentation by Dr. Andrews we saw interesting evidence that baboons change the configuration of their vocal tracts so as to produce something like formant transitions and, further, that such transitions may convey information from one baboon to another. If it is indeed the formant transitions that carry the information, and if the transitions are as brief and rapid as they sometimes are in human speech, then we should not be surprised to find feature detectors specialized to track them. And in working with baboons we might, of course, expect to get at such devices more directly than we can in research on human beings.

Though baboons may produce and respond to rapid transitions, we have as yet found no reason to believe that they (or, indeed, any creatures other than man) produce or perceive phonetic strings. I should doubt, therefore, that we would find the specialized phonetic processor to which I referred. But what I doubt is surely not important. What is important, I should think, is that we can find out whether baboons do have something like transition detectors and also whether they behave toward speech as if they make a phonetic interpretation. Dr. Andrews has given us a good start in that direction.

The experiments that Philip Morse described are a model of how to learn about the biology of language. To select some interesting characteristic of human speech perception and then look for that characteristic in prelinguistic infants and nonhuman primates is surely one of the best ways to uncover whatever there may be of biological predisposition, specialized process, and species-specificity. The experiments are certainly hard to do, but they are very much worth doing, and Dr. Morse does them very well indeed.

The results Dr. Morse told us about this evening were interpreted by him in terms of the possibility that there are devices like transition detectors. In his view, such devices might explain categorical perception of the place distinction for stop consonants in infants and the somewhat in-between tendency toward categorical perception he got in monkeys. I think it quite reasonable to suppose that the output of such detectors would be categorical. I doubt, however, that the concept of feature detector could take us very far toward explaining the perception of stop consonants, except by a kind of metaphorical extension. Some of the reasons for my doubt will, perhaps, become clearer in connection with the examples I mean to develop when I discuss Dr. Warren's paper in a few moments, so I will say no more about those reasons now. In fairness to Dr. Morse, however, I should emphasize that he was not trying to explain the perception of stop consonants, nor even the perception of the place feature, but only some data on discrimination and tendencies toward categorical perception in infants and monkeys.

As for Dr. Morse's experiment, I should say that in using three formants instead of two he gained the advantage of greater realism, but at the cost of some added difficulty in interpretation of the results. That difficulty arises because, when second- and third-formant transitions are both varied, it is harder to scale physical similarity and therefore that much harder to assess tendencies toward categorical perception. If one nevertheless prefers to use the three-formant patterns because they are closer to what occurs in speech, he might reduce the difficulty I referred to by coupling the transition cues with a variety of vowels, thus randomizing the acoustical similarities; if the discrimination functions nevertheless come out the same way they did in Dr. Morse's experiment, the conclusion would be quite compelling.

Still, the results so far obtained with infants are impressive. The infants of Morse's study did show a strong tendency toward categorical perception of the place distinction in the stops, and, as Morse pointed out, that result accords with those obtained by other investigators. In the case of the monkeys, however, it is a good deal less clear that perception of the stops is categorical. There was, in the monkeys of Dr.

Morse's experiment, some tendency in that direction, though less apparently than with the infants. In that connection, we should keep in mind the results of the earlier study by Sinnott,[13] to which both Morse and Warren referred. Using reaction time as the measure, Sinnott found that her monkeys, like those of Morse, discriminated within phonetic categories; but they did not discriminate better across phonetic boundaries than within them. That is, Sinnott's monkeys did not show any appreciable tendency toward categorical perception, although her human subjects did.

Since the experiment on discrimination of the voicing distinction by chinchillas[14] was several times referred to by our speakers, I should also comment on that. It is surely of interest that the chinchillas "classified" the speech stimuli so as to put the boundary in much the same place that human listeners do. Given that the relevant acoustic cue is the relative time of onset of two parts of the pattern, it is also of interest that research with nonspeech sounds has found a categorical "notch" in the auditory system at a relative displacement appropriate to the speech-sound boundary.[15] In the case of the voicing distinction, it may be, therefore, that in the development of language, nature took advantage of a categorical distinction characteristic of some mammalian auditory systems, although special adjustments in the articulatory mechanisms would presumably have been necessary to get them to produce accurately just that small difference in timing required to put the sounds within the preset (and rather narrow) constraints of the ear.

I nevertheless have several reservations, even about this apparently simple case. Using an expanded range of the same stimuli that were used in the chinchilla experiment, Wilson and Waters[16] found that variations in stimulus range caused rhesus macaque monkeys to shift their "boundary" from 28 msec, which happens to be about where the chinchilla boundary was, to about 66 msec. (They also found some tendency toward categorical perception, wherever the boundary was.) That kind of change, which implies that the monkeys may have been splitting the range, does not occur in human subjects. (See, for example, Sawusch, et al.[17]) The possibility that such a change might occur in chinchillas was not controlled for.

My other reservation arises from the fact that the human boundary is not fixed at either of the boundaries so far found with animals and with nonspeech sounds, but rather varies (together with the categorical notch) from about 18 msec to as much as 45 msec as a function of the duration of the transitions and the frequency at which the first formant begins.[18,19] (The variation with duration of the transitions may reflect a normalization for rate of articulation.) I would be interested to know if the chinchilla's boundary moves in the same way. It would also be interesting to know if the chinchilla, or indeed any other animal, appreciates that the voicing distinction is, indeed, the same in those cases in which the relevant acoustic cues are entirely different. What happens, for example, when the distinction is moved from initial position (e.g., [bɪ] vs. [pɪ], which is the kind of distinction so far studied in animals) to intervocalic position following a stressed syllable (e.g., [raɛbɪd] vs. [raɛpɪd]), where a sufficient cue is the time interval between the two syllables; or to final position [e.g., [raeb] vs. [raep], where a sufficient cue is the duration of the preceding vowel (plus consonant-vowel transition)]. To "understand" that such distinctions have something in common despite gross difference in the acoustic cues would constitute an impressive demonstration of phonetic interpretation.

We come now to that part of this session that touched more directly on the matter of specialized phonetic processes. The relevant paper was given by Richard Warren. He reminded us of his earlier experiments—very important experiments, in my view—in which he found that the auditory system does not measure up to one of the requirements of phonetic perception. The requirement is that the order of the phonetic segments be preserved; the word "bad" is different from the word "dab."

Now if we measure the rates at which speech is produced and perceived, we find that the durations we can allot to the phonetic segments are often very short. Indeed, those durations can be as little as 50 msec/segment or, for brief periods, even less. But Dr. Warren has found with nonspeech sounds that the ear cannot properly cope with segments of those temporal dimensions. At the very short durations that we can assign to phonetic segments, the ear can discriminate one order of segments from another—that is, it can hear distinctively different patterns—but, as Dr. Warren told us, it is unable to identify the separate components in the order of their occurrence. Now I will not here review or comment on Dr. Warren's solution to this very real problem. I will rather offer an alternative solution, which is that in perceiving the order of the phonetic segments we need not—and indeed do not—rely on the temporal order of acoustic segments. Indeed, I would argue that even if the ear were able to identify the order of very short-duration acoustic segments, it could hardly make use of that ability in perceiving speech. That would be so because the string of phonetic segments is drastically restructured in the conversion to sound, with the result that segmentation of the sound does not correspond directly to the segmentation of the message; accordingly, the segments are not signaled simply by acoustic events in ordered sequence. But, fortunately for the integrity of the message, information about segment order is nevertheless conveyed, though by acoustic cues that could be interpreted, I should think, only by a device that "knows" the secret of the code—that is, by a phonetic device.

Let us consider, for example, the matter of segment order in the syllables [ba] and [ab] and see how information about the phonetic structure is carried in the sound. In producing those syllables, the gestures for the segments [b] and [a] are not made discretely and in turn. Rather, as we well know, the gestures are organized into units larger than a segment—something like a syllable, perhaps—and then coarticulated. If the [ba] and [ab] syllables had been produced at a moderately high rate of articulation, we should then see for [ba] an acoustic signal lasting perhaps 70 or 80 msec and containing three formants that rise from the beginning of the acoustic syllable to the end. For [ab] we should see the mirror image—that is, three formants that fall. If we search out the information about [b], we find that it exists not just at the beginning (for [ba]) or at the end (for [ab]), but throughout the acoustic syllable. Information about the vowel is also carried from one end of the sound to the other. It is as if the coarticulation had effectively folded consonant and vowel into the same piece of sound. As a result, there is no acoustic criterion by which one can divide the speech signal into segments corresponding to the segments of the phonetic message. A further consequence is that the cues for the segments must necessarily exhibit a great deal of context-conditioned variation: the transition cues for the consonant, for example, are rising in the one case and falling in the other. (It should be remarked that when we listen to those transitions in isolation we hear rising and falling glissandos, just as our knowledge of auditory psychophysics would lead us to expect.)

To explain how a listener might recover the identity of the segments—that is, know that there is a consonant [b] and a vowel [a]—we might suppose that there is a specialized phonetic device that can "hear through" the context-conditioned variation in the acoustic cues and arrive at the canonical forms of the segments. If so, then that same device could use the same context-conditioned variation to discover the order of the segments: for if the rising pattern contains a [b], then it could only be a syllable-initial [b]; and if the falling pattern contains a [b], it could only be a syllable-final [b]. Thus, I would suppose that perceiving the order of the phonetic segments does not depend on the ability of the ear to deal with discrete sounds of short duration, but rather on the operation of a very special phonetic device that is able to cope with the fact that information about order is often encoded in the sound as variations in acoustic shape. Indeed, I would suppose that such encoding would seem nicely designed to evade just those limitations of the ear that Dr. Warren's research has revealed.

I should comment finally on the paper by Philip Lieberman. His work is especially interesting from my point of view because it offers evidence for a specialization associated with the production of speech that is, in an important sense, analogous to the transition detectors of the auditory system. To see the analogy, we should consider what might have occurred as grammar—hence language—evolved. The view I want to present has been developed elsewhere,[5] so I will only outline it here.

If, as in an agrammatic system of acoustic communication, the messages were directly linked to sounds, the number of messages we could communicate would be limited to the number of holistically different sounds we can produce and perceive. And that is a relatively small number. But grammar drastically restructures the information in the message, making it appropriate, at the one end, for the great message-generating capabilities of the brain and, at the other, for the relatively limited abilities of the vocal tract and the ear to produce and perceive sounds. Viewed this way, the processes underlying grammar evolved as a kind of interface between two different kinds of structures, adapting the potentialities of the one to the limitations of the other. (My earlier comments on evading the auditory limitations described by Dr. Warren are an example of this kind of grammatical function at the very lowest level of the linguistic system—that is, at the conversion from phonetic message to sound.) But it is also possible that in this evolutionary process the structures being linked by the grammar might themselves have changed. On the perception side of the process an example would be the development of transition detectors in the auditory system to extract just that information which the phonetic (grammatical) system uses in carrying out its peculiar function. And on the production side there are the changes in the vocal tract that Dr. Lieberman has told us about. Those changes have apparently made the vocal tract less limited for phonetic communication, and so have reduced the mismatch between that organ and the message-generating intellect, a mismatch otherwise taken care of by the grammar. We might suppose that if we had to speak with the vocal tract of a nonhuman primate, the grammatical interface would have to be even more complex than it is.

I think I can justifiably end my comments on a hopeful note. Those of us who care about speech and the biology of language have reason to be encouraged. We now know enough about speech to be able to identify some of its most distinctive characteristics—those characteristics, that is, that most clearly imply the existence of specialized linguistic processes. As a result, we can fruitfully make comparisons with nonlinguistic processes in man and with any processes at all in prelinguistic infants and (presumably) nonlinguistic animals. Indeed, the comparisons are, for obvious reasons, easier to make at the level of speech than at the level of syntax, especially with infants and animals. Moreover, we have started to make those comparisons. But we have only just started. There are hundreds of experiments out there waiting to be done. Until we see what results they produce, we would be well advised, I think, to suspend judgment.

REFERENCES

1. STUDDERT-KENNEDY, M. 1974. The perception of speech. *In* Current Trends in Linguistics, T. A. Sebeok, Ed. (Mouton, The Hague, The Netherlands.). (Also in *Haskins* Laboratories Status Report on Speech Research SR-23. 1970. 15–48.)

2. COOPER, F. S. 1972. How is language conveyed by speech? In Language by Ear and by Eye. J. F. Kavanagh and I. G. Mattingly, Eds.: 25–45. MIT Press, Cambridge, Mass.
3. STEVENS, K. N. & A. S. HOUSE. 1972. The perception of speech. In Foundations of Modern Auditory Theory, Vol. 2. J. Tobias, Ed.: 3–62. Academic Press. New York, N.Y.
4. FANT, C. G. M. 1962. Descriptive analysis of the acoustic aspects of speech. Logos 5: 3–17.
5. LIBERMAN, A. M. 1974. The specialization of the language hemisphere. In The Neurosciences: Third Study Program. F. O. Schmitt and F. G. Worden, Eds.: 43–56. MIT Press. Cambridge, Mass.: 43–56. (Also in Haskins Laboratories Status Report on Speech Research SR-31/32. 1972. 1–22.)
6. ELLIOTT, L. L. 1971. Backward and forward masking. Audiology 10: 65–76.
7. LESHOWITZ, B. & E. CUDAHY. 1973. Frequency discrimination in the presence of another tone. J. Acoust. Soc. Amer. 54: 882–887.
8. KAY, R. H. & D. R. MATTHEWS. 1972. On the existence in human auditory pathways of channels selectively tuned to the modulation present in frequency-modulated tones. J. Physiol. (London) 225: 657–677.
9. EIMAS, P. D. & J. D. CORBIT. 1973. Selective adaptation of linguistic feature detectors. Cog. Psychol. 4: 99–109.
10. COOPER, W. E. 1975. Selective adaptation to speech. In Cognitive Theory. Vol. 1. F. Restle, R. M. Shiffrin, N. J. Castellan, H. R. Lindman and D. B. Pisoni, Eds.: 23–54. Lawrence Erlbaum Assoc. Hillsdale, N. J.
11. DARWIN, C. J. The perception of speech. In Handbook of Perception. Vol. 7. E. C. Carterette and M. P. Friedman, Eds.: 59–102. Academic Press. New York, N.Y. (Also in Haskins Laboratories Status Report on Speech Research SR-42/43. 1975.: 59–102.)
12. GANONG, W. F. 1975. An experiment on "phonetic adaptation." Quart. Progress Report (Res. Lab. Electronics. MIT) 116: 206–210.
12a. LIBERMAN, A. M. How abstract must a motor theory of speech be? Paper delivered at the 8th Int. Congr. Phonetic Sciences. Leeds, England. August 21, 1975. (Also in Haskins Laboratories Status Report on Speech Research SR-44. In press).
13. SINNOTT, J. M. 1974. Human versus monkey discrimination of the /ba/ /da/ continuum using three-step paired comparisons. J. Acoust. Soc. Amer. (Suppl.) 55: S55(A).
14. KUHL, P. K. & J. D. MILLER. 1975. Speech perception by the chinchilla: Voiced-voiceless distinction in alveolar plosive consonants. Science 190: 69–72.
15. MILLER, J. D., R. E. PASTORE, C. C. WIER, W. J. KELLY & R. J. DOOLING. 1974. Discrimination and labeling of noise-buzz sequences with various noise-lead times. J. Acoust. Soc. Am. 55: 390(A).
16. WILSON, W. A. & R. S. WATERS. 1975. How monkeys perceive some sounds of human speech. Paper read at a meeting of the Amer. Psychol. Chicago, Ill. Sept.
17. SAWUSCH, J. R., D. B. PISONI & J. E. CUTTING. 1974. Category boundaries for linguistic and nonlinguistic dimensions of the same stimuli. Research on Speech Research (Department of Psychology, Indiana University) 1: 162–173.
18. LISKER, L., A. M. LIBERMAN, D. ERICKSON & D. DECHOVITZ. 1975. On pushing the voice-onset-time boundary about. J. Acoust. Soc. Amer. (Suppl.) (Also in Haskins Laboratories Status Report on Speech Research SR-42/43. 1975. 257–264.).
19. STEVENS, K. N. & D. H. KLATT. 1974. Role of formant transitions in the voiced-voiceless distinction for stops. J. Acoust. Soc. Am. 55: 653–659.

DISCUSSION

Jan Wind, *Moderator*

Anthropological Institute
Vrije University
Amsterdam-1011, The Netherlands

DEAN FALK (*University of Michigan, Ann Arbor, Mich.*): I'd like to address this to Professor Lieberman. This is about the placement of the hyoid bone in the Lachapelle. Professor DuBrul earlier pointed out that the hyoid bone has been placed above the inferior edge of the mandible, and according to Professor DuBrul, this would prohibit opening of the mouth.

In July I published an article in the American Journal of Physical Anthropology, where I said that this would prohibit swallowing. You did respond earlier a little bit, and now I agree with DuBrul that, yes, if I'd step on its head it would swallow or open its mouth. I would like to hear your response to our criticisms of this placement of the hyoid bone, but first of all I would like to say that in my article I did demonstrate that in fetal chimpanzees, adult chimpanzees, infant humans, and adult humans, placement of the hyoid bone is below the inferior edge of the mandible, not above it. So I think the evidence would support an inferior placement of the hyoid bone. And you have to look at the function of the hyoid bone for whatever it is, opening of the mouth or swallowing.

DR. LIEBERMAN: First of all, the Neanderthal mandible, as it develops, tends to get very much more massive. If you look at the infant Neanderthals, the adolescent and Neanderthals in Vleck's work, you see a much more gracile form of mandible in which the hyoid placement would essentially be that of an infant. As the mandible gets more massive to support this very elaborate array of teeth, you just get more elaboration at the back.

Now, so far as the study about the function of the hyoid, your point in your paper was that the hyoid placement would prevent motion of the hyoid in the vertical plane in Neanderthal. In human swallowing, the hyoid goes up and down quite a bit: that's necessary for swallowing. However, this is not the motion of swallowing in an animal like the newborn. In the Trube and Bosma data on swallowing, the hyoid moves in the anterior posterior dimension. Of course Negus noticed this. This is also the case with chimpanzee. The low placement of the hyoid could no more have interfered with swallowing in Lachapelle than it does in swallowing in chimpanzee, gorilla, dog, and so on. In other words, they don't swallow the same way, they don't have to swallow the same way. It's sufficient for the hyoid to move in the anterior posterior dimension.

DR. FALK: Could I just make a brief response to that? 1. The hyoid bone of newborn humans has been located below the inferior edges of the mandible. 2. In Lachapelle as you have reconstructed it, the hyoid bone has been placed a full half-length of the mandible forward. I maintain that this would mess up swallowing in chimpanzee-like organisms but that's relative to my *own* interpretation of how chimps swallow.

3. Maybe if you just lower it a little bit it wouldn't make too much difference. But I would hope that maybe you'd do that, go ahead and reconstruct and reinterpret. That's what I would like to see done.

DR. LE MAY: I wanted to speak about Dr. Lieberman's work. I think the search for the beginning of vocalization is very interesting, but I feel strongly that one should use all possible pertinent data from modern man when speculating about the functional abilities of fossil man. As a radiologist I frequently see x rays of skulls of persons who have led successful, vocal lives but come in for films of the head because of injuries or recent onset of neurological symptoms. It is not rare to see in x rays of such individuals that the length of the hard palate is shorter than the distance between the palate and the basion; i.e., the anterior margin of the superior end of the spinal canal—a finding Professors Lieberman and Crelin described as occurring mainly in newborns and Neanderthal man (rarely in modern man), and which they used in designing the vocal tract of Neanderthal man. Modern, normally intelligent and successful adult persons do not rarely have a hard palate longer than the distance from the palate to the basion.

In addition, we know that the face continues to develop after the endocranial portion of the vault no longer enlarges. I measured the length of the palate and the palatal-basion distance on skull films of 64 children between the ages of 5 and 15 years studied at Boston's Children's Hospital. Of this group, 51 of the 64 had hard palates which were shorter than the P-B distances. So we see that not just Neanderthal and newborn individuals but some normal adults and most children have a throat of this configuration.

Another factor used by Lieberman and Crelin in their design of the vocal tract of Neanderthal man was the location of the larynx as determined by the direction of the styloid process from the skull. The main skull they used for their model of the level of the larynx was that of La Chapelle-aux-Saints. The base of this skull, I have been told, was broken and has been rebuilt; and the styloid processes project less than 1 cm from the vault. By studying x-ray films of the pharynx of modern man, we must conclude that we could not with certainty determine the exact level of the hyoid bone and larynx by using the angle of the styloid process, because the base of the styloid often extends fairly horizontally from the skull and then the styloid turns downward. At other times, on films of the pharynx of modern man we see the styloid extending sharply downward from the skull and then turning forward; so I do not believe it is possible to locate the larynx by a short styloid process, such as that portion remaining on the La Chapelle-aux-Saints skull, and I feel that Professors Lieberman and Crelin need more hard evidence than they have presented to date to provide a convincing basis for their hypothesis.

DR. LIEBERMAN: Dr. Le May has, unfortunately, not followed the continuing discussion of the reconstruction of the supralaryngeal vocal tract that was reported in Lieberman and Crelin in 1971; cited in this volume. The points that she raises have been answered before, and the basis for the reconstruction is reviewed in the paper that I presented at this meeting. I'll attempt, however, to summarize the discussion.

1. The reconstruction is not based on comparing a few isolated features in newborns and classic Neanderthal. The particular skeletal features that were noted were cited as examples of the total skeletal complex that is similar in newborn humans and classic Neanderthal skulls. We noted in 1971 that some of the skeletal features that always occur in newborn humans and classic Neanderthal sometimes occur in adult humans. We specifically noted that some adult humans also have a long palate-to-basion distance. This simply reflects the fact that the course of human development is not uniform and that in the process of maturation some individuals retain some of the skeletal features that are typical of newborns. Normal adults, however, do not retain the total skeletal complex that correlates with the soft tissue of the newborn supralaryngeal vocal tract. If Le May wants to replicate our reconstruction the appropriate animal is the human newborn, where the total complex is preserved. The palate-to-basion distance never was offered as a "crucial" factor that in itself would suffice to reconstruct a vocal tract.

2. Dr. Le May's comments on the small fragments of the styloid process on the La Chapelle skull and the changes in angulation of the styloid, etc., reveal that she has also missed the fact that Crelin determined the angulation of the styloid from the base of the styloid. The base is present in the fossil remains of La Chapelle-aux-Saints and other classic Neanderthal fossils. There is plenty of other fossil evidence available as well as statistical studies like those of Howells and Berglund that demonstrate that normal adult humans and classic Neanderthal fossil skulls fall into two metrically different populations.

Part XII. Neural Parallels and Continuities (I)

INTRODUCTION

Karl H. Pribram

Department of Psychology
Stanford University
Stanford, California 94305

We have heard many references to the brain during this conference. Thus a good deal needs to be reviewed in discussion of this first session on brain function *per se* to point out the relevance of the data presented to the themes of the conference as a whole. My remarks will be organized around three areas of inquiry: 1) clinical observation; 2) results of neuropsychological experimentation; and 3) philosophical analysis.

First, briefly, a clinical observation. The issue has been raised as to whether the ability to speak is merely a reflection of cognitive competence in general. Clinical evidence clearly indicates that speech can be dissociated from intelligence, whether that is measured by tests or in daily adaptive living. Any visit to an institution harboring the mentally retarded will reveal retardates who speak fluently with all of the sytactic and semantic structures so dear to the linguist in full display. Just as the idiot savant whose astounding mathematical abilities are imbedded in an otherwise vacuous mentality, the fluent retardate makes one take seriously the old-fashioned idea—shocking to most of us but expressed without hesitancy in this conference by Professor Chomsky—that language as expressed in speech may indeed be an isolatable "faculty" of the mind. Thus we must pursue the themes of this conference—the origin of language and speech—without diluting them, and ask whether the demonstrations of other cognitive competencies, be it through fossil remains or pongoid performances, are in fact relevant to this issue. My own inclination is that they are most relevant, but that this relevance must in each instance be demonstrated; it cannot just be assumed by identifying other cognitive abilities with linguistic ability, even though they may to a large extent have developed together. I have been impressed with the care that has been taken at this conference by those who have presented the data on fossils and on nonhuman primate communication to establish the connection between various cognitive performances and linguistic competence, not just to assume their identity.

Second, and with more direct bearing on the presentations of this session, some results of neuropsychological experiments. Dr. Warren has given us a thorough and critical review of data that clearly separate man's brain functions from those of his nonhuman relatives. Hemispheric specialization, a left-right difference in processing, has until now been demonstrably a characteristic of the human brain, which is not present in other primates (or any mammal, for that matter). But recently Dewson and Burlingame[1] have put this avowedly species-specific characteristic to severe test. Dewson's point of departure has been that we have until now failed to confront the nonhuman primate with tasks demanding processing of comparable complexity to that involved in linguistic speech and hearing. He has thus spent a good portion of the past decade training monkeys to respond to complex auditory signals in a delayed matching from sample paradigm. The auditory signals are various sounds and sequences of those sounds. Cautiously, and with great pain to himself, he has allowed these highly trained animals to come to surgery. He has shown with Cowey and Weiskrantz[2,3] that in monkeys a unilateral resection of cortex which on the basis of earlier experiments in my laboratory[4,5] we believe to be homologous to Wernicke's area in man, will drastically impair performance on such auditory tasks. More

728

recently, he has asked my collaboration[6] and in a dramatic initial demonstration on five monkeys has shown that when such *unilateral* resections are made in the right hemisphere of the monkey they have no effect, but when made in the left hemisphere of the monkey, the effect is severe and long-lasting despite attempts at retraining. Our tentative conclusion: the rudiments of hemispheric specialization may already be found in monkeys when adequate testing procedures are used. As in the beautiful demonstrations of communicative capacities of chimpanzees and gorillas, the awesome gap between man and nonhuman primates has been narrowed to some extent.

Where Warren addressed right-left differences in brain function and hemispheric specialization, Myers and Robinson have addressed front-back differences, or more accurately, frontomedial (i.e., frontolimbic) vs. lateral-posterior-convexity differences. Their argument has been that speech comes under the control of two separate brain mechanisms—one frontolimbic and the other posterior convexity in location. They and several other speakers and discussants at this meeting (e.g. Lamendalla) have suggested that in primate evolution there has been a shift from limbic to convexity control, and that this shift accounts for the linguistic capacities of *Homo*. I have wrestled with this possible interpretation ever since our initial report in 1949[7] of the production of vocalization by electrical stimulation of the motor portions of the limbic cortex. My conclusions are somewhat different and are summarized in Chapters 17, 18, and 19 of *Languages of the Brain* and reviewed in a paper submitted for publication as part of the proceedings of this conference. Briefly, I review the evidence that the relationship between Broca's (i.e., expressive) aphasia and Broca's area is untenable. The left third frontal convolution of man has been damaged by disease and by design in literally hundreds of patients without any resulting aphasia. Expressive aphasias are consequent, by all reports, on damage to the foot of the precentral convolution. Yet, deep lesions in the vicinity of the ventral portion of the frontal lobe do produce changes in cognitive and linguistic processes that have as yet been poorly specified. Possibly such lesions involve the limbic forebrain, areas that contribute to the uncinate fasciulus which joins the orbitofrontal and temporal polar (including amygdala) formations. My hypothesis, therefore, based mainly on data obtained in the laboratory on nonhuman primates, has been that *both* frontolimbic and posterior convexity contribute to man's linguistic competence. Formally, this hypothesis states that frontolimbic processing leads to the use of symbols defined as context-sensitive constructions, whereas posterior convexity processing leads to signs, defined as context-free constructions. Other terms for context that have been presented here, by Fillmore, for example, are frame, prototype, or schemata. Those who work on problems of memory speak of context-sensitive constructions in terms of relation categorizing, episodic, or incidental memory as opposed to event categorical or lexical storage, which is relatively context-independent. This hypothesis derives from the fact that frontolimbic lesions impair delayed response and alternation type task performance but not discrimination, but posterior convexity lesions impair discrimination but not delay-type tasks. Further, a long series of experimental analyses has shown that the delay-type tasks tap context sensitive, incidental, episodic processes, whereas discrimination procedures tap the ability to categorize events.

The hypothesis states further that linguistic competence stems from the joining of the ability to construct signs to that involved in constructing symbols, the joining of event-categorizing and relation-categorizing or episodic processes. Under current investigation are two alternative anatomical suggestions as to how the join is effected: Geschwind holds to the common view that corticocortical association paths are critical, but I have proposed that subcortical pathways by way of the basal ganglia are specifically involved. The point to be made here is not which of these views is correct, but that brain research has come to the point of stating precise hypotheses that can be tested at the neuroanatomical, electrophysiological, and neurobehavioral levels. We no longer need rely on vague speculations regarding the relationship between linguistic competence as an organ of mind and the embodiments of this organ in certain systems of the brain.

This brings me to my final area of inquiry, that of the philosopher. Sometimes this conference has taken on the airs of an eighteenth century meeting in the disputations between primatologist-empiricists and linguistic-rationalists. We heard from Dr. Fouts that "the Cartesians have had it"; that "the *evidence* is on the side of the empirical evolutionist." I have heard such claims before—from radical behaviorists of which at one time I was one. During this period Lashley kindly turned to me one day and said, "That's all right, Dr. Pribram; I had my Watson period; you'll grow up one day." He was, of course, correct, and my prognosis is that the evolutionary empiricism will, when its time is ripe, also find its own maturity.

There has been a considerable debunking of Descartes at this meeting. I cannot share this sentiment. The *evidence* is on his side. The linguists and philosophers in their reliance on intuition (an important scientific step explicable by a holographic logic;[8]) have not done him complete justice. Two evidential points framed within the empiricist tradition can be presented on his behalf. 1) With regard to the mind-body problem and cogito ergo sum: we today infer mind both from verbal reports of introspection and from instrumental behavior. Discrepancies arise that make it imperative to take seriously the introspections and not ignore them as was recommended by the radical behaviorists. Recently Weiskrantz et al.[9] have studied a patient with a restricted unilateral resection of occipital cortex. Using the technique of verbal report, the patient was found to have a homonymous hemianopia. When given instrumental discrimination tasks, however, this patient responds reliably (85% criterion) to the position and shape of objects displayed in his blind hemisfield. Despite repeated testing, with the excellent results of his performance made known to him, the patient insists that he sees nothing in the blind field, that he is merely guessing and at best has some vague feel of the presence or absence of something in the blind visual field. This example of blindsight, as Weiskrantz calls it, is not unique. Patients with medial temporal lobe lesions such as those reported by Milner[10] have also shown a remarkable dissociation between verbal introspection and testing procedures on the one hand and instrumentally acquired skills on the other. The dissociation is not between a verbal report and instrumental technique, however, but between what is tapped by the different procedures (e.g. contextual cues aid verbal as well as pictorial recall). There is thus in man a dissociation between reports of awareness and performance. The question arises as to where the major ape stands in this respect, since he has been shown able to recognize himself in mirrors (Gibbons— minor apes—and monkeys do not). Perhaps Dr. Rumbaugh, Dr. Fouts and especially Dr. Bever and Dr. Terrace will have an answer for us on this point one of these days. The *question* is an important one and is *Cartesian*, even though the answer may come from experimental techniques framed in an empiricist tradition.

2) But, you may still ask, do you go so far as to suggest that Descartes was correct in his view on the pineal gland as the seat of the spiritual in man? The question is Cartesian, but the answer again can be derived within the empiricist and even the positivist tradition. Let us look at the evidence. Jung defined "spiritual" as the collective term for processes determined by feeling, in distinction to "consciousness" which he defined as the collective term for processes determined by perception. (Jung uses the concept "collective" where today we would use "universals"). In Descartes' day feelings were determined by "humors"; today the evidence points additionally to the brain amines, catechol (norepinepherine and dopamine), and indole (serotonin)

*neuro*humors that are responsible for states of alertness and mood. The master gland that regulates endocrine (humoral) processes is the pituitary; however, the pituitary, in turn, is under the control of melatonin, a secretion of the pineal gland that is sensitive to light and other neurally mediated determinants of feeling states.

I present this evidence not so much to praise Descartes as to caution against burying the questions he raised prematurely. This conference especially should be sensitive to the wisdom of the ages and the continuity of the issues that have concerned man since he became human. The issues have been dealt with according to the technologies available at the time—but the issues have changed remarkably little. My own interest in the data presented here devolves on this remarkable fact (one that has emerged repeatedly during the conference): Man is recognizably *human* for the period of his existence. Of course, he shares his animal heritage with the primates, and especially the apes. Much of what is to become the human animal is expected to be common to man and ape alike, and in these days of search for identity and return to primitives, we are all delighted to learn just how much in common there is. Further, the theory of evolution demands that humanity is achieved incrementally and not at one stroke; thus scientific understanding depends on identifying these increments. It is on these increments that we should focus our inquiry and not be deflected from the problem they present by polemics on the definition of language. The issue for this conference is clear; it was enunciated by Aristotle, given precision by Descartes, and structure by Kant. Now we are engaged in acquiring empirical evidence relevant to this age-old issue, "What is it that makes man human?"

References

1. Dewson, J. H. III & A. C. Burlingame. 1975. Auditory discrimination and recall in monkeys. Science **187:** 267–268.
2. Dewson, J. H. III, A. Cowey & L. Weiskrantz. 1970. Disruptions of auditory sequence discrimination by unilateral and bilateral cortical ablations of superior temporal gyrus in the monkey. Exp. Neurol. **28:** 529–548.
3. Cowey, A. & J. H. Dewson, III. 1972. Effects of unilateral ablation of superior temporal cortex on auditory sequence discrimination in *Macaca mulatta*. Neuropsychologia **10:** 279–289.
4. Dewson, J. H. III, K. H. Pribram & J. Lynch. 1969. Effects of ablations of temporal cortex upon speech sound discrimination in the monkey. Exp. Neurol. **24:** 579–591.
5. Weiskrantz, L. & M. Mishkin. 1958. Effect of temporal and frontal cortical lesions on auditory discrimination in monkeys. *Brain* **81:** 406–414.
6. Dewson, J. H. III, A. C. Burlingame, K. Kizer, S. Dewson, P. Kenney & K. H. Pribram. 1975. Hemispheric asymmetry of auditory function in monkeys. Pres. 90th Mtg. Acoustical Soc. Amer. San Francisco, Calif. Nov.
7. Kaada, B. R., K. H. Pribram & J. A. Epstein. 1949. Respiratory and vascular responses in monkeys from temporal pole, insula, orbital surface and cingulate gyrus. A preliminary report. J. Neurophysiol. **12:** 347–356, 1949.
8. Yevick, M. L. 1975. Holographic or Fourier logic. *In* Pattern Recognition. Vol. 7. Pergamon Press. London, England.
9. Weiskrantz, L., E. K. Warrington, M. D. Sanders & J. Marshall. 1974. Visual capacity in the hemianopic field following a restricted occipital ablation. *Brain* **97**(4): 709–728.
10. Milner, B. 1974. Hemisphere specialization: scope and limits. *In* The Neurosciences Third Study Program. F. O. Schmitt and F. G. Worden, Eds.: 75–89. The MIT Press. Cambridge, Mass.
11. Miller, G. A., E. H. Galanter & K. H. Pribram. 1960. Plans and the Structure of Behavior. Henry Holt and Co. New York, N.Y.
12. Pribram, K. H. 1971. Languages of the Brain: Experimental Paradoxes and Principles in Neuropsychology. Prentice-Hall. Englewood Cliffs, N.J.

THE SEARCH FOR CEREBRAL DOMINANCE IN MONKEYS*

J. M. Warren and A. J. Nonneman†

Department of Psychology
The Pennsylvania State University
University Park, Pennsylvania 16802

In the human clinical literature cerebral dominance refers to two different sorts of phenomena: handedness and cognitive skills. Most humans are right-handed, so in most people the left hemisphere is dominant for language behavior and for handedness, and the right hemisphere is dominant for nonverbal cognitive skills.[1,2]

At the time the present research was begun it was reasonable to assume that rhesus monkeys have cerebral dominance for handedness[3] and to ask if the cerebral hemispheres of rhesus macaques, like those of humans, are also functionally asymmetrical in their contributions to cognitive behavior.

The plan of the experiment was simple. A group of rhesus monkeys was extensively adapted to the laboratory and tested on two series of handedness tasks. A subset of animals with strong and consistent hand preferences was selected as experimental subjects. Half were given unilateral lesions on the hemisphere (contralateral to the preferred hand) that was dominant for handedness, and half lesions on the hemisphere (ipsilateral to the preferred hand) that was not dominant for handedness. They were then trained for almost two years on a series of learning experiments to see if injuries to the dominant and nondominant hemispheres produced differential impairments in performance.

METHOD

Subjects

A group of 25 intact young rhesus monkeys was tested for six months on two series of handedness tests and on visual discrimination problems.[4,5] On the basis of their handedness scores and judgments of their emotional stability, 17 of the 25 animals were selected for postoperative study: 5 sham operated monkeys, the normal (N) control group; 4 with unilateral frontal lesions, 2 with lesions on the dominant (DF) and 2 with lesions on the nondominant (NF) hemisphere; 8 with ablations of the posterior foveal prestriate cortex, 4 on the dominant (DP) and 4 on the nondominant (NP) hemisphere. Lesion effects were evaluated primarily by testing the subjects on series of discriminations between different kinds of visual pattern stimuli. Bilateral foveal prestriate ablations frequently impair pattern discrimination performance, but bilateral frontal lesions do not.[6] The frontal preparations were therefore treated as operated controls in all of the experiments on visual discrimination learning.

*This research was sponsored by grant M-04726 from the National Institute of Mental Health, U.S. Public Health Service.
†Present address: University of Kentucky, Lexington, Ky., 40506.

Apparatus

All of the behavioral tests were carried out in the Wisconsin General Test Apparatus (WGTA), illustrated in Harlow.[7]

Procedure

The sequence of postoperative tests is given in TABLE 1. Relevant details concerning each test are provided in the appropriate section of the Results.

TABLE 1

SYNOPSIS OF POSTOPERATIVE TESTING PROGRAM

Tests	Postoperative Weeks
Handedness Retest	7–9
Five Color Discrimination Experiments	10–43
Shape Discrimination	44–56
Object Discrimination	57–66
Mirror-Image Pattern Discrimination	67–74
Delayed Response	75–80

Surgery

The monkeys were anesthetized with sodium pentobarbital (37 mg/kg), and decorticated by gentle subpial aspiration under aseptic conditions. The frontals incurred unilateral ablations of the dorsolateral prefrontal cortex, including the banks and depths of the principle sulcus. The posterior animals were deprived of the foveal prestriate cortex on one hemisphere.

Histology

At the end of the experiment the monkeys were deeply anesthetized with sodium pentobarbital and perfused intracardially with physiological saline followed by 10% formalin in saline. The brains were photographed before being dehydrated, embedded, and cut in 40-micron sections. Two series of every tenth section were prepared, using thionin and Weil stains. The cortical lesions were reconstructed from the cross sections, supplemented by photographs of the whole brains; retrograde degeneration was mapped on standard sections of the macaque thalamus.

RESULTS

Anatomy

The variations among monkeys in the same lesion group were small in respect to extent, depth, and other lesion parameters. No appeal is made to individual

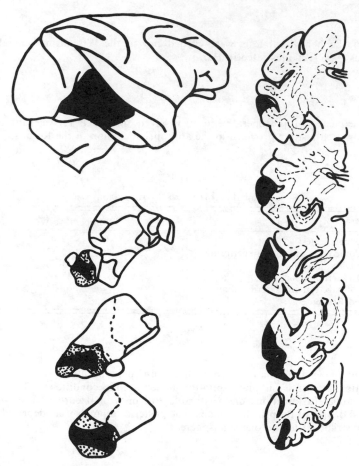

FIGURE 1. Synopsis of histological findings in the median foveal prestriate case, Monkey NP 12.

differences in ablations in considering the behavioral results, because there was no significant correlation between either extent of cortical damage, or severity of thalamic degeneration, and performance by the posterior cases on the tasks which revealed a deficit in this group. The anatomical results are therefore summarized by showing the reconstruction of the cortical lesion and representative coronal sections of the cerebrum and thalamus for the median posterior and frontal cases in FIGURE 1 and 2, respectively.

Handedness Tests

The monkeys' hand preferences in taking raisins or peanuts from the left, center, and right food-wells in the test tray of the WGTA were observed under three conditions. In the Reach test the subjects simply took a visible bit of food from one of the food wells. In the Block and Card tests they had to displace a small wooden object or three-inch square of posterboard to uncover food in an underlying well in the tray. The position of the food incentive was varied from trial to trial in a balanced irregular sequence as a control for environmental biases, and the monkeys' responses were scored by recording the hand used to carry the food to the mouth on each trial.

There were three series of handedness tests. Twenty-five animals were tested on Series 1, just after their arrival in the laboratory, and again on Series 2, six months later. The 17 monkeys selected for postoperative study were also tested on Series 3, four months after Series 2. The monkeys were always given 25 trials a day in the handedness tests. They were tested for 500 trials on Reach and Block and 100 trials on Card in Series 1; all of the tests were presented for 200 trials in Series 2 and 3.

The test-retest correlations for the three tests are presented in TABLE 2 and the correlations between preference scores on pairs of tests are given in TABLE 3.

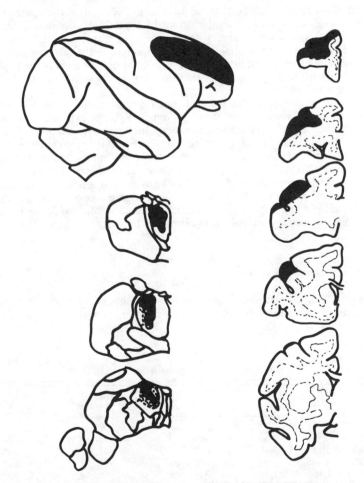

FIGURE 2. Synopsis of histological findings in the median dorsolateral frontal case, Monkey NF 11.

TABLE 2

RETEST RELIABILITY OF HANDEDNESS TESTS

	Series 1 and 2	Series 2 and 3
N	25	17
Tests		
Reach	.62*	.96*
Block	.62*	.86*
Card	.73*	.98*

*$p < .01$

Although the absolute values of these product-moment correlations are somewhat variable, every one of them is significant at the 1% level of confidence. There is, in other words, a significant tendency for monkeys to respond in the same way on successive repetitions of the same test, and to respond in the same way on different tests given at the same point in time. This means, for the purposes of the experiment, that the tests used to diagnose handedness in our subjects satisfy two of the essential requirements for adequate selection tests.

The hand preference scores for each experimental monkey on the immediately preoperative set of tests (Series 2) are set out in TABLE 4, which shows that every experimental case had a statistically significant preference for using one hand rather than the other on all three manipulation tests. Each of these monkeys thus appears to be a suitable subject with which to investigate the existence of cerebral dominance.

Inspection of TABLE 4 also reveals that half the members of the DP (dominant posterior) and NP (nondominant posterior) groups had lesions on the right hemisphere, and half on the left. This allowed us to evaluate the possibility of a difference between the right and left hemispheres, independent of dominance for handedness. No evidence of such a difference between the right and left halves of the brain was found.

Color-Discrimination Experiments

Two kinds of discriminanda were used in these five experiments. Both were two dimensional patterns made by fixing squares of colored construction paper to three-

TABLE 3

INTERCORRELATIONS BETWEEN HANDEDNESS TESTS

	Series		
	1	2	3
N	25	25	17
Tests			
Reach and Block	.64*	.92*	.80*
Reach and Card	.62*	.94*	.96*
Block and Card	.90*	.98*	.85*

*$p < .01$

inch squares of white posterboard. Whole cards are completely covered with the differential color cues. Part-cards are made by mounting 1.5-inch squares of colored paper in the center of the background card, so that only 25% of the plaque provided differential cues compared to 100% in the whole card situation. Whole cards are considerably easier for monkeys to discriminate. Information on the parameters that affect rhesus monkeys' performance on visual pattern discrimination tasks of the sort used in this series of tests may be found in Meyer *et al.*,[8] and Warren.[9]

TABLE 4

PERCENTAGE OF PREFERENCE SCORES ON PREOPERATIVE HANDEDNESS TESTS

Group	Monkey	Preferred Hand	Reach	Test Block	Card
DP	9	L	85	100	98
	17	R	96	100	100
	24	R	100	100	100
	33	L	97	100	100
Median			96	100	100
NP	12	L	99	100	100
	21	R	91	97	100
	26	R	96	99	100
	39	L	99	100	100
Median			96	99	100
DF	28	R	87	100	100
	32	L	98	99	100
NF	11	R	100	100	100
	38	R	77	99	100
Median			92	99	100

Experiment 1. Each day for 36 days the monkeys were given 25 trials of discrimination training with one of 36 different pairs of part-cards.

Experiments 2 and 3. Whole-cards were used in both experiments. In Experiment 2, the subjects were trained 40 trials a day, to a criterion of 36 correct responses in a single session, on four different pairs of colored squares. In Experiment 3, the animals were tested on four 10-trial problems per day for 36 days, for a total of 144 problems.

Experiment 4. This experiment was intended to see if the groups differed in their ability to transfer the effects of training on an easy whole-card discrimination to a difficult part-card discrimination task. The monkeys were trained on 20 two-stage problems. Each problem consisted of a block of 15 trials with a pair of whole-cards, followed by training, to a criterion of 10 consecutive correct responses, with the same colors presented as part-cards, and with the original cue-reward relation maintained.

Experiment 5. This experiment compared the responses of the normal and brain-injured monkeys to changes in irrelevant contextual cues. The subjects were trained 50 trials a day to a criterion of ten consecutive correct responses and were required to choose a part-card with a central red square rather than a green one under five conditions. The background on which the red and green patches were both presented was (1) white, (2) yellow, (3) pink, and (4) blue. In the fifth condition the red square was presented on a green background, and the green square on a red background. This last condition was intended to maximize conflict between the two stimulus alternatives.

The results of Experiments 1 through 4 are summarized in TABLE 5, which gives the median scores for the four groups of monkeys as well as the medians for the combined normal and operated (frontal) controls and for the dominant and nondominant posteriors. The relatively small size of our samples and the considerable variation within groups dictate that we use the median as the measure of central tendency, and use nonparametric significance tests to evaluate all the results of this experiment.

None of the differences between groups was significant in Experiments 1, 2, and 3, nor in the transfer stage of Experiment 4.

TABLE 5

MEDIAN PERFORMANCE ON COLOR-DISCRIMINATION PROBLEMS

	Experiment				
	1	2	3	4-Learning	4-Transfer
Group	% Correct	Errors	% Correct	% Correct	Errors
N	53	20	82	91	170
F	62	20	84	90	130
Control	55	20	82	90	155
DP	59	34	79	83	162
NP	57	18	84	87	133
Posterior	57	19	80	84	135

The results of the initial training stage of Experiment 4 are summarized in the left panel of FIGURE 3, which shows the percentage of correct responses on trials 1 through 15, averaged over all 20 problems, for the posterior and control groups. The intraproblem learning performance of the posterior cases is consistently inferior to that of the controls; the difference between groups is significant at the 5% level of confidence ($U = 16$).

The mean percentage of errors by individual posterior monkeys is given on the right in FIGURE 3. It is readily apparent that it made no difference for performance on Experiment 4 whether the animals suffered injuries to the hemisphere that was dominant or nondominant for handedness ($U = 5$, $p = .243$).

The results of Experiment 5 are presented in FIGURE 4, where median errors to criterion by the posterior and control groups are plotted against successive transfer problems. The groups did not differ significantly on problems 1 through 3; the posterior group made significantly more errors than the controls on problem 4 ($U = 17.5$, $p < .05$) and problem 5 ($U = 7.5$, $p < .01$), when the subjects had to discriminate a red square on a green background from a green square on a red background.

The panel on the right side of FIGURE 4 presents the sum of the errors on problems 4 and 5 for the eight posterior preparations. These data reveal no significant differences between the animals with lesions in the dominant and nondominant hemisphere. ($U = 4$, $p = .171$)

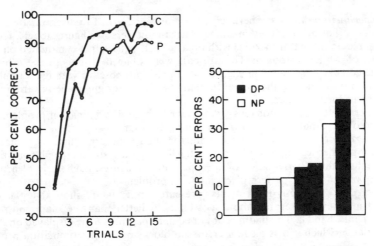

FIGURE 3. *Left:* Intraproblem learning curves for control (C) and posterior (P) groups on 20 colored pattern-discrimination problems. *Right:* Percentage of errors made in this experiment by individual posterior cases.

Shape-Discrimination Learning

The training procedure and criterion were the same in the following three experiments. The subjects were trained to a criterion of 10 consecutive correct responses in a single session on each problem, with a maximum of 50 trials given in a single day.

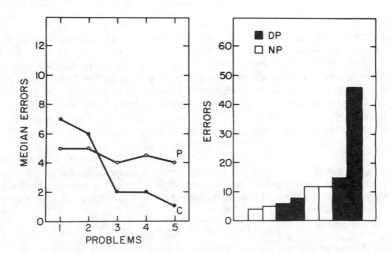

FIGURE 4. *Left:* Errors by control (C) and posterior (P) groups on red-green discrimination with varying backgrounds. *Right:* The sum of the errors made on problems 4 and 5 by individual posterior monkeys.

Experiment 6. In this experiment, the monkeys learned to discriminate 20 pairs of patterns that differed only in shape. The stimuli were five figures (circle, triangle, square, rectangle, and trapezoid) with areas of 2.25 square inches mounted on 3 inch squares of white cardboard. The animals were obliged to choose the arbitrarily designated correct stimulus in each of the 10 pairings possible with five stimuli, and were then retested on the same 10 pairs, with the original cue-reward relation reversed in each problem.

Experiment 7. The monkeys were trained on 20 discrimination problems with wooden objects that differed only in external contour.

Experiment 8. The stimuli were mirror image patterns, made by mounting identical geometrical figures on three-inch white squares, so that the plaques differed only in the right-left orientation of the superimposed figures. Each subject learned six of these mirror image pattern discrimination problems.

The results of these experiments, presented in TABLE 6, show that the brain-injured monkeys performed about as well as or better than the sham controls on Experiments 7 and 8. The findings obtained in Experiment 6 are displayed on the left in FIGURE 5, which shows median errors on blocks of five discrimination problems

TABLE 6

MEDIAN ERRORS TO CRITERION ON SHAPE-DISCRIMINATION PROBLEMS

	Experiment		
Group	6	7	8
N	558	27	555
F	580	24	389
Control	558	27	504
DP	1312	36	431
NP	911	24	305
Posterior	1009	24	444

for the control and posterior groups. The posterior cases were grossly inferior to the controls on problems 1 through 10 when they were tested on the ten pairs of discriminanda for the first time ($U = 13$, $p = .025$). The gap between the posteriors and controls was narrowed on the second presentation of the stimulus pairs, on problems 11 through 20, and the ordinate scale required to represent the first half of the experiment magnifies the "catching up" effect so it is a little hard to see that the posteriors continued to make significantly more errors than the controls ($U = 17$, $p < .05$). If one sums errors over all 20 problems, the difference between the posterior and control groups attains the 1% level of confidence ($U = 7$).

The total number of errors made by each monkey with a posterior lesion is shown in the right panel of FIGURE 5. The monkeys with lesions on the dominant hemisphere made more errors than animals with lesions on the nondominant side of the brain, but the difference between groups does not attain an acceptable level of statistical significance ($U = 3$, $p = .100$).

Delayed Response

Experiment 9. The monkeys were tested on twenty 25-trial sessions of delayed response, with each session consisting of five trials with 0-sec, 10 trials with 5-sec, and 10 trials with 10-sec delays.

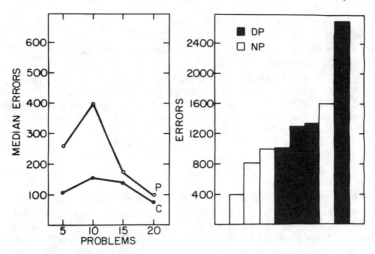

FIGURE 5. *Left:* Median errors by control (C) and posterior (P) groups on 20 discriminations of patterns differing in shape. *Right:* Total errors made on this experiment by individual posterior cases.

The median percentage of correct responses at the three delays by the sham control, frontal and posterior groups is given in the left hand panel of FIGURE 6. None of the differences between groups is statistically reliable. The percentage of errors by individual frontal cases is shown in the right panel of FIGURE 6. These data do not suggest that lesions in the dominant and nondominant hemispheres have differential effects on delayed response performance by frontal monkeys.

DISCUSSION

This experiment yields two main conclusions. First, unilateral lesions in the posterior association cortex produce significant deficits in performance on some visual discrimination learning problems. And, second, there is no evidence that

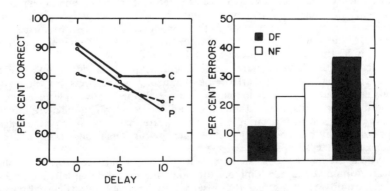

FIGURE 6. *Left:* Performance on delayed response by intact control (C), frontal (F) and posterior (P) groups. *Right:* Percentage of errors by individual frontal cases.

lesions of the hemispheres which are dominant or not dominant for handedness differentially affect learning performance by monkeys.

Both results are in good agreement with the findings of previous research. It is now pretty well established that unilateral lesions in association cortex produce significant deficits in learning and problem-solving by monkeys, although the defects are milder than those resulting from bilateral lesions. Warren, et al.[10] showed that unilateral lesions in the posterior association cortex impair the performance of monkeys on visual discrimination tasks. The evidence that unilateral frontal dysfunctions impair problem-solving by monkeys is more varied and, hence, more convincing. Performance on tasks like delayed response, delayed alternation, and delayed matching has been significantly impaired by unilateral ablation,[11,12] by unilateral electrical stimulation,[13] and by unilateral cooling[14,15] of the dorsolateral frontal cortex.

Our failure to find a defect in delayed response performance in the frontal monkeys of the current study does not disconfirm the results of the experiments just cited, because they are not comparable in one important respect. In all of the experiments that yield positive evidence of a loss in delayed response by unilateral preparations, the monkeys were tested very soon, within eight weeks at the most, after the frontal cortex was removed or rendered dysfunctional. In this experiment,

TABLE 7

MEDIAN PERCENTAGE CORRECT RESPONSES ON DELAYED RESPONSE

Group	Delay		
	0	5	10
N	91	80	80
DF	87	74	70
NF	81	77	71
Frontals	81	76	71
Posteriors	89	78	68

we waited almost two years before testing the unilateral frontals on delayed response and observed no loss. Meyer et al.[19] also tested monkeys with unilateral frontal lesions on delayed response two years after surgery. They too found no evidence of impairment in their subjects with unilateral frontal damage. Duration of postoperative recovery has a strong effect on delayed response performance by unilateral frontal monkeys, suggesting that the losses resulting from unilateral frontal lesions may be transient and fade completely in 18–24 months.

The conclusion that unilateral cortical lesions produce significant defects in learning performance should therefore be qualified in two respects. First, the effects of unilateral frontal ablations in monkeys are evidently recoverable in cases with prolonged postoperative survival times. Second, studies in which unilateral preparations have been tested on a variety of tasks indicate that only some of the learning skills disrupted by bilateral lesions are affected by unilateral posterior[10] or frontal ablations in monkeys.[12]

The data are entirely consistent regarding the possibility that the hemispheres which are dominant and nondominant for handedness are differentially important in learning by monkeys. Warren et al.[12] observed no difference in the delayed response impairments shown by monkeys with unilateral dorsolateral frontal lesions on the dominant and nondominant hemispheres. Hamilton[16] compared the learning performance of the dominant and nondominant hemispheres in a large series of split-brained monkeys, and found no interhemispheric differences related to dominance for handedness in either the retention of preoperatively learned habits or the acquisition of new habits postoperatively. Stamm *et al.*[17] recorded averaged steady potential shifts from both frontal cortices while their monkeys worked on delayed response. They could detect no difference in the activity of the hemispheres which were dominant and nondominant for handedness. Bauer and Fuster[14] did not determine hand preferences in their monkeys, but they were unable to see any major differences between the two hemispheres in any of their subjects in the effects of unilateral cryogenic cooling of the frontal cortex.

The evidence thus indicates that it is very unlikely that cerebral dominance for cognitive behavior exists in rhesus monkeys.

Recent evidence also forces us to regard with great scepticism the position[3] that handedness in monkeys is much like handedness in humans. Repeated administrations of a battery of 10 manipulation tasks show that hand preferences in monkeys are strongly influenced by practice and are task-specific; initial preference scores may have very low or zero-order correlations with hand preference scores obtained several months later.[19] These data are compatible with an experiential than with an organismic account of development of handedness in monkeys. Deuel[18] has reported more direct experimental evidence against the existence of permanent and generalized handedness in monkeys. Her subjects exhibited contradictory preferences on the same task in different situations (WGTA and primate chair), and manifested antagonistic preferences on different motor tasks (dexterity, pursuit, etc.) in the same situation (primate chair).

Rhesus monkeys also lack a conspicuous anatomical asymmetry that is present in man and may be related to handedness. Dr. Norman Geschwind examined the brain stems of 13 monkeys that had served in one of our long-term studies of handedness and could see no appreciable difference in the cross sectional areas of the pyramidal tracts in any of the monkeys, even those which had very strong and consistent manipulatory preferences. As Dr. Le May pointed out in her presentation to this conference, when the pyramidal tracts are measured rostral to the pyramidal decussation in man one finds the tract on the left is larger in about 80% of the cases.

There are then tolerably good grounds for doubting if rhesus monkeys exhibit cerebral dominance for either handedness or for cognitive behavior.

SUMMARY

Twelve monkeys with statistically significant and consistent manual preferences on three handedness tests were subjected to unilateral ablations in the association cortex. Eight received lesions in the foveal prestriate cortex, and four lesions in the dorsolateral frontal cortex; half the subjects in each group were operated on the dominant, and half on the nondominant hemisphere for handedness.

The unilateral posterior preparations were significantly inferior to the control group of four unilateral frontals and five sham operated monkeys on three series of visual pattern discrimination problems. No evidence was obtained that lesions in the dominant hemisphere produces more severe deficits in learning capacity than lesions in the nondominant hemisphere.

The results of this and four other experiments indicate that there is no cerebral dominance for problem-solving in monkeys. Recent research indicates that handedness in rhesus monkeys is only superficially similar to handedness in humans; thus, monkeys appear to lock cerebral dominance for handedness as well as for cognitive behavior.

ACKNOWLEDGMENT

The authors are grateful to Dr. Ivan Divac for making the lesions in the experimental monkeys.

REFERENCES

1. HÉCAEN, H. & J. DE AJURIAGUERRA. 1964. Left-Handedness. Grune & Stratton. New York, N.Y.
2. PENFIELD, W. & L. ROBERTS. 1959. Speech and Brain-Mechanisms. Princeton University Press. Princeton, N.J.
3. WARREN, J. M., J. M. ABPLANALP & H. B. WARREN. 1967. The development of handedness in cats and monkeys. *In* Early Behavior. H. Stevenson, E. H. Hess & H. Rheingold, Eds. John Wiley & Sons. New York, N.Y.
4. WARREN, J. M. & H. B. WARREN. 1969. Two-cue discrimination learning by rhesus monkeys. J. Comp. Physiol. Psychol. **69:** 688–691.
5. WARREN, J. M. & H. B. WARREN. 1973. Pretraining and discrimination reversal learning by rhesus monkeys. Animal Learning Behav. **1:** 52–56.
6. GROSS, C. G. 1973. Visual functions of inferotemporal cortex. *In* Handbook of Sensory Physiology. Vol. 7/3. Central Visual Information. Part B. Springer. Berlin, Germany.
7. HARLOW, H. F. 1949. The formation of learning sets. Psychol. Rev. **66:** 51–65.
8. MEYER, D. R., F. R. TREICHLER & P. M. MEYER. 1965. Discrete-trial training techniques and stimulus variables. *In* Behavior of Nonhuman Primates. A. M. Schrier, H. F. Harlow & F. Stollnitz, Eds. Academic Press. New York, N.Y.
9. WARREN, J. M. 1953. The influence of area and arrangement on visual pattern discrimination by monkeys. J. Comp. Physiol. Psychol. **46:** 231–236.
10. WARREN, J. M., R. GRANT, K. HARA & R. W. LEARY. 1963. Impaired learning by monkeys with unilateral lesions in association cortex. J. Comp. Physiol. Psychol. **56:** 241–253.
11. MEYER, D. R., H. C. HUGHES, D. J. BUCHHOLZ, A. D. DALHOUSE, L. J. ENLOE & P. M. MEYER. Effects of successive unilateral ablations of principalis cortex upon performance of delayed alternation and delayed response by monkeys. Brain Res. In press.
12. WARREN, J. M., P. R. CORNWELL & H. B. WARREN. 1969. Unilateral frontal lesions and learning in rhesus monkeys. J. Comp. and Physiol. Psychol. **69:** 498–505.
13. WEISKRANTZ, L., L. MIHAILOVIC & C. G. GROSS. 1960. Stimulation of frontal cortex and delayed alternation performance in the monkey. Science **131:** 1443–1444.
14. BAUER, R. H. & J. M. FUSTER. Delayed-matching and delayed-response deficit from cooling dorsolateral frontal cortex in monkeys. J. Comp. Physiological Psychol. In press.
15. FUSTER, J. M. & R. H. BAUER. 1974. Visual short-term memory deficit from hypothermia of frontal cortex. Brain Res. **81:** 393–400.
16. HAMILTON, C. R. Perceptual and mnemonic lateralization in monkeys. *In* Lateralization in the Nervous System. S. R. Harnad, Ed. New York: Academic Press. New York, N.Y. In press.
17. STAMM, J. S., S. C. ROSEN & A. GADOTTI. Lateralization of functions in the monkey's prefrontal cortex. *In* Lateralization in the Nervous System. S. R. Harnad, Ed. Academic Press. New York, N.Y. In press.
18. DEUEL, R. K. 1975. 30 monkeys without cerebral dominance. Neurology **25:** 389.
19. WARREN, J. M. & A. NONNEMAN. Handedness and cerebral dominance in monkeys. *In* Lateralization in the Nervous System. S. Harnad, Ed. Academic Press. New York, N.Y. In press.

COMPARATIVE NEUROLOGY OF VOCALIZATION AND SPEECH: PROOF OF A DICHOTOMY

Ronald E. Myers

Laboratory of Perinatal Physiology
National Institute of Neurological and Communicative
Disorders and Stroke
National Institutes of Health
United States Public Health Service
Bethesda, Maryland 20014

The existence of a dichotomy between those behaviors and body movements which are volitional and those which are emotional has been recognized in clinical neurology for many years. The neurologist, in examining his patient, requests him to "show his teeth" with all his strength. In response to this command, the patient strongly bares his teeth. If a weakness appears in the action of one or both sides of the face the neurologist concludes the patient has a paralysis of volitional use of the face—if no evidence exists of a lesion of the facial nerve or its nucleus. The neurologist also waits for occasions when the patient smiles or laughs in response to any amusing situation. He again takes care to determine whether the patient shows any asymmetry in action of the two sides of his face. If such an asymmetry appears and the patient does not also show evidence of a volitional paralysis, the neurologist concludes that the patient has a weakness in the emotional use of the opposite side of the face. Again, such a paralysis can be bilateral or entirely one-sided. These time-honored methods of investigating the motor activity of the face may serve us as the basis for an operational definition of the terms "volitional" and "emotional." Those unintended facial movements (or vocal utterances) which arise as a part of an instinctual reaction to an appropriately evocative situation may be regarded as emotional or involuntary, whereas those facial movements (or vocal emissions) which are clearly intended by the individual or requested of him may be considered volitional.

The neurologist has long recognized that large lesions which affect the precentral gyrus, the internal capsule, or the corticospinal tracts of one or the other hemisphere may cause a paralysis of the voluntary use of the opposite side of the body. If, however, such lesions are restricted to inferior portions of the precentral convolution or to a small part of the internal capsule, they may cause a paralysis restricted to the opposite side of the face. Lesions affecting the left hemisphere in such locations also often cause disorders of speech. The association of right facial weakness with speech difficulties is common and excites no special attention in the literature, particularly since such right-sided motor symptomatologies associated with speech disorders have been described since the early 1800s. See, for example, Broca's 1865 description of the occurrence of speech disorders following lesions of the posterior portion of the left inferior frontal convolution.[1]

It took neurologists a longer time to recognize that isolated paralyses of the emotional use of the face may occur. However, by the middle 1800s, the possibility of such paralyses was well recognized, and from that period through the 1920s numerous papers describing this phenomenon appeared under a variety of titles.[2-4] In contrast to the ready recognition of a relation between paralyses of volitional movement and the corticospinal system, it has been difficult to define a precise neurologic basis for paralyses affecting emotional expression. This has been true partly because isolated paralyses of emotional expression are uncommon and because they result from a diversity of pathologic processes. Also, the neurologic mechanisms that underlie emotional expression are widely distributed in the brain and often encompass structures which are small in size and which occur intermixed with diverse other brain tracts and nuclei. Generally speaking, however, the mechanisms that underlie emotional expression are located in or near the midline, and they occupy ventral regions of the brain. Brain loci, lesions of which cause paralyses of emotional expression, include the orbitofrontal region of frontal lobes, the area innominata, the medial aspect of the tip of temporal lobes, the anterior ventral thalamus, the subthalamus and hypothalamus, and restricted regions of the brain stem. Thus, the clinical neurologist has clearly recognized and documented a dichotomy of function in the use of the face, and he has provided information regarding the locations in the brain of mechanisms that underlie the two types of function.

If a clear-cut dichotomy has been defined with respect to facial expressions, such a distinction remains less clear with regard to functions of the vocal apparatus. In part, this lack of definition of a distinction between vocalizations results from the major attention that has been paid in man to aphasic difficulties. However, because of this preoccupation with aphasia, we now know a great deal about the cerebral mechanisms that underlie the use of the human voice for symbolic communication. Several specific cortex regions of the left hemisphere have been positively identified as supporting speech function, as illustrated in FIGURE 1. A detailed discussion of these regions and their functions are available in Penfield and Roberts[5] and Nielsen.[6]

One branch of the dichotomy in the use of the vocal apparatus in man is symbolic communication; i.e., speech. The use of words in verbal communications is clearly volitional. The existence of a second type of use of the voice, i.e., in emotional expression, remains uncertain, and its neurology poorly defined. Indeed, the neurologist, when confronted with the proposition of an emotional use of the voice, inevitably thinks of the use of curse words or interjections. Such an interpretation is particularly reasonable, since the use of curse words may be preserved in aphasics who have otherwise lost all evidences of speech. Still, it must be remembered that curse words are symbolic utterances which denote specific meanings and which, in their normal, nonpathologic use are tied in with volitional communication. Thus, from a biologic view, the other branch of the dichotomy in the use of the human vocal apparatus is likely restricted to such phenomena as laughing, screaming, or shouting and other nonsymbolic utterances that may arise involuntarily during the expression of mirth or joy in happy situations, or of fear, surprise, or anger in less pleasant situations. To my knowledge, no publications are available that bear upon the neurology of such emotional uses of the voice except insofar as they may become exaggerated following diffuse or bilateral lesions within the hemispheres.[7]

What are the relations that exist between the use of the face and voice? The almost total absence of information as to the neurology of the emotional use of the voice makes this question difficult to answer. However, in agreement with others,[8] we would like to suggest that strong functional ties bind those uses of the face and voice which are emotional in character. Thus, a high probability exists that when the face is used to express emotion, the voice also participates. On the other hand, such close relations between face- and voice-use in volitional acts are not obvious. The close links that bind emotional face- and voice-use lead us to suggest that the neurology underlying emotional face-use is similar to that which controls emotional use of the voice. Further evidence supporting this assumption is described below.

The presence of two distinct uses of the face in man (volitional and emotional) and of a clear separateness in the underlying neural mechanisms raises questions with respect to the significance of facial expressions and vocalizations in animals and of their relations to facial expressions and speech in man. Are the vocalizations and facial expressions of animals to be identified with the emotional or with the volitional use of the voice and face in man? Or, are the vocal responses of animals still differently organized than either of the uses of the voice in the human?

Several theories have been proposed to relate the vocalizations of animals and speech in man. The most obvious of these suggests that animal vocal responses gradually evolved into the speech of man. Hockett has advanced a view that suggests such an interpretation.[9] Another interpretation proposes that human speech originated not from the vocalizations of animals but from gestures and other body movements.[10] Still a third interpretation views human speech as having evolved *de novo* and as bearing little relation to animal vocal responses. This interpretation has been advocated most recently by Lancaster[11] and by Myers.[12] Though hypotheses supporting the *de novo* origin of speech have not enjoyed widespread acceptance, the data which support such an evolution are considerable. The remainder of the present discussion reviews the lines of evidence from neurology which bear upon this question.

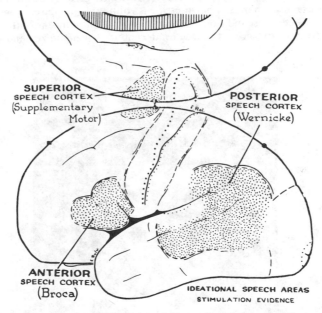

FIGURE 1. Left-hemisphere schema of man illustrating those areas of cortex electrical stimulation of which interferes with ongoing speech. (By permission of Princeton University Press.[5])

A dichotomy exists in the use of the face and voice in man. Both the face and the voice may be activated by two separate brain mechanisms, one related to volition and the other to emotion. What is the situation of the monkey with respect to its use of face and voice? It is a difficult task in observing animals to draw inferences with respect to the nature of their actions vis-à-vis volition versus instinct. It is possible only to suggest that the use of both the face and the voice by rhesus monkeys in their natural habitat seems to be restricted to circumstances that connote emotion. Their facial expressions and vocalizations typically appear as components of behavior patterns which themselves are best characterized as emotional or instinctual in nature. For example, this species uses its facial expressions and vocalizations as component parts of attack reactions, of defense reactions, of fear reactions, or in the expression of loneliness or isolation from the group, or of hunger. FIGURE 2 shows an example of the rhesus monkey's use of facial expression as a component part of a reaction pattern that expresses hostility or aggressiveness. At the same time, the rhesus monkey does not seem to utilize its facial expressions or vocalizations outside of such patterns of emotional reaction. Thus, observations of rhesus monkeys in a natural setting encourage the view that this species uses its face and voice almost exclusively as component parts of instinctual patterns of reaction.

The transfer of the rhesus monkey to experimental situations in the laboratory permits more direct inferences to be drawn as to the presence or absence of a volitional use of its face and voice. The rhesus monkey (and other animals) may be taught to carry out a variety of movements to receive food reward or to avoid punishment. Thus, the rhesus monkey easily learns to press a lever with its hands, and within a short time this response is performed with great speed and accuracy. We believe this use of the hands in bar-pressing is volitional, and the ease and rapidity of learning of this response indicates that the volitional mechanisms of the brain of the monkey have a ready access to those brain centers that organize hand movements.

FIGURE 2. Facial threat expression of rhesus monkey. Rhesus monkeys use facial expressions and vocalizations almost exclusively to communicate socially and to express emotion. (Courtesy of Dr. John Vandenbergh of Dorothea Dix Hospital, N.C.)

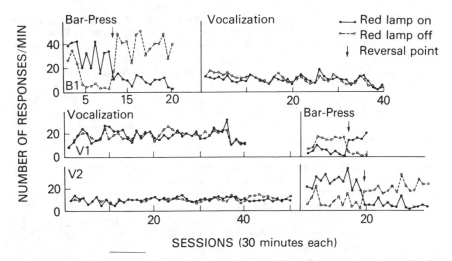

FIGURE 3. Performance of three rhesus monkeys on differential bar-press and vocalization conditioning. At the arrows, the reward-punishment values of the two conditions were reversed. Differential responses according to whether a red lamp was on or off easily emerged in relation to bar-press behavior but not vocalization. (From Yamaguchi and Myers.[15])

Can the rhesus monkey similarly be taught to utilize its facial expressions or its vocalizations mediately to achieve food reward or to avoid punishment? Unfortunately, to the knowledge of the writer, no such studies have been carried out with respect to utilization of facial expressions. Such studies, however, have been accomplished with regard to vocalizations, and the results are conflicting.

Skinner was the first to suggest that marked difficulties may arise when attempts are made to condition the vocal responses of animals.[13] Very interestingly to us, he explained this refractoriness to the fact that animal vocalizations are tied in with emotion or instinct and are not volitional. Thus, he states: "Well-defined emotional and other innate responses comprise reflex systems which are difficult, if not impossible, to modify by operant reinforcement. Vocal behavior below the human level is especially refractory."

The results of work carried out by Shirley Myers and coworkers[14] appear to conflict with this point of view. These workers seem to have succeeded in establishing definite instrumental vocal responses in cebus monkeys. However, careful study of this work indicates that the cebus monkeys' acquisition of these responses proceeded with difficulty, and only three of the original six animals studied succeeded in showing evidence for such a response. Yamaguchi and Myers, on the other hand, failed to be able to establish discriminative vocal responses in six rhesus monkeys despite prolonged efforts at conditioning utilizing several different experimental approaches.[15] FIGURE 3 compares the ease with which differential bar-pressing responses were developed depending on the presence or absence of a red light and the difficulties encountered in establishing comparable differential responses using their vocalizations. These latter authors emphasize the need for the animals' responses to be discriminative in nature to distinguish more definite conditioning of vocal responses from enhancements of vocalizations that may develop in association with acquired anticipatory sets. That is, the animals come to expect to be fed or to receive electric shocks when they are placed into a specific setting at a specific time. Such expectations induce certain tensions or emotional states in the animals which states are associated with enhanced facial expressions or vocal responses. Increases or decreases in number or prominence of vocal responses in different situations thus need not be adjudged to be examples of the use of vocalizations as instrumental responses but, rather, may indicate only enhanced or aroused feelings in the animals.

Sutton *et al.* have also attempted to condition the vocal responses of rhesus monkeys.[16] They described what they interpreted to be a definite success. However, they used an experimental paradigm which lacked a clear-cut discriminative aspect to the emission of the vocal responses and, from the set-up of the experiment, it is possible to interpret what enhanced vocal responses they could demonstrate to an anticipatory set. Furthermore, they used only three animals in their study and, allowing the widest leeway possible in their interpretation of the results, only one of the three behaved in a way that could be interpreted as suggestive of conditioning.

A further study describes the results obtained using 15 rhesus monkeys in a conditioning situation where individual vocal responses were food rewarded.[17] These animals were studied during from 17–37 30-minute sessions. Under these conditions, 4 of the 15 animals increased the numbers of vocal responses which they emitted over the first 4–7 sessions of testing. This early response enhancement suggested that these animals had, indeed, acquired conditioned vocal responses. However, after this brief initial period, all of these animals stabilized at new rates of responding. These new rates would easily have permitted these animals to further enhance their responses should they have been so inclined. The remaining 11 animals failed to show any definite enhancements of their vocal responses over the numerous sessions of testing. Despite the giving of food reward, one of these animals progressively decreased the numbers of vocalizations it emitted over the sessions of testing. FIGURE 4 presents the vocalization curves of two animals, one of which showed an incremental and the other a decremental pattern of responding during testing. These overall results are interpreted as indicating that, if rhesus monkey vocal responses are available for instrumental use and therefore, can be brought under volitional control, they are poorly so. The overall experience with vocal conditioning in rhesus monkeys supports the view that the vocal apparatus (and, in all likelihood, the facial musculature as well) of nonhuman primates is poorly accessible to those mechanisms of the brain that organize and control voluntary movements.

Until recently, little information has been available to identify those mechanisms of the brain that control the vocal responses of nonhuman primates. The earliest data bearing on this topic came from the brain stimulation studies of Robinson using rhesus monkeys[18] and of Jurgens *et al.* using squirrel monkeys.[19,20] The results of these studies show that it is the stimulation of white-matter tracts and subcortical grey-matter structures that are related to the limbic system that produce vocalizations. Robinson also indicates that direct stimulation of corticospinal fibers at the level of the internal capsule or of the pes pedunculi fails to elicit vocal responses. Jurgens[21] and Walker and Green[22] also failed to produce vocalizations when the lower precentral gyrus (the motor face area) was stimulated in monkeys, although movements of the vocal folds have been observed by others.[23,24] It is generally held that the precentral gyrus and the corticospinal tracts are intimately tied up with voluntary movements, whereas the various structures of the limbic system regulate instinctive behavior. If these suppositions are true, then these stimulation studies suggest that the vocalizations of rhesus monkeys are controlled by brain structures having to do with instinctual or emotional behavior, and they afford no positive evidence of a linkage with neural mechanisms having to do with volition.

What contributions have ablation studies made toward elucidating the brain mechanisms that underlie animal vocalizations? Again, few studies have been carried out in this area utilizing nonhuman primates. Nonetheless, studies with cats have demonstrated the presence of mechanisms in the midbrain—located particularly in the periaqueductal grey substance—which are involved in organizing faciovocal activity.[25-27] These results remind us that humans also may develop paralysis of the emotional use of the face following lesions at the level of the midbrain or pons.[2,28,29]

Regions can be identified over the hemispheral surfaces of monkeys that correspond in their general positioning to the speech areas of man. These regions include the inferior third of the precentral gyrus, the supplementary motor face area located on the medial surface of the hemisphere, the supraangular, and the supramarginal regions. Myers,[11] and Yamaguchi and Myers[30] have described studies in which these individual monkey "speech" areas have been removed bilaterally alone and in

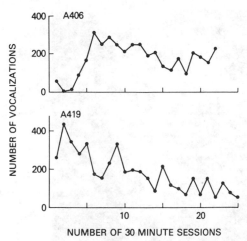

FIGURE 4. Two patterns of rhesus monkey vocalization that emerged in association with food reward. In the incremental pattern (above), the vocal responses progressively augmented over the early sessions of testing and then, despite continued food reward, slowly declined. In the decremental pattern (below), the numbers of vocal responses emitted progressively declined despite food reinforcement. The incremental pattern occurred in 4 and the decremental in 1 of 15 monkeys tested. The remaining 10 animals showed essentially no change in numbers of vocalizations from beginning to end of testing despite food reward.

various combinations. These studies failed to identify any clearly defined deficits in vocal responses following lesions of any single one of these zones of cortex. On the other hand, as one after the other of these "speech" areas were removed bilaterally in sequence in the same animal, the vocal responses did decline in number. The depressions following removal of all four areas averaged 49% and ranged between 18% and 77% of the initial rates. These depressions might suggest some specific relation of these areas to vocalization, but they also may be part of a generalized depression of neurologic function that results from such extensive bilateral cortical removals. Sutton, Larson, and Lindeman also were unable to demonstrate any significant deficits in vocal responses following "speech" area lesions in monkeys.[31]

The motor homunculus of Penfield and Jasper[32] and the corresponding simunculus of Woolsey *et al.*[33] importantly contribute to our knowledge of the cortical mechanisms underlying movement. The boundaries of the projections of the homunculae upon the cortical surface have been carefully defined from electrical stimulation. It might be anticipated from the conformation of the simunculus that lesions of the lower one-third of the precentral gyrus should cause a weakness of the opposite side of the face. Such a result would correspond with the findings observed in humans who sustain pathologic lesions in this region. However, specific surgical topectomies restricted to this zone and, indeed, ablations of the entire precentral gyrus in rhesus monkeys fail to produce such striking contralateral facial weaknesses.[13,34] Rather, deficits in contralateral facial motor activity were observed only in animals following removal of the temporal lobe, of the entire frontal lobe, or, surprisingly, of the prefrontal-orbitofrontal cortex alone. The lack of the definite facial weakness following precentral gyrus removal in monkey is illustrated in FIGURE 5. These findings suggest that the rhesus monkey controls its facial movements not through precentral gyrus mechanisms having to do with volitional movement, but rather through mechanisms in areas of the brain that regulate instinctual and emotional behavior. The identification of the involvement of the orbitofrontal, the anterior temporal, and the cingulate cortex in the control of instinctual and emotional behavior is described elsewhere.[34-38]

FIGURE 5. Facial expression of juvenile rhesus monkey following removal of right precentral gyrus eight days earlier. Note the absence of any asymmetry of expression.

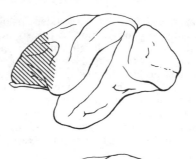

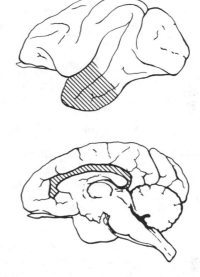

FIGURE 6. In monkeys, lesions of prefrontal-orbitofrontal cortex bilaterally (above) markedly and permanently reduced all facets of social-emotional behavior and largely abolished vocalizations and facial expressions. Lesions of anterior temporal cortex (middle) produced similar but less marked deficits, whereas cingulate cortex ablations (below) exerted a variable effect on vocalizations.

The unimpressive effects of lesions of inferior precentral gyrus (the cortical area for volitional control of face in man) on movement of the opposite side of the face and of the "speech" areas on vocalizations of rhesus monkeys coupled with the multiple suggestions that monkey facial expressions and vocalizations are regulated by brain centers concerned with social behavior and emotion have led to a more specific examination of the relations between those neural mechanisms that control emotion and the emission of vocal responses by rhesus monkeys. These studies were carried out with animals that were vocalizing at stable and predictable rates within a specific test situation. Zones of cortex that have been earlier identified as controlling social behavior and emotion were then removed (see FIGURE 6). In contrast to the mildly depressive effects of removals of the "speech" areas as described above, the lesions in zones of cortex controlling social behavior and emotion produced marked and often permanent deficits in vocalizations.[17] Of the three areas of cortex that regulate social behavior, it was the lesions of the prefrontal-orbitofrontal region*

* It is removal of the orbitofrontal component of the prefrontal-orbitofrontal region that accounts for the deficits in social behavior and vocalization that follow lesions of the prefrontal-orbitofrontal region, as has been demonstrated by further work in this laboratory (see also Ervin et al.[39]).

which produced the most marked deficits. In many instances, the effects of this lesion on spontaneous vocalizations were so devastating as to cause near total and permanent muteness, as illustrated in FIGURE 7. The removals of anterior temporal or cingulate cortex produced less marked and temporary but, nonetheless, significant deficits. The declines in vocalization were observed not only in the formal testing situation in the psychologic laboratory, but they also showed up in studies of the social behavior and emotion of monkeys maintained in the free-ranging situation[35,36] or held in small social groups in enclosures.[37] Furthermore, not only did these lesions produce major deficits in the vocalizations of these animals, but they also significantly diminished their use of facial expressions as tested in appropriately evocative situations.

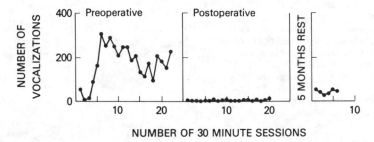

FIGURE 7. Effects of removal of prefrontal-orbitofrontal cortex on vocalizations in monkeys. The losses of vocal responses were sometimes nearly total and seemingly permanent as illustrated above. It is the removal of the orbitofrontal cortex that largely accounts for the social behavioral and vocalization deficits which are seen following removal of the entire prefrontal lobe.

What do studies using nonhuman primate species other than rhesus monkeys contribute to our knowledge regarding the volitional use of the face and voice? Of major interest have been the recent studies on the chimpanzee's use and nonuse of hand gestures and vocal utterances. The Hayes were the earliest to rear a chimpanzee in a familial setting and to attempt exhaustively to teach it to use its voice to communicate.[40] The Hayes generally failed to be able to teach their chimpanzee to use word sounds although, in retrospect, they did report that the chimpanzee had expended considerable effort (without success) to teach them (the Hayes) to communicate with it (the chimpanzee) not through imposed word forms but through hand gestures.[41]

Others have taken up this pursuit.[42-44] What has generally emerged from these studies is that the chimpanzee is a highly intelligent animal that can communicate ideas very well with the human provided it is not required to use its vocal apparatus. The chimpanzee has shown a particular cleverness in using its hands to communicate both by means of sign language or by depressing levers. These overall results fit well into the schema evolved in the present paper. That is, the chimpanzee, like the monkey, tells us: "If you want me to communicate with you don't ask me to do so using my vocal apparatus and word forms but rather ask me to communicate using any system you may want which requires the manipulation of levers or the use of hand gestures." The chimpanzee confirms that it, like the rhesus monkey, has excellent volitional control over its hands and body movements but only meager volitional control over its vocal apparatus. This view reminds us of the ease with which the rhesus monkey can be taught to bar-press for food reward and of the enormous difficulty encountered when attempts are made to condition it to utilize its vocal apparatus according to a discriminative schedule in instrumental responding.

In conclusion, the face and voice of nonhuman primates are poorly under volitional control. Rather, in these species, the face and voice function primarily as signaling systems, but apparently only within the realm of social and emotional behavior. Both brain stimulation and lesion studies support this view. The facial expressions and vocalizations of nonhuman primates are closely akin to man's emotional use of the face and voice. It remains unclear whether or at what level the nonhuman primate has developed even rudimentary mechanisms in its brain that can support any voluntary control of its face or voice. Certainly, if further work does demonstrate the existence of such mechanisms, it must be concluded from the present review that the magnitude of their influence must be small.

What do the present considerations suggest with respect to the origins of speech in man? If the present interpretations are valid, it is apparent that the speech of man has evolved not from the vocal responses of lower primates, but rather speech has developed *de novo* in man during his evolutionary development beyond the level of monkeys or, indeed, apparently, of the apes. From a neurologic view, the evolution of speech must represent the evolution of those mechanisms of the cerebrum located posteriorly in zones of cortex that function to analyze the information of the senses, to establish memories thereof, and to organize voluntary responses which proceed from these analyses or memories. The separate and distinct mechanisms of the cerebrum that control emotional and instinctive behavior still remain in the human to link us phylogenetically with our lower primate forebears. For the proper study of language, however, one would do well to focus on the physiologic properties of the posterior cerebrum of man himself and to avoid speculation as to similarities between the vocal responses of animals and speech in man.

References

1. BROCA, P. 1865. Sur la faculte du langage. Bull. Soc. Anthropol. **4:** 493–494.
2. SPILLER, W. G. 1912. Loss of emotional movements of the face with preservation or slight impairment of voluntary movement in partial paralysis of the facial nerve. Am. J. Med. Sci. **CXLIII:** 390–393.
3. MONRAD-KROHN, G. H. 1924. On the dissociation of voluntary and emotional innervation in facial paresis of central origin. Brain **47:** 22–35.
4. FEILING, A. 1927. A case of mimic facial paralysis. J. Neurol. Psychopath. **8:** 141–145.
5. PENFIELD, W. & L. ROBERTS. 1959. Speech and Brain Mechanisms: 119–137. Princeton University Press. Princeton, N.J.
6. NIELSEN, J. M. 1946. Agnosia, Apraxia, Aphasia: Their Value in Cerebral Localization. 2nd edit: 1–201. Paul H. Hoeber, New York, N.Y.
7. WILSON, S. A. K. 1929. Modern Problems in Neurology. Ch. XII. Pathological Laughter and Crying: 260–296. Williams Wood & Co. New York, N.Y.
8. MAGOUN, H. W., D. ATLAS, E. H. INGERSALL & S. W. RANSON. 1937. Associated facial, vocal, and respiratory components of emotional expression: An experimental study. J. Neurol. Psychopath. **17:** 241–255.
9. HOCKETT, C. F. 1960. The origin of speech. Sci. Am. **203:** 88–96.
10. HEWES, G. W. 1973. Primate communication and the gestural origin of language. Current Anthropol. **14:** 5–24.
11. LANCASTER, J. B. 1968. Primate communication systems and the emergence of human language. *In* Primates. J. C. Jay, Ed.: 439–457. Holt. New York, N.Y.
12. MYERS, R. E. 1969. Neurology of social communication in primates. Proc. 2nd Int. Congr. Primat. Karger. Basel, Switzerland. **3:** 1–9.

13. SKINNER, B. F. 1957. Verbal Behavior: 463. Appleton-Century-Crofts. New York, N.Y.
14. MYERS, S. A., J. A. HOREL & H. S. PENNYBACKER. 1965. Operant control of vocal behavior in the monkey Cebus albifrons. Psychonomic Sci. **3:** 389-390.
15. YAMAGUCHI, S. & R. E. MYERS. 1972. Failure of discriminative vocal conditioning in rhesus monkey. Brain Res. **37:** 109-114.
16. SUTTON, D., C. LARSON, E. M. TAYLOR & R. C. LINDEMAN. 1973. Vocalization in rhesus monkey: Conditionability. Brain Res. **52:** 225-231.
17. YAMAGUCHI, S. & R. E. MYERS. 1975. Cortical mechanisms underlying vocalization in rhesus monkey: prefrontal-orbitofrontal, anterior temporal, and cingulate cortex. Neuropsychologia In press.
18. ROBINSON, B. 1967. Vocalization evoked from forebrain in *Macaca mulatta*. Physiol. Behav. **2:** 345-354.
19. JURGENS, U., M. MAURUS, D. PLOOG & P. WINTER. 1967. Vocalization in the squirrel monkey (Saimiri sciureus) elicited by brain stimulation. Exp. Brain Res. **4:** 114-117.
20. JURGENS, U & D. PLOOG. 1970. Cerebral representation of vocalization in the squirrel monkey. Exp. Brain Res. **10:** 426-434.
21. JURGENS, U. 1974. On the elicitability of vocalization from the cortical larynx area. Brain Res. **81:** 564-566.
22. WALKER, A. E. & H. D. GREEN. 1938. Electrical excitability of the motor face area: A comparative study in primates. J. Neurophysiol. **1:** 152-165.
23. HAST, M. H. & B. MILOJEVIC. 1966. The response of the vocal folds to electrical stimulation of the inferior frontal cortex of the squirrel monkey. Acta Oto-Laryng. (Stockholm) **61:** 196-204.
24. HAST, M. H., J. M. FISCHER, A. B. WETZEL & V. E. THOMPSON. 1974. Cortical motor representation of the laryngeal muscles in *Macaca mulatta*. Brain Res. **73:** 229-240.
25. KELLY, A. H., L. E. BEATON & H. W. MAGOUN. 1946. A midbrain mechanism for facio-vocal activity. J. Neurophysiol. **9:** 181-189.
26. KANAI, T. & S. C. WANG. 1962. Localization of the central vocalization mechanism in the brain stem of the cat. Exp. Neurol. **6:** 426-434.
27. SKULTETY, F. M. 1963. Stimulation of periaqueductal gray and hypothalamus. Arch. Neurol. **8:** 608-620.
28. MILLS, C. K. 1912. Preliminary note on a new symtom complex due to a lesion of the cerebellum and cerebello-rubro-thalamic system, the main symptoms being ataxia of the upper and lower extremities of one side, and on the other side deafness, paralysis of emotional expression in the face and loss of the senses of pain heat and cold over the entire half of the body. J. Nerv. Ment. Dis. **XXXIX:** 73-76.
29. WILSON, S. A. K. 1924. Pathologic laughing and crying. J. Neurol. Psychopath. **IV:** 299-333.
30. YAMAGUCHI, S. & R. E. MYERS. 1975. Effects of "speech" area lesions on vocalization in monkey. Brain Res. In press.
31. SUTTON, D., C. LARSON & R. C. LINDEMAN. 1974. Neocortical and limbic lesion effects on primate phonation. Brain Res. **71:** 61-75.
32. PENFIELD, W. & H. JASPER. 1954. Epilepsy and the Functional Anatomy of the Human Brain: 52-106. Little, Brown & Co. Boston, Mass.
33. WOOLSEY, C. N., P. H. SETTLAGE, D. R. MEYER, W. SPENCER, T. PINTO-HAMUY, & A. M. TRAVIS. 1952. Patterns of localization in precentral and "supplementary" motor areas and their relation to the concept of a premotor area. Res. Pub. Ass. Res. Nerv. Ment. Dis. **30:** 238-264.
34. MYERS, R. E. 1972. Role of prefrontal and anterior temporal cortex in social behavior and affect in monkeys. Acta Neurobiol. Exp. **32:** 567-579.
35. MYERS, R. E. & C. S. SWETT, JR. 1970. Social behavior deficits of free-ranging monkeys after anterior temporal cortex removal. A preliminary report. Brain Res. **18:** 551-556.
36. MYERS, R. E., C. SWETT & M. MILLER. 1973. Loss of social group affinity following prefrontal lesions in free-ranging macaques. Brain Res. **64:** 257-269.
37. FRANZEN, E. & R. E. MYERS. 1973. Neural control of social behavior: Prefrontal and anterior temporal cortex. Neuropsychologia **11:** 141-157.

38. MYERS, R. E. 1975. Neurology of social behavior and affect in primates: A study of prefrontal and anterior temporal cortex. *In* Cerebral Localization. K. J. Zulch, O. Creutzfeldt, & G. C. Galbraith, Eds.: 161–170. Springer Verlag. New York, N.Y.
39. ERVIN, F. R., M. RALEIGH, H. D. STEKLIS, 1975. The orbital frontal center and monkey social behavior. 5th Ann. Mtg. Soc. Neurosci.: 554. New York, N.Y.
20. HAYES, K. J. 1950. Vocalization and speech in chimpanzees. Am. Phycol. **5:** 275–276.
41. HAYES, G. 1968. Spoken and gestural language learning in chimpanzees. Paper read at meeting of Psychomonic Society. November.
42. GARDNER, R. A. & B. GARDNER. 1969. Teaching sign language to a chimpanzee. Science **165:** 664–672.
43. PREMACH, D. 1971. Language in chimpanzee? Science **172:** 808–812.
44. RUMBAUGH, D. M. & T. V. GILL. 1976. Language and the acquisition of language-type skills by a chimpanzee (*Pan*). K. Salzinger, Ed. Vol. 270. Annals New York Acad. Sci. In press.

DISCUSSION OF THE PAPER BY R. E. MYERS

E. W. Menzel

Department of Psychology
State University of New York
Stony Brook, New York 11794

Several times in Dr. Myers' talk and many other times at this conference we have heard the statement that monkeys or apes are incapable of using one or another humanoid mode of communication. In listening to Dr. Myers' talk it struck me that actually in most of these cases the data showed an incapacity in either the production of signals or in the understanding of the "same" signals when someone else gave them, but not in both. Might it not be important, especially from the standpoint of physiological psychology and speech pathology, to specify whether one is talking about the production vs understanding aspect of the communicative process, or animals as signalers vs. animals as receivers? (I must admit that in my own papers I have not always been careful about this distinction.) Some examples in which one gets different results according to how one looks at the communication process are as follows:

1. The Hayes and Kellogg chimps and other home-raised chimps were not, in my opinion, "total failures" at learning human verbal language. They failed only in producing words. All of these animals were reported to understand many (up to 100) words when the words were spoken by the trainer or parent surrogate, and they could "answer" with nonverbal signals. (Incidentally, I have never seen any evidence that wild-born, group-living chimps have this degree of understanding. Even a pet dog seems more acute. The only calls that wild-born chimps, or untamed dogs for that matter, seem to attend to much are the calls of conspecifics.)

2. My own studies of wild-born, group-living chimps revealed some, but not much, propensity to produce manual gestures; but the same animals, even on trial 1, readily used our manual pointing gestures as a cue to the location of a distant, hidden object, and they could respond appropriately even after a delay of several minutes between our signal and their opportunity to respond. Indeed, almost any relatively iconic bodily or locomotor cue that we (or another chimp) gave could be used as a cue to the relative desirability and general location of a hidden, distant object. My guess is that a receiver's ability to use a signaler's general eagerness and orientation or direction of focused attention as a cue of objects comes first; and the receiver's attention to more specialized indicators of eagerness and orientation (e.g., manual gestures, visual direction of gaze) comes later, as a result of experience with particular individual signalers. In this regard even von Frisch's studies have been misinterpreted: the dances of honeybees do not constitute *the* system by which honeybees get to distant resources; they constitute *one* system and there are other alternative specialized signals that can be used if the occasion demands. (Cf the Wenner-von Frisch controversy. Wenner seemed to assume that any demonstrable use of a nondance cue system as a sufficient basis for response disproves the dance language hypothesis—which is about like saying that if a man can get along with gestures he is not competent in English.)

3. The Gardner and Fouts chimps and other home-raised chimps initially seem to produce relatively few spontaneous manual gestures unless they are prompted, molded, or reinforced for so doing; but they do seem very acute at picking up and understanding almost any gross motor cues and many manual cues that their trainers give. That is, they are better at understanding humanoid cues than at (spontaneously)

producing them. Almost surely they get "tuned in" to manual signals more than wild chimps would because their human social companions are much more manually inclined than chimps.

4. The isolation-reared chimps studied at Yerkes and the isolation-reared rhesus monkeys studied at Wisconsin spontaneously produced all or essentially all of the major vocal calls of normal conspecifics; but they did not seem to respond appropriately to the vocalizations or other species-typical signals of others until they had had considerable social experience with conspecifics. (Incidentally, Gordon Stephenson's work with wild Japanese monkeys suggests that some signals have somewhat different meanings in different social groups—which is one more line of evidence that even though one or both aspects of the communicative process, taken separately, might be innate, the total communicative process, or the meaning of a specific signal in a specific situation, might not be innate.)

5. The Myers and Yamaguchi studies showed a relative lack of ability on the part of rhesus to produce certain facial expressions voluntarily in an operant training situation, but Robert Miller has shown that the same species is capable of using the facial expressions of others as cues to impending food or electric shock. (I should add that when Miller used isolation-reared rhesus in the same test, he found them poor both at sending appropriate facial cues to other animals and at understanding the facial expressions of others.)

6. Dr. Myers cited studies that suggest no lateralization in the ability of rhesus to produce vocal calls; but Dr. Pribram, in his discussion, cited a recent, unpublished study that shows lateralization in the auditory system of the same species.

I am no physiologist, and I am prepared to stand corrected on the basis of other evidence, but to me these data suggest considerable modifiability and social learning; and, more important, the data also suggest that when one is trying to train animals on human-type rather than species-typical signal systems the failures are more frequent on the production (signaler) rather than the understanding (receiver) aspect of the communicative process.

It is my opinion that the major reason wild primates do not more often use humanoid methods of communication is that they already have very good alternative communication systems and can "say" just about everything they care to say or need to say as long as their companions are familiar conspecifics and they can choose the conditions under which they live. It is principally when the individuals with whom they are trying to communicate do not know or refuse to reinforce the signals that they are already giving that they are likely to switch to an alternative (less preferred or less well-developed) system. In the case of language-trained animals I would add that there is as yet no evidence that these animals can communicate any more effectively *with each other* using our signal systems than they could communicate using the signal systems of their own devising. The fact that they can communicate better with people probably tells us more about humans as receivers than it tells us about animals. Obviously, if a man and a chimp are trying to communicate and the man does not respond to the chimp's signals, someone must try something else. The radical null hypothesis in language-training experiments has been stated by David Premack, who maintains that he has not taught the chimp any new modes of thought but only provided them with a new system for translating their thoughts into terms which we (as receivers) can understand.

One final point, and this is on Dr. Myers' discussion of voluntary and involuntary communication systems. In several of the conference papers, including the one I coauthored with Marcia Johnson, it was stressed that the meaning of particular animal signals does not lie in the signals as such but in the total communication situation, including the individual identities of the participants, their physical states and characteristics, and the environmental context. Further, probably no one doubts that monkeys are capable of voluntary, intentional, and purposive changes of their location in space, whether they sit, stand, or lie down, and so on. Now: even if one can show that some monkeys do not have direct voluntary control over their finer musculature or molecular aspects of their communicative behavior (e.g., the movements of their vocal cords and facial muscles), couldn't they still be said to have direct voluntary control over their overall communicative messages? Indeed, might they not even be said to have (indirect) voluntary control over their molecular responses? For example, all they have to do to voluntarily avoid making an "involuntary" fear grimace is to stay far enough away from the "fear stimulus," or turn their head so that they don't have to look at it, or run to a protector. Similarly, all they have to do to voluntarily produce an "involuntary" response is to put themselves in whatever situation "automatically" elicits that response. (This is surely a common method of self-control in humans, and almost surely it evolved before more peripheral or central methods of self-control.) The distinction between voluntary and involuntary communications systems (which I agree is an extremely important distinction) thus takes on new dimensions as soon as one is dealing with a free-moving animal, or looks at the hierarchical organization of communicative behavior rather than the more molecular aspects of that organization. Is it possible that we see animal behavior in general (and animal communication systems in particular) in more deterministic terms than our own in part because scientists, at least from the time of Descartes, have been more apt to study animals under restricted circumstances and to examine more molecular aspects of their behavioral organization?

LIMBIC INFLUENCES ON HUMAN SPEECH*

Bryan W. Robinson

Tallahassee Neurological Clinic and
Tallahassee Neurological Foundation
Tallahassee, Florida 32303

The history of the modern study of human communicative disorders began in the latter half of the last century with the studies of Broca,[1] of Wernicke,[2] and of other neurologists. Their discovery and description of critical areas of neocortex located in a dominant hemisphere set the context of discussion and theory for the next one hundred years. Studies and experiments on human speech have, to a large extent, been confined to these areas of the neocortex and to their relationship to human propositional speech.

Apparently forgotten for many years has been the comparative neurology of vocalization and vocal communication. It is known now that animal vocalization is generated and supported by tissue lying exclusively, or nearly so, within the limbic system. But, at the time of the discoveries of Broca and Wernicke, this was not known. The limbic system was not yet defined, and techniques for studying the subcortical and basal parts of the brain were a number of years away. Therefore, most workers assumed that the neural apparatus supporting animal vocalization was related to the human speech areas, that the latter developed or evolved out of the former, and that human speech was itself a highly developed form of animal vocalization.

However, evidence gathered in the past fifteen years has suggested strongly that animal vocal communication is limbic in origin [3,4] and that human speech arose from new tissue.[4-6] If this is true, and if human speech did not evolve out of animal vocalization but represents an independent development, it then becomes important to inquire whether the limbic system, essential for vocal communication in subhuman species, has lost this function in man or whether it still plays a significant role in human communication.

THE LIMBIC SYSTEM

In view of the broad interests of the members of this society, it may be useful to define briefly the limbic system and its functions.

It was Broca[7] who defined the *limbic lobe* to include that cortex which encircles the corpus callosum, basal ganglia, and thalamus. Specifically, the limbic lobe included the subcallosal, cingulate, and parahippocampal gyri as well as the underlying hyppocampal formation and dentate gyrus. Modern authorities,[8-13] using functional and anatomical evidence, have developed the broader and more extensive concept of the *limbic system*. This term is used to include not only the structures of the limbic lobe, but also the associated subcortical nuclei and regions, such as the hypothalamus, preoptic region, amygdala, septum pellucidum, and important parts of the thalamus, basal ganglia, and brain stem. Other authors[14] include, in addition, certain regions of the cortex, such as temporal lobe, anterior insular region, and posterior orbitofrontal cortex.

*Part of this work was supported by a grant from the Knight Foundation.

A wide and at times bewildering variety of responses has been elicited from limbic structures by several techniques, most prominently by electrical stimulation with surface and depth electrodes, often in awake and sometimes in unrestrained animals in natural social groups. These responses defy simple categorization but fall into three broad groups.

First, there are a number of simple or fragmentary responses that can be evoked from virtually all limbic tissue. Various autonomic reactions such as urination, defecation, penile erection, ejaculation, piloerection, salivation, and changes in heart rate, blood pressure, pupillary size, body temperature, and respiratory rate and depth are frequently seen. There may be long-lasting hormonal and endocrine changes affecting thyroid, gonads, and adrenal cortex. Fluctuations in the level of consciousness can be produced and range from extreme activation to placidity. Finally, a general change in motor tone or even inhibition or arrest of certain somatic movements has been described.

Second, at a higher level of complexity, more organized behavioral patterns can emerge from limbic system activation, particularly if the animal is unrestrained and is in an appropriate environmental and social setting with other animals. Organized aggression, fighting, fear reactions, defensive and escape responses, sexual activity with mating and ejaculation, feeding, and drinking can all be seen in full natural complexity. The areas of the limbic system from which such behaviors can be evoked are more restricted than for the more simple responses, but representation is still widespread through the limbic system. Some truly remarkable phenomena can at times be seen hinting at the potential of limbic system manipulation to modify fundamental behavior patterns. For example, in free-ranging primates, persistently evoked aggression can change, apparently permanently, a submissive male into a dominant one.[15] This capability of the limbic system to produce long-lasting changes in behavior and perhaps in brain organization has not been adequately studied by behaviorists and sociologists, and its role in recovery of function after damage has not yet been explored.

Third, an even more complex class of behaviors elicitable from the limbic system is demonstrated by giving the experimental animal the ability to turn the electrical stimulation on or off.[16] These motivational behaviors, termed self-stimulation, escape-from-stimulation, and avoidance-of-stimulation, may be related to feelings of pleasure or displeasure and may represent primary reinforcement accompanying basic drives for food and sex. It should be noted, however, that the exact nature of the subjective feelings associated with self-stimulation and escape-from-stimulation is not clear. The correlation between behaviors that are presumably pleasurable, such as sexual activity and self-stimulation, is not perfect, although this lack of correspondence may be the result of the artificiality of electrical brain stimulation rather than denoting something fundamental about brain organization.

Regardless of the subjective nature of these motivational responses, all workers agree that they are powerful modifiers of behavior and can be used to greatly accelerate learning. They are apparently the most effective reinforcers known, and in the proper experimental arrangement compete effectively with behaviors necessary for survival itself.

There have been many attempts to incorporate these many diverse limbic responses and behaviors into an overall concept. No scheme is fully satisfactory, but the notion that the limbic system is closely allied to adaptive behavior is plausible. MacLean[9] has pointed out the particular relationship of the limbic system to those responses and behaviors important for species preservation and self-preservation. Sexual, feeding, and aggressive behaviors, together with the appropriate autonomic and hormonal reactions, supplemented with powerful elemental reinforcers, combine to suggest the vital role of the limbic system in adaption and in producing long-lasting and permanent modifications in behavior.

The Limbic System and Vocal Communication

Deliberately omitted from the above discussion is the relationship of the limbic system to vocal communication. There are many experiments that show the limbic system to be important, perhaps essential, for vocal communication in cats, birds, and monkeys. The pioneer work of Hess[17] in awake, unrestrained cats identified many loci in the brain from which vocalization could be reliably evoked. These studies, confined primarily to the diencephalon, showed that the most effective areas were in the lateral and posterior hypothalamus.

In the sea gull and pigeon, Delius[18] has performed electrical brain-stimulation studies with implanted depth electrodes. The most consistent area from which vocalization could be elicited was located in the midbrain in an area encompassing the nuclei intercolliculari and mesencephalicus lateralis dorsalis. This area appeared to be primarily efferent in function, since latencies were quite short, the responses were not extinguished by anesthesia, reliability was extremely high, there were few after-effects, the sounds were abnormal and did not correspond to natural sounds, and there were no associated behavioral changes or postures. However, vocalizations were also elicited from portions of the hypothalamus and from the archistriatum, occipitomesencephalic tract, and some septal nuclei. These latter structures appear to be homologous with certain mammalian limbic structures, such as the amygdala, stria terminalis, and septal bed nuclei. In these areas, a more central organization of communication was suggested by a number of findings. The vocalizations were often accompanied by natural posturings and sounded natural. Further, behavioral after-effects and long latencies were often seen, and the reliability of evoking the calls was influenced markedly by the stimulus context.

The most extensive mapping and behavioral analysis of electrically evoked vocalization has been performed in the squirrel monkey[3] and the rhesus monkey.[4] Thousands of stimulations in dozens of awake and at times unrestrained animals in a variety of stimulus contexts combined with careful mapping demonstrated beyond doubt that the vast majority of effective stimulation sites are in the limbic system and closely allied regions in the rostral brain stem. The loci responsible were primarily in the anterior gyrus, amygdala, diagonal band-substantia innominata, anterior perforated area, stria terminalis, ventral septum, preoptic areas, all portions of the hypothalamus, nucleus accumbens, nucleus ventralis anterior, midbrain nucleus of the thalamus, zona incerta, and tegmentum. Virtually every type of vocalization described by naturalists was elicited. Different types of vocalizations were not randomly distributed anatomically in this system. Specific vocalizations often occurred in definite loci and zones. The data suggested four neural subsystems[4] mediating the different types of vocalizations, indicating a complex organization in limbic vocalization circuitry which lacked geometrical simplicity.

Two noteworthy features of the mapping should be emphasized. First, loci producing vocalization were distributed equally on both the right and the left side of the brain. There is, thus, no dominant side of the limbic system as regards vocalization. Second, there was no evidence that the neocortex participates in limbic vocalization. Several hundred neocortical sites in the precentral area were stimulated without the production of any type of sound. Kaada,[14] similarly, resected the lower precentral areas bilaterally without modifying vocal responses.

Other conclusions were reached from the data. Of these, the most important was that the vocalizations were natural and arose from a central organization intimately related to behavior. Not only did the vocalizations sound natural to human observers, but other animals reacted to them with appropriate behavioral responses. Spectroscopic analysis[3] also showed these sounds to be virtually identical to natural sounds and calls.

SPEECH IN MAN

The situation with regard to human speech contrasts strikingly with that described above. Data on human speech have been derived primarily from clinical material, since the performance of experimental brain lesions is not feasible. The most valuable information has been obtained from patients with vascular occlusions producing localized cerebral infarcts. Supplementary information has been obtained from patients with penetrating head wounds with restricted brain injury[19] and from brain stimulation during surgery.[20,21] Detailed neuropsychological testing of epileptics before and after cortical surgery[22] has provided knowledge concerning the functions of certain regions of the brain. Language lateralization and the phenomenon of dominance have been extensively studied by unilateral carotid injections of sodium amytal.[23,24]

All these approaches suffer from an unavoidable but regrettable lack of adequate experimental planning and control. Most of the brains studied are abnormal and, in addition, anatomical correlations are often imprecise. Nonetheless, nearly a century of study has led to widespread acceptance of the theory of Broca-Wernicke, which dealt with disorders of human speech not related to the mechanical functions of the production and enunciation of word sounds. Their formulation was based on clinical evidence and noted the peculiar dependence of propositional speech on highly circumscribed and specific areas of neocortex located unilaterally in a dominant hemisphere, usually the left. Elaborations by other investigators[25-28] divided the aphasias generally into the basic categories of sensory and motor (or fluent and nonfluent in more modern operational terms) and identified other characteristic features. Geschwind[29] has reviewed this complex literature and has cogently summarized the evidence that the various aphasic syndromes result from lesions which either affect Wernicke's or Broca's area directly, or which disconnect them from each other or from other sensory neocortical areas.

THE LIMBIC SYSTEM IN MAN

There are many fundamental anatomical similarities between the limbic system of the human brain and that of lower forms, particularly the subhuman primates.[30] The limbic system shows progressive elaboration as one ascends phylogenetically. The changes appear to be related primarily to the developing neocortex and to the necessarily more complex thalamus and basal ganglia. Still, the various divisions and interconnections of the primate limbic system are readily identified in man. The amygdala, septum pellucidum, preoptic regions, hypothalamus, habenula, hippocampus, dentate gyrus, hippocampal gyrus, cingulate gyrus, posterior orbitofrontal cortex, temporal polar cortex, anterior insular cortex, limbic nuclei of the thalamus, limbic midbrain areas, various interconnecting pathways and tracts, and other limbic structures are not only present but have closely similar topographic relationships as in lower forms.

There are a number of interconnections between the limbic system and cerebral cortex which could be of importance in human speech mechanisms.[31] Limbic-neocortical circuitry is complex, and any summary is oversimplified. However, it is worth noting that the temporal polar region and the posterior orbitofrontal cortex are heavily interconnected by the uncinate fasciculus, which itself lies closely subjacent to Broca's area and to the anterior limb of the arcuate fasciculus arriving from Wernicke's area. Lesions in and near Broca's area must frequently involve this pathway. The amygdala is intimately related to temporal polar structures that are connected to the dorsomedial nucleus of the thalamus. This latter structure, in turn, is connected not only to the lateral hypothalamus, but to prefrontal cortex, which is adjacent to Broca's area. The anterior cingulate cortex, after receiving fibers from the anterior nuclei of the thalamus, sends fibers via the cingulum bundle to the hippocampal gyrus, where transcortical connections are made to temporal neocortex, the hippocampus and back into the core of the limbic system.

Thus, wide expanses of frontal and temporal cortex lying near Broca's area are heavily connected to the limbic system.

Physiological studies on the intact human limbic system are rare. Depth-stimulating electrodes have been implanted in abnormal brains, usually in psychosis or epilepsy.[32] Tumors and trauma cases also have provided information. Typical functions of autonomic responses, complex behavioral responses (fear, rage), and motivational responses (self-stimulation, escape from stimulation) have been elicited from the human limbic system. Based on a consideration of the anatomical and functional similarities of the human and subhuman limbic systems, most workers feel that the human limbic system subserves an emotional and adaptive role in man similar to that in animals.

And what of speech? As indicated above, the neocortex is highly important for human speech and is generally considered the only integrative brain tissue of importance in human speech. On the other hand, the limbic system is necessary for the generation of vocal communication in animals. The question arises as to whether the capacity of the limbic system for vocal communication has been lost in man.

As long as human speech is considered to have evolved "out of" primate vocalizations, then it is reasonable to suppose that limbic speech functions have been subsumed into neocortical speech and are indeed "lost." Itani[33] has given evidence for this view. But if, on the other hand, human speech represents a new development arising from new circuitry, then it may be asked whether the limbic system still retains its ancient potential for communication and in what form limbic communication appears in man.

Based on the above considerations, it has been suggested[4,6] that

> ... human speech normally depends on two systems rather than one. The first and phylogenetically older system is located in the limbic system, is bilaterally represented without hemispheric dominance, antedates primate development, is closely related to emotional, motivational, and autonomic factors, and is capable of transmitting only signals of low informational content. The second system is supplementary to the first, was developed in man, is neocortical, lateralized, and usually dominant in the left hemisphere. As is so often true in the central nervous system, it did not arise "from" or "out of" the old system but from new tissue, namely, the neocortical association areas. This new tissue permitted speech greater independence from emotional factors and provided it thereby the means and circuitry to carry compact, dense, and precise informational loads. This system arose in parallel with the old, surpassed it, and relegated the old system to a subordinate role.

THE LIMBIC SYSTEM AND HUMAN SPEECH

In inquiring as to the role of the limbic system in human speech, it is instructive to identify first those aspects of human speech not adequately explained by the Broca-Wernicke theory. Clinical neurology presents at least four aspects of speech disorder that are not readily accountable by a strictly neocortical theory and that may be more understandable if consideration is given to the limbic system.

First, it is a common observation in neurology that precise correlation between the extent of neocortical damage and the type and severity of the resulting aphasia cannot be established. Apparently identical cortical lesions do not necessarily produce identical speech deficits. This problem has been partially solved by Geschwind's [29] revival of Wernicke's theory of neocortical disconnections, in which attention has been given to the depth of a lesion and not just to its surface extent. Wernicke,[2] as well as others, pointed out that the cortical regions described by Broca and himself must not only be interconnected, but must necessarily be connected to other areas of sensory and motor cortex to give speech content and expression. Thus, the observation that neocortical lesions outside of Broca's and Wernicke's areas could produce aphasic speech defects found a partial explanation. However, major discrepancies still exist, implying the presence of still unidentified neural structures of importance in speech.

Some of the lack of correlation between the neocortical lesion and the resulting dysphasia may be due to damage to neighborhood limbic structures and pathways. As has been seen, wide areas of temporal and frontal cortex are closely related to the limbic system and are also proximate to Broca's area. The uncinate fasciculus, interconnecting the temporal polar and orbitofrontal cortex, lies just deep to the arcuate fasciculus interconnecting Wernicke's and Broca's area. All of these structures must be frequently damaged in infarcts, penetrating wounds, and other lesions producing aphasia. Attention should be given to these structures as well as to other limbic areas in clinicopathological studies of aphasia.

Second, the occurrence of mute states in alert patients who do not have specific neocortical damage is not readily explained by the Broca-Wernicke theory of speech. These syndromes are characterized by the partial or complete absence of speech. However, burst of linguistically normal speech may occur from time to time. For example, the dysphasic syndrome associated with anterior cingulate lesions has an element of mutism with intermittent bursts of speech.

Lesions associated with mutism are typically not neocortical. The best documented areas of damage are in the anterior cingulate cortex and in the rostral brain stem, especially the central tegmentum and the central gray substance. These areas contain important limbic pathways. As has been described, the anterior cingulate cortex is related to the hippocampal gyrus and hippocampus via cingulum bundle, to the septum via the fornix longus of Forel, and to the mamillary bodies of the hypothalamus and the anterior nuclei of the thalamus. The midbrain areas contain important limbic pathways that form the limbic midbrain area.[11] Bilateral lesions in these midbrain areas, as well as in the paraventricular gray surrounding the third ventricle, also an important limbic area, may result in the syndrome of akinetic mutism, in which an awake and visually attentive patient rarely speaks or moves.

The intriguing possibility exists that these mute states may result from specific effects of limbic lesions that remove facilitation from the neocortical speech circuits. Since vocalization is bilaterally represented in the limbic system without unilateral dominance, such lesions would in most cases be bilateral, would affect other vital functions, including consciousness, and would therefore be uncommon. These syndromes may be termed *limbic aphasias*, since the word "aphasia" literally means "not speaking," and its use in this context would appear to be appropriate.

Third, the selective preservation of vulgar and profane speech and the temporary improvement of speech in nonfluent aphasics who are under emotional stress[34] are phenomena that have no ready explanation in a theory of speech restricted to the neocortex.

The speech most commonly retained in aphasia is that related to emotional expression, such as words or phrases of deep personal significance, affirmation, denial, profanity, and ejaculation. The return of such language is noteworthy in that it is apparently not related to one's training, since it is readily seen, for example, in individuals who rarely use profanity in their normal speech. It therefore does not represent the nonspecific activation of habitual language forms but the specific facilitation of neural tissue associated with emotion, presumably the limbic system. It may represent vestigial limbic speech reflecting the role of the limbic system in emotionally charged vocalization and mediated by connections between the limbic system and the brain stem. The fact that such vulgarisms are selectively preserved implies that this older pathway still functions in neocortical aphasia.

The facilitation of nonfluent dysphasic speech by excitement is also not a new observation. The present author[6] has briefly reported such a case, which illustrates not just the greater quantitative production of linguistically impaired speech but qualitatively improved speech with less linguistic impairment. The case was remarkable in that a sustained state of emotional excitement was brought about by the manic phase of a manic-depressive psychosis. A more complete report is being prepared (manuscript in preparation).

Briefly, the patient was a 45-year, right-handed male who suffered a right hemiparesis and a nonfluent dysphasia secondary to a left convexity meningioma, despite successful removal of the tumor at craniotomy. Some four or five years after operation he developed a manic state. Neurological testing showed no evidence of recurrence of the meningioma. During the mania, there was significant improvement both in speech and in use of the right extremities. Treatment with chlorpromazine was effective in reducing the mania but with concomitant reappearance of both the nonfluent dysphasia and the right hemiparesis. By cycling the dosage of medication, the beneficial effects of the mania on speech was observed several times.

The improvement in speech during the sustained manic excitement was linguistically noteworthy. Although the content of the speech was paranoid and psychotic, there was marked return to prosody and rhythm. More normal use was made of all grammatical forms, including articles, modifiers, connectives and other filler words. Nonfluency was replaced by fluency; indeed, volubility was seen at times.

The case suggests some interesting possibilities. The *qualitative* improvement in speech under the influence of emotional excitement implies that the essential neocortical circuitry for speech, though damaged, was still partially intact and, under sufficient facilitation, could function successfully. This implication should be distinguished from that suggested by the mere increase in the use of dysphasic or profane speech during excitement. This, in turn, suggests that some cases of nonfluent aphasia may be due to loss of specific facilitation as well as to neocortical damage. Temporary improvements in aphasia, therefore, may be made possible by pharmacological or physiological means of activating specific portions of the limbic system.

Fourth, the rate and amount of recovery of speech in aphasic patients is quite unpredictable from the extent of neocortical damage. Patients who begin with linguistically identical speech disorders may achieve widely diverse levels of recovery at differing rates. While it is true in general that aphasics with small lesions tend to recover somewhat faster and more completely than those with large lesions, there are many exceptions. Every neurologist has seen permanent aphasia result from lesions too small to identify with certainty. Conversely, Smith[35] has reported speech preservation and partial recovery in a case of a surgical hemispherectomy. Geschwind[36] cites a case of ongoing recovery over an 18-year span after a lesion that destroyed the entire perisylvian region.

Some factors influencing recovery in aphasia have been identified. *Age* of the patient is a critical factor. Aphasia is rarely permanent in children, and recovery is the rule under the age of twelve. Recovery of speech from a single, abruptly occurring insult is less likely than from *serial lesions* of the same ultimate anatomical extent. *Left-handedness* is a beneficial factor with regard to aphasia. Although left-handed persons are more likely to become aphasic than right-handed individuals,[37] presumably since speech may be disordered by damage to either hemisphere, they also recover speech more completely than right-handers with left-hemisphere damage.

Other factors commonly believed to be of importance, such as overlearning and speech therapy, seem actually to play minor roles. Regarding the former, Geschwind[36] has pointed out that some aphasics may retain the ability to write their own names, but that this ability is often lost despite the fact that signing one's name is a highly overlearned response. As for the latter, Sarno[38] has presented evidence that a program of speech rehabilitation produces no more improvement than if the patient had been left alone.

However, even after these multiple factors are considered, the degree of recovery in an individual patient remains quite unpredictable. A major difficulty, of course, is that the mechanisms of long-term recovery from central nervous system damage remain unknown.[39] However, central to the idea of recovery in the central nervous system, given the inability of neurons to regenerate, is some type of anatomical or functional reorganization. Suggested mechanisms of recovery have included disinhibition of long-lasting diaschistic influences,[40] neuronal sprouting and denervation hypersensitivity,[41-43] and the use of alternative pathways.[44,45] There is evidence that each of these mechanisms may be important in specific situations.

There is also evidence that the use of certain drugs may hasten or extend recovery. Luria[46] has maintained that the stimulation of cholinergic mechanisms is helpful. Watson and Kennard[47] have reported that the use of stimulants such as the cholinergic carbaminol choline, strychnine, and amphetamine can accelerate recovery and make it more complete, whereas sedatives, including anticonvulsants, may have the opposit effect. Pretreatment with α-methyl-p-tyrosine (AMPT) seems to protect an animal partially against the effects of a lesion in the lateral hypothalamus,[48] and the use of nerve growth factor given subsequent to such a lesion is reported to improve recovery.[49]

Geschwind[36] has made the perceptive suggestion that, whatever the mechanism, unused pathways might be "opened up" or reorganization "stimulated" by specific patterns of synaptic activation of the neural elements undergoing the rehabilitative changes. Noting that subclinical seizures are not uncommon after cerebral lesions, the hypothesis is advanced that epileptic discharges might supply the needed synaptic activation.

Whether an epileptic discharge can result in specific patterns of synaptic activation necessary for recovery is debatable. The very universality of aphasia recovery in childhood argues against this being the primary mechanism of recovery, since minor or subclinical seizures occurring and persisting after the onset of aphasia is surely not universal. In addition, bursts of epileptic synaptic activity would be nonphysiologic and nonspecific.

Recalling the patient described above and the transient recovery of speech and movement in that case, the possibility exists that facilitation resulting from limbic activation is a more likely source of specific patterns of synaptic activity. This hypothesis is testable in properly designed animal and human experiments. The possibility was raised in the preceding paragraphs that temporary improvements in dysphasic speech might result from limbic activation. The additional possibility is raised in this section that appropriate limbic manipulation might enhance the rate or degree of permanent recovery from neural damage.

CONCLUSION

Almost a century has passed since the initial formulation of the modern neocortical theory of speech. This theory has been quite successful in explaining and predicting various clinical syndromes of aphasia. Yet, as has been noted, there remain unexplained discrepancies related to (1) the lack of prediction of the exact nature of aphasia from a specific neocortical lesion and vice versa; (2) the occurrence of mutism in awake patients without lesions of the neocortical speech areas; (3) the selective preservation of emotionally charged words and phrases; (4) the temporary qualitative linguistic improvement of nonfluent dysphasic speech under certain conditions; and (5) the inability to predict the rate and degree of recovery of speech from a given neocortical lesion.

The concept of the limbic system was developed a number of years after the neocortical theory of speech. Studies have shown that this system is intimately concerned with adaptive and motivational behaviors. Through the reticular activating and other systems, it provides powerful facilitation to a wide variety of other neural systems and, under proper conditions, can act as a most effective reinforcer. Its presumed role in supplying motivation for volitional acts has come to be accepted along with the notion that the triple factors of motivation, sensory input, and motor output are necessary for the performance of any act.

Investigations into the comparative neurology of vocal communication in animal species have shown that it is the limbic system which serves as a neural substrate for vocalization and that the neocortical speech areas in man are not homologous to this more primitive tissue. The limbic system is, however, anatomically related to the neocortex by means of forebrain connections, as well as to the cranial nerve nuclei needed in vocal communication. Thus, the neurological foundation of animal vocalization would appear to be fundamentally different from that of human speech.

It was Hughlings Jackson [50,51] who pointed out that when one neural system is supplanted by a newer and more highly evolved substitute, the functions of the old system are rarely lost or completely changed but are usually retained in modified form and serve to supplement the newer system. It is the position of the present author that the limbic system in man still retains some of its ancient capacity for vocal communication and is a significant factor in the neural functioning of human speech. The concept is presented that human speech normally depends on two systems working harmoniously together. The one system is phylogenetically older, is subordinate, and is supplementary to the other. Anatomical and clinical considerations suggest that the older system normally functions through the newer by means of forebrain connections but that vestigial limbic speech is still possible through its brain stem connections. In rational and logical discourse, the neocortical system is predominant, but in times of emotional stress the limbic system may reclaim its old primacy.

Lesions affecting speech provide an insight into the *modus operandi* of the two systems. The resulting model supplies an explanation for the discrepancies noted above in the neocortical theory of speech. Namely, lesions of limbic structures neighboring the neocortical speech centers account for the lack of one-to-one mapping between neocortical lesions and the type and degree of aphasia; vestigial limbic speech appears as the selective preservation of emotionally charged or vulgar words and phrases; withdrawal of limbic facilitation produces mutism; and heightened limbic facilitation results in transient qualitative and quantitative improvement in the nonfluent dysphasias and may increase the rate and degree of ultimate recovery.

References

1. IN JOYNT, R. J. 1964. Cortex **1**: 206.
2. WERNICKE, C. 1874. Der aphasische Symptomen-complex. Franck und Weigert. Breslau, Germany.
3. WINTER, P., D. PLOOG & J. LATTA. 1966. Vocal repertoire of the squirrel monkey (Samiri scuireus), its analysis and significance. Expl. Brain Res. **1**: 359–384.
4. ROBINSON, B. W. 1967. Vocalization evoked from forebrain in *Macaca mulatta*. Physiol. Behav. **2**: 345–354.
5. ROBINSON, B. W. 1969. *In* Primate Communication. D. Ploog and T. Melnechuk, Eds. Neurosciences Research Bull. Vol. 7.
6. ROBINSON, B. W. 1972. Anatomical and Physiological Contrasts between Human and other Primate Vocalizations. *In* Perspectives on Human Evolution 2. S. L. Washburn and P. Dolhinow, Eds.: 438–443. Holt Rinehart and Winston, Inc., New York, N.Y.
7. BROCA, P. 1878. Anatomie comparee circonvolutions cerebrales. La grand lobe limbique et la scissure limbique dans la serie des mammiferes, Rev. Anthropol. Ser. 2. **1**: 384–498.
8. MACLEAN, P. D. 1952. Some psychiatric implications of physiological studies on fronto-temporal portions of limbic system (visceral brain). Electroenceph. Clin. Neurophysiol. **4**: 407–418.
9. MACLEAN, P. D. 1958. The limbic system with respect to self-preservation and the preservation of the species. J. Nerv. Ment. Dis. **127**: 1–11.
10. NAUTA, W. J. H. & D. G. WHITLOCK. 1954. An anatomical analysis of the nonspecific thalamic projection system. *In* Brain Mechanisms and Consciousness. V. F. Delafresnaye, Ed.: 81–98. Blackwell. Oxford, England.
11. NAUTA, W. J. H. & H. G. J. M. KUYPERS. 1958. Some ascending pathways in the brain stem reticular formation. *In* Reticular Formation of the Brain. H. H. Jasper *et al.*, Eds.: 3–30. Little, Brown and Company. Boston, Mass.
12. NAUTA, W. J. H. 1962. Neural associations of the amygdaloid complex in the monkey. Brain **85**: 505–520.
13. NAUTA, W. J. M. & W. R. MEHLER. 1966. Projections of the lentiform nucleus in the monkey. Brain Res. **1**: 3–42.
14. KAADA, B. R. 1951. Somatomotor, autonomic, and electrocortical responses to electrical stimulation of "rhinencephalic" and other structures in primates, cat, and dog. Acta Physiol. Scand. **24**: (suppl.) 83.
15. ROBINSON, B. W., M. ALEXANDER & G. BOWNE. 1969. Dominance reversal resulting from aggressive responses evoked by brain telestimulation. Physiol. Behav. **4**: 21–45.
16. OLDS, J. & P. MILNER. 1954. Positive reinforcement produced by electrical stimulation of septal area and other regions of the rat brain. J. Comp. Physiol. Psych. **47**: 419–427.
17. HESS, W. R. 1956. Hypothalamus and Thalamus. Georg Thieme. Stuttgart, Germany.
18. DELIUS, J. D. 1971. Neural substrates of vocalization in gulls and pigeons. Exp. Brain Res. **12**: 64–80.
19. LURIA, A. R. 1969. Traumatic Aphasia, Mouton. The Hague, The Netherlands.
20. FOERSTER, O. 1936. Handbuch der Neurologie. O. Bumke and O. Foerster, Eds. **6**: 1–448, Springer. Berlin, Germany.

21. PENFIELD, W. & L. ROBERTS. 1959. Speech and Brain Mechanisms. Princeton Univ. Press. Princeton, N.J.
22. MILNER, B. 1962. In Interhemispheric Relations and Cerebral Dominance. V. B. Mountcastle, Ed.: 177–195. Johns Hopkins Press. Baltimore, Md.
23. WADE, J. & T. RASMUSSEN. 1960. J. Neurosurgery 17: 266.
24. BRANCH, C., B. MILNER & T. RASMUSSEN. 1964. J. Neurosurgery 21: 399.
25. DEJERINE, J. 1892. Mem. Soc. Biol. 4: 61.
26. LIEPMANN, H. 1908. Drei Aufstze aus dem Apraxiegebiet. Karger, Berlin, Germany.
27. GOLDSTEIN, K. 1917. Die Transkortikalen Aphasien. Fischer, Jena. East Germany.
28. GESCHWIND, N. & E. KAPLAN. 1962. Neurology 12: 675.
29. GESCHWIND, N. 1965. Disconnexion syndromes in animal and Man. Brain 88: 237–294, 585–644.
30. SARNAT, J. B. & M. G. NETSKY. 1974. Evolution of the Nervous System, Oxford Univ. Press. New York, N.Y.
31. TRUEX, R. C. & M. D. CARPENTER. 1969. Human Neuroanatomy. 6th edit. Williams and Wilkins Company. Baltimore, Md.
32. SHEER, D. E., Ed. 1961. Electrical Stimulation of the Brain: 477–556. Univ. of Texas Press. Austin, Texas.
33. ITANI, J. 1963. Vocal communication of the wild japanese monkey. Primates 4: 11–66.
34. MONRAD-KROHN, G. H. 1924. On the dissociation of voluntary and emotional innervation in facial parasis of central origin. Brain 47: 22–35.
35. SMITH, A. 1966. Speech and other functions after left (dominant) hemispherectomy. J. Neurol. Neurosurgery Psychiatry. 109: 95–150.
36. GESCHWIND, N. 1974. In Plasticity and Recovery of Function in the Central Nervous System. D. G. Stein, J. J. Rosen & N. Butters, Eds.: 467–508. Academic Press. New York, N.Y.
37. GLONING, I., K. GLONING, G. HAUB & R. QUATEMBER. 1969. Comparison of verbal behavior in right-handed and non right-handed patients with anatomically verified lesion of one hemisphere. Cortex 5: 43–52.
38. SARNO, M. T. 1970. Speech therapy and language recovery in severe aphasia. J. S. H. R. 13: 607–625.
39. STEIN, D. G., J. J. ROSEN & N. BUTTERS, Eds. 1974. Plasticity and Recovery of Function in the Central Nervous System. Academic Press. New York, N.Y.
40. MONAKOW, C. V. 1914. Die Localisation in der Grosshirnrinde und der Abbau der Function durch korticale Herde. J. F. Bergmann, Wiesbaden, Germany.
41. COTMAN, C. W., D. A. MATTHEW, D. TAYLOR & G. LYNCH. 1973. Synaptic rearrangement in the dentate gyrus: Histochemical evidence of adjustments after lesions in immature and adult rats. Proc. Nat. Acad. Sci. USA 70: 3473–3477. 1973.
42. EIDELBERG, E. & D. G. STEIN, Eds. 1974. Functional Recovery after Lesions of the Nervous System. Neurosciences Research Program Bulletin, vol. 12.
43. GUTH, L. 1956. Regeneration in the mammalian nervous system. Physiol. Rev. 36: 441–478.
44. LASHLEY, K. S. & D. A. MCCARTHY. 1926. The survival of the maze habit after cerebral injuries. J. Comp. Psychol. 6: 423–433.
45. BRINKMAN, J. & J. G. J. M. KUYPERS. 1973. Cerebral control of contralateral and ipsilateral arm, hand, and finger movements in the split-brain rhesus monkey. Brain 96: 653–674.
46. LURIA, A. R. 1963. Restoration of Function After Brain Injury. Macmillan. New York, N.Y.
47. WATSON, C. W. & M. A. KENNARD. 1945. The effect of anticonvulsant drugs on recovery of function following cerebral cortical lesions. J. Neurophysiol. 8: 221–231.
48. GLICK, S. D. 1972. Changes in amphetamine sensitivity following frontal cortical damage in rats and mice. Eur. J. Pharmacol. 20: 351–356.
49. BERGER, B. D., C. D. WISE & L. STEIN. 1973. Nerve growth factor: Enhanced recovery of feeding after hypothalamic damage. Science 180: 506–508.
50. JACKSON, J. H. 1874. On the nature of the duality of the brain. Medical Press and Circular 1, reprinted in Brain 38: 80–103, 1915.
51. JACKSON, J. H. 1958. Selected Writings. J. Taylor Ed.: Basic Books. New York, N.Y.

DISCUSSION

Karl Pribram, *Moderator*

Department of Psychology
Stanford University
Stanford, California 94305

DR. EDWARD WEINSTEIN: I want to make some comments on both Dr. Myer's and Dr. Robinson's papers. It's interesting that the monkey already has available the anatomical apparatus for laughter, even though one rarely sees monkeys laugh in the usual sense. Some observers in earlier times have seen grimaces in chimpanzees that might be interpreted as laughter. Stimulation of the brainstem two to three millimeters on either side of the midline in the reticular substance of the lower midbrain, pons, and medulla, i.e., between the midline and the central tegmental fasciculus, produces a series of facial, respiratory, and vocal synkinesias which mimic many of the complex, self-preservatory functions of the animal. Stimulation in the lower midbrain produces components of the lid-closure reflex. The eyes close, the eyes roll up, and the pupils contract, much as happens during sleep. Stimulation of other loci produces synkinesias similar to those of laughter, in which the eyes narrow, the tongue thrusts forward, the face spreads, and respiration stops in expiration. Still other synkinesias exist for swallowing, defecation, and other functions. Thus, even though the monkey may need other conditions and other kinds of brain development to laugh in a social setting, he has the neural apparatus for its expression.

DR. WILLIAM WILSON: Several years ago we were stimulated by the paper of Yamaguchi and Myers[*] which described their failure to establish discriminative vocal conditioning in rhesus monkeys. Their results struck us as remarkable, and we set out to find out how they could have gone so wrong. We believed, contrary to their conclusions, that it should be possible, perhaps with some procedural changes, to bring about a discriminative conditioning of primate vocalizations. We proceeded to demonstrate the possibility of such conditioning in two lemurs without too much trouble.[†] This last year Peter Aitken and I have turned our attention to rhesus monkeys. We were sure it would be still easier to show that Yamaguchi and Myers were wrong in using the rhesus monkey. So far, however, we haven't made any headway in that direction. In other words, we have completely confirmed their findings of the great difficulty, or, perhaps, the impossibility, of training rhesus monkeys using food reward to vocalize to an arbitrary signal such as presentation of a light. Nonetheless, the animals did seem to learn a complex set of contingencies. We could enhance their rates of response by rewarding all vocalizations, just as Yamaguchi and Myers did, in the preliminary stages of their experiment. When the situation was changed so that they were rewarded if they vocalized when a light was on and not when it was off, the monkeys maintained the same rate of vocalization to both the light-on and the light-off situations, displaying the same lack of discriminative conditioning that Yamaguchi and Myers have already described. However, when the light was on they advanced to the food cup as if they knew that only during *that* period would they receive food. Observing the animals which did vocalize in this test

[*]Yamaguchi, S. & R. E. Myers. 1972. Failure of discriminative vocal conditioning in rhesus monkey. Brain Res. **37:** 109–114.
[†]Wilson, 1975.

situation, it seemed that their vocalizations were very *effortful*. They seemed to experience difficulty in vocalizing.

So I have three questions that are all variations of "what does it mean?" What does it mean that lemurs *can* be trained in this discriminative conditioning situation to vocalize? What does it mean that the monkey seems to understand that "I get food only when the light is on," and that "I get food only when I vocalize," but is unable to put these two concepts together to realize that "I should vocalize only when the light is on." Finally, what is the meaning of the effortfulness evident in the animal's behavior when he vocalizes as a result of training?

DR. MYERS: Your clear-cut establishment of discriminative vocal conditioning in lemurs along with evidence for some discriminative vocal conditioning of cebus monkeys by Shirley Myers *et al.*‡ and of a chimpanzee by Randolph and Brooks§ serve as a caution to all of us not to overgeneralize results with rhesus monkey to all primate species. It is gratifying to hear you have replicated our results which show that rhesus monkey vocalizations are refractory to discriminative instrumental conditioning. However, reading between the lines, one senses that you are still committed to the proposition that rhesus monkey vocalizations can be conditioned. You base this belief on the fact that some of your animals increased their vocal responses during the early days of testing in the training apparatus. Unfortunately, other interpretations are possible. Overall, we have worked with nearly 20 monkeys attempting to teach them to vocalize for food reward. In the simple instrumental conditioning situation, only four of these animals increased their vocalizations early over successive days. The remainder either showed no long-term change in frequency of vocalization as training proceeded, or, indeed, a few diminished rather than increased their vocal responses. The behavior of the four animals that increased their vocalizations can be considered as only one minor variant—which happens to be incremental—of several possible patterns of vocalizing in the training box. Thus, the animals as a whole do not seem to show evidences of simple conditioning. Furthermore, even if all animals increased their vocalizations in the box, that is no proof that they were using their vocalizations instrumentally. Such increases in vocalizations can equally well result from their recognition that the training box is also a feeding box. When hungry monkeys are placed in feeding boxes they may tend to vocalize prominently, just as they do in their home cages when the animal caretaker enters the room at feeding time and rattles the lid of the food box. This vocalizing is not carried out *in order to* bring the caretaker but because the animals *are* hungry and they are reminded of and anticipate food. In this respect we agree with Skinner¶ when he says that the cat meows not to be let out of the house but because he hasn't been let out. Thus, no clear evidence has been uncovered thus far to show that rhesus monkey vocalizations have been conditioned in any *instrumental* sense either in simple or discriminative conditioning situations.

You have observed evidences that your monkeys understand that they get food reward only when the signal light is on. You suggest that they also possibly understand that they get food reward only when they vocalize. This realization, however, if it does exist, is apparently not of any help to them for the reason that they lack the capacity to control or modulate their vocalizations voluntarily. Perhaps it is just this discrepancy between their realization of a relation between their emission of

‡Myers, S. A., J. A. Horel & H. S. Pennybacker. 1965. Operant conditioning of vocal behavior in the monkey. *Cebus albifrons*. Psychonomic Sci. **3:** 389–390.

§Randolph, M. C. & B. A. Brooks. 1967. Conditioning of a vocal response in a chimpanzee through social reinforcement. Folia Primat. **5:** 70–79.

¶Skinner, B. F. 1957. Verbal Behavior: 463 ff. Appleton-Century-Crofts. New York, N.Y.

vocalizations and their reception of food reward combined with their inability to control their vocalizations that causes effort or strain in their voices.

One source of misunderstanding our interpretation of the emotional basis of vocalization in rhesus monkeys revolves around the meaning of the term "emotion." Our interpretation that rhesus monkey vocalizations arise almost entirely in relation to emotional states has been rejected on the grounds that rhesus monkeys often vocalize in situations that are "outside fear or threat."‖ However, we find the definition of emotion implied in such a statement to be too limited. Rather, we believe emotion encompasses many states of being which do not necessarily imply any extreme states of arousal or agitation such as is implied in "fear or threat." We believe emotion also includes many other, more moderate feeling states, including, for example, feelings of isolation, hunger, sex drive, playfulness, and maternal protectiveness. These emotional states which are often mild in tone are, nonetheless, associated with their own particular types of vocalization.

The suggestion that rhesus monkey vocalizations are almost exclusively tied in with and expressive of emotion is entirely unpopular in a society such as ours which emphasizes free will and individual responsibility. In a genuine sense we have been shunned personally by our professional colleagues for holding such unacceptable views. As scientists, however, we are bound to respond to our experimental findings. When we began our studies of rhesus monkey vocalizations we, ourselves, had no doubt whatsoever that they could be easily and rapidly taught a variety of instrumental types of vocal conditioning. It seemed obvious that rhesus monkeys can and regularly do voluntarily control their voices. Thus we, like everyone else, were absolutely shocked and incredulous of our findings.

DR. JASON BROWN (*New York University, New York, N.Y.*): I'd like to speak just briefly on the question of limbic aphasia and the possible relation of akinetic mutism to aphasic states. Firstly, I think that Ed Weinstein is perfectly correct in drawing attention to the possible relationship of certain types of jargon, specifically semantic jargon and an unusual kind of paraphasia which he himself ascribed, to bilateral limbic lesions. I would like to suggest that this need for bilateral lesions might be more characteristic of young aphasics, since we can see semantic jargon with unilateral lesions in older patients. With respect to the posterior aphasias, attention has classically been focused on the possible role of Insula in aphasia. As many of you know, this was a theme that concerned Kurt Goldstein most of his life, and I think that at the present time we have to say that the subject is still open. The surgical extirpation and stimulation studies haven't really supported the idea of an insular role in language, but the possibility of an insular aphasia, something that Dejerine suggested many years ago, still remains open. Even up until 1948, in his last book, Goldstein was still speaking of a possible relation of Insula to what he called central aphasia, what many of us now call conduction aphasia. For him this limbic transitional cortex was a central anatomical zone mediating central processes in a kind of hierarchic language structure.

With respect to anterior aphasia, I think that I would have to disagree with Dr. Weinstein on the lack of relationship of mute states to aphasic states, and thus agree with Dr. Robinson on that point. Particularly with respect to bilateral cingulate gyrus lesions, one finds a kind of mutism, actually a selective mutism with or without akinesis. That is, one can see mutism without generalized akinesia, a mutism that is a little different from true akinetic mutism, which is a more persistent affair. This type

‖Sutton, D., C. Larson, E. M. Taylor & R. C. Lindeman. 1973. Vocalization in rhesus monkey: Conditionability. Brain Res. **52**: 225–231.

of selective mutism may be punctuated at time by excited outbursts that may simulate in some ways catatonic mutism with excitement. I would like to suggest that there might be transitions between this type of mutism and Broca's aphasia, and one transitional syndrome that comes to mind is the so-called transcortical motor aphasia, where one sees markedly reduced spontaneous speech, essentially no spontaneous speech in many patients, in fact a greater reduction in spontaneous speech than one usually finds in the true Broca's aphasic, but repetition is often quite well preserved. One could argue that this syndrome is transitional between true Broca's aphasia with neocortical lesion and the selective mutism of bilateral cingulate gyrus lesions. This particular syndrome is usually caused by occlusion of the anterior cerebral artery, and I think the pathology might not be as it's been claimed in the past, cortex neighboring Broca's area, but rather cingulate or other transitional cortex.

Finally, with regard to Dr. Pribram's remarks on Broca's area, one is always reluctant to engage Dr. Pribram in a debate of any type, but I don't think we can dispense with the importance of Broca's area so cavalierly. If one examines closely the cases of the *topectomy* project, *Burckhardt's* cases, Penfield's cases of extirpation around Broca's area, one finds that these are, by and large, very young patients. Burckhardt's patient was 27. The average age of Penfield's cases is in the early 20s, and of course we know that younger patients who become aphasic show better recovery than older aphasics. One could argue that what we have in these cases is more diffuse language representation, anteriorly and posteriorly, so that when one does an extirpation relatively early in life the overall effect on language is much less than if the same operation was done at a later stage.

We should also keep in mind that the topectomy is a limited cortical removal, natural pathology is rarely so well-demarcated and also involves subcortex. Moreover, for clinicians, Broca's area is not just the pars opercularis of F3, which was removed in the topectomy cases. There has been a lively debate as to whether pars triangularis, anterior insula, or part of the inferior Rolandic region is involved. Even Broca himself thought part of F2 should be included in the Frontal speech zone. Another factor concerns the possibility of a difference in the effects of a natural and a surgical lesion. Perhaps this boils down to a difference between destroying an area and cutting it out. We have the same controversy, though on a larger scale, surrounding the work on dominant hemispherectomy; that is, why do natural lesions of left hemisphere produce at times more severe aphasic states, global aphasias, than does total left hemispherectomy? Here the question of diaschisis comes into play. There is also the fact that the hemispherectomy is done for gliomas, so that the left hemisphere is in a way "prepared" for removal; that is, the hemispherectomy is like the final stage of a multistage operation, early stages of which were accomplished by tumor growth. Single and multistage procedures in man, as in animals, have quite different consequences. I think that the parallel between the hemispherectomy and the topectomy findings suggests that this is not a crucial factor, that perhaps this difference between destruction of an area and its removal is more decisive.

DR. BRYAN ROBINSON: I want to thank Dr. Weinstein and Dr. Wilson for their comments. I don't want to make a big case for the use of the word "aphasia" to denote what I have tried to describe. Perhaps it is improperly used. The word "aphasia" is rather technical and has certain meanings for certain people, but I think that the disturbance in language and communication that occurs from limbic lesions needs to be described somehow. Perhaps we need a word that will include the mute states as well as the classical aphasic states. To my mind, it is quite natural that the effects on speech from two systems that are so different would themselves be quite different. One wouldn't expect the same linguistic deficits to occur in the two cases.

With regard to the second point concerning recovery from childhood aphasia, a symposium†† has been published on the general phenomenon of recovery in the central nervous system. Many possible mechanisms for recovery discussed extensively. Geschwind's concluding discussion concerns childhood aphasia and he points out that one quite viable hypothesis is that speech is learned by both hemispheres, and that the phenomenon of language dominance is a maturational event that leaves speech latently in the right hemisphere. When a child becomes aphasic due to left-hemisphere damage, the right hemisphere, in some fashion, may become stimulated so that speech is recovered. In an older person, for reasons which are not known, this is rarely seen.

††STEIN, D. G., J. J. ROSEN & N. BUTTERS, EDS. 1974. Plasticity and Recovery of Function in the Central Nervous System. Academic Press. New York, N.Y.

Part XII. Neural Parallels and Continuities (II)

LATERALIZED TEMPORAL-LIMBIC DYSFUNCTION AND PSYCHOPATHOLOGY*

P. Flor-Henry

Department of Psychiatry
University of Alberta and Alberta Hospital
Edmonton, Alberta, Canada T5J 2J7

Impressed by the fact that rabies, with its predilection for hippocampal structures, presents with prominent mental symptoms: fear, terror, rage, insomnia, struck by the psychological changes accompanying tumors of the corpus callosum which encroached on the mesial aspect of the hemisphere and by the dysphoric states occurring with ischaemic lesions of the anterior cingulum, Papez,[1] in 1937, stated his celebrated hypothesis. The hippocampus, fornix, mamilloanterior thalamic tract and its projections to the cingulate gyri formed the anatomical substrate for emotion. MacLean[2-4] in 1949 expanded the Papez circuit, showing that the septal nuclei, their brain stem connections via the medial forebrain bundle, the amygdaloid nuclei, and the insula were all, anatomically and functionally, part of the same complex neurophysiological system. This system he labelled "the limbic system" in 1952, emphasizing that the anterior cingulate and orbital-frontal components had important inhibitory functions as well as being crucial to autonomic regulation. MacLean also separated the amygdaloid subdivision of the limbic system, related to aggression and defense from the septal subdivision, related to sexuality. Importantly, he stressed that the frontotemporal region, (posteroorbital-insular-temporopolar-pyriform-amygdaloid-rostral-hippocampal) was essentially a closed physiological system where discharges induced by electrical or strychnine stimulation tended to be confined to these limbic circuits. MacLean in 1970, because of the common symptomatology often seen in "smouldering limbic epilepsy" and schizophrenia, concluded that perturbations of the frontotemporal limbic regions might be responsible for the affective, delusional, and perceptual abnormalities encountered in the endogenous and toxic psychoses.

The critical importance of the frontotemporal areas in the organization of the limbic system has been subsequently confirmed by the studies of Jones and Powell[5,3] on sensory convergence in the cerebral cortex. By neuronal degeneration techniques in the cerebral cortex, it was demonstrated in the monkey's brain that the sensory areas of the neocortex establish, by an orderly step-by-step progression, reciprocal connections in the parietal and frontal cortex, finally converging in the superior temporal and orbital frontal cortex; from which they project into the cingulate gyrus, the amygdaloid, and hypothalamus.

In this paper some of the evidence which suggests that the major psychopathological syndromes are the reflection of the lateralized, asymmetrical dysfunction of the anterior limbic system will be discussed, and new observations on the functional psychoses derived from neuropsychological tests and Power Spectral analysis of the EEG will be presented. Noteworthy in this context is the fact that as early as 1937 Papez quotes the earlier observations of Dandy,[7] who concluded in 1931, on the basis of neurosurgical evidence, that the "seat of consciousness" was localized to a brain stem-left mesial-frontal-cingulate axis. Removal of the right hemisphere, of the left

*The neuropsychological part of this research was made possible by a grant from the Medical Services Research Foundation of Alberta.

frontal lobe, left temporal or occipital regions were without effect on consciousness, whereas ligation of the left anterior cerebral artery produced loss of consciousness, as might brain stem injuries, but right anterior cerebral artery ligation did not influence consciousness. Papez again refers to Alford,[8] who in 1933 published observations on 33 cases of left hemiplegia, not one of whom exhibited confusion and only three, emotional instability. On the other hand, 27 of 55 cases of right hemiplegia had "definite and permanent confusion of consciousness and emotional instability." This last was essentially of the catastrophic reaction type. It is remarkable that in 1965 Serafetinides et al.,[9] using the intracarotid amytal technique, made similar observations, finding in 21 patients that loss of consciousness followed only dominant injections.

Review of Evidence for Localization

From the outset, clinical observations of certain forms of the schizophrenic syndrome emphasized the presence of language abnormalities as Kraepelin emphasized the presence of "speech confusion" in dementia praecox. It was Kleist who first drew attention to the localization and lateralization implications of the paragrammatical misconstructions, and of the finer disorders of speech understanding found in schizophrenia. Kleist writes in 1928,[10] "we found that a defect of comprehension combined with paralogias or a defect of speech combined with paraphasic phenomena was very rare in confusional or motility psychoses. It was never absent however in the schizophrenias and was very frequently seen in catatonic and hebephrenic dementia, even in the initial stages of these two disorders." In 1960, Kleist[11] concluded that the linguistic formulation and understanding of abstract and insignificant thoughts, themselves connected with speech, was one of the outstanding features of schizophrenia and implied "sensory aphasic impairments similar to those found in focal brain lesions of the left temporal lobe." In schizophrenia, however, higher levels of speech, those responsible for word derivations, word constructions, sentence formation, and abstract meaning of speech conceptions are perturbed—rather than more primitive levels of speech: sounds, word sequences, names, encountered with focal lesions of the left fronto-temporal regions. A number of contemporary reports have documented the presence of abnormalities and defects of speech perception in schizophrenia: Lawson, et al,[12] in relation to contextual constraint, observed that schizophrenics "have a deficiency in perceiving words in meaningful relation to each other as part of an organized pattern" and moreover have a particular defect in auditory verbal memory; Mefferd et al.,[13] comparing schizophrenics with carefully matched controls found that the former significantly failed to reproduce stimulus words, irrespective of distractibility; Moon et al.,[14] noted that the "loosening of associations" of schizophrenia was the result of the mishearing of the stimulus words, and vanished when this was controlled for; Walker and Birch[15] reported that the development of right-left preference was significantly impaired in schizophrenic children, compared to normals. Bull and Venables[16] recently found impairment of speech perception in schizophrenics compared to normals and depressed patients. This effect was independent of stimulus intensity, although with a dichotic listening paradigm they were unable to demonstrate that it was due to a left hemisphere effect. Maher[17] reviewed in 1972 empirical studies on language and schizophrenia. These show that schizophrenics fail to utilize the semantic and syntactic redundancies of language, use a restricted vocabulary (hence repetitions), and also repeat at the level of syllables apparently because of an active tendency of words, or parts of words, once pronounced, to intrude again. Geschwind,[18] discussing mutism, akinetic mutism, echolia, palilalia and schizophrenic word salad, the so-called non-aphasic disorders of speech, considers the neurological evidence which relate this symptomatology to a disconnection of the language areas in the dominant hemisphere from the rest of the cortex, notably by large frontal or parietal lesions. He draws attention to the similarity existing between Wernicke's fluent aphasia and schizophrenic word salad, although graphorhea, common with the latter is almost never found in the former. It is striking that the 'non-aphasic disorders of speech' are all classical symptoms of catatonic and chronic forms of schizophrenia.

For several years observations derived from surprisingly diverse investigative techniques have been published, all of which demonstrate dysfunction of the dominant hemisphere in schizophrenia. It has been shown by Fitzgerald and Hallspike,[19] Cawthorne et al.,[20] that abnormalities of directional preponderance to caloric stimulation of the vestibular system were ipsilateral to the side of the lesioned temporal lobe. Fitzgerald and Stengel,[21] studying 50 schizophrenics, found completely normal responses in 10, diminished or absent responses in 6, and 18 with abnormal directional preponderance. In 16 of these the direction of the slow nystagmic component was to the left. The remainder were normal on first, but abnormal on second examination. Monakhov,[22] in the interareal analysis of in-phase alpha synchronization by toposcopic techniques, showed that normals had a preponderance of·alpha synchronization on the dominant hemisphere, whereas this was reversed, or reduced in paranoid schizophrenia and in paranoid hallucinatory phases of the illness. Vinar and Skalickova,[23] comparing 100 schizophrenics, 20 manic-depressives and 220 normals, found neurological evidence implicating the dominant hemisphere in the schizophrenics. Luria and Homskaya[24] published observations demonstrating that the lateral asymmetry of electrodermal responses, with attenuation or absent responses during the orienting response, were ipsilateral to lateralized frontal and/or temporal lesions. In addition, they found that nonresponders with temporal lesions might respond to signal tones, although they did not respond to neutral tones as opposed to frontal lesions who responded neither to signal nor neutral tones. Pribram[25] has provided evidence that the orienting and habituation characteristics of the orienting response hinge on a reciprocal hippocampal-amygdaloid interaction: amygdaloid stimulation inducing the response, hippocampal stimulation provoking its habituation. On these bases, Gruzelier and Venables[26-28] reported lateralized abnormalities of the electrodermal characteristics of the orienting reflex in a large number of schizophrenics which implied dominant, or left-temporal dysfunction in this group. A smaller number of depressed patients, on the same parameters, had dysfunction of the nondominant temporal systems, whereas a group of psychopathic personality deviants showed left-sided effects. Both opthalmodynometric[29] and gamma irradiation techniques,[30] with radioactive Iodine, reveal that the cerebral circulation is asymmetrical and increased in the nondominant hemisphere. Nonetheless, Ingvar and Franzen,[31] investigating the regional cerebral blood flow of the dominant hemisphere in 20 schizophrenics report that, compared to normals or demented patients, although the mean cerebral blood flow is normal, there is in the schizophrenic significant hypocirculation in the left frontal and hypercirculation in the postcentral regions. This, the authors suggest, might reflect a defect in mediothalamic-fronto-cortical projection systems. In normal monozygotic twins, some 20–35% are discordant in terms of lateral preference. Gottesman and Shields[32] reported that a similar proportion (2 out of 10) was found in their twins concordant for schizophrenia. However, eight out of eleven in the pairs discordant for schizophrenia differed in laterality. This difference was statistically significant. Boklage[33] has analyzed in detail this aspect of the data of Gottesman and Shields. Taking all monozygotic twins, 64% are concordant for schizophrenia.

Considering dextral-dextral (MZ) pairs, 93% are concordant for schizophrenia. Of the eight dextral-dextral pairs, 7/8 are concordant, both for schizophrenia and subtype, but of the 13 sinistral-dextral pairs, only three are concordant for schizophrenia and none for subtype. In addition, the dextral-dextral pairs have the most severe illness, whereas in the sinistral-dextral grouping the sinistral twin has a more severe illness than the dextral, although still less severe than in the affected dextral-dextral pairs. The parallel with aphasia and sinistrality is striking. In strictly lateralized dextrals, damage to the dominant hemisphere induces severe dysphasic disturbances, whereas sinistrals who are more likely to have imperfect lateralization or bilateral speech representation, suffer a milder dysphasic handicap, from which they recover more rapidly after lateralized cerebral injuries. In the same manner, those twins (MZ) who are strictly lateralized, left-hemisphere dominant dextral, have the most concordant, and the most severe schizophrenia. In the mixed laterality pairs, the sinistral twin is the most likely to have the schizophrenic illness which is much more benign than in the dextral-dextral, strictly lateralized pairs, although more severe than if the mixed laterality dextral twin is affected. It would appear that similar laws govern left-hemisphere speech specialization, dextrality, mixed laterality and dysphasia, on the one hand, and lateral preference, dextrality-sinistrality, concordance for, and severity of schizophrenia, on the other.

Posttraumatic Psychoses

Hillbom and Kaila[34] extracted 81 cases of psychosis from 1,821 brain-injured soldiers. Of these, 20 were schizophrenic-paranoid psychoses, 17/20 had temporal lesions, with a significant excess on the left side. Subsequently, Hillbom,[35] having expanded his series to 3,552 cases, took a random sample, (n = 415) and established a temporal localization and a left-sided association with psychosis. In cases without psychiatric disabilities the incidence of right and left wounds was comparable, but as psychiatric disability increased, there was a regular trend by which left-sided wounds outnumbered right-sided injuries; this became significant when left temporal lesions alone were considered. Remarkably similar were the findings of Lishman,[36] who studied 670 patients with penetrating head injuries, extracted from an initial cohort of 1,024 on the basis of documentation for adequate analysis. Psychiatric disability and intellectual disorders correlated with brain damage and involvement of the left hemisphere but was independent of generalized intellectual impairment, physical disability, posttraumatic amnesia, and posttraumatic epilepsy. Left temporal lesions showed a strong association with psychiatric disability. Affective disorders were associated with right-hemisphere damage and there was a trend for right frontal lesions to lead to the "post-traumatic syndrome" and left frontal lesions to sexual and psychopathic changes. Davison and Bagley[37] selected 40 cases of schizophrenic psychoses associated with closed head injuries and with skull fracture from the international literature, on the basis of adequacy of information provided. They found significant associations between temporal lesions, left-hemisphere injuries, closed head injuries, and unconsciousness of more than 24 hours.

Cerebral Tumors

Bingley,[38] studying mental symptoms in temporal lobe gliomas, reported that in 198 dextral patients there was a moderate association between mental symptoms and papilloedema. If the lobes were considered separately, however, there was no association with the dominant, but a marked association between papilloedema, mental symptoms, and the nondominant lobe. Furthermore, with dominant lesions mental symptoms occurred before the appearance of papilloedema, and in cases without papilloedema dominant gliomas had more psychic symptoms. Also, blunting of affect was strongly associated with dominant gliomas. These remarkable relationships again emphasize the importance of dominant temporal pathology in the genesis of psychiatric symptomatology. Davison and Bagley[37] culled 77 cases of schizophrenic psychoses associated with cerebral tumors and found that, compared to unselected series of cerebral tumors, the tumor site in the psychotic group had a temporal localization, (p < .001). In a correlational analysis made between individual symptoms and lesion site in 80 cases with circumscribed lesions, the most significant statistical relationships that emereged related primary delusions and catatonic symptomatology to left hemisphere, particularly left temporal localization (p < .001).

Temporal Lobe Epilepsy

The study of psychopathological manifestations encountered in temporal lobe epilepsy, as this writer has already extensively discussed,[39-42] demonstrates very significant laterality effects with respect to psychosis, psychopathic personality deviation, and affective disturbances. There is a very strong association linking dominant temporal epilepsy with schizophrenic and paranoid psychoses and with psychopathy. There is a weaker, but nevertheless quite definite, relationship between nondominant temporal epilepsy and manic-depressive psychoses, and, more generally, with dysphoric states of neurotic type. Interestingly, Mnoukhine and Dinabourg,[43] investigating 139 children with cerebral palsy, hemiparesis, and epilepsy observed that cerebral insult lateralized to the dominant hemisphere produced profound intellectual retardation and blunting of affectivity, whereas lateralization to the nondominant hemisphere led to "distinct intensification of emotional manifestations, abrupt excitability, melancholic depressions."

Neuropsychological Investigation of Psychopathy and Depression

Dr. L. T. Ycudall and this writer have reported[44] evidence derived from 70 patients: depressed, (neurotic, psychotic, with and without structural brain damage) and psychopaths, (primary and "neurotic" criminals) chosen simply because they had, consecutively, been referred for neuropsychological testing. Hence, in this respect, it was a biased sample. They were subjected to a neuropsychological test battery, organized by Yeudall and consisting of 25 indicators of localized and lateralized cerebral dysfunction, evaluating frontal, temporal, and parietal functions. Blind neuropsychological interpretations showed that psychopathy was related to dominant and depression to nondominant frontotemporal dysfunction (r = .76; p < .001). What is more, for the depressed patients the nondominant lateralization held irrespective of the presence, or absence, of brain damage. It was noteworthy that primary psychopaths alone exhibited dominant effects, the "neurotic" criminals showing nondominant dysfunction. Systematic analysis of the verbal and performance scales of the Wechsler (W.A.I.S.), confirmed these laterality effects, the psychopaths exhibiting a decrement of verbal, over performance I.Q. and the depressed a decrement of performance over verbal I.Q. scores. It is well established that the vocabulary and similarities subtests of the WAIS are sensitive indicators of dominant hemispheric dysfunction, and the object assembly and block design subtests, of dysfunction of the nondominant hemisphere. These observations are in agreement with a large body of psychometrical data on psychopathy and depression. It is suggested, however, that it is not because they "act out" that psychopaths have a diminished verbal I.Q. and that it is not "because they are depressed" that affective patients have a lowered performance I.Q., but rather that these lateralized decrements and the corresponding psychopathological states are different reflections of underlying lateralized cerebral disorganization.

NEUROPSYCHOLOGICAL AND POWER SPECTRAL EEG ANALYSIS OF THE FUNCTIONAL PSYCHOSES

Neuropsychological Investigation

Method

Consecutive patients (n = 114) who fulfilled our research criteria for schizophrenia, mania, hypomania or depression (unipolar and bipolar) were subjected to neuropsychological testing, under blind conditions. The criteria for schizophrenia were strict, following Schneiderian, rather than Bleulerian formulations. Two or more Schneiderian symptoms of the first rank had to be present, in a setting of clear consciousness, without a history of exogenous factors, in the absence of structural disease of the Central Nervous System and where the abnormal mental symptoms could not be understood as being derivative of an underlying morbid mood. When the above constellation appeared to be reactive to adverse life events and showed a well-marked affective coloring, they were classified as "schizophreniform." Acute psychoses, even if thought disordered, hallucinatory, and with florid symptoms of the first rank which were periodic in course, and which exhibited either at the time of examination or in previous episodes definite clinical depression or mania, were labeled "schizo-affective" and classified with the affective psychoses. The affective syndrome of depression was characterized by dysphoric mood, present for at least two weeks, with subjective sadness, anorexia, loss of weight, insomnia, or hypersomnia, loss of energy, diminished libido, impaired concentration and delusions of unworthiness. The diagnosis of mania, or hypomania, was established when euphoria or irritability was found, accompanied by motor overactivity, pressure of speech, flight of ideas, delusional grandiosity, distractability and diminished sleep requirements. The diagnostic criteria were related to those advocated by Feighner et al.[45]. The mental state was documented by the Present State Examination Schedule, developed by Wing et al.,[46] which was also completed by a second psychiatrist* to allow for the reliability of the psychiatric symptomatology elicited and for a subsequent correlational analysis between psychic symptoms and neuropsychological variables. Approximately half the schizophrenia series belonged to the nuclear syndrome and half to the "schizophreniform" variety. Ninety percent of the nuclear group satisfied the criteria of Feighner et al. There was 90% agreement on subdiagnosis between the two psychiatrists. The average duration of illness was nine years. Including the "schizophreniform" class the agreement on diagnosis fell to 50%, 64% being Feighner positive. The distinction between the nuclear and schizophreniform varieties was made retrospectively. Similarly the agreement on diagnosis for the

---

* Dr. B. Howarth, Consultant Psychiatrist, Alberta Hospital, Edmonton, Canada.

affective psychoses was 78%, 75% fulfilling the criteria of Feighner.[45] The patients were then tested, under blind conditions, with the "laterality" neuropsychological test battery, devised by Yeudall.† In addition, the Wechsler Adult Intelligence Scale was administered (WAIS). In about half the series the testing was carried out before the administration of psychotropic drugs. Because the psychopathological syndromes selected were severe, the testing, undertaken by a specially trained assistant,‡ took on the average five to eight hours, but not infrequently had to be done over two days, taking 13–16 hours. The neuropsychological "pattern" analysis was interpreted under double blind conditions at the end of the two years of study by two neuropsychologists§ to permit an interreliability assessment. Neither the tester, nor the neuropsychologists knew the patients nor their diagnosis.

Results

The psychotic series consisted of schizophrenia (n = 54), and affective psychoses (n = 60). The two psychotic groups did not differ significantly in age, (schizophrenia x̄ = 36.3; affective x̄ = 38.6) nor in years of education. Sixty-one percent of the schizophrenic series were male, but only 48% of the affectives. Of the total psychosis series, 7.3 percent were sinistral or ambidextrous. This was assessed by the Marrion Annet[47] questionnaire, consisting of 12 items of hand preference. Dextral choice reported on eight or more was considered dextral; similarly for sinistrality, intermediary preferences viewed as ambidexterity were allocated to the sinistral group. One-way analysis of variance, T-test analysis, multiple step-wise discriminant function analysis, and canonical variate analysis were carried out. TABLE 1 shows the mean scores on the 75 patients who were able to complete all the neuropsychological tests. It is clear that the schizophrenics, compared to the affectives, are significantly impaired on those variables that reflect dominant frontal and temporal functions: aphasia, speech sounds, Oral Word Fluency, and Trail-Making B. Examining these variables for all patients, similar findings emerge, schizophrenics having significantly impaired scores on aphasia (p < .04), ideomotor apraxia (p < .005), Oral Word Fluency (p < .005), and Trail-Making B (p < .01).

The two psychotic groups did not differ significantly from each other on Memory For Designs, Tactual Formboard, Purdue-Pegboard, and Constructional Apraxia, all tests senstive to dysfunction of the nondominant hemisphere. It should be noted, however, that both groups, in these tests, differed from normal scores and were impaired. It was also noteworthy that bilaterally, on both fingertip writing and finger localization the schizophrenics were poorer than the affectives, but very particularly for responses from the left hand (R. hand = p < .02 vs. L. hand = p < .009). The clinical memory scales, both for verbal and nonverbal, learning were similar in both categories.

---

† The "Laterality" neuropsychological battery consists of 27 variables which were derived from the following tests: Wepman-Jones Aphasia Screening Test, Trail-Making A and B, sensory-perceptual integration: auditory, visual, somesthesic, and visual fields, Dynamometer, Seashore Speech Sounds, Graham-Kendal Memory for Designs, Raven's Colored Progressive Matrices, Organic Integrity Test, Finger-Oscillation, Oral Word-Fluency, Purdue-Pegboard, Tactual Formboard astereognosis, Seashore Rhythm, Finger localization, and William's clinical memory evaluating both verbal and nonverbal learning.

‡ Mr. W. Stefanyk, Psychologist, Alberta Hospital, Edmonton, Canada.

§ Dr. L. T. Yeudall and Mr. D. Faux.

Multiple step-wise discriminant function analysis performed on the 75 patients who had completed all the tests yielded an 85% correct classification for schizophrenia and a 94% correct classification for the affective syndromes. In order of diminishing discriminatory power the variables were: (1) Speech Sound Perception; (2) Oral Word Fluency; (3) Purdue-Pegboard Assemblies; (4) Wepman-Jones Aphasia tests and (5) Finger-Oscillation-preferred hand.

Interestingly, although the Full Scale WAIS I.Q. was comparable in both groups (schizophrenia $\bar{x}$ = 90; affective $\bar{x}$ = 94), the mean verbal I.Q. for the schizophrenics was lower, (93 vs. 98, p < .07) but the mean performance I.Q. was similar with schizophrenia x ⁻ 87, and affective $\bar{x}$ = 89. Analysis of the subtests revealed that the schizophrenics were significantly more impaired on vocabulary, (p < .05) and digit span (p < .04). Curiously, a stepwise discriminant function analysis on the WAIS subtests yielded a 70% correct separation for schizophrenia and 74% for affectives. In order of diminishing importance the subtests were: (1) digit span; (2) object assembly; (3) digit symbol; (4) vocabulary, and (5) block design (Mahalanobis' D-square-22.04, 13 d.f.; p < .05).

TABLE 1

"T-Tests": Schizophrenia, (n = 35) & Affective, (n = 40)*

Variable	$\bar{x}$: Schiz.	$\bar{x}$: Affective	P-1-tail
Speech Sounds	12.40	6.65	0.0004
Trail, (A+B)	284.40	184.12	0.005
Trail, A	66.60	46.15	0.02
Trail, B	217.80	137.97	0.005
Ravens, C. M.	10.91	7.10	0.02
Finger Localization, Preferred Hand	11.31	7.92	0.02
Finger Localization, Nonpreferred	11.80	7.75	0.009
Tactual Form Board, Preferred Hand	699.66	561.30	0.02
Seashore Rhythm	9.00	6.55	0.008
Oral Word Fluency	8.86	12.42	0.0004
Aphasia Screening	9.29	7.78	0.05

*Subjects who Completed all Tests. Means of neuropsychological variables for schizophrenia and affective psychoses.

The clinical pattern analysis (TABLE 2) showed that both psychotic groups exhibited bilateral frontotemporal dysfunction, but that, very dramatically this was asymmetrical, predominantly left frontotemporal for schizophrenia and predominantly right frontotemporal for the affectives.¶ It is worth noting here that not a single case of affective or periodic schizoaffective psychosis proved to have predominantly left-hemispheric dysfunction, and that in the schizophrenias the three lateral-

¶The table shows the pattern analysis evaluated by the senior neuropsychologist (L.T.Y.). The second neuropsychologist (D.F.) found that 90% of the affectives had predominantly right-hemisphere dysfunction, whereas 80% of the schizophrenics had predominantly left-hemisphere dysfunction, excluding those cases with symmetrical dysfunction.

TABLE 2

FRONTOTEMPORAL DYSFUNCTION*

	L	L > R	=	R > L	R	Normal
Schizophrenia: (n = 53)	4	41	2	3	0	3
Affective: (n = 49)	0	0	3	41	4	1

*Sinistrals excluded

ity misclassifications, all with pronounced affective features, fell into the "schizophreniform" variety. The three schizophrenics with normal neuropsychological profile were the only three of the series that were of superior intelligence. This is of interest in view of the recent evidence[48] that intelligence and schizophrenia are independently transmitted, and that high I.Q. has a favorable action on the schizophrenic process.

Examining the interactions existing between severity of cerebral dysfunction, laterality, lobe, and diagnosis (TABLES 3, 4) it is seen that mild degrees of cerebral disorganization appear to occur randomly and bilaterally in both groups. Laterality effects emerged only in the presence of severe dysfunction, and were stronger in the frontal than in the temporal regions. The strongest association was between severe left frontal dysfunction and schizophrenia.

There were six affectives and two schizophrenics who proved to be sinistral. Of these, all but one (affective), on the basis of finger oscillation, dynamometric strength and preferred hand for exploration on the formboard, appeared to have remained left-hemisphere dominant. On these premises, all six affectives had predominantly nondominant dysfunction, and the two schizophrenics, predominantly dominant dysfunction. In a separate analysis (Scheffes Multiple Comparisons) of the affective psychoses, the pure depressive (n = 13), the pure hypomanic and manic types (n = 26), the periodic schizoaffectives (n = 21), the unipolar (n = 31), and the bipolar cases (n = 29) were compared with each other. The severity of cerebral dysfunction was similar in all these subcategories, and they could not be distinguished in terms of neuropsychological characteristics. The neuropsychological evidence presented thus suggests that the endogenous psychoses reflect lateralized, asymmetrical dysfunction of the anterior limbic structures, more particularly of the orbital frontal-anterior

TABLE 3

LATERALITY AND SEVERITY OF CEREBRAL DYSFUNCTION

Frontal			
Schizophrenics			
	Left	Right	
Mild	18	35	$\chi^2 = 17.45$
Severe	33	10	$p < 0.001$
Affectives			
	Left	Right	
Mild	33	23	$\chi^2 = 8.95$
Severe	9	25	$p < 0.01$

temporal regions, anatomically and functionally linked through the uncinate fasciculus. It is notable that a threshold effect seems to operate, milder degrees of neuropsychological dysfunction occur bilaterally in both psychoses. The schizophrenic syndrome appears to be crucially dependent on disorganization of those neuronal assemblies in the dominant frontotemporal regions that are also critical for language processes. The affective psychoses, and the periodic schizoaffective psychoses, reflect perturbation of the homologous, nondominant cerebral areas. The significance of disturbance in the anterior rather than the posterior aspects of the limbic system is further suggested by the fact that the strongest associations between diagnosis and lateralized disturbance hold in the frontal regions and are still evident in the temporal, but disappear in the parietal areas. In addition, it is perhaps worthy of emphasis that the 27 neuropsychological variables discussed, quite independently of psychic symptoms, provide an objective diagnostic technique that correctly classify the endogenous psychoses with an accuracy of the order of 90%.

TABLE 4

LATERALITY AND SEVERITY OF CEREBRAL DYSFUNCTION

Temporal Schizophrenics			
	Left	Right	
Mild	26	28	$\chi^2 = 3.05$ n.s.
Severe	21	10	($\chi^2 = 3.8$, $p < 0.05$)
Affectives			
	Left	Right	
Mild	22	19	Yates Corr.
Severe	4	21	$\chi^2 = 7.71$ $P < 0.01$

Power Spectral EEG Analysis

This research was made possible through the collaboration of Dr. Z.J. Koles,[**] who was responsible for the design of the hardware and software components of the system and the analysis of the spectral data, with the technical assistance of Mr. P. Bo-Lassen.[††] The initial findings have been reported in an abstract.[49] Twenty-eight schizophrenics, 18 manic-depressive, and 19 normal controls were studied. The psychiatric groups were not medicated and had not received ECT. Needle electrodes in the right and left temporal and parietal regions were used in a unipolar montage against a vertex reference. A Tektronic type RM122 preamplifier and cascaded band-pass amplifiers were also used to provide additional gain in the 3–50 Hz region. The overall amplification, determined by the ± 2.5V input range of the data acquisition system ranged between 30,000 and 50,000. The data acquisition and analysis system consisted of a Hewlett-Packard 2100S minicomputer. Each subject was analyzed in ten three-minute situations: at rest, eyes open and closed, and during verbal and visuospatial tasks both motor and nonmotor. During each situation three-minute

[**] Dr. Z. J. Koles, Associate Professor, Division of Biomedical Engineering and Department of Surgery, University of Alberta, Edmonton, Alberta, Canada.

[††] Mr. P. Bo-Lassen, Graduate Student, Faculty of Electrical Engineering, University of Alberta, Edmonton, Alberta, Canada.

recordings consisting of 10 bit samples (at a rate of 120/second), were collected simultaneously from the four electrodes. The data was analyzed with a Fast Fourier Transform in consecutive segments of 256 samples. A raw spectral estimate was obtained by averaging the transforms from all the segments, and refined spectrum by smoothing the raw estimate with a digital low pass filter.

Results

The schizophrenics showed significantly more power in the 20–30 Hz band in the left temporal region than normals ($p < .05$). Power in the right temporal region was similar in schizophrenics and normals. The schizophrenics had significantly more power in the 20–30 Hz band in the left, than in the right temporal areas ($p < .05$). In normals the right/left power ratios calculated in the alpha frequencies reflected the relative lateralized suppression of cerebral energy expected during verbal and spatial tasks, as originally reported by Galin and Ornstein.[50] The ratios were greater during verbal than during spatial tasks. The psychotic groups showed the same effect as normals, but more weakly ($p < .05$ vs. $p < .001$, respectively), and the schizophrenics failed to show it in the parietal regions. The manic-depressives had more power in the 20–30 Hz band than normals, in both right and left temporal regions. The excess energy was however significantly greater on the right side (Left, $p < .1$; Right, $p < .05$, Mann-Whitney U-test, one tailed test). Examined at two-second intervals for three-minute periods, the time-course deviations of right/left energy ratios of both psychotic groups behaved similarly and were markedly different from normals. In normals there are frequent fluctuations of the ratios over time, above and below unity, but they are small. In both psychoses these shifts, on either side of unity, are often of much greater magnitude and of much longer duration.

Conclusion

These results appear to indicate bilateral, although predominantly right temporal abnormality in the affective psychoses and predominantly left temporal dysfunction in the schizophrenics. In addition the "sluggish" right/left energy shifts in different cognitive tasks and the abnormal time course deviations of these ratios in the psychoses suggest perhaps a defect of interhemispheric integration.

Discussion

It is tempting to relate the defect of interhemispheric integration to the observation that showed that the only structural difference differentiating the brains of chronic schizophrenics from normal brains was the larger width and volume of the corpus callosum in the former.[51] In this perspective it is fascinating to recall that Kurt Goldstein in 1927,§§ describing a patient with section of the corpus callosum had the following to say on the psychopathological consequences of disturbed interhemispheric connections:
"The separation of so large a part of the brain and the resulting impossibility of evaluating stimuli perceived with the right hemisphere . . . surely cannot be without

§§ Quoted from Geschwind, N.[18]

effect on the total personality . . . I have pointed out the presence in my patient of a feeling of strangeness in relation to movements of the left hand, which she described with such curious expressions, (she would say someone was moving her hand and that she was not doing it herself), that she was regarded at first as a paranoiac. It appears to me not to be excluded that on this basis and under certain conditions there may develop paranoid states, perhaps also the experience of double personality and above all the experience of being influenced from without. . . ."

The diverse evidence reviewed and the original neuropsychological and electrophysiological data presented, shows that one of the crucial parameters leading to the schizophrenic syndrome relates to abnormal events which occur in the dominant frontotemporal circuits. Numerous studies of mean integrated amplitude in chronic schizophrenia, pioneered by Leonide Goldstein,[52-55] were almost always derived from left occipital electrodes. These revealed that hypovariablity was characteristic of chronic schizophrenia. More recently these workers[56] found that the total integrated amplitude was higher on the left side in 173 psychiatric patients; and that anxiety and euphoriants (15 mg d-amphetamine) produced a shift to the right, whereas chlorpromazine a shift to the left, in normals. Similarly, Serafetinides[57,58] reports a voltage increase, lateralized to the dominant hemisphere in schizophrenia, which correlated with improvement, spontaneous or as the result of chlorpromazine. Again recent spectral studies[59,60] confirm that the abnormally high energy between 18 and 30 Hz is a striking feature of schizophrenia. The composite spectral curves averaging schizophrenics and normals (from an ongoing study) illustrate the abnormal left temporal energy in the 20–30 Hz, characteristic of schizophrenia (FIGURES 1, 2).

D'Elia and Perris[61] have shown that integrated amplitude from parietooccipital leads is higher on the stimulated side after unilateral ECT. They also conclude[62] that because of a significant increase in the variance of the amplitude on the left side, after bilateral ECT, the left hemisphere is implicated primarily in depression. It should be noted that the coefficient of variation, the more usual index of variability, did not significantly differ on the right or left in their 18 patients. Marjerrison,[63] who replicated this last investigation, found a bilateral, not unilateral, increase in variance after bilateral ECT and "could not support their conclusion of more pronounced involvement of the dominant hemisphere in depressive states." Perris[64] found further evidence for his view, reporting Visual AER, which are smaller on the left than on the right in depression, with a majority inverting after treatment. Since it has been shown that the visual AER in normals is larger over the nondominant than over the dominant hemisphere,[65] this conclusion is certainly questionable, since his study lacked a normal control group.

It is apparent the association between schizophrenia and the left hemisphere is more powerfully established than that of the lateralization to the right hemisphere of the affective syndromes. The problem, perhaps, is that it would seem that bifrontal and nondominant frontotemporal disorganization, both may be translated into dysphoric morbid states, whereas perturbation of the dominant frontotemporal system alone modulates the schizophrenic syndrome (which may, of course, occur with bilateral disorganization). The formulation would explain why transitions from chronic manic-depressive psychosis to schizophrenia is possible, and also why the converse, chronic schizophrenic syndromes transforming themselves into manic-depressive states, never occurs.

Some of the evidence that suggests that affective responses are a function of the nondominant hemisphere is as follows:

1. It is an old neurological observation that euphoric indifference is a feature of cerebral tumors of the non-dominant hemisphere.[66] Anosognosia for hemiplegia, found with left, but not with right paralysis, is an analogous phenomenon.

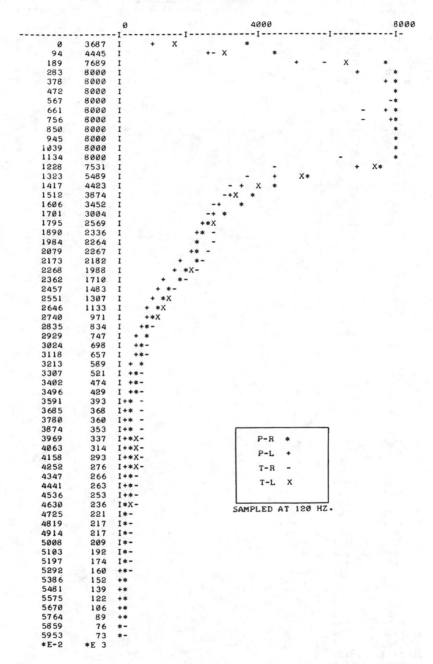

FIGURE 1. Composite spectrogram: 7 normals (eyes open).

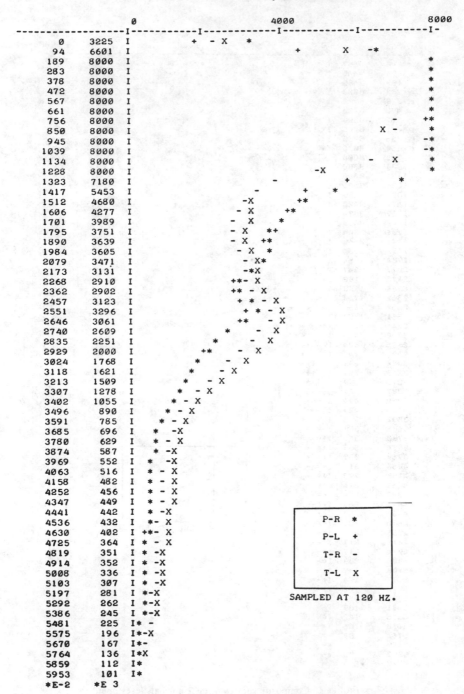

FIGURE 2. Composite spectrogram: 11 schizophrenics (eyes open).

2. Dysphoric states after penetrating head injuries are lateralized to the right,[36] as are manic-depressive psychoses in temporal epilepsy.[39]

3. It is now accepted that unilateral nondominant ECT is as effective as bilateral ECT in certain pathological depressions. There are a number of recent studies that suggest that unilateral nondominant induction may be therapeutically more effective than bilateral.[67,68] Notwithstanding, assuming bilateral and unilateral nondominant seizures to be equivalent, unilateral seizures to the dominant hemisphere are therapeutically less effective. Since the majority of unilaterally induced seizures are asymmetrically bilateral, both at the motor and neurophysiological level, and implicate more the stimulated side,[61] it would follow that the nondominant hemisphere is critically involved in depression.

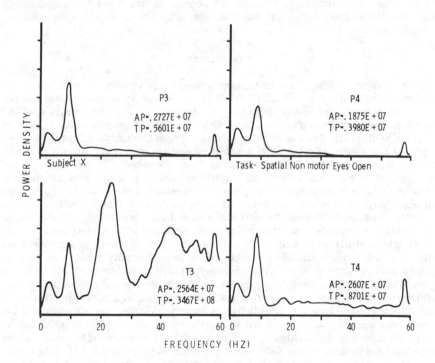

FIGURE 3. Characteristic spectral EEG found in schizophrenia.

4. It has been shown[69] that in normals intracarotid injection of amytal to the nondominant hemisphere produces euphoria and injections to the dominant side, depression. However, in depressed patients both dominant and nondominant injections induce euphoric responses. Further, there is an inverse relationship between speech laterality and depth of depression: the more depressed the patient, the more he appears to exhibit the organization of the nondominant hemisphere in both hemispheres. These findings may imply that with increasing intensity of depression the nondominant hemispheric dysfunction progressively leads to contralateral frontal disorganization expressed as reduced lateral specialization on that side.

5. It will be recalled that observations in the thirties [7,8] on hemiplegics found that emotional instability of the "catastrophic reaction" type was associated with right, but not left hemiplegia; in other words, with severe insults lateralized to the dominant hemisphere. This has been confirmed by Gainotti,[70] in a study of 160 lateralized cerebrovascular lesions, 80 to the left and 80 to the right hemisphere. A strong association was found between "depressive-catastrophic" reactions and lesions with Broca-type aphasia, i.e., dominant frontal. Abnormal mood reactions were characteristic of ischaemic lesions to the right hemisphere. It should be emphasized that "catastrophic-depressive" reactions are quite different from endogenous psychoses that do not occur in the wake of massive cerebral insults accompanied by hemiplegia, right or left. As dominant frontal lesions produce blunting of affect,[38,43] the following hypothesis is suggested: affective responses are determined by nondominant fronto-temporal limbic circuits, but are regulated by frontal mechanisms in the dominant hemisphere. With increasing intensity of depression, the frontal disorganization becomes increasingly bifrontal, and this may also modulate the schizoaffective symptomatology.[71]

Conclusion

The evidence reviewed implies that the schizophrenic syndrome and psychopathy are manifestations of neuronal disorganization in the dominant orbital frontal-temporal regions. The manic-depressive syndromes reflect disorganization of the nondominant anterior limbic structures. Quite apart from the relationships existing between hemispheric dominance, language and speech abnormalities, thought disorder, and blunting of affect another association perhaps emerges. If one accepts that, for the reasons outlined earlier, subjective "consciousness" is a function of brain stem-mesial frontal connections on the left side, then it seems possible that the insidious feeling of personality change and "depersonalization" often seen in schizophrenia may also be the reflection of lateralized hemispheric dysfunction. On neuropsychological evidence the periodic schizoaffective psychoses, like the manic-depressives, have predominantly nondominant dysfunction, but some power spectral EEG data is available that shows that during the acute psychotic phase these have more extensive bitemporal involvement. How these laterality effects can be integrated with the gender-related differential hemispheric organization of the male and female brain and thus immediately account, in a developmental perspective, for the different sex incidence of the major psychopathological syndromes has been discussed elsewhere.[72] Infantile autism, aggressive psychopathy, and schizophrenia are overrepresented in males, compared to females, who, on the other hand, are more liable to affective disturbances, both psychotic and neurotic. The male, whose dominant hemisphere is relatively more vulnerable, but who, compared to the female has a more efficient nondominant hemispheric organization, will thus be more susceptible to syndromes of dominant dysfunction: autism, schizophrenia, psychopathy. The female, with relative dominant hemispheric superiority and nondominant vulnerability will have an increased susceptibility to syndromes of nondominant dysfunction: pathological disturbances of mood. Developmental aspects are of fundamental importance, for these phenomena are most prominent early in ontogenesis and progressively diminish with maturation.

References

1. Papez, J. W. 1937. A proposed mechanism of emotion. Arch. Neurol. Psychiatry 38: 725–743.

2. MacLean, P. D. 1949. Psychosomatic disease and the "visceral brain." Psychosom. Med. 11(6): 338–353.
3. MacLean, P. D. 1952. Some psychiatric implications of physiological studies on fronto-temporal portion of limbic system (visceral brain). Electroencephalogr. Clin. Neurophysiol. 4: 407–418.
4. MacLean, P. D. 1970. The limbic brain in relation to the psychoses. In Physiological Correlates of Emotion. P. Black, Ed. Chapt. 7: 129–146. Academic Press. New York, N.Y.
5. Jones, E. G. & T. P. S. Powell. 1970. An anatomical study of converging sensory pathways within the cerebral cortex of the monkey. Brain 93: 793–820.
6. Powell, T. P. S. 1973. Sensory convergence in the cerebral cortex. In Surgical Approaches in Psychiatry. L. V. Laitinen & K. E. Livingston, Eds. Chapt. 36: 266–281. Medical and Technical Publishing Co. Lancaster, England.
7. Dandy, W. E. 1931. The brain. In Practice of Surgery. D. Lewis, Ed. Chapt. 1(12): 53–54. W. F. Prior Company, Inc. Hagerstown, Md.
8. Alford, L. B. 1933. Localization of consciousness and emotion. Am. J. Psychiatry 89: 789–799.
9. Serafetinides, E. A., R. D. Hoare & M. V. Driver. 1965. Intracarotid sodium amylobarbitone and cerebral dominance for speech and consciousness. Brain 88: 107–130.
10. Kleist, K. 1928. Uber zykloide, paranoid und epileptoide Psychosen und uber die Frage der Degenerationspsychosen. Schweiz. Arch. Neurol. Psychiatr. 23: 1–35. In Themes and Variations in European Psychiatry. S. R. Hirsch & M. Shepherd, Eds. Transl. by H. Marshall. Chapt. 12: 295–331. John Wright & Sons Ltd. Bristol, England.
11. Kleist, K. 1960. Schizophrenic symptoms and cerebral pathology. J. Ment. Sci. 106: 246–255.
12. Lawson, J. S., A. McGhie & J. Chapman. 1964. Perception of speech in schizophrenia. Br. J. Psychiatry 110: 375–380.
13. Mefferd, R. B., J. W. Lester, B. A. Wieland, G. A. Falconer & A. D. Pokorny. 1969. Influence of distraction on the reproduction of spoken words by schizophrenics. J. Ner. Ment. Dis. 149(6): 504–509.
14. Moon, A. F., R. B. Mefferd, B. A. Wieland, A. D. Pokorny & G. A. Falconer. 1968. Perceptual dysfunction as a determinant of schizophrenic word associations. J. Ner. Ment. Dis. 146(1): 80–84.
15. Walker, H. A. & H. G. Birch. 1970. Lateral preference and right-left awareness in schizophrenic children. J. Ner. Ment. Dis. 151(5): 341–351.
16. Bull, H. C. & P. H. Venables. 1974. Speech perception in schizophrenia. Br. J. Psychiatry 125: 350–354.
17. Maher, B. 1972. The language of schizophrenia: A review and interpretation. Br. J. Psychiatry 20: 3–17.
18. Geschwind, N. 1964. Non-aphasic disorders of speech. Int. J. Neurol. 4: 207–214. Reprinted In Selected Papers on Language and the Brain. 1974. N. Geschwind, Ed.: 549. Synthese Library. D. Redel Publishing Co. Dordrecht, Holland.
19. Fitzgerald, G. & C. S. Hallpike. 1942. Studies in human vestibular function: I. Observations on the directional preponderance ("Nystagmusbereitschaft") of caloric nystagmus resulting from cerebral lesions. Brain 65(2): 115–137.
20. Cawthorne, T. E., G. Fitzgerald & C. S. Hallpike. 1942. Studies in human vestibular function: II. Observations on the directional preponderance of caloric nystagmus ("Nystagmusbereitschaft") resulting from unilateral labyrinthectomy. Brain 65(2): 138–160.
21. Fitzgerald, G. & E. Stengel. 1945. Vestibular reactivity to caloric stimulation in schizophrenics. J. Ment. Sci. 91: 93–100.
22. Monakhov, K. K. 1971. The Pavlovian theory in psychiatry, some recent developments. In Modern Perspectives in World Psychiatry. J. G. Howells, Ed.: 531–555. Transl. Dr. R. Pos. Brunner Mazel. New York, N.Y.
23. Vinar, J. & O. Skalickova. 1965. Neurologieke Hodneceni Schizofrenniho Onemocneni. Cesk. Psychiatr. 61: 373–377.
24. Luria, A. R. & E. D. Homskaya. 1966. Disturbance of action control in frontal lobe

lesions. *In* Human Brain and Psychological Processes. A. R. Luria, Ed. Chapt. 10: 530–556. Harper and Row. New York, N.Y.

25. PRIBRAM, K. H. 1967. The limbic systems, efferent control of neural inhibition and behaviour. *In* Progress in Brain Research. W. Adey & T. Tokizane, Eds. Vol. 27: 318–336. American Elsevier Publishing Co. New York, N.Y.

26. GRUZELIER, J. & P. VENABLES. 1974. Bimodality and lateral asymmetry of skin conductance orienting activity in schizophrenics: Replication and evidence of lateral asymmetry in patients with depression and disorders of personality. Biol. Psychiatry. **8**(1): 55–73.

27. GRUZELIER, J. H. 1973. Bilateral asymmetry of skin conductance orienting activity and levels in schizophrenics. Biol. Psychol. **1**: 21–41.

28. GRUZELIER, J. H. & P. H . VENABLES. 1973. Skin conductance responses to tones with and without attentional significance in schizophrenic and nonschizophrenic psychiatric patients. Neuropsychologia **11**: 221–230.

29. CARMON, A. & G. M. GOMBOS. 1970. A physiological vascular correlate of hand preference: Possible implications with respect to hemispheric cerebral dominance. Neuropsychologia **8**: 119–128.

30. CARMON, A., Y. HARISHANU, E. LOWINGER & S. LAVY. 1972. Asymmetries in hemispheric blood volume and cerebral dominance. Behav. Biol. **7**: 853–859.

31. INGVAR, D. H. & G. FRANZEN. 1974. Abnormalities of cerebral blood flow distribution in patients with chronic schizophrenia. Acta Psychiatr. Scand. **50**: 425–562.

32. GOTTESMAN, I. I. & J. SHIELDS. 1972. Maudsley schizophrenic twin series. *In* Schizophrenia and Genetics. I. I. Gottesman & J. Shields, Eds. Chapt. 3 & 8: 60 & 296. Academic Press. New York, N.Y.

33. BOKLAGE, C. E. 1974. Embryonic determination of brain programming asymmetry: A neglected element in twin-study genetics of human mental development. Proc. First Intern. Congr. Twin Studies. Gregor Mendel Institute for Medical Genetics and Twin Studies. Rome, Italy.

34. HILLBOM, E. & M. KAILA. 1949. Psychoses after brain-trauma. Nord. Psykiatr. Medlemsbl. **3**: 102–117.

35. HILLBROM, E. 1960. After-effects of brain-injuries. Research on the symptoms causing invalidism of persons in Finland having sustained brain-injuries during the wars of 1939–1940 and 1941–1944. Acta Psychiatr. Neurol. Scand. **35**(Suppl. 142): 112–125.

36. LISHMAN, W. A. 1968. Brain damage in relation to psychiatric disability after head injury. Br. J. Psychiatry. **114**: 373–410.

37. DAVISON, K. & C. R. BAGLEY. 1969. Schizophrenia-like psychoses associated with organic disorders of the central nervous system: A review of the literature. *In* Current Problems in Neuropsychiatry. R. N. Herrington, Ed.: 113–184. Royal Medico-Psychological Association. Headley Brothers, Ltd. Ashford, Kent, England.

38. BINGLEY, T. 1958. Mental symptoms in temporal lobe epilepsy and temporal lobe gliomas. Acta Psychiatr. Neurol. Scand. **33**(Suppl. 120): 136–151.

39. FLOR-HENRY, P. 1969. Psychosis and temporal lobe epilepsy. A controlled investigation. Epilepsia **10**: 363–395.

40. FLOR-HENRY, P. 1972. Schizophrenic-like reactions and affective psychoses associated with temporal lobe epilepsy: Etiological factors. Am. J. Psychiatry **126**: 400–404.

41. FLOR-HENRY, P. 1972. Ictal and interictal psychiatric manifestations in epilepsy: Specific or non-specific? Epilepsia **13**: 773–783.

42. FLOR-HENRY, P. 1976. Epilepsy and psychopathology. *In* Recent Advances in Clinical Psychiatry. 2nd edit. K. Granville-Grossman, Ed. Churchill Livingstone. Edinburgh, Scotland.

43. MNOUKHINE, S. S. & E. Y. DINABOURG. 1965. Epileptiform manifestations in early right sided and left sided lesions of the brain in children. Zh. Nevropatol. Psikhiatr. im S. S. Korsakova. **65**: 1073–1077.

44. FLOR-HENRY, P. & L. T. YEUDALL. 1973. Lateralized cerebral dysfunction in depression and in aggressive criminal psychopathy: Further observations. IRCS. 5-0-4.

45. FEIGHNER, J. P., E. ROBINS, S. B. GUZE, R. A. WOODRUFF, G. WINOKUR & R. MUNOZ. 1972. Diagnostic criteria for use in psychiatric research. Arch. Gen. Psychiatry **26**: 57–63.

46. WING, J. K., J. E. COOPER & N. SARTORIUS. 1974. The Measurement and Classification of Psychiatric Symptoms. Cambridge University Press. New York, N.Y.

47. ANNET, M. 1967. The bilateral distinction of right, mixed and left handedness. J. Exp. Psychol. **19:** 327–333.
48. JONES, M. B. & D. R. OFFORD. 1975. Independent transmission of IQ and schizophrenia. Br. J. Psychiatry **126:** 185–190.
49. FLOR-HENRY, P., Z. J. KOLES, P. BO-LASSEN & L. T. YEUDALL. 1975. Studies of the functional psychoses: Power spectral EEG analysis. IRCS Med. Sci. **3:** 87.
50. GALIN, D. & R. ORNSTEIN. 1972. Lateral specialization of cognitive mode: An EEG study. Psychophysiology **9:** 412–418.
51. ROSENTHAL, R. & L. B. BIGELOW. 1972. Quantitative brain measurements in chronic schizophrenia. Br. J. Psychiatry **121:** 259–264.
52. GOLDSTEIN, L., A. A. SUGERMAN, H. STOLBERG, H. B. MURPHREE & C. C. PFEIFFER. 1965. Electro-cerebral activity in schizophrenics and non-psychotic subjects: Quantitative EEG amplitude analysis. Electroencephalogr. Clin. Neurophysiol. **19:** 350–361.
53. SUGERMAN, A. A., L. GOLDSTEIN, H. B. MURPHREE, C. C. PFEIFFER & E. H. JENNEY. 1964. EEG and behavioral changes in schizophrenia. Arch. Gen. Psychiatry **10:** 340–344.
54. GOLDSTEIN, L. & A. SUGERMAN. 1968. EEG Correlates of Psychopathology. Proc. 58th Am. Psychopathol. Assn. Mtg. New York, N.Y.
55. MARJERRISON, G., A. E. KRAUSE & R. P. KEOGH. 1968. Variability of the EEG in schizophrenia: Quantitative analysis with a modulus voltage integrator. Electroencephalogr. Clin. Neurophysiol. **24:** 35–41.
56. SUGERMAN, A. A., L. GOLDSTEIN, G. MARJERRISON & N. STOLTZFUSS. 1973. Recent research in EEG amplitude analysis. Dis. Nerv. Syst. **34:** 162–166.
57. SERAFETINIDES, E. A. 1972. Laterality and voltage in the EEG of psychiatric patients. Dis. Nerv. Syst. **32:** 622–623.
58. SERAFETINIDES, E. A. 1973. Voltage laterality in the EEG of psychiatric patients. Dis. Nerv. Syst. **34:** 190–191.
59. GIANNITRAPANI, D. & L. KAYTON. 1974. Schizophrenia and EEG spectral analysis. Electroencephalogr. Clin. Neurophysiol. **36:** 377–386.
60. LIFSHITZ, K. & J. GRADIJAN. 1974. Spectral evaluation of the electroencephalogram: Power and variability in chronic schizophrenics and control subjects. Psychophysiology **11**(4): 479–490.
61. D'ELIA, G. & C. PERRIS. 1970. Comparison of electroconvulsive therapy with unilateral and bilateral stimulation. I. Seizure and post-seizure electroencephalographic pattern. Acta Psychiatr. Scand. **46**(Suppl. 215): 9–29.
62. D'ELIA, G. & C. PERRIS. 1973. Cerebral functional dominance and depression. Acta Psychiatr. Scand. **49:** 191–197.
63. MARJERRISON, G., J. JAMES & H. REICHERT. 1975. Unilateral and bilateral ECT: FEG findings. Can. Psychiatr. Assoc. J. **20:** 257–266.
64. PERRIS, C. 1974. Averaged evoked responses, (AER) in patients with effective disorders, Acta Psychiatr. Scand. **50**(Suppl. 255): 89–98.
65. SCHENKENBERG, T. & R. E. DUSTMAN. 1970. Visual, auditory and somatosensory evoked response changes related to age, hemisphere and sex. Proc. 78th Ann. Convention Am. Psychological Assn. **5:** 183–184. New York, N.Y.
66. HECAEN, H. & J. de AJURIAGUERRA. 1952. Meconnaissances et Hallucinations Corporelles. Masson et Cie. Paris, France.
67. GALIN, D. 1974. Implications for psychiatry of right and left cerebral specialization: A neurophysiological context for unconscious processes. Arch. Gen. Psychiatry **31:** 572–583.
68. COHEN, B. D., S. B. PENICK & R. E. TARTER. 1974. Antidepressant effects of unilateral electric convulsive shock therapy. Arch. Gen. Psychiatr. **31:** 673–675.
69. HOMMES, O. R. & L. H. H. M. PANHUYSEN. 1971. Depression and cerebral dominance. Psychiatr. Neurol. Neurochir. **74:** 259–270.
70. GAINOTTI, G. 1972. Emotional behavior and hemispheric side of the lesion. Cortex **8**(1): 41–55.
71. FLOR-HENRY, P. 1973. Psychiatric syndromes considered as manifestations of lateralized temporal-limbic dysfunction. *In* Surgical Approaches in Psychiatry L. V. Laitinen & K. E. Livingston, Eds.: 22–26. Medical and Technical Publishing Company. Lancaster, England.
72. FLOR-HENRY, P. 1974. Psychosis, neurosis and epilepsy. Br. J. Psychiatry **124:** 144–150.

DISCUSSION OF THE PAPER BY FLOR-HENRY

Maureen Dennis

Department of Psychology
The Hospital for Sick Children
Toronto, Canada

Dr. Flor-Henry has presented evidence of an association between psychopathological state and lateralized temporal lobe dysfunction: schizophrenic psychoses are associated with left temporal disturbance, affective disorders with right-sided malfunction.

What are the underlying relationships expressed by these correlations? Consider the left temporal lobe—schizophrenia association. One interpretation is that left temporal lobe dysfunction produces, independently, language impairments and schizophrenia. In that case, schizophrenia and aphasia are parallel but separate effects of the same neurological disturbance. A second possibility is that the language disturbances of left temporal lobe disorder are part of the basis on which patients are diagnosed as schizophrenic. In this view, schizophrenia and aphasia are partly overlapping symptom clusters, and so it would not be surprising to find schizophrenics showing left temporal EEG abnormalities, auditory-verbal memory defects, and a parallel genetic incidence. A systematic comparison of the speech and language defects of schizophrenia with those of left temporal lobe-damaged individuals not diagnosed as schizophrenic would help clarify the meaning of the presented correlation. A comparable question of interpretation can be raised for the association between right temporal damage and affective states. Impulsivity, expressed as poor maze-planning, is found in psychopaths.[1] Maze-planning is also disrupted by right-hemisphere damage[2] and by bilateral frontal lobectomy.[1] Interestingly, Dr. Flor-Henry's affectives show both right-sided and bilateral anterior EEG abnormalities. Perhaps the impulsivity associated with these kinds of cerebral disturbance is one of the diagnostic criteria for affective disturbance?

Whatever their interpretation, the described results give evidence of a cerebral lateralization of psychopathological states. The described effects may reflect subcortical as well as cortical asymmetries. Meier and Story[3] found that right but not left subthalamotomy impaired maze-planning behavior. This suggests that the subcortical centers sensitive to dopamine levels may be asymmetric in terms of the control of behavioral functions like impulsivity. Some evidence does exist for a connection between dopamine level and schizophrenic symptoms (there are psychomimetic effects of dopamine-facilitating drugs, and some tranquilizers produce side effects resembling the symptoms of Parkinsonism[4]) but it remains to be shown that these relationships are asymmetric at a cerebral level.

Dr. Flor-Henry suggested that his results might explain the sex difference in the incidence of schizophrenic and affective disorders. One corollary of this suggestion is an effect of sex on the lateralized functioning of the temporal lobe. Lansdell[5] has shown that lateralized temporal lobe removal produces different effects in males and females.

REFERENCES

1. PORTEUS, S. D. 1959. Porteus Maze Tests: Fifty Years Application. Pacific Books. Palo Alto, Calif.

2. KOHN, B. & M. DENNIS. 1974. Neuropsychologia, **12**: 505–512.
3. MEIER, M. J. & J. L. STORY. 1967. Neuropsychologia **5**: 181–189.
4. MATTHYSE, S. 1974. *In* Brain Dysfunction in Metabolic Disorders. F. Plum, Ed. Res. Pub. Ass. Res. Nerv. Ment. Dis. Vol. **53**: 305–314. Raven Press. New York, N.Y.
5. LANSDELL, H. 1962. Nature **194**: 852–854.

LANGUAGE IN A SOCIOBIOLOGICAL FRAME*

Karl H. Pribram

Department of Psychology
Stanford University
Stanford, California 94305

THE STRUCTURE OF LANGUAGE

In an earlier paper published by The New York Academy of Sciences I addressed the contributions that comparative neurobehavioral research had made to delineating the structure of language.[1] That report distinguished two quite separate aspects of animal communication, each of which has at its disposal a different neural mechanism. One form, the *symbolic*, relates the communicative act to the internal state of the animal and is in a sense arbitrary and synthetic with respect to the situation in which it occurs. The other constructs *signs* by differentiating the features distinctive to the situation, thus assigning attributes and characterizing it.

Further, the earlier report developed the thesis originally proposed by Vowles[2,3] and amplified by Beer (Ref. 4 and this volume) that three levels of neural mechanisms could be identified in the production of both sign and symbol. At the deepest level, which is shared by vertebrates and invertebrates alike, presymbolic processes are based on recurring regularities such as those that make up circadian and ultradian rhythms. Rudimentary significations, by contrast, are at this level based on stochastic finite-state Markov-type mechanisms. In vertebrates, presymbolic and presignificant communications are constructed from these primitive operations by phrase structure hierarchies, which in man are subject to still another type of operation leading to the transformational capacities necessary to the construction of linguistic signs and symbols.

SIGN AND SYMBOL IN HUMAN LANGUAGE

On this occasion I want to concentrate on the relevance of these grammatical distinctions to the origins of human language. The first of a series of questions that stems from the earlier analysis is whether symbolic or signifying processes are more rudimentary and pervasive in the development of man's linguistic abilities. The logical possibilities are, of course, four: Human language is derived from 1) symbolic expression, 2) from assigning features, 3) from both, 4) from neither. Let us explore these alternatives.

The facts supporting biological evolution make it unlikely that human language has sprung *de novo* with no relationship to subhuman primate forms of communication. I shall therefore, as an act of faith, dismiss this alternative and bolster the decision by arguments to be made in favor of the other possibilities.

Human language is nothing if not arbitrary. The sheer variety of languages, the different forms of expression used within a language to convey a meaning, the almost universal use of an alphabet (an arbitrary code), and the variety of alphabets all attest to the fact that the form of human language is symbolic.

*Supported by NIMH research career award MH15214-14.

Equally apparent is the fact that the content of human language is much more developed and richer in signifying, characterizing the attributes of the environment than in expressions relating the dispositions of the communicants. The likelihood is therefore remote that human language is derived exclusively from either the symbol or the sign aspect of animal communication. Somehow, both have become fused in the process by which man communicates.

The linguistic analysis of language and its development in the human infant make it imperative to view human communication as a fusion of symbolic and significant operations. Man's languages have two primary characteristics: they provide a prolongation of reference[5] and they are productive.[6] Both these characteristics are found in primordial form in the signs and symbols of nonhuman primates, but the extent to which they are developed in man is hardly foreshadowed by these rudiments. Even a retarded child before he is a few years old will spin sentences that are so far beyond the nonhuman level[7] that he can easily be identified as a member of the genus *Homo* by this action alone.

A child begins verbalization, just as does the nonhuman primate, with what are called holophrases: single utterances signifying something or symbolizing some state. Linguists have not classified holophrases in this fashion, but my own observations make clear to me that holophrases are of two kinds: more or less continuous grunts, coos, and explicatives which refer to the baby's internal state, and shorter, repetitive syllablelike sounds often accompanied by directive gestures that indicate something about the world the baby sees, hears, touches, or tastes.

At about the age of two years the holophrases become more precise and their referent more readily distinguishable, until couplings of holophrases occur. Such couplings—and later strings—are also observed in chimpanzee utterances. But the child quickly goes on to make *propositions*, something which, at the time this is written, has not been observed in ape-language.

Propositions or sentences develop around predication. Predication implies another function, that of nominalization or noun-formation. The line of development from sign to nouns as found in human utterances seems to be straightforward enough. Verbs such as *run, catch, flow,* and so on, and other parts of speech such as adjectives and adverbs give somewhat more trouble, until one realizes that they also signify existences and are therefore forms of nominalization. In a sense, such verbs are names for actions rather than things, the adjectives and adverbs are names for attributes—and the difference lies in the number of transformations over which things, attributes, and actions remain invariant.

Predication, however, is premised on more than existence. Predication makes a statement about occurrences, the truth or falsity of a proposition, the rules that proclaim the is-so and the is-not of such occurrences. *Black sand water* is a string of holophrasticlike utterances that a chimpanzee might make pointing to a beach in Hawaii. I should understand him. A child would say, "Look, the sand *is* black *next to* the water." He would be very upset if you explained to him that he is subject to an illusion caued by the heating of the air over an asphalt landing strip. It would be foolhardy to try to communicate the difference between propositions "The sand is black next to water" and "The illusion of water is produced on asphalt by heat" to a chimpanzee.

The point here is that predication is premised on symbolization. Predication is an expression by the human organism that this is the way it is (or is not). According to this view, predication is derived from the ordering of events into a temporal structure (a rule) that groups occurrences in terms of equilibrations and disequilibrations of the brain. Some groupings are right, others wrong. And sometimes the grouping becomes rather complicated before it feels right.

Nominalization derived from signifying (through predication) provides the extended referent in human language: "purple people eaters," for example. Predication derived from symbolizing (and utilizing nomination) provides human language with its productivity: the variations of groupings (purple people or purple eaters?) that can feel right could be almost infinite.

How is this fusion between symbol and sign performed? How do the parts of the brain involved in symbol construction and those involved in the construction of signs come to interact? Is a new cortical formation responsible for the fusion, do corticocortical connections develop that are poorly, or not at all, functional in subhumans, or is the transformation accomplished subcortically? Each of these possibilities has been seriously entertained by brain scientists, and there is some evidence in support of each. Again, let us examine them in turn in order to obtain some grasp regarding where inquiry must go to resolve the problem.

WHAT IS NEW IN MAN'S BRAIN?

There is little question that in the human cerebral cortex, areas can be found that are either absent in subhumans or present only in rudiment. The large development of frontal cortex in terms of man's vaulting forehead was already noted by the early phrenologists. Equally impressive is the growth of the posterior nonprojection cortex centering on the angular gyrus, the confluence of parieto-, temporal, and occipital cortical formations.[8] Does the quantitative increase in these cortical structures herald the qualitative transformational change expressed as human language?

My answer to this question is a tentative no. I reason as follows: if the cortical growth is *per se* to be responsible for the development of human language, evidence should lead to two major language "centers": one well forward in the frontal cortex, the other in the tissues around the angular gyrus. The evidence for and against a major category of aphasia centered on the third frontal convolution is critical. If Broca's[9,10] aphasia is to be given weight equal to Wernicke's (see Pribram[15]), the idea that new cortical accretions are responsible for human language is tenable. So let us look at the problem handed us by Broca.

All of the evidence[11-15] shows that expressive aphasia does not result from damage as far forward as Broca's part of the third frontal convolution. Further, to fit the facts of a cortical topography peculiar to man, even the third frontal convolution is too ventral and posterior a location for a new language "center" to be developed in tissue not present in subhuman primates. Electrical stimulation of the third frontal convolution, in all primates including man, yields tongue movements. This is not the locus of the new cortical accretion.

The place of the territory around the angular gyrus in the development of human language is not so easily disposed of. Aphasic symptoms, as we have seen, result when the cortex of the angular gyrus is damaged. But again the match is imperfect (see Bogan and Bogan, this volume). All of the evidence points to the posterior part of the superior temporal gyrus as the locus involved in Wernicke's syndrome and holds that Wernicke's is the major, central, or primary aphasia. Also, as in the case of the frontal cortex, although the fit is better, the angular gyrus is not exactly the place of maximum new accretion of cortex in man; it is somewhat too close to the Sylvian fissure to be equated with the considerable anatomical development of intrinsic nonprojection cortex.

These mismatches, although some of them are slight, give me an uneasy feeling when the origin of human language is attributed simply to the growth of new areas in the frontal and posterior intrinsic cortex.

CONNECTIONS AND DISCONNECTIONS

If not the new areas directly, perhaps their development brings with it new functional pathways that allow symbol and sign aspects of communication to interact. This possibility is detailed in the aphasia literature under the heading of disconnection syndromes most recently advocated by Geschwind.[16] Earlier versions of the disconnection view were voiced by Freud,[17] Liepman,[18] and Dejerene.[19] All these authors adduce specific case histories in support of their suggestion that one or another major pathway is pathologically involved in the production of a language (or language-related) disorder. Unfortunately, to date, comprehensive and quantitative behavioral analyses such as those produced by Bay[20] and Hecaen and Angelergues[21] have not been performed on such patients. Often the anatomical verification of the lesion also leaves a good deal to be desired: multiple damage is often reported when a single focus is held responsible for the disorder; histological serial analysis of the entire brain is seldom performed.

Arraigned against the corticocortical disconnection hypothesis are all of the subhuman primate experimental findings I reviewed in my earlier paper. In the monkey it appears that intrahemispheric corticocortical connections play a minor, if any, role in the organization of the psychological process. But monkeys do not talk the way men do. Is the difference in importance of corticocortical pathways the critical reason why they do not? Or do the corticosubcortical connections shared by all primates, which, up to now, have been ignored, play the critical role?

THE CENTRENCEPHALIC HYPOTHESIS

Convergence of significant and symbolic processing at some subcortical locus or loci is, on the basis of subhuman evidence, a serious contender as an explanation for the emergence of human language. Subcortical formations are rarely given more than cursory inspection when the brains of aphasics are studied. When the lesion is caused, as it so often is, by disease of the middle cerebral artery, the basal ganglia, parts of the thalamus, and many fiber tracts are affected. Penfield, among others, has opted, on the basis of his experience, for a centrencephalic mechanism in the production of human language (Ref. 13; cf. Robinson, this annal). Careful surgical excisions of cortex so rarely produce lasting changes in man or monkey that one is literally driven to the subcortical formations for an answer to questions of localizing the site of disturbances.

The one exception to this is, of course, Wernicke's zone in the posterior part of the superior temporal gyrus (see Bogen and Bogen, this volume). Here, because neurosurgeons tread with extreme caution, data are hard to come by, but opinion is strong and to the point: in the adult, at least, damage is not to be hazarded.

The centrality of Wernicke's zone and the possibility that subcortical convergences are critical to the production of human language make up the centrencephalic hypothesis. This hypothesis takes strength from the subhuman primate experimental results that show that the nonprojection cortex associated with the auditory mode lies in the midtemporal region;[22] that most likely, this cortex exerts its role in audition through efferents coursing to subcortical stations in the auditory projection systems;[23,24] that removal of this cortex results even in monkeys in the inability to discriminate vowel sounds;[25] and that, contrary to any other cortical removals in subhuman primates, unilateral damage plays havoc with certain types (sequences) of auditory discriminations.[25,26]

The subcortical locus upon which the symbolic and signifying processes can conveniently converge has not yet been established. From the results of experiments on nonhuman primates, however, the basal ganglia and related nuclei in the upper midbrain are the best candidates. These are motor structures involved in producing the muscular settings necessary to action. It should therefore not be too surprising that communicative and linguistic acts also depend on the function of these motor structures.

Thus both the corticocortical disconnection and the centrencephalic hypotheses continue to be tenable though unproven. Techniques to test them are available. Quantitative behavioral evaluations of aphasic patients and serial histological reconstructions of their lesions and resulting degeneration (e.g. retrograde change in the thalamus) will go a long way toward supporting or disproving the disconnection hypothesis. Especially important is a comprehensive evaluation of whether language-related and nonlanguage disturbances are correlated or whether they are separable when a disconnection syndrome is suspected.

With regard to the centrencephalic hypothesis, the current vogue in electrical stimulations of deep brain structure should uncover evidence regarding possible subcortical language mechanisms. Such studies should, over the next decade, provide the necessary crucial facts to test the centrencephalic hypothesis.

THE INSIDE AND THE OUTSIDE OF LANGUAGE

Finally, the alternative must be entertained that *the convergence of sign and symbol does not take place primarily in the brain at all.* It is possible, and indeed likely, that the auditory mechanism in primates, because of the development of cerebral dominance, has extended to encompass such a large share of the cortical and subcortical process that all but the purely symbolic aspects of human language are accounted for, as suggested by Piere Marie,[27] Bay,[20] and Hecaen and Angelergues[21] (Ciba Foundation Symposium, 1964). A central language processor based on the auditory projection system and its associated cortex would account for the signifying aspects of language. With use of adjacent accessory "poles" in the precentral, parietal, and occipitotemporal cortices, expressive, somatic, and visual communication could be established simply by an overlap of functional areas. The primary auditory projection is ideally placed for such overlap. The derivation of the acoustic system from gill and jaw is reflected in the cortex by the fact that auditory projections encompass both somatic area II superiorly and motor face and mouth areas anteriorly.[28] Even when such proximity does not exist, "associations" within the primary projection are present innately or established through learning.[29] Electrocortical evidence obtained in the visual mode shows cells to be present that react to auditory stimulation,[30] to the presence or absence of reinforcement, and to the intention of making a specific movement.[29,31]

The route by which such "associations" are established is unknown, but in the auditory cortex the path need not at least be long.

These considerations, however, apply only to significant communication. How, then, does the symbolic aspect of human language become involved in communication? It is possible that this occurs only through the environment— that there is no corticocortical connection nor subcortical convergence involved in all. When the neural sign system becomes sufficiently powerful (i.e., has sufficient memory and coding capability), it can treat the tokens of expression (of others and of self) as signs, signifying social rather than physical situations. This power, of course, would be immensely enhanced when memory is augmented externally; i.e., when symbols become recorded and treated as signs.

Should this cultural hypothesis of human language development prove to be correct (and I believe there is much to be said for it), the brain problem of human language production would be immensely simplified. First, the fact that aphasics can still express their feelings through gestures, expletives, and "emotional" language and simple song (which elsewhere in this annal have been shown to be related to the limbic forebrain (e.g., Robinson, Myers, this annal) would fit the conception that the human language system is primarily sign-based. Second, the fact that the arbitrariness of human language is so culture-bound would tend to validate the cultural hypothesis. Third, the overwhelming evidence of the central place of Wernicke's syndrome in the aphasic complex would support a sign-based view of the problem. The several dimensions along which the aphasic syndrome may vary would be attributable to invasion of areas adjacent to Wernicke's. The operation of the language-producing mechanism would involve the subcortical connections by way of which Wernicke's area operated on the auditory projection system. Lesions of such connections would impair language processing. Still to be tested is the possibility that more remote corticocortical connections might also be important, especially in rare and unusual syndromes—perhaps even idiosyncratically with patient-to-patient variation dependent on the particular experience of the individual.

According to this view, then, human communication, just like animal communication, is in the first instance bimodal. Only through culture do the symbolic and significant aspects of language become interwoven, and the evidence from aphasia suggests that the interweaving takes place mostly within the neural systems serving communication by signs.

BRAIN ORGANIZATION AND MEANING

In addition to insights into the development of the grammatical structure of human language, studies of brain function can teach us a good deal about the fundamental issues of the organization of meaning. In Chomsky's terms (this annal), what has been discussed so far concerns the relation between superficial and deeper structure. If the analysis has been correct that this relationship initially devolves on the formation of prelinguistic signs through hierarchical phrase-structuring, the question to be explored is the nature of features and what makes them distinctive.[6,32,33]

Units in the nervous system have been discovered that are sensitive to features of the environment (e.g., Mountcastle;[34] Werner;[35] Evarts;[36] Hubel & Wiesel;[37] Barlow & Hill;[38] Spinelli et al.[39]). Further, these features appear to be organized into different configurations in each of the hemispheres of the human brain. Thus after the age of seven or thereabouts, damage to the right hemisphere of most people impairs primarily spatial relationships, whereas damage to the left hemisphere impairs the linguistic abilities, which are the concern of this paper. Sperry,[40] in an elegant series of experiments, has demonstrated the separateness of these functions in patients whose hemispheres have been severed from one another by sectioning of the major commisure, the corpus collossum, that ordinarily connects them.

But these important contributions also pose problems of interpretation to neurolinguists. Are we to search for a different brain cell for each distinctive feature of language? If so, do these brain cells respond to the feature innately, or do they become responsive only through experience? Further, most of the feature-sensitive units that have been discovered so far deal with the spatial aspects of input. How do such feature-sensitivities relate to linguistic structure in a hemisphere that supposedly does not process these features?

Many of these puzzling problems are resolved if we look at the evidence from a somewhat different theoretical perspective. The ordinary interpretation that feature-sensitive cells in the brain serve as "detectors" for that feature has been found wanting. Thus, for instance, Pollen and Taylor[41] have shown that the output of "complex" cells of the visual cortex (which are assumed to be detectors of lines of specified length and orientation) is not invariant across all transformations of input other than orientation. In fact, changes of luminance, width of line, number of lines and their spacings all influence the cell's output. Thus only a network of neurons could separate their orientation specificity from that to luminance, for example. Several groups of investigators[41-43] have shown that such cells are in fact more accurately stated to be sensitive to spatial frequencies than to lines *per se*, and that it is therefore in error to think of them as simple line "detectors."

The change from sensitivity for lines to one for spatial frequency has major consequences. As discussed elsewhere,[15,44-46] a spatial frequency analysis of light just like the temporal frequency analysis of sound (by the auditory system) is accomplished in the domain of continuous oscillations and not in the digital domain in which present-day computers operate almost exclusively. This shift in emphasis allows alternate hypotheses to be formulated regarding what might distinguish a feature in speech and what the organization of deep structure might look like in the brain.

Phoneticians have in fact already made it clear that the distinctive features of spoken language are most readily analyzed in terms of the wave forms generated by the vocal apparatus—the vocal cords, larynx, oral cavity, tongue, and lips. For example, one recent study was able to decompose speech sounds into some six to eight components by performing a Fourier analysis, taking into account both spatial and temporal relations.[47] And the Haskins group has for years been simulating sounds by using spectral techniques (e.g. Liberman *et al.*[48]).

If, in fact, the distinctive features by which linguistic communications take place are to be identified as wave forms, perhaps the deep structure of such communications is to be found in the wave mechanical domain. The computer, with its programmable digital information-processing capabilities, has been of great service both as a model and in data analysis with regard to syntactic superficial structure. Is there not an information-processing system that can serve with equal value as a model (and perhaps in due time in data analysis) in our search for the deep semantic structure of meaning?

Optical information-processing systems are just beginning to be recognized as useful analogues in studies involving the oscillatory domain. Aside from their image-constructing capacity, they partake in organizations characterized by the distribution of information produced by interference among wave fronts. This distributed aspect of their organization makes them attractive to brain scientists who have been puzzled for years by the apparent distribution of input for storage over reaches of brain surface, rendering their functions resistant to local damage.

Organizations of optical information-processing systems in which information is distributed are called *holograms*.[49,50] The proposal has therefore been made that the spatial and temporal frequency analyses performed by the brain are indicative of a holographiclike brain process.[51,15,46] But it must be borne in mind, of course, that for neural holograms only the organization of the paths taken by light in optical systems serves as the model. The energy involved in neural excitation is electrical, not photic.

The suggestion to be entertained here is therefore that deep structure is, in the final analysis, semantic structure and that semantic structure derives from a distributed neural organization akin to that found in the holograms of optical information-processing systems. Note that deep structure is conceived to be derived from a holographic organization and is not synonymous with it. Syntactic structures, as delineated in the earlier paper, partition—map—the holographic-distributed store of information into useful, meaningful organizations.

In biology, this mapping of a distributed, more or less homogeneous matrix into useful hierarchical and heterarchical organizations is commonplace. Thus the morphogenetic field becomes organized into useful structures by the action of inducers that derepress the potentialities of DNA molecules embedded in those fields. Thom[52] has recently developed a topological mathematics to describe the mappings of the morphogenetic field. Applying this to language, each distinctive feature would be occasioned by continuous interactions (i.e., wave forms generated in the vocal apparatus), but the ensuing stabilities, the distinctive features *per se*, would result when the interactions—the relationships—temporarily gel into nonlinearities, a process Thom calls a "catastrophe."

The difference between right and left hemisphere function is ordinarily conceptualized in terms of whether processes leading to image formation or to nonlinear catastrophic processes are emphasized. But more likely a simpler distinction based on sensory-motor (e.g., auditory-verbal vs. visuosomatic) mode is responsible. Reynolds[53,54] has suggested that differential use of the hands by primates has necessitated specialization of function between their cerebral hemispheres (see also Steklis & Harnad, this annal). Abler[55] has suggested further that when such specialization occurs, a problem arises for innervation of midline structures such as the tongue. He has experimentally demonstrated that one innervation (usually the right in right-handed persons) must dominate, or conflicting signals from the two hemispheres disrupt function. In short, once hemispheric specialization has occurred, dominance must follow if the midline structures involved in speech are to function harmoniously. And dominance entails some catastrophic-like "decisional" mechanism which more or less stably "takes over" the innervation of the midline. In discussion, we have even entertained the possibility that the left hemisphere has the edge in achieving dominance because the heart is located on the left side of the body and thus provides some slight advantage to the embryo's circulation. Wada *et al.*[56] (see also LeMay, this annal) have shown that asymmetries in the size of the cortex of the supratemporal plane already exist at birth—although some puzzling sex differences also emerge in these studies: the difference is greater in males. There are, however, as yet only anecdotal data on differences in early cerebral circulation to support such a hypothesis.

CONCLUSION: RESOLUTION OF THE PARADOX

To summarize these arguments, two views of human language production have been presented. One holds that the symbolization of signs takes place within the brain. The other proposes that symbols must be externalized in culture to be operated upon by the neural process that produces signs. The latter view makes the production of ordinary human language a more or less unitary process and has substantial support. The view that the brain is involved in bringing together sign and symbol depends on the presence of corticocortical connections or corticosubcortical convergences the function of which in language have yet to be firmly established as existing.

I am thoroughly convinced of both views and believe that resolution of the paradox lies in making a distinction between two uses of human language: the communicative and the thoughtful. When we restrict ourselves to testing the communicative capacity of brain-damaged man, we come to an essentially unitary position on aphasia (cf. Marin & Saffran, this volume). When, however, we ask questions about the *structure* of language disturbed by brain damage, or when we introspect and study our own and other people's verbal reports of introspection, we find a rich internal commerce between sign and symbol that at any moment, at least, needs no external crutch (though such a crutch may well be necessary to the development of this commerce).

I believe that the communicative use of human language is to a considerable extent an elaboration of animal sign communication, a relatively unitary process based on constructions of features from invariances occurring in stochastic events. Such significant communications are dependent on culture for their connectivity with symbolic processes; however, a parallel cultural elaboration of context-dependent symbolic communication based on recurring variances also occurs, and this is manifest through nonverbal (gestural-kinesis) and nonlinguistic (tonal quality, intensity) verbal channels.[57] The significant (cerebral convexity) and symbolic (frontolimbic) communicative processes most likely develop separately and can be maintained separately or brought together through experience and thought. Bateson has, in fact, suggested that in every human communication these two types of processes must be and are attended and that psychopathology results when the significant and symbolic messages continuously conflict[58,59] (see also Tanner, this annal).

Thus the thoughtful, reasoned use of language appears to be structurally multidimensional. The question remains an open one, whether this multidimensionality depends primarily on brain connectivity or whether it is largely the result of cultural factors external to the brain. Evidence in support of both possibilities exists and has been reviewed here.

I have therefore come to the conclusion that man's linguistic complexity must be due to the type of brain connectivity that has made possible the richness of all his culture. Culture is composed—made—by successions of acts. Thus the brain's motor mechanism must be involved with production of culture, and so I look to them for the necessary connectivity. Both the frontolimbic and posterior intrinsic cortex, so highly developed in man, have been shown in nonhuman primates to exert their influence via subcortical motor structures. I thus place my faith in the centrencephalic hypothesis as the most likely to account for the fact that the complexity of language is determined both by man's superior brain and his superior culture (which, in turn, is fashioned by actions guided by his superior brain).

ACKNOWLEDGMENTS

To Jacob Bruno Bronowski, Ursual Bellugi-Klima, Edward Klima, and Roman Jakobson for their attentive encouragement and criticisms, and to the Salk Institute, where some of these ideas were first formulated and expressed.

REFERENCES

1. PRIBRAM, K. H. 1973. The comparative psychology of communication. Ann. N.Y. Acad. Sci. 223: 134–143.
2. VOWLES, D. M. 1970. The psychobiology of aggression. Lecture delivered at the University of Edinburgh. University Press. Edinburgh, Scotland.
3. VOWLES, D. M. 1970. Neuroethology, evolution and grammar. *In* Development and Evolution of Behavior: Essay in Memory. T. C. Schneirla, Ed. W. H. Freeman and Co. San Francisco, Calif.

4. BEER, G. 1974. Ethology—the Zoologist's Approach to Behavior. Parts 1 and 2. Tuatara. Vol. **2**: 170–177; Vol. **12**: 16–39.
5. BRONOWSKI, J. 1967. Human and animal languages. *In* To Honor Roman Jakobson, Essays on the Occasion of his Seventieth Birthday. Vol. **1**: 374–394. Mouton. Paris, France.
6. JAKOBSON, R. 1956. Two aspects of language and two types of aphasic disturbances. Part II. *In* Fundamentals of Language. R. Jakobson and M. Halle, Eds.: 53–82. Mouton. The Hague, The Netherlands.
7. KLIMA, E. & U. BELLUGI, 1972. The signs of language in child and chimpanzee. Communication and Affect: A Comparative Approach T. Alloway, L. Kramer and P. Ploner, Eds.: 67–96. Academic Press. New York, N.Y.
8. BLUM, J. S., K. L. CHOW & K. H. PRIBRAM. 1950. A behavioral analysis of the organization of the parieto-temporo-preoccipital cortex. J. Comp. Neurol. **93**: 53–100.
9. BROCA, P. 1861. Remarques sur le siége de la faculté du langage articule suiviés d'une observation d'aphemie (perté de la parole). Bull. Société Anatomique de Paris **36**: 330–357.
10. BROCA, P. 1878. Anatomie comparée des circonvolutions cerebrales. Le grand lobe limbique et la scissure limbique dans la serie des mannifères. Rev. Anthrop. **1**: 385–498.
11. LURIA, A. R. 1964. Factors and forms of aphasia. *In* Disorders of Language. A. V. S. de Reuck and M. O'Connor, Eds.: 143–161. Ciba Foundation Symposium. Little Brown and Co. Boston, Mass.
12. LURIA, A. R. 1966. Higher Cortical Functions in Man. Basic Books. New York, N.Y.
13. PENFIELD, W. & L. ROBERTS. 1959. Speech and Brain Mechanisms. Princeton Univ. Press. Princeton, N.J.
14. TEUBER, H. L. 1960. *In* Handbook of Physiology: Neurophysiology, Vol. **3**: 1595–1668. J. Field, H. W. Magoun, V. E. Hall, Eds. American Physiological Soc. Washington, D.C.
15. PRIBRAM, K. H. 1971. Languages of the Brain: Experimental Paradoxes and Principles in Neuropsychology. Prentice-Hall, Inc. Englewood Cliffs, N.J.
16. GESCHWIND, N. 1965. Disconnexion syndromes in animals and man. Brain **88**: 237–294.
17. FREUD, S. 1953. On Aphasia. Authorized and translated by E. Stengel. International Univ. Press. New York, N.Y.
18. LIEPMAN, H. 1912. Anatomische befunde bia aphasischen und apraktischen. Neurol. Zbl. **31**: 1524–1530.
19. DEJERENE, J. 1914. Semiologie des Affections du Systeme Nerveux. Masson et Cie. Paris, France.
20. BAY, E. 1964. Principles of classification and their influence on our concepts of aphasia. *In* Ciba Foundation Symposium on Disorders of Language. A.V.S. de Reuck and M. O'Connor Eds.: 122–142. Little Brown and Co. Boston, Mass.
21. HACAEN, H. & R. ANGELERGUES. 1964. Localization of symptoms in aphasia. *In* Ciba Foundation Symposium on Disorders of Language. A. V. S. de Reuck and M. O'Connor, Eds.: 223–246. Little Brown and Co. Boston, Mass.
22. DEWSON, J. H. III, K. H. PRIBRAM & J. LYNCH. 1969. Effects of ablations of temporal cortex upon speech sound discrimination in the monkey. Exp. Neurol. **24**: 591–597.
23. DEWSON, J. H. III, K. W. NOBEL & K. H. PRIBRAM. 1966. Corticofugal influence at cochlear nucleus of the cat: Some effects of ablation of insulartemporal cortex. Brain Res. **2**: 151–159.
24. NOBEL, K. W. & J. H. DEWSON III. 1966. A corticofugal projection from insular and temporal cortex to the homolateral inferior colliculus in cat. J. Aud. Res. **6**: 67–75.
25. DEWSON, J. H. III & A. COWEY. 1969. Discrimination of auditory sequences by monkeys. Nature **222**: 695–697.
26. DEWSON, J. H. III & A. C. BURLINGAME. 1975. Auditory discrimination and recall in monkeys. Science **187**: 267–268.
27. MARIE, P. 1926. Travaux et Memoires. Vol. 1. Masson. Paris, France.
28. PRIBRAM, K. H., B. S. ROSNER & W. A. ROSENBLITH. 1954. Electrical responses to acoustic clicks in monkey: Extent of neocortex activated. J. Neurophysiol. **17**: 336–344.
29. PRIBRAM, K. H., D. N. SPINELLI & M. C. KAMBAK. 1967. Electrocortical correlates of stimulus response and reinforcement. Science **157**: 95, 96.
30. SPINELLI, D. N., A. STARR & T. BARRETT. 1968. Auditory specificity in unit recording from cat's visual cortex. Exp. Neurol. **22**: 75–84.

31. SPINELLI, D. N. & K. H. PRIBRAM. 1970. Neural correlates of stimulus response and reinforcement. Brain Res. **17:** 377–385.
32. JAKOBSON, R. 1964. Towards a linguistic topology of aphasic impairments. *In* Ciba Foundation Symposium on Disorders of Language. A. V. S. de Reuck and M. O'Connor, Eds.: 21–42. Little Brown and Company. Boston, Mass.
33. JAKOBSON, R. 1966. Linguistic types of aphasia. *In* Brain Function. Vol. 4. Speech, Language and Communication. E. C. Carterette, Ed.: 67–91. Univ. California Press. Los Angeles, Calif.
34. MOUNTCASTLE, V. B. 1967. Modality and topographic properties of single neurons of cat's somatic sensory cortex. J. Neurophysiol. **20:** 408–434.
35. WERNER, G. 1974. Neural information with stimulus feature extractors. *In* The Neurosciences; Third Study Program. F. O. Schmitt and F. G. Worden Eds.: 171–183. MIT Press. Cambridge, Mass.
36. EVARTS, E. V. 1967. Representation of movements and muscles by pyramidal tract neurons of the precentral motor cortex. *In* Neurophysiological Basis of Normal and Abnormal Motor Activities. M. D. Yahr and D. P. Purpura, Eds.: 215–254. Raven Press. Hewlett, N.Y.
37. HUBEL, D. H. & T. N. WIESEL. 1962. Receptive fields, binocular interaction and functional architecture in the cat's visual cortex. J. Physiol. **160:** 106–154.
38. BARLOW, H. B. & R. M. HILL. 1963. Selective sensitivity to direction of movement in ganglion cells of the rabbit retina. Science **139:** 412–414.
39. SPINELLI, D. N., K. H. PRIBRAM & B. BRIDGEMAN. 1970. Visual receptive field organization of single units in the visual cortex of monkey. Intern. J. Neuroscience **1:** 67–74.
40. SPERRY, R. W. 1970. Perception in the absence of the neocortical commissures. *In* Perception and Its Disorders. Res. Public. ARNMD. Vol. **48:** 123–138.
41. POLLEN, D. A. & J. H. TAYLOR. 1974. The striate cortex and the spatial analysis of visual space. *In* The Neurosciences: Third Study Program. F. O. Schmitt and F. G. Worden, Eds.: 239–247. Cambridge, Massachusetts: MIT Press. Cambridge, Mass.
42. CAMPBELL, F. W. & J. B. ROBSON. 1968. Application of Fourier Analysis to the visibility of gratings. J. Physiol. **197:** 551–556.
43. GLEZER, V. D., V. A. IVANOFF & T. A. TSCHERBACH. 1973. Investigation of complex and hypercomplex receptive fields of visual cortex of the cat as spatial frequency filters. Vision Res. **13:** 1875–1904.
44. PRIBRAM, K. H. 1974. How is it that sensing so much we can do so little? *In* The Neurosciences: Third Study Program. F. O. Schmitt and F. G. Worden, Eds.: 249–261. MIT Press. Cambridge, Mass.
45. PRIBRAM, K. H. 1974. Holonomy and structure in the organization of perception. *In* Proc. Conf. Images, Perception and Knowledge. University of Western Ontario. London, Canada. In press.
46. PRIBRAM, K. H., M. NUWER & R. BARON. 1974. The holographic hypothesis of memory structure in brain function and perception. *In* Contemporary Developments in Mathematical Psychology. R. C. Atkinson, D. H. Drantz, R. C. Luce, and P. Suppes, Eds.: 416–467. W. H. Freeman and Co. San Francisco, Calif.
47. PORT, R. 1973. Oral presentation on speech mechanisms and Fourier analysis at Univ. Minnesota Conf. Cognition, Perception and Adaptation. Minneapolis, Minn.
48. LIBERMAN, A. M., F. S. COOPER, D. P. SHANKWEILER & M. STUDDERT-KENNEDY. 1969. Perception of the speech code. *In* Brain and Behavior. Vol. 4. Adaptation. K. H. Pribram, Ed.: 105–148. Penguin Books. Harmondsworth, Middlesex, England.
49. GABOR, D. 1969. Information processing with coherent light. Optica Acts **16:** 519–533.
50. STROKE, G. W. 1969. An Introduction to Coherent Optics and Holography. Academic Press. New York, N.Y.
51. PRIBRAM, K. H. 1966. Some dimensions of remembering: Steps toward a neuropsychological model of memory. *In* Macromolecules and Behavior. J. Gaito, Ed.: 165–187. Academic Press. New York, N.Y.
52. THOM, R. 1972. Stabilite Structurelle et Morphogenese. W. A. Benjamin, Inc. Reading, Mass.
53. REYNOLDS, P. C. 1974. Handedness and the evolution of the primate forelimb. Presented at Conf. Human Brain Function. Neuropsychiatric Institute. U.S.C.A.

54. REYNOLDS, P. C. Play, language and human evolution. *In* Play: Its Evolution and
      Development. J. Bruner, A. Jolly and K. Sylva, Eds. Penguin Books. London, England.
55. ABLER. Personal communication.
56. WADA, J., L. CLARK & I. HAMM. 1973. Asymmetry of temporal and frontal speech zones.
      Presented 10th Inter. Congr. Neurology. Barcelona, Spain.
57. BIRDWHISTELL, R. L. 1954. Introduction to Kinesics. Washington, D.C. Department of
      State. Foreign Service Institute. Reprinted Univ. Louisville. 1954. Louisville, Ky.
58. BATESON, G. 1963. Exchange of information about patterns of human behavior. *In*
      Information Storage and Neural Control. W. S. Fields and W. Abbott, Eds.: 1–14.
      Charles C Thomas. Springfield, Ill.
59. BATESON, G. *In* Pragmatics of Human Communication. P. Watzlawick, J. Beavin and D.
      Jackson, Eds. W. W. Norton & Co. New York, N.Y.

EVOLUTION OF LANGUAGE LATERALIZATION AND COGNITIVE FUNCTION

Jerre Levy

Department of Psychology
University of Pennsylvania
Philadelphia, Pennsylvania 19174

STRUCTURAL LATERALIZATION IN APE AND MAN

The living hominids and pongids appear to be unique among the primates in having structurally asymmetric brains in the region of the Sylvian fissure. Wada,[1] Geschwind and Levitsky,[2] and Witelson and Pallic[3] have all shown the planum temporale to be larger in the left than in the right hemisphere in the majority of human brains. LeMay and Culebras[4] and Hochberg and LeMay[5] observed a relative expansion of the parietal operculum in the left hemisphere of right-handers, but not in left-handers, and Rubens[6] has found the posterior ramus of the Sylvian fissure to be longer on the left, and the occipital cortex to be larger on the right.

Very recently, LeMay has reported similar asymmetries in the chimpanzee and orangutan brain (this volume), as have Yeni-Komshian and Benson.[7] They examined 25 human, 25 chimpanzee, and 25 Rhesus monkey brains, finding a longer Sylvian fissure on the left in ape and man, but not in monkey. Consistent with the anatomical symmetry of the monkey brain, Hamilton[8] has concluded, after a number of studies in split-brain monkeys, that there is no evidence of functional asymmetry.

LATERALIZATION AND GESTURE

Functional Lateralization in the Ape?

Given the recent remarkable achievements of Washoe, Sara, Lana, Bouie, and Nim in manual communication, one is led to wonder whether the high-level cognitive ability displayed by these apes is associated with functional lateralization of their brains. To date, there are no adequate studies in the literature that would allow conclusions to be drawn regarding the presence or absence of functional asymmetry in the chimpanzee hemispheres, but the discovery of anatomical lateralization offers a very strong suggestion for its presence.

Although Locke (this volume) maintains that neuroanatomical asymmetries provide insufficient grounds for concluding that functional asymmetries exist, when the anatomy has already been shown to have functional correlates in one species (*Homo sapiens*), it would seem to require only a minor inductive leap to conclude that similar correlates exist in another species (*Pan troglodytes*).

The neuroanatomical asymmetries of the ape brain are surely homologues of those in man, and it is extremely likely that they have the same functional significance. Jerison[9] has pointed out that the vertebrate brain reveals its specialized capacities by the relative development of various portions of the central nervous system, a correlation he calls the *principle of proper mass*. The recognition of the validity of this principle is of enormous importance for understanding the fundamental relationship between neuroanatomy and behavior, and is as basic to neuropsychology as is the principle of natural selection to biology. In the particular case of anatomical asymmetries of the hemispheres, not only have empirical observations demonstrated correlated asymmetric functions in the human species, but there is a theoretical expectation of such functional lateralization on the basis of the principle of proper mass, and we predict it for ape, as well as for man.

Is Gestural Communication Language?

It has been known for over a hundred years that in the vast majority of right-handers, the left cerebral hemisphere is the main integrative organ for language and that the critical language integration regions surround the Sylvian fissure.[10-12] It is not unlikely that in the chimpanzee these regions are also critical for the cognitive capacities underlying their learned communicative skills. Katz (this volume) denies that apes like Washoe display true language, and attributes their complex gestural behaviors to simple, conditioned reactions. From the point of view of a nonlinguist, it would appear that the creativity shown by Washoe and other communicating apes is at least as fluent and complex as that shown by the very young human child, and it seems doubtful that any linguist would deny that a fifteen-month-old human baby who points to his teddy bear and says, "Bear," has language, while suddenly attributing it to him at age two when he says, "Give me bear." The criteria set by linguists for language in apes seem significantly more stringent than those they set for human children.

The desire by the human species to find some characteristic that qualitatively sets man apart from all other animals may finally result in his claim that language is language only if it permits vocalization of thoughts. Both Hewes (this volume) and Montagu (this volume) have emphasized the close association in evolution between the development of manual skill, gesturing, and speech. It is difficult to doubt their conclusions.

Neurological investigation reveals that even in the twentieth century variety of *Homo sapiens*, this evolutionary heritage can be seen. The patterning and sequencing of manual movements is disrupted by lesions to the left cerebral hemisphere, a syndrome known as ideational apraxia.[13] Recent work by Kimura[14,15] shows that in right-handers, the right hand moves and gestures during speech to a greater extent than the left, while in left-handers the association between speech and gesturing of the dominent hand is less clear. Also, of course, in literate human beings, the control of the writing hand necessarily arises from the language hemisphere. I do not believe that it is accidental that the linguistically specialized hemisphere is also specialized for the temporal sequencing of hand movements. It is more likely that this is a manifestation of the fact that the first forms of language to emerge in human evolution were gestural in nature and arose in an animal with a laterally specialized brain.

THE ASSOCIATION BETWEEN COGNITION AND LATERALIZATION

Why do hominoids, but no other primates, manifest language or protolanguage, as well as cerebral lateralization? Is there an intimate association between the two, or, as Kinsbourne has proposed[16] is the correlation accidental? Kinsbourne suggested that it is not cerebral asymmetry that must be accounted for, but rather, cerebral symmetry.

The Advantage of Symmetry

Kinsbourne has quite correctly pointed out that bilateral symmetry of organization can develop only in consequence of selective pressures for symmetry. Bilaterally symmetric animals evolved and typify all advanced species because of the powerful adaptive advantages brought with such organization. Given that an animal's body is left-right symmetric, and given that he lives in a world that is randomly asymmetric on the left and right, then, in the usual environment, he would suffer rather serious disadvantages if his capacity to move in one or the other direction, or to perceive stimuli on one or the other side of space, were relatively deficient. It is for this reason, suggests Kinsbourne, that the motor and sensory systems of animals, including man, are symmetrically organized.

The lateralization of cognitive function, on the other hand, Kinsbourne hypothesizes, has no adaptive consequences, and it developed simply because of a relaxation in selective pressure for symmetry. If Kinsbourne is correct, cerebral asymmetry should have no particular consequences for either cognitive structure and ability or for motoric and perceptual responses. Further, it would be expected that all mammals would have laterally organized cognitive abilities, since selective pressures for symmetry would be just as relaxed for them as for the anthropoids.

The Disadvantages of Cognitive Lateralization

The evidence to date, as mentioned, leads to the conclusion that only the hominoids among primates have laterally asymmetric brains. More importantly, however, lateral specialization of cognitive function leads, as Kinsbourne himself has shown,[17-19] to both perceptual and motoric asymmetries, precisely the traits which he says must be under strong *negative* selection, and functions which ought to be, on adaptive grounds, symmetrically organized.

Activation of one or the other side of the brain, by whatever means, produces both an orientation toward and a perceptual bias for the contralateral half of space. This is obviously an adpative response if the asymmetric activation has been produced by sensory stimulation, for it will tend to bring the source of stimulation into the central visual field and will selectively direct attention toward the stimulus. If, however, as is the case in human beings, asymmetric hemispheric activation can occur independently of stimulation from the external world, and strictly as a function of cognitive processing, the resulting motoric and perceptual biases can have dire consequences.

Split-Brain Patients

Evidence from split-brain patients strongly suggests that simple, nonverbal visual processing is a sufficient condition for activating the right hemisphere and producing a bias of attention to the right.[20] Even on visual discrimination tasks in which the left hemisphere is equal or superior to the right, the very fact that it is pure visual recognition which is required appears to direct attention to the left visual field, and it is the right hemisphere which assumes control of behavior. When this occurs, patients behave as if their left hemispheres had no awareness whatsoever of stimuli appearing in the right visual field.

Normal Populations

This leftward perceptual bias during the act of visual perception occurs for normal populations, even under nontachistoscopic, normal viewing conditions. Gilbert and Bakan [21] found that when subjects are given photographs of faces to inspect in free vision and are asked to say whether the original or a mirror-reversed photograph looks more like pictures constructed of two left or two right halves, right-handed subjects almost always select the construction composed of the half-face which is on the subject's left in the inspection figure. This was true of Israelis, as well as of North Americans. No such effect was found in left-handers. The authors interpreted their results to mean that dextral subjects were attending more to the left than the right side of space. Nelson and McDonald [22] found that when told to select the best title possible from available sets for various pictures, subjects selected titles descriptive of the left half of pictures.

This bias apparently has effects even on aesthetic taste. In a recently completed study, [23] I found that when subjects were shown pairs of vacation slides, one in the original and one in mirror orientation, and asked to choose the one they preferred, right-handers preferred those slides in which the more important content or greater heaviness, as judged by a second group of subjects, was located on the right. The correlation between preference and the direction and degree of judged asymmetry was 0.72 for right-handers and nonsignificantly above zero for left-handers on picture-pairs showing strong preference asymmetry for dextrals. About 60% of left-handers preferred the same versions as right-handers, whereas 40% preferred the opposite versions. Perceived asymmetry was significantly stronger on left asymmetric slides than on right asymmetric slides, and on basically symmetric pictures, there was a slight, though highly significant, perceived left asymmetry.

These results strongly suggest that there was a perceptual bias to the left in viewing the pictures, producing a slight perceived leftward asymmetry in basically symmetric slides, summating with actual stimulus asymmetry when a slide was left asymmetric, and subtracting from perceived asymmetry when a slide was actually right asymmetric. In consequence, subjects preferred those slides which they perceived to have more aesthetic balance, and these were slides in which a right stimulus asymmetry compensated for an inherent left perceptual asymmetry. (See FIGURE 1.)

Thus, a number of investigations demonstrate that lateralization of cognitive function does not merely organize processes asymmetrically in the brain, but that, because of this, in human beings, and possibly great apes also, the motoric and perceptual systems are functionally asymmetric. It is exceedingly difficult to believe that such behavioral asymmetries would not carry with them precisely the same sort of disadvantages that would result from lack of symmetry in the peripheral sensory and motor apparatuses themselves.

One is forced to the conclusion that lateral specialization of the brain did not result from a mere relaxation of selective pressure for symmetry, but rather, that the cognitive advantages of lateralization outweighed the perceptual and motoric disadvantages. This implies, of course, that the cognitive advantages of lateral specialization must be very great indeed.

Advantages of Cognitive Lateralization

I have suggested that since the processes and strategies involved in language and all its cognitive correlates and prerequisites are so different from those needed for high-level visuospatial capacities, it is reasonable to suppose that the underlying neural organizations must also be equally different.[24,25] I believe that if this is true, lateral specialization of the brain is a necessary consequence.

Overwhelming evidence from the neurological literature suggests that within a single cerebral hemisphere, although symptoms may be localized, it is invalid to think of various functions being organized into neat packets, each separately located in particular, restricted regions of the cortex. Electroencephalographic studies show that there are widespread changes all over the brain prior to a motor act or following sensory stimulation. We do not move with the motor cortex nor see with the striate cortex, though the normal operation of these regions may be necessary for normal function. Kurt Goldstein was not very distant from the truth when he maintained that the organ of mind functioned as an integrated whole, and he was certainly more

FIGURE 1. Examples of preferred and nonpreferred pictures.

correct than those extreme localizationists who believed that various functions were due solely to the patterns of neural activity occurring in small, circumscribed regions of the brain. As Marin has discussed (this volume), normal cerebral function depends on a dynamic equilibrium among all brain regions, and the symptoms resulting from brain lesions are as often, if not more often, due to a release from inhibition of an intact area, as from loss of excitation from the damaged area. Although certain symptoms of cerebral disequilibrium are seen in split-brain patients, the symptoms are extremely subtle, and, as Sperry[26] has said, the only explanation for the fact that severing of the most massive bundle of fibers in the brain produces such extremely minor symptoms, is that each hemisphere is a whole and complete brain within itself.

Given the premises that two very different neurological patterns are needed to integrate the functions associated with the left and right hemispheres, that the neural computers integrating these functions involve organizational networks extending throughout the occipital, temporal, parietal, and frontal lobes of the brain, and that each hemisphere functions as a complete brain within itself, lateralization of the computers seems to be a logical consequence. Were the brain constrained to be symmetric, this would mean either that each neural computer would have half the neural elements (neurons) of each hemisphere, or that each element could be controlled by and form a part of either computer. If the former were the case, each hemisphere would simply duplicate the functions of the other, and no extension of capacity would be gained by virtue of having two hemispheres. Each computer would, in effect, be half as large as that in the lateralized brain. If every neuron were an integral part of two differently organized neural patterns, activation of any neuron in the system would be almost certain to engage both computers, producing interference in the activity patterns of each.

Lateralization appears to provide for a minimization of interference effects in neural activity patterns and a maximization of the complexity of the computers integrating those patterns. If two very different kinds of cognitive capacities are to be present, then joint optimization of the level of those capacities seems to require lateralization.

This is not to suggest that confining one set of functions to one side of the brain optimizes that set of functions alone, but rather that, if both sets of abilities are to be present, this is best achieved by lateralization. It is conceivable, and possibly even likely, that if both sides of the brain could be fully devoted to the same set of processes, the skills and capacities based on them might exceed those in the fully lateralized person. This would, in fact, be the case if performance on some task depended not only on the adequacy of the organization of a specialized hemisphere, but on the adequacy of the selective activation of that hemisphere and the selective inhibition of the other. Clearly, no matter how well organized may be the visuospatial hemisphere for visuospatial tasks, performance will be poor if it is the language hemisphere that attempts to handle the task. No such problems would arise if both sides of the brain were identically organized to serve the same set of functions.

One might expect great variability in performance in a group of people having only minimally asymmetric brains. If both hemispheres are well organized for verbal abilities, verbal performance might be excellent and visuospatial skills relatively poor. If both hemispheres are well organized for visuospatial abilities, the reverse might occur. And if the tendency toward cerebral symmetry results from an intermixture of neural patterns in both hemispheres, performance may be poor in both sets of abilities.

As cognitive capacities evolve to higher and higher levels, lateralization is likely to show a correlated increase. If the ape brain is laterally specialized, and in the same direction as that of man, then, if the association I have proposed between lateral organization and cognitive ability is correct, the cognitive prerequisites to language were probably present prior to the divergence of the hominids and pongids, and the enormously complex processes that allow for human speech have been under selection for 25,000,000 years.

If it can be demonstrated that variations in lateral organization of the brain are correlated with variations in cognitive structure, there can be little doubt that variations in the former were, during our evolutionary history, also correlated with fitness.

Lateralization: Varieties and Cognitive Correlates

In a recently completed investigation, in collaboration with Marylou Reid, I examined the relationships among brain lateralization, handedness, hand position in writing, and performance.[27] I had postulated some years ago that hand position in writing was predictive of the direction of brain lateralization, specifically that individuals whose pencil is held below the line of writing, the pencil pointing toward the top of the page, had language organized in the hemisphere contralateral to the writing hand, the typical writing position and the normal organization. However, some 60% or so of left-handers and less than one percent of right-handers have an inverted hand position. I have been informed by two Israeli psychologists (Gur and Gur, personal communication) that the same is true in Israel, where writing proceeds from right to left. Such people typically have the hand above the line of writing, and the pencil points toward the bottom of the page (FIGURE 2). These, it was postulated, had language organized in the hemisphere ipsilateral to the writing hand and visuospatial functions in the contralateral hemisphere. The study that will be described aimed at testing this hypothesis, but, as will be seen, the differences among the groups extended well beyond mere differences in direction of lateral organization.

Two tachistoscopic tests were administered to all subjects, one requiring identification of a nonsense consonant-vowel-consonant syllable, vertically oriented, and projected to the left or right visual field, and the other requiring the location on a matrix, of a dot projected to the left or right field. In both tests, a number was also projected at fixation and subjects were required to name the number prior to identification of the syllable or location of the dot, and all stimulus presentations were followed by an immediate mask. No more than 2% of the trials of any subject had to be thrown out because of misidentification of the central number.

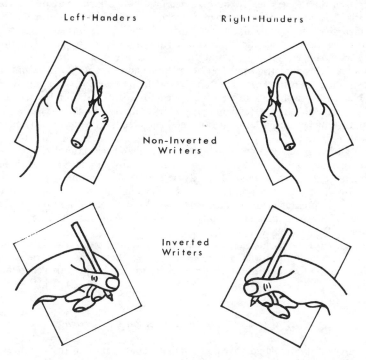

FIGURE 2. Typical writing postures of noninverted and inverted writers.

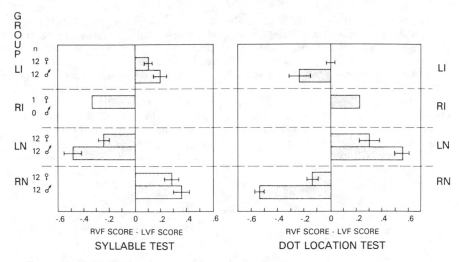

FIGURE 3. Field difference scores as a function of handedness, hand posture, sex, and task.

Potential subjects were pretested for left and right visual field exposure thresholds for a simple dot detection task, and only those subjects having equal thresholds for the two fields were selected for further testing. Out of 77 people tested, only four had unequal thresholds for the two fields. The exposure durations for the Syllable and Dot Location Tasks were determined individually for each subject in order to maintain performance between floor and ceiling. The performance score for each subject was measured by the proportion of correct responses multiplied by the reciprocal of the exposure duration and a constant. The constants for the Syllable and Dot Location Tasks were so chosen that the mean performance of dextrals across both visual fields for one test was the same as that for the other test. The purpose of this normalization was to enable comparison of the Syllable and Dot Location scores for males and females and for other groups of subjects, relative to the dextral mean. The scores, it should be noted, represent a measure of the amount of information correctly processed per unit time.

There were a total of 73 subjects, 24 dextrals, all of whom write in the noninverted position (Group RN), 24 left-handed writers who also write in the noninverted position (Group LN), 24 left-handed writers who write in the inverted position (Group LI), and one dextral who writes in the inverted position (Subject RI). Half of the three groups were male and half female. Subject RI is female, has a left-handed sister, and a left-handed father who is an architect.

The predictions were completely confirmed. FIGURE 3 shows the field differences for the three groups of subjects, as well as for Subject RI. Groups RN and LN appeared to be exact mirror images of each other, each having language organized in the hemisphere contralateral to the writing hand and visuospatial functions in the ipsilateral hemisphere. Both groups were well lateralized on both tests as measured by field differences. Group LI and Subject RI had verbal functions in the hemisphere ipsilateral to the writing hand and visuospatial functions in the contralateral hemisphere and were less lateralized than the other two groups. Females in all groups were less lateralized than males on the Dot Location Test and on the Syllable Test for Groups LN and LI, but not Group RN.

In addition, on the Syllable Test, total performance was poorer for Group LI and Subject RI (FIGURE 4). Interestingly, poor performance on this test was significantly associated with weak lateralization on the Dot Location Test ($r = .40$). In other words, bilateralization of spatial function seemed to interfere with language function.

Although total performance did not differ among the groups summed over sexes on the Dot Location Test, the variability in performance was significantly greater in Group LI than in Groups RN and LN. A majority of subjects were extremely poor in Group LI, but a significant minority of males outperformed all other subjects. Possbily, people having only weakly lateralized brains do poorly on both verbal and spatial function if the neurological organizations for both have developed bilaterally, but extremely well in one set of abilities if its neurological substrate is dominant on both sides of the brain.

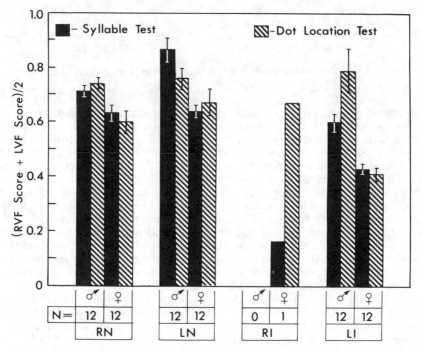

FIGURE 4. Performance scores as a function of handedness, hand posture, sex, and task.

CONCLUSION

These data, although possibly raising more questions than they answer, add much weight to the view that performance on cognitive tasks is associated with both direction and degree of lateral specialization of the brain, and with the relationship between manual and cerebral dominance. It can hardly be accidental that indices of brain organization such as handedness and hand position in writing are predictive of performance levels on verbal and spatial tests.

Clearly, much more work is called for to investigate in detail the various types of brain organization that can occur and their cognitive correlates. Nevertheless, research to date can leave little doubt that such correlates exist, and offers confirmation for the view that lateral specialization, far from being an accidental consequence of the relaxation of selective pressure for symmetry, has profound adaptive implications—biological, psychological, and sociological—for the whole of the human species.

REFERENCES

1. WADA, J. 1969. Interhemispheric sharing and shift of cerebral speech function. Paper presented at 9th Intern. Cong. Neurol. New York, N.Y.
2. GESCHWIND, N. & W. LEVITSKY. 1968. Human brain: left-right asymmetries in temporal speech region. Science **161:** 186–187.
3. WITELSON, S. F. & W. PALLIE. 1973. Left hemisphere specialization for language in the newborn: neuroanatomical evidence of asymmetry. Brain, **96:** 641–647.
4. LeMAY, M. & A. CULEBRAS. 1972. Human brain-morphologic differences in the hemispheres demonstrable by carotid arteriography. New Engl. J. Med. **287:** 168–170.
5. HOCHBERG, F. H. & M. LeMAY. 1975. Arteriographic correlates of handedness. Neurology **25:** 218–222.
6. RUBENS, A. 1975. Anatomical asymmetries of human cerebral cortex. Paper presented at Lateralization Symp. Soc. Neuroscience. New Jersey Chapter, Rutgers Medical School. Piscataway, N.J. To be published *In* Lateralization in the Nervous System. Academic Press. New York, N.Y.
7. YENI-KOMSHIAN, G. & D. A. BENSON. 1976. Anatomical study of cerebral asymmetry in the temporal lobe of humans, chimpanzees and Rhesus monkeys. Science **192:** 387–389.
8. HAMILTON, C. R. 1976. Perceptual and mnemonic lateralization in monkeys. Paper presented at Lateralization Symp, Soc. Neuroscience. New Jersey Chapter. Rutgers Medical School. Piscataway, N.J. To be published *In* Lateralization in the Nervous System. Academic Press. New York, N.Y.
9. JERISON, H. 1973. Evolution of the Brain and Intelligence. Academic Press. New York, N.Y.
10. DAX, M. 1836. Lésions de la moitié gauche de l'encéphale coincidant avec l'onbli des signes de la pensée. Read at Montpellier, France.
11. BROCA, P. 1861. Perte de la parole, ramollissement chronique et destruction partielle du lobe anterieur gauche du cerveau. Bull. Soc. Anthrop. Paris **2:** 235–238.
12. WERNICKE, C. 1874. Der aphasische Symtomenkomplex. Cohn and Weigert. Breslau, Poland.
13. DE AJURIAGUERRA, J., H. HÉCAEN & R. ANGELERGUES. 1960. Les apraxies: variétés cliniques et latéralisation lésionnelle. Rev. Neurol. **102:** 566–594.
14. KIMURA, D. 1973. Manual activity during speaking. I. Right-handers. Neuropsychologia **11:** 45–50.
15. KIMURA, D. 1973. Manual activity during speaking. II. Left-handers. Neuropsychologia **11:** 51–55.
16. KINSBOURNE, M. 1976. Lateral orientation and the lateralization of cognitive function. Paper presented at the Lateralization Symp. Soc. Neuroscience. Rutgers Medical School. Piscataway, N.J. 1975. To be published *In* Lateralization in the Nervous System. Academic Press. New York, N.Y.
17. KINSBOURNE, N. 1970. The cerebral basis of lateral asymmetries in attention. Acta Psychol. **33:** 193–201.
18. KINSBOURNE, M. 1972. Eye and head turning indicates cerebral lateralization. Science **176:** 539–591.
19. KINSBOURNE, M. 1974. The interaction between cognitive process and the direction of attention. *In* Attention and Performance. V. P.M.A. Rabbit and S. Dornic, Eds. Academic Press. New York, N.Y.

20. LEVY, J., C. TREVARTHEN & R. W. SPERRY. 1972. Perception of bilateral chimeric figures following hemispheric deconnection. Brain **95:** 61–78.
21. GILBERT, C. & P. BAKAN. 1973. Visual asymmetry in perception of faces. Neuropsychologia **11:** 355–362.
22. NELSON, T. & G. MACDONALD. 1971. Lateral organization, perceived depth, and title preference in pictures. Percept. Mot. Skills **33:** 983–986.
23. LEVY, J. 1976. Lateral dominance and aesthetic preference. Neuropsychologia. In press.
24. LEVY, J. 1969. Possible basis for the evolution of lateral specialization of the human brain. Nature **224:** 614–615.
25. LEVY, J. 1974. Psychobiological implications of bilateral asymmetry. *In* Hemisphere Function in the Human Brain. Dimond, S. and J. G. Beaumont, Eds. Paul Elek, Ltd. London, England.
26. SPERRY, R. W. 1967. Split-brain approach to learning problems. *In* The Neuroscience, A Study Program. The Rockefeller University Press. New York, N.Y. G. C. Quarton, T. Melnechuk & F. O. Schmitt, Eds.
27. LEVY, J. & M. REID. 1976. Variations in writing posture and cerebral organization. Science. In press.

CEREBRAL ASYMMETRY: CHANGES IN FACTORS AFFECTING ITS DEVELOPMENT*

Dennis L. Molfese, Virginia Nunez,
Sylvia M. Seibert, and Nerella V. Ramanaiah

Department of Psychology
Southern Illinois University at Carbondale
Carbondale, Illinois 62901

During the past century a great deal of research has focused on the relationship between language abilities and hemisphere functions. The results of these efforts suggest that many language abilities may be controlled by mechanisms within the left cerebral hemisphere, whereas the right hemisphere may control quite different functions in the adult human brain. However, although the presence of such relationships has long been studied in adults, researchers have only recently turned their attention to the development of the hemispheric differences in infants and children. To date a number of researchers employing remarkably diverse procedures have reported finding some indications of hemispheric differences within the first year of life. Such procedures have included the use of evoked potential recording techniques,[1-5] photic driving procedures,[6,7] EEG power distributions analyses,[8,9] anatomical analyses,[10,11] and dichotic listening procedures.[12] This paper will briefly review the use of electrophysiological techniques to assess hemispheric differences and then will report several recent attempts by our lab to isolate the acoustic determinants of laterality.

An early indication of hemispheric differences in infants was reported by Molfese.[1,13] Molfese recorded the auditory evoked potentials (AEP) of 10 infants (mean age: 5.8 months), 11 children (mean age: 6 years) and 10 adults (mean age: 25.9 years) to a series of speech syllables, words, a piano chord, and a white noise burst. Twenty-seven of the 31 subjects responded to the speech material with a larger amplitude left-hemisphere (LH) evoked potential. Thirty subjects responded to the piano chord with the largest amplitude change occurring in the right hemisphere (RH), and 29 subjects responded to the white noise stimulus with the largest AEP occurring in the RH. The proportion of subjects who responded with differential hemispheric activity did not differ across age groups. This was interpreted as support for the hypothesis that hemispheric differences are present during infancy. A recent AEP study conducted by Barret et al.[5] with marasmic and normal infants generally supports these earlier findings. They presented a series of clicks and a second series containing repetitions of the child's own name to a group of infants ranging in age from five to twelve months (mean age: 8 months). The AEPs were recorded from the anterior parietal locations C_3 and C_4 from the left and right hemispheres, respectively. When the hemisphere responses of the normal children were compared, 11 of

*Supported in part by a grant (RR81) from the General Clinical Research Centers Program of the Division of Research Sources, National Institutes of Health, and by a grant (2-15-87) from the Office of Research and Projects, Southern Illinois University at Carbondale. The permission of Dr. Philip Sunshine (Department of Pediatrics, Stanford Medical School) and Dr. John B. Taylor and Dr. William R. Hamilton (Doctor's Memorial Hospital, Carbondale) to work with their newborn infant populations is gratefully acknowledged. Special thanks is also extended to Dr. Gordon Pitz for his development and modification of several computer routines.

16 comparisons showed a LH predominance, whereas three reflected a larger RH response. A clear RH amplitude predominance emerged from the infants' responses to the click stimulus.

Several other procedures have been employed to assess hemispheric differences in infants. Gardiner et al.[8] and Gardiner and Walter,[1] analyzing changes in the EEG power distributions, reported finding hemispheric differences in four six-month old infants in response to continuous segments of speech and music. The infant EEGs were recorded from four locations over each hemisphere and referred to linked mastoid electrodes. The EEG epochs were recorded from stimulus onset to offset. Continuous plots of the laterality ratio versus time for each pair of symmetrical channels were then calculated for each epoch. Only the parietal and temporal locations (P_3-P_4 and W_1-W_2, respectively) yielded hemisphere differences, with the largest changes occurring at the W leads. For all infants, the power spectrum between 3 and 5 hertz (Hz) decreased at the LH leads during the speech condition and at the RH leads during the music condition.

Hemispheric differences have also been found in response to visual stimuli. Crowell et al.[6] found evidence of differential hemispheric driving in the right hemisphere of newborn human infants in response to presentations of rhythmic visual stimuli. Subjects were 97 newborn full-term infants. Crowell et al. placed electrodes over the left and right occipital areas (O_1 and O_2, respectively) and referred these areas to the right ear. Repetitive light flashes were presented at three/second for four seconds. Recorded responses were later tested for photic driving—an increase in the EEG spectral frequency to the same frequency as the stimuli. Photic driving was found in 36 infants (37% of the total). Of these infants, 50% showed unilateral driving. Sixteen infants showed greater activity in the RH; two infants had more activity in the LH. Eighteen infants showed bilateral driving. Given that adults in a similar situation typically show bilateral driving, the presence of unilateral driving was thought to be due to a more advanced development of the RH occipital area.

A more recent study by Crowell et al.[7] with 217 infants supported these earlier findings for unilateral driving and reported a decrease in asymmetrical responding with age. At two days of age, 12% of the infants showed bilateral driving, but at 30 days, 48% of the infants had bilateral driving. This decrease in differential hemispheric responding may be comparable to that reported by Molfese[2] and Molfese et al.[4] They reported that the degree of laterality, as indicated by amplitude differences of the AEPs, was greater in the infants than in the adults in response to both the speech syllables and the nonspeech stimuli. The authors hypothesized that such decreases in laterality might be due to changes in the corpus callosum and various commissures which interconnect the two cerebral hemispheres.[14]

All the studies reviewed report the presence of hemispheric differences during infancy. Interestingly, all those studies involving auditory stimuli were generally consistent in their findings that speech materials triggered a large LH response, but nonspeech stimuli such as clicks, white noise bursts, and music produced a greater RH response.[1-5,8,9,13]

Given that infants at birth are generally thought to have only a reflex-based cognitive system[15] and little or no linguistic skills,[16] it would appear that the asymmetrical responses of infants to auditory stimuli must be based, at least initially, on certain physical characteristics of the acoustic stimuli. Researchers, however, have only recently turned their attention to this problem. Cutting,[17] in a study with adults, isolated several elements that triggered differential hemispheric responding. Using a modified dichotic listening procedure, Cutting presented a series of vowel (nontransition) and consonant-vowel (transition) syllables which were synthesized with either narrow bandwidth formants or with "normal" formants. Cutting reported that both the broad-band and transition stimuli resulted in a right-ear advantage (greater LH than RH processing), but the narrow bandwidth and nontransition stimuli did not elicit any differences between hemispheres. In an attempt to assess the contribution of these acoustic elements in eliciting differential hemispheric activity in infants, Molfese[3] presented stimuli similar to those employed by Cutting to a group of 16 newborn infants. Half the stimuli contained a transitional element and half were steady state sounds. Of these sounds, half were composed of three formants with bandwidths comparable to those for speech and half with bandwidths of only 1 Hz. The AEPs were recorded from the T_3 and T_4 electrode locations and referred to linked ear lobes.[18] An analysis of the amplitude changes across hemisphere and stimulus conditions indicated that bandwidth was a determining factor for producing hemisphere differences. When a normal bandwidth stimulus was presented, a larger amplitude AEP occurred in the LH than in the RH. However, when a narrow bandwidth stimulus was presented, the RH amplitude change was larger than that for the LH. The presence of transitional elements did not appear to have any effect on the AEP amplitude across hemispheres. Consequently, it was concluded that bandwidth, rather than transitional elements, was a critical acoustic element responsible for triggering differential hemispheric activity. These analyses, however, like those for many EP studies, involve only a relatively small proportion of the AEP response. In this case, only two time points out of nearly 200 were set aside for analysis, and the bulk of the data was discarded. If the AEP does reflect changes in brain-processing over time, as some writers have suggested,[19] the analysis of the entire waveform over time would be of critical importance in attempts to understand the underlying processes that generate these waveforms. Recently, a technique has been developed that not only allows one to analyze the entire waveform, but in addition, allows for the possibility of identifying the processes reflected by different components of the evoked potential waveform.[20]

The following study represents initial attempts to evaluate the suitability of such analyses for studying hemispheric differences in newborn human infants. This study, like Reference 3, was again designed to assess what acoustic characteristic of speech sounds would trigger a LH response. The work of Molfese[3] and Cutting[17] both suggested that bandwidth was a decisive factor in triggering LH processing. Although Molfese had not found any indication that transitional elements were critical to lateralization of responses, it was hypothesized that the measure used (AEP amplitude) may not have been sensitive enough to this manipulation. Given the continuous nature of the AEP response, the transition element could have been coded in another part of the AEP waveform. If the factor analysis would be sensitive to changes throughout the AEP, perhaps it could isolate such an element. An additional acoustic stimulus, a pure tone, was added to assess possible contributions to a lateralized response by number of formants.

METHOD

Subjects

Fourteen neonates (seven males and seven females) were tested within 48 hours of birth. Mean birth weight was 7.01 lbs (range: 5.90–8.47) for males and 7.19 lbs (range: 5.00–8.30) for females. Demerol was the chief anesthetic administered to the mother during labor. Two infants (one male and one female) were delivered by Caesarian section.

Stimuli

Five sounds were used as stimuli: two synthetically produced speech syllables gæ and æ and two nonspeech stimuli which were constructed from pure tones corresponding exactly to the central frequencies of the formants for the speech syllables. These stimuli were constructed by Dr. James Cutting on the parallel resonance synthesizer at the Haskins Laboratories. For additional information concerning the construction of the stimuli, the reader is referred to Cutting.[17] A fifth stimulus, a 500-Hz tone, was also presented. This stimulus was similar to the æ syllables in that it was a steady state sound. It was, however, composed of one formant rather than three, and the formant bandwidth was 1 Hz. The four multiple formant stimuli are depicted in FIGURE 1. The broad-band "speech" stimuli are presented on the left side of the

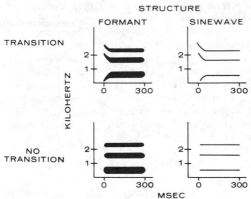

FIGURE 1. The acoustic structure of the syllables gæ and æ. Stimuli with normal broad-band formant structure are on the left of the figure and narrow-band sinewave structure are on the right. Stimuli with transitions (gæ) are represented at the top of the figure, and steady state stimuli (æ) are at the bottom. All stimuli were 300 msec in length. (After Cutting.[17])

figure; the narrow bandwidth nonspeech stimuli are on the right. The formants of the broad-band stimuli were 60, 90, and 120 Hz in width for formants 1, 2, and 3, respectively. All formants of the narrow-band stimuli were 1 Hz in width. Both stimuli at the top of the figure contain transitional elements that generally characterize a consonant sound. Two steady state sounds that typify vowel sounds are at the bottom of the figure. All stimuli were 300 msec in duration and were presented at equal peak intensity levels.

Twenty random orderings of these stimuli were recorded on one channel of a stereo tape recorder. The time interval between stimuli was randomly varied between 4 and 8 seconds. A 50-Hz square wave was recorded on a second channel of the tape recorder 30 msec before each stimulus. This pulse served as a signal to a PDP-12 computer to begin averaging the AEPs.

Procedure

Each infant was tested individually in a room adjoining the hospital nursery. The infant was placed in a semireclined infant seat and scalp electrodes were placed over the left and right temporal areas (T_3 and T_4, respectively). These electrodes were referred to linked ear leads. A fifth recording lead was placed on the forehead to serve as a floating ground. A mean resistance of 4.55 kHz was maintained throughout the testing. The electrodes were then plugged into two isolation amplifiers (Analogue Devices, model 273J). This output was connected to two modified differential amplifiers (Tektronix AM 502), with the bandpass flat between .1 and 30 Hz. After approximately a five-minute period had elapsed following application of the recording electrodes, the stimuli were presented. The AEPs elicited in response to these sounds were recorded on a Cassette FM tape recorder (Vetter model C-4). These responses were later averaged on a PDP-12 computer.

Data analyses

Following Chapman *et al.*,[20] the data analyses were performed with use of factor-analytic and analysis of variance techniques. The raw data consisted of 140 EP measurements in microvolts (mV) obtained from both hemispheres of 14 infants, during five experimental conditions. A 70 (variables) × 140 (cases) input data matrix was obtained from these 140 EP measurements by taking the recordings at each of 70 time points (with an interval of 13 msec) from each EP measurement over a 900-msec period.Intercorrelations among the 70 variables were submitted to principal components analysis, and factors with eigen values greater than 1.0 were rotated by the varimax method,[21,22] with the BMD × 72 computer program.[23] This was done to obtain latent components of EPs, which would provide a parsimonious representation of complex data.

To obtain exact temporal and amplitude measures of the factors, it was necessary to convert the factors to the original metric (mV). The rotated factors were expressed by multiplying the factor loading at each time point first with the standard deviation of all EP values at that point, and then with the factor score appropriate for a particular stimulus condition. For interpreting each factor, factor scores were submitted to mixed design analysis of variance,[24] using the BMD 08V computer program.[23]

RESULTS

Four factors accounted for 96.08% of the total variance. The centroid (the average EP of the entire data set) and the four factors (in the original metric) are plotted in FIGURE 2.

Factor 1 was characterized by a negative-going waveform which peaked approximately 600 msec after stimulus onset. Factor 2 was marked by a late positive wave which reached its peak 884 msec following stimulus onset. Factor 3 was initially characterized by a negative deflection which peaked 533 msec after stimulus onset and a subsequent positive wave which reached its maximum at the end of the 900-msec period. Factor 4 was characterized by an initial positive wave which peaked after 300 msec. This was followed by a negative wave which peaked at 624 msec and a subsequent smaller positive peak at 832 msec.

Analyses of variance were performed to investigate the effects of four independent variables (sex, hemisphere, transition, bandwidth) on each of the four factors.

Factor scores were first analyzed by a 2 (sex) × 2 (hemisphere) × 2 (bandwidth) × 2 (transition) analysis of variance. A significant main effect for sex ($F = 4.75$, $df = 1, 12$, $p < .05$) was present for factor 1. A significant transition effect ($F = 5.28$, $df = 1, 12$, $p < .05$) indicated differences between the gæ stimuli and the æ stimuli for factor 2. A significant hemisphere effect ($F = 6.66$, $df = 1, 12$, $p < .05$) revealed differential hemispheric responding for factor 4. Inclusion of the fifth stimulus, the

500-Hz tone, resulted in a 2 (sex) × 2 (hemisphere) × 5 (stimulus condition) design. An analysis of variance indicated no significant main effects. Using Schefféplanned comparison tests, in which the tone was grouped first with the steady state stimuli and then with the narrow bandwidth stimuli, the transition and bandwidth variables were further examined. A significant transition effect ($F = 4.34$, $df = 1$, 48, $p < .05$) was represented by factor 2 and a significant bandwidth effect ($F = 4.40$, $df = 1$, 48, $p < .05$) was reflected by factor 3.

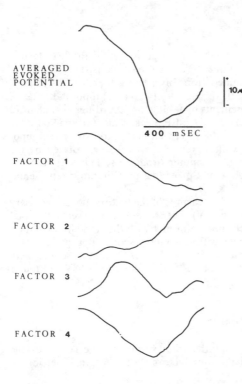

FIGURE 2. Centroid and four factors over all stimulus conditions. The centroid at the top is the average EP of the entire set of data. The calibration scale is 10 μV. Below are the four factors obtained from the varimax principal components analysis and returned to the original metric. In this and all other figures, positive is up and the time course is 900 msec. This and the following figures were constructed from points at 52-msec intervals.

A group-averaged AEP and four factors were then reproduced for each stimulus for both hemispheres. The group AEP and the four factors elicited in response to gæ are shown in FIGURE 3. The group AEPs at the top of the figure reflect an overall amplitude difference between hemispheres with a larger AEP occurring in the LH than in the RH in response to this broadband, transitional speech syllable. The LH response was approximately 6.5 V larger than the RH. Factor 1 reflected the sex difference in the AEPs of newborn infants; therefore, discussing its differences across hemispheres and stimuli is of little value and will not be developed in this or the following figures. Factor 2, which was sensitive to steady state (nontransition) elements, was characterized by a late positive component for the RH but almost no change in potential for the LH. Factor 3, which differentiated between narrow and broadband stimuli, was characterized by a negative deflection. Factor 4, which reflected hemisphere differences, was represented by components that were opposite in polarity for the two hemispheres.

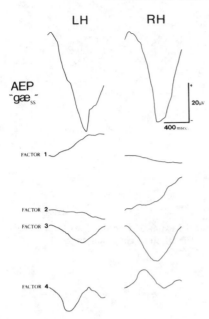

FIGURE 3. Reproduced EPs and factors for stimulus condition gæ$_{ss}$. For this and the following figures the left hemisphere plots are shown on the left, and those for the right hemisphere on the right. The four factors for each hemisphere were obtained from the rotated factor loadings returned to the original metric and multiplied by the factor score for that condition. Consequently, factors in the two hemispheres differ only by their appropriate condition factor scores. The reproduced EPs shown at the top are the sums of the four factors plus the centroid. At the right is a 20 μV calibration scale.

FIGURE 4 represents the group AEPs and factors elicited in response to æ$_{ss}$—a steady state, broad bandwidth stimulus. A larger change in AEP amplitude (16 μV) occurred in the LH than in the RH in response to this stimulus. In contrast to factor 2 for gæ$_{ss}$, the LH was marked by a large positive waveform. The RH component was similar to that for the gæ$_{ss}$ stimulus. As indicated earlier, factor 2 occurred when a

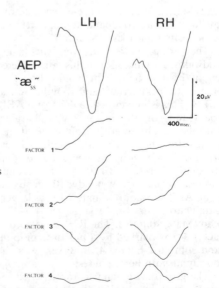

FIGURE 4. Reproduced EPs and factors for stimulus condition æ$_{ss}$.

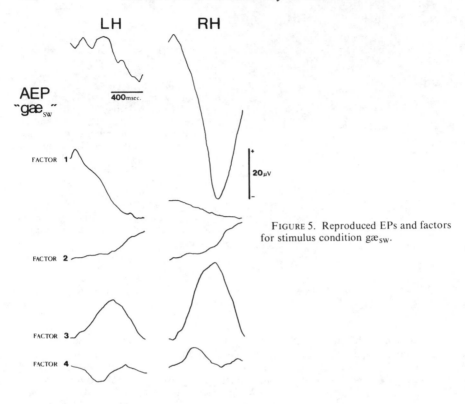

FIGURE 5. Reproduced EPs and factors for stimulus condition gæ$_{SW}$.

steady state stimulus was presented. Factor 3 was again marked by a negative-going waveform for a broadband stimulus. Hemisphere differences are again reflected by the opposite polarities of factor 4.

The group AEPs and components elicited in response to gæ$_{SW}$, a narrow bandwidth transitional stimulus, are depicted in FIGURE 5. This stimulus differs from that of FIGURE 3 only in bandwidth. The RH amplitude of the group AEP in response to this narrow band stimulus was approximately 47 μV larger than that for the LH. This is in contrast to the group AEPs elicited in response to the two previous broad-band stimuli. Factor 2 was characterized by a late positive wave for both hemispheres, although the amplitude of the LH is greatly reduced from the level it reached for the preceding stimulus. Factor 3 was characterized by a positive waveform for both hemispheres. Factor 4 again reflected opposite polarities for the two hemispheres. In FIGURE 6, the group averaged AEPs and factors elicited in response to the narrow bandwidth steady state stimulus æ$_{SW}$ are presented. The RH group AEP was approximately 19 μV larger than the LH response. The LH was once again characterized by a large, late positive deflection for factor 2 in response to a steady state stimulus. The RH was also marked by this late increasing component. Factor 3 was marked by a positive component in both hemispheres for this narrow band stimulus. Factor 4, however, was characterized by components with similar polarity in both hemispheres.

The group AEPs and factors elicited in response to the 500-Hz tone (a steady state, narrow bandwidth, single formant stimulus) are illustrated in FIGURE 7. The

RH group AEP was approximately 12 μV larger in amplitude than the LH. Factor 3, however, like that for the two preceding narrow bandwidth stimuli, was marked by a positive wave. The hemisphere polarities as reflected in factor 4 were again opposite to each other. Intriguingly, these polarities were opposite to those for the four other stimuli.

In general the degree of laterality as indicated by amplitude differences between hemispheres was approximately twice as great for the narrow bandwidth stimuli in the RH (mean amplitude difference = 26 μV) than for broadband stimuli in the LH (mean amplitude difference = 11.25).

DISCUSSION

The use of the factor analysis to isolate the minimum number of AEP components that account for the majority of the variance appears to have been successful. Four factors were found that accounted for 96% of the total variance. The factor analysis also gave some indication of the temporal relationships between the different factors. Factor 1 occurred during the initial portion of the AEP, factor 2 increased over the final third of the response, and factor 3 was marked by a prominent wave midway through the AEP response. Factor 4 was the only factor that appeared to undergo change throughout the temporal period of the AEP. In light of these temporal differences, it would appear that the coding and processing of different experimental elements occurred at different times following stimulus onset.

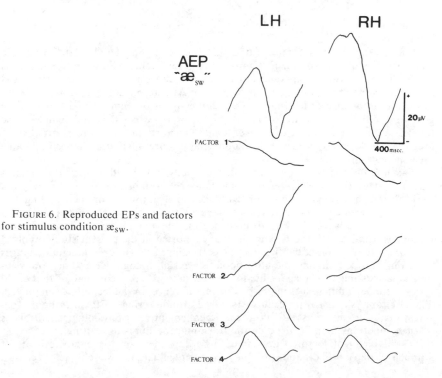

FIGURE 6. Reproduced EPs and factors for stimulus condition æ$_{SW}$.

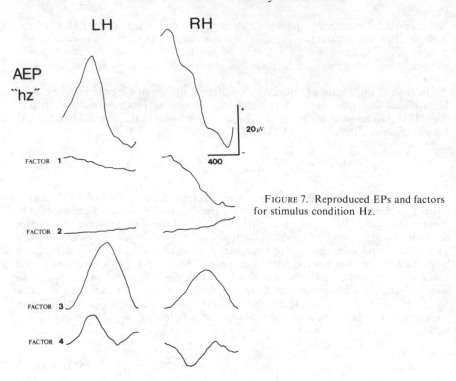

FIGURE 7. Reproduced EPs and factors for stimulus condition Hz.

Subsequent analyses demonstrated that each component did relate to specific characteristics of the experimental situation. Factor 1 reflected a sex difference. This factor differed between male and female infants across all stimulus conditions and appeared as a larger component in the female AEP responses. This could reflect a more advanced stage of neurological development for the female infants or a more general difference in the neurological processes between males and females. The former case is in agreement with several anatomical studies which report that some areas of the female cortex are developmentally more advanced than comparable areas in male infants.[10,11]

Factor 2 increased in amplitude when a steady state multiple formant stimulus was presented. However, a stimulus that contained a transition element in which a rapid change in frequency did occur (gæ) failed to elicit this factor. This finding is in contrast to Cutting's[17] report that the presence of transitional elements produced a right ear (LH) advantage. This discrepancy may be due in part to developmental factors. Cutting tested adults, and the work reported in the present study involved newborn infants. Consequently, it is possible that various developmental changes occurring between infancy and adulthood as a result of cognitive and neurophysiological factors might be responsible for these differences. A second factor that could account for such differences might be due to differences in the techniques employed. The electrophysiological procedures involved in monitoring AEPs in response to a set of stimuli might be assessing quite different cognitive or physiological correlates of these functions than do the dichotic listening procedures of Cutting.

The polarity of factor 3 appeared to be dependent on the bandwidth of the stimulus. When a broad-band stimulus was presented, factor 3 was characterized by a negative waveform, but a positive waveform occurred in response to a narrow-band stimulus.

Hemisphere differences were reflected in factor 4 by opposite polarities for the two hemispheres. The hemispheres of the newborn infants responded differently from each other to all stimuli. Although this is in agreement with earlier studies of hemisphere differences in infants, the lack of an interaction of hemisphere with transition or bandwidth suggests that no specific acoustic factor was responsible for producing the differential hemispheric activity reflected in factor 4. When the more traditional measures of hemispheric differences such as amplitude measures are considered, the situation becomes even more confusing. Several researchers have reported changes in AEP amplitude [1-5] or activity [6-9] across hemispheres as a function of different stimuli. Such differences have previously been interpreted as an indication of differential hemispheric involvement in the processing of particular stimuli.[25,19] However, given that there was some overlap between the different factors in time, the amplitude or activity of the AEP at any single time point could reflect the influence of more than one factor. Thus, the overall amplitude differences between the left and right hemispheres for the group AEPs (cf., FIGURES 3–7) could reflect the contributions of sex and stimuli factors in addition to the influence of the hemisphere differences. Consequently, the overall amplitude differences between hemispheres that have been previously reported may reflect both general differences in the types of processing available to each hemisphere [26] as well as differences in the utilization of more general mechanisms common to both hemispheres.[27]

The failure of the present study to find acoustic factors that might trigger differential hemispheric responding may also be due to the limited nature of the stimuli. The one stimulus that appeared to affect the polarity of factor 4 was the 500-Hz tone. The polarity here for both hemispheres was the reverse of that for the first four stimuli. This stimulus, it was noted, differed from the other sounds in that it was composed of one formant, rather than three. Perhaps if the number of formants were varied more systematically, some acoustic factors affecting laterality might emerge.

At this point, it no longer seems surprising to find indications of hemispheric differences in human infants, even though less than a decade ago some individuals had argued that such differences would not appear until sometime between two and three years of age as the child develops his language skills.[28] Nevertheless, questions still remain unanswered as to the role of cerebral asymmetry in language and cognitive functions. Lenneberg[28] had argued that man differed from lower organisms because of basic biological differences that allowed him to use language. A basic element that contributed to these differences was lateralization. Over the past several years, however, researchers have found indications of such hemispheric differences in other species.[29]

In a recent study conducted at the University of Konstanz (West Germany), Molfese *et al.*[30] found indications of hemispheric differences in cats to stimuli that differed in bandwidth, transition, and number of formants. Bipolar recordings were made of AEPs over the primary auditory area (A1), the visual area (V18), and the insular temporal cortex (IT) across hemispheres. Only the insular temporal leads reflected a hemisphere difference. No differences between hemispheres occurred across the primary auditory or visual areas. An example of the AEP responses is presented in FIGURE 8. The AEPs elicited in response to both the broad-band and narrow-band stimuli from the IT cortex are marked by positive deflections during the initial period following stimulus onset. Consequently, the two hemispheres responded differently to these stimuli. The visual area, however, was not characterized by such a deflection. The two hemispheres in this region were apparently responding in a similar fashion, and no hemisphere differences were present. In addition, no changes in the direction of laterality appeared as a function of bandwidth. However, these data have not yet been submitted to the types of analyses used by the present authors in this paper. It is possible that the use of factor analytic techniques supplemented by other analyses might reflect some differences across hemispheres and stimuli. In any case, it is clear that lateralization of function is not unique to man. Consequently, the specific role of hemispheric differences in determining or influencing language abilities remains open to speculation.

SUMMARY

The present study offered further support for the notion that hemispheric differences are present during early infancy. Moreover, in addition to finding evidence of electrophysiological differences between male and female infants, discrete components of the AEP response were identified and isolated that were responsive to specific aspects of the acoustic stimuli. Information concerning temporal differences in the processing of these elements was also obtained.

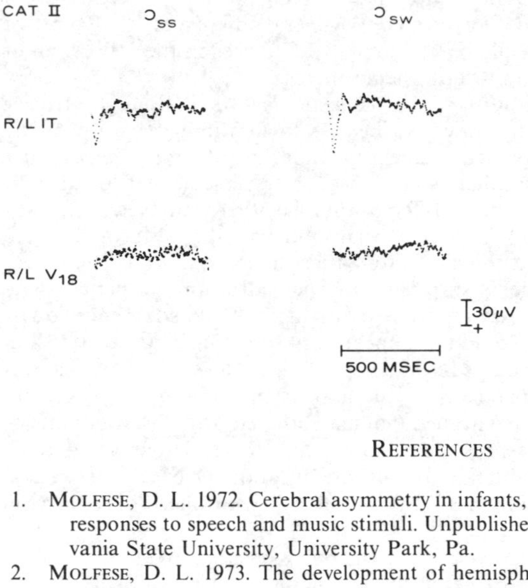

FIGURE 8. AEPs of Cat II to a broad-band steady state vowel ($\supset_{ss}$) and a narrow-band steady state vowel ($\supset_{sw}$). AEPs in response to $\supset_{ss}$ are depicted on the left and those to $\supset_{sw}$ are on the right. The top row of AEPs are responses recorded from the insular temporal region (IT), and responses from visual area 18 (V18) are presented at the bottom. AEPs were recorded for 500 msec following stimulus onset. The calibration is 30 V with negative up.

REFERENCES

1. MOLFESE, D. L. 1972. Cerebral asymmetry in infants, children and adults: auditory evoked responses to speech and music stimuli. Unpublished doctoral dissertation. The Pennsylvania State University, University Park, Pa.
2. MOLFESE, D. L. 1973. The development of hemispheric asymmetry for speech and nonspeech stimuli. Paper presented to the Midwestern Psychol. Assn. Chicago, Ill.
3. MOLFESE, D. L. The ontogeny of cerebral asymmetry in man: auditory evoked potentials to linguistic and non-linguistic stimuli. In Recent Developments in the Psychobiology of Language: The Cerebral Evoked Potential Approach. J. E. Desmedt, Ed. Oxford University Press. London, England. In press.
4. MOLFESE, D. L., R. B. FREEMAN & D. S. PALERMO. 1975. The ontogeny of brain lateralization for speech and nonspeech stimuli. Brain Lang. 2: 356–368.
5. BARNET, A. B., M. V. DE SOTILLO & M. CAMPOS. 1974. EEG sensory evoked potentials in early infancy malnutrition. Paper presented at Soc. Neuroscience. St. Louis, Mo.
6. CROWELL, D. H., R. H. JONES, L. E. KAPUNIAI & J. K. NAKAGAWA. 1973. Unilateral cortical activity in newborn humans: an early index of cerebral dominance. Science 180: 205–208.

7. CROWELL, D. H., L. E. KAPUNIAI & J. A. GARBANATI. Hemispheric differences in human infant rhythmic responses to photic stimulation. *In* Cerebral Evoked Potentials in Man. J. E. Desmedt, Ed. Oxford University Press. London, England. In press.

8. GARDINER, M. F., C. SCHULMAN & D. O. WALTER. 1973. Facultative EEG asymmetries in infants and adults. *In* Cerebral Dominance. BIS Conf. Rep. Vol. 34: 37–40.

9. GARDINER, M. F. & D. O. WALTER. Evidence of hemispheric specialization from infant EEG. *In* Lateralization in the Nervous System. S. Harnad, R. W. Doty, L. Goldstein, J. Jaynes & G. Krauthamer, Eds. Academic Press. New York, N.Y. In press.

10. WITELSON, S. F. & W. PALLIE. 1973. Left hemisphere specialization for language in the newborn: anatomical evidence for asymmetry. Brain 96: 641–646.

11. WADA, J. A., R. CLARKE, A. HAMM. 1975. Cerebral hemispheric asymmetry in humans. Arch. Neurol. 32: 239–246.

12. ENTUS, A. K. 1974. Hemispheric asymmetry in processing of dichotically presented speech and nonspeech sounds by infants. Unpublished doctoral dissertation. McGill University. Montreal, Canada.

13. MOLFESE, D. L. 1972. Cerebral asymmetry in infants, children, and adults: auditory evoked responses to speech and non-speech stimuli. Paper presented to 84th mtg. of Acoustic Soc. Amer. Miami, Fla.

14. SELNES, O. A. 1974. The corpus callosum: some anatomical and functional considerations with special reference to language. Brain Lang. 1: 111–139.

15. PIAGET, J. 1970. Piaget's theory. *In* Carmichael's Handbook of Child Psychology. P. Mussen, Ed. Vol. 1: 703–732. John Wiley & Sons. New York, N.Y.

16. MACNAMARA, J. 1972. Cognitive basis of language learning in infants. Psych. Rev. 79: 1–13.

17. CUTTING, J. E. 1974. Two left-hemisphere mechanisms in speech perception. Percept. Psychophys. 16: 601–612.

18. JASPER, H. H. 1958. The ten-twenty electrode system of the international federation of societies for electroencephalography: Appendix to report of the committee on methods of clinical examination in electroencephalography. Electroencephalogr. Clin. Neurophysiol. 10: 371.

19. REGAN, D. 1972. Evoked Potentials in Psychology, Sensory Physiology and Clinical Medicine. John Wiley & Sons, Inc. New York, N.Y.

20. CHAPMAN, R. M., J. W. MCCRARY, H. R. BRAGOON & J. A. CHAPMAN. Latent components of evoked potentials functionally related to information processing. *In* Cerebral Evoked Potentials in Man. J. E. Desmedt, Ed. Oxford University Press. London, England. In press.

21. HARMAN, H. H. 1967. Modern Factor Analysis. 2nd edit. Univ. Chicago Press. Chicago, Ill.

22. MULAIK, S. A. 1972. The foundation of factor analysis. McGraw-Hill, Inc. New York, N.Y.

23. DIXON, W. J., Ed. 1972. BMD Biomedical Computer Program: X-series supplement. Univ. Calif. Press. Berkeley, Calif.

24. MYERS, J. L. 1972. Fundamentals of experimental design. 2nd edit. Allyn & Bacon. Boston, Mass.

25. BARNET, A. B. & A. LODGE. 1967. Click-evoked EEG responses in normal and developmentally retarded infants. Nature 214: 252–255.

26. NEBES, R. D. 1974. Hemisphere specialization in commissurotimized man. Psychol. Bull. 81: 1–14.

27. BROADBENT, D. E. 1974. Division of function and integration of behavior. *In* Neurosciences: IIIrd Study Programs. F. O. Schmitt and F. C. Worden, Eds.: 31–42. MIT Press. Cambridge, Mass.

28. LENNEBERG, E. H. 1967. Biological foundations of language. John Wiley & Sons. New York, N.Y.

29. WEBSTER, W. G. 1972. Functional asymmetry between the cerebral hemispheres of the cat. Neuropsychologia 10: 75–87.

30. MOLFESE, D. L., R. B. FREEMAN, JR. & V. J. JONES-MOLFESE. 1975. Electrophysiological indices of hemispheric differences in cats. In preparation.

WERNICKE'S REGION—WHERE IS IT?

J. E. Bogen and G. M. Bogen*

Ross-Loos Medical Group
Los Angeles, California 90026

In this subject, the first question both logically and chronologically was and is: Can a lesion (focal damage) of the cerebrum cause a loss of language without causing a loss of intelligence? That is the original question, still debated hotly by many people. Much of the heat is attributable to the way in which the question is phrased. Suppose we phrase it relatively, as follows: Can a lesion of the cerebrum produce a deficit in language that is *far in excess* of the concomitant deficit in intelligence? Asked in this way, almost everyone would answer yes. There are worthy persons who are still arguing that anyone who has a loss of language from a cerebral lesion must have some accompanying loss of intelligence. Similarly, there are equally worthy persons recurrently showing us that intelligence can be preserved in spite of severe aphasia. Both parties are undoubtedly correct. But the force of either argument is largely dissipated when the question is rephrased in the relative way. Of course, how much intelligence is lost (or retained) depends upon how one goes about measuring intelligence; but with almost any measures, except those strictly linguistic, the answer will be yes. Indeed, if the answer were *not* yes, there would not be such a thing as aphasia, since a "selective loss of language from a cerebral lesion" is what the word "aphasia" means in contemporary usage.

Once we all understand that there *is* such a thing as aphasia, we come to a second question. It is: Can one indicate those places in the cerebrum where an aphasiogenic lesion is likely to occur? Again the answer is yes—an aphasiogenic lesion occurs in right-handed people in the right hemisphere 1% of the time, perhaps 2% at most. If you have a person who is definitely right-handed, and he has a cerebral lesion that produces a loss of language far out of proportion to the loss of intelligence, the odds are about 50 to 1 that the lesion is in the left hemisphere. Indeed, one can localize better than that. It is rather unlikely that the lesion will be in the left occipital pole. It is even less likely that it will be in the left temporal pole and it is very unlikely, although not impossible, that it will be in the left frontal pole. So, in this negative way, we can narrow down to some extent where an aphasiogenic lesion will occur.

There is a third question, raised by Wernicke[1] about 1874: Is there more than one kind of aphasia? In other words, when a person suffers linguistic loss with relative preservation of general intelligence, can the linguistic loss be of more than one kind? When we look at the patients, it is obvious that they are different. The question is, should those differences be emphasized, and how? There are almost as many classifications of aphasia as there are aphasiologists. Rephrasing this third question does not seem to help with this argument, which has continued unabated for over a century. In the words of Lhermitte and Gautier:[2]

> For the present there is no satisfactory classification of aphasias. (page 97)

The characterization of aphasias is not a central concern here, but we would suggest that in order to deal with the question in a precise manner, it will be necessary to use the mathematics of multidimensional vector spaces; that is, we could characterize a patient's condition with a vector, each of whose coordinates represent

*Supported in part by The Foundation for the Realization of Man. San Francisco, Calif.

the degree of some specific deficit such as anomia, nonfluency, phonemic disintegration, syntactic confusion, and the like. Or we might incline to the system of Hécaen and Angelergues,[2a] who semiquantified the language deficit in their aphasic patients in terms of seven features: disturbance in articulation, fluency, verbal comprehension, naming, repetition, reading, and writing. Until there is a more widespread acceptance of this (vector) approach, it will be difficult to decide upon a system of independent dimensions. What we want eventually is a function describing the changes (including rotation as well as a decrease in vector norm) over time, as the patient recovers. This approach introduces a quantification in the place of arbitrary boundaries for categories of aphasia; and it can precisely represent the qualitative variability of aphasic syndromes with time.

There is another familiar question: If there *are* different kinds of aphasia, are the respective lesions in different places? It's at this point that such agreement as may exist among aphasiologists seems to vanish altogether. Of course, there could not be much agreement on *where* the loci would be for lesions that produce different kinds of aphasia if people cannot agree on what *kinds* of aphasia there are to begin with.†

But let us consider a particular, single dimension: verbal comprehension. It was emphasized by Wernicke, and is considered important by almost all authors. There are patients who have trouble comprehending spoken language. They vary as to whether they can read out loud, or whether they can repeat what they hear, or whether they can do this or that. But whatever else they can or cannot do, they cannot comprehend spoken language very well. Suppose we ask: Is there a region in the cerebrum where a lesion will produce a serious deficit in comprehension of language which is all out of proportion to the loss of nonlinguistic abilities? It was Wernicke who first raised this question, and he gave an answer. He gave, in fact, *several* answers, and we will refer to three of them.

Before we get to the whereabouts of Wernicke's region, we should take note of the fact that this question does not arise with respect to Broca's area. Broca's area is defined anatomically. It is the foot, that is, the posterior third of the inferior frontal gyrus (See FIGURE 1). The question about Broca's area is not "where is it?"—there is no question about *where* it is. The question about Broca's area is "what good is it?" At this time we consider only Wernicke's region, of which the question is *not* "what good is it?" because it's defined in terms of what it's good for—it's the area where a lesion will cause language comprehension deficit. The question with Wernicke's region is "where is it?"

There is, first of all, Figure 3 in Wernicke's classic monograph of 1874.[1] What does one see in this picture? For one thing, he shows the right hemisphere, rather than the left; but this is more in the nature of a printer's error than anything else, and we all now understand that we are talking about the left hemisphere. The feature that requires discussion is his little circle labeled "a_1," in the middle of the superior temporal gyrus (also called "the first temporal gyrus" or "T_1"). He obviously doesn't mean that the brain substance covered only by that little circle does all the comprehension. Rather, the little circle represents the "center," somewhat in the sense of a center of gravity. He does not delimit the entire region, but only localizes the center of it. One naturally asks, is the little circle right in the middle of the entire region or closer to one end? After all, the center of gravity of a thing does not have to be right in the geographic middle; it might be at one end. Wernicke gave us some idea of what he thought. He wrote in 1874 (on page 45):[1]

---

† There is also the fact that people's brains differ. (See the article by Whitaker and Selnes in this volume.)

We will direct our attention to that gyrus of the cerebral convexity which circles around the Sylvian fissure in an arc directed superiorly and posteriorly. Anterior to the central fissure it runs longitudinally (as the first frontal gyrus, in Leuret's nomenclature), while its posterior limb is in the longitudinally coursing first temporal gyrus. That this entire structure is to be regarded as a single gyrus is evident from comparison with the brains of animals, e.g., those of dogs. Comparative anatomy has shown it to be a general law for the formation of the convolutions of the brain that they describe an arc around the fossa Sylvii, the peak of which is directed toward the occipital pole and both limbs of which run more or less parallel to the fossa Sylvii in the frontal and temporal portions of the brain. This law holds for humans as well."

Then on page 47:

The entire region of the first convolution, which circles around the fossa Sylvii serves in conjunction with the insular cortex as a speech center.

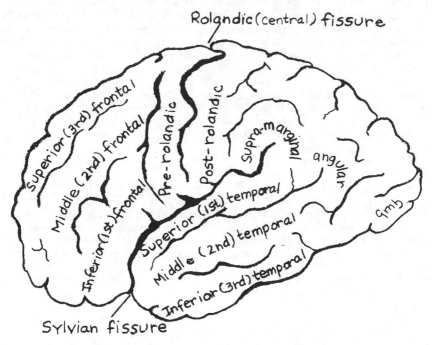

FIGURE 1. Lateral surface (convexity) of the left cerebral hemisphere, showing the more prominent fissures (sulci) and convolutions (gyri). The frontal gyri are numbered from below upward to conform with the concept of a "primeval first gyrus." But the overwhelming majority of neurologists number these gyri in reverse direction, so that the inferior frontal gyrus is called "the third frontal gyrus" or "F_3".

We all know that the word "center" is troublesome, and it is just as easy to talk about the speech "region." Also, Wernicke used the word "speech" instead of "language"; but he meant "language" the way we mean it now. So what Wernicke is telling us is that the primeval first convolution, together with the insula, acts as a language region or language zone. (Following the advice of E. A. Weinstein, we generally avoid the two-dimensional word "area," since it incorrectly implies that the depth of the lesion is irrelevant).

As you may know, Wernicke did not believe that the language zone was all the same; some of it was more important for comprehension and some of it for expression and what not. So, where did he think was the region for comprehension? There is another picture, in his big text on neurology of 1881,[3] seven years later. This picture (Figure XX on page 205) shows the area for language comprehension to be almost synonymous with the first temporal gyrus. It seems to lap over a little bit, though, just barely into the second gyrus. Why does it lap over just a little bit? Probably, because he wasn't sure; he was rather fudging a little bit over the sulcus, so he couldn't be accused of using the sulcus as the boundary. That raises the question: does Wernicke's region (the region within which a lesion disturbs comprehension of language) include part of the second temporal gyrus?

One answer is in Charcot's opinion of 1888, as reproduced in an article by Pierre Marie,[4] his devoted student. Charcot definitely included the second temporal gyrus. Furthermore, Charcot included the angular gyrus. By this time Dejerine had pointed out that language comprehension deficits can occur from lesions in the angular gyrus. Just because Wernicke did not know that a lesion back there would cause a comprehension deficit does not mean that the angular gyrus is not part of Wernicke's region.

But then an instructive thing happened. Pierre Marie began to see patients for himself. And in the course of twenty years he came to realize that Charcot was not entirely correct. In 1906, Pierre Marie[5] said,

> The only cerebral territory whose lesion produces aphasia is the so-called territory of Wernicke (gyrus supramarginalis, gyrus angularis, and feet of the first two temporals).

That's what he says; it is explicit. Among other things, it completely excludes the middle parts of the first and second temporal gyri as well as any frontal cortex. But then came the war (World War I), and Marie softened his attitude in the face of new evidence.

Before we consider Marie's opinion after his observations during World War I, we should consider Dejerine's view as illustrated in his textbook of 1914.[6] This is of particular interest, since Marie and Dejerine were such implacable opponents. (They were not even able to agree, in the great debate of 1908,[7] which questions to debate). There are several notable things in Dejerine's picture of Wernicke's region. First, there is a vague suggestion of what we eventually must have; that is, an awareness that there is no sharp boundary on one side of which a lesion causes aphasia and on the other side of which it does not. What we will eventually need is a picture that indicates the *probability* of a language deficit as being higher or lower. Dejerine indicated more heavily in his picture the places in which a lesion is most certain to cause aphasia; and then he has a dotted line that takes in considerably more territory: most of the parasylvian area including the second temporal gyrus. But there is another feature of note. He did not include, within the dotted line, the inferior Rolandic region, although it is part of what Wernicke called the primeval first gyrus. Why was this excluded by Dejerine? It probably reflects a usage that has reappeared from time to time ever since; that is, to call by the term "language area," not an area within which a lesion disturbs language, but within which a lesion disturbs language without disturbing something else even more, such as making the person hemiplegic. It is nearly certain that a lesion in the inferior Rolandic area will cause aphasia. Well, then, why isn't this included in the "language area"? It is because there is also paralysis. So some people have tended to use the term "language area" to mean "language and only language." This is a serious misconception, because it happens that almost all cerebrocortical tissue serves more than one function. So here is a rather peculiar convention, appearing clearly for the first time; it has reappeared from time to time ever since.

Now we consider Marie and Foix (1917).[8] Before World War I, people who had aphasia were usually older folks with strokes. But during the War, neurologists saw many young men with shrapnel wounds, free of any uncertainty as to whether the patient's deficit was the result of an aphasiogenic lesion superimposed upon generalized atherosclerosis or some previous, silent stroke. What Marie and Foix ended up with is illustrated in their paper of 1917 (as reprinted in Lhermitte and Gautier[2]). This picture shows the zone within which one can expect a lesion to cause difficulty in comprehension of language. (We note parenthetically that, according to Marie, if you have trouble talking it is not necessarily a sign of aphasia—it is the failure to *comprehend* language which Marie considered definitive). The region outlined by Marie and Foix definitely takes in most of the second temporal gyrus as well as the angular gyrus and the supramarginal gyrus. It also includes the inferior Rolandic cortex, which Dejerine wanted to exclude for the terminologic reasons previously mentioned. There are two details about the region indicated by Marie and Foix which are peculiar; first, they left out Broca's area—there is a funny little dent anteriorly because Marie had very strong feelings about Broca's area. He believed that it "plays no special role in aphasia," an extreme view which is agreed to by hardly anyone else before or since. There is a similar funny little dent at the top of the language area. If you have had much experience with aphasia patients you know that this dent is misleading, since lesions there do occasionally cause aphasia.

Next we consider Lewandowsky's textbook of 1923[9]; an important authority in those days. In his picture, Wernicke's area comes a short way into the second temporal gyrus; but for some reason, he leaves out part of the angular gyrus. In fact, he leaves out most of the parietal operculum. But what is most important about his picture is that it shows us something that no one else bothers to show us. He has opened up the Sylvian fossa and shows the language zone extending medially into the Sylvian fossa to include the insula and then back out underneath the frontal operculum to include Broca's zone. This resembles what Wernicke said, but which no one else has bothered to indicate in a picture before or after Lewandowsky. If there is a *confluent language zone* (as Wernicke said and as Lewandowsky illustrated forty years later), where does the posterior part end and the anterior part begin? Perhaps the division is somewhere in the middle, half-way across the insula? It is apparent that when the actual anatomy is exposed, and the Sylvian fissure no longer looks as if it were a bottomless chasm, a sharp division between anterior and posterior language areas can be drawn only arbitrarily. This is certainly worth remembering—that there is no big gap between the posterior and anterior language areas, as suggested by so many other pictures.

Next we come to Henry Head (1926).[10] He studied British soldiers instead of French soldiers; and he concluded that there are four kinds of aphasia. These four types of aphasia are shown in a picture (IV-5), which Penfield and Roberts[11] based on Head's verbal description. This picture looks somewhat like Wernicke's primeval first gyrus, except that it stretches out posteriorly into the angular gyrus; it includes the parietal and frontal opercula. In fact, we are beginning to realize that whenever people try to present a comprehensive view of the matter, they commonly show a picture of the entire parasylvian region.

Well, then, one might ask, why is there so much confusion about the language zone? One answer is that many people are unduly influenced by certain textbook errors. Fulton's textbook of neurophysiology[12] was the *only* American textbook of neurophysiology for many years. In that book it says (on page 395) that Wernicke's area is the angular gyrus of the left hemisphere. Where did he get this strange idea? We don't know. But he does say on the next page that there is an alternative view he attributes to Pierre Marie; namely, Wernicke's area is the angular gyrus together with the base (i.e. the posterior third, or foot) of the first and second temporal convolutions. *That* is what Fulton ascribed to Marie: but is not what Marie[5] said (in 1906), because it does not include the supramarginal gyrus. How is it that someone with the reputation of being as scholarly as Fulton leaves out the supramarginal gyrus (besides not mentioning the Marie and Foix picture of 1917)?[8] We may never know how this came about; but we do know that vast numbers of people have read this, and believed it, because it was in Fulton's textbook. One thing seems clear: Fulton did not rely on Schilder[13] (1923), who said that Wernicke's area was the posterior one-third of the first two temporal gyri.

Let us look at another famous authority, MacDonald Critchley.[14] This is what (on page 16) he says:

> In the dominant hemisphere the inferior parietal lobule (supramarginal and angular gyri) together with the posterior third of T_1, make up what is often termed by continental neuro-anatomists, "Wernicke's area."

In other words, Critchley leaves out entirely the second temporal gyrus. He gives a definition of Wernicke's area which is no more accurate than what Schilder said, or what Fulton said, or what Fulton said that Marie said, which is *not* what Marie said.

Let us consider now our first teacher, J. M. Nielsen.[15] According to Nielsen, Wernicke's region has shrunk, and consists of a tiny raisinlike area in the middle third of T_1. When this picture was shown to some medical students (after they had seen the previous pictures), one of them said, "It looks like the side pocket of a pool table." But there is a really important part of the Nielsen scheme: what he called the "language formulation area." This is a region in which a lesion causes comprehension troubles, and it includes the posterior part of the *inferior* or third temporal gyrus. Why did Nielsen believe that this was an area in which a lesion causes language deficit? First of all, he believed it because Mills asserted this fact on the basis of several cases. Furthermore, Nielsen also saw people who had aphasia from lesions there. And the reason we emphasize this at the present time is because we also have had a couple of aphasic patients whose lesions were in the posterior part of the inferior temporal gyrus.

A somewhat different picture appears in the book of Percival Bailey.[16] This picture obviously came from Marie and Foix,[8] because Broca's area is left out. Furthermore, Bailey's picture has the other funny little dent in the superior aspect. What is notable about Bailey's picture (which is done with dots instead of just drawn lines) is that his picture suggests that the edges are not sharp; they seem to fade out, instead of having the sudden discontinuity of a sharp line beyond which nothing happens. This is a crucial concept.

Next we can look at a picture from World War II instead of World War I (and from Russian soldiers, rather than British or French soldiers). The data, from Luria,[17] are quite informative. The picture indicates that 95% of people with a lesion within the first temporal gyrus are going to have what Luria calls phonemic acoustic perception deficits. In the posterior part of the inferior temporal gyrus, the probability is 37%. The probability is essentially zero in the frontal pole and in the occipital pole. In the parietal operculum, it is 53%. It is important to note this because there are some people such as Lewandowsky[9] and Nielsen,[15] whose pictures totally omit the parietal operculum. It is also noteworthy that Luria shows the probability to be 19% for phonemic acoustic deficit with a lesion of Broca's area.

With the picture of Luria, we have the beginnings of an appropriate map. It is the *probability* of a deficit which should concern us. What is the probability that a lesion, here or there, will cause a language deficit? And the answer is that it is very high in or near the first temporal gyrus, and fades out with different gradients (varying among individuals) toward the poles. And by the time it gets to any pole (occipital, temporal, or frontal) the probability is essentially zero.

Next we can consider some World War II soldiers from England. Sir Ritchie Russell[18] shows a picture labeled "the limits of the area within which a small wound will cause aphasia." This takes in Broca's area and the entire second temporal gyrus. Furthermore, the dent in the superior aspect, which looked rather peculiar in the picture of Marie and Foix (and of Bailey), is entirely missing. The work of Russell is widely respected. But surely it is unreasonable to show a distinct boundary beyond which a lesion will not cause aphasia, and within which it always will. We already know about the data of Luria. Furthermore, we know about the "language formulation area," which includes the posterior part of the third temporal gyrus. So why does Russell show a distinct line of demarcation? Probably because it is easier to draw a distinct line.

Next we consider a book by Penfield and Roberts,[11] a book which has been cited as widely as any on the subject, and rightly so. But the book is a little confusing, because it contains several different versions of Wernicke's area in one book. One of these pictures is the Penfield and Roberts version of the literature (figure IV-8 on page 81). This is not *their* version of Wernicke's area—it is their version of everybody else's version. They do include Mills' and Nielsen's inferior area. They show a "writing center," not because they believe in it (nobody believes in it), but because it is part of the literature. But a strange thing about this picture is the inferior Rolandic and parietal areas! There is just a big empty space! Another surprise is that "Wernicke's area" in this picture consists of the posterior half of the first temporal gyrus and the angular gyrus. This is again unique! We have no other picture of Wernicke's area consisting of the first temporal gyrus and the angular gyrus alone; there is only this picture, which purports to describe the literature up until this time.

Well, what do Penfield and Roberts themselves believe? What did they conclude from their own evidence on the basis of stimulating or excising the exposed cortex of the locally anesthetized human? First, there is the stimulation evidence. On page 135 (figure VIII-14)[11] the area in question includes the foot of the first temporal gyrus, the posterior half of the second, a bit of the third, and it takes in the angular gyrus and the supramarginal gyrus; but it does not include the inferior Rolandic area. Why not? Apparently, they excluded *that* area because stimulation there not only produced interruption of speech but also caused a behavioral deficit which they interpreted as a motor disorder. So they followed the peculiar convention of Dejerine.[6] But is this region not important for language? Of course! Picture VIII-14 is not a picture of their data (which is shown on page 122); it is a picture of a theory. The data picture (VIII-3) is particularly notable for showing something new; no one before this pointed out the role of the posterior part of the third (superior) frontal gyrus. It turns out that there is not only no dent in the superior aspect (as shown in the picture of Marie and Foix) but, in fact, there is a bulge.

Penfield and Roberts show another picture (X-4 on page 201)[11] from stimulation evidence; but, to our consternation, it is slightly different! The first temporal gyrus is not even included. Wernicke's area (as shown in this picture) omits the third or inferior temporal gyrus. Indeed, the mystery here (as on page 135) is that the first temporal gyrus is not included, although everyone else agrees that it should be included except for Fulton. Why have Penfield and Roberts left it out? It is not because stimulation there did not interfere with speech, as we can see by looking at their data (picture VIII-3 on page 122). The data picture really looks a great deal like Bailey's version of Marie and Foix.[8] And it looks very much like the picture of Russell.[18] In fact, we are beginning to come to the conclusion that when we have a picture of the data, rather than someone's theory, that we will have a picture that looks pretty much like all the other pictures of the data.

Next is a Penfield and Roberts[11] picture of their excision evidence (Figure X-10).[11] They left out the first temporal gyrus again! This picture is not the same as those on pages 135 and 201, where they also left it out, because in this picture Wernicke's area goes all the way down to the inferior surface of the hemisphere.

In another picture (IX-23) from Penfield and Roberts, based on excision, the first temporal gyrus is finally included, which is a great relief, since otherwise it might suggest (as does X-10) that if excision of this gyrus were done, it would not cause aphasia, which, of course, it usually does.

We consider next a picture from Masland,[19] an eminent figure in contemporary neurology. His representation of the language regions does not include the supramarginal gyrus at all. What happened? He has there only a blank space in the very place where Henry Head[10] said a lesion causes semantic aphasia and where, according to Luria,[17] you have a 53% chance of losing phonemic acoustic perception. And it is the same place where, according to Geschwind[20] (as we will see later) a lesion causes "conduction aphasia." Small wonder that the student can easily become confused.

A student might also be confused by the book of two other eminent authorities, Espir and Rose.[21] They give, in three different places, three different definitions of Wernicke's area.

Let us look at a picture drawn by a linguist, Harry Whitaker,[22] until now, at least, a good friend of ours. This was written for linguists by a linguist; he learned some neurology and summarized it for the linguists who would like to know something about the neurology of language. So he went back, all the way back, and what he showed them looked very much like Wernicke's picture of 1881; it is mainly the first temporal gyrus. But Whitaker's picture[22] is a little bit different from Wernicke's picture,[3] because it does not creep across the sulcus and, therefore, it does not include *any* of the second temporal gyrus. What happened to all of the intervening data in the preceding hundred years? Here we find the linguists starting all over again, right from the beginning. Perhaps that is a good idea, if the neurologists are as confused as they sometimes seem. In Whitaker's favor, it might be said that at least he did not draw sharp lines around his labels.

Next we have a picture from another good friend, Norman Geschwind (or he was a good friend until now). This picture (Figure 4.1 in Ref. 20) is sometimes called the Boston version. What he shows us consists only of the posterior fourth of the first temporal. He just leaves out everything else we have mentioned so far, the past century of investigation. He has Wernicke's area so shrunk down and so pushed up in a corner that it looks like the corner pocket of Nielsen's pool table. Why does he do this? It is because he is not drawing a picture to represent data. It is intended to represent what he considers to be the preferable theory, or, at least, the theory to which beginners should first be introduced. This is what we might call "a picture for the people."

The simplication by Geschwind goes even further, later.[23] In a 1972 article his figure shows Wernicke's area just as shrunken as before, but now it is peculiarly reniform. He does this, apparently, to illustrate a physiological theory; he is not giving a picture of the data, nor a picture intended to have literal anatomical significance. The trouble is that, given this simplistic version, many people then carry it with them the rest of their lives. There are a lot of molecular biologists and quantum physicists and mathematicians who are educated, sophisticated people, and who are now taking an interest in language; if you teach them this simple-minded version, how will they feel several years from now when they realize they have been talked down to?

We are nearing the end now, with a picture from Jason Brown.[24] His "Wernicke's area" is beautifully egg-shaped; but it seems a little small (although it is certainly larger than Geschwind's). One reason it is so small is that he redefines it as the area in which a lesion will produce jargon aphasia if you are past middle-age. This certainly is one way of solving the problem of where Wernicke's region is, to define it in a different way. But the picture does have the virtue of suggesting gradients; it seems to indicate that the further away the lesion is from the first temporal gyrus, the less likelihood there is of something happening.

We can conclude with a picture from Benson.[25] His Figure VII shows what he calls Group B aphasia; that is, those patients who have a comprehension deficit but are fluent. This is not quite a picture of the data, because the numbers indicate the centers rather than the entireties of the various lesions. But the picture does indicate, to some extent, the locations of the lesions that cause comprehension deficit. And these locations are where one would expect them to be, from all of the previous pictures, with the exception that there are no cases with lesions in the posterior end of the inferior temporal gyrus. But that is just a sampling error. If Benson had had a larger sample, he would have had some cases down there.

CONCLUDING COMMENTS

Is there *any* way to draw a satisfactory picture of Wernicke's region? One answer would be that we need a picture, resembling a topographic map, that shows a probability distribution; that is, a map which shows the likelihood at any particular locus of a comprehension deficit from a lesion at that locus. A probability distribution of the sort suggested here may provide one approach toward resolving the long-standing issue of topism versus holism. In order to construct the real thing, we will require a vast amount of quantitative information. But this requirement should not be a weighty argument against the probability approach. Indeed, we should welcome an approach that can make use of a vast amount of data which has heretofore been conveniently ignored by the simplified schemes with which we have struggled in the past.

REFERENCES

1. WERNICKE, C. 1874, 1968. The symptom complex of aphasia (1874). Reprinted in English in Proc. Boston Colloq. Philos. Sci. **4:** 34–97.
2. LHERMITTE, F. & J.-C. GAUTIER. 1969. Aphasia. Handbook of Clin. Neurol. **4:** 84–104.
2a. HÉCAEN, H. & R. ANGELERGUES. 1964. Localization of symptoms in aphasia. In Disorders of Language. A. V. S. DeReuck & M. O'Connor, Eds. Little, Brown U Co., Boston, Mass.
3. WERNICKE, C. 1881. Lehrbuch der Gehirnkrankheiten. Theodore Fischer. Kassel, Germany.
4. MARIE, P. 1888, 1971. On aphasia in general and agraphia in particular according to the teaching of Professor Charcot. Le Progres Medical, Ser. 2, **7:** 81–84. Reprinted in Pierre Marie's Papers on Speech Disorders. Hafner. New York, N.Y.
5. MARIE, P. 1906, 1971. The third left frontal convolution pays no special role in the function of Language. Semaine Medicale **26:** 241–247. Reprinted in Pierre Marie's Papers on Speech Disorders. M. F. Cole and M. Cole, Eds. Hafner, New York, N.Y.

6. DEJERINE, J. 1914. Sémiologie des Affections du Système Nerveux. Masson. Paris, France.
7. MARIE P. & J. DEJERINE *et al.* 1908, 1971. Discussion on aphasia. Soc. of Neurol. of Paris. Rev. Neurol. **16:** 611, 1025. Reprinted in Pierre Marie's Papers on Speech Disorders. M. F. Cole and M. Cole, Eds. Hafner. New York, N.Y.
8. MARIE, P. & C. FOIX. 1917. Les aphasies de guerre. Rev. Neurol. **24:** 53–87.
9. HIRSCHFELD, R. 1923. M. Lewandowsky's Practische Neurologie für ärzte. 4th edit. Springer. Berlin, Germany.
10. HEAD, H. 1963. Aphasia and Kindred Disorders of Speech. Vol. I (1926):441. Hafner. New York, N.Y.
11. PENFIELD, W., & L. ROBERTS. 1959. Speech and Brain-Mechanisms. Princeton Univ. Press. Princeton, N.J.
12. FULTON, J. F. 1938. Physiology of the Nervous System. Oxford Univ. Press. New York, N.Y.
13. SCHILDER, P. 1923, 1953. Medical Psychology. (English version, 1953):129. Internat. Univ. Press. New York, N.Y.
14. CRITCHLEY, M. 1966. The Parietal Lobes (1953). Hafner. New York, N.Y.
15. NIELSEN, J. M. 1944. Aphasia Due to Cerebral Trauma. Bull. Los Angeles Neurol. Soc. **9:** 52–60, 1944.
16. BAILEY, P. 1948. Intracranial Tumors. 2nd edit. Chas. C Thomas. Springfield, Ill.
17. LURIA, S. 1958, 1972. Brain disorders and language analysis. Language and Speech **1:** 14–34. Reprinted in Aphasia: Selected Readings. M. T. Sarno, Ed. Appleton-Century-Crofts. New York, N.Y.
18. RUSSELL, W. R. 1963. Some anatomical aspects of aphasia. Lancet i: 1173–7.
19. MASLAND, R. L. 1968. Some neurological processes underlying language. Ann. Otol. Rhinol. Laryngol. **77:** 787–805.
20. GESCHWIND, N. 1969. Problems in the anatomical understanding of the aphasias. *In* Contributions to Clinical Neuropsychology. A. L. Benton, Ed. Aldine, Chicago.
21. ESPIR, M. L. E. & F. C. ROSE. 1970. The Basic Neurology of Speech. Blackwell. Oxford, England.
22. WHITAKER, H. A. 1971. On the Representation of Language in the Human Brain. Linguistic Res. Edmonton, Canada.
23. GESCHWIND, N. 1972. Disorders of higher cortical function in children. Clin. Proc. Children's Hospital Nat. Med. Cent. **28:** 261–272.
24. BROWN, J. W. 1975. On the neural organization of language: thalamic and cortical relationships. Brain and Language **2:** 18–30.
25. BENSON, D. F. 1967. Fluency in aphasia: correlation with radioactive scan localization. Cortex **3:** 373–394.

ANATOMIC VARIATIONS IN THE CORTEX: INDIVIDUAL DIFFERENCES AND THE PROBLEM OF THE LOCALIZATION OF LANGUAGE FUNCTIONS.

Harry A. Whitaker and Ola A. Selnes

Departments of Neurology and Psychology
University of Rochester
Rochester, New York 14627

The controversy concerning the localization of brain functions, particularly speech and language, is well known. The overwhelming statistical support for the classical position[1] has been challenged from a number of points of view: contradictory case histories, limitations of the behavioral analysis, difficulties inherent in localizing lesions, and behavioral instabilities of patients with central nervous system disease. With rare exceptions, individual anatomic variations in the brain have not been considered in this context, which is somewhat surprising in view of the recent surge of interest in interhemispheric asymmetries of the brain. The only explicit remark on the relationship between anatomic variability and language functions that we know of is Bolton:[2]

> Such variability with regard to the individual distribution of the special parts of the psycho-motor area which subserve the evolution of speech is ... the only possible explanation of the widely divergent views which are held by equally competent observers. (p. 35)

From our review of the literature, the conclusion seems inescapable that each person's brain may be as individual as his physiognomy. This conclusion should come as no surprise if one extrapolates from the large number of animal studies which suggest that the biochemical and morphological structure of the brain is modified by experience, since clearly, no two individuals share an identical set of experiences. As expressed by Gray:[3]

> No cortex is an exact duplicate of another, either in the number or size of its convolutions. Indeed, it seems likely that each roof brain is as individual to its possessor as his face ...

Early interest in anatomic variation was concerned primarily with topography and brain weight and size. The early studies typically attempted to correlate these gross measures with factors like sex, race, intellectual achievment, criminality, and other deviant social behavior. Although we might question whether the external morphology of the brain directly reflects any of these factors, the physical measures themselves provide clear evidence of the extent of individual variation in brain morphology.

The average weight of the human brain, after fixation in formalin, is about 1400 grams; the coefficient of variation of weight is slightly less than ten percent.[4] However, as noted by Frontera (cited in Ref. 4), factors relating to the fixative agent, to the techniques of fixation, and to the tissue itself may influence measurements of weight by as much as 50 percent. Not surprisingly, a rather wide range has been observed. Tompkins[5] reported a human brain weighing 1938.8 grams, and Wilder[6] reported a brain weighing only 680 g. As an aside, Wilder's patient was 5'6" tall and weighed 145 pounds. Of his premorbid behavior, Wilder says: "There was nothing defective or peculiar about him, either mentally or physically." (p. 95)

Comparable differences exist in the overall dimensions of the brain, which in turn implies differences in surface area. Wilder[7] refers to a study of the cortical surface in which the difference between the smallest and largest brain was on the order of 310 square centimeters.

The most apparent variation from one brain to another is in the pattern of gyri and sulci. Von Bonin[8] noted:

> The fissural pattern of the human brain has been studied for almost a century with great assiduity without, however, proving much more than its great variability.

Recent studies by Sanides,[9] however, indicate that there is fairly good correspondence between boundaries of cytoarchitectural fields and the fissures and sulci of the brain. This suggests to us that the gyral pattern may have a functional significance, not as yet explored. This suggestion is not inconsistent with a recent theory proposing that one of the mechanisms underlying the formation of gyri and sulci is the differential growth rate of the inner and outer cortical layers.[10]

It is generally accepted that the minor sulci and gyri show large variations from one brain to another, but that the major fissures (Rolandic, Sylvian) do not. Even these landmarks, however, are subject to considerable variation. In approximately 60 percent of the brains examined by Cunningham,[11] the upper end of the fissure of Rolando reached over the dorsal margin to the mesial surface of the hemisphere. In approximately 24 percent it just reached the top margin of the hemisphere, and in the remaining 19 percent, the fissure fell short of the top margin. In approximately 19 percent of the brains in this same series, the Fissure of Rolando showed a shallow connection with the fissure of Sylvius. (See also Ref. 7.)

The fissure of Rolando develops in two parts; its lower $\frac{2}{3}$ appear first, and the upper $\frac{1}{3}$ appears later, and independently, in fetal life. Occasionally, the two parts fail to connect, leaving a gyrus connecting the ascending frontal with the ascending parietal convolutions. This configuration has been found in both the left and right hemisphere, and in rare cases it has been found to be present bilaterally,[12] as seen in FIGURE 1.

In addition to supporting Cunningham's observation,[11] Mickle[13] also noted that the fissure of Rolando may be positioned more forward or backward, and may also variously connect to other fissures in the frontal and parietal lobes.

Concerning the fissure of Sylvius, Eberstaller[14] noted that the number of secondary gyri originating from this fissure varies from one brain to another. He identified as many as five secondary sulci; some of these are not so common, occurring in only 13–22% of the brains examined. Cunningham[11] also pointed out the extreme variability of the configuration of the anterior limbs of the fissure of Sylvius, of interest because they partially delineate Broca's area. There may be one, two, or three branches present. Connolly[15] found that a single branch occurred more frequently in the right than in the left hemisphere.

Finally, it has been noted that the gyral pattern in the cingulate region has several variants,[14,16] some examples of which are shown in FIGURE 2.

It is generally agreed that there are distinct cytoarchitectural areas in the neocortex, although the number and precise boundaries of these areas have been a source of dispute. The classical maps of Brodmann, von Economo and the Vogts were based on a small number of brains,[17] and these and other investigators used different techniques as well as different criteria of classification. It is nevertheless possible that some of the differences between these maps are due to individual variations. Whenever the question of the boundaries, and therefore the size of a specific cytoarchitectural area, has been specifically addressed, striking individual

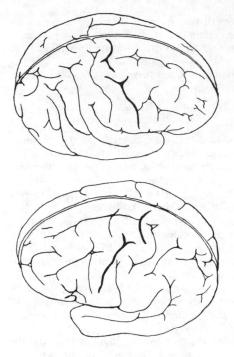

FIGURE 1. Left and right hemisphere of a brain showing complete, bilateral interruption of the Fissure of Rolando. (By permission of Cambridge University Press.[12])

variations have been discovered. Sarkisov[17] has summarized the results of several studies assessing the variability of cytoarchitectural areas, represented diagrammatically in FIGURES 3-5. Sarkisov's study supports the earlier work of Stengel,[18] who observed individual differences in both the gyral pattern and the cytoarchitecture of Broca's area. Stengel states:

> In reviewing our findings, one of the most important appears to be the regular relationship between cytoarchitectonic and convolutional patterns, which we found to be particularly clear in the foot of the third frontal convolution and somewhat less clear in the region of the pars triangularis. This confirmation appears to us of importance, since there has been a tendency, stemming from the Vogt school, to ascribe little or no importance to the convolutional pattern with respect to the physiology of the brain. (p. 674)

Stengel analyzed brains from both deaf-mutes and normal subjects, and summarized his findings of the gyral patterns as shown in FIGURE 6.

Although not the first (cf. Refs. 19, 20, 21), Filimonoff's[22] cytoarchitectural study of the variability in the occipital lobe is one of the most extensive documentations of the large degree of individual differences in this region of the brain, two examples of which are shown in FIGURE 7. There is also an interesting practical consequence of the variation in the striate cortex (area 17). Stimulation of this area in man produces phosphenes—sensations of spots of light. Recent research on visual prostheses for the blind, involving stimulation of the striate cortex with an electrode array connected to a TV-camera, has demonstrated that the pattern of phosephenes is stable enough to be associated with patterns of visual stimuli.[23]

In a study of 52 hemispheres, Stensaas et al.[24] found a threefold difference in the total amount of striate cortex (between 359 and 1308 square millimeters). There was a fourfold difference in the amount of exposed striate cortex into which the electrode array of the visual prostheses would be inserted. In practial terms, this means that about 50 electrodes could be placed in some brains, while in others about 200 could be placed in the striate cortex, obviously with consequences for the amount of visual information that could be transmitted with such prosthetic devices. Dobelle and Mladejovsky[23] also found that the phosphene map produced by the electrode array varied considerably from subject to subject (in a total of 15 volunteer patients). Electrodes that were adjacent to each other on the surface of the striate cortex might or might not produce phosphenes that were adjacent. For each subject, however, the phosphene map was quite stable during the course of the experiment—up to 2½ days in one subject. These data clearly show that a physiological variability from person to person exists concomitantly with the anatomic variation.

The receptive language areas have also been studied, and in the opinion of von Economo and Horn,[25] these may exhibit the largest degree of individual variation of any cortical region. Their study addressed both the gyral and the cytoarchitectural pattern, looking at both individual and interhemispheric differences. Some of their principal observations include:

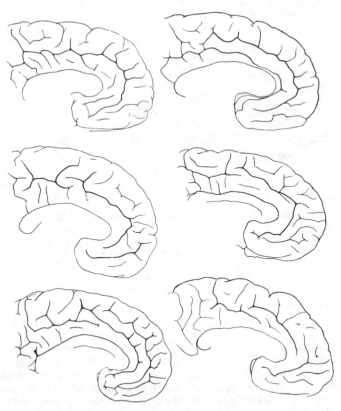

FIGURE 2. Some variations in the configuration of the cingulate gyrus and its surroundings. (From Retzius.[16])

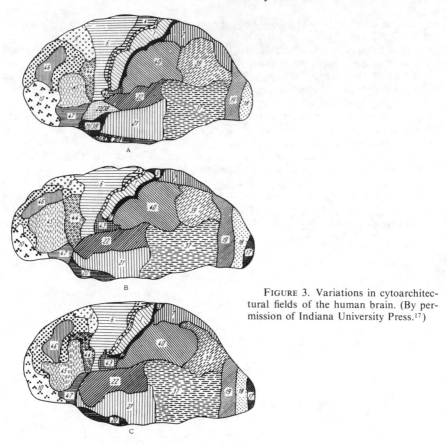

FIGURE 3. Variations in cytoarchitectural fields of the human brain. (By permission of Indiana University Press.[17])

The superior temporal lobe (planum temporale) shows a large degree of individual differences from one brain to another in the pattern of gyri, which implies a seemingly larger variability of this region than other regions of the cortex (p. 755). . . . Individual differences in the finer architectural structure were particularly noted in Heschl's gyrus in each brain. Well defined sub-fields in one brain could not be found in others, or they were shifted in their position. The most conspicuous difference concerned the degree or distribution of complete granulation, which varied from one brain to another. (p. 756)

A recent study by Campain and Minckler[26] further elaborates the variability in gyral patterns in the auditory cortex; they identified five typical patterns in a series of 30 brains.

A substantial portion of the data base for the localization of higher cortical functions derives from studies of vascular lesions. It is therefore important to note that the blood supply to the brain is, if anything, even more variable across individuals than the variations just reviewed of cytoarchitecture, convolutional pattern, brain size and weight. Indeed, the location of large arteries and veins on the surface of the cortex is so variable that they cannot be reliably used as neurosurgical landmarks. An elegant treatise of cerebral angiography has recently been published by Waddington.[27] This study clearly documents the extent of variation for each of the major vessels, in terms of both number and branching patterns. The configurations of the orbitofrontal and operculofrontal arteries (shown in FIGURES 8 AND 9) are pertinent examples of the extent of variability found in the blood supply of the brain. It is clear from an inspection of these configurations that an occlusion of any of the branches of these arteries would result in impairment of widely different amounts of brain tissue in the vicinity of Broca's area.

Two dramatic examples of individual variations in cortical topography were brought to our attention by Dr. George Ojemann.[28] These observations were from two patients undergoing right temporal-parietal craniotomies for control of epilepsy. During electrical stimulation of the Rolandic cortex in the first patient, it was found that the motor responses (lip and jaw opening) and the sensory responses (tingling of left tongue and cheek) were all evoked from the top of a single gyrus with no sulcus in between.

In the second patient, similar stimulation produced motor responses (lip and tongue movements) and sensory responses (tingling of the tongue, sensations of pressure and numbness of teeth) as expected. The motor responses, however, were evoked from points in the cortex posterior to those evoking sensory responses; in other words, a complete reversal of the normal pattern. Both patients are neurologi-

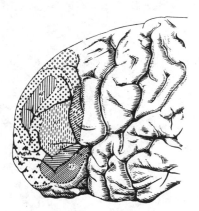

FIGURES 4 & 5. Variations in cytoarchitectural fields in the frontal lobe. (By permission of Indiana University Press.[17])

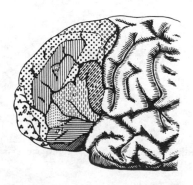

cally normal except for the visual field cuts subsequent to the temporal lobectomies; both engage in normal activities and are gainfully employed.

We conclude by recognizing the fact that there are well documented differences between the left and right hemispheres, perhaps a feature of the primate brain, rather than an exclusive property of the human brain, as noted by LeMay and Geschwind.[29] There are, of course, individual differences in the degree of asymmetry between the two halves of the brain. In this regard, we note with interest that Ojemann's two

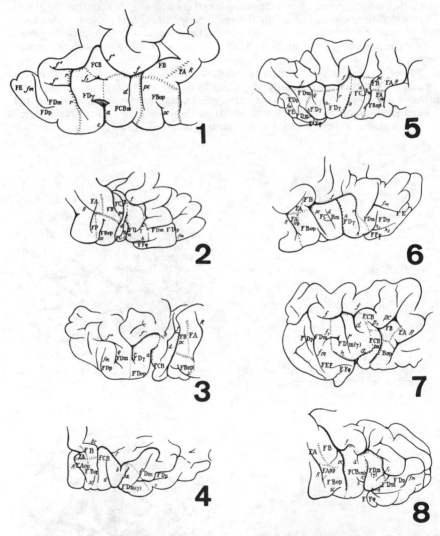

FIGURE 6. Gyral pattern of Broca's area and its immediate surroundings. 1, 3, 5: left hemisphere of normal brains; 2, 4, 6: right hemisphere of normal brains; 7: left hemisphere of a brain from a deaf-mute; 8: right hemisphere of the same brain. (By permission of Springer-Verlag, New York, N.Y.[18])

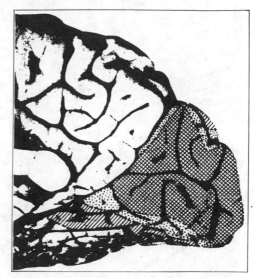

FIGURE 7. Examples of the extremes of variations in the size of the Striate Area (crosshatched). (By permission of Akademie Verlag.[22])

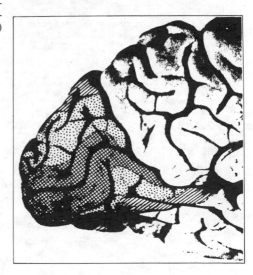

patients exhibited anomalies of the right hemisphere, reminding us of the remark made by Mickle:[13]

> On the whole, unusual and deviating states of the cortical architecture appear more frequently in the right than in the left cerebral hemisphere, even after due allowance is made for the degree of difference existing between the normal standards of right and of left cerebral hemisphere in man.

Nonlocalizationists have frequently remarked upon the lack of correspondence between the site of lesion and behavioral deficits. In the future, rather than being

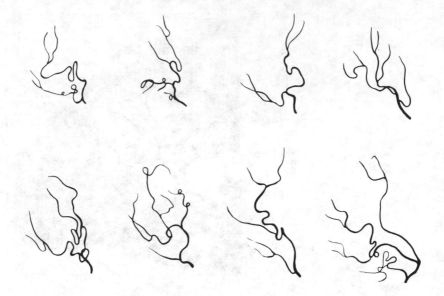

FIGURE 8. Some variations in the configuration of the orbitofrontal artery. (By permission of Little Brown & Company.[27])

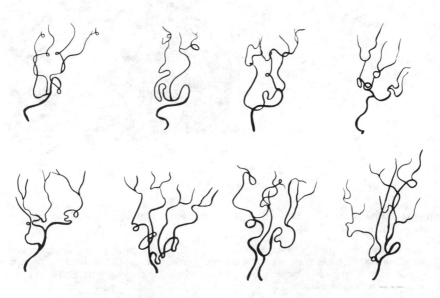

FIGURE 9. Some variations in the configuration of the operculofrontal artery. (By permission of Little Brown & Company.[27])

impressed by such incongruities, one might well reflect upon the striking degree of agreement despite substantial individual differences. If proper account is taken of the wide range of possible variations in cortical morphology, these incongruities can no longer be considered to refute a theory of localization.

ACKNOWLEDGMENT

We are grateful to Dr. George Ojemann for permission to use his unpublished case materials.

REFERENCES

1. HENSCHEN, S. E. 1922. Ueber Motorische Aphasie und Agraphie. *In* Klinische und Anatomische Beiträge zur Pathologie des Gehirns. Almquist & Wiksell. Uppsala, Sweden.
2. BOLTON, J. S. 1911. A Contribution to the Localization of Cerebral Function based on the Clinico-Pathological Study of Mental Disease. Brain 33: 26–148.
3. GRAY, G. W. 1948. The Great Ravelled Knot. Scientific American 179(4): 26–39.
4. BLINKOV, S. M. & I. I. GLEZER. 1968. The Human Brain in Figures and Tables. Plenum Press. New York, N.Y.
5. TOMPKINS, C. 1882. Virginia Med. Monthly. (Cited in Ref. 7.)
6. WILDER, B. G. 1911. Exhibition of, and Preliminary Note upon, a Brain of About one-half the average Size from a White Man of Ordinary Weight and Intelligence. J. Nerv. Ment. Dis. 38: 95–97.
7. WILDER, B. G. 1889. The Brain. Anatomy. *In* A Reference Handbook of the Medical Sciences. A. H. Buck, Ed. Vol. 8: 107–164. William Wood & Co. New York, N.Y.
8. VON BONIN, G. 1949. Architecture of the precentral motor cortex and some adjacent areas. *In* The Precentral Motor Cortex. P. C. Bucy, Ed. Univ. Illinois Press. Urbana, Ill.
9. SANIDES, F. 1962. Die Architektonik des Menschlichen Stirnhirns. Mon. Gesamtgeb. Neurol. Psychiat. (no. 98). J. Springer. Berlin, Germany.
10. RICHMAN, D. P., R. M. STEWART, J. W. HUTCHINSON & V. S. CAVINESS, JR. 1975. Mechanical Model of Brain Convolutional Development. Science 189: 18–21.
11. CUNNINGHAM, D. J. 1892. Contribution to the Surface Anatomy of the Cerebral Hemispheres. Royal Irish Academy. Dublin, Ireland.
12. WATERSTON, D. 1906–07. Complete Bilateral Interruption of the Fissure of Rolando. J. Anat. Physiol. 41: 143–146.
13. MICKLE, W. J. 1898. Atypical and unusual brain-forms, especially in relation to mental status: A study of brain surface morphology. J. Ment. Sci. 44: 17–45.
14. EBERSTALLER, O. 1890. Das Stirnhirn. Urban & Schwarzenberg. Leipzig, Germany.
15. CONNOLLY, C. J. 1950. External Morphology of the Primate Brain. Charles C Thomas. Springfield, Ill.
16. RETZIUS, G. 1896. Das Menschenhirn. Norstedt & Sons. Stockholm, Sweden.
17. SARKISOV, S. A. 1966. The Structure and Functions of the Brain. N. Raskin, Ed. Indiana Univ. Press. Bloomington, Ind.
18. STENGEL, E. 1930. Morphologische und Cytoarchitektonische Studien ueber den Bau der Unteren Frontalwindung bei Normalen und Taubgestummen. Z. Neurol. Psychiat. 130: 631–677.
19. BOLTON, J. S. 1900. The exact histological localisation of the visual area of the human cerebral cortex. Phil. Trans. R. Soc. Lond. (Biol. Sci.) 193: 165–222.
20. SMITH, G. E. 1907. A new topographical survey of the human cerebral cortex, being an account of the distribution of the anatomically distinct cortical areas and their relationship to the cerebral sulci. J. Anat. Physiol. 41: 237–254.
21. BRODMANN, K. 1918. Individuelle Variationen der Sesphäre und ihre Bedeutung für die Klnik der Hinterhauptschüsse. Allg. Z. Psychiat. 74: 564–568.

22. FILIMONOFF, I. N. 1932. Ueber die Variabilität der Grosshirnrindenstruktur. Mitteilung II. Regio Occipitalis beim Erwachsenen Menschen. J. Psychol. Neurol. **44:** 1–96.
23. DOBELLE, W. H. & M. G. MLADEJOVSKY. 1974. Phosphenes produced by electrical stimulation of human occipital cortex, and their application to the development of a prosthesis for the blind. J. Physiol. **243:** 553–576.
24. STENSAAS, S. S., D. K. EDDINGTON & W. H. DOBELLE. 1974. The Topography and Variability of the Primary Visual Cortex in Man. J. Neurosurg. **40:** 747–755.
25. VON ECONOMO, D. & L. HORN. 1930. Ueber Windungsrelief, Masse und Rindenarchitektonik der Supratemporalflache, ihre Individuellen und Seitenunterschiede. Z. Neurol. Psychiat. **130:** 678-757.
26. CAMPAIN, R. & J. MINCKLER. 1975. A note on the gross configuration of the human auditory cortex. Brain & Language. In press.
27. WADDINGTON, M. M. 1974. Atlas of Cerebral Angiography with Anatomic Correlation. Little Brown & Co. Boston, Mass.
28. OJEMANN, G. Personal communication.
29. LEMAY, M. & N. GESCHWIND. 1975. Hemispheric differences in the brains of Great Apes. Brain Behav. Evol. **11:** 48–52.

DISCUSSION

Stevan R. Harnad, *Moderator*

Department of Psychiatry
Institute of Mental Health Sciences
CMDJ-Rutgers Medical School
Piscataway, New Jersey 08854

STEVAN HARNAD: As anyone who is a declared enthusiast of the right hemisphere rather than the left hemisphere is likely to be, Dr. Bogen, you're not too fond of boundaries, and that's surely part of your complaint against Wernicke's area; but unless your object is to cause a moratorium (not unlike the moratorium that they had on meetings of this sort) on any positive declarations concerning the locus of Wernicke's area (and I know anyone who likes hemisphere differences and lateralization can't be altogether inimical to localization in general), what *do* you propose?

DR. BOGEN: We frequently localize lesions; but I do not "localize functions." I wouldn't use that phrase any more, but rather the phrase "representation of function." This may sound like a quibble, but it turns out to have important consequences. When we have a localized lesion, then what we would say is that for any locus, there is some likelihood (with respect to a particular function) that a lesion at that locus will produce a deficit in the function which we have indicated. In other words, for each particular function, there is a probability density associated with every locus. Well, if you do it that way, what you obtain is a map that looks like a topographic map of the countryside with peaks and valleys which represent the probability densities instead of altitudes. Now, the probability density for a deficit in speech comprehension falls off away from the sylvian area to reach essentially zero at the three poles: occipital, temporal, and frontal. If you continue the same map across the other side of the brain you are going to find out that you have very low probability. It's not a completely flat countryside over there (not all at "sea level," in other words) because there are a few elevations, but they are all pretty low. Now, suppose somebody has a lesion as a result of which he has aphasia; what's the likelihood you're going to find the lesion in the right hemisphere? The answer is, very little. This is because if you do a double integration of the entire right hemisphere it's going to be 1% or less of the total probability.

S. HARNAD: Are we to take that probability distribution, based on many individuals, to be true of each person's *individual* cortex, despite the fact that we know it's different for everybody?

DR. BOGEN: Everybody is going to be different, and sometimes these differences are very important; that is why they often have to be reemphasized. We have this proclivity for making rules, and somebody has to keep reminding us that the rules are an intellectual tool and not reality.

DR. E. WEINSTEIN (*Mt. Sinai Medical School, New York, N.Y.*): We get into these traps of language. I mean, after we say "area" often enough, we stop thinking about the third dimension; in other words, we stop thinking about the depth of the lesion. Or take another example: I think for years we've talked of "higher cortical function" because it happened to be highest in the head, although we heard some evidence that you get pretty high limbic functions. I do think that the depth of the lesion is extremely important in determining the behavior in so-called "Wernicke's aphasias" and a lot of other behavioral disturbances, for example, in patients with Broca's aphasia. I think that this should always be an anatomical and physiological consideration.

855

DR. BOGEN: You are absolutely right.

DR. MARTIN GARDINER (*Children's Hospital, Boston, Mass.*): Directing the question to Dr. Bogen, what about the problem of what is sometimes called "diaschisis"—the indirect and temporary aphasic reactions due to injuries in another area that cause secondary malfunction in an area. To what extent do your data reflect that, as compared to individual differences?

DR. BOGEN: I didn't have time to cover everything, but in case I never see most of you again, I do want to call your attention to something Wernicke said. He did not call it "diaschisis," but he was talking about the same thing. It subsides with time. Meanwhile, while you wait long enough to get rid of the diaschisis, you have the appearance of a variety of compensatory features, which gums up the situation with additional variables. So Wernicke said (and this is really crafty) that in order to know what kind of aphasia the patient has, you have to examine him at "just the right time."

DR. DENNIS: I have a comment and/or question for Dr. Bogen and Dr. Whitaker. The kind of variations in localization and in individual differences that you described are extremely interesting. I just wonder about the application of the term "individual difference." The *massa intermedia*, a commissure associated with a certain nonverbal skill, is absent in about 35% of the population; so a lot of what you are saying may be just the tip of the iceberg in terms of the kinds of variation that exist.

DR. WHITAKER: As far as I know, the variation of anastomoses between the cortical arteries is the only well-established cortical variability comparable to the *massa intermedia* variation.

DR. BROWN: To Dr. Bogen's two spatial dimensions of variation and Dr. Weinstein's third, I would like to add a fourth: *time*. If we look at a patient with a lesion of Wernicke's area on the left side we find striking differences in the *type* of aphasia we see, according to the *age* of the patient. Localization, if you want to use that term, is really a two-phase process, both phases of which occur simultaneously. We see lateralization to the left side and at the same time intrahemispheric localization or specification: that is, we see *inter*hemispheric and *intra*hemispheric specification occurring simultaneously such that diminished lateralization goes along with more diffuse intrahemispheric organization while increasing lateralization tends to go along with increasing focalization or specification of function.

To conclude these remarks, I think that in the long haul we're not really going to be able to move very far in this whole question of localization unless we change our notion of anatomy and come to think of structure, anatomical structure, not as some sort of rigid skeleton on which function is superimposed but as an active dynamic form-building process equally active in the kinds of psychological processes that we study.

Part XIII. Language and the Human Brain

THE ROLE OF LANGUAGE IN THE MEMORY
DISORDERS OF BRAIN-DAMAGED PATIENTS*

Laird S. Cermak and Nelson Butters

Psychology Service
Boston Veterans Administration Hospital
Boston, Massachusetts 02130
and
Aphasia Research Unit
Neurology Department
Boston University School of Medicine
Boston 02215

The relationship between verbal memory and linguistic processing has now been fairly well established. A number of memory theorists have emphasized that the ability to retain verbal information is in large part dependent upon the extent to which the individual can analyze the information as it is being presented.[1-4] The more features of the verbal information an individual can detect and store, the greater will be his likelihood of retrieving the information at some later time. However, of even greater import than the "number" of features analyzed is the "nature" of the features that are stored.[2] A subject's analysis of the semantic features of information increases his probability of retrieval beyond that which occurs when only the phonemic and/or visual features of information are analyzed. This superiority of semantic analysis is demonstrable even in cases where subjects need more time to process complicated phonemic features of the information than they need to perform semantic feature analysis.[5] Limited semantic analysis provides a far more permanent memory trace than even prolonged sessions of phonemic rehearsal. This difference in the product of semantic and phonemic analysis becomes apparent when an individual attempts to retain a telephone number by rote rehearsal. Although he may practice for several minutes, the number is forgotten almost as soon as rehearsal ceases. In contrast, retention of a novel, even when read at a rapid rate, is generally retained for some time after the novel has been completed. The individual's ability to retain the story plot is related to the fact that it has been processed on a semantic rather than phonemic or visual level.

The dependence of memory upon semantic analysis implies that individuals who are profoundly amnesic might be incapable of efficient analysis of verbal information. Conversely, individuals who lack proficiency in language skills (i.e. aphasic patients) may also have an underlying defect in semantic analysis and, as a consequence, in verbal memory. To assess these two hypotheses, the memory and information-processing abilities of patients with alcoholic Korsakoff's syndrome and of patients with Broca's (anterior) aphasia have been studied. Since the alcoholic Korsakoff patient is unable to retain verbal information for more than a few seconds, the possibility that this severe anterograde amnesia might be correlated with failures in semantic analysis has been investigated. On the other hand, since patients with Broca's aphasia have difficulty using language, investigations of their information-processing abilities have focused on assessments of their verbal memory deficits.

*The research reported in this chapter was supported in part by NIAAA grant AA-00187 and NINDS grant NS-06209 to the Boston University School of Medicine.

AMNESIA AND SEMANTIC ANALYSIS

The extent of the Korsakoff patients' memory impairment has been fully documented. Clinically, Talland[6] described these patients as having a severe anterograde amnesia manifested by their inability to remember day-to-day events, current information, or hospital personnel. It has also been shown by Seltzer and Benson[7] that Korsakoff patients' retrograde amnesia is especially severe for events that have occurred during the past ten to twenty years. Finally, using a contemporary information-processing model of memory,[3] Cermak and Butters[8] have demonstrated that these patients are impaired in all three storage systems believed to exist in normals: long-term memory, short-term memory, and immediate (iconic) memory.

The possibility that these memory deficits may be related to inefficient utilization of language skills began to emerge in a report by Cermak and Butters.[9] These authors discovered that Korsakoff patients' recall of an eight-item list of words, containing two words from each of four categories, could not be aided through introduction of the category names as cues. If anything, these cues tended to diminish rather than facilitate the patients' retrieval (see FIGURE 1). In contrast to normal subjects, the Korsakoff patients retrieved more items during free recall than they did during cued recall. It appeared that the patients were retaining the information in a rather raw, uncategorized, state sufficient for "spewing out" the words but not for the more complex, cognitive mental manipulations needed when they had to respond to the category names with the appropriate items.

Further evidence supporting the validity of this interpretation emerged in a later study[10] in which the patients were shown 60 words at the rate of one word every two seconds. The patients were instructed to indicate whenever a word was repeated. Within the list, six words were actually repeated, but six others bore a homonym relationship (e.g., *bear* and *bare*) with others in the list, while six other pairs bore an associate relationship (e.g., *table* and *chair*), and six a synonym relationship (e.g., *boat* and *ship*). The rationale was that the more fully the subject analyzed the features of each word the less likely he would be to recognize "falsely" a related word as a repetition. However, if his level of analysis were meagre, the Korsakoff patient might indicate that a homonym had previously been presented when, in fact, only the word's phonemic feature had previously occurred. The patient might also indicate

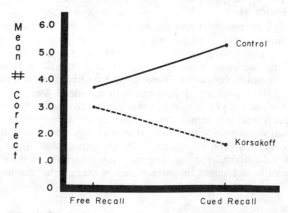

FIGURE 1. Mean number of words correctly recalled during a free recall and a cued recall task.

TABLE 1

MEAN NUMBER OF FALSE RECOGNITIONS AS A FUNCTION OF THE TYPE OF RELATIONSHIP WITH A
PREVIOUSLY PRESENTED WORD*

Patient Population	Relationship with Prior Word				
	Homonym	Associate	Synonym	Neutral	Repeat
Korsakoff	2.3	2.3	0.7	0.8	3.3
Alcoholic controls	0.5	0.2	0.3	0.0	4.2

*Repeats represented correct responses.

that an associate had been presented when actually it may only have been implicitly evoked by the prior occurrence of its associate.[11] Such results did occur for the Korsakoff patients, who, although detecting nearly as many actual repetitions as did their controls, falsely recognized far more homonyms and associates as being repeats (TABLE 1). Synonyms and unrelated words were not falsely recognized, indicating again that the patients were probably relying on their phonemic and rather automatic associative levels of analysis to compare and contrast verbal information in memory.

The distractor technique, which has had an extensive history in normal memory literature, has also frequently been employed in analyses of amnesic short-term memory deficits.[12-14] This paradigm, originally developed by Peterson and Peterson,[15] involves the presentation of a very short list of stimulus items (e.g. three words), followed immediately by a distractor activity (such as counting backwards) designed to prevent the patient from rehearsing the just-presented material until such time as recall is signaled, usually 10–20 seconds later. Korsakoff patients perform very poorly on this test (FIGURE 2), usually losing verbal information after only 9- or 18-sec delay intervals. This finding does not in and of itself imply any relationship between initial analysis of the material and eventual retrieval, for a pure "storage-deficit" hypothesis could also account for the data. However, a modification of this procedure, developed by Wickens,[16] allowed us to investigate further the role of semantic analysis in Korsakoff patients' memory abilities.

Wickens demonstrated that after a normal adult subject has received four distractor task trials on which the stimulus words are all drawn from the same semantic category (e.g. animal names), his recall will drop from a 95% probability of being correct on trial 1 to a probability of 40–50% on the final trial. Wickens attributes this decrement to the influence of the interference generated by having analyzed and categorized each word in the task similarly. With each successive trial, more and more similarly analyzed words are being stored in memory, and the probability becomes less and less that the subject will be able to separate the most recently presented items from those presented on prior trials. If, however, words from a distinctly different category are presented on Trial 5 (e.g. vegetable names), the probability of recall for a normal subject will again approximate 90–95%. Presumably this increase occurs because the subject analyzes and stores these new items on the basis of a different class inclusion than the words from prior trials. Since the interference generated during the first four trials is specific to the semantic category represented by the words presented on those trials, the new items are recalled easily. If for any reason the subject does not detect this shift in class inclusion, then no increase in performance would occur. Thus the technique can be used to determine what features of verbal stimuli Korsakoff patients normally analyze in the course of their attempts to retain information.

Two of Wickens' more easily discriminated dimensions were adapted for use with Korsakoff patients.[17] The first task involved a shift between letters and numbers. Since the inclusion of numbers as stimuli negated the use of counting as a distraction, rapid color-naming was used to prevent rehearsal. Following four trials, during which the patient was asked to try to retain consonant trigrams, a trial containing a three-digit number was introduced. This alpha-numeric shift was also performed in the opposite direction (numbers to letters) for half the total number of test sessions. The results, which can be seen in FIGURE 3, indicate quite clearly the Korsakoff patients' ability to detect and profit from this change in class inclusion. When a shift occurred (Experimental Condition), recall increased; when it did not (Control Condition), recall decreased. The next step involved conducting an experiment involving more abstract, semantic classes of verbal material.

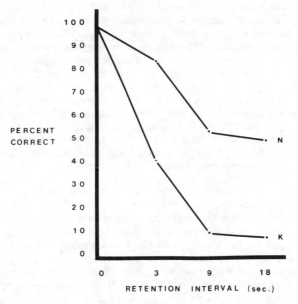

FIGURE 2. Percentage of words correctly recalled following 0, 3, 9, or 18 seconds of distractor activity for Korsakoff patients (K) and Normal controls (N).

In the second experiment, words drawn from four taxonomic categories (e.g. animals, vegetables) were used instead of letters and numbers. Again the same procedure of shifting from one category of stimuli to another represented the crucial feature of the experiment. For example, on each of the first four trials a patient may have been presented with three animal names. Then, on the fifth trial, he may have received three food names (Experimental Condition) or three more animal names (Control Condition). As can be seen from FIGURE 4, the Korsakoff patients did not demonstrate any release from interference when the taxonomic shift occurred on the fifth trial. By contrast, alcoholic control patients examined under identical experimental and control conditions evidenced considerable release when the semantic categories were changed (FIGURE 5). It appears that the Korsakoff patients' lack of

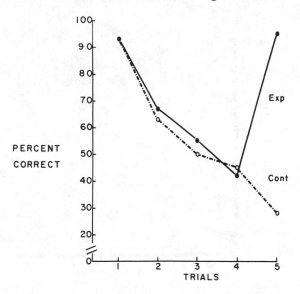

FIGURE 3. Probability of recall following an alpha-numeric shift for Korsakoff patients.

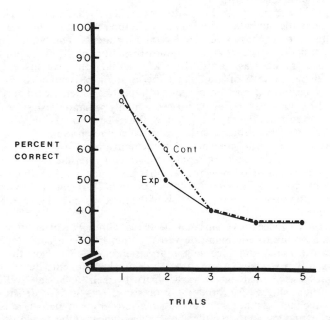

FIGURE 4. Probability of recall following a taxonomic shift for Korsakoff patients.

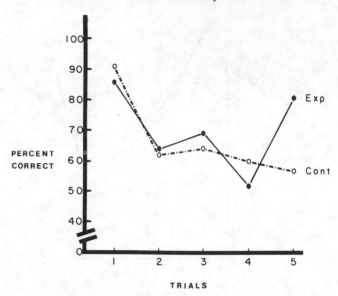

FIGURE 5. Probability of recall following a taxonomic shift for alcoholic controls.

semantic analysis leaves them more susceptible to the effects of proactive interference than is the case for the controls.

Further evidence that Korsakoff patients tend to rely more upon their phonemic than their semantic analysis of information is found in a study by DeLuca et al.[18] This investigation also assessed the Korsakoff patients' ability to retain words following distraction except that in this study the nature of the distractor task rather than the memoranda was varied. In one condition the patients engaged in a nonverbal distractor task of scanning patterns for a particular configuration; in another they performed an acoustic task of repeating letters heard through headphones; and in yet another they performed a highly semantic task of searching for words, some even from the same category as those they were trying to remember. It was discovered that the acoustic task interfered with retention of the words for the Korsakoffs, but not for the controls, while the nonverbal distraction interfered with neither group's retention and the semantic distractor interfered (as expected) with both groups' retention. However, the fact that an acoustic task, unrelated semantically to the memoranda, interfered with the Korsakoff's retention implied that they were relying upon their phonemic analysis of the three words to a greater extent than were the controls.

The bulk of evidence thus seems to indicate that although Korsakoff patients have retained their ability to communicate verbally, they have either lost their language competence when analyzing incoming information or they have lost the motivation for utilizing such a strategy. At any rate, the Korsakoff patients' dense anterograde amnesia can be accounted for, at least in part, by their inefficient level of analysis during the initial stages of information processing. This analytic deficit might also account for the finding that Korsakoff patients' retrograde amnesia is most dense for recent decades and less so for remote, if one can assume that the development of their analytic inefficiency was progressive across time.

APHASIA AND VERBAL MEMORY

If verbal memory impairments can be related to inefficient verbal analysis, then it follows that aphasic patients who are known to have impaired verbal skills might have poor verbal memories. Evaluation of such verbal memory defects in aphasics has always been difficult, since direct recall tests rely upon the patients' ability to verbalize the word (which he often cannot do), and recognition tests tend to tap only the most rudimentary levels of feature analysis, such as direct visual matches. Tests are needed that encourage the aphasic patient to rely upon his phonemic or semantic analysis of a word in order to retain the information but do not require overt recall to demonstrate retention.

One solution to this problem would be to have the patient "demonstrate" his retention of particular features of a word by detecting similar features in subsequently presented words. Such a task has been developed [19] with normal subjects, and it has been adapted for use with brain damaged patients by Cermak and Moreines.[20] Briefly, the task requires that the patient listen to a list of words read at a constant rate (e.g. one word every sec) and detect when a word has been repeated; or, in another condition of the task, detect when a word rhymes with a previous word; or, in yet another condition, detect when a word is a member of the same category as a previous word in the list. The patient does not have to indicate the previously presented word; instead, he has only to raise his hand whenever a match does occur. Memory for particular features of words can then be determined by plotting the number of correct matches detected as a function of the number of words intervening between the initial and probe member of each match.

Anterior aphasics with good comprehension, as assessed by the Boston Diagnostic Aphasia Battery,[21] participated in this experiment along with a group of alcoholic Korsakoff patients and a group of nonorganic control patients. The results, which can be seen in FIGURE 6, showed that the aphasic patients were able to detect as many repetitions as the normal controls and as the Korsakoff patients when no words intervened between repeated words. However, as soon as two words intervened, the aphasics were somewhat worse than the other two groups, and when four words intervened their detection rate was far below the performance of the normals and even below the Korsakoffs. The explanation for this dramatic retention loss can be seen in the second and third panels of FIGURE 6. The aphasic patients were impaired

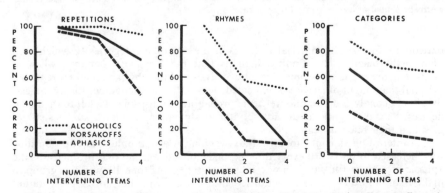

FIGURE 6. Percentage of target words correctly identified by aphasics, Korsakoffs, and alcoholic control patients on each of the three tasks as a function of the number of intervening words presented at a one-word/sec rate.

in their ability to detect rhymes even when the rhyming words occurred in succession. This aphasic deficit became even more apparent when two or more words intervened between members of the rhyming pair. To insure that the aphasic patients understood the concept of rhyming, the patients were read a list of 20 pairs of rhyming words, one pair at a time. One-half of the pairs were rhymes; one-half were not. The patients were asked to indicate, by shaking their head, which pairs rhymed and which did not. The aphasic patients were correct more than 90% of the time. Apparently, then, the aphasics' deficit in the previous rhyme-detection task must have been related to an inability to retain a running memory load of phonemically analyzed information. It should be noted in FIGURE 6 that Korsakoff patients are also impaired in the detection of rhymes. The Korsakoffs' impairment, however, approaches that of the aphasics only after four words have intervened between rhymes.

The results for semantic detection show that this task is the most difficult one for aphasic patients. However, given their severe difficulty retaining the phonemic representations of a word, it is not too surprising that more sophisticated analyses are so difficult. Although the performance of the Korsakoff patients is relatively good on this semantic task, it must be noted that the nature of the instructions encouraged the

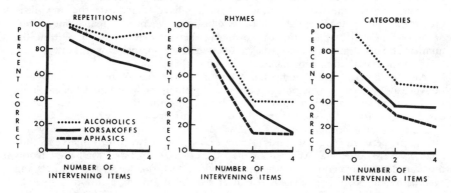

FIGURE 7. Percentage of target words correctly identified by aphasics, Korsakoffs, and alcoholic control patients on each of the three tasks as a function of the number of intervening words presented at a one-word/three-sec rate.

patients to analyze the material in terms of the semantic categories to which each item might belong. This finding suggests that the Korsakoff patients, when so instructed, are capable of some semantic analysis and thereby can retain more verbal material than might otherwise be expected. This outcome strengthens the hypothesis that level of analysis determines retrieval probability. Unfortunately, left to their own devices, Korsakoff patients do not spontaneously employ semantic analysis strategies, and their retentive capabilities suffer accordingly.

An interesting sidelight to this study was that when stimulus presentation time was increased to one word every three seconds, the only group that profited was the aphasic group. As FIGURE 7 shows, increased processing time allowed this group to make many more category detections than occurred with the shorter presentation rate. In fact, they now performed nearly on a par with the Korsakoff group, but still inferior to the controls. Apparently the aphasic patients are capable of some semantic analysis, but the rate at which they make these analyses is much slower than is normally the case. Korsakoff patients did not improve with increased processing time, indicating that they probably performed as much semantic analysis as they could in the shorter time interval and performed no more in the longer. The normals showed little improvement, but were probably affected by a ceiling level of performance. In the more difficult task originally devised by Cermak and Youtz,[19] normals did improve as presentation rate was slowed.

The aphasics' performance on the phonemic portion of this experiment did not improve, implying that their ability to recirculate phonemic features (i.e. rehearse by rote) is impaired, as well as their ability to analyze this feature. Since increased presentation time did not enhance the strength of the product of this analysis, it must be concluded that the patient is not utilizing this time to strengthen the trace through rehearsal. Unlike semantic analysis, phonemic analysis seems not only to be slower for aphasics than for the other groups but more limited as well.[22]

Similar results have been reported by Goodglass, et al.[22] who also devised a test to measure the memory ability of anterior aphasics. In their task the patient viewed a series of two to four pictures for five seconds each. The pictures were then turned over and the patient was asked to pick up each picture card, still face down, and place it on a display card containing the same pictures as those now face down before the patient. The patient had to "remember" which picture before him was that of a hat in order to pick it up and place it on top of the picture of a hat seen on the display. Patients' memory for pictures was tested for nonverbal designs, nonhomophonic pictures (such as pipe, bus, clock, and hand) and homophonic pictures (such as tag, bag, cat, and bat). It was hypothesized that if the patient used some form of verbal encoding of the items in order to remember them, recall of the verbalizable items should exceed that of the nonverbal. Furthermore, if such encoding was based on a phonemic analysis, and recirculation of the product of that analysis, then recall of the nonhomophonic test list should exceed that of the homophonic, because less interference would be present during retention. This is precisely what occurred for the nonaphasic, brain-injured control group, but for the aphasic patients no significant differences in recall occurred among any of these three types of material. Furthermore, while the aphasic patients performed normally on the nonverbal task, they fell far behind the nonaphasics on the verbal tasks because they failed to improve, whereas the nonaphasics' performance rose dramatically. This led the authors to conclude that the nonaphasic patients used verbal mediation to help them retain the pictures. This verbal mediation probably involved some form of phonemic recirculation, since the nonhomophonically related pictures were recalled better than the homophonically related pictures. The aphasics did not use such mediation, as evidenced by their poor performance on the verbalizable tasks and by the lack of a difference between homophonic and nonhomophonic conditions. As in the previously described Cermak and Moreines[20] study, it again appeared that aphasic patients' inability to analyze the phonemic features of a stimulus led to rapid forgetting of the stimulus by these patients.

CONCLUSION

The dependence of memory upon proficiency in the use of language has now been investigated from both directions. Several studies have demonstrated that patients whose primary deficit is an inability to remember new information also have severe analytic deficits. Similarly, patients whose primary difficulty is linguistic also suffer from verbal memory deficits. It is tempting to conclude from this research that memory is dependent upon an individual's initial analysis of incoming information, a conclusion that is presently in favor among theorists of normal information processing. However, such a conclusion must remain tentative at this time, because most of the present set of experiments have been rather indirect tests of the hypothesis. They have been designed to demonstrate the simultaneous occurrence of the two deficits within a set of brain-injured patients and have been successful in attaining this limited goal. What must now be devised is a method of assuring an improvement in an amnesic's analytic processing and then correlating this increment with an observed improvement in his retrieval performance. Or, similarly, it will be necessary to correlate improvements in aphasics' verbal memory with recovery of their linguistic skills. Such procedures are necessary for direct tests of the hypotheses set forth in this paper. It is hoped that the framework of the theory proposed here will serve to stimulate research in this direction.

REFERENCES

1. ATKINSON, R. C. & R. M. SHIFFRIN. 1967. Human memory: A proposed system and its control processes. Technical Report No. 110. Stanford University. Stanford, Calif.
2. CRAIK, F. I. M. & R. S. LOCKHART. 1972. Levels of processing: A framework for memory research. J. Verbal Learning, Verbal Behav. **11**: 671–684.
3. CERMAK, L. S. 1972. Human Memory: Research and Theory. Ronald Press. New York, N.Y.
4. CERMAK, L. S. 1975. Psychology of Learning: Research and Theory. Ronald Press. New York, N.Y.
5. CRAIK, F. I. M. & E. TULVING. 1975. Depth of processing and retention of words in episodic memory. J. Exp. Psychol. General **104**: 268–294.
6. TALLAND, G. 1965. Deranged Memory. Academic Press. New York, N.Y.
7. SELTZER, B. & D. F. BENSON. 1974. The temporal pattern of retrograde amnesia in Korsakoff's disease. Neurology **24**: 527–530.
8. CERMAK, L. S. & N. BUTTERS. 1973. Information processing deficits of alcoholic Korsakoff patients. Quart. J. Studies on Alcohol **34**: 1110–1132.
9. CERMAK, L. S. & N. BUTTERS. 1972. The role of interference and encoding in the short-term memory deficits of Korsakoff patients. Neuropsychologia **10**: 89–95.
10. CERMAK, L. S., N. BUTTERS, & J. GERREIN. 1973. The role of verbal encoding ability of Korsakoff patients. Neuropsychologia **11**: 85–94.
11. UNDERWOOD, B. J. 1965. False recognition by implicit verbal responses. J. Exp. Psychol. **70**: 122–129.
12. MILNER, B. 1970. Memory and the medial temporal region of the brain. *In* Biology of Memory. K. H. Pribram & D. E. Broadbent, Eds.: 29–50. Academic Press. New York, N.Y.
13. BADDELEY, A. D. & E. K. WARRINGTON. 1970. Memory Coding and Amnesia. Neuropsychologia **11**: 159–165.
14. CERMAK, L. S., N. BUTTERS, & H. GOODGLASS. 1971. The extent of memory loss in Korsakoff patients. Neuropsychologia **9**: 307–315.
15. PETERSON, L. R. & M. J. PETERSON. 1959. Short term retention of individual verbal items. J. Exp. Psychol. **58**: 193–198.
16. WICKENS, D. D. 1970. Encoding categories of words: An empirical approach to meaning. Psychol. Rev. **77**: 1–15.
17. CERMAK, L. S., N. BUTTERS & J. MOREINES. 1974. Some analyses of the verbal encoding deficit of alcoholic Korsakoff patients. Brain and Language **1**: 141–150.
18. DeLUCA, D., L. S. CERMAK & N. BUTTERS. 1976. The differential effects of semantic, acoustic and nonverbal distraction on Korsakoff patients' verbal retention performance. Inter. J. Neurosciences **6**: 279–284.
19. CERMAK, L. S. & C. YOUTZ. 1976. Retention of phonemic and semantic features of words. Memory and Cognition **4**: 172–175.

20. CERMAK, L. S. & J. MOREINES. 1976. Verbal retention deficits in aphasic and amnesic patients. Brain and Language 3: 16–27.
21. GOODGLASS, H. & E. KAPLAN. 1972. The Assessment of Aphasia and Related Disorders. Lea & Febiger. Philadelphia, Pa.
22. GOODGLASS, H., G. DENES & M. CALDERON. 1974. The absence of covert verbal mediation in aphasia. Cortex 10: 264–269.

DISSOCIATIONS OF LANGUAGE IN APHASIA:
IMPLICATIONS FOR NORMAL FUNCTION*

Oscar S. M. Marin, Eleanor M. Saffran,
and Myrna F. Schwartz

*Departments of Neurology
Baltimore City Hospitals
The Johns Hopkins University School of Medicine
Baltimore, Maryland 21205*

The language disorders that result from organic brain disease have mostly been used to answer anatomical questions: which areas of the brain subserve language? The concern of this paper is to show that pathological data can also be used to study the normal language process; that they are relevant for a theory of language function, as well as for the eventual ascription of that function to the brain. We hope that this will emerge from the data that comprise the second part of the paper. The first part, a general consideration of the neuropsychological approach to the study of language function, is included here in an effort to correct some prevailing misconceptions.

DO PATHOLOGICAL DATA HAVE ANY RELEVANCE TO THE NORMAL LANGUAGE PROCESS?

Many psycholinguists are skeptical that pathological data have any use in the study of normal language (e.g. Ref. 1, p. xiv). In our own forays among them, we almost invariably meet with the same invective: "What can you possibly learn about the way a car works (or a vacuum cleaner, or a computer) by pounding it with a sledgehammer!" We submit that the argument is not equal to its devastating intent: random decomposition *can* result in potentially instructive dissociations of function.† In the case of the car, it might be possible to discover, say, whether the steering mechanism functions independently of the engine. This example seems banal, but only because, having designed the machine in the first place, we already have a good theory of automotive function. The same cannot be said for language; here, the suggestion, from pathology, of dissociations in language function can help to build the theory.

The car analogy makes another point: that we would derive little useful information from the behavior of the disabled machine if we did not know what questions to ask about its performance; i.e., is the power source working? how about the steering mechanism? and so on. It is only recently that advances in linguistics and psycholinguistics have provided a comparable framework for the specification of language functions.

There *are* some difficult problems facing the neuropsychologist, but these are problems inherent in the study of brain mechanisms through pathology and are not touched upon by mechanical analogies. First of all, the human brain is a vastly complex instrument; its operating principles with respect to language, and in-

*The preparation of this paper was aided, in part, by grant no. 12160-01 CMS from N.I.N.D.S; and by N.I.M.H. fellowship no. 00560-01 to M.F.S.

†The method is clearly acceptable in other sciences; perhaps the best example is the use of the nuclear accelerator in atomic physics.

deed, to behavior in general are practically unknown.[2] It is conceivable that it is put together in such a way as to defeat any attempt to study its function by removing one of its parts (a conclusion that did seem to emerge from Lashley's[3] classical study of maze learning in rats). Furthermore, in brain-damaged man we are dealing with an adaptive organism which will strive to accomplish its functions as best it can. In his effort to communicate, the patient might conceivably resort to mechanisms that are quite different from those employed in the normal state. It is reasonable to conclude from these arguments that pathology will tell us little about normal language function.

However, we have been convinced by our observations of aphasic patients that such pessimism is not warranted. We contend that an altogether different set of assumptions can reasonably be adopted: (1) that the nervous system is organized in terms of functionally meaningful subsystems, and that there is some degree of parallelism between functional organization and anatomical organization; (2) that at least some of these subsystems can be selectively impaired by neurological disease; and (3) that while organic pathology gives rise to a large variety of symptoms that reflect various mechanisms of inhibition, release, isolation, and so on, in no way do they represent the creation of new subsystems; rather, they reflect a reorganization that emphasizes intact subsystems.

The first two of these working assumptions seem clearly justified. Whatever the history of the localizationalist debate (see, e.g., Ref. 4, Chap. 1), it is now generally accepted that the human cerebral cortex is not equipotential for all the cognitive operations it performs; focal brain damage can at the very least affect some functions more than others (the rest of Luria's book is testimony to this assertion). Assumption (3) has less empirical force; it is difficult to prove that the injured brain has *not* invented a new mechanism. But we would argue that it is a reasonable assumption: in the first place, because adult nervous systems are limited in their plasticity;[5,6] second, because the behavioral manifestations which we study often emerge too soon after brain damage to be reasonably considered the product of new functional systems. To be sure, there is so much that is bizarre in aphasic language that one could easily doubt that it reflects anything about normal function. What has to be appreciated is that functional impairment or absence can alter the ways in which *intact* processes emerge in behavior. Thus, when, for example, a patient reads "carpenter" as "nails,"[7] it is unlikely that his error reflects an *addition* to the language mechanism; rather, compromise at some stage of the reading process has caused preexisting lexical structure to manifest itself more obviously in behavior (this is, in essence, the classical argument of Hughlings Jackson, 1884[8]). It is therefore more cautious to adopt the position that aphasic behavior reflects a "reorganization which emphasizes the remaining intact subsystems" than to assume that mechanisms are created *de novo* in the injured brain. That an occasional exception may be claimed does not, in our view, seriously undermine the usefulness of our third assumption.

We are arguing that the behavior of the patient with organic brain disease largely reflects capacities that existed in the premorbid state. We should therefore be able to make some inferences about the organization of normal language function from *patterns of functional preservation and impairment*: if process X is intact where process Y is severely compromised or absent, and especially if the converse is found in other patients, there is reason to believe that X and Y reflect different underlying mechanisms in the normal state. At the very least, the resulting matrix of intact and impaired functions should yield a taxonomy of functional subsystems. It may not tell us *how* these subsystems interact to produce normal language behavior, but it should identify and describe *what* distinct capacities are available to the language user (e.g., it might, to take a hypothetical instance, describe a semantic process that is distinct from a syntactic process). The method is, of course, limited by the functional topology of the brain. Because functions may overlap in their anatomical substrates, we cannot state with assurance that every functional system that *could* be observed *will* be observed. But *positive* evidence that functions are organized independently should be significant for a theory of the language process.

There are other uses to which the dissociations of function in aphasia can be put. In the normal state, many cognitive operations are performed in parallel; they are usually synergistic and redundant; to complicate their analysis, they are frequently recursive; i.e., there is feedback. The challenge of psycholinguistics is to develop experimental methods that tease apart these operations, to penetrate into this cohesive machinery to discern how signals progress from one level of encoding to another. So far, this methodological armamentarium has been quite limited.

An advantage of studying pathological cases is that some of this complexity is eliminated. Lesions may strike quite specifically at processes that are virtually impossible to manipulate independently in normals (for examples, see below). In some cases, information processing is arrested prematurely, so that the results of early encoding operations can be observed more directly than in the normal state, where they are masked by subsequent operations. "Word deafness" is a good example: the speech signal cannot be analyzed phonetically and is perceived, instead, on the basis of earlier auditory operations.[9]

The objective stated here, to learn something about the organization of the normal language process from the analysis of pathological states, has some methodological implications. The aphasias can be studied from several different points of view. As noted earlier, they have principally been used to answer anatomical questions; for this purpose, patients are grouped on the basis of lesion site, and the groups are then compared in their performance of various language tasks. It is also legitimate, and important for clinical purposes, to study aphasia as a phenomenon in its own right; here, groups are selected on the basis of diagnostic category, as determined by performance on a battery of language tests. Often, this is done with the assumption that the diagnostic category accurately reflects the localization of the lesion (e.g., "fluent" patients generally have posterior lesions and "nonfluent" patients anterior ones).

The problem with anatomy as a fixed parameter is, first of all, its imprecision. The brain lesion is almost always an accident of nature, quite outside experimental control; in most cases, brain damage cuts across many functional subsystems. And in addition to the fact that the lesion rarely provides a neat functional dissection, we can usually localize it only very grossly (except where cases come to autopsy, or in some instances of surgical intervention). Thus, any collection of patients chosen on the basis of lesion site is likely to be quite heterogeneous with respect to basic language function.

The same difficulty applies when aphasia is the fixed parameter. Performance on a diagnostic battery is the product of a complex interaction between intact and impaired functions. The same level of performance can be achieved in many different ways: for example, a patient might fail to repeat sentences accurately because he has a decoding problem, an expressive problem, a memory deficit, a syntactic disorder or any of these in combination. It is not surprising, therefore, that when groups so constituted are tested on a particular variable (e.g., syntax, phonology) there often seems to be very little difference among them.[10,11] To recover information about functional organization, it is necessary to choose appropriate units of analysis for both the independent and dependent variables; groups should be selected on the basis of their performance on a particular language function and then tested on other parameters which some hypothesis specifies as related to or independent of that function. But this optimal method is usually not possible, both because there are rarely sufficient numbers of similar cases, and because the appropriate units of analysis have yet to be formulated.

It is our contention that at this stage in the endeavor, more useful insights into normal language function will be provided by the detailed consideration of privileged cases, cases where there is still sufficient language to study language behavior, and where there are rather clean dissociations of function. It is here that patterns of functional integrity and impairment can be seen most clearly, and where differences between quite similar patients can serve to inform rather than to obscure. There are, of course, dangers in generalizing from these unusual cases; rarity may point to uniqueness of cognitive organization rather than, as we would have it, a serendipitous lesion. But we are not suggesting that the single case should be the final testing ground for theory; rather, that it can serve a useful hypothesis-generating function. And some confidence in the results can be sought in the consistency with which cases relate to one another; put together, they should overlap and interlock to provide, eventually, a comprehensive picture of the language process.

It is possible that the aphasis, observed in a sophisticated manner, will give us a fresh look at normal language, perhaps directing our attention to processes (e.g., lexical operations) which "normal science"[12] has somewhat neglected. The pathological data may yield a description that differs from prevailing views in linguistics and psycholinguistics. Further experiments are then necessary to reconcile differences, but the hypotheses generated by pathology should not be dismissed out of hand. Who is to say, *a priori*, that brain lesions will fractionate the language process more arbitrarily than the artifices of psycholinguistic experiment? It is altogether possible that the natural experiment will bring us closer to psychological reality.

And while we might agree with Fodor *et al.*[1] that "remarkably little has been learned about the psychology of language processes in normals from over a hundred years of aphasia study" (p. xiv), this conclusion must be put in historical perspective. The language disorders have been studied primarily for anatomical and for pragmatic clinical purposes; we have argued above that these are not the appropriate frames for the recovery of information about normal language function. It should also be said that we are just now learning what the appropriate questions are to ask about language, in normals as well as in aphasics. Given the early stage of the inquiry, it is surely premature to preclude the use of facts that may emerge from the study of pathology. We hope that the data to be presented below will affirm this position.

DISSOCIATIONS OF LANGUAGE FUNCTION IN APHASIA

We wish briefly to describe several of the studies performed in our laboratory that have an obvious relevance to the normal language process, and then to discuss in more detail the work currently in progress that bears on the organization of lexical and syntactic functions.

Auditory Short-Term Memory and Language Comprehension

Auditory short-term storage has been exhaustively studied by psychologists, at least with respect to its function in memory. But it is also thought that short-term storage must be essential to language comprehension (e.g. Ref. 38) that sentences must be preserved at the level of surface structure until they can be given a deep-structure interpretation. This assertion is difficult to test directly in normal subjects. It is essentially impossible to manipulate auditory short-term memory independently of other variables.

Several years ago, Warrington and Shallice (1969) pointed out that a classical syndrome in aphasia—"conduction aphasia": the inability to repeat spoken language despite grossly intact comprehension and production—might profitably be viewed as a specific disorder of auditory verbal short-term memory. They analyzed the mnestic capacities of their patient in some detail, with an eye toward the prevailing view in psychology that short-term storage is the essential precursor to long-term memory. In our own study of a similar case (I.L.), we looked in addition, at the effect of the memory impairment on language comprehension.[13]

It was first demonstrated, using a variety of experimental techniques, that the patient's deficit was virtually restricted to auditory verbal short-term memory: I.L. could speak, read, and comprehend language (at least grossly), but had difficulty recalling more than two unrelated items presented auditorily (although his span for equivalent materials presented visually was within the normal range). None of the effects normally attributed to auditory short-term memory was evident in his behavior (e.g., terminal-item superiority, improvement with vocalization-at-presentation, etc.), and, in general, his performance in immediate memory tasks seemed to reflect storage in semantic rather than phonological form. This was seen most dramatically in a sentence-repetition task, in which he was instructed to repeat, verbatim, sentences presented auditorily. His performance was accurate with sentences up to four or five words in length; beyond that, he would deliver what were in most instances perfectly adequate paraphrases of the original sentence: e.g., for "The residence was located in a peaceful neighborhood," he said, "The residence was situated in a quiet district." The paraphrases tended to be adequate as long as sentence structure was straightforward: sentences of the subject-verb-object (SVO) type, even when extended by left-branching clauses, were paraphrased correctly. However, embedded sentences and semantically reversible sentences were frequently misinterpreted: e.g., for "The boy the dog chased went home," "The boy chased the dog home," for "The soldier was watched by the man in the car," "The soldier watched the man in the car." Zurif and Caramazza (personal communication) have obtained strikingly similar results with conduction aphasics in a rather different kind of task. These data suggest that, except when syntax gets complicated, preservation of surface structure may not be essential for the extraction of meaning; semantic constraints, plus a serial assignment of the lexical items to SVO categories may suffice (for a similar argument from normal data see Bever.[14]) But whatever conclusions are to be drawn from these observations, the virtues of such a preparation should be evident.

It should also be noted here that both Warrington's patient and our own represent rather pure examples of this clinical syndrome, and it is most unlikely that the acoustic storage hypothesis would have emerged out of group data. Armed with this hypothesis, however, it is possible to find evidence of auditory short-term memory impairment in patients who appear rather diverse clincially (Warrington *et al.*[15] and Schwartz *et al.*, unpublished data).‡

‡In one of our own cases, we have found that the auditory storage deficit is expressed in terms of phonological rather than semantic deviation from the input. Apparently unable to rely on semantic mechanisms, as I. L. was able to do, the patient has to work with a degraded phonemic record, and his repetition errors are phonetically, rather than semantically related to the target.

Reading without Phonology

One's intuition is that some issues in psycholinguistics should prove easier to resolve than others; one of those is the problem of basic mechanisms in reading. But it remains the subject of intensive debate. Is it, for example, possible to access lexical entries directly from the orthography, or is it necessary first to convert graphemic information to phonological form? (see, e.g., discussions in Refs. 16 and 17.) The problem with addressing this question in the normal subject is that, whatever other strategy he might be using, he is also capable of converting grapheme to phoneme, and we are hard put to prevent him from doing so.

It is possible, however, to find patients with brain lesions that fractionate the reading process at various stages, permitting us to study certain operations in isolation.[18] One of these forms of acquired dyslexia seems to represent a specific impairment of grapheme-phoneme conversion; these patients are nonetheless able to read, albeit with some restrictions. One of our patients (V.S.) retained an impressive reading vocabulary (in excess of 16,500 words) despite the visuophonological dissociation.[19]

The impairment of grapheme-phoneme conversion in this patient was demonstrated in a variety of experiments (e.g., failure to identify rhymes and homophones when visually presented, although rhyming words were recognized when presented auditorily; inability to use auditory codes in short-term memory for verbal materials presented visually, etc.), but perhaps most dramatically, in the patient's inability to access lexical entries from phonetically correct but unfamiliar spellings (e.g., "kote," "hite," "rayne," seeling," and others); these words posed no problem when spelled normally.

The failure to transform grapheme into phoneme except by lexical mediation made possible a number of interesting experiments. 1) We were able to ask what kinds of reading performances are possible without direct grapheme-phoneme conversion. For example, it is normally difficult to separate the effects of orthographic structure from phonological structure; orthographic dependencies obviously reflect phonological dependencies (i.e., "wfle" is an unacceptable orthographic sequence in English because it is an unacceptable phonological sequence). Normal performance in reading tasks could depend on one, or the other, or on both. The patient can be used to show whether certain phenomena observed in normal subjects (e.g., the superior recognition of phonologically permissible sequences in tachistoscopic experiments (see McClelland and Johnston[20]) could possibly be mediated by knowledge of orthographic structure alone (Saffran *et al.*, unpublished data). 2) The impossibility of direct phonological encoding is at least contributory to an intriguing phenomenon in the oral reading performance of these patients: their tendency to produce errors that are semantically related to the target word.[7,18] Whatever else is involved in this "semantic paralexia," it is unlikely that the patients would produce such substitutions if they were capable of encoding the graphemic information directly into phonological form. Typical errors are the following: "tulip" read as "crocus"; "robin" as "bird"; "grass" as "lawn." These substitutions are quite similar to the kinds of errors normal subjects make in reading discourse aloud, an exercise which, at least in the skilled reader, is also unlikely to depend heavily on phonological strategies.[21,22]

It has been suggested that such error patterns in normals can be used to make inferences about abstract levels of representation.[1] We would argue that the aphasic data can serve a similar purpose. This point will be taken up again in *Lexicon without Syntax*, below.

Syntax without a Lexicon

One of the most intriguing observations to be made in aphasia is that lexical and syntactic functions can, to a large extent, be disrupted independently, especially in speech production. Thus it is possible to find patients who are virtually asyntactic in their spontaneous speech; in the extreme, their utterances are holophrastic and consist almost entirely of referential nouns. At the other extreme, there are patients whose output is fluent, prosodic, and well-structured syntactically; inflections and function words are spared. What is lacking in this second group is an adequate lexicon.

The lexical problem can be manifested in several different ways. The patient may grope for the word he wants, and his output may be marked by frequent pauses and circumlocutions; this is the case in the set of clinical syndromes labeled as "anomia." Other patients, perhaps less aware of the lexical problem because of severely impaired language comprehension, speak copiously and without hesitation, but insert incorrect lexical items or even neologisms into the syntactic frame; clinically, this pattern belongs to "Wernicke's aphasia."

These radically different patterns of language breakdown in aphasia would seem to have obvious significance for a theory of the language process. But except for the linguist Jakobson,[23] who has written extensively on this polarity of aphasic disorders, these striking findings have penetrated very little into the consciousness of "normal science," i.e., psycholinguistics. What we hope to do in this section and the next is to show how these disorders might be used to reveal relationships between syntactic function and lexical structure.

As mentioned above, the lexical disorder is usually manifested in two abnormal patterns of sentence production: in the anomic patient there is much hesitation and circumlocution; in the Wernicke's aphasic, content words are replaced by semantic or phonemic substitutions that often verge on neologism. In this section we will describe a patient (S.B.) who fits into this general category of lexical disturbances, but in the extreme: although almost devoid of specific content words, her sentence production was otherwise normal—prosodically, phonologically and syntactically.§

To give some indication of her speech pattern, we include an excerpt of S.B.'s description of a picture story that we often use to elicit production in our patients (the "broken window picture" from Wells and Reusch.[24]) In this picture, a man has just run out of his house to remonstrate with a girl passerby, thinking that she must be responsible for his broken window. We also see a boy in baseball garb hiding behind a fence and can reasonably assume that he, not the girl, is the culprit. The patient (S.B.) comments to the interviewer (I.):

S.B.: "This guy did something, right there . . . He ran . . . and she's there like she didn't even know."
I.: "Who broke it?"
S.B.: "She would never do it—she looks like a really nice kid. He's really getting mad (pointing to the man) . . . *He* did it (pointing to the boy); he broke it."
I.: "How?"

§ There are some unusual features about this case which probably explain the relative purity of the disorder. It is the result of an extensive lesion of the posterior region of the right hemisphere in a left-handed individual with a family background of sinistrality. Comparable destruction of the left hemisphere in a right hander would undoubtedly have produced a more severe aphasia, with a profound comprehension disturbance and, most likely, fluent but neologistic production.

S.B.: "I can't tell you but I know what it is. It is just broken. 'Cause this kid did it."

I.: "What kind of 'kid' is that?"

S.B.: "Him."

It is apparent from this sample that the patient does not invent neologisms or make inappropriate lexical substitutions; instead, she relies on a small number of content words, most of them rather unspecific, and strongly on the use of pronouns. The impression we get from this excerpt, that within the category of contentives there are more verbs and adjectives than nouns available, is borne out by quantitative analyses of extended samples of her output. We do not have the appropriate normal sample for comparison, but the numbers seem striking in and of themselves. The following tabulation comes from a conversation with the patient before most of the effort to restore her lexical capabilities had begun. In a rough classification according to syntactic category, we find: nouns, 55 occurrences; verbs, 340 (excluding auxiliaries and "to be" in all its forms); adjectives, 82; adverbs, 80; pronouns, 267.¶ Of the nouns, more than 50% were occurrences of the words "thing," "place," and "people"; most of the remainder were other general terms like "time," "way," "kind," and so on.** This pattern of relative preservation and loss of items according to syntactic category is diametrically opposed to what we see in the asyntactic patients to be described in the next section: their spontaneous speech is characterized by an overwhelming use of nominal forms for specific reference; many fewer verbs and adjectives, and a virtual absence of function words.††

Unlike some anomics,[26] this patient's difficulty did not seem to lie in accessing lexical entries from other levels of representation, but rather in using these entries for the purpose of speech production. S.B. was able to comprehend the referential words she was completely unable to produce. At some level, she was even able to evoke the phonological form of the word although she could not express it overtly. This was demonstrated by her ability to select pairs of objects with names that rhymed (e.g., "tree-key"; "whale-scale") with a fair degree of success; when she ran into trouble, it was usually because the entry *she* accessed (e.g., "stones") was different from the one *we* intended (e.g., "rocks"—to rhyme with "sox"). But in no case could these words be articulated. S.B. was totally incapable of specific nominal reference. Not even the most common and earliest acquired nouns in the language, nor even her own name, were spared. She was also unable to repeat these words, although she understood their meaning. It appeared that most of the lexicon had become isolated from the mechanisms of speech production. The syntactic machinery was thus left to operate with an extreme narrow lexical base, especially with respect to nouns.

The speech pathologists worked intensively to restore S.B.'s vocabulary, and a number of intriguing phenomena emerged during this period of therapy. The teaching process was laborious, since, except for most vowel sounds, S.B. could repeat very little of what was said to her. Words had to be pieced together from disparately elicited phonological elements (e.g., /aU/ by pinching the patient; "shoe"

¶ Recognizing that we do not have an appropriate normal sample for comparison, it may still be instructive to look at an analysis from a sample of normal text: nouns, 35%; verbs, 32%; modifiers, 15%; pronouns, 18%; (From Wepman *et al.*[27])

**There were only two specific nouns in this sample, "mom" and "weight," and the transcript suggests that these words had been taught by the therapist.

†† In a corpus derived from one such patient, Myerson and Goodglass[25] found seven times as many nouns as verbs.

from "ssh" and /u/). But for some period after these reconstructed lexical items could be produced at will and in proper referential context, they could not be inflected, nor could they be inserted into syntactic frames. When shown two shoes she could not say "shoes," but responded "shoe—two of them". The following excerpt illustrates this difficulty rather dramatically; here the patient even seems to have some awareness of the problem. This sample is taken from a conversation that occurred shortly after S.B. had mastered a few proper names, including those of a fellow patient ("Noah"), a therapist ("Terry"), and, finally, her own (let us call her "Susan"), and also the word "Dad":

"Noah, Susan, Terry, Susan. How do you do the other one? . . . Yeah, Noah . . . He goes to sleep and everything . . . Noah. He goes to sleep all the time. Dad did . . . dad, go to sleep. Go to sleep, dad. No, how do you do that? . . . Susan—eat, drink and sleep . . . Who is Susan? Me. That was better . . . Susan. I am Susan. Noah. And Daddy . . . Dad is better. I didn't know how to do that. Susan, Noah, Terry . . . Terry's really . . . she's all right." These observations make the notion of lexical insertion almost palpable.

The case of S. B. suggests that syntax can operate quite normally in sentence production despite isolation from most of the lexicon.‡‡ It also suggests a hypothesis that will be explored in more detail below: that at least for purposes of speech production, the lexicon is organized in close association with syntactic function; thus, when a lesion compromises the lexicon but spares syntax, the nominal referents, which rely very little on syntax for their phonological specification, are most affected, verbal forms less so. The reverse pattern should be observed in cases where syntax is impaired.

Lexicon without Syntax

Let us turn now to the aphasic disorder that seems to be the obverse of the previous one: the patient who has a much wider referential lexicon but who is essentially asyntactic. These patients produce short, halting phrases consisting almost entirely of concrete nouns and specific verbs. The function words of the language are used infrequently and inappropriately. Nouns are improperly inflected for number and verbs either uninflected or used in the progressive form. Speech melody is flat. Such patients have been extensively described in the literature under a variety of labels (agrammatism, nonfluency, Broca's aphasia, anterior aphasia, disorders of encoding, disorders of contiguity), but there is general agreement on the basic syntactic impairment.

Incapable of generating well-formed sentences, the output of these patients becomes primarily holophrastic and concrete, biased toward specific reference and the naming of people, objects, and situations known to the listener. The following is an excerpt from one such patient's description of the "broken window picture" (see *Syntax without a Lexicon*, above). Asked to describe what is happening in the picture, the patient (H.T.) replied:

H.T.: "Like the door . . . crash . . . like, pants . . . shirt . . . shoes . . . the boy . . . the dress . . . I dunno."

‡‡ With some qualifications: early in S.B.'s recovery, there was some tendency to use pronouns and auxiliaries improperly; e.g., "did" instead of "was"; "anybody" instead of "anywhere."

When pressed to explain the action, he could only assume the roles of various characters, as follows:

H.T.: "'Do . . . you do window?' . . . 'Does . . . you do the window?' . . . 'No I did'" (laughs). "Like, the boy is hidin . . . there."

I.: "Why?"

H.T.: "Because, well . . . the man is trying . . . man . . . like, the man . . . because the boy . . . the boy . . . the window . . . like, hidin' out, see . . . O.K., like the girl . . . 'Was do the window?' and 'No, sir' . . . like this . . . 'the boy.'"

This picture interpretation task elicits in normals, and indeed even in S.B., above, complex sentences referring to thoughts, expectations, and emotions of the characters. Constructions of this sort are impossible for the asyntactic patient, who is forced to rely on the uninformative recital of the elements of the scene.

Even in more structured situations, the patients are unable to produce well-constructed sentences. When, for example, the experimenter supplies the declarative form of the sentence, the patients cannot use this information to formulate questions or negative assertions, relying for the former on rising intonation and for the latter on the insertion of "no" or "not" somewhere in the utterance, e.g., "No the boy is studying"; "I not can sing." Others have reported similar observations.[10] And, contrary to earlier views, there is growing evidence that these patients are also impaired in the comprehension of certain syntactic structures.[10,28] Semantically reversible sentences, particularly when in passive form, seem to pose particular difficulty (Hamill, unpublished observations).

The syntactic disorder is reflected in oral reading performance as well. Thus we were impressed by the fact that two of our asyntactic patients, H.T. and V.S. (whose reading difficulties are discussed in detail in *Reading without Phonology*) made errors with precisely those kinds of words which were absent or inappropriate in their spontaneous speech. In reading sentences, they produced the following:

(Dinner is on the table.)   "Dinner . . . dinner is . . . the table."
(They walk to school.)   "This walkin to school."

This reading pattern was in sharp contrast to that of a third patient, J.D., a fluent aphasic whose reading of sentences also reflected his difficulties in spontaneous speech. Thus:

(Dinner is on the table.)   "Wendy is on the trip."
(They walk to school.)   "They work to school."

These observations suggest that, in these three patients at least, the difficulties in reading and in speech production may reflect common underlying pathology. The reading task, with its tight specification of input and output, provides us with a better experimental paradigm than the elicitation of spontaneous speech. We are therefore using oral reading performance to elucidate the relationship between syntax and the availablity, for production, of various classes of words.

Our first task was to document the dissociation of word classes in reading. To do this we composed a list of word pairs in which one member of the pair was a function word and the other a content word. Function words were drawn from pronouns, prepositions, articles, various forms of the copula "be," conjunctions, and particles. Content words consisted of nouns, uninflected verbs and adjectives. The words in

TABLE 1

FUNCTION VS. CONTENT WORD READING

| | | Number of Errors: | |
	V.S.	H.T.	J.D.
Function Words	43	37	17
Content Words	12	13	34

each pair were matched, insofar as possible, for frequency of usage and for phonology; whenever possible, the members were homophones, e.g.:

would—wood
which—witch
be—bee

Other examples are:

us—bus
and—end
through—throw

There was a total of 60 such pairs. Patients were presented one word at a time for oral reading. Members of pairs were presented in different test sessions.

Results of this study dramatically supported our initial observations of dissociations according to word type: the two nonfluent patients, H.T. and V.S., made three times as many errors on function words as on content words, while the fluent patient, J.D., showed just the reverse pattern of errors (see TABLES 1 and 2).

Performance on homophone pairs eliminates the possibility that these patients are unable to pronounce those words on which they make errors; H.T. was able to read "four" but not "for"; V.S. read "sum" but not "some"; and J.D. read "for" and "some" but not "four" or "sum." Thus the required articulatory pattern is *possible*, but is not reliably specified by the grapheme.

We already know this to be the case for patients like V.S. and H.T. These patients are incapable of encoding the graphemic information directly into phonological form (see *Reading Without Phonology*). The same may not be true of J.D., however. The pattern of his reading performance suggests that he *is* able to extract some limited information about the sound of the target word, and constructs the most likely response from this partial information. Thus he reads short, high-frequency words, i.e., function words, better than longer, lower frequency words, i.e., content words.

TABLE 2

FUNCTION VS. CONTENT WORD READING:
WORD-PAIR COMPARISONS

| | | Number of Errors | |
	V.S.	H.T.	J.D.
Content Word Correct Function Word Incorrect	33	28	5
Function Word Correct Content Word Incorrect	2	4	20

In addition, his errors are generally substitutions of words phonologically related to the target but of higher frequency (e.g., "when" for "week"; "here" for "heel"; "no" for "note"; "why" for "wish"). It may be the case, then, that the dissociation in word-reading in patient J.D. simply reflects a word-frequency effect coupled with limited decoding of the grapheme. Notice, however, that such an explanation will not suffice for the asyntactic patients. It predicts a dissociation in word-reading precisely the reverse of theirs, and it sheds no light on their frequent production of errors semantically, rather than phonologically, related to the target (e.g., "clothes" for "wear"; "bee" for "hive.") But such errors *are* consistent with our earlier suggestion that these patients access the lexical entry directly from the orthography, i.e., without prior phonological encoding. In fact, we can further suggest, in light of these errors, that their output is mediated by the semantic information in the lexical entry.§§

Does this strategy also explain their difficulty with function words? It does if the lexical entry of function words cannot be accessed directly, in the manner of content words. If so, it supports our contention, made earlier in the case of S. B., that the organization of the lexicon reflects syntactic function. This possibility was further explored in reading studies with the asyntactic patients, V.S. and H.T.

Aware that our previous function-content dichotomy grouped together highly disparate elements,[29] we prepared a large battery of reading materials designed to delimit the boundaries of the dissociation. The following facts emerged.

1. All function words are difficult for these patients, but not to the same degree. Personal pronouns (regardless of case), relative pronouns, and prepositions were read at approximately 50% accuracy by both patients. Articles, conjunctions, and particles, however, were more difficult, resulting in 80–100% errors.

2. A majority of the errors with pronouns involved the substitution of other pronouns. These substitutions were typically unrelated to the target in number, gender, or case, but it was possible to demonstrate that at least some of this information was available to the patients by having them indicate to whom the word referred. Thus, in a typical instance, the patient read "me" as "him" while pointing to himself. It appears from this that not all the information that can be extracted from the grapheme is reflected in phonological output.

3. In a more detailed look at the reading of content words we found that both patients had far more difficulty with verbs than with nouns, but much of this added difficulty reflected a problem with inflection. Thus a majority of their errors in verb-reading were instances in which they read the verb stem correctly but substituted an incorrect ending. Patient H.T. was particularly interesting in this regard. His reading of verbs invariably took one of two forms; whenever there existed a nominal form for the verb, he read that form (i.e., "love" for "loving"; "smile" for "smiled"; "dance" for "dances"). Otherwise he read all verbs in their progressive aspect (or as gerunds ¶¶) (e.g., "sitting" for "sits"; "eating" for "eats"; "wanting" for "wanted"). V.S. exhibited a similar tendency to produce the gerundive.

---

§§ We use the term "lexical entries" to describe, in shorthand fashion, the wealth of information about words available to the speaker of the language. We think of each lexical entry as representing the convergence of information about what a word means, how it is used, and how it sounds. But, we make no commitment to the form this information takes, i.e., whether it is specified abstractly, as a list features, or more concretely, in terms of sensorimotor and acoustic images.

¶¶ It seems likely that this overuse of the -ing form in both reading and spontaneous speech represents a further example of the bias toward naming, here, by use of the gerund, or nominal form of the verb. Goodglass has made the same point.[10]

4. These patients have great difficulty specifying number by means of the plural inflection (or lack of it) of noun forms. In general, the pattern of their errors is idiosyncratic, with approximately 40% of plurals read as singular forms, and a similar percentage of singulars read as plurals; a given plural might on one occasion be read as singular, on another as plural. The fact that these patients would often spontaneously indicate correct number by holding up one or two fingers, even when simultaneously producing the incorrect inflection, indicated to us once again that these patients know more about the target than is evident in their spoken output.

We attempted to determine whether failure to pluralize appropriately was related to articulatory difficulties involving the /z/ inflection or to its linguistic function as a marker of number. We composed a list of ten nouns that are comparable in form to regular plurals but which, by convention, have no singular nominal form (e.g., trousers, clothes, news, suds). We compared the reading of these words to regular plural nouns of comparable frequency and phonological structure (e.g., misers, mouths, clues, buds). The results were quite dramatic: both H.T. and V.S. made only one error on the list of irregular words that end in /z/, and those errors did not reflect omission of the final /z/; on the control list, however, they made a total of 11 errors, of which 6 were omissions of the plural inflection. Thus the patients' inconsistent specification of number in the reading of nouns is not due to a failure to attend to this feature of the grapheme, or to the inability to articulate final /z/. Instead, it is a problem with the phonological specification of number.

5. The difficulty in specifying such features as number, tense, and aspect is not found with irregular forms. Both irregular plural nouns and verbs with irregular past tense forms are read several orders of magnitude better than their regular counterparts. The problem relates, then, to the specification of such features by means of phonological rules.

6. An additional datum of interest: It was mentioned above that the asyntactic patients show a strong tendency to read inflected verbs as either nominal forms of those verbs or in the gerundive. This tendency parallels their spontaneous production and suggests again that their output is strongly biased toward the function of naming. (See also Refs. 18, 25, and 30.)

We therefore hypothesized that identical graphemes would be read more successfully in a nominal than in a verbal context. To test this hypothesis, we gave the patients 60 sentences of the following kind:

The baby is *sleeping*. vs. *Sleeping* is good for babies.
They were *fighting* yesterday. vs. Please stop the *fighting*.
The bird will *fly* away. vs. The *fly* buzzed in my ear.
They *fight* at school. vs. There was a *fight* at school.

The patients were asked to read the sentence to themselves and then to read aloud the underlined word. Both patients made twice as many errors on targets used in verbal context compared with the same targets used in a nominal context. This result confirms our view that the phonological output in these patients is particularly well-suited to the function of naming.

Let us summarize what we know about reading in these patients:

1. Phonology is not extracted directly from the orthography, but is instead mediated by lexical entry.
2. Patients appear to know much more about the target word than they are able to express in phonological output.
3. Function words are read very poorly.
4. Nouns, and verbs in a nominal context, are read very well.
5. Content words are not appropriately inflected for such features as number, tense, and aspect.

Given these facts, we propose the following hypothesis: (1) that at least for the purpose of speech production, the lexicon is organized on the basis of linguistic functions, among which are (a) naming or making reference, and (b) the expression of relations, propositions, et cetera, via syntax; (2) that entries which serve the latter function exclusively (i.e., function words or grammatical morphemes) are closely tied to the syntactic machinery*** and are expressed only through its operation. Other lexical entries are less closely related to the syntactic machinery and, given certain referential contexts, can be expressed directly. Output via this pathway will not be appropriately inflected for such features as tense and number, since these require phonological specification by the syntax.

The first part of this hypothesis, which postulates two distinct subsystems of language, receives impressive support from a series of studies on first language acquisition. Nelson [31] has uncovered interesting individual differences in children at the same level of mean length utterance (MLU); some children (termed *referential*, by her) have extensive naming vocabularies but make little syntactic use of this lexicon; others (termed *expressive*) show a more syntactic usage of a smaller vocabulary. The aphasic data suggest that these developmental patterns may reflect different rates of maturation of two neurologically distinct systems.

The second part of the hypothesis states that lexical entries differ in the degree to which their phonological expression is determined by syntactic operations, and that the lexical structure reflects these differences. This formulation is not inconsistent with the descriptive framework provided by standard transformational grammar. Chomsky, [32] for example, has differentiated between "lexical" and "non-lexical" or "grammatical" formatives, the latter probably corresponding to our syntax-bound morphemes. Jacobs and Rosenbaum [33] account for the dependence of certain phonological features on syntactic operation by positioning two lexical passes, one before, and one after, the application of all transformations. Postal [34] describes a direct phonetic-semantic coupling for lexical entries and suggests that these *inherent phonological properties* (his stress) are operated upon by the phonological component of the syntax to specify aspects of pronounciation such as stress, intonation, and inflection. We assume that in a holophrastic, referential context, these phonological operations may be bypassed.

Consistent with this hypothesis, we propose that the reading impairment in our asyntactic patients reflects the following factors: (1) an inability to specify phonology directly from the orthography, which precludes "sounding out" the written word; (2) the availability of an alternative strategy for reading, namely, accessing the lexical entry directly from the orthography; (3) the impairment of syntax and, along with it, the relative inaccessibility of the phonological elements which it specifies and the lexical entries most closely associated with its functioning.

According to the hypothesis presented above, the dissociation data reveal a lexical organization based upon linguistic function. But the fact that the lexicon can be described in functional terms does not guarantee that this is in reality its defining dimension. Consider, as an alternative possibility, that the lexicon is organized with regard to the representational derivation of its entries; that is, the degree to which their meaning can be specified by sensorimotor images and contextual memories and associations. This organizing principle, too, would account for our dissociation data; it would polarize concrete nouns and verbs, on the one hand, and abstract words, including function words, on the other.

*** We are using the term "syntactic machinery" to refer to whatever algorithmic operations contribute to the generation and comprehension of well-formed sentences of English. These may be conceived of as related to the transformational operations described by linguists, but we must keep in mind that evidence for the psychological validity of these operations is scanty. [1]

There is evidence that patients who have difficulty reading function words also have difficulty with abstract nouns,[18,35,36] and we have found supporting evidence in our asyntactic patients as well. Furthermore, the responses of our patients to abstract targets frequently suggested mediation by imagery. For example, in reading the word "success," patient V.S. said "son . . . college . . . doctor . . . ," raising her hand to indicate successive levels of achievement.

But the fact that abstract nouns are as difficult as function words for our patients is not inconsistent with the "linguistic function" hypothesis. Like function words, abstract nouns rarely occur in a holophrastic context; they generally depend upon a syntactic frame for an elaboration of meaning. Thus performance on abstract words does not differentiate between the two hypotheses presented here. A more adequate test might be provided by fictitious proper names. These words serve the linguistic function of making reference and are frequently used in holophrastic utterances. Thus, according to our "linguistic function" hypothesis, they should be read as well as content words. On the other hand, since they lack concrete referents and cannot be represented in terms of images, associations, and the like, the "representability" hypothesis predicts that they should be as difficult as abstract nouns and function words. We are currently investigating this question.

The hypothesis that lexical organization reflects the concreteness of its entries has certain attractions. It explains the fact that dissociations similar to that described here can be seen in patients whose spontaneous speech does not suggest a syntactic impairment.[36] It may be that the inability to encode phonology directly from the grapheme makes these patients more dependent on other levels of representation; i.e., they "name the image" evoked by the grapheme.[35] Function words should thus be impaired relative to concrete words apart from any syntactic impairment.

Furthermore, the "representability" hypothesis may put us on more secure ground from a biological perspective. The acquisition of concrete meanings may follow a course that is phylogenetically, ontogenetically, and neurologically distinct from abstract meanings, and it would not be surprising to find that lexical organization reflects these differences. Thus, concrete words, but not abstract words, can be learned by the association of symbol and referent, a form of learning of which nonhuman species are also capable. Concrete words are also acquired earlier in development, at which point they may be used holophrastically and in a nonlinguistic sense, as an elaboration by the child of his contact with the environmet.[29] Finally, as meanings that can take a variety of sensory forms, they might have a more redundant representation in the brain and therefore be less vulnerable to brain damage. Gardner[38] has invoked this redundancy factor to account for naming performance in children and aphasics.

This "representability" hypothesis, however, does not account so readily for the reciprocal dissociation in the anomic patient S.B. (*Syntax without a Lexicon*), who tended to preserve in her production just those kinds of words that disappear with syntactic impairment: verbs and adjectives (which have been given a verbal derivation in transformational grammer,[33]) along with the various function words. In addition, it sheds no light on the failure of our asyntactic patients to inflect properly in reading tasks, or on their reliance upon a nominal context for reading. These data are more consistent with a lexicon organized with reference to syntactic function.

Thus we are left with a number of open questions. But we believe that we have demonstrated the feasibility of answering these questions through the study of aphasia. We maintain that dissociations in language behavior of the magnitude we have described can be seen only in cases of language pathology, and that the existence of these dissociations justifies the study of such cases, with an eye toward implications for normal language function.

ACKNOWLEDGMENTS

We thank Arna Rubman, Rose Calini, and Clara Marin for their help in the preparation of this manuscript.

REFERENCES

1. FODOR, J. A., T. G. BEVER AND M. F. GARRETT. 1974. The Psychology of Language. McGraw-Hill. New York, N.Y.
2. MATURANA, H. 1970. Biology of Cognition. Report #9.0. Biological Computer Laboratory. Dep. Electrical Engineering. University of Illinois at Urbana-Champaign. Urbana, Ill.
3. LASHLEY, K. 1929. Brain Mechanisms and Intelligence. University of Chicago Press. Chicago, Ill.
4. LURIA, A. R. 1966. Higher Cortical Functions in Man. Tavistock. London, England.
5. ROSNER, B. S. 1974. Recovery of function and localization of function in historical perspective. *In* Plasticity and Recovery of Function in the Central Nervous System. D. G. Stein, J. J. Rosen and N. Butters, Eds. Academic Press. New York, N.Y.
6. LeVERE, T. E. 1975. Neural stability, sparing and behavioral recovery following brain damage. Psychol. Rev. **82:** 344–358.
7. SAFFRAN, E. M., M. F. SCHWARTZ & O. S. M. MARIN. 1976. Semantic mechanisms in paralexia. Brain and Language 3: 255–265.
8. JACKSON, J. H. 1884. Croonian lectures on evolution and dissolution of the nervous system. *In* Selected Papers. Vol. 2. Basic Books. New York, N.Y.
9. SAFFRAN, E. M., O. S. M. MARIN & G. H. YENI-KOMSHIAN. 1976. An analysis of speech perception in word deafness. Brain and Language 3: 209–228.
10. GOODGLASS, H. 1968. Studies on the grammar of aphasics. *In* Developments in Applied Psycholinguistics Research. S. Rosenberg, and J. H. Koplin, Eds. MacMillan. New York, N.Y.
11. BLUMSTEIN, S. 1973. Some phonological implications of aphasic speech. *In* Psycholinguistics and Aphasia. H. Goodglass and S. Blumstein, Eds. Johns Hopkins Univ. Baltimore, Md.
12. KUHN, T. S. 1970. The Structure of Scientific Revolutions. University of Chicago Press. Chicago, Ill.
13. SAFFRAN, E. M. & O. S. M. MARIN. 1975. Immediate memory for word lists and sentences in a patient with deficient auditory short-term memory. Brain and Language 2: 420–433.
14. BEVER, T. G. 1970. The cognitive basis for linguistic structures. *In* Cognition and the Development of Language. J. R. Hayes, Ed. John Wiley & Sons. New York, N.Y.
15. WARRINGTON, E. K., V. LOGUE, & R. T. C. PRATT. 1971. The anatomical localization of selective impairment of auditory short-term memory. Neuropsychologia **9:** 377–387.
16. LEVIN, H. & J. WILLIAMS. 1970. Basic Studies in Reading. Basic Books. New York, N.Y.
17. KAVANAUGH, J. F. & I. G. MATTINGLY. 1972. Language by Ear and by Eye. M.I.T. Press. Cambridge, Mass.
18. MARSHALL, J. & F. NEWCOMBE. 1973. Patterns of paralexia: a psycholinguistic approach. J. Psycholinguistic Res. 2: 175–199.
19. SAFFRAN, E. M. & O. S. M. MARIN. Reading without phonology: evidence from aphasia. Quart. J. Exp. Psychol. In press.
20. McCLELLAND, J. & J. JOHNSTON. 1975. Familiar units and orthographic structure in the word-letter phenomenon. In preparation.
21. KOLERS, P. A. 1970. Three stages of reading. *In* Basic Studies in Reading. H. Levin & J. Williams, Eds. Basic Books. New York, N.Y.
22. LaBERGE, D. 1972. Beyond auditory coding. *In* Language by Ear and by Eye. J. F. Kavanaugh and I. G. Mattingly, Eds. M.I.T. Press. Cambridge, Mass.
23. JAKOBSON, R. 1971. Linguistic types of aphasia. *In* Roman Jakobson, Selected Writings II. Mouton. The Hague, The Netherlands.

24. WELLS, F. L. & J. REUSCH. 1945. Mental Examiner's Handbook. The Psychological Corporation. New York, N.Y.
25. MYERSON, R. & H. GOODGLASS. 1972. Transformational grammar of three agrammatic patients. Lang. Speech 15: 40–50.
26. GESCHWIND, N. 1967. The varieties of naming errors. Cortex: 3: 97–112.
27. WEPMAN, J. M., R. D. BOCK, L. V. JONES & D. VANPELT. 1956. Psycholinguistic studies of aphasia: a revision of the concept of anomia. J. Speech Hearing Disord. 21: 468–477.
28. ZURIF, E., A. CARAMAZZA & R. MYERSON. 1972. Grammatical judgments of agrammatic aphasics. Neuropsychologia 10: 405–419.
29. BROWN, R. 1973. A First Language: The Early Stages. Harvard Univ. Press. Cambridge, Mass.
30. WHITAKER, H. A. 1972. Unsolicited nominalizations by aphasics: the plausibility of the lexicalist model. Linguistics, 78: 62–71.
31. NELSON, K. 1975. Individual differences in early semantic and syntactic development. Ann. N.Y. Acad. Sci. 263: 132–139.
32. CHOMSKY, N. 1965. Aspects of the Theory of Syntax. Harvard Univ. Press. Cambridge, Mass.
33. JACOBS, R. A. & P. S. ROSENBAUM. 1968. English Transformational Grammar. Ginn. Waltham, Mass.
34. POSTAL, P. 1968. Epilogue. In English Transformational Grammar. A. A. Jacobs and P. S. Rosenbaum, Eds. Ginn. Waltham, Mass.
35. RICHARDSON, J. R. E. 1975. The effect of word imageability in acquired dyslexia. Neuropsychologia 113: 288–291.
36. SHALLICE, T. & E. K. WARRINGTON, 1975. Word recognition in a phonemic dyslexic patient. Quart. J. Exp. Psychol. 27: 187–200.
37. GARDNER, H. 1974. The naming of objects and symbols by children and aphasic patients. J. Psycholinguistic Res. 3: 133–149.
38. GLANZER, M. 1972. Storage mechanisms in recall. In The Psychology of Learning and Motivation. G. H. Bower, Ed. Academic Press. New York, N.Y.
39. WARRINGTON, E. & T. SHALLICE. 1969. The selective impairment of auditory verbal short-term memory. Brain 92: 885–896.

STRATEGIES OF MASTERING A VISUAL
COMMUNICATION SYSTEM IN APHASIA*

Lynn Davis and Howard Gardner†

Aphasia Research Center
Boston University School of Medicine,
Boston Veterans Administration Hospital
Boston, Massachusetts 02130
† Harvard Project Zero
Cambridge, Massachusetts 02138

INTRODUCTION

The recent devising of a new form of aphasia therapy has provided an opportunity to investigate the ability of the severely aphasic patient to communicate in other than his natural language. In this therapeutic innovation called VIC (for *VIsual Communication*), messages are written on index cards which are laid down from left to right. The patient initially observes others as they communicate with the system; eventually he is drawn into the interchanges, first as a "comprehender," later as a "producer" of messages. Goals of the VIC program, methods of instruction employed in daily therapy sessions, and the degree to which patients have demonstrated success in mastering the system have been detailed elsewhere (e.g. Refs. 1–3). A few points about VIC should nonetheless be noted here.

First of all, two levels of language use are entailed in the system. At Level 1, three communicative functions are taught in the following order: 1) carrying out commands; 2) answering questions; 3) describing events. For patients who master these tasks, Level 2 training explores their ability to express feelings and immediate needs via this alternative mode of communication. The degree of success achieved by patients has been documented both in quantitative terms[3] and by means of case studies.[3,4] Finally, in what follows, the various ideographic and arbitrary geometric designs which refer in VIC to particular objects and elements have been termed *symbols*; as symbols, they carry the *semantic* or *referential* portions of the VIC system. The formal relations that obtain among these symbols when they are organized into messages have been considered the *syntax* of VIC.

Given that patients can master one or both of the levels of VIC, and that the system has a place in rehabilitation, questions of fundamental theoretical importance remain. To begin with, just what are the patients learning: an elaborate game (cf. Brown,[5] Lenneberg,[6]), a genuine language-like communicative system, or perhaps some hybrid? And relatedly, by what means do those successful with VIC acquire its basic components:[6] by sudden insights, trial-and-error, or a gradual series of steps? By examining the ways in which principal features of VIC are acquired, insight can be gained into the function served by the system, patients' grasp of the essential features of the system, and the relationship between VIC and other systems of communication employed by primates, infrahuman as well as human.

*The research reported herein was supported in part by grant NS 11408-02 from the National Institute of Neurological Diseases and Stroke.

Given our interest in communication within a language framework, we shall deal with the questions posed above by focusing on the acquisition of four constructions generally deemed central to language. In doing so, we shall use a vocabulary and a framework drawn from work on semantic relations.[7,8] This approach has become regarded increasingly as a useful way of describing adult language and, in recent years, has been applied as well to early language use by young children.[5] By tracing through the events that mark the acquisition by aphasics of these semantic relations, we expect to gain insights about the general processes involved in acquiring a new symbol system, as well as the particular demands and problems posed by specific semantic relations.

It must be noted that, in describing various configurations of VIC as semantic relations, we are making an assumption about the functions assumed by particular symbols. It may well be that patients can utilize the system without possessing a genuine grasp of the relevant semantic relations. However, for the purposes of exposition, and with the understanding that we are propounding a testable hypothesis, we shall continue to refer in what follows to four basic semantic relations.

The following VIC utterance illustrates the semantic relations to be discussed here:

John put pencil in glass and give comb (to) Brian.

The *agent-action relation* obtains between the symbols for "John" and "put," as well as the symbols for "John" and "give." The *action-object relation* obtains between the symbols for "put" and "pencil," and the symbols for "give" and "comb." The *action-location relation* obtains between the symbols for "put" and "glass." The *action-beneficiary relation* obtains between the symbols for "give" and "Brian." Patients who master these semantic relations and can employ them flexibly and productively may be said to use VIC as an effective means of communication. Because of our interest in detailing the processes of VIC acquisition, we will focus in this account on patients who did not initially apprehend the system but who eventually came to master the system in an apparently appropriate manner.

To determine the manner in which VIC patients come to appreciate these semantic relations, a simple recording of number of correct and incorrect responses is clearly insufficient. Accordingly, protocols describing each VIC session include detailed descriptions of strategies by which patients arrive at various responses, types of errors committed, and reactions by patients to negative feedback. Such descriptions constitute the principal source on which patient mastery of the various semantic relations is assessed.

PLAN OF PAPER

In the following sections we first examine some general patterns of symbolic mastery observed in a variety of patients and then focus on the course of mastery of each of the four semantic relations. Whenever a particularly revealing strategy demonstrated by a single patient is described, his initials will be noted; otherwise, descriptions pertain to progress or regression typifying a majority of VIC learners. A general discussion section will review the findings as they bear upon the question of whether the system is being utilized as a legitimate vehicle of communication. Throughout the paper, and particularly in the final sections, a comparative perspective vis-à-vis two other groups learning first symbol systems will be maintained.

Literature describing early language use by normal and abnormal children and the recent developments in teaching of symbol systems to infrahuman primates will be considered. By means of this discussion, the central issue of whether the various populations are learning a language or a game will once again be confronted.

GENERAL BEHAVIORAL STRATEGIES

The patient entering the VIC program brings with him—and employs—a raft of earlier schemes, or behavioral patterns, for dealing with new situations. His attention in initial encounters with the system is focused on *random exploration of cards and objects*, with little or no evidence exhibited for appreciation of the cards' potential value as symbols. Cards and objects are manipulated indiscriminately; cards placed on top of, underneath, next to, or inside various objects may or may not depict those objects.

In these early encounters with VIC, the patient bears a certain resemblance to the young child in the latter half of the sensorimotor stage of cognitive development (cf. Piaget[9]). Certainly, knowledge of the substantiality of objects independent of his own experience is an integral part of the patient's schemes for dealing with VIC. Yet, unaware of the cards' symbolic value, the patient displays no need to "make sense" of the cards. More generally, the patient exhibits a lack of differentiation among the major components of symbolic communication: the addresser, the addressee, the vehicle (or symbol), and the referent (or object to which it refers).[10]

Following a period in which he observes accomplished VIC users employing the system, the patient is gradually drawn into the "conversation." Paralleling Piaget's description of early symbol use by the child, the patient's first attempts to find meaning in the cards are typically demonstrated through *use of gestures*. Presentation of the "comb" symbol card may be met by a combing gesture over the head, the "pencil" symbol card by a writing gesture, and so on.

As the patient becomes more experienced in the use of VIC cards as symbols, the initially observed gestures tend to drop out of his response pattern. Even at this point, however, the patient exhibits an *incapacity to differentiate between the cards as objects and the cards as symbols*. Instructed to "pick up the comb," he may instead pick up the "comb" symbol card used in the utterance, and thereafter continue to make errors of this type, even though each error is corrected immediately and the appropriate response demonstrated. As the patient acquires more experience with the system, however, confusion of card and object also tends to drop out of his response pattern.

Concomitant with, and facilitated by, gradual *appreciation of the object cards as distinct from their symbolic function*, the patient comes to accept the potential symbolic value of the other cards to which he is exposed. Indeed, he comes to expect that each card has its own symbolic function; when confused about the "meaning" of a particular card, he may point to it and, via gesture, facial expression, or stereotyped speech (e.g. "I don't know"), designate it as the source of his confusion.

Eventually the patient's appreciation of the symbolic function of VIC cards reaches a level of sophistication at which he appreciates, and can use as such, the symbol cards as members of "VIC form classes" (i.e., names, verbs, objects, and grammatical morphemes—conjunction and prepositions). As noted in Gardner *et al.*,[3] the bulk of errors committed by patients in the production of VIC utterances is of the "same category" type—i.e., the patient substitutes for the correct symbol another member of the same form class (e.g., verb A for verb B). "Different category" errors (such as use of a verb symbol where a name or object symbol is required) constitute across patients only about 3% of the total number of errors committed. Errors committed in the execution of commands also consist of confusing one verb for another, one object for another, and so on; however, the demand characteristics of the situation—i.e., "do something"—make this necessarily the case and therefore of limited interest.

Further support for *appreciation of form classes* is found in the skill of successful VIC patients in sorting systematically their own sets of cards into piles that define the various form classes. In addition, a number of instances have been noted in which patients, having observed the use in commands of new VIC symbols (e.g., name cards for communicators new to the VIC sessions; verb and preposition cards seen for the first time), place the cards without hesitation in the appropriate form class piles.

This level of sophistication precedes the final step necessary for successful VIC mastery—*appreciation of the formal relations obtaining among symbols* when they are organized into meaningful utterances. Required here is the capacity to perform certain computations or procedures of the sort specifically entailed in natural language—e.g., attending to syntax, or word order, so as to apprehend the various grammatical and semantic relations between the verb and the accompanying nouns in a given utterance. Put differently, given that the patient can respond to and utilize the referential function of individual symbols, successful VIC mastery requires, in addition, appreciation of the predicative function of utterances comprised of these symbols—i.e., the use of VIC utterances not only to refer to various elements (topic) but to make certain statements (comment) about those elements (cf. de Laguna[11]).

The foregoing discussion has outlined a typical pattern of strategies as it emerges during the course of VIC mastery. It is not the case, however, that a strategy makes an appearance at an appointed time and then is replaced smoothly and permanently by a more sophisticated pattern of behavior. Rather, exemplifying a well-documented pattern among brain-damaged patients,[12] VIC acquisition is marked by repeated regressions to earlier and more primitive modes of dealing with the system. Particularly when a new and more complex utterance or utterance type is introduced, patients may fall back on earlier strategies, sometimes indeed acting as if they had completely forgotten their most recent level of understanding. Evidence of general progress in VIC does come, however, from the observation that patients who have mastered a substantial portion of the system are more likely to regress to a fairly sophisticated level of mastery than to one of the earlier and more primitive modes of response.

Having reviewed some of the general response patterns which characterize VIC users as they attain the basic levels of the system, we move now to a discussion of strategies employed by patients in coming to grips with the predicative function of the various semantic relations expressed in VIC.

STRATEGIES ASSOCIATED WITH SPECIFIC SEMANTIC RELATIONS

The Action-Object Relation

The early stages of VIC acquisition consist for the most part of readily discernible actions that require gross manipulations of a specific set of familiar objects. As such, the action-object relation receives first and primary focus and continues thereafter to be of crucial importance in successful mastery of the system. The patient John confronted with the command "John pick-up spoon" must appreciate not only the symbolic function of the action and object cards, but the relation between the two—i.e., that the object referred to is to undergo a change of state *as a result* of the action referred to.

Typically, early patient strategies exhibit a tendency to respond to each card separately. Instructed to "pick-up the spoon," the patient locates the spoon, places it below its symbol card, and then raises his empty hand over his head. The symbolic function of each card is appreciated; the predicative function of the formal relation between them is not. The patient successfully interprets each "topic" referred to in the utterance; however, he demonstrates little or no awareness of the "comment" realized in the utterance by virtue of the relations among the elements contained therein.

Patients often display a rather obvious and instructive strategy that proves unique to the mastery of this and, later, the action-location relations. Requested to pick up the spoon, the patient locates the spoon, places it below its symbol card, looks to the verb card, and *then* picks up the spoon. Unlike the earlier strategy of locating the spoon and raising an empty hand, this strategy demonstrates that the patient has now successfully processed the comment as well—and in fact does so in an orderly fashion. However, he remains unable to combine topic and comment in a single seamless action; he must still execute the command in steps.

Eventually, this "two-step" execution of the command tends to be replaced by a single smooth execution. However, the less advanced strategy may reappear when a new construction is introduced. For example, the patient may return briefly to the strategy of responding to each symbol card separately, as did one patient (J.S.) when first confronted with the newly demonstrated command "give fork (to) Brian" (a third party in the room). After locating the fork and placing it beneath its symbol-card, J.S. then swept his empty hand over the table and into the hand of a rather startled Brian. Other analogous regressions may also occur. However, the incidence of errors due to generalized regression tends to decrease as the patient becomes more familiar with the system, much as the child learning to ride a bicycle falls off less frequently, even though he may be mastering more difficult riding techniques.

The Agent-Action Relation

The patient's initial encounter with VIC includes assignment of an arbitrary design representing his VIC "name" and parallel exposure to the names of other VIC communicators. Unlike the young child, for whom a confusion among proper names is common,[13] the patient generally experiences little difficulty in appreciating the symbolic function of these cards. Further, the patient generally learns quickly that the name symbol card appearing at the beginning of a command utterance designates the person who is to perform the indicated action, and attains a high degree of success in responding only to those commands directed to him. Inappropriate responses (e.g., patient executes a command directed to another VIC communicator) are easily corrected by pointing out the name symbol card at the beginning of the utterance, and indeed, often corrected by the patient himself before he has completed the indicated action.

In the face of what might appear to be almost immediate appreciation of the agent-action relation, the following question arises: Does the ability to respond only to those commands with the patient's name symbol card at the beginning of the utterance necessarily indicate appreciation of the agent-action relation? That is, can one infer appreciation of the predicative function of the formal relation as one that implies, in the notion of agent, a motivating force that causes or instigates the action? Clearly, the patient could respond in the appropriate manner by responding to the symbolic function of the name and verb cards separately, perhaps even perceiving the name card to be a sort of attention-getting signal on the order of "You! Pick up the spoon."

A firmer index of the patient's mastery is provided by his performance when instructed to describe an action by another VIC communicator, or to answer a question about a similar event (e.g., "Who is-picking-up the-spoon?"). Most patients succeed at these tasks; moreover, use of the wrong name symbol card in describing an action by another VIC communicator is easily corrected by simply pointing out the name tag of the person executing the action indicated in the utterance.

One patient (G.S.), however, experienced continuing difficulty in determining the correct name symbol card to use in describing an event that had just occurred in his view. With apparently no insight into what was expected, he would place at the beginning of an otherwise correct utterance an incorrect name symbol card—for example, one referring to a VIC communicator in the room who had not committed the action in question or sometimes even to himself or a VIC communicator who was not present at the time. When corrected, he would shrug his shoulders and point to the other people present, to himself, or to an empty chair that had been occupied previously by another person. To be sure, he could respond appropriately to commands directed to him and could match as many as five name symbol cards with their appropriate referents, even when these referents were not wearing their name tags. However, his difficulty in determining the agent of a particular action and expressing it in an utterance of his own persisted, suggesting a fundamental difficulty in either his concept of agency, *per se*, or his ability to capture this concept in symbolic form.

The Action-Beneficiary Relation

More complex constructions of the type "John give spoon (to) Brian" are not introduced until the patient has demonstrated mastery of the relations described above. As a result, and perhaps due also to the fact that the concept of "beneficiary" is an integral part of the action "to give," several examples of such commands, directed to another VIC communicator, generally suffice to convey to the patient the expected response—that of giving the object or objects denoted to another VIC communicator.

An utterance of this type contains two name symbol cards that relate by virtue of their respective positions in different ways to the action symbol card. Accordingly, it is incumbent upon the patient to rely on syntax, or word order, to determine the predicative function of the various relations that comprise the utterance as a whole. In this respect, the action-beneficiary relation proves more demanding than the two discussed above.

Early difficulty in dealing with such a condition is of a specific and not unexpected variety; that is, the patient responds to commands directing another VIC communicator to give an object to the patient by locating the object himself and giving it to the person to whom the command was directed. Thus, rather than failing to appreciate the action-beneficiary relation, the patient is unable to use the respective positions of the name symbol cards to determine which is the agent of the action and which the beneficiary. It might be said that confusion of this sort exemplifies the generalized regression described above—i.e., introduction of a new construction undermines previously indicated mastery of an old construction.

In most cases, appropriate response to the previously mastered construction (agent-action) recovers quickly and in fact proves instrumental in solidifying success with the action-beneficiary relation. The patient demonstrates this success by giving an object to the indicated person when directed to do so and by waiting, sometimes impatiently with his hand outstretched, when another VIC communicator is directed to give an object to him. One patient (J.S.), in an apparently inadvertent but instructive error, exemplified his use of word order to determine the beneficiary of the action "to give." Responding to a command directing another VIC communicator to give an object to him, he located the object himself, looked to see which name symbol card was at the end of the utterance, and attempted—by passing the object from his left hand to his right hand and then holding it against his chest—to "give" the object to himself.

The patient's use of word order in mastering the action-beneficiary might be challenged, inasmuch as the utterances directed toward the patient are semantically constrained. That is, shown the cards "spoon" and "Brian," the patient naturally hands the spoon to Brian, rather than attempting to hand Brian to the spoon. Firmer determination of such mastery can be forthcoming if other verbs entailing a beneficiary relation are used, or utterances in which the object and beneficiary might be interchanged—e.g., "Give the baby dog to Raggedy Ann." We have not yet had the opportunity to attempt such modifications.

The Action-Location Relation

Constructions of the type "John put spoon in glass" and "John put spoon in box" are similar in two ways to the action-beneficiary constructions. First, they are not introduced until the patient has demonstrated sufficient mastery of the action-object and agent-action relations and, indeed, has come to expect the predicative function of VIC utterances. Second, attention to syntax is necessary for a determination of which of the two objects referred to in the utterance is the location of the indicated action. However, correct performance may sometimes come about as a result of the cards considered independent of word order. This is because the compelling concavity of the glass and the box allows the patient to rely on the identifying features of the objects rather than the positions of their respective symbol cards to determine the appropriate response. Whether this strategy is in fact being utilized can be tested in various ways.

First, the patient may be directed to place the glass inside the box, or the box inside the glass. Because either object can serve as the container for the other, the appropriate response to each command must be based on the word order of that particular utterance. Second, prepositions other than "in" may be introduced. Correct response to commands that direct the placement of one object on top of, to the left or right of, and in front of or behind, another object also requires that syntax be used to determine which object is the location.

In dealing with the various commands just described, the patient typically evolves a strategy that indicates his awareness that word order signifies which VIC object is to be considered the location. First, reminiscent of an earlier strategy successful in dealing with the action-object relation, the patient locates all objects indicated in the utterance and places them below their respective symbol cards. He then "fixes" the object referred to last—i.e., to the right of the preposition—by holding it firmly on the table below its symbol card, and then places the other object in relation to it as indicated by the action and preposition cards. Thus, directed to place the fork to the right of the spoon, the patient first fixes the spoon beneath its symbol card and then places the fork to the right of it. Response to this particular command proves an especially telling indication of the patient's strategy because the correct response requires placement of the indicated objects in a left-right orientation opposite to that occupied by their symbol cards in the utterance. In watching a patient go through such a sequence, one cannot help feeling that one is watching—in externalized form—the kinds of mechanisms that underlie comprehension of all sorts of symbolic messages (cf. Vygotsky[14]).

DISCUSSION

What Has Been Learned in VIC

The strategies utilized in the patient's attempts to deal with the specific semantic relations described above present a relatively consistent picture of how the predicative function of semantic relations in general are dealt with, differing primarily to the extent that a two-step treatment of the symbols that comprise each relation precedes a smooth, seemingly automatic response to the relation as a whole. Ranging from an obvious demonstration of the two-step treatment of the action-object relation to a simple noting of name symbol cards before responding to an utterance that includes the action-beneficiary relation, patient strategies indicate that mastery of each relation evolves gradually.

That this course of mastery reflects many of the general properties of learning— e.g., error rates go down as patients acquire familiarity with the system; regressions occur; isolated acts eventually become combined—is not surprising. At issue, however, is the *nature* of that learning. Is the successful VIC patient fully aware of the communicative impact of the symbol cards when organized into messages, or is he responding to them, albeit in an apparently appropriate fashion, simply on the basis of such correlated but communicatively irrelevant conditions as length of utterance, presence or absence of the "box" or "glass" symbol card, and so on?

One might sketch out three possible levels of understanding of VIC. One extreme is represented by the view that VIC is simply a card game. A patient of this persuasion would simply learn which cards should be laid out, or which responses made, when the therapist has laid out certain other cards. While some patients have indeed regarded VIC in this manner, they cannot have passed through the steps outlined here, for even these steps invariably require at least some attention to elements other than the therapist's cards.

The opposite extreme in understanding would entail a genuine appreciation of VIC as a viable means of communication. Here the patient is aware that the cards can be used to capture his ideas and feelings, and can also be read as indices of the thoughts and intentions of others.

An intermediary degree of understanding is also possible and indeed may characterize some of the patients in the VIC program. Such a patient is aware that the cards relate to events in the external world; and so, in producing and reading VIC messages, the patient carefully correlates the cards with the objects and actions in his view. However, the exercise of VIC ceases for such patients once they have left the VIC session. The possibility that the cards might be used universally as a viable mode of communication is foreign to them.

It is extremely difficult to make a decisive determination about the level of understanding of VIC patients, understanding which indeed may alter or remain in flux over the course of training. Nonetheless, some indices can be noted. In a case of genuine appreciation of VIC's potential for communication, for example, card use by the patient is prompted not only by situations that demand such a response, but by his own needs, wants, fears, and so on. Patients falling into this category would include those who have proceeded to Level 2 of VIC and, in the process, have spontaneously used their cards to request cigarettes and matches when they wanted to smoke, to ask when they would be going home when that was their foremost concern, and so on.

On the other hand, indications of purely game-like strategies are revealed by the following forms of patient behaviors:

1. Slavish matching of *specified* elements in VIC questions (e.g., in answer to the question "Who put what in what?", the "put" and "in" symbol cards are located first and placed directly underneath their niche in the question).

2. Responding to commands by matching them with cards from the patient's own set.

3. Consistent use of the strategy for ordering elements in a "put in" utterance (i.e., the "box" or "glass" symbol card occurs generally in the final position) in the case of utterances where such ordering is irrelevant (e.g., "Brian give comb and glass (to) John").

4. Use of habitual answers to questions without regard for the consequences. For instance, in answer to the question "John want cigarette?," the patient may answer "yes," yet indicate no interest in smoking the cigarette given to him. Or the patient may respond with "John feel happy" to the question "John feel what?," even when he is manifestly in a depressed mood.

5. Persistent inability to place symbol cards in their appropriate form class piles.

6. Excessive and inappropriate reliance on social cues (e.g., facial expression of therapist or other VIC communicators); focusing on the positive or negative feedback rather than other consequences of the responses.

Intermediate between response to VIC as a card game and its use as a genuine means of communication lies a broad, less easily delineated mode of behavior. Clearly, the patient who, upon presentation of the "Write It" card, describes correctly an action carried out before him has sampled the real world in determining his response. His use of VIC cards in this case reveals none of the game-playing strategies described above, relying instead on communicatively relevant conditions particular to the situation. It may, in fact, be the case that the vocabulary available to the patient in Level 1 of VIC leaves little room for a more sophisticated view of the system. Perhaps only in Level 2 can the patient appreciate the possibility of using VIC as an effective and versatile means of communication.

The mark of the successful VIC subject, then, is a full appreciation of the nature of the system. Unlike the normal person, to whom the system can be explained, and unlike the child whose appreciation of language as a means of communication appears to develop gradually and naturally, the patient entering VIC is confronted immediately with a new situation which itself must be decoded—i.e., he must learn how and what to learn in the context defined by the VIC scenario. Learning of this type, variously called set learning, learning to learn,[15] and deuterolearning,[16] must be a totally bootstrap operation for the severely impaired aphasic. Inevitably ignorant at first of VIC's potential value as an alternative to his vitiated language, he is unable even to isolate the "meaning" of a particular symbol or symbols as the source of his confusion. His challenge is to figure out the system on his own through observation of other individuals using VIC, feedback to his own responses, and spontaneous use of the system, as well as whatever additional clues may emerge from this process.

The strategies described above speak to the question of what the successful VIC patient has learned. His ability to learn four basic semantic relations certainly counts as evidence that a certain communicative aspect of the system has been appreciated. Yet, even though the typical patient eventually demonstrates an ability to respond to and utilize these relations, it cannot be categorically stated that he regards particular constructions as *expressive* of those relations. Nevertheless, to the extent that the patient can successfully generalize strategies for particular semantic relations to utterances containing newly introduced name, verb, object, or preposition symbol cards, at least some appreciation of the predicative function of those semantic relations may be assumed.

Regarding this point, it is instructive to note that a patient's performance on the "picture arrangement" subtest of the Wechsler Adult Intelligence Scale, which requires that eight sets of pictures be arranged in such a way that each set depicts a logical sequence of events, has generally proved to be a reliable indicator of the patient's success in VIC. It is tempting to speculate that the patient who is at least able to *think* about sensorimotor patterns as forms of action in the real world, and can demonstrate as much via the sequencing of pictures, is perhaps better equipped to deal with VIC utterances as *expressions* of forms of action realized in the formal relations obtaining among the symbols that comprise those utterances.

Yet, mastery of these semantic relations proves to be only the first in a series of steps necessary in acquiring a fuller appreciation of the system's potential for communication. Of great importance is the ability to respond to interrogative particles in VIC questions (e.g., "who," "what") as requests for specification of constituents, and, further, to specify those constituents even when they are not explicitly asked for, as when the "Write It" card is employed by the therapist. Only as patients have the opportunity to utilize the system to express semantic relations under a variety of conditions can we gain strong evidence that they are appreciating the *full* significance of each particular relation.

At present, VIC contains only a limited number of the grammatical morphemes and sentence types that constitute the later stages of language development in the child. And even this small set of properties that extend beyond the basic semantic relations has been mastered in their entirety by only a few VIC patients. It is therefore premature to speculate about the degree of symbolic complexity and understanding of the system which might eventually be acquired by VIC subjects. Nonetheless, it is interesting to note that, with few exceptions, patients have experienced considerable difficulty in learning the grammatical morphemes in the system: and/or, in/on, in front of/behind, to the left of/to the right of, and verb tenses. There are various possible reasons for these difficulties, some of which may be quite apart from the linguistic facets of these constructions. Yet it is at least tempting to speculate, even as it is consistent with recent findings in aphasiology,[17] that the ability to handle the more purely computational aspects of a symbolic system—be it natural language or VIC—is particularly devastated in the case of a severe aphasia.

COMPARISON WITH OTHER SUBJECTS LEARNING A FIRST SYMBOL SYSTEM

In a way, the young child represents an ideal in the acquisition of a new symbol system because he epitomizes both facets under consideration here: an obvious communicative facility, coupled with eventual mastery of the computational mechanisms that govern symbol use. Within a few years, he evolves from communication which is entirely unmediated (e.g., crying when hungry or uncomfortable), to communication which utilizes a variety of symbol systems.

With respect to language, the normal child acquires early on the operation of matching names and referents and an appreciation of the semantic relations described above, demonstrating these capacities in a proliferation of spontaneous utterances. And in an overwhelming majority of cases, the word order of such utterances parallels adult usage of word order, assuming that the child intends to express the semantic relations suggested by context (cf. Brown[5]). Further, as the child's use of language extends to include modulations of meaning within the simple sentence, various sentence modalities, embedding of one sentence within another, and coordination of simple sentences—the milestones of Brown's Stages II through V—the linguistic abilities reflected in the use of such operations become increasingly complex. In these respects, aphasic patients in the VIC program could do no better than to emulate the child.

Unfortunately, instances of spontaneous VIC use are at a minimum. Whether due to age, personality change, or the effects of cortical damage, aphasic patients characteristically demonstrate little curiosity or interest in the world around them or in communicating via whatever skills remain at their disposal (e.g., simple gesturing). Carried over into the VIC program, insufficient motivation can preclude success at even the simplest level—recognition of VIC cards as symbols. In the absence of spontaneous VIC use by patients who have otherwise demonstrated proficiency with the system, we have in this paper discussed two alternative indices: the patient's capacity and intention to convey various semantic relations in utterances of his own, and the dearth of "different category" and word order errors evidenced in those utterances.

Although even the most successful VIC patient does not use the system as productively or spontaneously as a child language-user, he is at the same time readily distinguished from the autistic child who, if he uses language at all, does so in a ritualistic and generally echolalic fashion. Slavish repetition of utterances like "I am eating my lunch" provides perhaps the purest example of language used solely as a game. It is intriguing that "echolalic" matching in VIC has occurred in only one patient who presented with the syndrome of transcortical (or "echoing") aphasia.

Until recently, the major attempts to teach new symbol systems to infrahuman primates have focused on either communicative facility or mastery of computational skills, the one in the absence of the other. Although the chimpanzee Washoe[18] has demonstrated mastery of over one hundred signs in American Sign Language and uses them spontaneously in various combinations, she apparently has indicated little proclivity to order her utterances in the same way her human teachers do, or to reflect a consistent ordering of her own design. Another chimpanzee, Sarah,[19] on the other hand, in her use of variously shaped and colored tokens, has demonstrated an impressive mastery of certain computational mechanisms entailed in natural language, while evidencing little interest in using her token-language spontaneously.

However, Lana's performance with Yerkish[20] seems relatively unexceptionable. She uses her newly acquired symbol system to ask spontaneously, and often, for food, movies, or whatever, and to comment on various elements of her environment; moreover, she reflects in her utterances a consistent use of word order. Such "invented" requests as "Please machine move into room" and "Please machine tickle Lana," while in one sense inappropriate, offer convincing evidence that she has indeed mastered the semantic relations described above.

To be sure, Yerkish incorporates little that is more complex and demanding than the semantic relations of Stage I, and therefore the extent to which her "final" symbol system will resemble natural language remains to be determined. Nonetheless, in view of the criteria for a communication system cited here, her performance is most noteworthy. Indeed, based on our findings and those of other investigators, it seems that the ideal learning situation may be one that combines a naturalistic setting—in which enjoyment and comfort is dependent upon use of the symbol system—and a relatively operant training procedure that reinforces only those utterances that honor the rules of the system.

CONCLUSION

The success of aphasic patients in mastering Level 1 of VIC, and the various strategies that provide a window onto how and what they have learned, suggest that at least some of the capacities necessary for language use may be spared in brain-damaged individuals, even when language itself is gone. In the course of the program thus far, we have adduced a moderate amount of evidence for communicative facility with the system and mastery of at least some of the computational mechanisms that govern VIC use. The challenge now is to expand the system itself to make it, on the one hand, more relevant to the patient's everyday life and, on the other, capable of carrying greater syntactic complexity.

Toward this end, we are currently exploring a provision for inflecting verbs with respect to tense, an operation that would allow at once for greater flexibility in VIC syntax, as well as communication about people, events, and so on, outside the immediate VIC context. In addition, we are experimenting with the use of "operators," plastic overlays which either modify object symbols (e.g., "large, yellow pencil") or change their semantic roles (e.g., an agent operator converts "letter" to "mailman"; a location operator transforms "football" to "stadium"). Strategies employed by patients in dealing with these and other semiotic functions hold much potential for revealing valuable clues into the aphasic patient's linguistic abilities beyond those indicated by his success with semantic relations. Only then can we better assess the extent to which an artificial symbol system like VIC actually can assume the basic communicative functions of natural language.

Acknowledgments

We are grateful to Errol Baker, Thomasin Berry, Nancy Foldi, Brian Mercer, Amy Veroff, and Edgar Zurif for their assistance with various phases of the therapy program; Dr. D. Frank Benson for his generous support of our effort; Dr. Wesley Woll and Patti Kurtz of the Lemuel Shattuck Hospital in Boston and Dr. Charles Bonner, Lydia Thayer, Jayne Jacobs, and Marilyn Carreiro of Youville Hospital in Cambridge for the use of their facilities and their continuing interest in the program.

References

1. ZURIF, E., H. GARDNER, E. BAKER, T. BERRY & D. BERKEY. 1974. Visual communication therapy. Paper presented to Academy of Aphasia. Warrenton, Va.
2. BAKER, E., H. GARDNER & E. ZURIF. 1975. Sparing of communicative functions in aphasia. In symposium Recovery of Function after Brain Damage. Presented at International Neuropsychol. Soc. Tampa, Fla.
3. GARDNER, H., E. ZURIF, T. BERRY & E. BAKER. 1975. Visual communication in aphasia. Neuropsychologia. In press.
4. BAKER, E., T. BERRY, H. GARDNER, E. ZURIF, L. DAVIS & A. VEROFF. 1975. Can linguistic competence be dissociated from natural language function? Nature [New Biol.] 254: 509–510.
5. BROWN, R. 1973. A First Language: The Early Stages. Harvard University Press. Cambridge, Mass.
6. PLOOG, D. & T. MELNECHUK, Eds. 1971. Are Apes Capable of Language? Neurosciences Res. Prog. Bull. Vol. 9(5).
7. FILLMORE, C. 1968. The case for case. In Universals in Linguistic Theory. E. Bach & R. Harms, Eds. Holt, Rinehart & Winston. New York, N.Y.
8. McCAWLEY, J. 1968. The role of semantics in grammar. In Universals in Linguistic Theory. E. Bach & R. Harms, Eds. Holt, Rinehart & Winston. New York, N.Y.
9. PIAGET, J. 1952. The Origins of Intelligence in Children. International Universities Press. New York, N.Y.

10. WERNER, H. & E. KAPLAN. 1963. Symbol Formation. John Wiley & Sons. New York, N.Y.
11. DE LAGUNA, G. 1927. Speech: Its Function and Development. Yale University Press New Haven, Conn.
12. GOLDSTEIN, K. 1948. Language and Language Disturbances. Grune & Stratton. New York, N.Y.
13. STERN, W. 1924. Psychology of Early Childhood. Henry Holt. New York, N.Y.
14. VYGOTSKY, L. 1965. Thought and Language. MIT Press. Cambridge, Mass.
15. HARLOW, H. 1959. Learning set and factor theory. In Psychology: A Study of a Science. S. Koch, Ed. 2: 492–537. McGraw-Hill. New York, N.Y.
16. BATESON, G. 1972. Steps to an Ecology of Mind. Ballantine Books. New York, N.Y.
17. ZURIF, E. 1975. Semantic and syntactic factors in impaired comprehension. Presented at International Neuropsychological Symposium. Crete.
18. GARDNER, R. & B. GARDNER. 1969. Teaching sign language to a chimpanzee. Science. 165: 664–672.
19. PREMACK, D. 1969. Language in chimpanzee? Science. 172: 808–822.
20. RUMBAUGH, D., E. VON GLASERFELD, H. WARNER, P. PISANI & T. GILL. 1974. Lana (chimpanzee) learning language: a progress report. Brain and Language. 1(No. 2): 205–212.

DISCUSSION

Earl Miner, *Moderator*
Department of Comparative Literature
Princeton University
Princeton, New Jersey 08540

UNIDENTIFIED SPEAKER: My question is for anyone who would like to answer it. From the evidence of the ability of aphasics to learn visual communication systems such as that used by Dr. Gardner or American sign language, what can we infer about differences in brain function with respect to visual vs. vocal auditory language?

DR. HOWARD GARDNER: It seems clear to me on the basis of the work we have done that it no longer makes any sense to assume that any language system *has* to operate in human beings through the auditory/oral channel. Now, in effect we already knew that from the experience of the deaf, but our studies attack this problem in a somewhat different way. We have somebody whose brain *was* normal and who learned language the normal way, so it would have been at least theoretically possible that by the time people were fifty or sixty (which is when they usually have a stroke) everything had somehow irrevocably migrated to a vocal-auditory area of the brain and there would be no other chance for the person ever to communicate again. I think our studies have certainly shown that that is not true, in a strict sense.

On the other hand, I wouldn't want anyone to leave thinking that we have patients who are writing periodic sentences or reading Plato. It is very, very primitive, even in relation to the sort of things going on with the chimpanzees. So if you have a normal brain and it's lesioned at age fifty or sixty, it is still very difficult for you to acquire a communication system like the one that we have developed.

UNIDENTIFIED SPEAKER: Do you feel that there are different areas in the brain responsible for visual vs. vocal communication, or that this cannot be determined?

DR. GARDNER: It would be nice to know what areas of the brain our patients are using, since we know from radiological studies that they are not using the areas that Dr. Bogen was sketching on the board. That means that it is very likely they are using certain portions of the right hemisphere; there is certainly massive evidence that visual-spatial processing is exactly what the right hemisphere does. This is why we designed the system on that basis, rather than on other ones that would have been theoretically possible.

UNIDENTIFIED SPEAKER: Dr. Gardner, it seems to be characteristic of primates that they generally *like* to be able to communicate. I just wondered if these people seem to enjoy using this system?

DR. GARDNER: That's a very good question. Our training atmosphere is entirely different from what I infer to be the atmosphere of the primate studies. That is, I think the idea there has been to completely immerse the subject in the new symbol system that he is learning. I gather that *Washoe* is being "signed" to around the clock, and so on. For ethical as well as for practical reasons we cannot devise a total VIC environment. I would say that our patients are generally happy with VIC even though they may not be aware that it is a communication system: at least someone pays attention to them for an hour or an hour and a half a day, and they are doing something. But that happens way before any of them get a clue as to just what is going on in this "game."

DR. BARRY KEATING: Why not either use pictures that the patients would draw, or, conversely, use American Sign Language?

898

Dr. GARDNER: As far as having them draw, the reason we don't have them draw is the same reason we don't use Sign Language. Patients who are this severely aphasic are invariably apraxic, and that causes lots of difficulties. There is some work going on in sign language in aphasics. Dr. Jane Holmes is going to report on it at the Aphasia Academy. One of the things we are hoping to do is teach the patient VIC well enough so that he can map what he knows in VIC onto Sign. We haven't yet done that. As far as a pure picture language is concerned, as we suggested in the paper, we're interested more than in just whether or not the patient can capture certain semantic relations. We want eventually to be able to ask the more sophisticated question: can the patient do linguistic transformations and solve problems where he has to be sensitive to much finer shades of meaning.

NEUROBIOLOGY OF LANGUAGE:
AN OVERVIEW*

Oscar S. M. Marin

Departments of Neurology
Baltimore City Hospitals
Baltimore, Maryland 21224
The Johns Hopkins University
School of Medicine
Baltimore, Maryland 21205

NATURE AND SCOPE OF THE PROBLEM

The essential question for a neurobiology of language is to define and give detailed description of the relationship between language, a complex symbolic communication system, and the brain, a biological organ. To a large extent, the evidence for the relationship between language and brain function has been inferred from the study of language disorders associated with brain damage in man. Although experimental techniques have begun to be available in the last two decades (i.e., cortical-evoked potential studies, dichotic listening experiments, etc.), it is likely that for some time to come the neuropsychological study of pathological clinical cases will continue to provide the bulk of the material for language-brain correlation. This raises in itself a series of methodological problems that have been discussed in greater detail elsewhere (Marin *et al.*[33]). We are concerned here with more general aspects of the problem.

The study of the relationship between language and brain obviously supposes some fund of knowledge in both these areas. I will therefore comment on the present state of the language disciplines (linguistics and psycholinguistics) and the brain sciences, with a view toward the problem of language-brain correlation. It is clear that an adequate neurobiology of language will require the integration of data from disciplines that diverge radically in goals, subject matter, and methodology. A serious problem, then, is the specification of levels of description and units of analysis on both sides of the brain-behavior equation. Is it, for example, reasonable to attempt to correlate a linguistic theory with the microstructure of the brain, or are other levels of analysis more appropriate? A concern with this question will be evident throughout this review.

Another recurrent theme will be the scope of the neurobiological question. Human language involves complex auditory processes, some of which may be unique, and delicate coordination of the vocal apparatus. Neurology has something to say about the localization of these processes in the brain, although, as has been pointed out at this conference, even this knowledge is scanty and equivocal.[4,55] But besides these extreme sensory and motor aspects of verbal communication, language also implies a complex set of mental processes: extraction of meaning from words and sentences; recalling verbal symbols from memory; associating verbal symbols with their referents; organizing sentences that convey specific meaning and that follow prescribed syntactic orders and precise phonological rules, and so on. In all these processes the brain is equally engaged. But how? The unconscious nature of

*The preparation of this paper was aided, in part, by grant no. 12160-01 CMS from N.I.N.D.S.

these central operations and their inaccessibility to direct observation constitute perhaps the most formidable barriers to the understanding of the relations between brain and behavior (see Chomsky[8] and Rozin[46]). We have no clear conception of the units of analysis utilized in these operations, and we possess incomplete notions of their physiological or anatomical substratum. However, a neurobiology of language that ignores these central processes, as some anatomical models have done (e.g. Geschwind[17]), is likely to be incomplete.

Our objective knowledge of the neurobiology of language is almost nil; the data are incredibly scanty. Hence, in the foregoing text I shall, for the most part, restrict myself to the review of some of the different methodological options that are open for the study of the language function of the brain. In doing this, I hope to be able to improve the conceptualization of the overall problem as well as to point to the limitations and preconceptions implicit in the areas of research it encompasses. An excursion into some evolutionary and phylogenetic aspects of language communication will also be made.

LANGUAGE DESCRIPTION, PSYCHOLINGUISTICS, AND THE NEUROBIOLOGY OF LANGUAGE

It seems to me obvious that the study of the language-brain relationship must begin with language, and not with the brain. We wish to explain how the nervous system serves language function; therefore, our description of the language process will necessarily determine what we look for in the brain (e.g., correlates of syntactic processes, phonological processes, etc.). Preserving what seems to be a logical sequence, we will look first at language, and then at the nervous system.

In the last two decades a great deal of progress has been made in the description of the language system. Contemporary transformational theories have had a prominent role in this advance. It is important, however, to keep in mind that, to a great extent, this advance has been the result of a deliberate exclusion from the theoretical body of many considerations that, biologically bounded, would have otherwise impeded the degree of formal description that has been required. Thus, Chomsky[8] states that "when we speak of a grammar as generating a sentence with a certain structural description, we mean simply that the grammar assigns this structural description to the sentence. When we say that a sentence has a certain derivation with respect to a particular generative grammar, we say nothing about how the speaker or hearer might proceed, in some practical or efficient way, to construct such a derivation." Judith Greene,[19] referring to the same general problem of abstraction and lack of empirical relevancy of some linguistic theories, comments that "the fact that the transformational theory postulates a generative syntactic component which initiates the input required for the semantic and phonological components carries no temporal implications about the order in which such operations might be performed by the language users." It is reasonable to expect, therefore, that many of these rules have no direct psychobiological reality and no predictive value for neuronal processing of the same information.

The gap between linguistic theory and biological reality is most evident in the relationship between language comprehension and language production. Speaker and hearer are symmetrical in Chomsky's theory, but would seem to have different requirements in actuality. The high degree of redundancy in spoken language allows for some imprecision in the decoding process (see Miller[37]). The guesswork and filling-in of missed items usually does not prevent successful comprehension; contextual information is available and, clearly, is used. By contrast, more precision is required in the case of instructions for the phonological specification of word utterance, for lexical insertion, and, by and large, for the syntactic programming necessary for sentence production. In this respect, the structural symmetry of the speaker-hearer suggested by linguistic theory contrasts with the asymmetry one would expect to find in the neural mechanisms of language reception and production.

The relative neglect, at least until recently, of semantic aspects of language organization, as compared with the emphasis on phonological and syntactic aspects, also tends to increase the distance between biology and linguistic theory. The adaptive significance of language must lie, after all, in its ability to communicate meaning. But much of the linguistic effort even within semantics (e.g., Katz[25]) appears to have little or no relevance for a neurobiological study of language. Of course, neurobiological applicability may not have been the goal in the first place; the concern has been with formal description. One cannot but hope, however, that other more empirically and semantically oriented linguistic approaches will provide a more solid base for the psychological and biological reality of language communication in man.[12,20] This task may turn out to be overwhelmingly complex, since the approach readmits to linguistic theory a multiplicity of parameters that, while clearly valid, complicates the description of language tremendously (e.g., see Osgood[43] for the relations between language and perception; see also Fillmore,[13] this volume; Bever.[2]).

In any case, demonstration of the psychological reality of the various aspects of the linguistic theory must be recognized as an indispensable prerequisite for the subsequent task of correlating those findings with brain structure and function; it would seem premature, at this stage, to try to plug linguistic theory into the brain.[6] The psycholinguistic data accumulated thus far are very limited. The complexity, seclusion, and near inviolability of the central processes of the brain have taxed the experimental ingenuity of contemporary psychology, with few results (see Fodor *et al.*[14] for summary and evaluation). The difficulties inherent in trying to discriminate parameters, operations, and levels of processing in an essentially redundant and coherent normal system make the task an extremely difficult one. Here, data from pathological cases have a unique value and their relevance for the clarification of even theoretical linguistic issues should be recognized [33]

The essential problem in the understanding of these central processes was alluded to earlier. We cannot be aware of them directly; we know them only by their reflections on the surface of sensory systems. Just as what we know of the properties of elementary particles strongly depends on the characteristics of the method of detection that reveals them, what we know of our inner mental processes inevitably depends on the characteristics and constraints imposed by the sensory-motor vehicles that make them manifest. Hence, in a neurobiological study of language, the relations between the acousticovocal or visuomotor vehicles of speech and the more central language processes are of the greatest importance. The modality-specific constraints are most dramatically evident in studies of the sign language of the deaf.[1,27] Studies of the communicative capabilities of other animals also contribute to the differentiation of central cognitive processes and those related to mode of communication.[36,44,47] Thus, these areas of research, as well as linguistic and psycholinguistic studies of spoken language, can be expected to contribute to a neurobiological understanding of human communication.

SEARCH FOR LINGUISTIC-PHYSIOLOGICAL CORRELATIVE UNITS

The attempt to relate language functions to physiological processes in the central nervous system, circumventing the limitations of gross anatomy, is tempting. Such an approach would proceed along the lines of the analytical studies being made in the motor system and in the optic tectum and cortex, and, on the whole, would conform with the microanalytical style of contemporary physiology. It would expand on the preliminary correlations of linguistic phenomena with brain activity, using gross evoked potentials (see for instance, Molfese[39]). It is perhaps premature to predict what such methods could contribute to the overall neurobiological understanding of language but, at present, one can see some fundamental problems with this approach:

(1) There are many obstacles to single-unit recording in human subjects, although it is occasionally possible.

(2) Although physiologists now routinely stimulate and record from single neurons or neuronal aggregates, we know very little about the integration of these activities into meaningful functional units, except perhaps for a few relatively simple instances (see for instance Refs. 11 and 22). In the case of the mammalian cerebral cortex, it has been practically impossible to penetrate its functional organization beyond the early stages of sensory feature detection, nor has it been possible thus far to discover neuronal patterns of activity that parallel the sequence of overt motor activity. The problem may not be solely one of methodological limitation, but, as Maturana[35] has pointed out, there may be unsuspected conceptual difficulties in describing overt behavioral function in terms of tissue correlates. This brings to mind Eddington's[10] description of the brown, wooden table in contrast to the "scientific" one constructed of electrically charged particles and the disproportionate amount of empty space which surrounds them.

Eddington's example may be extreme, but it does illustrate rather dramatically that descriptions of the same phenomena at different levels can involve totally different referential systems. The perceived table with its color, its shape, its solid consistency, its wooden composition, its joints, nails, ornaments, belongs to a system in which its use, its categorical value as object, are integral parts of its definition. The "scientific" reductionist description, on the other hand, utilizes the radically different parameters of the physical theory of one's choice. Von Glasersfeld,[18] from a cybernetic point of view, and Maturana,[35] from a biological perspective, have stressed the conceptual distance that may exist between our descriptions of functions and behavior, and the inner code utilized by the nervous system. Blum[3] has shown how even the point-to-point visual representation of a real object may suffer enormous spatial modification in its neuronal representation; the mind-brain problem would be a good deal easier to conceptualize if we could hold to the earlier Gestalt views on psychophysical isomorphism. The naturalistic description of language, the abstract descriptions of linguistics, and even the description of psycholinguistic process are already not totally correspondent with each other. Still, these differences may be minimal as compared with the distance between our account of language structure, units and processes, and the correlative internal code.

But perhaps the most serious obstacle to the search for a satisfactory neuronal unit for language representation is the lack of adequate linguistic, or better, psycholinguistic unit(s) of analysis. We have not yet specified the units for an adequate theory of speech perception, much less comprehension and production. And, as I have argued above, it is useless to look for physiological units unless we know what, functionally speaking, they are the units of. If, for example, we have a system that encodes only the relationships between two stimuli, we would expect it to have very different physiological properties than a system that encodes the stimuli discretely and absolutely. Nelson[42] has utilized Cassirer's[7] distinction along these lines in a discussion of concept development and language acquisition, and we can recognize its importance for the characterization of linguistic operations to be correlated with brain processes.

CLASSICAL NEUROLOGICAL AND NEUROANATOMICAL APPROACH
TO LANGUAGE FUNCTION OF THE BRAIN

But while we lack an adequate description of the language process, and we do not as yet know how to characterize neuronal activity in relation to function, there is, nevertheless, a body of evidence that correlates brain anatomy and the language process: the studies of brain pathology and language function. Following the classical tradition of neurology, attempts to correlate language and brain structure have been based on the general assumption that brain functions as well as language can be analyzed by decomposing the total into components that represent processes of a simpler or possibly more general nature. It is further assumed that linguistic components can be directly correlated with subsystems of the neurological machinery. The hope is that the level of fragmentation will be such as to permit, without great distortion, a subsequent resynthesis of the overall function.

From the neurological standpoint, this set of presumptions has confirmed its usefulness by a long tradition and has proved to be, clinically and experimentally, most rewarding. To a large extent, these assumptions constitute the major working hypothesis of clinical neurology, which looks at the nervous system as a hierarchical organization of interdependent subsystems, many of which can be observed and studied in some lesser or greater degree of isolation. Thus, although we know that the organization of movement involves a series of structures and functional processes, the cerebellar or the cerebral cortical components can be analyzed in relative isolation from the rest; similarly, we may presume that the thalamic sensory processes can, at least to some extent, be differentiated from lower sensory mechanisms and also from higher cortical ones. In the case of language, we believe that the brain deals with the various perceptual, cognitive, and executive tasks, at least to a certain extent, by assigning them to different neural subsystems. If these systems can be disrupted independently by focal brain lesions, the clinical syndromes should provide a general picture of language-brain interactions. The method seems to be a plausible one, in view of our experience in the field of aphasia. The lateralization and relative circumscription of the so-called speech area is a promise for further success in the studies of language-brain correlations. The fact that some brain lesions can selectively disrupt some language functions, leaving others intact, has further proved the value of the approach (for instance, see Refs. 15 and 31).

Let us look at the problem in more detail. The following statements can serve as starting points for an analysis of some anatomical and clinical aspects of language:

(1) The medium of natural language is predominantly acoustic.

(2) The anatomical substrata for speech function are, for the most part, concentrated in a particular region of the left hemisphere.

(3) It is possible to recognize in language performance an acoustic-phonetic afferent system as well as an articulatory effector. The two poles of the language system are fairly well circumscribed in the cerebral cortex, and appear to be connected by means of a fiber tract. The receptor-effector polarity constitutes a familiar pattern of neural organization for many functions and is, of course, reminiscent of the reflex arc which, in various forms, combinations, and complications, serves as one of the predominant building blocks of nervous function.

Thus, one would be tempted to try to establish a parallel between language and the organization of other sensorimotor functions. What, for example, can this receptor-effector apparatus do in isolation? In this circumstance, speech is well articulated, but no spontaneous production is observed. Speech activity is virtually restricted to a faithful imitation of what is heard (echolalia). No traces of comprehension are noted.[16] The complexity of the repetition performance can be surprising:

One patient, recently presented to me at the University of Pennsylvania, although giving no evidence of language comprehension, was nevertheless able to repeat sentences in French, a language he did not know. With long sentences, the echolalic patient would wait for a pause (which might or might not signal end of the sentence) and then proceed to repeat the last few words. This strongly suggests that what operates here is an auditory verbal short-term memory, isolated from a long-term semantic counterpart.

Under other circumstances the opposite dissociation may occur. Such is the case in some forms of conduction aphasia where repetition is limited to one or two letters, words, or numbers. In these cases, however, it is surprising that in spite of the difficulty in retaining phonological information, the patient is usually able to comprehend sentences and even to render a paraphrase that contains the essential meaning of the original[54] (for a critical view see also Brown[5]).

Other patients have a somewhat similar disorder in reading: they may be completely unable to convert the graphemic stimulus to phonological form. In reading aloud, these patients make errors that are unrelated to the phonology of the word, reflecting its meaning instead (e.g., "shoulder" read as "arm"[48]). Finally, in cases where there is a severe deficit in speech perception ("word deafness"), residual comprehension is strongly influenced by semantic context and occurs despite the phonetic impairment.[49]

The point that I wish to make with these examples is the following: While a "reflex arc" can be demonstrated for the speech mechanism as elsewhere in the nervous system, its function with respect to language appears to be limited. With the exception of imitation and the role of auditory feedback, there is little direct coupling between mechanisms of speech perception and speech production. The circuit serves language mostly as a transduction device: it converts an external signal into a form that can be comprehended, and converts thought into external signals. This is a crucial point because it once again points to a distinction between language as a cognitive process and speech as the mechanism of actualization which in man has taken an acoustic-vocal form.

But even if we could agree that the anatomical correlations described by the classical aphasia studies constitute a satisfactory level of analysis for language function, the question would remain as to how often the central nervous system organizes itself in discrete and distinct anatomical territories. How far in the exploration of language processing can we expect to find the territorial discreteness one seems to observe in word deafness, an isolated impairment of the phonetic perceptual apparatus,[49] or perhaps in some cases of articulatory speech defects? In other words, what are the biological constraints that compel the neurological machinery to set aside for certain functions, specialized cortical or subcortical territorial analyzers? In general one sees that greater physiological and structural discreteness are common features of neurological organization when homogeneous, well-defined modalities or spatial or sequential parameters, are essential components of the function. When such parameters do not constitute the axis of the process, strict anatomical localization is no longer as obvious. In the case of human communication, gross anatomical correlation is valid insofar as modality (acoustic) and need for detailed temporal sequence are indispensable to the encoding or decoding mechanisms. On the other hand, it is less likely, and indeed no evidence can be given, that anatomical discreteness is a necessary condition for central language processes that are related to the retrieval of items from storage, for paradigmatic lexical selection processes, or, as the case seems to be, for the lexical storages themselves.

In this respect it is interesting to observe that while certain aspects of perception and production of speech are fairly localizable, there is a surprising evasiveness of an anatomical locus for the lexicon. Anomia, an aphasic disorder that specifically affects the access to dictionary items, has proved to be the most difficult type of aphasia to localize. The occurrence of anomia in association with diffuse cortical disorders (as in cases of dementia) contrasts further with the more circumscribed lesional loci of some perceptual, phonological, and perhaps syntactic processes of language.

GENERAL EVOLUTIONARY ASPECTS OF LANGUAGE

From different perspectives, the origins and evolution of language have been discussed by Montagu,[40] Isaac,[23] Jaynes,[24] Steklis and Harnad,[51] Hewes,[21] and Marshack[34] (all in this volume). These are problems that, despite their theoretical biological interest, are nevertheless so devoid of objective data and so difficult to recapture in their natural history, that only very limited empirical study seems to be possible.

Language has obviously segregated man from other primates in such a dramatic way that it suggests an evolutionary development that has been almost explosive. But the impossibility of retracing the evolutionary history of language is at least partly due to the fact that speech and language are not the only functions that create a gap between man and other primates. In the motor sphere, for instance, the problem of handedness has been repeatedly mentioned. To this one should add the obvious advances and at least quantitative differences in other functions, such as cross modality perception, perceptual and cognitive generalizations, concept formation, memory capabilities, logical operations, symbolization, and so on.

It is, in short, very difficult to analyze the evolution of language in isolation from other cognitive functions, and, surely, language has been influenced by other cognitive structures that may have parallel or even identical evolutionary histories. It might be of some interest, however, to review some of the biological prerequisites for acoustic communication.

From an evolutionary standpoint, phylogenesis can be viewed as a progressive expansion of the organism's spatial and temporal relations with the environment. One can conceptualize this biological trend in three main stages that can still be traced in man. The first deals with biochemical and biophysical homeostasis, the crucial safeguard of the stability of the internal milieu, which, in mammals, is primarily subserved and regulated by hormonal systems, but also by metabolic, immunological, and even by servomechanisms at the cellular level. These systems are essential for the survival of cells, tissue, and organism, but their scope is limited to the relations between the organism and its immediate physical environment. Furthermore, in this relation, the environment is active and the organism reactive.

The second stage, which still engages large proportions of the neural machinery of mammals, also deals with the relations between the organism and its surrounding environment, but of a kind that is not only evaluated in units of biophysical change but also in sensory units that are peculiar to the organism itself. It is represented in us by the sensations of pain, temperature, propioception, position, and touch; it deals with the adaptation of the organism with respect to the immediate environment and allows for withdrawal from harmful changes as well as for the regulation of position, equilibrium, and posture. Thus it sustains the basic mechanisms of locomotion and permits reactive movements in response to environmental changes to outer and inner stimuli.

Some general properties are of great biological interest. Essentially, this is the first internal evaluative system of reference that the organism acquires for its relations with the environment. In this sense the second stage constitutes a typical autoreferential system in which the equation "organism: environment" places the former as an essential part of the balance. It also deals almost exclusively with a regulation that is spatially organized and in which the topography of environmental change with respect to the sensory surface is of crucial interest. Such a spatial system has necessarily to be organized in a symmetrical fashion and many neuronal mechanisms are therefore organized in terms of spatial symmetry.

At still relatively low levels of evolution the nervous system has already greatly enriched the inventory of physiological mechanisms and function. One can witness, for example, a gradual independence between input and output; an increasing dependency of the final output results from inner physiological states; an increase in the cumulative recording of singular events that condition and influence future responses; a decreasing tendency to trigger action on the basis of single feature detection, and, conversely, stronger dependency on composite sensory information as the effective stimulus for action.

A crucial stage in biological evolution came with the development of the telereceptive sensory systems (visual, auditory, and, in lesser proportion, smell) and the functional and anatomical reorganization at the level of the cerebral cortex. The interposition, between the receptors and effectors, of increasingly more complex central processors becomes now an outstanding feature of higher nervous processes. Vision still conserves greatly the spatial characteristics of earlier stages of evolution and reinforces the need for bilaterality of function and structure. It adds, however, a new dimension that opens a great new path: vision not only reached far beyond the organism's immediate environment, increasing the spatial and temporal scope of its adaptive behavior and, hence, its motor functions, but, at the same time, it allowed the organism to evaluate features of the external world in detachment from the direct concern or active participation of the organism itself. It permitted judgments of size, color, distance, and shape; objects could be judged relative to each other, the seeing organism remaining a rather detached witness. The autoreferential equation, "organism: environment" is transformed into the triangular relationship of "environment: environment: organism," in which the latter could be passive observer. This step to objectivity and alloreferential behavior seems crucial for the development of cognition: images, percepts, memories of the external world can be gathered in independence, or brought together; properties and features can be abstracted and generalized; details can be discriminated. In short, a whole repertoire of representations of the world can be now accumulated in the vast memory storages; a new independent chemistry of these data can be realized not solely for better planning of adaptive behavior, but for its own sake. In this respect, in what concerns man and perhaps also superior mammals, sole fulfillment of immediate survival needs is probably insufficient explanation for this cognitive development, in which asthetic gratification and probably other factors may also figure.

But how could this inner template of the world, this iconic set of images and abstracted concepts and ideas, this inner world of a painter, be transmitted and communicated to others and even to oneself?

Premack[45] has written that a symbol is an item that represents another item. Language as a symbolic system thus provided a way to rerepresent man's experience. But it is necessary for a symbol to be independent of the referential system to which it refers, and this independence could have been one of the outstanding advantages offered by the auditory system.

Most of the organism's contact with the environment was visual. The auditory system served principally as an alerting system for rather indiscriminative recognition and detection of location of visually hidden targets; cognitively, it was the secluded cradle in which a symbolic system could operate independently of the environment. It cannot be a passing coincidence that the two major acoustic systems used by man, speech and music, share a highly abstract and symbolic nature. The importance of a secluded modality for the organization of a symbolic system is reinforced by the very interesting observations on communication systems that employ modalities more central to the organism's relations with the external world. Bellugi[1] has stressed the almost palpable struggle that the American Sign Language for the deaf has gone through to acquire symbolic independence from the inherent iconic nature of the visual-motor system. Her description of the genesis of some more abstract symbols such as "home" (a brief movement of fingers from the mouth to the cheek) is most dramatic. The gesture "home" derives, according to Bellugi, from the fusion of two iconic movements of "eating" (oscillating movements of fingers in front of mouth) and those for "sleeping" (extended fingers along the cheek).

The temporal nature of the acoustic stimulus reinforced the trend toward temporal expansion that the larger circle of environment was imposing in the organism. From a primarily reactive motility, the motor systems began to organize themselves in more and more temporally organized programs that would involve centrally patterned units of organization, ballistic movements, and feed-forward controls, and would open roads to spontaneous, voluntary motility. These roots can be seen, as Sherrington[52] pointed out, in spinal reflex mechanisms such as the scratch reflex and stepping movements. As in the case of cognition, manipulative motility dealt with the environment in an objective, detached, and nonautoreferential manner. In the case of language it became obvious that the temporal dimension imposed additional constraints to the extant spatial ones: an emphasis on what is first and then next, on temporal sequencing of what leads and what follows. The bisymmetrical representation would not serve for the direction of a unitary, temporally organized act, and the need for concentration of the central processors for speech and language and for purposeful movements became a logical solution. This concentration, hemispherical lateralization, was organized, as Levy[29,30] rightly points out, despite some sacrifice of the bilaterality required by spatial functions.

At the effector-motor-vocal end there is another compelling reason for concentrating the innervatory motor instructions on one side. The vocal tract moves symmetrically, in the course of speech utterances, pulling or relaxing muscles in an equal manner on either side. This is an unusual situation: other axial muscular structures are bisymmetrically innervated in such a way that excitation of the agonist on one side results in inhibition of the contralateral homolog that then becomes functionally antagonistic. When, as it happens in face innervation, the contralateral functional balance is not organized in such strong antagonistic terms and contraction of one group of muscles may require homolateral relaxation in another of the same side, there is a tendency for bilateral representation at the cortical level. In the case of innervation of the vocal tract it is obvious that bilateral motor control would have been a redundancy that, given the speed and variability at which movements are required in speech performance, would have created inconvenience and disadvantages.

The recognition of language as the vehicle of expression of inner desires and emotional states cannot be denied, and many, in fact, have suggested that it is in these inner urges that one can find the origins of speech and language. The position taken here is opposite to that view, since it recognizes, for cognition and manipulative movements, and the subsequent development of symbolic communication mechanisms, the need for independence and detachment from inner emotional states. This is not to deny relations between emotions and language and the value of speech and language in emotional expression, but to emphasize that even in the fully developed individual, the expression of such inner states remains still the most difficult to verbalize; more often than not, we cast our emotional expression in strongly esthetic and referential terms, using images, metaphors, and figurative resources.

The partial segregation of this predominantly autoreferential system from objective cognition and the language mechanism that serves it finds confirmation not only in the apparently similar separation of these aspects of behavior in the structure of the central nervous system but also in the different vocal systems employed in emotional expression. Traditional neurology has recognized for a long time similar dissociations in the emotional and voluntary expression of facial gestures (e.g., Wilson[56]). Myers[41] has given further evidence in the same direction by pointing out that emotional vocalization in primates can be substantially reduced or abolished by resection of the frontal lobes but remains unmodified by posterior lesions. In man, posterior frontal and retrorolandic temporoparietal lesions of the left hemisphere have the well-known devastating effect upon voluntary speech, whereas emotional expressions of laughing, crying, screaming, weeping, sobbing tend to remain intact. In frontal lobe lesions in man, overall activity becomes depressed, and the blunting of affect also involves speech production in the form of different degrees of lack of spontaneity, down to mutisms; the vocalic machinery, however, remains unimpaired (e.g. Luria[32]).

Concluding Remarks

About a decade ago, Teuber[53] reviewed the state of our knowledge of the brain mechanisms underlying speech and language. It was clear then, as it is today, that there is still a vast distance to go. Teuber pointed to our ignorance in the area of general brain mechanisms, of those that subserve language as well as other functions, and was optimistic that advances in our understanding of the general properties of input, output, and central brain processes would increase our insight into speech and language mechanisms. This can hardly be doubted. Any knowledge of the intimate work of the nervous tissue will certainly refine the correlative study of the brain and its functions. But even if we had a more adequate understanding of basic neuronal mechanisms, a successful neurobiology of language would require an adequate understanding of language function as well. While it is not clear to me that the last ten years have witnessed any radical breakthrough in the area of basic brain processes, I do think that we have at last begun to make significant inroads into the understanding of human language.

Teuber rightly commented that our greatest ignorance is in the area of output mechanisms, of speech and language production. Here he was giving only another instance of a situation that obtains throughout vertebrate neurophysiology: our understanding of sensory-perceptual mechanisms is far better than our understanding of motor functions. Incomplete as our knowledge of apraxias (disorders of the organization of voluntary movements without paralysis) may be, we have better insight into those apraxic disturbances that clearly have a perceptual component (e.g., constructional and dressing apraxias) than into the seemingly simpler apraxia of gait; and although it is clinically easy to recognize a motor aphasic we have better insight into disorders of speech perception than into the more common production disturbances of Broca's aphasia. Some of the reasons for these disparities have been alluded to earlier, but in addition there is one of overriding importance: we can hope to obtain reasonable answers to our research questions only when we have some degree of control over the input of the system we are analyzing. As long as we have been able to analyze and manipulate the properties of sensory stimuli, we have been able to formulate testable hypotheses about the brain mechanisms that process them.

Recent progress in the area of speech perception supports this statement; it has been the fragmentation of the speech signal into clauses, phonemes, distinctive features, etc., that has given us some insight into the sensory processes that may be involved.

The case of speech output shows us the obverse situation: almost total lack of understanding of the central processes that may take place in speech and language, and hence ignorance of the factors that generate the syntactic or phonological instructions. Thus, we cannot yet formulate the proper questions that would permit analysis of the motor aspects of language function. This situation prevails in general for the motor organization of the nervous system. But, for example, once it was recognized that movements could be classified as either of ballistic type (no sensory-motor feedback control—preprogrammed) or rampant (slow—with continuous feedback control), it became possible to discriminate two different mechanisms at the physiological level.[9,28]

Almost a decade after Teuber reviewed the problem, I would therefore like to take a rather different perspective and propose that greater insights into the neurobiology of language require, first, a deeper knowledge of language and its performance mechanisms. This will encourage the formulation of better questions about the relationships of brain and language and prescribe the units of the neuronal mechanisms that subserve language function.

Finally, this overview of some aspects of the neurobiological approach to language should have made us aware of how much this field extends beyond human speech and how relevant are the studies of other communication systems in man and in animals. Previously unrecognized cognitive capacities were revealed when the chimpanzee was equipped with an adequate communication system. The brain may manifest other unsuspected capabilities when provided with a system of expression. In man, arbitrary developments such as music, art, and, even, perhaps, mathematics are such instances of potentiality awaiting a means of realization. The nervous system therefore appears capable not only of meeting the increasing requirements of biological adaptation, but, given an appropriate mode of expression, it may reveal capacities as yet untapped.

ACKNOWLEDGMENTS

I wish to thank most sincerely for her invaluable help my collaborator, Dr. Eleanor M. Saffran, who, by wrestling with my "Spanglish" and some of my arguments, was almost always able to clarify my ideas.

REFERENCES

1. BELLUGI, U. This volume.
2. BEVER, T. 1970. The influence of speech performance on linguistic structure in Advances in Psycholinguistics. G. B. Flores d'Arcais and W. J. M. Levelt, Eds. North Holland-Am. Elsevier.
3. BLUM, H. 1973. Biological shape and visual science. Part I. J. Theor. Biol. 38: 205–287.
4. BOGEN, J. E. & O. O. BOGEN. This volume.
5. BROWN, J. W. 1975. The problem of repetition: a study of "conduction" aphasia and the "isolation" syndrome. Cortex 11: 37–52.
6. CAPLAN, D. & J. C. MARSHALL. 1975. Generative grammar and aphasic disorders: a series of language representation in the human brain. Fdn. of Language Vol. 12: 583, 593.
7. CASSIRER, E. 1923. Structure and function and Einstein's theory of relativity. W. B. Swaby and M. C. Swaby, transl. Dover Publications. 1953.

8. CHOMSKY, N. 1965. Aspects of the Theory of Syntax. Mouton. The Netherlands.
9. DeLONG, M. R. 1974. Motor functions of the basal ganglia: single-unit activity during movements. In The Neurosciences, Third Study Program. F. Schmidt and F. G. Worden, Eds. MIT Press. Cambridge, Mass.
10. EDDINGTON, A. S. 1929. The Nature of the Physical World. Macmillan Co. New York, N.Y.
11. EVARTS, E. V. 1974. Sensorimotor cortex activity associated with movements triggered by visual as compared to somesthetic inputs. In The Neurosciences. Third Study Program. F. Schmidt and F. G. Worden, Eds. MIT Press. Cambridge, Mass.
12. FILLMORE, C. J. 1968. The case for case. In Universals in Linguistic Theory. Bach, Emmon and Harms, Eds. Holt Rinehart and Winston Inc. New York, N.Y.
13. FILLMORE, C. J. This volume.
14. FODOR, J. A., T. G. BEVER, & M. F. GARRETT. 1974. The Psychology of Language. McGraw-Hill Inc. New York, N.Y.
15. GESCHWIND, N. 1965. Disconnexion syndromes in animals and man. Brain 88: 237–294 (Part I); 587–664 (Part II).
16. GESCHWIND, N., F. QUADFASEL & I. SEGARRA. 1968. Isolation of the speech area. Neuropsychologia 6: 327–340.
17. GESCHWIND, N. 1970. The organization of language and the brain. Science 170: 940–944.
18. VON GLASERSFELD, E. This volume.
19. GREENE, J. 1972. Psycholinguistics. Penguin Books, Inc. New York, N.Y.
20. HALLIDAY, M. A. K. 1970. Language structure and language function. In New Horizons in Linguistics. J. Lyons, Ed. Penguin Books, Inc. New York, N.Y.
21. HEWES, G. W. 1976. This volume.
22. INGLE, D. 1975. Some unresolved issues concerning the optic tectum. In sensorimotor functions of the midbrain tectum. Neurosciences Res. Prog. Bull. Vol. 13(2): 258–266.
23. ISAAC, G. L. This volume.
24. JAYNES, J. This volume.
25. KATZ, J. J. 1972. Semantic Theory. Harper and Row. New York, N.Y.
26. KATZ, J. J. This volume.
27. KLIMA, E. S. & U. BELLUGI. 1975. Perception and production in a visually-based language. Ann. N.Y. Acad. Sci. 263: 225–235.
28. KORNHUBER, H. H. 1974. Cerebral cortex, cerebellum, and basal ganglia: An introduction to their motor function. In The Neurosciences. Third Study Program. F. Schmidt and F. G. Worden, Eds. MIT Press. Cambridge, Mass.
29. LEVY, J. 1973. Lateral specialization of the human brain: Behavioral manifestations and possible evolutionary basis, In The Biology of Behavior. J. Kiger, Ed. Oregon State Univ. Press. Eugene, Ore.
30. LEVY, J. This volume.
31. LURIA, A. R. 1966. Higher Cortical Functions in Man. (English translation by B. Haigh). Basic Books, Inc. New York, N.Y.
32. LURIA, A. R. 1973. The frontal lobes and the regulation of behavior. In Psychophysiology of the Frontal Lobes. K. H. Pribram and A. R. Luria, Eds. Academic Press. New York, N.Y.
33. MARIN, O. S. M., E. M. SAFFRAN & M. SCHWARTZ. This volume.
34. MARSHACK, A. This volume.
35. MATURANA, H. R. 1970. Biology of Cognition: Biological Computer Laboratory. Reprt 9.0 Dept. Electrical Engineering. University of Illinois. Urbania, Ill.
36. MENZEL, E. 1975. Natural language of young chimpanzees. New Scientist 65: 127–130.
37. MILLER, G. A. 1951. Language and Communication. McGraw-Hill Inc. New York, N.Y.
38. MOFFITT, A. R. 1971. Consonant cue perception by twenty-to-twenty-four-week-old infants. Child Dev. 42: 717–731.
39. MOLFESE, D. L. This volume.
40. MONTAGU, A. This volume.
41. MYERS, R. E. This volume.
42. NELSON, K. 1974. Concept, word, and sentence: Inter-relations in acquisition and development. Psych. Rev. 81: 267–285.

43. OSGOOD, C. E. 1971. Where do sentences come from? *In* Semantics: An Interdisciplinary Reader in Philosophy, Linguistics and Psychology. Cambridge University Press. Cambridge, England.
44. PREMACK, D. 1971. On the assessment of language competence in the chimpanzee. *In* Behaviour of Non-Human Primates. Vol. **4**. A. M. Schrier and F. Stollnitz, Eds. Academic Press. New York, N.Y.
45. PREMACK, D. 1972. Two problems in cognition: symbolization and from Icon to Phoneme. *In* Communication and Affect. A Comparative Approach. T. Alloway, P. Krames, and P. Pliner, Eds. Academic Press. New York, N.Y.
46. ROZIN, P. 1974. The psycho-biological approach to human memory. Conference on Current Research Approaches to the Neural Mechanisms of Learning and Memory. In press.
47. RUMBAUGH, D. M. & T. V. GILL. This volume.
48. SAFFRAN, E. M., M. F. SCHWARTZ & O. S. M. MARIN. 1976. Semantic mechanisms in paralexia. Brain and Language. In press.
49. SAFFRAN, E. M., O. S. M. MARIN & G. H. YENI-KOMSHIAN. 1976. An analysis of speech perception in word deafness. Brain and Language. In press.
50. SAFFRAN, E. M. & O. S. M. MARIN. 1976. Immediate memory for word lists and sentences in a patient with deficient auditory short term memory. Brain and Language. In press.
51. STEKLIS, H. D. & S. R. HARNAD. This volume.
52. SHERRINGTON, C. S. 1906. The integrative action of the nervous system. Yale University Press. New Haven, Conn.
53. TEUBER, H. L. 1967. Lacunae and Research: Approaches to them. *In* Brain Mechanism Underlying Speech and Language. C. Millikan and F. Darley, Eds. Grune and Stratton. New York, N.Y.
54. WARRINGTON, E. K. & T. SHALLICE. 1969. The selective impairment of auditory verbal short-term memory. Brain **92**: 885–986.
55. WHITAKER, H. & O. A. SELNES. This volume.

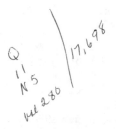

CONCLUDING REMARKS

Robin Fox

Department of Psychology
Rutgers University
New Brunswick, New Jersey 08901

First of all, let me thank those of you who have seen it through to the end, for still being with us. Part of the joy of this conference has been the enormous determination of the audience, the pleasure of seeing rows upon rows of full chairs through some of the most daunting sessions. We have heard constant references to the famous declaration of the Linguistic Society of Paris, and someone has unearthed an actual facsimile. This has been put up on the screen, and I have been asked to call your attention to Article 2. Anything coming from such an extraordinarily authoritative source, of course, I suppose has to be taken seriously, and the Linguistic Society of Paris decided to rule out discussion concerning "the origin of language or the creation of a universal language." We have offended, certainly seriously, against the first canon, and I suppose we have talked about universal grammar, which goes close to offending against the second. I am not told what the sanctions are, but we can expect, no doubt, the finger of God to point down at us, and something quite terrible in consequence.

While I am speaking of the splendid nature of the audience, I think that this is also a good opportunity to thank the organizers of the conference, not only The New York Academy of Sciences but the three people who worked so incredibly hard to put on this extraordinary display of talent and discussion, namely Jane Lancaster herself, who will be joining us, Horst Steklis, and Stevan Harnad. It's very rare, I think, that three such young, talented people have got together and worked so hard to put on anything quite so remarkable.

When they first asked me to chair this final session, I was told that I was to sum up the entire conference. You can imagine the reaction I had in at least seeing the absolute impossibility of this task. It is quite impossible to sum up such a conference. What the conference has done, I think for all of us, is to raise some extraordinary questions. We will go away, I think, not with any sense that we have taken a great step forward, but that we've aroused in our minds a lot of propositions about what steps we ought to be taking. What struck me about it is that in some areas the differences between theories is quite extraordinary, so that, for example, the origins of language have been placed either with the early australopithecines or in the upper Pleistocene. Lord knows what happened in between! It gets a little wild and woolly, it seems, when one tries to plug in anything about language to the actual archeological record. Theoretical divergences become quite staggering. Someone pointed out to me that the only consolation is that astronomy is in a worse mess.

Other areas, it seems to me, have been much more promising. At least for me, as an absolute amateur in that area, the papers on lateralization have been most striking. When one considers the kind of discussion we had on the cost benefit analysis between symmetry and asymmetry in the evolution of the brain—what we had to give up in order to provide ourselves with asymmetry as it were—and the enormous selection pressures that there must have been in that direction, and when one puts that together with what Steklis and Harnad say about the localization of fine motor functions and the way language, as it were, hitched onto this, one begins to get some sense of a coming together in evolution that could, in fact, be plugged into a lot of other things.

What made me particularly sad about this conference, since I'm a social anthropologist, was the complete nonrepresentation of the social sciences. I think some of the other speakers in this final session might raise some of the areas that they felt should be represented, but when one considers that language must have had both its origin and its evolution in a context of increasing social complexity, the fact that it was difficult to drum up any speakers from the social sciences who could say anything about this at all, I think borders on disgrace. It makes me personally quite ashamed, and particularly because it seems to me that somewhere or other that's where the synthesis has got to come. However, as I say, I give these merely as examples of questions that the conference has raised in my mind and things that we can go ahead and do.